THE

READER'S COMPANION TO

MILITARY HISTORY

THE READER'S COMPANION TO

MILITARY HISTORY

ROBERT COWLEY
AND
GEOFFREY PARKER
EDITORS

SPONSORED BY
The Society for Military History

HOUGHTON MIFFLIN COMPANY
BOSTON · NEW YORK

Copyright © 1996 by Houghton Mifflin Company
All rights reserved

For information about permission to reproduce selections from
this book, write to Permissions, Houghton Mifflin Company,
215 Park Avenue South, New York, New York 10003.

For information about this and other Houghton Mifflin trade
and reference books and multimedia products, visit
The Bookstore at Houghton Mifflin on the World Wide Web
at http://www.hmco.com/trade/.

Library of Congress Cataloging-in-Publication Data

The reader's companion to military history / Robert
Cowley, Geoffrey Parker, editors.
p. cm.
"Sponsored by the Society for Military History."
Includes indexes.
ISBN 0-395-66969-3
1. Military history. I. Cowley, Robert. II. Parker,
Geoffrey, 1943– . III. Society for Military History (U.S.)
U27.R348 1996
355'.009 — dc20   96-8577   CIP

Printed in the United States of America

Book design by Robert Overholtzer

HWK 10 9 8 7 6 5 4 3 2 1

Contents

Maps

Contributors

Thomas B. Allen
Bethesda, Maryland

Thomas F. Arnold
Yale University

Jere L. Bachrach
University of Washington, Seattle

George Baer
Naval War College

Tami Davis Biddle
Duke University

David Birmingham
University of Kent at Canterbury,
England

Jeremy Black
University of Exeter, England

Michael Blow
Greenwich, Connecticut

Eugene N. Borza
The Pennsylvania State University

Clare Brandt
Rhinebeck, New York

Marshall Brement
Middleburg, Virginia

Malcolm Brown
The Imperial War Museum,
England

David Buisseret
University of Texas at Arlington

William Caferro
University of Tulsa

D'Ann Campbell
Austian Peay State University

Caleb Carr
*MHQ: The Quarterly Journal of
Military History*

Eliot A. Cohen
The Johns Hopkins University

Philippe Contamine
University of Paris-Sorbonne,
France

Theodore F. Cook, Jr.
William Paterson College

James S. Corum
USAF School of Advanced
Airpower Studies

Robert Cowley
*MHQ: The Quarterly Journal of
Military History*

David Culbert
Louisiana State University,
Baton Rouge

Carlo W. D'Este
New Seabury, Massachusetts

Malcolm Deas
St Anthony's College,
Oxford, England

Robert A. Doughty
United States Military Academy

William J. Duiker
The Pennsylvania State University

R. David Edmunds
Indiana University

Stanley L. Falk
Former Chief Historian,
U.S. Air Force

Steven Fanning
University of Illinois at Chicago

Byron Farwell
Hillsboro, Viginia

R. Brian Ferguson
Rutgers University

Arther Ferrill
University of Washington, Seattle

Caroline Finkel
Istanbul, Turkey

Thomas Fleming
New York, New York

M. R. D. Foot
London, England

General Sir David Fraser
Alton, Hampshire, England

Karl F. Friday
University of Georgia

David Fromkin
Boston University

William C. Fuller, Jr.
Naval War College

John Gillingham
The London School of Economics
and Political Science, England

Carroll Gillmor
Salt Lake City, Utah

David M. Glantz
Journal of Slavic Military Studies

Joseph T. Glatthaar
University of Houston

Anthony Goodman
The University of Edinburgh,
Scotland

Stewart Gordon
Los Angeles, California

David A. Graff
Bowdoin College

Molly Greene
Princeton University

Ira D. Gruber
Rice University

Bruce I. Gudmundsson
The Institute for Tactical
Education

John F. Guilmartin
The Ohio State University

Paul G. Halpern
The Florida State University

Michael I. Handel
Naval War College

Victor Davis Hanson
California State University, Fresno

Kenneth W. Harl
Tulane University

Ross Hassig
University of Oklahoma

Daniel R. Headrick
Roosevelt University

Holger H. Herwig
The University of Calgary, Canada

Don Higginbotham
University of North Carolina,
Chapel Hill

Thaddeus Holt
Point Clear, Alabama

Alistair Horne
Turville, Oxfordshire, England

Donald D. Horward
The Florida State University

Samuel Hynes
Princeton, New Jersey

Keith Jeffery
University of Ulster at Jordantown,
Northern Ireland

Francis Jennings
Newberry Library Emeritus

W. Scott Jessee
Appalachian State University

Robert W. Johannsen
University of Illinois
at Urbana-Champaign

Timothy D. Johnson
David Lipscomb University

Robert J. T. Joy
Uniformed Services University
of the Health Sciences

Walter E. Kaegi
The University of Chicago

David Kahn
Newsday

David Kaiser
Naval War College

Alvin Kernan
The Andrew W. Mellon Fund

Richard M. Ketchum
Former Editor,
American Heritage Books

Bernard Knox
Center for Hellenic Studies

Glenn LaFantasie
Warrenton, Virginia

A. D. Lambert
King's College, England

David Clay Large
Montana State University

J. F. Lazenby
University of Newcastle, England

Bradford A. Lee
Naval War College

Bernard Lewis
Princeton University

Edward N. Luttwak
Center for Strategic and
International Studies

John A. Lynn
University of Illinois
at Urbana-Champaign

Angus MacKay
The University of Edinburgh,
Scotland

Lawrence Malkin
New York, New York

John H. Maurer
Naval War College

Adrienne Mayor
Princeton, New Jersey

William H. McNeill
The University of Chicago

James M. McPherson
Princeton University

Ira Meistrich
New York, New York

Bruce W. Menning
U.S. Army Command and
General Staff College

Allan R. Millett
The Ohio State University

Daniel Moran
Naval Postgraduate School

Ted Morgan
New York, New York

Eric Morris
South Glamorgan, Wales

Lance Morrow
Millbrook, New York

Susan Brind Morrow
Millbrook, New York

Williamson Murray
Marine Corps University

Scott Hughes Myerly
Los Angeles, California

Larry Neal
University of Illinois
at Urbana-Champaign

Robert L. O'Connell
National Ground Intelligence
Center

Stephen B. Oates
Amherst, Massachusetts

Josiah Ober
Princeton University

Jane H. Ohlmeyer
University of Aberdeen, Scotland

Geoffrey Parker
The Ohio State University

Rod Paschall
Carlisle, Pennsylvania

Mark R. Peattie
Hoover Institution on War,
Revolution and Peace

Joseph E. Persico
Guilderland, New York

Peter O'M. Pierson
Santa Clara University

Daniel Pipes
Middle East Quarterly

Douglas Porch
Naval War College

Barbara Nevling Porter
Chebeague Island, Maine

John Prados
Washington, D.C.

Paul Preston
The London School of Economics
and Political Science, England

Theodore K. Rabb
Princeton University

Jeffrey T. Richelson
Alexandria, Virginia

N. A. M. Rodger
National Maritime Museum,
England

Clifford J. Rogers
United States Military Academy

Alex Roland
Duke University

Elihu Rose
New York University

Gideon Rose
Council on Foreign Relations

Morris Rossabi
City University of New York

Gunther E. Rothenberg
Purdue University

Edward J. Schoenfeld
University of Pittsburgh

H. M. Scott
University of St Andrews, Scotland

Patricia Seed
Rice University

Dennis E. Showalter
Colorado College

Charles R. Shrader
Carlisle, Pennsylvania

Neil Asher Silberman
Branford, Connecticut

John Masson Smith, Jr.
University of California, Berkeley

Paul Sonnino
University of California,
Santa Barbara

Roger J. Spiller
U.S. Army Command and
General Staff College

Gale Stokes
Rice University

Brian R. Sullivan
Falls Church, Virginia

Jon Sumida
University of Maryland,
College Park

Jon Swan
Columbia Journalism Review

Tim Travers
The University of Calgary, Canada

Noah Andre Trudeau
Washington, D.C.

Ulrich Trumpener
University of Alberta, Canada

Robert M. Utley
Moose, Wyoming

Martin van Creveld
The Hebrew University of
Jerusalem, Israel

Hans J. van de Ven
University of Cambridge, England

Hans Vogel
University of Leiden, Netherlands

Arthur Waldron
Naval War College

Joanna Waley-Cohen
New York University

Geoffrey Ward
New York, New York

Gerhard L. Weinberg
University of North Carolina,
Chapel Hill

Stanley Weintraub
The Pennsylvania State University

Bernard A. Weisberger
Evanston, Illinois

James Scott Wheeler
United States Military Academy

Tom Wicker
New York, New York

Simon Winchester
New York, New York

J. M. Winter
Pembroke College, Cambridge,
England

Editors' Note

We believe that *The Reader's Companion to Military History* is the most accurate reflection available of the current state of the art. In this book you will will find what the foremost practitioners of military history, including our advisory board and the more than 150 authorities who have written entries, consider most important. The 570 entries are a distillation: here are the concepts, personalities, organizations, wars, battles, and general phenomena that seem both basic and indispensable.

The study of military history has undergone drastic changes in recent years. The old drums-and-bugles approach will no longer do. Factors such as economics, logistics, intelligence, and technology receive the attention once accorded solely to battles and campaigns and casualty counts. Words like "strategy" and "operations" have acquired meanings that might not have been recognizable a generation ago. Changing attitudes and new research have altered our views of what once seemed to matter most. For example, several of the battles that Edward Shepherd Creasy listed in his famous 1852 book *Fifteen Decisive Battles of the World* rate hardly a mention here, and the confrontation between Muslims and Christians at Poitiers-Tours in 732, once considered a watershed event, has been downgraded to a raid in force.

The subject matter of this book ranges from the origins of war to ethnic cleansing, from Thutmose III to H. Norman Schwarzkopf, from the War of the Triple Alliance in Paraguay to the Battle of Khalkin-Gol on the border of Mongolia and Manchuria. Here you will find the unexpected, the surprising. What is the only major engagement fought between Chinese and Arabs? The Battle of Talas River, 751. Who originated the term No Man's Land? Ernest Swinton, 1909. What is the truth about Roland? The hero of legend was actually an incompetent leader. Who first used ironclad ships in battle? The Korean admiral Yi Sun-Shin, in the 1590s. Were the fearsome Amazons purely a myth? Perhaps, but remains of women warriors have been unearthed in the Black Sea region. What may have been the largest naval battle in history? Not Leyte Gulf, in 1944, but Ecnomus, in the First Punic War, 256 B.C.

Although the *Reader's Companion* runs to 542 pages, it does not — cannot — provide equal coverage for all countries and all centuries. To elucidate and explain all the wars that have taken place, absorbing the energies and resources of humankind for millennia, would be impossible in a single volume; this book does not pretend to be an encyclopedia. But how can military history be reduced to manageable proportions? Two obvious options, to deal only with the modern world or only with the West, immediately fell by the wayside, because they would have excluded many fascinating precedents and parallels. For example, the entry on "Drill" would have been confined to modern "square-bashing," instead of drawing attention to the remarkable coincidence that only two societies, China and the West, invented drill, and that both did so twice, at precisely the same time — in the fifth century B.C. and again, drawing on those classical precedents, in the sixteenth century A.D.

We therefore adopted two working principles in selecting entries and allocating relative lengths: (1) given that the Western way of warfare has come to dominate armed conflict all over the globe, we have "privileged" Western matters; and (2) given that many readers will be more interested in recent wars, we have also given more weight to the conflicts, personalities, and developments that shaped warfare in the twentieth and, to a lesser degree, the nineteenth century. Thus we have two entries entitled "Korean War," one dealing with the conflict of the 1950s, the other with that of the 1590s. The first is far more substantial, however, and the leading participants have entries of their own, whereas the second is far shorter, and only the Japanese leader who launched the invasion and the Korean admiral who destroyed the invasion fleet receive separate notice. So although "non-Western" phenomena feature in our volume, they receive proportionately less attention. Likewise, although World War II and Rome's Punic Wars are both included, the former is one of the longest entries in the book, with separate treatments for each major battle and prominent commander, whereas the latter is much shorter, with separate treatment of only a few leading players.

Readers can find entries on subjects that interest them in one of three ways: by going straight to the relevant place in the main text, which is alphabetically arranged; by following up cross-references in those texts; and by checking the index for the location of additional topics. Inevitably, however, as stated at the outset, some will search in vain, since our selection, even though informed by a distinguished advisory board, could not include everything. We would be delighted to hear of any glaring omissions; perhaps gaps can be filled in a future edition. Meanwhile, we hope that every reader will find unfamiliar material — even on familiar subjects — that will provoke and challenge as well as inform, for as Sir Walter Raleigh observed in the early seventeenth century, "The ordinary theme and argument of all history is war."

ROBERT COWLEY
GEOFFREY PARKER

THE
READER'S COMPANION TO
MILITARY HISTORY

A

Abd el-Krim

1881?–1963, Moroccan Berber Leader

Born the son of a Berber tribal leader, Abd el-Krim (Mohammed Abd el-Karim el-Khattabi, "Wolf of the Rif") became a Muslim judge at Melilla, the chief town in Spanish Morocco, where he also edited a newspaper. A quarrel with a Spanish officer landed him in prison, but he escaped and, joined by his tribesmen, launched a revolt against Spanish rule. Throughout 1921–1922, he led raids on Spanish outposts and ambushed Spanish patrols. On July 21, 1921, he scored a victory over a Spanish army under General Fernández Silvestre in the Battle of Anoual and then advanced to the outskirts of Melilla.

In 1923 he declared a republic of the Rif and created a modern army, equipped it with machine guns and mountain howitzers, and hired numbers of mercenaries, including deserters from the French Foreign Legion.

When the French advanced against him, he successfully attacked them too, advancing almost to Fez before he was defeated in 1925 by French general Louis Lyautey. Harassed by French and Spanish forces, he surrendered on May 26, 1926, to the French and was exiled to the Indian Ocean island of Réunion. He was released in 1947 and went to Egypt, where he continued his anti-French campaign until his death.

BYRON FARWELL

Accommodation for Troops

The accommodations made available for soldiers reflect the nature of armies and the resources of governments. Strong, centralized states prefer keeping at least the core of their armies well in hand. The camps of Rome's legions (q.v.) tended to evolve into permanent communities. The Ottoman Empire's janissaries and some of its technical troops lived in barracks. In practice, however, such forces tended with time to acculturate to their civilian environments. In the field, the subsistence nature of preindustrial economies, whether Asian, European, or African, guaranteed that large forces seldom stayed long in any one place. Quartering was correspondingly ad hoc, usually involving soldiers lodged with civilians or in public buildings at community expense.

The rise of large, permanent standing armies in Europe during the late sixteenth and seventeenth centuries created new problems. No state was willing to spend its limited military budget on infrastructure. The result was a systematic extension of billeting. Soldiers were assigned to private homes, taverns, empty buildings, and stables — usually in small groups and usually on a temporary basis, to prevent both affinities and hostilities from developing between the soldiers and their unwilling hosts. In theory, the men were supposed to receive rations or subsistence allowances; however, "free quarters" tended to be the rule. Under this system, property owners received receipts that could later be redeemed from the appropriate authorities, though delay and discounting often soured relations between the state and its subjects.

The worst effects of billeting were modified by the common practice of allowing soldiers to seek jobs in their extensive off-duty hours. From a military point of view, however, the negative effects on training, discipline, and unit cohesion outweighed the system's advantages. In the aftermath of the Seven Years' War (q.v.), Europe's armies were increasingly concentrated in barracks financed by governments' steadily improving ability to tax and borrow. By modern standards the accommodations were primitive, with men sleeping two to a bed, latrine facilities consisting of a tub somewhere on the floor, and married quarters defined by blankets hung from ropes. These conditions, however, did not differ significantly from the standard lifestyles of the peasants and casual laborers who made up the armies.

Risks of contagious diseases were more than balanced by the utility of having concentrations of reliable men in case of civic disorder or natural catastrophes. At the same time, troops in barracks were initially kept isolated, as much to protect middle-class sensibilities from the sights, sounds, and smells of a "brutal and licentious soldiery" as to seal off the soldiers from the revolutionary ideas that swept Europe in the late eighteenth and early nineteenth centuries. Success in both endeavors was limited. During the revolutions of 1848 in particular, units often refused to act against civilian crowds that included sweethearts and drinking companions.

As short-term conscription became the principal means of recruitment, barracks life was accurately perceived as the only way to socialize draftees into military systems in an acceptable period of time. One result was a steady improvement in living conditions. By 1914 the average European soldier ate and slept about as well as he could expect to at home when times were good. This fact contributed not a little to the relative acceptability of military service among young adults.

World War I (q.v.) and its aftermath changed significantly the pattern of military accommodations. During the war, billeting made a temporary comeback, particularly in Britain. Permanent facilities, however, were so overcrowded that they deteriorated significantly. After 1918 funding for repair and replacement was limited. The result was a growing gap between living conditions in the army and those in civilian life. The German Wehrmacht owed a good part of its initial popularity to the new buildings that sprang up after 1935 to house the new generations of conscripts.

Post–World War II affluence combined with the growing importance of long-service volunteers, even in ostensibly conscripted forces, led armies in the 1970s increasingly to abandon Western communal barracks in favor of accommodations more like college dormitories or efficiency apartments. The Soviet Union retained the traditional system — a decision that contributed to the growing disaffection that led to its collapse. In increasingly privatized societies, where separate rooms and separate televisions are becoming norms for adolescents, barracks may become as obsolete as billets.

DENNIS E. SHOWALTER

Reginald Hargreaves, "Bivouacs, Billets, and Barracks," *Army Quarterly* (January 1963): 231–242.

Actium, Battle of

September 2, 31 B.C.

At Actium, Octavian (the future Roman emperor Augustus) and his general Marcus Vipsanius Agrippa defeated Mark Antony and Cleopatra VII of Egypt, ending the Roman Civil War. In the name of the republic, Octavian declared war in 32 B.C. on Cleopatra, to whom Antony was both husband and ally. Each army numbered thirty legions. Antony enjoyed a superiority in cavalry furnished by eastern allies, but Octavian possessed more veteran legions; at sea, Octavian's fleet of six hundred quinqueremes outclassed the five hundred belonging to Antony. Antony blundered in allowing himself to be besieged on the Actium promontory in western Greece. During the summer of 31 B.C., hungry Antonian soldiers deserted in droves. On September 2, 31 B.C., Antony risked a desperate breakout with his remaining two hundred seaworthy quinqueremes, and it ended in fiasco. Cleopatra's squadron of sixty ships escaped, followed by Antony in his flagship; but the rest of the fleet, pursued by Agrippa, fled in disorder to Actium's harbor. On the next day, Antony's army and fleet surrendered.

Actium closed a century of revolution that had wracked the Roman world. In 30 B.C. Octavian annexed the eastern provinces after Antony and Cleopatra, each in turn, committed suicide. In naval warfare, Actium was the last clash of great warships in classical antiquity. For the next four centuries, the Roman navy faced no rival, and so concentrated on transports, river flotillas, and swift coastal craft to suppress piracy.

KENNETH W. HARL

Aerial Weapons

The advantages of discharging missiles from a height were understood from the dawn of time, and appreciation of the military potential of aerial weaponry predated human-carrying flying vehicles. Visionary schemes foresaw destruction raining down from balloons, and Austrian forces suppressing a rebellion actually attacked Venice with unmanned balloons carrying incendiary bombs in 1849.

But as a practical matter, aerial weaponry had to await the development of the airplane and dirigible. Rifles and machine guns were carried aloft almost from the beginning and were used with limited effect by Italian aviators against Ottoman forces in Libya in 1911. The Italians also dropped crude bombs, which showed more promise.

Aerial weaponry came of age during World War I (q.v.), following a brief period in which aircraft were used almost exclusively for reconnaissance (q.v.); the aviators defended themselves with pistols and rifles. Pusher aircraft, with the crew seated ahead of the engine and propeller for a clear forward field of fire, were armed with machine guns even before the war, but these airplanes were slower than "tractor" scouts with forward-mounted engines. The seminal event, the development of synchronization gear, made it possible to mount a machine gun to fire through the propeller arc ahead of the pilot, making the entire aircraft a gun mount and vastly simplifying aiming. Defensive machine guns on flexible mounts soon followed. Machine gun–armed aircraft were used to strafe ground troops, and from 1917, the Germans and then the Allies fielded specialized ground-attack aircraft. After experiments with steel flechettes, highly explosive bombs fitted with fins and impact fuses became the staple of aerial bombardment. In 1915, the Germans launched zeppelins capable of carrying two tons of bombs, and by war's end the largest conventional bombers carried bomb loads of more than a ton. Such aircraft, however, were exceptional, and primitive aiming and navigation systems limited their effectiveness. Zeppelin raids were briefly effective as a terror weapon, and attacks on London by conventional bombers in 1917 forced the British to hold back large numbers of aircraft from the Western Front for defense — but bombing had little effect on the war. Aerial reconnaissance, artillery spotting, and denying the enemy use of the air remained far more important than bombardment. Techniques and technologies developed in World War I reached maturity during the interwar period and played important roles in World War II (q.v.), notably dive-bombing, torpedo attacks on

ships, and cannon- and rocket-armed fighters. On fighters, ring-and-bead gun sights gave way to an illuminated display projected on a ground glass plate in front of the pilot, controlled by a gyroscopic mechanism that automatically computed the lead angle; these would revolutionize air-to-air combat by making average fighter pilots adequate marksmen.

In 1918, rifle-caliber machine guns were the standard aircraft armament — twin synchronized guns on fighters for attack and manually aimed flexible guns for defense. By 1939–1940, British fighters carried as many as eight rifle-caliber machine guns, the Americans were standardizing .50-caliber weapons, German fighters carried 20-mm shell-firing cannon, and newer American and British bombers had hydraulic and electrically powered multiple-gun turrets. Radar, first used to direct ground-controlled intercepts of attacking bombers and then mounted in night fighters and bombers to permit attacks in darkness and through clouds, completely reshaped the face of aerial warfare from 1940 to 1945.

Ground and naval forces proved vulnerable to aerial attack from the beginning of World War II, and air superiority became an essential ingredient of victory. Carrier-based dive-bombers and torpedo-bombers replaced the guns of capital ships as arbiters of naval combat. Fighters carried heavier cannon; rockets supplemented guns for ground attack and, in German service, for attacks on bomber formations. German aircraft dropped radio-controlled, visually guided bombs and missiles in attacks on ships from 1943, and the Americans used radio-controlled bombs against bridges in 1944–1945. American forces introduced napalm (jellied gasoline) firebombs as an antipersonnel weapon.

Advances in aircraft speed, range, and load-carrying capability made long-range aerial bombardment a major factor in World War II, although problems in accuracy and navigation had to be solved before attacks on cities, transportation nets, and industry could have strategic impact. The destruction by firestorm of Guernica at the hands of German and Italian bombers in the Spanish civil war (q.v.) provided a foretaste of the vulnerability of cities to incendiary bombs. Japanese attacks on Chinese cities from 1937 and German raids during the Battle of Britain (q.v.) hinted at the potential of long-range strategic bombardment; however, only the British Royal Air Force and the U.S. Army Air Forces realized that potential, and then not until 1943–1945. By war's end, heavy bombers routinely carried two to seven tons of bombs, and the British on occasion employed enormous bombs of twelve thousand and twenty-two thousand pounds, known as "blockbusters." The defining expression of strategic bombardment came with the atomic bombs, which destroyed Hiroshima and Nagasaki in August 1945, though, ironically, incendiary attacks on cities — notably Hamburg, Dresden, and Tokyo — caused far more deaths.

The appearance of jet aircraft late in World War II introduced unprecedented speed to aerial combat, demanding air-to-air weapons with increased range and single-shot lethality. In response, guided missiles began to enter service in the middle to late 1950s. The first to achieve combat success was the U.S. Navy's heat-seeking Sidewinder in 1958; with progressive improvements, it remains in service. Radar-guided missiles offered the advantage of being able to attack through clouds, but they were more complex than heat-seekers and took longer to mature technically. The replacement of vacuum tubes with transistors from the 1970s in the West — but, significantly, not in the Soviet Union — enormously improved reliability and introduced an ongoing revolution in miniaturization. The first heat-seekers homed in on engine heat and flew up the tailpipe to achieve a kill; current infrared missiles are all-aspect — that is, they can acquire the target from the front or sides as well as from the rear, homing in on the jet exhaust plume and using sophisticated lead-computing gyros to determine target location and laser proximity fuses to detonate the warhead.

Radar missiles have undergone comparable improvement and now encompass several basic types, each with its particular advantages: active homing missiles, which carry their own transmitters and receivers; semiactive homing missiles, which carry only a receiver and depend on the launching aircraft's radar to illuminate the target; and passive homing missiles, which lock onto enemy radar transmissions. Active missiles operate autonomously once launched, that is, they require no external commands, but are comparatively large and complex. Semiactive missiles are smaller and simpler, but require the launching aircraft to continue transmitting and remain pointed generally toward the target until missile impact. Passive radar missiles operate autonomously, but can home in only so long as the enemy

radar is transmitting. Active radar homing is widely used in antiship missiles, often with infrared terminal homing. Semiactive radar missiles are the most common type of air-to-air missile next to infrared. Passive radar missiles are widely used to attack radar-controlled, surface-based antiaircraft guns and missiles.

Air-to-ground weaponry was revolutionized by the development in the United States of television, laser, and autonomously guided aerial munitions in the late 1960s. These munitions proved enormously effective in destroying discrete targets such as bridges and power plants late in the Vietnam War (q.v.). The lesson was reinforced in the Gulf War (q.v.) of 1990–1991. Although laser-guided bombs took most of the plaudits in the Persian Gulf, autonomously guided Tomahawk cruise missiles, using on-board, terrain-mapping radar for orientation, demonstrated that air-breathing cruise missiles could evade sophisticated antiaircraft defenses and inflict significant damage on small, high-value targets.

More exotic aerial weapons include aerially sprayed defoliants, used extensively by the United States in Vietnam; fuel-air bombs, in which an aerosol-sprayed explosive agent such as butane detonates in combination with atmospheric oxygen; and aerially dispensed micotoxins, highly lethal organisms related to fungi, used by Soviet and Soviet client forces in the Middle East and Southeast Asia.

JOHN F. GUILMARTIN

Christopher Campbell, *Air Warfare: The Fourth Generation* (1984); Charles H. Gibbs-Smith, *Aviation: An Historical Survey from Its Origins to the End of World War II* (1970); John H. Morrow, Jr., *The Great War in the Air: Military Aviation from 1909 to 1921* (1993).

Agincourt, Battle of

October 25, 1415

Had Henry V of England been less strong-willed, the Battle of Agincourt — thanks to Shakespeare, probably the most famous clash of the Hundred Years' War (q.v.), although it was less politically significant than Poitiers (q.v.) and far less innovative in terms of tactics and weaponry than Crécy (q.v.) — would never have taken place. During the five-week siege of the Norman port of Harfleur, which opened the fifteenth-century phase of the war, Henry's army suffered heavily from disease. Once the city fell to hunger and Henry's twelve large bombards, the king's advisers recommended that he end the campaign and return to England. He refused. Proclaiming (perhaps disingenuously) his willingness to face battle, Henry insisted on leading his one thousand men-at-arms and five thousand archers across northern France toward the English base at Calais. Delayed by difficulties in crossing the Somme, he was cut off near Agincourt by a French force of about twenty thousand. Tactically, the ensuing battle was virtually a repetition of Poitiers. The English archers repulsed a preliminary cavalry attack, sending wounded horses crashing back into the advancing French men-at-arms. Fighting dismounted on constricted ground where their superior numbers hindered more than helped, the French were checked by the English center and taken in flank by the wings of archers (first with arrows, then hand to hand). By the end, French losses may have approached ten thousand killed or captured, compared to a few hundred English casualties.

The French never again dared to challenge Henry in the field. This greatly facilitated his conquest of Normandy (1417–1419), which led to the triumphant Treaty of Troyes (1420) by which Henry was recognized as the heir and regent of Charles VI of France.

CLIFFORD J. ROGERS

Airborne Troops

Proposals to bring troops unexpectedly into battle by aerial transport were made in World War I (q.v.), and the Soviet Union formed a sizable corps of parachute troops during the interwar period. However, the first airborne troops used in combat were the German *Fallschirmjäger* (literally, "parachute light infantry") during the 1940 invasions of Norway and the Low Countries. Made up of rigorously trained volunteers, these troops entered battle by jumping at low altitude from transport aircraft, wearing parachutes deployed automatically by a cord (or static line) attached to the aircraft, or by assault glider. Each method had advantages and disadvantages. Large numbers of paratroops could be quickly dropped on or near an objective and could land on rough terrain but were inevitably dispersed by wind and the interval between jumpers; they landed as individuals rather than in formed units and carried only pistols and submachine guns (heavier

weapons and reserve ammunition were parachuted separately). Gliders, however, could release their tows some distance from an objective, arriving swiftly and silently to deliver their troops in formed units with machine guns, mortars, and light antitank weapons; but they required a reasonably smooth landing surface and demanded great piloting skill. These tactics enjoyed considerable initial success — most spectacularly in the German capture of Crete (May 1941) (q.v.), the only battle fought and won entirely by airborne troops. They set the pattern for subsequent developments. The *Fallschirmjäger*'s basic kit — helmet with chin strap, camouflaged smock, and baggy trousers with large pockets bloused into high leather jump boots — distinguishes airborne troops to this day.

American and British airborne units were formed with carefully selected volunteers in 1941–1942 and were used with considerable success, though often with high casualties, in World War II (q.v.) — notably in the Normandy invasion (see *D-Day*) and in crossing the Rhine. As parachutes improved, paratroops routinely jumped carrying all personal weapons and ammunition; by 1944, British and American gliders could carry jeeps and light field howitzers. The paratroop ethos was defined during World War II, and by war's end, the term *paratrooper* — a volunteer who jumped from airplanes — was synonymous with *elite*. Parachute units were the cream of the French forces during the Indochina War (q.v.) and the Algerian War (q.v.); the Soviet Union organized a large, elite airborne establishment during the Cold War (q.v.).

Helicopters and methods for extracting extremely heavy loads from the ramps of transport aircraft by parachute rendered assault gliders obsolete in the 1950s, and helicopter assault operations largely supplanted mass parachute assaults in the 1960s. The U.S. Army pressed these developments to the limit in Vietnam (q.v.), fielding whole helicopter-mobile divisions; significantly, however, infantry in these units were generally parachute trained. Specialist units began to exploit skydiving techniques such as HALO (high altitude, low opening), using manually deployed, steerable parachutes to insert small patrols and raiding parties precisely and silently behind enemy lines. Although the distinction between airborne troops and line infantry has been blurred by the helicopter, parachute infantry units are universally regarded as a corps d'élite and are fielded by every major military establishment. In addition, the speed, range, and carrying capacity of jet and turbojet transports continue to give parachute operations strategic relevance for mass operations far from home on short notice.

JOHN F. GUILMARTIN

Aircraft

The potential advantages of being able to fly over an enemy and rain destruction from above or gain information about hostile dispositions have long been instinctively understood. The means of doing so had to await the invention of the airplane by the Wright brothers, experiments with balloons during the Wars of the French Revolution (q.v.) notwithstanding. Early military use of heavier-than-air aircraft was severely limited by the constraints imposed by feeble power plants and the consequent need to use light, but aerodynamically inefficient, structures of wood, wire, and canvas. In August 1914, few airplanes could carry more than a pilot and an observer, yet for all that they brought back the vital reconnaissance (q.v.) that produced Allied victory on the Marne (q.v.). Wartime priorities spurred steady increases in engine power, and as World War I (q.v.) progressed, airplanes carried increasingly heavier payloads of ordnance and — of at least equal importance — radios for artillery spotting and cameras for photographic mapping and reconnaissance.

By 1915 the importance of aerial reconnaissance was evident, and single-seat fighter planes were developed to deny it to the enemy. Armed with synchronized machine guns mounted ahead of the pilot and firing through the propeller arc, these raised aerial combat to new levels of lethality. The year 1915 also saw the first serious attempts at strategic aerial bombardment, notably in zeppelin raids on Britain by the German Naval Air Service. By mid-1916, it would have been unthinkable to mount a ground offensive on the Western Front without aerial artillery spotting, and, since artillery spotting required air superiority, fighter aircraft became arbiters of battlefield victory and remain so today. By war's end, the Germans had subjected London to sustained attack by heavy bombers, and the newly formed British Royal Air Force was attacking industrial targets in western Germany.

The interwar years witnessed revolutions in engine power, aerodynamic sophistication, and, particularly in the United States, structural efficiency. Externally braced biplanes gave way to streamlined monoplanes with retractable landing gear, and Japan and the Soviet Union developed world-class aviation industries. By the mid-1930s, the ratio of useful load (fuel, passengers, and cargo) to empty weight of the most efficient American transports was approaching 60:40, whereas most European designs remained in the 40:60 range. The American advantage applied to bombers, and although British bomber design caught up during World War II (q.v.), only the United States fielded a land-based transport with global range.

By 1939, the major powers — the United States, Britain, France, the Soviet Union, Germany, Japan, and Italy — all possessed bombers capable of destroying an undefended city. Britain, Germany, and Japan fielded heavily armed fighters of superior performance. Japan, the United States, and, with qualifications, Britain, possessed carrier-based naval air arms able to devastate an enemy fleet. The Luftwaffe had applied voice radios to revolutionize air-to-air tactics in the Spanish civil war (q.v.), and the Royal Air Force had developed an air defense system based on ground-controlled radar interception. All of these technologies proved pivotal in World War II, in which American and British design engineering, tactical ingenuity, strategic prioritization, and scientific perceptiveness overcame an early Axis lead and German success in fielding an efficient radar-controlled night fighter system and a brutally effective jet fighter. Aerial reconnaissance was even more important to the outcome of World War II than to that of World War I, and strategically rather than tactically. Bombers destroyed defended cities in Japan and Germany, and the German oil industry and rail net as well. Carrier-based bombers also destroyed the Imperial Japanese Navy.

The postwar years saw a remarkable increase in the importance of military aircraft, not only because of the potential — and, as it turned out, deterrent — use of jet bombers to deliver nuclear weapons (q.v.), but also in their roles as high-flying reconnaissance platforms; in an American military air transport net that circles the globe; in the use of aircraft in antisubmarine warfare; and in the increasing effectiveness of aerial intervention in ground combat, especially in the ill-fated American venture in Vietnam (q.v.). Helicopters, developed in Germany and the United States during World War II, came of age with jet turbine power during the 1960s and proved themselves in

Vietnam as assault transports, gunships, and frontline resupply and casualty evacuation vehicles.

In the years following the collapse of the Soviet Union, the importance of military aircraft has, if anything, increased. The reasons include the increased effectiveness of "smart" weapons (q.v.); the development of highly sophisticated, remote-controlled aircraft for reconnaissance and target designation; and the continued need for fighter aircraft to provide air superiority over the battlefield.

JOHN F. GUILMARTIN

Christopher Campbell, *Air Warfare: The Fourth Generation* (1984); Charles H. Gibbs-Smith, *Aviation: An Historical Survey from Its Origins to the End of World War II* (1970); John H. Morrow, Jr., *German Air Power in World War I* (1982).

Air Strategy

The emergence of air power theory came as a direct result of World War I (q.v.); the horrifying casualties of that conflict resulted in a search for a means to avoid the costly stalemate in the trenches. Although the experiences with air war in the Great War were ambiguous, German attacks on London and British attacks on the Rhineland did suggest a promising avenue of approach.

The first theorist to emerge as an advocate of "air strategy" was the Italian soldier Giulio Douhet. His central, single-minded argument was that the decisive mission of air power must be "strategic bombing" — a direct attack on the enemy's population. According to him, all other missions (such as interdiction, reconnaissance [q.v.], air superiority, sea control, and close air support) represented fundamental misuses of air power. At the heart of his argument lay a belief that the bombardment of population centers would shatter an enemy nation's morale and lead directly to the rapid collapse of its war effort.

Douhet exercised relatively little influence on developments in Britain and the United States until a commercial translation of his work became available in 1943; his position as a prophet of air power largely reflects the fact that the Anglo-American experience with air power before and during World War II (q.v.) was largely dominated by doers rather than theorists. Sir Hugh "Boom" Trenchard, the first chief of Air Staff in Britain in the interwar period, molded his service within an intellectual framework similar to Dou-

het's. In a 1923 conference dealing with a conjectural air war against the French, Trenchard underscored his faith in strategic bombing (q.v.) and his belief that "the French in a bombing duel would probably squeal before we did."

American theories of air strategy moved in a different direction. The first and most controversial American theorist was General Billy Mitchell (q.v.), whose intemperate attacks on senior American military leaders eventually resulted in his richly deserved court-martial. Like Douhet and Trenchard, Mitchell was a true believer in air power and argued that armies and navies would play little role in future conflicts; but unlike other air theorists, Mitchell believed that air superiority was an essential element in any future air war. Unfortunately, Mitchell's successors within the U.S. Army Air Forces developed an air strategy that virtually eliminated the fighter as a major factor in future air war.

By the end of the 1930s, American air power theorists had evolved a theory of air war that represented a precisely articulated body of interconnected assumptions. They based their strategy on the belief that well-led, disciplined bomber formations could fight their way through enemy-controlled airspace unaided by fighter escorts and suffer relatively low levels of casualties. Once these formations had made their high-altitude, deep penetrations, they would be able to hit precise targets that would ensure the destruction not only of major weapons-producing factories, but also a significant sector of the enemy's economy. This would lead to widespread dislocations and difficulties throughout the enemy's economic structure. The full impact of such bombing would eventually destroy the means and will of the enemy to resist.

Significant thinking about air power occurred in the German military during the interwar period as well. With Adolf Hitler's (q.v.) appointment as chancellor in January 1933, the Nazis set out to create a massive air force to further their megalomaniacal goals. From the first, the Germans were interested in strategic bombing, but the fact that they had conducted a thorough and honest study of air power's impact on World War I provided them with a more realistic conception of the future role of air power in war. Moreover, Germany's position in the center of Europe forced German airmen to recognize that air strategy must include a substantial supporting element of ground forces, while the Spanish civil war (q.v.) provided salient lessons on the difficulties in-

On a low-altitude mission over Europe in June 1943, B-17s are attacked by German Me 109s.
The painting, entitled Chariots of Fire, *is by Loren Blackburn.*

volved in strategic bombing. The Luftwaffe, therefore, developed a broader and more thorough conception of air power — one that included air superiority, interdiction, reconnaissance, and close air support as well as strategic bombing.

Although it ran into substantial problems — many of which were of its own making — in developing a long-range strategic bomber, the Luftwaffe did develop navigational and all-weather bombing aids that would allow it to hit targets under any conditions — capabilities that the Royal Air Force (RAF) and the U.S. Army Air Forces (USAAF) would not possess until the midpoint of the war. But, like the Americans and the British, the Germans failed to understand the enormous complexities that strategic bombing would involve.

In the first years of World War II, German air strategy allowed the Luftwaffe to support the lightning campaigns of the German army in conquering most of Europe. The RAF did possess radar and well-equipped

Fighter Command — both of which the British government had forced on a most unwilling Air Staff — and on a very slim margin it was able to win the Battle of Britain (q.v.). But its bomber offensive against the Third Reich floundered through to 1943, doing minimal damage to the Germans at great cost to its aircraft and crews. The American effort began against German targets in 1943 and, like the British effort, achieved rather little at first, also at great cost.

But in 1944 the huge resources that the British and American governments lavished on the RAF and USAAF began to pay large dividends. Supported by long-range escort fighters, the P-51 Mustang in particular, the U.S. Eighth and Fifteenth Air Forces broke the Luftwaffe fighter force and established general air superiority over the European continent. By midyear they were in the process of destroying the Reich's petroleum industry. American and British aircraft also interdicted the German army's logistical support structure in France before and after D-Day (q.v.); over the winter of 1944–1945, strategic bombing then destroyed the German transportation network. By 1944, over half a million soldiers and fifteen thousand flak pieces were defending the Reich from Allied air attacks. But both British and American air commanders persisted in costly and less effective attacks that raised the cost of the air campaigns — the British Bomber Command lost over 50 percent of its air crews over the course of the war.

The terrible cost of the Combined Bomber Offensive, as well as the ambiguity of its results, should have raised serious questions about prewar strategies, but the appearance of the atomic bomb at the end of the war, especially given its decisive results at Hiroshima and Nagasaki, seemed to provide a new legitimacy to those strategies. That was certainly how the newly created U.S. Air Force felt in the immediate years after World War II. But America's new opponent in the Cold War (q.v.), the Soviet Union, soon acquired its own atomic bomb. Moreover, shortly after the Korean War (q.v.) had ended, scientists developed thermonuclear weapons with almost unlimited destructive potential — weapons that threatened not only to obliterate one's opponents, but the entire world as well.

The strategic question then centered on whether weapons, whose use would most probably result in the destruction of both sides, actually possessed any utility. From the mid-1950s, air strategy bifurcated into strategic theories of nuclear power and its deterrent value and those concerning the conventional use of air power. In the first case (led by two prominent thinkers, Bernard Brodie and Herman Kahn), nuclear strategy became the preserve of the academic world, which worried about issues such as the first use of nuclear weapons, "counterforce" strategies aimed at attacking the enemy's military structure, and "countervalue" strategies aimed at attacking the enemy's population centers. The final iteration of the latter resulted in the strategy of "mutually assured destruction" (MAD). There is little evidence that these theoretical musings by academics had any substantial influence on those charged with the actual planning of nuclear war in the United States and the Soviet Union. The American plan, the Single Integrated Operating Plan (SIOP), appears to have involved a massive laydown of nuclear weapons that equated nuclear strategy and target selection with the number of weapons available. But at least the academic writings may have worried the politicians on both sides.

The United States and the Soviet Union also expended enormous resources on the creation of conventional air forces. Soviet air strategy tied air power to the support of Soviet ground forces. American conventional air strategy, however, became a battleground between academics and the military. In particular, American political scientists became enthralled with ideas of graduated escalation and signal sending — theories that exercised a disastrous impact on the conduct of the air campaign against North Vietnam, when American political leaders skewed the planning process in favor of such strategies. But no evidence suggests that U.S. Air Force leadership had anything more to offer than the absolute destruction of North Vietnam by conventional weapons. In the Gulf War (q.v.), allied air planners showed considerably greater sophistication in developing an air strategy that sought to gain wide effects with minimal collateral damage through the use of conventional precision munitions, cruise missiles, and stealth aircraft. But in the end, the coalition had to wage a ground war to gain the full fruits from the successes of the air campaign — not exactly what the early air theorists had hoped for.

WILLIAMSON MURRAY

Williamson Murray, *Luftwaffe* (1985); Sir Charles Webster and Noble Frankland, *The Strategic Air Offensive Against Germany* (1961).

Alba, Duke of

1507–1583, Spanish General and Statesman

Fernando Alvarez de Toledo, third duke of Alba, was the most famous European soldier of his day. A member of a prominent warrior dynasty of Castile, he had memorized the military treatise of Vegetius (q.v.) by age thirteen, and from 1532 he served his Hapsburg sovereigns in Hungary, Germany, North Africa, Italy, and the Netherlands. His early campaigns taught him two lessons. On the strategic level, he learned to avoid battles, preferring to use greater resources and superior discipline to wear his adversary down by attrition. On the tactical level, he came to appreciate the value of firepower and in the 1550s pioneered the introduction of muskets to the Spanish infantry.

Alba's most celebrated military achievements took place in the early stages of the Dutch Revolt (q.v.). In 1567 his methodical preparations nipped an initial rebellion in the bud, and in 1568 he defeated another invasion by insurgents; but in 1572, despite mobilizing more than seventy thousand soldiers — the largest Christian army of the day — and despite the widespread use of terror (hanging all captured enemies and sacking selected captured towns), he failed to extinguish a second revolt and was recalled in 1573. Seven years later, however, at the age of seventy-three, he commanded the army raised to enforce Spain's claim to Portugal, and he died at the height of his military reputation. A determined enemy of uniforms, which he felt reduced the soldier's fortitude, Alba habitually dressed from head to toe in bright blue when he led his troops on campaign.

GEOFFREY PARKER

Albigensian Crusade

1208–1229

In 1208 Pope Innocent III issued a call for a "holy war" against the Albigensian heretics (Cathars) in southern France. The Albigensians preached that an inseparable gulf existed between the material world, which was evil, and the spiritual world, which was good. The crusade quickly devolved into a savage guerrilla war, however. Although intended to fight heresy, it became a war of conquest, providing an opportunity for the northern barons to plunder the richer south. In one of the few pitched battles of the campaign, the crusaders, commanded by Simon de Montfort, inflicted a defeat on the Albigensians at Murat in 1213. In a brilliant ruse, Montfort induced Peter of Aragon, the Spanish monarch who had taken up the Albigensian cause, to lift his siege of the city and attack its lightly guarded southeastern gate. Montfort and his forces then escaped through the northern gate and engaged the pursuing enemy in the open field. There Montfort won a decisive victory over his larger, but confused and disorganized, foe. Several years later (1218), Montfort met an ignominious death, killed during the siege of Toulouse by a rock hurled by a machine purportedly operated by women. By crusade's end (1229), the south was damaged economically; the French crown had acquired Toulouse, thus extending its influence to the Mediterranean; and the church, in order to extirpate the remaining vestiges of heresy, had established one of its most potent weapons, the Inquisition.

WILLIAM CAFERRO

Albuquerque, Afonso de

1453–1515, *Portuguese Soldier*

Afonso de Albuquerque was second viceroy (1509–1515) of the Portuguese forts and fleet in the Indian Ocean and implemented an aggressive policy, which, by combining politics and military force, aimed at seizing the lucrative spice trade between Asia and Europe. The strategy consisted of developing ports and forts along the Western Indian coast; in addition, Albuquerque conquered emporia at the entry to the Red Sea, in the Persian Gulf, and in Indonesia. Further, he used military force to monopolize the production of certain Asian spices (pepper, mace, and nutmeg). Albuquerque was successful because the Portuguese had important advantages in navigation and cannon technology, and no single power had before tried to control trade across these broad regions by force. Though the Portuguese effort came to include over one hundred forts from Sofala to Macao, and a fleet of more than one hundred ships, within fifty years it was clear that Albuquerque's grand plan had failed; the cost of the forts and the fleet began to exceed the profits of the trade. The Portuguese could never completely control local rivals, nor could they exclude the Ottomans from the Red Sea or European interlopers who were eventually armed with superior guns and ships from the Indian Ocean.

STEWART GORDON

Alexander, Harold

1891–1969, *British Field Marshal*

Harold Alexander served in the Irish Guards on the Western Front in World War I (q.v.), where he had a most successful combat career. By 1939, he had risen to division command and at Dunkirk commanded the rear guard. Posted to India, he commanded the retreat from Burma, although evidence now suggests that much of the credit for this accomplishment should go to William Slim (q.v.).

In 1942, Winston Churchill (q.v.) selected Alexander for command of the Middle East after the disaster at Gazala and the collapse of Tobruk. His assumption of command coincided with Bernard Montgomery's (q.v.) takeover of Eighth Army. As the theater commander, Alexander provided the logistical and strategic support that enabled Montgomery to win at El

Alamein (q.v.) and push through to Tunisia, where Eighth Army linked up with the forces of Operation Torch. Under Dwight Eisenhower's (q.v.) overall command, Alexander was responsible for combined operations against Sicily and mainland Italy. He proved adept at making the Anglo-American partnership work at the operational level, but found it difficult to control his subordinates, whether American or British.

In late 1943 Alexander assumed control of the Mediterranean from Eisenhower; he was responsible for the moves that eventually resulted in Rome's liberation in June 1944, but the deliberate disobedience of Mark Clark (q.v.) resulted in the escape of most of the German troops. The advance then stalled short of the Po River Valley until April 1945, when the last Allied offensive in Italy took place and broke the back of German forces.

Alexander, like Eisenhower, was well liked and able to get along with subordinate commanders of different nations. But many faulted him for being too urbane and lacking in that command authority over subordinates required in a theater commander. Nevertheless, he proved an immensely popular governor-general of Canada (1946–1952) and served as minister of defense (1952–1954) before retiring.

WILLIAMSON MURRAY

Alexander the Great

356–323 B.C., *King of the Macedonians*

Cavalry commander at age eighteen, king at twenty, conqueror of the Persian Empire at twenty-six, explorer of the Indian frontier at thirty, Alexander the Great died before his thirty-third birthday: neither the ancient sources nor the modern literature take sufficient note of this brilliant commander's extreme youth. What permanent accomplishments resulted from this whirlwind of activity?

Alexander's defeat of the Persian Empire removed the bloc that had prevented the spread of Greek settlements into the East. Although no surviving evidence suggests that Alexander himself promoted a policy of Hellenization, Greek culture undoubtedly penetrated into western Asia as the result of his conquests, and western Asia, up to the Mesopotamian frontier, became for the first time a part of the Greek world. This

is Alexander's most certain, though unintended, historical achievement.

Alexander's military genius is undisputed. He improved the fine army inherited from his father, Philip, by the addition of allied forces; he strengthened the cavalry arm, utilized weapons specialists, and employed a corps of engineers; he was invincible in both siege warfare and set battles. His movements were marked by speed; his logistical, intelligence, and communications operations were flawless; and his ability to improvise was unrivaled. Yet he was careful in strategy: rather than strike deep into Asia immediately, he spent nearly two years securing the coastal areas of Asia Minor and the Levant in order to ensure that Persian naval forces would not interdict his lines to Europe. Bit by bit he wore away the western sections of the Persian Empire before driving into Mesopotamia and the Iranian plateau.

Only three setbacks checked his progress. Along the Indian frontier his officers refused to march farther east, and, after his return to Babylonia, his Macedonian troops mutinied against the integration of Asian troops into the ranks. The third episode was the horrible loss of personnel in the Makran desert on the return march from India to the Persian Gulf, where lack of water and food accomplished what no enemy army had been able to do.

Alexander's conquests created a legend that would provide the standard by which other leaders measured their careers. Kings, generals, and emperors discovered that they were unable to compete with the legend and turned to emulation — Antiochus the Great, Pompey the Great, Nero, Caracalla, Severus Alexander, and Charlemagne (q.v.), to mention a few — and Alexander's career as a metaphor for achievement has reached even into modern times.

But the ruler who is arguably the most famous secular figure in history was little admired in his own lifetime. Although we lack sufficient details about his character, there was no doubt that he was an inspiring leader and personally a very brave soldier. He was ruthless toward those who opposed him — even from within his own ranks — but fair and honest toward those who exhibited courage and skill. He probably suffered from an overwhelming ambition and an uncontrollable temper that often arose from drinking excessive amounts of wine. He was widely despised by many of the subject Greeks, whose attitude might best be summed up by the comment attributed to one

Alexander (left) charges the Persian king Darius III at the Battle of Issus (333 B.C.). Although made more than three centuries later, this Pompeii mosaic is considered a near-contemporary illustration because it was based on a painting, attributed to Philoxenus of Eretria, that was completed within a generation of the event.

Athenian orator who, when informed of Alexander's death, replied, "What? Alexander dead? Impossible! The world would reek of his corpse!" In the end, his achievement appears to have been a grand adventure tied to his own personal ambitions — conquest for its own sake.

EUGENE N. BORZA

Donald W. Engels, *Alexander the Great and the Logistics of the Macedonian Army* (1978).

Algerian War

November 1954–March 1962

Although nationalist agitation and rebellion had often marked the history of Algeria, the series of attacks on police stations and government offices that occurred on the night of November 1, 1954, chiefly in remote areas of Constantine Province, passed almost without notice in Paris. By 1956, however, large tracts of the countryside had fallen under rebel control, and a terrorist campaign had paralyzed Algiers.

The French response to the crisis was hamstrung by the one million Algerians of European extraction, the *pieds noirs*, who sabotaged reforms designed to give

Muslims a stake in French Algeria. Backed by an important section of the French army, the *pieds noirs* locked French policy into a sterile search for a "military" victory over the insurgents.

On an operational level, the French army applied counterinsurgency (q.v.) techniques with brutal efficiency. Barriers built along the frontiers of Morocco and Tunisia blocked resupply and reinforcement of the Armée de libération nationale (ALN) commands. Inside Algeria, over one million Muslims were "resettled" in government camps, while French officers organized militias to deny remote villages to the insurgents. Meanwhile, helicopter-borne elite units of paratroops and foreign legionnaires swooped down on ALN companies, often guided to their targets by French-led Muslim commandos who stalked ALN units in the countryside. Successful offensives in 1959 demonstrated beyond doubt that the French army had the military situation well in hand.

The impression of French military victory was deceptive, however, for torture and "collective responsibility" — random executions carried out in villages where "terrorist" activity had taken place — drove moderates and many ordinary Muslims into the arms of the Algerian National Liberation Front (FLN). Outgunned on the battlefield, the FLN won the political and diplomatic war hands down as Arab states recognized the Provisional Government of the Algerian Republic. The United Nations rejected Paris's contention that Algeria was an internal French problem and voted to debate the issue. Even France's "Anglo-Saxon" allies, concerned that the Algerian situation was pushing France to the brink of civil war, pressed Paris to end the conflict.

On May 13, 1958, a *pieds noirs* rebellion in Algiers supported by the army and the threat of civil war brought General Charles de Gaulle (q.v.) to power in Paris; as a last resort he initiated negotiations that led to the signing of a peace accord at Évian on March 18, 1962. The war cost the French army 15,000 dead, whereas Muslim casualties were estimated to be between 300,000 and 400,000. Another 30,000 to 150,000 Muslims perished in the civil war that followed independence.

DOUGLAS PORCH

Allenby, Edmund

1861–1936, British World War I Field Marshal

Nicknamed "the Bull" for his famous outbursts of temper, Edmund Henry Hynman Allenby originally joined the Inniskilling Dragoons. After service in colonial campaigns, he attended staff college, led a cavalry column in the Boer War (q.v.), and by 1909 was promoted to major general and inspector general of cavalry.

On the Western Front, Allenby became commander of the Third Army in 1915 and directed the ill-fated Gommecourt diversion at the Somme (q.v.) on July 1, 1916. The following spring his army took part in the Arras offensive. Allenby's aggression had little scope in this structured offensive, which bogged down after three days. Douglas Haig (q.v.) then advised caution, but Allenby ordered "relentless pursuit" of the now heavily reinforced enemy; the attacks suffered severe losses, resulting in complaints by divisional commanders to Haig. Allenby was removed and sent to the Middle East.

Away from the operational confines of the Western Front, Allenby became a changed man. He kicked to life the slumbering Palestine campaign against Turco-German forces; his dramatic arrival at units was preceded by the warning signal BBA — "Bloody Bull's About." In late 1917 Allenby accepted the clever deception plan of his staff for a left feint against Gaza, while actually turning Beersheba (q.v.) on the right wing. Again Allenby ordered relentless pursuit. This time it worked, as did another deception plan in 1918 when a right feint east of the Jordan enabled the left wing to succeed. Allenby captured Jerusalem and Damascus, and after the war was appointed high commissioner in Egypt, where he displayed some political skills.

Allenby was lucky to be sent to Palestine, where he had room to maneuver with cavalry, twice as many troops as the enemy, air superiority, and good logistics. He took advantage of these assets. Yet Allenby remains enigmatic — a failure in France, successful in the Middle East — capable of furious rages but a humanist who was well read, a student of nature, and a keen historian of the Crusades (q.v.).

TIM TRAVERS

Amazons

Amazons, fierce warrior women who lived at the fringes of the "civilized" world, were the mythical arch-enemies of the ancient Greeks. Their exploits and lifestyle represented a reversed image of Greek society in which men dominated "weaker" women and prided themselves on military prowess in well-disciplined hoplite (q.v.) phalanxes. According to legends enjoyed by men and women of classical Greece, Amazons were expert horsewomen-archers who gloried in hunting, fighting, and sexual pleasure. It was said that they raised their daughters on mares' milk; the word *a-mazon* probably means "those who were not breast-fed." Their virtues mirrored those of Greek men — personal bravery, loyalty, and skill in the martial arts — but Amazons specialized in ambush and lightning cavalry raids, and like the real-world Parthians, their aim was deadly even in retreat. In some versions of the myth, Amazons were credited with the inventions of cavalry and iron weapons. Formidable in hand-to-hand combat with swords and battle-axes, they fought the best Greek heroes, including Hercules, Achilles, and Theseus. Scenes of Greek warriors pitted against valiant Amazons were popular in art: more than one thousand ancient vase paintings depict Amazons, and the famous Parthenon sculptures commemorated the Athenians' legendary defeat of the Amazon general Oreithyia and her forces at the Acropolis.

Various traditions place the Amazon homeland in North Africa or on the steppes of south Russia, but all

This bronze statuette (Etruscan, about 500 B.C.) portrays an Amazon archer on horseback. Amazons were notorious for their deadly aim, even in retreat.

ancient writers agree that imperialistic armies of bloodthirsty women swept across entire continents until they were finally repelled by the Athenians (Homer, eighth century B.C.; Herodotus, fifth century B.C.; Strabo and Diodorus Siculus, first century B.C.; and Plutarch and Pausanias, first and second centuries A.D.). The empire-builder Queen Myrina amassed an army of thirty thousand horsewomen and three thousand infantrywomen to cut a swath through what is now Libya and Egypt, through Syria and Asia Minor. Tombs of illustrious Amazons were pointed out in these regions in antiquity, and several great cities, many named for their commanders, were supposed to have been founded by Amazons: Myrina, Cyme, Priene, Cyrene, Smyrna, Mytilene. At Ephesus, at the great sanctuary of Artemis, goddess of the hunt, women performed war dances, rattling shields and beating the ground to the music of pipes.

The exploits of the Amazons were stunning. Queen Myrina's sister Mytilene led naval campaigns in the Aegean Sea as the Amazons poised to conquer Greece. Meanwhile, Queen Lysippe and her *Oiorpata* (Man-killers) invaded the Black Sea area from south Russia. During the Trojan War, King Priam hired Penthesilea and her twelve Amazon mercenaries "hot for war and battle-grim" to fight Achilles and the Greeks. When Hercules set out for his Ninth Labor, to capture the golden belt worn by the reigning Amazon champion Hippolyta, it was a chance for his band of Greek heroes to quench Amazon power before they could threaten Greece. In the "dust and gore" that ensued, Hippolyta was defeated, and Hercules and his men sailed off with captive women and rich booty. But the Amazons overpowered the sailors and took over the ships; Herodotus says that they landed on the shore of the Sea of Azov, headed inland on foot with their bows and arrows, captured some wild horses, and set off in search of loot in the territory of the Scythians.

Some young Scythian warriors fell in love with the band of marauding women and proposed marriage. The young women were not averse to an alliance but prized their independence. Herodotus records their proud answer: "Our business is with riding and the bow and javelin — we know nothing of women's work. We must be free to hunt and make war." The lovers decided to form a new tribe and vowed to raise both girls and boys to hunt, ride, and do battle. They became the Sarmatians, a real tribe of nomadic, war-like horsepeople of southern Ukraine.

In the 1950s, Soviet archaeologists excavated warriors' tombs in the territory of the ancient Sarmatians, who had traded with the Greeks in Herodotus's time. Of the graves that contained weapons and armor, nearly a quarter belonged to women. Typically, the young women's skeletons were surrounded by large iron lances, daggers, and spears; bows and triple-barbed arrowheads; metal-plated armor; and horse trappings. Clear evidence of battle wounds — severe skull injuries, bronze arrowheads embedded in bone — shows that Sarmatian women were indeed warriors. These finds lend credence to Herodotus's story of the "new" tribe of equals, a notion that continues to fascinate men and women today.

ADRIENNE MAYOR

J. H. Blok, *The Early Amazons: Modern and Ancient Perspectives on a Persistent Myth* (1994); Herodotus, *The Histories*, book 4, trans. David Grene (1987); Adrienne Mayor and Josiah Ober, "Amazons," *MHQ: The Quarterly Journal of Military History* (summer 1991): 68–77.

Ambuila, Battle of

October 29, 1665

The Portuguese penetration of West Central Africa began in the Kongo kingdom in 1483, continued with the colonial conquest of Angola starting in 1574, and culminated in the great battle of Ambuila fought on October 29, 1665. A colonial army raised in the Angolan fortress-city of Luanda, commanded by a Luso-African soldier of mixed Portuguese and African parentage, Luis Lopes de Sequeira, with his elite of 450 musketeers, opposed the royal Kongo army, which included a musket regiment of 380 men including 29 Portuguese expatriates and a Luso-African commander, Pedro Dias de Cabral. The Luanda force also hauled two pieces of light field artillery into the mountainous battle zone. The Kongo king, Antonio I, mobilized an irregular force of peasant conscripts (improbably estimated at 100,000 in local lore) and took with him to the battle fourteen chests of precious possessions that he did not dare leave in his capital. He also carried the state archives to prevent rivals from making a bid for power and legitimacy during his absence. Despite his preparations and the size of his army of archers stationed in the wooded hills, the king was killed, along with his African Capuchin chaplain. The Kongo crown and scepter were sent to Lisbon as trophies, and the king's severed head was buried at Luanda with great pomp. His kingdom was laid waste by civil war for the whole of the next generation.

DAVID BIRMINGHAM

American Civil War

1861–1865

The Civil War marked the history of the United States more indelibly than any conflict that preceded or followed it. In fact, not until the end of the Vietnam War (q.v.) did the combined total casualties in all U.S. wars equal the Civil War's totals. The root cause of the conflict lay in the South's economy, which depended on a system that utilized the labor of Black slaves to grow certain crops, particularly cotton and tobacco. As the United States expanded in the nineteenth century, the contrast between the economic systems of the North and South exacerbated tensions. The election of Abraham Lincoln (q.v.), leader of the Republican Party (which possessed strong abolitionist sentiments), brought the quarrel to a head in late 1860.

The states of the Deep South immediately seceded; Lincoln's call for volunteers after the South Carolina militia shelled the federal garrison of Fort Sumter in early April 1861 caused Virginia, North Carolina, Tennessee, and Arkansas to join the rebellion.

A superficial comparison of the opposing sides seemed to favor the North. The former possessed a population of twenty-six million, far exceeding the South's nine million; moreover, nearly three million of the South's population were slaves — unavailable for military service and representing a serious threat of insurrection. The North also possessed nearly all the industrial resources in the United States, most of the nation's financial resources, and most of its railroads.

But the South, which remained on the defensive for much of the conflict, enjoyed some substantial advantages. Its vast geographical expanse played a major role in its lengthy resistance. Taken together, Mississippi and Alabama by themselves are slightly larger than the entire area of the former West German state. The distance from central Georgia to northern Virginia is approximately the same distance as that from East Prussia to Moscow, and the distance from central Texas to Richmond exceeds the distance from the Franco-German border to Moscow, a distance that Napoleon (q.v.) traveled in 1812. The fact that substantial portions of the South were primeval wilderness exacerbated the problems of distance. To supply the North's military operations in the West, railroads had to transport the industrial production of the East fifteen hundred miles to Cairo, Illinois, where its operations down the Mississippi and into Tennessee only *began*.

At the start, neither side had any sense of the magnitude of the tasks on which they were embarking. The tiny army of the United States was a constabulary force that barely provided enough soldiers to intimidate the Indians. The United States had waged a war against Mexico (see *Mexican War*), but that conflict had provided only a glimmering of the problems of mobilization and conducting war over long distances. Following secession, most Southern officers resigned their commissions and returned to their states to join the Confederate militia. In the North, however, the federal army maintained control over most of its officers, leaving the volunteer regiments for the most part in the hands of amateurs. This situation gave Southern forces an advantage, particularly in the East, during the war's first year.

"The Home of a Rebel Sharpshooter, Gettysburg" (1863) was taken by Alexander Gardner, a member of Mathew Brady's famed photographic corps that brought the camera to the battlefield. For many Americans, the reality of the war was and still is defined by the work of these photographers.

But what remains inexplicable is the considerable contrast between the eastern and western theaters in terms of the performance of the opposing forces. Unfortunately, the disparity in the military effectiveness of the armies has to a great extent eluded historians. All too often, histories of the war have depicted Southern troops as an idealized country folk, trained and prepared for war by their youth on farms, whereas Northern troops, living in dank factory slums, were incapable of fighting. In fact, 85 percent of the North's population lived on farms; and if Northern armies had a difficult time against Confederate forces in the eastern theater, their comrades in the West dominated their Southern opponents throughout the war. The performance of Northern and Southern armies had less to do with the makeup of the armies — they were all drawn from similar backgrounds — than with the particular styles of leadership and battle effectiveness

that resulted from idiosyncratic factors, such as the ability of senior leaders including Ulysses S. Grant (q.v.), Robert E. Lee (q.v.), George B. McClellan (q.v.), and Braxton Bragg to impose their personalities on the character of the armies they led.

At the start of the war, General Winfield Scott (q.v.) proposed the "Anaconda Plan" to defeat the South by imposing a blockade, opening up the Mississippi River (thus splitting the South in two), and capturing the Confederacy's capital, Richmond. Although these lines of approach played an important role in the eventual Union victory, they provided no means to strike at the will of the Southern population, nor did they threaten the South's heartland. Nevertheless, the North came off much better in 1861, the first year of the war, because it maintained control over the border states. In Maryland and Missouri, Lincoln and his supporters disregarded the most basic constitutional

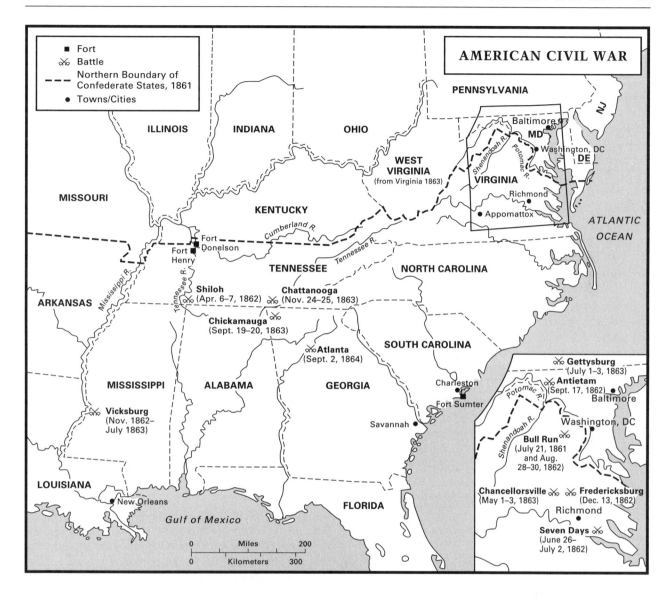

AMERICAN CIVIL WAR

Legend:
■ Fort
⚔ Battle
— — Northern Boundary of Confederate States, 1861
● Towns/Cities

protections, including habeas corpus, in order to crush Southern sympathizers; in Kentucky, Northern political skill and Southern mistakes preserved the state for the Union. On the battlefield, matters were less successful for the North: Union politicians and the president pushed General Erwin McDowell to advance on Confederate forces in Virginia before his troops were ready. The result was the closely fought Battle of Bull Run. But at the end of the day, Union forces fell apart, the first of many defeats in the East.

The first crucial move of the war came in early 1862, when troops under command of Grant captured Forts Donelson and Henry. Grant was a West Pointer with an impressive record in the Mexican War who had fallen on hard times, partially because of a drinking problem. But the call-up of volunteer regiments gave him his opportunity; appointed to command an Illinois volunteer regiment, Grant's extraordinary clarity of mind and unruffled leadership moved him rapidly up the chain of command in the West. By seizing these forts, Grant's forces gained control of the mouths of the Tennessee and Cumberland Rivers near their confluence with the Mississippi. Now Union gunboats could project naval power all the way up the Tennessee to Muscle Shoals in Alabama, thus cutting the only east-west railroad in the South and allowing the Union to reach deep into central Tennessee, the heartland of the Confederacy.

By early April, Grant's army, still learning the rudiments of military service, came under a murderous Southern counterattack at Shiloh, Tennessee. Caught by surprise, Grant's forces came close to defeat, but the Confederates proved as badly trained. Reinforced over the night, Union forces were able to drive the Confederates off the field. But the casualty bill for the two-day battle was terrible. Grant himself claimed in his memoirs that the ferocity of Shiloh convinced him that only a war of "complete conquest" would settle the conflict. But the advantages that Grant had gained at Donelson, Henry, and Shiloh were frittered away by the senior leadership in the West, who possessed neither drive nor strategic wisdom. Nevertheless, the North had already established the basis for future campaigns to open up the Mississippi and drive through Tennessee into Georgia.

In the East, General McClellan regrouped and retrained what became known as the Army of the Potomac. After a long delay, he finally moved against Richmond in April 1862; but after arriving close enough to see its church spires, he found himself under a series of savage attacks organized by General Lee, the new commander of the Confederate Army of Northern Virginia. Union troops gave as good as they got, but McClellan lost what little nerve he possessed, and the Peninsular campaign collapsed. That stinging defeat was followed by the defeat of Union forces at the Second Battle of Bull Run at the end of August.

Lee next determined to invade Maryland. McClellan, now defending, possessed every advantage, including a copy of Lee's strategic planning; never-the-less, he botched the battle. At Antietam (q.v.) the Army of the Potomac launched three massive assaults, each of which almost succeeded: but Lee's forces held, and when the day was over the casualties were higher than on any other day in U.S. military history. At least the draw allowed Lincoln to issue the Emancipation Proclamation, which freed the slaves. Not many weeks after the battle, Lincoln replaced McClellan with Ambrose Burnside (q.v.). It proved to be a disastrous choice. Burnside threw his troops against Lee's entrenched army at Fredericksburg that December, and another slaughter resulted.

The year 1863 did not bring much better results in the East. Another new general, "Fighting Joe" Hooker, launched the Army of the Potomac into the Wilderness in northern Virginia and caught Lee by surprise. But the Confederates recovered quickly: Lee held greatly superior Union forces at bay, while "Stone-wall" Jackson (q.v.) outflanked Hooker at Chancellorsville (q.v.). The resulting attack nearly shattered the Army of the Potomac, broke Hooker, and gave Lee his greatest victory. But Lee's ablest lieutenant, Jackson, was mortally wounded. Lee then invaded the North in pursuit of a "decisive" victory to end the war. The outcome was a three-day battle at the Pennsylvania town of Gettysburg (q.v.) on July 1–3, which finally brought the Army of the Potomac a success — an achievement due more to the spirit of its soldiers than the intelligence of its leaders.

Union forces in the West in 1863 were more successful. In May, Grant moved south of Vicksburg and then launched one of the most brilliant campaigns of the war, driving Confederate forces back into the city. On July 4, the day after Gettysburg ended, he received the surrender of the city and its army, a victory that split the South in two and opened up the Mississippi. Unfortunately, General Henry Halleck, chief of staff in Washington, D.C., then dispersed Grant's forces. Meanwhile, a second great western army rolled through central and western Tennessee toward Georgia; but at the Battle of Chickamauga, Union mistakes combined with Confederate reinforcements from the East to result in a major defeat.

Lincoln immediately responded by giving Grant command of the western theater. Major reinforcements from the Army of the Potomac, twenty-five thousand men and all their equipment, moved twelve hundred miles west in less than two weeks. Grant quickly struck to relieve Chattanooga and in late November at Lookout Mountain gained a victory that scattered Confederate forces and secured Union control of Tennessee. Lincoln quite rightly rewarded him with the command of all Union forces.

Grant's strategy for 1864 involved a concentric advance by Union armies into the South; several of the moves failed because of the incompetence of political generals, but Grant understood their importance for maintaining support back home. The Army of the Potomac came under Grant's overall direction, while General William T. Sherman (q.v.) led the western armies. Beginning in May the Army of the Potomac launched a series of costly assaults on Lee's forces; casualties on both sides were horrific. Nevertheless, by summer's end Grant had pinned Lee to Richmond and destroyed the Army of Northern Virginia's offensive capabilities.

The war's decisive campaign came in the West. Sherman drove Confederate forces back on Atlanta;

frustrated by retreat, Richmond placed the aggressive John Bell Hood in command. Hood launched a series of attacks around Atlanta that wrecked his army. At this point Sherman made one of the crucial decisions of the war. With Grant's permission, he left a portion of his forces to cover middle Tennessee. With the rest he cut loose from his supply lines and struck across a defenseless Georgia. By now Union strategy had reached its final, pitiless conclusion: an outright war on the South's population. Sherman's troops carried out a wholesale wrecking of the South's infrastructure as they advanced toward Savannah. Similarly, in August Grant sent General Philip Sheridan to turn Virginia's Shenandoah Valley into "a barren waste . . . so that crows flying over for the balance of the season will have to carry their provender with them." In the end, the combination of Union victories on the battlefield with the destruction of the South's economic and political infrastructure finally led to the collapse of Southern morale.

The Civil War was the first modern war — one in which military power, resting on popular support and the mass products of industrialization, approached the boundaries of "total war." Neither the strategic vision nor the military capabilities to project military power over continental distances existed at the beginning. As the war continued, its conduct became steadily more savage; by 1865 Union armies had destroyed much of the South, leaving a collection of "Chimney-villes," in the derisive words of Sherman's soldiers. It would take the South over one hundred years to rejoin the Union fully, and a part of the war's legacy would be the vicious racism that marks much of the history of the United States. But in the end Lincoln and military leaders like Grant and Sherman had maintained the Union; in Lincoln's words, "the last best hope of earth" had survived.

WILLIAMSON MURRAY

Shelby Foote, *The Civil War: A Narrative History* (1958–1974); James McPherson, *Battle Cry of Freedom* (1988).

The American Revolution

1775–1781

The dates are misleading. Those years between Lexington and Yorktown (q.v.), or even the culminating Treaty of Paris, do not begin to encompass the process that became known as the American Revolution. As

John Adams suggested, it was in the hearts and minds of the colonists for a decade and more before 1775, and it was not complete until a constitution had been written and a president inaugurated. Even then, of course, there was no real denouement, because what we tend to think of narrowly as the war of the Revolution was in fact much more than a series of military campaigns — it was a profound social as well as political upheaval, and a force that has inspired the people of other countries until this day.

Before, during, and immediately after the military conflict, a ferment of ideas — argued and discussed by an assemblage of remarkable men whose likes have rarely been seen — produced an innovative combination of republicanism and federalism that would serve as a model form of government for humankind, offering fresh political opportunities.

What erupted in America in 1775 was something altogether novel in the world — the specter of a colonial people revolting against authority, with freedom as their goal. That was what made it so very difficult for the British to comprehend, for they believed they already *were* the freest people on the face of the earth (dangerously so, it was thought by their European rivals). Before it came to blows, London saw its fractious colonists grow ever more unruly and uncompromising in their demands for more freedom and less governmental control. This was a day when the family was a unit, its structure patriarchal, its authority unchallenged and sacrosanct, and the symbolic father of the family that comprised the British Empire was George III, against whom no threat could be tolerated. Indeed, for a long time most colonists considered their quarrel to be with Parliament, not their king.

The American Revolution had two faces — one intellectual, the other military — and the second had to succeed if the ideas and ideals of the first were to survive. Beginning with the outbreaks of violence in and around Boston, what was at first little more than a police action by the British military became a full-scale war on sea and land, from the coastal plain to the far reaches of the frontier. At its core was the electrifying document known as the Declaration of Independence, proclaimed by Congress in July 1776, which transformed the struggle into what was at once a war of liberation and a civil war, a conflict that set friends and family members against one another and eventually became a worldwide conflagration.

No one knows for certain how many of the two and one-half million to three million provincials (600,000 of them slaves) took up arms, but at no time did the number approach what would today be considered a reasonable percentage of the available able-bodied men. In ideological terms, contemporaries estimated that one-third of the Americans supported the rebellion, another third opposed it, and the final third remained neutral and took no side.

After the almost accidental exchange of shots on Lexington Green, the countryside for miles around was aroused, with men and boys off the farms harrying the king's troops through Concord and all the way back to Boston. This had the unexpected effect of rallying support beyond the borders of Massachusetts, and two months later a rebel army threw up an earthen fort on Breed's Hill. When General Thomas Gage's redcoats rose to the challenge and attacked, they came within a hair's breadth of defeat. What was known ever after as the Battle of Bunker Hill proved to the British that the Americans would fight. The engagements at Trenton and Princeton showed that they *could* fight. And Saratoga (q.v.) demonstrated that they could win. But the rebel military triumphs were few, and whether they won the war or the British lost it is a trade-off.

As much as anything else, monumental logistical problems cost Britain its American colonies. On the eve of the conflict, the British Empire was the greatest empire since Rome, but in the absence of any real wish on the part of the king and his cabinet for reconciliation, the exacting laws of time and distance soon took their toll on the chances for victory. Despite the odds favoring a quick triumph, every redcoated soldier, every item of the army's food and equipment and weaponry, had to be shipped across three thousand miles of ocean — a voyage that often took three months — and the wastage and delays were appalling.

When France, followed by Spain and the Netherlands, entered the war on the side of America, Britain was forced to confront a threat it had always managed to avoid: an alliance of maritime foes undistracted by a conflict in Europe. That fact severely limited the resources that could be arrayed against the rebels, and London elected to move the focus of the war to the South, where the British could rely heavily (it was thought) on Loyalist support. The plan very nearly succeeded, but as a Frenchman observed, even if well-disciplined British troops did subdue the American people, "the country of America was unconquerable." George Washington (q.v.) and his generals capitalized on that advantage by substituting a guerrilla-style war of maneuver for the European battle tactics in which two armies met head to head. As Nathanael Greene (q.v.) put it, "We fight, get beat, rise, and fight again," and in 1781 he proved his point by winning a major campaign without ever really winning a battle.

For the Americans who fought the war — and only a handful stuck it out with the army from start to finish — it was a miracle of survival. Theirs was, after all, a predominantly agricultural society in which farmers had to till their fields and harvest their crops whether a war was being fought or not, and because of that all-important fact, it was all but impossible to keep an army in existence. How close the war came to ending in defeat was never clearer than on what may have been its darkest day — December 30, 1776. George Washington and the ragged, hungry remnants of the Continental army had surprised and defeated the enemy garrison at Trenton. Now all but a handful had one day of service remaining before their enlistments were up and they headed for home. Washington desperately wanted a few more weeks from them, to give the country one more victory. But when he rode out in front of these dirty, suffering men standing bare-legged in the snow and appealed to them to stay with him, not one soldier moved. The general wheeled his horse around and made one last, impassioned request, saying that only they could surmount "the crisis which is to decide our destiny." Then, and only then, did one man, then another and another, step forth, pledging to stay for another month.

In the final analysis, the ability of America's militiamen to come together quickly at a certain locale for a limited period of time was enough to confound and defeat the British. That is what occurred most notably at the siege of Boston and at Saratoga, accounting for victory at both places. By remaining alive long enough to convince the king of France that revenge against the British was finally possible, the ordinary citizen soldiers of America were the agents responsible for the French commitment of ships and money and the matériel of war that made possible the final military triumph at Yorktown (q.v.).

With or without the aid that finally came, the Americans knew all along that they had everything to gain from victory and everything to lose from defeat. In the face of every conceivable discouragement, they fought on, and with each passing month the possibility grew that independence could be achieved. Although it was truly a wonder that anything resembling unity among the states was possible, given the rivalries and profound differences between them, a good part of the answer lies in a line written in a soldier's diary after the Battle of Saratoga: "We had Something more at Stake than fighting for six Pence Pr Day."

Across the Atlantic, the people of Britain lost the will to keep going, for the cost became too high. As George III's former prime minister, Lord North, sorrowfully admitted in 1783, the war in America had been popular at the beginning, "eagerly embraced by the people and Parliament. . . . Nor did it ever cease to be popular until a series of unparalleled disasters and calamities caused the people wearied out with almost uninterrupted ill-success and misfortune, to call out as loudly for peace as they had formerly done for war."

RICHARD M. KETCHUM

John R. Alden, *A History of the American Revolution* (1989); *American Heritage History of the American Revolution: The History of America's Struggle for Independence*, rev. ed. (1984).

Amiens, Battle of

August 8–11, 1918

Following the failure of the 1918 German spring offensives and the successful French counterstroke on the Marne in July, the Allies turned to their own offensive on August 8 in the Amiens sector. The Amiens offensive finally ended Erich Ludendorff's (q.v.) hopes for further attacks and indeed persuaded the German high command that the war must be ended. Amiens was therefore a turning point on the Western Front. But Amiens is also significant because this battle was a well-prepared combination of several arms.

The Fourth Army commander, Henry Rawlinson, combined for this attack eleven divisions (three British, four Canadian, four Australian) comprising 75,000 men, more than 500 tanks, 1,900 aircraft (including French planes), and 2,000 guns. Against this formidable array, the German defenses consisted of 37,000 men, 530 guns, and 369 planes. Moreover, German defenses were not well prepared, whereas Rawlinson achieved surprise through wireless deception (including periods of radio silence and fake messages from other parts of the line), the last-minute deployment of the Canadian Corps, and movement of troops and matériel entirely by night.

The offensive opened at 4:20 A.M. on August 8 and achieved immediate success. The troops and tanks

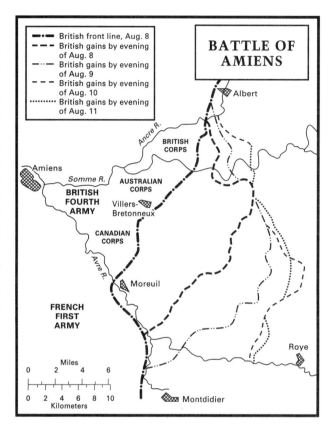

BATTLE OF AMIENS

- ━·━·━ British front line, Aug. 8
- ━ ━ ━ British gains by evening of Aug. 8
- ━·━·━ British gains by evening of Aug. 9
- ─ ─ ─ British gains by evening of Aug. 10
- ·········· British gains by evening of Aug. 11

Albert

Ancre R.

BRITISH CORPS

Amiens

Somme R.

AUSTRALIAN CORPS

BRITISH FOURTH ARMY

Villers-Bretonneux

CANADIAN CORPS

Avre R.

Moreuil

FRENCH FIRST ARMY

Roye

Miles
0   2   4   6

Kilometers
0 2 4 6 8 10

Montdidier

advanced eight miles, capturing 400 guns and causing 27,000 casualties, including 12,000 prisoners. In contrast, the spearhead of the attack, the Australians and Canadians, suffered but 6,500 casualties. The success of the first day had been due to surprise, the drive and firepower of the infantry, the large number of tanks, and counterbattery dominance.

The offensive was resumed over the next three days, but disorganization and stiffening German resistance limited the advance, and Rawlinson was convinced to end the battle by the Canadian Corps commander, Arthur Currie. Nevertheless, the offensive dealt a fatal blow to the German cause. For Ludendorff, "August 8th was the black day of the German Army in the history of the war."

TIM TRAVERS

Anglo-Dutch Wars

1652–1654, 1665–1667, 1672–1674, 1780–1784

The first Anglo-Dutch conflict originated when the aggressive new Republican regime in Britain, following victory in the English Civil Wars (q.v.), began to stop and search any merchant ship, even if neutral, and to confiscate any Royalist goods found aboard. The Dutch Republic, with the largest carrying trade in Europe, found these practices unacceptable and in 1652 resolved to challenge them, even though, in the pessimistic assessment of one of their leaders, "The English are about to attack a mountain of gold, while we are about to attack a mountain of iron."

In a series of bloody battles in the North Sea and English Channel, and through the capture of more than one thousand Dutch vessels within a year, Britain forced recognition of its claims. However, even as they admitted defeat in 1654, at the instigation of M. H. Tromp (q.v.) the Dutch government laid down sixty new warships to form the core of a standing navy. It intervened effectively in the Baltic to maintain a balance of power favorable to Dutch commercial interests in 1658 and 1660, and in 1665 went to war against Britain, which had attacked Dutch shipping in the Mediterranean and captured Dutch colonies in West Africa and North America (including New Amsterdam, taken in 1664 and renamed New York). This time Britain faced a better-armed adversary: indeed, in 1667 a daring raid by the Dutch navy caught the British fleet at anchor in the river Medway, burned six ships, and towed away the flagship. At the peace that followed, Britain kept only New York. Again, from 1672 through 1674, British aggression failed in the face of superb Dutch seamanship and combat effectiveness.

These naval actions involved huge fleets. Although more men and ships had fought in 1571 at Lepanto (q.v.), the firepower involved in the battles of the Anglo-Dutch wars was far greater (4,233 guns aboard seventy-five Dutch warships at the North Sea battle of Kijkduin in 1673). Moreover, during the twenty battles fought, the two sides perfected a new basic naval tactic: two fleets blasting away in a single line of battle that stretched up to ten miles.

One hundred and ten years later, in 1780, Britain declared war on the Dutch again, through frustration at the quantity of goods carried to the rebellious American colonies (see *American Revolution*) and their French allies by neutral Dutch shipping. After one indecisive battle, the Dutch fleet stayed in port until peace was signed in 1783.

GEOFFREY PARKER

Animals

Animals have been humanity's wartime allies since the dawn of history — and probably before. A surprisingly wide range of species — horses, elephants, dogs, and birds among them — have served in a variety of roles: as beasts of burden, mounts, guards and alarms, messengers — even as weapons.

Doubtless the most important animals of war have been the least remarkable: the necessary legions of pack and draft animals. Before the internal combustion engine, armies depended on animals in staggering numbers. In the seventeenth century an authority calculated that a modest artillery train of 15 cannon required 490 horses to pull the equipment alone — more would be required for the 239 wagons carting powder, shot, odd tools and supplies, and the officers' personal effects. And these horse-drawn wagons represented only one-quarter of the 944 needed by even a small European army of 15,000 men. In 1799 a joint Anglo-Indian army traveled with at least 85,000 bullocks, their route of march covering an area of eighteen square miles; in 1897 another British force in India, of 44,000 men, still required 60,000 draft animals. And what was an army's single greatest supply item, by volume? Fodder for all the animals — a logistical fact through World War I (q.v.).

But animals have also served in the front lines. Before the medieval invention of the horse collar made it an efficient draft animal, the horse was bred almost exclusively for war, hunting, and racing — the horse was considered the war animal par excellence from the end of the Bronze Age (when the chariot revolutionized warfare) through the nineteenth century. Armies only grudgingly gave up horses after World War I and still retain them for crack ceremonial units.

Other animals have carried men into battle. The armies of the Arab conquest found that strong-smelling camels spooked opposing Byzantine cavalry horses and could carry them through deserts impenetrable to their enemies in order to deliver surprise attacks. Elephants — aggressive as well as huge — with crews of archers, javelin throwers, and pikemen — terrorized the battlefields of the ancient world from Numidia to Burma. Their mahouts often carried a hammer and spike to pierce the animal's spinal cord should the beast, maddened by wounds, dust, noise, and strange smells, swerve from the enemy and plunge toward friendly ranks.

The dogs of war have been more than a phrase. Ancient Greeks occasionally used dogs in battle, and Spanish conquistadores (q.v.) hunted Peruvian Indians with mastiffs. In World War II (q.v.) the Soviet army trained dogs, with antitank mines strapped to their backs, to seek out Nazi tanks; but when released on the battlefield, the dogs indiscriminately aimed for Russian tanks as well. Dogs have been more successfully trained to sniff out land mines and have most often been used as guard animals. During the Peloponnesian War (q.v.) the barking of a dog named Sorter alerted Corinth to a sneak attack: the grateful citizens erected a monument to Sorter and forty-nine other canine guards, all civic heroes.

Birds have a surprisingly full war record. In 386 B.C. a flock of geese warned Rome of a Gallic attack; two millennia later, the U.S. Army experimented with alarm geese in Vietnam (q.v.). The homing pigeon has long been used for wartime communication. During the 1870 siege of Paris, pigeons carrying microphotograph dispatches (allowing each bird to carry the equivalent of over twenty thousand messages) reached the city from as far away as London. Lacking radios, some World War I tanks carried pigeons to release through miniature armored trapdoors, and ground troops advanced with portable pigeon lofts to supplement field telephones.

Finally, animals have also been used as weapons. An eleventh-century Viking, Harald Hardradi, besieging a town in Sicily, noticed that birds nesting in the eaves of the city's thatched houses foraged in the surrounding fields. He had some captured; daubed them with an inflammable mixture of fir shavings, wax, and sulfur; and then set them alight — whereupon they flew to their roosts and set the town ablaze. This story has a twentieth-century parallel. During World War II, American scientists developed the bat bomb: an aerial munition designed to release thousands of live bats, each equipped with a tiny incendiary device (one of the first applications of napalm), high over a highly combustible target, a Japanese city of paper and wood houses. Amazingly, before the program folded, field trials showed some promise, accidently torching a newly finished barracks and water tower. Pentagon opposition included one officer who confused the bat bomb program with the atom bomb project.

THOMAS F. ARNOLD

The third-century Vietnamese heroine Trieu Au rides an elephant to war against China. Intelligent, trainable, and the largest land animal in the world, the elephant has been used in warfare since ancient times.

An Lu-shan Rebellion

A.D. 755–763

Led by An Lu-shan, a Chinese frontier commander, this military revolt nearly brought down the T'ang dynasty and marked a major watershed in Chinese history. The rebellion was made possible by the establishment of permanent frontier armies composed of long-service professional troops, many of non-Chinese origin, who felt more loyalty toward their own immediate commanders than to the distant imperial court. But its immediate cause was the deadly rivalry between An Lu-shan, who commanded some 200,000 men from his headquarters near today's Peking, and Yang Kuo-chung, the dominant minister at the capital, Ch'ang-an. An set his army in motion on December 16, 755. With few troops in the interior of the empire capable of standing against them, the rebels gained possession of Ch'ang-an by the autumn of 756. This was the high-water mark of the rebellion. Increasingly violent and unstable, An was himself murdered at the beginning of 757; by the autumn of that year, loyalist troops recalled from other sectors of the frontier recaptured Ch'ang-an. Fighting continued to rage back and forth across the North China Plain until 762, when loyalist forces broke the back of rebel resistance in a climactic battle at Lo-yang.

Although the T'ang dynasty would survive for another century and a half, the power of the imperial court was a pale shadow of what it had been in the prerebellion years. Centralized rule was replaced by provincial autonomy as many loyalist commanders joined the ex-rebels in setting themselves up as regional warlords. The ravages of war spurred the migration of population from North China to the Lower Yangtze region, contributing greatly to its economic growth, and the postrebellion scene was distinguished by new patterns of land tenure, social mobility, and commercial activity that would provide the basis for the great social and economic changes of the Sung period (960–1279). The events of the An Lu-shan rebellion also had a significant impact on Chinese literature. When the aged emperor Hsüan Tsung fled his capital in 756, mutinous guardsmen forced the execution of both Yang Kuo-chung and his cousin Yang Kuei-fei — who happened to be the emperor's favorite concubine — in an episode that has provided endless fascination for Chinese poets and dramatists.

DAVID A. GRAFF

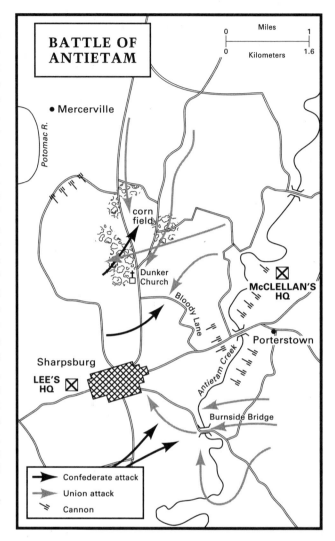

Antietam, Battle of

September 17, 1862

Fought along Antietam Creek, at Sharpsburg, Maryland, this battle brought about America's bloodiest day, the product of Confederate audacity and Union command failure. Following Second Manassas, General Robert E. Lee (q.v.) advanced into Maryland, believing that the potential strategic and political gains justified his defiance of the avowed Confederate defensive policy. Lee's complex operational plan divided his outnumbered force; disaster loomed when a lost copy of that plan came to the Union commander, Major General George B. McClellan (q.v.). Slow, cautious, and defensive-minded, however, McClellan wasted all the advantages of his lucky discovery and his two-

to-one numerical superiority. The battleground Lee selected was well suited for defense but dangerous as well, having the Potomac River behind him. McClellan planned to overwhelm Lee's left flank but failed to exercise command control, so the combat diffused south along the battle line. The first four hours of fighting, much of it across farmer David Miller's thirty-acre cornfield, were indecisive. Next came a series of bloody head-on attacks against Lee's center that finally overran the area afterward called Bloody Lane. The last action of the day was against Lee's right, where Union troops pierced the line (weakened to reinforce other sections) but were stopped by late-arriving Confederate reinforcements. Lee withdrew across the river on September 18, suffering 10,318 casualties (of 38,000 engaged) to McClellan's 12,401 (of 75,000). The draw that the Union claimed as a victory provided the Lincoln administration enough justification to issue the preliminary Emancipation Proclamation. A series of graphic battlefield photographs of the dead, taken by Alexander Gardner, brought to the home front "the terrible earnestness of war."

NOAH ANDRE TRUDEAU

Anzio, Battle of

January 22–May 23, 1944

By the end of 1943 the Italian campaign had become a stalemate as Field Marshal Albert Kesselring's (q.v.) German army group stopped the Allied advance cold at Cassino. The Allied ground commander in chief, General Sir Harold Alexander (q.v.), concluded that he could not take Rome unless the Allies initiated an amphibious end run and weakened the Cassino front by drawing off German troops manning the Gustav Line. Operation Shingle, one of the most ill-conceived operations of the war, took place thirty-five miles southwest of Rome on January 22, 1944, when a corps-sized Anglo-American expeditionary force commanded by U.S. major general John P. Lucas landed at Anzio and Nettuno.

Alexander believed that if the expeditionary force seized the Alban Hills northeast of Anzio, it could block German resupply of Cassino, thus compelling Kesselring to abandon the Gustav Line and retreat to the Apennines. Lucas recognized that the Anzio force could not hold both the Alban Hills and a vital logistical lifeline to the port of Anzio, and elected merely to establish a beachhead outside Anzio and Nettuno.

Kesselring quickly contained the Allied threat and massed German troops. In mid-February, they carried out Adolf Hitler's (q.v.) order to "lance the abscess south of Rome" with a massive counteroffensive aimed at destroying the beachhead. A series of furious attacks failed to break the Allied line in what one historian has described as "a charge of the Light Brigade without the horses... sheer slaughter."

Lucas was relieved of command even though he had been given a mission he had no practical possibility of carrying out. After a four-month stalemate during which British and American losses totaled seven thousand killed, thirty-six thousand wounded or missing, and forty-four thousand hospitalized from various nonbattle injuries and sickness, the siege of Anzio finally ended on May 23, 1944, when the Allies launched a breakout offensive.

CARLO W. D'ESTE

Appeasement

Appeasement is among the most protean and the most controversial concepts of international politics. The word came into common currency in Britain during the era between the two world wars of the twentieth century. Those who coined it had in mind a policy of reducing tensions and averting a new war by addressing the grievances of powers dissatisfied with the status quo. From this perspective, appeasement represented the elevation of considerations of morality and justice over considerations of power. It resonated with liberal concepts of international politics that had become prominent since the mid–nineteenth century and that seemed to have been vindicated by the lessons of the war of 1914–1918. It played upon a sense of guilt over the putative harshness of the Treaty of Versailles (q.v.) of 1919. Neville Chamberlain and other policy makers in Britain (and elsewhere) were conditioned by this climate of opinion.

After Chamberlain, along with French premier Édouard Daladier, endorsed the transfer of Czech territory to Adolf Hitler's (q.v.) Germany at the Munich Conference of 1938, appeasement took on a quite different meaning. Now it amounted to a capitulation to threats or, more broadly, a failure to use force to combat aggression, all in a vain effort to avoid war. Critics of appeasement drew this lesson from the 1930s: efforts to appease dictators by democracies operating from a position of weakness served only to encourage further aggressive behavior and make a world war more likely.

This lesson has cast a long shadow. The desire to avoid appeasement, or charges of appeasement, cut short the Roosevelt administration's search for a modus vivendi with Japan before the attack on Pearl Harbor (q.v.) in 1941. Later the charge of appeasement was leveled against Franklin Roosevelt (q.v.) for the concessions that he made to Joseph Stalin (q.v.) over Eastern Europe and China at the Yalta Conference in 1945. When Harry Truman made the decision to intervene in the Korean War (q.v.) in 1950, he was inspired by the experience of the 1930s. When General Douglas MacArthur (q.v.) heard of proposals to curtail his drive to the Yalu River in the autumn of 1950, he retorted that they were tantamount to appeasement. British prime minister Anthony Eden invoked memories of the 1930s to justify his use of force in 1956 against Egyptian leader Gamal Abdel Nasser's nationalization of the Suez Canal (see *Arab-Israeli Wars*). In unleashing Operation Desert Storm in the Gulf War (q.v.), President George Bush, having tried unsuccessfully to appease Saddam Hussein before Iraq's invasion of Kuwait in August 1990, drew an analogy between Saddam and Hitler. In 1995, seeking more effective military action in Bosnia, French president Jacques Chirac likened Western policy there to appeasement in the 1930s.

A number of scholars, meanwhile, had long since grown uneasy with the historical understanding of appeasement that informed public discourse and policy debates. Some historians pointed out that the concept had, over time, lost any precise meaning. Others suggested that Chamberlain's appeasement of Hitler in the 1930s was not extraordinary when seen in historical perspective. A few noted that sometimes, as with British appeasement of the United States at the turn of the twentieth century, concessions had led to reconciliation, not war.

Of course, the United States of William McKinley's era had virtually nothing in common with the Germany of Adolf Hitler. That is precisely the point of historical scholarship: each instance of appeasement must be judged in its own context. At any given time and place, appeasement is one diplomatic strategy that must be compared to other diplomatic and military strategies in terms of their likely risks and rewards and in light of an assessment of the intentions and capabilities of the power to be appeased or resisted. Chamberlain had many good political, economic, and military reasons to try to appease Hitler in 1938. What Chamberlain failed sufficiently to appreciate was that Hitler was determined to fight for hegemony over Europe sooner or later. Appeasement was almost certainly the worst possible policy for dealing with the German dictator, but there was probably no diplomatic or military strategy that could have deflected or deterred Hitler from the war that he so ardently desired. After World War II (q.v.), Western leaders were fortunate to have more potent instru-

ments of deterrence and, in most cases, more deflectable adversaries.

BRADFORD A. LEE

Martin Gilbert, *The Roots of Appeasement* (1966); Williamson Murray, *The Change in the European Balance of Power, 1938–1939* (1984).

Arab-Israeli Wars

1947–1948, 1956, 1967, 1973, 1982

The extension of European nationalism to Jews yielded Zionism, a movement to re-create a Jewish nation in the lands of the Bible. Jewish immigration to Palestine grew steadily and took on added meaning — and gained added external support — in the wake of the Holocaust. The Arab world strongly opposed these developments, however, and when the British decided to wash their hands of Arab-Israeli skirmishing in 1947–1948, the stage was set for a direct confrontation.

The United Nations proposed the creation of both a Jewish and an Arab state in Palestine, but the Arabs refused; when the state of Israel was proclaimed in May 1948, forces from the surrounding countries attacked together. The results surprised many: the Israelis proved that loose militias fighting for a cause could be swiftly transformed into a competent army, whereas the Arabs found that without military professionalism, initiative, or a unified command, their superior numbers and equipment meant little. The Israelis stalemated the Syrians and the Iraqis, as well as the impressive Arab Legion from Jordan, while simultaneously defeating the Egyptians outright.

In 1956 conflict erupted again. The Israelis, threatened by Soviet arms sales to Egypt, and the British and the French, outraged at the nationalization of the Suez Canal, joined forces to attack Egypt by land and sea respectively. Israeli armor performed well, helped by an ill-managed Egyptian withdrawal. Although the British and French actions stopped humiliatingly short under American pressure, Israeli operations gained the Sinai peninsula.

In the late spring of 1967, Gamal Abdel Nasser pushed tensions to the brink again until, responding to the mounting threat, the Israelis unleashed a devastating preemptive air attack. Superb intelligence, planning, and execution resulted in the swift destruc-

Israeli mechanized infantry pass a dead Syrian tank crewman as they move across the Golan Heights during the Yom Kippur War of 1973.

tion of the air forces of Egypt, Jordan, and Syria, accompanied by equally successful blitzkriegs on the ground. The "Six-Day War" ended with Israel in possession of the West Bank and Golan Heights in addition to the Sinai. Arab-Israeli combat was now sophisticated enough for the world to pay attention to its military lessons, and observers noted how tanks and planes still dominated modern warfare.

In the aftermath of the 1967 disaster, Nasser took a different tack, harassing the Israelis with raids and artillery strikes in what became known as the War of Attrition. Arab revenge of a sort came in 1973, when Egypt and Syria struck in unison on Yom Kippur. Strategic and tactical surprise, combined with an overwhelming ratio of forces, led to initial Arab victories in both theaters. Nevertheless, Israeli counterthrusts regained the lost ground and more, and the war stopped when the superpowers intervened to prevent further Arab losses. Once again the world learned military lessons, this time about how surface-to-air missiles and antitank weapons could humble even Israeli planes and armor. (Differential Arab and Israeli performance throughout these wars has also driven home the importance of the human element in war.)

Egypt's postwar peace moves brought back the Sinai (the Camp David accords), and the removal of Egypt from the Arab-Israeli conflict changed the balance irrevocably. Then in 1982 Israel attacked Lebanon: pushing through Palestine Liberation Organization forces with ease, the Israelis soon engaged the Syrians there, crushing their air defenses with methods anticipating the "information warfare" or "military-technical revolution" demonstrated in the Gulf War (q.v.) a decade later.

Ironically, for all their military success against Arab armies, in the late 1980s the Israelis found themselves at a loss when confronted with the spontaneous uprising of Palestinian civilians known as the Intifada. In the wake of the Gulf War and the collapse of the Soviet Union, these events, combined with grudging Arab recognition of Israel's lasting presence, sparked new developments in the peace process. The signing of the Declaration of Principles in 1993 inaugurated a new era of relations between Israelis and Palestinians, followed in 1994 by the Israeli-Jordanian peace treaty. Negotiations between Israel and the Palestinians, Syrians, and Lebanese continue, holding out the prospect that the age of the Arab-Israeli Wars may finally be over.

GIDEON ROSE

Trevor N. Dupuy, *Elusive Victory: The Arab-Israeli Wars, 1947–1974* (1992); Chaim Herzog, *The Arab-Israeli Wars: War and Peace in the Middle East* (1984).

Armada, Spanish

1588

Philip II of Spain's attempt to conquer England in 1588 had been long premeditated. He had already been king consort of England from 1554 to 1558 and had endeavored to secure a Catholic succession in 1558–1559 and 1570–1571, but the Turkish onslaught following Lepanto (q.v.) in 1571 and the outbreak of the Dutch Revolt (q.v.) in 1572 diverted the king's resources for more than a decade. However, Elizabeth of England became alarmed by Spain's growing power — Portugal and her empire were annexed in 1580 and much of the southern Netherlands reconquered after 1582 — and in 1585 she dispatched Sir Francis Drake (q.v.) with a fleet to raid the Spanish Caribbean and an army to assist the Dutch Republic.

Philip II and his ministers now decided that the fate of the entire Spanish monarchy depended upon the destruction of Elizabeth's regime and worked both to secure its diplomatic isolation and to mobilize the ships, men, and munitions necessary for invasion. Because Spain lacked a permanent navy, the fleet was not ready to sail until 1588; and because Philip II's best troops served in the southern Netherlands, the king devised a strategy that required the fleet from Spain to sail up the English Channel and collect his elite forces from the ports of Flanders before landing near Dover.

The plan almost worked. For thirty-six hours in August 1588, the 130 ships of the Armada, carrying twenty thousand reserve troops, lay at anchor off Calais while, twenty-five miles away at Dunkirk, thirty thousand veterans embarked on their transports. The English, however, sent in fire ships, which broke the Armada's order, allowing the twenty or so battleships of the Royal Navy to use their superior firepower to inflict serious damage on the Spaniards and to force them out into the North Sea. Strong winds prevented the Armada from returning to the Channel, and so they returned to Spain by circumnavigating Britain and Ireland. Storms delayed them, damaging the ships further so that some sank and others ran out of supplies. In the end, perhaps one-third of the fleet and one-half of the men aboard perished.

Spain learned several lessons from her errors. Almost immediately, twelve purpose-built warships were laid down in the royal dockyards, and the design of naval guns was improved. Two subsequent attempts at invasion (in 1596 and 1597) involved forces only from the Iberian Peninsula — although storms drove both back before they reached the invasion area. But the cost of open war with England proved crippling: Elizabeth's navy now made regular and costly raids on the coasts of Spain, destroying property, seizing ships, taking hostages; on the high seas and in America, English privateers preyed on Spanish shipping and outposts, causing huge losses and paralyzing trade; and, in the Netherlands, English troops helped the Dutch struggle for independence. When peace with England came in 1604, six years after Philip II's death, Spain's decline as a great power was evident.

GEOFFREY PARKER

Armies

The Western world has come to believe that the words *armed forces* are synonymous with military organizations that possess a high state of discipline and loyalty to the constituted polity. It has not always been so in the Western world (the Middle Ages being a case in

The Ten Most Important Land Battles

Châlons (France, A.D. 451)
Hastings (England, October 14, 1066)
Yorktown (United States, October 1781)
Waterloo (Belgium, June 18, 1815)
Gettysburg (United States, July 1–3, 1863)
Marne (France, September 6–13, 1914)
Khalkin-Gol (Mongolia, August 20–31, 1939)
Battle of Britain (England, July–September 1940)
Stalingrad (Russia, September 1942–February 1943)
D-Day (France, June 6, 1944)

point), nor for the most part have other societies been able to guarantee such a fundamental civil-military relationship (q.v.).

Western military traditions of discipline reach back to the Greeks and Romans; the former created military service that rested on the social cohesion of the *polis*, whereas the Romans developed a far more complex system that depended on a ruthless discipline applied throughout their military forces. As the republic reached for control over the Mediterranean basin, the basic building block of Roman military power — the legion (q.v.) — evolved into a form that Julius Caesar (q.v.) used to subdue Gaul and that enforced the Pax Romana for over two hundred years. Roman soldiers endured perhaps the most ferocious discipline (q.v.) that any army has endured. Their officers and centurions possessed absolute power of life and death over them; day in and day out they practiced the serious business of preparing for war. As the Jewish historian Josephus suggested, "The Romans are sure of victory . . . for their exercises are battles without bloodshed, and their battles bloody exercises." Edward Gibbon was equally to the point: "So sensible were the Romans of the imperfections of valor without skill and practice that, in their language, the name of an army was borrowed from the word [*exercitus*] which signified exercise." Above all, the Romans developed an efficient and effective battle drill (q.v.) — one on which all modern parade ground drill is based — that allowed them to maneuver large numbers of men in close proximity to the enemy so that they could inflict maximum killing on their opponents.

But in the third and fourth centuries A.D., the discipline that had made the Roman army an unparalleled force in military history collapsed. The Romans lost the secret that had allowed them to conquer and maintain an empire across the entire Mediterranean basin. Despite increasingly large forces, their armies could no longer stand up to the barbarians. With the disappearance of the legion, military forces in the West came to resemble armed mobs rather than trained, disciplined military forces.

The warrior culture of the conquering German tribes gradually mutated into the feudal (q.v.) system, which was based on a highly trained and enthusiastically pugnacious class of nobles. Europe's rulers and nobility engaged in a seemingly endless series of wars throughout the Middle Ages. The basis of war was the knight, trained from childhood for combat alone. But though the individual knight constituted a formidable fighting machine, he was fractious, undisciplined, and likely to rebel against his lord; thus he was a thoroughly unreliable instrument.

In fact, the warrior mobs of medieval Europe reflected the norm throughout the history of war outside the West. There were some differences: Chinese armies tended to rely on the empire's numbers; the minimal number of military leaders within the Chinese system enhanced internal peace at the price of effectiveness against external enemies. Arab armies depended on the religious fury of the faithful warrior; the Turks attained greater discipline by employing the warrior caste of janissaries, but obedience to civil authorities always remained a problem. Only the Mongols (q.v.) managed to combine the warrior ethos with a ferocious discipline.

Such warrior forces could achieve considerable feats under extraordinary leadership, but they were largely incapable of acting in a disciplined fashion to further the policies of the state. And that was the problem that the warring Europeans confronted at the end of the Middle Ages. In 1576 the Spanish army, which had almost broken the Dutch Revolt (q.v.), mutinied and sacked Antwerp in an orgy of violence. The Dutch (not surprisingly, considering that Antwerp was friendly to the Spanish cause) decided to continue the revolt. But it was the Thirty Years' War (1618–1648) (q.v.) that displayed in clearest form the unsuitability of Europe's military institutions to serve either the internal or external purposes of the state. By the time that the fighting between the various armed mobs was over, the war had wrecked all of Germany from the Baltic Sea to the Alps.

In his classic, *The Prince*, Niccolò Machiavelli put

his finger on the heart of the problem: "The principal foundations of all states are good laws and good arms; there cannot be good laws where there are not good arms." And in the *Discourses* he noted: "It is necessary to revive the discipline of the ancients, cherish and honor it, and give it life, so that in return it may give reputation to the state." In the seventeenth century, the Europeans set about rectifying the ill discipline of their armed forces. The process began with Maurice of Nassau (q.v.), leader of the Dutch Republic, who explicitly studied the Roman way of war, as Machiavelli had suggested. By using old texts such as those of Vegetius (q.v.), the Dutch re-created the Roman legion in modern form. Roman drill, down to the two-stage command, reappeared, and discipline became the foundation on which military science now revolved.

It was not an easy process — how to introduce discipline where none existed represented a fundamental challenge to military reformers. The fact that the Swedish articles of war, introduced in the 1620s, indicated that soldiers must dig when told to by their officers underlines the fact that obedience had not been the prevailing practice. Gustavus Adolphus's (q.v.) improvements on Maurice's reforms were crucial to the creation of an army in the sense of what the Romans meant by the word, a force disciplined to serve the civil and military authorities. The Swedes also introduced a system of taxation and local recruiting (q.v.) to support the new structure.

But the French were the great translators of the Swedish reforms in the mid–seventeenth century. Under Louis XIV's (q.v.) driving leadership, they created a highly disciplined army that allowed Louis to impose absolutism on France and threaten his neighbors with French hegemony. The difficulty in incorporating the Roman way of war into an armed force involved the state's responsibility to ensure payment and food for the soldiers in the ranks (no matter what their training, if soldiers are not fed and paid, discipline will collapse); this in return required a complex and efficient bureaucracy to collect taxes and pay the soldiers. And out of that relationship arose the creation of the modern bureaucratic system and the state itself. France's success in this process threatened Europe's stability. Not only was the French army a threat, but the French state now possessed undreamed-of resources. With their survival on the line, the English, the Dutch, and the Hapsburgs adapted.

By the early eighteenth century, the Europeans pos-sessed disciplined, organized military forces, capable of projecting the state's power externally and maintaining order within. The Europeans transferred the discipline of their armies to the seas and soon had navies that could reach out across the world's oceans. The new military system, controlled by Europeans, was exportable. In the eighteenth century, the East India Company organized and trained a force of local Indians, sepoys (q.v.), in European methods. The conquest of India soon followed.

But in 1793 the French Revolution changed the nature of European politics and armies. Confronted in 1793 by a war that they had ignited (which would eventually turn into the Wars of the French Revolution [q.v.]), the French assembly decreed a *levée en masse* and, invoking the spirit of French nationalism, rallied their people to the defense of the nation. Within a year they had put an additional one million soldiers in the field and overturned the strategic and operational framework in the Low Countries, the Rhineland, and Italy. Initially, the French ran into considerable problems in disciplining their new forces, but by combining experienced old regiments with enthusiastic new troops, they gained the best capabilities of both. The revolutionary French army was soon a disciplined, effective battle force, but it derived its spirited dedication from the ideals of revolutionary nationalism.

The French Revolution provided a model of the army of the future: one that combined nationalism, discipline, and ideological commitment. The model would become applicable even to the armies of non-Western nations in the twentieth century, as those enthusiastic pupils of the French — the Vietnamese — so aptly proved in the struggle against their tutors and the Americans. For much of the nineteenth century, European nations fought this influence in an effort to return to the armies of the ancien régime. But the success of the Prussian armies in the Seven Weeks' War (q.v.) and the Franco-Prussian War (q.v.) proved the deadliness of armed, disciplined force combined with the power of industrial might and nationalism.

The triumph of the Prussian General Staff under Helmuth von Moltke (q.v.) also demonstrated that the professionalization of the officer corps would have to figure prominently in the transformation of Europe's armies in response to the Industrial Revolution. It was not enough to have honorable, well-born officers; officers with brains who had spent long hours inside and outside of military schools studying their profession were now needed. Some armies managed this transition smoothly; the Germans, for example, were all too successful at institutionalizing professional values in the officer corps and among their NCOs. Others managed the transition less smoothly and paid a heavy price on the battlefields of World War I (q.v.) and World War II (q.v.). In the twentieth century, the profession of arms came more and more to involve complex management, supply, and administrative issues as conflicts were fought across the globe; the Americans proved to be the masters of such worldwide conflicts. All armies found the process of balancing the demands for support with the demands of preparing for and fighting on the terrifying battlefields of the twentieth century to be increasingly complex and difficult. That process of professionalization is clearly not yet complete.

WILLIAMSON MURRAY

John Keegan, *The Face of Battle* (1976).

Armor

Armor protection has played an important role in warfare for the past three millennia. Use of body armor was evident in the Western military tradition beginning with the hoplite warrior (q.v.) of ancient Greece. By 600 B.C., Iron Age Greeks had developed sophisticated bronze body armor, single-piece bronze helmets, and shin greaves. In addition, hoplites carried a large round shield *(hoplon)*, a twenty-foot pike, and an iron sword. This expensive array of armor *(hopla)* reflected Greek wealth and technical skill, and the high value placed on warriors' lives. Fighting in a phalanx, these soldiers were remarkably successful against their far less protected Persian enemies: only superior Roman tactical organization ended their sway in battle.

Roman use of armor reflected a different political and economic outlook than that of Greece. By 250 B.C., Roman legionnaires were protected by body armor (cuirass) made of individual iron hoops that were hinged at the back and clasped in front. These hoops, supported by a leather tunic, were cheaper than Greek bronze armor and easier to maintain. Roman iron helmets were also simpler than Greek bronze helmets and provided better neck protection. Legionnaires carried a javelin *(pilum)*, a sword, and an iron-ribbed,

Albrecht Dürer's 1498 engraving shows an armored knight with a lightly protected horse and long spear, which may indicate that he fought dismounted, as English knights often did in the major battles of the Hundred Years' War. Cavalrymen equipped in full body armor were approaching obsolescence as gunpowder weapons and massed formations of pikemen gave foot soldiers an advantage on the battlefield. By the early seventeenth century in western Europe, lightly armored cavalry carrying a heavy saber and a pair of pistols dominated the field.

oblong shield with a metal boss for additional protection. Rome's less expensive equipment served its mass armies well into the fifth century A.D., when political crisis and leadership failure ended Roman military supremacy.

With the collapse of the Western Roman Empire, use of armor declined dramatically in Europe until the age of Charlemagne (q.v.). Germanic warriors fought protected with only metal-reinforced wooden shields and iron-rimmed boar-tusk helmets. However, by the ninth century the Carolingians and Normans had developed the chain mail suit, the conical iron helmet, and the body-length shield that protected the individual warrior into the thirteenth century. Then, with the increasing lethality of projectiles (arrow and bullet), an "arms race" between plate armor protection and projectile effectiveness ensued, until sixteenth-century gunpowder weapons made the plate-armor-equipped warrior obsolete. Armor protection in European warfare remained largely insignificant until the twentieth century.

Ancient Chinese use of body armor followed a different pattern. By the Spring and Autumn periods (about 700 B.C.), a suit of overlapping rectangular leather plates, sewn to a wool mantle, was in use. The leather plates in this armor were replaced with iron squares by wealthy warriors in the Han dynasty (200 B.C.), but the general pattern of Chinese armor continued for the next sixteen hundred years, until the advent of Western firearms.

The Japanese adopted Chinese armor and military forms in about the sixth century. However, with the introduction of Western firearms to Japan by the Portuguese (in about 1540), plate-steel armor suits were adopted to protect the samurai (q.v.) in battle. The rise of the Tokugawa Shogunate (1600) brought 250 years of domestic peace, relegating armor in Japan to a ceremonial role.

The term *armor* today describes military units composed of tanks, armored infantry carriers, reconnaissance vehicles, and armored, self-propelled artillery pieces. Modern armored warfare began in World War I (q.v.) when the American invention of the caterpillar tractor was married to the armored car and given high-caliber weapons. The combination of mobility, armor protection, and firepower continues to be the hallmark of armored vehicles and units.

The British and French were the first to deploy armored units when they developed tanks in World War I, providing a technological solution to the tactical impasse imposed on warfare by defensive weapons and tactics. Most historians give credit to the Englishmen Sir Ernest D. Swinton (q.v.) and Winston Churchill (q.v.) for the impetus needed to develop the tank. However, the French simultaneously stumbled upon the idea of combining armored cars with caterpillar tractors.

During the 1920s and 1930s, military leaders disagreed as to the tactical importance of tanks and their role in future warfare. Most senior American, French, and British generals concluded that tanks were best employed as infantry-support vehicles, and they relegated armor development to the supervision of infantry officers. Some German and Russian officers, however, accepted General Erich Ludendorff's (q.v.) view

The armor of a daimyo officer in mid-fifteenth-century Japan was made of tiny metal plates, which were lacquered and then sewn together with colorful silk. The antler-like embellishments on the helmet recall the water buffalo horns worn by samurai.

that tanks operating alone had been decisive in 1918 and that they should be developed as a separate branch of the army and used in units composed entirely of armored vehicles.

By the mid-1930s, tanks and armored units became important elements of land warfare, and their use promised to restore tactical mobility and the relative weight of offensive operations to the battlefield. Among the military commentators and officers advocating the use of all-mechanized armor units were the Englishmen J. F. C. Fuller (q.v.) and Basil H. Liddell Hart (q.v.), the Frenchman Charles de Gaulle (q.v.), and the German Heinz Guderian (q.v.). The British, French, and Russian armies experimented with some of their ideas, but Germany developed the combined arms division — built around tank regiments — that became the most powerful offensive formation on twentieth-century battlefields.

The Germans created the first three panzer (armored) divisions in 1935–1937 by combining two regiments of tanks, one regiment of infantry mounted in armored half-tracks, and one regiment of artillery towed by half-tracks. Radio-equipped signal units, reconnaissance troops, and engineers mounted in armored vehicles rounded out this "combined arms team," which proved to be extraordinarily flexible, fast, and powerful against Poland, France, and Russia in 1939–1941.

Allied armies copied Germany's successful armor organization. They also attempted to emulate German doctrinal use of mission-oriented orders (in German, *Auftragstaktik*), so as to give subordinate-unit leaders tactical latitude and flexibility. During World War II (q.v.), armored doctrine evolved because of the development of new armored vehicles (especially the Russian T-34/85 tank and the German Panther tank), and tactical developments such as the Russian use of operational maneuver groups (composed of armor, self-propelled artillery, and mechanized infantry units) and Erwin Rommel's (q.v.) deep attacks in Africa. A combination of tanks, armored infantry, and self-propelled artillery, supported closely by aircraft, became the standard method of employing armored task forces. These armored formations proved to be dominant on the Eastern Front in massive armored battles such as Kursk (1943) (q.v.), where Russian tank armies under Marshal Georgii Zhukov (q.v.) crushed much of the Nazi army. From mid-1943, Russian superiority in tank design and armor doctrine became clear, resulting in the Red Army's (q.v.) conquest of eastern and central Europe by May 1945.

Most major conflicts since 1945 have reemphasized the importance of the tank and the need to employ it properly with infantry and artillery. In the Korean War (q.v.), American infantry units were at the mercy of North Korean tanks until American tank units were rushed to the peninsula to protect them. The Arab-Israeli Wars (q.v.) of 1948, 1956, 1967, and 1973 reconfirmed the value of combined arms teams and doctrine.

More recent U.S. operations indicate that the heavily armored tank continues to have an important role in combined arms operations in urban, jungle, and desert environments. In Grenada, the U.S. Marine Corps had to send M60A1 tanks in to destroy Grenadine armored cars that the American infantry could not eliminate. The massive use of armored divisions in Kuwait (see *Gulf War*), closely supported by jet fighters and helicopters, demonstrated the advantages enjoyed by modern armored vehicles and units

over dismounted infantry at night and in conditions of limited visibility. And the need to send two companies of heavy tanks and three companies of M2 Bradley-mounted infantrymen to Somalia in October 1993 to protect infantry from heavily armed bandits reaffirmed the importance of armor to modern armies in peacekeeping operations.

Military technology is currently undergoing phenomenal changes that will result in significant shifts in the mix of the armored team, but not in the importance of combining the three main elements of land combat power. The emphasis among Western nations on keeping casualties low ensures that armies will continue to use armored vehicles to protect soldiers, as was evident in the NATO deployment of armor in Bosnia in the 1990s. Heavy tanks combining high speed, tremendous protection from Cobham and depleted-uranium armor, heavy firepower from 120-mm cannon, and digital battlefield arrays will continue to be used in combat, accompanied by armored infantry and artillery vehicles. These vehicles will be equipped with thermal-imagery sights and driving devices that eliminate the visibility differences of day and night, giving the armored task force a dramatic advantage over dismounted infantry. With such technologies, armored units will continue to provide an efficient and effective means of conducting military operations.

JAMES SCOTT WHEELER

Robert H. Scales, ed., *Certain Victory: The United States Army in the Gulf War* (1993); Martin van Creveld, *Technology and War from 2000 B.C. to the Present* (1989).

Arms Control

See Disarmament.

Arms Race

Over the past century, the arms race metaphor has assumed a prominent place in public discussion of military affairs. But even more than the other colorful metaphors of security studies — balance of power, escalation, and the like — it may cloud rather than clarify understanding of the dynamics of international rivalries.

An arms race denotes a rapid, competitive increase

in the quantity or quality of instruments of military or naval power by rival states in peacetime. What it connotes is a game with a logic of its own. Typically, in popular depictions of arms races, the political calculations that start and regulate the pace of the game remain obscure. As Charles H. Fairbanks, Jr., has noted, "The strange result is that the activity of the *other* side, and not one's own resources, plans, and motives, becomes the determinant of one's behavior." And what constitutes the "finish line" of the game is the province of assertion, rather than analysis. Many onlookers, and some participants, have claimed that the likelihood of war increases as the accumulation of arms proceeds apace.

A close examination of the historical evidence reveals a different picture. Political purposes almost always drive and govern arms races. It is common for a major race to be initiated by a state interested in changing the political status quo. In some cases, the response of states content with the status quo is swift and resolute, but in other cases it is constrained by domestic political or economic considerations or diverted by diplomatic calculations. The course of an arms race has frequently exacerbated a sense of rivalry and occasionally even determined the timing of a war; but most often it has ended in a political settlement between rivals or in a decision by one side to moderate its buildup.

The first competitive buildup in which contemporaries used the arms race metaphor seems to have been the naval rivalry in the late nineteenth century, in which France and Russia challenged Britain in the context of acute tensions over colonial expansion. The British responded with a determination to remain masters of the seas. The ultimate result was not war, but rather an Anglo-French political settlement in 1904 and an Anglo-Russian rapprochement in 1907 against the background of a rising German threat.

The German challenge to Britain in the early twentieth century involved the most famous naval arms race of all. As the post-Bismarck political leadership decided that Germany must become a world power, Admiral Alfred von Tirpitz (q.v.) was able to justify building a large German battle fleet. When the British finally responded, the upshot was a competition that fit an action-reaction model more closely than any other arms race. The Germans in the end could not keep up, because of domestic difficulties in raising taxes and pressures to give greater priority to spending on the army. Though the naval arms race did poison Anglo-German relations, it was the actions of the German army, not the German navy, that ultimately produced war in 1914.

A third major naval arms race, involving the United States, Britain, and Japan, erupted at the end of World War I (q.v.). It was fueled by Japanese efforts to expand their political influence in East Asia and by an American attempt to gain greater political leverage over Britain. This was a race that, for financial reasons, none of the participants wanted to run very far. It ended at the Washington Conference of 1921–1922 with the first major arms-limitation treaty ever and a new political settlement for East Asia.

Was there, then, no truth at all in the 1925 verdict of a former British foreign secretary, Sir Edward Grey, that "great armaments lead inevitably to war"? In fact, an arms race among European armies had some part in the outbreak of World War I. In the July crisis of 1914, German chancellor Theobald von Bethmann-Hollweg took greater risks in brinkmanship than he might have otherwise done, because of a presumption that Russia's stepped-up efforts to improve its military capability meant Germany would be in a stronger position to win a war in 1914 than later.

Similarly, Adolf Hitler (q.v.) was in a rush to attack France in 1940 and the Soviet Union in 1941, partly because of the dynamics of an arms race that he had started in the 1930s. Held back by domestic financial constraints, Britain and France had lagged behind. But they, and Germany's other adversaries, had accelerated their rearmament in the late 1930s, and Hitler moved forward his program of conquest lest the German lead be overtaken.

Japan, too, succumbed to "now or never" calculations in 1941. Its naval leaders appreciated that the Japanese navy had gained a lead over the U.S. Pacific Fleet in every class of warship, but that a massive American naval program begun in 1940 would leave them far behind by 1943. Coupled with the effects of an American oil embargo against Japan, this playing out of the dynamics of an arms race helped to prompt an attack on the United States in December 1941 (see *Pearl Harbor, Attack on*). But in this case, as in the two European wars, hegemonic political ambitions fueled the conflict.

Leads and lags in an arms race against a background of a hegemonic struggle characterized the Cold War (q.v.) as well, but the deterrent effect of weapons of mass destruction made "now or never" calculations much less tempting for the superpowers of the nuclear age. The arms competition between the United States and the Soviet Union did not fit an action-reaction model very well. For domestic political and economic reasons, the United States was slow to rearm in the late 1940s even as it perceived hegemonic ambitions on the part of the Soviets. After the United States did greatly increase its nuclear and conventional arms during the Korean War (q.v.), the Soviet leadership for its own domestic reasons made only a partial response. When from the mid-1960s the Soviets undertook the most massive peacetime military buildup in history, the United States chose to disengage somewhat from the race. Not until after 1979 did it reassess its posture. The new qualitative improvements embodied in the last American arms spurt of the Cold War made Soviet military leaders nervous and helps explain why they were willing in the mid-1980s to accept the new ideas promoted by Mikhail Gorbachev in hopes of raising the technological level of Soviet society. The arms race that had produced the greatest anxiety among contemporaries ended in the most astonishing political settlement of the past century.

BRADFORD A. LEE

Charles H. Fairbanks, Jr., "Arms Races: The Metaphor and the Facts," *The National Interest* (Fall 1985); Patrick Glynn, *Closing Pandora's Box: Arms Races, Arms Control, and the History of the Cold War* (1992); Paul Kennedy, *Strategy and Diplomacy, 1870–1945* (1983).

Arnhem, Battle of

September 1944

In September 1944, after the victorious end of the Normandy campaign, Field Marshal Bernard Montgomery (q.v.) devised a daring operation to open the way to the Ruhr by seizing a bridgehead north of the Rhine, at Arnhem. On September 17, Operation Market, the largest airborne and glider operation in history (five thousand aircraft) was carried out by three Allied airborne divisions. Operation Garden was the ground side in which the Thirtieth (British) Corps was to link up with the British First Airborne at Arnhem by thrusting north along a narrow corridor opened by the U.S. Eighty-second and 101st Airborne Divisions. Then, the remainder of British Second Army would rapidly assault the Ruhr, thus hastening the collapse of the Third Reich and likely ending the war in 1944.

Although the airborne landings initially went well, Allied intelligence had failed to heed reports from the Dutch underground that a German panzer corps was bivouacked nearby. The Second Parachute Battalion was the only First Airborne unit to reach the key Arnhem bridge over the Rhine. The remainder of the division was soon pinned down by the panzer corps in and around Arnhem.

Congestion and German resistance along the single narrow road to Nijmegen and Arnhem delayed the British ground advance. The attempt to relieve Arnhem failed even though Lieutenant Colonel John Frost's gallant paratroopers held the northern end of the Arnhem bridge against the Ninth SS Panzer Division for four days before finally being overrun and captured.

Of the ten thousand men who had landed at Arnhem, fourteen hundred were killed and over six thousand captured; only twenty-four hundred paratroopers safely crossed to the south bank of the Rhine in small rubber boats.

Market-Garden was a military disaster during which the ground force was unable to breach the River Waal at Nijmegen in time to establish a bridgehead north of the Rhine in what became popularly known as "a bridge too far."

CARLO W. D'ESTE

Arnold, Benedict

1741–1801, American Revolutionary War General and Traitor

The leitmotif of Benedict Arnold's life was conflict. Arguably the greatest battlefield general on either side in the American Revolutionary War (q.v.), he also waged unending inner warfare between the two opposing sides of his nature: the honorable and the corrupt.

When Arnold was fourteen years old, his father's alcoholism precipitated the family's financial and social overthrow, leaving young Benedict with an insatiable craving for security of status and of income. He devoted the rest of his long life to an all-consuming quest for unconditional approval and what he deemed its logical outcome, remuneration.

Like most Whigs in the 1760s and 1770s, Arnold adhered to the patriot cause for financial rather than ideological reasons. Nevertheless, during the first three years of the American Revolutionary War, he fought for the cause with such valor and devotion — as commander of the legendary march up the Kennebec River in 1775 and during the failed assault on

Quebec that ensued, at the naval battle at Valcour Island on Lake Champlain the following year, and at the second Battle of Saratoga in 1777 — that he became a national hero. As a result, his treason, when he attempted in 1780 to betray the fortress of West Point, came as a terrible shock to the country and to his fellow soldiers, from commander in chief George Washington (q.v.) down to the lowliest militia man.

The underlying factor in Arnold's turnabout was his keen sense of being underappreciated and underrewarded by his own country. The catalysts were a sense of alarm at his imminent exposure for malfeasance and his infatuation with Margaret Shippen, the beautiful young Philadelphia belle and closet Tory who became his second wife.

Arnold's last twenty years were spent mostly in London, desperately trying to support his family but barred from all employment by the British establishment, who despised him. He had joined the British because he considered America ungrateful. What he never recognized was that nobody — on either side — thanks a traitor.

CLARE BRANDT

Arnold, Henry H. "Hap"

1886–1950, U.S. General

"Hap" Arnold graduated from West Point in 1907 and after a short period in the infantry switched to the aviation section of the Signal Corps where he became one of the army's first officers to win his wings. Arnold did not see active service in World War I (q.v.), but became one of Billy Mitchell's (q.v.) strongest supporters in the early 1920s. Mitchell's court-martial taught Arnold the importance of working with others to achieve his goals.

Arnold possessed extraordinary gifts as an administrator and leader, which have tended to obscure his considerable conceptual skills. In 1938 he became head of the army air corps, and the appointment of George C. Marshall (q.v.) as army chief of staff in September 1939 provided him with strong support throughout World War II (q.v.).

Arnold was an unabashed advocate of strategic bombing (q.v.), and that mission provided the primary focus for his effort to mobilize U.S. industry and air forces for the conflicts in Europe and in Asia. Like most Allied airmen, Arnold underestimated the threat that Luftwaffe fighters represented to bombers flying in great unescorted formations. He applied considerable pressure to Eighth Air Force's commanders in 1943 that contributed to the second disastrous attack on Schweinfurt. Nevertheless, when supported by escort fighters in 1944, Eighth Air Force was able to destroy the Luftwaffe's fighter force, wreck the German oil industry, and interdict the flow of supplies to Normandy. Never an ideologue, Arnold provided air force units that could support the army and navy campaigns in Europe and the Pacific. In the end the forces he mobilized, trained, and then deployed, and the leaders he picked to conduct the air war, played a major role in Allied victory.

WILLIAMSON MURRAY

Arsenals

Places for the centralized manufacture and storage of the tools of war, arsenals appeared in Europe late in the middle ages. The fact that *arsenal* comes from Arabic words meaning "house of manufacture" bears witness to the Mediterranean origins of the institution. Today the word has been generalized so that it can mean the total assemblage of arms held by a state or even by an individual. In Europe, but not in the United States, the term applies to naval yards as well as to weapons plants and depots.

Venice boasted the first great European arsenal to support its galleys in the Adriatic and the Mediterranean from the twelfth century. Initially it produced and warehoused naval stores but later built ships as well. The management of fleets, particularly galley fleets, could not be improvised like feudal armies, and for this reason, state-supported arsenals provided for forces at sea before they were created to arm forces on land. In the Venetian arsenal, galleys were built in prefabricated sections and stored disassembled, ready to be put together when needed. Other states followed the Venetian lead; from the thirteenth century, France created *clos de galères* as naval yards for its galleys. After the neglect of its navy during the sixteenth century, and with the attempt to build a great ocean-going fleet in the seventeenth century, the French founded substantial naval arsenals at Toulon, Brest, and elsewhere along the coast.

Military arsenals also took form primarily in the seventeenth and eighteenth centuries. French small arms production centered around St.-Étienne and Charleville by the late seventeenth century, whereas other centers cast cannon, notable among them Douai, Metz, and Tournai. The Royal Arsenal at Woolwich in England came into existence around 1720. Greater centralization of arms production fostered greater uniformity among weapons. The tremendous growth of armed forces during the early modern period also called for better coordination of arms production and increased capacity to maintain and store weapons. The permanent magazines that dotted Europe in the late seventeenth and eighteenth centuries held not only grain but also functioned as arsenals, storing small arms and artillery. In about 1697, Metz held five hundred artillery pieces and enough small arms for twenty thousand men.

The first U.S. arsenal dates from the American Revolution (q.v.), when George Washington (q.v.) decided to set up a powder factory at Springfield, Massachusetts, in 1777. The historic arsenal at Harpers Ferry was established in the 1790s; it would become the target of John Brown's raid in 1859. Although great numbers of weapons have been produced by U.S. arsenals in the past two centuries, the United States has perhaps placed a heavier reliance than other nations upon private industry to supply its armed forces with the tools of war. During the American Civil War (q.v.), the Springfield arsenal, the largest U.S. facility, produced one thousand rifled muskets per day. During World War II (q.v.) the Springfield arsenal manufactured the famous M1 Garand rifle in huge quantities, although it closed after the war. Today U.S. arsenals continue to design, test, and produce weapons.

JOHN A. LYNN

Oliver Hogg, *The Royal Arsenal* (1963).

The high, curved trajectory of the mortar enables these seventeenth-century artillerymen to fire into a fortified town, which may be several thousand yards away. A slow-burning fuse, lit upon firing, ignited the gunpowder that filled the round projectiles.

Art

See Representation of War in Western Art.

Artillery

The term *artillery* was used in antiquity to designate all the impedimenta of combat, but today it is generally applied to guns larger than small arms and, by extension, to the projectile-throwing engines of classical and medieval times too large to be carried and fired by an individual. The earliest artillery in this sense was the Greek *gastraphetes* (belly bow) of the fourth century B.C., in essence a large crossbow cocked by the downward pressure of the user's weight. The *gastraphetes* inspired larger tension engines drawn by windlasses and held in the cocked position by ratchets and pawls, but tension engines were limited in power by the strength of their wooden bows. Greek engineers turned to torsion, the rotational force developed by bundles of tightly twisted skeins of sinew, hemp, and perhaps — no one is sure — human hair. Torsion engines were of two basic types: catapults, featuring a single arm rotating in the vertical plane with a spoon-like recess at the end which threw projectiles in a looping arc; and ballistae, with two horizontally opposed arms rotating in a horizontal plane, mounted on

This fifteenth-century print demonstrates the use of a counterpoise trebuchet to throw a dead, diseased horse into a besieged town in order to introduce plague.

either side of a stock and connected by a cord that drove the projectile in a comparatively flat trajectory. Both types threw spherical stones, and ballistae also shot finned arrows and javelinlike projectiles. Roman siege ballistae could throw stones of fifty pounds or more some 300–350 yards and had sufficient power to strip fortress battlements of their outer walls, depriving the defenders of cover. Though warships occasionally carried ballistae and Roman legions had a contingent of cart-mounted *carrobalistae* from the second century B.C., the first field artillery — torsion artillery — was used primarily for defending and attacking fortifications. Classical artillery technology was almost entirely lost after the fall of Rome, and only small catapults survived.

The Asian equivalent to these engines was the trebuchet, a Chinese invention that exploited the force of gravity as a source of propulsive energy. The trebuchet threw its projectiles in a high, looping arc from a sling mounted on the long end of a wooden pole pivoting about an axle, which was suspended from a frame and worked by pulling the short end downward. Trebuchets were originally worked by traction, that is, by gangs pulling downward on ropes attached to the short end of the pole, and fired relatively small projectiles in the range of two to ten kilograms. The

traction trebuchet was used in Europe by the sixth century. The much larger counterpoise trebuchet, in which a large counterweight replaced human traction, was a European development of the middle to late twelfth century. These could be very large, and some were capable of throwing horses into the walls of a besieged fortress. Spherical stones were the most common projectile, and modern experiments affirm that although the trebuchet's range was no more than 150–200 yards, it was capable of considerable accuracy.

Artillery in the modern sense stems from the discovery of gunpowder in China by the tenth century A.D. By the eleventh century the Chinese had learned to exploit gunpowder's energy to propel spherical projectiles from tubular barrels, but used gunpowder primarily in firecrackers, rockets, and — apparently — catapult projectiles. Gunpowder reached Europe with the Mongol invasions of the thirteenth century, and its exploitation fell to European smiths. The first European cannon appeared in the 1320s, and the 1350s saw the development of wrought-iron guns with tubular barrels capable of imparting militarily significant velocities to spherical projectiles of stone or iron. In the 1380s immense stone-throwing bombards appeared, notably in Flanders, which could breach masonry walls with ease . . . if they could be dragged to the spot.

Cast bronze replaced wrought iron as the gun founder's metal of choice in the fifteenth century, and cast iron projectiles began replacing those of cut stone. By the early 1500s, bronze muzzle-loaders suspended in their carriages by integrally cast trunnions — cylindrical projections extending laterally from the barrel, just forward of the center of gravity — were the preferred form of artillery and remained so on land until the 1850s. Cast iron muzzle-loaders, heavier than bronze and less safe but much cheaper, replaced bronze at sea from the mid-1500s. Mobile land carriages with limbers and dished wheels (with spokes angling outward from the hub in a shallow cone for strength) appeared in France by the 1490s, and the four-wheeled naval truck carriage was in English and perhaps Portuguese service by the 1580s; these gave artillery its definitive form until the 1850s.

The distinction in land service between field artillery on the one hand and siege and fortress artillery on the other became increasingly clear-cut during the seventeenth and eighteenth centuries, but artillery changed little save in efficiency and standardization until the mid–nineteenth century, when rifled cannons firing elongated projectiles appeared in Europe. These proved superior in range, accuracy, and penetration — the demands of attacking armored warships were an important stimulus — and quickly grew in size and power. Bronze proved too soft for rifling, and gave way to cast iron, wrought iron, and steel in turn. Breech-loaders had important advantages in rate of fire and ease of loading, particularly in enclosed naval and fortress mounts, but became practical only at the end of the nineteenth century with the development of methods of effectively sealing the breech mechanism during firing, with expanding pad obturation for very large guns and brass shell casings for smaller ones. The general adoption of nitrocellulose-based propellants came at about the same time and dramatically increased both ballistic performance and the wear and strain on chambers, barrels, and carriages. Finally, the development of efficient hydropneumatic recoil absorption mechanisms, beginning with the Model 1897 French 75-mm rapid-fire field piece, the famous French '75, made it possible to combine great accuracy with high rates of fire.

Highly explosive shells magnified artillery's destructive capacity; illuminating, gas, white phosphorus, and flechette ammunition have given artillery a wide range of capabilities; and improved materials and carriages have made for lighter and more efficient pieces. But basic artillery technology has changed little since World War I (q.v.). Both the Soviet Union and the United States fielded nuclear artillery shells in sizes as small as 155 mm, but these have never been used in combat. More recently, artillery shells have been fitted with terminal-guidance mechanisms that home in on a spot of laser light placed on the target by a forward observer. Although these devices permit pinpoint accuracy, they are expensive, and their combat utility is uncertain.

JOHN F. GUILMARTIN

Shelford, Bidwell and Dominick Graham, *Fire-Power: British Army Weapons and Theories of War, 1904–1945* (1982); Carel de Beers, *The Art of Gunfounding: The Casting of Bronze Cannon in the Late Eighteenth Century* (1991); B. P. Hughes, *Firepower: Weapons Effectiveness on the Battlefield, 1630–1850* (1974).

Assurnasirpal II

r. 883–859 B.C., *Assyrian King and General*

Assurnasirpal's conquests laid the foundations for the vast Assyrian Empire (q.v.), which would grow in the next two centuries to encompass all the lands from the Persian Gulf in the east to Egypt in the west. His predecessors had struggled to build an army and reestablish control of Assyria's homeland in northern Iraq. Assurnasirpal first consolidated their gains, campaigning in the northern and eastern mountains and down the Euphrates River to create a ring of security around Assyria. When a Syrian city assassinated its pro-Assyrian governor, Assurnasirpal made it a public example, flaying its leaders, installing an Assyrian governor, and accepting the submission of nearby city-states. With this territory secured by garrisons, his army thrust west, seizing the trade routes to the eastern Mediterranean, claiming its rich cities as tributaries, and laying the basis for Assyrian wealth and power for the next two centuries.

BARBARA NEVLING PORTER

Assyria

The ancient Assyrians are remembered today as the brutal creators of a huge empire in the Middle East between the ninth and seventh centuries B.C. The biblical prophet Isaiah called them "the rod of [God's] anger" and the prophet Hosea recalled that "mothers were dashed in pieces with their children" by Assyrian soldiers, while the poet Byron described their armies as coming down "like the wolf on the fold." The biblical prophets' descriptions reflect their nation's direct experience (Assyrian armies had conquered Israel in 722 B.C. and swept through Judah in 701 B.C.), but the violence they depict must be understood as only one aspect of a complex people, whose kings were also skillful diplomats, whose rule conferred some genuine benefits, and whose empire helped to create and spread a sophisticated culture throughout the Middle East.

The royal library at Nineveh, for example, assembled by the Assyrian king Ashurbanipal (668–627 B.C.), reflects the complex intellectual life of which Assyrian kings were patrons. Its thousands of cuneiform documents range from treatises on astronomy and mathematics, and poems such as the famous Epic of Gilgamesh, to handbooks for doctors, collections of hymns, and foreign dictionaries for scribes. It also included thousands of letters to the palace from administrators, army officers, and advisers all over the empire, reporting on everything from enemy troop movements to the repair of temple statues and the storage of horse feed — evidence of the palace's close supervision of a vast administrative network. Although Ashurbanipal's library reflected centuries of Mesopotamian literary and technical achievement, the techniques developed for administering the empire — and for conquering it in the first place — had been in large part uniquely Assyrian inventions.

Originally an agricultural state and then a trading center, Assyria was driven to systematic warfare by three factors: its homeland, in what is today northern Iraq, was rich in grain but lacked other natural resources; its trading routes to the Mediterranean were increasingly blocked by powerful city-states holding key roads and fords; and its homeland's lack of natural barriers left it constantly vulnerable to conquest. After three centuries of rule by the kings of Mitanni, Assyria emerged in the mid–fourteenth century B.C. determined to build a powerful army. A century later, King Tukulti-Ninurta I demonstrated that army's effectiveness by briefly conquering the long-renowned city of Babylon. His later assassination inaugurated another period of weakness, but Assyria gradually reemerged to begin serious conquest under Assurnasirpal II (r. 883–859 B.C.) (q.v.), whose annual campaigns amassed tribute while confirming Assyria's

expanding boundaries, and whose spectacular success in forcing his way west to the Mediterranean opened the road for future trade and conquest. Assurnasirpal decorated his new palace at Calah (modern Nimrud) with massive wall carvings depicting his campaigns in gory detail, and his inscriptions report that in city after city, "I slew many of their inhabitants, I destroyed, I devastated, I burned with fire; [their] men I took alive, I impaled them on stakes over against their cities. . . ." Assurnasirpal's carvings and inscriptions, memorable for their proud assertions of Assyrian forcefulness, inaugurated the widespread use of a violent propaganda that became a standard tool of Assyrian kings and still shapes our image of Assyria today.

Despite reverses, the empire rapidly expanded until Sargon II's conquest of the mountain fortresses of nearby Urartu, in 714 B.C., freed Assyria from the last direct threat to its security, leaving it in control of an empire that stretched over fifteen hundred miles from the Persian Gulf to the borders of Egypt. But at the same time Assyria became economically dependent on tribute, booty, and captive labor from this empire to support both its growing cities and the increasingly large army needed to prevent revolts and repel attacks from outside the empire.

Assyria's empire was held together partly by force and fear, and partly by the benefits it conferred: safe roads for a growing trade, protection from rivals, relative freedom of religion under the umbrella of Assyria's gods, and in some cases, direct gifts from the Assyrian king, including tax privileges and public works projects. In the end, this was not enough: overextended by the sheer size of its empire and beset by internal problems, Assyria fell in 612 B.C. to a coalition of Babylonians, Medes, and Palestinians. Its ruined cities lived on only in legends until nineteenth-century archaeologists began to piece together the forgotten history of one of the most powerful states of the ancient Near East.

BARBARA NEVLING PORTER

H. W. F. Saggs, *The Might That Was Assyria* (1984).

Atatürk, Mustafa Kemal

1881–1938, *Turkish General and Statesman*

Mustafa Kemal, known since 1934 as Atatürk (meaning "Father of Turks"), first came to public attention in April 1915 as a young lieutenant colonel commanding the Ottoman Nineteenth Division. By his energetic action during the opening days of the Gallipoli campaign (q.v.) he prevented Anzac (Australian and New Zealand Army Corps) troops from gaining possession of a strategic ridge. He later served as a corps commander and army commander, first in eastern Anatolia against the Russians and then in Palestine and Syria against the British.

In 1919, Mustafa Kemal became the leading spokesman for the defense of Turkey's territorial integrity and independence against the Allies. He eventually established himself in Ankara as president of the Grand National Assembly and de facto head of a separate government. Although he initially left the actual conduct of military operations to friends and associates, in the summer of 1921 Mustafa Kemal assumed direct command of the Turkish "Western Front." In an extended and bloody campaign (Battle of the Sakarya), he stopped the advance of the Greek army on Ankara and eventually forced the Greeks back to their original positions. Eleven months later, on August 26, 1922, the Turks launched a massive strike against the Greeks and drove them out of Asia Minor within three weeks.

Elected president of the Republic of Turkey in October 1923, Mustafa Kemal spent the remainder of his life on the consolidation and modernization of the country, occasionally resorting to ruthless methods. He died in Istanbul on November 10, 1938.

ULRICH TRUMPENER

Atlantic, Battle of the

See North Atlantic, Battle of the.

Attila

406?–453, *King of the Huns*

Attila became king of the Huns sometime after A.D. 435 and ruled until his death in A.D. 453. The Huns were fierce warriors who struck terror into the hearts of the inhabitants of the Roman Empire. Living in the Great Hungarian Plain, they dominated the northern frontier of the Roman Empire, extracting tribute from the emperors of the Eastern and the Western Empires, especially from the wealthier East. The Romans considered the Huns to be savage barbarians, and tales of

---

The Ten Most Overrated Commanders

Attila the Hun
Joan of Arc
Louis-Joseph de Montcalm
Robert E. Lee
Heinz Guderian
Douglas MacArthur
Bernard Montgomery
George S. Patton, Jr.
Vo Nguyen Giap
H. Norman Schwarzkopf

Hunnic cruelty abound in late Roman literature. By the time of Attila, the Huns were no longer nomadic horse archers. Settled in Hungary, they had developed an infantry army, and they differed from other barbarian tribes on the Roman frontier in their ability to conduct successful sieges of fortified cities.

By the late 440s, Attila was looking west, and in 451 he moved across the Rhine and into Gaul, taking Reims, Mainz, Strasbourg, Cologne, and Trier. Paris held out, while the Huns marched on into central Gaul and put Orléans under siege. At that point the Roman general Aetius mobilized a force of Romans and barbarian allies and moved out to meet the Huns. They met at the Battle of Châlons (q.v.) in A.D. 451. Aetius drove Attila back into his camp, and by nightfall Roman arms were victorious. Aetius, in the face of considerable criticism, allowed Attila to withdraw across the Rhine, but for the moment the Western Roman Empire had been saved.

In the following year Attila and the Huns crossed the Alps and moved into Italy, unleashing a fury of destruction. The great city of Aquileia, at the head of the Adriatic, was wiped off the face of the earth. (Its surviving inhabitants later founded the modern city of Venice.) Major towns of the Po Valley fell to the invaders — Milan, Verona, Padua. It appeared that all of Italy would be overrun.

According to legend, at this point Pope Leo I met Attila in northern Italy and overwhelmed him with a show of bravado and sacerdotal robes. We are told that a great miracle occurred, that Saints Peter and Paul presented themselves to Attila and threatened the Hunnic leader with death if he ignored the appeals of the pope. More likely, Attila decided to withdraw from Italy because his troops were beginning to suffer from disease and were running short of supplies. In any event, Attila did abandon the invasion, and Italy was saved.

Attila died the next year from a nosebleed, we are told, while celebrating his marriage to a new, young wife. His name and that of the Huns have become synonymous with savagery, and in modern times the German army, especially in World War I (q.v.), was compared with the Huns. (The term was first used in modern times when the German kaiser sent troops to help quell the Boxer Rebellion [q.v.], encouraging them to fight like Huns.) Attila left no strong leader to replace him, and the Huns quickly disappeared from the pages of history.

ARTHER FERRILL

Attrition

Wars of attrition have been common to history, yet the term has almost defied definition — except in the narrow sense of suggesting the defeat of an adversary's matériel and manpower reserves over time. Most dictionaries of military terms avoid the word *attrition* altogether, for it has no precise or legal connotation.

The concept of attrition was acknowledged by many ancient writers, but most associated it with prolonged wars, such as the twenty-seven-year Peloponnesian War (q.v.), or with individual great captains such as Hannibal (q.v.), who sought not to conquer Rome but rather to wear it down by attacking its sources of power and supply. Military writers accepted that a strategy of attrition was at all times accompanied by the danger that it could lead to extreme caution and even inertia on the part of commanders who would succumb to the temptation to avoid bold but risky decisions.

At the end of the nineteenth century, the German military historian Hans Delbrück coined the phrase "strategy of attrition" as the opposite of Carl von Clausewitz's (q.v.) expression "strategy of annihilation." Delbrück recognized that attrition strategy could be misconceived as pure "maneuver strategy," and hence invented the accompanying term "bipolar strategy" to define his meaning further. Under bipolar strategy, the commander was free to achieve a goal by choosing between battle or maneuver, "now swinging toward one pole and then to the other," as the situation and the moment demanded. Above all, Del-

brück stressed what he called the "politico-military counterbalancing relationships" that drove strategies of attrition. Clean, crisp borders between politics and strategy evaporated under attrition. "Strategy becomes politics and politics strategy."

The classic case of the strategy of attrition was the German operation before Verdun (q.v.) in 1916. General Erich von Falkenhayn (q.v.), in his Christmas Memorandum of 1915, eschewed defining a specific target and simply planned an operation "in the direction of Verdun" first and foremost as a "suction cup" designed to "drain" the French lifeblood. The "operation limited to a narrow front" was to consist of a conventional assault, hurling men against entrenched positions; superior artillery would ensure a favorable kill ratio of five French to every two German soldiers. Falkenhayn boldly identified the ancient fortress salient of Verdun as an object "for the retention of which the French General Staff would be compelled to throw in every man they have. If they do so, the French will bleed to death." If the French refused battle, then the "moral effect" of this on France "will be enormous." It was "immaterial," Falkenhayn crowed, "whether we reach our goal" of Verdun. But after six months of battle and about 200,000 soldiers killed or missing in action, the kill ratio was 1:1.1 in favor of the Germans. Few strategists thereafter dared pursue strategies of attrition openly.

HOLGER H. HERWIG

Aurangzeb

1617–1707, *Mughal Emperor*

Aurangzeb was the sixth in the line of Mughal emperors of India (see *Mughals*). In the political and cultural realm, he is best known for turning the empire away from the secularism of his predecessors; Aurangzeb, from a position of his own personal faith in Islam, favored Muslims over indigenous Hindus, even those with long records of service to the empire, such as Rajputs and Bundelas. He launched vigorous military campaigns on all frontiers: into the foothills of the Himalayas, current-day Assam, Afghanistan, unconquered tribal areas adjoining the Mughal heartland, and the southern half of the Indian peninsula. Ironically, several of these campaigns were against Muslim kingdoms (Bijapur and Golconda) and Muslim groups (Pathans). On level, open terrain, no contemporary force could stand against Mughal heavy cavalry backed by musketeers and the most efficient artillery in the whole region (staffed, in part, by Portuguese and other Europeans). In hilly or waterlogged areas, however, it was difficult to mass the cavalry or bring the heavy artillery to bear. Long supply lines proved to be even more of a problem. Indigenous groups, especially the Marathas, used the superior mobility of their light cavalry to cut off supplies of the slower-moving Mughal armies, as well as to raid deep into Mughal territory. For more than a quarter-century, Mughal armies, often led personally by Aurangzeb, tried unsuccessfully to subdue the Marathas. At his death, the Mughal Empire encompassed virtually all of the Indian subcontinent, but factional rivalries, regional revolts, and crises of legitimacy and loyalty would effectively dismember the empire within a generation.

STEWART GORDON

Austerlitz, Battle of

December 2, 1805

In exile on St. Helena, Napoleon (q.v.) was notably sparse in his comments on this battle of the 1805 campaign. To some companions, Napoleon never mentioned Austerlitz at all. This is remarkable in that historians typically picture Austerlitz as Napoleon's most spectacular victory. Indeed, it seems that Napoleon himself also thought of the battle in this way, because he referred to it repeatedly at critical moments later in his military career, for example, at Borodino, where Napoleon told associates he felt he could see "the sun of Austerlitz."

The Battle of Austerlitz came about after Napoleon had seized Vienna in the wake of his encirclement of an Austrian army at Ulm earlier in this campaign (October 1805). The French were in pursuit of Austrian forces; the latter reconstituted their army by making a junction with an approaching Russian force. The combined Russo-Austrian army under General Mikhail Kutuzov (q.v.), with 85,000 men and 278 guns, advanced through Moravia toward Vienna. Kutuzov was accompanied by both the Austrian emperor Francis I and the Russian tsar Alexander, resulting in command conflicts that reduced the effectiveness of the combined army. A plan for an outflanking movement by the right wing was adopted despite Kutuzov's opposition. That became the gambit attempted on December 2.

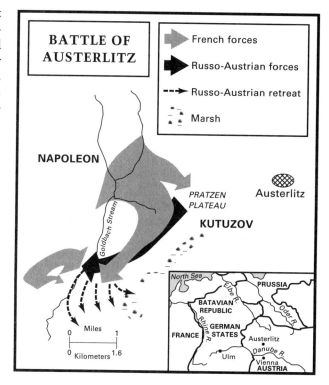

Anticipating such a move, Napoleon massed the bulk of his army, which totaled seventy-three thousand troops and 139 guns, on the opposite flank and in his right center, and sent these forces in to attack when he judged the Russo-Austrian army had become overextended and had denuded its center. The French attack broke the allied left wing and gained key heights behind the Russo-Austrian attack force, which was then pinned against marshland. The allied army disintegrated, obliging Emperor Francis to negotiate peace with the French. French losses totaled nine thousand against allied casualties of twenty-seven thousand, including the loss of 180 guns and forty-five colors.

Austerlitz has gained a reputation as a classic example of operational art. It is arguable, however, that Ulm, where twenty-nine thousand Austrians were forced to surrender with virtually no battle at all, represents an even greater achievement.

JOHN PRADOS

Austro-Prussian War

See Seven Weeks' War.

Austro-Turkish Wars

1526–1791

The capture of Belgrade in 1521 allowed Ottoman forces to advance into Hungary, most of which they overran in 1526, following the battles of Mohács (q.v.). The Hapsburg rulers of Austria and Bohemia now became directly involved in holding back the Turks. However, with both sides distracted by internal and external concerns, neither was able to engage its full military resources for prolonged periods, and hostilities therefore consisted primarily of border raids. When major forces became engaged, Austria possessed the advantage, for by the 1530s Hapsburg infantry had already learned to combine shock and fire, a tactical combination to which the Turks never found an answer.

In 1529 the Turks appeared before the gates of Vienna (q.v.). Forced to withdraw, they advanced again in 1532, but major imperial forces drove them back. Both sides now began to fortify all strategic locations along the frontier, creating a defense in depth that prevented substantial gains by either side. An armistice, permitting frontier raiding, was concluded in 1547; although fighting intensified again between 1555 and 1562, stalemate returned until the indecisive "Long War" of 1593–1606.

The revival of Turkish power brought a renewed confrontation in 1663–1664 and another major Turkish offensive culminating in the siege of Vienna in 1683 (q.v.). But Vienna held, and the Turks were badly defeated by a European coalition, including Catholic and Protestant forces, and expelled from Hungary in 1699. Eager to gain further territory, Austria went to war from 1716 to 1718 and allied itself with Russia against the Turks in 1737, but suffered a major defeat. In 1788 Austria once again joined Russia against the Turks, but following setbacks and facing threats in the West, made peace in 1791.

After 1600, the Turks seemed unable to innovate, only to imitate: most new techniques (such as use of pistols, musketry volleys, and bastion fortifications) were introduced by, and remained largely confined to, European defectors. However, the enormous size and the combat effectiveness of Turkish armies sufficed to keep the West at bay until the nineteenth century, when industrial production provided Christian forces with a decisive advantage.

GUNTHER E. ROTHENBERG

'Ayn Jalut, Battle of

September 8, 1260

The Mamluks, Turkish slave soldiers from Egypt, inflicted the first irretrievable defeat and territorial loss on the "invincible" Mongols (q.v.). The victory reinspired Muslims demoralized by the Mongols' recent (1258) destruction of Baghdad, the caliph, and the Caliphate; it also marked the end of Mongol westward expansion. Many scholars erroneously claimed that huge numbers enabled the Mamluks to win against the qualitatively superior Mongols, counting 120,000 Mamluks that mistranslation inflated from 12,000. The Mamluks marched north after seasonal water and pasture shortages had forced withdrawal of 50,000 Mongols and their 250,000 mounts. The armies met in the Jezreel Valley of Palestine and Israel, and fought, with 10,000 to 20,000 cavalry each, to a conclusion showing the Mongols' comparative limitations.

The Mongols repeatedly charged to shoot at the approaching Mamluks, avoiding hand-to-hand combat for which they were inadequately armed and mounted. They shot the horse of Qutuz, the Mamluk ruler; they broke the Mamluk left. But after Qutuz restored order, the Mamluks stood fast, shooting faster and farther than the galloping Mongols. The Mongols' commander, Kedbuqa, was killed, and their Syrian allies deserted. The Mamluks, armored and riding larger, fresher horses, charged the dismayed Mongols who were riding tired ponies. The Mongols broke and lost many men, much of their reputation, and all of Syria.

JOHN MASSON SMITH, JR.

Aztecs

The Aztecs (Mexicas) migrated into the Valley of Mexico from the north at the end of the twelfth century and founded their capital, Tenochtitlan, in 1345. Overthrowing the Tepanec Empire in 1428, they became the largest empire in Mesoamerica until they were conquered by Hernán Cortés (q.v.) less than a century later, in 1521.

War in Aztec society was professionally planned and professionally fought, and it benefited virtually all segments of society. Expansion occurred for many reasons, including religion, since ritual human sacrifices were required. But expansion also brought ma-

Aztecs in war costume besiege Spaniards who have taken refuge in the palace at Tenochtitlan in 1519. The Aztec in front is an eagle knight; the others are unit commanders, indicated by the tall black headdresses that enabled warriors to recognize them at a distance. Their obsidian-tipped weapons were no match for the Spaniards' state-of-the-art crossbows and firearms.

terial gains in tribute and in wider trade networks, which, in turn, undergirded the state, directly supporting the king and, through him, nobles, commoners, and religious cults. Thus, the primary imperial goals were economic and political, inextricably woven into Aztec society.

Wars clustered between December and April, during the dry season when marching was easiest, postharvest supplies were at their height, and farm laborers were available for service. The Aztec army probably marched no more than 1.5 miles per hour, or 12 miles per day, with each army (eight thousand elite and commoner warriors, all professionally trained) departing on sequential days or traveling by parallel routes. Since there were no draft animals or wheeled vehicles in Mesoamerica, everything was carried by human porters at a ratio of one for every two soldiers, providing a total of eight days' food, or a combat radius of about 36 miles — three days coming and going, one day fighting, and one day recuperating.

To march farther, the Aztecs demanded supplies from tributaries en route, but logistics still constrained marches beyond the empire, profoundly affecting strategy. City-states were vulnerable to outright conquest, but confederacies or empires controlling large hinterlands were not, as the defenders had time to marshal their armies and meet the enemy at the borders. Such battles could be decisive, but victory meant the conquest of only that particular place: confederated and imperial armies could withdraw into their interiors beyond the Aztecs' logistical ability to follow. Thus, although city-states could be conquered in toto, complex polities fell only through a gradual process of chipping away at their peripheries.

Battles typically began at dawn with a slingshot and arrow barrage at a range of about sixty yards, covering the advance of soldiers armed with stone-bladed broadswords and thrusting spears. All soldiers carried shields, but accomplished soldiers also wore protective quilted cotton armor that novices had yet to earn. While closing, members of military orders and other veteran soldiers led, hurling darts from spear-throwers in an effort to disrupt the opposing formations. But once the two sides closed, the barrages largely ceased and combat became hand to hand. Aztec ranks sought to maintain a solid front, but only the first few ranks could bring their weapons to bear. If the opposing formations were not breached, the Aztecs often extended their front to envelop them and cut off reinforcements and resupply.

Usually, forces clashed in the open, but defenders sometimes awaited attack behind city walls, although this maneuver was not common in Mesoamerica during Aztec times because many cities were too large to be adequately fortified, and their surrounding hinterlands still lay vulnerable. But when fortifications were encountered, entry was gained by deceit or treason, by breaching the walls, by scaling them with ladders, or, less often because of logistical problems, by besieging the town. In most cases, the enemies' submission, not their destruction, was the Aztecs' primary objective, since their foes' primary value was as tributaries.

When confronting an enemy too powerful for easy conquest, the Aztecs initiated a "flower war" (*xochiyaoyotl*), whose first stage was a limited battle that demonstrated prowess. At that point many opponents conceded, but if they remained undaunted, the conflict escalated in size and ferocity, becoming a war of attrition. While thus tying down their opponents, the Aztecs continued their expansion, ultimately encircling them and severing outside support, until they could be crushed outright.

The Aztecs did not replace vanquished rulers, station troops in conquered territories, or otherwise alter local customs. Rather, the empire was held together by each local ruler's awareness that noncompliance was rebellion justifying reconquest and the imposition of heavier tribute demands. Because the system depended on local cooperation, tribute was modest but very cost effective. The system's continuation, however, depended on the tributaries' belief that the Aztecs could and would impose their will, and thus the Aztecs relied on strong leadership, selecting their kings from among a small group of upper nobles with established military prowess. Rather than a territorial system linked by administrative hierarchies and imperial troops, the Aztec Empire was a loosely integrated series of tributary states, united only by their acquiescence to Tenochtitlan.

ROSS HASSIG

Ross Hassig, *Aztec Warfare: Imperial Expansion and Political Control* (1988).

B

Babur

1483–1530, Warrior and Founder of Mughal Empire

Zahir-ud-din Muhammad Babur, a Chaghadai Turk, founded the Mughal Empire in India (see *Mughals*). At the death of his father, Babur (at age twelve) inherited a band of cavalry and disputed rights to an area centered on the Fergana Basin, southeast of present-day Tashkent. Forced out of his homeland, Babur and his band led a pillar-to-post existence for more than two decades, the band surviving on a mixture of plunder and occasional collecting of taxes in a particular area. In good times, Babur was the master of a large city such as Samarkand or Kabul; in bad times, he had barely fodder for the horses. What held the band together was the personal charisma and fighting prowess of Babur, and his willingness to share all he had to maintain a common "table," at which plans and tactics were discussed. Babur's troops were exclusively heavy, mailed cavalry, and all were consummate archers, trained in the use of the reverse-curve Persian bow while on horseback. Early battle formation consisted of the center (always Babur's own band), the vanguard, and left and right wings (often allied bands or units). Tactics consisted of frontal charges using arrows, which resolved into hand-to-hand combat with sword and battle-ax. Babur later developed "sweeping" tactics, which relied on disciplined mobility. In these early years, Babur had no artillery and could take a fort only by scaling.

From his base at Kabul, Babur began raiding the Indian plains in the early years of the sixteenth century. Over the course of two decades, he acquired some light, camel-mounted swivel guns, but the decisive weapons in the defeat of the reigning Afghan sultans of Delhi (Panipat, 1526 [q.v.]) and the indigenous Rajputs (1527) were the same as those of earlier years — heavy cavalry with bow and arrow, and sword.

Babur's extraordinary achievement was founding the Mughal Empire in India from a base of a few hundred troops in a disputed territory of Central Asia. Babur's successors would expand the territory of the empire to include almost all of the South Asian subcontinent over the following two hundred years.

STEWART GORDON

Balkan Wars

1912–1913

In the first years of the twentieth century, Russia and Austria-Hungary cooperated to gain control of southeastern Europe, aiming to fill the vacuum left by the decline of Ottoman powers in the region. After the Bosnian crisis of 1908–1909, however, their policies diverged. Russia tried to create an alliance of Balkan states to cut off Austria to the south, but they lost control of the negotiations. In 1912, Serbia, Greece, Montenegro, and Bulgaria signed military alliances for the purpose of driving the Ottomans out of their last holdings in the Balkans. Despite warnings from the great powers of Europe, in October 1912 the four Balkan allies attacked the Ottomans with 700,000 men in the First Balkan War. The Ottomans, under pressure from a war with Italy and in the throes of reorganization after the Young Turk Revolution, could put only 320,000 troops in the field. Early in 1913 the great powers imposed a peace, but the main territorial questions remained open. Both Greece and Serbia had hoped to take parts of Albania; however, to maintain a balance of power in the Balkans, the powers insisted on preserving the new Albanian state. One of the only parts of their former European possessions that the Ottomans did not lose was the Gallipoli Peninsula (q.v.). Serbs, Bulgars, and Greeks also coveted Macedonia. The Bulgars, who from the time of their independence in 1878 claimed that Macedonia was Bulgarian, decided to attack Serbia and Greece. In the ensuing Second Balkan War of 1913, Bulgaria was utterly defeated. The Treaty of Bucharest (1913) gave slightly more than half of Ottoman Macedonia to Greece, about a third to Serbia, thus almost doubling its size, and the remainder to Bulgaria. Serbia and Montenegro split the Sandžak region, establishing a common border; Romania took Southern Dobruja; and the Ottomans recovered Adrianople (Edirne).

The struggle over Macedonia, the increase in Serbian power, and the large number of atrocities committed on the basis of ethnic criteria created a heated atmosphere in which the assassination of Archduke Franz Ferdinand at Sarajevo in 1914 led Austria to declare war on Serbia, thus touching off World War I (q.v.). Many of the ethnic issues that surfaced in the two Balkan wars remain on the agenda today.

GALE STOKES

Ballistic Weapons

A ballistic weapon inflicts damage by means of a projectile whose point of impact is determined by the direction and velocity with which it is launched or thrown. Examples of ballistic projectiles include sling stones, arrows, and thrown spears in antiquity, and cannon balls, rifle and machine-gun bullets, and conventional artillery shells in modern times. Unguided rockets become ballistic projectiles after the rocket motor has ceased firing (after motor burnout). Such a projectile is said to follow a ballistic trajectory. It may damage its target by kinetic energy (by definition, the mass of the projectile multiplied by the impact velocity squared) or by some other means, such as an explosive or incendiary warhead or the release of poison gas. Outside the atmosphere, ballistic projectiles are affected only by gravity and follow a parabolic arc. Trajectories within the atmosphere are affected by aerodynamic drag, the resistance of the air to movement. At subsonic velocities, drag is a product of the velocity squared; atmospheric density; and the size, shape, and surface texture (relative smoothness) of the projectile. At supersonic velocities, drag is further influenced by Mach number, that is, the velocity of the projectile as a multiple of the speed of sound. Drag increases sharply as the velocity approaches and exceeds the speed of sound, and supersonic drag is particularly sensitive to projectile shape.

Although Galileo identified the shape of a ballistic trajectory in a vacuum as a parabola in the 1630s, mathematical equations capable of accurately predicting trajectories in the atmosphere were not developed until the twentieth century, and even now depend on empirically derived data giving the subsonic and supersonic drag of specific projectile shapes. Several basic concepts, however, were understood empirically from the beginning and explained scientifically in the mid–eighteenth century: elongated projectiles such as arrows or javelins that move through the air parallel to their longitudinal axes encounter considerably less aerodynamic resistance than spherical projectiles of the same mass, and they carry farther. Similarly, pellets or balls of a relatively massive substance such as lead carry farther than those of iron or stone; and, because the mass of a sphere increases as a function of the diameter cubed while drag increases as a function of the diameter squared, large spherical projectiles carry farther than small ones for the same initial velocity.

The earliest ballistic weapons were no doubt thrown rocks. These were replaced as serious weapons in pre-Neolithic times by hand-thrown spears and javelins, the throwing stick for darts (the atlatl), the sling, and, above all, the bow. Hand-thrown objects have been replaced in modern times by hand grenades with fragmentation, incendiary, blast, or gas warheads. The bow reached a plateau of technological sophistication in the form of the composite recurved bow of wood, horn, and sinew by the third millennium B.C., utterly outclassing the early modern European cavalryman's wheel lock or flintlock pistol in range, accuracy, and rate of fire, and remained the premier missile weapon of mounted combat until the appearance of the Colt revolver in 1835. Greek engineers developed an array of ballistic weapons worked by tension and torsion, and these were inherited by the Romans. Firing spherical stones and a variety of fin-stabilized, javelinlike projectiles, the more powerful of these were serious engines of war; knowledge of them was almost entirely lost in the Dark Ages.

The crossbow, a short, stiff bow mounted permanently on a stock with a sear and release mechanism to hold the drawn string in preparation for firing, was developed by the Chinese in antiquity. Transported from China to Europe in classical times, the crossbow was all but forgotten in Europe for a thousand years. Rediscovered — or perhaps reintroduced — in the tenth century, it became the most important European ballistic weapon of medieval times and gave way to gunpowder arms only in the sixteenth century. The dominant medieval crew-served ballistic weapon was the trebuchet, a siege engine worked by human traction or the force of gravity. Anticipating cannon balls, spherical stones were the trebuchet's principal ammunition (see *Siege Weapons*).

Gunpowder, known in China by the ninth century and transported to Europe during the thirteenth century, radically changed the development of ballistic weaponry. The pivotal event was the development by European smiths in the early 1300s of tubular barrels that could fire spherical projectiles. These quickly grew to large dimensions and by the 1350s were throwing stone balls rivaling those of counterpoise trebuchets in size. In the 1420s, European gunners began firing directly at fortress walls to bring them down, rather than firing over them, trebuchet-style, for harassment. By the fifteenth century, gun founders understood the relative merits of projectiles of lead, stone, and iron: lead was used for small arms, stone and iron for artillery. Stone balls could be fired from less massive cannon and were economical of gunmetal, but required immense amounts of skilled labor to make and had given way to iron cannonballs by the eighteenth century. Cannon were also used to fire dice or scatter shot for antipersonnel effect. Exploding cannonballs appeared in the sixteenth century, but the fragility of the cast iron projectiles and the unreliability of slow match fuses limited their use to short-barreled mortars. By the seventeenth century, rifled barrels were used to impart spin to the projectile and dramatically improved accuracy by eliminating the unpredictable lateral drag forces, which cause a slowly spinning spherical projectile to dart and wobble in flight like a baseball pitcher's knuckle ball. But of projectile materials, only malleable lead could be forced into the rifling. In consequence, only small arms were rifled, and complex loading procedures limited their tactical utility. Smoothbore, black-powder weapons firing spherical projectiles remained the dominant ballistic weapons until the 1850s.

The perfection of case and canister ammunition, rounds containing multiple spherical subprojectiles, gave artillery awesome lethality against massed formations on the battlefield. Improved metallurgy, casting methods, and fuses made exploding shells a common presence on the battlefield, first fired from short-barreled field howitzers and, beginning in the 1820s, from naval and field guns. The shrapnel shell, invented in 1748 by an English artilleryman, Henry Shrapnel, dispersed its load of case shot with a small bursting charge, increasing the effective range of case. Shrapnel became a basic artillery munition, and the term is still applied to the fragments of an exploding shell or bomb. Dramatic change commenced in 1847 with the invention of the minié ball, an ellipsoidal lead bullet with a flat base that expanded on firing to fill the rifling grooves; this eliminated the smoothbore's advantages in simplicity and rate of fire and made the infantry rifle dominant on the battlefield. Next came the self-contained brass cartridge, making breech-loading, repeating arms practical. The technical problems posed by rifled artillery were more difficult, but were ultimately solved by fitting elongated iron and steel projectiles with copper driving bands to engage the rifling. The appearance of armored warships in the 1850s led to the development of specialized armor-piercing ammunition for warships and coastal fortifications. Scientific internal ballistics emerged in the United States and Europe at the same time, leading to larger, more powerful, and more efficient artillery. The 1870s saw the operational debut of rifled, breech-loading artillery.

The development of high explosives and nitrocellulose-based (smokeless) propellants in the final decades of the nineteenth century produced a revolution in ballistic weaponry. The maximum muzzle velocities and ranges of gun systems increased enormously, and high-explosive shells gave artillery an order-of-magnitude leap in destructive capacity. Advances in aerodynamic knowledge were applied to the projectile design, enhancing accuracy, range, and terminal effect. The development of hydropneumatic artillery recoil systems in the 1890s enormously improved rates of fire and accuracy, particularly for field artillery. Poison gas and smoke rounds joined high-explosive and shrapnel artillery ammunition as standard in World War I (q.v.). Smoothbore mortars firing finned projectiles proved able to deliver more close-in firepower than tube artillery of equivalent weight and thus became a standard infantry-support weapon. Finally, smokeless propellants and high-explosive warheads made battlefield bombardment rockets, used mostly for incendiary and psychological effect in the black-powder era, a useful supplement to tube artillery in World War II (q.v.). The Germans also used bombardment rockets against bomber formations, and unguided air-to-surface rockets became a standard ground attack weapon.

Tube artillery approached a plateau of tactical effectiveness with the development in the early twentieth century of fire-control systems attached to the gun, which produced the proper elevation and lead angle for moving targets when the estimated range was entered. The first of these were mechanical analog systems (that is, working on the same principles as a slide rule) for long-range naval gunnery. By World War II, electro-mechanical analog fire-control systems were the norm for naval and antiaircraft artillery, and fighter aircraft were fitted with gyroscopic lead-computing gun sights. Currently, artillery of all kinds is directed by digital electronic fire-control systems using inputs from electronic-sensor and target-acquisition systems. Radar-activated fuses, developed by American and British scientists during World War II, increased the lethality of antiaircraft and field artillery, in the latter case with precisely controlled low-altitude air bursts. A wide array of ballistic antitank weapons and munitions appeared in World War II, including rounds using a "shaped" high-explosive charge for penetration and high-velocity subcaliber projectiles (penetrators with a significantly smaller diameter than that of the bore, encased in a light shell or discarding sabot) of titanium carbide and other hard, dense substances.

The most recent major ballistic weapons are the aerial bomb and intermediate- and intercontinental-range ballistic missiles, IRBMs and ICBMs. Aerial bombs were used widely in World War I and have played an important role in every major conflict since (see *Aerial Weapons*), though precision guided bombs and missiles have been used in preference to free-fall munitions in attacks on point targets since the final stages of the Vietnam War (q.v.). During World War II, German engineers developed large, liquid-fueled rockets that could loft militarily significant payloads above the atmosphere, achieving range by eliminating aerodynamic drag. One of these, the V-2, was the first operational IRBM. Though not used militarily to date, nuclear- and thermonuclear-tipped IRBMs and ICBMs have been an underlying strategic and geopolitical reality since their appearance in American and Soviet arsenals in the late 1950s.

JOHN F. GUILMARTIN

Ian. V. Hogg, *The Illustrated Encyclopedia of Ammunition* (1985); Werner Soedel and Vernard Foley, "Ancient Catapults," *Scientific American* (March 1979): 150–160; W. T. S. Tarver, "The Traction Trebuchet: A Reconstruction of an Early Medieval Siege Machine," *Technology and Culture* (January 1995): 136–167.

Baltic Crusade

Twelfth to Sixteenth Centuries

The Baltic crusade, a series of military expeditions aimed at converting the pagan people of northern Europe, began in the twelfth and ended in the sixteenth century. The era officially began in 1147, when the Saxons, Danes, and Poles, responding to Pope Eugene III's call, initiated a crusade against the Wends of the southern Baltic. This was followed by crusades against the Livonians, Estonians, Finns, Prussians, and Lithuanians. By the thirteenth century much of the responsibility for sustaining these crusades fell to the Teutonic Knights (see *Knightly Orders*), a military order formed in the Holy Land in 1190. They were aided by constant support from the Roman pontiff and by a steady flow of mercenaries from throughout Christendom, including King John of Bohemia, King Lewis of Hungary, and Henry Bolinbroke, the future Henry IV of England. The battles with the Lithuanians, exacerbated by forbidding terrain and extreme weather, were some of the most bitter of the crusades (see *Tannenberg, Battle of*). Fighting consisted of both winter and summer campaigns (*Reisen*, "journeys"), which often became search-and-destroy missions inflicting heavy casualties on civilians.

By the start of the sixteenth century, the impetus for the crusades had ceased; religious objectives gave way to more overtly political ones. Though less spectacular and expensive than the Crusades (q.v.) to the Holy Land, the achievements of the northern crusaders were more enduring. In addition to Christianity, the crusades brought to the north many of the typical features of medieval Western civilization, including castles, manors, parliaments, and feudal law codes.

WILLIAM CAFERRO

Bannockburn, Battle of

June 24, 1314

Robert the Bruce, king of Scotland, besieged Stirling as part of the war to establish his kingdom's full independence from the English crown. Edward II, "always lily-livered and luckless in war," advanced with roughly seventeen thousand troops to rescue the stronghold. Encouraged by successful skirmishes on June 23, Robert boldly chose to meet the English army (three times larger than his own) in open battle —

contrary to his normal strategy. Edward's vanguard charged prematurely and in disorder, making no impact on the tightly arrayed Scots, whose pikes disemboweled the English horses. Fighting on difficult ground, the English main body barely checked the Scottish advance. After Robert the Bruce's reserve flanked the English, Edward fled, and his troops broke. Pinned against a treacherous stream, the Bannockburn, thousands perished. Never again did the English seriously challenge Robert's rule of Scotland. This glorious victory over a more powerful foe solidified the Bruce's military reputation and helped make him Scotland's foremost national hero.

Shocked by their dramatic defeat, the English adopted the Scots' practice of fighting on foot. Bannockburn, like Courtrai (q.v.), twelve years earlier, marked the beginnings of a new style of infantry-dominated warfare.

CLIFFORD J. ROGERS

Barton, Clara

1821–1912, U.S. Civil War Nurse and Humanitarian

A one-woman relief agency and the outstanding Union battlefield nurse in the eastern theater of the American Civil War (q.v.), Clara Barton served in field hospitals at or near the battlegrounds of Second Bull Run, Antietam (q.v.), Fredericksburg, Battery Wagner, the Wilderness, and the Richmond-Petersburg siege. Often under fire, she showed a skeptical military establishment that women could serve in the field with bravery and competence and thus cleared the way for other Northern women to follow her to the Virginia front. The Civil War was the central, defining event in Barton's life: it gave her the opportunity to reach out and seize control of her destiny in the relief of the suffering. She later served in military hospitals in Europe and Cuba and founded and became first president of the American Association of the Red Cross.

STEPHEN B. OATES

Battle Fatigue

A successor to the "shell shock" of World War I (q.v.), battle fatigue denoted the psychophysiological state of Anglo-American soldiers in World War II (q.v.) who were no longer able to function in combat. Like shell shock, battle fatigue was a term used by troops but

Clara Barton, the American Civil War's "Angel of the Battlefield" and founder of the American Red Cross Society, works at her desk in about 1904.

considered suspicious by medics and brass hats. Early campaigns extinguished official belief that psychological screening would eliminate recruits who might become mentally unhinged by the prospect of being blown up or crippled.

Even so, many commanders embraced medieval attitudes about how men should comport themselves in the face of danger. Many preferred to believe in the "baptism of fire," a rite of initiation during his first combat that supposedly hardened the soldier against future stresses.

Combat soldiers were naturally the first to understand that there was no such thing as "getting used to it." If a soldier stayed on the line long enough, he would succumb to mental stresses if he was not physically injured first. A veteran could as easily suffer battle fatigue as the greenest soldier. A brief rest might restore the victim's soldierly capacities, or he might require permanent evacuation.

Battle fatigue encompassed any number of symptoms: the loss of one or more of the senses, various forms of paralysis, loss of memory, or dramatic "startle reactions," such as trying to dig a foxhole in one's hospital bed after hearing a loud noise.

No fighting arm or geographical part of World War II was free of battle fatigue, although various terms were conceived to describe the condition. In the Pacific, one was said to have "gone Asiatic." Combat airmen could suffer from "the clanks." In one command, a physician catalogued over sixty different terms to describe battle fatigue.

Medics began the war largely ignorant of the neuropsychiatric history of World War I. They confined themselves to symptomatic treatments designed to return soldiers to the fighting forces promptly, a course of action that was often medically and militarily counterproductive. Once broken by combat, soldiers who returned to the lines tended not to last very long or perform very well.

By the war's end, social psychology had supplanted psychiatry as the preferred means by which to understand the phenomenon. Fixing upon the context in which the soldier's mental trauma had occurred, Western armies saw the social bonding common to small, or "primary," groups as the proper antidote to neuropsychiatric casualties. Armies began to pay attention to how the psychological support provided by primary groups might contribute to the sturdiness of combat formations. Still, there remains a certain mysterious quality to battle fatigue and its modern variants that medical science has done little to dispel.

ROGER J. SPILLER

William S. Mullins and Albert J. Glass, eds., *Neuropsychiatry in World War II: The Overseas Theaters* (1978).

Beersheba, Battle of

October 31, 1917

Remembered as an outstanding example of tactical deception, the Battle of Beersheba paved the way for the British conquest of Palestine in World War I (q.v.). Following two costly, unsuccessful assaults on Gaza (March 26 and April 17–19, 1917), General Edmund Allenby (q.v.) assumed command of the Egyptian Expeditionary Force. With the war bogged down in the west, a breakthrough on the Ottoman front seemed a morale-building necessity. Allenby planned a surprise eastward movement to capture the desert town of Beersheba and thereby outflank the Ottoman-German-Austrian defenses at Gaza on the coast. Concealing his battle plan through diversionary naval shelling, surreptitious transfer of forces eastward, and the intentional "loss" of documents detailing an imminent attack on Gaza, Allenby's cavalry forces achieved a quick if hard-fought victory at Beersheba and proceeded northwestward to the coast. With the defenders of Gaza encircled and forced to surrender, a wholesale Ottoman retreat began.

NEIL ASHER SILBERMAN

Belisarius

A.D. 500?–565, *Byzantine General*

Probably the greatest Byzantine general, Belisarius was born in the Balkans, of unknown ethnic origin. After serving as one of Emperor Justinian's personal bodyguards, he became governor of Mesopotamia in the eastern provinces (A.D. 527–529). Appointed master of the soldiers in the Orient (529–531), he led Byzantine forces unsuccessfully against the Persians in frustrating actions. He crushed a rebellion (the Nika Revolt) at Constantinople against Justinian in 532, commanded an expeditionary force that reconquered North Africa from the Vandals (whose kingdom he annihilated) from 533 to 534, and reoccupied Sicily in 535. He was directing the reconquest of Italy from the Ostrogoths (536–540) when he came under suspicion and was recalled to Constantinople. He brought the captured Ostrogothic king to Constantinople, was then sent against the Persians (540–541), and later returned west to Italy (544–549) to fight, in protracted, difficult warfare, the resurgent Ostrogoths under their resourceful king, Totila. Belisarius exploited Ostrogoth vulnerabilities (including their neglect of horse archery) to reconquer much of Italy and reoccupy Rome and Ravenna, but he failed to end the war. After another recall to Constantinople, he successfully defended it against Kotrigur Huns (559–560). His victories greatly enriched him, but accusations of conspiracy caused his brief arrest in 562. An astute observer, he innovatively used craft, dissimulation, and psychology to accomplish victories with a minimum of soldiers (seldom more than eighteen thousand). His adviser (and superb historian) Procopius made him the hero of his *History of the Wars.*

WALTER E. KAEGI

Bismarck-Schönhausen, Otto von

1815–1898, Prussian Prime Minister and German Chancellor

"Red reactionary, smells of blood, to be used only when the bayonet reigns," King Frederick William IV had noted of Otto von Bismarck in 1848. Yet Bismarck was first and foremost a Prussian, convinced that the struggle with Austria for mastery in central Europe could be settled only by war. In fact, Bismarck is widely known for his ready recourse to war and his militant speeches. He directed wars against Denmark in 1864, Austria in 1866, and France in 1870–1871, whereby Prussia unified the German states. He spoke often of letting the guns do the talking and habitually wore his honorary general's uniform in Parliament. His famous "iron and blood" speech in 1862 marked him as a dangerous militarist. "After all," he once declared, "war is, properly speaking, the natural condition of humanity." Yet in later life the "Iron Chancellor" developed a healthy distrust of the military and of what he termed the "demigods" in the General Staff, based largely on his experiences in the wars of German unification. The carnage in Bohemia and France sobered his early enthusiasm for armed violence, and he came to see that one could never "anticipate the ways of Divine Providence securely enough" to entrust a nation's fate to its generals and war.

Bismarck's celebrated clashes with General Helmuth Karl von Moltke (q.v.), chief of the Prussian General Staff, laid bare the uneasy relationship between political and military leadership in time of war. Moltke drew a distinct boundary between politics and strategy: diplomacy was paramount until the start of hostilities; thereafter, military necessity reigned supreme. The generals resented Bismarck's heavy-handed interference in military operations, found him to be "ill-mannered" and "domineering," and were infuriated by what they considered to be his "infantile counsels." Bismarck, for his part, saw war as but a means to political ends and demanded that statecraft remain supreme at all times. He found the generals to possess the acumen of blinkered professionals, ignorant in diplomacy and politics. Although Bismarck never digested Carl von Clausewitz's (q.v.) *On War* ("the one great book I never read"), he understood that armed violence was but the "extension of politics by other means." Egotism rather than roman-

ticism, and *Realpolitik* rather than *Idealpolitik*, dictated his actions. The dualism between political and military authority remained unresolved; it would plague a future generation under Kaiser Wilhelm II.

Bismarck's statecraft was brilliantly revealed in the Bad Kissingen Dictate of 1877. The chancellor rejected the military's demand for new wars of conquest and instead settled for what the historian Ludwig Dehio called "semihegemony" on the Continent. He maintained 1 percent of the populace in the army and spun a web of alliances radiating out from Berlin: to Vienna in 1879, Rome in 1882, and St. Petersburg in 1887. In the process, Bismarck created a brief period of *pax germanica*. "We, situated in the center of Europe," he decreed, "must not be exposed to isolation." Two cardinal goals drove his policy: to allow no conflicts among the major powers in central Europe and to sustain German security without seeking German hegemony in Europe. None of his successors were wise enough to follow this sage counsel. Kaiser Wilhelm II dismissed Bismarck in April 1890 so that he could assume the post of "officer of the watch on the ship of state.... Full steam ahead!"

HOLGER H. HERWIG

Lothar Gall, *Bismarck, The White Revolutionary*, 2 vols. (1986); Otto Pflanze, *Bismarck and the Development of Germany*, 3 vols. (1990).

Blacks in the Military

In the ancient world, Black Africans constituted a significant element within the Egyptian population and played an important part in the pharaohs' armies. Later, Blacks played a vital military role in states in or bordering on Africa, including Yemen, the Maghrib states, Egypt, Sudan, and Ethiopia. With the rise of Islam in the eighth-century Arab world, Blacks served as slave soldiers — ironically, servile yet also honorable. Visibly different from their masters, Blacks were unlikely to succeed in intrigue against the state, a factor that made them attractive as slaves. Still, Black slave generals sometimes commanded armies and might become rulers. African states south of the Sahara also maintained powerful armies, the most notable in Ethiopia and the many states of West Africa.

European conquest of the Americas led to the importing of Blacks as servile labor; administrators

The all-Black 369th Infantry returns from France after the longest frontline service of any U.S. regiment in World War I — 191 days in the trenches. The regiment served with the French army, and more than 170 were awarded the croix de guerre or Legion of Honor.

thus feared their use as soldiers, but expediency and Blacks' greater immunity to tropical diseases led to their use as soldiers in New Spain as early as the sixteenth century. They later served in segregated militia units and, in Brazil, sometimes under Black officers.

Severe manpower problems in the New World led to the wider military use of Blacks (for example, a Black militia was founded in the Danish West Indies [U.S. Virgin Islands] in the 1720s, with a Black captain). They also played a most significant role in the development of martial music — Blacks were still thought to be exotic in eighteenth-century Europe, and they served as percussionists in military marching bands, dressed in elaborate, sumptuous "Oriental" costumes that mixed Turkish and European martial styles.

During the American Revolution (q.v.), Blacks served on both sides in segregated corps under white officers; whereas the rebel Blacks' status was not improved by this service, those fighting for England were ensured free status and passage to West Africa (helping establish the Sierra Leone colony). In the 1790s, high disease rates among whites led Great Britain to raise twelve Black West India regiments; slave dealers supplied early "recruits," but after 1808, captured illegal slave-trade ships provided manpower. The West India regiments fought with distinction in the Caribbean and West Africa until 1926. Blacks constituted a significant element as British Royal Navy sailors. During the Napoleonic Wars (see *Napoleon*), Britain raised the ancestor unit of the Ceylon (Sri Lanka) regiment partly from slaves purchased from Portuguese Mozambique; in Egypt, French general Jean-

Baptiste Kléber in 1799 bought slaves from Ethiopian slave dealers to form new battalions.

In the American Civil War (q.v.), Blacks helped to tip the balance in favor of the Union, serving in segregated units in which the first Black officers were commissioned. They struggled against Northern racist attitudes opposed to their service and proved themselves determined and able in battle. Ironically, the Confederacy, shortly before its defeat, out of desperation was forced to accept Black soldiers as well. Black units remained in service after 1865; the military constituted a source of employment for the Black poor.

The dramatic African colonial expansion of European powers after 1880 resulted in the creation of a number of Black units. Regiments of the British Gold Coast (Ghana), Nigeria, and Sierra Leone — together with the Gambia Company — united to form the West African Field Force in 1899; in East Africa, the King's African Rifles likewise amalgamated other local units in 1902, and southern African colonies also raised Black corps. Recruits came only from "warlike" ethnic groups; such regiments served with distinction in World War I (q.v.).

France utilized African soldiers in Louisiana from 1736 (to repress an Indian uprising) and in Senegal from 1765; in the early twentieth century, French colonial Black soldiers, the "Tirailleurs sénégalais," were renowned as assault troops on the Western Front during World War I. The United States also sent Black units to Europe.

In World War II (q.v.), Blacks served in all the U.S. military forces — but still in segregated units that were subject to institutionalized discrimination — and in European forces from those states possessing African and Caribbean colonies. This wider military service by Blacks tended to broaden veterans' horizons and encourage later demands for better treatment, contributing to political movements for equality in America and to African demands for independence from colonialism.

The Korean War (q.v.) was especially important for American Black soldiers; General Matthew Ridgway (q.v.) got permission in 1950 to integrate all his Far East command's units; later, a special army report stated that integration had benefited the army. All units were integrated in 1952, putting this traditionally Southern-dominated, conservative institution in the forefront of American racial integration. Until then, Black units suffered discrimination by commanders and received inferior equipment and conditions.

The Vietnam War (q.v.) saw the widespread drafting of American Blacks into the military, whereas wealthier whites often evaded the draft through college deferments. But on a positive note, increased numbers of Black officers served in Vietnam. In the 1992 Persian Gulf operation (q.v.), for the first time the highest-ranking American officer, the commander of the Joint Chiefs of Staff, General Colin Powell, was himself Black; he held more power than any Black soldier in U.S. history.

SCOTT HUGHES MYERLY

Roger Norman Buckley, *Slaves in Red Coats: The British West India Regiments, 1795–1815* (1979); Bernard C. Nalty, *Strength for the Fight* (1987); Benjamin Quarles, *The Negro in the Civil War* (1953).

Blenheim, Battle of

August 13, 1704

This battle was the duke of Marlborough's (q.v.) first important victory in the War of the Spanish Succession (q.v.) and also the first major battle in which he exercised independent command. It climaxed a remarkable march by an Anglo-Dutch army of forty thousand men, covering 250 miles in twenty-one days from the Low Countries to the Danube — notable not because of the difficulties of the terrain nor serious military opposition, but because of the distance involved and the immense logistical effort required. Superior logistics ensured that the allied troops arrived in central Europe in prime condition, which sharply contrasted with their French adversaries, who were in a bedraggled state after a much shorter march. Marlborough's purpose was to remove the threat that France and its ally Bavaria were believed to pose to Britain's partner Austria, though it now seems more likely that French strategy instead aimed only at securing communications with Bavaria and laying waste to southwestern Germany.

When the duke reached central Europe, his army joined Austrian troops led by Prince Eugène of Savoy to create a combined force of sixty thousand men. The two commanders decided upon an aggressive strategy and forced the French and Bavarian armies to a decisive battle that took place around the village of Blen-

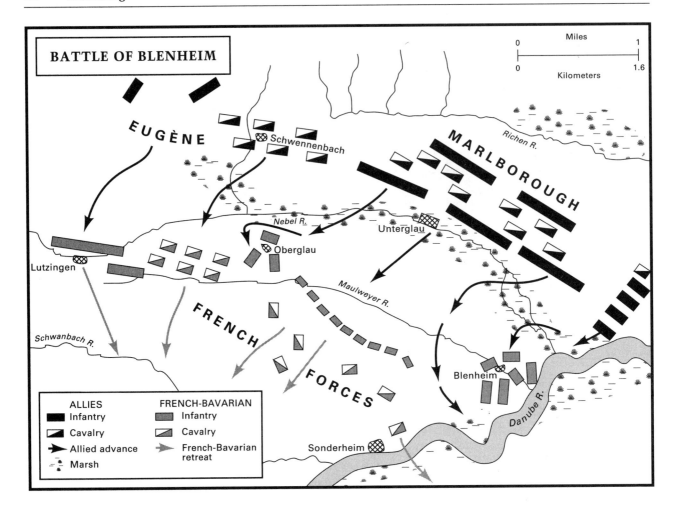

BATTLE OF BLENHEIM

EUGÈNE

Schwennenbach

MARLBOROUGH

Richen R.

Nebel R.

Unterglau

Oberglau

Lutzingen

Maulweyer R.

FRENCH

Schwanbach R.

FORCES

Blenheim

Danube R.

ALLIES
Infantry
Cavalry
Allied advance
Marsh

FRENCH-BAVARIAN
Infantry
Cavalry
French-Bavarian
retreat

Sonderheim

heim (Blindheim) on the Danube. Though the allies were numerically inferior, Marlborough's energetic leadership and his skill in creating a local superiority in one part of the battlefield, together with Eugène's bravery and spirited contribution, brought about a famous victory commemorated in the name of the duke's palace of Blenheim, near Oxford in his English homeland.

H. M. SCOTT

Blitzkrieg

Conventional wisdom traces blitzkrieg, "lightning war," to the development in Germany between 1918 and 1939 of a body of doctrine using mobility to prevent repetition of the attritional deadlock of World War I (q.v.). Soldiers such as Hans von Seeckt (q.v.) and Heinz Guderian (q.v.) allegedly perceived more clearly than their counterparts elsewhere in Europe the military potential of the internal-combustion engine combined with modern communications technology. Large formations moving on tracks and wheels, directed by radios, could rupture an enemy's front and so disorganize its rear that countermeasures would be paralyzed. First tested in Poland, the concept reached perihelion in France and the Low Countries in 1940, when in less than six weeks the German army crushed the combined forces of four nations. Applied a year later against the Soviet Union, blitzkrieg purportedly brought the Wehrmacht to the gates of Moscow in six months. Some accounts insist that only Adolf Hitler's (q.v.) incompetent interference tipped the war's balance so far against Germany that even blitzkrieg's most sophisticated re-

The 1939 Nazi blitzkrieg vanquished Poland in less than a month.

finements could do no more than stave off the Reich's collapse.

Seldom in the history of military thought have such elaborate interpretive structures been built on a more limited foundation. The term *blitzkrieg* was in fact never used in the title of a German military manual or handbook. Nor is it to be widely found in the memoirs or correspondence of German generals. The word was used in the Wehrmacht during World War II (q.v.) but was commonly considered to be of foreign origin. Guderian wrote in *Panzer Leader* that "our enemies coined the word." The first known use of the word *blitzkrieg* in an English publication occurred in an article in *Time* magazine in September 25, 1939, discussing the Polish campaign. From there the word came into general circulation as a shorthand description of a form of war that seemed to have no convenient existing frame of reference. From Western sources it expanded into German popular military literature, and from there into history. The transmission process was facilitated by the British theorists J. F. C. Fuller (q.v.) and Basil Liddell Hart (q.v.), who insisted that their concepts of mobile war were fundamental to the German victories of 1939–1941.

Reality is at once more limited and more complex.

On one level, mobile warfare was a faute de mieux improvisation that arose from the restrictions on conventional forces stipulated by the Treaty of Versailles (q.v.). The German high command in the 1920s and 1930s also sought inspiration for the future in its own past — specifically in the ideas of Helmuth Karl von Moltke (q.v.) and Alfred von Schlieffen (q.v.). Tanks, aircraft, and motor trucks were regarded as force multipliers facilitating traditional operational approaches. The aim of German military planners in both the Weimar Republic and the Third Reich was to achieve victory by enveloping enemy armies, threatening their lines of supply and communications, and forcing them to fight in an unexpected direction. The anticipated result would be quick, decisive victories for a state that since the days of Frederick the Great (q.v.) had been convinced of its inability to win a drawn-out war of attrition.

These concepts remained tactical and operational. Grand-strategic and economic planning in Adolf Hitler's Reich were not shaped by a doctrine of lightning war. A familiar argument is that Nazi Germany deliberately rearmed in breadth rather than depth, proposing to tailor its force mix to specific situations in the context of a diplomatic strategy designed to keep Germany's enemies isolated from one another. However, no significant data support such a grand design. Instead, the best evidence indicates that Hitler sought rearmament in both breadth and depth, with an economy oriented to military needs as completely as possible. Instead, far from coordinating their specific preparations, the army, navy, and air force competed so intensely for scarce raw materials that as early as 1938 their demands seriously overheated the ramshackle Nazi economy. Throughout the war the Wehrmacht's inability to cooperate internally was one of Germany's most significant military weaknesses — a far cry from the smoothly working machine that is the essence of blitzkrieg in popular myths.

Revisionism must not be taken to extremes. German operational successes in the early years of World War II were by no means the product of sheer good fortune. But neither did they reflect a coherent, planned approach to the diplomatic, economic, and military challenges that after 1918 confronted a state unwilling to accept the consequences of its defeat in World War I. What are commonly called blitzkrieg operations developed out of experiences gained on the field between 1939 to 1941. In that sense blitzkrieg is best understood as a post facto construction for explaining a complex structure of events and ideas.

DENNIS E. SHOWALTER

James S. Korum, *The Roots of Blitzkrieg: Hans von Seeckt and the German Military Reform* (1992).

Blockade

Blockades are attempts by one belligerent state to obstruct a port or an entire coast of another state to prevent shipping or communication by sea with that state by allied or neutral powers. Blockades come in two categories, military and commercial. Military (or naval) blockades try to prevent an enemy's armed forces from leaving port, to bring them to action before they can carry out the mission for which they left port. Their ultimate purpose is to secure command of the sea, and their executors usually are battle squadrons. Commercial blockades have no immediate military objective but seek first and foremost to halt the enemy's seaborne trade by denying it the use of the

sea-lanes of communications, ultimately forcing the adversary to surrender. Commercial blockades usually are conducted by cruisers, or in some cases, submarines. Blockades may encompass the whole enemy coast or part of it, and they often combine military and commercial blockades.

Blockades may also be "close" or "open." The former, as exercised by Britain when it bottled up French naval forces in ports and denied merchants access to seaborne shipping and communication during the rule of Napoleon (q.v.), are exhausting in terms of wear and tear to both ships and men; they demand a force greater than that against which they act and require large reserves for their relief. Close blockades became impractical with the development of mines and submarines — naval commanders declined to risk expensive capital ships to patrol lethal waters close to hostile shores. Open blockades, as executed by Britain against Germany from 1914 to 1918 and again from 1939 to 1945, strive to protect one's own trade and communications and deny command of home waters to the enemy. The penalty for blockade violators is usually loss of ship and cargo.

Modern common law has defined five conditions of blockade. First, it must be established by authority of a belligerent government. Second, under Article 4 of the Declaration of Paris (1856), it must be effective and not simply a "paper blockade" — that is, an enemy's shores must be actively patrolled at all times; a mere declaration of intent to blockade is unlawful. Third, it must be continuously maintained and impartially enforced against all vessels. Fourth, there must be some violation by egress or ingress before a neutral vessel may be seized (London Naval Conference, 1909). And fifth, a vessel about to be seized must have knowledge of the blockade.

In modern times, famous blockades include those by Britain against French and Spanish ports, 1803–1814; by the United States against the Confederacy, 1861–1865; by Britain against Germany, August 1914–June 1919; by German U-boats against Britain and its allied and associated powers, February–June 1915, March–April 1916, and, more rigorously, February 1917–October 1918; by Britain against Germany, November 1939–May 1945; by German U-boats against Britain and the Allies, 1939–1945; and by the republics of the Western Hemisphere against all actions "contrary to [their] security" in January 1942 (Rio de Janeiro Foreign Ministers' Declaration). Most effective among these blockades were those by the

United States against the Confederacy in the 1860s and against Japan in World War II (q.v.). More recent U.S. naval blockades were maintained against Cuba in 1962 and Vietnam in 1965. The United Nations in 1966 authorized Britain to blockade Rhodesian oil — an example of an internationally authorized commercial blockade.

Perhaps most severe in human terms was the open blockade of Germany in World War I (q.v.) by Britain and its allied and associated powers. According to the German Health Office in 1919, the "hunger blockade" and its attendant malnutrition resulted in 763,000 deaths, raised child mortality by 50 percent, increased tubercular-related deaths by 72 percent, and caused a 51 percent surge in women's mortality. The blockade led to rampant cases of rickets, influenza, dysentery, scurvy, keratomalacia, and hunger edema. It also destroyed civilian morale in Germany, thus helping the Allies achieve victory in 1918.

HOLGER H. HERWIG

Julian Corbett, *Some Principles of Maritime Strategy* (1988).

Boer War

1899–1902

The Boer War began when Sir Alfred Milner, the British high commissioner in South Africa, goaded the Boers in the South African republics into declaring war on October 12, 1899. The Boers, a people of mixed Dutch, German, French, and British ancestry who spoke their own language (Afrikaans), had strong feelings toward independence. They were understandably wary of British intentions. They had armed themselves with modern weapons from Europe, and with the help of these they enjoyed initial success, besieging Mafeking, Kimberley, and Ladysmith.

A large expeditionary force under General Redvers Buller was sent from England to overwhelm them. A part of this army moved to relieve Kimberley and Mafeking; another part attacked the Boers who had invaded Cape Colony; and the remainder, under Buller's personal command, attempted to relieve Ladysmith. All came to grief within one week ("Black Week," December 10–15, 1899). Under Lord Roberts, with Lord Kitchener (q.v.) as his second in command, however, Kimberley was relieved on February 15, 1900, and soon after, some four thousand Boers were

trapped at Paardeberg on the banks of the Modder River.

On March 13, Roberts entered Bloemfontein, capital of the Orange Free State, and annexed the country as a British province. After a delay caused by typhoid among his troops, he marched into the Transvaal, occupying Johannesburg and Pretoria. By August all of the major towns, railways, mines, and factories were in British hands. The Transvaal was annexed, and in November, considering his work completed, Roberts returned home, leaving Kitchener to mop up.

But the Boers refused to surrender, fighting a guerrilla war that lasted until May 31, 1902. Only by organizing a blockhouse system and carrying out a scorched earth policy was Kitchener able to bring the stubborn Boers to heel.

BYRON FARWELL

Bolívar, Simon

1783–1830, *South American Soldier and Political Leader*

Born in Caracas, Venezuela, into a rich Creole family, Simon Bolívar became the main protagonist in the struggle for the independence of South America. His military knowledge came through reading authors such as Julius Caesar (q.v.) and Raimundo Montecuccoli, and he placed it at the disposal of the independence movement against Spain that began in 1810. Bolívar soon became the military and political leader of the Venezuelan independence struggle, fighting first and foremost for liberty. But in 1814, Bolívar withdrew to the Orinoco plains: the revolution became consistently victorious only after the plainsmen (*llaneros*), superb mounted warriors, had joined Bolívar's cause. The year 1817 brought a decisive victory for the insurgents in the Battle of San Félix, and, with Venezuela temporarily secured, Bolívar led his troops across the Andes into Colombia, defeating the royalists who upheld the cause of Spain, at Boyacá in 1819. After crossing the Andes once more, Bolívar defeated the remnants of royalist opposition in Venezuela in the Battle of Carabobo (1821). He died in 1830 after seeing the disintegration of the state of Gran Colombia (consisting of Venezuela, Colombia, Ecuador, and Panama) that he had helped to create.

HANS VOGEL

Bouvines, Battle of

July 27, 1214

Ever since King Philip II of France had driven him out of Anjou, Normandy, and Poitou in 1203–1204, King John of England had been planning the grand — and expensive — strategy by which he hoped to recover his lost territories: he set out to pit an Anglo-German-Flemish army financed by King John himself and commanded by the Emperor Otto IV and Count Ferrand of Flanders against Philip.

In 1214, John (an erratic and uninspiring leader) campaigned in the west of France, and although his army fled (July 2) from the siege of La-Roche-au-Moine (near Angers) at the approach of Philip's son Louis, the strategy had succeeded in making his enemies divide their forces. In consequence, Philip's own army in the northeast was outnumbered when Otto IV attacked. Unable to withdraw safely, Philip decided to fight. It is impossible to reconstruct the course of the battle or estimate the numbers involved with any certainty. But it is certain that the outcome was disastrous for the count of Flanders (who was captured) and for Otto IV and John, both of whom quickly lost control of their own states. In England, rebellion led to the signing of Magna Carta. In France, Bouvines ensured that the crown would remain what Philip Augustus had begun to make it — the dominant power in the kingdom.

JOHN GILLINGHAM

Boxer Rebellion

1899–1900

This struggle against foreigners and foreign influence in north China was initiated by warriors of the I-ho-ch'üan ("righteous and harmonious fists" — hence the western name "Boxers") and related secret martial arts societies and was joined by the Ch'ing dynasty (see *Manchus*).

The long lineage of the Boxers went back to traditional underground political-religious organizations such as the Eight Trigrams sect and the White Lotus Society. But mobilization of masses of traditional fighters against well-equipped foreign forces was something new — ultimately a consequence of the empress dowager's success in ending the "hundred days' reform" of 1898 by placing its patron, the young Kuang-hsü emperor, under house arrest. By halting

In 1900, international forces suppressed the uprising of antiforeign Chinese traditionalists that became known as the Boxer Rebellion. Here, Italian soldiers watch over captured Boxers.

this reform, she prevented China from rapidly acquiring the modern institutions and armaments required to deal with foreigners on their own terms. Therefore she and her supporters at court had to turn to traditional means to confront mounting foreign pressure for territorial and other concessions.

The Boxers, who were strongest in the capital region and Shantung, had initially called for overthrow of the Ch'ing, which they considered an alien dynasty, and restoration of the Ming; court patronage, however, which was hastened by reports of the Boxers' immunity to bullets, led the Boxers to support the Ch'ing and concentrate on expulsion of foreigners. Their attacks began in 1899 and included the murders of foreign missionaries, numerous Chinese Christians, the chancellor of the Japanese legation, and the German minister, as well as the destruction of railways, churches, and other "foreign" structures. With support from regular Ch'ing troops, Tientsin was captured and the Legation Quarter in Peking besieged in the summer of 1900. Seven powers dispatched a relief force some 18,000 strong: the largest detachment was Japan's (8,000); the smallest, Italy's (53). They quickly drove the Ch'ing forces from Tientsin; in Peking they relieved the legations, freed the foreigners, and systematically sacked the Chinese capital (from which the court had fled). Russia took the opportunity to occupy Manchuria, which foreshadowed war with Japan four years later (see *Russo-Japanese War*). Hostilities with China remained limited to the north, however, because of the neutrality and reassurances of the viceroys of the south, as well as the decision of the commander of Chinese besieging troops not to overrun Peking's Legation Quarter, as he could have.

The punitive Boxer Protocol of 1901 required execution of ten high officials and punishment of a hundred others, as well as destruction of Chinese fortifications and demilitarization of railways in the Peking region; it established a system of foreign garrisons, reaffirmed foreign privileges and immunities, and imposed a massive indemnity of 67.5 million pounds sterling, whose payments stretched to 1940. Foreign diplomats considered the Boxer Protocol the capstone of the "Treaty System," which had regulated China's international relations since the mid–nineteenth century. But for Chinese nationalists, this most onerous of the "Unequal Treaties" was as hateful as was the Treaty of Versailles (q.v.) in interwar Germany. The United States' indemnity share was devoted to an educational fund; payment to other powers was suspended in 1917 when China joined the Allies in World War I (q.v.), and it never resumed.

ARTHUR WALDRON

Boyne, Battle of

July 1, 1690

The "Glorious Revolution" of 1688 may well have been a bloodless one in England, but in Ireland it precipitated a lengthy and bitter struggle — known as the "war of the three kings" — between the ousted English monarch James II, supported by Louis XIV of France, and his nephew and successor to the English throne, William III of Orange. In 1689 James mobilized a Catholic army that numbered about twenty-five thousand men, but, since it had few cannon and remained ill trained and poorly equipped, it proved no match for William III's superior force of thirty-five thousand. After failing to capture Derry and Enniskillen, the Jacobites succumbed as they tried to cross the river Boyne, near Drogheda. The battle left one thousand Jacobites and five hundred Williamites dead.

Even though the war did not end until October 1691, with the conclusion of the Treaty of Limerick, William's decisive victory at the Boyne not only gave him control of Dublin and much of the east coast of Ireland but also forced James to flee to France. The war shifted the balance of power in Ireland from the Catholics to the Protestants for over two hundred years, and its effect is still to be seen in Northern Ireland today, when the Protestant community marches to celebrate the anniversary of William's victory and toasts his "glorious, pious, and immortal memory."

JANE H. OHLMEYER

Bradley, Omar N.

1893–1981, General of the U.S. Army

Omar Nelson Bradley was born in rural Missouri and spent his boyhood impoverished, with no thought of a military career, until someone suggested that he might qualify for an appointment to West Point, where he could receive a paid education. Bradley seized the opportunity, qualified for admission in 1911, and graduated in the class of 1915, later acclaimed as "the class the stars fell on."

During World War I (q.v.), while most of his contemporaries were serving in the American Expeditionary Force in France, Bradley's infantry regiment was guarding copper mines in strike-ridden Montana. Cast into the backwater of the army of the interwar period, he was apprehensive, needlessly as it turned out, that his lack of combat service would harm his career.

Bradley graduated from the Command and General Staff College at Fort Leavenworth, Kansas, in 1929, and subsequently served as an instructor in tactics at the Infantry School. He deeply impressed the assistant commandant, Lieutenant Colonel George C. Marshall (q.v.), who rated him "quiet, unassuming, capable, [with] sound common sense. Absolute dependability. Give him a job and forget it." Bradley, in turn, emulated the future chief of staff's leadership qualities, later observing, "From General Marshall I learned the rudiments of effective command. . . . When an officer performed as I expected him to, I gave him a free hand. When he hesitated, I tried to help him. And when he failed, I relieved him."

In 1938, Bradley was assigned to the War Department General Staff, where one of his duties was to present decision papers orally to Chief of Staff Marshall, who promoted him directly to brigadier general in 1941 and sent him to Fort Benning as commandant of the Infantry School. In 1942, Bradley was promoted to major general and first given command of the Eighty-second Division, and later of the Twenty-eighth (National Guard) Division. With the efficiency and ruthlessness that was to characterize his later performance, he rapidly turned the understaffed, clique-ridden, demoralized Twenty-eighth Division into a first-class fighting unit.

In February 1943, Marshall assigned Bradley to North Africa to assist Dwight D. Eisenhower (q.v.) in the aftermath of the disastrous American defeat at Kasserine Pass. He was sent first as an observer to Second Corps under Lloyd Fredenthall, but on the recommendation of the new commander, George S. Patton, Jr. (q.v.), Bradley was appointed deputy commander and later succeeded Patton in command of the corps, which he led with distinction during the final days of the campaign in Tunisia and in the short but difficult Sicilian campaign in July and August 1943.

Eisenhower next selected Bradley to command the U.S. First Army in Operation Overlord, the cross-Channel invasion of Normandy, on June 6, 1944. Bradley was the architect of Operation Cobra, the American breakout from the Cotentin Peninsula that unleashed the First Army and Patton's newly activated Third Army into Brittany and across southern Normandy, precipitating the collapse of the German army that ended the campaign.

As an army group commander from August 1, 1944, to V-E Day in May 1945, Bradley commanded more troops than any general in American history: four armies, twelve corps, forty-eight divisions — in all, over 1.3 million troops.

Despite earning the nickname "the GI General" from correspondent Ernie Pyle, Bradley's low-key style of command made him little known among his troops. The only serious criticisms of his generalship are that he acted indecisively during the battle of the Falaise gap and uncharacteristically insisted on attacking through the Hürtgen Forest in the autumn of 1944. In all other circumstances, Bradley was a resourceful strategist and tactician who earned high praise from Eisenhower as "the master tactician of our forces" and "America's foremost battle leader." In 1950, when Bradley became one of only five U.S. Army officers promoted to the five-star rank of General of the Army, President Harry S. Truman praised Bradley as "the ablest field general the U.S. ever had."

In August 1945, Bradley was appointed to head the Veterans Administration, and until February 1948, when he succeeded Eisenhower as U.S. Army Chief of Staff, he helped overhaul an organization responsible for seventeen million veterans. In August 1949 he became the first-ever chairman of the Joint Chiefs of Staff, serving two terms during the difficult period of the Korean War (q.v.).

Omar Bradley retired in 1953 after thirty-eight years of distinguished military service; when he died at the age of eighty-eight, his reputation as one of the giants of the U.S. Army of World War II, and an exemplar of the American military tradition of producing superior leaders, was secure.

CARLO W. D'ESTE

Britain, Battle of

July–September 1940

On June 17, 1940, the defeated French signed an armistice and quit World War II (q.v.). Britain now stood alone against the power of Germany's military forces, which had conquered most of Western Europe in less than two months. But Prime Minister Winston Churchill (q.v.) rallied his stubborn people and outmaneuvered those politicians who wanted to negotiate with Adolf Hitler (q.v.). But Britain's success in continuing the war would very much depend on the RAF Fighter Command's ability to thwart the Luftwaffe's efforts to gain air superiority. This then would be the first all-air battle in history.

In fact, Britain's situation was more favorable than most of the world recognized at the time. Britain possessed an effective air defense system, first-rate fighter pilots, and a great military leader in Air Marshal Hugh Dowding (q.v.). On the other hand, the Germans had major problems: they had no navy left after the costly conquest of Norway, their army was unprepared for any form of amphibious operations, and the Luftwaffe had suffered heavy losses in the west (the first two factors made a seaborne attack on the British Isles impossible from the first).

Even more serious, the Germans had poor intelligence and little idea of British vulnerabilities. They wasted most of July in waiting for a British surrender and attacked only in August. Although air strikes did substantial damage to radar sites, on August 13–15 the Luftwaffe soon abandoned that avenue and turned to attacks on RAF air bases. A battle of attrition ensued in which both sides suffered heavy losses (an average loss of 21 percent of the RAF's fighter pilots and 16 percent of the Luftwaffe's fighter pilots each month during July, August, and September).

For a time the advantage seemed to swing slightly in favor of the Germans, but a combination of bad intelligence and British attacks on Berlin led the Luftwaffe to change its operational approach to massive attacks on London. The first attack on London on September 7 was quite successful; the second, on September 15, failed not only with heavy losses, but also with a collapse of morale among German bomber crews when British fighters appeared in large numbers and shot down many of the Germans. As a result, Hitler permanently postponed a landing on the British Isles and suspended the Battle of Britain.

WILLIAMSON MURRAY

Brunswick, Karl Wilhelm, Duke of

1735–1806, Prussian Field Marshal

Nephew of Frederick the Great (q.v.) of Prussia and an exponent of his methods of warfare, Karl Wilhelm, duke of Brunswick, served in the Seven Years' War (q.v.) and became a Prussian general in 1773. Promoted to field marshal in 1787, he commanded the Prussian army that successfully and rapidly invaded the United Provinces (Dutch Republic) that autumn, in order to restore the authority of the house of Orange.

In 1792 he was appointed commander of the Prussian forces sent to suppress the French Revolution, and the "Brunswick Manifesto" warned that Paris would be subject to exemplary vengeance if Louis XVI was harmed (see *French Revolution, Wars of the*). Yet Brunswick's army was not prepared for a major campaign, and it was arguably too late in the year to attempt one. At 108 miles from Paris, Brunswick met the French at Valmy (q.v.): heavily outnumbered, he turned back without a full-scale engagement and evacuated France. In 1793 he counterattacked against the French, who had invaded Germany, and recaptured Mainz, but resigned in 1794 in protest at interference by Frederick William II of Prussia. He returned to command the Prussian army in 1806 but was routed by Napoleon (q.v.) at Auerstedt and died of his wounds soon after. Brunswick symbolized the problems that ancien régime warfare faced in dealing with the French Revolution.

JEREMY BLACK

Brusilov, Aleksei

1853–1926, Russian General

Russia's most successful general of World War I (q.v.) made his initial reputation as an instructor and commander of the army's cavalry school. Promoted to corps command in 1914, he led the Eighth Army against the Austrians during the advance into Galicia, and then in 1915 on the long retreat after Gorlice-Tarnów. He established himself as both a skillful tactician and a commander able to inspire and control his subordinates. Assigned in March 1916 to command the Southwestern Front, Brusilov brought to his new post not only an offensive spirit, but also a set of offensive techniques well adapted to the Eastern Front. In June 1916, when Russia's allies called for an attack to relieve Austrian pressure on Italy, Brusilov responded not merely by concentrating on a single sector, but by sending his four armies forward simultaneously, using local reserves to exploit local successes. The result was a series of breakthroughs on a front of over two hundred miles that virtually destroyed the Austro-Hungarian army's fighting power. German reserves drawn from the west (see *Somme, Battle of the* and *Verdun, Battle of*) eventually halted an attack already slowed by supply shortages and hampered by command rivalries that even Brusilov could not overcome. After the revolution of March 1917, Brusilov became commander in chief of a Russian army no longer equal to the offensive the provisional government demanded. Relieved of his post, Brusilov subsequently joined the Red Army (q.v.) in 1920, but, serving in an advisory capacity, his role was largely symbolic.

DENNIS E. SHOWALTER

Bulge, Battle of the

December 16, 1944–January 28, 1945

In December 1944, in an all-out gamble to compel the Allies to sue for peace, Adolf Hitler (q.v.) ordered the only major German counteroffensive of the war in northwest Europe. Its objective was to split the Allied armies by means of a surprise blitzkrieg (q.v.) thrust through the Ardennes to Antwerp, marking a repeat of what the Germans had done three times previously — in September 1870, August 1914, and May 1940. Despite Germany's historical penchant for mounting counteroffensives when things looked darkest, the Allies' leadership miscalculated and left the Ar-

BATTLE OF THE BULGE

dennes lightly defended by only two inexperienced and two battered American divisions.

On December 16, three German armies (more than a quarter-million troops) launched the deadliest and most desperate battle of the war in the west in the poorly roaded, rugged, heavily forested Ardennes. The once-quiet region became bedlam as American units were caught flat-footed and fought desperate battles to stem the German advance at St.-Vith, Elsenborn Ridge, Houffalize and, later, Bastogne, which was defended by the 101st Airborne Division. The inexperienced U.S. 106th Division was nearly annihilated, but even in defeat helped buy time for Brigadier General Bruce C. Clarke's brilliant defense of St.-Vith. As the German armies drove deeper into the Ardennes in an attempt to secure vital bridgeheads west of the River Meuse quickly, the line defining the Allied front took on the appearance of a large protrusion or bulge, the name by which the battle would forever be known.

A crucial German shortage of fuel and the gallantry of American troops fighting in the frozen forests of the Ardennes proved fatal to Hitler's ambition to snatch, if not victory, at least a draw with the Allies in the west. Lieutenant General George S. Patton's (q.v.) remarkable feat of turning the Third Army ninety degrees from Lorraine to relieve the besieged town of Bastogne was the key to thwarting the German counteroffensive. The Battle of the Bulge was the costliest action ever fought by the U.S. Army, which suffered over 100,000 casualties.

CARLO W. D'ESTE

Burnside, Ambrose E.

1823–1881, *American Civil War General*

Perhaps the most unfortunate Union officer to rise to top rank, Ambrose Burnside possessed a West Point imprimatur, genial behavior, personal courage, and unwavering dedication, which prompted steady promotions; but his command irresolution, weak grasp of operational matters, lack of self-confidence, and poor leadership techniques portended eventual disaster. Following his spectacular defeat at Fredericksburg in December 1862, he candidly admitted his failings but was kept on by Abraham Lincoln (q.v.). He commanded the Ninth Corps for much of the war, most notably at Antietam (q.v.), where his failure to carry the Rohrbach Bridge in a timely fashion limited the Union victory. Burnside could be brilliant, as shown in his creation of what is arguably the first major amphibious force in U.S. history for his small-scale but successful 1862 North Carolina expedition; he could also experience a fatal torpor under stress, reducing him to drawing lots to select the lead division for his July 30, 1864, assault at Petersburg when his initial plan had been rejected. The resulting fiasco at the Crater ended his military career. He remains a figure large in image but distressingly shallow in substance.

NOAH ANDRE TRUDEAU

Byzantium

The Byzantine Empire experienced wars in every century of its history, often both internal and external ones. The greatest external ones were those of Julian's (q.v.) invasion of Persia (A.D. 363), Justinian's wars to reconquer the western provinces of the former Roman Empire (Sicily, Italy, North Africa, and Spain) in the sixth century (see *Belisarius*), those of Justinian and his successors (especially Heraclius, 610–641) with the Sassanian Persians, and those with the Muslim Arabs starting in the seventh century. Wars with Slavs and Bulgars and then the Altaic steppe horsemen in southeastern Europe lasted from the seventh century through the eleventh century. Struggles with the Seljuk Turks occupied the empire's leaders in the east from the late eleventh century through the middle of the thirteenth century, followed by wars with new Turkish entities, capped by the Ottomans (q.v.), who conquered Byzantine territory rapidly in the late thirteenth and early fourteenth centuries and then seized Constantinople in 1453.

Despite its wars, Byzantium endured by seldom attempting to risk everything in one engagement, often preferring diplomacy, conspiracy, and bribery to open combat. After the end of the fourth century, Byzantine field armies seldom exceeded 20,000 in a particular campaign, and total forces were probably something over 100,000 from the seventh century to the tenth century; their numbers fell rapidly to total only a few thousand by the fourteenth century. They relied on their Hellenistic and Roman military heritage, including its siege and ballistic machines. Byzantines made extensive use of updated strategic and tactical manuals of warfare and created pyrotechnic solutions (for example, Greek fire, an igneous petroleum mixture), which aided them especially in naval engagements. Fear of ambitious military commanders discouraged political leaders from entrusting adequate matériel and human resources to them. Total casualties and costs of these wars are unknown.

WALTER E. KAEGI

C

Caesar, Julius

100–44 B.C., Roman Statesman and General

Gaius Julius Caesar, one of the world's greatest military leaders, was born into a senatorial, patrician family and was the nephew of another famous Roman general, Marius. After the death of Marius and the rise of Sulla, Caesar's life was for a time in jeopardy, but in the early 60s B.C. he launched his own successful political and military career. Rising rapidly, he campaigned successfully for the consulship in 60 B.C. and struck a deal with two of Rome's leading figures, Pompey the Great and Crassus. Together the three of them became known as the First Triumvirate and controlled Rome throughout the 50s B.C., until Caesar and Pompey, after Crassus's death, went to war against one another in 49 B.C.

During the heyday of the First Triumvirate, Caesar devoted his energies to the conquest of Gaul (modern France). After serving as consul in 59 B.C., Caesar became governor of Cisalpine and Transalpine Gaul (northern Italy and southern France, respectively). In 58, when the Helvetii in Switzerland attempted to migrate into central Gaul, Caesar decided that they would be a threat to the Roman province, and in a great battle he stopped their advance and sent them back into their homeland. In the meantime he had become friendly with the chieftains of central Gaul, and they urged him to protect them against a German invader from across the Rhine, Ariovistus. So, in the summer of 58, after defeating the Helvetians, Caesar marched against the Germans and drove them out of Gaul.

Caesar was by then inextricably involved in the affairs of Gaul. Over the next several years, in a series of brilliant campaigns, the Roman general conquered all of Gaul and made it a Roman province. The conquest required several difficult battles in northern Gaul and the crossing of the Rhine over a trestle bridge constructed by Roman engineers. In the summers of 55 and 54 B.C., Caesar sailed across the English Channel, thereby securing his northern flank along the Rhine in Gaul by precluding a Celtic attack from across the Channel, though Britain did not become a Roman province for another hundred years. After dealing with a major revolt by Gallic chieftains, including Caesar's famous siege of Vercingetorix's bastion at Alesia in 52 B.C., the Roman leader brought resistance to an end in 51 and 50 B.C.

Early in 49, as his command in Gaul was coming to an end, Caesar began civil war with his old associate, Pompey the Great, who had allied himself with the Roman Senate against Caesar. In a surprising blitzkrieg, Caesar invaded Italy and drove Pompey into Macedonia in less than seventy days. Since Pompey had a fleet and Caesar did not, Caesar decided to attack Spain, where Pompey had strong support, while Caesar's men constructed warships. Victorious in Spain, Caesar then sailed to Macedonia, but he could not dislodge Pompey from his base at Dyrrhachium (modern Durazzo). Caesar finally raised the siege, fell back into central Greece, and defeated Pompey, who had pursued him, at the Battle of Pharsalus in 48 B.C.

Caesar was then drawn into an affair with Cleopatra in Egypt and finally had to fight two more battles with the Pompeians, one in North Africa (Thapsus, 46 B.C.) and another in Spain (Munda, 45 B.C.). Triumphant all over the Mediterranean, the great general was assassinated by political rivals on the Ides of March in 44 B.C., as he prepared an invasion of the Parthian Empire. His generalship was characterized by boldness, decisiveness, and a sometimes reckless willingness to move ahead of his supply lines.

ARTHER FERRILL

Çaldıran, Battle of

August 23, 1514

In this field battle, the army of the Iranian Safavid shah Ismail was defeated by that of the Ottoman sultan Selim I (q.v.) in the plain of the same name to the northeast of Lake Van on the present Iran-Turkey border.

Selim made the settling of scores with Ismail his first priority on securing the throne: Ismail's support of the heterodox Shi'ite elements proselytizing in Ottoman Anatolia, who were known as Kızılbaş from their red headgear, represented a profound challenge to the Sunni Ottoman dynasty's claims to religious and political legitimacy in the area.

Selim left Istanbul in April. Ismail, his own army weakened by recent defeat near Bokhara at the hands of the Özbek khans of Transoxania, hoped that a scorched earth policy in eastern Anatolia would retard Selim's advance; although the provisioning of Selim's troops proved difficult and they arrived exhausted and without enthusiasm for a fight, Ismail's lack of field cannon and harquebuses, whose impor-

tance was well appreciated by Selim, consigned his army to defeat. However, losses were high on both sides, most significantly among the Ottoman military command.

Selim advanced to the Safavid stronghold of Tabriz, apparently intending to winter his troops in the area and consolidate his victory the following spring, but dissent among the janissaries forced him to withdraw to Amasya.

In territorial terms the immediate gains by the Ottomans from their victory were small: their frontier was pushed further eastwards, and subsequent diplomacy won over Kurdish chiefs in the borderlands, thus establishing a buffer between Ottoman and Safavid domains and preventing the Safavids from controlling Mesopotamia.

The victory of Selim at Çaldıran signaled the success of a protoimperial state increasingly divorced from its Anatolian Turkish base over one that relied on these same seminomadic and syncretist populations for support.

CAROLINE FINKEL

Cambrai, Battle of

November 20–December 7, 1917

Cambrai was famous for two things: it saw the first great tank attack in history and, of equal importance, the first preregistration of artillery for an offensive. The idea for the large-scale use of British tanks started in early August 1917, when J. F. C. Fuller (second general staff officer, Tank Corps) (q.v.) and H. J. Elles (general staff officer, Tank Corps) put in a tank raid scheme for the Cambrai sector to General Headquarters. Eventually, headquarters agreed, and nine infantry divisions, five cavalry divisions, and three brigades of tanks were made available for the offensive under Julian Byng, general officer commanding, Third Army.

The key to the success of the Cambrai attack of November 20, 1917, was threefold. First, some 376 Mark IV fighting tanks were committed to the assault, to crush lanes through the wire and to protect the infantry as they advanced. Second, the artillery was able to do counterbattery and suppression work, and fire a barrage, without previous registration. This worked because the guns' targets had been plotted on maps beforehand, while each gun had previously been fired behind the lines to establish its accuracy. Third,

BATTLE OF CAMBRAI

Cambrai
Bourlon
Fontaine
Canal de St. Quentin
Graincourt
Noyelles
Boursies
SIXTH CORPS
Flesquières
Havrincourt
Marcoing
Masnières
Les Rues Vertes
FOURTH CORPS
CAVALRY DIV.
THIRD CORPS
La Vacquerie
Canal de St. Quentin
BRITISH THIRD ARMY
Gouzeaucourt
Banteux
Bantouzelle
Fins
Villers-Guislain
Cavalry Corps HQ

▪▪▪ British front line, Nov. 20
‐ ‐ ‐ British gains, Nov. 20
🔲 British tank battalions
→ Direction of attacks
‐·‐ British front line, Nov. 30
→ German counterattacks, Nov. 30

SEVENTH CORPS

0 1 2 3 Miles
0 1 2 3 4 5 Kilometers

because of the first two factors, the Cambrai offensive would be a complete surprise.

At 6:20 A.M. on November 20, tanks and infantry advanced with great success against an astonished German defense. By nightfall, gains of two to three miles had been achieved. However, cavalry exploitation was slow to develop, and although more gains were made in the next nine days, German reserves halted the attack. Then, on November 30, a German blitzkrieg (q.v.) counterattack recaptured much of the ground lost. The surprise storm troop tactics used here anticipated the methods of the German 1918 spring offensives (see *Ludendorff, Erich* and *Ludendorff Offensive*). However, the original tank and artillery combined attack at Cambrai had forever altered the modern battlefield.

TIM TRAVERS

Camouflage

Camouflage hides or disguises the appearance of troops, weapons, ships, airplanes, equipment, or structures. The military art has long emphasized deception, but although warriors and soldiers in some situations, such as ambushes, tried to conceal themselves, forces marshaled for battle in ages past put little premium on blending into the surroundings. A general who wished to keep the presence of units from the enemy could simply put them out of sight behind some convenient topographical feature. By and large, camouflage is a modern phenomenon, for it took a number of advances in military technology to make it essential.

In the age of black powder, weapons produced such obvious clouds of smoke that there was little hope of disguising them after they came into play. In addition, officers more concerned with seeing and controlling their men than with hiding them emphasized colorful uniforms rather than ones that would help a soldier disappear into the background. Moreover, weapons were not lethal enough to prohibit units from standing in the open (see *Uniforms and Military Dress*).

A number of factors radically altered this situation. The introduction of small-bore repeating rifles, machine guns, and rapid-fire artillery toward the end of the nineteenth century increased the rate, range, and accuracy of fire. Its increased lethality made cover and concealment in battle more valuable while the advent of smokeless powder made it possible. Battle dress came to hide rather than advertise a soldier's presence. The British donned khaki uniforms for colonial campaigns in the 1880s and for home service as well in 1902. The Germans went to field gray in 1910, whereas the French changed later, replacing their blue and red uniforms for horizon blue only after World War I (q.v.) began. This trend for more camouflaged clothing led to the mottled utilities worn today.

World War I greatly increased these impulses toward the use of camouflage. By then concealment of land forces required an added dimension — hiding them from aerial observation. Nets woven with various patterns of colored cloth cloaked gun positions, storage facilities, and so on. On the front line, armies showed considerable ingenuity. Modern artists served their countries by devising camouflage schemes; the French called upon cubist painters, while the Germans made use of the expressionist Franz Marc, among others. In World War II (q.v.), belligerents put a great deal of effort not only into hiding what was actually there, but also in displaying dummy equipment to make the enemy believe that something was there that was not. On the home front, the threat of aerial bombardment also caused authorities to camouflage civilian targets, such as oil storage tanks and factories. One U.S. aircraft factory in California disappeared under an artificial town built on its roofs.

At sea, camouflage had little purpose when ships stood at only a cable's length to blast away at each other, but the growing range and power of naval guns and the use of fast, long-range torpedoes available by the close of the nineteenth century changed this situation. By the 1890s the French and Germans painted their warships gray, and in 1903 the British followed suit. The German use of submarines in World War I further increased the need for camouflage. A number of naval advisers and artists argued that ships could not literally be hidden but that patterns painted on them could confuse an enemy as to the type, size, and direction of a vessel. After much debate, the British adopted "dazzle painting" in garish colors and shapes. After the war, the U.S. and British navies abandoned camouflage, but they returned to deceptive color schemes again in World War II. Some, like the dazzle painting of World War I, broke up the shape of the vessel; some attempted to make ships less visible against the horizon; and some were meant to make a ship appear to be of another class or type.

With limited exceptions, warplanes made little use

of camouflage in World War I, but after that conflict, studies demonstrated the value of using light gray or blue on the bottom surfaces of an aircraft to make it less visible from the ground, and varying earth tones or sea tones on the upper surfaces to allow it to blend in when seen from above. Simple black best cloaked an airplane at night. Although radar has diminished the importance of aircraft camouflage, it is still employed. Of course, in a sense, certain high-tech countermeasures provide a kind of electronic camouflage by confusing and distracting enemy radar or infrared sensors, or, in the case of stealth technology, so reducing an aircraft's visibility to radar that it cannot be spotted at all.

Many of the visual camouflage practices of the World War II era retain their relevance today, but modern imaging technology pierces the darkness of night and also requires that soldiers be aware of the heat signatures of their vehicles, which stand out vividly in infrared scopes. Camouflage must now be even more than meets the eye.

JOHN A. LYNN

Guy Hartcup, *Camouflage: A History of Concealment and Deception in War* (1980).

Camperdown, Battle of

October 11, 1797

This battle was fought during the Wars of the French Revolution (q.v.) off the coast of North Holland near Kamperduin between a British squadron under Admiral Adam Duncan and the (French-controlled) Dutch fleet under Vice Admiral Jan Willem de Winter. Both sides had sixteen ships of the line and some frigates; the Dutch formed a line of battle heading northeastward, parallel to the coast and about nine miles off shore, when Duncan's squadron appeared from the north, directly to windward. Fearing that the Dutch were edging to leeward into shallow water, where he could not follow, Duncan attacked in two groups without waiting to get his squadron in line, achieving a concentration on the Dutch vanguard and rear. Though the Dutch fought with great gallantry, this concentration overwhelmed them, and they lost nine ships of the line and two frigates. De Winter had been ordered to sea against his protests for political rather than military reasons, and Duncan's victory had limited strategic significance, but tactically it was the

first of a new style of crushing victories. By bold improvisation rather than careful planning, Duncan had escaped the limitations of the traditional line of battle and demonstrated that the British at sea could win as decisively as the French on land.

N. A. M. RODGER

Cannae, Battle of

August 216 B.C.

Hannibal (q.v.) won his third great victory of the Second Punic War (see *Punic Wars*) by encircling and annihilating an entire Roman army near the small village of Cannae in southern Italy. Hannibal himself met the initial murderous Roman charge head-on, his personal presence ensuring that the crescent of mercenary Spanish and Celtic infantry would bend but not break until his Africans at the flanks and rear could tie the knot. Cannae was thus a startling reversal of the usual Western military paradigm: Carthaginians, not Romans, were the invaders — outnumbered, relying largely on the skill of their general and the discipline of the troops, arrayed against a numerically superior but poorly led Western army.

Cannae itself was more than a tactical masterpiece; it was also a human story of abject carnage and mayhem. Nearly fifty thousand Romans were butchered in a single afternoon, a prodigious task of organized killing, where nearly six hundred legionaries were slaughtered each minute until darkness curtailed the bloodletting. The work continued on into the next morning, when thousands of parched Roman wounded, begging for a quick end to their misery, were systematically dispatched. Hannibal walked through the debris of the battlefield as Carthaginian looters collected gold senatorial rings by the bushel.

Hannibal has been faulted for not following up his great victory and marching on Rome. But his troops were exhausted, and Rome was a fortified city with plenty of resolute defenders. And although Cannae was proof of Hannibal's tactical genius, it was also a telling indication of the weakness of the entire Carthaginian strategic plan. Without steady reinforcement and logistical support, even spectacular victories like Trasimene, Trebia, and Cannae remained isolated phenomena, never integrated into a comprehensive design to occupy territory and detach Roman allies.

The idea that by sheer tactical brilliance an entire

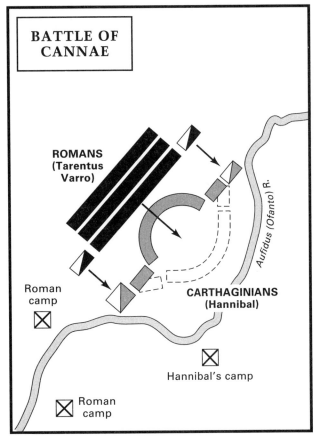

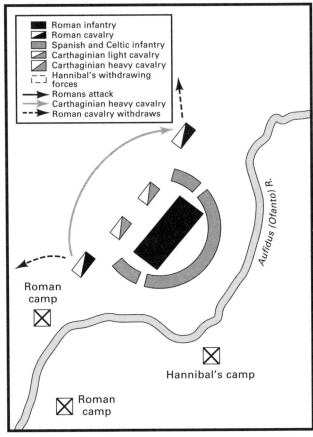

army could be encircled and annihilated has held an obvious fascination for subsequent Western strategists — Frederick the Great (q.v.), Helmuth von Moltke (q.v.), and Alfred von Schlieffen (q.v.) come quickly to mind — who searched for their own Cannae to end the fighting in a single stroke, without serious loss to themselves.

VICTOR DAVIS HANSON

Caporetto, Battle of

October 24–November 7, 1917

By September 1917, after eleven battles along the Isonzo, the principal theater of war ever since Italy entered World War I (q.v.), both the Italian and the Austro-Hungarian armies were exhausted. Russia's collapse, however, enabled the Austro-Hungarian command to strengthen the Italian front and plan offensive operations. Lacking faith in the capability of its allies, the German high command reinforced the plan with seven divisions and heavy artillery, while insisting on operational control. The plan called for an assault along a twenty-mile front on the upper Isonzo, with the village of Caporetto at the center and the Tagliamento River some thirty miles west as the objective.

The attack force, designated as the Fourteenth Army, two German and two Austro-Hungarian corps under General Otto von Below, jumped off on October 24. Using new infiltration tactics, a brief saturation bombardment combining high-explosive and gas shells followed by swift penetration at weak points, the attack routed the surprised Italians. Exploiting success and discarding its initial objective, the offensive continued until November 7, when it reached the Piave (an advance of some seventy-five miles), where the Italians, stiffened by six French and five British divisions rallied. Vividly pictured in Ernest Hemingway's 1929 novel, *A Farewell to Arms*, Caporetto was one of the most famous routs in history.

A test of the new German offensive doctrine, Caporetto inflicted 300,000 casualties, including 265,000 prisoners, and temporarily improved Austria-Hun-

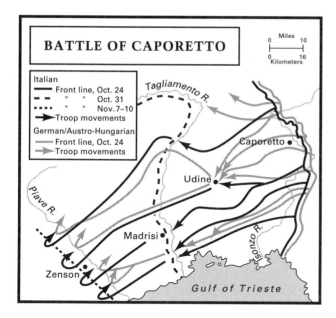

BATTLE OF CAPORETTO

Italian
— Front line, Oct. 24
– – " " Oct. 31
···· " " Nov. 7–10
➡ Troop movements
German/Austro-Hungarian
— Front line, Oct. 24
➡ Troop movements

Miles 0—10
Kilometers 0—16

Tagliamento R.
Caporetto
Udine
Piave R.
Madrisi
Isonzo R.
Zenson
Gulf of Trieste

after a coup in 1797. He came back under Napoleon (q.v.), whom he served as minister of the interior and minister of war at different times. The return of Louis XVIII in 1815 forced Carnot into exile. He traveled to Poland and settled in Prussia, where he occupied himself with writing and mathematics until his death.

JOHN A. LYNN

Carrhae, Battle of

53 B.C.

Marcus Licinius Crassus, member of the First Triumvirate with Julius Caesar (q.v.) and Pompey the Great, became governor of the Roman province of Syria in 55 B.C. as part of a deal he had made with his two colleagues. From Syria he hoped to launch a successful invasion of Parthia, and in 53 B.C. he crossed the Euphrates with an army of nearly forty thousand. The Parthians attacked him at Carrhae, not far beyond the Syrian border. Caught by surprise, the Romans were surrounded by Parthian mounted archers and forced to retreat at the end of the day.

Crassus approached the Parthians under a flag of truce but was captured and beheaded. Seven legions were destroyed, and only about ten thousand Romans escaped. Crassus's head was displayed in the Parthian court, and the standards of the Roman legions were set up in Parthian temples. Three decades later, in 19 B.C., the emperor Augustus negotiated the return of the standards and of the surviving captives.

ARTHER FERRILL

gary's strategic position. The defeat also contributed to the formation of the Allied Supreme War Council. In the end, however, Caporetto could not change the outcome of the war.

GUNTHER E. ROTHENBERG

Carnot, Lazare

1753–1823, French Military Administrator

Lazare Carnot sat on the ruling Committee of Public Safety during the height of the French Revolution (q.v.) in 1793–1794; he provided his valuable military knowledge and experience to the committee and earned the title of "organizer of victory."

Although of middle-class origins, Carnot rose to the rank of captain of engineers in the old royal army but threw in his lot with the Revolution and eventually won election to the governing assemblies, where his military background and ability catapulted him to the fore. In August 1793 he joined the twelve-member Committee of Public Safety; there he coordinated the raising, equipping, arming, and feeding of an army of one million men, by far the largest army ever raised in Europe. He also directed French strategy and even played a role in tactical development; he was a partisan of the bayonet attack. He continued in office after the execution of the committee's most famous member, Maximilien Robespierre, and remained active in revolutionary government until forced to flee France

Castles

Castles are distinguished from other fortifications by their primary purpose: the protection of a feudal lord, his family, and his loyal retainers. Any protection of a wider community was a distinctly secondary concern. Though a castle might shelter the humble, with their cattle and movables, in time of trouble, castles more characteristically served feudal magnates as intimidating power bases, aiding them, in the words of one chronicler, in "defending their own districts, or rather plundering them." The castle stood aloof, the symbol and the instrument of the lord's absolute local power. Besides its military utility, the castle invariably doubled as the lord's living quarters. The great hall was not only a banquet room, but also the court

The solidity of this fourteenth- or fifteenth-century fortified castle in Combourg, France, demonstrates advances in technology and stonecutting. But the advent of gunpowder and the cannon soon rendered its kind obsolete. Note the heavy curved towers, the arrow slits or "murder holes," and the crenellated battlements that protected archers.

where the lord exercised his considerable legal rights of justice; here as well the lord or his seneschal collected and recorded manorial rents and dues. Meanwhile, prisoners moldered in the dungeon below. The castle more than dominated the countryside in a military sense: it secured the entire political, social, and economic order, in peace as well as in war.

In western Europe, the appearance of the castle in the tenth and eleventh centuries followed the atrophy of centralized kingdoms (such as that left by Charlemagne [q.v.]) and the emergence of a distinctive political system: feudalism (q.v.). The feudal superior — the king, a duke, even a bishop — distributed land, the all-important fief, to a vassal in return for that vassal's military support, often forty days' active service. Each vassal promptly erected a castle to mark and protect his fief; typically, at first, a modest motte and bailey. The motte was a conical mound of earth crowned with a wooden tower and adjoined by the bailey, a defendable courtyard with hall, stables, barns, and other buildings. A palisade and ditch surrounded both. These simple earth and timber castles controlled their world, and their ubiquity can

hardly be overestimated: by one count some 625 dotted the landscape of late-eleventh-century England and Wales.

From the twelfth century, kings and the more powerful barons could increasingly afford the materials and skilled labor to build more grandly. A large stone tower, the keep, replaced the motte, and stone curtain walls ringed the bailey. Projecting wall towers bolstered the curtain, and the barbican, a detached double-tower with portcullis and drawbridge, protected the main gate. Ditches grew bigger, and hydraulic projects filled some with water, making moats. By the High Middle Ages the greatest castles were architectural marvels, the secular equivalents of the great cathedrals, and their builders were international experts: the thirteenth-century master mason who directed the construction of Edward I of England's (q.v.) castles in Wales had previously built similar castles for Count Philip of Savoy in southern France.

Properly garrisoned and victualed, such castles were almost impervious to the siege techniques of the day. Attackers used wheeled towers, battering rams, and a variety of hurling engines (see *Ballistic Weapons* and *Siege Weapons*) to overcome castle walls. Defenders displayed a cruel ingenuity in the objects dropped on mining and assault parties: boiling oil, wagon wheels, beehives, even noxious pots of sulfur. Successful sieges took months, and often depended on exceptional resolve and guile: in 1204 the Angevin castle of Château Gaillard fell to King Philip Augustus of France only after a particularly intrepid attacker climbed up through the garderobe — a lavatory chute.

Given such tactical defensive strength, it is often forgotten that castles were aggressive tools of conquest and subjugation. In 1066 William the Conqueror's (q.v.) first act was to build two castles on the English coast; near one of these, at Hastings (q.v.), he won the crown of England. A century later, the Anglo-Norman invaders of Ireland sailed with prefabricated timber castles to delimit their expanding presence in a hostile land. The contemporary Norman conquests of Sicily, Naples, and Greece similarly relied on vassals, fiefs, and castles. The same strategic triad furthered the Crusades (q.v.). In Iberia, Christian castles marked the southward-creeping religious frontier, while in the Baltic, stone castles gave a decisive military advantage to the Teutonic Knights in their struggle against the pagan Letts and Prussians (see *Baltic Crusade*). Castle building as an offensive strategy reached

The walls of Osaka Castle, completed in the early seventeenth century, stand up to nineteen yards thick — possibly the thickest walls anywhere in the world. Although their angular design resembles that of European bastions, it almost certainly evolved independently.

its zenith in the Holy Land. Here a mosaic of feudal lordships enforced the "Frankish" beachhead; anchoring each was a castle, among them the formidable Hospitaller stronghold of Krak des Chevaliers in Syria, described by one Saracen as "a bone stuck in the throat of the Muslims."

Three developments ended the reign of the castle. First of all, kings with centralizing political ambitions came to see nonroyal castles as potential threats to their own power. In England, by the thirteenth century a baron needed written permission, a "license to crenellate," to improve or found a castle. Second, as court culture — and the competition for royal honors and offices — replaced the rude martial independence of an earlier day, so the bright, sunny villa replaced the damp, drafty castle as the rural ideal. Social domination continued; but now it was enforced by lawyers, not armed retainers. Third, in the fifteenth century gunpowder revolutionized warfare. The first effective siege cannon, huge bombards belching stone balls of many hundredweight, though slow firing and awkward to transport, could easily smash the stoutest medieval wall. Castle builders responded by constructing enormous towers — those at Ham in northern France had walls thirty-five feet thick — with vaulted internal chambers to mount cannon of their own. Few could afford such monster castles; and besides, though massive, their brittle stone towers remained vulnerable to an ever-improving artillery.

Thus military, political, and social change killed the castle. Nevertheless, it remained a symbol of feudalism down to the end of the old regime, which is why — like the angry peasants of a medieval jacquerie — the citizens of Paris in 1789 seized and destroyed a castle, the Bastille, to open their revolution.

As feudalism decayed in Europe, on the other side of the world, in Japan, a similar political system flourished. Japanese feudal warlords — daimyo — built increasingly large and complex castles beginning in the sixteenth century. As architecturally impressive as anything in the West, these castles depended on enormous masonry walls, towering keeps with distinctive tiers of tiled gables, wide and deep moats, and mazelike internal passages to confuse intruders and channel them into murderous cul-de-sacs. As in the West, these castles were the symbols, as much as the instruments, of feudal control. And, also as in the West, central authority distrusted these local power bases; from 1615 the shogun (the de facto ruler of all Japan) decreed that warlords could enjoy only one castle each — all others had to be destroyed. Thus the decline of the Japanese castle mirrored the decline of those in the West.

THOMAS F. ARNOLD

J. Bradbury, *The Medieval Siege* (1992); N. J. G. Pounds, *The Medieval Castle in England and Wales* (1990); M. W. Thompson, *The Decline of the Castle* (1987).

Cavalry, Ancient and Medieval

Cavalry tactics involve the deployment of horsemen to achieve the advantages of mobility and shock. As early as 1400 B.C., mounted warriors fought in the armies of the ancient Near East, but it was the Assyrians (850? B.C.) (q.v.) who instituted mounted archers and spearmen as an integral part of their regular standing army. The mobility of the horse, combined with the long-range missile capability of the bow, endured across centuries of Near Eastern warfare, notably among the Scythians, Parthians, Huns, Turks, and Mongols (q.v.). Dispersed in small groups, mounted archers avoided closing with the enemy, always seeking to envelop the flanks or rear, as exemplified at Carrhae (53 B.C.) (q.v.) and Mantzikert (A.D. 1071) (q.v.).

A mounted archer provided a more stable firing platform than did a chariot. Without a suspension mechanism to stabilize the vehicle, a chariot could overturn easily when negotiating sharp turns or running over uneven ground. These drawbacks, combined with the depredations of horse archers from Mongolia and Turkestan, forced China in the fourth century B.C. to replace its chariots with horsemen and infantry. This shift was also accompanied by a dramatic change in the composition of the armies: a standing army of peasantry supplanted the chariots of the noble lineages. Chariot warfare nevertheless continued until about A.D. 500 in India, where a lack of grasslands prevented the breeding of horses of sufficient size and stamina for mounted operations.

In Greece in the fourth century B.C., a new coordination between infantry and cavalry emerged, with cavalry forces integrated fully into the battle plan. At Leuctra (371 B.C.), experienced cavalry drove the weak Spartan (q.v.) horsemen back into their hoplites (q.v.), creating a gap for the Theban cavalry to penetrate and thus disrupt the formation. The Macedonians (q.v.) developed an even closer coordination between infantry and cavalry. Acting as a hammer and anvil, infantry fixed the position of the enemy while cavalry served as the principal striking force.

The imperial Roman legion (q.v.) did not fight as an isolated formation; the Roman tacticians Arrian and Vegetius (q.v.) intended that infantry and cavalry would interact in a combined arms capacity. Traditional European military history has maintained that a tactical shift occurred between the Roman and medieval eras, dispensing with the infantry of the Roman legion in favor of the medieval mounted knight; such scholars cite the shock tactics of Germanic cavalry at the Battle of Adrianople (378) as the catalyst for this development. Recent research, however, indicates that this engagement cannot serve as a clear dividing line between ancient and medieval warfare. In that engagement, a confederation of Visigoths, Huns, and Alans attacked and dispersed the Roman cavalry, leaving the flanks of the legions vulnerable. But the allied cavalry attack apparently was more accident than innovation.

Actually, the trend toward mounted operations had emerged earlier as part of the Roman military response to a series of third-century invasions. To dispatch forces readily to any point along a threatened frontier, Emperor Gallienus (r. 260–268) upgraded the status of cavalry in the Roman army, creating special detachments that patrolled the area just inside the borders. Within this combat zone, regional field reserves intercepted enemy incursions. These forces became the tactical cavalry units of the mobile field armies of Diocletian, which later constituted the central field force of Constantine.

New research has undercut the entire idea of a mid-eighth-century military revolution aimed at an expansion of cavalry in the West, especially of mounted shock combat. This mode of cavalry warfare depended upon the combined effectiveness of the charging horse and its technological accoutrements: the lateral support provided by the stirrup, the couched lance, and the elongated shield. These features of medieval shock cavalry developed slowly, not coalescing fully until the eve of the Crusades (q.v.).

Traditionally, the tournaments of the twelfth and thirteenth centuries have been regarded as military exercises designed to train knights for pitched battles. Indeed, tournaments did teach knights to fight in tactical units, but the infrequency of set battles in the period 1050–1300, and the relative unimportance of mounted knights when set battles did occur, meant that shock cavalry was practiced almost exclusively in tournaments. If anything, the frontal charges practiced in tournaments put mounted knights at a disadvantage and in part explain the late medieval defeats of cavalry forces, especially at Courtrai (1302) (q.v.), Bannockburn (1314) (q.v.), Crécy (1346) (q.v.), and Agincourt (1415) (q.v.).

The predominance of siege warfare in medieval Europe provided few opportunities for medieval knights to be tactically decisive. During the frequent stalemates, however, tournaments often served to relieve the monotony for the besiegers. Also, the medieval rural landscape (networks of castles typically separated by the distance a horse could cover in a day) enabled horsemen to maintain lines of communication and patrol the countryside against raids and skirmishes, thus carrying out logistical wars to reduce the material resources of rivals.

CARROLL GILLMOR

Bernard S. Bachrach, "On Roman Ramparts, 300–1300," in *The Cambridge Illustrated History of Warfare*, ed. Geoffrey Parker (1995); Carroll Gillmor, "Practical Chivalry: The Training of Horses for Tournaments and Warfare," *Studies in Medieval and Renaissance History* 13 (1992): 7–29; I. G. Spence, *The Cavalry of Classical Greece* (1993).

Cavalry, 1500–1945

Despite the warning that English longbows and Swiss infantry had conveyed by their victories over aristocratic armies in the late Middle Ages, the armored man on his horse remained the idealized hero of Europe's upper classes right up to the beginning of the twentieth century. However, this great period of Western military development saw the slow, steady marginalization of cavalry, as infantry (q.v.) and artillery (q.v.) came to play increasingly dominant roles on the battlefield.

Something along the same lines occurred in Asia as the great threat of steppe horsemen to both China and India — one largely based on nomad (q.v.) cavalry — began to dissipate in the eighteenth century. The Mughal (q.v.) conquest of most of northern and central India in the sixteenth century had rested largely on the cavalry of the emperors, but by the early eighteenth century the empire's political structure had collapsed. No further waves of conquering cavalry issued forth from Asia; instead, the threat now came from Europe and its armies and navies.

The exalted position of the horseman in European military tradition rested on the fact that undisciplined infantry had little chance of standing up against the charge of armored cavalry. But in the late sixteenth century, Maurice of Nassau (q.v.) reintroduced the ferocious discipline of the Romans to the training, drill, and order of infantry formations. Gustavus Adolphus (q.v.) picked up this development in the 1620s, and it soon spread. But during conflicts in which the new highly disciplined infantry forces were not yet available, or available only in small numbers, such as the English Civil Wars (q.v.), cavalry could still play a larger, if not decisive, role.

But massed, well-trained infantry that would stand unyielding in the face of a cavalry charge could not be broken. There was, in fact, never such a thing as the "shock" value of cavalry. A horse will not ride into a brick wall, nor will it ride into a wall of bristling bayonets. Throughout the Napoleonic Wars an infantry square, deployed and ready, was broken by a cavalry charge only once — and, in this case, rider and horse were killed before the horse could shy away, and both smashed into the square to make a hole for the other horses to follow.

If cavalry could not break deployed infantry, what purpose did they serve? They could hope to catch infantry before they were deployed, raid the enemy's interior, scout the enemy's positions, and, as one wag put it in the eighteenth century, keep the infantry from deserting. Such tasks did keep cavalry busy until, by the late nineteenth century, increasing firepower made the horsemen of doubtful utility.

The complexities of deploying from march into battle line — never satisfactorily solved until Napoleon's (q.v.) time — provided a significant role for the cavalry. Horse units were still important enough in the duke of Marlborough's (q.v.) time for that great commander to lead them into battle and, at Blenheim (1704) (q.v.), to separate the French right wing from its main body and win one of the greatest military victories in European military history. But this was unusual; cavalry's main role involved scouting out the enemy's dispositions and at times raiding its rear. It also proved useful when an enemy formation was on the point of breaking. Individual infantrymen made ideal targets for the smashing hooves of the horses and the slashing sabers of the cavalrymen.

Cavalry reached its apotheosis under Napoleon. At the beginning of his campaigns, cavalry played two crucial roles. First, they screened off the movement of Napoleonic armies from enemy spies or opposing cavalry formations. Consequently, the enemy never knew where the emperor's forces were moving. Second, the French cavalry identified the enemy's location in detail and prepared the ground for the concentration of the French army at whatever point the emperor believed would be decisive. In the Ulm and Austerlitz (q.v.) campaigns of 1805, French cavalry fulfilled this role to the hilt. An equally important role was pursuit. After the double victory of Jena and

Polish cavalrymen at Końskie, May 1939. Although cavalry could not stand up to tanks and machine guns, the use of horses continued through World War II, particularly in Eastern European countries.

Troops of the First Cavalry Division (Airmobile) descend from a CM-47A "Chinook" helicopter during an operation near Pleiku, Vietnam, on January 20, 1966.

Auerstedt in October 1806, Napoleon launched his cavalry under its commander, Marshal Joachim Murat. Two weeks later, having captured Berlin and driven on to the Baltic coast, Murat reported that "the pursuit ends for a lack of enemies."

But when Napoleon lacked cavalry, his system of war ceased to exhibit the nearly flawless execution that had marked the great victories of 1805 and 1806. In 1812 he lost most of his cavalry in Russia. In the next year he fought what may have been his greatest campaign, but with an ill-trained, greatly weakened cavalry. Blinded by the inability of his mounted troops to do reconnaissance (q.v.), Napoleon was never able to catch his enemies as he had once done. Moreover, his cavalry could not follow up on battlefield victories to turn them into strategic successes, as happened at Dresden in September 1813.

In the American Civil War (q.v.), cavalry played its traditional roles. General Robert E. Lee (q.v.) depended greatly on "Jeb" Stuart's cavalry to spy out the movement of Union forces. When Stuart was not available (such as during the Gettysburg [q.v.] campaign), Lee ran into significant difficulties. In the western theater of operations, the Confederate cavalry commander, Nathan Bedford Forrest, proved particularly effective at using his troops as a raiding force of mounted infantry. So swift were Forrest's movements that William Tecumseh Sherman (q.v.), who feared few, recorded that Forrest terrified him. By the end of the war, Union cavalry, equipped with carbines, were executing the Union's "hard war" policy by destroying whole sections of the South, from the Shenandoah to Alabama and Mississippi.

In the early twentieth century, most senior military leaders refused to recognize that cavalry no longer had a role. But the first campaigns of World War I (q.v.) in the west and the ensuing stalemate ended any significant role for the cavalry in that theater. In the east, given the distances and dispersal of forces, cavalry continued to be of use. Similarly, in the Middle East, Edmund Allenby (q.v.) used cavalry to great effect against the Turks in campaigns that conquered Palestine and Syria.

But the increasing motorization and mechanization of armies even during World War I spelled the doom of the mounted horseman. By the late 1930s, the horse itself was playing a relatively insignificant role in the economic structure of Western nations. The German army, however, clung to the horse as a means of supply for its formations — a reflection of the Reich's economic weaknesses (lack of oil and rubber) rather than military choice. The Soviets also held on to horses, again because of the economic and technological backwardness of Soviet society as much as for military reasons. But the Red Army (q.v.) eventually rode to victory in World War II (q.v.) on a logistics system supported by American trucks, while the Germans were still using horses. In the end, only the traditions of the cavalry have survived in the armored cavalry regiments and scouting forces of modern mechanized armies.

WILLIAMSON MURRAY

Censorship

Military censorship dates from the Crimean War (q.v.), which by no coincidence also marks the appearance of the first war correspondents, previous reports from the battlefield having been dependent on letters from serving officers or their books, starting with Thucydides, who fought on the Athenian side in the Peloponnesian War (q.v.). Censorship as such can be said to exist only in countries with a relatively free and nonpartisan press, principally those in America and Great Britain and certain other Western European countries; others, especially in non-Western countries, generally censor themselves or respond to official guidance in war and peace.

The most celebrated of the first war correspondents, William Henry Russell of *The Times* of London, encountered limitations of access as soon as he reached the Crimean peninsula in 1854. Officers disdained him, and the commander, Lord Raglan, refused to speak to him. That did not prevent him from reporting the failures of an ill-fed and ill-led expeditionary force, leading to a reform of the British army. Raglan's successor, Sir William Codrington, issued history's first censorship order on February 25, 1856, prohibiting the publication of reports on morale and criticism of the high command as well as military movements.

This set the stage for the Boer War (q.v.) and World War I (q.v.), when censorship reached its apogee to shield the home front (q.v.) from the horrifying spectacle of mindless, mechanized, unprecedented slaughter. The few correspondents permitted by the British on the Western Front were kept under close surveillance, but in the last analysis, iron control was imposed on the press by appeals to patriotism. When the United States entered the war in 1917, its more energetic correspondents filed stories on the American Expeditionary Force's lack of clothing, weapons, and munitions, but they were heavily censored.

Censorship in World War II (q.v.) was easily justified by the public consensus behind the war. Allied correspondents felt they were an essential part of this great crusade against tyranny, and many found it professionally useful because it meant commanders could confide tactical information, secure in the knowledge that the censor provided a necessary backstop, while correspondents were attached to military units and roamed freely. In Europe, the supreme commander, Dwight D. Eisenhower (q.v.), said, "Public opinion wins war," and in the Pacific his opposite number, Douglas MacArthur (q.v.), was no less solicitous of the press (although he more overtly used them to reinforce his image).

During the first six chaotic months of the Korean War (q.v.), a lack of censorship permitted the full reporting of the defeat of the ill-trained and poorly led American troops. The army proposed self-censorship, but reporters pleaded for a less arbitrary formal regime, which was installed on December 21, 1950. By late spring of 1951, the front had stabilized and the war became tactically routine. The military command nevertheless remained baffled by the problems that arose in dealing with propaganda by the Communist side to affect truce negotiations as they dragged on for more than two years of military stalemate, a situation in which censorship offered little help.

During the Vietnam War (q.v.), journalists were uncensored and had virtually unlimited access. The military came to believe that this was a principal factor in their failure in Vietnam; reports of the gruesome battlefield details helped drain away public support. During the Gulf War (q.v.) of 1991, the American military restored censorship, imposed military escort officers (reviled as "minders" by the journalists), and severely limited access, realizing that advances in technology freed the press from dependence on military communications. Written dispatches or television images could be computerized and sent in seconds over public telephone lines or relayed by satellite, posing a powerful new challenge to the military control of information — a challenge left unresolved at the end of that conflict.

LAWRENCE MALKIN

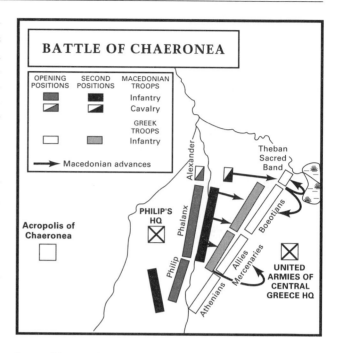

Chaeronea, Battle of

August 2, 338 B.C.

The dream of the Athenian leader Demosthenes of a pan-Hellenic rebuff to Philip II of Macedon (q.v.) was nearly realized when thirty thousand Greeks in the plain of Chaeronea blocked the southward march of the Macedonians (q.v.). The victorious Athenians on the left wing at first ran wildly after Philip and his retreating hypaspists, the royal guard of mobile infantry. But the king was most likely feinting, not retreating, and all the Athenians accomplished was to split open their own allied line. On cue, the eighteen-year-old Alexander (q.v.) rushed into the resulting gap, his Macedonian cavalry encircling the Thebans on the right wing, causing a general collapse throughout the army. The startled Greeks fled south into the mountains before Philip's renewed onslaught.

Chaeronea was not proof of the superiority of the Macedonian phalanx with its lighter body armor and lengthier spears. Rather, it was a more fundamental reassessment of the entire nature of Greek warfare, a preview of a new military to come, wherein light infantry, cavalry, and the phalanx worked in concert, incorporating feints, reserves, encirclements, and oblique advances to confuse and tear apart less imaginative and slower-moving infantry.

In the Greek mind, Chaeronea marked the end of the entire idea of an autonomous and free city-state and the invincibility of its amateur militia. Philip

himself must have recognized the significance of his victory: he allowed a magnificent stone lion to rest over the bodies of the Theban Sacred Band, the elite corps of three hundred lovers, annihilated, to the man, by the cavalry charge of his son.

VICTOR DAVIS HANSON

Châlons, Battle of

451

In 451 Attila the Hun (q.v.) descended in fury upon the Roman cities of northern Gaul. The Roman warlord Aetius rushed north from Italy and convinced Theodoric, king of the Visigoths, to rally to the Roman cause. Their combined might forced Attila to make a fighting retreat to the Catalaunian Plains in northeastern France near Troyes, ideal country for Hun cavalry tactics. The Visigoths on the right seized a sloping hill that dominated the field, while Aetius's best troops held the left. Attila's cavalry drove so deep into the weak Roman center that they were nearly cut off by Roman and Visigoth counterattacks. Attila fought his way back to his fortified camp as night fell, and he prepared to commit suicide rather than surrender. Aetius, however, allowed Attila to retreat to Hungary, where he died in 453.

Although many argue that the importance of Châlons has been exaggerated, there is no doubt that contemporaries saw it as an epic combat with un-heard-of losses. A Hun victory might have profoundly altered the history of medieval Europe.

W. SCOTT JESSEE

Chance

Early in his writing career, Winston Churchill (q.v.) suggested, "Countless and inestimable are the chances of war." Numerous other military historians have remarked on the crucial, central role that chance plays in war and in battle.

At Gallipoli (q.v.), Mustafa Kemal Atatürk (q.v.) happened by the Anzac landing site at precisely the right moment to form a defense on the ridgeline over-looking the cove. The line held, and the Anzacs never gained the ridge. Writing after the war, Churchill commented concerning Gallipoli, "The terrible ifs accumulate." At Gettysburg (q.v.) an obscure colonel with barely one year of military service found himself and his regiment on the far left of the Union line on the second day of the battle. Joshua Chamberlain saved the position on Little Round Top and probably the battle when, with his troops out of ammunition and heavily outnumbered, he ordered a bayonet charge on the oncoming Confederates. In 1914 a Brit-ish fishing trawler recovered a lead-lined chest with a German naval code inside — the chest had been cast into the North Sea by a heavily damaged German naval vessel. This gave British codebreakers some of the cribs they needed to gain access to the enemy's naval codes for the rest of the war. In June 1944, General Dwight D. Eisenhower (q.v.) gambled that the weather would change on the next day; without that break in the weather, the D-Day invasion (q.v.) might have been postponed to the end of the month, with incalculable consequences. In the mid–thirteenth century, Mongol (q.v.) armies, having completely wrecked Kievan Russia and smashed the armies of Hungary's nobility, were poised to destroy central and western Europe; Mongol spearheads were approach-ing Vienna and Venice. But a hurried message brought news of the Great Khan Ögödei's death, and Mongol leaders returned home to elect a new khan. The Mon-gol tide receded, never to return.

Such examples are innumerable in the history of war. The two greatest commentators and historians of conflict in the Western world, Thucydides and Carl von Clausewitz (q.v.), give heavy emphasis to the role

---

Ten Military Might-Have-Beens

Xerxes' Fleet Avoids the Athenian Trap at Salamis, and Greece Becomes Part of the Persian Empire (480 B.C.)

Alexander the Great Lives to Old Age (323 B.C.)

Mongol Khan Ögödei Lives to Old Age, and His Armies Conquer Western Europe Instead of Withdrawing to Elect a New Khan (1240)

The Ottoman Empire Captures Vienna and Goes On to Conquer Western Europe for Islam (1529)

The Wind Blows the Armada Back into the English Chan-nel (1588)

Benedict Arnold Captures Quebec, and Canada Joins the Colonies in Revolt (1776)

Napoleon Does Not Go to Moscow and Expels the Brit-ish from the Iberian Peninsula (1812)

The Schlieffen Plan Works (1914)

Successful Assassination of Adolf Hitler (1938)

Operation Sealion Succeeds, and Germany Conquers England; Hitler Takes Moscow and the Caspian Oil Fields; Rommel Takes Cairo and Palestine, and Nazi Forces Join Hands in Iraq; Meanwhile, the Japanese Navy Rules the Indian Ocean as Far as Africa (1940–1942)

---

that chance plays in war — Thucydides' emphasis on the role of accident is so heavy that most trans-lators have tended to omit many of his references to chance.

In fact Thucydides was on target — since the 1950s, research from fields as diverse as meteorology, ecol-ogy, physics, and mathematics has underlined that we live in a nonlinear universe in which the behavior of variables in all areas, including such simple phenom-ena as dripping faucets, is so complex as to be literally unpredictable, or fundamentally "chaotic." Not sur-prisingly then, war, which is the interaction of thou-sands, if not tens of thousands, of random actors and factors, reflects this reality. Chance dominates the interplay between the various contestants. Like all human affairs, war is nonlinear in character and there-fore dominated by chance. And that is why theories of war based on linear conceptions, and all attempts to make a "science" of war, are doomed to failure. As Clausewitz quite correctly commented: "No other human activity is so continuously or universally bound up with chance. And through the element of chance, guesswork and luck come to play a great part in war."

WILLIAMSON MURRAY

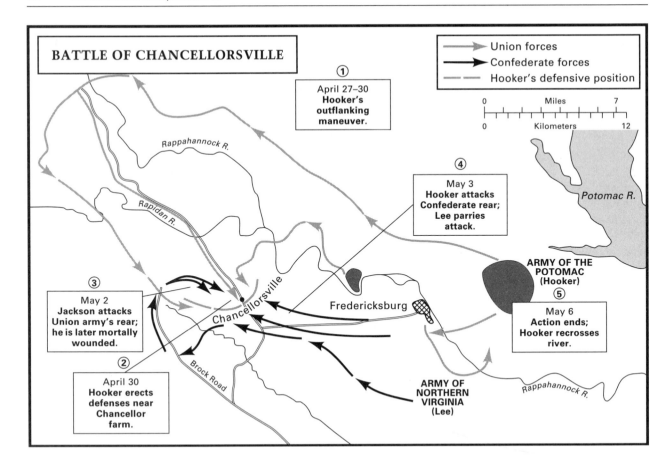

Chancellorsville, Battle of

May 1–3, 1863

Fought in the Wilderness region of Virginia, Chancellorsville was General Robert E. Lee's (q.v.) greatest defensive victory, an outstanding example of command partnership and the misuse of strategic initiative. On April 30, Lee (whose 60,000 men occupied the Fredericksburg heights) found 80,000 enemy troops behind him, thanks to a brilliantly executed march and river crossing by Union major general Joseph Hooker, who proclaimed Lee could either "ingloriously fly" or give "battle on our ground." Unnerved by sharp counterattacks delivered by the outnumbered Confederate rear guard, Hooker squandered his advantage by halting to erect defenses near the Chancellor farm. Lee arrived on May 1, and together with his able subordinate Thomas J. "Stonewall" Jackson (q.v.), planned his own flank movement.

Early on May 2, Jackson and 30,000 men followed a circuitous route that brought them against Hooker's weak right flank. Jackson's attack, begun in late afternoon, was a brilliant tactical success that destroyed half of Hooker's line; only nightfall prevented a complete victory. Jackson, scouting in the dark, was mortally wounded by his own pickets. The most intense combat of the battle took place on May 3, with Hooker now defending against Lee's attack. In masterful crisis management, Lee simultaneously parried a thrust against his rear by the 27,000 troops Hooker had left behind. On May 6, Hooker recrossed the Rappahannock, having lost 17,278 casualties to Lee's 12,826, including the irreplaceable Jackson. Lee now possessed the strategic initiative, which in a few weeks would lead him north to Gettysburg (q.v.).

NOAH ANDRE TRUDEAU

Chandragupta Maurya

r. 321?–296? B.C., *Indian Emperor*

The founder of the Mauryan dynasty, Chandragupta Maurya succeeded where Alexander the Great (q.v.)

had failed — he united all of northern India for the first time under one rule. An ambitious young commoner with royal ambitions and the shrewd, ruthless counsel of a Brahmin named Kautilya (who has been called India's Machiavelli [q.v.]), he first seized the kingdom of Magadha in modern Bihar and then, one by one, engulfed his neighbors until his empire encompassed both the Ganges and Indus Valleys and stretched all the way to Afghanistan. His empire lasted some 140 years — about as long as British India survived. Little is known of Chandragupta's last years, but Jains hold that he converted to their faith, abandoned his throne to his son, Bindusara, and fled to south India where he starved himself to death in the manner of their saints.

GEOFFREY WARD

Charlemagne

A.D. 742–814, *King of the Franks and Western Roman Emperor*

Charles the Great (Charlemagne) expanded the Carolingian realm until it dominated western Europe extending from the river Ebro to the Elbe, and from central Italy to the North Sea. Intervention in local Roman affairs led to his coronation as emperor by Pope Leo III in 800, reviving an independent Roman Empire in the west.

Charles's most important wars included the conquest of Lombard Italy in 773–774, the conquest of Saxony in 772–804, and the destruction of the Avar Khanate in 791–796. Charles also led significant expeditions into Spain, southern Italy, and against internal opposition in Bavaria. He sometimes personally led operations in two widely separated regions (Saxony and Italy, for example) during the same year. Charles last commanded in the field in 810 at age sixty-eight against the Danes.

Charles matched energy and persistence with strategic vision. Winter campaigns turned the tide of the Saxon war, whereas incremental advances combined with diplomacy secured a buffer zone, or mark, in northern Spain. During the Avar campaign of 791, Charles's army advanced in two independent columns kept in communication by a fleet on the Danube River. Charles used fortifications to protect lines of advance, pontoon bridges and water transport to increase operational mobility, and naval squadrons to protect his coasts against piracy.

This image from the cathedral treasury at Aachen shows Charlemagne and his soldiers using the military equipment designed for mounted shock combat (high-cantled saddles, long lances, great helms, and mail armor covering the entire body) that was current in 1215 when the piece was produced. But in the time of Charlemagne, four centuries earlier, cavalry typically fought their opponents hand to hand while seated on horseback.

More remarkable was his ability to maintain command control and achieve strategic objectives when he himself was not in direct command; in one year (806), Charles's armies fought five independent campaigns. Capable surrogate commanders (including his sons) led expeditions, while a system of envoys *(missi)* made sure that royal orders were carried out. Margraves — officials who combined civil and military authority in designated border zones called marks — contained local frontier problems, leaving Charles free to concentrate on more urgent affairs.

Charles did not always attain his objectives, in part because his ambition sometimes exceeded the material capabilities of his era. One example was the canal with which he wanted to connect the Rhine and Danube Rivers (a feat not achieved until the 1840s). Another was his attempt to coordinate strategy against Umayyad Spain with Harun al-Rashid, which failed because of the distances involved. Also, the administrative structures that Charles established relied on his personal attention — enforced by constant travel throughout the realm — to function well. When he settled at Aachen because of declining health after 810, Carolingian strategy became reactive and prone to inactivity; this was particularly evident in attempts to contain piracy on the Mediterranean and North Seas.

Any assessment of Charles must balance his personal successes against the breakup of the Carolingian Empire two generations after his death. Once Charles's grandsons divided the territory among them in 843 (see *Fontenoy, Battle of*), the new kingdoms lacked the resources necessary to match his achievements. Europe in his day was as much Roman as medieval — counts were royal officials rather than hereditary magnates, and heavily armored soldiers fought on foot as often as on horseback. Still, Charles has captured the imagination of the nations that have supplanted his empire, and his name has been the touchstone of a united Europe from Napoleon (q.v.) to the European Union.

EDWARD J. SCHOENFELD

Donald Bullough, *The Age of Charlemagne* (1973).

Charles XII

1682–1718, Swedish King and Military Commander

Charles XII became king in 1697 at age fifteen and, only three years later, was attacked by Russia, Saxony-Poland, and Denmark. The resulting conflict, the Great Northern War of 1700–1721 (q.v.), was not concluded until three years after his death, when the Peace of Nystad forced a defeated Sweden to hand over almost all of the Baltic empire conquered during the preceding century and a half. Charles XII's personal responsibility for this catastrophe has been debated ever since his death. Many have seen him as a reckless military adventurer whose unthinking pursuit of further victories placed intolerable burdens upon his people. Recently it has been recognized that Sweden's imperial position was precarious, that it was surrounded by predatory enemies, and that there was little real alternative to his military campaigns. The Great Northern War's (q.v.) first decade saw Charles XII win a series of impressive victories, but an attempted invasion of Russia came to grief at Poltava (July 1709) (q.v.). This effectively decided the conflict's outcome. Charles XII was forced to take refuge in the Ottoman Empire (1709–1714). Although he returned to the Baltic and resumed personal direction of the fighting, he died in mysterious circumstances (with allegations of a murderous conspiracy by discontented subjects) while besieging the Norwegian fortress of Frederiksten in December 1718.

H. M. SCOTT

Cheng Ch'eng-kung

See Koxinga.

Chiang Kai-shek

1887–1974, Chinese General and Political Leader

Born in Chekiang and trained in part in Japan, Chiang Kai-shek was an early recruit to the Kuomintang, or Nationalist movement, of Sun Yat-sen, the revolutionary still revered in China as "father of the country." Sun's movement sought initially to overthrow the Ch'ing dynasty; when that was accomplished in 1912 — but with Sun excluded from power — the target shifted to the new, dictatorial regime in Peking. Most important, Chiang served as commandant of the Kuomintang's Whampoa military academy, located near Canton in South China. He won real preeminence, however, as commander of the victorious Northern Expedition of 1926–1928, a remarkable feat of arms that saw a Kuomintang force of only 100,000, moving up from China's deep south, overthrow greatly superior Peking government armies and establish the new Nationalist Government at Nanking. As that government's leader, Chiang consolidated his domestic power while preparing for inevitable war with Japan. When his hand was forced by Japanese attacks near Peking in 1937, Chiang led heroic Chinese resistance in the general war, which lasted until 1945 and devastated his own forces while reviving the Communists, who had previously been nearly eliminated (driven to remote northwest China by the "anti-bandit" campaigns of the 1930s and the subsequent Long March). Defeat in the ensuing Chinese Civil War (1945–1949) (q.v.) drove Chiang and two million followers to Taiwan, where the Republic of China government survived and indeed prospered.

Long compared unfavorably to Mao Tse-tung (q.v.), Chiang has yet to find his biographer, and until recently most assessments of him have been closer to that of Joseph Stilwell (q.v.), who ridiculed him as "the peanut," than to that of Owen Lattimore, who considered him "a great man." But recent confirmation of the staggering human cost of Chinese Communism has vindicated Chiang's judgment of its threat, while the corruption and disorder of post-Mao China serve as reminders of how intractable were the problems he faced.

ARTHUR WALDRON

Ch'i Chi-kuang

1527–1587, *Chinese General*

Ch'i Chi-kuang initiated reforms of tactics and training that allowed Chinese troops to move safely across the steppe lands of East Asia and use their superior numbers to defeat nomad horsemen decisively and permanently in ensuing decades.

Two changes in older Chinese practice lay at the heart of Ch'i's reforms. First of all, he took to heart the precepts of Sun Tzu's (q.v.) classic text *On War* written in the fifth century B.C. and required his soldiers to drill incessantly. This created obedient, proficient troops with high morale. Second, he devised a new formation that may be called a "cart division," by equipping his armies with carts that both carried supplies and, in case of sudden attack, could also form laagers around the troops, thus protecting them from the arrows of nomad horsemen. After some experimentation, Ch'i standardized these formations by assigning 125 heavy carts and 216 light carts to each division, along with three thousand cavalry and eleven thousand infantry. Individual weapon training with crossbows and halberds was then supplemented by unit training, which required moving from march to laager and back again, and practicing offensive sallies through gaps left in the laager. In addition, large-scale army maneuvers coordinated the movement of separate divisions, which totaled sixteen by the time General Ch'i surrendered his command on the northwest frontier in 1574.

Prolonged drill along these lines gave Chinese forces the capability of moving safely across the open steppes. Their superior numbers could thus be brought to bear against nomad confederacies as never before; and in the following 150 years, the military power of steppe nomads in East Asia was forever erased. The Chinese state as we know it today thus came into existence, largely on the strength of the improvement in tactics and training that General Ch'i instituted.

Ch'i's mode of training remained normative for Chinese armies long after his death in 1587, thanks in large part to the fact that he wrote two books, *A New Treatise on Disciplined Service* (1570) and *A Practical Account of Troop Training* (1571). These were reprinted from time to time, translated into Korean and Japanese, and as recently as 1939, Chiang Kai-shek (q.v.) had them reprinted for use by his armies.

WILLIAM H. MCNEILL

Ch'ien-lung

r. 1736–1795, *Fourth Manchu Emperor of Ch'ing China*

By glorifying his military exploits and promoting martial spirit, Ch'ien-lung sought to strengthen the military element in Chinese culture. In 1792 he claimed "Ten Great Victories," although several were hollow or pyrrhic. These included the conquest of Xinjiang (1755–1759), the crushing of two Chin-Ch'uan rebellions (1747–1749, 1771–1776) and one in Taiwan (1787–1788), and the defeat of the Burmese (1766–1770), the Vietnamese (1788–1789), and the Gurkhas (twice in 1790–1792) (q.v.). Further, he suppressed five major rebellions — by Yunnan and Kuei-chou Miao (1735, 1795), Kansu Muslims (1781, 1784), and Shantung millenarians (1774) — and numerous minor uprisings.

Obsessed by warfare, Ch'ien-lung read dispatches immediately, interrogated visitors about foreign warfare, and sought the advice of Western missionaries in China on weapons' use and production. He commemorated his victories by installing the Hall of Military Merit adorned with battle scenes and portraits, by erecting memorials engraved with his own compositions, and by commissioning numerous, often documentary, paintings with military themes. He sometimes personally greeted returning commanders outside Peking and staged spectacular triumphs.

Unlike many Chinese rulers, Ch'ien-lung considered permanent military readiness essential; but, despite his fascination with technology, the absence of a militarily equal or superior opponent in East Asia rendered extensive modernization unnecessary.

JOANNA WALEY-COHEN

Children in War

Children have never been strangers to war. But what is a child? The idea of childhood as an innocent, sheltered time is a very recent novelty. Even in the West, well into the twentieth century the child was everywhere considered little more than a small adult. Children worked in mines, lost fingers and hands in mill machinery, and starved with their peasant parents as dearth stalked the countryside.

Through most of history a boy became a man, and a soldier if need be, when he was tall enough to pass — especially when his elders were already dead or

Dressed in samurai war costume, young Japanese boys march in a patriotic procession on Empire Day in Tokyo, in 1934.

drafted. After his catastrophic invasion of Russia in 1812, a desperate Napoleon (q.v.) prematurely called up the annual levies of France and French-occupied Europe, filling his armies' gaping ranks with *les Marie Louises* — beardless teenage boys so young they looked like girls. Another disastrous invasion of Russia compelled another dictator, Adolf Hitler (q.v.), to do the same, remaking his Hitler Youth from boy scouts to crack soldiers (in a touch of the macabre, on field service Hitler Youth members under age eighteen received a candy ration rather than cigarettes). But boys have served with full official approval in normal times as well. In the premodern Muslim world, the

heart of a professional army was often a special corps of slaves purchased in boyhood (and converted to Islam, if necessary); the Ottoman (q.v.) sultans raised their elite slave corps, the janissaries, with a special tax on Christian households in the Balkans: a tax of sons. The eighteenth-century British army regularly provided the youngest recruits with too-large uniforms they could grow into, and in the Royal Navy down to World War I (q.v.) small boys, affectionately known as powder-monkeys, fetched ammunition for the guns. In America and Europe, regimental drummer boys and bugle boys, half mascots and half brothers-in-arms, served through the nineteenth century

— and their presence on the field of battle seemed somehow romantic.

Evil dictators and callous governments are not the only forces that push the young into war: the eager young recruit, lying about his age, is all too common. Adolescents — enthusiastic, easily indoctrinated, fearless in their innocence — make some of the best soldiers. A fourteenth-century chronicler noted the ferocity of the boy-man soldier: "hot and impetuous, quick with weapons, careless of safety." This adolescent passion for blood did not change with mass education or the electric light. Ernst Jünger, who as a nineteen-year-old lieutenant commanded a German platoon on the Western Front in World War I, in 1929 knowledgeably concluded that "troops composed of boys of twenty, under experienced leadership, are the most formidable." The crack Hitler Youth formations of the next world war confirmed this dark truth. Should this effectiveness be surprising? The squad, the atomic unit of war — be it the Roman *contubernium* or the Napoleonic *ordinaire* — is built around an adolescent comradeship (called "primary group cohesion" by the social scientist) unalloyed by the emotional claims of adulthood: wives, offspring, and the steady, boring peacetime job. Even the technical vocabulary of modern war betrays an original association of youth with organized violence: *infantry* comes from the Italian *fanti*, "the boys"; and *brigade* from *brigate*, the adolescent street gangs, complete with "colors," that caroused in the streets and squares of Renaissance Italian cities.

Sadly, child warriors are not yet remotely historical. In the guerrilla wars of today's Third World, too many too-young soldiers carry rifles designed for taller, stronger frames. From the Iran-Iraq War (where Iranian "volunteers" might be as young as age eleven) (q.v.), to the jungles of Sri Lanka and Burma, to the hills of Bosnia and Guatemala, boy soldiers fight on. And in Cambodia in the 1970s, the Khmer Rouge proved that children, far from being natural lambs, can easily be made the most vicious lions, loyally undertaking a program of genocide — against adults.

But no discussion of children in war can omit their participation as victims. War's dangers (malnutrition, disease, destruction of property, and the death of family members even more than in actual combat) have typically left children starved, orphaned, turned to the roads as refugees, and generally helpless. For every older boy attracted by the dark excitement of war, dozens of sisters, younger brothers, and cousins have experienced war only as fear, hunger, and loss. Thus while for some boys World War II meant comradeship (manning antiaircraft batteries in Germany, organizing scrap drives in the United States) and patriotism (following battles in newsreels and newspapers), for many more children war brought horrifying days and nights in bomb shelters, anxious separations from parents, meager meals, and sometimes death. Even minor sufferings could leave their mark: how many Europeans of a certain age still crave sweets, or butter, in memory of wartime shortages? The suffering of children in war, far from being a marginal issue, has for many people become war's symbolic definition: for Vietnam, a naked girl fleeing in terror along a country road.

THOMAS F. ARNOLD

Chinese Civil War

1945–1949

This struggle between the forces of Chiang Kai-shek (q.v.) and Mao Tse-tung (q.v.), which gave birth to the People's Republic of China, was the culmination of a conflict having its origins in the rivalry between China's two revolutionary parties, the Nationalists (Kuomintang) and the Communists. Early Communist attempts to win power, first by infiltrating the much larger Kuomintang and then by direct military rebellion, had failed in the 1920s, while their subsequent strategy of operating from remote rural base areas proved unable, in the 1930s, to withstand Nationalist encirclement campaigns. By 1937, the Chinese Communists, at Yenan in the distant northwest, seemed to be on the verge of extinction.

Japan's full-scale invasion of eastern China after 1937 changed all this by bleeding white the forces of the National Government of Chiang Kai-shek and the Kuomintang, while the Communists prospered: their guerrilla tactics cost few casualties, appealed to patriotism, and swelled their ranks.

Even more important, the occupation of Manchuria by Soviet armies in August 1945 provided the Communists with an unprecedented strategic opportunity. The territory was self-sufficient and easily defensible; historically it had proven a good base for conquering the rest of China. With Soviet acquiescence, the Communists transferred some 20 central committee members, 20,000 cadres, and 100,000 troops to Manchuria from elsewhere in China by

CHINESE
CIVIL WAR

Shantung
Province

January 1946. And the Communists expected to take over peacefully, at least to judge by the way they concentrated on building up a civil administration rather than preparing defenses.

This proved a false hope. Reoccupation of the territory received high priority from the National Government, and in November 1945 it threw its crack American-equipped divisions into Manchuria, while winning Soviet diplomatic agreement to withdraw Soviet troops in the following year. Divided from their Soviet patrons and unequipped for mechanized warfare, the Communists were forced slowly to retreat north, while their leaders protested vigorously at the United States–sponsored peace talks brokered by General George C. Marshall (q.v.) then in progress. In May 1946, National Government troops looked set to complete the conquest, only to be halted by order of their own government, evidently because of pressure from the Americans, who feared damage to the peace talks.

The halt changed strategic calculations for both sides. The National Government had been counting on a rapid victory that would accelerate its reconsolidation of power in the rest of China. The Communists above all feared loss of Manchuria, for prewar experience had demonstrated that, given time, the National Government could isolate and destroy their base areas anywhere else. So the halt saved them. With sanctuary in northern Manchuria and their main forces still intact, they were well placed to mount a counter-

offensive. They sought to draw away National Government forces from Manchuria by launching offensives in Shantung and central China. In responding, the National Government proved incapable of assigning priority to strategic objectives and divided its forces reactively, while pursuing impressive but strategically unimportant victories, culminating in March 1947 with the capture of the old Communist capital at Yenan. Meanwhile, the Communists focused on the key Manchurian theater.

Summer 1947 saw a major Communist attempt to break through southward along the railway in Manchuria, leading to a major battle at the key junction of Ssu-p'ing-k'ai. Firepower was the key to the victory won by well-equipped Nationalist troops; in response, the Communists quickly began acquiring heavy artillery of their own.

The turning point came in 1948. By then, Communist firepower had become formidable; manpower ratios were beginning to favor the Communists. Most important, however, National Government overextension was turning into stalemate. Its forces were strong almost everywhere but had decisive superiority nowhere. When Communist victory in Manchuria broke the stalemate, its momentum proved irresistible.

The breakthrough offensive began in March 1948. Ssu-p'ing-k'ai was finally taken; when Chin-chou fell in October, the remaining National Government positions in Manchuria were irretrievably isolated and quickly collapsed. The crucial Huai-Hai battle in east central China began in early November 1948, and half a million National Government troops were eventually committed. The Communist victory in early December rendered Peking and Tientsin untenable. Communist troops moved south across the Yangtze River in April; Shanghai fell peacefully in May, and the People's Republic of China was proclaimed in Peking in October. On December 10, 1949, Chiang Kai-shek flew from Ch'eng-tu, in the southwest, to Taiwan. The fighting was effectively over, although the political contest continued between Taipei and Peking.

Traditionally, the Chinese Civil War has been interpreted as a prototypical Asian peasant revolution of rural masses against a corrupt government. Some of the picture fits, but not all. The National Government, exhausted by the Anti-Japanese War, was beset by political rivalries and riddled with corruption, and the Chinese economy was consumed by spiraling inflation. The Communists made a democratic-sounding appeal that persuaded much moderate opinion at least to remain neutral and won support from important sectors of the intelligentsia as well as the poor peasantry (although the soldiers on both sides were overwhelmingly peasants). Alliance politics were critical: the Soviets helped the Communists even while seemingly accommodating the Nationalists; ineffective U.S. intervention deeply alienated both Chinese parties. Ultimately, however, this was not a social war; its outcome was determined militarily and could have gone either way. Revolution, as the most recent scholarship has underlined, was much more its consequence than its cause.

ARTHUR WALDRON

Stephen I. Levine, *Anvil of Victory: The Communist Revolution in Manchuria, 1945–1948* (1987); Suzanne Pepper, *Civil War in China: The Political Struggle, 1945–1949* (1978).

Ch'in Shih-huang-ti

259–210 B.C., *Chinese Emperor*

The future unifier of China succeeded in 246 B.C. to the throne of the northwestern kingdom of Ch'in, one of the seven "warring states" into which the Chinese cultural area was divided. He maintained and strengthened his predecessors' attempts to harness all of the state's resources for the purpose of war making and continued their drive for territorial expansion. Exploiting divisions between their opponents, the Ch'in armies conquered and annexed the six rival kingdoms in a series of campaigns between 230 and 221 B.C., and their leader, King Cheng, now assumed the title of Shih-huang-ti, or "first august emperor."

Ch'in Shih-huang-ti never led his armies in battle, but he did take a hands-on approach to the governance of his realm and was said to be in habit of working his way through some sixty pounds of bamboo-strip documents at a single sitting. The Ch'in Empire could not survive without him. Within a few years of his death, it had been torn apart by uprisings led by dispossessed local elites and backed by a populace pushed to the brink by labor exactions for grandiose projects such as the Great Wall and the imperial tomb complex at Li-shan. Although the first emperor's harsh rule was condemned by generations of Confucian scholars, his system of centralized administration in fact provided the blueprint that was followed by the Han dynasty (202 B.C.–A.D. 220) and all of its successors down to 1911.

Since 1974, excavations at the tomb of Ch'in Shih-huang-ti have uncovered a mortuary army of some seven thousand life-size terra-cotta warriors deployed to guard the emperor in the afterlife. The figures include spear-armed infantrymen, archers, crossbowmen, cavalry (with terra-cotta horses), and chariot-mounted troops. They are an important source of information concerning the armor, weapons, small-unit organization, and even uniform colors of the Ch'in army, and their dense formation suggests both the sternness of Ch'in discipline and the sophistication of Ch'in tactics.

DAVID A. GRAFF

Chu-ko Liang

A.D. 181–234, *Chinese Statesman, General, and Strategist*

For the Chinese, Chu-ko Liang is the archetype of the scholar-general who wins victories by clever stratagems rather than brute force. He was the great strategic adviser to Liu Pei, the founder of the state of Shu-Han, one of the "Three Kingdoms" into which China was divided at the end of the Han period. In A.D. 207 he persuaded Liu to make his base in Szechwan and form an alliance with the state of Wu on the lower Yangtze in order to resist Ts'ao Ts'ao (who held de facto power in North China), initiating the tripartite division that would last until 263.

The historical Chu-ko Liang has been largely eclipsed by the image created by popular fiction, particularly the fourteenth-century *Romance of the Three Kingdoms*, which endows him with superhuman wisdom and even occult powers. On one occasion in this text, when Chu-ko is surrounded in an undefended town by a large enemy force, he has the gates left open; so great is his reputation for cunning that the enemy commander, fearing a trap, immediately retreats.

DAVID A. GRAFF

Churchill, Winston S.

1874–1965, *British Statesman*

Winston Churchill's greatest contribution — one acknowledged by all but the most perverse of his critics — was his animation of the resistance of Great Britain, the English-speaking world, and indeed all free peoples in the struggle against Adolf Hitler (q.v.) and

Nazi Germany. His archaic-seeming but magnificent oratory rallied Nazism's enemies before the war and inspired his nation and its allies through nearly six weary years of struggle.

So much is known. But Churchill's career as a war leader and manager has excited far more controversy. Should he receive credit, for example, as first lord of the Admiralty (1911–1915) for the modernization of the Royal Navy and its concentration opposite Germany (see *Fisher, John Arbuthnot*), or should attention focus on the failed Gallipoli (q.v.) operation of 1915, which was his pet scheme? As the driving force, in 1919, of the rolling extension (that is, automatically extended each year) of the Ten Year Rule, which instructed British planners not to expect a major conflict for a decade to come, did he cripple British defense planning? Were his estimates of the German military buildup in the 1930s greatly exaggerated, and above all, was his direction of Britain's war machine in 1939 capricious and unfocused?

These accusations, leveled ever more frequently against Churchill by historians who seek (vainly) to dim the glow of unqualified admiration that his name still evokes, have yet to alter the fundamental picture of greatness. Indeed, even the particular criticisms mentioned above can be rebutted. There were strong arguments to be made for the attempts to force the Dardanelles, which came heartbreakingly close to success on several occasions. The Ten Year Rule, several researchers now note, did *not*, in fact, limit the amount of British defense spending in the 1920s, and in any event, Churchill insisted that it should be reviewed annually by the Committee on Imperial Defence. Churchill's estimates of German strength came straight from British intelligence. Above all, a careful examination of Churchill's record as war leader in the period 1940–1945 shows a master of war statesmanship equal or superior to any other democratic war leader.

Churchill's genius went far beyond a grasp of the fine phrase. His probing intelligence — revealed most wonderfully in the memoranda with which he bombarded his subordinates — kept hordes of bureaucrats alert to their duties. His military subordinates began reading signal intelligence summaries in order to keep up with their chief, an avid reader of intelligence material, who threw the full force of his patronage behind British cryptanalysts. He had a particular talent for focusing governmental energies on immediate or looming crises. In the Battle of Britain (q.v.), the Battle of the North Atlantic (q.v.), and the V-weapon assault on London, to take only three cases, he drew together all parts of the British government to parry potentially mortal threats to Britain's continuance in the war. He managed Anglo-American relations with subtlety and skill, yielding where necessary, but successfully coaxing, imploring, and persuading the U.S. president regarding important matters such as the decision to postpone an invasion of France until 1944. Despite his reputation as a bully of generals, he almost never overruled them outright. He would hound them, cross-examine them, demand justification for their positions, but except in the gravest extremity would not (unlike Hitler) issue orders in opposition to the united opinion of his military advisers. At the same time, a perusal of the diaries of his chivvied and resentful field marshals and admirals suggests that without Churchill's aggressive drive, British strategy would have been impossibly cautious and passive.

Churchill deserves more attention than he has received as a student of war, not merely a practitioner of it. Churchill's six-volume biography of his ancestor Marlborough (q.v.), together with his multivolume memoir and histories of the two world wars, contains absorbing meditations and brilliant aperçus on operational art, military technology, coalition strategy, and many other subjects. Churchill combined experience at the highest level in war leadership with a capacious historical understanding and extraordinary skill in exposition. Even the works of his youth, such as *The River War*, repay reading by the student of military affairs.

"There are times when I incline to judge all historians by their opinion of Winston Churchill — whether they can see that, no matter how much better the details, often damaging, of man and career become known, he still remains, quite simply, a great man." Thus British historian Geoffrey Elton. It remains an appropriate judgment.

ELIOT A. COHEN

Martin Gilbert, *Churchill: A Life* (1991); John Lukacs, *The Duel* (1990); John Wheeler-Bennett, ed., *Action This Day: Working with Churchill* (1968).

Chu Teh

1886–1976, Chinese Communist General

When in the late 1920s the Chinese Communists began to build up their own army, Chu Teh was one of the very few party members who had received a military education at the Yunnan Military Academy in south China. Having participated in the fighting of the 1911 Revolution and served in warlord armies, Chu also had substantial experience as a military commander. In the summer of 1927 in central China, the first Communist efforts at armed struggle were carried out by formerly Nationalist army units infiltrated or won over by the communists. Appalled with warlordism, Chu Teh joined these mutinies on the Communist side. Following defeat, he led the several hundred men under his command into the hill country of south China where together with Mao Tse-tung (q.v.) he began to build up a soviet and expand its forces. He defended the soviet from four attacks by Chiang Kai-shek's (q.v.) armies. By 1934 the Chinese Red Army numbered around 100,000 troops.

Chu Teh served as commander of all Communist forces during the Anti-Japanese War (1937–1945) and the Chinese Civil War (1945–1949) (q.v.), yet he has received little credit for developing Communist strategy or for leading Communist forces during important battles. Chu was a "soldier's general": an approachable and earthy man without intellectual or ideological pretenses. Given that he was a member of the highest military and political decision-making bodies, Chu no doubt played a more important role than is usually acknowledged in the making of Communist war. Nonetheless, it is probably true that he was most important as a general with whom ordinary Communist troops could readily identify. That made him the ideal commander in chief.

HANS J. VAN DE VEN

Civil-Military Relations

"Civil-military relations" is essentially a modern, Western concept involving the doctrines of nationalism, popular sovereignty, and military professionalism. Thus it is difficult to distinguish the civilian and military aspects of earlier societies in the same terms with which we analyze the past two centuries.

In general, premodern military forces remained intrinsically bound to their host societies. Soldiers could and sometimes did rebel and overthrow existing governments, for example when the janissaries deposed the Ottoman sultan in 1622 and installed a successor. However, early agrarian societies seldom produced sufficient surplus to maintain truly professional standing armies such as the janissaries. The Mongols (q.v.) owed their vast numbers of cavalrymen to the fact that the skills and equipment of mounted warriors were the same as those of herdsmen on the steppe; there was no difference between soldiers and civilians.

The same was true for the ancient Greeks. In Athens and Sparta, every citizen was a soldier and every soldier a citizen. The Roman republic followed a similar pattern, at least until the reforms of Marius early in the first century B.C. created armies of professional soldiers for an empire that had grown beyond the bounds of a city-state (see *Legions*). But the Marian system proved vulnerable to manipulation by political generals; one hundred years of civil war resulted. Only after Augustus placed control of the legions in the hand of a single man (himself and his successors) did stability return to the Roman world. The succeeding two hundred years of peace rested on the willingness of a relatively small group of professional soldiers (barely 300,000) to protect the great civilian world (over one hundred million). But in the words of Tacitus, the soldiers eventually discovered the secret of the empire — namely, that they controlled all the power. The structure could not then support their extravagant demands, and anarchy resulted — combined with other factors, it destroyed the empire.

Medieval Europe was a warrior society; there was consequently no separation between those who ruled and the military. Even the leaders of the church could prove as fierce in battle as any knight. Not until the seventeenth century did military organizations with the civil discipline of the Romans return to Europe. In effect the nobility was co-opted by the monarchies by being given the premier positions of command in the emerging military organizations. The French Revolution (q.v.), however, brought a fundamental change with the destruction of the nobility and the creation of a ferocious civilian authority that demanded the absolute obedience of all citizens, regardless of age, to the needs of the *Republic* — the first embodiment of the modern nation-state. While the revolutionaries threw the military career open to those with the most talent, they also closely monitored the performance of generals: those who failed faced trial for treason and then the guillotine. Napoleon (q.v.) removed some of the ambiguities for a short period by returning to the earlier model in which civil and military were embodied in his sole command as emperor — a state of affairs that undoubtedly contributed to the collapse of the First Empire.

The British and the Americans developed a view of civil-military relations that differed from that of their cousins on the Continent. Oliver Cromwell's (q.v.) dictatorship, established in seventeenth-century England with the support of his grim Puritan army, resulted in a profound suspicion of standing armies among most British and Americans. Because of their geographic position, protected by the ocean, both countries largely minimized the role of armies except in times of national emergency. In the War of Spanish Succession (q.v.) and the Napoleonic Wars, British armies played crucial roles in the defeat of states with hegemonic dreams; but these successes hardly altered national prejudices against standing armies.

In the nineteenth century the roles of civilian and military began to radically diverge with the increasing technological complexity of war. Officership became a demanding and complex profession, which grew increasingly suspicious of a civilian world that did not share many of its values. Abraham Lincoln (q.v.), confronted with the secession of the Southern states, mobilized a great army to put down the rebellion. There were tense moments between the president and his generals. In one case Lincoln wrote to a new commander of the Army of the Potomac, George B. McClellan (q.v.): "I have heard . . . of your recently saying that . . . the Government needed a dictator. Of course it was not *for* this, but in spite of it, that I have given you the command. Only those generals who gain successes, can set up dictators. What I now ask of you is military success, and I will risk the dictatorship." Lincoln's common sense and the strong tradition of civilian control over the military largely insulated the United States, as it did Britain, from the struggles between generals and politicians that marked affairs on the Continent.

The pattern of civil-military relations in Europe in the late nineteenth century followed a harsher track. In France, the Dreyfus affair came close to ripping the army and the country apart. In Germany, the successes of German arms in 1866 and 1870 led the military as well as many civilians to miss entirely the crucial role that Otto von Bismarck's (q.v.) civilian control had exercised in creating the strategic and political context necessary for victory. But the leaders of Wilhelmine Germany wrote off Carl von Clausewitz's (q.v.) dictum that "war is a continuation of politics by other means" and embarked on an approach that consistently placed pure operational expediency above strategic and political concerns.

Ironically, there was a curious reversal of the imbalance in German civil-military relations in the next war. In World War I (q.v.), the military had essentially eclipsed the civilian government; in World War II (q.v.), however, Adolf Hitler (q.v.) completely dominated and overruled his military. In either case, a more balanced division of authority might have allowed Germany to avoid its worst strategic mistakes. In contrast, in both wars, Britain and the United States demonstrated a far superior relationship between civilian and military authorities — consequently, their fundamentally sounder war aims and strategies ultimately compensated for weaknesses at the operational and tactical levels.

According to the Western model of representative government that dominates much of the world, the military must remain ultimately subordinate to civilian control. In order for armed forces to function effectively, however, political leaders must also grant considerable autonomy to military professionals in the planning and execution of operations. At the heart of the problem remains the difficulty in drawing any clear, conclusive boundary between military and political affairs, for as Clausewitz observed, the two realms are inextricably related.

WILLIAMSON MURRAY

Thucydides, *History of the Peloponnesian War*, trans. Rex Warner (1954).

Clark, Mark W.

1896–1984, U.S. General

A career infantry officer, Mark W. Clark was best known for his remarkable physical courage and for his controversial command of the multinational U.S. Fifth Army in Italy from September 1943 to December 1944.

A 1917 graduate of West Point, Clark was wounded on his first day of combat while serving with the Fifth Division in France in June 1918. In 1942, George Marshall (q.v.) sent Clark to England, where he so impressed Winston Churchill (q.v.) that the prime minister nicknamed him "the American Eagle." Shortly thereafter he was appointed as Dwight Eisenhower's (q.v.) deputy supreme commander for the invasion of French North Africa. Clark's most famous exploit was a hazardous mission by submarine in October 1942 to negotiate secretly with Vichy French officers near Algiers prior to the Operation Torch landings the following month.

His appointment to command Fifth Army made him the youngest lieutenant general in the U.S. Army. Despite a well-earned reputation for bravery, Clark earned considerable criticism for the Salerno landings, the ill-fated Rapido River operation in January 1944, the Battle of Anzio (q.v.), a series of unsuccessful and costly assaults against the town of Monte Cassino (q.v.), the destruction of the abbey of Monte Cassino by Allied bombers, and his failure to encircle the German Tenth Army during the drive on Rome.

Clark ended the war in command of the Allied Fifteenth Army Group in Italy. From 1945 to 1947 he was the U.S. high commissioner in occupied Austria. During the final months of the Korean War (q.v.), Mark Clark was commander in chief of the United Nations Command and ended a distinguished thirty-six-year career shortly after signing the armistice for the UN in July 1953.

CARLO W. D'ESTE

Clausewitz, Carl von

1780–1831, Military Strategist and Prussian General

Carl Philip Gottlieb von Clausewitz joined the Prussian army at the age of twelve and saw active service against the French in 1793–1794 before entering the Berlin Military Academy. He then joined the General Staff and fought (and was captured) at Jena (1806) and in the Waterloo campaign (1815) before becoming director of the Berlin Staff College (1818), where he devoted himself to writing about war. Between 1806 and 1815 he left the Prussian army, and he served against Napoleon (q.v.) in Russia in 1812.

Clausewitz is best known for his book *On War*, published posthumously in 1832. Despite its philosophical and epistemological dimensions, *On War* is a book written for the practical military reader as well as for strategists, political leaders, and students of war in general. Clausewitz wrote about war not as an armchair expert, but as one who had witnessed and participated in numerous campaigns during the Napoleonic Wars.

Narrowly focused on how to wage war in the most effective way, *On War* is not concerned with broader ethical questions, the causes and origins of war, and other questions that concern the modern student of war. Indeed, no less than 50 percent of *On War* is dedicated to purely operational, even tactical, matters.

Unfortunately, this practical book has failed to appeal to many military readers because it lacks concrete, manual-type answers. In fact, it raises as many questions as it answers. Unlike Antoine-Henri Jomini, Basil Liddell Hart (q.v.), or J. F. C. Fuller (q.v.), Clausewitz never claimed to develop universally valid recipes, rules, or principles that would guarantee success in war. Moreover, he carefully showed the exceptions to every general principle or rule. *On War* forces serious readers to wrestle with Clausewitz's concepts and then to develop their own critical ideas of what war is all about.

Much like Niccolò Machiavelli's (q.v.) *The Prince*, *On War* is neither moral nor immoral in focus but an amoral, "objective" study. Although Clausewitz studied war systematically, he did not think that war could be waged as an exact science. He stated "that the term 'art of war' is more suitable than 'science of war.'"

The most important chapter of *On War* is Chapter 1 of Book 1, "What Is War?" The only fully edited chapter in the book, it is the most definitive, encapsulating most of Clausewitz's key ideas. Had he written only this chapter, it would still stand as the foremost exposition on war. Chapter 1 begins with an important yet simple definition of war: "War is thus an act of violence [force] to compel our enemy to do our will." Thus, war serves an instrumental purpose; it is distinguished from other human activities by the use of physical violence or force, and cannot serve any purpose unless one side can compel the enemy to do its will. War is "... a clash between major interests which is resolved by bloodshed — that is the only way in which it differs from other conflicts."

Clausewitz then discussed the inherent tendency of war, *in theory*, to escalate. Once war begins, each side will force the opponent to use the maximum available physical force, which in turn compels the other to do the same. Each side will try to disarm the other — to impose its will rather than be forced to submit. Once this escalation commences, war acquires its own momentum, which operates independent of political logic and rational cost-benefit calculations. Instead, it obeys an inherent tendency toward violence and securing an ultimate victory.

Clausewitz, of course, knew that *in reality* wars do not always escalate out of control and are not always fought nonstop to the end. The enemy's strength is usually known at least in part, and therefore not *all* of the available force needs to be brought to bear; and even if either side would like to employ all of its forces at one point at one time, this would be physically impossible, given the available space and time. Moreover, the belligerents realize that even the most decisive victory is never final, since the enemy may rise again. Thus, each war must also involve diplomatic and political efforts to make victory acceptable in the long run. Even when a total and decisive victory is achievable, limited goals are often more practical. This observation led Clausewitz to conclude that war *in reality* is not exclusively based on dynamics of escalation; it is instead moderated by political calculations, uncertainties, the limits of strength, and psychological factors.

In order to serve the interests of a group or state, war must be guided by political leaders. But they must not ignore the imperatives of military action. Clausewitz delineated a division of labor between political leaders and the military, in which the military influences the political leaders by explaining what type of action (and at what cost) is feasible.

> The political aim . . . must adapt itself to its chosen means, a process which can radically change it; yet the political aim remains the first consideration. Policy, then, will permeate all military operations, and, in so far as their violent nature will admit, it will have a continuous influence on them. War . . . is not merely an act of policy but a true political instrument, a continuation of political intercourse, carried on by other means. What remains peculiar to war is simply the peculiar nature of its means. . . . The political object is the goal, war is the means of reaching it, and the means can never be considered in isolation from their purpose.

But after establishing that war should be controlled by the political authorities, Clausewitz never examined the motives, rationality, or ultimate objectives of the political leaders. His position is thus amoral.

Clausewitz concluded Chapter 1 with two central ideas. First, before any nation goes to war, its political and military leaders must understand the *nature* of that particular war. Will it be short or long? conventional or unconventional? total or limited? What are the enemy's motives or interests, and how intense is its commitment to achieving its goals? How will this affect the relative effort, endurance, and commitment of each side?

The second central idea is known as the "Clausewitzian trinity." The three elements of the trinity are primordial violence and hatred, which are a blind natural force; chance and probability, which are in the realm of the creative spirit; and subordination, calculation, and reason, which are the instruments of policy. These three dimensions are represented by the people, the military, and the government. The passions and motivation of the people constitute the nonrational aspects of war; the planning and execution of the war are carried out by the military; the government determines the political goals, the purpose of the war, and the allocation of resources. Although each of these elements is present in every war, their relationships and relative importance vary. A correct analysis of their interaction *within* each state and *between* warring states is critical for understanding the nature of a given war. Clausewitz's simple, elegant framework synthesizes ideas familiar to others before him (Sun Tzu [q.v.], Thucydides, Machiavelli [q.v.]) in a more explicit and hence more effective manner.

The three elements of the trinity are all nonmaterial, or intangible. Though it can be argued that the nature of war is also defined by economic strength and military technology, Clausewitz on the whole deliberately ignored the material aspects of war. This omission might be seen as a flaw in his work. It could, however, be argued that (1) Clausewitz thought that material and technological factors on each side tend to cancel each other out; (2) the trinitarian analysis was conducted against the backdrop of a given material environment; or (3) Clausewitz underestimated the importance of these factors because he lived before the Industrial Revolution, in a world of relatively static military technology. What may have been true for his time is not, however, correct today. It is impossible to understand modern warfare without due consideration of material and technological factors.

For Clausewitz, all other things being equal, the shortest, quickest, and most effective way to win a war is through destruction of the opponent's army in a decisive battle. This conviction explains his emphasis on the need "always to be very strong: first in general and then at the decisive point." Numerical superiority (all other things being equal) is the key to victory. (Also, despite his preference for the offensive, Clausewitz was the first modern theorist of war to emphasize the superiority of the defense.)

The last book of *On War* includes a look at the circumstances under which limited war can or should be waged. This contrasts with the beginning of *On War*, where Clausewitz emphasized the inherent tendency of war to escalate and the desirability of winning decisive military victories. Although many readers believe that the discussion of limited war constitutes a significant, unfinished reexamination of his entire theory of war, this is probably not the case. Clausewitz stressed the "moderating" role of politics and the rational calculus of war in Book 1, where he explicitly discussed the possibilities of limiting war in various ways.

More than any other theorist on war, Clausewitz emphasized the roles of uncertainty, chance, friction, and luck. Part of Clausewitz's search for the most effective way to wage war involved the development of methods to reduce uncertainty. Thus, for example, he believed that in the absence of intelligence, a commander who seizes the initiative and takes high risks can reduce uncertainty by increasing it for the enemy. "With uncertainty on one scale," he noted, "courage and self-confidence must be thrown into the other to correct the balance." He discussed extensively the military genius, whose artistic intuition in the midst of the chaos and uncertainty of battle can impose a measure of order and arrive at the necessary decisions instantaneously.

The passage of time and the development of military technology since Clausewitz's death have rendered some of his ideas obsolete. Still others were wrong to begin with. For example, Clausewitz regarded the achievement of surprise (q.v.) on the strategic level and even on the higher operational level as very unlikely. Modern military technology and the Industrial Revolution have undisputedly changed the validity of this observation. Also, Clausewitz consistently underestimated the role of deception (q.v.) in support of military operations. He viewed deception and diversions as mere distractions or wasted effort. Although this conclusion probably reflects the lessons of the Napoleonic Wars, Napoleon (q.v.) himself never underestimated the value of intelligence and deception. Clausewitz also neglected economic and material factors in war. In light of this criticism, it is obvious that although Clausewitz's work is of inestimable value for the student of war, it must always be read with a critical eye.

MICHAEL I. HANDEL

Azar Gat, *The Origins of Military Thought: From the Enlightenment to Clausewitz* (1989); Michael I. Handel, *Masters of War*, 2nd rev. ed. (1996); Michael Howard, *Clausewitz* (1988); Peter Paret, *Clausewitz and the State* (1976).

Coen, Jan Pieterszoon

1587–1629, Dutch Colonial Administrator and Conqueror

Born in Holland, Jan Pieterszoon Coen first sailed to Indonesia in the service of the Dutch East India Company in 1607 and rose to become its governor-general in Asia in 1617. Like Afonso de Albuquerque of Portugal (q.v.) a century before, Coen aimed to monopolize the production and trade of certain luxury goods (especially spices) and to control the rest. But, he wrote, in Asia "you cannot have trade without war nor war without trade," and so he burned down the Javan city of Jacatra, building the fortified stronghold of Batavia on its ruins (1619), and slaughtered or enslaved the people of the spice-producing Banda Islands (1621). By the time he returned to Holland in 1623, the Dutch maintained trading bases from Japan to India. Coen had laid the foundations of a seaborne empire in Asia that would last until the Japanese conquests of 1942.

GEOFFREY PARKER

Cold War

1946–1991

The Cold War is one of the strangest chapters in the long, bloody history of international conflict. For forty-five years it drove the politics and devoured the resources of the United States and the USSR. It twisted the fates of smaller nations sucked into the orbits of the superpowers and multiplied the violence of civil wars. Through the space race it extended into the heavens themselves and even threatened to end earthly life in nuclear devastation. It was longer and more far-reaching than the wars of 1914–1918 and 1939–1945 out of which it grew. Yet not a single shot was ever exchanged directly between Soviet and American soldiers. To call it war violates conventional definitions. To call it anything less flouts reality. It was, from beginning to end, unique.

The Cold War was conducted in phases, swinging between crises of mortal danger and "thaws" that offered reprieves from the terrifying prospect of full hostilities between the Soviet and American giants. The opening development (1945–1947) was the swift collapse of the wartime alliance against Adolf Hitler (q.v.). The roots of disagreement lay in the failure to agree on peace terms. The "temporary" division of Germany into Soviet and Western occupation zones

West Berliners welcome one of the American aircraft that, along with French and British transport planes, flew in supplies around the clock for nearly ten months in 1948–1949. One of the earliest and most dramatic Cold War tests between the superpowers, the Berlin airlift overcame the Soviet blockade of land access that attempted to starve into submission the city's two million residents.

froze into permanence as Joseph Stalin's (q.v.) demands for reparations and a paralyzed German industrial machine clashed with American and British fears of leaving a power vacuum and economic chaos in the heart of Europe. The USSR likewise refused to permit free elections in the eastern European nations still garrisoned by its troops, and they soon fell under the control of Communist autocrats and became isolated behind what Winston Churchill (q.v.) called an "iron curtain." Old American suspicions of Communist designs on the entire world were revived. So were

Soviet fears of capitalist "encirclement," exacerbated by ongoing U.S. development of the atom bomb. Cracks in the partnership became fissures during 1946, and when a Communist-led insurrection in Greece gained momentum, the United States reacted strongly. President Harry Truman asked for and got from Congress four hundred million dollars to help both Greece and neighboring Turkey to defend their independence. The importance of the Truman Doctrine was its identification of the USSR as a clear threat to peace.

A second phase now began (1947–1950) in which the Cold War became consolidated and incorporated into the institutions of both superpowers. In the United States during 1947 the armed forces were reorganized and partly unified, and the Central Intelligence Agency (CIA) was created, as was the National Security Council, whose aim was to coordinate military, diplomatic, and economic policies in the interests of "defense." One example of such linkage was the Marshall Plan, proposed in 1947 and passed by Congress in 1948, which pledged seventeen billion dollars to aid the economic recovery of western European nations, and so forestall Communist political exploitation of postwar miseries. The underlying assumption was that all Communist parties were guided from Moscow in programs of subversion and espionage. The same mind-set brought about a search for suspected "Reds" in government that peaked early in the 1950s with the witch-hunts of Senator Joseph R. McCarthy.

The year 1948 brought crisis and testing of the new machinery. In March the USSR forced a Communist regime on Czechoslovakia, which had been partly independent until then. The United States responded with renewal of conscription and plans to rehabilitate the Western-held portions of Germany despite Soviet objections. Moscow's counterstroke was to cut off road and rail access to Berlin, forcing the West to choose between dropping its new German policy or seeing the city starve. War seemed only an incident away in June, until a brilliant escape hatch was found in the Berlin airlift. Fleets of American and British planes supplied Berlin for eight months, and it was the Soviets who backed away. In the summer of 1949 the United States recognized the new "state" of West Germany and led in the creation of the North Atlantic Treaty Organization (NATO), pledging itself to help defend western Europe against any attack. The USSR later (1955) organized its satellite nations into the Warsaw Pact, so the metaphorical iron curtain became an actual armed frontier between East and West.

Stalin, meanwhile, had set in motion a crash program to make the USSR a modern military colossus. Its first notable success was the achievement of a Soviet atomic bomb in 1949. This led the United States to expedite work on developing the more powerful hydrogen bomb, first tested in 1954. The USSR matched the feat, and the nuclear arms race began in earnest.

The permanence of the Cold War was assumed in both sides' thinking, especially after Chinese Communists won their long civil war in 1949 (q.v.) and allied their huge nation with the USSR. Early in 1950, a secret American strategic planning document, NSC-68, called for permanent mobilization for a "long, twilit struggle." That struggle erupted in Asia on June 25, 1950, with the start of the Korean War (q.v.). This conflict was another novelty of the post-1945 era, a superpower war by proxy. American forces fought North Koreans merely as "agents" of the United Nations. But when Chinese "volunteers" entered, the reality of Sino-American battle threatened to destroy the facade. World War III loomed afresh. It would not come so close again until the Cuban missile crisis of 1962. But the high tension of winter 1950–1951 lingered through 1956.

The "globalization" of the Cold War continued during the first term of Dwight D. Eisenhower's (q.v.) presidency (1952–1956) as his militant secretary of state, John Foster Dulles, forged the Southeast Asia Treaty Organization to parallel NATO and encouraged the CIA to plot the destablization and overthrow of allegedly Communist regimes in Iran (1953) and Guatemala (1954). Dulles also hinted at the possibility of moves to liberate the "captive nations" of eastern Europe and indicated willingness to "go to the brink" of war as a tool of his foreign policies. In the Middle East, Arab resentment of U.S. support for the newly created (1948) state of Israel was exploited by the USSR, which became an ally and arms supplier to Egypt and Syria. In October 1956, tension in the region exploded. Egypt nationalized the Suez Canal. Britain and France, in a last bid for influence in a postcolonial world, joined Israel in a surprise paratroop operation that seized the canal. The USSR threatened to step in — but its only actual intervention anywhere that month was in Hungary, where

Soviet troops brutally suppressed a Budapest uprising. The United States, meanwhile, secured the voluntary departure of the Israeli, French, and British forces, and did nothing for Hungary except deliver angry speeches in the United Nations. The brink had been reached, and neither side wanted to go beyond it.

In fact, some events of the early 1950s generated a countertrend to "brinkmanship." In 1953 Stalin died. In 1954 Eisenhower overruled Dulles by refusing to send aid to French armies besieged at Dien Bien Phu (q.v.) in Indochina (which led to France's abandonment of the colony that year). A number of Asian and African nations showed reluctance to support either of the warring Western camps at the Bandung Conference of 1955. They included Communist China, moving steadily away from linkage to Moscow, and India, long a friend of the West. In that same year, the almost unthinkable took place — a summit conference at Geneva, unproductive but civil, between Eisenhower and Stalin's temporary successors. So, following the Suez and Hungarian crises, a "thaw" set in. The successful launch of a Soviet space satellite in 1957 opened a new "front" in the Moscow-Washington rivalry, but a space race between American and Soviet technicians was not an immediate threat to peace. The warmest point was reached in 1959 when the Soviet leader Nikita Khrushchev toured the United States. Eisenhower was supposed to make a return visit to the USSR in the summer of 1960, but in May the bottom fell out of the seeming truce. A CIA spy plane, the U-2, was shot down deep in Soviet territory while on a high-altitude photoreconnaissance mission that violated fast-fading "norms" of international law. Khrushchev raged against the bad faith of the United States, and inevitably the peace trip was scrubbed.

The pendulum now took a violent two-year swing toward war, with Cuba and Berlin as flashpoints. The revolutionary victory of Fidel Castro in 1959 spurred the United States into clandestine measures to topple him. The CIA planned an "invasion" by anti-Castro exiles at the Bay of Pigs in April of 1961. Inherited and approved by President John F. Kennedy, it was a disaster whose result was to tighten the links between Castro and Khrushchev, to whom he turned for protection against further "Yankee" assaults. Seizing on a moment when Kennedy seemed vulnerable, Khrushchev now threatened once more to isolate Berlin, but the young president responded with a partial mobilization and an unambiguous pledge of support for the city. Once again, as in 1948, the Soviets did not push the issue to confrontation. But in August 1961, the Communist East German government built the Berlin Wall, a palpable symbol of its desire to isolate its citizens from the magnetic pull of the thriving West. In the long run, that prosperity was to prove the winning card in the strange struggle that the Cold War became.

But the threat of "hot war" came closest to reality in 1962. Khrushchev raised the stakes by shipping medium-range offensive missiles to Cuba. The discovery of these by U.S. intelligence in October prompted a dramatic, ten-day game of nuclear "chicken." Kennedy ringed Cuba with a U.S. naval blockade against further missile shipments and warned that any challenge to it would meet with a "full, retaliatory response upon the Soviet Union." Meanwhile, a U.S. invasion was readied. It was the Soviet leader who blinked first, ordering USSR freighters to accept U.S. search parties. Ultimately a face-saving solution was reached: a strictly unofficial U.S. promise of no invasion and NATO's removal of some offensive missiles in Turkey, in return for which Khrushchev took his rockets home from Cuba. But few Americans (and presumably Russians) who lived through that week could forget the feeling that fire might rain from the skies at any moment.

Sobered, both leaders now reacted away from belligerence and sought some accommodation by signing the Nuclear Test Ban Treaty of 1963. It forbade airborne bomb tests that spread dangerous radiation through the entire atmosphere of the earth, literally involving millions of innocents in the Cold War's "fallout." The assassination of Kennedy and the 1964 ouster of Khrushchev ended this brief "honeymoon." But in the ensuing ten years there were revolutionary developments in the Cold War that can now be seen in hindsight as the "beginning of the end."

First came the United States' deepening involvement in the Vietnam War (q.v.). American participation began with sending military hardware and advisers to Saigon; escalated in 1965 to the commitment of U.S. ground, naval, and air forces; was reduced during peace talks from 1968 to 1972; and proved unavailing to avert final defeat in 1975. Costly and divisive, the Vietnam experience made the postwar United States aware at last that no power is unlimited.

Meanwhile, the USSR was also encountering iden-

tical limits. It had "lost" Yugoslavia in 1949 and China in 1959. Its Syrian and Egyptian clients were beaten by Israel in the Six-Day War of 1967 (see *Arab-Israeli Wars*). In 1968 it could keep Czechoslovakia in its grasp only by suppressing a liberalized government in Prague. The cost of supporting Communist governments or insurrectionary movements in Africa was burdensome and yielded little return.

The moment was therefore ripe for the astonishing turnaround of 1972, engineered by President Richard Nixon and his Machiavellian adviser, Secretary of State Henry Kissinger. For twenty-three years the United States had officially recognized only the Nationalist government of China, isolated on Taiwan, and ignored the mainland Red regime. Now, forsaking Taiwan, Nixon journeyed to Peking for a state visit that started a gradually warming relationship. This, as Kissinger knew, put pressure on the USSR to be more accommodating to the United States to avoid isolation: the United States, in short, was the "balancing" power between the two rival Communist states. Nixon soon traveled to Moscow for an equally amicable summit, during which important trade and arms limitation agreements were signed.

The Cold War continued, but as it was now driven by pragmatic power considerations and institutional inertia more than by ideology, there was ample opportunity and incentive for continued "warming." The arms race, for example, had assumed fantastic proportions and expense as both sides modernized and enlarged their arsenals. Intercontinental ballistic missiles with multiple warheads, some undetectably carried in submarines, were hideously destructive and expensive. Neither side dared to use them, but neither could risk the possibility of the other gaining an advantage, so the warheads multiplied by thousands, the potential casualties by millions, and the costs by billions (see *Ballistic Weapons*). Though Britain, France, and China joined the "nuclear club," the true "balance of terror" lay between the USSR and the United States. The Strategic Arms Limitation Talks that both entered in 1972 led to treaties that attempted not the elimination of nuclear weapons but the preservation of that balance. Both sides throughout the 1970s shared an interest in "stabilizing" the arms race, and their discussions led to further cultural, scientific, and commercial exchanges that culminated in the Helsinki Accords of 1975, agreed to by President Gerald Ford and Soviet premier Leonid

Brezhnev. These included unenforceable pledges to respect human rights in exchange for recognition of existing frontiers.

This period of "détente," in which moral rhetoric kept flowing but actual policies rested on practical power considerations, came to an end in 1979, the start of a final Cold War revival that lasted through 1985. The Soviet Union invaded Afghanistan at the "invitation" of a satellite Communist government threatened by rebellion. Like the U.S. intervention in Vietnam, it turned out to be a disaster, abandoned by Moscow after eight years of futile and exhausting battle against popular resistance. But at the start, the invasion gave fresh momentum to American critics of détente who branded it as a fatal abandonment of U.S. principle and resolve.

The critics triumphed with the election of Ronald Reagan in 1980. The new president unswervingly denounced the USSR as an "evil empire" seeking world domination and won support for a gigantic, costly program of U.S. "rearmament." Reagan also began a covert war against the leftist Sandinista regime in Nicaragua, invaded Grenada to oust another leftist government in 1983, and in other ways made it appear that the United States had returned to the brinkmanship of the 1950s.

Yet ironically, during his second term Reagan showed flexibility when the USSR suddenly and dramatically began to fold its hand. The turning point came in 1985 with the accession of Mikhail Gorbachev to Soviet leadership. The Soviet Union's economy was in ruins, and dissidence was boiling throughout its realm; the sixty-eight-year-old Communist system was on its last legs. Gorbachev wanted to bring about a peaceful transition to a more open society, and an indispensable first step was to end the bankrupting Cold War. Accordingly, in summit meetings, he struck up a surprising rapport with Reagan that ultimately resulted in arms reduction. Gorbachev and Reagan flirted with the idea of eliminating nuclear weapons altogether, but were dissuaded from so destablizing a move. However, the Strategic Arms Reduction Treaty of 1991, built on this momentum, actually provided for supervised destruction of some missiles in both countries.

In the end these steps came too late to save the USSR. One by one a series of upheavals took place between 1988 and 1991. A newly elected Soviet Parliament dissolved the Communist Party and, in 1991,

the Soviet Union itself (which broke into eleven constituent republics). The Baltic states occupied by Soviet troops during World War II seceded; the Communist regimes established in eastern European nations in 1945 were overthrown, and in the most dramatic symbolic moment of all, East Germans tore down the Berlin Wall in 1989. East Germany itself disappeared soon after, and Germany was reunified after forty-five years. The Cold War was over. Time has yet to reveal its consequences and its assessment by future generations.

BERNARD A. WEISBERGER

Bernard A. Weisberger, *Cold War, Cold Peace* (1985).

Collins, Michael

1890–1922, Irish Republican Army Leader

Michael Collins — "the Big Fellow" — is credited with masterminding the nationalist guerrilla effort against the British during the 1919–1921 Irish War of Independence. He combined a sharp political awareness and considerable personal charm with utter ruthlessness in pursuit of his military aims. During 1919, as director of organization and adjutant general of the Republican forces, he set up both an intelligence network and an assassination squad that became known as the "Twelve Apostles," which began its work by targeting plainclothes police. Collins's most dramatic operation occurred on "Bloody Sunday," November 21, 1920, when nineteen British army officers, mostly working in intelligence, were shot at eight different locations in Dublin. Collins, however, appreciated that the British Empire could not be defeated militarily, and he accepted the Anglo-Irish settlement of December 1921 as providing, as he said, enough freedom "to achieve full freedom." But irreconcilable Republicans rejected the treaty because it partitioned Ireland and did not provide complete independence. During the bitter civil war that followed, Collins, by now chairman of the new Irish Free State government, was shot dead in an ambush mounted by his former comrades. He was the modern prototype of the terrorist leader whose techniques, especially of urban guerrilla warfare, have influenced a number of subsequent revolutionary campaigns.

KEITH JEFFERY

Combined Operations

A term coined by the British military in the early twentieth century, "combined operations" are expeditions that "combine" land armies and naval forces in the pursuit of one strategic objective, supplemented by aviation elements of a separate air force or from the army and naval air components. In contemporary American usage, a multiservice force is called a "joint" force; a "combined" force includes elements of different national military establishments. To the degree that the term "combined operations" implies a type of military activity rather than a type of military organization, it means that an army-navy expeditionary force forms at a friendly port of embarkation, sails to a defended objective area, conducts air and sea operations designed to ensure the safety of the expeditionary force, and then puts a landing force ashore to capture the objective of the campaign by direct assault or siege.

Combined operations are as old as the history of warfare. They occurred in the wars of the Greeks and the Persians (499–448 B.C.) and during the Peloponnesian Wars (q.v.). The Romans took Carthage in the same way in 202 B.C., and William, duke of Normandy, defeated the English after a landing at Hastings (q.v.) in A.D. 1066. The Mongols (q.v.) failed to capture Japan in the thirteenth century with an invasion fleet and army. The Japanese invaded Korea in the late sixteenth century but suffered two defeats at the hands of the Korean "turtle boat" navy of Admiral Yi Sun-Shin (q.v.).

The institutional development of armies and navies in western Europe, however, gave combined operations their special character by the eighteenth century. In addition to enemy resistance, combined operations now faced a high level of organizational tension; because of their different perspectives and responsibilities, admirals and generals found it hard to cooperate. Admirals put the safety of the fleet first and worried about storms, enemy naval forces, shoal waters, and coastal fortifications; generals feared that fleet safety would deprive them of naval cannon bombardments and supplies and reinforcements. Fleet safety, for example, might dictate landings too far from the objective (a port city, a naval anchorage) in difficult terrain. A prolonged siege might doom the landing force to epidemic diseases, which ruined British expeditions against the Spanish at Cartagena (1740) and Havana (1762).

By the early part of the twentieth century, advances in military and naval technology and the development of a maritime strategic doctrine (sea power) brought renewed interest in combined operations, especially in Great Britain and the emerging naval powers, Japan and the United States. As the unchallenged naval power of the nineteenth century, Great Britain found it relatively easy to send amphibious expeditions to Russia, China, and Egypt. Japan placed armies in Korea and China without much interference from enemy fleets or storms. The United States defeated three major British combined operations in the War of 1812 (q.v.) and then mounted several of its own in the Mexican War (q.v.); it also conducted successful riverine and inshore operations in the defeat of the Confederacy (1861–1865) (see *American Civil War*). The ingredients for successful landings became apparent: freedom from enemy naval attack, overwhelming naval gunfire, rapid ship-to-shore movement against the least defended location compatible with the military mission, and the timely buildup of an army ashore. Steam-powered, armored, and heavily armed warships, coupled with steam-powered transports, made these conditions obtainable.

The accumulated experience of World War I (q.v.) suggested that combined operations remained a difficult military task, but might not be impossible, even against a defended beachhead. The most ambitious and dramatic expedition of the war, the campaign at Gallipoli (q.v.) by Australian, British, French, and New Zealand forces in 1915, proved a costly disappointment. The Japanese mounted several successful amphibious expeditions against weak German forces in China and the South Pacific, and the United States, whose navy and marine corps had already experimented with major landing exercises since 1900, watched everyone else. In the twenty years between the world wars, Japan and the United States, planning to fight each other, led the world in developing amphibious doctrine and forces, even creating specialized amphibious shipping (Japan) and landing craft and vehicles (the United States). Both nations provided aviation support for their amphibious forces.

As a complex global conflict, World War II (q.v.) made combined operations an unavoidable necessity, especially after Nazi Germany overran western Europe. Only the Russo-German theater of the war did not require major amphibious operations. After a successful campaign of conquest in 1941–1942, the Japanese armed forces lapsed onto the strategic defense and allowed their amphibious capability to dwindle. In the meantime, the Fleet Marine Force (FMF) of the U.S. Marine Corps and comparable U.S. Army divisions brought the amphibious assault to a high art in collaboration with very effective U.S. Navy amphibious forces. Anglo-American amphibious forces landed in North Africa (1942), Sicily (1943), Italy (twice in 1943), and France (twice in 1944) to create a second front against Germany. These landings incorporated the complementary assault by paratroopers and air-landing formations beyond the beachhead. The combination of mobility and air and naval firepower from the sea prevailed over the beach defenders.

After World War II, amphibious operations diminished in importance, but not usefulness, in a wide range of military expeditions. Only the United States maintained a landing force of World War II scale and modern technical capability, the FMF, which conducted only one essential landing in the Korean War (q.v.) at Inchon (1950) but added a major threat in the Vietnam War (q.v.) and the Gulf War (q.v.). Amphibious forces contributed to the resolution of the Cuban missile crisis (1962) and spearheaded the Dominican intervention (1965). British amphibious forces, which had diminished to one commando brigade and four vessels by 1994, led the Suez intervention (1956) and the reconquest of the Falkland Islands (1982) (q.v.). Both NATO and the Warsaw Pact organized amphibious forces for flanking operations in the Norwegian Sea, the Baltic approaches, the Black Sea, and the Mediterranean as part of their planning for World War III. Military theorists have proclaimed the death of combined operations for most of the twentieth century, and they have invariably been wrong. The ability to mount an amphibious assault, however small, remains an attractive operational capability.

ALLAN R. MILLETT

Merrill L. Bartlett, *Assault from the Sea* (1983); L. E. H. Maund, *Assault from the Sea* (1949); Allan R. Millett, *Semper Fidelis: History of the United States Marine Corps*, rev. ed. (1993); Masao Suekuni, *Amphibious Operations in Military History and Their Background* (1982); Alfred Vagts, *Landing Operations* (1946).

Command

No function in war has undergone more change over the centuries than that of command. In Homeric war-

The Ten Most Underrated Commanders	
Aetius	Charles Cornwallis
Saladin	George Thomas
Suleiman I	Ferdinand Foch
Maurice of Nassau	K. K. Rokossovsky
George Washington	Matthew Ridgway

fare, command was a function of the strongest, meanest, and toughest: the single warrior himself determined the fate of armies (and tribes) in single combat. By the fifth century B.C., the Greeks had evolved a disciplined military formation, the phalanx — but it had only a primitive command function. Generals were responsible for lining everyone up and then launching themselves and the formation at their opponents. The Romans developed disciplined formations as well — legions (q.v.) subdivided into ten cohorts with smaller subunits. The system allowed considerable flexibility, and Roman generals could command from the rear. Through a sophisticated system of signals they could even order complex maneuvers in battle.

But the collapse of the Roman Empire brought with it a collapse of Rome's military institutions. European feudal armies were no different than armies elsewhere in the world — only as good or bad as their warrior king or chieftain. The best of the lot were undoubtedly the Mongols (q.v.) who seem to have been able to control their armies over hundreds of miles. But they also were only as good as their leaders, and when Genghis Khan (q.v.) and Tamerlane (q.v.) disappeared, the Mongols melted back into the steppe.

When the Europeans rediscovered the Roman system after the Middle Ages, they mixed highly disciplined formations with command elements able to coordinate the movement of several formations. Although eighteenth-century generals, such as the duke of Marlborough (q.v.), were often involved in the fighting, they had minuscule staffs and generally remained in the rear, where they could coordinate changes of alignment through those staffs.

The armies of revolutionary and Napoleonic France, partially driven by the great increase in manpower, produced a number of improvements in the system of command. First, the French introduced the division and then the corps, which allowed the com-

Supreme commander of the Allied Expeditionary Force General Dwight D. Eisenhower encourages paratroopers in England on June 5, 1944, before the Allied invasion of Europe.

mand and control of sizable forces over considerable distances. Moreover, a combination of arms — infantry (q.v.), artillery (q.v.), cavalry (q.v.) — in each formation allowed these formations to fight independently under a separate command element. Napoleon's (q.v.) masterful coordination of his corps in the 1805 Ulm campaign allowed him to envelop the Austrians and then destroy them (see *Austerlitz, Battle of*). The movements, however, largely took place out of the range of the emperor's watchful eyes; he had to depend on couriers and on the competence and initiative of his subordinate commanders.

But the increasing size of armies created a situation in which even the great Napoleon could no longer control the vast forces under his command. The increasing pace of technological change in the mid–nineteenth century only added to the problems of command. The Prussians found a unique answer: the education and use of highly trained staff officers to control and manage the information flow between commander and combat formations. The appearance of the telegraph mitigated some of the problems, but telegraphic lines always remained subject to disruption. Moreover, the information they transmitted could be misleading, as occurred in the Seven Weeks' War (q.v.) in 1866.

There the Prussian staff system overcame the difficulties resulting from the breakdown in communications. Count Helmuth von Moltke (q.v.), chief of the Prussian General Staff, managed to concentrate three separate armies on the field at Königgrätz (1866) (q.v.) almost simultaneously and destroyed his Austrian opponent. The Prussian command system worked to even greater advantage in the 1870 Franco-Prussian War (q.v.). But the principle problem that the Prussians confronted has survived into the twentieth century: how to command organizations without depriving subordinate commanders of the initiative and authority to react in response to unforeseen events.

The answer, pushed by the Germans in the Ludendorff offensive (q.v.) of March 1918 in World War I (q.v.), was to devolve responsibility and command authority to the lowest level possible; this emphasis on "mission-oriented" tactics gave the Germans a great tactical advantage in the next war. When combined with the tank, aircraft, and the radio, German tactics returned maneuver to the battlefield. Nevertheless, a number of German generals still led from the front. The Allied performance of 1940, in which their commander in chief, General Maurice Gamelin (q.v.), sat ensconced in his comfortable headquarters far behind the front lines with no radio, stands in stark contrast to the German example.

The command problem late in the twentieth century is rather too much than too little of a good thing. Revolutionary changes in technology — which allow senior officials in Washington to talk to company commanders on the ground — enable a multiplicity of command authorities to intervene in situations that they cannot possibly understand. Moreover, the vast flow of information, during the Gulf War (q.v.) for example, threatens to choke commanders with irrelevant information. The increasing complexities of sensors and means of communications are thus steadily and rapidly exacerbating the problems of command. It will not get better.

WILLIAMSON MURRAY

Ulysses S. Grant, *Personal Memoirs* (1885); William Slim, *Defeat into Victory* (1956).

The Common Soldier

The notion that some soldiers have higher social status than others, that some are more "noble" than the others, and that, at least by inference, the remainder are "common," is a long-standing one. In many cases, this distinction was related to whether or not a soldier rode into battle. Those who fought from chariots, on horseback, or in aircraft tended to be accorded higher status than those who fought on foot. The term "common soldier" is thus closely related to that of "foot soldier." However, the notion that the vast majority of soldiers in an army are "common," and of necessity or right ought to be, is an artifact of conditions that may not survive the twentieth century.

In the mercenary armies (q.v.) of the late Middle Ages and the early modern period, the soldier retained a great deal of his individuality. As personally owned weapons were replaced with mass-produced, government-issued ones, as eclectic and often outlandish costumes were replaced by uniforms, and as "on-the-job training" was replaced by minutely regulated drill, soldiers became increasingly characterized by their resemblance to robots. Indeed, by the early eighteenth century, the ideal of a military unit as a well-oiled machine composed of a large number of identical and largely interchangeable parts had been firmly established in most European armies.

This process had the (often intended) effect of making service as an ordinary soldier odious to all but the least fortunate members of society. The adventurous sons of noble and wealthy families were, in the sixteenth century, still willing to serve as spearmen (hence the modern rank of lance corporal) or cavalrymen. By the middle of the eighteenth century, such men would deign to serve only as officers. Even if, as in the case of France until the Revolution of 1789 or Prussia during the Wars of Liberation against Napoleon (1813–1815), some of these men served as foot soldiers, they were given the status of officers or, at the very least, of officer candidates. Indeed, through the end of the twentieth century, the notion that someone from the upper classes might serve in the ranks and that someone from the lower classes might serve as an officer was considered anathema in most armies. The occasional "ranker officer" (like the British field marshal William Robertson) or "gentleman ranker" (like the anonymous hero of Rudyard Kipling's "Baa Baa Black Sheep") were but the exceptions that proved the rule.

In the latter half of the nineteenth century, the introduction of universal military service in many nations greatly reduced the social stigma attached to service in the ranks. In those countries where the system was most successful, notably Germany and France, two or three years of service as a common soldier became, for all but the most privileged members of society, an important rite of passage. However, as universal military service increased, rather than diminished, the distinction between (professional) officers and (time-serving) soldiers, it tended to strengthen the dichotomy between officers and common soldiers.

The great explosion in military gadgetry that took place during World War I (q.v.) introduced a more complex, three-class hierarchy. Officers and common soldiers in the ranks were joined and, indeed, partially replaced by a bewildering variety of technicians who served in, behind, and even above the trenches. Some of these technicians — particularly those associated with flying machines — quickly attained status far greater than that of common soldiers and, in many armies, were accorded noncommissioned or even commissioned officer rank. Even those who bore the same titles and drew the same pay as common soldiers found that they suffered far less from the forces of sameness and anonymity that pressed so hard upon the "rank and file."

By World War II (q.v.), the great need for technicians resulted in a strong tendency to assign the most intelligent recruits to the technical branches. The result, which was particularly marked in the United States but also visible in other technologically sophisticated armies, was that the infantry had to make do with soldiers who, in many cases, lacked the ability to learn the many skills needed by modern riflemen. At the same time, the proliferation of technicians in some armies was such that, for the first time since the Middle Ages, men who fought on foot were greatly outnumbered by other sorts of soldiers. The ironic result of this was that the combat infantrymen who had, in World War I, formed a vast military proletariat, became, in World War II, and particularly in America's wars in Korea (q.v.) and Vietnam (q.v.), a minority underclass. As members of such groups often do, these "uncommon common soldiers" took a perverse pride in their condition, and terms such as "dogface" and "grunt" took on a certain panache.

The guerrilla forces that fought against American and other Western powers during the second half of the twentieth century did a far better job of preserving the status of the combat infantryman. This largely resulted from the material poverty of guerrilla armies, which, lacking sophisticated equipment, had little need for technicians. At the same time, the fact that most guerrilla armies contained large numbers of unarmed porters and laborers meant that the infantryman was not at the bottom of the social ladder. Indeed, it was a common practice in many non-Western guerrilla armies to reward the faithful service of a porter or a laborer with the gift of a rifle and transfer to an infantry unit.

Many Western armies have reacted to the decline in the quality and number of infantrymen by inventing, in the form of the commando, a new sort of infantryman that, though his tasks were little different from those of the common soldier, possessed a higher degree of skill and enjoyed far greater status. Recruits who might otherwise avoid service in the infantry units were, and continue to be, attracted to elite forces. In some modern armies, such as that of Germany, elite parachute and mountain infantry units contain the only true infantrymen in the active duty force. In others, such as that of Russia in the period after the fall of Communism, there are serious proposals to replace the existing mass army with professional units trained in the style of commandos. Indeed, in a world in which policy makers most frequently require "surgical strikes," it is questionable whether there will be much for a common soldier to do.

BRUCE I. GUDMUNDSSON

Byron Farwell, *Mr. Kipling's Army* (1981); Samuel Stouffer et al., *The American Soldier* (1949); Martin van Creveld, *Fighting Power* (1981).

Communications Technology, Military

Military communication serves two purposes: to convey information so that commanders can make informed decisions and to carry orders from commanders to subordinates. As armed forces have become larger and warfare more complex, the need of commanders to be well informed and promptly obeyed has grown in proportion; hence, the increasing importance of communication.

For every urge to communicate, however, there is a reason to desist. In war, each side tries to obtain information about the enemy while hiding information about itself. But information is especially vulnerable to espionage while it is being communicated; hence, military communication is inextricably linked with secrecy, intelligence (q.v.), and counterintelligence. The explosion of communications technology during the past two hundred years has both increased the scope of warfare and complicated the tasks of information gathering, secrecy, and control.

Before the 1790s, military communications relied largely on messengers on foot, on horseback, or on shipboard. Attempts to communicate faster than a person could travel were few and limited. Fire signals were used for simple, unidirectional, prearranged messages, such as a victory or the sighting of enemies; from the Romans to Paul Revere's signal — "one if by land, two if by sea" — little progress occurred. Naval flags and codes also served mainly for simple one-way commands.

The late eighteenth century saw important innovations in military communications. New signal flags and codebooks introduced into the Royal Navy during the wars of the American and French revolutions permitted the transmission of unanticipated messages in both directions. At Trafalgar (q.v.) in 1805, Horatio Nelson (q.v.) used Sir Home Popham's code of flags, first issued in 1800, to encourage his fleet with the message "England expects every man to do his duty." In 1794, the Frenchman Claude Chappe began placing semaphores on hilltops and tall buildings; this network, reserved for military and administrative uses, eventually linked Paris to all the important towns in France and, under Napoleon (q.v.), even reached Amsterdam and Milan. The British Admiralty built a similar system to communicate with its naval bases. In Sweden, Germany, and the United States, short lines near major ports gave advance notice of the arrival of ships.

The revolutionary communications systems of the nineteenth century — telegraphs, submarine cables, and railroads — were designed for civilian uses and taken over by the military only in wartime. The exception was radio. As early as 1897, the Royal Navy subsidized Guglielmo Marconi's experiments, and the British War Office and Admiralty and the Italian navy became Marconi's first customers. Similarly, the German armed forces were among the first buyers of AEG and Siemens radio equipment.

In World War I (q.v.), navies used radio to control widely dispersed fleets. Until 1916 German U-boats, too cramped to carry bulky long-wave transmitters, could only communicate within two hundred to three hundred miles from home; beyond that range, they acted like the lone commerce raiders of centuries past. In 1917, when vacuum tubes permitted more distant communication, submarine attacks moved out into the Atlantic.

Armies seldom used radios after the war of movement ended in September 1914. On the Western Front, telegraph and telephone lines linked army units down to the battalion level. However, artillery barrages severed telephone wires between the front and rear trenches, no matter how deeply they were buried; hence, during battle, command and control depended on runners, as in ancient times. Only late in the war did forward units obtain field radios.

Because radio waves spread beyond borders, seas, and battlefields, they required codes and ciphers. To penetrate enemy secrets, the belligerents, especially the British, developed direction-finding receivers and sophisticated traffic analysis and codebreaking methods. With the help of codebooks seized from the German cruiser *Magdeburg* and other ships, the British Admiralty's "Room 40," or cryptanalysis section, was able to decrypt German naval signals. At Jutland (q.v.) and in other battles, however, the admirals failed to make the best use of such information. Until the end of the war, cryptography remained a handicraft and codebreaking a mental exercise poorly integrated into operational practice.

Two inventions of the 1920s transformed not only military communications, but strategy and tactics as well. The first was the shortwave transmitter, which could communicate cheaply at great distances, yet remained small enough to fit into a submarine, a plane, or a tank; by the 1940s, there were even suitcase sets for spies. Commanders could now control warships and submarines, armored divisions, or fleets of bombers spread over enormous areas. The introduction of shortwave, however, did not eliminate the need for enormous long-wave transmitters that could broadcast to the entire world at once. Submarines could receive messages while submerged but had to surface in order to transmit.

The second invention of the interwar period was cipher machines, such as the German Enigma, the American Sigaba, and the British Typex, which could be operated by hastily trained personnel, yet were considered invulnerable to codebreaking.

World War II (q.v.) demonstrated the potential of the new technologies. Although there were instances of radio silence, most of the time the belligerents filled the ether with their radio traffic, for the need to command and control took precedence over the risks of interception. Shortwave radio allowed tactics such as submarine wolf packs, massive bombing raids, and coordinated blitzkrieg attacks. FM radio was used for local communication, for instance, between ships in convoy. By the end of the war, every tank and aircraft carried a transceiver, and ships and army units had several.

Improved communications tempted high commands to micromanage battles, a temptation to which Adolf Hitler (q.v.) increasingly succumbed as the tide of war turned against Germany. More insidious was the race between secrecy and communications intelligence. Although all sides relied on machine encryption to protect their communications, British and American cryptanalysts developed techniques to read enemy messages almost as quickly as their intended recipients. Thus in June 1942, Admiral Chester Nimitz (q.v.), the U.S. commander in chief in the Pacific, learned of Japanese plans to attack Midway Island (see *Midway, Battle of*) and thus was able to catch the Japanese fleet by surprise.

Since World War II, developments have continued apace. In the Korean War (q.v.), walkie-talkies put infantry platoons in constant communication with regimental headquarters. Since the 1960s, communications satellites have allowed instantaneous communication with remote parts of the world, whereas navigation satellites allow small units to fix a position within a few yards — although, of course, only the great powers can afford such technologies.

The United States and the Soviet Union spent enormous sums on security, espionage, and counterintelligence with, at best, temporary advantages. Lesser challengers, such as terrorist organizations and guerrilla fighters, use human messengers instead of electronic communications whenever possible. Even the finest communications technologies do not guarantee either superiority in war or security in peacetime.

DANIEL R. HEADRICK

Daniel R. Headrick, *The Invisible Weapon: Telecommunications and International Politics, 1851–1945* (1991); Arthur Hezlet, *The Electron and Sea Power* (1975).

Condé, Louis II de Bourbon, Prince of

1621–1686, French General

Though headstrong and rash, Louis II de Bourbon, prince of Condé, still stands near the top of any list of the outstanding captains of France. He bore the title duke of Enghien until he inherited the rank of prince of Condé upon the death of his father in 1646. He won his first great battle at Rocroi (q.v.) in 1643, when he was barely twenty-two years old. There Condé seized the initiative, led the French cavalry of the right wing in a spirited assault that decided the battle, crushed the Spanish (believed to be virtually invincible at the time), and established his reputation as a great, if rash, tactician and leader. He gained further glory at the battles of Freiburg (August 5, 1644) and Lens (August 29, 1648). His victories earned him the title "the Great Condé."

As cousins of the king, the Condés stood very close to the French throne. The family's great pretensions to power and privilege eventually led the Great Condé to join the rebellion of the Fronde by 1651. This revolt against the royal government directed by Cardinal Jules Mazarin severely challenged the monarchy, but it was eventually defeated. Even after the end of the Fronde, however, Condé still led Spanish troops against Louis XIV (q.v.). The remarkable transfer of allegiance that saw the victor of Rocroi commanding the troops of his erstwhile enemy resulted from Condé's pride, which was deeply wounded at not receiving rewards he believed were owed him by the French monarchy. The princely rebel was finally defeated in 1658 by Turenne (q.v.) at the Battle of the Dunes.

Following the Peace of the Pyrenees, Condé returned to France. Although the king did not welcome Condé back into his good graces, loyalty among the well born was still more important than loyalty to country and Louis tolerated actions that would be considered treason today. With the outbreak of the War of Devolution (1667–1668), Condé once again received a French command and led a successful invasion of Franche Comté. In the Dutch War (1672–1678), he took part in the initial invasion of the United Provinces. Condé tended to rush headlong into battle, and this tendency cost him dearly at Senef (August 11, 1674), when the French lost ten thousand men in a largely indecisive action. In 1675 he maneuvered very successfully against Raimundo Montecuccoli and forced him back over the Rhine, but shortly afterwards he retired: although only fifty-four years of age, decades of hard campaigning had battered and weakened him. He spent the last decade of his life at his estate in Chantilly.

Condé, like his contemporary Turenne, was an independent commander, prone to follow his own course of action; also like Turenne, Condé advocated coming to grips with the enemy in battle. The passing of these two great generals in the same year gave a different character to French warfare, which Louis XIV wished to control personally and which came to emphasize sieges over battles.

JOHN A. LYNN

Eveline Godley, *The Great Condé* (1915); John B. Wolf, *Louis XIV* (1968).

Congress of Vienna

1814–1815

This conference brought the Napoleonic Wars to a close and laid the diplomatic foundations for a century in which Europe avoided a general war. The representatives began to arrive in September and October 1814; the conference included three of Europe's great monarchs, Tsar Alexander I of Russia, Emperor Francis II of Austria, and King Frederick William III of Prussia. High-ranking diplomats also attended: Castlereagh for Great Britain, Metternich for Austria, Hardenberg for Prussia, and Talleyrand for France.

At first, the major victorious powers — Great Britain, Russia, Austria, and Prussia — expected that the several smaller states invited would play little part in drafting a settlement and that France would remain docile, as befitted a defeated country. But the course of events frustrated both expectations, as disputes over the fates of Poland, Saxony, and Italy created rifts among the allies. In particular, Tsar Alexander's demands caused the other three major victors to band together to resist Russia. Dissension among the allies allowed Talleyrand to break the isolation of France and maneuver the country into a more influential position. The return of Napoleon (q.v.) in March 1815 helped to bring the allies back together, and on June 9, 1815, a week before the emperor met defeat at Waterloo, the powers at Vienna signed the final instrument of the conference.

The main territorial adjustments agreed upon by the Congress of Vienna included the following: Austria received Lombardy, Venetia, the Dalmatian coast, and part of Poland; Prussia gained parts of Saxony and Poland; the Russian tsar became king of Poland, which contained most of the grand duchy of Warsaw; and England retained Malta, Heligoland, and various colonial prizes seized during the war. The congress did not set French borders, which were established by the separate Treaty of Paris in November 1815. It returned France to the frontiers of 1790; thus Napoleon's military triumphs and the sacrifice of millions of lives succeeded only in losing the territories that the revolutionary armies had won for France.

The great question concerning the Congress of Vienna is this: why was it so successful? Many have responded by arguing that the congress respected and established a balance of power in Europe. However, balance-of-power thinking was hardly original; it had underlain treaty settlements for the preceding century and a half, and they had not brought lasting peace. Something else was involved. Rather than create a balance among hostile forces, the statesmen of Europe created an international system based on compromise and consent. Twenty-five years of war had taught them that countries must recognize one another's interests in order to ensure order and stability. These would be regulated through a series of periodic international conferences. In short, the Congress of Vienna did not bring a return to the old international politics of the eighteenth century, but accepted and furthered new approaches to the international system that could serve as an inspiration, if not as a model, for future international accords.

JOHN A. LYNN

Paul Schroeder, *The Transformations of European Politics, 1763–1848* (1994).

Conquistadores

Conquistador is the Spanish word meaning "conqueror." Spain conquered the Americas and for most of the sixteenth century considered its military conquest (*conquista*) a valid title to rule. Although *conquista* was abolished in 1573 and officially replaced by the term *pacification*, nevertheless many continued to refer to the Spanish victories as conquistas and its leaders as conquistadores.

The two most famous conquistadores were Hernán Cortés (q.v.) and Francisco Pizarro, the victors in Mexico and Peru. Both men led small Spanish forces but shrewdly manipulated traditional native jealousies in order to enlarge their numbers and to defeat large indigenous armies. Relying upon struggles over succession to the Inca (q.v.) throne, Pizarro gained control over most of Peru, and, utilizing traditional enemies (the Tlaxcalans) in Mexico, Cortés moved to conquer the Aztecs (q.v.) centered in present-day Mexico City. Participants in both expeditions realized huge riches from booty in precious metals and stones; these riches too came to be associated with conquistadores.

Militarily the Spaniards held a decisive technological advantage — iron-based weapons. Although several peoples of the Americas used copper ornaments, and a few (including the Incas) had copper weapons, none possessed the lethal edge of iron and steel. Iron helmets proved formidable defenses against even the most powerfully hurled stones, giving the Spaniards a decisive advantage in the Andes. Although harquebuses and other gunpowder weapons were impressive in demonstrations, iron and steel swords, knives, and helmets proved far more effective militarily. Once victorious, the Spaniards successfully prevented native people from acquiring the iron-based weapons that had been the principal agents of their defeat.

Animals provided a second, intermittently important technological advantage. Horses enabled Spanish conquistadores besieged in Peru to launch lightning raids for food while otherwise blockaded by Inca forces. Dogs were used to track and attack humans in jungle or forest settings.

Equally important to the conquistadores' victories was the unwitting introduction of European diseases. Introducing infections against which native communities had no natural immunities both weakened native troops at crucial stages in the fighting and produced widespread disorganization in the military, as native troops scrambled to replace both leaders and field commanders.

Spanish warfare in the Americas, like all European warfare, was far bloodier and involved more warriors than the conflicts most Indians were familiar with. Iron and steel swords and knives produced far greater

In a mid-sixteenth-century drawing, the "Lienzo de Tlaxcala," Hernán Cortés (left), one of the greatest conquistadores, fights alongside native warriors against Aztecs during the sixteenth-century Spanish conquest of Mexico. Horses, swords, and firearms gave the Europeans an advantage over the otherwise formidable native armies.

bloodshed than the traditional native weapons — even their poison arrows. Also, many (although not all) native peoples did not actually kill people on the battlefield, reserving that for a subsequent ceremonial occasion. Hence, European practices of battlefield killing appeared far more brutal than indigenous practices in many parts of the Americas. This, coupled with official renunciation of the term *conquistador,* made the name synonymous with bloody events. But the term is also associated with the great riches of gold and silver that only a few of those who fought in the Americas ever realized.

PATRICIA SEED

Ross Hassig, *Mexico and the Spanish Conquest* (1994); John Hemming, *Conquest of the Incas* (1970).

Constantinople, Sieges of

Other than civil wars and rebellions, Constantinople experienced many sieges, blockades, and assaults by land and sea at the hands of external foes. This coveted city constituted the nerve center and capital of the Byzantine Empire and ranked as Europe's largest city for many centuries. Situated at the crossroads of Europe and Asia, Constantinople overlooked the wa-

terways between the Black Sea and the Mediterranean. The land walls (more than three and a half miles long and thirty-six feet in height) constructed by Emperor Constantine I and elaborated by Emperor Theodosius II in 413, and the sea walls of Emperor Anastasius I (r. 491–518), helped in defending the city. Its defenders varied in number, from at least several tens of thousands in the seventh and eighth centuries to less than ten thousand in 1453. Belief in supernatural assistance from various religious relics, reinforced by convictions that the Virgin Mary and God guarded it, strengthened the defenders psychologically.

The first siege and blockade occurred in 626 at the hands of Avars and allied Slavs from the Balkan side and Sassanian Persians on the Asiatic side, but they abandoned it. From 674 to 678, Arab Muslims blockaded and besieged the city in the first Arab siege. The Byzantines used an igneous petroleum mixture called Greek fire to destroy their ships, causing them to retire with heavy loss. The second Arab siege (from August 15, 717, to August 15, 718) marked the zenith of Arab expansion against the Byzantine Empire. The crafty Emperor Leo III misled the Muslim commander Maslama in negotiations. The Muslims abandoned the siege with heavy losses.

Bulgars threatened Constantinople in the years 813, 913, and 924, but these were not formal sieges. There were three unsuccessful Russian naval attacks, each of them brief, against Constantinople — in 860, 907, and 941 — each probably involving efforts to compel the Byzantines to concede better trade terms. Crusaders of the Fourth Crusade blockaded and threatened Constantinople from June to August 1203, and then, after negotiations failed, stormed it — the first foreigners to succeed in doing so — on April 13, 1204, with enormous loss of Constantinopolitan life and property. The Byzantines easily recovered Constantinople in 1261.

The first Ottoman Turkish threat to Constantinople was Sultan Bayezid's blockade from 1394 to 1402, which was especially intense from 1394 through 1397. Bayezid's rival, the Turkic leader Timur (see *Tamerlane*), intervened and ended it at the Battle of Ankara in 1402. Ottoman sultan Murad I's siege failed in 1422. The final siege, by Sultan Mehmed II the Conqueror, started on April 6, 1453, and was aided by excellent cannonry. On May 29, 1453, the walls and the city (reduced to less than fifty thousand persons from its several-hundred-thousand maximum) were stormed, and the breach made by Turkish assailants resulted in the end of the Byzantine government and the death of Emperor Constantine XI. The new artillery made the existing walls obsolete, although the gunpowder revolution was only one of several causes for Constantinople's fall. Its defeat terminated the Byzantine Empire and consolidated Ottoman Turkish control of the Balkans and Anatolia, giving the Ottomans (q.v.) an appropriate imperial capital.

WALTER E. KAEGI

Convoys

Traveling together for purposes of security — forming a convoy — precedes written human history, but it must be seen as a temporary and expensive solution. The ancient Chinese, Greeks, Persians, Egyptians, and Romans escorted their supply wagons, making up convoys. The fundamental concept was simple: seek the safety of numbers against would-be predators. Often, Rome had to supply armed escort craft to accompany its merchant ships in the pirate-plagued Mediterranean. But there was a price. Awaiting the assembly of enough merchantmen to make up a convoy cost time, and thus money. Eventually, Rome solved its problem by simply capturing all the land in and around the Mediterranean Sea, thereby depriving raiders of sanctuary. During much of its later history, Rome needed no maritime escorts, no convoys.

Since Rome, the naval convoy has been a staple of European conflicts. In 1639, a large escorted fleet dispatched by Philip IV, carrying troops and supplies from Spain to the Netherlands, was almost totally destroyed by the Dutch under Admiral Tromp (q.v.). Three months later, another Spanish convoy en route to Brazil was mauled off Recife. Spain had been receiving silver-laden convoys from its New World possessions since the early sixteenth century, and these treasure ships were prey to French and English pirates. However, the greatest Spanish prizes, the Manila Galleons that crossed the Pacific between Mexico and the Philippines, were largely unescorted during their voyages from 1565 until 1815. The vast expanse of that ocean provided an inherent improbability of interception. In all that time, the English took only four of them. The first shot in the dozen-year struggle between Great Britain and Napoleon's (q.v.) France was fired by a Royal Navy frigate against a French convoy in the English Channel.

In the same era, American convoys were more likely to be found on the ground. In the 1820s and 1830s, infantry (mounted rangers and dragoons) provided escort service through Comanche Indian country on the Santa Fe Trail. Columns of supply wagons and teamsters were accompanied and protected throughout the Mexican War (q.v.). Confederate cavalry raiders marauding in the Union rear provoked escorted wagon trains during the American Civil War (q.v.). Later, there were Sioux, Apache, and Cheyenne raiders. By 1890, both convoy doctrine and terminology were well understood in the U.S. and British armies.

Nineteenth-century army doctrine usually advised dividing the escort into an advance guard, main body, rear guards, and flank guards. The escort was mostly made up of infantry, but its advanced party was largely composed of cavalry. The main body, about one-third of the escort, was responsible for supplying flank guards, but its bulk was usually located midway within the column, ready to move anywhere to beat off an attack. The advance guard was well to the front and was expected to scout out the path, inform the column of an enemy's presence, and disperse opponents so the convoy could get through. Defeated attackers were not to be pursued; the mission was protection. If the defense was not successful, the escort was expected to get away with at least some of the wagons, preferably the forward elements in which the high-value items — ammunition, money, and rations — were located.

Convoys at sea became vital to the Allies in both world wars. By early 1917, Germany's unrestricted submarine warfare had increased sinkings by 30 percent each month, outstripping the Allied ship construction program. The ineffective zone defense on the transatlantic route was scrapped for convoy tactics. A ring of destroyers or other such escort craft was placed around merchant or troop transport ships. The most important vessels — ammunition transports, oil tankers, and so on — were situated in the middle of the group. Proceeding at the rate of the slowest ship, the convoy made its way across the ocean, zigzagging in dangerous areas to foil a U-boat captain's necessarily painstaking alignment for torpedo firing. By stopping the unending stream of single merchantmen, the Allies, in both wars, decreased the number of U-boat firing opportunities.

Convoy tactics protected American supply trucks in Vietnam (q.v.) in the 1960s and UN vehicles in

Bosnia during the 1990s. Convoys may sometimes be necessary, but they are an expensive response to an enemy's capabilities. They are, in essence, defensive and therefore cannot win wars. A winning strategy should negate the need for escorts, overhead cover, advance guards, and the like. The troublesome opponent should be left with no forces to menace one's supplies, no airfields to harbor aerial attackers, no ports to spawn raiding craft. The Romans had it right.

ROD PASCHALL

Denis H. Mahan, *Advanced Guard, Out-Post, and Detachment Service of Troops* (1869); Chester G. Starr, Jr., *The Roman Imperial Navy, 31 B.C.–A.D. 324* (1941).

Coral Sea, Battle of

May 4–8, 1942

The first air-sea battle in history and an engagement in which the lead role was played by aircraft launched from ships at sea, this battle resulted from Japanese efforts to make an amphibious landing at Port Moresby in southeast New Guinea. Unknown to the Japanese, Allied codebreakers had learned enough about enemy communications to discern Japanese plans in time for Allied fleets to assemble in the Coral Sea. Rear Admiral Frank J. Fletcher commanded American task forces, including two large aircraft carriers and other ships, and a British-led cruiser force mounted surface opposition. The Japanese used many more ships but divided them into a number of widely separated groups, one of which contained a light carrier. The Japanese covering force (led by Vice Admiral Takagi Takao) also contained two large carriers.

There were a number of missed opportunities as carrier airmen learned their trade. Air strikes from both sides either missed their targets or found them only after using up their ordnance. Americans connected first, sinking the light carrier *Shoho*. When the main forces traded air strikes, the Americans lost the carrier *Lexington* (*Yorktown* was also damaged), and the Japanese suffered damage to the carrier *Shokaku*. Without air cover, however, the Japanese invasion force turned back, leaving the strategic victory to the Allies. The results had an important impact upon the Battle of Midway (q.v.) a month later, reducing Japanese forces available at that key battle.

JOHN PRADOS

Corbett, Julian

1854–1922, *British Naval Historian*

Sir Julian Corbett was born in London, the son of a rich architect. Initially he chose law as a career but spent much of his youth traveling and following a number of dilettantish pursuits. His first forays into the literary world came with the publication of a series of swashbuckling novels. But in 1889 and 1890, Corbett tried his hand at history and, after publishing popular histories, followed up with a thoroughly researched two-volume work, *Drake and the Tudor Navy*. In the 1890s Corbett became a founding member of the Navy Records Society.

Although he had never served in the military, Corbett found himself drawn into the circle of naval reformers and their advocacy of professional military education. By the first decade of the twentieth century, he was playing an important role not only in the education of senior officers but also in the public debates over naval policy. He was a strong supporter of Admiral Jackie Fisher's (q.v.) efforts to reform the Royal Navy, and that in turn further increased his influence within Fisher's inner circle. Corbett's influence over policy, his championship of Fisher, and his historical arguments that battle for its own sake was not necessarily the best approach earned him bitter enemies among that group of naval officers (and civilian commentators as well) who regarded "thinking as a form of mutiny" — to use David Lloyd George's phrase. In his participation in policy debates, it is worth noting that Corbett was not always on target; he became a strong opponent of the convoy (q.v.) system during World War I (q.v.) and seriously underestimated the submarine threat.

Corbett's claim to fame does not rest only on his participation in the policy-making debates of his day. Unlike Alfred Thayer Mahan (q.v.), he was a first-rate historian rather than a publicist. His great work on naval theory, *Some Principles of Maritime Strategy*, although less original than Carl von Clausewitz's (q.v.) *On War*, still remains one of the great classics on the subject of conflict. Drawing much from the Prussian thinker, Corbett placed naval war within the larger framework of human conflict.

According to Corbett, land and maritime operations did not represent separate theaters existing independently of each other, but rather were together intertwined with the political, strategic, and operational framework within which conflicts take place. Unlike Mahan, Corbett understood that naval warfare occurred within this larger context. The storm-tossed squadrons of the Royal Navy may have played a crucial role in Napoleon's (q.v.) defeat, but only the great armies fighting on the Continent finally accomplished the emperor's overthrow.

Consequently, navies were not the independent executors of national policy with strategies divorced from other concerns. Moreover, control of the sea did not necessarily translate into a "seek out and destroy" strategy. The key was to have the use of sea lines for communications, while denying that use to the enemy. Naval strategy was not an end in itself; it was a means to an end, and that end was determined by national strategy. His formulation of ideas, closely connected with historical reality, makes much of Corbett's writing still of relevance today (see *Naval Warfare, Theorists of*).

WILLIAMSON MURRAY

Cornwallis, Charles

1738–1805, *British General*

The eldest son of the first earl Cornwallis, Charles Cornwallis saw military service in Germany during the Seven Years' War (q.v.), fighting at Minden (1759). He became major general in 1775, served under Sir Henry Clinton during the American Revolution (q.v.) in the successful campaign to capture New York (1776), and led the pursuit across New Jersey. Although surprised by George Washington's (q.v.) crossing of the Delaware and outmaneuvered at the Battle of Princeton (January 3, 1777), he outflanked Washington's defensive position at the Battle of Brandywine (September 11, 1777). Promoted to lieutenant general and second in command of the army in America in 1778, Cornwallis played a major role in command of the British rear guard in the inconclusive Battle of Monmouth Courthouse (June 28, 1778). Second in command when Clinton captured Charleston in May 1780, Cornwallis was left in command in the South when Clinton departed for New York on June 8. He defeated Horatio Gates at the Battle of Camden (August 16): American militia had proven unable to confront British regulars, and North Carolina was left exposed to the British. Cornwallis felt that he should conquer North Carolina, but he was delayed by sick troops, the enervating summer heat, and partisan attacks on his supply lines. His invasion of North Carolina in September 1780 was cut short by the defeat of subordinate Patrick Ferguson at King's Mountain (October 7).

In early 1781, unable to control South Carolina in the face of a vicious local war waged by American partisans, Cornwallis again thought of moving north to cut American supplies and drive back their regular forces, leading to the settlement of the South. On March 15, 1781, Cornwallis defeated Nathanael Greene (q.v.) at Guilford Courthouse in North Carolina with about two thousand men, but this was no rout, and over one-quarter of the earl's force were casualties.

On May 13, 1781, the British crossed the Roanoke. Cornwallis marched to the Chesapeake to seek a decisive battle in Virginia and to cover the Carolinas. However, lack of Loyalist support made the conquest of Virginia impossible, and Cornwallis instead established his army in an unfortified, low-lying, poor defensive position at Yorktown (q.v.). He was surprised by the buildup of American and French military and, crucially, naval strength. Besieged by land, he could not be relieved by sea because of the strength of the French navy, and on October 18, 1781, the British army at Yorktown surrendered.

Cornwallis's reputation did not suffer as it should have from this defeat. He was sent on a special mission to Frederick the Great (q.v.) in 1785 and appointed governor-general and commander in chief in India in 1786, a post he held until 1794. He reformed the organization of the East India Company, emphasizing the need for officers to understand native languages and customs. After the unsatisfactory 1790 campaign against Tipu Sultan of Mysore, Cornwallis took personal charge of the war. He sought a methodical invasion of Mysore and in 1791 stormed Bangalore. It was too near the rainy season to attempt a siege of Tipu's capital, Seringapatam, but in 1792 Cornwallis did so, forcing Tipu to surrender and cede much of his territory. As commander in chief and governor-general of Ireland (1797–1801), Cornwallis defeated the Irish rebellion and the limited French invasion of 1798.

JEREMY BLACK

Cortés, Hernán

1485?–1547, *Spanish Conquistador*

Born in Medellín, Spain, Hernán Cortés emigrated to the West Indies in 1506, led an expedition to Mexico in 1519, and is credited with conquering the Aztec

Empire in 1521, ultimately becoming a wealthy land-holder in Mexico. With a force of some 450 men, Cortés landed on the coast of the mainland at present-day Veracruz, allied himself with the local Totonacs, and then marched inland. After first fighting and then becoming allied with the Tlaxcalans, Cortés marched to the Aztecs' lake-island capital of Tenochtitlan and was peacefully received. Eight days later, however, he seized the ruler, Montezuma, and effectively governed the Aztec Empire until April 1520. Cortés then learned that Pánfilo de Narváez had reached Veracruz, intending to capture and return him to Cuba for violating the orders under which he commanded his expedition. However, Cortés and a force of 266 Spaniards marched to Veracruz and defeated Narváez.

In Cortés's absence, the Spaniards remaining in Tenochtitlan massacred thousands of Aztecs during a monthly festival and were, in turn, besieged in their own quarters. Cortés returned with a force of over 1,300 men (including Narváez's) but was soon besieged as well. Montezuma was killed during the siege, and with food and water running short, Cortés escaped during a night storm in June 1520, but lost over 860 Spanish soldiers, 5 Spanish women, and more than 1,000 Tlaxcalans. The survivors reached Tlaxcala and were nursed back to health. Too weak to attack Tenochtitlan, they began assaulting Aztec tributaries near Tlaxcala. Meanwhile, small-pox brought by Narváez's men reached the Valley of Mexico in October, killing tens of thousands; strengthened, Cortés returned to the valley in late December. There, he found allies in the city of Tex-coco, and, ultimately, with the entire eastern side of the valley, as well as farther south. Cortés had thir-teen brigantines built and launched them in April 1521, sweeping the lakes around Tenochtitlan of Aztec canoes. The Spaniards then severed the aque-duct supplying fresh water to the capital and launched attacks along the city's three major causeways. For-tunes ebbed and flowed, but with most food and water cut off from Tenochtitlan, the Spaniards wore down the Aztecs, who finally submitted on August 13, 1521.

Given the uneven contest — a few hundred Span-iards versus an empire of millions — many reasons have been offered for Cortés's success: his leadership, Christianity, Western civilization, European technol-ogy, and the western European mind-set. At the same time, Aztec vulnerabilities are suggested: their belief that Cortés was a god, their experience in fighting ritual wars only, a flawed imperial system, and their

susceptibility to smallpox. All of these explanations assume Cortés's role to be pivotal and accept the es-sential accuracy of the Spanish accounts. However, these European accounts are not dispassionate histo-ries, but pleas for royal support in which the petition-ers placed their own actions in the most favorable light possible. Viewing the conquest from an Aztec perspective, however, suggests a strikingly different interpretation.

Much of Cortés's success doubtless depended on his own personal determination and ability; only by suc-ceeding could he gain royal support and avoid trial by the governor of Cuba, whose orders for the expedi-tion Cortés repeatedly violated. Nevertheless, once inland, Cortés never took the initiative, despite his claims; rather, the native peoples asserted themselves for their own purposes.

Cortés was on the verge of defeat by the Tlaxcalans when they, not he, opted for an alliance: encircled by the Aztecs, Tlaxcala's kings saw the Spaniards as ef-fective allies against the Aztecs. They were too few to be decisive in themselves, but the Tlaxcalans imme-diately grasped the advantages of Spanish technology — cannon, harquebuses, crossbows, steel swords — and horses. Thus armed, the Spaniards could serve as shock troops to breach enemy lines with a consis-tency that native arms could not match. And once the Aztec lines were breached, the Tlaxcalans could pour through the enemy front, turn their flanks, divide their forces, and rout them.

Cortés also claimed numerous allies, but this too was a native, not Spanish, initiative. Ignorant about the Indian political system and especially about local politics, Cortés did not, and could not, use these to his advantage.

Native rulers were selected from among a group of eligibles, typically one with strong local alliances. The Tlaxcalan-Spanish presence, however, signifi-cantly altered the political equations. When Mon-tezuma's successors failed to secure the allegiance of his tributaries, Aztec control slipped drastically. Be-cause of their internal political turmoil, the Aztecs did not take the offensive against Cortés, and when they finally sent reinforcements to their tributaries after the harvests, they were too few to stop the Span-iards. Unable to secure their tributaries, the Aztecs waited in Tenochtitlan, which was a sound decision, based on known technology and patterns of warfare, but it gave the Spaniards a convenient single target.

The loss of their allies, the ship blockade of Tenoch-titlan, and the severing of the causeways led to the eventual defeat of the Aztecs. This was not a victory of a handful of Spaniards, but of tens of thousands of Indians who took advantage of the Spaniards' presence to use them as shock troops in a war in which the Indians supplied the vast majority of troops and played the largest part in battle. However, once the Aztecs were defeated by the other Indians, Cortés played one ally off another and, in the absence of a dominant indigenous group, seized control.

ROSS HASSIG

Ross Hassig, *Mexico and the Spanish Conquest* (1994).

Cossacks

The Cossacks were frontiersmen who originally inhabited lands north of the Black and Caspian Seas and whose descendants evolved to form a military caste in imperial Russia. Two traditions blended to produce the various Cossack communities and groupings of Russian and Ukrainian history. The first sprang from free migrants of mixed Slavic and possibly Tatar origins, who in the fourteenth and fifteenth centuries settled on the frontiers of Poland, Lithuania, and Muscovy to discharge mounted military service. In exchange for various rights and privileges, including retention of status as free men and conditional land tenure, these service-obligated "town" Cossacks defended advancing settlement lines from nomadic and Tatar incursion. During the sixteenth and seventeenth centuries, Cossacks in what is now Ukraine figured prominently in Polish military service, but also fought stubbornly to retain autonomy, for which purpose in 1654 they sought alliance with the Muscovite tsar. Autonomy proved ephemeral, however, as Muscovite and imperial Russia successively absorbed, abolished, or transplanted various service-obligated Cossack groupings, including the Ukrainians.

A second and related tradition sprang from fugitives, wayward Russian and Ukrainian peasants, and adventurers of sometimes uncertain ethnic origins who fled beyond state frontiers to the open steppe, where they formed truly autonomous military societies in the great river valleys of the region. Free Cossack communities began to appear during the second half of the fifteenth century, and by the mid–sixteenth century, they counted six distinct groupings, the roving bands of which plundered traditional Islamic enemies and Orthodox allies alike. Nevertheless, these same free Cossacks, like their nominal service-obli-gated brethren, gradually came to serve as Muscovite allies, fielding light cavalry for tsarist campaigns, pressing Russian colonization into the Caucasus and Siberia, and standing as bulwarks against invasion from the south and east. Free Cossacks were also sensitive to infringements of their rights and privileges, and, from the revolt of Stepan Razin in 1670–1671 until the rising of Emelian Pugachev in 1772–1774, they periodically reacted explosively to encroachments against their status and freebooting ways.

The two Cossack traditions melded during the eighteenth and early nineteenth centuries, when the former free Cossack groupings were either abolished or brought under the complete control of imperial St. Petersburg. Regardless of origin, by the time of the Crimean War (q.v.), all Cossacks had been transformed into a closed military caste subject to mandatory mounted service in exchange for collective title to their lands and superficial reaffirmation of traditional rights and privileges.

While modernizing the Russian army during 1861–1874, War Minister D. A. Miliutin further regularized Cossack governance and cavalry service, thus ensuring the existence of the Cossacks as an anachronism in an age of smokeless powder weaponry and mass cadre and conscript armies. The Cossack population base of 2.5 million enabled them to satisfy approximately 50 percent of the cavalry requirements of the Russian army, and Cossacks usually performed reliably as mounted troops in the suppression of popular disturbances. But, by the beginning of the twentieth century, despite reform, traditional Cossack communities teetered on the verge of disaster, thanks to a heavy burden of military service, overcrowding in communal holdings, usurpation of land by the Cossack nobility, and an influx of non-Cossack population.

The two revolutions of 1917 and the Russian Civil War of 1918–1920 (q.v.) divided the Cossacks, with majorities in the Don and Kuban supporting the White movement. Following Bolshevik victory, many Cossacks fled abroad, while those who stayed were persecuted, gradually disappearing as an identifiable group. During World War II (q.v.), the Red Army (q.v.) resurrected Cossack formations, but they had little in common with their earlier namesakes, save perhaps geographical affinity.

BRUCE W. MENNING

Philip Longworth, *The Cossacks* (1970).

Counterinsurgency

Counterinsurgency, a 1960s-era U.S. politico-military doctrine aimed at defeating Marxist-supported "wars of national liberation," differed from European versions that over the years had been variously called "small wars," "antiguerrilla operations," or "counterrevolutionary warfare." European experience in this field included British efforts during the Boer War (q.v.), the "Malayan Emergency," and campaigns in Kenya and Cyprus in the 1950s. Germany had practiced fighting guerrillas during World War II (q.v.); France constantly tried to suppress colonial insurgents for most of the nineteenth and twentieth centuries; the United States, too, had a background in such conflicts, notably in the Philippines immediately following the Spanish-American War (q.v.). But, in the 1960s, Washington faced a situation that was not like either its own battle against Filipino guerrillas (1900–1902), or the European experience.

U.S.-style counterinsurgency excludes many of the earlier European counterguerrilla techniques. The latter included the brutal Roman-style, scorched earth extermination methods used by the Nazis in World War II and the concentration camps employed by the British during the turn-of-the-century Boer War and the Malayan campaign of the 1950s. The U.S. approach did, however, borrow from the oil-spot methods of the late-nineteenth-century French antiguerrilla expert General Hubert Lyautey. In Indochina and North Africa, Lyautey would choose a centrally located village, isolate it from all contact with insurgents, secure it, and then slowly push the zone of security outward, encompassing surrounding villages. Gradually, the guerrillas would be shut off from the population, their source of food and recruits. U.S. counterinsurgency mainly relied on a few of the more humane, military-style techniques of these earlier doctrines: constant patrolling, continuous pressure on insurgent bands, and strict control of population and resources. But it also went beyond these measures and penetrated deeply into economic and political spheres, an approach deemed necessary because counterinsurgency was not intended only to destroy a sophisticated rural and urban Communist movement possessing considerable appeal for many Third World peoples, but also to supplant that appeal with a desire for Western norms. Counterinsurgency was aimed at building a native society whose members had a stake in its future while waging a highly mobile battle against armed insurgents and simultaneously rooting out the opponent's clandestine, village-level political and military infrastructure.

Counterinsurgency, aggressively pushed by the Kennedy administration from 1961, involved at the village level as many U.S. civilian agencies and programs as it did military entities and operations. Its goal was to identify the indigenous government with positive programs provided by the United States (such as medical clinics and agricultural development) in order to erode support for guerrilla groups, whose main aims seemed to be little more than death, destruction, and disruption.

While the conventional war against North Vietnamese regulars was being lost in Vietnam (q.v.), U.S.-supported counterinsurgency campaigns were succeeding in Latin America. During the 1960s and early 1970s, Communist guerrilla organizations were defeated in Bolivia, Venezuela, Colombia, Peru, and Guatemala — all by governments heavily aided by the United States. In Bolivia, Che Guevera (q.v.), the most famous Latin American Marxist insurgency advocate, was hunted down and killed by U.S.-supported counterguerrilla forces. In part, counterinsurgency succeeded in the Western Hemisphere because the Communists were never able to create the regular forces demanded by Mao Tse-tung's (q.v.) phased doctrine of protracted war. And anti-Communist Latin American governments mustered more popular support than did South Vietnam's distasteful U.S.-backed regime.

ROD PASCHALL

Douglas Blaufarb, *The Counterinsurgency Era: U.S. Doctrine and Performance, 1950 to the Present* (1977).

Courage

A disease, most frequently encountered in soldiers but not unknown among civilians, that causes its victims to be heedless of danger or death. The word derives from the Latin *coraticum*, "heart," and appears first in Middle English as *corage*. The anatomic referent suggests that its true provenance lies in the ancient past.

Homer's *Iliad* held up courage as the ultimate manly quality, one that achieves its greatest height when the warrior fights for a lost cause. Hector's courage won the gods' approval when he realized he was doomed to die in combat against Achilles, but pressed on: "Let me at least not die without a struggle, inglorious, / but do some big thing first, that men shall come to know of it."

By exercising courage, Hector may have become a secular god celebrated in memory, but his sacrifice served no tawdry military object. In fact, in the wake of his own death lay that of Troy itself. Thus, even from this early date, courage was considered a supramilitary mode of behavior, one that subordinated all else to personal action.

Homer defined a beautiful and poetic courage to excite aspiring heroes, implying that courage springs from qualities already present in its host, a manifestation of character. But a contrary opinion might say that courage is hardly possible without a looming disaster to call it forth. Or that, like a principle, courage is meaningless without its test. This perspective wrenches courage from its dalliance with the gods and places it on a par with its baser relatives, bravery and heroism, which the classical school would regard as acts rather than qualities.

Whether by virtue of character or circumstance, when courage appears its context is singularly personal. One is therefore given to wonder at the long and intimate association of courage with collective military action. For the longest time, too, when battle captains fought in the front rank, courage was deemed the sine qua non of leadership. This ideal has persisted well into the modern age, in which leaders have been wont to pose in battle as if choreography alone would inspire the troops. The habit attained a certain burlesque quality during the age of limited war (the eighteenth century), when the general and his coterie would prance about on distant heights, well removed from the slaughterhouse below.

This practice was among the many perversions that transformed the classical ideal of courage during the Napoleonic Wars, when every soldier was seen as making a full investment toward victory. At a time when even defeats could redound to the benefit of social power, courage in the masses became an important national asset. The innocent, the romantic, and the suicidal were enlisted alike in the quest for victory, and courage was of necessity democratized.

Courage had thus become a ward of the state, and as a consequence more demands were made upon it. The new social context worked a subtle and gradual change in the classical view of courage: an assumption that courage could be instilled by some means, that this mode of behavior once remarkable for its rarity could now be manipulated to convey its supposed benefits to official doings, and further, that once

instilled, it could be commanded at will. Courage was in danger of being domesticated.

Yet courage resisted these mutations. Courage was discovered to be far from common. Worse yet, it proved to be rather inconstant, present in full flood one day, only to desert its hero on the next. So held the old Spanish proverb "He was a brave man that day."

In the classical view, courage was very nearly a state of perpetual grace, and throughout the nineteenth century, armies and their combatants held stubbornly to it at horrendous cost. Some armies went as far as to suppose that courage might compensate for a lack of good sense, or training, or weaponry; enemy lines, it was hoped, could be swept away merely by the force of élan. Eventually, even professional soldiers noticed that the purchasing power of courage was declining precipitously. One machine gun could bring to a dead halt a whole battalion's worth of courage.

World War I (q.v.) gave courage a bad press. Human behavior had become a serious field of scientific and medical study and had conceived explanations for human action in battle that bore no relationship to the sentimental and romantic traditions that courage had carried through the centuries. Both the world wars, taken together, effectively brought all talk of death-defying courage to an end. Death was altogether too strong to be denied in industrial-age warfare.

Steeped in such traditions, westerners were confounded when in the nineteenth century they encountered a form of courage so different that it was often dismissed by the ignorant as pathological behavior. Yet in Japan a rich undergrowth of courageous tradition had evolved, which served cultural and social existence much more literally than that of the West. This tradition was also relentlessly martial, and it was within this context that the shape of courage was most thoroughly articulated. In its earliest forms the concept of a martial spirit, known in China as *Wu* but rendered by the Japanese as *Bu*, framed a view of courage that would not have seemed foreign to Homer. Here again we see the fight against preordained disaster. "Heaven decrees their fall: the dread Powers / are angry," wrote the Chinese poet Ch'u Yuan of warriors in the third century B.C. And, again, the dead of battle were invested with the grace of the demigod. Ch'u called them "captains among the ghosts."

Ch'u composed his lines on the way of the warrior, or *Bushido*, well before its embodiment appeared in the form of the legendary samurai (q.v.). As if in imitation of the cherry blossom conceit, Bushido achieved its fullest literary expression during the Tokugawa era (1603–1868), just as the samurai class lapsed into decadence.

By the time Yamamoto Tsunetomo's *Hagakure* appeared in 1716, Japanese martial philosophy had taken an extravagant, extreme road, one that diverged substantially from corresponding Western developments. Not only had the samurai come to personify Bushido, but also the ideal of Bushido had become the samurai's personal property. The samurai ideal found in *Hagakure* and other texts held that upon entering service, the warrior should assume that he was in effect already dead. All that remained was the consummation of that fact. One was therefore obliged to comport oneself in a righteous manner, so as not to dishonor oneself or one's master.

This ideal made of the samurai a formidable warrior and was the engine of an intense individual courage. Texts made plain that mere externalities — such as events of state or even the fates of battle — could not be allowed to interrupt the play of courage. In the *Hagakure,* as elsewhere, one finds few concessions to reason or materialism; on the contrary, the samurai was charged to divest himself of any influence that threatened to interpose between self and act. The study of tactics, for instance, was forsworn by some masters as unworthy of a samurai because it introduced deliberation and circumspection to the act of combat, which righteousness demanded must transcend such vulgar considerations. Ultimately, failure was impossible because death always waited to absolve the warrior who behaved courageously. Death was therefore intrinsic to the warrior's behavior, and if the warrior was not killed in action, he could supply the death himself by means of ritual suicide, hara-kiri.

The constellation of ideas that made up the Japanese ideal of courage, though centuries old, survived with some alteration into twentieth-century wars. Like its Western counterpart, the tradition of courage in Japan made a substantial investment in the conduct of modern industrial war. Having imbibed centuries of this ideal, the Japanese raised armies full of soldiers who were trained to reconcile tradition with modernism. When tradition and modernism clashed, tradition reigned supreme: one result was the infamous banzai charge, a form of deliberate, collective courage that Japan's Western enemies were hard put to fully comprehend.

Reductionism is as appealing as ever when one contemplates the matter of courage. Bromides abound and bromides predominate. Reason has not yet driven them out, which is to say that humankind has come to value an ideal of courage that is yet to surrender all its mysteries.

ROGER J. SPILLER

Philippe Contamine, *War in the Middle Ages* (1984); Arther Ferrill, *The Origins of War: From the Stone Age to Alexander the Great* (1985); Ivan Morris, *The Nobility of Failure: Tragic Heroes in the History of Japan* (1975).

Courtrai, Battle of

July 11, 1302

In 1302, the people of Flanders drove out the governor the French had installed after conquering the county in 1297–1300. King Philip the Fair quickly dispatched an army to break the siege of Courtrai castle and crush the rebellion, but to do so, the French had to attack eight thousand well-equipped Flemish militiamen, tightly arrayed on marshy, trap-filled ground behind two brooks. Twenty-five hundred French men-at-arms, considered the finest heavy cavalry of their day, crossed the brooks and charged, but failed to break the Flemish infantry's formation. Outnumbered and without room to maneuver properly, the cavalrymen were pushed back into the brooks by Flemish arms. A rout ensued, and more than one thousand noble men-at-arms perished, "the glory of French made into dung and worms." Flanders regained its freedom, and the urban craft guilds — whose members formed the core of the communal militias — rose to political prominence.

This unprecedented victory of common infantry over chivalric cavalry sparked the "infantry revolution" of the fourteenth century. The Scots at Bannockburn (1314) (q.v.) emulated the Flemings in fighting on foot, and their victory led the defeated English to do the same at Crécy (1346) (q.v.) and elsewhere. By Poitiers (1356) (q.v.), even the French knights dismounted to fight.

CLIFFORD J. ROGERS

Crécy, Battle of

August 26, 1346

After the first nine years of the Hundred Years' War (q.v.), Edward III of England was still far from achieving his war aims. So, in July 1346, he invaded Normandy with a strong army of roughly thirty-two hundred men-at-arms, seventy-eight hundred archers, and twenty-four hundred Welsh spearmen, and then launched a great *chevauchée,* a mounted raid intended to draw Philip VI of France into battle and "make an end to the war." After burning his way from Cherbourg via the suburbs of Paris to Crécy-en-Ponthieu, he halted to meet Philip's much larger army.

The English longbowmen, arrayed in wings angling forward from the central body of dismounted men-at-arms, easily dispersed Philip's Italian crossbowmen. The vanguard of the huge French army then prematurely charged the English center, riding down their own fleeing auxiliaries. As the English archers shot arrows "like thunderbolts" into their flanks, killing and wounding men and horses, the French chivalry lost any semblance of order. By the time they reached the enemy, they were in no shape to break the English formation. The piles of dead simply grew higher as charge after charge met the same fate. Philip, wounded, fled the field, leaving upwards of three thousand of his force — including two kings, nearly a hundred barons and counts, and more than fifteen hundred noble men-at-arms — dead on the field, and many others captive. "The realm of France," as Froissart says, "was afterward much weakened in honor, strength and counsel." Edward was so covered in glory that he was offered the throne of the Holy Roman Empire, which he declined.

Although the Valois monarchy was shaken by this crushing English victory, it did not collapse, partly because the arrival of the Black Death in 1348 gave the French a respite from the war, however unwelcome. Still, the Crécy campaign did set the stage for the Treaty of Brétigny, by which Edward gained a third of France to rule in full sovereignty. It also served notice to all of Europe that an "infantry revolution" had overturned the dominance of chivalric cavalry.

CLIFFORD J. ROGERS

Crete, Battle of

May 20–31, 1941

In April 1941, Germany began a lightning campaign that conquered Yugoslavia and mainland Greece. But a great threat remained: Crete, an island from which the British could unsettle the Balkans and launch air attacks on the critical Romanian oil fields. Worried by that threat, Adolf Hitler (q.v.) accepted the plans of General Kurt Student for an airborne assault on the island. After German paratroopers captured the main airfields, Ju 52s would fly in reinforcements.

Despite decryptions of German radio traffic that a massive assault was coming against Crete's airfields, the local Allied commander deployed his troops to meet a seaborne invasion because he refused to believe that a major military operation would depend almost exclusively on airborne forces.

Nevertheless, the German attack almost failed. German paratrooper drops on May 20 were slaughtered; yet despite the enemy's desperate situation, the New Zealand battalion commander overlooking Máleme airfield withdrew his troops during the night. Able to airlift reinforcements to Máleme, the Germans pushed back the defenders until they withdrew.

By seizing Crete, the Germans protected their Balkan flank and Romanian oil fields. But paratrooper losses were so heavy that Hitler never authorized another major drop; on the other hand, the Anglo-Americans, impressed by Crete, established the great airborne armies of 1943 and 1944.

WILLIAMSON MURRAY

Crimean War

1854–1856

The Crimean War was a result of Russian pressure on Turkey; this threatened British commercial and strategic interests in the Middle East and India. France, having provoked the crisis for prestige purposes, used the war to cement an alliance with Britain and to reassert its military power.

Anglo-French forces secured Istanbul before attacking Russia in the Black Sea, the Baltic, the Arctic, and the Pacific, supported by a maritime blockade. In September 1854 the allies landed in the Crimea, planning to destroy Sevastopol and the Russian Fleet in six weeks before withdrawing to Turkey. After victory on the River Alma, they hesitated; the Russians then reinforced the city and attacked the allied flank at the battles of Balaklava and the Inkerman. After a terrible winter, the allies cut Russian logistics by occupying the Sea of Azov; then, using superior sea-based logistics, they forced the Russians out of Sevastopol, which fell on September 8–9, 1855.

In the Baltic, also a major theater, the allies captured the Åland fortress of Bomarsund in 1854, and destroyed Sveaborg, the Helsinki dockyard, in 1855. These operations detained 200,000 Russian troops in the theater. The British prepared to destroy Cronstadt and St. Petersburg in 1856, using armored warships, steam gunboats, and mortar vessels.

Forced to accept defeat, Russia sought peace in January 1856. It had lost 500,000 troops, mostly to disease, malnutrition, and exposure; its economy was ruined, and its primitive industries were incapable of producing modern weapons. Allied war aims were limited to securing Turkey, although for reasons of prestige Napoleon III wanted a European conference to secure his dynasty.

The Peace of Paris, signed on March 30, 1856, preserved Ottoman rule in Turkey until 1914, crippled Russia, facilitated the unification of Germany, and revealed the power of Britain and the importance of sea power in global conflict. It had a major influence on the conduct of the American Civil War (q.v.). The use of the term *Crimean* and a fascination with striking events such as "the Charge of the Light Brigade," have obscured the scale and significance of the conflict.

A. D. LAMBERT

Cromwell, Oliver

1599–1658, English General and Lord Protector of Great Britain and Ireland

Although he became one of the most famous figures in English history, Oliver Cromwell began life as an ordinary country gentleman; when the English Civil War (q.v.) broke out in 1642, he was a middle-aged father of five children with no military training. Yet within a decade, according to one leading Royalist statesman and historian, he "mounted himself into the throne of the three kingdoms [England, Wales, and Scotland] without the name of a king but with greater power and authority than had ever been exercised or claimed by any king."

Cromwell's power stemmed from his military ability and his unique relationship with his troops. As soon as the war began, the creation of a pious and professional army to serve the English Parliament became his principal concern, and in 1645 he pushed for the formation of a standing army, with central funding and central direction. Under the command of Thomas Fairfax, with Cromwell as his deputy, this "New Model Army" quickly routed the main Royalist force at the Battle of Naseby (June 14, 1645), marking the beginning of a string of remarkable victories that within a year forced Charles I to surrender. Cromwell always led his cavalry from the front, although it

took its toll: he sustained combat injuries and often laughed hysterically immediately before and after action. But close contact with his troops paid dividends, for Cromwell managed to lead his "Ironsides" back into battle when other units paused to plunder.

The decision to execute the king in 1649 provoked a Royalist reaction in Ireland and Scotland that threatened the security of the new republic in England and forced Cromwell back into the field. He began his Irish offensive with a massacre of the combined forces of the Catholic Confederates and the Protestant Royalists at Drogheda (September 1649); the following month the town of Wexford, base of the Irish navy, met a similar fate. Scotland's decision to invade England in support of Charles II in 1650 forced Cromwell to leave the completion of the reconquest of Ireland to others while he focused his efforts on subduing the Scots. His stunning victories first at the Battle of Dunbar (September 3, 1650) and then at Worcester (September 3, 1651) not only forced Charles II to flee to the Continent for nearly ten years, but also effected the political integration of the three kingdoms — ruled after 1653 by Cromwell as lord protector, advised by the Council of State, and with a single Parliament meeting at Westminster — for the first time in their history.

Cromwell, a committed Puritan, and his godly "Ironsides" attributed their successes on the battlefield to divine intervention and now set out to create a godly society by establishing a body of evangelical preachers, by reforming the legal system, and by introducing legislation such as the Blue Laws (1650) against blasphemy, cursing, drunkenness, and adultery. Cromwell believed in liberty of conscience for his fellow Christians — "I meddle not with any man's conscience"; a truly revolutionary concept for the day — but in every other respect he remained a social conservative. He feared the democratic ideas of the so-called Levellers (English radicals); he believed in rule by the godly, not by the people in general. After 1649 he genuinely strove to reconcile the traditional political nation to his regime; yet in 1657 he rejected a proposal, known as the "Humble Petition and Advice," which implored him to become king.

That the Protectorate rested on a bed of pikes — with a standing army of some sixty thousand men, together with a large navy — is no myth; but it was not until a Royalist rising broke out in March 1655 that Cromwell finally resorted to blatant military rule, placing the various regions of England and Wales under the command of senior army officers. In addition, his government pursued an aggressive foreign policy, fighting wars first against the Dutch (1652–1654) (see *Anglo-Dutch Wars*) and then against Spain (1656–1659).

Excoriated as a usurper and hypocrite by his adversaries and venerated as a savior and hero by his supporters, Cromwell died on September 3 — the anniversary of two of his greatest victories — in 1658 of "a bastard tertian ague" (probably malaria). Almost as soon as his son, Richard, took over the reins of power, his subordinates in Scotland and Ireland began to plot the restoration of Charles II. The "British Republic" gave way to monarchy again in 1660.

JANE H. OHLMEYER

C. H. Firth, *Oliver Cromwell and the Rule of the Puritans* (1900).

Crusades

1095–1291

In its broadest sense, the term *crusades* refers to a series of endeavors by the church to promote various religious and moral causes. In the popular imagination, the Crusades have come to be associated with the series of wars waged by Western Christians against Muslims in the Near East from 1095 to 1291. The causes for the wars are complex. In addition to standards such as piety, adventure, and greed, historians have adduced numerous other explanations, including the desire of the still-weak papacy to extend its authority and seize the moral leadership of Christendom and, ironically, the culmination of the peace movement aimed at limiting private warfare among the nobility of northern Europe. From the Muslim perspective, the appearance of Christian crusaders in their lands was a perplexing but hardly novel event. Muslim chroniclers tended to see the Crusades as a continuation of the Christian expansionist imperialism that they had experienced previously in Spain and in southern Italy and Sicily.

The initial conflict was sparked by the movement of the Seljuk Turks into the Holy Land. Originating in central Asia and recently converted to Islam, they had swept through Persia, reduced the Abbasid caliphs to clients, and inflicted a humiliating defeat on the Byzantines of Mantzikert (1071) (q.v.). According to the traditional and often disputed version, the Byzantine emperor Alexius issued an urgent plea to the West for assistance. This in turn led Pope Urban II to issue a call for "holy war" at Clermont in 1095. Amid shouts of "God wills it," the best of the Frankish nobility went forth.

There were altogether eight official Crusades. The most successful was the first (1095–1099), led wholly by nobles. Their victories led to the capture of Jerusalem and the establishment of a series of Latin states in the Holy Land, known collectively as Outremer. The remainder of the Crusades failed to achieve the success of the first. The recapture of the county of Edessa by the Muslims in 1144 led to the Second Crusade (1147–1148). Promoted by the great Cistercian monk Bernard of Clairvaux, the Crusade was an ambitious affair that included simultaneous expeditions against the Moors in Spain and Portugal and the Wends in Pomerania (see *Baltic Crusades*). Although some successes were achieved in the Baltic and Iberian theaters, the expedition to Palestine was a dismal failure. Betrayed by the Byzantines, King Louis VII of France and the Holy Roman Emperor Conrad III were constrained to make hasty retreats. Louis suffered the further indignity of losing his queen, Eleanor of Aquitaine, to an adulterous affair with one of his generals. The ensuing divorce removed the important territory of Aquitaine from the control of the French crown and, with Eleanor's subsequent remarriage to Louis's rival, Henry II, brought it under the sway of the English. The Third Crusade (1189–1193) saw the spectacle of the three most illustrious Western rulers setting out for the Holy Land: Richard the Lion-Heart of England (q.v.), Philip Augustus of France, and the Holy Roman Emperor Frederick Barbarossa. Philip Augustus, who disliked both the environment of the Middle East and the role of warrior, soon returned to France, whereas Frederick Barbarossa died en route, swept away by the tide as he stopped to take a drink. Only Richard the Lion-Heart distinguished himself in battle. The dashing English king made a lasting impression on the Muslims, who would later invoke his name to rally errant troops and strike fear into the hearts of naughty children. Richard found a worthy adversary in the great Muslim leader Saladin (q.v.). After seizing political power in Egypt and Syria (1171), Saladin embarked on a campaign to liquidate the crusader kingdoms, culminating in the defeat of the crusaders at Hattin (q.v.) and the reconquest of Jerusalem (1187). Richard and Saladin fought their fiercest battle at Acre, where the English king eventually scored an impressive victory (1191). Richard failed, however, to take Jerusalem.

The thirteenth century saw continued calls for cru-

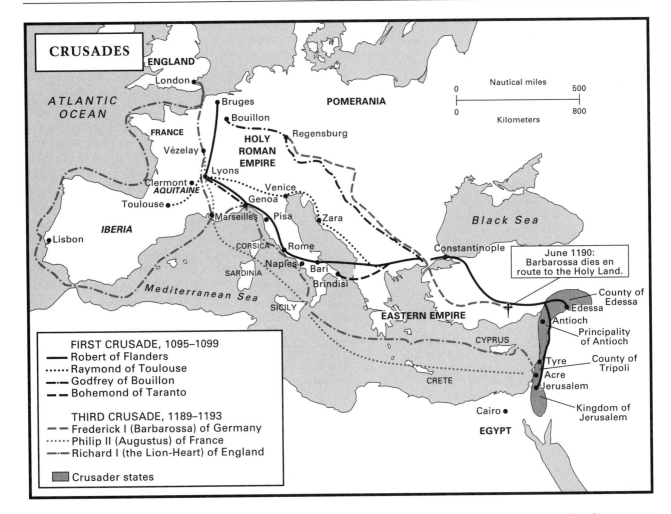

FIRST CRUSADE, 1095–1099
— Robert of Flanders
····· Raymond of Toulouse
—·— Godfrey of Bouillon
— — Bohemond of Taranto

THIRD CRUSADE, 1189–1193
— — Frederick I (Barbarossa) of Germany
····· Philip II (Augustus) of France
—·— Richard I (the Lion-Heart) of England

▨ Crusader states

sades not only against Muslims in the Middle East, but also against the Slavs in the Baltic and Albigensian heretics in southern France. The contest in the Middle East induced notables such as Emperor Frederick II, Louis IX (St. Louis) of France, and Edward I of England to take up the cross. Frederick II had the audacity to recapture Jerusalem by negotiation (1229) rather than battle, a maneuver that earned him the further enmity of the pope, who had excommunicated him some years earlier. The Sixth (1248) and Seventh Crusades (1270) were led by the saintly French King Louis IX, who accomplished little. Louis's first expedition resulted in his capture, the second in his death. By the time of Louis's arrival, however, new players had entered the fray. The Mamluks, who formed the elite core of Ayyubid armies, seized power themselves in Egypt (1250). Their ascendancy made them a formidable new antagonist, and they would ultimately emerge victorious. Meanwhile, the Mongols (q.v.), led by Genghis Khan (q.v.), had moved rapidly from their

home in Central Asia to occupy much of Persia. In 1258, they defeated Muslim forces, took Baghdad, and were poised to strike at the very heart of Islam. Louis, for his part, tried hard to make alliance with the Mongols, who had alleged Christian sympathies The advance of the Mongols was abruptly stopped by the Mamluks at 'Ayn Jalut (q.v.) in 1260.

The eastward movement of Latin armies brought conflict with the Byzantines, who came to despise their crude allies. These tensions culminated in the conquest of Constantinople (q.v.) during the Fourth Crusade (1201–1204). The capture of the city, for which the Venetians have absorbed much of the blame, led to the establishment of a Latin regime that lasted until 1261.

The Crusades officially came to an end when the city of Acre, the last Christian stronghold, fell to the Mamluk sultan Baibars in 1291. This did not, however, mark the end of calls for crusades, which continued for hundreds of years. In the modern era, the Nationalist insurgents in Spain (1936–1939), imitating the earlier epoch, referred to their movement as "the crusade" (see *Spanish Civil War*).

The conflicts brought to the battlefield two very different styles of warfare. The Christian crusaders favored the frontal charge, led by mailed knights on horseback. The Muslims relied on maneuverability, employing light cavalry of mounted archers to harass crusader troops. Muslim tactics, which included shooting frequent volleys of arrows and employing the so-called feigned retreat, were designed to cause confusion and break the enemy line. A potent weapon used by the Muslims, "Greek fire," was borrowed from the Byzantines. The mixture exploded on impact and could not be extinguished with water. To aid in reconnaissance, the Muslims employed carrier pigeons. The Christian and Muslim battles also saw some of the most protracted sieges of the Middle Ages. Richard the Lion-Heart's siege of Acre lasted two years, from June 1189 to July 1191.

The overall impact of the Crusades has been much debated. There were indeed few enduring political results. Militarily, the most apparent effect was on European fortifications. Impressed by the Byzantine fortifications, with their double or triple concentric lines of turreted walls, crusaders brought the style back to the West. Richard the Lion-Heart's mammoth Château Gaillard was inspired by what he had seen during his stay in the Holy Land. The Crusades also witnessed the birth of the three great knightly orders (q.v.): the Templars, Hospitallers, and Teutonic Knights. Economically, the greatest beneficiaries were the Italian seaports Venice, Genoa, and Pisa, which established permanent bases in Syria and enlarged their role in international commerce.

WILLIAM CAFERRO

Jonathan Riley-Smith, *The Crusades: A Short History* (1987); R. C. Smail, *Crusading Warfare, 1097–1193* (1956).

Custer, George Armstrong

1839–1876, U.S. General

After two years as a Union staff officer in the Civil War (q.v.), George Armstrong Custer, a West Point graduate, was appointed brigadier general of volunteers at the age of twenty-three. From Gettysburg (q.v.) to Appomattox, he excelled as a bold and aggressive cavalry leader, first of a brigade, then a division. With long blond hair and gaudy uniform, he also captured the popular fancy. He ended the war a major general.

In the postwar regular army, Custer served as lieutenant colonel of the Seventh Cavalry and gained fresh fame as an Indian fighter. His reputation rested primarily on the Battle of the Washita, on November 27, 1868, in which he attacked and destroyed the Cheyenne village of Chief Black Kettle. He campaigned successfully against the Sioux in Montana in 1873 and explored the Black Hills in 1874. At the Battle of the Little Bighorn, on June 25, 1876, he attacked a large Sioux and Cheyenne village, but he and all 212 men of his immediate command were surrounded on a treeless ridge and wiped out by superior numbers of Indians. "Custer's Last Stand," celebrated in folklore as well as history, awarded the commander immortality. He was controversial in his own time and has been ever since. He was a superior leader of horse in the Civil War, less so, because of a different style of war, on the western plains. Always he was good press and made the most of it.

ROBERT M. UTLEY

Cyrus the Great

r. 559–530 B.C., Great King of Persia

Cyrus was founder of the Achaemenid dynasty. The greatest conqueror until Alexander the Great (q.v.), he overthrew his lord, King Astyages of Media, in 550 B.C. and consolidated Iran, Afghanistan, and Central Asia into a single empire. In 546 B.C., he conquered Anatolia (Turkey) upon defeating the cavalry of King Croesus of Lydia by cleverly deploying camel forces. The Lydian horses bolted at the smell of camels, and the dismounted Lydians were easily routed. In 539 B.C., he captured Babylon. Killed while fighting nomadic Massagetae in Transoxiana, Cyrus left the task of conquering Egypt to his son Cambyses (r. 530–522 B.C.). Cyrus welded the Iranian horsemen into the world's first great cavalry army (Assyrian kings had deployed cavalry only as an auxiliary to chariots) and perfected siegecraft (well seen in his swift capture of the Lydian capital, Sardes). Cyrus, a tolerant and judicious ruler, united Persian and Median aristocrats into an imperial ruling class, won the admiration of the conquered, and thus ensured Persian domination of the Near East for the next 250 years.

KENNETH W. HARL

D

Dardanelles Campaign

See Gallipoli Campaign.

Darkness

Prior to the twentieth century, warfare in darkness was exceptional. Lacking the nighttime visual acuity of some members of the animal world, humans from the earliest times preferred hunting and fighting in daylight. Resting and defensive activities took place between sundown and dawn, a period of psychological apprehension. On occasion, an opponent's anxiety might be exploited. The biblical tale of Gideon's outnumbered three hundred and their triumph over the Midianites (in about 1250 B.C.) is an unusual night attack story involving torches and trumpets to strike fear into the hearts of bewildered defenders. Gaining surprise and inducing panic in the dark was also used by the English against the Spanish Armada (q.v.) in a devastating fire ship raid at Calais in 1588.

Firepower and darkness have long been tactically linked. Those with a firepower disadvantage might stage nighttime raids or ambushes, disappearing during the day. An inferior army or fleet might refuse combat during daylight and escape at night. Since the eighteenth century, European sieges usually featured a "night cordon," a tighter ring around the besieged during hours of darkness, thereby protecting against unobservable extension of trenches and gun movements. And darkness has been used to cover the approach march of forces. For example, George Washington's (q.v.) crossing of the Delaware River, a movement that brought on the Battle of Trenton in 1776, occurred on Christmas night. But for the most part, warfare on land and sea remained a daytime affair until 1914.

World War I (q.v.) changed this, largely because of the enormous firepower available to the participants. Darkness nullified observation, thereby undermining the effectiveness of an opponent's guns. During 1914–1918, darkness, therefore, became a great equalizer. German zeppelins, having a better chance of avoiding discovery and reaction by Allied defenders, attacked at night. U-boats often made their deadly strikes under the cover of darkness. On land, troop movements, raids, attack preparations, and some attacks were often nighttime activities, shielded from the enemy's observation and crippling fire.

In World War II (q.v.), nighttime military activities expanded. The employment of paratroopers contributed to this growth. Lightly armed and vulnerable in daylight, their introduction on a darkened battlefield created confusion among their enemies and offset some of their relative weakness in armaments. The Allied nighttime parachute assault that preceded the Normandy landings in June 1944 (see *D-Day*), for instance, gained vital terrain and temporarily mystified German defenders. The advent of radar greatly extended the use of darkness for attacker as well as defender. Night antiaircraft defenses were considerably enhanced by radar detection devices. On the other hand, radar served as a navigation aid for bombers in conditions of low visibility and during night raids.

Since World War II, military use of the dark has continued. Some American riflemen were equipped with infrared night scopes during the Korean War (q.v.), and by the 1960s, a wide variety of passive, nonemitting night-vision devices and gun sights were emerging. Today, nighttime may be of little use to those facing a well-equipped adversary. And, for the well-equipped, there is little difference between daylight and the dark.

ROD PASCHALL

Under heavy German fire, American soldiers leave a Coast Guard landing boat on D-Day and wade to the beaches of Normandy.

D-Day

June 6, 1944

Almost immediately after their ignominious withdrawal from Dunkirk in 1940, the British promised that they would return to the Continent. The German attack on the Soviet Union and declaration of war on the United States in December 1941 set the strategic preconditions for such an effort. Nevertheless, it required the development of complex capabilities of amphibious warfare — doctrine, interservice cooperation, landing craft, and so on — before an invasion of the Continent became possible. Moreover, the failure at Dieppe in 1942 had taught the Allies the difficulty of capturing a port. They knew they would have to support their landing forces over the beaches.

Through 1943, none of the preconditions for a successful invasion were in place: the U.S. Army was not ready, the Allies had not gained air superiority, there were not enough landing craft, and the Battle of the North Atlantic (q.v.) prevented any major buildup of forces in Britain. But the pieces came to-gether at the end of the year. Winston Churchill (q.v.) and Franklin D. Roosevelt (q.v.) selected Dwight D. Eisenhower (q.v.) as supreme commander of the invasion, with Air Marshal Arthur Tedder as deputy and Bernard Montgomery (q.v.) as ground commander. Both Eisenhower and Montgomery demanded an increase in resources so that they could land five divisions and three armored brigades by sea and three more divisions by air.

By May 1944, Allied air forces had gained air superiority; the strategic air forces had wrecked the French transportation network on which the Wehrmacht depended. The Allies had selected Normandy for the invasion site; German intelligence never picked up where the attack would come, but Allied deceptions convinced German leaders until the end that Pas de Calais would be the most likely place.

A stint of bad weather set in at the beginning of June, but a break allowed the Allies to go on June 6. On the east side, British airborne drops and seaborne landings went very much according to plan. In the west, U.S. airborne drops scattered all over the

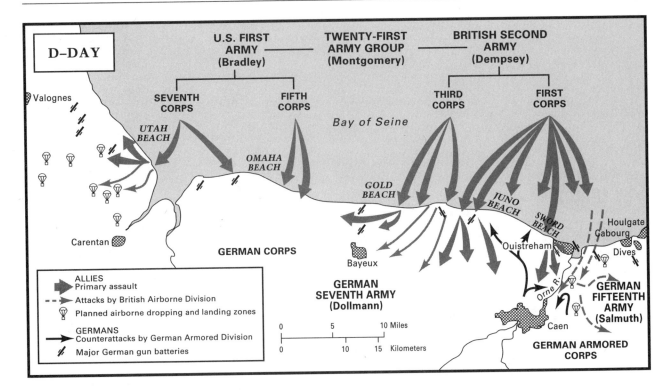

Cotentin Peninsula, but that confused more than helped the Germans. The landings at Utah Beach, aided by the paratroopers inland, quickly broke German defenses. Only at Omaha Beach did the Allies encounter effective German defenses, and for much of the morning it was touch and go whether the landing would succeed; Omar Bradley (q.v.) even considered sending the next waves into Utah rather than reinforce what appeared to be a failure on the Omaha beaches, but the Germans were not reinforced and eventually broke. By the end of the day, the Allies had gotten 156,000 men ashore in France, supported by thousands of vehicles. Everywhere the German response was hesitant and uncertain: Adolf Hitler slept in; Erwin Rommel (q.v.) was at home visiting his wife; Seventh Army was running a war game for its senior commanders at Rennes. Once ashore, however, Allied success in Normandy was assured though costly. Outnumbered on the ground, against an enemy possessing total air superiority, the hard-pressed Germans nevertheless hung on in the face of impossible odds.

German troops proved both extraordinarily well trained and fanatical; Allied forces had much to learn; and the *bocage* country's hedgerows proved to be a nightmare for an attacker. Montgomery's forces, de-

spite several opportunities, failed to break out, but became involved in a series of battles around Caen. But eventually, relentless pressure in the air and on the ground resulted in a breakthrough to Avranches at the end of July. The liberation of France followed within a month.

WILLIAMSON MURRAY

Deception

Deception can be defined as follows:

1. The process of influencing the enemy — by supplying or withholding information — to make decisions disadvantageous to the enemy.
2. A purposeful attempt by the deceiver to manipulate the perceptions of the targets' decision-makers in order to gain a competitive advantage.

Deception has never been a principle of war. Deception is only a means to achieve surprise (q.v.) (which *is* a principle of war) and not an end in itself. Although the *principles* of deception have not changed throughout history, deception itself has, in this century, changed in magnitude and scope. Formerly considered an improvised tactical method, it has evolved into a complex activity occurring on all levels of war.

More than two millennia have passed since Sun Tzu (q.v.) stated unequivocally that "all warfare is based on deception," and four hundred years since Niccolò Machiavelli (q.v.) asserted, "Force without fraud is not enough." Both of these strategists elevated deception close to the level of a panacea when extolling it as the key to victory. Admittedly, deception might have been relatively more important in premodern history, when firepower and mobility were limited. For example, the Bible, Greek mythology, and Chinese and Byzantine history alike abound with detailed accounts of the primarily tactical use — though often with strategic consequences — of deception in war. Even the oldest recorded histories of war, from the conquest of Jericho (q.v.) to the story of the Trojan horse exhibit all of the basic patterns of deception as they exist today. Such diversions, feigned withdrawals, acclimatization, and double agents are ultimately based on manipulating enemies' perceptions and reinforcing their preexisting beliefs or wishful thinking.

Reinforcement of the intended victim's existing perceptions is often considered the most critical ingredient for success. Deception operations are unlikely to be exposed because they reinforce, rather than attempt to change, the enemy's perceptions. Even the most sophisticated intelligence organizations will seldom expose a deception operation indicating the accuracy of their analyses. When Adolf Hitler (q.v.) expected the Allies to attack the Balkan and Romanian oil fields in 1943, the Allied deceivers obliged by passing along information indicating that such an attack was to begin in Greece and Sardinia; the Allies actually intended to invade Sicily. In much the same way, Hitler and the German high command believed that the expected Allied invasion of northwest Europe had to take the shortest possible route and would depend upon the availability of a port. The British then reinforced their beliefs by suggesting that such an invasion would take place at the Pas de Calais.

The second most important factor in effective deception is supplying the opponent with largely accurate (though typically obsolete or trivial) information that can be verified "independently." Third, the victim must not obtain the information easily. The greater the investment required to win the "prize," the more the target will trust in its veracity. To achieve this end, therefore, the deceiver must be intimately acquainted with the intended victim's level of sophistication, beliefs, and methods of collecting intelligence. This brings us to the fourth important factor — determining whether the proposed victim has "swallowed the bait."

Deception is never a game played for its own sake: it is always a means to achieve surprise. It gives the deceiver a significant advantage over the opponent through an attack in which the time, place, or methods are unexpected. Defenders can also use deception to lure an attacker into striking at their strongest point, thereby causing the attacker to waste time and resources. By helping to achieve surprise, deception thus acts as a valuable force multiplier.

Weakness and military inferiority produce a particularly strong incentive for the use of deception: the "underdog" is only too happy to seize upon ways to use his forces more effectively and weaken his opponent at a lower cost. Conversely, stronger forces tend to rely less on deception and fraud because they expect to emerge victorious anyway. Consequently, the stronger side must make a greater conscious effort to incorporate deception into its strategic repertoire in order to achieve a less costly, more decisive victory.

Always dependent on strict secrecy, deception can be passive (concealing) or active (disseminating misleading information). The means of passing on deceptive information include using unwitting agents and double agents; exposing some force concentrations while concealing others; and, in modern times, making extensive use of radio traffic (allowing the enemy to intercept and decipher messages or detect bogus transmission activity representing nonexistent headquarters and troops). Although deciphering the enemy's encoded radio messages is the most reliable method of verifying the success of deceptions operations, other methods might include aerial observation of troop movements and concentrations, or the use of double agents.

Deception can be very convincing when used to "inflate" the strength of a weaker side, as illustrated in the classic paradigm of the "Potemkin village" ruse. In 1936–1937, the Luftwaffe managed to impress the chief of the French air force with the numbers and quality of the aircraft ostensibly at its disposal by surreptitiously flying its aircraft from one field to the next on his itinerary. The weaker side can also exaggerate the order of battle to pin down some of the opponent's forces with nonexistent troops. Thus, the Allied threat to the Pas de Calais in 1944 was maintained by FUSAG, a fictitious army group that succeeded in projecting as much additional strength (or more) as was involved in the invasion of Normandy; in this way, FUSAG "attracted" a substantial number of German troops that would otherwise have been able to reinforce those fighting the invasion in Normandy.

Even if the deceivers intend, as an overall strategic threat, to project a larger number of troops than they actually have available, most military deception efforts on the operational level want to conceal the number and location of troops available for an attack: this would include "exposing" notional or real troops at a point where the attack will not occur while camouflaging the troops concentrating for the real attack.

Better intelligence, especially of the technological sort, should make the use of traditional deception more difficult. Deception should not be confused with electronic warfare per se, although the two are often related. The principles of deception, that is, its objectives as well as its basic method of manipulating and reinforcing the opponent's perceptions, are not likely to change. As long as human beings go to war, deception will play a pivotal role as an inexpensive, effective measure that allows the achievement of the decisive factor of surprise.

MICHAEL I. HANDEL

Donald C. Daniel and Katherine L. Herbig, eds., *Strategic Military Deception* (1982); Michael I. Handel, ed., *Strategic and Operational Deception in the Second World War* (1987); J. C. Masterman, *The Double-Cross System* (1972); Ewen Montagu, *The Man Who Never Was* (1954) and *Beyond Top Secret ULTRA* (1978).

Declaration of War

War is not simply a matter of physical force. It involves moral and legal considerations, both playing significant roles in the process of initiating war. Conflict's nonmaterial aspects depend heavily on rituals (q.v.). War is a sufficiently uncertain process that few individuals and fewer societies feel comfortable engaging in it without all the help, material and otherwise, they can solicit. A declaration of war is among the most common means of invoking higher powers, both by its contents and in its own right. Cultures as discrete as those of American Indians, Pacific islanders, and the great powers of twentieth-century Europe shared a pattern of initiating hostilities through some kind of formal process. Successive Chinese empires couched aggrandizement on various frontiers in terms of violations of moral or legal requirements to pay homage and tribute to the Middle Kingdom. Greek warfare, when waged against other Greeks, could be extremely cruel, yet increasingly the convention governing such conflicts was that a state of war should be formally declared before opening hostilities.

Rome too believed war needed justification. Against organized states, Rome usually began with formal declarations of intent. Against barbarians, however, such niceties were deemed unnecessary — and it was in that context that much Christian thinking on the subject of war developed. Augustine, believing as he did that peace was not possible in a fallen world, spoke for increasing numbers of Christian theorists in the late empire when he justified wars fought to secure justice and order. Such wars had to be declared and conducted by a legitimate ruler or ruling body. Acting in that capacity, individuals became instruments of divine will while those who obeyed them were freed of all responsibility for the nature of their cause.

The Germanic peoples who moved into western Europe had their own independent notions of war as a judicial process in which the gods (or later, God) oversaw the right. Sometimes rulers themselves or their designated champions would settle an issue; sometimes major battles were fought by mutual agreement. In either case, causes of offense and claims for redress were expected to be clearly stated beforehand. Often as well, general declarations would be supplemented by direct gestures such as sending heralds to bear defiance to the enemy.

Christian and German cultures combined for half a millennium to sustain both the legitimacy of war and the need for its formal initiation. Nor was the process confined to states. Individual aristocrats followed the same pattern of declaring war on enemies in a "feud." By the sixteenth century, however, going to war without government sanction brought with it the risk of outlawry: private warfare survived only in areas like Germany and Scotland, where central authority was weak or nonexistent. On the other hand, sovereign bodies had not only the right to make war, but also by the seventeenth century virtual carte blanche in that regard. Although formal declarations remained important, the fast-developing body of international law also recognized significant exceptions: savages, infidels, and heretics. European expansion into Asia, Africa, and the Americas combined with the Catholic and Protestant reformations in providing ample opportunity to test the limits of these categories. Against the Dutch and the English, Spanish theorists indulged in a rhetoric of blood regularly translated into action. In New England, outnumbered and frightened settlers applied to American Indians rules developed in Queen Elizabeth's Irish wars — which usually meant there were no rules.

Particularly as their subjects clashed informally outside of Europe, the major powers also agreed, tacitly or officially, not to regard such conflicts as causes of war. Whatever happened "beyond the line" was the affair of individuals and private trading companies.

This did not mean abandonment of the principle that a just war must be formally initiated. In the aftermath of the Thirty Years' War (q.v.), such rough-and-ready rules of thumb gave way to an increasing emphasis on formal, public observations. Louis XIV (q.v.) set the pattern by putting lawyers to work unearthing and developing French territorial, commercial, or political rights. This pattern was copied throughout Europe: it became important for governments to justify policies. Frederick the Great (q.v.) cloaked his invasion of Silesia in 1740 with at least a fig leaf of legality. Revolutionary France emphasized ideology in justifying war, but was never quite willing to dispense entirely with formalities. Napoleon (q.v.) too began even his most open aggressions with elaborate statements of their justification.

The continued development of international law as the nineteenth century progressed made declaring war an even more attractive option, at least in theory. The exercise of force in peacetime not only required sudden, overwhelming need with no time for deliberation, but the force used by the aggrieved party was required to be proportional to the threat posed by the attack. By declaring war, a state could free itself from these and similar restrictions. At the same time states could still fight one another without a formal declaration of hostilities, as the United States demonstrated from 1797 to 1801 in the Quasi War with France. As Otto von Bismarck (q.v.) discovered in the Franco-Prussian War (q.v.), moreover, even a declared war fought within accepted ground rules might defeat its own purposes by destroying the opposing government, leaving no one with whom to make peace.

Despite such contretemps, nations remained reluctant to accept the final logic of international anarchy. The Hague Convention of 1907 required "formal and explicit warning" of the intent to open hostilities. Even Adolf Hitler (q.v.) began his wars by the rules until Operation Barbarossa (q.v.), in which he invaded the Soviet Union without warning. Japan took extreme pains to ensure, however, vainly, that its "final note" reached the intended recipients before the first bombs struck Pearl Harbor (q.v.). The end result was to make declarations of war seem nothing but fig leaves for aggression.

After 1945, paradoxically, the United Nations charter forbade states to use or threaten force against other states without UN sanction, even limiting the right of self-defense. This too contributed significantly to the decline of formal declaration of war. In Vietnam (q.v.), the U.S. government argued that such declarations of war now tended to imply the need to destroy the enemy totally—which it did not advocate in this case. In other cases, notably the Arab-Israeli conflicts, wars remained formally undeclared because one side did not officially recognize the other. The result has been a growing tendency for international law to adjust to pragmatic realities by rendering the right to use force almost independent of the existence of a formal state of war. Such a state of anarchy would have shocked the Greeks and bodes ill for stability in the future.

DENNIS E. SHOWALTER

Geoffrey Best, *Humanity in Warfare: The Modern History of the International Law of Armed Conflict* (1980); Frederick H. Russell, *The Just War in the Middle Ages* (1975).

de Córdoba, Gonzalo

1453–1515, Spanish General

Known as the "Great Captain" for his peerless martial skill, Gonzalo de Córdoba was one of the first men systematically to adapt the late medieval army to the realities of the gunpowder battlefield. He learned his trade in the last campaigns of the Reconquest (q.v.), but his international reputation was won when he captained the Spanish armies that intervened in Italy from 1495. Largely ignoring the heavily armored lancers that remained the most prestigious arm of battle, Gonzalo instead concentrated on reforming his infantry. He firmly established the pike in Spanish service, increased the proportion of men armed with the harquebus, and also mixed sword-and-buckler men with his pikemen. In the fearsome clash of pike squares, these swordsmen could slip under the enemy's spears to eviscerate their formation. Besides rearming the infantry, Gonzalo championed the use of harassing light horsemen. The Great Captain's reforms — and his excellent generalship — proved their worth in the 1503 Spanish victories over the French at Cerignola and, more decisively, at the Garigliano River, which secured the kingdom of Naples for Spain. With these victories the Spanish infantry began to win their reputation as the best foot soldiers in Europe, a reputation that lasted until the Thirty Years' War (q.v.).

THOMAS F. ARNOLD

Defense

An anecdote from the American Civil War (q.v.) has a Confederate asking his Northern counterpart to explain the Union victory at Gettysburg (q.v.) after so many defeats. The Yankee's answer was "Well, Johnny Reb, every rooster fights best on his own manure pile!"

The story may be apocryphal; the message is accurate. From the Spartans (q.v.) at Thermopylae to the French at Verdun (q.v.) in 1916 and the Germans in Berlin in 1945, armies tend to do their best on ground of their own choosing. Nevertheless, armed forces, at least their senior planners and commanders, tend consistently to denigrate the defensive as leading to stalemate. Defensive operations are typically thought to be at best a temporary expedient, a preliminary to the attacks considered as decisive by theorists from Sun Tzu (q.v.) to Carl von Clausewitz (q.v.) and field soldiers from Alexander the Great (q.v.) to Norman Schwarzkopf (q.v.). Aggressiveness, the capacity to take action when common sense dictates the wisdom of remaining passive, is a quality as highly prized by armed forces as it is naturally rare. Training is focused heavily on its development; generals and admirals are reluctant to risk its loss. The British army's costly and largely unproductive trench raids of World War I (q.v.) were prefigured by John Bell Hood's battering an entire Confederate army to pieces in front of Atlanta in order to restore fighting spirit allegedly diminished by his predecessor's caution.

Yet conventional wisdom is challenged on every level by operational reality. From the beginning of organized warfare, defense has been recognized as su-

perior to offense by a factor of about three to one, based on both rule-of-thumb experience and elaborate theoretical simulations. The strength of the defense may well begin in physiology and psychology. Human beings as a species are anatomically better configured for defense than attack; nor does it require full acceptance of the concept of a territorial imperative to recognize that soldiers can become intensely proprietary about pieces of ground with which they have no previous connection. The German army of World War I had emotional as well as doctrinal justification for holding the ground of Belgium and northern France; official insistence that terrain meant nothing did its share to diminish U.S. morale in Vietnam (q.v.).

It is, however, not necessary to leave the battlefield in order to understand both the power and the appeal of the defensive in warfare. Defensive operations are cost effective. They facilitate maximizing human and material resources — both of which are ultimately in limited supply. Defensive operations make fewer physical demands than offensive ones; in 1916 the British military attaché to tsarist Russia was chagrined to see the splendid Russian Guardsmen defeated by weedy German physical specimens with the advantage of trenches, barbed wire, and machine guns. In material terms as well, the defense is less demanding. Scarce resources, technical or human, can be husbanded either to reinforce threatened points or to launch a general counterattack.

The defense is also a force multiplier. Properly constructed fortifications can channel an attack into killing zones or encourage enemies to exhaust themselves in frontal attacks. Japanese defense systems of World War II (q.v.) in the central Pacific remain an outstanding example on a tactical level. Operationally, defensive tactics provide an opportunity to concentrate numerically or materially weaker forces in critical sectors — a technique whose potential was maximized by the German army on the Eastern Front from 1943 to late 1944.

Properly planned defensive operations can also transform the often vaunted initiative to an illusion by forcing the enemy to attack specific points. The mutually supporting castles of medieval Europe or Tokugawa Japan could not be bypassed with impunity. The fortress networks of post-Renaissance Italy and seventeenth-century Flanders shaped the conduct of war in those crucial regions for almost three centuries.

Defensive warfare can also facilitate counterpunching. Active defense involves maneuvering an enemy into committing forces in order either to overwhelm them with shock and firepower or to strike a weakened position of the line. The horse archers of Central Asia, from the Scythians to Tamerlane (q.v.), were masters at encouraging their enemies to overextend themselves. Active defense can succeed as well by encouraging misplaced concentrations. At Austerlitz (q.v.) in 1805, Napoleon (q.v.) used a weak right flank as bait. Then, when the Russians and Austrians had worn themselves out, he broke through their front in the center.

The defense is an equalizer in that it puts less stress on commanders and soldiers alike. The strain of waiting for an attack is never lightly borne. Nevertheless, once the attacker is committed to a course of action, what Napoleon called "good ordinary generals," like George Meade at Gettysburg, have corresponding opportunities to respond effectively, as Meade did in destroying Pickett's charge on July 3, 1863. Naval history shows a similar pattern: between 1652 and 1815, first against the Dutch and later against the French, British admirals tended to concede the first moves, increasingly and legitimately confident in their ability to win the endgames.

Finally, defensive warfare gives its practitioners the moral high ground. Even at places and in periods dominated by martial values, few cultural or political systems have been completely comfortable with aggression. The Chinese, the Persians, the Romans, and even the Mongols (q.v.) of Genghis Khan (q.v.) took pains to justify their wars in defensive terms. They invited surrender before striking. They employed preemptive self-defense, describing their enemies as deserving what they were about to receive. In seventeenth-century Europe, Louis XIV (q.v.) kept international lawyers busy justifying — or rejecting — his territorial and dynastic claims. The concept of *jus ad bellum* (see *Laws of War*) was stretched and extended to cover almost every contingency, yet consistently emphasized moral reasons for fighting, such as supporting allies and suppressing groups or states acting outside international law.

As the American Revolution (q.v.) and the Wars of the French Revolution (q.v.) extended both the scope of warfare and the nature of participation in armed forces, new generations of citizen-soldiers demanded increasing assurances of the righteousness of their cause and the legitimacy of their sacrifice. Liberals like Friederich List, nationalists like Jefferson Davis,

and socialists like Jean Jaurès made the same response: just wars were defensive wars, fought to protect borders and identity.

The initiators of World War II — Germany, Japan, and Italy — allowed their people no such delusions. Axis behavior, however, proved anomalous. The principle implemented at Nuremberg and Tokyo that aggressive war is an international crime may have produced no international trials between the 1940s and the 1990s. Nevertheless, departments and ministries of defense have replaced their more martially titled predecessors throughout the globe. Even professional armed forces are uncomfortable with "surgical strikes" except on the smallest of scales. The United States justified intervention in Indochina as a response to aggression. Saddam Hussein insisted Kuwait had initiated hostilities in 1989, even though none of its forces had crossed the frontier. And for states that remain tempted by offensive war, Israel, Vietnam, and Afghanistan stand as contemporary reminders that roosters do in fact fight better on their own manure piles!

DENNIS E. SHOWALTER

Archer Jones, *The Art of War in the Western World* (1987).

de Gaulle, Charles

1890–1969, French Soldier and Statesman

The son of a schoolmaster, Charles André Joseph Marie de Gaulle was commissioned in 1914 into the infantry. Wounded and captured at Verdun (q.v.) in 1916, his unusual height defeated his various attempts to escape. In 1934 his book *Vers l'armée de métier* (translated as *The Army of the Future*, London, 1940) called for the creation of an army of 100,000 professional soldiers organized in mechanized divisions that would force a war of movement on the enemy. The French high command, however, preferred a defensive doctrine (see *Maginot Line*).

In 1940 when, despite a few successes with his armored brigade, Germany overwhelmed France, de Gaulle fled to England to take command of the "Free French" forces and prepare for the liberation of his country. In 1944, after D-Day (q.v.), he returned to France. Rejecting the plans for a postwar order devised by his allies, Franklin Roosevelt (q.v.) and Winston Churchill (q.v.), he entered Paris in triumph on August 26 and later served briefly as president of France.

Finally, in 1958, when the Algerian War (q.v.) caused the collapse of the Fourth Republic, de Gaulle again became president (of the Fifth Republic) and, during his eleven years in office, reformed the constitution, ended the Algerian War, and created an independent French nuclear capability.

GEOFFREY PARKER

Demobilization

A fighting retreat may be the most difficult of military operations, but demobilization runs a close second. Military organizations grow phenomenally in time of war. Germany in World War I (q.v.), for example, mobilized some thirteen million men, whereas its largest peacetime establishment had been considerably less than one-tenth that size. When wars end, the presence of excess soldiers poses several potentially grave difficulties for the governments that have called them forth from their civilian occupations.

The picture Americans usually have is that of draftees eager to return to civilian life. The example par excellence of American demobilization is the Review of the Armies on May 23–24, 1865. After parading through Washington, D.C., the vast armies of the Union simply dissolved and returned to their civilian occupations. In such cases (and they would apply to many of the victorious armies of World War II [q.v.], for example) one difficulty is reconciling the demands of equity (releasing first those who have served the longest or in the most difficult circumstances), administrative efficiency, and military effectiveness. In practice, the first criterion usually dominates. As a result, demobilizing countries experience an implosion of military strength, as units are suddenly gutted of experienced personnel, junior leaders, and technical experts, and the few new recruits or career soldiers are shunted hither and yon in a state of administrative chaos. The results can be seen, for example, in the dismal performance of American forces in the opening months of the Korean War (q.v.): five years after World War II, the first units to fight bore but superficial resemblance to the divisions that had overcome fanatically defended Japanese island strongholds and the disciplined skill of the Wehrmacht.

Governments in the modern period have tried, with varying degrees of success, to provide demobilized soldiers with jobs, housing, medical care, and even, in some cases, educational benefits. The American GI bill of World War II gave millions of veterans the opportunity to gain a higher education and thereby transformed American academic life. In earlier periods military service tended to lead to an expansion of suffrage as well. Those who fought often claimed a share in governance, although they might not always receive it. Modern wars of mass mobilization bring new social groups into political life, often with incalculable consequences. North African veterans of the French army from World War II and Indochina helped lead the war against France in Algeria a decade later.

The longer the war, the greater the risk of antagonism from veterans who no longer fit in with civil society. Their sacrifices might seem disproportionate to anything gained by their country, and certainly to any personal reward they have gained. They may miss as well the camaraderie of the front and even (more or less openly) the excitement of battle. During the interwar period, groups such as the Croix de Feu in France and the veterans' groups associated with the various political parties in Germany thrived for these reasons. Veterans' parties may simply be interested in pensions, or, far less healthily, they may lose themselves in unattainable quests for patriotic unity or military adventure.

Some soldiers may not, in fact, look forward to demobilization. The first order of business for Carthage after the First Punic War (see *Punic Wars*) was disposing of troublesome mercenaries (q.v.) suddenly unemployed by the cessation of the struggle with Rome. The Cold War (q.v.) demobilization of the American and Soviet militaries posed awkward problems for both societies. The United States, being infinitely wealthier, managed to trim its forces by two-thirds of a million men and women in the space of five or six years without excessive pain. A program of carefully adjusted financial incentives, together with normal attrition, slowly brought the force down in size. The Soviet military faced an infinitely more difficult task. Draftees may have been only too eager to leave the brutal conditions of the Red Army (q.v.), but officers, particularly those stationed in eastern Europe, found themselves shivering in tents, waiting for housing and contemplating looming unemployment. Still, on balance it is remarkable how quickly large armies can be absorbed by even moderately healthy industrial economies.

In the developing world, however, demobilization often brings with it mass unemployment, brigandage, and (if the war has been severe) a major problem of caring for those touched in body and mind by the horrors of war. Uganda in the early 1990s, for example, found itself coping with the task of demobilizing tens of thousands of veterans of a long and bloody civil war who were, for the most part, young, married (often with children), semiliterate, and propertyless, with a 30 percent chance of suffering a major medical disability. Vietnam and Iran in the early 1990s confronted similar problems.

Demobilization extends beyond the discharge of soldiers. Perhaps the most impressive demobilization of all time involved not merely individual soldiers but an entire branch of military technology. In 1600 the Battle of Sekigahara brought to a culmination the unification of Japan under the strong, centralized rule of the Tokugawa Shogunate. In short order Japan severely reduced its interaction with the outside world. The Tokugawa managed to tame by various means the hundreds of thousands of warriors who had suddenly lost their function, incorporating some of them into the ruling structures of society. More remarkably, the shogunate also made firearms (which in late-sixteenth-century Japan were numerous, well made, and increasingly effective) a rarity and gradually redirected the martial practices of the samurai (q.v.) into the athletic, ethical, and aesthetic disciplines that became known as "martial ways." Thus, the martial spirit persisted but was consciously remolded by a powerful government that could afford to ignore international politics.

In the world wars, demobilization meant the reconversion of industry to civilian production, and in all conflicts it means the abolition of some agencies (particularly those associated with a war economy) and the radical shrinkage of others (military intelligence organizations, for example). Demobilization, however, like an economic recession, causes other organizations and enterprises to flourish and indeed acquire enormous resources. Veterans' bureaus and hospitals expand enormously in the wake of demobilization. In 1895, thirty years after the American Civil War (q.v.), the U.S. government spent more on veterans' compensation and pensions than on the army, the navy, and the public debt combined. After the Cold War, the dismantling of advanced weapons (nuclear-powered submarines, for example) and the closure of large military bases actually increased certain government expenditures.

Finally, demobilization has a psychological dimension as well. Total war in particular focuses a nation's energies on narrow and often heroic purposes; the natural response after the crisis is a kind of social relaxation. This includes changes in social mores (wars often bring in their wake a loosening of sexual morality, for example) as well as in policy, wherein warfare is often followed by a period of turning inward. All wars leave legacies more subtle than anniversaries, monuments, graveyards, and veterans' hospitals. A country's mental and spiritual fabric and the political and military institutions formed by it will never quite regain their former shape, however much they appear to return to normalcy. In this respect, at least, no demobilization ever restores the *status quo ante bellum*.

ELIOT A. COHEN

Noel Perrin, *Giving Up the Gun: Japan's Reversion to the Sword, 1543–1879* (1979); Bruce D. Porter, *War and the Rise of the State: The Military Foundations of Modern Politics* (1994).

Desertion

Desertion is the act of leaving military service, or a place of duty, without permission and with the intention not to return. It is the *intention not to return* that differentiates desertion from the less serious offense of absence from duty. Desertion has been the bane of virtually every organized military force throughout history, and few armies, from the most egalitarian to the most authoritarian, seem to be immune: it takes place in war and peace, in garrison and at the front.

Given the sheer dimension of the phenomenon, desertions have unquestionably undermined the efficiency of military organizations. In Napoleonic France, deserters numbered hundreds of thousands: as many as half of the draftees from the Haute-Loire district could be expected to absent themselves from the army at the earliest opportunity. Similarly, in the first year and a half of the American Civil War (q.v.), the Army of the Potomac alone had 85,000 desertions. However, the advent of peace brought no lessening of the number of desertions in the U.S. Army. To the contrary, the harsh conditions of peacetime service on the western frontier encouraged whole regiments to virtually evaporate: in 1867, desertions from George Custer's (q.v.) famous Seventh Cavalry Regiment reached 52 percent, and between 1867 and 1891, almost one-third of the troops discharged themselves. In more contemporary times, the practice continued, although at somewhat diminished rates. In World War II (q.v.), the U.S. Army reported 40,000 deserters and the British Army over 100,000, the apparent discrepancy being accounted for by the more lenient American interpretation of "desertion" as opposed to mere absence without leave.

The omnipresence of desertion suggests that the underlying causes vary. The fear of death or injury in battle is one obvious factor, but more widespread motives are likely to be less dramatic: simple discontent with military life, homesickness, boredom with garrison duty, personal or financial problems. Indeed, studies of British and American deserters in World War II indicate that soldiers who were less well adjusted as civilians were more likely to desert. Opportunity also plays a part. In the French Foreign Legion, desertion rates varied with locale: in Algeria the problem was less acute if only because there was no place to desert to. Weather can also be a consideration; in the post–Civil War American army, the nickname for a deserter was "snowbird," a reference to those soldiers who preferred to serve only through the winter, deserting in the spring when travel was easier and jobs in the mines or on the transcontinental railroad became available.

Traditionally, desertion was among the most serious of military crimes, but punishment — as other aspects of military life — was subject to wide variation. In the army of Frederick the Great (q.v.), a deserter, especially one from the battlefield, could expect death; but over the years, punishment seems to have been lessened. In the pre–Civil War U.S. Army, a deserter was flogged; after 1861 the practice was discontinued in favor of tatooing or branding. In World War II the U.S. Army frequently charged troops as Absent Without Leave (AWOL) who would have been classified as deserters in most other armies. However, the problem of absence from duty, by whatever name, became so acute in the European theater in 1944 and 1945 that one hapless soldier, Private Eddie Skovik, was executed as an example to others.

ELIHU ROSE

Deterrence

The Royal Navy's Admiral Jackie Fisher (q.v.) may have been "the heartiest, merriest, and smartest delegate at The Hague" attending the conference on war limitation in 1899, but he scandalized his colleagues with what one observer described as his not uncommon notion . . . that nations are deterred from going to war by fear of the atrocities which accompany conflict. He exclaimed impatiently . . . "What you call my truculence is all for peace. If you rub it in, both at home and abroad, that you are ready for instant war with every unit of your strength in the first line, and intend to be first in, and hit your enemy in the belly, and kick him when he is down, and boil your prisoners in oil (if you take any!), and torture his women and children, then people will keep clear of you."

Herein lies the central dilemma of deterrence: in the name of peace, and in order to secure it, one threatens awful deeds. And indeed, as Fisher would argue, the more awful the deeds threatened, the more likely a country is to secure its objective.

A common distinction is drawn between deterrence by *punishment* and deterrence by *denial*. The former operates by threat, the latter by precluding opponents from actually accomplishing their desires. In both manifestations, deterrence is a phenomenon as old as human conflict. The practice in the ancient world of taking hostages, for example, reflected widespread practice of deterrence by punishment; the construction of border fortifications (Hadrian's Wall and indeed all of Rome's elaborate border fortifications come to mind), deterrence by denial. Deterrence sometimes succeeded and sometimes failed. The distinction between forces useful for deterrence and those useful for actual combat is critical in the nuclear age, but less clear regarding conventional warfare throughout the ages. By and large, the best deterrent was the best fighting force, and vice versa.

Matters began to change in the 1920s and 1930s because of the growing prospects of aerial bombardment, a form of warfare that seemed particularly devastating, and against which it would be impossible to devise defenses. These anxieties merely foreshadowed those of the early nuclear age. In 1946, Bernard Brodie, in the first volume written on nuclear strategy *(The Absolute Weapon)*, wrote, "Thus far the chief purpose of our military establishment has been to win wars. From now on its chief purpose must be to avert them. It can have almost no other useful purpose." Atomic weapons could devastate cities instantaneously, and there appeared to be no reasonable defense against them. And, in 1950, there was an enormous and pressing foreign policy crisis: how would the United States prevent the Soviet Union from overrunning western Europe, should it choose to do so?

The combination of these fundamental facts and an

immediate policy problem gave birth to modern deterrence theory in its various forms. Over the years theorists spun out ever more refined webs of argument. Some of these formulations became mathematical, particularly among social scientists exploiting the new tools of game theory. Deterrence theory was also heavily psychological, examining the nuances of perception and misperception, not real capability, which was often hidden from view by layers of secrecy.

Deterrence hinged on credibility, one party's apparent willingness to perform actions that might appear irrational, and which certainly could be very costly. Thomas Schelling, one of the foremost theorists of deterrence, argued that leaders would occasionally have to make threats that "leave something to chance." He pointed out that it sometimes proved advantageous to leaders to appear to be slightly — but only slightly — out of control and prone to react excessively to a provocation. President Richard Nixon understood the value of this reputation, and particularly after ordering the Christmas bombings of Hanoi in 1972, he exploited it well. The North Vietnamese yielded on the final points of their negotiations, knowing that they were dealing with a man not altogether unhappy to be called "The Mad Bomber" in the U.S. press.

At the same time, deterrence also required communication, so that neither side would fail to understand the stakes for the other side. For the deterrence theorists, the greatest worry was inadvertent war, a cataclysm that might follow from misperception. Political and military leaders agreed, with the result that hot-line agreements became a mainstay of early U.S.-Soviet arms control. The hot-line has been used sparingly (the occasions are classified) at moments of crisis, including during the Arab-Israeli conflicts (q.v.). As a practical matter too, politicians put great stress on the words and actions that made commitments to fight under certain conditions both clear and credible. The rhetoric of the North Atlantic Treaty Organization (NATO), with its endless, near-obsessive repetition of American affirmations of willingness to fight a nuclear war, reflected the importance deterrence had assumed for Europeans and Americans.

By the 1980s, classical deterrence theory had run its course; as more detailed knowledge of how armed forces actually operated nuclear weapons became available, the theory became less satisfying. Despite the clamor of academics and even some civilian politicians for graduated nuclear options to bolster deter-

rence, for example, the military planning bureaucracies in the United States appeared (at least for some decades) to have developed plans calling for massive use of nuclear weapons at the outset of a conflict. Extended deterrence — which rested on a willingness by the United States to risk New York City to save Hamburg — seemed increasingly threadbare. The premise of rationality on both sides was shaken by revelations and studies that suggest that neither side understood the other very well at all. At the same time, the imminence of a Soviet threat to western Europe seemed ever more remote.

Deterrence remains, in the post–Cold War world, something real. When the United States deployed tens of thousands of troops to Kuwait in 1994, it did so to deter a repetition of the Iraqi invasion of that country in 1991. But it was deterrence by denial, not deterrence by punishment at work here. Even where deterrence by punishment was used or threatened — for example, in Yugoslavia in 1993–1994, when American and European air power was brandished against Serb nationalists — its force was far less than that of the older nuclear threats. Possession of nuclear weapons did not save Great Britain from the insult of an Argentine lunge for the Falkland Islands (q.v.) in 1982, nor, for that matter, Israel from a barrage of Iraqi high-explosive-tipped missiles in 1991. Deterrence still succeeds, to be sure, and indeed one of its peculiarities is that evidence of its success is often ambiguous, because successful deterrence is usually manifested by a chain of nonevents. But deterrence in the modern period, like that of earlier times, is likely to be a chancy business, in which the actual use of military power, and not merely its threat, will constitute the substance of strategy.

ELIOT A. COHEN

Robert Jervis, Richard Ned Lebow, and Janice Gross Stein, *Psychology and Deterrence* (1985); Thomas C. Schelling, *The Strategy of Conflict* (1960).

Dien Bien Phu, Battle of

November 1953–May 1954

The battle that settled the fate of French Indochina was initiated in November 1953, when Viet Minh forces at Chinese insistence moved to attack Lai Chau, the capital of the T'ai Federation (in Upper Tonkin), which was loyal to the French. As Peking had hoped, the French commander in chief in Indochina,

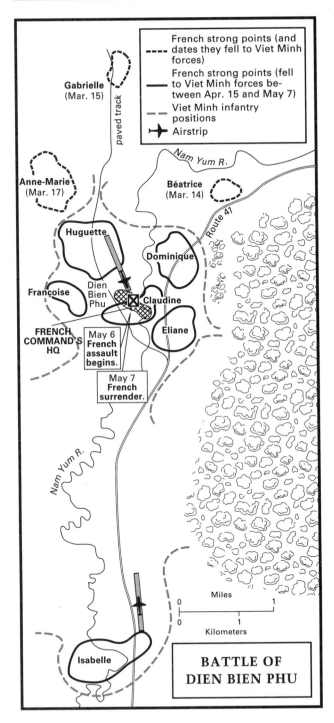

BATTLE OF DIEN BIEN PHU

Viet Minh sweep into Laos. Because he considered Lai Chau impossible to defend, on November 20, Navarre launched Operation Castor with a paratroop drop on the broad valley of Dien Bien Phu, which was rapidly transformed into a defensive perimeter of eight strong points organized around an airstrip. When, in December 1953, the T'ais attempted to march out of Lai Chau for Dien Bien Phu, they were badly mauled by Viet Minh forces.

Viet Minh commander Vo Nguyen Giap (q.v.), with considerable Chinese aide, massed troops and placed heavy artillery in caves in the mountains overlooking the French camp. On March 13, 1954, Giap launched a massive assault on strong point Béatrice, which fell in a matter of hours. Strong points Gabrielle and Anne-Marie were overrun during the next two days, which denied the French use of the airfield, the key to the French defense. Reduced to airdrops for supplies and reinforcement, unable to evacuate their wounded, under constant artillery bombardment, and at the extreme limit of air range, the French camp's morale began to fray. As the monsoons transformed the camp from a dust bowl into a morass of mud, an increasing number of soldiers — almost four thousand by the end of the siege in May — deserted to caves along the Nam Yum River, which traversed the camp; they emerged only to seize supplies dropped for the defenders. The "Rats of Nam Yum" became POWs when the garrison surrendered on May 7.

Despite these early successes, Giap's offensives sputtered out before the tenacious resistance of French paratroops and legionnaires. On April 6, horrific losses and low morale among the attackers caused Giap to suspend his offensives. Some of his commanders, fearing U.S. air intervention, began to speak of withdrawal. Again, the Chinese, in search of a spectacular victory to carry to the Geneva talks scheduled for the summer, intervened to stiffen Viet Minh resolve: reinforcements were brought in, as were Katyusha multitube rocket launchers, while Chinese military engineers retrained the Viet Minh in siege tactics. When Giap resumed his attacks, human wave assaults were abandoned in favor of siege techniques that pushed forward webs of trenches *à la Vauban* (q.v.) to isolate French strong points. The French perimeter was gradually reduced until, on May 7, resistance ceased. The shock and agony of the dramatic loss of a garrison of around fourteen thousand men allowed French prime minister Pierre Mendès-France to muster enough parliamentary sup-

General Henri Navarre, came out to defend his allies because he believed the T'ai "maquis" formed a significant threat in the Viet Minh "rear" (the T'ai supplied the French with opium that was sold to finance French special operations) and wanted to prevent a

port to sign the Geneva Accords of July 1954, which essentially ended the French presence in Indochina.

DOUGLAS PORCH

Disarmament

Disarmament has its origins in the nineteenth-century development of liberal doctrines about international politics. Many advocates of disarmament thought that major wars occurred because the great powers competed with one another in armaments. The outbreak of World War I (q.v.) seemed to confirm this explanation because major increases in armaments preceded that conflict. For example, Sir Edward Grey, Great Britain's foreign secretary (1906–1916), said in an oft-quoted statement on the conflict's origins, "The enormous growth of armaments in Europe, the sense of insecurity and fear caused by them — it was these that made war inevitable." This theory of why conflicts occur had its policy corollary: disarmament would provide a way to reduce international tension and preclude war. In an attempt to promote a liberal international order, President Woodrow Wilson (q.v.) called for disarmament as part of his peace program known as the Fourteen Points.

Perhaps the most important role played by disarmament in world affairs has occurred at the end of major wars, when the winning side imposed restrictions on the armed forces of the countries it defeated. In classical antiquity, for example, the Romans tried to disarm their long-standing rival Carthage (see *Punic Wars*). Napoleon (q.v.) also dictated limits on the military strength of Prussia and Austria after he defeated them in war. In the twentieth century, the victorious powers insisted on limiting the German army and navy as part of the peace settlement that ended World War I. This step was intended to prevent Germany's military from posing a serious offensive threat to its neighbors. After World War II (q.v.), both Germany and Japan were disarmed. Although more than fifty years have elapsed since the end of World War II, both countries still observe important limitations on their armed forces. Neither country has tried to reassert its independent status as a great power by developing nuclear weapons.

One of the best examples of disarmament before the twentieth century occurred in Japan. For almost two hundred years, beginning in the middle of the 1600s, the Japanese eschewed the use of firearms as weapons for combat. Throughout this period of self-imposed disarmament, the sword remained the dominant weapon. This changed in the middle of the nineteenth century, when outside great powers threatened intervention in Japanese affairs. With the end of Japan's isolation within the international political system, disarmament also came to an end.

The term *disarmament* is often used interchangeably with *arms control,* but the two terms should be considered separate concepts. General disarmament is a utopian doctrine, unlikely to be realized as long as competing states strive to promote their own security in an anarchic international environment. No country is likely to disarm completely as long as other states do not renounce war and armaments as well, for fear that it would be committing suicide. Disarmament is thus often considered a long-range goal, associated with a fundamental reordering of the international political environment that aims at ending its anarchic nature by establishing world government or an effective system of collective security.

Arms control, on the other hand, provides decision-makers with a more pragmatic policy approach. The objectives of arms control are to promote international stability by reducing the likelihood of war, the costs of weaponry, and the damage of fighting once conflict occurs. All major states seriously consider arms control as part of their security policy. The U.S. Congress, for example, established the Arms Control and Disarmament Agency (ACDA) in 1961 to provide a bureaucratic institution for dealing with arms control issues.

Examples of arms control can be found before the modern era. In twelfth-century Europe, for example, the church worked to ban crossbows in warfare among Christians. This attempt at premodern arms control failed, and crossbows remained in widespread use throughout Europe. Arms control negotiations have played a major role in international politics during the past century. Between the two world wars, the major naval powers made a considerable effort to negotiate relative force levels between them: the Washington Conference (1921–1922) and the London Conference (1930) achieved notable success in limiting naval armaments. The League of Nations also attempted to advance international disarmament; its efforts culminated in the Geneva Conference (1932–1934), where an attempt was made to distinguish between "defensive" and "offensive" weaponry and then to eliminate those forces categorized as offensive. But the rise of German, Italian, and Japanese imperialism during the 1930s, and the fear that this engendered in the Western liberal democracies, temporarily doomed arms control.

The advent of atomic weapons during World War II gave further impetus to advocates of disarmament. Many prominent writers, intellectuals, and policy activists supported efforts to "ban the bomb," even if this entailed unilateral disarmament. Nuclear disarmament became for many a moral imperative, for the stakes at risk seemed nothing less than the extinction of the human species. Movies and television popularized this apocalyptic vision, helping to garner widespread support for the disarmament movement.

The leaders of the superpowers meanwhile gave considerable attention to arms control during the Cold War (q.v.). A relaxation of tensions in superpower relations, or détente, was widely viewed to coincide with arms control agreements, such as the conclusion of the first round of SALT (Strategic Arms Limitation Talks) in 1972, the INF (intermediate nuclear forces) agreement in 1987, and START (Strategic Arms Reduction Talks) in 1991. To many analysts of international relations, the superpower experience showed that arms control can play a useful (if modest) role in helping rival states to manage the uncertainty of their armaments competitions. Ardent advocates of disarmament, however, came to view arms control as a subterfuge employed by the leaders of the great powers to frustrate genuine disarmament.

Although disarmament had its origins in the liberal democracies, nonliberal regimes have also sought to exploit disarmament to achieve their foreign policy and strategy goals. Tsar Nicholas II of Russia, for example, called for the convening of the Hague Conference (1899) to prevent wealthier great powers from modernizing their armed forces. Adolf Hitler's (q.v.) regime used the failure of other powers to disarm after World War I as an excuse for German rearmament in the 1930s. The Soviet Union also abetted disarmament as a way of causing domestic political embarrassment for the governments of its principal adversaries, the liberal democracies.

The end of the Cold War, and the successes of superpower arms control, has not dampened interest in disarmament and arms control. In the liberal democracies, organizations promoting disarmament retain considerable clout in the domestic political arena. A current view holds that modern liberal democracies can achieve effective disarmament among themselves, because they seem less prone to make war on one another. The Rush-Bagot Agreement (1817), which led to the demilitarization of the border between Canada and the United States, is used to illustrate the way disarmament between modern democracies can be achieved. The spread of democracy, then, conceivably advances the cause of disarmament.

In the aftermath of the Cold War, attempts to limit the geographical spread of nuclear weapons and ballistic missiles, and to eliminate the use of chemical and biological agents as weapons of mass destruction, have also emerged as important policy concerns. Paradoxically, disarmament has even been used as a justification for resorting to war. The coalition that fought Iraq in 1991 (see *Gulf War*), for instance, aimed not only at restoring Kuwait as an independent, sovereign state, but also at eliminating Iraq's ability to manufacture and use nuclear, chemical, and biological weapons. The prospect for a major war in northeast Asia, brought about by North Korea's desire to build a nuclear arsenal, and the determination of the United States and South Korea to prevent this development, is also part of an attempt to further international disarmament. The establishment of a liberal world order could therefore entail fighting wars for the sake of disarmament. Hence the plea of disarmament advocates — namely, that weapons themselves cause war — might come to have a new, more ominous meaning.

JOHN H. MAURER

Discipline

Among the early citizen militias of the Greek city-state and Roman republic, complex codes of discipline were nonexistent. Yet hoplites (q.v.) and republican legionaries usually fought superbly: they were not part of expeditionary armies bent on conquest and aggression, but men in arms for a few days or weeks with a high degree of morale and group solidarity. The presence of family and lifelong friends in the ranks and the knowledge that their own dependents were helpless to their immediate rear usually provided incentive enough to stand and fight.

Abandoning position and failure to muster were the most frequent charges, and the accused usually received a public trial. If convicted, the guilty was subject to property confiscation, exile, and occasionally public stoning. Public disgrace prevented routine infractions: soldiers of questionable loyalty and courage were informally snubbed by members of the community, their records repeatedly dredged up in lawsuits and public debate — a process of public odium that worked quite well in maintaining a fully staffed and effective militia.

Off the battlefield such yeomen in arms were often unruly. In literary accounts, we hear that Greek militiamen could be unsteady, even abusive on the march and in camp, arguing openly with officers and experiencing sudden states of both group exultation and abject depression. Most classical armies were mirror images of the civic body itself: citizen-soldiers assumed the army to be their own and thus guided by popular will. They saw themselves as privileged beneficiaries of the same rights as all adult males of the community, and so had no desire or need to abide by a corpus of distinct military justice executed by a single grandee.

An exception to informal early Greek and Roman practice was the Spartan (q.v.) code of chastisement, shrouded in secrecy and mystique. Usually corporal punishment was rare — thanks to lifelong rigorous training in the barracks and at group messes. The more common charge was the entirely subjective notion of faintheartedness in battle, or even chance survival in the midst of the mass extinction of comrades round about. Shunning was the most frequent punishment for the unlucky survivor; records indicate that often a Spartan under suspicion was not spoken to, his entire family equally ignored by the community — his only recourse was suicide by hanging.

The rise of Hellenistic professional armies, enormous in number and multicultural in the broadest sense, for the first time brought in systematic codes of military discipline, including careful guidelines concerning pay, dependents, and terms of service, and buttressed by complicated hierarchies of rewards and punishments. After Alexander (q.v.), soldiers were under contractual agreement to a king, emperor, or tyrant and were not patriots who fought of their own free will in answer to a state call-up. They owed allegiance to individual generals who guaranteed their pay and assumed absolute ownership of their labor.

Commanders naturally turned to systematic corporal punishment — even execution — once the old restraints of kinship and family shame were lost. Individual acts of cowardice in the Roman army — desertion, conspiracy to commit mutiny, and coward-

ice — officially warranted execution, in the most severe cases through hanging or confinement with wild beasts. Yet despite the rhetoric of Roman reactionary literature, leniency was commonplace. Extenuating circumstances, such as length of service and previous conduct, might lead to lesser chastisement: beating with rods, reduction of rank, and fines. Humiliation was a favorite Roman punishment, as errant soldiers might be forced to stand in public all day holding poles or dirt.

Entire units in the Roman army who fled in battle were occasionally decimated — the macabre practice of selecting every tenth legionnaire by lot to be stoned or clubbed by fellow soldiers of other cohorts. Centurions of the disgraced cohort bore personal responsibility and were frequently executed. The 90 percent who survived were often then reduced to barley rations. During the empire, however, mutiny and widespread cowardice often resulted in disbandment of the entire cohort or legion, a disaster for professional legionaries who lost lifelong employment and retirement stipends.

Although the severity of Roman military discipline is a favorite topic in ancient literature, under the real conditions of the campaign all sorts of circumstances continued to mitigate actual enactment of sentences, not the least of which was the growing importance of the army itself as an arbiter of imperial succession. Decimation, for example, seems to have become rare by late imperial times, and commanders often seemed overwhelmed by insubordinate and unruly troops stationed in garrisons and forts. Donatives, stipends, and outright bribery were the more common methods of ensuring legionary loyalty.

Uniform discipline in medieval armies fell far short of classical standards and was completely antithetical to the fragmented and dynastic nature of European society. Family quarrels might destroy coalitions of knights in the midst of campaigning, and musters of the lower classes could dissolve if pay was not forthcoming or promises of loot and booty exaggerated.

The end of feudalism and rise of the nation-state in the fifteenth and sixteenth centuries brought new attempts to institute codes of military conduct — along with uniforms, pay, and regular provisions — among armies that were often conscripted rather than purely mercenary. Frederick the Great (q.v.) created a codified system of strict punishment that marked the dawn of Prussian militarism, whose entire ideology rested on absolute respect and deference to a professional military caste — a tradition to survive among the German armies even during the darkest moments of both world wars. Frederick's innovations were widely emulated, and by the early nineteenth century most Western nations had instituted military academies, such as Sandhurst, West Point, and St. Cyr, where codes of military justice and adherence to international norms of military behavior became part of the official curriculum of the officer corps. During the nineteenth and twentieth centuries, military courts that dispensed imprisonment for insubordination and capital punishment for desertion began to convince the men under arms of the power of state authority.

Despite the successful subjection of the army to legal statutes, the gradual elimination of hired troops, and success in supplying regular wages and rations, Western armies on occasion were still prone to insubordination and revolt in mass — if the conditions of service became unduly barbaric — by aggrieved soldiers who saw themselves ultimately as free men in a constitutional society. The duke of Wellington (q.v.) temporarily lost control of many corps (mass drunkenness was common) during the Peninsular War of 1812. Discipline was a constant problem amid the trench slaughters of World War I (q.v.): 263 British soldiers were shot for desertion or cowardice. After the French army mutinied in 1917, 23 ringleaders were executed and another 23,000 punished for dereliction of duty. (In the same year, whole German divisions refused to return to the Western Front.) Though the German army executed only 48 men in World War I, in the next war between 13,000 and 15,000 were victims of a draconian military justice system. On the Russian front, the Nazis maintained discipline in the face of horrendous losses by encouraging atrocities: shared guilt and the knowledge that prisoners were often killed in retaliation were powerful incentives to fight to the last. An absence of domestic support, inability to distinguish combatant from civilian, and military stalemate in Vietnam (q.v.) caused some American units to refuse assignments, threaten officers, and rely on both drugs and alcohol on a regular basis. Sometimes there were actual murders, called "fragging."

Non-Western armies showed nearly the same variations in the application of discipline. Morale and obedience were high under commanders who demonstrated a record of victory and showed little hesitation in ordering execution — Tamerlane (q.v.), Saladin (q.v.), Genghis Khan (q.v.), and Mehmed II rarely faced dissension among their well-rewarded followers. On other occasions, weakness in leadership or military setbacks led to mass collapse and desertion rarely seen in the West; the Aztec, Muslim, and Zulu armies of Montezuma, Mahdi, and Cetewayo seemed to have largely disintegrated in the wake of a leader's defeat or death and subsequent slaughter of troops. In general, it is a fair generalization that non-Western armies have relied more on religious and political fervor — emperor worship, Islam, Bushido, or Marxism — or on the personal magnetism of an individual grandee than on codified statutes to ensure recruitment and obedience to command.

Yet the trend in Western society toward individualism and the integration of military and civilian justice suggests that an army's traditional and legal recourse of punishing insubordination — immediate discharge, corporal punishment, lengthy imprisonment, and execution — will increasingly be found unacceptable by the population at large.

VICTOR DAVIS HANSON

Anthony Babington, *For the Sake of Example* (1983); Omer Bartov, *Hitler's Army* (1991); Brian Campbell, *The Roman Army, 31 B.C.–A.D. 337: A Sourcebook* (1994); W. K. Pritchett, *The Greek State at War* (1971–1991); A. Vagts, *A History of Militarism* (1959).

Disposal of the Dead

All armies confront the need to dispose of the dead. For the small city-states of Greece, the winning side would usually return the dead to their homes for proper attention; the fallen of the defeated would be stripped — to be claimed after their city had asked for a truce. Only in special circumstances, such as the Athenian victory over the Persians at Marathon (q.v.), would the victors honor the dead with a great burial mound. At Trasemine Lake the Carthaginians apparently dumped the Roman dead in pits, while incinerating their own with honors — but they were, after all, the victors. Given the lowly position of soldiers in Chinese society, common soldiers in China who died in battle got short shrift; even on the winning side their fate was to be thrown into trenches, holes, or lake beds, or even immured within the Great Wall, a

The remains of Union soldiers of the American Civil War are gathered for burial in April 1865, almost a year after the failed assault on Cold Harbor, Virginia.

singular mark of disrespect. Chinese generals who died in battle did not receive funerary honors as military leaders, but rather were honored for their Confucian (that is, civilian) virtues.

In the ancient and medieval periods, the value of armor ensured that the victors would strip the dead — though at the Battle of Visby in Sweden in the fourteenth century so many knights died and the weather was so hot that the bodies decomposed before the victors could strip them of their armor. The putrefying remains, armor and all, were then dumped in pits; they were excavated six centuries later. Whatever the prospects of loot, armies tended to leave the depressing environs of battle as quickly as possible — leaving the peasants, undoubtedly also busily engaged in looting the dead, the business of disposing of the bodies. As late as the early nineteenth century, Napoleon's (q.v.) soldiers — on their way back from Moscow — passed the dismal sight of the rotting corpses of their fallen comrades at Borodino, a sight hardly calculated to lift their morale.

In the American Civil War (q.v.), such age-old practices began to be abandoned. The great Civil War cemeteries of the Northern dead underline a significant change in sensibilities. The Southern dead, however, were largely treated in the traditional fashion — anonymously buried in trenches or even flung down wells. World War I (q.v.) continued the swing toward the memorialization of the dead. Moreover, at least on the Western Front, soldiers introduced a system of identification: French soldiers wore "dog tags" on their wrists at the start of the war and later around their necks. British and American armies followed their example. At the war's end, the contenders gathered the dead together in great national cemeteries in northern France. But vast numbers remained unidentified: the British memorial on the Somme (q.v.) lists the names of 73,412 missing. The French, less sentimental, deposited the bones of hundreds of thousands of their dead, intermingled with German remains, in ossuaries, the greatest of which is at Verdun (q.v.).

In World War II (q.v.) the contestants on the Western Front again created great cemeteries for their fallen. But in the east (not surprisingly, given the crimes perpetrated by the Nazis) the Soviets displayed scant concern for the German dead or their graves. The steppe around Stalingrad (q.v.) remains littered with the bleached bones of the German dead. For their own dead, the Soviets had no coherent burial plan except mass interment and great Stalinist memorials. In the post–World War II world, the limited numbers of war dead at least allowed the Americans to bring bodies home. But for the enemies of the United States, there was no such luxury; the dead of North Korea, China, and North Vietnam lie in unmarked sites with few, if any, memorials to mark their passing.

WILLIAMSON MURRAY

Doctrine

There are at least two general understandings of doctrine. The broadest is that offered in the 1965 *Soviet Dictionary of Basic Military Terms:*

> A nation's officially accepted system of scientifically founded views on the nature of modern wars and the use of armed forces in them, and also on the requirements arising from these views regarding the country and its armed forces being made ready for war.

One perhaps may question the phrase "scientifically founded" in the quotation above, but the definition remains a useful one, particularly for countries like the former Soviet Union that actually concocted formal doctrine at this high strategic level. It also offers a frame of reference for understanding the approach to war making of countries that do not have as formal a process for codifying doctrine, but which do, in fact, make coherent strategic choices of the kind implied by the Soviet definition. Israel is a good example. Before 1967 that country's acute geographical vulnerability, coupled with the natural aptitude of its army for offensive warfare, led to a coherent doctrine for preemptive offensive action in the event of political crisis. Few countries, however, codify their strategic doctrine in more than platitudes, and even fewer have policy-making mechanisms for imposing it on their defense establishment.

A second understanding of doctrine, narrower but more practical (and prevalent), looks at the operational level of war. In this understanding, doctrine means a certain common approach to the fighting of battles, which leaves details of implementation to a commander's judgment of circumstances. Doctrine reflects an army's way of war, its habitual way of fighting, the mind-set that it seeks to cultivate in commanders and their subordinates. The official definition of the Joint Chiefs of Staff in the United States includes these statements: "Fundamental principles by which the military forces or elements thereof guide their actions in support of national objectives. It is authoritative but not directive." Note how the last sentence captures the internal tension in doctrine, between the desire to prescribe a common way of fighting and the imperative of adjusting particular military actions to circumstances.

The modern development of doctrine is often traced to the German army in the mid–nineteenth century, particularly to the work of the pioneering chief of the General Staff Helmuth von Moltke the Elder (q.v.). His "Instructions for Large Unit Commanders" of 1869 is perhaps one of the best formulations of an army's doctrine. In addition to general precepts for corps commanders and observations on organization and even tactics, it states clearly the spirit of the Prussian (later, the German) army: senior commanders assign missions to subordinate commanders but leave the manner of completing those tasks to their discretion. The lineal descendants of this pamphlet may be found in the operations manuals of most Western militaries.

A common doctrine of war allowed German generals to coordinate their activities even when out of range of direct communications; indeed, this was the genius of Moltke's system and that of the German General Staff. Moreover, the animating spirit of German doctrine — the belief in mission-type orders, the allowances made for the fog of war and unforeseeable mishaps — was fundamentally in accord with the nature of modern combat. A comprehensive but ill-founded doctrine, however, can have calamitous results. The French army in the interwar period, which adopted a disastrous concept of "methodical battle" utterly incompatible with armored warfare, offers an instructive example.

Some military establishments, such as that of Britain before World War II (q.v.), thought that doctrine smacked either of meaningless abstraction, on the one hand, or mindless rigidity on the other. These misconceptions fed off a disdain for the glutinous quality of German philosophical prose and a (misplaced) belief that the Germans possessed excessive rigidity, as opposed to the pragmatic creativity of the sturdy Anglo-Saxon. The common and cynical definition of doctrine as "the opinion of the senior officer present" is indicative of a more general attitude. The evolution of British tactics in World War I (q.v.), however, indicates the weakness of a military system without any doctrinal core. Some individual army or corps commanders adapted well to the shifting demands of both defense and offense in trench warfare. The successful approaches, however, were not systematically explored or diffused throughout the army, in sharp contrast to those of the Germans.

It is, of course, possible to have a doctrine without realizing it. Horatio Nelson's (q.v.) fighting instructions to his captains embodied a naval tactical doctrine that served the Royal Navy well in the Napoleonic Wars. But in recent years more militaries have come to believe in the necessity of having formal, written doctrine. Even the U.S. Navy, historically an organization deeply, even morbidly, suspicious of doctrine, has created a doctrine command and begun to publish doctrinal manuals. Of all the American services, however, the U.S. Army has devoted the most attention to doctrine.

The U.S. Army's fascination with doctrine had roots in the intensification of military competition with the Soviet Union after the Vietnam War (q.v.). Influenced by Soviet writers, and seeking ways to overcome numerical inferiority on the Central Front in Europe, the army turned to doctrine, which had the further benefit of contributing to a restoration of discipline and professional qualities following the debacle of the Indochina war. In theory, and to a large measure in practice, operational doctrine drives the army's training and procurement programs and informs all levels of professional military education as well. Other services (the marines, for example) have adapted doctrine to a more moderate degree and as a result may retain greater flexibility.

Yet doctrine has a darker side. It degenerates easily into platitude or dogma, exciting thereby the derision of officers who think, and providing altogether too much comfort to those who do not. Doctrine can become a substitute for creative thinking about warfare, particularly in a time of revolutionary change in the means of its conduct. And in the absence of a clear connection between an army's philosophy of war and the political rationale for its employment — a matter that doctrine in the narrower view rarely provides —

it can pave the way for civil-military friction. Doctrine, in other words, may drive soldiers to insist on fighting in ways incompatible with the political objectives of statesmen. This problem too reminds us that in war, more than in any other human activity, orthodoxy is a perilous cast of mind.

ELIOT A. COHEN

Dudley Knox, "The Role of Doctrine in Naval Warfare," *U.S. Naval Institute Proceedings* (March–April 1915): 325–365; Helmuth von Moltke, "1869 Instructions for Large Unit Commanders," in *Moltke on the Art of War* (1993).

Dönitz, Karl

1891–1980, German Grand Admiral

Karl Dönitz was born on September 16, 1891; he entered the German navy in 1910 and was depth-charged in the U-boat *UC68* late in World War I (q.v.). Returned to Germany from a British prison camp in 1919, Dönitz commanded torpedo boats by 1928 and the light cruiser *Emden* six years later. In January 1936, Dönitz was appointed commander of U-boats in the German navy; in January 1943, he replaced Erich Raeder as head of the navy; and on April 30, 1945, he briefly succeeded Adolf Hitler (q.v.) because of his sycophantic adoration of the führer. In October 1946, the War Crimes Tribunal at Nuremberg (q.v.) sentenced Dönitz to ten years' incarceration for war crimes and crimes against peace. He denied all knowledge of the Holocaust, showed no remorse for the slave labor empire that built his U-boats, and remained an unrepentant Nazi: in April 1945, shortly before the führer's suicide, he deemed Hitler "the single statesman of stature in Europe"; in 1969 he described Hitler's personal style of command as the "best method of military leadership."

Dönitz commanded Germany's U-boat force in the Battle of the North Atlantic (q.v.). His submarines sank 175 Allied warships and 2,603 merchant ships, but lost 784 boats and 28,000 men. In April 1943, convoy HX231 drove off all attacking U-boats. Allied convoys, radar, aerial patrols, depth charges, special naval "killer groups," and Ultra electronic intercepts blunted the German underseas campaign. Dönitz conceded defeat in the battle on May 24, 1943, when he recalled his boats. After 1943 more than thirty-five hundred Allied ships in sixty-two convoys crossed the Atlantic without a single loss.

Dönitz's strengths included his ruthless application of the wolf-pack technique, his iron-willed determination to fight to the last boat, and his unbounded enthusiasm. But his command was deficient in staff training, lacked a naval air arm, and lagged in operations research. Above all, Dönitz never decided whether to conduct a simple tonnage war or to direct attacks against specific targets with the greatest potential for decisive impact.

HOLGER H. HERWIG

Dowding, Hugh

1882–1970, *British Air Marshal*

The most crucial figure in the British armed forces during World War II (q.v.) was the improbable Air Marshal "Stuffy" Dowding, developer and leader of Fighter Command in the Battle of Britain (q.v.). Dowding had a successful enough career in World War I to be noticed by Lord Trenchard, the "father" of the Royal Air Force (RAF), and by 1932 he headed the RAF's research and development establishment. There, Dowding pushed two crucial developments: first, he set the specifications and then approved the contracts for development of what eventually became the Hurricane and Spitfire fighters; second, in 1935 he provided both money and encouragement for experiments that led to the development of radar systems capable of identifying and tracking attacking enemy aircraft. In 1937, passed over as chief of Air Staff, he took over Fighter Command — considered by most RAF officers to be a backwater of little importance — where Dowding spent the next three years creating a highly responsive and effective air defense, based on radar, high-speed fighters, and well-designed command and control systems (all of them developments he had set in motion during his previous assignment). Despite considerable opposition from the Air Ministry, he emphasized single-seat fighters as the cornerstone of Britain's air defense.

When war broke out in 1939, Dowding, although due for retirement, stayed on. As the French collapse began to suck Fighter Command's strength into a hopeless struggle, Dowding stood up to Winston Churchill (q.v.) and warned that his command could not lose any more fighters and still accomplish its mission to defend Britain. Churchill, always respectful of strong individuals and good arguments, accepted Dowding's position and even quashed a cabal in the Air Ministry that attempted to remove him early in the summer. Dowding then fought and won the Battle of Britain, the first and only defeat the Germans suffered at British hands in the first three years of the war. Nevertheless, Dowding received small thanks: not only did the RAF remove him from his command at the end of the battle, but also it failed to give him any further significant assignment — despite Churchill's urgings.

WILLIAMSON MURRAY

Dragoons

Moving on horseback but fighting on foot, dragoons first appeared in the mid-sixteenth-century French army. In the 1620s the Swedish and French armies created regiments of dragoons, who wore no armor, rode small horses, and fought with musket and saber. In 1690 the French army included forty-three dragoon regiments, while in 1710 the Russian army contained twenty-four; but by then, although the term survived, dragoons operated both on and off the battlefield as medium cavalry and no longer fought on foot. In the twentieth century, however, the original concept reemerged: during World War I (q.v.), the British cavalry used their horses for mobility but fought on foot with rifles and machine guns; during World War II (q.v.), infantry divisions were all motorized so that foot soldiers again rode into battle but fought dismounted; and since the 1950s, helicopters have extended the infantry's mobility still further.

GEOFFREY PARKER

Drake, Francis

1542?–1596, *English Pirate, Privateer, and Admiral*

The dazzling career of Sir Francis Drake, who rose from humble beginnings to win fortune and knighthood, reflects the fluidity of society and warfare in his era. Professional in his craft, he proved a bold commander and fine strategist; sensitive to morale, he promoted health and was curt with the pretensions of gentlemen aboard ship.

Drake was stirred by conviction of Spanish treachery and Protestant zeal to wage a private war against Spain. He understood the strategic vulnerability of Spain's maritime empire and treasure routes, which he plundered between 1571 and 1580; on the expedition of 1577–1580, he sailed around the world, the first Englishman to do so. He believed his depredations lawful; Spaniards considered him a pirate.

War with Spain became open in 1585, and Drake dominated its early years. He raided the Caribbean, disrupting the flow of treasure, and in 1587 he attacked Cádiz, "singeing the King of Spain's beard" and delaying the Armada (q.v.), assembled for the invasion of England, by a crucial year. Vice admiral of Queen Elizabeth's navy in 1588, he prompted its concentration at the western entrance to the Channel, which contributed much to the Armada's defeat. He failed with his Counter-Armada of 1589 to detach Portugal from Spain. Losing influence, he shared with John Hawkins command of an expedition to the Caribbean in 1595. Frustrated by Spain's repaired defenses, Drake died in January 1596. As Hawkins had also died, the expedition returned to England.

PETER O'M. PIERSON

Drama

See Representation of War in Drama.

Drill/Marching

Marching in step multiplied the battle effectiveness of shield-carrying spearmen, allowing them to move about the battlefield, support one another, and maintain an unbroken shield wall as long as they fought in open, more or less flat terrain. The ancient Sumerians discovered this simple fact, proven by a surviving bas-relief from about 2450 B.C., and they must have invented some form of drill to teach spearmen how to maintain their places in the ranks. But from the beginning, the flanks and rear of massed infantry formations were vulnerable to missiles, launched by nimble, unarmored troops; and when archers learned to use the speed of horseflesh to move about the battlefield — first as charioteers (1800? B.C.), then as cavalry (after 875 B.C.) — even well-drilled heavy infantry ceased to be effective.

Nevertheless, for several centuries in China, as well as in ancient Greece and Rome, foot soldiers equipped with shields and spears continued to dominate battlefields even after cavalry had eclipsed such tactics in the Middle East. Surviving texts tell us

This etching of a pikeman comes from a 1607 military manual on Maurice of Nassau's drill system. Pikemen anchored the pike with a foot when lowering the weapon to oppose a cavalry charge. Soldiers moved together in response to a shouted word of command to prevent entangling the pikes, which could be twelve feet in length or longer.

something about the drill that prepared Chinese, Greek, Macedonian, and Roman troops for battle. Sun Tzu (q.v.), in *The Art of War* (composed in about 400 B.C.), and other writers make it clear that Chinese infantry were taught to march in cadence and were trained to deploy themselves into different formations obedient to signals conveyed by drumbeats, gongs, and (for large units) the display of pennants. Among the Greeks, only the Spartans (q.v.) are known to have marched in step and to have practiced deployment from march formation to battle line. We know more about Macedonian drill, thanks to a brief text by an otherwise unknown author, Aelianus Tacticus, who wrote in the second century A.D. He tells us that Alexander's (q.v.) foot soldiers were drilled to obey conventional "words of command," allowing them to move about the battlefield in different formations while keeping their spears in diverse positions, all according to the will of their officers. According to another otherwise unknown author, Flavius Renatus Vegetius (A.D. 400?) (q.v.), Roman drill began with individual training in the use of sword and javelin, went on to small-unit marching and deployment, and climaxed in legionary exercises involving a march of about ten miles, construction of a fortified camp, and then a return to base, all in a single day.

The ability of cavalry to outmaneuver foot soldiers and attack unprotected flanks and rear eventually disrupted the classical Chinese and Roman infantry armies and their respective forms of drill. But the memory lingered, and in modern times, when infantry regained importance in battle as part of combined arms deployment in which cavalry, artillery, and infantry each played a role, the old texts inspired military reformers to revive and modify classical drill.

General Ch'i Chi-kuang (1527–1587) (q.v.) revived old forms of drill in China, securing his infantry from cavalry harassment by using wagon laagers that carried supplies needed for long-distance campaigning on the open steppes. The result was spectacular — China was able in the ensuing two centuries to conquer and annex about half of the Eurasian steppe, dividing it with the Russians, whose success against nomad cavalry rested on their adaptation of new European forms of armament and drill, pioneered by Maurice of Nassau (1567–1625) (q.v.), who set out to revive and revise the classical teachings of Aelianus and Vegetius.

Ch'i Chi-kuang made scant use of gunpowder weapons, even though China had invented them; but the infantry drill that Maurice of Nassau introduced to the Dutch armies in the 1590s relied as much on the fire of matchlocks as on pikemen for offensive capability, and on digging trenches and erecting other field fortification for defense. Like the Macedonians, Maurice and his collaborators worked out "words of command" for each motion needed to handle weapons efficiently, and devised other commands for march and deployment in battle. Incessant practice filled soldiers' idle hours and made the motions of loading and firing almost automatic. Maurice's drill — and still more drill — paid off in an increased rate of fire and superior precision of movement on the battlefield. Other European armies hastened to adopt the Dutch methods, and the resulting rituals

of close-order drill became hallmarks of European armies thereafter and remain alive to the present, even after breech-loading rifles and machine guns banished older forms of drill and deployment from actual battle.

One reason for the survival of old-fashioned close-order drill is that prolonged movement in unison arouses a strong psychological response and creates an esprit de corps among those who drill together that pays off even on modern battlefields. The same sort of group cohesion undergirded spectacular European military successes in the centuries between 1650 and 1900, against Asian and African armies that did not emphasize prolonged close-order drill. But when Asian and African soldiers were subjected to European-style drill, they quickly came to equal European troops, as Indians serving the French and British East India Companies (the sepoys [q.v.]) proved as early as the eighteenth century, and as Japanese, Chinese, and many other soldiers have shown in the nineteenth and twentieth centuries, when European forms of drill and equipment reached them.

Close-order drill and effective soldiering are therefore likely to remain closely associated, even though marching erect into battle ceased to be feasible after 1866, when the Prussians introduced breech-loading rifles, and permitted their soldiers to crawl across the battlefield and fire from a prone position.

WILLIAM H. MCNEILL

William H. McNeill, *Keeping Together in Time: Dance and Drill in Human History* (1995).

Dunant, Jean Henri

1828–1910, Swiss Philanthropist and Pacifist

Scion of a bourgeois Geneva family, Jean Henri Dunant was horrified by the carnage of nearly forty thousand casualties he witnessed on the battlefield at Solferino, Italy, in 1859. He organized emergency care for wounded French and Austrian troops, to whom he became known as "the man in white."

In a memoir published in 1862, he proposed the organization of relief societies in time of peace to care for the wounded in wartime, which led in 1864 to the foundation of the Red Cross and the drafting of the first international code of rules for war, the Geneva Convention. Neglecting his affairs, this tireless pacifist went bankrupt in 1867 campaigning against

By the early seventeenth century, arduous sieges dominated European warfare. The Spanish siege of Dutch Breda lasted almost one year, from July 1624 to June 1625. Here, in Diego Velásquez's The Surrender of Breda, *the Dutch commander surrenders the city to victorious Spanish general Ambrogio Spinola.*

slavery, against "new and frightful weapons of destruction," and in favor of disarmament, international arbitration, humane treatment for prisoners of war, and the purchase of land in Palestine for the resettlement of Jews — well before the rise of the Zionist movement. Dunant shared the first Nobel Peace Prize in 1901 with Frédéric Passy, another Swiss.

The International Red Cross, staffed by Swiss and functioning as a trusted go-between during armed conflicts, nevertheless engenders a certain amount of cynicism in Switzerland, where, in an allusion to one of the nation's principal arms exporters, it is sometimes wryly referred to as "the Oerlikon-Bürhle after-sales service."

LAWRENCE MALKIN

The Dutch Revolt

The longest-lasting revolt in modern European history began in a region that was both economically prosperous and politically unstable. The seventeen provinces either inherited or conquered by the

Hapsburg dynasty in the Low Countries had an export trade worth almost double that of England's in 1548, the year in which (for the first time) they became a single federative state within a Hapsburg monarchy dominated by Spain. Provincial customs, often guaranteed by charter against central government interference, nevertheless survived, and when Philip II (1555–1598), who tried to rule his entire empire from Madrid, attempted to override them — first to persecute heretics and then to raise taxes — he provoked insurrection.

The decision to send an army from Spain under the duke of Alba (q.v.) stifled an uprising led by Calvinist activists in 1567, but the cost of his troops (which Philip II insisted should be supported by the Netherlands) provoked a second rebellion in 1572. Although Alba moved swiftly and managed to regain almost all the rebel areas within the year, some twenty cities in the provinces of Holland and Zealand sustained rebellion until the financial strain of fighting on two fronts (see *Lepanto, Battle of*) compelled Philip to withdraw his troops in 1577, leaving the rebels in control of almost the entire Netherlands.

Dissension within the ranks of the rebels (some of whom were Calvinists and others Catholics) soon encouraged Philip II to reassert his authority, and until 1587 his forces systematically besieged and captured the towns of the southern Netherlands. However, the diversion of resources to the Spanish Armada (q.v.) and to the war with France led to some losses until the frontier came to rest near the rivers Maas, Waal, and Rhine, which bisect the Netherlands: areas to the south (the core of modern Belgium and Luxembourg) remained Catholic and loyal to Spain, and those to the north (the modern kingdom of the Netherlands) formed the Calvinist-led Dutch Republic. The two sides concluded a twelve-year truce in 1609 and, although hostilities recommenced in 1621 during the Thirty Years' War (q.v.), in 1648 the Dutch gained full recognition of their sovereignty.

The density of towns in the Low Countries largely determined the nature of the war. Between 1572 and 1648, some twenty-seven miles of new fortifications were constructed, all in the "modern" style, with bastions, ravelins, hornworks, and crownworks (see *Fortifications*), which made a long blockade of each one essential. Sieges therefore far outnumbered battles, and each year's campaign generally consisted of investing one or more towns. Some sieges lasted more than a year (Ostend resisted for almost three years, 1601–1604), and the major commanders, such as Maurice of Nassau (q.v.), made their reputations through siegecraft. However, the close proximity of the various fortified centers created, in effect, a "defense in depth" that limited any gains from the capture of individual towns. In military terms, neither side could win; nevertheless, the war continued for ideological reasons — above all through Spain's reluctance to harm the Catholic faith by conceding toleration to Protestants and to "lose face" by granting independence to rebels.

GEOFFREY PARKER

E

Economic Warfare

Economic warfare involves the use of force to attack some vulnerable aspect of an adversary's economy in order to achieve the policy objectives of the conflict. Its main attraction lies in the hope that it can bring war-winning results at a relatively low cost to the victor, in money or casualties. The historical record suggests that such hopes are not easily realized.

Economic warfare has its best chance of success when the policy objectives are themselves primarily economic. If one belligerent aims simply to take from another belligerent its control over trade routes or valuable raw materials, the ends suggest the means for doing so in a straightforward manner. Such was the case, for example, with the Portuguese in the Indian Ocean in the early sixteenth century and with the British in the Anglo-Dutch Wars (q.v.) of the third quarter of the seventeenth century. If, by contrast, the stakes of a war involve national survival or regional hegemony, attacks on the economy of an adversary usually become effective only over an extended period and in conjunction with other uses of force that have put that adversary's means to resist under ever greater pressure.

An ancient conflict — the Peloponnesian War (q.v.) fought between Athens and Sparta from 431 to 404 B.C. for primacy in the Greek world — provides the best example of effective economic warfare in a high-stakes conflict. Capitalizing on the costly failure of an Athenian expedition to Sicily (see *Sicilian Expedition*), Sparta and its allies in 413 B.C. established a fort near Athens at Decelea, from which they managed to interdict the Athenian supply of silver, slave labor, and food. But even that did not suffice to end the war, for Athens still had access to its maritime empire and other overseas sources of supply. Only after Sparta captured the Athenian fleet in 405 B.C. could it starve Athens into submission — twenty-seven years after the war had begun.

In modern history, the closest strategic analogue to ancient Athens was Britain and its empire. From the late seventeenth century to the mid–twentieth century, its main adversaries tried to use economic warfare to cut it off from its overseas sources of wealth and food. None ever succeeded. One important reason was that, unlike Athens, Britain did not lose sea control. In the 1690s, the France of Louis XIV (q.v.) adopted a naval strategy of *guerre de course*, commerce-raiding without a prior knockout blow against the British battle fleet. That remained a major element of both French and Spanish strategy against Britain for over a century, but never with the crippling results that its advocates expected. Finally, in 1806, Napoleon (q.v.) tried something new, his Continental System, decreeing a closure of European markets to British exports. The result was ultimately more painful to him than to his foe: in an effort to plug leaks in the system, he launched his ill-fated invasions of the Iberian Peninsula and Russia.

In the two world wars of the twentieth century, Germany waged economic warfare against Britain with a new weapon, the submarine. The German unrestricted U-boat campaign of 1917 backfired by bringing the United States into World War I (q.v.) on Britain's side. In World War II (q.v.), Germany's submarine campaign made Britain's sea lines of communication to key sources of supply more tenuous than ever before, but by the second half of 1943, the British, the Americans, and the Canadians had won the Battle of the North Atlantic (q.v.).

Britain, meanwhile, had for centuries tried to use its naval prowess to wage economic warfare against adversaries in continental Europe. Spain, because of its dependence on transatlantic treasure from the sixteenth to the eighteenth centuries, seemed a prime target for such warfare, but the British suffered chronic disappointment in their designs on Spanish bullion. France was less dependent on overseas sources of supply. Britain managed to impose an unprecedentedly tight naval blockade on Napoleon, but he compensated for many of its economic effects through control of a large European empire. In World War I, a British naval blockade (q.v.) reached a new modern peak of effectiveness in economic warfare by starving Germany over four years, but it was immensely aided by German mismanagement of domestic production and distribution of food. And what above all made possible the efficacy of the naval blockade was the demands placed on the German economy by a massive ground war fought on multiple fronts.

Indeed, in all the total wars of the industrial era, the interaction of different forms of military power brought about the economic attrition of the losing side. In the first such war, the American Civil War (q.v.), the effects of the Northern naval blockade on the Southern economy were magnified by the thrust of the Union army into eastern Tennessee and then by William T. Sherman's (q.v.) famous march to and along the Atlantic seaboard, which struck not only at Confederate morale but also, as it was designed to do, at Confederate economic resources.

World War II added a dramatically new form of military power — bombing from airplanes — to the mix. Early enthusiasts of air power supposed that "strategic" bombing (q.v.) would have such a quick and decisive impact on the infrastructure of industry or the morale of industrial workers that no other forms of military power would matter. Such expectations proved illusory in the war against both Germany and Japan. Until the last year of the European conflict, British and American bombing failed to depress the level of German war production, and the cost of trying to do so proved high. Only after the Luftwaffe was suppressed and Allied armies had penetrated into Western Europe did the combined bomber offensive pay major dividends. And, meanwhile, not until the last nine months of the Pacific war could American bombers readily reach the home islands of Japan. By the time that the air campaign began taking a terrible toll on Japanese cities in March 1945, the interdiction by American submarines of the flow of oil and other raw materials from Southeast Asia to Japan was already paralyzing the Japanese war economy. Air power thus proved to be a supplement to, not a substi-

tute for, other means of waging economic warfare. And even with all means combined, crippling an enemy's economy proved a long and expensive process.

Such lessons of historical experience escaped many American political and military leaders. The irrepressible advocates of strategic air power after World War II were surprised to find that even heavy bombing of the meager economic assets of North Korea and North Vietnam did not necessarily produce decisive political results.

The idealistic advocates of finding ways to achieve the fruits of war without actually waging it were disappointed to discover that economic sanctions were usually not cost-effective. Imposed on weak states, sanctions have sometimes helped achieve modest results, as against Rhodesia in the 1970s and Serbia in the 1990s. But against adversaries with the will and capability to respond militarily, they have run the risk of triggering war, as happened with Athens against the Spartan alliance; with China against the Mongols in the fifteenth century; and with the United States against Japan in 1941. If major powers see high stakes in a conflict, there is rarely a cheap or risk-free way to make them capitulate.

BRADFORD A. LEE

Paul M. Kennedy, *The Rise and Fall of British Naval Mastery* (1976); Mancur Olson, *The Economics of Wartime Shortage* (1963); R. J. Overy, *The Air War, 1939–1945* (1981).

Economy of Force

Like so many other important concepts related to war, the idea of *the economy of force* was first developed by Carl von Clausewitz (q.v.) in his classic work, *On War*. Clausewitz formulated this concept, as he states, to provide commanders with a simple rule for guidance amid the confusion and complexity of battle. This is one of the few occasions on which Clausewitz explicitly developed a rule, or "principle," of war, a practice he generally avoided as too mechanical.

Clausewitz's initial description of the concept of the economy of force is also the most succinct:

Always . . . make sure that *all forces are involved* [in battle] — always . . . *ensure that no part of the whole force is idle*. If a segment of one's forces is located where it is not sufficiently busy with the enemy, or if troops are on the march — that is, idle — while the enemy is fighting, then these forces are being managed uneconomically. In this sense they are being wasted, which is even worse than using them inappropriately. When the time for action comes, the first requirement should be that *all parts must act*.

In the broader context of his ideas concerning the operational level of war, Clausewitz saw as most critical the achievement of numerical superiority, particularly the superior concentration of forces at the decisive point. To achieve this numerical superiority, the maximum possible number of troops should always be engaged in battle, even to the extent of not holding troops in reserve, a practice Clausewitz was convinced made sense only under exceptional circumstances.

Thus, the principle of the economy of force to some extent contradicts the common recommendation that some troops be held in reserve for unexpected situations or for the exploitation of fleeting opportunities. But, given the uncertain nature of war, Clausewitz held that the precise amount of strength required to achieve victory can never be calculated in advance; therefore he suggested always to concentrate as many troops as possible rather than to economize and use the minimum necessary.

Later discussions of the principle of the economy of force have indeed incorporated the wider context Clausewitz had in mind. One example can be found in Ferdinand Foch's (q.v.) chapter on economy of forces in his book *The Principles of War* (1903):

Modern war knows but one argument: the tactical fact, battle. In view of this it asks of strategy that it should both bring up *all available forces* together and engage in battle *all these forces* by the means of *tactical impulsion* in order to produce *shock*.

The art of achieving numerical superiority at the decisive point of engagement, even if one's own forces are numerically inferior overall, was then directly identified by Foch with the concept of the economy of force: "The art consisted in *securing the numbers*, in having the numbers on the selected point of attack; the means of doing this was *an economy of force*." By this point, then, the concept of the economy of force had been expanded to include many if not all of the pivotal guiding principles of operations. Having grown so broad, it lost the simpler, original meaning assigned it by Clausewitz, namely, the simultaneous use of all forces. This may not have been noticed by the framers of the U.S. military doctrine, who, beginning in the "Combat and General Principles" of 1923,

distinguished between the concept of the economy of force and that of mass, or numerical, superiority. This distinction has remained in U.S. operational doctrine to this day. Unfortunately, in the process, the specific meaning of the economy of force changed once again, as evidenced by a comparison of the definitions listed in the 1949 and 1978 versions of the U.S. Army's "Principles of War":

The principle of economy of force is a corollary to the principle of mass [herein always presented in conjunction with or preceding the definition of the economy of force]. In order to concentrate superior combat strength in one place, economy of force must be exercised in other places. This situation will frequently permit a strategically defensive mission to be effectively executed through offensive action. [1949]

Economy of force is the reciprocal of the principle of mass. Minimum essential means must be employed at points other than that of the main effort. Economy of force requires the acceptance of prudent risks in selected areas to achieve superiority at the point of decision. [1978]

The U.S. doctrine has thus developed a third definition of Clausewitz's broader usage of the concept, which indicates that only the minimum number of forces should be used in engagements or areas of secondary importance. Although the simplification of Foch's version by the United States may have distorted the original Clausewitzian meaning of the concept, it at least had the advantage of clarity and simplicity. However, as the idea of accepting higher risks on secondary fronts was added to the latest version of the manual, Clausewitz's concept as originally set forth was muddled once again.

MICHAEL I. HANDEL

John I. Alger, *The Quest for Victory: The History of the Principles of War* (1982); Carl von Clausewitz, *On War*, Books 3, 5, 6, trans. Michael Howard and Peter Paret (1976); Ferdinand Foch, *The Principles of War*, trans. Hilaire Belloc (1921).

Education, Military

Until at least the sixteenth century, "military education" was an oxymoron in most parts of the world. At least in theory, Chinese officers of the Ming and Ch'ing dynasties were educated in accordance with Confucian bureaucratic principles. In practice, whether in China, Mughal India, or the Ottoman Em-

West Point cadets take a test in 1952, under the watchful eye of an officer-teacher.

pire, warfare was a craft best mastered like any other craft — by a process of apprenticeship. Europe was no exception. The tribunes who served in Rome's legions (q.v.) as senior officers were expected to take their cues from the veteran centurions. In the Middle Ages, although military treatises existed and were widely read, studying them was in no way a requirement for high rank. The emergence of systematic military education in early modern Europe depended heavily on technology. The printing press facilitated large-scale production of books and pamphlets. The development of the *trace italienne* and its complicated successors made both constructing and capturing fortresses a process too complicated to depend entirely on rules of thumb. In the sixteenth and seventeenth centuries, an increasing number of individual entrepreneurs and private academies provided formal instruction to young men preparing for military careers.

This process expanded in the eighteenth century, a period shaped by the aim of integrating social phenomena into an order taking its rationale from the world of mathematics. Soldiers sought to woo Bellona by understanding her. As Europe's major military systems grew more alike in their ways of making war,

even a slight edge could prove significant. Frederick the Great (q.v.) in particular, whose kingdom had approached collapse in the Seven Years' War (q.v.), insisted that war could no longer be treated as a matter of improvisation. Instead it had to be understood theoretically.

This mind-set resulted in a spate of works on military theory and history. Prussia, however, took the next major step in producing educated soldiers. Johann von Scharnhorst sought around 1800 to develop an officer corps informed not only by formal technical instruction, but also by the cultivation of individual character and understanding through open, systematic exchange of ideas and information.

The Prussian War Academy initially offered a program combining general and professional study and emphasizing students' independent work and thought. Similar schools were created throughout Europe and North America in the nineteenth century. The education of junior officers became formalized. The cadet schools of Prussia-Germany, St. Cyr in France, Sandhurst in Great Britain, and West Point in the United States derived from a growing conviction that subalterns could no longer learn their trade by osmosis, reflecting the nineteenth-century emphasis on professionalization and credentials. Also, the exponential growth of armies in the industrial age precluded that officers be drawn only from a small group, based on wealth and birth.

The changing nature of war also fostered a belief in the utility of military education. The Prussian victories in 1866 and 1870–1871 (see *Franco-Prussian War*) were widely perceived as triumphs of preparation over improvisation. Naval education, while retaining its emphasis on practical experience at sea, also became increasingly formalized in the nineteenth century. Dartmouth, Annapolis, and their counterparts supplanted, without ever quite replacing, the "salt horses" of earlier eras. In the succeeding decades, states and armed forces propounded short, decisive wars, which in turn encouraged concentration on details and specializations in the curricula of war academies; their graduates were *schooled* rather than broadly educated. The result during World War I (q.v.) was comprehensive tunnel vision. C. S. Forester's image (in *The General*) of people who had never seen a screw attempting to remove one from a block of wood by applying direct force is a perfect metaphor for the mass slaughters of 1914–1918.

The period from 1918 to 1945 was no less limited in its approach to military education. The Germans taught officers how to command in war, but seldom rose above the operational level to the strategic. The Soviet Union sought to integrate operations and politics, but doctrinal innovations such as combined arms and deep-penetration operations were stifled by the Great Terror of the late 1930s. U.S. service schools suffered from limited curricula and doctrinal disputes between advocates of mass and supporters of mobility. Despite this, the United States would produce an amazing number of competent general officers for the size of its peacetime army.

Paradigmatic change began only in 1945. Particularly in the West, officers were now encouraged to take degrees in nonmilitary subjects from civilian institutions. Military school programs became more open as well, though the service academies in the United States continue to suffer from a misplaced emphasis on engineering. At the same time, nuclear weapons and guerrilla warfare presented challenges not listed in standard syllabi. The Cold War (q.v.) and the principal wars of national liberation ended before military educational systems fully adapted to the new situations. Nevertheless, armed forces face the twenty-first century with at least the prospects of greater intellectual flexibility than previously manifested.

DENNIS E. SHOWALTER

Martin van Creveld, *The Training of Officers: From Military Professionalism to Irrelevance* (1990).

Edward I

1239–1307, *English King*

Though Edward I's reputation among modern historians rests primarily on his contributions to the development of Parliament and the common law, he was also an important military figure. During his long reign (1272–1307), his wars in England, Wales, France, and Scotland marked him as an energetic, tricky, and sometimes brilliant commander. Edward's campaign against the baronial rebels in 1265, when he outmaneuvered and defeated three enemy forces over three weeks, demonstrated truly Napoleonic flair. His methodical conquest of Wales, secured by an expensive system of state-of-the-art castles (q.v.), showed an equal mastery of economic and positional warfare. Elsewhere, his military ambitions exceeded his successes. His invasion of France in 1297, like his Crusade (q.v.) of 1271–1272, was a moderate success at best. In Scotland, he won several victories, captured many strongholds, and repeatedly seemed to have conquered the kingdom; but his overbearing treatment of the defeated led to constant rebellions, and he never really secured this conquest.

Edward's frequent, costly, and large-scale campaigns forced England to develop more sophisticated techniques of military administration and finance. His effective use of Welsh spearmen and archers in combination with English troops, all serving for pay, laid the foundations for the dominant English infantry tactics of the following century.

CLIFFORD J. ROGERS

Eisenhower, Dwight D.

1890–1969, *U.S. World War II General and President*

Dwight D. Eisenhower was born to a poor family in Denison, Texas, and there was little about Ike (his boyhood nickname, based on a guttural shortening of his last name) that suggested his future as a victorious commander in a world conflict and the political leader of a superpower.

Graduating from West Point (the navy had been his first choice) in 1915, Eisenhower ranked 61st academically and 125th in discipline out of a total of 164 graduates — not a sterling record by any measure; but at the academy, he learned that leadership was not an innate talent. "The one quality that can be developed by studious reflection and practice is the leadership of men," he wrote in 1943.

Eisenhower's practical education as a military officer advanced slowly and without great distinction. During World War I (q.v.), he failed to receive the combat experience he wanted and served instead as the commander of Camp Colt, a tank training center in Gettysburg, Pennsylvania. From 1922 to 1924, he was stationed in the Panama Canal Zone and came under the tutelage of Brigadier General Fox Conner. Conner recommended Eisenhower for the command and general staff school in Fort Leavenworth, Kansas, where he was graduated first in his class in 1926. He became an aide to General Douglas MacArthur (q.v.), and in 1933 went with MacArthur to the Philippines where he helped reorganize the republic's army. His relationship with MacArthur was nothing like his friendship with Conner. Late in life, Eisenhower said that "probably no one has had more, tougher fights with a senior than I had with MacArthur."

In March 1941, Eisenhower was promoted to colonel, and three months later he was named chief of staff of the Third Army. His rise up the army career ladder suddenly accelerated. After coming to the attention of General George C. Marshall (q.v.), the army chief of staff, Eisenhower was promoted to brigadier general and, after the Japanese attack on Pearl Harbor (q.v.), was transferred to the army's war plans division. In a few months, he was promoted again — this time to major general — and placed in charge of the operations division of the War Department. Marshall, who liked and trusted Eisenhower, decided in June 1942 to appoint him to be commander of all U.S. troops in Europe. One month later he won another promotion to lieutenant general and took command of Operation Torch, the Allied invasion of French North Africa.

It was his first assignment as a combat commander, and his lack of battlefield experience bothered other officers. To Sir Bernard Montgomery (q.v.), the British Eighth Army commander, Eisenhower seemed like "a very nice chap" who knew "nothing whatever about how to make war or to fight battles." The invasion of North Africa, and especially the American defeat at Kasserine Pass, revealed that some of the criticism of Eisenhower was justified. The early campaign, which lasted from November 1942 to March 1943, was poorly coordinated and badly implemented. On the battlefield, the Allied command structure was confused and inadequate. Eisenhower, who spent much of his time focusing on political and logistical problems, could not galvanize his forces.

But Ike learned quickly from the lessons of Tunisia. He was promoted to full general in February 1943, and in the summer he launched an Allied invasion of Sicily and in September an amphibious assault on the Italian mainland at Salerno. Thinking the risks too high, however, he called off an airborne operation intended to capture Rome. The invasion of Italy turned into a stalemate, with the Allied armies a long way from Rome. It also underscored how caution and uncertainty plagued Eisenhower in situations that called for audacity and decisiveness. For all his failures, though, Eisenhower had learned how to be a general.

In December 1943, he was appointed supreme commander of the Allied Expeditionary Forces, and he soon arrived in England to direct plans for an invasion of France across the English Channel. Eisenhower became the very real power behind Operation Overlord in nearly all its complicated aspects. His experience in Africa and Italy gave him the foundation for building and maintaining a massive coalition army. In preparing for D-Day (q.v.), Eisenhower demonstrated his true talent for diplomacy and for forging agreements among the Allied leadership.

But the stress of being the supreme commander, of always trying to remain optimistic in the face of what actually seemed to be impending disaster, took its toll on Eisenhower. His blood pressure soared, and his doctors worried that his hypertension was worsening. Their concern was well founded: he regularly smoked four packs of cigarettes and drank fifteen cups of coffee a day. "I seem to live on a network of high tension wires," he wrote to his wife.

In the campaigns that followed D-Day, Eisenhower wrestled with ambitious and contentious generals under his command. Montgomery hoped to be named the sole ground commander. Two American generals, George Patton (q.v.) and Omar Bradley (q.v.), could not abide Montgomery and sought to undercut his role in the campaign.

Particularly irksome to Eisenhower and the other American generals was Montgomery's slowness in the field. During the months following Normandy, Montgomery delayed before Caen and failed to take Antwerp and Arnhem. To make matters worse, Montgomery insisted that Eisenhower's strategy was faulty. Eisenhower had ordered the Allied forces to move along a broad front toward the Rhine, while Montgomery argued strenuously for a pencil-line thrust along a narrow front through Belgium and into the Ruhr. Eisenhower refused to waver.

Historians would later debate the merits of this strategy. Some scholars have argued, as did Montgomery after the war, that a narrow-front thrust into Belgium could have ended the war with Germany six months earlier, thus saving thousands of lives. Eisenhower resented such accusations and speculations, especially since victory over Germany ultimately proved to be more difficult — and took longer to achieve — than anyone in the Allied leadership had anticipated.

Other critics have also complained that Eisenhower failed to take Berlin and allowed the Soviets to gain possession of the valuable German capital. In Eisenhower's estimation, winning the race to Berlin might have fulfilled a political objective but it would have forfeited the aims of the Allied military policy — to make sure that a German defeat ended in unconditional surrender. A political challenge to the Soviets over who should rightly capture Berlin would, Eisenhower believed, prolong the war and damage the agreements already hammered out at Yalta by Franklin Roosevelt (q.v.), Joseph Stalin (q.v.), and Winston Churchill (q.v.).

Eisenhower was not a perfect general. His grasp of battlefield strategy and tactics was feeble at best, but his understanding of how a coalition army must function kept the Allied forces together and brought about the disintegration of the Third Reich. Over the course of the war, Eisenhower grew as his responsibilities increased; he learned from his mistakes, and he was able to control his personal shortcomings — such as his volatile temper — for the sake of sustaining unity and cohesion. Out of necessity, Eisenhower became a modern warrior — a general who waged war by managing the movement of large armies, coordinating large-scale campaigns, balancing the delicate relations in sensitive multilateral alliances, and keeping everyone focused on the final objective.

In November 1952, Eisenhower ran successfully as the Republican candidate for the U.S. presidency. As commander in chief, Eisenhower drew heavily and constructively on his experience as a military commander. Throughout his two terms as president, he succeeded in keeping the United States out of major conflicts. In July 1953, the new president negotiated a truce for the Korean War (q.v.). A year later, Eisenhower forged the Southeast Asia Treaty Organization (SEATO), an alliance aimed at thwarting the spread of Communism in that region. Accepting the division of Vietnam into two nations, North and South, the president kept the United States from becoming embroiled in the disputes over Indochina. His response to the Suez crisis, which effectively blunted the plans of Great Britain and France to invade Egypt, resulted in the Eisenhower Doctrine, which called for U.S. assistance in the Middle East against any Communist aggression. In summer 1958, during his second term, the president sent troops to Lebanon to keep the government out of leftist hands.

It was Communism, in fact, that drove much of the president's "New Look" foreign policy. The modern commander had become a cold warrior. As such, Eisenhower's military acumen enabled him to fight Communism at every turn, but to do so without bringing the world to the brink of destruction. Instead, he resorted to covert actions rather than overt military interventions, particularly in countries in which the Soviet Union seemed to be gaining influence and power. Eisenhower supported or approved several operations carried out by the Central Intelligence Agency in Iran (1953), Guatemala (1954), and Tibet (1959), and the plans for the Bay of Pigs invasion in Cuba. Yet he took no action when an uprising occurred in East Germany (1953) or when the Soviet Union invaded Hungary (1956). As commander in chief, Eisenhower knew which wars to stop and which ones to fight.

Despite the rising threat of Communism around the world and his firm resolve to prevent its expansion, Eisenhower did not embrace a national security policy based on military buildup or increased defense spending. It did no good, said Eisenhower, to fight Communism by turning the United States into a "garrison state." In his farewell address, he warned against such a future and the growth of "an immense military establishment." The nation, he said, "must guard against the acquisition of unwarranted influence, whether sought or unsought, by the military-industrial complex." When he retired to his farm in Gettysburg, Congress restored him to the rank of General of the Army.

GLENN LAFANTASIE

Stephen E. Ambrose, *Eisenhower: Soldier, General of the Army, President-Elect, 1890–1952* (1983); David Eisenhower, *Eisenhower: At War, 1943–1945* (1986); Dwight D. Eisenhower, *Crusade in Europe* (1948).

El Alamein, Battle of

October 23–November 4, 1942

The Battle of El Alamein marked the culmination of the North African campaign between the forces of the British Empire and the German-Italian army commanded in the field by Erwin Rommel (q.v.) in World War II (q.v.). Having taken Tobruk in June 1942, Rommel advanced into Egypt but had been checked and beaten at Alam Halfa in September; thereafter the initiative had passed.

Rommel mined and fortified a forty-mile line in considerable depth and strength — unusually, in a desert war, both flanks were sealed, by the Mediterranean in the north and by the Qattara Depression in the south. To break this line and destroy the Axis forces was the task of Bernard Montgomery (q.v.), commanding the British imperial forces. The battle would be a set-piece affair — there could be little opportunity for maneuver.

Rommel (on sick leave when the battle began but having personally planned the defense) commanded thirteen divisions and five hundred tanks, totaling about 100,000 men. Montgomery disposed of approximately double the number of tanks and men — an army of British, Australians, New Zealanders, Indians, and South Africans, together with some French and Greek units; Allied air superiority stood at about the same proportion. Battle began on October 23, and the result, after ten days of ferocious pounding, was complete Allied victory, although Rommel's army escaped annihilation and slipped away from an unenterprising pursuit.

El Alamein was a battle of World War I character — methodical, using massed artillery, with limited advances made good and counterattacks defeated until breakout. Its significance was great. The *Panzerarmee* withdrew, ultimately to Tunisia; within days of El Alamein, Anglo-American forces landed in Morocco. By May 1943 the campaign was over and the

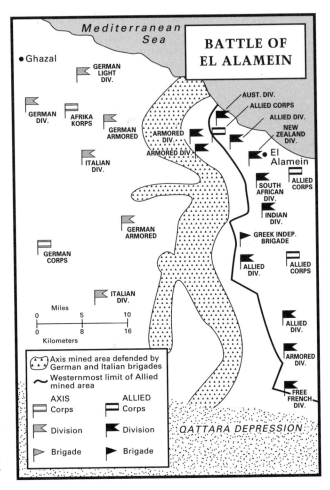

Mediterranean dominated by the Allies. Meanwhile, in Russia the Germans were suffering disaster at Stalingrad (q.v.): the two battles — Stalingrad and El Alamein — proved to be the watershed of the war against Germany.

GENERAL SIR DAVID FRASER

El Cid (Rodrigo Díaz)

1040?–1099, *Spanish Military Leader*

The Spanish epic hero Rodrigo Díaz was born in Vivar (to the north of Burgos). He was and still is more commonly referred to as El Cid, a title derived from the Arabic *sid*, meaning "lord." His exploits are most famously celebrated in the *Poema* or *Cantar de Mío Cid*, which in its surviving form was probably composed or written down in about 1207 (although there may well have been an earlier oral tradition, which came into existence after his death in Valencia in 1099). Another anonymous poem, the *Carmen Campidoctoris*, extolled his deeds during his lifetime, and within fifteen years of his death a cleric wrote the biographical *Historia Roderici*.

The Cid rose to favor during the reign of Sancho II of Castile (1065–1072), becoming the king's chief military commander. Sancho, however, was assassinated, being succeeded by his brother Alfonso VI (d. 1109) who grew increasingly jealous of Rodrigo's military prowess and fame.

Sent to collect tribute money from Muslim Seville in 1079, the Cid defeated its ruler and his Christian allies at the Battle of Cabra. Some of his captives were distinguished members of the Castilian court, and, falling out of favor, the Cid was exiled by the king and departed with his military retinue for eastern Spain. Though he remained loyal to Alfonso during his exile, he entered the service of the Muslim ruler of Zaragoza as a mercenary for five years, defeating and capturing the Christian count of Barcelona in a battle near Tamarite in 1082, and winning another victory somewhere on the lower valley of the Ebro against a combined Aragonese and Muslim army in 1084.

The arrival of powerful Almoravid armies from North Africa in 1086 led to a reconciliation between the Cid and Alfonso VI. After defeating the Catalans at Tévar in 1090 and temporarily checking their ambitions south of the Ebro River, the Cid turned his attention to Muslim Valencia. Systematically cutting off the city's supplies, he entered Valencia as its conqueror in June 1094. Immediately, however, he had to face the threat of a large Almoravid army, which he defeated in a remarkable victory in October at the Battle of Cuarte, using the classic ruse of a feint followed by an attack, and again at Bairen in 1096.

Although the loyal relationship between a lord or king and his vassal formed an important facet of the Cid's career, it is also clear that he was a professional mercenary motivated by an endless quest for money. During his harsh rule of Valencia, for example, he literally held its richest citizens to ransom.

The Cid died in his bed in Valencia in July 1099, and his body was subsequently returned to Castile for interment at the monastery of Cardeña. Inevitably, a cult and legends grew up. In the thirteenth-century *Estoria de Cardeña*, for example, the Cid's death was reportedly followed by the embalmment of his body, after which his armed and clothed corpse was taken on his famous charger Babieca to Castile. The legend that the dead Cid actually led his troops into victorious battle was an even later invention, graphically depicted by Charlton Heston in the film about the hero.

ANGUS MACKAY

Engineers/Pioneers/Sappers

Engineers are troops that specialize in using physical obstacles to slow down the enemy, removing similar obstacles that stand in the path of friendly units, and the ancient art of attacking and defending fortresses. As the skills and attitudes necessary for these tasks are essentially the same as those possessed by inventors, engineers have often proved far more innovative than their comrades in the infantry, cavalry, and artillery. Indeed, many of the weapons, devices, and techniques used by other branches of the service were either first employed by combat engineer units or, at the very least, designed by military engineers.

Though the attack and defense of fortresses date back to the beginnings of organized warfare, engineers are a relatively new type of soldier. The military classics of medieval Europe, as well as those of the ancient Chinese, Roman, Greek, Arab, and Persian civilizations, make much of the various machines ("engines") used in sieges and provide advice to the officers ("engineers") who supervised their construction and use. They make little mention, however, of the craftworkers and laborers who did the actual work. Indeed, the idea that these men were proper soldiers, rather than civilians who had been hired or impressed into temporary service, took a long time to develop. The notion that the men with the picks, shovels, and axes in their hands were themselves worthy of the title "engineer" took longer still.

In the late seventeenth century and throughout the course of the eighteenth century, permanent units of military engineers were first formed in European armies; engineer officers were generalists, highly educated men of science equally capable of designing fortresses, laying out new cities, casting cannon from the bells of captured towns, and mapping uncharted territories. The men who filled the ranks of eighteenth-century engineer units, on the other hand, were highly specialized. Pioneers, whose characteristic tool was the ax, created and cleared obstacles such as *abbatis* (fallen trees whose branches had been sharpened). Miners dug under the walls of fortifica-

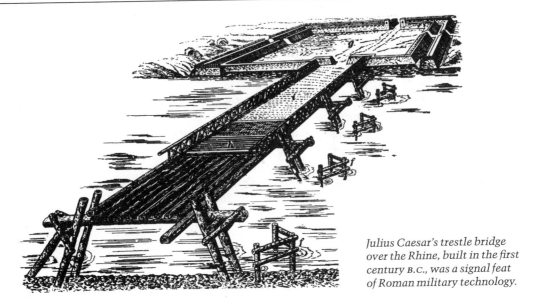

Julius Caesar's trestle bridge over the Rhine, built in the first century B.C., was a signal feat of Roman military technology.

tions, with the aim of either "undermining" those walls or placing an explosive charge. Those who dug open trenches (saps) were called sappers, whereas those who built improvised (pontoon) bridges became known as pontoniers.

The nineteenth century brought increased specialization. The military exploitation of railroads, the telegraph, balloons, electric power, and construction equipment was largely the work of engineers. As the engineers who dealt with these new machines tended to be formed into specialized units, this expansion created a distinction between the technicians serving in rear areas and the "combat engineers" who performed traditional duties at the front. This contrast was enhanced by the replacement of sappers, pioneers, pontoniers, and miners with a single type of combat engineer, a soldier who was expected to be able to fell a tree, set an explosive charge, drain a marsh, or build a bridge with equal facility.

The Russo-Japanese War (1904–1905) (q.v.), a conflict whose central campaign on land was the struggle for the Russian fortress of Port Arthur, saw a vast increase in the repertoire of engineers. New or revived devices such as barbed wire, the hand grenade, trench mortar, and improved explosives required a soldier who combined the traditional skills of the engineer with the ability to use (or overcome) these new weapons in close combat. The German army paid particular attention to these innovations. "Fortress pioneers" (*Festungspioniere*), as they were called, came to form a permanent part of many ar-

mies by the end of World War I (q.v.). The fighting techniques developed by the assault engineers of World War I, moreover, became part and parcel of the infantry tactics of all but the most backward twentieth-century armies. Though the spectacular breakthroughs of 1940 — Eben Emael, Dinant, Monthermé, and Sedan (q.v.) — were led by assault engineers, their most common task during World War II (q.v.) was the clearing of fields that other engineers had sown with land mines. This was sometimes done by tanks, such as the "funnies" of the British Seventy-ninth Armored Division (equipped with giant flails, plows, or rollers), or by robots, such as the German "Goliath." Most of the time, however, the painstaking and dangerous work of locating and digging up containers filled with high explosives was done by hand.

In both world wars, the combat engineers of most armies were greatly outnumbered by those who did engineering work behind the lines. Some of these undertakings, such as the building of the Alaska-Canada Highway in 1941 or the maintenance of the European railroad networks during World War I, were hard to distinguish from civilian projects. Others, such as the construction of the Atlantic Wall in German-occupied France between 1942 and 1944, or the enormous Soviet effort involved in erecting a thick belt of minefields and tank traps around the Kursk (q.v.) salient in 1943, had a purely military character.

Only a minority of the people involved in rear-area military engineering served in the armed forces sponsoring the work, and these soldiers, sailors, and airmen, moreover, tended to be skilled technicians. The vast majority of workers, men and women who wielded picks and shovels rather than slide rules or bulldozers, were unfortunates who worked under some form of compulsion. During World War I, for example, poverty induced scores of thousands of Asian laborers to go to France to build the vast infrastructure of trench warfare. During World War II, the Germans, Japanese, and Soviets used armies of slave laborers — political prisoners, conscripted civilians, and prisoners of war — for construction projects such as the famous "Bridge over the River Kwai."

In the many wars that were fought in the half-century after World War II, modern construction techniques greatly reduced the role of manual laborers in military engineering. (The vast underground fortresses built at the behest of the Vietnamese Communists form the most prominent exception.) As yet, however, no mechanical substitute has been found for the combat engineer. Indeed, with the proliferation of land mines around the world, combat engineers often find that they have much work to do long after the last shots have been fired.

BRUCE I. GUDMUNDSSON

Paul W. Thompson, *Engineers in Battle* (1942).

English Civil Wars

1642–1646, 1648, 1650–1651

The civil wars of seventeenth-century England also involved the two other kingdoms ruled by the Stuart dynasty, Scotland and Ireland. The invasion of England by a Scottish army seeking religious concessions in 1639 and again in 1640 precipitated political deadlock in London, which paved the way for a rebellion by Catholic Ireland (October 1641). The struggle between King Charles I and his Westminster Parliament over who should control the army needed to crush the Irish insurrection in turn provoked the outbreak of civil war in England (August 1642). Initially northern and western England, together with much of Ireland, stood for the king, while the southeast (including London), the Royal Navy, and Scotland fought for Parliament. However, at Marston Moor (July 2, 1644) Charles lost control of the north; and the following year, at Naseby (June 14, 1645) the Parliamentary forces led by Oliver Cromwell (q.v.) routed his main field army.

Having won the war, Parliament failed to secure a satisfactory peace settlement, enabling the king to mobilize an army of disaffected Scots. Cromwell quickly defeated this force at the Battle of Preston (August 17–20, 1648), and, determined to bring "Charles Stuart, that man of blood, to an account for that blood he had shed, and mischief he had done . . . in these poor nations," the victorious army took control of Parliament and, in January 1649, had Charles I executed.

Having pacified all England, Parliament turned to the conquest of Ireland and Scotland. Since 1642 the Catholic Confederation of Kilkenny had controlled Irish affairs and periodically aided Charles. However, any chance of rekindling the Royalist cause in Ireland ended in September 1649, when Oliver Cromwell massacred the combined force of Irish Confederates and Royalists at Drogheda and, the following month, captured the Confederate fleet in Wexford.

The Cromwellian reconquest of Ireland dragged on until the fall of Galway in April 1652 because of the outbreak of the third English Civil War. Early in 1650, Charles II, son and heir of the executed Charles I, cobbled together an army of English and Scottish Royalists, which prompted Cromwell to invade Scotland;

at the Battle of Dunbar (September 3, 1650) he won control of most of Scotland. The following year at Worcester (September 3, 1651) Cromwell shattered the remaining Royalist forces and ended the "wars of the three kingdoms."

The English conflict left some 34,000 Parliamentarians and 50,000 Royalists dead, while at least 100,000 men and women died from war-related diseases, bringing the total death toll caused by the three civil wars in England to almost 200,000. More died in Scotland, and far more in Ireland. Moreover, the trial and execution of an anointed sovereign and the presence of a standing army throughout the 1650s, combined with the proliferation of radical religious sects, shook the very foundations of British society and ultimately facilitated the restoration of Charles II in 1660. This was the last civil war fought on English — though not Irish and Scottish — soil.

JANE H. OHLMEYER

J. P. Kenyon, *The Civil Wars of England* (1988).

Espionage

Espionage, usually defined as the illegal acquisition of information about an individual, group, or organization, has been called the second oldest profession. There are two types of espionage: The first is human intelligence, which involves sending spies into a group or country or suborning individuals working for a target group or nation. A second, long-established type of espionage, cryptology, involves intercepting coded or ciphered messages and decoding them.

Perhaps the oldest example of human intelligence operations, allegedly based on God's advice, was Moses' decision to send secret agents "to spy out the land of Canaan." Cryptology also proved useful before the modern era — the deciphering of several messages in 1628 allowed France's Cardinal Richelieu to prevent the English navy from coming to the aid of the Huguenot bastion of La Rochelle. In the U.S. Civil War (q.v.), both sides practiced the traditional forms of espionage; Union forces explored the possible advantages of balloon reconnaissance.

But espionage would change drastically as the result of the technological advances of the late nineteenth and early twentieth centuries — particularly Guglielmo Marconi's development of radio (see *Communications Technology, Military*) and the Wright brothers' invention of the airplane.

Those advances were evident in World War I (q.v.). Of course, traditional human intelligence operations remained important; the British train-watching network in Belgium provided valuable intelligence on German troop movements. But the use of radio by military organizations meant that those communications could be intercepted by the enemy simply by placing an antenna in the right place. Thus, the German victory at Tannenberg in 1914 (q.v.) was aided by the interception of Russian messages. Meanwhile, Britain, Germany, and Russia all found communications intelligence important in conducting naval operations. Britain benefited from the acquisition of three codebooks seized from German ships (see *Jutland, Battle of*). Most dramatically, Britain intercepted a telegram containing German foreign minister Arthur Zimmermann's proposal of a Mexican-German alliance that would lead to Mexico's recovery of the southwestern United States. This telegram helped coax the United States into the war before it was too late for His Majesty's forces.

Aircraft carrying either observers or cameras monitored and reported on troop movements early in World War I. When the conflict settled into one of trench warfare, the planes photographed trench systems and gun emplacements, and spied on the arrival of new troops.

During World War II (q.v.), individual agents and networks made significant contributions — particularly Soviet spies in Germany, Japan, and Britain. The grayness of the Soviet regime stood in sharp contrast to the flamboyant lifestyles of some of its best agents, such as Richard Sorge in Tokyo and Kim Philby in Britain. At the same time, the British succeeded in turning the entire German spy network in Britain into a vehicle for disinformation.

The war also illustrated the growing role of technology in espionage activities. The dramatic advances in the sophistication of coding and ciphering devices was often matched by the advances in deciphering technology. Britain's ability to read German communications enciphered with the sophisticated Enigma machine (thought by its users to be totally secure) represented the most important intelligence coup of the war and paid significant dividends in the Battle of the North Atlantic (q.v.).

Aerial reconnaissance units owed much to the vision and initiative of Theodor Rowel of Germany and

Sidney Cotton of Britain, who established special squadrons for aerial reconnaissance. British photographic aircraft played a crucial role in assessing the impact of bombing raids, monitoring fleet movements, and spotting the facilities associated with the V-2 terror weapon.

But perhaps the most dramatic change in espionage that occurred in World War II was that it clearly became part of a larger field — intelligence (q.v.). The need for information about an enemy nation's social life, domestic politics, leadership, economics, as well as its military capabilities and plans, resulted in the creation of organizations that relied on the products of espionage as well as newspapers, magazines, radio broadcast transcripts, and other open material to broaden the intelligence enterprise.

The transition from hot war to cold war among the superpowers stimulated the growth of intelligence and espionage activities (see *Cold War*). On occasion, spies had dramatic effects on world events. Colonel Oleg Penkovsky, who spied for the CIA and the British, provided the United States with key information on Soviet missiles that proved critical during the Cuban missile crisis; the information acquired by Israeli agents Eli Cohen and Wolfgang Lotz on Egyptian and Syrian weapons systems and tactics significantly aided Israeli forces during the Six-Day War in 1967 (see *Arab-Israeli Wars*).

Technological developments in the 1950s and particularly the 1960s revolutionized the nature of espionage. First, the U-2 spy plane allowed the United States a deep look into Soviet territory and helped dispel the fear of a bomber gap. Subsequently, the satellites developed by both superpowers allowed continual monitoring of each other's military activities, as well as those conducted elsewhere in the world.

The 1970s and 1980s brought technological developments such as the SR-71 spy plane, capable of flying at over 2,100 miles per hour, and the KH-11 satellite, able to detect objects as small as six inches in size from about 150 miles in space and to send those images back to earth instantaneously. In addition, the United States deployed several satellites to intercept foreign communications and radar signals, and telemetry from missile tests. Advanced Soviet imaging and signals intelligence satellites followed the American ones.

Such developments helped break down the barriers between "strategic intelligence" — used to support national leaders — and "tactical intelligence" — used to support military commanders. Satellites that returned images in film capsules (all did so prior to 1976) provided vital information on other nations' military programs but did not allow an up-to-date assessment of battlefield conditions. But satellites that could return images instantaneously could provide intelligence relevant to an ongoing battle. By the time of the Gulf War (q.v.) in 1991, the United States was able to employ an extensive network of instantaneous imaging and signals intelligence satellites to monitor the battlefield, along with a variety of intelligence aircraft. At the same time, human intelligence sources provided valuable information about potential targets for coalition aircraft.

The continuing possibility of military conflict ensures that human and technological espionage will not fade away.

JEFFREY T. RICHELSON

David Kahn, *Hitler's Spies: German Military Intelligence in World War II* (1978); Jeffrey T. Richelson, *A Century of Spies: Intelligence in the Twentieth Century* (1995).

Ethiopian War

October 1935–May 1936

The Italian-Ethiopian War began on October 3, 1935, when an invading army of 100,000 Italian and Eritrean troops crossed the Mareb River separating Italian Eritrea from Ethiopia, a proud African empire that had never been colonized by Europeans. Benito Mussolini (q.v.), the Italian dictator, ordered the invasion in order to consolidate Italy's empire in the Horn of Africa and to avenge the humiliating defeat of an earlier Italian invasion force at Adowa (March 1, 1896). Mussolini expected the war to be very short, for his forces were far better trained and equipped than the Ethiopian armies under Emperor Haile Selassie. Yet it took the Italians seven months to complete their invasion with the conquest of Ethiopia's capital, Addis Ababa, in May 1936. Rome's control over Ethiopia lasted only five years; in May 1941, a British army drove the Italians out and restored Haile Selassie to his throne.

As the last effort by a European power to build a colonial empire in the Third World, Italy's conquest of Ethiopia was one of the most brutal campaigns in the history of modern warfare. Frustrated by the slow pace of the invasion, Italian forces resorted to terror tactics, including the bombing of undefended villages and the widespread use of poison gas. The war also had momentous political consequences. It pointed up the ineffectiveness of the League of Nations, which responded weakly to the appeal of Ethiopia, a member state, for help against the aggressor. Yet even the mild sanctions that Geneva imposed on Rome estranged Mussolini from Britain and France and pushed him toward his fateful alliance with Nazi Germany. This bloody colonial conflict was therefore an important milestone on the road leading toward World War II (q.v.).

DAVID CLAY LARGE

Ethnic Cleansing

"Ethnic cleansing" is a new euphemism for the expulsion of racial groups, generally but not always minorities, who are feared or despised, whose property is coveted, or whose rule is resented. They are dispatched through harassment, rape (q.v.), police or military violence, mass roundups, murder, or all of these. Such outrages are conducted on populations seen as alien or "other." Jews, Armenians, and Kurds are historically the best-known victims, although the practice was also common in sub-Saharan Africa.

Since every occasion of "ethnic cleansing" differs, each deserves and in modern times usually receives its own name. Such terms are often designed to conceal rather than to reveal, depending on whether they have been assigned by the perpetrators or the victims. Adolf Hitler's (q.v.) "final solution" was the term applied by the Nazi bureaucratic apparatus for what a Polish-Jewish researcher in America almost simultaneously described, in a new coinage, as "genocide" (q.v.). Armenians still call their mass expulsion from the crumbling Ottoman Empire "the massacres," a term rejected by Turks to this day. The classical euphemism "put to the sword" for the mass murder of a conquered people is as old as the Roman destruction of Carthage in 146 B.C.

The term *ethnic cleansing* is primarily associated with the disintegration of the nation of Yugoslavia in violence after 1990. The practice was adopted principally by the dominant Serbs to segregate by civil terror and military force the ethnic populations of the successor states of the former Yugoslavia within their "appropriate" territories. The main difference among these peoples is religion; language and culture had been relatively homogeneous under Communist rule.

Although the most notorious example is the eviction by Serbs of hundreds of thousands of Muslims from their homes in Bosnia-Herzegovina, Catholic Croatians began the practice on a smaller scale in July 1991 by forcing Orthodox Serbs out of Croatia; there were more mass expulsions of Serbs and massacres of Bosnian Muslims in 1995. The practice gained inadvertent sanction by Germany's speedy recognition of Croatia as an independent state before it had guaranteed minority rights. In Bosnia-Herzegovina, the Serbs represented one-third of the population but quickly gained the upper hand against the Muslim majority with arms supplied mainly by the government of neighboring Serbia, based in Belgrade. Villages were shelled and attacked, and a deliberate policy of rape was used by Serbs to terrorize Muslim women into fleeing with their families, thus creating Serbian villages. In the early part of the campaign, men and women alike were put into concentration camps for systematic beating, rape, and execution.

Like the "final solution," the phrase "ethnic cleansing" itself appears to be of totalitarian origin. Slobodan Milosevic, the Serbian Communist leader, used the term "ethnically clean" in April 1987, in accusing Albanians of trying to force minority Serbs from Kosovo (q.v.), a battle site with a crucial role in Serbian nationalist lore. The phrase has also been traced to the former Soviet Union, where in 1988 Armenians and Azerbaijanis tried to force each other out of the enclave of Nagorno-Karabakh in an operation that Soviet officials described variously as *etnicheskie chistki* — "ethnic purges" and *etnicheskoye chishcheniye* — "ethnic cleansing." The phrase first appeared in English in a Reuters dispatch on July 31, 1991, quoting Croatia's Supreme Council as accusing the Serbs of expelling Croats from the border areas of Croatia with the aim of "the ethnic cleansing of the critical areas . . . to be annexed to Serbia." The phrase was also used by the Bosnian foreign minister in 1993, lamenting that the world had stood aside from both the disintegration of Yugoslavia and the Nazi atrocities of the 1930s.

LAWRENCE MALKIN

F

Fabius Maximus Cunctator ("The Delayer")

d. 203 B.C., *Roman Dictator*

Respected scion of a noble Roman family, Fabius was elected to the extraordinary office of dictator in 217 B.C., following Hannibal's (q.v.) stunning victories early in the Second Punic War (see *Punic Wars*). Realizing that Hannibal's strengths were battlefield brilliance, mobility, and the psychological and economic impact of his presence in Italy on Rome's allies, Fabius dogged Hannibal's tracks but refused battle. This prevented Carthaginian troops from dispersing and plundering, thereby pressuring Hannibal's mercenary army while limiting the war's effect on Rome's Italian allies. Despite frequent setbacks and recurrent criticism by political enemies, Fabius's conservative strategy paid off: the core of Rome's confederacy held firm.

Later in the war, Fabius was apparently blinded by his own successes. He employed constitutional maneuvers in an unsuccessful attempt to stymie bolder strategic initiatives by Scipio Africanus (q.v.). Yet Fabius deserved both his nickname and Rome's thanks: his delaying tactics saved Rome from losing a war and preserved the manpower resources necessary to win it.

George Washington (q.v.) was later nicknamed "the American Fabius." The deeply conservative "Delayer" might have been surprised to find his name borrowed by progressive British socialists, who founded the Fabian Society in 1884.

JOSIAH OBER

Falkenhayn, Erich von

1861–1922, *German General*

Commissioned into a line regiment, Erich von Falkenhayn served with the German military mis-

sion in China, from which his dispatches during the Boxer Rebellion (q.v.) caught the kaiser's attention. Imperial favor led to rapid promotion until Falkenhayn became Prussian war minister in July 1913. On September 14, 1914, six weeks after the outbreak of World War I (q.v.), he succeeded Helmuth Karl von Moltke (q.v.) as chief of the General Staff. After directing the bloody "race to the sea" in the west that ended in stalemate, Falkenhayn in 1915 strove for victory in the east and supervised the German breakthrough at Gorlice-Tarnów and the defeat of Serbia. His hopes for a separate peace with Russia were not shared by the German government, however, and as a result, Falkenhayn opted for a strategy of attrition: against France along the Meuse, and against Britain through submarine warfare.

Falkenhayn's name is forever associated with Verdun (q.v.), where he ordered a German assault designed to "bleed white" the French armies — but it was not to be. The "Meuse mill" ground up French and German forces alike. A British assault across the Somme (q.v.) in July 1916, another grinding man-consumer, sealed Falkenhayn's fate: on August 28, 1916, he was replaced. Not even a brilliant operation against Romania late in 1916 could salvage Falkenhayn's reputation.

HOLGER H. HERWIG

Falkland Islands, Battle for the

April 2–June 14, 1982

In perhaps the final military action of Britain's four centuries of imperial history, a formidable British force was sent across more than eight thousand miles of ocean to retake its sparsely settled colonial possessions in the South Atlantic — the Falkland Islands and their Antarctic dependencies — after their occupation by seaborne troops from nearby Argentina, which had claimed sovereignty.

Parliament in London voted to dispatch a task force to the region within hours of receiving news in early April 1982 that a substantial Argentine force had landed on what its leadership called Las Islas Malvinas and had expelled the British governor and commander in chief, and a small party of Royal Marines.

The subsequent action, which commenced with the recapture of the Dependency of South Georgia on April 25, involved the deployment of two aircraft carriers and numerous destroyers (two were sunk), frigates (two sunk), submarines, other naval and supply vessels (including the ocean liner QE2), and naval aircraft. Seventeen Royal Air Force squadrons, one commando brigade, and one infantry brigade also took part.

The opposing Argentine forces — mostly conscripts — were well dug in by the time of the first engagements on the Falkland Islands proper; they were supplied by ships, naval bases, and air bases less than two hundred miles away, on the Patagonian mainland. However, many of the troops were young and poorly trained, and their morale was unusually low (poor food and intolerably bad winter weather contributed to their lack of fighting spirit).

British forces were landed some eighty miles away from the colonial capital, Port Stanley, and walked — or "yomped," a word that subsequently entered the English vocabulary — across the freezing moorlands to engage in brief but bitter battles. Port Stanley was eventually entered by British troops on June 13, and the formal surrender was taken the next day.

The little war, which briefly fascinated the entire world — "like two bald men fighting over a comb," commented the Argentine writer Jorge Luis Borges — cost 255 British and at least 652 Argentine lives. It led to reforms in the design of the Royal Navy's vessels, which had shown themselves unexpectedly vulnerable to fire following missile attacks, and to a new consideration of supply problems in remote rural environments, which proved a near-fatal flaw in British tactics, causing some artillery detachments to run down to their last few shells.

There is still considerable friction over the Falklands — but despite renewed Argentine agitation for talks about the still-disputed sovereignty issue, the islands are not the subject of substantive discussion and remain under British rule, with a large and costly British resident military presence to prevent any recurrence of the events of 1982.

SIMON WINCHESTER

Farragut, David G.

1801–1870, American Civil War Naval Officer

David G. Farragut, a nautical Ulysses S. Grant (q.v.), operated with fixed purpose and flexible tactics. The Tennessee-born officer was rescued from desk service by his foster brother, David D. Porter, to command the 1862 New Orleans expedition. After Porter's mortar fleet failed to subdue Forts Jackson and St. Philip, Farragut led his wooden vessels past the guns, hastening the capitulation of New Orleans (April 28) and closing the lower Mississippi. Throughout early 1863, Farragut was an unhappy partner in federal designs against Port Hudson. An attempt to run these guns on March 14 failed; for it he employed the somewhat novel tactic of lashing smaller gunboats to the unengaged side of his saltwater warships to power them through. When the fort surrendered (July 9), Farragut targeted Mobile. His fleet fought its way into Mobile Bay on August 5, 1864, in what he described as "one of the fiercest naval contests on record." Farragut, directing operations from his flagship's maintop platform, ordered his vessel into an area of the bay he knew to be seeded with underwater explosives (usually encased in wood or tin, they are today referred to as mines, but were then called torpedoes). The command Farragut gave on that day has entered legend as "Damn the torpedos! Full speed ahead!" His victory contributed greatly to Abraham Lincoln's (q.v.) reelection. Farragut was the first to hold the U.S. ranks of rear admiral, vice admiral, and admiral.

NOAH ANDRE TRUDEAU

Feeding Armed Forces

Soldiers, sailors, and airmen must be fed before they can fight; in a day-to-day sense, food is more essential to armed forces than ammunition. The provision of food is a major matter of concern to logisticians, although armies in the past have also supplied their own food on the march by living off the country in one manner or another (see *Logistics*).

Food is not simply a matter of survival — it is also a part of culture, and different forces have eaten different foods prepared in different manners consistent with the agriculture, economies, and values of the regions that gave them birth. In western Europe, wheat bread was long the staple food of armies. Roman soldiers consumed between $1\frac{1}{2}$ and 2 pounds of bread or biscuit daily. As punishment, commissaries issued to soldiers barley instead of wheat, since barley was considered to be animal food. The diet of the Roman soldier also included meat, poultry, cheese, vegetables, and olive oil. Pork was a special favorite. In the seventeenth century, regulations set the daily food allowance for a European infantryman at $1\frac{1}{2}$ to 2 pounds of bread (made of wheat and rye), $\frac{1}{2}$ pound of meat, and 1 pint of wine or 1 pot of beer or cider — whichever was the local drink. By the end of the eighteenth century, blocks of dried, pressed vegetables were added to the normal fare.

One of the key advances in the evolution of modern military administration was the greater care that states took in feeding their troops. This was symbolized by the creation of permanent magazines for the storage of grain and other foodstuffs in the seventeenth century. Beginning in the seventeenth century, field armies brought along their own field ovens to produce the bread they needed, since the local facilities found en route were most often inadequate. From these ovens, well-regulated trains of wagons brought the bread to the troops. The actual work of stockpiling essentials and preparing and transporting rations, however, was often left to private contractors. For most armies, uniformed personnel did not take over the daily provision of food until the nineteenth century.

Soldiers drew bread rations; sailors managed on hardtack, which could be stowed for long periods on shipboard. Bread became inedible after eight days in dry cool weather, and sooner when it was damp or particularly hot; but hard biscuit, since it contained no moisture, was nearly eternal. However, biscuit was less palatable than bread, and it was more expensive because it required more fuel to cook it into its bricklike state. For Mediterranean galleys and Atlantic men-of-war alike, biscuit served as the essential fuel for humans. In addition to hardtack, sailors ate salted meats, which could also survive long voyages, although weevils and maggots often infested foodstuffs. In the late eighteenth century, citrus fruit or juice was added to the sailor's diet to ward off scurvy.

Navies accepted the full responsibility of feeding their men long before army administrators did so, since on shipboard sailors could not forage.

In Europe, religious dietary restrictions did not complicate the feeding of armed forces, but in other parts of the world, the type and preparation of food were wrapped up in religious practice and taboos. Nowhere was this more the case than in India. Dietary restrictions concerning the animal fat used to seal cartridges in India are said to have contributed to the outbreak of the mutiny in 1857 (q.v.), since Muslims regarded it as sinful to bite cartridges smeared with pork fat, and Hindus those with beef fat. Not only were there dietary taboos, but also sepoys (q.v.) generally cooked for themselves, since there were caste restrictions on who could cook for whom, and contact with eating or drinking vessels by those considered impure or improper rendered the utensils polluted.

Industrial progress brought great changes in feeding armed forces, as prepackaged rations such as canned foods made their first appearance during the nineteenth century. Napoleon (q.v.) even offered a prize for developing canned meat for his troops. Refrigeration later played a great role in preserving food for sailors, although its use is more limited for land campaigns.

U.S. armed forces have traditionally expected high food standards. Even during the American Civil War (q.v.), soldiers received coffee and sugar as rations, items that in Europe were regarded as luxuries. On the other hand, European soldiers and sailors drew alcoholic beverages that were not given to the American troops. The tendency for elaborate rations continues in the current Meals Ready to Eat, or MREs; still, soldiers in the field can become less than fond of these. In contrast, troops from other cultures have often been able to subsist on the most meager diets and have taken pride in it. Spartan (q.v.) food was purposely simple and unappetizing; Zulu (q.v.) marched rapidly with each man carrying only his weapons and a sack of corn; and the Viet Cong could get along for some time on little more than rice balls.

Although it might be tempting to imitate simplicity in rations, it would be a mistake to fail to meet a soldier's or sailor's expectations of food, for it is one of the foundations of morale. Historically, troops fed poorly, either in absolute terms or measured by their own standards, have turned to marauding or have mutinied (see *Looting/Plunder/Booty* and *Mutiny*).

Certainly this was an endemic problem in early modern Europe, and one of the grievances of French troops during the 1917 mutinies was the quality, if not the quantity, of food.

It can also be argued that the way in which soldiers eat can influence morale. Eating together in small mess groups has often been a conscious or unconscious method of fostering small group cohesion. The Roman *contubernium*, the Spanish *camarada*, and the French *ordinaire* were mess groups that served as fundamental units in military life. Differences in style of food and eating often separate officers from enlisted men. In early modern European armies, officers often tried to maintain a style of cuisine close to elite civilian standards. Louis XIV (q.v.) even tried to limit the number of courses at officers' tables, because culinary competition among officers proved expensive and inefficient. Some contrasts in standards of eating still exist; whereas modern U.S. army officers eat the same rations in much the same conditions as their soldiers, naval officers enjoy meals in wardrooms staffed with waiters.

JOHN A. LYNN

John A. Lynn, *Feeding Mars* (1993); Martin van Creveld, *Supplying War* (1977).

Feudalism

So many theories, revisions, and counterrevisions have been proposed to explain the term *feudalism* that it has become like Potter Stewart's definition of pornography: we may not know what it is, but we know it when we see it. Some, taking a broad definition of feudalism, have seen it everywhere from ancient Egypt to the American South. Others, using a narrow definition, have seen feudalism only in medieval western Europe, Japan of the shoguns, and, possibly, nineteenth-century Ethiopia. A very strict definition is required for the term to have any real meaning or for a discussion of it to have any coherence.

Feudalism in this narrow sense is based on the historical reality of the area between the Loire and Rhine Rivers during the tenth and eleventh centuries. From this heartland feudalism spread to western Germany, parts of Italy and Spain, and above all, England. It is only by analogy that the term applies to other societies, such as that of Japan. Feudalism was essentially the extreme privatization of the government functions of defense, administration, and justice. The mechanism for putting these functions into private hands and paying for them was the fief, usually an estate with dependent peasants to work it, granted to the holder, or vassal, by a lord, or seigneur, in return for military service. The fief could sometimes be a cash payment, hence our word *fee*. In either case the fief was central to the concept of feudalism, the term itself coming from *feudum*, the medieval Latin word for "fief." Having parceled out land, the right of command (the *ban*), and considerable military force, the only thing that could prevent total anarchy was an interlocking series of oaths tying all vassals to their lords in a contract of mutual protection and cooperation. Theoretically at least, all vassals had a lord, except for the king, the ultimate lord.

Several historical factors account for this development. After the death of Charlemagne (q.v.), during the ninth century Carolingian governance broke down in a series of vicious civil wars, leaving the realm prey to devastating attacks from Vikings (q.v.), Magyars (q.v.), and Saracens that lasted through the tenth century. Under these blows the economy was so disrupted that Carolingian rulers had little means to pay for defense, or anything else. Defense from hit-and-run attacks had to be local in any case, and power began to pass into the hands of local nobles who could provide the people under their care with protection and justice.

During the tenth century these nobles increasingly relied on heavily armored horsemen to provide the protection. The expense of such an arm was enormous. It takes about 120 hours of skilled labor to construct a coat of mail (hauberk) and up to 200 hours to produce a sword. To support men armed with hauberk, shield, helmet, sword, and lance required specially bred and trained horses, and each cavalryman would need several of these expensive beasts. The skill to handle horse and arms in combat demanded intensive training from childhood. ("He who has stayed at school till the age of twelve and never ridden a horse is fit only to be a priest" was the medieval assessment.) The most powerful lords needed many cavalry men, and the answer to providing for them was the fief, an estate with peasants numerous enough to provide for at least one armored horseman. In return for the fief the horseman swore an oath of homage and fealty to his lord, thus becoming his vassal. Possessing the wealth necessary to fight in this style elevated the status of the cavalryman so that he became a member of a military and social elite, a true "knight."

If the knight was the blood of the system, the castle (q.v.) was the skeleton. Local fortifications (q.v.) were expensive, and by the early eleventh century a major feature of medieval warfare. The typical military operation was the siege (q.v.), not the cavalry charge. Consequently the lord who held a castle was powerful, whereas the great counts and dukes who controlled many such lords were so powerful that they could usually ignore their own lord, the king.

Such a system is generally seen pejoratively as barely controlled anarchy or a large-scale protection racket. Yet it provided the armed might to protect the still-fragile civilization of Europe and to throw the Muslims out of Sicily and Spain, seize the Holy Land, and begin the drive against the Slavs in the East. The long process of restoring public power, moreover, involved considerable give-and-take between monarchs and their most powerful vassals. The carefully modulated oaths that required the lord, even the king, to respect the privileges and rights of his vassals did much to shape the development of the modern European state, in which a sovereign's power is restricted by law. In this sense the Magna Carta is a very "feudal" document.

Strengths are also apparent in Japanese feudalism, the closest analogy to the European model. As imperial government declined after the ninth century, power devolved to a class of warriors, the samurai (retainers) (q.v.). Like European vassals, samurai owed allegiance to their daimyo (lord), not to the central government. In return the daimyo provided his samurai with land, status, and protection. By the sixteenth century the daimyos used their powerful armies and strong castles to become independent rulers of autonomous states. When united under the Tokugawa Shogunate in 1603, the samurai governed the country and imposed their own chivalric ethos on much of Japanese society. Japanese feudalism thus provided the strength necessary for Japan to fend off foreign rule until it could be modernized by the Meiji Restoration in 1867.

This sketch of European feudalism is something of a caricature: recognizable, but simplified and exaggerated. No one living during the so-called Age of Feudalism used the term, nor would recognize what we mean by it. The idea of a universal "system" is simply a modern construct meant to help us understand a complex society whose worldview was alien to ours.

Even theoretically, feudalism involved only the aristocracy. At all times major elements of society had little to do with our concept of the feudal. These included peasants of every degree of status, townspeople and merchants who always played an underrated role, and members of the church. Even among the warrior aristocracy holding fiefs, family was probably of overwhelming importance. Even that most feudal of rulers, William the Conqueror (q.v.), relied on kinsmen, most notably his half brother and a pair of cousins, as his most trusted lieutenants. Their loyalty owed as much to blood as to fiefs and oaths. Within the realm of warfare — the raison d'être of feudalism — infantry, engineers, and mercenaries played important roles throughout the Middle Ages. Although elements of feudalism lasted until the French Revolution (q.v.), by the end of the thirteenth century feudal institutions had lost whatever predominance they once had.

W. SCOTT JESSEE

Marc Bloch, *Feudal Society* (1964); Elizabeth A. R. Brown, "The Tyranny of a Construct: Feudalism and Historians of Medieval Europe," *American Historical Review* (1974): 1063–1088; Archibald R. Lewis, *Knights and Samurai: Feudalism in Northern France and Japan* (1974); Jean-Pierre Poly and Eric Bournazel, *The Feudal Transformation: 900–1200* (1991).

Fisher, John Arbuthnot "Jackie"

1841–1920, Admiral and Naval Reformer

Jackie Fisher, first Baron Fisher of Kilverstone, was born in Ceylon, the son of an English planter. He joined the navy in 1854, was made captain in 1874, and reached flag rank in 1890. Fisher served as commander of the Royal Navy's gunnery school (1883–1886), director of naval ordnance (DNO) (1886–1891), superintendent of the Portsmouth Dockyard (1891–1892), third sea lord and controller (1892–1897), commander of the North America and West Indies station (1897), commander of the Mediterranean Fleet (1897–1901), second sea lord (1902–1903), commander of the Portsmouth Dockyard (1903–1904), first sea lord (1904–1910 and 1914–1915), and chairman of the Board of Invention and Research (1915–1918).

While at the gunnery school and as DNO, Fisher was involved with the development of breech-loading big-guns, quick-firing guns, and naval range finders. As third sea lord and controller, he invented the destroyer and encouraged the introduction of water-tube boilers. As second sea lord, he reformed naval education. As first sea lord, Fisher changed the management of the dockyards, the manning system, gunnery training, the warship reserve, and the distribution of the fleet. These initiatives concentrated the main strength of the Royal Navy in home waters, increased the navy's ability to mobilize its full strength rapidly and fight more effectively in case of a short war, and produced large reductions in naval spending.

The Fisher administration also introduced the first all-big-gun battleship, HMS *Dreadnought*, and built additional units of similar design that laid the foundations for an all-dreadnought battle fleet. Ironically, Fisher opposed the building of *Dreadnought* and its successors. What he actually wanted, for a variety of strategic, tactical, technical, and financial reasons, was to replace the conventional battleship and armored cruiser with a navy based on the battle cruiser and submarine. Submarines were meant to prevent invasion, which would free battle cruiser squadrons, whose deployments were to be coordinated and controlled by the new wireless, to sweep the seas of enemy commerce raiders, and to defend outlying colonies from hostile battle fleets. Fisher's efforts to implement his radical strategy were defeated, but not before he had secured the construction of large numbers of battle cruisers and submarines, fostered the development of improved gunnery matériel and oil propulsion, and influenced the strategic thinking of many senior officials, including that of Winston Churchill (q.v.).

The radicalism of Fisher's strategic, tactical, and technical views, and the ruthlessness of his leadership, produced serious discord within the navy, which drove him from office in 1910. His opposition to the formation of an effective naval staff weakened the organization of the navy's leadership, which was to have serious consequences during World War I (q.v.). He made crucial mistakes over procurement of advanced methods of aiming naval artillery that compromised his battle cruiser scheme, which in turn contributed to the loss of three British battle cruisers at the Battle of Jutland (q.v.) in 1916. And Fisher's resignation over the Dardanelles campaign in 1915 (after his return to the Admiralty for a second term as service chief) precipitated a general reconstruction of the government that, among other things, forced Churchill out of office as first lord of the Admiralty. Fisher's successes were nonetheless remarkable, and

his impact on naval policy greater than that of any contemporary.

JON SUMIDA

Foch, Ferdinand

1851–1929, French General

Ferdinand Foch was the most inspired of the Western Front generals in World War I (q.v.), sometimes to his detriment. He could be almost mystically reckless with lives, initiating attacks when restraint would have served him better or prolonging offensives beyond all hope of success. His own pronouncements had a tendency to catch up with him. Fortunately for his permanent reputation, he will be remembered more for his presiding role in the victory of 1918 than for his sanction of the futile hecatombs of 1915 and 1916.

He was born in 1851, the son of a civil servant. In the summer of 1870, during the Franco-Prussian War (q.v.), he enlisted as a private in the French infantry but never fought. (But he did gain peacetime fame for massing 100,000 men at a review in a rectangle of 120 by 100 meters.) He rose steadily in rank and in 1885 became a professor at the École Supérieure de Guerre, the command college in Paris that he would eventually head. He was now in his element, and his pronouncements would influence a generation of French officers, as well as the opening events of 1914. Foch wrote two widely read paeans to the offensive, *The Principles of War* (1903) and *The Conduct of War* (1905). "A lost battle," he proclaimed, "is a battle which one believes lost. . . . A battle won is a battle we will not acknowledge to be lost. . . . The will to conquer sweeps all before it. . . . Great results in war are due to the commander." In argument, Foch tended to win by intimidation and deliberate arrogance — irresistible, perhaps, because he never admitted to doubts.

August 1914 found him in command of a crack, two-division corps on the Lorraine border. While his disciples disastrously pressed *offense à outrance*, the apostle of attack soon found himself on the defensive. At Morhange on August 20, the rocklike stand of his Twentieth Corps helped avert a French catastrophe. It may have been the only time in his life — he was just short of sixty-three — that he saw action. Put in charge of the French Ninth Army during the Battle of the Marne (q.v.), he blocked the German advance at the marshes of St.-Gond. "My right is driven in, my center is giving way, the situation is excellent, I attack," he is supposed to have said. He probably never uttered these legendary words, but he surely would have done so had he thought of them.

Foch next took charge of the French armies of the north; he now coordinated moves with the British and Belgian armies during the so-called "race to the sea." If he did not succeed in going on the offensive, he did help check the German drive for the last true prizes of 1914, the Channel ports. Several times he was forced to brace up the nervous British commander, Sir John French (q.v.), with what his biographer, B. H. Liddell Hart (q.v.) calls "an injection of Fochian serum." But when the Germans ruptured the line at the Second Ypres (q.v.) in 1915, Foch's insistence on counterattacks produced only unnecessary Allied losses. Death on an even larger scale was the most visible result of Foch's Artois offensives in the spring and early fall of the year; casualties approached 150,000. After the Artois the *élan* of the French common soldier, which he so prized, would never be the same.

In 1916, he directed the French part of the 141-day offensive at the Somme (q.v.). He gained more territory and lost fewer men than his British opposite, General Sir Douglas Haig (q.v.), but the costly lack of a decision seemed to have permanently tarnished his career. Foch was relieved of command. He bided his time, a perfervid phoenix waiting to soar from the ashes, and gradually worked his way back to a position of influence. He had the good fortune not to have played a part in the Allied disasters of 1917.

On March 21, 1918, Erich Ludendorff's (q.v.) German armies broke through on the Western Front (see *Ludendorff Offensive*) and seemed ready to split the French and British armies asunder. Desperate prospects demanded desperate measures — and on March 26 the Allied leaders did what they should have done long before: they named a supreme commander. Their choice was Foch. His reaction was characteristic. "Materially, I do not see that victory is possible. Morally, I am certain that we shall gain it." Foch's optimism was infectious. He unselfishly lent French troops to the beleaguered British, and the Allies weathered Ludendorff's unremitting spring storm until American troops began to arrive in significant numbers. By midsummer the worst German threat was over. Henceforth, as Liddell Hart writes, "Foch beat a tattoo on the German front, a series of rapid blows at different points, each broken off as soon as its initial impetus waned."

By the late fall, the German army was on the point of disintegration. Foch felt that the war had gone on long enough. On November 8–11, 1918, in a railway carriage at a forest siding near Compiègne, he personally dictated armistice terms to a German delegation. At last, but not too late, he had learned when to stop.

ROBERT COWLEY

Fontenoy, Battle of

June 25, 841

During wars over the inheritance of Charlemagne's (q.v.) empire, his grandsons Charles the Bald and Louis the German defeated their elder brother Emperor Lothar I at Fontenoy near Auxerre in central France. After one wing of Lothar's army broke and fled, the rest of his forces withdrew with heavy losses. The exact number of combatants cannot be determined, but forces from every region of the Frankish Empire took part.

Defeat at Fontenoy ended Lothar's chance to impose his rule on a united Frankish Empire. He eventually was forced to divide the realm with his brothers, accepting the Treaty of Verdun in 843. After the civil war, the Frankish aristocracy likewise split into regional groups.

Tactics at Fontenoy foreshadowed later medieval practices, such as mutually agreeing on a battle site, avoiding combat on holy days, and treating battle as a ritual "Judgment of God." As in later conflicts, actual adherence to such customs had more to do with the military and political objectives of the combatants than with religious feeling or a lack of military capability.

EDWARD J. SCHOENFELD

Force/Violence

Obviously fundamental features of human life, force and violence have nevertheless proved very difficult to interpret and understand. There are two sets of problems. One is whether forcible or violent behavior, and hence by extension the making of war, is a natural, perhaps genetically determined, human characteristic. The other is exactly what role force and violence have played in the development of human societies, particularly as compared to economic and social influences. The simple fact is that the development of Western civilization has been propelled to a very large degree by war.

That genetic endowment is at the root of certain

violent behavior is now beyond doubt. But such behaviors are increasingly understood as being relatively constrained both by environmental factors and by the logic of cost and benefit. For example, many animal species use violence to defend territory or create hierarchies; such violence, however, usually ceases once the immediate aim has been achieved or the cost of the attempt becomes too high.

Some anthropologists argue that similar restraints on the use of force existed in some primitive human societies; but what seems to distinguish the human employment of violence is the lack of such restraints, particularly once the state begins to organize it. Carl von Clausewitz (q.v.) noted that the "natural tendency" of conflict was to "approach its abstract concept" (i.e., the pure use of force) or in today's terms, to escalate, and much of his work is devoted to how political means must be used to restrain it in the waging of war.

History was once little more than a recital of feats of arms. Since the eighteenth century, however, the primary role attributed to force and violence has been gradually undermined, most significantly by the recognition of economic factors. Adam Smith did not attempt to present a monocausal analysis of the development of society and agreed that force had a place, although he did not specify what it was. But when Karl Marx attempted to explain all human history and action through economic mechanisms, he created a set of still-controversial intellectual problems.

Because the admission of any autonomous role for force necessarily vitiates economic determinism, Marxists have sought, first, to explain how conflictive phenomena can be determined by, and emerge from, economic processes that are stipulated to be noncoerced, and second, to reveal how even patent examples of autonomous violence, such as enslavement and imperialism, are at base economic. Friedrich Engels attempted these tasks in *Anti-Dühring* (1894). The German philosopher Karl Eugen Dühring had pointed out that, without a sword, Robinson Crusoe could never have enslaved his man Friday, and argued that violence must therefore be considered an independent factor in the creation of oppression. Engels's intricate counterargument shows at most that economic interests often direct the employment of violence, but he does not rule out its use for other noneconomic purposes. The debate, however, made Dühring's approach, tagged "the idealism of violence," a recognized heresy within Marxism. Independently strengthening the tendency among analysts to minimize the role of force and violence as independent historical factors has been the stress, characteristic of modern French historiography and ultimately inspired by sociology, on vast ecological, demographic, and economic processes as the drivers of history.

Fascist theories, with their exaltation of force, clearly suggest a conviction that force and violence are independent historical factors capable of overriding social, economic, and other influences. The same is true of the practice of communist power seizures (as opposed to their self-justifications) and of terrorism (q.v.) and insurgency, which although often rationalized in economic and other terms, in fact rely ultimately on violence.

New approaches are suggested by sociobiology (which has undermined anthropology's premise that human cultures and behaviors are potentially of infinite diversity, and therefore that the use of force might be no more than an optional, culturally conditioned choice) and by the development of rational choice theory (which accounts for those aspects of war that seem most irrational — escalation out of proportion to goals, for example, or attrition — rather as economists account for consumer behavior by looking at the play of perfectly plausible sets of human preferences). These developments are matched, in historical writing, by a renewed attention to force and violence. The new approach, moreover, increasingly resembles that of biologists and ethologists: the status of force as an independent variable is accepted, while the constraints of context and environment are explored. Still imponderable, however, are the roles of human imagination and will, which, equipped with the means to coerce, look likely to remain wild cards of history (see *Militarism*).

ARTHUR WALDRON

Jo Groebel and Roberta A. Hinde, eds., *Aggression and War: Their Biological and Social Bases* (1989).

Fortifications

Although the first defenses built by humans to protect themselves from their enemies were surely temporary, the earliest extant archaeological evidence concerns permanent works. Archaeologists date stone walls and towers at Jericho (q.v.), clearly built to repel

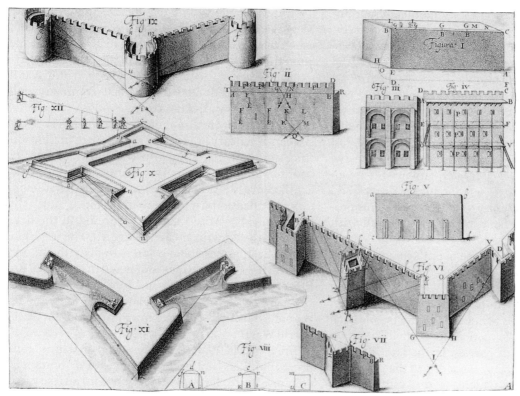

This illustration from Matthaes Dögen's L'Architecture militaire *(1647) shows the evolution in Europe from the vertical defenses of the Middle Ages to the low-lying bastion first developed in Italy in the early sixteenth century — the* trace italienne.

human assailants, to about 8000 or 7000 B.C. By late Neolithic times, settlements of stone or mud brick in the Fertile Crescent were built with the outermost dwellings joined together to form a defensive perimeter, the rooftops serving as observation and firing platforms similar to those of Native American pueblos in the southwestern United States. By historical times, cities were routinely surrounded by walls of stone or brick sufficiently high to discourage escalade, topped by a walkway or fighting platform and supported by towers projecting above and forward of the wall to cover it with defensive fire. The walkway was shielded by an outer wall, crenellated, or notched, to provide cover for observation and missile fire, and often featured overhanging galleries from which projectiles and unpleasant substances could be dropped or poured on an enemy below. Ditches gave the wall greater height and made the approach to it more difficult. So close was the relationship between fortifications and civilization that the Chinese characters for *wall* and *city* are the same.

Permanent linear defenses also appeared in antiquity, the most famous being Hadrian's Wall and the Antonine Wall of Roman Britain and the Great Wall of China. Some of these, notably the Great Wall of China for much of its length, were normally used not to stop attackers outright, but to channel their movements. Similar, though less massive, defenses called *letzi* were used by the Swiss to control access to populated valleys. Armies on the march defended their camps with ditches and earthen ramparts, often topped with timber palisades and firing towers. Roman legionaries were renowned for their industrious work with spade, mattock, and axe; fortified Roman camps were famous for their size and sophistication, and some formed the nucleus of later cities.

Forts and cities protected by Roman stone walls remained after the fall of Rome, but many in the West were abandoned. The collapse of Charlemagne's (q.v.) empire in the ninth century saw the emergence of a decentralized political and economic system based on local chieftains' strongholds, generally timber palisades atop earthen mounds. This type of fortification, closely associated with the rise of feudalism (q.v.), reached a peak of sophistication in the motte and bailey fortress of the eleventh century, with a high conical keep for the lord and his retinue and an outer enceinte, or bailey, for lesser retainers.

Motte and bailey castles in economically peripheral areas were progressively abandoned, and surviving examples were replaced by permanent stone castles with an inner keep and high curtain walls and round corner towers surrounded by a wet or dry moat. The entry way, an obvious point of vulnerability, was protected by gate, drawbridge, portcullis, and outer works, which became increasingly elaborate with time. Walls and towers grew progressively higher, and sophisticated provisions were made for the defensive firepower of crossbows and, later, gunpowder weapons. Machicolations, overhanging stone galleries, and hoardings, their temporary wooden equivalent, provided platforms to defend the base of the wall with dropped objects and missile fire.

The development in Europe of efficient siege artillery and the explosive, subterranean mine turned the medieval castle's strengths into weaknesses: unobserved "dead space" at the bases of round towers represented opportunity for gunners and miners, and high walls brought down by cannon fire filled the ditch with rubble for assault parties. In the late fifteenth century Italian engineers responded to the challenge with earthen ramparts, which absorbed cannon balls; with walls and towers cut down in height, protected from escalade by a ditch and from battery by a raised outer slope, or glacis, swept by defensive cannon and harquebus fire; and with the *trace italienne* plan, which featured projecting angular bastions of "arrowhead" shape with straight walls, swept by artillery firing in enfilade from protected casemates. (Interestingly, the Japanese developed the angle bastion independently.) Progressively reinforced with outlying ravelins, hornworks, and crownworks by Dutch and French engineers, the *trace italienne* fortress with stone-clad earthen ramparts and sunken profile set the standard for permanent fortress design from about 1500. In the eighteenth century it was challenged by "vertical" systems, which employed layers of heavily casemated guns piled several stories high to drive the enemy back with sheer firepower.

Both systems were rendered obsolete overnight by heavy rifled siege guns in the 1860s and gave way to works of reinforced concrete, sunk in the earth and defended by steel-armored gun ports and turrets. These were made obsolete in turn — or so it seemed — by highly explosive, armor-piercing shells in the early days of World War I (q.v.) and gave way to trenches, bunkers, and other semipermanent earthworks protected by barbed wire entanglements. The lesson was reinforced by the presumed failure of the Maginot line in 1940, but in fact, pronouncements of the demise of reinforced concrete fortifications were premature. These proved a useful means of magnifying the power of the tactical defense in World War II (q.v.) and are used today for strategic command-and-control centers and ballistic missile silos.

The advent of effective gunpowder weaponry in the sixteenth century produced a renaissance in field fortification that culminated in the elaborate lines of countervallation and circumvallation of formal eighteenth-century European sieges. Thereafter, temporary fortifications waned in importance until the rifled musket forced infantry to ground in the final stages of the American Civil War (q.v.). The tendency of European professional soldiers to deny the importance of field fortifications foundered in the face of fire from breech-loading rifles, machine guns, and quickfire artillery in the Russo-Japanese War (q.v.) and received a terminal setback from the same forces in World War I.

Since World War II, cannon- and machine gun–armed bunkers and pillboxes of earth or reinforced concrete with overhead protection from artillery fire, connected by communications trenches and protected by minefields and barbed wire (in static operations) and foxholes and quickly scraped out and sandbagged shelters for men and vehicles (in mobile warfare) — all carefully camouflaged, at least when built by professionals — have been a constant feature of land warfare and are likely to remain so for the indefinite future.

JOHN F. GUILMARTIN

Christopher Duffy, *Siege Warfare: The Fortress in the Early Modern World, 1494–1660* (1979); Anthony Kemp, *The Maginot Line: Myth and Reality* (1982); Charles W. C. Oman, "Fortification (1100–1300)," in *A History of the Art of War in the Middle Ages*, vol. 1 (1924).

Franco-Prussian War

1870–1871

The first war fought by a united Germany and the last by an imperial France, the Franco-Prussian War created the European order that would last until World War I (q.v.); drastically altered the way most states raised, trained, and equipped their armies; and was largely responsible for the spread of an ideal of military professionalism that is still very much in evidence around the world. Ostensibly fought over the issue of whether the German prince Leopold von Hohenzollern would be permitted to accept the vacant throne of Spain, the Franco-Prussian War was really a dispute about German unification.

Led by the brilliant Helmuth Karl von Moltke (q.v.), the fast-moving Germans managed, within seven weeks of starting to mobilize their armies (July 16, 1870), to force the personal capitulation of Emperor Napoleon III as well as the surrender of the bulk of the French forces in the field at the first Battle of Sedan (September 2, 1870) (q.v.). In this short campaign, soldiers on both sides displayed similar degrees of courage and self-sacrifice. However, French efforts were marred by indecision at the highest levels, failure to concentrate forces, mutual jealousy among corps commanders, and gross inefficiency in the fields of transport and supply. The German armies, on the other hand, benefited from rapid and efficient mobilization, a faultless railroad deployment, and a spirit of cooperation that caused commanders at all levels to take bold measures in the service of common purposes.

Although the loss of the main French army caused the demise of the Second Empire, it did not end the war, for the newly created Third Republic decided to continue fighting. The second phase of the war consisted largely of a German siege of Paris, the beating back of French attempts to relieve the capital, the taking of a number of French fortresses (such as Metz and Strasbourg), and considerable activity on the part of *francs tireurs* (French guerrillas) behind German lines. The fighting between the Germans and the French ended with the surrender of Paris on January 28, 1871. A few weeks later a long-feared revolt erupted in the French capital — the Paris Commune — and the Franco-Prussian War gave way to a short but bloody French civil war.

The lesson drawn by most governments from the Franco-Prussian War was the efficacy of the German way of warfare. As a result, most of the world's armies began to imitate, with varying degrees of success, German uniforms, equipment, administration, military literature, organization, and training. This enthusiasm for methods that promised swift and decisive victory was so great, in fact, that most observers forgot that the initial German victory, though swift, had been far from decisive and that the French Republic was only brought to terms because it was less afraid of the Germans outside the gates of Paris than of the revolutionaries within.

BRUCE I. GUDMUNDSSON

Michael Howard, *The Franco-Prussian War* (1989); Dennis E. Showalter, *Railroads and Rifles* (1975).

Frederick II (the Great)

1712–1786, King of Prussia

Frederick II of Prussia ranks simultaneously as one of history's greatest and most misunderstood captains. He is best presented as a master of war limited in arms, conduct, and effects. Some restraints on warfare were military. Eighteenth-century societies could generate neither the human nor the material surpluses necessary to wage sustained war on a large scale. Eighteenth-century governments possessed neither the power nor the legitimacy to mobilize even the resources theoretically available to them. Eighteenth-century armies were high-cost, complex institutions whose men and equipment were essentially nonreplaceable assets.

Other restrictions on warfare were political. Most accounts of European international relations in this period stress the balance of power: the invisible hand that kept any state from getting too far ahead of its neighbors. Yet the balance of power was intended to prevent empire rather than preserve peace. Nor did it guarantee the position of lesser players. Alliances were intended for expansion and acquisition as well as security. Prussia, "a mollusk without a shell," was spread in fragments from the Rhine to the Memel and was a correspondingly obvious target in an international system clearly suffering from structural tensions likely to destabilize it.

Frederick II seemed ill-equipped to cope with the challenges facing him when he assumed the throne in 1740. Years of bitter feuding with his father, Frederick William I, had given him vaulting ambitions. To date, however, the new king had done little beyond compose theoretical treatises on statecraft. The death of Austrian emperor Charles VI was for Frederick an opportunity. The Prussian king legitimately expected the Hapsburg Empire, now ruled by the young, inexperienced Maria Theresa, to be challenged on all of its frontiers by all of its neighbors. In such a context Prussia must become either hammer or anvil. To stand aside was to invite Brandenburg's fate in the

Thirty Years' War (q.v.): ravaged by all, respected by none. War, moreover, offered a tempting prize. The Austrian province of Silesia possessed human and material resources that, properly utilized, would enable Prussia to become a European power of the first rank.

This achievement would depend heavily, if not entirely, on the army — and an army of a particular kind. Prussia's army was trained and organized to maximize its efficiency under existing conditions of warfare. In an age when battles were decided by the firepower of linear formations, and victory was completed by cavalry charges, Prussian infantry could deliver more rounds per minute than any of its European counterparts. Prussian cavalry could strike harder, rally more completely, and appear more quickly where needed than any other horsemen on the Continent. Frederick's battalions could change from columns of march into lines of battle so rapidly that the process seemed almost magical. The famous oblique order, with one flank of the army weighted heavily and echeloned forward to roll up the enemy, depended as much on quickness of deployment on the field as on prebattle planning (see *Leuthen, Battle of*). The Prussian army, ready for war from a standing start, should have been able to secure Silesia and hold it against all comers while Frederick legitimized his state's new status by negotiations.

This plan determined the course of Prussian policy for over two decades because it proved such a spectacular miscalculation. On the surface, all went well. Silesia was quickly overrun. From Mollwitz in 1741 to Hohenfriedeberg in 1745, the Prussian army established itself as the master of central Europe's battlefields. Frederick was still learning the craft of generalship — he left the field of Mollwitz during the fighting. Prussia's king, however, displayed the diplomatic virtuosity of a riverboat gambler, making and abrogating treaties, concluding and abandoning alliances with breathtaking audacity. Yet Austria and its empress, Maria Theresa, remained unreconciled to the new status quo. The king's behavior created enough mistrust among his neighbors that by 1756, France, Russia, and Austria formed a grand alliance whose major aim was, if not to destroy Prussia completely, then to reduce it permanently to the status of a middle-ranking German state. By 1756 Frederick stood alone in a sea of enemies, his only support a British connection that never became more than a relationship of convenience.

Frederick initiated the Seven Years' War (q.v.) with exactly the same assumptions that had shaped his behavior in 1740. By striking first, he hoped to win battlefield victories decisive enough to encourage his adversaries to negotiate a durable peace. The history of the war is the history of that strategy's failure. Between 1756 and 1763, Frederick confirmed his reputation as one of history's great battle captains. His oblique order decided the Battle of Leuthen (1757) but was less important than the king's use of combined arms tactics (Rossbach, 1757), his ability to recover from the shock of defeat (Kolin, 1757; Kunersdorf, 1759), and not least the Prussian army's own formidable fighting power. Frederick might have been a misanthrope, but his repeated condemnations of his army's rank and file were balanced again and again by public recognition such as restoring the swords of a previously disgraced regiment after its performance at Leignitz (1760). Frederick shared the hardships of campaign and the risks of battle without fanfare. If he was not beloved in the fashion of Robert E. Lee (q.v.), he was respected as a man and a general.

For all Frederick's triumphs in the field, political success eluded him. If Prussia's armies were seldom outfought, they were defeated often enough to keep the anti-Prussian coalition in the field despite its increasing internal conflicts.

The indecisive nature of the Seven Years' War reflected to a degree the nature of eighteenth-century armies. Armed forces tend to learn from each other, copying and adapting behaviors and techniques. Nothing essential to Frederick's way of war was inherently unique to Prussia. The Austrians, the Russians, and even the French were able to overhaul their military systems to a point where Frederick's undoubted gifts as strategist and commander could do no more than force a long endgame against superior forces. Prussia was ultimately saved from defeat, perhaps destruction, less by the military genius of its ruler than by the death of Russia's Empress Catherine and her temporary replacement by the Prussophilic Peter III. Once Russia left the war, the remaining combatants collapsed from mutual exhaustion.

This outcome confirmed Frederick's essential goal. From the beginning of his reign, he had sought not to overturn the European system but to secure Prussia's place as an accepted major player in that system. In the second half of his reign, Frederick sought aggrandizement in the context of the great power relationships established after the Peace of Hubertusberg in

1763. By the Bavarian succession crisis of 1778–1779, indeed, Prussia's king emerged as an elder statesman, sustaining a German and European order apparently threatened by the vaulting ambitions of Austria's young emperor, Joseph II.

After 1763 the Prussian army functioned as a strategic deterrent. Its purpose was less to wage war than to demonstrate Frederick's readiness and capacity to make war when necessary. The parades, the maneuvers, the mythology that developed around Prussia's great battles — all were designed to highlight the risks of trying conclusions with Old Fritz and his faithful grenadiers. The deterrent of the army proved successful for twenty years after the king's death. Even then it required the ambition and the genius of Napoleon (q.v.) to challenge it. Frederick the Great did not transcend his milieu either as soldier or as statesman. Nevertheless, by establishing Prussia as a great power and by encouraging the definition of such status in military terms, he decisively shaped the next two centuries of Europe's history.

DENNIS E. SHOWALTER

Christopher Duffy, *Frederick the Great: A Military Life* (1985).

French and Indian War

See Seven Years' War.

French, John

1852–1925, *British World War I field Marshal*

John Denton Pinkstone French's unorthodox early career may explain some of his later difficulty in commanding the British Expeditionary Force (BEF) in 1914–1915. He began by training for the navy, but transferred to the Suffolk artillery militia in 1870, and then transferred again to the cavalry in 1874. By these unusual means, French joined the regular army. At the start of the Boer War (q.v.) in 1899, French's talents fitted the old-fashioned cavalry opportunities of the campaign. Clearing the Cape Province of Boers in 1899, French led the relief of Kimberley.

The Boer War made French's reputation and led to increasingly senior staff positions, culminating in promotion to field marshal in 1913. Along the way, French's career had been assisted by various influential officers, including Douglas Haig (q.v.), who saved

him from bankruptcy. This protective system helped French, for despite his resignation from the army in 1914 over Irish home rule, he was appointed to command the BEF in the same year. In France, during the BEF's retreat in 1914, French's personality proved vulnerable under pressure and swung sharply between optimism and pessimism. Initially, French acted aggressively, but he became discouraged after Mons and advocated taking the BEF out of the line. He was dissuaded by Horatio Kitchener's (q.v.) intervention. Then, at Le Cateau, Horace Lockwood Smith-Dorrien's Second Corps successfully stood fast, in opposition to French's orders (French never forgave this and later dismissed Smith-Dorrien.) finally, at first Ypres (q.v.) in late 1914, French at first issued attack orders, but again became pessimistic and once more wished to take the BEF out of the line; this time he was dissuaded by Ferdinand Foch (q.v.).

With the line stabilized in 1915, a series of stalled BEF offensives led to doubts about French's competence. False stories about his handling of the reserves at Loos led to his dismissal in late 1915. Subsequently, French commanded the Home Forces and then became lord lieutenant of Ireland. Despite recent attempts to give French's strategic thought some coherency, he must be judged as unfit to command at the highest level.

TIM TRAVERS

French Revolution, Wars of the

1792–1799

Although revolution struck France in 1789, the Wars of the French Revolution actually began with a French declaration of war on April 20, 1792. After the French let the armed genie out of the bottle, it did not really return to safe confinement until 1815; however, the era of the revolutionary wars proper lasted only until General Napoleon Bonaparte (q.v.) seized power by coup on November 9, 1799. The most important and interesting campaigns of this many-faceted struggle were those fought to defend and extend the Revolution (1792–1794), Bonaparte's Italian campaign (1796–1797), and his expedition to Egypt (1798–1799).

The French began the war badly, with embarrassing reverses; however, at Valmy (September 20, 1792) (q.v.) the French turned back a Prussian invasion and launched a period of conquest. French general Charles-François Dumouriez defeated the Austrians at Jemappes (November 6, 1792) and chased them from what is today Belgium, while other French forces seized much of the Rhineland. But after weathering this first crisis, the army disintegrated during the following winter, and in 1793 the Austrians and their Prussian and English allies regained what they had lost in the previous year. Yet French victories at Hondschoote, Wattignies, Kaiserslautern, and Fröschwiller in the fall stabilized the line and bought time. Spring and summer campaigns in 1794 pushed the allies back on all fronts; the key Battle of fleurus (June 26, 1794) won back the Austrian Netherlands for France. The French went forward to occupy the Dutch Netherlands, the Rhineland, and parts of Italy as well in 1795.

The fortunes of war influenced the onset and decline of the most radical period of the Revolution, the Reign of Terror, which was to a large degree a response to the military crisis. A month after French victory at fleurus, the radical Maximilien Robespierre went to the guillotine, and the Revolution shifted back toward the center.

The French triumphed because they created a new kind of army, driven by a new spirit. At the start of the war, the French fielded not only the old regiments of the royal army, but also new battalions of the Volunteers of 1791 and the Volunteers of 1792. Some of the latter were compelled to enroll, but most were genuine volunteers, inspired by a love of their country and a desire to preserve their revolution. By 1793 the flood of volunteers did not provide sufficient manpower, and the French turned to outright conscription. In August of that year the government decreed a *levée en masse,* which ordered young men ages eighteen to twenty-five to the front, while enlisting the labor of other able-bodied men, women, and children in the war effort. This provided the classic example of a nation-in-arms. The revolutionary army now climbed to one million men, at least on paper, dwarfing any preceding army in history.

Although not all of France rallied behind the new regime, the army of the Revolution displayed real patriotic devotion. Officered by talented commoners and filled with a rank and file who could be expected to show enthusiasm and initiative in the field, the army proved its superiority over the mechanically trained armies it faced. Many have concluded that the French simply overwhelmed their enemies by sheer numbers and employed crude "horde" tactics. In fact, the French did not always possess the advantage in numbers, and rather than simply rushing at their foes, the French developed a flexible tactical system incorporating line, column, and skirmishers backed by mobile artillery that could adjust the style of fighting to ground and circumstance better than the tactical systems of their opponents could. Although doubtless the rapidly trained revolutionary levies could not match Prussian or English regulars in formal drill, battles were not won by the side with the neatest alignment.

Benefiting from the new soldiers, spirit, and tactics created by the revolution, Napoleon Bonaparte added his own genius to demonstrate the full potential of French arms in Italy in 1796. This young general, only twenty-six years old when he took command, transformed a small, badly supplied army into conquerors. Driving a wedge between the Piedmontese and their Austrian allies, he separated the two and forced the Piedmontese out of the war. Then he turned on the Austrians and drove them east with a series of brilliant flanking maneuvers and hard-fought battles. The Austrians held tenaciously to Mantua and sent armies to its relief through the summer, the fall, and into the winter. The fortress finally capitulated on February 2 and freed Bonaparte to advance into Austrian territory, where his success led the Austrians to conclude the Peace of Leoben, on his terms, in April 1797.

Having driven one enemy from the war, the victorious Bonaparte next hatched a romantic but ill-considered scheme to weaken another by threatening British colonial possession of India by seizing Egypt. His army of about thirty-six thousand troops began landing near Alexandria on July 1, 1798. He took the city the next day and marched up the Nile to confront the Mamluks at the Battle of the Pyramids on July 21, a victory that won him all of Egypt. However, Horatio Nelson (q.v.) smashed the French fleet at the Battle of the Nile on August 1, which effectively isolated the French in Egypt. When Bonaparte attempted to march north into Syria in February and March, the French wave of conquest broke upon the walls of Acre, which Bonaparte failed to take. After returning to Egypt, he defeated a Turkish army at Abukir, but he realized that his gamble had been lost militarily. Still, he might cash in on the political capital he had won by victories in Italy and Egypt, so he embarked for France on August 24.

When Bonaparte arrived, he found the army transformed from a loyal supporter of the government into a force that could be mobilized for a coup against the corrupt politicians in Paris. When he used regiments under his command to purge the revolutionary councils, the final casualty of the Wars of the French Revolution became the revolutionary government itself.

JOHN A. LYNN

Jean-Paul Bertaud, *The Army of the French Revolution*, trans. R. R. Palmer (1988); John A. Lynn, *The Bayonets of the Republic* (1984).

French Wars of Religion

See Religion, French Wars of.

Friendly Fire

"Friendly fire," an ironic term for casualties in combat inflicted by one's own armed forces, has been a constant feature of warfare. It became a political and organizational issue only in the twentieth century, principally in the armed forces of western Europe, Canada, and the United States. Operating under media scrutiny and dependent upon public support, these military establishments cannot ignore the phenomenon of "fratricide" or "amicicide." Friendly fire is a serious problem: estimates of such casualties run from a low of 2 percent of all casualties to more plausible highs of 10–15 percent of all combat casualties. Friendly fire incidents are especially demoralizing since they destroy confidence in one's own comrades, commanders, and supporting arms.

The heat of battle has always created problems in distinguishing between the enemy and one's own forces. When battles were fought in classical and medieval times, distinctive insignia and tight formations simplified killing the right people, but arrows and thrown spears surely did not discriminate when launched into a melee. In some struggles, mounted knights trampled their own bowmen and men-at-arms. The introduction of firearms complicated identification problems by adding dense smoke and opening distances between the combatants. Artillery, even fired at short distances at visible targets, could kill friendly infantry when foot soldiers joined in close combat; such an incident occurred among British troops at the Battle of Guilford Courthouse in the American Revolution (1781) (q.v.). In the American

Civil War (q.v.), Confederate infantry killed Generals "Stonewall" Jackson (1863) (q.v.) and Micah Jenkins (1864), mistaking their mounted staffs for Union cavalry.

The revolution in weaponry in the twentieth century made friendly fire more likely and more destructive. Foot soldiers could still kill their comrades through error in battle or (more likely) in nighttime mistakes in security and patrolling operations, but the chief culprits became field and antiaircraft artillery, and aircraft, especially those attacking ground targets. Also, warships shot down friendly aircraft, and aircraft destroyed friendly aircraft; these problems led to the development of electronic transponders that communicated identification-friend-or-foe (IFF) signals. Tanks and other armored fighting vehicles, lacking adequate observation capacity, added to the sources of danger. The whole art of fire support coordination developed not only to inflict damage on the enemy, but also to prevent friendly fire. The fielding of automatic geographic-position-sensing devices from the 1980s onward through satellite communications should reduce friendly fire casualties that occur through position misreporting. Nevertheless, the use of infrared sights, hypervelocity munitions, terminal-guidance systems, and whole groups of standoff weapons that depend on electronic target identification increases the potential for accidental deaths.

The experience of the American armed forces reveals the changing dimensions of the problem. Artillery barrages that fell on friendly infantry units were commonplace in World War I (q.v.). Although artillery forward observers improved this situation in World War II (q.v.), the far greater involvement of aircraft made matters worse. U.S. Navy ships shot down twenty-three transports and killed about one hundred paratroopers in the invasion of Sicily (June 1943); bombers of the U.S. Army Air Forces made two major bombing errors in the Normandy campaign (July 1944) and killed over six hundred American soldiers, including the highest ranking U.S. casualty of World War II, Lieutenant General Leslie J. McNair. In the war with Japan, artillery, naval gunfire, and airplanes killed marines and soldiers in relatively small numbers in almost every operation. U.S. Navy ships sometimes destroyed fighters of their own combat air patrols, but the development of fighter-direction techniques reduced these incidents late in the war. Friendly fire incidents plagued subsequent operations in Korea (q.v.) and Vietnam (q.v.), especially (in the latter conflict) attacks by armed helicopters. One of the worst incidents in Korea occurred when U.S. Air Force aircraft attacked and killed or wounded seventy-six British soldiers (August 1950).

The Gulf War of 1990–1991 (q.v.) again proved the persistence of the friendly fire problem. Of the 146 coalition troops killed in combat, 35 died in friendly fire incidents; of 467 wounded, 72 fell in such incidents. In April 1994, two air force fighters shot down two army helicopters over the Kurdish enclave in northern Iraq and killed 26 crew and passengers.

The friendly fire issue raises the longstanding dilemma of reconciling realistic training of troops with concern for safety. Some armed forces do not consider this a problem; the pre-1945 German army and the Soviet armed forces conducted field training notorious for resulting in casualties. In the United States, training deaths are controversial and taken seriously; between 1988 and 1995, 170 service personnel have died in combat and over 4,000 in on-duty accidents. Finding technological aids and operational techniques to reduce friendly fire casualties should also curb training accidents, but war and realistic training will still take their toll of accidental deaths.

ALLAN R. MILLETT

Charles F. Hawkins, "Friendly fire: Facts, Myths, and Misperceptions," *Naval Institute Proceedings* (June 1994): 54–60; Charles F. Shrader, *Amicicide: The Problem of Friendly fire in Modern War* (1992).

Fulk Nerra

971–1040, *Count of the Angevins*

Fulk Nerra came to power in 987 and made Anjou the leading power of the middle Loire in the kingdom of France. Fulk's greatest reputation was as the "Great Builder" (*"le grand bâtisseur"*) of stone fortifications, most of them castles (q.v.), which he introduced in the west of France. He built at least thirty major fortifications, mostly of stone, and he eventually controlled at least seventy strongholds. Some formed a perimeter around the Angevin heartland in a system of defense in depth, choking off incursions into his territories, whereas others served as points of attack and encirclement.

Fulk also won two of the bloodiest pitched battles of his age: Conqéreuil, against Count Conan of Rennes in 996, and Pontlevoy, against Count Odo II of Blois in 1016. When necessary, Fulk could assemble an army of four thousand to six thousand effectives, one third of them mounted men. His tactics and strategy indicate an awareness of the principles found in the late Roman text of Vegetius's (q.v.) *De re militari*. Fulk's determination, ruthlessness, and innovative and sophisticated military policies enabled Anjou to become the dominant power in the west of France.

STEVEN FANNING

Fuller, J. F. C.

1878–1966, *British Soldier and Military Theorist*

After service in the Boer War (q.v.), John Frederick Charles Fuller studied at the British Staff College at Camberley and during World War I (q.v.) became chief of staff of the Tank Corps. He planned the Battle of Cambrai (q.v.) in 1917, the first offensive in history spearheaded by tanks, and then drew up "Plan 1919," which envisaged ending the war through massive concentrations of tanks and bombers. Although Germany's collapse rendered this redundant, Fuller now became, together with his close friend B. H. Liddell Hart (q.v.), the foremost advocate of mechanized warfare, propagating his views relentlessly through teaching (as chief instructor at Camberley), writing (he published over thirty books), and lobbying (he became military assistant to the chief of the Imperial General Staff). Although he failed to convince the British army, leading to his resignation in 1933, the chief German advocate of mechanized warfare, Heinz Guderian (q.v.), hailed Fuller (whose virulent anti-Semitism and membership of the British Union of Fascists at the time no doubt made his ideas yet more seductive to the Nazis) as his mentor.

GEOFFREY PARKER

G

Gallieni, Joseph-Simon

1849–1916, Marshal of France

A veteran of the heroic defense of Bazeilles during the Franco-Prussian War (q.v.), Joseph Gallieni enjoyed a brilliant colonial career that took him to West Africa, Tonkin, and eventually Madagascar, where he served as resident general from 1896 to 1905. While in Tonkin, Gallieni is credited with developing the "oil spot" method of pacification, through which French troops expanded outward from a series of interlinked strong points.

A member of the Supreme War Council, in 1911 Gallieni was instrumental in the appointment of Joseph Joffre (q.v.) as commander in chief. Retired in 1913, Gallieni was recalled on the outbreak of World War I (q.v.) and appointed military governor of Paris, where he made history during the First Battle of the Marne (q.v.) when he requisitioned Paris taxis and buses to ferry French troops to the battlefield — the first operational employment of motorized transport.

Named war minister in October 1915, Gallieni's growing doubts about Joffre's abilities peaked as he observed the French commander in chief's inadequate response to the German buildup before Verdun (q.v.). However, Gallieni resigned when none of his cabinet colleagues would agree to sack Joffre. He died on the operating table in May 1916. In 1921, Gallieni was posthumously promoted to marshal of France.

DOUGLAS PORCH

Gallipoli Campaign

February–March 1915 and April 1915–January 1916

A British naval raid on the Dardanelles during World War I (q.v.) was conceived as a diversionary action in aid of a Russia unnerved by the Ottoman invasion of the Caucasus (December 1914). Although the Otto-

man invaders were annihilated in January 1915, the Dardanelles proposal had by then assumed a life of its own and went forward. The British War Ministry insisted that troops were unavailable, but the admiral on the spot advised London that he could force the Straits and reach Constantinople with the navy on its own, and his plan was adopted.

A month after penetrating the Straits, the British-led Allied naval armada was poised to win, because the unprepared Turkish defenders had run out of ammunition. But unaware of that, and having lost several vessels to mines, the fleet turned around and steamed away. Now troops were sent in, and a month later, an Allied army of a half million men, many of them from Australia and New Zealand, landed at a handful of beaches on the Gallipoli Peninsula in the largest amphibious invasion in history. An additional British force landed more than four months later at another spot on the peninsula called Suvla Bay.

Heights dominated Gallipoli, and ably led Turkish troops held control of them throughout the campaign. Throwing away one opportunity after another, Allied officers let their troops be pinned down on their several invasion beaches. Fighting was fierce, and the opposing armies were evenly matched in numbers and courage. By the time the Allies withdrew, 259 days after landing, each side had suffered a quarter of a million casualties.

The failure of the Gallipoli campaign brought down Britain's military and civilian leaders: Horatio Kitchener (q.v.), John Arbuthnot Fisher (q.v.), Herbert Henry Asquith, and Winston Churchill (q.v.). It also brought to prominence one of the Turkish defenders, Mustafa Kemal Atatürk (q.v.). The Allied fiasco became a paradigm of military folly: heroic soldiers sent to senseless deaths by incompetent commanders. It remains a tragedy; for, just as Germany's hopes for a quick knockout ended at the Marne (q.v.), so Britain's ended at the Dardanelles, dooming Europe to the long

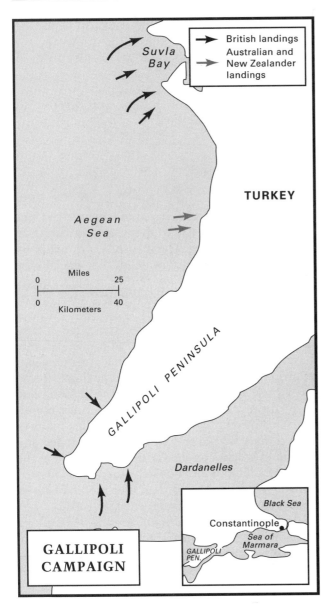

British landings

Australian and
New Zealander
landings

*Suvla
Bay*

TURKEY

*Aegean
Sea*

Miles
0   25

0   40
Kilometers

GALLIPOLI PENINSULA

Dardanelles

Black Sea

Constantinople
*Sea of
Marmara*

GALLIPOLI
PEN.

**GALLIPOLI
CAMPAIGN**

war of attrition that would lose the Continent its wealth, its position in the world, and the lives of a generation of its young.

DAVID FROMKIN

Gamelin, Maurice

1872–1958, French Military Leader

Top graduate of his 1893 St.-Cyr class, Maurice Gamelin served in various positions on the French General Staff between 1911 and 1916 and subsequently com-

manded a division on the Western Front. Following World War I (q.v.), he led the French military mission to Brazil, served in Syria, and commanded the Twentieth "Iron" Corps at Nancy before becoming deputy chief of staff in 1930.

As chief of staff (1935–1940), Gamelin is associated with the policy of appeasement and the fall of France in 1940. Recent historiography, however, has argued that his influence on policy remained limited and that he skillfully guided French rearmament and modernized French forces in a political climate deeply hostile to military reform. Unfortunately, in 1940 Gamelin's ill-fated decision to push his forces into Belgium and Holland created the opportunity for the German breakthrough in the Ardennes. His hands-off command style, combined with the French army's inability to match the Germans in speed and maneuverability once their lines had been pierced, made it virtually impossible to redress the situation (see *World War II*).

DOUGLAS PORCH

Gaugamela, Battle of

September 30, 331 B.C.

Following his campaigns securing Egypt and the Levantine coast, Alexander the Great (q.v.) turned inland and followed the ancient caravan routes through Syria into upper Mesopotamia. The Persian king, Darius III, whose forces had already been defeated twice by Alexander, assembled a huge multinational army in the area north of Babylon. Alexander chose his ground carefully and forced Darius to move north to meet him. Alexander was now close to the heart of the Persian Empire, and only Darius's army stood between the young Macedonian and the fabled centers of Babylon, Susa, and Persepolis.

The Macedonian tactics at Gaugamela had been tested on earlier grounds. The Macedonian left stood firm in a defensive position, even yielding in order to draw and extend the Persian right. The Macedonian center gave way before a charge of Persian scythed chariots and then closed ranks to surround and decimate the drivers. Alexander led the Macedonian cavalry on the right against the Persian left and center, and exploited gaps created in the Persian line. Speed of movement and superior discipline marked the Macedonian effort. When Darius, seeing his lines in disarray, fled the scene, the Asian forces collapsed.

Although neither king knew it at the moment, this

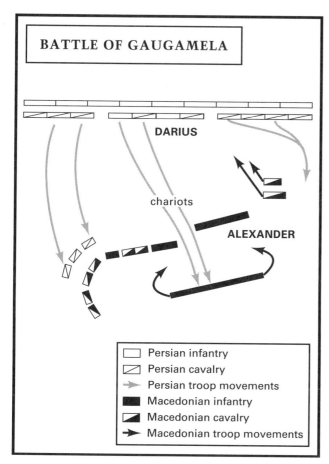

BATTLE OF GAUGAMELA

DARIUS

chariots

ALEXANDER

☐ Persian infantry
◩ Persian cavalry
→ Persian troop movements
■ Macedonian infantry
◪ Macedonian cavalry
➤ Macedonian troop movements

antithetical to either battlefield courage or the maintenance of discipline and was viewed instead as an understandable expression of male aggression and desire among a sizable minority of the army and navy.

The nature of such homosexual bonds ranged widely and depended for the most part on local custom and tradition. Athenian black- and red-figure vases routinely portray infantrymen naked or in half dress, where the clear intent is to highlight — even exaggerate — the physique of the young male: the artists assume that military scenarios are innately a part of male sexuality. At Sparta, senior hoplites (q.v.) developed conspicuous relationships with young trainees, where military exercise and the transmission of battle expertise were ostensibly central to the pederastic relationship. And at Thebes, a select unit of 150 paired lovers, the so-called Sacred Band, fought heroically for decades until they were annihilated at Chaeronea (338 B.C.) (q.v.). Elite units — from the Sacred Band, the Praetorian Guard, and the janissaries to the Waffen SS (q.v.) — have frequently entertained the reputation for both military excellence and physical ties among the soldiers themselves.

Among the Macedonian warring elite, the youth of both sexes were permanent fixtures at banquets and feasts, where drunken captains routinely squabbled over attractive lovers; the Hellenistic Greeks likewise assumed that an active bisexuality was normal behavior among their Persian and Eastern opponents. Depilation, interests in fashion, and open homosexual activity are portrayed negatively in Roman literature as symptomatic of extended duty in garrisons and of corruption by Asian practice and custom.

Nor were such homosexual interests limited to the rank and file. The Spartan king Agesilaus, Alexander and the Successors, Caesar ("every woman's man; every man's woman"), and the later emperors such as Hadrian were all known to have developed male liaisons, understood as a natural element of life in the field. In the twelfth century A.D., Richard the Lionheart (q.v.) purportedly sought a physical element in his ubiquitous male companionship, and we know that many of the close cadre of military advisers that surrounded Frederick the Great (q.v.) in the eighteenth century were primarily homosexual. In more modern times, a number of senior officers — Baron Steuben, Stephen Decatur, Lord Kitchener (q.v.), and Sir Douglas Haig (q.v.)—were all alleged to have preferred the select company of men, and there is no reason to doubt that this was true of a few of the

was the final battle between them. Darius failed in an attempt to form another army and was eventually assassinated by his own men. Gaugamela marked the end of two and a half centuries of Persian overlordship in western Asia and initiated the introduction of Greek culture into the area west of the Mesopotamian frontier.

EUGENE N. BORZA

Gays in the Military

Homosexuality among soldiers is rarely discussed in either ancient or modern military histories. Yet there is enough evidence in our sources to assume that group solidarity and unit morale, together with sequestered life in the barracks and on campaign, historically have encouraged physical relationships between men-at-arms. In classical antiquity, the overt expression of male affection per se was not seen as more anonymous commissioned and noncommissioned officers as well.

The modern notion in many armies that *all* types of homosexual expression are both shameful and injurious to military discipline is perhaps an outgrowth of Christianity in general and in particular American Protestant thought, which has seen the army as a nation-in-arms, a moral force protecting the traditional values of the majority of its citizenry. In that sense, the contemporary and absolute (though often unenforced) prohibition of all homosexual activity in some armies is perfectly logical, but there is no historical precedent that physical affection between those of the same sex has either undermined morale or diminished the fighting capacity of the army at large.

There is scant historical evidence of female homosexuality in the military, largely because women took part in fighting generally only during sieges and in times of national catastrophe. Scholars argue whether Greco-Roman accounts of Amazon (q.v.) societies were exaggerations of real military castes in Africa and Asia where lesbianism, hunting, and military gallantry became feminine ideals (see *Women in War*).

Modern military forces have adopted various attitudes toward homosexuality. The American military's policy of "don't ask, don't tell" bridges the gulf between absolute acceptance and prohibition. Although such halfway measures inevitably pose bureaucratic and legal challenges, the tolerance for homosexuals, but not overt homosexual acts, is actually consistent with most past armies' practice.

VICTOR DAVIS HANSON

K. J. Dover, *Greek Homosexuality* (1978); Randy Shilts, *Conduct Unbecoming* (1993).

General Staff

No organized army has ever taken the field without a body of assistants to the commander. From ancient times to the eighteenth century, their primary responsibilities lay in administration. Staff officers coordinated supply arrangements and legal systems, assisted in deploying troops for battle, and carried messages once the fighting started. Staffs were small, functioning as military households as much as formal organizations. Special training was not a prerequisite for appointment. Commanders like Frederick the Great (q.v.) preferred to rely on their own reason and intuition rather than turn to subordinates for counsel on anything but matters of detail.

The General Staff in a modern sense first took shape in the Napoleonic Wars. The French Revolution, with its improvised mass armies and rapidly promoted generals, put a premium on men who could bring order out of well-intentioned chaos. One of them, Louis Berthier, was assigned to the Army of Italy in 1795. When Napoleon (q.v.) took command, he saw the value of Berthier's emphasis on organization and centralization. In its ultimate elaboration of Berthier's system, Napoleon's headquarters combined the functions of a personal household, an imperial administration, and a military planning staff. The planning staff, under Berthier's direct control, was responsible for troop movements, supply, and personnel matters. By 1812 at the latest, the limitations of this model were clear. Depending essentially on a single directing mind, its efficiency diminished as the scale of warfare increased.

Prussia took a different track. Initially its General Staff officers were technicians, expected to give advice only when asked. In the "pre-reform" period prior to 1806, however, it was reorganized, and its functions were expanded to include administering intelligence, making contingency plans, and studying the theory and practice of war. A policy of rotating officers between staff and line assignments was adopted as well. After 1806 a war academy provided a steady supply of trained middle-ranking officers. Arguably even more important was the creation of permanent staffs for the divisions and army corps organized under the Defense Law of 1814.

This linking of the General Staff in Berlin with the staffs of the fighting formations greatly facilitated the process of creating a nervous system for an army of citizen conscripts. Prussia, and later Germany, could count on a substantial body of officers with a common intellectual experience who also did regular turns of troop duty. This encouraged formation commanders to view their chiefs of staff as colleagues rather than subordinates or rivals.

The Prussian-German General Staff's essential mission was preparing for war. Mapmaking, gathering intelligence, preparing mobilization plans, coordinating railway schedules — these routine tasks were the material from which careers were made. The eventual result was tunnel vision: a focus on tactical and operational concerns to the eclipse, then the virtual exclusion, of strategic and grand-strategy issues. By the beginning of World War I (q.v.), the General Staff had become the nodal point of German policy making. This, however, was a role for which it was in no way prepared.

Despite its successes in 1866 and 1870–1871 (see *Seven Weeks' War* and *Franco-Prussian War*), the German model's political implications meant it found few imitators. Both Britain and the powers of the Continent significantly restricted their General Staffs' functions to military affairs and kept their duties subdivided. Navy and air force staffs followed a similar pattern, in good part because of the higher levels of technical demands made by their respective services.

Tsarist, then Soviet, Russia came closest among the twentieth century's great powers to imitating the German model, but the Red Army (q.v.) was kept throughout its existence firmly under the supervision of the political authorities. Under Adolf Hitler (q.v.) the German General Staff was similarly and systematically limited in its functions. The Federal Republic of Germany eschewed any equivalent organization when creating the Bundeswehr. The United States has also continued to resist the concept of a supreme General Staff, favoring instead a committee system in which the service chiefs of the army, navy, air force, and marine corps serve on an equal basis. Often criticized as cumbersome and tending to the lowest common denominator in decision making, the Joint Chiefs of Staff, with some modifications in the aftermath of Vietnam (q.v.), demonstrated a high level of efficiency during the Gulf War (q.v.). For all the praise heaped on the German system, in short, the Napoleonic model of a General Staff, with limited military functions and under strict political control, appears to have had a longer and more successful life.

DENNIS E. SHOWALTER

Martin van Creveld, *Command in War* (1985).

Genghis Khan (Temüjin)

1162?–1227, Founder of the Mongol Empire

Born into a family that was part of the minor Mongol nobility, Temüjin's formative years were shaped by the murder of his father when he was nine years old. His mother took on the duties of teaching him how to ride a horse, shoot a bow and arrow, and tend the animals. She instructed him that allies were most essential in the harsh environment they inhabited. From his earliest days, he set about forming an association of trustworthy and reliable allies who were drawn to him by his intelligence, bravery, and persuasive abilities. By the 1180s, he had organized a group of utterly loyal retainers *(nököd)* with whom he shared wealth or spoils that resulted from successful campaigns against other tribes. With more powerful leaders such as Jamukha, a childhood friend, and the Ong Khan of the mighty Kereyid tribes, he established relations of blood brotherhood *(anda)*. Yet when he no longer needed these blood brothers, his pattern was to break with or betray them. He would eventually turn against and kill both Jamukha and the Ong Khan.

Temüjin continued to strengthen his army and his position until he was accepted as leader of all the Mongols (q.v.). He divided his forces into units of one thousand and then ten thousand men and scattered the tribes into different units so that each individual would develop a loyalty to the army, not to his original tribe. Temüjin promoted men of ability, not necessarily the old tribal chieftains, and the grateful new leaders became devoted to him. By 1204, he vanquished the Naiman, his last and most tenacious opponents, and in 1206, an assemblage of the Mongol nobility *(khuriltai)* ratified him as their leader and granted him the title "Genghis Khan," meaning "Oceanic Ruler" or "Fierce Ruler."

Genghis Khan's successes owed much to his military acumen and his administrative abilities. He imposed tight discipline on his troops, punishing them severely for infractions. He planned his campaigns meticulously and developed a sophisticated intelligence network. He devised tactics and strategy carefully to capitalize on the information about the enemy that he obtained from his spies and allies. Frequently, the mere threat of Genghis's attacks and devastating invasions induced opponents to capitulate. His superb cavalry offered the mobility he required in battle, and their ability to shoot a bow and arrow while riding gave them the upper hand in combat with ordinary foot soldiers.

Before an attack, Genghis dispatched envoys to foreign states with "orders of submission," demanding acquiescence to his rule. If the foreigners yielded, he would permit their rulers to govern as long as they provided taxes and performed labor and military service. If they refused to succumb, he would attack. The

A Chinese fantasy version of Genghis Khan shows him in battle gear.

Tanguts of Northwest China were the first non-Mongols to reject his orders of submission. Since they controlled the oases vital to trade with Central Asia and the Middle East, Genghis was eager to compel their submission in order to dominate this lucrative commerce. In 1209, his troops trekked across parts of the Gobi desert and engaged the enemy. They did well in the open field but encountered obstacles in inducing towns to surrender, as they had not developed the techniques of siege warfare. Nonetheless, their relentlessness finally caused the Tanguts to sue for peace.

Genghis Khan's campaigns spread to North China and Central Asia. Commercial and tributary disputes had bedeviled relations with the Chin dynasty of North China and eventually resulted in war. The cul-mination of the conflict occurred in 1215 with the successful siege of the Chin dynasty's capital in the area of modern Peking. The Mongols' ability to prevent the resupply of the city and their use of catapults revealed a growing sophistication in sieges. Genghis's expeditions in Central Asia showed an even greater ability to besiege and capture large cities. Commercial and diplomatic conflicts with the Khwarazmian shah of Central Asia, who made the mistake of killing Genghis Khan's envoys, erupted into a full-scale war. In 1219, Genghis set forth toward the west with an army of about 200,000 men. Within the next two years, his forces besieged and then, in rapid succession, took Bukhara, Samarkand, Herat, Nishapur, and Merv, sizable towns that put the Mongols' skill in siege warfare to a test. Genghis remained in Central Asia for four years, but then headed eastward to punish the suddenly rebellious Tanguts. En route, he died in August of 1227.

Aside from his conquests and his military innovations, Genghis Khan bequeathed policies that proved invaluable in ruling the diverse ethnic and religious groups in the domains he had subjugated. First, he adopted a policy of religious toleration, which ingratiated the Mongols to the native clerics. Second, he recruited and employed foreigners in his army and in his administration. Without foreign assistance, he and his successors could not have governed the vast territories they dominated. Third, he issued the Jasagh, a set of orders and rules for his people. It imposed capital punishment for horse theft and severe sanctions on disobedient soldiers, prescribed a specific way of butchering animals, and legitimized the practice of the levirate, the marriage of a widow to her husband's brother. Fourth, by promoting trade, he and his descendants set the stage for an increase in travel across Eurasia, permitting European envoys, merchants, and craftworkers to journey, for the first time, as far as China.

The career of Genghis Khan defies easy characterization. A man who unleashed terrible destruction and death on his way to conquest, he paved the way for a peaceful era that resulted in the first direct contacts between Europe and China. An illiterate nomad, he ordered the development of the first Mongol written language, supported craftworkers and artists, and patronized a variety of religions. A military man prone to use violence, he nonetheless devised rules designed to resolve conflicts peacefully. He was neither a monster, as he is often depicted in the West, nor the greatest military genius of all times, as the Mongols perceive him to be.

MORRIS ROSSABI

Paul Ratchnevsky, *Genghis Khan: His Life and Legacy*, trans. T. N. Haining (1991).

Genocide

The term *genocide* was coined from the Greek word *genos*, meaning "race, nation, or tribe," followed by the Latin suffix for "killing," in order to define a specific class of mass murder. Prompted by the German racial killings under the Nazi regime, Raphael Lemkin coined the word in his book published during World War II (q.v.) entitled *Axis Rule in Occupied Europe*. Lemkin cited cases of genocide that occurred as far back as the Roman destruction of Carthage, when a city-state was physically destroyed and its entire population either put to the sword or sent into slavery (see *Punic Wars*).

In the shock of the full disclosure of the Holocaust (as Germany's destruction of European Jewry later became known), the United Nations General Assembly quickly defined genocide as a crime in 1946, although the international convention against it did not go into effect until 1951 and lacked enforcement powers. In drafting the convention, Communist nations succeeded in eliminating political motives from the official definition of genocide, which is par excellence a crime of intent. The convention nevertheless retains Lemkin's principal categories of a national, ethnic, racial, or religious group as designated victims of genocide. It also specifies the means as murder and serious bodily or mental harm, as well as the deliberate imposition of physical conditions calculated to destroy a group (for example, concentration camps). The convention also forbids measures to prevent births within the proscribed group and the forcible transfer of children outside of it.

The unprecedented application of technology and the modern bureaucratic state to the task of racial mass murder was unique in history and justified the invention of a new word. Attempts were then made by researchers, polemicists, and especially by interested groups to backdate the concept of genocide to the Albigensians (q.v.) in the thirteenth century, the American Indians in the nineteenth century, and the Armenians killed or forcibly exiled by the Turks in

1915. Others have also attempted to broaden the word's meaning to include the atomic bombings of Hiroshima and Nagasaki and the entire Vietnam War (q.v.). Its devaluation as a concept was ensured when the word *genocide* began to be applied by authors to abortion, medical research, and even the regulation of native languages in schools.

Genuine cases of genocide did appear again in Cambodia in 1975, the tribal wars of Rwanda and Burundi in 1972 and 1994, and the disintegration of Yugoslavia early in the 1990s when various cultural groups, but principally Serbs, attempted to force out minority populations, mainly Muslims in Bosnia, using terror, concentration camps, rape, and murder (see *Ethnic Cleansing*). In the first international legal action against a clear-cut case of genocide, specific Serb commanders were accused of "crimes against humanity" before the International Court of Justice in The Hague. The concept was developed by the Allied prosecutors at Nuremberg, who applied it to the wartime behavior of the German leaders and successfully convicted them of what were essentially war crimes (q.v.). This legal precedent has proven more precise and durable than the scholarly concept of genocide.

LAWRENCE MALKIN

Geography

We tend to overlook how much military history has been shaped by geography — the study of terrain, climate, vegetation, soils, and geology that we now lump under the rubric "earth sciences." Geographical factors go far to explain why, for example, the English victory at Crécy (1346) may have resulted less from the indiscipline of the French than from the judicious placement of English archers on the terraced walls of a small ravine. Or why, in the mid–eighteenth century, the wilderness-backed French fortress of Quebec, dominating the St. Lawrence River and blocking access to the interior, was the choke point of North America (see *Quebec, Sieges of*). Once the British took it in 1759, the French and Indian War was as good as over. As Francis Parkman noted of the final surrender of the French the following year, "Half the continent had changed hands at the scratch of a pen" (see *Seven Years' War*).

Those same geographical factors also explain why a principal cause of Sir Douglas Haig's (q.v.) failure at Passchendaele in 1917 was a combination of unex-

The Best Western Military Sites

We have listed here the twenty military sites that we consider, in the words of the Michelin guides, most "worth a visit." We use the word *site:* not all are battlefields. We have also limited our choices to the West, recognizing that we are omitting what may be the greatest military site in the world, the Great Wall of China.

Megiddo (Israel). Archaeologists have counted twenty levels of civilization, almost all of which have ended in siege and destruction. This once-strategic road junction near the port of Haifa is the original Armageddon.

Masada (Israel). A.D. 73–74. One of history's most famous last stands, Romans against Jewish Zealots, took place at this shiplike butte overlooking the Dead Sea. The Roman camps and siege ramp, as well as the ruins on top, have the eerie look of recent abandonment.

Hadrian's Wall (England). A.D. 122–126. This Roman buffer against northern invasions, running seventy-three miles across the spine of England's uplands, with excavated forts (including luxury loos) and breathtaking views, was built on the orders of the emperor Hadrian. It remained operational for almost three centuries.

Cadbury Castle (England). Fifth–sixth centuries. This five-hundred-foot-high hill fort broods over the Somerset countryside in southern England. Early in the sixth century, a military leader of great wealth and influence, possibly King Arthur, built walls and large but impermanent buildings on Cadbury's eighteen-acre summit. The Arthurian tradition took root early on. Seventeenth-century antiquarians believed that Cadbury Castle was Camelot.

Aigues-Mortes (France). Thirteenth century. Some may prefer Carcassonne or Caernarvon Castle in Wales, but this walled "new town" (or so it was when Louis IX built it) near the mouth of the Rhone is one of the most perfect (and perfectly preserved) examples of medieval fortress architecture.

Lützen (Germany). 1632 and 1813. In the countryside near Leipzig, an excellent museum commemorates the place where Gustavus II Adolphus fell in the Thirty Years' War (a second museum is located in the castle that served as headquarters for his opponent, Wallenstein). Here, too, Napoleon made a late show of tactical brilliance.

Neuf-Breisach (France). 1698. Vauban's masterpiece, the most complete and unspoiled of his fortresses, stands on the Rhine near Colmar. Neuf-Breisach is less a product of restoration than of three centuries of benign neglect.

Louisbourg (Canada). 1745 and 1758. The French fortress on Cape Breton Island was twice besieged — and twice captured — first by an improbable force of New England irregulars and thirteen years later by a British army commanded by Generals Jeffrey Amherst and James Wolfe. This is one of the most accurate restorations of a major military site anywhere.

Saratoga (United States). 1777. Fortunately, perhaps, the heights above the Hudson where John Burgoyne surrendered to Horatio Gates are off the beaten track, but historians and archaeologists have done their share to impede the march of progress. Fields, tree lines, and fortifications have the location — and the look — of the original.

West Point (United States). 1780 to the present. You can still see the forts that Benedict Arnold tried to betray to the British — along with the United States Military Academy, situated above the Hudson on one of the most dramatic river bluffs in North America.

Valmy (France). 1792. There is something eerily empty about the plains of Champagne where the artillery duel that saved the French Revolution took place. Here the informed imagination needs few aids.

Austerlitz (Czech Republic). 1805. We nominate the Emperor's personal favorite as the best of the Napoleonic battlefields. Just the view from the Pratzen Heights will make the trip to the Czech Republic worthwhile. The town once called Austerlitz is now Slavkov, in Moravia.

Antietam (United States). 1862. Farmers grow corn in these Maryland fields, as they did during the Civil War. Is there a better preserved battlefield on the continent? You can look at the stone bridge across which Ambrose Burnside funneled his men and marvel at his dimness: Antietam Creek was then, and is now, shallow enough to wade in.

Gettysburg (United States). 1863. For many Americans, a visit to this Pennsylvania town is a rite of passage. Some may find all those Victorian monuments a distraction — but to dismiss them is to ignore Gettysburg's meaning.

Vicksburg (United States). 1863. The Civil War's most important city siege took place here, and the military park, with its sixteen miles of roads, still holds the Mississippi city in its jaws. Siegeworks remain; so does the USS *Cairo,* the Union gunboat brought up from the bottom of the river in 1964.

Verdun (France). 1916. As many times as you clamber over the shattered concrete on the Meuse Heights or, armed with a good map and a modicum of caution, wander into Verdun's haunted woods, you will inevitably come on something unexpected. Be careful of unexploded shells. Don't pass up side trips to a pair of 1915 battlefields, the mine-riven buttes of Les Éparges and Vauquois (where you can hire a guide to take you into the old German tunnels).

The Somme (France). 1916. Its monuments are its mine craters and its myriad cemeteries (which tend to pop up where the fighting was hottest). With its busloads of visitors, it is becoming as popular with the British as Gettyburg is with Americans. Don't rush through the Somme battlefield. There is more to this wide-open landscape than first meets the eye.

The Maginot Line at Hackenberg (France). 1930s. Quite simply, this is one of the most amazing military sites you will ever see. Inside a hollowed-out hill are dormitories, dining halls, shell storage chambers, and an electric train that will take you through a mile of tunnels. Up top there is evidence of battle — between the Germans and Americans in the winter of 1944–1945.

The Churchill War Rooms (England). 1940. In the heart of Whitehall in London, Churchill's underground operational headquarters can be seen, almost as government janitors left them when they locked up after Japan's surrender in 1945.

The D-Day Beaches (France). 1944. They are not remarkable so much for the battered relics of June 6, 1944 — though enough remain — as for the wondering question that the landscape itself will inevitably provoke: How did the Allies bring it off?

Robert Cowley

pected rainfall and a poor choice of battlefield, with its impervious clay base. "Shellholes filled with water, which could not drain away," the geographer Douglas W. Johnson wrote, turn[ed] the battlefield into an almost impassable morass which blocked the advance for which the bombardment was supposed to be a preparation." Haig might well have heeded the teaching of Vegetius (q.v.) fifteen centuries earlier: "The nature of the ground," the Roman military theorist wrote, "is often of more consequence than courage."

Armies have always chosen the paths of least resistance staked out by geological features. One can point to such natural encounter areas as the Bosporus, northern Italy, what is now Israel, the passes from Afghanistan into the northwest Indian plain, Flanders and the North Sea dune belt ("the cockpit of Europe"), or the great grassland troughs of Asia through which the horsemen of the Mongols (q.v.) and Tatars poured.

If certain areas are combat-intensive, it follows that military actions have converged repeatedly on a handful of places. One could point to the key high point of Vimy Ridge, where the duke of Marlborough (q.v.) campaigned — and that later played a part in both world wars. Panipat (q.v.), on the river plain north of Delhi, is another such locus of contention. Sweeping out of Afghanistan, Tamerlane (q.v.) and his Tatar cavalry destroyed an Indian army there in 1398, and Babur (q.v.) did the same in 1526, establishing the Mughal Empire (q.v.) in the process. (Thirty years later, the Mughals had to fight to regain power in a third Panipat.) Jerusalem, sitting atop the Judaean Hills and dominating the principal north-south roads of the Holy Land, may be the most august of the world's military magnets. A cultural and religious choke point as well, it has endured more than a hundred sieges in the three thousand years (and more) of its history — nearly all of the attacks on its walls being mounted in the relatively flat and open area to the north of the city. (The oldest choke point was Megiddo [q.v.], sixty miles away, which was besieged as early as 2700 B.C. It may be no accident that the original Armageddon was a road junction.) But the dubious honor of being the world's most fought-over place is held by Adrianople (now the Turkish city of Edirne), west of the Bosporus. A city at the confluence of three rivers and their strategically important valleys, Adrianople has witnessed no fewer than fifteen major battles and sieges between 323 and 1913.

But in fact the greatest part of the earth's surface has been hardly, if at all, touched by war. Most of history's major naval battles, for instance, have been fought inshore, often as an adjunct to land campaigns. Opposing naval forces had trouble finding one another in the open ocean, and even as late as World War II (q.v.), distance invariably humbled surveillance systems. There have been exceptions, of course: the Glorious First of June 1794, when the British intercepted a huge French naval convoy four hundred miles off Ushant; Midway (q.v.), a mid-Pacific encounter triggered by the American breaking of Japanese codes; and the North Atlantic (q.v.) convoy battles of 1942–1943.

"Almost seventy per cent of the world's 60,000,000 square miles of dry land," John Keegan has written, "is either too high, too cold, or too waterless for the conduct of military activities." The so-called desert warfare of World War II rarely took place more than a hundred miles from the Mediterranean. "Jungle" warfare is generally fought along well-established roads or trails such as the path across the Owen Stanley Range in New Guinea, scene of desperate struggles between the Japanese and the Australians and Americans in 1942. As for the forests of the temperate zone, military history teaches that if they cannot be put to advantage — as Heinz Guderian (q.v.) did with his surprise crossing of the Ardennes in 1940 — they are best left alone. "To groves always men come both to their joy and their undoing," wrote the poet David Jones, who was wounded in one, Mametz Wood, in 1916.

Commanders must also deal with the happenstances of geography. "The British may harass us and distress us," Nathanael Greene (q.v.), the American Revolutionary War (q.v.) general, wrote in 1781, "but the Carolinas alone can subdue us." The Nazi failure to take into account the twice-yearly mud months in Russia — the *rasputitsa* (roadless period) of the spring and the fall — may have denied them their ultimate prize, Moscow, in 1941, even more than the famous winter. On a local level, ignorant of the geological structure of the Somme (q.v.) area, both sides experienced serious problems with flooded tunnels and dugouts in 1916. As Douglas W. Johnson put it, "An army may find the waters beneath the earth more dangerous than the fire above." There is, too, the example of the Israeli operations officers Yigael Yadin and Yitzhak Rabin, both aware of the country's ancient landscape. In the Negev Desert at the end of 1948, in a maneuver worthy of Stonewall Jackson's (q.v.) swing along a forgotten woodland road at Chancellorsville (q.v.), they directed Israeli troops to outflank and thereby surprise an Egyptian force by taking a Roman caravan route unmarked on most maps. They knew not only their history but also their geography.

Johnson, a Columbia University professor and a major in American military intelligence in 1917–1918, produced one of this century's essential books of military science and history, *Battlefields of the World War*. He spoke of "the fallacy of the contention that modern methods of warfare have reduced to insignificance the role of terrain as a factor in strategy and tactics." Though he was writing in 1920, some things have not changed. In war, as in so much else, geography can be destiny.

ROBERT COWLEY

Robert G. Albion, *Forests and Sea Power: The Timber Problem of the Royal Navy, 1652–1862* (1926); Douglas W. Johnson, *Battlefields of the World War* (1921); John Keegan, *A History of Warfare* (1993).

Gettysburg, Battle of

July 1–3, 1863

Involving 90,000 Union soldiers and 75,000 Confederates and resulting in combined casualties of approximately 50,000 (23,000 Union and an estimated 24,000–28,000 Confederate), Gettysburg was the largest and most important battle of the American Civil War (q.v.). Coinciding with the capture of Vicksburg (q.v.) by Union forces (July 4) and an advance by the Union Army of the Cumberland that drove Confederate forces out of middle Tennessee (June 23–July 4), Gettysburg proved to be crucial in securing ultimate Union victory.

Gettysburg is located in central Pennsylvania, a few miles north of the Maryland border. It had no intrinsic military significance; the battle occurred there because a dozen roads converged in the town from every point on the compass. Commanded by General Robert E. Lee (q.v.), the Confederate Army of Northern Virginia had invaded Pennsylvania in June to capture supplies, destroy a vital railroad bridge over the Susquehanna River at Harrisburg, encourage antiwar activists in the North, and gain a military triumph on Northern soil that, coming on top of the Confederate victory at Chancellorsville (May 1–6, 1863), might force Abraham Lincoln's (q.v.) government to conclude peace. When Lee learned on June 28 that the Union Army of the Potomac had crossed its namesake

river and was threatening to cut off part of the divided Confederate invasion force, he ordered all units to use the convenient road network to concentrate in the vicinity of Gettysburg.

On the morning of July 1, a Confederate infantry

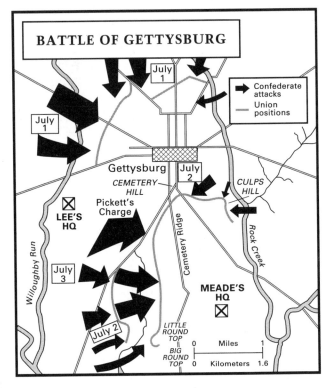

BATTLE OF GETTYSBURG

division clashed with two Union cavalry brigades fighting dismounted a mile northwest of Gettysburg. Couriers pounded down the roads to summon reinforcements. Outnumbered Unionists held on until late afternoon, when they were driven back through town to Cemetery Hill and Culps Hill, a mile south of the village. On the next day Union troops dug in on those hills and on Cemetery Ridge, running two miles southward to Little Round Top. The Confederates attacked both the Union left and right on July 2 and achieved some gains but no victory. The Union commander, Major General George Gordon Meade, and his subordinates fought a skillful defensive battle. But an overconfident Lee thought that, having reinforced both flanks, Meade would be weak in the center. On July 3 Lee ordered an assault on that center, spearheaded by Major General George Pickett's fresh division. Thirteen thousand Confederates went forward in the attack; fewer than half of them came back. Lee had made his supreme effort and come up short. On the next day (July 4) he began a retreat to Virginia. Meade followed cautiously and failed to cut off the Confederates before they recrossed the Potomac. Nevertheless, the North celebrated Gettysburg as the biggest Union victory of the war.

JAMES M. MCPHERSON

Edwin B. Coddington, *The Gettysburg Campaign: A Study in Command* (1968).

Giap, Vo Nguyen

1912–, *Vietnamese Military Leader*

Vo Nguyen Giap was born in Quangbinh Province, in Central Vietnam, of an impoverished Mandarin family. Educated in a French *lycée* in Hue and at Hanoi University, he joined the Indochina Communist Party in the 1930s. On the outbreak of World War II (q.v.), he fled to China to join Vietnamese Communist leader Ho Chi Minh at Chingsi, where, in May 1941, the Vietnamese Independence League, abbreviated to the name Viet Minh, was formed. In autumn 1944, Ho gave his blessing to the formation of armed propaganda teams under Giap's command, which, in April 1945, became the People's Liberation Army.

Giap served as interior minister in the revolutionary government that Ho Chi Minh created on the surrender of the Japanese in 1945; he is alleged to have directed brutal purges against non-Communist elements. In 1946, as tension mounted between the Viet Minh and the French (see *Indochina War*), Giap became defense minister. An avid student of military history, he emerged as a major Communist strategist and military organizer of the Vietnam wars (q.v.). He was influenced by Mao Tse-tung's (q.v.) theories of a three-stage escalation of revolutionary war from guerrilla warfare, to parity with the incumbent forces, and finally to the third phase, in which the insurgents would overwhelm the occupiers. Giap's strengths as a military commander lay in his meticulous attention to organization, particularly logistics. His weakness was his impatience to reach the Maoist "third phase," which caused him to undertake campaigns, or persist in costly actions, beyond the capabilities of his forces.

The Communist victory in China (see *Chinese Civil War*) and Mao's decision to aid the Viet Minh caused Giap to conclude in February 1950 that the time had come to move to the third phase of revolution. The spectacular collapse under Viet Minh pressure of a series of French posts along the Chinese frontier in October 1950 appeared to give credibility to Giap's analysis. However, when Viet Minh forces assaulted the Tonkin Delta in 1951, they were driven back with significant losses. Although the French defeat at Dien Bien Phu (q.v.) in 1954 enhanced Giap's military reputation, it appears that most of the major strategic decisions of the Indochina War were taken by the Chinese, often over the objections of Giap.

Following the Geneva Conference, which partitioned Vietnam at the seventeenth parallel, Giap remained a voice for reunification by military means, even in the face of escalating U.S. involvement in South Vietnam in the early 1960s. Given the collective nature of Communist decision making, it is impossible to know exactly how far Giap was responsible for the decision to attack Khe Sanh in 1967, for the Tet offensive (q.v.) of 1968, or for the 1972 Easter offensive, for which he was a primary advocate. By the time South Vietnamese resistance collapsed in 1975, much of the direction of the war had passed to General Van Tien Dung. After the war, Giap was given short-term assignments until he retired as defense minister in 1980, and from the politburo in 1982. Critics feel that Giap's military reputation has been inflated by his self-promotion, which contrasts markedly with the usual anonymity of Communist commanders, and by the adulation of his adversaries, particularly the French.

DOUGLAS PORCH

Grand Alliance, War of the

1688–1697

This conflict goes by several names: the French term it the War of the League of Augsburg, whereas others label it the Nine Years' War. It was one of a series of conflicts (1667–1714) by which Louis XIV (q.v.) sought to add new territory to France and new glory to his name. In the 1680s he became obsessed with securing his northeastern frontiers by buttressing natural obstacles with fortresses and by seizing certain key areas to give his kingdom more defensible borders. In September 1688, Louis XIV precipitated the War of the Grand Alliance by laying siege to Philipsbourg, a fortress commanding an important Rhine crossing that Louis regarded as a potential invasion route to Alsace. He hoped for a limited war along the banks of the Rhine, but when he met unexpected opposition,

Louis ordered the devastation of the Palatinate (1688–1689) to deny its assets to the enemy, and this act shocked Europe. Resentment against Louis's brutal aggression and fear that Louis intended to dominate Europe united a great coalition against the French and escalated the conflict. Small German states banded together; then in 1689 the English and the Dutch, united under William III, joined the fray, as did Spain, Brandenburg, Bavaria, Hanover, Saxony, and Savoy.

The French at first enjoyed an unusual naval advantage over the English, winning the Battle of Beachy Head (July 10, 1690), but they profited little from it, and the English and Dutch defeated the French at the Battle of La Hogue (May 29, 1692). This defeat, added to the drain on French resources as Louis assembled an unprecedented army of 400,000 men, caused the French to abandon further large-scale naval action and to turn instead to privateers.

As in the preceding wars, the major seat of fighting soon shifted to the Spanish Netherlands, where the French armies led by Marshal Luxembourg scored important victories at Steenkerke and Neerwinden, while Sébastien Le Prestre de Vauban (q.v.) successfully directed sieges against Mons, Namur, and Charleroi. Luxembourg died in 1694, and William III scored some notable successes after his rival disappeared; however, Louis accepted the unfavorable Treaty of Ryswick in 1697 not because French arms had been bested, but because his state was driven to the brink of bankruptcy by the war.

JOHN A. LYNN

Grant, Ulysses S.

1822–1885, *American Civil War General and President of the United States*

Born in a two-room cabin at Point Pleasant, Ohio, Ulysses S. Grant attended district schools and worked at his father's tannery and farm, where he developed a love for horses. In 1839 Grant's father secured his appointment to West Point, where Grant excelled in horsemanship but was an indifferent student in most academic subjects, graduating in 1843 near the middle of his class. He joined the Fourth Infantry as a lieutenant and in 1846 went with his regiment to Texas, serving first under General Zachary Taylor (q.v.) and then General Winfield Scott (q.v.) in the Mexican War (q.v.). As a line officer and regimental quartermaster, Grant fought in most of the battles in Mexico and emerged from the conflict as a brevet captain.

After the war Grant served at a variety of bleak army posts, winding up at dreary Humboldt Bay, California, in 1853. Lonely for his family (he had married Julia Dent in 1848), the taciturn captain began drinking and resigned from the army in 1854. Joining his wife and two sons on a farm south of St. Louis, he tried a variety of occupations with marginal success. In 1860 Grant moved to Galena, Illinois, and went to work in his family's leather goods store, where the outbreak of the American Civil War (q.v.) in April 1861 found him.

Grant helped recruit and organize Illinois regiments and in June 1861 became colonel of the Twenty-first Illinois. Through the influence of Galena congressman Elihu Washburne, Grant was promoted to brigadier general in August. He took charge of Union troops at the supply base of Cairo, Illinois, at the confluence of the Ohio and Mississippi Rivers. These rivers — with the Tennessee and Cumberland Rivers, which flowed into the Ohio a short distance above Cairo — were keys to unlocking the Confederate heartland. Recognizing the strategic importance of this river network, Grant in February 1862 launched a campaign in cooperation with a fleet of ironclad gunboats to capture Confederate Forts Henry and Donelson, which protected the Tennessee and Cumberland Rivers just south of the Kentucky-Tennessee border. Fort Henry fell to the gunboats on February 6; Grant then marched his small army to invest Fort Donelson. After repulsing a gunboat attack, the Confederate garrison tried a breakout assault on February 15. Union forces contained it and sealed up the Confederates in their works. The Confederate commander asked Grant for his terms of surrender; Grant replied with words that made him famous: "No terms except an unconditional and immediate surrender can be accepted. I propose to move immediately upon your works." These words illustrate Grant's straightforward, no-nonsense style of leadership, without vainglory, that left no one in doubt of his purpose and his determination to achieve it.

After capturing Fort Donelson, Grant was promoted to major general and began preparing a campaign against Corinth, Mississippi, an important Confederate railroad junction. Before he could launch that campaign, however, Confederate general Albert Sidney Johnston surprised Grant with an attack on his camps at Pittsburg Landing on the Tennessee River, bringing on the bloody two-day Battle of Shiloh (April

6–7, 1862). Grant's Army of the Tennessee hung on grimly during the first day and, reinforced overnight by troops from the Army of the Ohio, counterattacked and drove off the Confederates on the second day. Despite this victory, Grant's reputation fell under a cloud for a time, but President Abraham Lincoln (q.v.) upheld him against criticism.

During the latter half of 1862, Grant commanded Union troops occupying a large area in western Tennessee and northern Mississippi, beating off efforts by Confederates to regain control of the area. Late in the year he began a campaign to capture Vicksburg (q.v.), a Confederate bastion on the Mississippi that was the largest remaining obstacle to Union control of the entire course of that great river. After several months of frustration that provoked renewed criticism and calls for Grant's dismissal, which Lincoln deflected, Grant in April 1863 launched a bold plan to take Vicksburg. While he marched his infantry past the fortress on the west side of the river, his cavalry carried out a brilliant diversionary raid through the whole state of Mississippi, and the river fleet ran past the guns of Vicksburg. The gunboats rendezvoused with Grant downriver and transported his troops to the east bank. Cutting loose from his supplies and living off the country, Grant confused the Confederates by rapid maneuvers and defeated them in a series of battles that by May 19, 1863, had driven them into the Vicksburg fortifications. After a siege of six weeks the garrison surrendered, yielding Grant thirty thousand prisoners and one of the most brilliant achievements of the war.

Given command of the vast theater between the Appalachians and the Mississippi, Grant went to Chattanooga, where he directed efforts that culminated in the spectacular Union victory at Missionary Ridge on November 25, which drove the Confederacy's second-largest army deep into Georgia. Having split the Confederacy in two with the capture of Vicksburg, Grant was now poised to cut it into three parts with a thrust through Georgia. But in March 1864 Lincoln promoted him to lieutenant general and called him to Washington to become general in chief of all Union armies. Putting General William T. Sherman (q.v.) in charge of the principal western Union army to command the strike through Georgia, Grant made his headquarters with the Army of the Potomac in Virginia and planned a campaign to destroy the Confederate Army of Northern Virginia and capture Richmond.

These objectives took a year to accomplish, largely because of Robert E. Lee's (q.v.) tactical prowess and his army's fighting power. In a titanic campaign of bloody battles and flanking maneuvers from the "Wilderness" of Virginia near Fredericksburg to Petersburg south of Richmond, with an important sideshow in the Shenandoah Valley, Grant finally overcame Lee and brought the enemy to bay at Appomattox, where a third major Confederate army surrendered to Grant on April 9, 1865, virtually ending the Civil War.

Grant remained general in chief until he was elected president in 1868. Serving two terms, he found his presidency plagued by the intractable problem of Reconstruction, by an economic depression that began in 1873, and by the corruption of several members of his administration. These events left a tarnish on the illustrious reputation Grant had carried out of the Civil War. But when he died of throat cancer on July 23, 1885, Grant's standing as the foremost military commander in American history remained firm, as it does today. Just days before his death, Grant had completed his two-volume *Personal Memoirs*, which is generally considered one of the greatest military autobiographies in the English language.

JAMES M. MCPHERSON

Bruce Catton, *Grant Moves South* (1960); Bruce Catton, *Grant Takes Command* (1969); William S. McFeely, *Grant: A Biography* (1981).

Great Northern War

1700–1721

In this wide-ranging and prolonged conflict, Russia replaced Sweden as the dominant power in northern Europe. Between 1560 and 1660, Sweden had conquered a substantial Baltic empire. Its heart was around the Gulf of Finland (Karelia, Ingria, Estonia, Livonia), but successful intervention in the Thirty Years' War (q.v.) also brought significant gains in Germany (Western Pomerania, Wismar, Bremen, and Verden), while southern Sweden was reconquered from Denmark (1645; 1660). This empire was a testimony to Sweden's impressive army and to its rulers' ambitions and military skill. But the Swedish Empire was too far-flung to be easily defended and also rested upon precarious domestic foundations: Sweden's population was no more than three million, less than one-third of Russia's, and Russia was its principal rival.

In 1617 Sweden's gains by the Peace of Stolbova had deprived the emerging Russian state of direct access to the Baltic, and during succeeding decades Russia's continuing domestic problems ensured that this territorial settlement remained unchallenged. During the second half of the seventeenth century, however, Russian power revived, especially after the accession of the energetic and ambitious ruler Peter the Great (1672–1725) (q.v.). Peter was anxious to reopen direct links with western Europe and to recover the territory lost in 1617. In the late 1690s he allied himself with Denmark and Saxony-Poland, and in 1700 the three powers attacked Sweden, ruled since 1697 by the youthful Charles XII (q.v.).

The war's early years witnessed a series of spectacular Swedish successes. In summer 1700, Denmark was rapidly defeated and forced temporarily out of the conflict, and three months later the Russians were routed at Narva (November 20). Charles XII then turned his attention to the third of his enemies, Augustus the Strong, ruler of Saxony-Poland. By 1706–1707, Augustus had been defeated and temporarily deposed as Polish king. But Charles XII's preoccupation with Poland had given Peter the Great a much-needed opportunity to rebuild his shattered armed forces: a modern-style army, based on infantry and manned by peasant conscripts, was created very rapidly in the years after Narva.

In 1709 Charles XII's attempted invasion of Russia came to grief at Poltava (July 8) (q.v.), after which his army was lost and he himself forced into exile (1709–1714) in the Ottoman Empire. This shattering defeat effectively decided the war's outcome. Peter the Great slowly conquered much of Sweden's Baltic empire, while Prussia and Hanover both entered the war in the hope of securing territory when peace was made. Though Charles XII returned from the Ottoman Empire and resumed personal control of the war effort, he accomplished little before his death in 1718.

Peace was concluded at Nystad in September 1721. Sweden lost all of its empire (apart from the extreme tip of Western Pomerania), whereas Russia secured the former Swedish possessions of Livonia, Estonia, Ingria, and Karelia. The war's main political consequence was the establishment of Russia as the leading military power in northern Europe, a position it was never to lose.

H. M. SCOTT

R. M. Hatton, *Charles XII of Sweden* (1968).

Greco-Turkish War

1919–1922

Hostilities between Greek troops and Turkish nationalists first erupted in May 1919, following the occupation of Smyrna (Izmir) and its hinterland by the Greeks as part of the price exacted from the Turks for their support of the Central Powers in World War I (q.v.). Carried out at the request of Britain, France, and the United States, the operation served to advance Greece's territorial ambitions in Asia Minor. After consolidating its control over a fairly large zone, up to the Allied-designated "Milne Line," the Venizelos cabinet in the spring of 1920 secured London's agreement to expand further the area of occupation. Starting on June 22, several Greek divisions advanced both northward and eastward against limited Turkish resistance, taking Panderma (on the Sea of Marmara) as well as Bursa and Uşak.

Once the sultan's government in Istanbul had signed the Peace of Sèvres (which gave Greece possession of Eastern Thrace and supreme authority in the Smyrna region for five years, to be followed by a plebiscite), the Turkish nationalist regime in Ankara, headed by Mustafa Kemal Atatürk (q.v.), vowed to fight back. In November 1920, a more conservative regime was established in Athens under the previously exiled Greek monarch, King Constantine. Early in 1921, the new Greek commander in Asia Minor, General Anastasios Papoulas, launched a reconnaissance in force toward the important rail center of Eskişehir, but Turkish troops repulsed them.

Despite growing dissatisfaction with the Greek role in Asia Minor in Paris, Rome, and other Allied capitals, Papoulas launched new attacks in March 1921, but once again his troops were forced back. Three months later, with his forces swollen to about 200,000 men, he advanced successfully, taking both Eskişehir and Afyon (another important rail center). The Greeks then slowly pushed eastward in the direction of Ankara.

Commanded by Mustafa Kemal in person, the Turks initially lost a lot of ground (Battle of the Sakarya), but by early September the tide had turned, and the Greeks eventually withdrew to a partially fortified line running from the Sea of Marmara to the region east of Eskişehir and Afyon, and thence southwest to the Menderes River. They would stay in those positions, far from their logistical bases, for the next eleven months.

With increasing resources, including war matériel from Soviet Russia, at his disposal, Mustafa Kemal on August 26, 1922, launched a series of major attacks against the central and southern sectors of the Greek front. Though they encountered fierce resistance in some places, the Turks soon made headway in several strategic locations. By September 5, they had reached Bursa; four days later their cavalry entered Smyrna.

The catastrophic rout of the Greek army in Asia Minor triggered a revolution in Athens that culminated in the expulsion of King Constantine and his brother Andrew, and the execution of two prime ministers, three other cabinet members, and the last Greek commander in Asia Minor, General Georgios Hatzianestis. The Greek defeat also led to a Turkish showdown with Britain and the eventual replacement of the Sèvres peace treaty by a new settlement acceptable to the Turks (the Treaty of Lausanne). In the aftermath of the Greco-Turkish War, most Greeks living in Asia Minor lost their ancestral homes, either by flight or, later, by a compulsory population exchange negotiated with Ankara.

ULRICH TRUMPENER

Greek War of Independence

1821–1829

The Greek War of Independence was the first successful attempt by a Balkan people to break away from the Ottoman Empire and establish a nation-state. Even so, the Greek insurgents were not strong enough to defeat the Ottoman Empire on their own, and European help proved decisive. By 1825, after four years of guerrilla warfare, the Ottomans appeared incapable of retaking the Peloponnesus, whereas the Greeks were not able to extend the area under their control. With some reluctance, the Ottoman sultan asked Muhammad Ali of Egypt for help. The Egyptian army had been the beneficiary of Muhammad Ali's military reforms, and its bayonet-wielding regulars scattered the disorganized Greeks wherever the two armies clashed. The Greek navy was also in disarray: Greek sailors, disgruntled over pay arrears, had simply quit their posts and gone home, allowing the Egyptians easy access to the Peloponnesus. European governments became alarmed by Egyptian successes against the Greeks, in part because they distrusted Muhammad Ali's intentions in the eastern Mediterranean. The balance-of-power concerns so characteristic of the whole Near East question also encouraged European involvement. Britain, in particular, was concerned that the Greeks might fall into the Russian sphere of influence. The Europeans therefore set up a naval blockade of the Peloponnesus. On October 20, 1827, the entire Egyptian-Ottoman fleet was sunk by the allied navy (of Russia, France, and Britain) in the Bay of Navarino. This proved a turning point in the war. A Greek kingdom was established by the London Protocol (1829), although the Greeks had to submit to the imposition of a foreign monarch.

MOLLY GREENE

Greene, Nathanael

1742–1786, *American Revolutionary War General*

Though Nathanael Greene was only thirty-two years old at the time of his appointment as a general in the Continental army in June 1775, the ex-Quaker from Rhode Island quickly gained the esteem of George Washington (q.v.) and emerged as his most trusted subordinate in the American Revolution (q.v.). To Washington, Greene's energy, intelligence, organizational skills, and mastery of geographical and topographical information, combined with his broad reading in military history and theory, more than made up for the fact that he had seen only brief service as an enlisted man in the colonial militia. After his promotion to major general in 1776, Greene served as a brigade commander in the northern campaigns of 1776–1777 before holding the post of quartermaster general from 1778 to 1780, a thankless task he performed particularly well, given the depreciated state of American currency.

Greene's fame as a general rests on his response to another difficult assignment: the command of the American Southern Department, a graveyard of previous commanders and a theater in which British Lord Cornwallis (q.v.) had the upper hand after sweeping through Georgia and most of South Carolina during 1779–1780. Calling out local partisan forces and at times dividing his army, Greene developed a strategy that kept the enemy off balance in a two-year campaign of hit-and-run attacks and a few pitched battles, which drained the British of irreplaceable manpower; he always withdrew in time to fight another day. This strategy of rapid movement and constant pressure wore out Cornwallis, who limped northward to Virginia and Yorktown (q.v.), leaving Greene to pick off one by one his isolated posts in South Carolina.

DON HIGGINBOTHAM

Grenadiers

Grenadiers owed their existence to the influence of the *trace italienne* (see *Fortifications*) on warfare in early modern Europe. Grenades, hollow iron balls filled with explosives and ignited by a slow-match fuse, were important in attack and defense of fortified places. They were also a high-risk weapon. The earliest grenadiers were often volunteers whose specialization logically fitted them to lead "forlorn hopes" and storming parties. Their accompanying reputation as shock troops survived the eclipse of the grenade as an infantry weapon. By the second half of the seventeenth century, most European infantry battalions included a grenadier company or two.

Grenadiers were usually not the biggest soldiers, but they boasted the best ones — long-service veterans with solid combat records. "Grenadier" also became an honorific assigned to larger units: the cream of Napoleon's (q.v.) Guard bore the title, while Britain's First Foot Guards took the appellation after Waterloo (q.v.). The twelve senior regiments of Prussia's infantry were also dubbed "grenadiers" without any improvement in the quality of their recruits. Halfway through World War II (q.v.), Adolf Hitler (q.v.) took this process to its logical conclusion by rechristening most German infantry as grenadiers — a recognition of their achievements, but unaccompanied by any improvement in armament or personnel.

DENNIS E. SHOWALTER

Gribeauval, Jean-Baptiste de

1715–1789, French Artilleryman and Reformer

Lieutenant General Jean-Baptiste de Gribeauval served as inspector general of French artillery; he significantly improved cannon to give French artillery an advantage during the Wars of the French Revolution (q.v.). By boring out the barrels instead of casting the bore into the piece, the Gribeauval system achieved finer tolerances, with less windage (the difference between the diameter of the cannonball and the diameter of the bore) to sap the power of gunpowder. A ball of a given weight thus required less

powder, and smaller powder charges allowed the walls of the chamber to be thinner. This alone lightened the pieces, but Gribeauval also shortened barrels, which further reduced their weight. The tube of a four-pounder in the previous French artillery system weighed 500 kilograms, but a Gribeauval four-pounder weighed only 290 kilograms. French guns also boasted elevation screws and graduated rear sights. In addition, Gribeauval also modified the construction and harnessing of gun carriages, giving France the most mobile artillery pieces the world had yet seen.

JOHN A. LYNN

Grotius, Hugo

1583–1645, Dutch Jurist, Diplomat, and Scholar

Born in Holland, Hugo Grotius (Hugo de Groot) wrote Latin elegies at age eight, went to university at age eleven, and began to practice law at age sixteen. He gradually became involved in politics until his opposition to Maurice of Nassau (q.v.) led to imprisonment (1618–1621), and he spent the rest of his life in exile, mostly in Paris, living from his writing (prose and poetry) and his work as a diplomat. His numerous books on history, law, and religion synthesized the material from an exceptional range of other writers and were presented with a compelling fluency that assured them wide circulation. His most famous book, *On the Law of War and Peace* (1625), attempted to set limits to destruction in war by asserting that governments and their troops are bound by natural law (see *Laws of War*). It also argued that states should resort to armed conflict only for good reasons; and that, once engaged in hostilities, they should respect — as far as possible — the same human rights as in peacetime. Thanks to his literary reputation, Grotius's ideas reached a broad audience.

GEOFFREY PARKER

Guadalcanal, Battle of

August 1942–February 1943

When Japanese troops arrived on Guadalcanal on June 8, 1942, to construct an air base, and then American marines landed two months later to take it away from them, few people outside of the South Pacific had ever heard of that 2,500-square-mile speck of jungle in the Solomon Islands. But the ensuing six-month Guadalcanal campaign proved to be the turning point of the Pacific war.

Strategically, possession of a Guadalcanal air base was important to control of the sea lines of communication between the United States and Australia. Operationally, the Battle of Guadalcanal was notable for the interrelationship of a complex series of engagements on the ground, at sea, and in the air. Tactically, what stood out was the resolve and resourcefulness of the U.S. Marines, whose tenacious defense of the air base dubbed Henderson Field enabled the Americans to secure air superiority.

By the end of the battle on February 9, 1943, the Japanese had lost two-thirds of the 31,400 army troops committed to the island, whereas the U.S. Marines and the U.S. Army had lost less than 2,000 soldiers of about 60,000 deployed. The ship losses on both sides were heavy. But by far the most significant loss for the Japanese was the decimation of their elite group of naval aviators. Japan after Guadalcanal no longer had a realistic hope of withstanding the counteroffensive of an increasingly powerful United States.

BRADFORD A. LEE

Guards

From the beginning of organized warfare, rulers and commanders have sought to create immediate entourages whose loyalty was absolute. In the seventeenth century, an increasing number of European states developed royal household troops into field formations. French, English, and German guard regiments served in the wars of Louis XIV (q.v.). Peter the Great (q.v.) created the Russian Imperial Guard partly to attract his turbulent nobility and partly as a training ground for officers, but its regiments earned solid reputations in battle. Until the nineteenth century, however, guard formations as a whole were not especially distinguished in comparison to the rest of their respective armies. That changed with the rise of Napoleon (q.v.), whose guard evolved into a combined arms force of shock troops with a strength of over eighty thousand. The emperor increasingly perceived this force as his instrument of last resort in a pitched battle, taking corresponding care to nurture and husband it.

Nineteenth-century states often followed the Napoleonic model. Guardsmen were usually taller and heavier than their counterparts of the line, but re-

ceived no special combat training. They might best be described as elites by designation, yet the mystique of their status did result in performances well above the average of their respective armies during World War I (q.v.). The divisions of the Prussian Guard in particular earned a solid reputation as shock troops.

After 1918, guards formations in the traditional sense declined with the monarchies that spawned them. Their elite status tended to be ensured by units of guards performing new specialized functions: tankers and paratroops. Nazi Germany's *Grossdeutschland* division and the senior divisions of the Waffen SS (q.v.) combined selective recruitment with high priorities for replacements and equipment. The Soviet Union took a different path by giving formations that performed especially well in combat the designation of "guards." Since World War II (q.v.), however, the decline in the size of armies and the general improvement in their personnel have tended to reduce the title of guards to an honorific, with no special connotations or expectations of unusual performance in anything except ceremonial duties.

DENNIS E. SHOWALTER

Guderian, Heinz

1888–1954, German World War II General

Heinz Guderian had served as an officer in World War I (q.v.) and in the 1920s. In the years after 1933 he pushed for the creation of separate armored units. After a period in charge of all German armor, he commanded a corps in the invasion of Poland.

Guderian played a key role in the armored thrust through the neutral Low Countries in May 1940 and the subsequent breaching of the French line south of the breakthrough. Promoted to full general, Guderian commanded the German Second Panzer Army on the central portion of the Eastern Front (see *Operation Barbarossa*). A man who held and voiced fixed ideas, he was frequently in conflict with his superiors. Though an admirer of National Socialism and an extreme nationalist, his conflicts with his army group commander, Field Marshal Günther von Kluge, as well as with Adolf Hitler (q.v.), contributed to his relief during the German defeat before Moscow in December 1941.

Hitler remained an admirer of a man devoted to himself. In addition to the monthly bribe Hitler arranged for field marshals and four-star generals,

Guderian was to get a huge estate to be stolen from its Polish owners; Guderian spent much of his involuntary relief looking over such properties. He was allotted an estate worth 1.25 million marks but did not consider it adequate. Soon he had other worries: in February 1943, Hitler called him to a new command.

German armor, like the country's whole military system, had been designed for war against the western powers, the assumption being that the Soviet Union could be conquered quickly and easily. But the Germans had miscalculated. Under the pressure of difficulties and defeats, they built tanks (the Mark V Panther and Mark VI Tiger) for the east; but Stalingrad (q.v.) showed that the new tanks were arriving none too soon. In hopes of pushing the new program forward, Hitler appointed Guderian as inspector general of armored forces in February 1943.

Guderian's enormous drive helped revive Germany's armored forces during 1943 and 1944, at a time of defeats. Two factors kept Guderian from getting the huge numbers of tanks he wanted: enormous allocations of resources to the building of submarines, and similar allocations to new weapons to destroy London (the V-1 pilotless plane, the V-2 ballistic missile, the V-3 supergun, and the V-4 rocket). Guderian's memoirs suggest that he never understood this.

Guderian was called upon in the crisis of the attempted coup of July 20, 1944 (he had had neither the good sense nor the moral judgment to join in that effort). On July 21, 1944, Hitler made him chief of staff of the German army to rebuild the crumbling Eastern Front. Guderian devoted his talents to this task. As he anticipated the final Red Army (q.v.) offensive, he struggled to secure reserves; instead, these were wasted in the Battle of the Bulge (q.v.).

When the Soviets began their 1945 winter offensive, the Eastern Front collapsed. The Germans slowed and briefly stalled the Red Army. Guderian hoped to assist the slowing down by evacuating German forces cut off in western Latvia. Hitler, following the advice of Admiral Karl Dönitz (q.v.), preferred keeping them there to protect the central Baltic as training ground for new submarines. Over this issue, Guderian repeatedly argued with Hitler, and over it the two parted company on March 28, 1945. Although deeply involved in the shooting of captured Red Army political officers and aware of other atrocities on the Eastern Front, Guderian was not tried after the war (see *War Crimes Trials*).

GERHARD L. WEINBERG

Guerrilla Warfare

"The guerrilla fights the war of the flea, and his military enemy suffers the dog's disadvantages: too much to defend, too small, ubiquitous, and agile an enemy to come to grips with." Robert Taber's 1965 warning of what America was about to face in Vietnam proved unfortunately accurate. But the efficacy of guerrilla warfare had not always been so formidable an obstacle to Western soldiers. British and French regulars met and defeated countless guerrilla groups throughout the colonial era. Americans had done the same in the Philippines at the turn of the century. In the last half of the twentieth century, most experts agreed that the difference was provided by the melding of a powerful communist political doctrine with a well-conceived military scheme, producing a seemingly new way of war. It seemed as though the West was in for a serious decline of fortune. Indeed, the publisher of Taber's book, *The War of the Flea*, made the somewhat immodest dust-jacket claim that the new brand of fighting being waged by Third World peoples ". . . could overrun the United States itself tomorrow!" But, two decades before the century was out, it was the Communist world that was beset with guerrillas while the West was thriving. Like the flea, the guerrilla did not appear to discriminate between its victims.

This form of warfare derives its modern name from Spanish. *Guerrilla* (little war) described the campaign of persistent, small-scale encounters waged by the people of Spain against Napoleon's (q.v.) ill-fated attempt at conquest during the early years of the nineteenth century. But this type of conflict has a long history. The Greek historian Herodotus described the difficulties faced by the Persian king Darius during his bloody invasion of Scythia (modern Bulgaria) in 512 B.C. The Persians were lucky to escape with most of their heads still attached after constant clashes with the nomadic and mounted Scythians, a people who vanished after lightning hit-and-run raids. More often than not, Rome was engaged in a military endeavor to put down yet one more group of guerrillas. There was the uprising of Salvius the soothsayer (109? B.C.) in Sicily, a countryside struggle lasting five years. The Thracian Spartacus (71? B.C.) managed a brutal conflict of ambush and raid against the legions in Italy itself for two years. And Julius Caesar (q.v.) had his hands full trying to subdue the elusive Britons. Caesar's description of this campaign bears a close resemblance to much of the guerrilla warfare writing of the 1960s. The Roman leader said his legions were incapable of countering guerrillas because "the enemy never fought in close array, but in small parties with wide intervals; and had detachments posted at regular stations, so that one party covered another in turn, and fresh, unspent warriors took the place of the battle weary."

Until the 1950s, the great bulk of these "small wars" had an identical outcome — the counterguerrilla force won. There were exceptions. For example, the American Revolutionary War (q.v.) guerrilla Francis Marion was successful against the British. T. E. Lawrence (see *Lawrence of Arabia*) and his band of Arabs triumphed against the Turks during World War I (q.v.). And Britain, the Soviet Union, and the United States successfully supported hundreds of thousands of guerrillas against the Axis powers in Eastern Europe, Yugoslavia, France, Italy, Burma, Indochina, the Philippines, China, and Malaya during World War II (q.v.). But in these cases, guerrilla campaigns were ancillary to the more conventional military and naval efforts sponsored by major powers. As in the case of popular Spanish resistance to Napoleon, the ultimate outcome depended more on allied regulars than on the farmer-guerrillas waiting to spring a cleverly concealed ambush. And plenty of guerrilla forces operated on losing sides. In the American Civil War (q.v.), John Mosby and William Quantrill's guerrillas represented the failed Confederate cause. From the Roman Empire until the mid–twentieth century, the deck appeared to be stacked against the guerrilla.

Mao Tse-tung (q.v.) brought change. His 1938 treatise, significantly entitled *On Protracted War*, advocated three novel tenets that gave guerrilla warfare new potential. First came an admission that guerrillas alone could not win. Mao therefore envisaged a progressive effort to create regular forces while the guerrillas waged their hit-and-run tactics. At a later phase, guerrillas and regulars would coordinate their campaigns against the opponent. Both styles of fighting, both organizations, were needed to win.

Second, and just as important, Mao demanded a mammoth effort in organizing popular political, logistical, and moral support for guerrillas and regulars. The entire population had to be enlisted in one organization or another, actively joining and giving to the cause. Youths, farmers, teachers, workers, artists, both men and women — every conceivable human group was pointed at the common cause of waging

Fidel Castro at his hideout in the Sierra Maestra mountains of Cuba. From here, he and his nine original supporters drew followers and initiated the guerrilla campaign that toppled the Batista dictatorship in 1959.

war. The Chinese leader envisioned a symbiotic relationship: he spoke of his guerrillas as being fish and the people as being water. It did not matter if the cause was truly desirable among the people; mass support was so vital that coercion and orchestrated hatred directed at selected scapegoats was encouraged from the start.

Finally, Mao's scheme depended on a refreshing piece of in-your-face honesty: the war would be a long one. There was no crowd-pleasing promise of quick victory, but only the idea that the goal was so worthy that it merited prolonged sacrifice — for generations, if necessary. The notions about not holding ground, concentrating for actions, and dispersing immediately thereafter had been germane to guerrilla warfare long before Mao's appearance. The Chinese Communist leader simply preserved what was worthwhile and added facets, such as developing a support structure among the peasantry and boldly acknowledging the length of the struggle, that gave this ancient form of armed conflict modern potency.

Remaining faithful to his principles, Mao survived

the Japanese threat of the late 1930s and early 1940s. By melding guerrilla operations with the efforts of regulars, he defeated Chiang Kai-shek's (q.v.) U.S.-supported Nationalists after World War II, and inspired emulation by many insurgent leaders in the postwar period. Time and again during the 1950s, 1960s, and 1970s, Third World guerrilla forces took on Western or Western-supported conventionally armed and organized forces; on occasion, they emerged victorious. French and Portuguese colonialism proved particularly vulnerable, mainly because these two nations failed to create extensive indigenous governmental organizations to produce a native class with a stake in the survival of the colonial regimes. Indochinese, Algerians, Angolans, and the people of Mozambique gained independence from France and Portugal after prolonged guerrilla campaigns. And Western-supported governments were not alone in experiencing severe trials at the hands of Marxist insurgents. Fidel Castro's guerrillas triumphed over Fulgencio Batista's regime in Cuba after the latter was abandoned by the United States. By the mid-1970s, Communist guerrilla warfare gave alarming indications of invincibility.

Politically, the tide turned, but militarily much stayed as the Chinese leader had left it. Marxist regimes themselves began either falling to or being besieged by guerrillas. In the late 1970s and early 1980s, Communist Nicaragua, Ethiopia, Angola, Afghanistan, Mozambique, and Vietnamese-occupied Cambodia became engaged in counterinsurgency (q.v.). These Marxist regimes proved as inept in dealing with insurgents as had the Western-supported governments a few decades earlier. What remains is the stark fact that Mao-style guerrilla warfare is a logical choice for those seeking to overthrow a government. Mao himself said, "Guerrilla strategy is the only strategy possible for an oppressed people."

ROD PASCHALL

Robert Asprey, *War in the Shadows* (1994); Mao Tse-tung, *On Protracted War* (1938).

Guevara, "Che"

1928–1967, *Revolutionary and Theorist of Guerrilla Warfare*

Ernesto Guevara Lynch, an Argentinian with Irish forebears, acted as one of Fidel Castro's chief lieu-tenants during the Cuban revolutionary struggle of 1956–1959. Drawing on his experience with Castro, Guevara developed a model of Latin American revolution, which asserted that in the countryside, elite guerrilla forces alone, working from an "insurrectionary center" (the *foco insurreccional*), could radicalize the people without (as Mao had taught) the careful development of a separate and parallel political organization. The success of the campaign against the corrupt and unpopular Batista regime in Cuba blinded Guevara to the weaknesses of this strategy. After a brief and unhappy excursion in 1965 to assist with the Kinshasa rebellion in the Congo (Zaire), he sought to bring his brand of revolution to south-central Bolivia. But his small and disparate band of guerrillas failed to elicit any response. In August 1967 he was tracked down and killed by Bolivian forces trained by the United States and implementing what was almost a textbook counterinsurgency campaign, for the government, unlike Guevara, had apparently won the "hearts and minds" of the local inhabitants.

KEITH JEFFERY

Gulf War

1990–1991

Seldom have so many gathered for a war eventually fought by so few. Five days after Iraq invaded Kuwait on August 2, 1990, the United States started to deploy army, navy, marine, and air force units to Saudi Arabia (Operation Desert Shield), while at the same time urging other countries to send their own forces to the scene. U.S. coalition-building efforts were so successful that by the time the fighting (Operation Desert Storm) began on January 17, 1991, twelve countries had sent naval forces, joining the local navies of Saudi Arabia and the Gulf states as well as the huge array of the U.S. Navy, with no fewer than six aircraft carrier battle groups; eight countries had sent ground forces, joining the local troops of Bahrain, Kuwait, Oman, Qatar, Saudi Arabia, and the United Arab Emirates, as well as the seventeen heavy, six light, and nine marine brigades of the U.S. Army, with all their vast support and service forces (including thousands of female reservists); and four countries had sent combat aircraft, joining the local air forces of Kuwait, Qatar, and Saudi Arabia as well as the U.S. Air Force, U.S. Navy, and U.S. Marine aviation, for a grand to-

A Kuwaiti man watches as one of more than six hundred oil wells, set afire by Iraqi troops as they retreated in defeat, burns in March 1991.

tal of 2,430 fixed-wing aircraft. Against them, the Iraqis deployed only a few gunboats and small missile craft to match the coalition's armada; but on the other hand, some 1.2 million ground troops with about 5,800 tanks, 5,100 other armored vehicles, and 3,850 artillery pieces made for impressive ground strength. With 750 fighters and bombers, 200 other aircraft, and elaborate missile and gun defenses, Iraqi air strength also seemed formidable.

As it happened, however, the Gulf War was the first war in history to be decided by air power. More specifically, victory was achieved by the guided-weapon bombardment of individual buildings and installations of Iraqi command and control facilities; electrical supply; telecommunication; air defense; weapons research, development, production, and storage; and oil refining and distribution. Air bases, rail and road bridges, and some 4,000 emplaced armored vehicles

were also targeted. Such was the cumulative result of the destruction of these fixed, well-defined targets that by the time the ground offensive started on February 24, Iraqi armed forces were paralyzed centrally, partly hollowed out, and thoroughly demoralized. Until cut short by the cease-fire unilaterally proclaimed by the U.S. government on February 28, the coalition's advance into Kuwait and turning movement into southern Iraq were almost unresisted. Heavily armored U.S. M.1 battle tanks rapidly penetrated the Iraqi front, but so did the jeeps of the French Foreign Legion, and even the rented cars of enterprising journalists.

But precision air power paralyzes much more than it destroys; even when applied on the largest scale, it amounts to mere acupuncture rather than drastic surgery. Long before February 24, Iraqi command and control was mute and deaf, the resupply of troops in Kuwait had broken down, and Iraqi forces were reduced to the options of retreat or surrender (except for laying some sea mines and a brief raid across the Saudi border, the only Iraqi action throughout the war was the launch of 94 Scud missiles against Israel and Saudi Arabia). But in spite of all the individual items of equipment destroyed or overrun (including some 110 aircraft plus 137 flown to Iran, 3,000 or so armored vehicles, and 2,000 artillery pieces, gunboats, and so on) and the many military installations and military-industrial facilities wrecked beyond repair, enough survived to allow the Iraqi regime to quickly reconstitute a large army. Saddam Hussein thus achieved what was probably his only strategic aim: to ride out the war with enough strength left over to remain in power. Insofar as President George Bush called off the ground offensive so quickly in order to keep Iraqi power as a counterweight to a more dangerous Iran, he too achieved his strategic aim.

EDWARD N. LUTTWAK

Gurkhas

Men from certain tribes in rugged and remote central and eastern Nepal have served in British and Indian armies for nearly two hundred years. The relationship began when in 1814–1816 the East India Company sent an army against the Nepalese for what they regarded as depredations, forays into British-ruled India, but in the fighting the British grew to admire the soldierly virtues of the little hillmen. Even before the war ended they had begun to enlist them.

Throughout British India, the Gurkhas occupied a special place in the army; they were numbered separately, wore their own uniforms, and carried, in addition to firearms, their sharpened, curved *kukri*. During the Indian Mutiny (q.v.), they remained loyal to the British; they fought on the Northwest Frontier, in both world wars, and more recently in the Falklands (q.v.). In all such conflicts they distinguished themselves by their endurance, bravery, and loyalty.

There is practically no desertion among the Gurkhas, and because no British soldier was allowed into Nepal until the 1950s, all recruiting before then was done by the Gurkha soldiers themselves, who regularly returned from furloughs accompanied by relatives or young men from their villages. The money they remit and the pensions of old soldiers constitute Nepal's largest single source of foreign exchange.

When the British rule over the subcontinent ended in August 1948, the Gurkha battalions were divided between the Indian and British armies. The Indians have increased their numbers; the British, whose Gurkha headquarters are based in Hong Kong, have decreased them and may phase them out, for reasons not readily apparent.

BYRON FARWELL

Gustavus II Adolphus

1594–1632, *King of Sweden and General*

Beginning in 1618 the revolt of the Bohemian and Austrian Protestant nobles against the efforts of the future Holy Roman Emperor Ferdinand II to impose Catholic absolutism in his lands escalated into a series of conflicts, the Thirty Years' War (1618–1648) (q.v.). In Germany this conflict pitted the Hapsburg emperor and his allies, the Catholic League, against a number of Protestant groupings supported by foreign powers including England, the Dutch Republic, and Denmark. By 1629, however, the imperial and Catholic forces, ably led by the experienced Bavarian Johann Tserclaes, count of Tilly, and the ambitious Albrecht von Wallenstein (q.v.), a Catholic noble and an innovative and ambitious military entrepreneur, had triumphed over their adversaries and established control over the German shore of the Baltic. This situation not only appeared to menace the German Protestants but also alarmed Sweden. Therefore, in 1630 a

Swedish army under Gustavus Adolphus invaded north central Germany.

The conflict that followed was not just a religious or political one. It also was, at least in its opening stages, a clash between two military systems. After almost one year of cautious maneuvering to establish a firm base, and forming alliances with German princes, on September 17, 1631, a Swedish-Saxon army under Gustavus Adolphus defeated a veteran imperial host under Count Tilly at Breitenfeld near Leipzig. In five hours of hard fighting (the Saxons fled at the outset), the Swedes defeated the stronger imperialists, demonstrating the superiority of their new battle tactics, based on mobility and firepower, over the older system based on massive pike squares.

Hailed as the "Lion of the North," Gustavus now was able to move through Germany at will. In 1632 he invaded Bavaria and again defeated Tilly, while the emperor called on Wallenstein to raise a new army. An able general, Wallenstein managed to draw the king into several months of inconclusive maneuvering around Nuremberg and then compelled him to move into Saxony to protect his ally and his lines of communication. On November 16, 1632, Gustavus fought his final battle at Lützen, defeating Wallenstein's army. But — the very model of a heroic combat leader — he was killed leading a cavalry charge. Although it may be argued that at the time of his death he had already passed his zenith, he was the outstanding commander during the Thirty Years' War.

Ascending the throne in 1611, he gained experience in wars against Denmark, Poland, and Russia. In the 1620s he began to reorganize the Swedish military establishment, which still was based on feudal obligations, and gradually built up a national conscript army — the first in modern Europe — though in the end, Sweden's limited manpower base compelled him to rely heavily upon foreign troops. When he came to rescue the beleaguered Protestant cause in Germany in 1630, he already had begun to recruit foreign regiments, and throughout his campaign in Germany these bore the brunt of the fighting while he hoarded his native troops to guard his vital line of communication with Sweden.

Although there can be little question about his Lutheran devotion, Gustavus's main objective in invading Germany was not religious, but secular — the establishment of Swedish hegemony over the Baltic, securing control over a powerful buffer zone in Germany, and extracting an indemnity to cover some of the costs of his intervention. Although Sweden lacked both the manpower and the logistical capacity to achieve Gustavus's maximum objectives at the Peace of Westphalia (q.v.), for some seventy years Sweden became the paramount power in the Baltic.

In the end, however, Gustavus's importance in the evolution of war rested on his perfecting of the Dutch fighting system developed by Maurice of Nassau (q.v.), which had never been fully tested in battle. Assisted by officers who had served in the Dutch Republic and with a firm grasp of classic as well as contemporary military literature, he increased the fighting potential of his infantry. He deployed it in battalions, six deep, with thirty-six files of pikemen equipped with shorter pikes in the center, and ninety-six musketeers on each side. Thanks to an increased rate of fire, made possible by introducing paper cartridges, this shallower deployment was enhanced by the "salvo," in which the musketeers closed up to three ranks in order to fire a heavy volley on command. He further increased infantry firepower by issuing his battalions small three-pounder cannon, weighing only six hundred pounds, which could be pulled by one horse or pushed by six men. Gustavus introduced clear distinctions between siege and field guns, the latter twelve-pounders made more effec-

tive by better casting, lighter tubes and carriages, and improved crew training. Even more important, he restored cavalry to a major role on the battlefield. Although he had met light lancers in Poland, he preferred heavy cavalry, albeit with reduced armor, and changed its doctrine, abandoning the futile reliance on pistol fire in favor of charging, three lines deep, with cold steel.

Gustavus experimented with new tactical combinations, shifting the deployment of battalions within brigades for greater firepower and mutual support, and attached small bodies of "detached musketeers" to work with his cavalry. Enhanced by strict discipline, good training, and regular pay and supply furnished by a home government operating with a regular budget, the result of the reforms was an army with high morale and a fighting system that others emulated. Wallenstein utilized elements of the new system at Lützen; France followed suit; Oliver Cromwell (q.v.) built his New Model of 1645 on similar lines. Gustavus Adolphus deserves to be called the father of modern warfare.

GUNTHER E. ROTHENBERG

Michael Roberts, *Gustavus Adolphus: A History of Sweden, 1611–1632*, 2 vols. (1953–1958).

H

Haig, Douglas

1861–1928, British Field Marshal and Commander in Chief of the British Expeditionary Force

Sir Douglas Haig remains the most controversial figure in the literature of the British army in World War I (q.v.). Some considered him callous, bungling, stupid, an intriguer, and a falsifier of documents. To others, he was the embodiment of the British nation during World War I, sternly following an undeviating course to victory on the Western Front. Others again have seen Haig as limited by the ideas and army structure of the late Victorian period and uncomfortable with the developing technology of World War I. The last view seems the most accurate.

Haig's previous battle experience in the mobile, colonial wars of the Sudan and South Africa did not prepare him well for the static nature of war on the Western Front. Neither did his Staff College training in the late nineteenth century. Taken together, these combined to produce a fixed image of war in Haig's mind. He conceived of battle as a structured, three-stage affair: first, the preparation, wearing down, and drawing in of enemy reserves; second, the rapid and decisive offensive; and third, exploitation. Essentially, Haig did not change his mind about this structure throughout World War I. He continued, therefore, to think of war as relatively simple, human-centered, dependent on morale, and requiring the determination of a commander to persist until victory.

In addition, Haig was a cavalryman, and he always optimistically anticipated breakthroughs (the decisive offensive), followed by cavalry exploitation. Hence at the Somme (q.v.), on July 1, 1916, Haig forced his army commanders to deepen their objectives, and he also wanted a short hurricane bombardment, followed by a rush through. The result was a mixed plan of lengthy bombardment and deep objectives that did not succeed. The same process occurred at Passchendaele on July 31, 1917, when Haig appointed an offensive-minded general (Sir Hubert Gough) to command, and pressed him to plan a decisive breakthrough, rather than a step-by-step advance.

Thus Haig's major offensives at the Somme and Passchendaele commenced with artillery preparations, followed by breakthrough attempts. But these failed, and so did not produce cavalry exploitation. When the breakthroughs failed, both battles turned into protracted efforts to wear down the enemy, resulting in the costly attrition warfare of 1916 and 1917. Larger casualties were sustained on the British attacking side than on the German defensive side. Haig has been criticized for this basic strategy; however, this attrition did eventually take its toll on the German army and undoubtedly contributed to victory in 1918.

Haig has also been criticized for his ignorance of conditions at the front. His distant but powerful personality (and the possibility of dismissal) tended to intimidate liaison officers, staff officers, and senior commanders, who often told Haig what he wanted to hear. Additionally, Haig's Staff College training decreed that a commander should set strategy and then step aside and leave tactics to subordinates. Together, these two factors detached Haig from reality at the front and from the tactical side of day-to-day action. In fact, tactics on the Western Front had swallowed strategy — thus Haig had removed himself from the changing nature of warfare on the front. This mind-set also tended to create a vacuum between Haig and his generals before major offensives, when free exchange of ideas proved difficult. Nevertheless, when Haig did intervene at the strategic level, it always led to pressure to break through rapidly, and when this failed, to unduly prolonged offensives.

As a cavalryman, Haig also did not fully appreciate

that technology had become central to the conduct of warfare. This can be seen in Haig's choice of battlefield at Passchendaele in 1917, which put his artillery at a severe disadvantage, while the terrain prevented the use of tanks. However, by late 1917 at Cambrai (q.v.), and through 1918, the many experts in the technical aspects of war had really taken over the preparation of battles, so that Haig, General Headquarters, and even army generals became less relevant. Thus the August 1918 Amiens (q.v.) offensive was really run at a lower level and did not require the supervision of Haig, except for his usual instruction to considerably deepen the objectives of the attack. In summary, as the offensives of 1916–1918 show, Haig expected technology to adapt to his offensive plans, rather than structuring his plans to accommodate his weapons. Thus he persistently pursued objectives that were technically beyond the capabilities of his forces.

Haig's persistence did eventually produce victory on the Western Front in 1918, when others were expecting the war to continue into 1919. Yet the question remains whether a more flexible and imaginative commander could have achieved the same results with less cost.

TIM TRAVERS

Gerard de Groot, *Douglas Haig, 1861–1928* (1988); Tim Travers, *The Killing Ground: The British Army, the Western Front, and the Emergence of Modern Warfare, 1900–1918* (1987).

Halsey, William F., Jr.

1882–1959, U.S. World War II Admiral

Mention Fleet Admiral William Halsey, and first should come recognition of his combat leadership in the South Pacific in World War II (q.v.), the victories off Santa Cruz Islands and Guadalcanal (q.v.), the offensive up the Solomons, and the battles of New Georgia, Vella Lavella, and Bougainville. Then may come discussion of his seamanship in two great typhoons in 1944 and 1945 that battered his ships more than the Japanese ever did. At last, you will come to the main argument, Halsey's decision in the Battle of Leyte Gulf (q.v.). Was he right, in October 1944, to pursue Vice Admiral Ozawa Jisaburo's carriers instead of staying on station to block an approaching surface fleet and prevent it from battering the American landing force? To take the chance that Raymond A. Spruance (q.v.) had foresworn in the Battle of the Philippine Sea (q.v.) to destroy the Japanese carrier force, Halsey left open the strait through which the Japanese center force steamed. It was to Halsey's, and the Americans', great good fortune that Vice Admiral Kurita Takeo did not press his advantage, and that, in a decision as controversial as Halsey's, Kurita ordered the Japanese force to retire before reaching gunshot range of the beachhead landing site.

Halsey, the son of a naval officer, a graduate of Annapolis, and a naval aviator by training, won a fifth star for his victories. In retirement he defended his action in the Battle of the Philippine Sea as in accordance with his orders — and, he might have added, in the tradition of Mahan (q.v.).

GEORGE BAER

Hannibal

247–182 B.C., Carthaginian General

Son of the distinguished Carthaginian general and empire-builder Hamilcar Barca, Hannibal presented the Roman republic with its greatest military challenge. Hannibal was convinced by diplomatic initiatives that Rome planned to undermine vital Carthaginian interests in Spain. He precipitated the Second Punic (Phoenician) War (see *Punic Wars*) by taking Spanish Saguntum by siege (219 B.C.). He then made a daring march from Spain to the Po Valley in northern Italy, across the Rhone and over the Alps. Although he lost thousands of men in the crossing and all but one of his elephants to pneumonia, Hannibal gained the allegiance of the Gallic tribes of the Po and inflicted a stunning series of defeats (Trebia, 218 B.C.; Trasimene, 217 B.C.; Cannae, 216 B.C. [q.v.]) on numerically superior Roman armies.

Styling himself a "liberator," Hannibal spared non-Roman Italian prisoners of war and agitated for a general uprising of Italian towns against Rome. Yet the grand revolt failed to materialize, and without it Hannibal's genius as a battlefield general meant little. Although he succeeded in killing tens of thousands of Romans, Rome's military manpower base remained vast. Moreover, unlike Hannibal's mercenaries, Roman soldiers were superb at siegecraft. Although unable to defeat him in open battle, Roman generals limited Hannibal's foraging by shadowing his army (the "exhaustion" strategy of Fabius Maximus [q.v.]) and inflicted punishments on towns swayed by Han-

---

The Ten Greatest Generals

Alexander the Great (356–323 B.C.)

Hannibal (247–182 B.C.)

Saladin (1138?–1193)

Genghis Khan (1162?–1227)

Oda Nobunaga (1534–1582)

Helmuth von Moltke (1800–1891)

Napoleon Bonaparte (1769–1821)

Arthur Wellesley, First Duke of Wellington (1769–1852)

William T. Sherman (1820–1891)

William Slim (1891–1970)

---

nibal's propaganda. Hannibal soon found himself in the no-win position of having to use his limited forces to defend towns loyal to him, yet being unable to requisition men or money in quantity from them without invalidating his "liberation" message. His appeals to the Carthaginians for reinforcements were ignored until too late; his brother Hasdrubal eventually followed him over the Alps with a new army but was defeated and killed at Metaurus (207 B.C.).

Hannibal withdrew his army from Italy under a negotiated settlement, but the war was not over. Scipio Africanus (q.v.) led a Roman army into Africa and handed Hannibal his first battlefield defeat at Zama in 202 B.C. At Zama, Hannibal's army included a full complement of war elephants, an ironic example of a general rule in ancient warfare: "the side with the most elephants loses." Hannibal fled to the Greek east where he was briefly military adviser to Antiochus of Syria. Having crushed Antiochus (190 B.C.), the vengeful Romans pursued Hannibal to the Black Sea coast, where he committed suicide. His career demonstrates how it is possible to win (almost) all the battles, but lose the war. Pro-Roman histories of the Hannibalic War were written by Polybius (in Greek) and by Livy (in Latin).

JOSIAH OBER

Han Wu-ti

156–87 B.C., *Chinese Emperor*

Wu-ti, meaning "the Martial Emperor," was the posthumous title assigned to Liu Ch'e, of the Han dynasty, who came to the Chinese throne in 141 B.C. His reign was one of the most aggressively expansionist periods in all of Chinese history. Abandoning the policies of his predecessors, who had sought to appease the nomadic Hsiung-nu of Mongolia, and drawing upon the resources accumulated during their relatively peaceful reigns, he launched the first of many offensive expeditions into the northern steppe in 129 B.C. Year after year, columns of tens of thousands of Chinese cavalrymen rode out to attack the nomads along a front that stretched from Manchuria to the oases of Central Asia. After major Chinese victories in 121 and 119 B.C., the Hsiung-nu were battered into quiescence (if not submission), leaving China's northern border free of nomad incursions for almost twenty years. During this period, Han Wu-ti's armies undertook campaigns that resulted in the conquest of Northern Vietnam (112–111 B.C.) and the Korean peninsula (109–108 B.C.). Perhaps the most ambitious expedition was that dispatched to the distant Central Asian state of Ferghana to seize its legendary horses; it took the Chinese general Li Kuang-li three years (104–102 B.C.) and many thousands of casualties to accomplish his mission.

Although these campaigns are often viewed as a glorious chapter in Chinese history, Wu-ti's relentless war making imposed heavy economic burdens on the Chinese people, and his victories had little long-term impact. In spite of his posthumous designation as "the Martial Emperor," Han Wu-ti never actually commanded his armies in the field; like most Chinese rulers, he remained in the capital and left battlefield leadership to his generals.

DAVID A. GRAFF

Harris, Arthur

1892–1984, *British Air Commander*

Arthur Harris enlisted in the British army at the start of World War I (q.v.), but switched to the Royal Flying Corps. After the war he remained in the Royal Air Force, where his acerbic wit, ambition, and enthusiastic support for strategic bombing ensured him a rapid rise. Harris was never known for concern for the traditional services; he came close to being dismissed from the Staff College at Camberley, where he suggested that the army would not buy a tank unless the vehicle ate hay and thereafter left deposits like a horse.

Harris began World War II (q.v.) as a group com-

This scene from the Bayeux Tapestry is thought to depict King Harold of England being mortally wounded in the eye at the Battle of Hastings. Above, the inscription reads, "King Harold Is Killed"; below, a border of dead men and horses indicates the heavy losses incurred in the fierce hand-to-hand combat.

mander in Bomber Command, which spent its time dropping propaganda leaflets — which he derisively referred to as "toilet paper." Harris took over Bomber Command in February 1942 when its fortunes were at a nadir, but with the arrival of new aircraft — the Halifax and especially the Lancaster — Harris pursued his vision of destroying German morale in great night attacks that would dehouse the German population, preferably while the Germans were inside. By 1943 his bombers were savaging the Ruhr and destroyed the heart of Hamburg in one night. (After the war, one of Hitler's inner circle claimed that if the British had achieved six more Hamburgs that summer, Germany would have collapsed.) But German night air defenses became more sophisticated, and in the Battle of Berlin, during the winter of 1943–1944, Harris nearly destroyed his command in his pursuit of victory. Instead, in April 1944 a battered Bomber Command turned to preparing for D-Day (q.v.), and it rendered crucial help in wrecking the French transportation network. In the end, Harris and his command played a major role in the Allied victory, but its contribution came at great cost to his crews, with 51 percent killed on operations, 9 percent in crashes in England; 3 percent maimed, 13 percent shot down, and less than 25 percent surviving unscathed. Postwar distaste over the campaign resulted in the govern-

ment's refusal to grant honors to Harris or even a medal to the men who had served in the effort.

WILLIAMSON MURRAY

Hastings, Battle of

October 14, 1066

The most famous battle on English soil, Hastings changed the destiny of England, and its sheer drama still astounds. It bore a resemblance to no other engagement of its time. It was, as a Norman knight said, "a strange kind of battle," pitting infantry against heavy cavalry.

In 1066 Harold Godwinson became king of England, despite a strong claim to the throne by Duke William of Normandy. The duke immediately raised a force of five thousand men and invaded England on September 28. Harold was distracted by a Norwegian invasion far to the north, which he defeated. Rushing south with only part of his army, he met the Normans at Hastings on October 13.

On the next morning the Norman infantry attacked the Saxon line. When they made no headway against the solid ranks of Saxon infantry, William sent in his cavalry. After their attack stalled, William deliberately staged several feigned "retreats" to lure the Saxons from their shield wall, where they could be slaughtered by his cavalry. When Harold was struck down late in the day by an arrow, Saxon resistance collapsed. William's leadership, particularly his flexible combination of infantry, archers, and heavy cavalry, had prevailed.

William was quickly crowned king of England. Norman rule would tie England firmly to the emerging civilization of mainland Europe, introduce castles (q.v.) and feudalism (q.v.), ensure the primacy of the Roman church, and inject a heavy dose of Latin and French into what would become modern English. In short, by blending Saxon and Norman institutions, the Normans laid the foundations of modern England.

W. SCOTT JESSEE

Hattin, Battle of

July 4, 1187

In one of Islam's most spectacular victories over Christian forces during the Crusades (q.v.), Muslim forces were led by the great sultan Saladin (q.v.), who, after unifying the two Islamic centers of power in Syria and Egypt, focused his attention on ridding the Holy Land of the crusaders. Saladin's hybrid force included Egyptian infantry and a Mamluk cavalry. The crusaders' army comprised Frankish knights, members of the Hospitallers and Templars (see *Knightly Orders*), and four thousand English mercenaries sent by King Henry II. Historians have long wondered why Guy, king of Jerusalem and head of the crusader forces, made the unwise decision to march across the hot, waterless plateau from Saffuriyah to Tiberias in the middle of the summer and risk everything in a pitched battle against Saladin's well-rested, well-provisioned army. Explanations have ranged from dissension within the crusader camp to the excessive cupidity of both the Templars and Reynald, lord of the great fortress of Kerak, who were anxious to fight. The crusaders set up camp on a rocky hill with twin volcanic outcroppings, known as the Horns of Hattin, from which the Sea of Galilee was visible. Saladin situated himself between the crusading army and the freshwater Lake Tiberias, the only available water source. He used his light cavalry to set off a torrent of arrows. The crusaders, going mad from thirst, were thrown into confusion and surrounded by the enemy. The annihilation of the crusaders' army left Christian lands open to Saladin, who followed up his victory with the capture of Acre (July 10, 1187) and Jerusalem (October 2, 1187). Saladin's success led directly to the calling of the Third Crusade (1189).

WILLIAM CAFERRO

Hawkwood, John

1320?–1394?, *English Soldier of Fortune*

The second son of a tanner in Essex, Sir John Hawkwood became the most famous mercenary captain of his day. His military career began in France in the Hundred Years' War (q.v.), but it was in Italy that he made his reputation. Hawkwood fought at the head of numerous mercenary companies ("free companies"), serving such masters as Milan, the Pope, and Florence. Using military tactics developed by the English in the Hundred Years' War (lance, longbow, infantry), Hawkwood gained impressive military victories (Castagnaro, 1389); between wars, he led companies on raids, extorting large sums of money from communites. His enduring fame rests as much on his military success as on his reputation as the one honest, reliable soldier among a treacherous lot — a reputation gained by his refusal to accept a Florentine bribe while employed by rival Pisa. Indeed, when Hawkwood died, the Florentines granted him burial in the cathedral, an honor denied their greatest poet, Dante Alighieri, a generation earlier.

WILLIAM CAFERRO

Hessians

Though the word *Hessians*, then and later, was often applied to all the German troops who fought for Britain in the American Revolution (q.v.), the fact is that George III purchased the services of soldiers from six German principalities. To be sure, Hesse-Cassel sent the largest contingent, 17,000, but five other German states dispatched another 12,800: Brunswick, 6,000; Hesse-Hanau and Ansbach-Bayreuth, each 2,400; Waldeck and Anhalt-Zerbst, each just over 1,000.

For the princes of Hesse-Cassel, selling the services of their citizens had a long history. Previous to this transaction with Britain, their most profitable ventures had been in Italy, where Venice had purchased Hessians to oppose the Turks; still other Italian states had turned to Hesse-Cassel for men to fight their immediate neighbors. The present ruler, Frederick II, sent none of his own one hundred children to risk death in America.

Although this trafficking in human flesh was still commonplace at the time, it nonetheless conflicted sharply with Enlightenment ideals. The writers Goethe and Schiller were among those who condemned German princes for exploiting their citizens in a cause of no concern to them; but these petty rulers, always hard up for cash, received handsome compensation from Britain. At least one of the treaties, with Brunswick, included an infamous blood-money clause: the ruler received an additional lump sum for each man killed or captured and for every three wounded.

The year 1776 saw the Hessians' reputation elevated by their effective use of the bayonet at Long Island and Fort Washington in New York City; but they demonstrated that they were hardly supermen after George Washington (q.v.) captured or killed virtually all of the Hessian garrison of nearly a thousand men at Trenton, New Jersey, the day after Christmas of that same year.

It is difficult to generalize about the quality of the German contingents. The landgrave of Hesse-Cassel's Bodyguards were equal to the best British regiments. The *Jäger* units, equipped with rifles and performing as light infantry, effectively engaged in scouting and patrolling duties. In contrast, some regiments were filled with the very old and the very young. Sometimes recruiters rounded up every stranger in sight. A student kidnapped into a Hessian regiment found himself with similar "enlistees": a merchant from Vienna, a monk from Würzburg, and a magistrate from Meninger, all "packed like sardines" aboard British transports.

The German troops probably equaled their British allies in abilities and performance. Certainly most were not the ogres described in school textbooks. They probably engaged in no more plundering and looting than did the redcoats. It would appear, however, that their desertion rates were especially high. Since they had no stake in the outcome of the war, many of them responded to inducements from the Continental Congress and the states to change sides in return for land and the blessings of liberty, which were enjoyed by German settlers in Pennsylvania and elsewhere. Assuredly, death in combat and from disease took a relatively small number of the twelve thousand German soldiers out of the thirty thousand in British service who failed to return to Europe after

the war. The countless mercenaries (q.v.) who remained behind added their ore to the great American melting pot and provide an early example of psychological warfare (q.v.) in American history.

DON HIGGINBOTHAM

Hindenburg, Paul von

1847–1934, German General and President

The "wooden titan" of the wartime empire and the Weimar Republic, Paul von Hindenburg saw action in 1866 and 1870–1871. Hindenburg is often dismissed by critics as lacking intelligence and imagination — "wooden" — but his career established him as a man of force and integrity who at the same time understood the difference between honor and intransigence. He spent most of his active service with troops, alternating command and staff appointments. Although regarded as a possible candidate for chief of staff and Prussian war minister, Hindenburg's talents were not sufficient to overcome his own well-founded opinion that he lacked the skills of the politician and the courtier required for success in the higher echelons of Wilhelm II's peacetime army. Hindenburg retired in 1911 as a corps commander. He was then sixty-four.

His career took an unexpected upturn three years later when Erich Ludendorff (q.v.) was appointed chief of staff of the Eighth Army, reeling from defeat at the hands of the Russians. Ludendorff was arrogant, touchy, and humorless, a man with more admirers than friends; someone calm and steady would be required to balance his mercurial temperament. Hindenburg's imperturbability, his good health, and his imposing physical presence all worked in his favor. On August 22, 1914, he was offered command of the Eighth Army. He promptly accepted.

The professional relationship between Hindenburg and Ludendorff became so close that Winston Churchill (q.v.) in *The Unknown War* consistently refers to them by the anagram H. In fact, the association began as a marriage of convenience. If a new command team joining the headquarters of a defeated army (whose staff officers feared for their own careers) did not watch each other's backs, no one could be expected to do it for them. Hindenburg also had the gift, rare among senior officers, of knowing his own limitations *and* his own best qualities. He could provide without resentment a base and a framework for a man more brilliant than himself and gave free play to Ludendorff's intellect, will, and energy. Hindenburg's calm kept Ludendorff steady during the battles of Tannenberg (q.v.) and the Masurian Lakes, two of Germany's brightest victories of the war. And it was Hindenburg, not his chief of staff, who became a household word as the savior of East Prussia and a symbol of Germany at war.

Hindenburg's wartime image was psychologically specific. It focused on mature male virility at a time when war was becoming a young man's province. Institutionally, the German army badly needed heroes in the aftermath of the Schlieffen Plan's (q.v.) collapse. Hindenburg also had the advantage of being isolated from the tensions proliferating in a high command forced by the battles of the Marne (q.v.) and First Ypres (q.v.) to rethink its basic views of war. For the first time in its history, imperial Germany had a hero independent of the royal house. By the end of 1914, former chancellor Bernhard von Bülow and Grand Admiral Alfred von Tirpitz (q.v.) were discussing the possibility of having Wilhelm II declared insane, his son appointed regent, and Hindenburg given the emergency post of imperial administrator. No one doubted where the real power would be.

Hindenburg's mystique increased during 1915 and 1916, both because of the achievements of his armies in the east and because of the continued loss of status by Chancellor Theobald von Bethmann-Hollweg, Chief of Staff Erich von Falkenhayn (q.v.), and not least the kaiser himself. His appointment as chief of the General Staff in August 1916 surprised few politicians and fewer soldiers. Hindenburg, once again working in tandem with Ludendorff, however, was in well over his head as the supreme commander of a total war effort in a state already stumbling from exhaustion. He lent his name and prestige to a series of policies ranging from inauspicious to disastrous. The munitions program, the Auxiliary Services Law, and the unrestricted U-boat campaign overstrained Germany's resources and, in the latter case, added the United States to Germany's enemies. Hindenburg participated in the intrigues that led to Bethmann's dismissal in July 1917 and saw to it that the chancellor's successors remained no more than figureheads. He accepted the increasingly unrealistic war aims of the militarists and nationalists. The shrewd common sense that had been a hallmark of his earlier career gave way to a passivity ironically replicating that of Wilhelm II.

Hindenburg came to life once more only as Germany stood on the brink of disaster. The great offensives of March 1918 so depleted Germany's human and material resources that the army proved unable to stop the battering Allied counterattacks. By October, the Second Reich was exhausted. While refusing to resign with Ludendorff, Hindenburg accepted the convictions of Ludendorff's successor, General Wilhelm Groener, that the army no longer supported the kaiser and the country needed immediate peace. Neither the abdication nor the armistice would have gone as smoothly as they did without Hindenburg's support. Even after his retirement in 1919, he remained a national hero — a fact made apparent in 1925 when he was elected president of the Weimar Republic. Hindenburg initially performed his new duties loyally and not ineffectually. However, the Great Depression, the rise of National Socialism, and his own advancing age robbed Hindenburg by 1930 of whatever effectiveness he still possessed. His appointment of Adolf Hitler (q.v.) as German chancellor in January 1933 gave the Nazi regime badly needed legitimacy. It thereby laid the groundwork for the destruction of the Germany Hindenburg loved after his fashion and served according to his best lights.

DENNIS E. SHOWALTER

Andreas Dorpalen, *Hindenburg and the Weimar Republic* (1964); Walter Gorlitz, *Hindenburg: Ein Lebensbild* (1953); Martin Kitchen, *The Silent Dictatorship* (1976).

History, Military

War decisively affects societies; it is one of the principal acts of a government. It is hardly surprising that systems with surplus intellectual resources have devoted good parts of them to the study of conflict. Herodotus and Thucydides, the founders of historical study in the West, were at bottom military historians. Military thought may have been in principle unpopular in Confucian China, but as early as the fifth century B.C., the history and nature of warfare were systematically analyzed in Sun Tzu's (q.v.) *Art of War*. The classical literature of India is largely shaped by martial themes, as are the orally based histories of sub-Saharan Africa.

Wherever it is studied, whatever its perspective, however, military history has never been an end in itself. Its purpose has been not only to discover what actually happened in war and why, but also to transmit that information to soldiers, governments, and not least, the people at large. Military history's functions in this context have been inspirational on one hand, didactic on the other. The "drum and trumpet" history so often disparaged today has been for centuries a means of integrating increasingly complex societies, linking generations, and inspiring common participation in the most difficult of all human efforts. It was not by accident that Socrates took pride in having earned Athens's equivalent of the Combat Infantry Badge. Nor did Samuel Johnson greatly exaggerate when he said that every man thinks meanly of himself for not having been a soldier or not having been to sea. In the nineteenth century, William James called for a "moral equivalent of war." Such an equivalent, however, remains undeveloped. Even the nonviolent resistance movements of the twentieth century tend to emphasize physical and moral courage, elevating protagonists such as Mohandas Gandhi and Martin Luther King, Jr., who were heroic enough *not* to strike back.

The didactic role of military history reflects the fact that, in Carl von Clausewitz's (q.v.) phrase, war is a chameleon. For centuries it was learned by apprenticeship — but, unlike the equivalent process of civilian life, war's apprenticeship offered little time for reflection. A cleric, a craftworker, and even a surgeon could pause in the middle of a process to explain or question. Battles wait for no one. Combat experience, moreover, was so intensely personal that even one's own memories could prove a snare and deceit. Military "families" such as the companions of Alexander the Great (q.v.) were useful in good part because they offered opportunities to cross-check individual stories promptly.

War, moreover, is an occasional occurrence. States and armies normally spend far more time planning and contemplating wars than fighting them. Apart from changes in opponents, terrain, and technology, the passage of time itself has limited the applicability of direct experience. It was scarcely accidental, therefore, that even before the development of the military as a profession, soldiers turned to history as a means of training and endeavor. Nor has the military sought its historians from its own ranks: whereas historians of law or medicine have traditionally been involved with these professions, the armed forces have both sought and accepted insights from outsiders with no direct experience in war. This anomaly can partly be explained by the relatively high degree of flexibility required in successful military establishments. It also reflects historians' willingness to produce functional accounts of military expertise and analytical frameworks for discrete events.

Until recently, even developed societies possessed relatively small literate classes, most of whom mediated with the gods or made policy decisions on earth. In that context, all history was produced for external purposes. Thucydides and Livy, Ibn Khaldun and Ssuma Ch'ien wrote to edify and instruct. The concept of history as valuable for its own sake is distinctively modern and distinctively Western, a nineteenth-century product of German idealism, expanded access to archives, and not least, economies prosperous enough to give historians a living at public expense, usually in educational systems.

The concept of history "as it really was" began changing both the motives for writing military history and its place in the intellectual world. The new criteria for history called not merely for objectivity, but also for detachment from the particular subject studied. The armed forces of the industrial age, on the other hand, deliberately emphasized history as an instrumental tool for understanding war's conduct. If intellectuals would not help them, the soldiers would do the work themselves.

Official histories — studies of campaigns or events prepared or commissioned by armed forces — made their first appearance in this context during the nineteenth century. Their original intent was arguably benign: to reconstruct, in detail, complex events that civilian historians lacked the interest or the technical knowledge to explore. Almost immediately, however, official historians encountered interrelated problems. The first might be called command influence. Objective evaluations of doctrine and performance meant embarrassing too many senior officers still serving or still influential. The second involved focusing on alleged lessons of history out of a desire to perform better the next time. The results could be anything from using historical evidence as a source of support for preconceptions to a present-mindedness relentlessly obsessed with forcing past wars into the procrustean bed of current doctrines and shibboleths.

Imperial Germany took a dubious lead in both fields. The General Staff's Historical Division merits the thanks of scholars for collecting a trove of data that would otherwise have remained inaccessible. What was done with the material is often another story. The official history of the Franco-Prussian War (q.v.) was designed to offend as few people as possible, with the result that it is often untrustworthy even as narrative. The volumes on the wars of Frederick the Great (q.v.) seek to make Old Fritz a precursor of nineteenth-century concepts of the "battle of annihilation." When civilian scholar Hans Delbrück suggested that Frederick instead practiced attritional war, he succeeded only in closing the uniformed historians' ranks against "amateurs."

Official military history reached its nadir after World War I (q.v.). British official historians arguably knew more about the Western Front than anyone but refused to tell the full story. Sir James Edmonds, the project's director, eschewed on principle "excessive" criticism, allowing participants in the events discussed not only to critique but also to influence the *Official History*'s presentation to the point of gross distortion in treating controversial operations such as the Somme (q.v.) and Passchendaele (see *Ypres, Battle of*). Matters were worse in Weimar Germany, where the government itself conspired in a systematic falsification of their country's military history between 1914 and 1918 as part of a general campaign against "war guilt."

Since 1945, some states and armed forces have backed away from using military history as a political weapon. In Japan and the former Soviet Union, the treatment of World War II (q.v.) has frequently combined equal parts of gilt and whitewash. British, U.S., and especially French official accounts of that conflict, however, are far more objective than their predecessors and incorporate far stronger critical dimensions. Still, triumphalism can remain a problem. The U.S. Army's history of the Gulf War (q.v.), for example, concentrates on victory won at the expense of lessons learned to a degree reminiscent of imperial Germany in the 1870s. Nevertheless the history of World War II (q.v.) compiled by Germany's *Militärgeschichtliches Forschungsamt* and the volumes on Vietnam emanating from the U.S. armed forces take commendable pains to present their respective stories "warts and all."

The nineteenth century also produced a new type of military writer: the historical strategist. Some were serving officers like Alfred Thayer Mahan (q.v.); others were civilian analysts like Sir Julian Corbett (q.v.) and Sir B. H. Liddell Hart (q.v.). They had in common a commitment to publicizing better ways of fighting wars in reaction to current errors. Mahan's concept of massed fleet actions reflected his distaste for what he perceived as a dilettantish approach to sea power in contemporary navies. Liddell Hart developed his strategy of the indirect approach in response to the stagnant butchery of 1914–1918: he himself had been gassed at the Somme (q.v.). These men and their counterparts share as well a tendency to perceive history as a source of support for their preconceptions. Mahan described the complex history of maritime warfare in the revolutionary and Napoleonic era as a series of decisive naval battles that remains seductive for its simplicity. Liddell Hart mustered commanders from Genghis Khan (q.v.) to T. E. Lawrence (q.v.) behind a vision of feint, deception, and maneuver that would ultimately produce victory without killing — in contrast to World War I, which reversed that equation.

Official historians and historical strategists dominated the writing of military history until after World War II. They did much as well to marginalize the discipline. Official historians and popular writers alike tended to become enmeshed in war's nuts and bolts: battles and commanders, weapons and logistics. Their work prefigured much "class, race, and gender" history in being interesting and intelligible only to increasingly limited audiences. On the other hand, historical strategists discredited military history by diluting it: putting data at the service of theory. Should the fit be imperfect, fact usually went to the wall. The pattern persists in think tanks, government and private, where clever ideas are at a premium and detailed research dismissed as pedantry — or at least as irrelevant to winning immediate battles for funding and prestige.

A change began during the 1930s, focused in educational institutions such as the universities of Oxford, Princeton, and Chicago. The intellectual godfather of this trend was Delbrück, whose emphasis on the relationship of strategy to policy and the relationship of military establishments to civilian institutions invited a shift from the study of war fighting to the analysis of war making. The nature of World War II, moreover, not merely invited but demanded a focus broader than the utilitarian, operational approach dominant for a century. Particularly for the United States, battlefield problems were ultimately functions of policy making and logistics. In order to fight anyone, President Franklin D. Roosevelt (q.v.) and his advisers had first to decide who, where, and how.

Makers of Modern Strategy, edited by E. M. Earle and published in 1942 by Princeton University Press, marked the beginning of what became the "new military history." A generation of scholars maturing after 1945 sought less to understand the specific aspects of war than to interpret the role of military affairs and military institutions in human development. To some degree this concern was fostered by a belief that nuclear weapons (q.v.) and revolutionary warfare had rendered the specific lessons of military history obsolete. The new military history was also fostered by new attitudes on the part of its traditional consumers. Armed forces after 1945 were increasingly influenced in the West by social science and management models, whereas the Soviet Union insisted in principle on war as a science in a Marxist-humanist context.

The result was a growing body of research focusing on the structural and intellectual aspects of armed forces, on policy making, on the impact of military institutions on their societies. Preparation for war was regarded as a secondary consideration. The study of combat itself was marginalized, left to popular writers and service-school historians. In the context of the Vietnam War (q.v.), whose battles appeared so ultimately sterile, this new military history acquired an academic legitimacy its predecessor never possessed. At the same time, historical approaches enjoyed enhanced respectability in the community of national security analysis. The relationship between military historians in uniform and those in the academic community became warmer and more comprehensive.

These gains were, however, bought at a price — the price of neglecting the special problems of waging war. Armed forces, whatever their social, cultural, and economic contexts, ultimately exist to fight and must ultimately pay primary attention to that basic function. Overlooking those facts produced military history often as incomplete, or as one-sided, as its discredited drum-and-trumpet predecessor. It was as though scholars of politics had decided to avoid discussing election processes. The problem was exacerbated during and after the Vietnam War, when it grew increasingly difficult to publish military history with both academic and general presses.

Beginning in the 1980s, the balance began swinging back to what has been called, only half facetiously, "the *new* new military history." Stripped of its accompanying jargon, this model recognizes the specific, unique nature and function of armed forces while analyzing them in the context of the wider issues introduced to the subject in the previous quarter-century. *The Making of Strategy* (1994), edited by Williamson Murray, MacGregor Knox, and Alvin Bernstein, is a benchmark anthology whose contributors — Robert A. Doughty, Holger H. Herwig, John A. Lynn, and Geoffrey Parker — have played major roles in military history's reorientation. *MHQ: The Quarterly Journal of Military History* has made the new approach available to general readers as well.

The result to date has often been confrontational as Young Turks and middle-aged Turks contest the intellectual high ground. The renewed debates among soldiers and scholars have nevertheless given military history a breadth and a stability previously unknown to the discipline and likely to continue into the next century.

DENNIS E. SHOWALTER

Hitler, Adolf

1889–1945, German World War II Leader

To avoid being arrested for evading military service in Austria-Hungary, Adolf Hitler left Vienna for Munich in May 1913 but was forced to return — then he failed the physical. He volunteered for the Bavarian army the following year and served during all of World War I (q.v.) on the Western Front. His experiences in the fighting affected his thinking about war thereafter.

After World War I, Hitler came to control the National Socialist German Workers Party, which he hoped to lead to power in Germany. When a coup attempt in 1923 failed, he turned, after release from jail, to the buildup of the party to seize power by means that were at least outwardly legal. He hoped to carry out a program calling for the restructuring of Germany on a racist basis so that it could win a series of wars to expand the German people's living space until they dominated and exclusively inhabited the globe.

He believed that Germany should fight wars for vast tracts of land to enable its people to settle on them, raising large families that would replace casualties and provide soldiers for the next war of expansion. The first would be a small and easy war against Czechoslovakia, to be followed by the really difficult one against France and Britain. A third war would follow against the Soviet Union, which he assumed would be simple and quick and would provide raw materials, especially oil, for the fourth war against the

United States. That war would be simple once Germany had the long-range planes and superbattleships to fight a power thought inherently weak but far distant and possessing a large navy.

Once Hitler had come to power in 1933, German military preparations were made for these wars. The emphasis in the short term was on weapons for the war against the western powers, and for the long term, on the weapons for war against the United States.

In 1938 Hitler drew back from war over Czechoslovakia at the last minute but came to look upon agreeing to a peaceful settlement at Munich as his worst mistake. When he turned to the war against France and Britain, he could not persuade Poland to subordinate itself to Germany to ensure a quiet situation in the east; hence, he decided to destroy that country before heading west. He was determined to have war and initiated it on September 1, 1939. To facilitate the quick conquest of Poland and break any blockade, he aligned Germany with the Soviet Union, assuming that concessions made to that country would be easily reclaimed when Germany turned east.

Hitler had originally hoped to attack in the west in the late fall of 1939, but bad weather — which would have hindered full use of the air force — and differences among the military led to postponement until the spring of 1940. During that interval, Hitler made two major decisions. Urged on by Admiral Erich Raeder, he decided to seize Norway to facilitate the navy's access to the North Atlantic and did so in April 1940. Urged by General Erich von Manstein (q.v.), he shifted the primary focus of attack in the west from the northern to the southern part of the force that was to invade the Low Countries. They might then cut off Allied units coming to aid the Belgians and the Dutch.

The new strategy at first appeared to work when the Germans in a few days broke through the French defenses and, within ten days, reached the Channel coast behind the Allied forces. Ordering their air force to destroy the cut-off Allied units, the Germans first wanted to turn south to prevent the buildup of a new defensive line, a decision on which the German commander, Gerd von Rundstedt, and Hitler agreed. As it became clear that many Allied soldiers might escape, the direction of the armor was reversed again, but too late to halt the evacuation of much of the British Expeditionary Force and many French soldiers. The thrust southward in early June 1940 brought a swift collapse of remaining French resistance, and this complete victory gave Hitler an aura of triumph, which assured him the enthusiastic support of almost all of Germany's military leaders, especially as he systematically tied them to himself by generous promotions and a system of mass bribery.

Because it looked as if this war was over, Hitler and the military began planning for the wars against the United States and against the Soviet Union. On July 11, the resumption of construction of the navy to defeat the United States was ordered; by July 31, after first hoping to invade the Soviet Union in the fall of 1940, Hitler, on the advice of his military staff, decided to attack in the east in the late spring of 1941.

As Britain refused to accept defeat, Hitler planned to combine three measures to knock it out of the war: the German air force would destroy the country's capacity to defend itself; there would be an invasion if Britain did not surrender; and the expected quick defeat of the Soviet Union would remove that country as a possible source of aid for Britain and, by ending any danger to Japan's rear, encourage that power to move in the Pacific and tie up the United States.

Hitler wanted Japan to join in the war with Britain and promised to join Japan in war with the United States if that was thought necessary by Tokyo, assuming that this would be the other way for Germany to acquire the navy for war with the United States. A short campaign in the Balkans was to secure what he believed might be a vulnerable southern flank; the last step in this, the airborne seizure of Crete (q.v.), proved so costly that the Germans attempted no major airborne operation thereafter.

The German invasion of the Soviet Union, begun on June 22, 1941, seemed at first to work as planned but quickly ran into trouble. The initial blows, which were supposed to bring the Soviet Union crashing down in a few weeks, did not have that effect. Thereafter, the question always was which sector to attack and whether to retreat. In this, Hitler was at times at odds with some generals, but others always took his position. As the war turned increasingly against Germany, disagreements became more frequent. Hitler still expected to win while some generals were trying to find a less messy way of losing. None advised against going to war with the United States. For the 1942 offensive in the east, Hitler and his military leaders agreed on striking in the south; this project ended in disaster at Stalingrad (q.v.). A new major offensive in 1943 not only ended in defeat at Kursk (q.v.) but also was followed by the first successful Red Army (q.v.) summer offensive.

Air Marshal Hermann Göring, General Wilhelm Keitel, Adolf Hitler (from left to right), and Foreign Minister Joachim von Ribbentrop (partial view) look over a map at German General Headquarters in Poland on September 23, 1939. Hitler at all times insisted on having the last word on military decisions.

When retreats were advocated, Hitler was always concerned about the loss of matériel that could not be hauled back, about the need to reconquer whatever had been given up, and about shorter lines, which released Red Army units for new offensives. Some generals, Erwin Rommel (q.v.) and Walther Model, for example, occasionally acted without or against orders to pull back and were not punished. Others were sent home to collect their monthly bribes in retirement.

As Hitler saw increasing danger from the western Allies, he relied more on Admiral Karl Dönitz (q.v.) to hold them off by submarine warfare. When that effort was blunted in 1943, he both supported the building of new types of submarines and geared strategy on the northern portion of the Eastern Front to protection of the Baltic area, where new submarines and crews could be run in. Enormous resources were also allocated to new weapons designed to destroy London. It was Hitler's hope that the Germans could drive any Allied troops who landed in the west into the sea and then move substantial forces east in the interval before any second invasion. When this plan failed, Hitler turned to holding all ports as long as possible, to hamper Allied supply lines and to prepare for a counterstroke that would defeat the western Allies. This counterstroke, the Battle of the Bulge (q.v.), would then provide the opportunity to move forces east after all.

As the Allies closed in on Germany, Hitler increasingly hoped for a split in the alliance he had forged against himself. He believed Germany had lost World War I because of the collapse of the home front and therefore assumed that establishment of a dictatorship and the systematic killing of all Jews would guarantee victory this time. When the end was near, he married his mistress and then committed suicide with her.

The term "Hitler's War," sometimes attached to World War II, is accurate at least to some extent;

obviously, only the massive energies of the German people, harnessed to his will, made the war possible and made it last so long. But there cannot be any doubt that in harnessing that energy to extraordinary projects and horrible crimes, Hitler placed his stamp on that war and on the twentieth century.

GERHARD L. WEINBERG

Karl Dietrich Bracher, *The German Dictatorship: The Origins, Structure and Consequences of National Socialism* (1971); Gerhard L. Weinberg, *Germany, Hitler, and World War II* (1995).

Holy War

See Crusades *and* Jihad.

Home Front

The "home front" is a phrase used first during World War I (q.v.) to describe the foundation of food, arms, and other munitions produced behind the lines, necessary for military units to exist and continue to fight. Such fundamental support was also required during mercenary expeditions in earlier periods, though it was less widespread. In the twentieth century, the home front was the democratic form of organizing military manpower and supplies.

Before the nineteenth century, the home front provided cash to pay soldiers and to provide them with arms. When such funds were in short supply, monarchs had to appeal to their subjects, at times with painful results. The downfall of the Stuart monarchy in the 1640s in England and the French monarchy in the 1780s was directly related to the inability of these regimes to finance war without the help of Parliament. Once convened, the "home front" took power.

After the *levée en masse* of the 1790s in France, the support of noncombatants for armed forces grew in amplitude and duration (see *French Revolution, Wars of the*). Revolutionary and Napoleonic armies had to be provisioned, whether on home soil or outside of metropolitan France. Here the home front provided a part of the costs of expeditions; the rest came from the unfortunate people whose homes lay in the invaders' path. Once again, we see the shadow of the past: the armies of Spain, central Europe, and Scandinavia scavenged at will in the Thirty Years' War (q.v.) of the seventeenth century. Two hundred years later, supply became the partial responsibility of the home population.

Starting in the American Civil War (q.v.), military leaders recognized the advantages of denying combatants supplies from home and of directly attacking and destroying civilian centers of production. This led to a second meaning of the term *home front*. It came to mean not only the material base of warfare, but also the locus of enemies who did not wear uniforms yet had to be smashed nonetheless. On September 8, 1870, the American Civil War general Philip Sheridan (q.v.) told the future German chancellor Otto von Bismarck (q.v.) that the "proper strategy" in wartime

consists in the first place in inflicting as telling blows as possible upon the enemy's army, and then causing the inhabitants so much suffering that they must long for peace, and force their Government to demand it. The people must be left nothing but their eyes to weep with over the war.

The behavior of sharpshooters (or *francs tireurs*) in the Franco-Prussian War (q.v.) of 1870–1871 further opened the definition of the enemy to include "irregular soldiers" — ordinary people indistinguishable from hundreds of other civilians. Once more, the old and the new are mixed here. Atrocities are as old as time, but the expansion of warfare to include as enemies those not in military units inevitably increased the incidence of civilian casualties in wartime.

From the beginning of World War I to the end of World War II, the home front came to define the entire population of combatant nations. There were four reasons for this change in the rules of military engagement, expanding exponentially the list of potential targets in wartime. The first is the scale of military activities, which dwarfed previous conflicts in terms of their magnitude and geographic spread. Roughly seventy million men served in uniform in the 1914–1918 conflict. Second, this was the first major war between industrialized powers, whose capacity to inject vast stores of arms and matériel into the conflict helped sustain it for fifteen hundred days. Third, from the invasion of Serbia, Belgium, and Prussia in 1914 by Austrian, German, and Russian troops, the war was characterized as a conflict of cultures and their values; each was deemed civilized by one side and barbaric by the other. The war was therefore not only a collision of national interests and aspirations, but also a clash of ways of life and beliefs.

This generalization of the terms of war led inevitably to the targeting of civilians, who shared responsibility with their armies for the carnage of war. Those ethnically different from the dominant power in a nation or empire risked extermination — witness the Turkish genocide against their own Armenian subjects, in a totally cynical exploitation of the fact that some Armenians were in the Russian army. And fourth, it was but a short step from the war of "Huns" versus civilized Britons and Frenchmen (from the Allied point of view) or of German "Kultur" against crass British materialism (from the other side) to the post-1917 demonization of the conflict in revolutionary Russia and beyond. The spread of the ideological element in warfare from the time of the Bolshevik revolution of November 1917 meant that enemies lurked everywhere, and everywhere deserved extermination.

These precedents of total war against the home front were evident in the form of military conflict in the interwar years — especially in the Spanish civil war (q.v.) of 1936–1939 — and in World War II (q.v.). The conflict of 1939–1945 followed World War I in each of the four elements listed above: It was the biggest, most heavily industrial war in history. It was perceived as the confrontation of incompatible "civilizations," and its ideological commitments were extended as far as the Nazi death camps, where six million Jews were killed. The fact that many of them could have aided the Nazi war effort is beside the point; the home front was newly defined as those social formations dedicated to the support of the army, which was now seen as merely the cutting edge of the nation at war. Front and home front became blurred in an irreversible way.

The major change in warfare since 1945 has been the progressive eclipse of wars between nations by wars between insurgent groups and constituted authorities, or between armed factions within a state unable or unwilling to stop the conflict. Once more, the old and the new have been combined. Insurgency was not invented in 1945; witness the terrible conflict in Spain during the Napoleonic Wars, immortally captured in the engravings of Goya. But since 1945, and partly in response to the existence of nuclear weapons (q.v.), most armed conflicts have not been conducted between states who have declared war against each other and signed a peace treaty when the will to fight of one side was broken; rather, in the second half of the twentieth century, warfare has remained ill defined.

In colonial war, it was frequently described as police activity against criminals or terrorists (terms used interchangeably), to deny opponents the dignity of combatant status or the protection of the Geneva Conventions about the treatment of prisoners of war (q.v.). One example among many is the Palestinian Intifada, or uprising against Israeli occupation of the West Bank of the Jordan River, from 1988 to 1995. In other subnational conflicts, such as the Tamil rebellion in Sri Lanka, the insurgents are so numerous as to place entire populations at risk. Here the distinction between combatants and noncombatants has vanished completely, as it has in the ethnic warfare in the former Yugoslavia from 1992 on. In Bosnia and Croatia, the concept of a home front realized the terrible promise implicit in Philip Sheridan's charge to Bismarck: since 1950, the people around whom wars of insurgency and counterinsurgency (q.v.) swirl are almost always left with nothing but their eyes to weep with. In dozens of cases, their eyes, and their lives, are forfeit as well.

J. M. WINTER

Geoffrey Best, *Humanity in Warfare: The Modern History of the International Law of Armed Conflict* (1983); Alan S. Milward, *War, Economy, and Society, 1939–1945* (1987).

Hoplites

Hoplites were the heavy infantry of the Greek city-states who fought in the columnar formation of the phalanx. Fighting in mass was hardly original — Mycenean and Near Eastern armies had done that for centuries. But from the eighth century B.C., the Greeks of the *polis* (city-state) refined the earlier loosely organized mob into neater lines and files, each propertied citizen now claiming an equal slot in the phalanx, a seat in the council chamber, and a plot in the countryside.

More radically, hoplites crafted sophisticated weaponry and armor to meet the new realities of formalized shock warfare. The helmet, breastplate, and greaves were constructed entirely of bronze, reaching a thickness of about a half inch, providing immunity from the attacks of most swords, missiles, and spears. An enormous three-foot shield — the *hoplon*, from which the infantryman derived his name — covered half the infantryman's own body. Each hoplite depended on the man next to him to shield his own

The conventions of early Greek vase-painting, which typically presented idealized forms and focused on individual rather than group experience, made the phalanx difficult to portray. This seventh-century B.C. *vase from Corinth — the earliest extant depiction of the phalanx — captures the essence of hoplite warfare among the front ranks. Note the prominent role of the flute-player in helping each side maintain cadence and formation until the moment when spears and shields collide.*

unprotected right side. A unique double grip allowed the oppressive weight to be held by the entire left arm, and the shield's concave shape permitted the rear ranks to rest it on their shoulders. Offensively, the hoplite depended on his nine-foot spear; should the shaft break, he might turn around what was left of its length to employ the reverse end, which was outfitted with a bronze spike. A reserve iron sword was carried in case the spear was lost altogether.

Hoplites until the fifth century B.C. fought almost entirely over land, usually border strips of marginal ground more important to a community's pride than to its economic survival. Careful protocol between the one thousand or so city-states governed the time, location, and conduct of such one-day wars. But the contrived nature of hoplite fighting should not suggest an absence of mayhem and savagery.

Columns eyed each other formally across flat plains, bronze glittering in the summer sun. The initial collision was horrific, as each side stumbled blindly ahead into the enemy mass, attempting to create some momentum that might shatter the opposing formation into fragments. Hearing was nonexistent. Dust, the crowded conditions of the battlefield, and crested helmets made sight nearly impossible. Descriptions of gaping wounds to the unprotected

neck and groin, involuntary defecation and urination, mistaken identity and panic all abound in descriptions in Greek literature. After not much more than an hour, the pushing ceased as one side collapsed and exited the field, allowing the exhausted victors to return the stripped dead, to erect an ostentatious trophy as testament to their prowess, and to annex or retain the disputed territory.

For nearly two and a half centuries, no army in the Mediterranean could withstand the charge of a hoplite phalanx. But after the Peloponnesian War (431–404 B.C.) (q.v.) its limitations became unmistakable. On rough terrain, in mountain passes, and on long marches, cavalry, light-armed troops, and archers were needed to provide cover, pursuit, and reconnaissance. But to incorporate the aristocratic horsemen, impoverished skirmishers, or hired mercenaries who made up those forces into the city-state's front ranks was antithetical to the whole idea of an agrarian community defended by its middling hoplite citizenry. Gradually military service of all types became divorced from social status, and the original idea of the hoplites' city-state was lost. Yet although the old hoplite phalanx was superseded by more sophisticated and integrated phalangite columns under Philip and Alexander of Macedon (q.v.), the ideals of hoplite warfare — the dominance of heavy infantry, the ideal of a citizen militia, the preference for direct confrontation, and a reliance on superior technology — remained strong in the West.

VICTOR DAVIS HANSON

Victor Davis Hanson, *The Western Way of War: Infantry Battle in Classical Greece* (1989).

Hostages

A hostage is a person held as a guarantee that certain actions or promises will be fulfilled. The practice of taking hostages dates back to antiquity; in ancient Rome, the sons of allied monarchs were required to live in the metropolitan capital as a guarantee of the ally's loyalty. Indeed, throughout much of history, the hostage, as the living symbol of the good faith of his ruler, was usually a person of considerable rank and title and was therefore treated more like an honored guest than a prisoner. Over the years, however, the role of the hostage has become considerably less benign, and in contemporary times a hostage is likely to be merely an unlucky pawn in the murky world of subnational or state-sponsored terrorism.

Historically, hostages came to be used in conjunction with military operations in an occupied country as a mechanism to discourage hostile acts, or to take reprisals for such acts committed by unknown persons. These hostages were typically drawn from the civil population, a practice that was generally condoned by international custom. Indeed, the taking of hostages was so widely observed that the international community found it necessary to differentiate between the prisoner of war and the civilian hostage. This was accomplished by the Geneva Convention of 1911, which specifically outlawed reprisals against prisoners of war for hostile acts performed by civilians. But this statute did not stop POW camp administrators from holding some individuals hostage to guarantee the good behavior of the entire group. In Japanese POW camps in World War II (q.v.), prisoners were divided into groups of ten; if one or more escaped, the lives of the remainder were forfeited.

Notwithstanding the traditional acquiescence to hostage taking, the treatment of hostages in both world wars became the subject of international concern and outrage. In the early months of the German occupation of Belgium under General Heinrich von Kluck in World War I (q.v.), posters usually warned the population that leading citizens — the burgomaster, the magistrate, the senator — or a number of men from each street picked at random, were to be held hostage against hostile acts. In the town of Andenne, 211 persons were thus executed, and 384 at Tamines. These acts, among many others, became the basis of a successful propaganda offensive concerning the Germans' "beastliness" mounted by Britain to influence American public opinion. In World War II, in their attempt to crush resistance movements in occupied European countries, German military authorities again executed many thousands of civilians. But by 1949, world opinion regarding the taking of civilian hostages had hardened to the degree that the Geneva Convention of that year outlawed the practice entirely.

The practice of taking hostages has been revived in recent years, particularly in the Middle East, where the interests of amorphous subnational groups often merge with those of state-sponsored terrorist organizations. Often hostages are taken simply to draw attention to the perpetrators and their political program or grievances; the effect of such activities has been enhanced by the power of modern media to disseminate news both widely and instantaneously. But contemporary hostage taking — that of the U.S. Embassy personnel in Teheran in 1979 or the numerous instances of airplane hijacking — has also been employed as a bargaining chip to induce a country to perform some specific act, such as the surrender of political prisoners. Although these actions have not been associated with military operations, specially trained military units have customarily been employed in rescue operations. The release of hostages held in Entebbe in Uganda in 1976 was dramatically accomplished by Israeli special forces operating at long range; an unsuccessful rescue operation was undertaken by specially trained U.S. units to recover American hostages in Iran in 1980.

ELIHU ROSE

Howe Brothers:

Richard, Earl Howe

1726–1799, *British Admiral*

Sir William Howe

1729–1814, *British General*

The Howe brothers were popular, experienced, and innovative commanders who are remembered not so much for their successes as for their failures. Both had risen to prominence in the Seven Years' War (q.v.) as aggressive and effective leaders, and both made important contributions to tactics during the ensuring years of peace. But as commanders in chief of British forces in the American Revolutionary War (q.v.), both allowed their hopes for a peaceful settlement to interfere with their conduct of the war.

During the campaigns of 1776 and 1777 in the middle Atlantic states, the Howes oscillated between efforts to destroy rebel forces in battle (as at White Plains and Brandywine) and to exert only enough pressure on them to promote negotiations (as on Long Island). Their alternately aggressive and cautious operations were well within the theoretical bounds of eighteenth-century warfare; and their reputations as aggressive, successful commanders with powerful friends in the British government forced critics to suspend judgment. By the time that the government began to question their performance, the Howes had forfeited Britain's best chance for ending the rebellion by force. The American war permanently blighted Sir William's reputation, but the admiral was able to regain a measure of respect by relieving Gibraltar in 1782 and winning a great victory over the French on the Glorious First of June in 1794.

IRA D. GRUBER

Hundred Days, War of the

March 20–July 8, 1815

The name given to the campaign of 1815 denotes the length of time King Louis XVIII was absent from Paris. The king fled as Napoleon (q.v.), who had left his island exile on Elba (off the Italian coast), approached the French capital. Successive French army units, posted to block the former emperor, either rallied to him or failed to act. By the time Napoleon reached Grenoble (March 7) he had acquired the political momentum that swept him into Paris and back to power. The French, dissatisfied with the apparent lack of direction of Louis XVIII's royal government, were willing to permit Napoleon another chance. In his own quest for power, however, Napoleon felt obliged to make political concessions he was not truly willing to deliver, posturing as a liberal constitutionalist. Subsequent retraction of these measures and recanting of promises eroded French political support for Napoleon and explain much about the brittle quality of French army morale in the Waterloo campaign (q.v.). Lapses of judgment in Napoleon's selection of ministers and military commanders also hampered the French.

Napoleon's enemies, who had been meeting throughout this period in Vienna and Brussels to reapportion Europe (see *Congress of Vienna*) swiftly agreed to put their armies back in the field. Like Napoleon, however, they too had to mobilize. Napoleon had some chance to defeat part of the allied forces before the others could coalesce, and he moved first into Belgium against the Anglo-allied army under the duke of Wellington (q.v.) (106,000 troops, 216 guns) and a Prussian army under Marshal Gebhard von Blücher (123,000 men, 296 guns). Napoleon attacked them separately in succession with 128,000 troops and 358 guns from June 15 to June 18 at Ligny, Quatre Bras, Wavre, and Waterloo; at Waterloo the French army was routed. French losses in the four battles totaled roughly 58,000, allied losses about 52,000.

Napoleon returned to Paris ahead of his army, subsequently abdicated, and then left on June 29 to be sent into exile on the island of St. Helena in the South Atlantic. Measured from when Napoleon had first left Elba, his 1815 adventure had actually lasted 123 days.

JOHN PRADOS

Hundred Years' War

1337–1453

The name the Hundred Years' War has been used by historians since the beginning of the nineteenth century to describe the long conflict that pitted the kings and kingdoms of France and England against each other from 1337 to 1453. Two factors lay at the origin of the conflict: first, the status of the duchy of Guyenne (or Aquitaine) — though it belonged to the kings of England, it remained a fief of the French crown, and the kings of England wanted independent possession; second, as the closest relatives of the last direct Capetian king (Charles IV, who had died in 1328), the kings of England from 1337 claimed the crown of France.

Theoretically, the French kings, possessing the financial and military resources of the most populous and powerful state in western Europe, held the advantage over the smaller, more sparsely populated English kingdom. However, the expeditionary English army, well disciplined and successfully using their longbows to stop cavalry charges, proved repeatedly victorious over much larger French forces: significant victories occurred by sea at Sluys (1340) (q.v.), and by land at Crécy (1346) (q.v.) and Poitiers (1356) (q.v.). In 1360, King John of France, in order to save his title, was forced to accept the Treaty of Calais, which granted complete independence to the duchy of Guyenne, now considerably enlarged to include almost a third of France. However, his son Charles V, with the help of his commander in chief Bertrand du Guesclin, by 1380 had succeeded in reconquering almost all the ceded territory, notably by a series of sieges.

After a hiatus, Henry V of England renewed the war and proved victorious at Agincourt (1415) (q.v.), conquered Normandy (1417–1418), and then attempted to have himself crowned as the future king of France by the Treaty of Troyes (1420). But his military successes were not matched by political successes: although allied with the dukes of Burgundy, the major-

A German lithograph of 1830 shows the captain of a hussar regiment of the Prussian guards. Light horsemen needing little protection, hussars typically wore fancy, heavily frogged short jackets and waistcoats and used a decorated sabretache (a leather case) to carry items on horseback — note the embroidered imperial Prussian crown and initials.

recaptured the duchy of Normandy (the Battle of Formigny, 1450), and then seized Guyenne (the Battle of Castillon, 1453). The end of the conflict was never marked by a peace treaty but died out because the English recognized that the French troops were too strong to be directly confronted.

English territory in France, which had been extensive since 1066 (see *Hastings, Battle of*) now remained confined to the Channel port of Calais (lost in 1558). France, at last free of the English invaders, resumed its place as the dominant state of western Europe.

PHILIPPE CONTAMINE

Hussars

The first hussars served as light cavalry in Hungarian armies from the later fifteenth century, specializing in raids and irregular operations. After the failure of a revolt against Hapsburg rule (1676–1681), many Hungarians took service in the armies of other states, and from 1692 hussar light cavalry regiments of Hungarian exiles served in the French army. Other states followed suit: hussars entered the armies of Prussia from 1721 and Russia from 1725. Gradually, however, the Hungarian component decreased: French units, for example, recruited deserters from enemy armies and, after 1750, Germans and Frenchmen. By 1786 the 6,320 hussars in French service included only 45 Hungarians. Nevertheless, the exotic uniforms of hussars all over Europe — with busby, cape, fur-lined pelisse, tight trousers, and boots — recall their Hungarian origins, and in the twentieth century they serve as light armored troops and retain their traditional roles of reconnaissance and raiding.

GEOFFREY PARKER

ity of the French refused English domination. Thanks to Joan of Arc (q.v.), the siege of Orléans was lifted (1429). Then Paris and the Île-de-France were liberated (1436–1441), and after the French army had been reorganized and reformed (1445–1448), Charles VII

I

Incas

One of the most thoroughly militarized societies on record, the Incas became a dominant Andean polity in the fourteenth century and progressively increased their military might and the geographic extent of their conquests until overthrown by Spanish conquistadores (q.v.) under Francisco Pizarro in 1532–1539. At its height, the Inca Empire controlled most of present-day Peru and Ecuador, as well as parts of Bolivia, Chile, and Colombia. Well organized for agricultural production, trade, and war, the Inca Empire was ruled by a hereditary theocracy under the aegis of the Sun God; legitimacy was traced through the mummies of the emperor's ancestors. These mummies were not entombed but remained active objects of ritual devotion; they were assigned retainers and palaces supported by the output of state-assigned lands, a practice that imposed a need for constant expansion — the number of royal mummies, and hence, lands assigned them, increased with each generation.

The organization of the Inca Empire was highly sophisticated, based economically on the exchange of agricultural products between climatic zones differentiated by elevation: fish from the coastal plain; bananas, other tropical fruits, and forest products from jungle regions; maize, squash, beans, and cotton from intermediate elevations; and potatoes and llama and vicuña wool from the Andean highlands. Politically, the empire was highly centralized, with all executive legitimacy residing in the person of the emperor, or Inca, and provincial authority discharged by a pyramidal structure of provincial and local officials. Military organization paralleled the political and was undergirded by universal conscription. The empire was bound together strategically by royal roads, which, though designed only for foot traffic, rivaled those of imperial Rome in extent and quality of construction and surpassed them in geographic obstacles surmounted.

By the sixteenth century, the Incas could simultaneously raise three armies numbering as many as thirty thousand each. Each contingent wielded the weapons of its native region and was led by a professional officer caste and headed by a professional imperial bodyguard of several thousand. The Incas possessed an advantage over lowlanders who opposed them: many of their troops, acclimated to the high altitudes of their native regions, were born with significantly greater lung capacity.

Though the Andeans could smelt bronze, they made no significant military use of metal and possessed no effective slashing weapons — a deficiency that cost them dearly in combat with Spanish conquistadores. The principal weapons were stone-headed clubs, stone- and bone-tipped spears, simple bows and arrows, and the sling. Armies were supported on the march by fortress-storehouses in which weapons, clothing, and provisions (including desiccated potatoes and llama meat) were stored. With these advantages, Inca armies could probably move faster than any others prior to the age of steam. Though not literate, the Incas were capable of sophisticated strategies but limited by the extreme centralization of command in the person of the Inca, a vulnerability of which the conquistadores took full advantage. Though Andean armies were, if anything, more vulnerable to Spanish steel and horses than those of the Mexica, the Spaniards required considerably more time to conquer the Incas than the Aztecs.

JOHN F. GUILMARTIN

Indian Mutiny of 1857

The Indian mutiny, the British name for the 1857 uprising against British rule, is remembered by Indians as the First War for Indian Independence. In fact, it was neither a mere mutiny nor a full-fledged revolution. Indian troops in British service at Meerut sparked it off on May 10, killing their British officers rather than bite off the tips of new, greased cartridges that they believed had been smeared with beef and pork fat in violation of both the Hindu and Muslim faiths. The Meerut garrison was soon joined by other forces all across northern India: Hindu princes eager to restore the past glories of their ancestors, Muslim Nawabs angered by British demands on their privy purses, and ordinary soldiers eager to restore the old Mughal Empire (q.v.). But, united only by their dislike of the British, these incompatible rebels never sought to join forces. The notion of an independent "India" seems never to have occurred to any of them.

The fourteen-month campaign that reimposed British rule was waged in a resolutely vengeful spirit. Atrocities had in fact been committed by Indians, but British officers committed atrocities of their own — blowing prisoners from cannon without trial, hanging innocent civilians from trees along their line of march — well before they had concrete evidence of the enemy's transgressions. And, although the notion of a united India was still decades away, memories of the brutality with which Britain reimposed its rule would help fuel the nationalist movement when it finally came.

GEOFFREY WARD

Indochina War

December 1946–July 1954

A strong Vietnamese nationalist movement, whose most dynamic element was the Indochinese Communist Party organized in 1930 under Nguyen Ai Quoc, the future Ho Chi Minh, had spawned unsuccessful uprisings in northern Annam and Tonkin in 1930–1931. But the Japanese occupation of Indochina following the fall of France in 1940, the complete suspension of French rule there in March 1945, followed by the Japanese surrender in August of that year, created a political vacuum that the Communists were well prepared to exploit — Ho Chi Minh's "August Revolution" of 1945 installed Viet Minh troops in Hanoi as a prelude for the declaration of the Democratic Republic of Vietnam on September 2, 1945. The Potsdam Conference (July 1945) called for the British to disarm Japanese troops south of the sixteenth parallel, roughly near Tourane (Da Nang) south of Hue, while Chinese Nationalists were assigned this task in the north. In the south, the British permitted the return of French troops in October, and in March 1946, Ho Chi Minh allowed French troops north of the sixteenth parallel in return for the departure of rapacious Chinese Nationalist forces. Inconclusive negotiations between France and Ho Chi Minh for independence continued over the summer. The uneasy peace between French and Viet Minh forces was shattered in November in Haiphong — on December 19, 1946, Viet Minh forces attacked several French garrisons in Tonkin. The war was on.

The first four years of the war were inconclusive, as the French tried unsuccessfully to decapitate the Viet Minh leadership. However, the victory of the Chinese Communists in 1949 (see *Chinese Civil War*), followed by Peking's decision to support the Viet Minh with arms and military advisors, led to a Viet Minh offensive that overwhelmed the French garrisons along the Chinese frontier in October 1950. Believing the French to be on the ropes, the Viet Minh commander, Vo Nguyen Giap (q.v.), attacked the Tonkin Delta in 1951 but was repulsed.

In 1952 and 1953, the French faced the classic dilemma of a conflict combining partisan and main force action. By January 1954, over 82,000 French troops were immobilized in 920 posts in the Tonkin Delta alone, to control an estimated 37,000 Viet Minh guerrillas. At the same time, the French had to respond to main force actions like that in November 1951–February 1952 around Hoa Binh, where Giap drew French forces out of the Tonkin Delta, and then made them fight their way back to base along roads strongly held by Viet Minh. The French staunched a Viet Minh thrust toward Laos at Na San in November–December 1952, in an action that witnessed the first use of the *base aéroterrestre* (a base established in enemy territory and supplied by air), a concept later applied at Dien Bien Phu (q.v.).

Although French arms registered some tactical successes, it was clear by early 1953 that French forces, whose 400,000 members were recruited principally from foreigners and among French colonial subjects, were seriously handicapped by declining morale, a serious shortage of officers, lack of mobility, limited air power, a constant turnover of senior leadership, and decreasing support for the war in France. More to the point, Paris refused to make the political concessions that would give the government of Emperor Bao Dai, the French-sponsored ruler of Vietnam, credibility in the eyes of the Vietnamese population and allow the emergence of a viable political alternative to the Viet Minh.

Although the French managed, with the aid of the well-armed Hoa Hao and Cao Dai religious minorities, and the underworld of Binh Xuyen gangsters who controlled Saigon, to hold their own in South Vietnam (Cochinchina), and despite the fact that military assistance from the United States increased to the point that Washington was projected to pay 75 percent of the war's cost in 1954, by the summer of 1953, France's situation in Tonkin was desperate. Under Chinese pressure, Giap abandoned his plans for an offensive against the Tonkin Delta in the autumn of 1953, and instead moved against Lai Chau, the last bastion of French influence in Upper Tonkin. As the Chinese had predicted, French commander Henri Navarre came out to fight — not, however, at Lai Chau, which he considered indefensible, but to the broad valley of Dien Bien Phu, which was occupied by French paratroops on November 20, 1953. While Giap built up his forces and supplies around the isolated French garrison, the Communist powers launched a "peace offensive," which culminated in a multipower agreement to open peace talks in Geneva in April 1954. With the goal of influencing these negotiations, Giap was prepared to pay a heavy price — as many as twenty thousand casualties — to overwhelm the French garrison; it was finally overrun on May 7. The shock of defeat was such that French prime minister Pierre Mendès-France signed the Geneva Accords of July 1954, which recognized Vietnamese independence, dividing the country at the seventeenth parallel and guaranteeing the integrity of Laos and Cambodia. French rule had come to an end.

DOUGLAS PORCH

Infantry

Since the first human beings fought in prehistoric times, the infantry has engaged in close combat with opponents. Though many aspects of the infantry have changed, its offensive missions of closing with and destroying the enemy and seizing and holding terrain and its defensive mission of denying key areas to the enemy have not. Infantry formations have comprised the bulk of all armies through much of recorded history and have largely determined their success or failure.

Across the centuries, the infantry has carried different weapons. The Greek hoplites (q.v.) carried the spear, the Roman legionaries the short sword, the English the longbow, the Spanish the harquebus, the Americans the long rifle, and so on. Modern infantry soldiers carry automatic rifles, machine guns, grenade launchers, mortars, and antitank weapons. For a brief period in the late 1950s and early 1960s, American infantry battalions also carried a short-range nuclear rocket, the Davy Crockett. As a consequence of numerous technological innovations, the infantry's ability to strike the enemy has extended far beyond the reach of a human being's arm or of a club, and today extends over thousands of yards.

Also, the infantry has always maintained its ability to travel by foot, but it has relied increasingly on other means of getting to the battlefield, including riding by horse or riding in wagons. Those who rode horses into battle were called dragoons (q.v.), but they usually expected to dismount and then fight. In the modern era, infantry moves by armored vehicles, airplanes, helicopters, trucks, trains, and ships. Those who drop by parachute from airplanes are known as airborne infantry, those who travel by helicopter are known as airmobile infantry (see *Airborne Troops*), and those who rely on armored vehicles are known as mechanized infantry. Light infantry are those easily deployable units that strategic airlift and sea lift can transport over long distances quickly and that can stabilize a situation before larger forces are required. When dismounted, these airborne, airmobile, mechanized, and light infantry fight in a similar fashion.

Formations used by the infantry have also changed. Alexander (q.v.) relied on the phalanx, Caesar (q.v.) the legion, Napoleon (q.v.) the division and the corps. In recent centuries, the infantry has evolved from employing close-order formations to open-order formations. Close-order formations experienced considerable difficulties against the accurate fire of rifles in the middle of the nineteenth century, particularly in the American Civil War (q.v.) and the Austro-Prussian War of 1866. In the twentieth century, the dispersion

The new and the old: In a Gulf War maneuver, foot soldiers have landed in the desert by helicopter. They now prepare to move in traditional formation.

of infantry has accelerated, as is evident from increased reliance on the platoon and squad, as well as the introduction of the fire team. The basic tactical maneuver element has evolved from the regiment to the squad. Today, an infantry company can occupy and defend an area that once would have required an army.

The infantry has rarely fought alone. Often supported by cavalry in the ancient period, the infantry gained additional assistance with the introduction of gunpowder and artillery. In the modern era, the infantry receives support from tanks, artillery, engineers, and aviation units. As support for the infantry has expanded, so have the complexity and weight of logistics. In the same sense, infantry units have become more unwieldy and less mobile. Whereas infantrymen once fought only with what they could personally carry, they now carry much additional equipment and are often followed by large, logistically cumbersome trains. In some recent wars, such as in Vietnam (q.v.), lightly armed and supported troops oftentimes have exploited their advantages in mobility and rapid striking power against their more heavily burdened opponents.

Command and control of the infantry have also evolved. For centuries, commanders remained within eyesight of their soldiers and communicated with them through shouts and hand signals or the use of drums and bugles. As the size of infantry formations and armies became larger, messengers became more important. As the increasing lethality of the battlefield caused greater dispersion, the introduction of the telephone and radio dramatically changed the way in which infantry commanders maintained contact with their soldiers. With improved electronics and smaller, lighter radios, commanders could communicate with their units, even though they were scattered widely across the battlefield. Over time, greater distances between soldiers and their leaders created a requirement for additional leaders and transformed the sergeant from an administrative and logistical specialist into a small-unit combat leader.

Through the ages, the infantry has worn an incredible variety of uniforms (q.v.). In addition to helmets and shields of dramatically different sizes and shapes, a veritable panoply of colors has covered the bodies of the infantry so that their commanders could see them and identify the units to which they belonged. In the

American Revolution (q.v.), the Americans fought against the "redcoats"; in the Civil War, blue and gray uniforms distinguished Northern from Southern soldiers, but the gaudy uniforms of the Zouaves (a Union group patterned after a French infantry unit that was originally composed of Algerian recruits and noted for colorful dress and precision drill) added other colors. As the battlefield has become more lethal, bright colors have tended to disappear. In 1914, the French went into battle with bright blue coats and red trousers, but by 1918 they wore a much more subdued blue. During that same period, the steel helmet became a permanent part of every infantry soldier's gear. Today, when in the field, the infantry wear camouflage (q.v.) uniforms that enable them to blend into their surroundings.

Thus, the role of the infantry has not changed over the centuries, but its arms, formations, logistics, uniforms, and command and control have. Despite the introduction of remarkable new technologies, no one doubts that the infantry still has a place on the modern battlefield, and most infantrymen believe they remain the "queen of battle."

ROBERT A. DOUGHTY

John A. English, *On Infantry* (1984); Steven T. Ross, *From Flintlock to Rifle: Infantry Tactics, 1740–1866* (1979).

Infantry Weapons

Individuals fighting on foot have wielded a variety of cutting, smashing, and missile weapons from the dawn of time: clubs, spears, bows, knives, swords, javelins, and so on. However, infantry in the modern sense — cohesive units of trained foot soldiers armed with a variety of weapons and able to engage mounted and dismounted enemies effectively in all kinds of terrain — are a comparatively recent phenomenon. The English longbowmen and Swiss halberdiers and pikemen of medieval times were precursors of infantry in Europe, and imitation of Swiss weapons and tactics by the Spanish and Germans led to the appearance of infantry in the modern sense. The seminal event was the development by the Spanish shortly after 1500 of mixed formations that combined "shock" with "shot." Shock was provided by pikes, in imitation of Swiss practice; shot, or missile fire, was provided by the harquebus, a matchlock shoulder weapon with a bore diameter of about 0.69 inch. The

resulting formations were capable of besting missile-armed cavalry in the open field, a feat beyond the capabilities of the Roman legion (q.v.) and the closest approximation of true infantry in premodern times. Parallel developments took place in Japan about a half-century later, spurred, as in Europe, by the introduction of handheld gunpowder weapons (see *Oda Nobunaga*); however, the Japanese abandoned gunpowder weaponry during the seventeenth century, and infantry was to remain an essentially European phenomenon until the twentieth century.

Progressive improvements in the efficiency of gunpowder shoulder arms rendered shock action increasingly costly, and the proportion of shot to shock increased accordingly. By 1600, pikemen served mainly to protect "shot" from cavalry while reloading. The Spanish musket, a large harquebus with a bore diameter of 0.82 inch or more, evolved as a means of penetrating body armor and engaging massed formations at long range. It slowly decreased in size as armor was abandoned and as opportunities for long-range fire diminished on increasingly densely populated and smoke-shrouded battlefields. By the late 1600s, the musket retained only its name and was no larger than the earlier harquebus. It was, however, far more efficient, for the matchlock had given way to the flintlock, and musketeers had acquired a means of protecting themselves against cavalry with the plug bayonet, a knife with a tapered handle that could be inserted into the musket's muzzle, turning it into a short pike. Around the turn of the eighteenth century, the replacement of the plug bayonet with the socket bayonet enabled musketeers to fire with bayonets fixed and produced the dominant infantry weapon for the next 150 years. The tactical superiority of this weapon and the trained soldiers who wielded it enabled the European powers to carve out vast colonial empires. The same period saw the rise and fall of the hand grenade, a black, powder-filled sphere of cast iron with a slow match fuse, as the weapon par excellence of shock infantry.

From about 1850, the reign of the smoothbore musket and bayonet ended with the general adoption among European armies of the minié ball, an ellipsoidal musket ball with a hollow base that expanded on firing to fill the grooves of a rifled barrel. Existing smoothbores could be easily converted to rifled muskets, and maximum effective ranges increased from 150 yards or less to 500 yards or more. The battlefield became far more lethal, and for a time small arms outranged field artillery, rendering the movement of artillery impossible once battle was joined. The flintlock gave way to the percussion cap at about the same time, giving more reliable ignition and simplified loading. The percussion cap also made breech-loading rifles, whose tactical advantages had long been appreciated, a practical proposition. The first of these was the Dreyse "needle gun," first issued by the Prussian army on a limited basis in 1835. The needle gun was general issue by the Danish War of 1864 and, with its French counterpart the chassepot, raised battlefield lethality to new levels in the Franco-Prussian War (q.v.) of 1870–1871.

More important, the percussion cap made possible the development of the self-contained brass cartridge. By expanding slightly during firing, the cartridge sealed the breech, preventing the escape of gas and powder fragments that endangered the user and eroded the mechanism. Moreover, by incorporating propellant, projectile, and primer in a sealed, watertight container, the brass cartridge made possible the repeating magazine rifle; the autoloading, or semiautomatic, pistol and rifle; and the machine gun. Repeating magazine rifles were used in small numbers by Union forces in the American Civil War (q.v.), as were manually operated machine guns, notably the Gatling.

Next came the development of nitrocellulose-based, or smokeless, propellants in the last decades of the nineteenth century. These cleared the battlefield's shroud of black powder smoke; they also permitted much higher muzzle velocities and longer effective ranges. By 1900, military institutions throughout the world had adopted as standard bolt-action, magazine rifles with bore diameters of 0.236 to 0.351 inch, firing a lead bullet from a necked-down brass cartridge. Though they demanded considerable strength and skill, these powerful rifles could deliver aimed fire at ranges of a thousand yards and beyond as the British learned, to their chagrin, in the Boer War (q.v.) of 1899–1902 and the Japanese and Russians demonstrated in the Russo-Japanese War (q.v.) of 1904–1905. Such rifles were the standard infantry weapon of World War I (q.v.). With the exception of the United States, which adopted the autoloading M-1 Garand in 1932, they were the basic infantry weapon of World War II (q.v.) and are still used as sniper rifles.

The autoloading principle, harnessing the energy of the exploding gunpowder within the cartridge to load and fire successive rounds, was first applied to semi-automatic pistols, but these were short-range arms for self-protection and had little impact. Next came machine guns firing rifle ammunition, worked by the rearward recoil of bolt, barrel, or both — or by high-pressure gas extracted from the barrel. The first machine guns were looked on more as artillery than infantry weapons: typically mounted on wheels or sledges and weighing seventy to eighty pounds or more, they dominated no-man's-land in World War I. Light machine guns weighing some twenty pounds appeared before World War I, but were largely unappreciated until the development of German shock troop (*Stosstrupp*) tactics in 1916–1918. These tactics also prompted the development in 1918 of the submachine gun, a light, full-automatic shoulder weapon firing pistol ammunition. The submachine gun proved well suited to jungle and urban combat and played a major role in World War II.

The hand grenade, now with high-explosive fillers and more or less reliable mechanical/pyrotechnic fuses, emerged as the premier weapon of shock combat in World War I. Armor reappeared in the form of the helmet, as did fighting knives. The need for firepower in the trenches led to the development of rifle-mounted grenade launchers and various patterns of trench mortar. Light mortars, notably the British 82-mm Stokes-Brandt, proved well suited to mobile operations and are still the basic infantry-support weapon. Heavy machine guns with bore diameters of about 0.5 inch appeared in the final days of World War I; though mostly vehicle-mounted since World War II, they too remain a standard support weapon.

With few exceptions, the infantry weapons of World War II differed little from those of World War I. All the major powers except the United States adopted a light machine gun as the standard squad-support weapon during the interwar period; the best of these were the Czech-designed British Bren, the German MG-34/MG-42, and the Soviet Degtyarev. The need for antitank protection, harkening back to the need for protection against cavalry in the sixteenth century, led during World War II to the development of weapons based on a high-explosive charge shaped into a hollow cone to focus the explosive energy into a narrow beam, which burns through armor like a hypervelocity acetylene torch (the "Monroe effect"). The first weapon to exploit this principle operationally was the American 2.36-inch rocket launcher, the "bazooka"; the definitive development was the German *Panzerfaust*, with its large warhead and expendable launcher. *Panzerfaust* derivatives, now termed rocket-propelled grenades (RPGs), remain a standard infantry weapon. Recoilless rifles, cannon that direct part of the propellant force rearward through a rocket nozzle to counteract recoil, provided infantry with human-portable, direct-fire artillery. Blast, smoke, and incendiary grenades joined fragmentation grenades as standard issue. Finally came the assault carbine, a full-automatic weapon that fires a cartridge of intermediate power. The first of these was the German MP 43. The Soviets followed suit, and the Kalashnikov AK-47 entered production in 1947. Enormously successful, the AK-47 was widely exported and played a major role in the American phase of the Vietnam War (q.v.) and various revolutionary struggles of the 1960s and 1970s. It also became a potent symbol of revolutionary war — it was brandished for the cameras by media-savvy worthies such as Jane Fonda (for North Vietnam) and Vanessa Redgrave (for the PLO).

JOHN F. GUILMARTIN

Charles W. C. Oman, *A History of the Art of War in the Sixteenth Century* (1937); John A. English, *On Infantry* (1981); Ian Hogg and John Weeks, *Military Small Arms of the Twentieth Century* (1973).

Innovation, Military

Over the five millennia of recorded history, warfare has seen the introduction of new and more effective weapons of destruction. But in the centuries before the early modern West began its drive toward world power, innovation was very much a haphazard affair. Developments such as iron weapons and the stirrup occurred by accident rather than design and then spread through the known world. But such innovations were rare. Stability rather than change characterized warfare.

But in the Middle Ages, gunpowder and then metal casting appeared in a Western society dominated by military competition and innovation, setting in motion a series of military revolutions that have inexorably pushed Western civilization to a position of world domination. Although military institutions by their basic nature possess a culture of obedience and a respect for tradition that do not always support innovation, in an environment of intense competition, Western military institutions have needed to innovate; the alternative all too often would have been catastrophic

military defeat. Such intense military competition did not mark the other centers of world civilization; as a result, they slowly fell behind until they were hopelessly out of the race. They could imitate, but could not innovate. Only the Japanese proved able to adapt to an environment in which change rather than stasis was the basic principle.

Perhaps the most important military innovations in Western history began with Maurice of Nassau (q.v.) and Gustavus Adolphus (q.v.). These two individuals reestablished the Roman system of disciplined obedience to military authority. This allowed their armies to spread out in linear formations without losing their cohesion and thus maximized the potential of handheld gunpowder weapons. This tactical innovation also helped states impose more coherent, effective governance on their populations.

By the early eighteenth century, innovations in sailing technology had given Western navies domination over the oceanic expanses of the entire world. Western ships had the seagoing capacity to survive almost any weather; but equally important, a host of technological aids, from compasses to chronometers and astrolabes, allowed Western sailors to determine where they were at any point in the world. Western navies were thus able to vie for world domination, while their counterparts on land struggled for control of Europe.

Until the end of the eighteenth century, military power remained the preserve of rulers who used it as a simple tool of government. In 1793, however, the entire context of Western war changed when French revolutionaries, about to lose a war of their own making, decreed the *levée en masse*. Everything in France — all men, women, and children, as well as their goods and wealth — was now at the disposal of the Republic. Inspired by fervid nationalism, the French waged a quarter-century war against the rest of Europe (see *French Revolution, Wars of the* and *Napoleon*). Only when the other European states replied in kind was Europe finally able to overcome French tyranny.

For the next century, Europe enjoyed an era of unprecedented peace, broken only by three relatively short major conflicts, the Crimean War (1854–1856) (q.v.), the Seven Weeks' War (1866) (q.v.), and the Franco-Prussian War (1870–1871) (q.v.). But the shortness of those wars obscured the emergence of an important new development: the impact of technological innovation on the strategic, operational, and tactical framework of conflict. The American Civil

---

The Most Important Military Innovations

Copper-headed mace (about 3500 B.C.). First use of metal for other than ornamental purposes; forced the development of helmets and body armor.

War-horse (domesticated in about 2000 B.C.). First source of energy to challenge human muscle as the determinant of success in combat.

Wheel (about 2000 B.C.). First applied to the war chariot. Caused a revolution in battlefield mobility and permitted the transport of weapons too heavy for pack animals or human porterage.

Composite bow (about 2000 B.C.). The first artificially engineered means of converting muscular energy into lethal projectile velocities and impact energies.

Gunpowder (eleventh-century China). The first storable source of chemical energy capable of doing work (by definition, force times distance) directly.

Full-rigged ship (about 1375–1475). In combination with nautical charts and celestial navigation, gave Europe mastery of transoceanic navigation.

Military maps (about 1550s–1750s). Accurate depiction of land masses, road nets, elevation information, and topographic detail including vegetation and humanmade features made possible realistic long-range tactical planning.

Steam power/propulsion (1780s–1840s). Expanded the scale of conflict through mass production and, in the form of steam locomotives and steamships, increased the speed, scale, and reliability of military movement.

Rifled musket (about 1850). Increased maximum effective ranges from less than 150 yards to over 300 yards, vastly increasing battlefield lethality.

Quick-firing artillery (late 1890s). Light, efficient, hydro-pneumatic recoil systems enormously multiplied the lethality of artillery.

Internal combustion engine (about 1880–1900). Expanded war into a third dimension by making submarines and aircraft practical realities, restored mobility to the battlefield (the tank), and vastly increased the speed and flexibility of overland maneuver (automobiles, trucks).

Radio and radar (late nineteenth century, late 1930s). Revolutionized operations by permitting instant communications between headquarters and subordinate units from 1914; revolutionized tactics (1938–1939) by permitting aircraft, ships, and small units to coordinate their actions in combat; revolutionized air and naval warfare from 1940 by permitting the detection of ships and aircraft beyond visual range.

Computers and transistors (1940–1945, 1960s). Used in World War II for Allied code breaking and as the guidance mechanism for German V-2 missiles: later applied to a wide range of analytical tasks, including weapons systems.

Nuclear weapons and nuclear power (1945, late 1950s). Made possible the instantaneous destruction of entire cities and development of the true submarine, capable of traveling indefinitely beneath the surface of the ocean all but free from detection.

John F. Guilmartin

War (1861–1865) (q.v.), however, displayed the new trends. The combination of technological change with mass popular support (as in the French Revolution) made the American conflict long and bloody. The Industrial Revolution provided both the economic strength to prolong the conflict and the weapons to increase the lethality of the battlefield. Railroads and steamboats allowed the Union to project its mobilized power over continental distances, while Northern ironclads made the blockade of the Confederate coast increasingly effective. Rifled muskets firing the minié ball allowed troops to kill at ranges of more than three hundred yards — nearly three times the range a Napoleonic infantryman could attain. And by the end of the war, Union cavalrymen were equipped with multishot carbines.

The Europeans, who generally ignored the American Civil War, had two more chances to observe the significant impact of modern technology on the battlefield: the Boer War (q.v.) and the Russo-Japanese conflict (q.v.). Although they understood some of the implications, only World War I (q.v.) hammered home the impact of modern technological innovation. On the ground, rapid-fire weapons, massed artillery — the great killer of the war, gas, tanks, flamethrowers, and barbed wire forced new tactical and further technological innovations on the combatants. World War I was the chemists' war, and their lethal innovations, from explosives to poison gas and petroleum, added to the terrible casualties of trench warfare.

Each side had to acclimate to an ever-changing battlefield; what worked in one year might not work in the next. In fall 1916, General Robert-Georges Nivelle (q.v.) launched a major offensive at Verdun (q.v.) to drive the Germans back; using innovative tactics, the French won a major victory. But the following spring,

Nivelle, now commander in chief of the French army, attempted a similar but larger offensive against the Germans. This time the attack not only failed with terrible casualties, but almost resulted in the collapse of France. Why? Because in one of the major tactical innovations of the war, the Germans had created a defensive system in depth. Placing the bulk of their infantry out of range of enemy artillery, they developed a sophisticated tactical system that utilized artillery, firepower, and movement to dominate the battlefield. The Germans created an offensive system of infantry tactics that by early 1918 had restored movement to the battlefield (see *Ludendorff Offensive*). In effect their innovations had created modern warfare.

But innovations occurred not only on land. The navies of the world had gone to war in 1914 with ships possessing capabilities unimagined when their admirals had joined up forty years before. Ship speeds had quadrupled, and their firepower, formerly effective only at point-blank ranges, could reach targets almost on the horizon. These radical changes in technology explain why admirals had so much trouble controlling their fleets. The appearance of the submarine further disturbed navies, as the undersea weapon threatened all the standard precepts of naval power. Finally, to add to the misery of military institutions, aircraft (q.v.) made their appearance in World War I in all the missions that are familiar to us today: close air support, reconnaissance (q.v.), air superiority, and strategic bombing (q.v.).

The end of the war brought no respite from rapid technological change. Moreover, war had underlined the fact that science and technology were inextricably linked to the battlefield. Few military organizations missed this essential point. Unfortunately for Europe, only the Germans proved willing to learn the tactical and operational lessons of the war as those lessons pertained to armies. Consequently, German military innovation during the interwar period pursued the course that the battles of 1918 had suggested — with an emphasis on speed and exploitation that positioned the Germans to innovate with armored warfare.

World War II (q.v.), whatever the impact of armored formations, proved to be a physicists' war, especially the war in the air. Even before the conflict began, Air Marshal Sir Hugh Dowding (q.v.) coupled the development of radar with the monoplane fighter and a modern command and control network to build an effec-

tive air defense system that enabled the Royal Air Force to triumph in the Battle of Britain (q.v.). Innovations came fast and furious in the air war: sophisticated navigational and blind-bombing devices, long-range escort fighters, airborne radar, radio-guided bombs, and eventually jet aircraft all played their part. By 1944 the Germans were firing ballistic (V-2) and cruise (V-1) missiles against their opponents. They flew the first jets in aerial combat. In the end, what won the air war for the Allies was their overwhelming productive superiority — based on the innovations in industrial manufacturing that set the United States apart from the rest of the world.

Innovations in the naval war equaled those in the air. The war against the submarine was won not only by technological innovations, such as sonar, radar, and direction finding, but also by intellectual innovations such as systems analysis. In the Pacific, by 1944 the American fleet was carrying with it a great air force based entirely on aircraft carriers. The conflict finally closed with the most terrifying technological innovation of history: the atomic bomb.

The Cold War (q.v.) ushered in the atomic age, in which the two superpowers deterred each other from another disastrous world war by building ever more frightening weapons of mass destruction. Both the weapons and their delivery vehicles proliferated — bombers, intercontinental ballistic missiles, and cruise missiles with pinpoint accuracy. The contest drew on the scientific knowledge of both societies, but there were spin-offs: ballistic missile development provided the launch vehicles for civilian communications and weather satellites, and the complexities of hitting targets at continental distances pushed the miniaturization of computers. But the Cold War had other spin-offs as well. The extended development of military aircraft resulted in the innovations that allowed civilian jets to shrink the world.

Conventional wars have accelerated the development of "smart" weapons (q.v.). Laser-guided bombs that so devastated Iraq in the Gulf War (q.v.) are now being replaced with weapons that will use the global-positioning satellites. Despite the increasing lethality of the battlefield, it seems unlikely that wars will stop or that military innovation will cease to contribute to military capabilities.

WILLIAMSON MURRAY

Williamson Murray and Allan Millett, eds., *Military Innovation in the Interwar Period* (1996).

Intelligence, Military

Intelligence is generally defined as information prepared for the use of policy makers. The information springs from a variety of sources, such as spies or codebreakers, and is analyzed and written up by evaluators, such as G-2 officers on army staffs. Policy makers, such as presidents or generals, then take it into account — or, in some cases, do not take it into account — in making their decisions and acting upon them.

The ultimate purpose of the information is to enable policy makers to optimize their resources, both physical and psychological. If intelligence can predict where an enemy will attack, a commander can then deploy forces more effectively. A commander who knows that a town ahead is free of the enemy can concentrate better on planning for the campaign beyond. If uncertainty reigns, the commander must will the unit to act. Intelligence thus replaces reserves in the physical area and determination in the psychological.

Intelligence was used from earliest days, as references in the Bible to scouting out the land of Canaan make clear, and as do the practices of tribal peoples such as the Jívaro of Ecuador who crept into enemy villages to count houses and thus estimate the size of the enemy force. In ancient China and India, Sun Tzu (q.v.) and Kautilya prescribed ways of gathering information. But intelligence reached its full potential only after the French Revolution (q.v.) and the Industrial Revolution. Mass armies, economies to support them, and railroads, which permitted mobilization by timetable, gave intelligence the targets it had never had: precise war plans and statistics of population and industry. The same revolutions gave intelligence the tools to expose these targets: the airplane to view them, the camera to fix and reproduce pictures of them, and the radio to overhear enemy messages. Intelligence first achieved permanent — not just transient — importance in World War I (q.v.). It attained great significance in World War II (q.v.).

Aside from open sources such as the press and parliamentary publications, which provide the most voluminous and often the most important information, intelligence sources may be conveniently grouped into three kinds: HUMINT, or human intelligence; IMINT, or imagery intelligence; and SIGINT, or signal intelligence.

HUMINT includes the most basic form of military intelligence: observation. Soldiers at the front lines watch their enemies. They see them marching, digging trenches, advancing in an attack. They hear their tank motors. They smell their fuel. All these details show what the enemy is doing, and where and when and how fast. They remain the backbone of information about the enemy as they percolate upward to higher commands.

More directed intelligence begins when frontline formations establish observation posts and dispatch patrols. Patrols discover the enemy machine-gun nests, strongpoints, dugouts. In fluid situations, armored cavalry or motorized scouts feel out the location and movement of enemy forces and determine which towns are occupied, which roads are blocked.

Prisoners (sometimes captured by patrols sent out for that purpose) and deserters provide, under interrogation, usually short-range, short-lived information: which units are in the enemy line, where the heavy guns are, whether reserves are present. Officers and men with more specialized information are often questioned in greater detail in rear areas.

The most glamorous but least reliable source of HUMINT is the spy. Usually the spy is little more than a clandestine scout, like members of the GREENUP team of the World War II U.S. Office of Strategic Services. Its members parachuted into Austria and reported Brenner Pass train departures for Italy. Rarely is he or she an agent in place, seated in the councils of the great and passing on vital information. In Tokyo in World War II, Richard Sorge, a Communist spy under cover as a German newspaper correspondent, and his main source, Ozaki Hotsuki, did have this access, reporting to their Communist masters in 1941 that Japan was not planning to attack the Soviet Union from the east while that country was fighting Adolf Hitler (q.v.). But spy information is fundamentally blighted by the fear that the agent is passing true information only to set up the recipient for a deception. And indeed, in 1944 GARBO, whom the Nazis thought a major source, was actually a double agent for Britain who played a major role in the D-Day (q.v.) deception.

IMINT is based on visible light, on infrared, or on radar. Pictures in light give fine detail; those taken by infrared or radar are coarser but penetrate darkness or cloud. They give, literally, snapshots of events, but a sequence can show which way a train is going or suggest when a fortification or a factory will be completed. Photo interpreters can tell, for example, how wide a bridge is. They have not always succeeded: they did not at first recognize the tall columns at Peenemünde in Nazi Germany as V-2 rockets. But in 1962 American photo interpreters detected the presence in Cuba of Soviet offensive missiles, enabling President John F. Kennedy to press for their withdrawal and leading to a backdown by the Soviet Union in the Cold War (q.v.).

SIGINT is the most important secret intelligence source. It is faster and more trustworthy than spies, more insightful than photographs, prisoner-of-war interrogations, or frontline reconnaissance (q.v.). SIGINT obtains information from enemy signals. Radio operators intercept these communications; direction-finding teams locate the enemy transmitters. Analysts then diagram the senders and receivers to infer an underlying organization; they graph quantities to predict enemy activity: more messages on the left flank than on the right may presage an attack on the left. When codebreakers solve encrypted messages and so disclose the actual words of the enemy, they reveal directly — without requiring inference — enemy capabilities, attitudes, and specific plans. So valuable is this that, during World War II, cryptanalysis contributed significantly to the Allied victory through its contributions to the Battle of Midway (q.v.) and the Battle of the North Atlantic against the U-boats (q.v.), to the destruction of the Japanese merchant fleet, and to various land battles in Europe in 1944 and 1945. Dwight D. Eisenhower (q.v.) called it "priceless." SIGINT's usefulness has grown in step with communications, so that the U.S. Army has added specialized communications-intelligence battalions to its divisions.

Intelligence officers assemble the data from these sources into a finished report. In armies, they serve as part of the General Staff of their unit. In the U.S. Army, this position is designated G-2, for the second officer of the General Staff. In the German army of World War II, the position was the Ic — roman numeral I for the operations portion of the staff, the lowercase c for the third General Staff officer.

Intelligence officers combine a hint from one source with a clue from another to draw a conclusion about a possible enemy action. Or, when sources conflict, they determine which is the more likely or seek an overlap where both could be true. They shape the facts and inferences into a report on enemy capabilities and, if possible, intentions. This goes to commanders, who normally incorporate its information in their decisions on their next moves. In the fall of 1942, for example, information from a variety of sources — primarily unglamorous, basic troop observation and enemy deserters — told Colonel-General Walther Model, commander of the German Ninth Army, at the tip of a salient jutting toward Moscow, that the Red Army (q.v.) would mount a massive attack to flatten the salient on November 25. Thus warned, the Germans braced themselves, repelled the attacks, and retained their position.

Some commanders ignore their intelligence officers. Sometimes they feel that lower echelons exaggerate the enemy threat to get more supplies; sometimes they insist, for what they regard as valid reasons, on acting on their own plan despite countervailing indications.

Intelligence doesn't win wars. Wars are won by the men and women in the trenches, on the ships, and in the airplanes. Intelligence is secondary to strength, morale, a commander's ability. But it can help commanders win. By optimizing resources, it can shorten wars and save lives.

Intelligence affects the defense more than the offense. The reason lies in the nature of these two forms of combat. The characteristic of the defense, as Carl von Clausewitz (q.v.) said, is "awaiting a blow." A blow can be awaited only through knowledge. Intelligence is thus integral to the defense. The offense, on the other hand, is "complete in itself," as Clausewitz said. It does not need information to carry out its function. This difference explains why more intelligence case histories consist of defenses than of attacks.

One example is the first decisive battle in the history of the world to be determined by intelligence. In 207 B.C., Rome was defending itself against the invading and rampaging forces of Carthage. The Carthaginian general, Hasdrubal, crossing the Alps with fifty-six thousand men and fifteen elephants, wrote to his brother Hannibal (q.v.) in southern Italy, telling him where they should meet. The Romans intercepted the letter, attacked, and defeated Hasdrubal at the Metaurus River before the brothers could join forces. Hannibal withdrew, and Rome advanced to become leader of the known world.

In 1756, Frederick the Great (q.v.) of Prussia learned through a spy of the plans, antagonistic to him, of Austria, Saxony, and Russia. He used this information to preemptively attack Saxony, launching the Seven Years' War (q.v.) in Europe. His victory moved

Prussia a major step closer to becoming a great power.

When World War I broke out, Russia attacked Germany with a northern and a southern army. They communicated in part by radio, in messages sent mostly in the clear because their cryptosystem had been distributed to only a few units. The Germans overheard these radiograms. One of them revealed that the northern Russian army was advancing so slowly that the German commanders, Generals Paul von Hindenburg (q.v.) and Erich Ludendorff (q.v.), could safely attack the southern army first. This they did. Helped by additional intercepts of Russian messages, they wiped it out. This battle, Tannenberg (q.v.), which began Russia's slide into revolution and ruin, was won in large measure with the help of intelligence and may be regarded as one of the most fateful in the twentieth century.

One of the most important intelligence coups of all time came in 1917 when the British cracked a German diplomatic message. The German foreign minister, Arthur Zimmermann, was faced with the probable hostility of the United States after Germany began unrestricted submarine warfare. To distract the United States, he proposed that Mexico declare war. As a reward, he promised Mexico the territory it had lost in the 1830s and 1840s: Texas, New Mexico, and Arizona. He transmitted his proposal to Mexico in a coded telegram, which Britain intercepted, solved, and revealed to the Americans. Six weeks later, an enraged U.S. Congress declared war on Germany, helping end the stalemate in the West, assisting in the Allies' victory, and making the United States a world power.

Another significant case history of the role of intelligence — again, in its defensive mode — began in the 1920s. Poland, carved in part out of territory that had been Prussian since the 1790s, feared that Germany would attempt to recover those lands. One way the new nation sought to discern the plans of Germany was to break German codes. Far-sightedly hiring mathematicians for this work, and aided by a German traitor, Poland reconstructed Germany's Enigma cipher machine — and passed its secret to the British just before World War II began. This led to the massive Allied solutions of German cryptograms called "the Ultra secret," which led to many Allied victories on land and at sea.

Though spies were dispatched and caught and sometimes exchanged during the Cold War, they seem not to have affected many events. An alleged American agent in the Kremlin revealed far less during the Cuban missile crisis than aerial photographs. The spy in the office of German chancellor Willy Brandt did not much change the course of East-West relations. The CIA's despicable Aldrich Ames, who revealed to the Russians American agents working against them — indeed cost them their lives — otherwise did not change the course of history.

Of course, intelligence is not omniscient. Pearl Harbor (q.v.) is, for many Americans, the primary case. The Japanese attack was a complete surprise. For Israelis, the failure to warn about the Arab attacks that began the Yom Kippur War (see *Arab-Israeli Wars*) demonstrates the fallibility of their otherwise excellent intelligence. And more recently, neither the U.S. Central Intelligence Agency, nor any other intelligence unit, predicted the end of the Cold War. But then, neither did anybody else.

DAVID KAHN

David Kahn, *The Codebreakers* (1967); Jeffrey T. Richelson, *A Century of Spies* (1995).

International Brigades

When the Spanish Republic was threatened by the military uprising of July 18, 1936, the Comintern (Communist International) took advantage of the spontaneous left-wing movement in its support to organize the International Brigades (IB) starting in mid-August. Italian, German, and Austrian refugees from fascism saw the Spanish civil war (q.v.) as their first chance to fight back. French (the most numerous contingent), British, and North American volunteers went to Spain out of concern about what defeat for the republic might mean for the rest of the world. Volunteers traveled via Paris, thence to be smuggled across the French border, arriving in Spain beginning in October; many had to trek over the Pyrenees. After rudimentary training at Albacete, the first units to reach a besieged Madrid on November 8 consisted of German and Italian antifascists, plus some British, French, and Polish left-wingers, a few of whom had fought in World War I (q.v.) or had experience of military service. They were sprinkled among the Spanish defenders at the ratio of one to four, boosting morale and passing on expertise to the civilians.

Led by the Soviet general Émil Kléber, the IB was vital to the defense of Madrid, although it was just one component of a heroic popular effort. In December and January, the IB played a decisive part in repelling efforts by the Nationalists (as the rebels became known) to encircle Madrid. The first American volunteers arrived in time to play a decisive part in these battles. In February, the rebels attacked through the Jarama valley on the Madrid-Valencia highway. Fiercely defended, the road was held at a cost of twenty-five thousand Republicans. Casualties among the IB were high since they were invariably used as shock troops.

In March, further Nationalist efforts to encircle Madrid by attacking Guadalajara were defeated by a counterattack involving the Italian Garibaldi Battalion of the IB. Thereafter, as the republic organized its Popular Army, and as the conflict turned into a more conventional war of large-scale maneuver, the Brigades played an important but less central role. After each engagement, there were fewer survivors, but, poorly clad, shod, and equipped, they fought on, held together by shared ideals rather than by conventional structures of hierarchy and discipline.

The Brigades played a substantial role in later offensives — the capture of Belchite and Teruel — and in the final defensive phase of the war. This followed Francisco Franco's great offensive through the spring and summer of 1938 after his recapture of Teruel in February 1938. Sweeping through Aragón and Castellón, 100,000 Nationalist troops reached the Mediterranean by mid-April, splitting the republic in two, and in July moved toward Valencia. Republican forces including the IB mounted a determined defense. Then, to relieve the threat against Valencia, the republic mounted a spectacular diversionary assault across the River Ebro in an attempt to restore contact with Catalonia. The Nationalist lines were breached, although at great cost to the IB. Francoist reinforcements were rushed in, and three months of fierce artillery bombardment and sweltering heat saw the Republicans pushed back.

In the hope of changing the attitude of the Western powers, the Republican government decided unilaterally to withdraw its foreign volunteers. A farewell parade was held in Barcelona for the International Brigades on October 29, 1938. In total, 59,380 of them had come from fifty different countries to fight fascism, including nearly 3,000 Americans. About one-third of the American volunteers were killed, and all the survivors had been wounded at least once. All told, 9,934 (16.7 percent) of all International Brigades had died, and 7,686 (12.9 percent) had been badly

wounded. In October 1938, 12,673 were still in Spain. They began the slow journey home or back into exile, often to fates more appalling than anything they had yet suffered. Those who survived were not to return to Spain until after the death of Franco, thirty-seven years later.

PAUL PRESTON

Iran-Iraq War

1980–1988

During the eight years between Iraq's formal declaration of war on September 22, 1980, and Iran's acceptance of a cease-fire with effect on July 20, 1988, at the very least half a millon and possibly twice as many troops were killed on both sides, at least half a million became permanent invalids, some 228 billion dollars were directly expended, and more than 400 billion dollars of damage (mostly to oil facilities, but also to cities) was inflicted, mostly by artillery barrages. Aside from that, the war was inconsequential: having won Iranian recognition of exclusive Iraqi sovereignty over the Shatt-el-Arab River (into which the Tigris and Euphrates combine, forming Iraq's best outlet to the sea), in 1988 Saddam Hussein surrendered that gain when in need of Iran's neutrality in anticipation of the 1991 Gulf War (q.v.).

Three things distinguish the Iran-Iraq War. First, it was inordinately protracted, lasting longer than either world war, essentially because Iran did not want to end it, while Iraq could not. Second, it was sharply asymmetrical in the means employed by each side, because though both sides exported oil and purchased military imports throughout, Iraq was further subsidized and supported by Kuwait and Saudi Arabia, allowing it to acquire advanced weapons and expertise on a much larger scale than Iran. Third, it included three modes of warfare absent in all previous wars since 1945: indiscriminate ballistic-missile attacks on cities by both sides, but mostly by Iraq; the extensive use of chemical weapons (mostly by Iraq); and some 520 attacks on third-country oil tankers in the Persian Gulf — for which Iraq employed mostly manned aircraft with antishipping missiles against tankers lifting oil from Iran's terminals, while Iran used mines, gunboats, shore-launched missiles, and helicopters against tankers lifting oil from the terminals of Iraq's Arab backers.

When Saddam Hussein, president of Iraq, quite deliberately started the war, he miscalculated on two counts: first, in attacking a country greatly disorganized by revolution but also greatly energized by it — and whose regime could be consolidated only by a long "patriotic" war, as with all revolutionary regimes; and second, at the level of theater strategy, in launching a *surprise* invasion against a very large country whose strategic depth he was not even trying to penetrate. Had Iran been given ample warning, it would have mobilized its forces to defend its borderlands; that would have made the Iraqi invasion much more difficult, but in the process the bulk of Iranian forces might have been defeated, possibly forcing Iran to accept a cease-fire on Iraqi terms. As it was, the initial Iraqi offensive thrusts landed in the void, encountering only weak border units before reaching their logistical limits. At that point, Iran had only just started to mobilize in earnest.

From then on, until the final months of the war eight years later, Iraq was forced on the strategic defensive, having to face periodic Iranian offensives on one sector or another, year after year. After losing most of his territorial gains by May 1982 (when Iran recaptured Khorramshahr), Saddam Hussein's strategic response was to proclaim a unilateral cease-fire (June 10, 1982) while ordering Iraqi forces to withdraw to the border. But Iran rejected a cease-fire, demanding the removal of Saddam Hussein and compensation for war damage. Upon Iraq's refusal, Iran launched an invasion into Iraqi territory (Operation Ramadan, on July 13, 1982) in the first of many attempts over the coming years to conquer Basra, Iraq's second city and only real port.

But revolutionary Iran was very limited in its tactically offensive means. Cut off from U.S. supplies for its largely U.S.-equipped forces and deprived of the shah's officer cadres who had been driven into exile, imprisoned, or killed, it never managed to reconstitute effective armored formations or its once large and modern air force. Iran's army and Pasdaran revolutionary guards could mount only massed infantry attacks supported by increasingly strong artillery fire. They capitalized on Iran's morale and population advantage (forty million versus Iraq's thirteen million), but although foot infantry could breach Iraqi defense lines from time to time, if only by costly human-wave attacks, it could not penetrate deeply enough in the aftermath to achieve decisive results.

By 1988 Iran was demoralized by the persistent failure of its many "final" offensives over the years, by the prospect of unending casualties, by its declining ability to import civilian goods as well as military supplies, and by the Scud missile attacks on Teheran. But what finally ended the war was Iraq's belated reversion to main-force offensive action on the ground. Having long conserved its forces and shifted to all-mechanized configurations to circumvent the reluctance of its troops to face enemy fire, Iraq attacked on a large scale in April 1988. The end came on July 18, when Iran accepted UN Resolution 598 calling for an immediate cease-fire, though minor Iraqi attacks continued for a few more days after the truce came into effect on July 20, 1988.

EDWARD N. LUTTWAK

Irish Republican Army (IRA)

This insurgent military organization is dedicated to the task of ending, usually by extreme means, British political authority in Ireland. In its more than two centuries of existence, the Irish Republican Army (IRA) has enjoyed varying degrees of popular support and consequently has displayed varying degrees of strength and competence. In recent years its tactical approach — directed by its Dublin-based political arm, Sinn Fein — has been largely that of terrorism, aimed both at damaging the economic well-being of those northern six counties of Ireland that in 1921 remained a part of the United Kingdom, and at wearying the popular commitment of the British to retain their hold on the territory.

The military wing, the Ogláigh na nÉireann, or Irish Volunteers, engaged in a variety of skirmishes against the British, most notably in the Dublin Uprising of 1916. They enjoyed their greatest triumph in 1921, when home rule was finally achieved for twenty-six of the thirty-two Irish counties (see *Collins, Michael*).

But at this point the movement divided. The Volunteers accepted the agreement that had been forged between London and Dublin and went on to form the core of the Irish Free State's new army; a breakaway body, the "Irregulars," was bitterly opposed to the agreement — because it did not include the six northern counties — and vowed, as self-styled patriots, to continue the struggle. A short-lived civil war erupted, which the Irregulars lost.

Although the IRA then engaged in several short-lived, desultory campaigns against the British in the North, they had become by the 1960s something of a

September 3, 1973: Wrecked cars and windowless buildings near London's Old Bailey bear witness to an IRA bombing, which caused heavy casualties.

joke: most of their weapons had in fact been sold to Welsh militant organizations. But with the sudden rise of civil rights fervor in Northern Ireland in 1968, what remained of the IRA leadership saw a chance for revival. Old-style IRA personnel and attitudes were promptly shunted aside, while a new and highly aggressive organization, the Provisional IRA (named to commemorate the Provisional Irish Government of 1916) was created, with links deliberately forged to other international terrorist organizations.

After a hesitant start, the Provisional IRA steadily evolved into a ferociously successful movement — unpopular, but highly effective and visible — which has kept the political situation in Northern Ireland in turmoil for more than a quarter of a century. More than three thousand people died violently between 1968 and 1994, including nearly seven hundred British soldiers and members of the security forces — making the Ulster campaign of the IRA one of the most effective and enduring of insurgent operations.

SIMON WINCHESTER

Isonzo, Eleven Battles of

June 23, 1915–September 15, 1918

When Italy entered World War I (q.v.) against Austria-Hungary on May 23, 1915, only the Isonzo valley at the southeastern end of the fortified mountain front offered prospects for a major offensive. Here a break through the enemy lines, capturing Gorizia and then Trieste, might lead to an advance across the Ljubljana (Laibach) Gap toward Vienna. General Luigi Cadorna, commanding the Italian army, concentrated two armies (about 200,000 strong) for this enterprise.

Recognizing the critical importance of this sector, the Austro-Hungarians had built fortifications and, despite setbacks in Serbia and Galicia, increased their troops to 100,000 men. In the first four Isonzo battles (June–August 1915), the Italians attacked but were repulsed. Reorganized and bolstered with more artillery, the Italians attacked again in October and yet again in November, also with little success.

In March 1916, Cadorna renewed his attacks in the

fifth battle, another failure, and, after having halted an Austro-Hungarian thrust from the Trentino, opened the sixth battle in August, expecting to find an opponent weakened because troops had been shifted to counter the Russian Brusilov (q.v.) offensive. This time Gorizia was taken, but there was no breakthrough. Three more battles followed, but they failed to improve on the initial success.

In 1917, French army mutinies and Russia's collapse demanded Allied diversionary measures. In response, Cadorna mounted the tenth and eleventh battles. The former stalled, but in the latter (August 18–September 15), shock troops drove the Austro-Hungarians off the strategic Bainsizza Plateau, though exhaustion and supply problems prevented exploitation. Shaken, however, Austria-Hungary requested German support, leading to the Italian disaster at Caporetto (q.v.), sometimes called the twelfth Isonzo battle.

The Isonzo battles illustrated that well-prepared positions could not be taken by conventional frontal assaults. Each time the Italians had superior numbers and fought bravely, but were held or made only minor advances with heavy losses. Though stretched to the limit, the Austro-Hungarians fought tenaciously on this front with remarkable unity, but they also suffered heavy casualties, which they could afford less than the Italians.

GUNTHER E. ROTHENBERG

Italian Independence, Wars of

1848–1870

These wars of the Risorgimento (national resurrection) unified Italy under the house of Savoy, previously rulers of the kingdom of Sardinia. Italy, dominated by Austria, had been divided into six states and two Austrian provinces. Italians call the wars of 1848–1849, 1859, and 1866 the First, Second, and Third Wars of Independence, stressing Italian-Austrian conflict. But fighting also occurred between the house of Savoy and other Italian dynasties and the papacy, and among Italian social and political groups. The French intervened to restore papal rule in 1849 and against Austria in 1859. The crucial war of 1860–1861 was all-Italian, uniting north, center, and south to form the kingdom of Italy. The Italian army captured Rome from papal forces in the final campaign in September 1870.

Giuseppe Garibaldi dominated these wars. Often mislabeled a guerrilla, Garibaldi built quasi-conventional forces from nationalist volunteers. His charisma inspired enthusiasm and individual initiative among his followers, who — at high cost — overwhelmed regular opponents. Although republican and democratic, Garibaldi accepted Italian unity under the house of Savoy as a political necessity. After conquering southern Italy in 1860, he surrendered it to Victor Emmanuel II of Savoy. Garibaldi advocated reorganizing the new Italian army to base it on self-motivated citizen soldiers, but the king preferred his obedient royalist army — although the Austrians had thrashed it in 1848–1849, and it had trailed behind its French allies in 1859; the Austrians would defeat it and the equally mediocre Italian navy in 1866 (although Prussian victories rescued Italy). But that army allowed the Savoys and their supporters to rule Italy. Only after the 1943–1946 collapse of the monarchy did Risorgimento military ideals materialize with the creation of a republican army.

BRIAN R. SULLIVAN

Italian Wars

1494–1559

The Italian Wars defy simple review. Politically complex, these wars made Italy the focus of European politics, the theater in which the king of France and the king of Spain competed for preeminence. The major Italian states — the Pope, Milan, Venice, Florence, and Naples — did their best to survive the wars with their independence intact. Few succeeded; instead, multifarious and shifting alliances became the rule, making ambassadors as important as generals. This marriage of permanent diplomacy with continual campaigning in fact marks the birth of modern strategic warfare. Just as modern was the new domination of gunpowder weapons: the harquebus and then the musket on the battlefield, heavy cannon and explosive mines in siege warfare.

The wars opened with King Charles VIII of France's seizure of Naples in 1494, ostensibly the first step in a crusade to the Holy Land. Alarmed at this easy conquest, an alliance of concerned states evicted France from Naples — but, thanks to the military skill of Gonzalo de Córdoba (q.v.), left southern Italy under permanent Spanish control. Attention duly shifted to the north, where the struggle for Milan brought the wars to a watershed in the 1520s. At the Battle of Pavia (1525), a Spanish army both decisively defeated the French and captured their king, Francis I. Despite furious attempts, France never avenged this great defeat or reversed Spanish ascendancy. Desperate French monarchs even allied themselves with the infidel Turks — a far cry from earlier crusading dreams. In the end, Spanish control of Naples and Milan proved unshakable, and King Henry II of France agreed to a comprehensive peace in 1559.

THOMAS F. ARNOLD

Iwo Jima, Battle of

February 19–March 26, 1945

The American amphibious invasion of Iwo Jima, a key island in the Bonin chain roughly 575 miles from the Japanese coast, was sparked by the desire for a place where B-29 bombers damaged over Japan could land without returning all the way to the Marianas, and for a base for escort fighters that would assist in the bombing campaign. Iwo Jima was defended by roughly 23,000 Japanese army and navy troops, and it was attacked by three marine divisions after elaborate preparatory air and naval bombardment (sixty-eight hundred tons of bombs, twenty-two thousand shells). The battle was marked by changes in Japanese defense tactics — troops no longer defended at the beach line but rather concentrated inland; consequently, the marines experienced initial success but then got bogged down in costly attritional warfare. The Japanese fought from an elaborate network of caves, dugouts, tunnels, and underground installations that were difficult to find and destroy. Except for 1,083 prisoners (two of whom did not surrender until 1951) the entire garrison was wiped out. American losses included 5,900 dead and 17,400 wounded.

Photographer Joe Rosenthal provided the U.S. Marine Corps with one of its most enduring images with his picture (restaged for the purpose) of Americans raising the flag over Mount Suribachi at the southwest corner of Iwo, an image replicated on postage stamps as well as on the memorial statue at the entrance to Arlington National Cemetery.

A damaged B-29 landed on Iwo as early as March 4; before war's end between 2,250 and 2,400 bombers did so. Fighters began to operate from Iwo Jima on March 11, 1945.

JOHN PRADOS

J

Jackson, Thomas J. "Stonewall"

1824–1863, *American Civil War General*

Few historical personages are known to posterity primarily by a nickname, but Confederate general Stonewall Jackson is a notable exception. He earned the name by which he is known and became a legend in his own time, as well as one of the three most famous American Civil War (q.v.) generals (with Robert E. Lee [q.v.] and Ulysses S. Grant [q.v.]), at the First Battle of Bull Run in 1861 (called First Manassas in the South).

In that first of the war's great engagements, Jackson commanded a brigade of Virginia troops that had arrived on the field by train from the Shenandoah Valley — the first example in combat history of troops being carried into battle by railroad. As federal attackers seemed about to win the day, Jackson's troops stood fast and helped turn the tide. Confederate general Bernard Bee is said to have exclaimed to his own troops: "Look! There stands Jackson like a stone wall!"

The nickname stuck. Jackson's fame was carried with it across the South and later the nation, and few would know him today by his real name — Thomas Jonathan.

Ironically, it was not as a "stone wall" but primarily as a lightning marcher, tactical and operational genius, and hard-striking offensive master that Jackson achieved greatness. In his "valley campaign" in 1862 — still studied by military officers today — he eluded, then defeated, superior federal forces; in August of the same year, he first marched entirely around the Union army of General John Pope, then stood on the defensive, luring Pope to the attack, until the rest of the Confederate army could join in a crushing counterattack and victory at the Second Battle of Bull Run (or Manassas).

Jackson commanded one of the two wings of Robert E. Lee's army at Antietam (q.v.) later in 1862 and held the right at Fredericksburg in 1863. At Chancellorsville (q.v.), later that year, he was the main instrument of Lee's innovative decision to divide his army; he sent the hard-marching Jackson around the rear of a much larger federal army, a daring surprise move that threw the Union troops into a panic and ultimately contributed to Confederate victory — but also in the untimely death of Stonewall Jackson, who was mistakenly shot by one of his own men as he was reconnoitering the front after darkness had fallen. The subsequent absence of Lee's "good right arm" at the Battle of Gettysburg (q.v.) is believed by many historians to have been a major factor in the Confederate defeat.

An ill-educated backwoodsman from western Virginia, Jackson stood seventeenth of fifty-nine in the class of 1846 at West Point. Though he had served with distinction in the Mexican War (q.v.), he was not highly regarded before the Civil War. As a teacher at the Virginia Military Institute, he was eccentric enough to be called "Fool Tom Jackson." A religious fanatic (it was said of him that "he lives by the New Testament and fights by the Old"), he had odd dietary habits, refusing to eat pepper, sucking on lemons, and maintaining a posture that would keep his alimentary canal straight. He was sensitive to a fault, often feuding with other generals; but he was revered by his troops. His greatest failure, during the Seven Days battles of 1862, was an aberration never satisfactorily explained.

Jackson's most effective military quality was decisiveness; he saw opportunities quickly, seized them at once, never hesitated to attack even superior forces if he saw the possibility of advantage, and marched to his objectives with relentlessness and speed unmatched by any other Civil War general. He may well have been, and some authorities consider him, the war's most remarkable soldier.

TOM WICKER

Jellicoe, John Rushworth

1859–1935, British Admiral

John Rushworth Jellicoe, first earl Jellicoe, entered the Royal Navy in 1872, became a captain in 1897, and reached flag rank in 1907. He served as director of naval ordnance (DNO) (1905–1907); second in command, Atlantic Fleet (1907–1908); third sea lord and controller (1908–1910); commander in chief, Atlantic Fleet (1910–1911); commander second division, Home Fleet (1910–1912); second sea lord (1912–1914); commander in chief, Grand Fleet (1914–1916); first sea lord (1916–1917); imperial envoy (1919–1920); and governor-general of New Zealand (1920–1924).

While DNO and third sea lord, Jellicoe played an important role in the development of naval matériel and tactics in the administration of Admiral Sir John Fisher (q.v.). In 1912, he took actions that retarded the development of an important new method of gunnery on the strength of an assessment of German tactical intentions that ultimately turned out to be mistaken, an error that was compounded in 1916 by his over-anxiety about the threat posed by long-range torpedoes, which inspired caution that adversely affected both fleet deployment and the effectiveness of British shooting at the Battle of Jutland (q.v.). Jellicoe's exhaustion after two years at sea, his inflexibility, and his unwillingness to delegate weakened his performance as first sea lord, which partially explains the inadequacy of the Royal Navy's response to the submarine crisis of 1917. Jellicoe's relations with politicians were often problematic, but he always enjoyed the deep respect and affection of his naval peers and subordinates.

JON SUMIDA

Jericho, Battle of

1400? B.C.

In the popular story of the Battle of Jericho, as related in the Book of Joshua, the Israelites, led by their prophet-general Joshua, captured the city by marching around it and blowing rams' horns until its for-

tification walls collapsed. Unfortunately, although there is plenty of archaeological evidence for the town, there is little for the battle. All that is known for certain is that the Jericho dating to the time of the Israelite conquest was relatively poor and unimpressive. But it controlled access to the Jerusalem plateau, itself vital to the security of the region. So the capture of Jericho would have been a major triumph for the invaders, a historical event likely to have been preserved in a strong oral tradition, eventually amplified and recorded in the Book of Joshua.

Most scholars date the Israelite invasion of Canaan somewhere between 1400 and 1200 B.C. The invaders approached the town from the Sinai. They would have been discouraged from taking a more direct route by the presence of several fortified positions protecting the main thoroughfare (called the "King's Highway"). Instead, they took a long loop around to the south of the town and circled back from the east.

This Jericho of the late Bronze Age had nowhere near the formidable defenses that had protected it during the earlier Middle Bronze Age. Its massive fortifications, built in about 8000 B.C., turned Neolithic Jericho into the world's first fortress, a key stage in humanity's shift from being nomadic hunter-gatherers to living in a sedentary, agrarian society.

IRA MEISTRICH

Jerusalem

Because it has been a strategic site in the Middle East for millennia, Jerusalem has been the object of numerous attacks and sieges. Perched on easily defensible Judaean hillsides less than thirty miles from the Mediterranean Sea, the city in antiquity controlled the principal highways that connected Egypt, Europe, and Africa. Whoever controlled Jerusalem was likely to control much of the economic, diplomatic, and military traffic of the ancient Near East. Another reason for Jerusalem's military significance has been its spiritual importance to the three primary sects of the region — Judaism, Christianity, and Islam — making it the object of wars for possession that have often far exceeded its strictly strategic value.

The first conquest of the city that can be documented was by the Israelites under King David, in about 996 B.C. In the centuries between that conquest in the tenth century B.C. and the end of the eighth century B.C., there were no fewer than six reconstructions of Jerusalem's fortifications, indicating the likelihood of minor, temporary occupations by local peoples such as the Edomites, Ammonites, and Moabites. In about 700 B.C., King Hezekiah of Judah led a rebellion against his Assyrian (q.v.) overlord, Sennacherib. Among Hezekiah's improvements of the city's fortifications was the famous underground Siloam water tunnel that ensured access to a reliable source of fresh water. This tunnel helped Jerusalem successfully withstand Sennacherib's siege.

Jerusalem fared less well against the Babylonians just over a century later. Nebuchadnezzar first took and partially destroyed the city in 597 B.C. He returned, following an unsuccessful revolt by his vassal Zedekiah in 586 B.C., and nearly razed the city. After Jerusalem was reoccupied by returning Israelite exiles in 538 B.C., it enjoyed a few centuries of relative peace and reconstruction before the next conquest, this one in 168 B.C. by Antiochus Epiphanes and the Seleucids. In the following year, Jerusalem was retaken by the Maccabees.

Two centuries later, during the First Jewish Rebellion (A.D. 66–70), Jerusalem suffered its most extreme destruction when it was captured by the Romans. It was completely obliterated in the following century when the Roman emperor Hadrian decided to build a new metropolis, Aeolia Capitolina, on the site of the old (see *Jewish Rebellions*).

The Arabs captured Jerusalem from its last Byzantine ruler in A.D. 636, lost it to the crusaders (see *Crusades*) in 1099, and recaptured it in 1187. The city's current fortifications were built in the sixteenth century by Suleiman the Magnificent (q.v.). General Edmund Allenby (q.v.) fought one of his toughest campaigns of World War I (q.v.) in the Judaean hills around Jerusalem, taking heavy casualties before finally capturing the city during his 1918 drive on Damascus.

Jerusalem became a divided city following bitter fighting in the 1948 war for Israeli independence. It remained divided until captured from Jordan by Israel in the Six-Day War in 1967 (see *Arab-Israeli Wars*).

IRA MEISTRICH

Jewish Rebellions

A.D. 66–73 and 132–135

The First Jewish War (A.D. 66–73) erupted because of Jewish outrage over Roman misrule. Cestius Gallus, governor of Syria, failed to restore order in Jerusalem

(q.v.) in 66, and the Jewish Zealots interpreted his ignominious retreat to his base at Ptolemais (Acre) as a sign from God to summon the populace to rebellion. In 67, Vespasian, a tough professional, assumed command, secured the Mediterranean ports, and overran Galilee with a sixty-thousand-man army spearheaded by four veteran legions. Vespasian halted operations against Jerusalem to seize the throne in the Roman civil war of 68–69, but in 70, his son Titus returned to capture and raze Jerusalem. Flavius Silva, in mopping up operations in 71–73, captured the last Zealot fortress, Masada (q.v.). Roman victory was never in doubt. Vespasian isolated Jewish insurgents, preventing an intervention by Vologeses, king of Parthia, Rome's rival empire in the East. Although Jews, despite their lack of arms and cavalry, fought valiantly, Zealot leaders foolishly warred among themselves and chose a strategy of defending strongholds, which the Romans could readily reduce by sieges because they excelled in this type of warfare. Defeat proved catastrophic for the Jews; half the population of Judaea and Samaria perished or was enslaved.

The Second Jewish War (132–135) was provoked when the emperor Hadrian commenced the refounding of Jerusalem as the Roman colony Aelia Capitolina. Hadrian waged a brutal war of pacification against tenacious peasants of Judaea, led by the Messianic figure Shimon bar-Kochba — who died in the massacre when the Romans took his fortified citadel, Betar. Hadrian established military colonies throughout Judaea, stationed two legions as permanent garrisons, and banned Jews from Jerusalem. His settlement helped shift the focus of Judaism from cultic worship at Jerusalem to the intellectual spiritualism of the synagogue.

KENNETH W. HARL

Jihad

Jihad is an Arabic word commonly translated "holy war," but literally meaning "striving," as in the Qur'anic phrase "striving in the path of God." Some Muslims, particularly in more recent times, interpret the duty of jihad in a spiritual and moral sense. The overwhelming majority of early authorities, citing relevant passages in the Qur'an, commentaries, and the traditions of the Prophet, discuss jihad in military terms. Virtually every manual of Islamic law has a chapter on jihad, which regulates in minute detail matters such as the opening, conduct, interruption, and cessation of hostilities and the allocation and division of booty. Fighters in a jihad are enjoined not to kill women and children unless they attack first, not to torture or mutilate prisoners, to give fair warning of the resumption of hostilities after a truce, and to honor agreements. Islamic law prescribes good treatment for noncombatants but accords the victors extensive rights over the property and also over the persons and families of the vanquished, who could be reduced to slavery.

According to Islamic law, it is lawful to wage war against four types of enemy: infidels, apostates, rebels, and bandits. Although all four types of war are legitimate, only the first two count as jihad. The rules for jihad are different from those regulating other forms of warfare; they are also different when fought against apostates and infidels. Renegade Muslims must be ruthlessly excised and, according to most authorities, put to death if captured. Some say they may be pardoned if they recant; others maintain that God may forgive them in the next world, but no human authority can do so in this world. As regards non-Muslims, there is a distinction between those who follow what Islam recognizes as a revealed monotheistic religion and the rest. Idolaters and polytheists must be given a choice between conversion and death; the latter sentence may be commuted to enslavement. Recognized monotheists — which in practice meant Jews and Christians — could be permitted to practice their own religions and run their own affairs, provided that they recognized the supremacy of the Muslim state and accepted certain restrictions.

Jihad is a religious obligation. In offense, it is an obligation of the Muslim community as a whole — that is, it may be discharged by volunteers or professionals; in defense, it becomes an obligation of every able-bodied individual. This obligation is, in principle, unlimited and will continue, interrupted only by truces, until all the world either adopts the Muslim faith or submits to Muslim rule. Those who fight in the jihad qualify for rewards in both worlds — booty in this one, paradise in the next. Those who are killed in the jihad are called martyrs.

The historical jihad began in the lifetime of the Prophet with the wars of the Muslims against the pagans in Arabia. It continued with the wars of conquest, which brought first the Middle East and then much of south and central Asia, North Africa, and, at different periods, parts of southwestern and south-

eastern Europe under Muslim rule. The jihad against Christendom eventually provoked a Christian response in kind, known as the Crusades (q.v.).

Like the word *crusade*, the word *jihad* is often used nowadays in a figurative sense, to denote a peaceful campaign for some good cause. Unlike the word *crusade*, it is still also used in many parts of the Muslim world in its original sense. In modern times, the term *jihad* has been used by the Ottoman Empire in its struggles against its European enemies and by religiously motivated independence movements in the British, French, Russian, Dutch, and Italian empires.

BERNARD LEWIS

Joan of Arc

1412?–1431, *French Military Leader*

Saint Joan of Arc (Jeanne d'Arc), canonized in 1920, was born in Domrémy in Lorraine to a peasant family. From 1425, she began having visions and hearing voices commanding her to leave her parents and village. Her task was to save France, which at this stage of the Hundred Years' War (q.v.) had two kings: the English Henry VI and the French Charles VII. Joan of Arc joined Charles VII at Chinon (March 1429) and was then sent to the aid of the town of Orléans, which had been besieged by the English for several months. Inspired by her prodigious energy, the French recaptured the fortified outposts that encircled the town, and the English abandoned the siege (May 8). The English then lost their other territories on the Loire and were defeated at Patay (June 18). Once again, Joan of Arc's military and religious power, combined with the abilities of the experienced French military commanders and soldiers, proved decisive. Joan of Arc then persuaded Charles VII to agree to the "sacred coronation ride," and she led the French as far as Reims (July 17). However, her attempt to recapture Paris (September 8) failed.

This marked the end of Joan of Arc's military successes; after this she encountered only defeat. Charles VII's advisers calculated that in order to recapture the kingdom it would first be necessary to make terms with the king's powerful relative, Philip, duke of Burgundy; but Joan of Arc did not agree. She went instead to the rescue of Compiègne, besieged by the Burgundian army, and was herself taken prisoner (May 23, 1430). She was handed over to the English govern-

In this representation created soon after her death, Joan of Arc carries a banner with the royal fleur-de-lis, signifying her role as savior of the French monarchy.

ment, tried by church tribunal, and condemned to death. On May 30, 1431, Joan of Arc was burned at the stake in Rouen.

Joan of Arc was not an experienced commander, but she possessed a good sense of the terrain and, dressed in her armor and with her standard at her side, she was an imposing figure. However, her greatest strength was her extraordinary courage, which imparted new life to all those she led.

PHILIPPE CONTAMINE

Joffre, Joseph

1852–1931, French Commander in Chief and Marshal

Born in Rivesaltes near the Spanish frontier, Joseph Joffre studied at the École Polytechnique. During the Franco-Prussian War (q.v.) of 1870–71, he fought in the defense of Paris. Commissioned in the military engineers, he served mainly in colonial postings in Formosa, Tonkin, and the Western Sudan. In 1903, he returned to France from Madagascar to command the Thirteenth Brigade, three years later the Sixth Division, and finally in 1908 the Second Corps at Amiens.

His limited command experience and the fact that he had never attended the *école de guerre*, virtually required for those who aspired to senior rank, made

Joffre a surprise choice for commander in chief in 1911. He owed his promotion to his proven organizational abilities and the fact that his main rivals were eliminated for reasons of age or political opinions. Joffre's main prewar achievement lay in strengthening the Russian alliance.

The opening battles of World War I (q.v.) in 1914 showed Joffre's war plan — Plan XVII — to have been based on flawed tactical and strategic concepts, and to have ignored enemy intentions. To be fair to Joffre, the demands of alliance politics, respect for Belgian neutrality, and a misplaced faith in offensive power shared by all armies desperately limited his options.

The victory won on the Marne (q.v.) in September 1914 was undoubtedly Joffre's crowning achievement. As the first French general in a century to defeat a German army, Joffre became a national hero, which, for better or worse, ensured his position as commander in chief for the next two and a half years. But he began to accumulate enemies in the Chamber of Deputies as the resolve and refusal to panic that had served him well on the Marne in 1914 hardened into stubborn pursuit of futile and bloody offensives in Artois and Champagne in 1915. His tardy response to the German buildup before Verdun (q.v.) in early 1916 further undermined his credibility. Promoted to marshal of France in December 1916, Joffre performed only perfunctory duties for the remainder of the war. He spent the postwar years mainly on writing his memoirs.

Joffre's historical reputation suffered in the post–World War I years at the hands of military historians such as Sir Basil Liddell Hart (q.v.), who saw him as a sphinx without a riddle, a tabula rasa who absorbed the imprint of offensive-minded "Young Turks" in the General Staff, with disastrous results. Modern historiography has been slightly more gentle, if only because it has sought to place Joffre more in the institutional and intellectual context of his time. His ability to rectify the numerous shortcomings of the French army before 1914 was circumscribed by republican politicians reluctant to accord the commander in chief the authority needed to resolve bureaucratic and technical disputes in the army. Though his 1915 offensives were costly, it is equally true that, until the French army mutinies of 1917, no French commander who failed to assault the German lines in France would long retain his post.

DOUGLAS PORCH

Julian

332–363, Roman Emperor

Julian (Flavius Claudius Julianus, "the Apostate") was the last of Rome's pagan soldier-emperors. Born into the Roman imperial family, Julian demonstrated bravery and strategic insight as a young man in border campaigns against Germanic tribes, notably at the Battle of Strasbourg in 357. Julian's troops declared him emperor in 360, and he renounced Christianity upon taking the throne. Perhaps inspired by tales of Alexander (q.v.) and other great pagan conquerors, Julian invaded Mesopotamia (March 363); his goal was to reassert Roman power against an ascendant Sassanian Persia. Julian's strategy — which depended on deception, speed, coordination of two armies and a large river fleet, and the execution of a complex pincers movement — proved overly complex. He failed to capture the Persian capital of Ctesiphon, lost momentum during a hungry retreat up the Tigris, and was killed (June 363) during a skirmish. Julian's failure led to long-term Persian gains in the East (see *Roman-Persian Wars*).

JOSIAH OBER

Justice, Military

Self-government by the fighting services is an ancient custom, growing out of the need for strict discipline, instant obedience, and the unchallengeable authority of the commander, reinforced in many societies by the notion of a warrior caste that upholds its own honor and with which outsiders must not meddle. Even in nations with unquestioned civilian control, the armed forces retain some of the characteristics of a state within a state.

Regulations for the governance of armed forces go at least as far back as scattered passages of Leviticus. In medieval England, military justice was carried out by the Court of the Constable and Marshal, enforcing articles of war proclaimed by the king. A code promulgated by Gustavus Adolphus (q.v.) of Sweden in 1621 is conventionally cited as the first of the modern codes. In English-speaking countries, the fountainhead of modern military law is the Mutiny Act, originally adopted by Parliament in 1689. In the United States, Articles of War were adopted by Congress for the governance of the Continental army during the American Revolution (q.v.). Under the present constitution, Congress enacted "Articles of War" with respect to the army, "Articles for the Government of the Navy," and "Articles for the Discipline of the Coast Guard." In 1951 these were replaced by the Uniform Code of Military Justice for all the services.

The Code covers serious offenses that are criminal under the general law, such as murder and robbery, as well as strictly military offenses such as fraudulent entry into the service, desertion, failure to obey orders, misbehavior before the enemy, conduct unbecoming an officer and a gentleman, and disorder and neglect to the prejudice of good order and discipline. Punishments can include, in appropriate cases, fine (including forfeiture of pay), imprisonment (including restriction to specified areas), or death; in addition, enlisted personnel can be given bad conduct or dishonorable discharges and can be reduced in rank, and officers can be dismissed from the service and can likewise be reduced in rank, including reduction to enlisted status. Historically, a court-martial could and did decree punishments such as flogging and branding. Flogging was abolished in the navy in 1846 and in the army in 1861; branding was not abolished by law until 1872 (though the branding of deserters in the "San Patricio Battalion" in the Mexican War [q.v.] may have been the last instance of its actual imposition).

The Code is administered through a hierarchy of tribunals. A commanding officer can decree simple punishment for minor offenses without a court-martial. A "summary court-martial," consisting of a single officer, cannot try officers and can administer only limited punishments. A "special court-martial" has at least three members and can impose punishments up to punitive discharge, six months' confinement, and forfeiture of not more than two-thirds of pay for not more than six months. A "general court-martial" consists of not less than five members together with a law officer whose function is somewhat like that of the judge in a civilian court; it can impose any authorized punishment. Under the Uniform Code, an enlisted accused can demand that at least one-third of the court consist of enlisted personnel.

The sentence of a court-martial is reviewed by the commanding officer who convened it or by some other commander authorized to convene a court-martial of the same type; he can disallow the sentence or reduce it but cannot increase it or reverse a verdict of not guilty. Serious sentences are reviewed by a board of not less than three officers, all qualified lawyers;

their determination can be examined by the Court of Military Appeals, a civilian court located in Washington, D.C.; its decisions are in turn reviewable by the U.S. Supreme Court.

The systems followed by other countries differ in detail but are generally similar overall. In the British army there are a "general court-martial" of at least five officers and a "district court-martial" of at least three officers. British officers can be not merely dismissed from the service but "cashiered"; a cashiered officer is ineligible to hold any appointment under the Crown. In France there is only one level of court-martial: unless convened in the field during active military operations, it consists of six officers, and a civilian judge of the locality in which the court is held presides over it.

THADDEUS HOLT

Jutland, Battle of

May 31–June 1, 1916

Jutland, which involved 250 ships and 100,000 men, was the only major naval surface engagement of World War I (q.v.); after 1918 it became the center of a great debate. The British Grand Fleet enjoyed a numerical advantage over the German High Sea Fleet of 37:27 in heavy units and 113:72 in light support craft. It also enjoyed the advantage of having broken German signal codes. There were two major phases of the battle. At 4:48 P.M. on May 31, 1916, the scouting forces of Vice Admirals David Beatty and Franz Hipper commenced a running artillery duel at fifteen thousand yards in the Skagerrak (Jutland), just off Denmark's North Sea coast. Hipper's ships took a severe pounding but survived due to their superior honeycomb hull construction. Beatty lost three battle cruisers due to lack of antiflash protection in the gun turrets, which allowed fires started by incoming shells to reach the powder magazines. Commenting that "[t]here seems to be something wrong with our bloody ships today," Beatty after this initial encounter turned north and lured the Germans onto the Grand Fleet.

The second phase of the battle started at 7:15 P.M., when Admiral John Jellicoe (q.v.) brought his ships into a single battle line by executing a 90-degree wheel to port. Gaining the advantage of the fading light, he cut the Germans off from their home base and twice crossed the High Sea Fleet's "T." Admiral Reinhard Scheer's ships took seventy direct hits, while scoring but twenty against Jellicoe: Scheer's fleet escaped certain annihilation only by executing three brilliant 180-degree battle turns away. By the full darkness at 10:00 P.M., British losses amounted to 6,784 men and 111,000 tons, and German losses to 3,058 men and 62,000 tons.

Kaiser Wilhelm II (q.v.) showered his sailors with Iron Crosses and his admirals with kisses; nevertheless, by early morning, June 1, Jellicoe stood off Wilhelmshaven with twenty-four untouched dreadnoughts and battle cruisers, while Scheer kept his ten battle-ready heavy units in port. Three German battle cruisers and three dreadnoughts required extensive repairs.

Strategically, Jutland proved as decisive as the Battle of Trafalgar (q.v.). The German High Sea Fleet had been driven home and would put out to sea only three more times on minor sweeps. Like the French after Trafalgar, the Germans now turned to commerce raiding. In his after-action report to the kaiser on July 4, Scheer eschewed future surface encounters with the Grand Fleet because of its "great material superiority" and advantageous "military-geographical position," and instead demanded "the defeat of British economic life — that is, by using the U-boats against British trade." Although the British public was disappointed with Jutland, Winston Churchill (q.v.) percipiently noted that Jellicoe was the one man who could have lost the war in an afternoon. Jutland instead proved Jellicoe's mettle.

HOLGER H. HERWIG

K

Kadesh, Battle of

1283? B.C.

Recent research suggests that the much-celebrated Egyptian victory at Kadesh was more a triumph of royal advertising than a military achievement. In his fifth year Pharaoh Ramses II, eager to advance beyond his father's Palestinian conquests, led the Egyptians against the fort-city of Kadesh in Syria, gateway to northern trade routes but allied with Ramses' rival, the Hittite ruler Muwatallis. Approaching Kadesh ahead of his army, Ramses learned from supposed defectors that the Hittites were far away; he was encamped before discovering that Muwatallis, actually nearby, had circled behind him, cut through Ramses' just-arriving first division, and was rapidly approaching. Ramses' inscriptions describe his single-handed triumph; other sources suggest the fortunate arrival of an Egyptian garrison protected Ramses until reinforcements arrived. Although both sides claimed victory, an Egyptian-Hittite alliance forged fourteen years later suggests the battle had actually been indecisive. Despite Ramses' claims, the Battle of Kadesh won little or nothing for the Egyptians and marked the end of Egyptian conquests in Palestine for many years.

BARBARA NEVLING PORTER

Kamikazes

Late in the Pacific war, the Japanese high command turned to an official national strategy of "special attack." The suicide airplane attacks were often referred to as "kamikaze" (divine wind), borrowing the name from the typhoons that reportedly blew up and swept away Kublai Khan's (q.v.) invading Mongol fleets in 1274 and again in 1281, in response to the fervent prayers of Japanese religious leaders.

The organization of the Divine Wind Special At-tack Corps was begun during the Japanese defense of the Philippines. Escorted to their target by fighters, the pilots were instructed to plunge their bomb-laden aircraft directly into enemy ships, creating a "man-guided bomb" of extraordinary power. The first such attack, involving five navy Zero fighters armed with 250-kilogram bombs, occurred on October 25, 1944, during operations off Leyte Island, following Vice Admiral Ōnishi Takijirō's (1891–1945) formal suggestion that such operations be planned. The tactic met with some success, and the army air force soon joined in.

Early advantages of surprise and the use of skilled pilots led to successes that encouraged repetition. Kamikaze forces grew and became a substitute method of attack in the Battle of Okinawa (q.v.), which began in April 1945; more than two thousand planes were employed using this tactic. American forces credited "suicide attacks" with sinking 34 Allied ships and damaging 288 others.

The notion of an enemy so dedicated, so fanatical, and so self-destructive chilled those who faced this threat, especially at the level of intensity encountered in the Okinawa campaign. But effective countermeasures soon minimized the chances that a kamikaze would slip through to the heart of the fleet — although picket ships often took the battering. At the same time, heedless of losses, the Japanese high command sought to whip the public into a frenzy of patriotic fervor as American forces approached the homeland, mythologizing the sacrifices of the kamikazes as the deliverers of a miracle that would keep enemy fleets from the sacred shores of Japan. By the summer of 1945, this spirit of utter sacrifice became a constant refrain in the remains of the empire. Army and navy units were raised to ram enemy planes in the sky, drive fast motorboats into landing craft, and leap from concealed positions to throw themselves under tanks. Heroic tales of the men who embodied the kamikaze

A Japanese kamikaze plane attacks the USS Missouri *in 1945.*

spirit were recounted everywhere in the final days of the war, fusing images of suicide and deliverance. Comrades and family members, however, now confirm that many of the "volunteers" were ordered to undertake such missions and harbored deep personal doubts and bitterness concerning the futility of their deaths.

Memorials to the kamikaze have continued to sprout throughout southern Japan, inviting visitors to pay respects to their spirit of self-sacrifice, which some feel is lacking in the present age. The terrible waste of talent is often woven into the tragic tale, although little criticism is directed at those who led Japan's armed forces into the hopeless straits that caused them to resort to such tactics.

THEODORE F. COOK, JR.

K'ang-hsi

r. 1662–1722, *Second Manchu Emperor of Ch'ing China*

K'ang-hsi overcame a major revolt, annexed Taiwan, and secured the border with Russia. In 1681 he sup-

pressed the Rebellion of the Three Feudatories (1673–1681). Wu San-kuei (1612–1678), a former Ming general who had materially aided the Manchu conquest in 1644 (q.v.), rebelled in southwest China together with two nearby satraps after K'ang-hsi declined to allow them virtual independence. Ultimately Ch'ing forces prevailed, but K'ang-hsi never fully trusted those regions again. In that war, rebels buried weapon stores that were unearthed only in the nineteenth century by Taiping (q.v.) insurgents.

Ch'ing suppression of this insurrection was followed in 1683 by Admiral Shih Lang's expulsion of the descendants of Koxinga (q.v.) from Taiwan, which became for the first time a prefecture of China. These victories completed the conquest phase of the Ch'ing dynasty (1644–1911).

K'ang-hsi then turned his attention northward. First he forcibly resisted Russian encroachment, concluding the Treaty of Nerchinsk (1689), which settled Sino-Russian border disputes for almost two centuries. Meanwhile the Western Mongols (Ölöds) under Galdan had invaded Mongolia; K'ang-hsi personally led Ch'ing troops to victory at Jaomodo in 1696, in 1697 forcing Galdan's suicide. Most of the three armies — totaling 107,000 men — returned, after 99 days during which they covered about 1,850 miles; compare Napoleon's (q.v.) Moscow campaign, in which only 2 percent of approximately half a million men returned from a 169-day campaign that covered somewhat shorter distances. This campaign was thus a triumph of Ch'ing military prowess and logistical brilliance; it was also aided by Western missionaries' cartography and advice on artillery. Before K'ang-hsi died, another Ölöd war erupted, and his armies also established indirect rule in Tibet. Thus many of his campaigns still resonate today.

JOANNA WALEY-COHEN

Kesselring, Albert

1885–1960, *German Field Marshal*

Albert Kesselring entered the Germany army as an artillery officer in 1904. He served as a General Staff officer in World War I (q.v.) and continued in that capacity in the armed forces of the Weimar Republic. But in 1933 Kesselring became one of those officers selected to move from the army to the Luftwaffe.

Learning to fly at age forty-eight, Kesselring made the transition to his new service smoothly. He soon became an enthusiastic advocate of air power and strategic bombing; in 1936 he became chief of staff of the Luftwaffe and moved on to field command in 1939. Kesselring led the Second Air Force in the 1940 campaign against France and the Battle of Britain (q.v.); for his performance in the former campaign, Kesselring was one of the Luftwaffe generals promoted to field marshal. In the latter battle he backed Adolf Hitler's (q.v.) fatal decision to refocus the Luftwaffe's effort against London in September, thus taking the pressure off the Royal Air Force.

In the 1941 invasion of the Soviet Union, Kesselring played a major role in supporting the army's advance, and at the end of the year he and his command transferred to the Mediterranean, where he also became theater commander. There, through to 1945, he showed considerable skill as both an air and a ground force commander, particularly in slowing down the Allied advance in Italy. But "smiling Albert," as he was known, also displayed an overly optimistic view that was increasingly at odds with reality; moreover, he maintained a slavish devotion to Nazism. His handling of Italian anti-Nazi activities lived up to the ferocious desires of his master, Hitler. In the end, his sycophancy explains why he was one of the few field marshals promoted in 1940 still on active duty in 1945.

WILLIAMSON MURRAY

Khalkin-Gol, Battle of

August 20–31, 1939

Few battles are less known or more significant than Georgii Zhukov's (q.v.) decisive defeat of a Japanese force of seventy-five thousand men on the Mongolian-Manchurian border in the waning days of August 1939, just as the Nazi-Soviet Non-Aggression Pact was being signed and World War II (q.v.) was about to begin. Handicapped by lengthy supply lines and facing crack units of the hitherto undefeated Japanese Kwantung Army, Zhukov, in a classic double envelopment and using his armor as a spearhead, first surrounded and then employed withering artillery to destroy his Japanese opponents. In doing so, according to Soviet sources, more than sixty thousand casualties and prisoners were inflicted on the Japanese — more than Tokyo received in that entire year in their concurrent war against China.

As a result, the Japanese warlords gave up forever their aspirations for an empire that would have in-

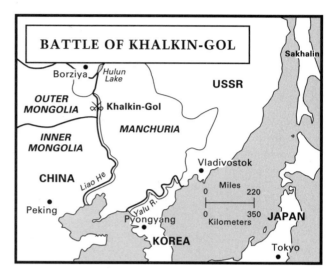

BATTLE OF KHALKIN-GOL

cluded both Inner and Outer Mongolia, the Soviet Maritime Provinces, and key portions of Siberia, and chose instead to focus on obtaining the resources of Southeast Asia, leading to war with the United States rather than with the Soviet Union. Thus Khalkin-Gol had the vital effect of keeping Tokyo neutral toward the USSR throughout World War II. Among other things, this allowed Joseph Stalin (q.v.) to transfer key divisions from Siberia to the West, which played a vital role in saving Moscow from the Nazi onslaught in December 1941 (see Moscow, Campaigns for).

MARSHALL BREMENT

King, Ernest J.

1878–1956, U.S. Naval Leader

Ernest J. King was abrasive, iconoclastic, tough, and brilliant by turns. He knew what he wanted and let no one stand in the way. King's daughter once recalled him as extremely even-tempered: "He's always mad."

Though trained in a "big-gun" navy, King supported submarines in the 1920s and aviation in the 1930s. He received pilot's wings in 1928 at age fifty. King commanded the Navy Bureau of Aeronautics, the carrier Lexington, and the air unit of the Battle Force, with which he conducted a maneuver prefiguring Japan's attack on Pearl Harbor (q.v.). Promoted to the navy's General Board before retirement, in December 1940 King was recalled to command in the Atlantic, and a year later President Franklin D. Roosevelt (q.v.) appointed him commander in chief of the U.S. Navy, soon adding duty as chief of naval operations. In late

1944, King was given five-star (admiral of the fleet) rank by an act of Congress.

Admiral King suffered early tragedy in World War II (q.v.) as unescorted merchant ships were sunk by U-boats off American coasts, but he made other contributions to U.S. strategy. King insisted upon a tactical offensive posture in the Pacific while the war in Europe was won, and he championed certain types of ship (destroyer escorts, landing ship tanks) that became crucial to Allied capabilities. He certainly lost bureaucratic battles, but it was often King's basic approaches that were carried out. King retired in 1946 and died a decade later.

JOHN PRADOS

Kitchener, Horatio Herbert

1850–1916, British Field Marshal and Secretary of State for War

Horatio Herbert Kitchener's long experience of colonial warfare and his solitary nature did not prepare him well for twentieth-century challenges. Brilliant in some judgments, he also made serious mistakes. A Royal Engineer by training, Kitchener rose to lead the Anglo-Egyptian force that recaptured Khartoum and then defeated the Mahdists at Omdurman (1898) in the Sudan. Originally chief of staff in the Boer War (q.v.), Kitchener later took over command and in a ruthless campaign defeated the Boer irregulars. Subsequently commander in chief in India, Kitchener was named secretary of state for war in 1914.

Against prevailing opinion, Kitchener correctly predicted the war would be lengthy, firmly argued for strong support of France when Sir John French (q.v.) wavered, and then set about successfully raising volunteer divisions (Kitchener's Army). However, Kitchener's judgment concerning the 1915 Gallipoli campaign (q.v.) was faulty, and he starved the expeditionary force of men and material until it was too late. He originally thought one or two brigades would be sufficient to support the navy at Gallipoli. He also forbade a landing on the Asiatic side of Gallipoli, only to reverse himself a few months later. Finally, when there was general agreement to evacuate, Kitchener still argued for a large combined army and navy offensive.

Kitchener also ignored the tank idea. But his chief difficulty was that he applied his colonial and Boer War experience to the War Office and refused to delegate responsibility. Hence, he treated the General Staff simply as personal advisers. Kitchener's one-man rule was resented and inefficient. Plans to replace him were under way when, while on a mission to Russia, he drowned in 1916 aboard HMS *Hampshire* when the cruiser hit a mine.

An enigmatic, isolated, and austere man, Kitchener was a very capable nineteenth-century administrator. But in the conditions of World War I (q.v.) he was often out of his depth.

TIM TRAVERS

Knightly Orders

Knightly orders, born in the martial religious enthusiasm following the First Crusade (1095–1099) (q.v.), were the conflation of two ideal medieval types: the monk and the knight. Even an ordinary knight who "took the cross" became a pilgrim fulfilling a holy contract; he was no longer just a warrior. But after marching or sailing to the Holy Land, crossing swords with the infidel, and visiting the holiest shrines of Christendom, most of these crusaders returned to their homes in Europe. The difficulties of maintaining a permanent armed presence in the Holy Land inspired some exceptionally pious knights to organize as formal religious communities. In Jerusalem in around 1119, eight or nine knights vowed themselves to chastity, obedience, poverty, and the military protection of ordinary pilgrims, often the victims of brigands and Muslim raiders. A decade later their leader met with the great Cistercian abbot Bernard of Clairvaux, who publicized their mission and influenced their strict monastic rule. The original handful of knights quickly became the powerful Knights of the Temple of Solomon, or Templars, and their castles, treasuries, and disciplined manpower became a mainstay of the crusader kingdoms. Meanwhile, the Order of the Hospital of St. John, or Knights Hospitaller, originally dedicated to nurturing the sick and wounded, evolved to include knight service as well. The third great knightly order founded in the East, the Teutonic Knights, similarly grew from a hospital charity. They were almost exclusively German. There were also several smaller orders.

Some in Western Christendom questioned these new orders. Their problematic combination of traditional, peaceful monastic devotion (habit and tonsure, communal living, meager and silent meals, indi-

A crusading Knight Templar — identifiable by the red cross on his shield — in a fresco (about 1175) at Cressac, France.

vidual poverty, frequent religious observance) with military training and campaign service deeply troubled some churchmen, who saw these knights as perverters of one of Christ's most basic messages: love thy neighbor, even thine enemy, as thyself. Other critics simply begrudged them their worldly success. Wealth flowed especially to the two most prominent orders, the Knights Hospitaller and Templar, as dying Christians (some of whom faced death without having fulfilled pilgrimage or crusading vows) bequeathed cash and properties to support the orders' crusading ventures.

Distrusted or envied by some Christians, the orders were frankly hated by their Muslim adversaries. Steadfast defenders of the "Frankish" presence in the Near East, the orders and their castles tenaciously guarded the perimeter of the Latin states, and in battle the orders were disciplined and ferocious warriors, calmly singing psalms as they prepared for the fray. Their charges several times scattered Muslim hosts. Captured knights faced short shrift: After the disastrous Christian defeat at Hattin (q.v.) in 1187, the victorious Saladin (q.v.) gave fifty dinars (a princely sum) for each captured Templar or Hospitaller, and then had them hacked to pieces.

With the fall of Acre in 1291, the last crusader stronghold in the Holy Land, the knightly orders had to shift their bases and reorient their missions. The Templars retreated to their rich network of fiefs and dependencies in Europe. This wealth — and a growing reputation for both indolence and insolence —

encouraged covetous fingers, and in 1307 King Philip IV of France seized their property. To justify this outrage Philip orchestrated show trials and tortured Templars into confessing the most heinous heresies. Reluctantly, the pope formally suppressed the order in 1312. Contrary to romantic legends of a surviving underground secret society, these blows killed the Knights of the Temple.

In 1310 the Knights of St. John settled at Rhodes and developed an expertise in naval warfare; their galleys came to terrorize the Muslim shipping of the Mediterranean. Whether they turned pirate or remained crusaders is entirely a matter of perspective. Their fortress island survived several Muslim sieges before an Ottoman effort evicted them in 1522 (see *Rhodes, Sieges of*). They eventually resettled at Malta, where they outlasted a massive Turkish siege in 1565. With a reputation for dash (and booty), the order continued to attract recruits, mostly French and Italian; besides proof of nobility, entrance requirements sensibly insisted that candidates know how to swim. The knights' final island fastness functioned as an independent state down to Napoleon's (q.v.) occupation of Malta in 1798. Thereafter landless, the Hospitallers nonetheless survived as an international honorary (and eventually charitable) organization, and international law still recognizes the order as a sovereign entity.

Least of the three major knightly orders in 1291, the Teutonic Knights subsequently became the most powerful. They relocated to Europe's northern frontier to direct a perpetual war against the still-pagan peoples of the Baltic littoral. Here they fought perhaps the bitterest crusade of all, riding from their castles to raid deep into the pine forests, exterminating those who would not convert — and enserfing those who did. In return, the snake-worshipping Lithuanians (among their most intractable opponents) roasted captured knights alive in their armor as human sacrifices. Undeterred, the Teutonic Knights carved out their own principality, the Ordenland, that at its greatest extent, in around 1400, included Prussia and present-day Latvia and Estonia. The Teutonic Knights' power subsequently withered, and the order's last Grand Master embraced Lutheranism in 1525, with the last of the order's lands secularized as his duchy of Prussia.

Even though crusading enthusiasm waned in the later Middle Ages, the knightly orders' idealism and ceremonial — the Hospitallers' crimson cloaks and white Maltese crosses, the Teutonic Knights' white cloaks and black crosses — inspired emulation. Feudal rulers founded their own, more purely chivalric orders with much reduced or superficial religious obligations, but greater pomp. Edward III of England created the Order of the Garter (1348), and the powerful dukes of Burgundy the Order of the Golden Fleece (1430). Membership conferred social cachet. A very few new orders did include active warfare — like the Knights of St. John, the Order of Santo Stefano of grand-ducal Tuscany raided Muslim shipping (and also Christian vessels, or so the Venetians alleged) — but in general these later orders aimed to flatter and reward participants, not to smite the infidel.

THOMAS F. ARNOLD

M. Barber, *The New Knighthood* (1994); D. Seward, *The Monks of War* (1972).

Konev, I. S.

1897–1973, Marshal of the Soviet Union

Ivan Stepanovich Konev was a superbly gifted officer who entered the tsarist army as a private in 1912 and then joined the Bolsheviks and the Red Army (q.v.) in 1918. He rose rapidly after the 1937 purges. At the beginning of Barbarossa (q.v.), he commanded Nineteenth Army (equivalent to a corps in Western armies) in the Ukraine, one of the few theaters where Soviet forces performed competently. By year's end he was in command of the Kalinin Front, which played a major role in the winter campaign that drove the Germans back from Moscow (q.v.).

Konev displayed enormous competence in manipulating large-scale forces in the complex operations that characterized fighting on the Eastern Front; like his fellow generals in the emerging Soviet leadership, he was a master of *maskirovka* (deception [q.v.]) and combined arms operations. In 1943 he was in command of the Steppe Front that remained on the defensive during the Battle of Kursk (q.v.) in July, but his troops then led the Soviet advances that reconquered most of the western Ukraine and hustled the Germans back across the Dnieper. In 1944–1945 he commanded the First Ukrainian Front, which played a major role in the destruction of the German Army Group North Ukraine.

Konev's forces then drove through central Poland and on into Silesia as the great winter offensive of 1945 unfolded. Joseph Stalin (q.v.) used Konev's ad-

vance to goad Marshal Georgii Zhukov (q.v.) in the attack on Berlin. Konev's troops got to the German capital, but the Soviet high command marked the boundary line between fronts just to the south of the Reichstag, so that Zhukov's men received the honor of hoisting the hammer and sickle over the shattered ruins. Konev served in the early Cold War (q.v.) period as commander in chief, land forces (1946–1955), and then briefly as deputy minister of defense and supreme commander of Warsaw Pact forces before ill health forced his retirement.

WILLIAMSON MURRAY

Königgrätz, Battle of

July 3, 1866

Königgrätz (Sadowa) — where 220,000 Prussians defeated a similar number of Austrians and Saxons — was the largest battle between Western armies before 1914. Its result determined the outcome of the Seven Weeks' War (q.v.).

The battle developed out of a Prussian attempt to envelop their opponents, which failed because of poor coordination between two Prussian armies and the failure of a third to advance at all, its orders having gone astray. By early afternoon the Austrians regarded the battle as won; all Prussia's reserves had been engaged, while the Austrian cavalry remained largely uncommitted. The outcome was reversed in shocking fashion, however, when the Prussian Second Army finally arrived to drive in the Austrian right and force a retreat. Prussia lost 10,000 men, the Austrians and Saxons 45,000, including 20,000 prisoners.

Königgrätz captured the imagination of Europe: in a single day, the London *Spectator* reported, "the political face of the world has changed as it used to change after a generation of war." Contemporaries attributed this result to the superior firepower of Prussian foot soldiers, armed with breech-loading rifles far superior in range and rate of fire to the muzzle-loaders of the Austrians. Modern historians accept the importance of this advantage in demoralizing the Austrian infantry, but attribute the overall outcome to other factors: the superior organization and planning of the Prussians, who moved large forces rapidly and independently by rail against a passive opponent; and also to the ability of Prussia's battlefield commanders and its brilliant chief of staff, Helmuth Karl von Moltke (q.v.), to improvise and persevere after all their plans had miscarried.

DANIEL MORAN

Korean War

1592–1593 and 1597–1598

In 1592 and 1597 Japanese invasions devastated Korea and seriously weakened Ming China, contributing to the fall of the Ming a few decades later. These campaigns, the first instances of organized Japanese aggression abroad since the seventh century and the last until the nineteenth, were born chiefly of personal ambition. Toyotomi Hideyoshi (q.v.), having made himself overlord of Japan, now sought to become suzerain of China as well. But when Korea, a vassal state of the Ming, refused his demands for safe passage for his armies, he determined to cut his way through the peninsula instead.

Initially the superiority of Japanese tactical expertise and weaponry — which included firearms — devastated the poorly prepared Koreans. But eventually a combination of guerrilla resistance and naval operations (led by the remarkable Admiral Yi Sun-Shin [q.v.]) against supply lines slowed the offensive, while a counterinvasion by Ming armies drove the Japanese back down the peninsula and generated a negotiated peace in 1593. Four years later Hideyoshi, accusing the Chinese and Koreans of reneging on their bargain, invaded again, but this time the defending forces proved more formidable. Hideyoshi ordered most of his commanders home in May 1598, effectively ending the war. His death three months later provided the excuse for the rest to withdraw as well.

KARL F. FRIDAY

Korean War

1950–1953

A postcolonial civil war between Korean political factions that began in 1945, the Korean War became an international struggle in June 1950. The conventional war ended with an armistice in July 1953, with Korea divided. A Communist government under Kim Il Sung (1912–1994) ruled on one side of the demilitarized zone (DMZ), and an authoritarian, capitalist regime under Syngman Rhee (1875–1965) on the other. The war gave a global dimension to the Cold War (q.v.)

by introducing American troops into Asia. The cost in lives made the war one of the worst since 1945: three million Korean civilian and military deaths (out of thirty million Koreans), one million Chinese soldiers, and about thirty-eight thousand battlefield deaths for the American and non-Korean military personnel of United Nations Command (UNC). Oppressed by Japanese colonial rule since 1905, Korea struggled against its historical curse as the battleground of the great powers.

The Korean War began in September 1945 when the United States and the Soviet Union forces, by prior agreement, entered a liberated Korea to keep order and to disarm the Japanese army of occupation at the end of World War II (q.v.). Above the thirty-eighth parallel, the dividing line established by the Americans and the Russians, the Communists received active Russian support at the cost of accepting a Soviet client, Kim Il Sung, as the dominant political leader. A Manchurian Korean, Kim had been a minor commander in the Northeast Anti-Japanese United Army. Fleeing the Japanese in 1940, Kim formed a Korean special operations unit in Siberia. He returned to Pyongyang as a captain in the Soviet army. His nemesis in the south, Syngman Rhee, was also born north of the thirty-eighth parallel of impoverished minor nobility. Rhee (Yi Sung Man) participated in the anti-Japanese resistance until forced into exile in 1905. He became a Christian, married a European wife, and earned three American college degrees. He served as president of a provisional government in exile and returned to Korea in 1945 under American sponsorship.

Both the Soviet Union and the United States preferred a unified Korea, but not one dominated by the protégé of the other. Russian sponsorship of Kim showed more purpose and organization than American sponsorship of Rhee, but the result was the same — the creation of two hostile, armed regimes in 1948 that divided the Korean peninsula and people. The United States tried to pass the Korean problem to the United Nations under a trusteeship agreement, but the South Koreans protested. In the meantime, Rhee supporters took control of the national police, the police auxiliaries, paramilitary youth groups, communal militias, and the Korean National Constabulary, which became the Korean army in December 1948. In all the security and military services, the leaders were Rhee loyalists or "professionals" (Koreans who had served in the colonial army or police). In

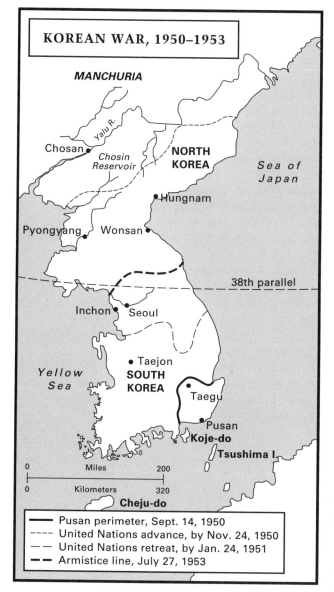

KOREAN WAR, 1950–1953

MANCHURIA

Yalu R.

Chosan

Chosin Reservoir

NORTH KOREA

Sea of Japan

Hungnam

Pyongyang   Wonsan

38th parallel

Inchon   Seoul

Taejon

SOUTH KOREA

Yellow Sea

Taegu

Pusan

Koje-do

Tsushima I.

| 0 | Miles | 200 |
| 0 | Kilometers | 320 |

Cheju-do

—— Pusan perimeter, Sept. 14, 1950
---- United Nations advance, by Nov. 24, 1950
– – United Nations retreat, by Jan. 24, 1951
▬▬ Armistice line, July 27, 1953

(ROK) security forces on Cheju-do in the Straits of Tsushima in April 1948. This vicious war soon spread to the mainland. Assisted by American advisers, the ROK army and national police crushed the revolt, which may have claimed as many as thirty thousand lives (1948–1950).

The guerrilla war also produced armed clashes along the border in 1949 and 1950. About half the ROK army of eight lightly armed divisions manned border positions while the other half fought the guerrillas. In the meantime, Kim built his own forces with Soviet arms and advisers; the North Korean People's Army (NKPA) reached 135,000 in early 1950. Kim hectored Joseph Stalin (q.v.) and Mao Tse-tung (q.v.) for assurances of military support for an invasion of South Korea and journeyed to Peking and Moscow to cajole his patrons. Pak promised more uprisings in the south. On June 25, 1950, the NKPA crossed the border with a combined arms force that outclassed the South Korean army (100,000) in discipline, tactical skill, and heavy weapons.

Much to the surprise of the Communists, the United States sent air, naval, and ground force units to Korea to stop the NKPA. Although the United States saw no vital national strategic purpose in defending Korea — and announced this in early 1950 — President Harry S. Truman saw many reasons to fight, not run. His administration could hardly stand to lose another civil war in Asia after the debacle in China (see *Chinese Civil War*); he needed a crisis to stir the nation to rearm and give military muscle to "containment"; he wanted to reassure the new allies of the North Atlantic Treaty Organization (NATO) that the United States believed in collective security; he wanted nothing to endanger the safe integration of Japan into the capitalist world; and he thought the United Nations should demonstrate its power to punish aggression. Truman, in fact, sought to legitimize intervention by UN resolutions, not a declaration of war, a decision that would later cause him political problems. The theater commander, General Douglas MacArthur (q.v.), saw the war in different terms; he envisioned an opportunity to reverse the Chinese revolution, forge a great anti-Communist alliance system in Asia, stimulate the Japanese economy, and embarrass the Soviet Union. MacArthur's public differences with the Truman administration on the war's purposes and conduct eventually led to his relief in April 1951.

For almost a year, the Korean War swept as far south

his regime, Kim also gave preference to fellow Communists, including Pak Hon Yong, chief of the Korean Workers' Party. Fleeing the south, Pak set up an organization of southern Communists to train guerrillas and organizers to subvert the Rhee regime. Other prominent leaders fell, both figuratively and literally, by the wayside.

The internal struggle for power in Korea involved violence from the start; two political assassinations occurred on the day U.S. troops first reached Seoul. The anti-Rhee forces, led by southern Communists, began a guerrilla war against the Republic of Korea as the Taegu-Pusan perimeter and as far north as the Yalu River. It then settled into a geographic stalemate in the mountains north of the thirty-eighth parallel. Both coalitions tasted victory and bitter, abject defeat. The initial NKPA offensive conquered three-quarters of South Korea, destroyed half of the ROK army, and allowed invading and domestic Communists to capture and execute South Korean Christians, government officials, landlords and businessmen, and thousands of true innocents. The three American infantry divisions sent from the U.S. Eighth Army (under Lieutenant General Walton H. Walker) in Japan performed indifferently and fell back to the Pusan perimeter. Army and marine reinforcements from the United States helped redress the balance, assisted by abundant air strikes from the U.S. Fifth Air Force. By the end of August, the NKPA had stalled at the end of a tenuous supply line.

MacArthur now directed a two-division amphibious landing deep behind the Communist army at Inchon, and this force (Tenth Corps) liberated Seoul in late September as Eighth Army broke out of the perimeter and struck north against the stunned NKPA. The campaign of exploitation surged north across the thirty-eighth parallel in October with ROK forces in the vanguard. The bulk of Eighth Army pushed into the northwestern provinces while Tenth Corps moved by land and sea along the eastern coast. Five ROK divisions fought with the Americans, now reinforced with other smaller UN contingents. The victory proved short-lived and the unification of Korea impossible, for the Chinese now intervened with an expeditionary force that eventually reached 600,000 soldiers.

Mao Tse-tung and his advisers, who had considered intervention as early as July 1950, saw no alternative to a war with the United States. They could not accept a unified, pro-Western Korea on China's border. They believed that the United States would extend the war to mainland China, first by partisan war (already under way), and then by an invasion by the rearmed Chinese Nationalist army. The U.S. Seventh Fleet already stood in their way in the Formosan Straits. Finally winning Stalin's promise of massive Soviet air support in Manchuria, the Chinese first tested Eighth Army in a week's fighting in late October and found UN Command (UNC) vulnerable to deep attacks and night actions.

In late November the Chinese struck again and drove a demoralized Eighth Army back across the thirty-eighth parallel, almost as far south as Taejon. The Tenth Corps extracted itself with an amphibious withdrawal. Punished by air strikes and suffering from logistical shortages as well as heavy casualties from the cold and combat, the Chinese People's Volunteer Force (CPVF) halted south of Seoul. In the meantime, the Eighth Army, now commanded by Lieutenant General Matthew B. Ridgway (q.v.), launched limited counterattacks in January–April 1951. Seoul was liberated again — for the fourth time in less than a year. Chinese offensives in April and May could not crack a restored Eighth Army, which had now reached a World War II level of competence. The UNC then pushed the joint Chinese–North Korean armies back into North Korea, but Ridgway rejected proposals to mount an amphibious landing on the east coast, designed to catch a substantial portion of the Communist armies. It was a lost opportunity.

Anxious to save their shattered armies, the Chinese and the North Koreans asked for negotiations, but these talks broke down in September through mutual provocation — some accidental, some intended. Further UN offensive operations in September and October proved costly for both sides. The truce meetings began again on October 25, 1951, and continued until the armistice of July 27, 1953. A superficial examination of the war's course over the intervening twenty-one months suggests that intransigence, ineptness, duplicity, and operational timidity doomed both sides to a "stalemated war."

The Korean War could have developed differently in 1952–1953, for both coalitions saw conditions to exploit. Both the Communists and the UNC held significant numbers of prisoners. American airmen may have been sent to camps in Russia, and they certainly went to China, coming under pressure to admit germ warfare charges, "immoral" air operations, atrocities, and racist policies. The UNC, on the other hand, found that many of its POWs did not want to be repatriated; many Chinese and Koreans had been dragooned into the Communist armies. So afraid of this ideological embarrassment were the Communists that they planted agents in POW camps in the south to terrorize the dissidents and start camp uprisings, the most dramatic at Koje-do in May 1952. The POW issue plagued the truce talks until both sides agreed to a system that would give the prisoners some choice regarding their futures. Both sides had much to hide about their treatment of POWs, especially the Communists, who had allowed 10,000 American and

Korean military prisoners to die from mistreatment. Eventually 82,500 POWs held by the UN returned to Communist control, but 22,000 chose to settle elsewhere. The United Nations accepted back about 14,000 POWs of all nationalities, whereas 359 captives (335 Korean) chose to stay in Communist hands.

As the truce talks continued, the Communists and the UNC sought advantages that might influence the course of the war. Communist guerrillas still harassed military and civilian camps and villages in the south; in 1952 the Communist underground may have attempted to assassinate Rhee, and political plotting plagued the ROK government and army. Conventional Communist military attacks often tried to inflict embarrassing casualties on American units, but the principal target remained the ROK army. A Communist offensive in July 1953 cost the ROK army almost twenty-five thousand casualties.

UNC air power appeared the most effective instrument of coercion. The U.S. Far East Air Forces pummeled not only Communist armies, but also targets throughout North Korea, inflicting thousands of civilian deaths, but only driving the Communist elite and logistical system underground or across the Yalu. Special operations forces had even less success in infiltrating the north and starting a guerrilla war against the Communists. The effort to subvert the Kim regime was not without reason, for his own government was torn by a coup attempt in 1952 organized by Pak Hon Yong. Kim unmasked the plot and executed Pak. Nevertheless, the Rhee regime, which had no taste for an armistice, hoped for a collapse in Pyongyang. Rhee also knew that he had external support from American "Asia Firsters" and anti-Communist leaders in Asia.

The armistice negotiations, however, reflected a more conservative appreciation of the war's costs and risks by the United States, the United Nations, Russia, and China. After Stalin's death in March 1953, Russia faced a succession crisis, unrest in eastern Europe, and a militant, expanded NATO. For China, the survival of Kim's regime seemed certain, and it needed to focus on its domestic agenda and relations with Russia, whose nuclear might it wanted to share. In Washington, a new Republican administration under Dwight D. Eisenhower (q.v.) sought economic stability, not high defense spending. Moreover, even with Indochina a lost cause, the security of Taiwan, the Philippines, and Japan looked promising. MacArthur's goal had been accomplished without Mac-

Arthur. With seven American divisions along the DMZ (eventually reduced to one, thirty years later), assisted by at least ten good ROK divisions, the ground defense of South Korea looked assured, supported by the U.S. Air Force, the U.S. Navy, and nuclear weapons. The United States concluded a mutual defense and assistance treaty with South Korea in August 1953, which was ratified by Congress early in 1954 and backed by concurrent UN pledges to protect South Korea.

Essentially, the United States accomplished its original war aims (to preserve the sovereignty of South Korea) and, thanks to the international crisis, increased defense spending threefold. The two Koreas survived in ruined form. The Chinese proved they had the will and the military capacity to blunt a Western effort to reverse their revolution. Conversely, the Chinese Nationalists received a reprieve through a new defense pact with the United States. The Soviet Union, however, had only awakened a sleeping American giant with its support of Kim. The real loser was Korea, which — as in the seventeenth century — had drawn in outside foreign powers to effect its own ruin.

ALLAN R. MILLETT

Clay Blair, *The Forgotten War: America in Korea, 1950–1953* (1987); Bruce Cumings, *The Origins of the Korean War*, 2 vols. (1981, 1990).

Kosovo, Battle of

June 28, 1389

On June 28, 1389, an Ottoman army of between thirty thousand and forty thousand men under the command of Sultan Murad I defeated an army of Balkan allies numbering twenty-five thousand to thirty thousand under the command of Prince Lazar of Serbia at Kosovo polje (Blackbird's Field) in the central Balkans. Both rulers perished in the battle, but the Ottomans (q.v.) won the day, thus sealing the eventual collapse of the medieval Serbian state.

The battle was one of several significant Ottoman victories in their two-hundred-year conquest of southeast Europe. However, because it became a central theme of Serbian oral epics, it remains a living memory for Serbs. Kosovo was the center of the Serbian medieval state and contains many ancient Serbian monasteries, but today its population consists primarily of Muslim Albanians. Thus the Serbian cult of Kosovo remains a source of ethnic conflict between Muslims and Serbs.

GALE STOKES

Koxinga

1624?–1662, Chinese Bandit Rebel or Resistance Hero

Koxinga (Cheng Ch'eng-kung) has been claimed by successive Chinese and Japanese regimes as a Confucian loyalist, Shinto nationalist (for expelling Westerners from East Asia), Chinese nationalist, anti-imperialist, and hero of the Taiwanese independence movement. A Sino-Japanese pirate entrepreneur imbued with self-interest, he alternately supported the defeated Ming dynasty (1368–1644) and negotiated with the conquering Manchu Ch'ing dynasty (1644–1911). Raised in Hirado, the Japanese port in which the Dutch maintained a trading post, he grasped the potential of the European weaponry he saw there and later used it effectively against both the Ch'ing and the Dutch. His father, Cheng Chih-lung, established a wide-ranging maritime empire and supported the Ming, but in 1646 he defected. Koxinga thereupon burned his scholar's robes and swore to wear armor until a Ming restoration. Such dramatic acts combined with his preference for martial values and his undoubted military talents to forge his legendary status.

His extensive military machine was based at Amoy (Hsia-men) on the Fukien coast and depended on sea power. During the 1650s Koxinga captured major portions of southeast and southwest China for the southern Ming regime, but failed to take Nanking, mainly through overconfidence, disregarding his generals' advice not to make the attempt. Relentlessly pursued, in 1661 he withdrew with many ships and men to Taiwan and besieged the Dutch Fort Zeelandia, eventually capturing it and establishing a stronghold on the island. He died shortly afterward.

Koxinga was sometimes so harsh that several subordinates defected to the Ch'ing, to whom they offered vital information and expertise. One such officer was Shih Lang, who in 1683 led the expedition that brought Taiwan under Ch'ing control; mainland governments have claimed jurisdiction over the island ever since.

JOANNA WALEY-COHEN

Kublai Khan

1215–1294, Mongol Khan and Emperor of China

Kublai Khan is known and revered for his civilian and administrative, not his military achievements. Grandson of Genghis Khan (q.v.), Kublai sought to govern rather than to exploit and devastate the vast domains bequeathed to him by two generations of Mongol conquests. He made the transition from a nomadic conqueror from the steppes to effective ruler of a sedentary society. Ironically, however, his reign witnessed the Mongols' (q.v.) most remarkable military success, the subjugation of the Southern Sung dynasty of China, and simultaneously their greatest military fiascos, the failed naval expeditions against Japan and Java.

Kublai's civilian achievements are impressive. Assuming the titles of Khaghan (Great Khan) and emperor of China in 1260, he set about consolidating Mongol rule in China. Appreciating the need to ingratiate himself to the Chinese if he was to rule a stable society, he restored central and local government institutions and agencies familiar to the Chinese and reinstated Confucian rituals and ceremonies at court. He shifted his capital from Karakorum, in Mongolia, to Tai-tu (near modern Peking), a signal that he recognized the importance of China to his empire. His attempt to accommodate Chinese culture persuaded many Chinese to act as counselors or to serve in his government.

His peaceful achievements have sometimes overshadowed Kublai's military expeditions, the most successful of which was the conquest of the Sung dynasty of China. Ever since his accession to the throne, Kublai had recognized that subjugation of the Sung would be invaluable both for Mongol reunification of China after more than three centuries of fragmentation and for access to the great wealth of South China. Yet such an expedition was far more demanding than other earlier Mongol campaigns. The Mongols' greatest strength, their cavalry, was not suited to South China's forested and agricultural lands. Horses could uncover little forage, could not traverse the dense underbrush, and found the heat oppressive. Moreover, crossing the Yangtze River to the south and attacking China's southeast coast required either the development or enlistment of a navy, and the huge and highly populated Chinese cities necessitated advances in siege warfare. Kublai's forces gradually built ships, recruited Chinese sailors, and lured Chinese naval defectors; they finally laid siege to the important crossroads at Hsiang-yang from 1268 to 1273. The Mongol troops eventually needed to import two Muslim engineers to build mangonels and catapults, which hurled huge boulders on the inhabitants, to overcome resistance. The fall of Hsiang-yang enabled the Mongols to move inexorably toward the Sung capital of Lin-an, which they occupied in 1276. Significantly, the final battle occurred at sea, off the island of Yai-chou, where the last Sung emperor drowned during the engagement (1279).

Other Mongol naval engagements were less successful. In 1274 and 1281, responding to Japan's unwillingness to accept even a pro forma tributary status, Kublai dispatched two expeditions overseas to pacify the Japanese. In the second expedition, a sizable flotilla transported about 40,000 troops from North China and 100,000 troops from South China. The two detachments converged off the island of Kyushu, but a disastrous typhoon (which the Japanese believed to be a kamikaze or "divine wind") hit the coast. Many of the Mongol vessels sank, and about one-half of the troops perished or were captured. The survivors fled back to China. In 1292, another ill-conceived overseas expedition set forth to subjugate Java. Within a year, Kublai's forces withdrew, as the semitropical heat, the jungles, and the parasitic and infectious diseases overwhelmed the Mongols, who were accustomed to a cooler climate and the spaciousness of the steppes. Kublai himself died the following year, with the disastrous Java campaign contributing a sour note to the end of his reign.

MORRIS ROSSABI

Morris Rossabi, *Khubilai Khan: His Life and Times* (1988).

Kursk, Battle of

July 5–16, 1943

In March 1943, a major German counterattack broke the back of the Soviet offensives that had isolated and crushed Sixth Army at Stalingrad (q.v.) and for a time threatened to destroy Army Group South. As the spring thaw halted operations, both sides pondered what to do next. Field Marshal Erich von Manstein (q.v.) urged an offensive against the Kursk salient as soon as the ground had dried out. The objective would be to wreck as much of the Soviet army as possible.

Adolf Hitler (q.v.) accepted Manstein's suggestion but postponed the attack until July so that a maximum number of newly produced tanks could reach the Eastern Front. But by delaying, Hitler allowed the Soviets to prepare their defenses, move in numerous reinforcements, and prepare the flanks of the Kursk salient with massive minefields and defensive works.

On July 5, the Germans struck on both sides of the salient to begin the biggest battle of World War II (q.v.). From the first they ran into trouble. Their Ninth Army, after initial success, became entirely bogged down in its attack from the north. In the south the Germans enjoyed greater success. But even here German armor failed to gain operational freedom; instead, Soviet defenses tied the Germans into a massive battle of attrition not only on the ground but also

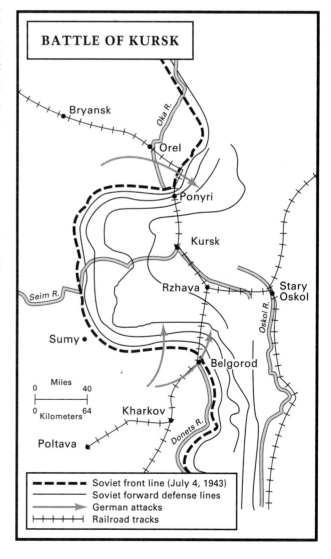

BATTLE OF KURSK

Bryansk · Oka R. · Orel · Ponyri · Kursk · Rzhava · Stary Oskol · Seim R. · Oskol R. · Sumy · Belgorod · Kharkov · Donets R. · Poltava

Miles
0   40
Kilometers
0   64

- - - - Soviet front line (July 4, 1943)
——— Soviet forward defense lines
——▶ German attacks
+++++ Railroad tracks

in the air. Then, on July 12, the Soviets attacked the Orel salient and threatened Ninth Army directly. Confronted by the Anglo-American invasion of Sicily and the threat of an Italian collapse, Hitler decided to call off the operation. At great cost, including the loss of much of their armor, the Germans had failed, and the operational balance on the Eastern Front had swung entirely in favor of the Soviets.

WILLIAMSON MURRAY

Kutuzov, Mikhail

1745–1813, Russian General and Field Marshal

One of eighteenth-century Russia's most famous soldiers, Mikhail I. Kutuzov fought in both of Catherine the Great's wars with the Ottoman Empire. Twice he survived Turkish bullets in the head.

Retiring from the army in 1802, he was recalled to service three years later and given command of the expeditionary corps that Alexander I was sending west against Napoleon (q.v.), but the crushing defeat of Russia and its Austrian allies on December 2, 1805, at Austerlitz (q.v.) resulted in Kutuzov's disgrace and relegation to petty administrative duties.

In June 1812, Napoleon invaded Russia. In early August, acting against his own inclinations, Alexander appointed Kutuzov commander in chief. Kutuzov's conduct of the campaign against Napoleon would make him a Russian national hero.

Kutuzov does not deserve full credit for Russia's victory in 1812. He did not develop the Fabian strategy of withdrawal used by the Russians that summer. In four respects, however, Kutuzov's contribution was vital. First, he recognized that as long as the Russian army remained intact, Napoleon could not win the war. He consequently refused to give battle after Borodino and permitted Napoleon to enter Moscow. Second, during the French occupation of Moscow, he bought time for the reinforcement and resupply of his own forces by pretending to negotiate with the French emperor. Then, too, he helped organize the partisan war that disrupted French lines of communication and ultimately compelled Napoleon to retreat. Finally, during that retreat, Kutuzov's parallel marches on both flanks of the Grande Armée confined it to the road, prevented it from foraging, and wore it down through starvation.

WILLIAM C. FULLER, JR.

L

Land Warfare, Theorists of

Attempts to understand the conduct of war on land, and to prescribe rules for it, probably started as soon as did warfare itself. The earliest codes must have been oral; fundamental principles such as surprise, mobility, and the need for protection cannot have been unfamiliar even to the leaders of prehistoric raiding parties. Judging by what is known about tribal societies that have survived until recently, such codes were neither comprehensive nor systematic. Possibly they took the form of poems, whose advantage is that they are easy to remember.

One of the earliest military writers whose name *is* known to us was the Chinese Sun Tzu (q.v.). Sun Tzu's starting point is the philosophical tradition known as Taoism. To its adherents, *tao* — best translated as "cosmic harmony" — presents an understanding of the world so perfect that the philosopher is able to bend it to his will without doing anything in particular; he glides through it, so to speak.

Accordingly, and contrasting sharply with many other authors on war, Sun Tzu advocates the use of minimum rather than maximum force. The stupid fights; the wise conquers without fighting. "The basis of all warfare is cheating." It is a question of using secrecy, speed, stratagem, and deceit in order to mislead the enemy, puzzle him, catch him off balance, and finally overwhelm him by a sudden concentration of strength against weakness ("throwing rocks at eggs") at the most unexpected time and place. All this is relatively simple if the war is short and conducted near home, but much harder if it is prolonged and fought far away.

Compared to those of Sun Tzu, most theories of war written in the West since classical times have been less philosophical and more technical. Among the earliest was the first-century A.D. rhetorician Onosander; his book describes the structure and tactical use of the Macedonian phalanx, which at that time was no longer in use. What Onosander did for the phalanx, Flavius Vegetius Renatus (see *Vegetius*) (fourth century A.D.) did for the Roman legion (q.v.); and again, it was a question of describing the operations of a formation that, during the author's life, was obsolete. However, Vegetius also has much to say about siege warfare, a field in which the Romans excelled.

Three other writers — the Roman Frontinus and the Byzantine emperors Maurice and Leo VI — belong to a different tradition. The first collected "stratagems" used by commanders of old; for him, as for Sun Tzu, the essence of war is deception (practiced, when necessary, against one's own troops as well as the enemy), but since he does not build this into theory, his work is merely a list of annotated tricks. Not so Maurice and Leo, whose books represent theory proper. In the *Strategicon*, the former analyzes the enemies facing the Byzantine Empire and suggests ways in which they may be overcome. In *Tactica*, the latter concentrates on various military formations, how to construct them, how to arm them, and how to use them.

The European Middle Ages produced no important theorists of war. The most popular handbook was that of Vegetius, translated into French and known to have been read by several princes. Though the Middle Ages did produce a number of works on *l'art de la chevalerie*, they did not deal with the conduct of military operations. Both Honoré Bonnet and Christine de Pisan focused on the law of war (q.v.) — in other words, the things that might and might not properly be done in a fight between knights.

The first modern theorist of war was Niccolò Machiavelli (q.v.) in *L'Arte della guerra*. An admirer of Rome, especially the republic, Machiavelli wanted to return to the citizen army, an idea that ran counter to the spirit of the age and that failed when tried by his native Florence. Compared to his insistence on the virtues of a citizen army, everything else that Machiavelli has to say — mostly about the best way to train troops and arrange them on the battlefield — is of secondary interest to the modern reader. His importance is rather that he is the first thinker in centuries to free himself both of theological considerations and of chivalrous ones that are rooted in right. His substitutes are force and trickery; but his thought on these subjects is political rather than military.

Between 1500 and 1789, writers such as Raimundo Montecuccoli, Sébastien Le Prestre de Vauban (q.v.), Jacques François de Chastenet Puységur, Count de Saxe (q.v.), Frederick the Great (q.v.), and Henry Lloyd had much of interest to say about the details of warfare, but little about the subject as a whole. Among them, the most systematic was Vauban; focusing on the relatively narrow fields of fortifications (q.v.) and siege warfare (q.v.), he advocated a methodical, step-by-step approach that would save casualties while guaranteeing the outcome. Montecuccoli discussed tactics, Puységur and Lloyd logistics; de Saxe "dreamt" of an army consisting of self-contained, independent, strategic units. Frederick the Great advocated iron discipline and short, lively wars; however, as a commander he was more successful in implementing the first than the second.

As the above makes clear, none of these writers dealt with strategy proper. The use of the word by Frontinus and Maurice was entirely different from our own, whereas Frederick, though he did have something to say about strategy (q.v.), never mentions the term. The first to do so was Joly de Maizeroy just before the French Revolution. The concept had a great future in front of it, and from 1800 on the most important works on war were really treatises on strategy.

The first to come to grips with strategy, meaning the art of conducting war rather than battle, was Dietrich von Bülow, who presented it in geometric terms. There were bases and there were objectives. The lines of operations connecting them could be single or double, parallel or converging or diverging, and the angles between them sharp or blunt; Bülow's aim was to examine which ones were the best. Antoine-Henri Jomini, who started writing in the same period, continued Bülow's work. Strategy was the art of moving armies over space, along lines of communications, amidst all kinds of obstacles both natural and ar-

tificial, and against the enemy. Victory depended on using speed and movement to concentrate strength against weakness at the decisive point. There were two main ways of doing so: cutting the enemy's communications on the one hand, and operations on internal lines on the other.

Until at least 1870, Jomini's book *Précis de l'art de la guerre* was considered the most useful guide ever to the conduct of war at the highest level. American Civil War (q.v.) commanders swore by it; both Helmuth von Moltke (q.v.) and Alfred von Schlieffen (q.v.) merely changed the details, the former by replacing internal with external lines and the latter by stressing the importance of one particular maneuver advocated by the Swiss theorist — outflanking and encircling the enemy. However, neither altered the definition of strategy, which remained a question of maneuvering armies against each other. This also applied to the British pundit Basil Liddell Hart (q.v.). To him strategy was primarily a question of deploying and moving forces on the ground in a way that would mislead the enemy, throw him off balance, and hit his vitals without exposing one's own.

In the 1930s the debate was carried on by Heinz Guderian (q.v.) and J. F. C. Fuller (q.v.), both of whom wished to use mechanized forces in order to conduct "strategy" as understood by Liddell Hart, Moltke, and Jomini. All, however, were overshadowed by the growing reputation of Carl von Clausewitz (q.v.), by far the greatest Western writer on war and the only one comparable in stature to Sun Tzu. Whereas others wrote of strategy, Clausewitz wrote of war; to him, its main characteristics were to be deduced from (1) its definition as a continuation of policy and (2) its nature as a *mutual* act of violence directed against the enemy's will. On these premises he built an impressive structure that emphasized massed force in order to crush the enemy as fast as possible. Although intelligence and maneuver were important, in the end war was a brutal business based on strength, including, above all, moral strength.

After 1860 Clausewitz's thought was developed by Ardant du Picq, Ferdinand Foch (q.v.), Rüdiger von der Goltz, and Theodor von Bernhardi, all of whom focused on the will to fight. Their work climaxed in the views of Erich Ludendorff (q.v.). From his time as de facto commander of the German army in World War I (q.v.), Ludendorff learned that modern war was a life-and-death struggle between entire social systems. In such a situation policy became a luxury; far from being the master of war, he saw policy as one of war's tools. Total mobilization of all national resources was the goal, military dictatorship the means. Moreover, since the struggle between nations was unceasing, and since modern war demanded long preparation, such dictatorship was to be permanent.

By the time Ludendorff demanded that "Clausewitz's theories be thrown overboard," large-scale land warfare itself was already on its way to abolishing itself. Translated into practice from 1939 on, total war culminated on August 6, 1945, when a single bomber flew over Hiroshima, dropping a single bomb. Since then war on land has been fought only between, or against, the weak; among first-rate powers (that is, those that own nuclear weapons), both Ludendorff's total war and Clausewitz's view of war as the instrument of policy became obsolete. More and more, war on land has taken the form seen in Bosnia in the 1990s. For that kind of war, no proper theory has yet been written.

MARTIN VAN CREVELD

Azar Gat, *The Development of Military Thought: The Nineteenth Century* (1992); Michael Howard, ed., *The Theory and Practice of War* (1965); Peter Paret, ed., *Makers of Modern Strategy: From Machiavelli to the Nuclear Age* (1986).

Las Navas de Tolosa, Battle of

July 16, 1212

As a consequence of the Christian victory at Las Navas de Tolosa, the power of the Almohads, the Berber regime that had dominated Muslim Spain (Al-Andalus) from the mid–twelfth century, was shattered, enabling the Christians to take over almost all of southern Spain in the ensuing forty years.

The battle was the result of a crusade against the Muslim infidel in Spain organized by Alfonso VIII of Castile, Rodrigo Ximénez de Rada, archbishop of Toledo (d. 1247), and Pope Innocent III (1198–1216). French, Provençal, and Italian knights and soldiers eventually arrived at Toledo to join up with crusaders brought by the kings of Aragón and Navarre, as well as the army assembled by Alfonso VIII of Castile.

Once the combined armies left Toledo and headed south, however, most of the "foreign" crusaders deserted, finding the heat and outbreaks of disease unbearable.

The Christian armies arrived at Las Navas de Tolosa, which lies to the northeast of Córdoba and Jaén, on Friday, July 13. During the ensuing Saturday and Sunday, only small skirmishes took place, but on the morning of Monday, July 16, the Christian armies attacked the Almohads. The Castilians and the Military Orders were flanked on the right by Sancho VII of Navarre with the Navarrese troops and urban militias from Ávila, Segovia, and Medina, and on the left by the king of Aragón and his army. Initially the Almohad vanguard had to retreat, but when the bulk of its army entered the battle, it seemed as if the Christians would be defeated. It was at this point that Alfonso VIII advanced and the kings of Aragón and Navarre converged from the flanks. The combined Christian attack was decisive, even reaching the chains and the guards defending the headquarters tent of the Almohad leader. A Muslim retreat quickly became a rout, and the Almohad leader, Muhammad an-Nasir, fled toward Jaén that same night. Among the enormous booty collected was the so-called Muslim "flag of Las Navas," which survives in the monastery of Las Huelgas in Burgos.

ANGUS MACKAY

Lawrence of Arabia

1888–1935, British Explorer and Military Leader

As one of the most colorful figures of the Near Eastern campaigns of World War I (q.v.), T. E. Lawrence was instrumental in promoting the "Arab Revolt" against Ottoman forces in Syria, Transjordan, and the Hijaz. Trained as an archaeologist at Oxford, Lawrence traveled widely in the Near East before the war, participating in excavations at Carchemish in Syria and a mapping expedition in the Negev Desert. Assigned to the headquarters of British Military Intelligence in Cairo at the outbreak of the war, Lawrence was dispatched to Arabia to forge a military alliance with Hussein, the sharif of Mecca. He subsequently became a trusted adviser of Hussein and accompanied his son Faisal in their protracted campaign, fought with irregular bedouin forces, against Ottoman rail lines and supply routes. Their most notable military achievements were the conquest of Aqaba (1917) and the occupation of Damascus (1918). With his exploits publicized throughout the world by the American journalist Lowell Thomas, Lawrence served as a diplomatic adviser to Hussein at the 1919 Paris Peace Conference. Though embittered by what he viewed as a British betrayal of the cause of Arab independence, Lawrence later served in the Middle East Division of the British Colonial Office. His autobiography, *Seven Pillars of Wisdom*, was published in 1926.

NEIL ASHER SILBERMAN

Laws of War

Most human societies develop permissions and prohibitions for the conduct of war. Tribal societies often equate "humankind" with members of their own tribe, evolving elaborate conventions to limit violence between members, sometimes even reducing it through ritual to a legitimized form of violent competition (much like team sports today). Nonmembers, however, were treated — or, rather, mistreated — as animals. Even the elaborate laws of chivalry in medieval Europe and the warriors' code of honor (Bushido) in Japan (see *Courage*) governed only the conflicts of kindred peoples and social equals. The process of applying the same rules to all combatants and civilians, whatever their social status and whichever side they supported, only began in sixteenth-century Europe.

The laws of war derive from five sources:

1. A series of prescriptive Christian texts (the Bible — above all, Deuteronomy 20:10–20 — Roman law, canon law), which laid down the permissions and prohibitions that should obtain in wars. As time passed, their findings were collected, codified, and developed by writers interested in the law of nature and (later) the law of nations.

2. Two movements in eleventh-century France. The peace of God movement, pioneered by the Roman Catholic Church, laid down the principle that the weak who could do no harm should not themselves be harmed, whereas the truce of God simultaneously attempted to restrict armed conflict between Christians to certain days of the week.

3. Legal codes enacted by armies themselves. These "articles of war" determined the rules of tolerable and intolerable conduct for all troops: duty to God, obedience to all superiors, vigilance and loyalty in camp and in action, humanity toward civilians (unless ordered otherwise), and so on. These codes also began to emerge in the eleventh century.

4. A collection of precedents drawn from the conduct of war itself. Most codes for the conduct of war left any offenses not specifically mentioned to "be punished according to the general customs and laws of war."

5. Reciprocity. Participants in armed conflict almost always came to appreciate, sooner or later, the advantages of mutual restraint. Honoring surrenders, sparing the wounded, and respecting flags of truce all reduced the danger and chaos of conflict for combatants on both sides by creating a predictable etiquette of belligerence.

The laws of war contain two parts: the *jus ad bellum* (rules concerning the legitimacy of war) and the *jus in bello* (rules concerning the conduct of war). The first — the criteria for waging a "just" war — excited debate in the West only at certain periods. Between the Middle Ages and the sixteenth century, a consensus developed in Europe that wars must be waged by a legitimate authority for a cause that was itself deemed just — to avenge an injury or to restore something wrongly seized. From the seventeenth century to 1914, however, following the lead of Hugo Grotius (q.v.), most writers accepted that war was a natural (if not a necessary) element in international politics and that every state was the sole judge of the justice of its own cause. World War I (q.v.) changed all that: in 1928 the Pact of Paris "for the renunciation of war" condemned recourse to war except in self-defense, and sixty-three states solemnly forswore war as an instrument of policy. "Planning aggressive war" became a "war crime" for which both German and Japanese leaders were arraigned after World War II.

Jus in bello has proved more difficult to regulate. A certain amount of brutality is of course inevitable in all armed conflicts, given that the business of the military in war is killing people and breaking things. Moreover, many atrocities take place in circumstances that have produced similar results in almost all societies at almost all times: when the sudden collapse of an enemy force turns one army into a cowardly crowd and the other into a murderous mob, when an adversary is completely broken in battle, or when a town is taken by storm. However, in most of the wars waged in Europe since the sixteenth century, breaches of the norms for military conduct have been subjected to scrutiny on three counts: first, proportionality (was the amount of force used, both strategic and tactical, appropriate to the end envisaged?); second, the avoidance of direct, intentional attack on noncombatants and on nonmilitary targets; and third, the renunciation of prohibited methods (ranging from genocide to chemical weapons that cause excessive, indiscriminate suffering).

The first attempts to establish universal prescriptions came in the mid–nineteenth century. In 1856 the Congress of Paris tried to limit naval warfare; in 1863 the U.S. Army's "General Orders, No. 100" *(Instructions for the Government of Armies in the Field)* established a rigorous framework for the proper behavior of soldiers toward others; in 1864 the first Geneva Convention, on the initiative of Jean Henri Dunant (q.v.), laid down rules to protect the wounded in war; and in 1868 the St. Petersburg Declaration outlawed the use of explosive antipersonnel bullets. The next two international conferences at The Hague in 1899 and 1907 codified and extended many of the existing laws of war on land (no agreement was reached, then or subsequently, on sea warfare). A number of further protocols followed World War I (for example, against the use of chemical gas), and in 1949 the entire corpus was reorganized into the four Geneva Conventions for the protection of war victims, ratified by 125 states. Finally, the 1977 Geneva Protocol extended these same rights and protection to "armed conflicts in which peoples are fighting against colonial domination and alien occupation and against racist regimes in the exercise of their right of self-determination."

This protocol deals with an area in which atrocities have most commonly occurred: civil wars, on the one hand, and the invasion of an area by armed forces that regard themselves as culturally superior, on the other. Such conflicts have been termed *bellum romanum,* or "wars of fire and sword" — the waging of war with no holds barred against those who (for either ideological or cultural reasons) do not belong to "our tribe" and who therefore deserve no special treatment. Examples include the slaughter of Native Americans by Europeans from the sixteenth century to the nineteenth century; the massacres of Ming loyalists in China after 1644 by the Manchus (q.v.); the conduct of the army of Morocco on its advance from Seville during the Spanish civil war (q.v.); the Japanese use of Chinese prisoners for bayonet practice in the 1930s; the policy of the German army toward Jews, Communists, partisans, captured enemy aircrew, and many other groups during World War II (q.v.); and the "ethnic cleansing" (q.v.) that accompanied the Yugoslav war.

However, enforcing the Geneva Conventions in such conflicts is even harder than in other wars, for neither those fighting for "national liberation" nor those opposing them have much incentive to respect the laws of war. International sanctions and the pressure of world opinion may make some impression, but because no world government exists, the primary responsibility for trying and punishing war criminals, whether soldiers or civilians, devolves upon the individual state. And states that begin hostilities without formal declaration of war — as Britain and France did against Egypt in 1956, as the Soviet Union did against Afghanistan in 1979, and as the United States did against North Korea, North Vietnam, and Iraq — rarely make the prosecution of their own war criminals a high priority (see *War Crimes Trials).*

GEOFFREY PARKER

Michael Howard, George Andreopoulos, and Mark Shulman, eds., *The Laws of War: Constraints on Warfare in the Western World* (1994); Michael Walzer, *Just and Unjust Wars: A Moral Argument with Historical Illustrations* (1977).

League of Augsburg, War of the

See Grand Alliance, War of the.

Lechfeld, Battle of the

August 10, 955

Responding to another in a sixty-year series of raids, approximately three thousand Germans under Otto the Great (q.v.) defeated about five thousand Magyars (q.v.) under the Karchas Bulksu near the Lech River northwest of Augsburg, Germany. Otto's personal guard stopped a Magyar encirclement, while a counterencirclement cleared the way for an attack that broke the main Magyar force.

The Magyars' use of siege machines against Augsburg on August 8–9 and the attempt of some to stand and fight against the German attack at the Lechfeld demonstrated a partial adoption of western combat techniques. Their defeat at the Lech led to permanent settlement in Hungary and eventual conversion to Latin Christianity. The Magyars were the last Central Asian nomads to invade western Europe.

Otto's ability to concentrate forces on the march and block escape routes during an extended pursuit on August 11–12 showed the effectiveness of the system, organized under his father Henry I, of combining fortifications with heavily armored troops. Otto exploited the propaganda value of the victory to solidify his rule in Germany and Italy and, in 962, became the first German king to be crowned Western Roman emperor.

EDWARD J. SCHOENFELD

Lee, Robert E.

1807–1870, Confederate General

Robert Edward Lee was born in Virginia, the fifth child of Henry "Light-Horse Harry" Lee (1756–1818) of Revolutionary War fame, by his second wife. In 1829 he was graduated second in his class at West Point without having incurred a single demerit in his four years there. Commissioned in the Corps of Engineers, he served as a captain under General Winfield Scott (q.v.) in the Mexican War (q.v.), in which he distinguished himself in the battles of Veracruz, Churubusco, and Chapultepec. He was slightly wounded in that war and earned three brevets to colonel. General Scott declared him to be "the very best soldier that I ever saw in the field."

In 1852 he was appointed superintendent of West Point. Three years later, with the approval of Jefferson Davis, then secretary of war, he transferred as a lieutenant colonel to the newly raised Second Cavalry and served in West Texas.

Although John Brown's raid on the U.S. Arsenal and Armory at Harpers Ferry, Virginia (now West Virginia), in October 1859 occurred while Lee was at his home on extended leave in Arlington, Virginia, he was placed in command of a detachment of marines and, with Second Lieutenant J. E. B. Stuart, captured Brown and his band.

On April 20, 1861, at the outbreak of the American Civil War (q.v.), he resigned his commission and three days later was appointed by Governor John Letcher of Virginia to be commander in chief of the military and naval forces of the state. When Virginia's troops were transferred to the Confederate service, he became, on May 14, 1861, a brigadier general, the highest rank then authorized. Soon after he was promoted to full general.

Lee's first field command was in the western part of the state, where he failed to hold back invading Union forces in an area of strong pro-Union sentiment. He was recalled to Richmond, and from March 1862 he was military adviser to President Davis. From this position he was able to influence some operations, notably those of General Thomas "Stonewall" Jackson (q.v.) in his Shenandoah Valley campaign.

When General Joseph E. Johnston was wounded at the Battle of Seven Pines on May 31, Lee took command of what became the Army of Northern Virginia. He successfully repulsed the efforts of Union general George McClellan (q.v.) in the Peninsular campaign,

concluding with the Battles of Seven Days: Oak Grove, Mechanicsville, Gaine's Mill, Garnett's and Golding's Farms, Savage's Station and Allen's Farm, White Oak Swamp, and Malvern Hill. Victories were won through Lee's aggressiveness and daring in the face of McClellan's timidity rather than by any comprehensive generalship on Lee's part, for he was unable to exercise control over his subordinate commanders, and the individual battles could be considered tactical defeats.

On August 29–30, he defeated General John Pope in the second Battle of Bull Run (Manassas), but when he invaded Maryland he was checked on September 17 by Union forces under McClellan at Antietam (q.v.). Here, even after the bloodiest day of the entire war, Lee held on and was willing to fight on the same field another day. On December 13, he defeated General Ambrose Burnside at Fredericksburg, and it was here that he made the remark to General James Longstreet that many of his admirers have tried to explain away: "It is well war is so terrible — we would grow too fond of it." Lee loved fighting a war.

Lee's most brilliantly fought battle was the defeat of Joseph Hooker at Chancellorsville (q.v.) on May 1–4, 1863. It is one of the most elemental rules of generalship, indeed one might feel it elemental common sense, that the general of a numerically inferior force refrain from dividing that force in the face of his enemy. Yet Lee had done that just before Antietam, detaching Jackson to capture Harpers Ferry; at Chancellorsville he did it not merely once, leaving part of his army at Fredericksburg, but twice, for he detached Jackson with the larger portion of his remaining force to come in on the Union right flank while he stood with only two divisions in front of the massive federal army. Such actions seemed so unthinkable to Hooker that he could not take it in. He paused to think about it, and his pause was fatal. The courteous, calm Lee was daring to the point of rashness.

Again invading the North, he was once more checked, this time at Gettysburg (q.v.), where his haste in insisting on what became known as Pickett's Charge, a massed infantry assault across a wide plain, cost the South dearly. The rifle, which had largely replaced the musket in the Union armies, had made such attacks hopeless. Lee failed to recognize the effect of improved weapons.

From the Battle of the Wilderness in May–June 1864 until the siege of Petersburg from July 1864 until April 1865, Lee fought what was essentially a rearguard action. In the winter of 1865, President Davis appointed Lee general in chief of the armies of the Confederate states. But by that time the Confederates had lost the war.

Lee has been charged with being too bloody-minded, of fighting on even when he must have known that his cause was lost. Viewed realistically, this was certainly true; but what the mind knows, the heart cannot always accept. Lee was not alone in failing to admit defeat in a cause to which he was emotionally attached. He fought to the bitter end, and that end came on April 9, 1865, when he surrendered to General Ulysses S. Grant (q.v.) at Appomattox Courthouse in Virginia.

After the war he became president of Washington College (today, Washington and Lee University) in Lexington, Virginia. He applied to have his citizenship restored, but the application was mislaid. It was found in 1970 and granted. He died in Lexington of heart disease on October 12, 1870. His last words were said to have been: "Strike the tent."

In the history of the world perhaps no general who failed so often has been so revered.

BYRON FARWELL

Douglas Southall Freeman, *Lee*, 1-vol. abr. of 4 vols. (1934), ed. Richard Harwell (1961); Emory M. Thomas, *Robert E. Lee: A Biography* (1995).

Legions

The legion — the Latin *legio* was derived from the verb *lego*, "to choose or select" — was the chief unit of the Roman army from the early republic to the end of the empire, a formation that underwent numerous structural and tactical changes over nearly a millennium to meet a variety of different challenges.

By the second century B.C., a legion was composed of about forty-two hundred infantry and three hundred cavalry, divided into three successive lines of ten maniples (each composed of about 140 legionaries), each maniple separated from its like counterpart by about the width of its own formation. So the ten independent maniples of each line — at least before they crashed against the enemy — had free space on both sides, as well as to the front and rear.

On an organizational level, Roman infantry were recruited into the legion by "centuries," groups of about sixty to seventy Italian farmers led by a skilled centurion, the mortar of the entire system for the next one thousand years. Two centuries fought together in a maniple, one stacked behind the other. In conventional Roman battlefield order *(triplex acies)*, imagine three successive lines of stacked infantry rectangles, a checkerboard a mile or two long, each maniple positioned behind the gap in the line ahead.

After initial skirmishing, the first line of ten maniples, the so-called *hastati* (anachronistically called "spear-men") approached to within about fifty to one hundred yards of the enemy, then ran and flung their javelins when about thirty yards distant. With sword and shield, the *hastati* followed their missiles and banged into the stunned enemy line, searching for pockets of collapsed men whom their missiles had just wounded or disarmed.

At this point, the second line of Roman swordsmen, the *principes* (leaders), followed up. They either pushed their advancing *hastati* on through the opponents' line, or — if the enemy proved formidable — served as a separate reserve, battering the enemy with a fresh assault of more slashing and thrusting blades, while the *hastati* retreated back through their advance.

If the *principes* did not break the enemy, the third and last manipular row, the *triarii* (third-liners) were waiting to the rear on their knees, covering with shields, spears extended. Rocklike, these last ten maniples were on the lookout for any wavering of the first two lines, giving rise to the dire proverb "Matters have come down to the *triarii*." More often, given the frequency of Roman legionary success, the *triarii* also advanced cautiously, and applied the coup de grâce to any battlefield stragglers or crumbling formations.

Obviously, the key to the early legion's success was coordination and adaptability, all made possible by reserves and the sheer diversity of forces. *Pila* (spears) gave Roman infantry an offensive reach unknown to a phalanx, its deadly shower of javelins superior in lethality to the slinger's bullets or bowman's arrows. Once inside the stunned enemy mass, the *gladius* (short sword) could make short work of phalangites, and the tall, ovoid *scutum* (shield) was handy for pushing in the manner of the phalanx, if maniples — once bunched together at impact — needed power at the enemy line. Spearmen to the rear prevented collapse. In a pinch, they could overwhelm confused and disorganized opposition. Of all ancient weaponry, the *gladius* was by far the most lethal; the Hellenistic Greeks were astounded at the carnage — severed limbs, decapitation, disembowelment — that Roman swordsmen could inflict on pike-wielding infantry with such a short sword.

Around 105 B.C., Marius, an experienced commander, bypassed the property qualification for Roman infantry service and, in a quest for greater manpower, equipped his legions at state expense. He also gradually normalized a sixteen-year, rather than an indefinite, tenure of service. Now military recruitment of Roman citizens, as in Hellenistic armies, was largely to be separated from status or wealth. This divorce ensured a much larger pool of potential soldiers, but marked a disastrous precedent whereby soldiers looked exclusively to a single grandee for pay and retirement benefits.

Marius also inaugurated a series of overdue (in the strictly military sense) logistical and tactical reforms. Cohorts (usually formed of about 480 men, three times larger than the maniple) evolved as the fundamental tactical unit of the legion, now to be redefined as ten cohorts of 4,800 soldiers. The ten (rather than the previous thirty) tactical segments of the legions were both more powerful and more versatile, better able to bring more legionaries, with all the respective arsenal of the army, to specific points in the enemy line: a Roman general need not necessarily follow the standard triple (and predictable) sequence of assault throughout the entire legion. Now he could diversify his attack, directing cohorts to the wings and rear where they could proceed with a phased charge on their own.

In line with this growing military sophistication, Marius also apparently issued broad edicts concerning training and equipment, seeking to standardize the more widely divergent manpower in the largely professional legions. The old skirmishers (the *velites*), the Roman poor armed with a ragtag assortment of light armament, were issued standard gear and brought into the formal apparatus of the legion; any nonlegionary light and missile troops, when needed, were now to be composed exclusively of allies. The third-rank *triarii* also gave up their *hasta* (lances) and were issued the standard short sword and javelin. With the reconstituted legion, Roman commanders slaughtered their opponents at will. Caesar massacred hundreds of thousands in Gaul with but minor losses of his own, subduing millions more with a force of less than ten legions.

The legion represented the entire culmination of existing Western military prowess. Drawing on an early Greek battle tradition of shock and decisive confrontation, coupled with the Macedonian legacy of integration and diversity of force, the pragmatic Romans achieved a marvelous balance between power and grace. With the support of their unmatched and elaborate governmental organization, and the capital of an expanding market economy, they surrounded the legionary with a rich infrastructure of war making — roads, camps, hospitals, arms and armor, support services, pensions, salaries, medical corps, officers — and thus crafted warfare as an enormous bureaucratic enterprise, its legions designed, if need be, to cope with any challenge far beyond the boundaries of Italy.

Throughout most of the empire, the legions remained about thirty strong, or between 150,000 and 200,000 paid men under arms. By the third century A.D., it was clear that the enormous expenditure required to support the army and its garrisons on the frontier was unsustainable. The peasantry was exhausted, the currency debased, but the legionaries ever more exacting of their salaries and retirement. Originally a militia of yeomen who kept Italy free, the legion and its demand for pay eventually devoured the very countryside it was supposed to protect.

VICTOR DAVIS HANSON

R. Davies, *Service in the Roman Army* (1989); L. Keppie, *The Making of the Roman Army: From Republic to Empire* (1987).

Legnano, Battle of

May 29, 1176

About four thousand cavalry from Milan and other towns in the Lombard League, with an undetermined number of Milanese infantry, defeated approximately thirty-five hundred Germans and allies from Como under Emperor Frederick I (Barbarossa) about twenty miles northwest of Milan. The Germans won an initial cavalry engagement, but were stopped by infantry formed around the *carrocio* (civic standard) of Milan. After receiving reinforcements, the Lombard cavalry rallied and returned to the fight, while the Germans lost cohesion when Frederick was unhorsed (though not killed).

Legnano, though not exclusively an infantry victory, was one of several medieval battles demonstrating that the tactical superiority of the heavily armored mounted trooper was never absolute. Although not a "national" victory for "Italy" over "Germany," Legnano marked a high point in the military and political power of the Lombard League, an association of northern Italian city-states, which Frederick had to dissipate by diplomatic maneuvering before gaining a favorable peace at Constance in 1183. Legnano also demonstrated the severe limits on German rulers' ability to sustain operations south of the Alps, which, when added to problems in maintaining political control within Germany, ensured their eventual failure to dominate Italy.

EDWARD J. SCHOENFELD

Leipzig, Battle of

October 16–19, 1813

This engagement, also known as the Battle of Nations, represented the climax of the campaign of 1813 in Germany (see *Napoleon Bonaparte*). In terms of numbers of troops engaged and amount of artillery, Leipzig was the biggest battle of the Napoleonic Wars. Separate but coordinated armies of Russians, Prussians, Swedes, and Austrians brought 370,000 troops and 1,384 guns to the battlefield, whereas Napoleon's strength stood at 198,000 men with 717 guns.

The battle developed when Napoleon seized the Leipzig position, intending to divide his opponents and attack them one by one. The French almost had that chance on the first day of fighting, when the Prussian army engaged while the Army of the North, a Russo-Prusso-Swedish force under Bernadotte (a former French marshal), hung back. However, Napoleon became the victim of his own repeated changes of operational focus during this campaign. With allied strength building up on the second day of Leipzig, Napoleon spent most of the day redeploying, while on the final day allied numbers and combat power proved simply too much. Even in withdrawal there was disaster for the French — a premature destruction of the major river bridge at Leipzig trapped the French rear guard. Casualties quoted for the battle are usually 73,000 French and 54,000 allies.

Leipzig was the first occasion on which Napoleon was clearly defeated in the field (the Austrian repulse of Napoleon at Aspern-Essling in May 1809 brought about a stalemate, not a clear victory, and its effects were soon reversed by the Battle of Wagram; French defeat in Russia in 1812 was the product of strategic factors, not an army in the field). The French Grande

Armée continued its westward retreat until, in 1814, the victors closed in on Paris and Napoleon abdicated.

JOHN PRADOS

LeMay, Curtis E.

1906–1990, U.S. World War II and Cold War General

Although he is known primarily for his devastating firebombing of Japan, which pressured the emperor to move toward surrender, and for his controversial advocacy of all-out air strikes during the Vietnam conflict (q.v.), Curtis LeMay was also a bold and innovative tactician, an inspiring and effective commander, and a key player in the development of the postwar air force.

During World War II (q.v.), LeMay quickly earned a reputation for daring and imaginative leadership in bombing attacks on German targets; he personally led some raids. He also introduced demanding new training practices and developed special flight formations, tactics, and bombing techniques that markedly increased the effectiveness of the air campaign. In 1945, commanding B-29 attacks on Japan, he devised and carried out punishing low-level incendiary raids that destroyed every major Japanese city and were a decisive element in forcing Japan's surrender.

After the war, LeMay was in charge of organizing and operating the 1948 American air supply of Berlin in the face of the Soviet blockade of that city, a task he successfully carried out with his usual aggressiveness and determination. He next took over the Strategic Air Command, then badly in need of strengthening and modernization, and raised performance standards and readiness to a high level of efficiency through a program of improved training, innovative management systems, and forceful example.

As vice chief and then chief of staff of the U.S. Air Force, LeMay was later involved in a number of Cold War (q.v.) crises, as well as in programs to improve air force weapons, systems, and operational procedures. He also expressed his strong disagreement with President John F. Kennedy and Secretary of Defense Robert S. McNamara (q.v.) over defense policy and strategy and was particularly outspoken in his criticism of President Lyndon B. Johnson's conduct of the war in Vietnam. Retiring in 1965, he supported conservative political causes and in 1968 made an ill-advised and unsuccessful run for the vice presidency on the independent ticket of George Wallace.

LeMay's reputation as a ruthless advocate of the indiscriminate use of military power is undeserved. He was a blunt military realist who believed in the proper application of force to achieve legitimate objectives. Asked about moral considerations, he replied, "Every soldier thinks something of the moral aspects of what he is doing. But all war is immoral, and if you let it bother you, you're not a good soldier."

STANLEY L. FALK

Leningrad, Siege of

August 28, 1941–January 27, 1944

German and Finnish forces besieged Lenin's namesake city after their spectacular initial advance during Operation Barbarossa (q.v.). After a precipitous advance during summer 1941, forces of German Army Group North struggled against stubborn Soviet resistance to isolate and seize the city before the onset of winter. In heavy fighting during August, German forces reached the city's suburbs and the shores of Lake Ladoga, severing Soviet ground communications with the city. In November, Soviet forces repelled a renewed German offensive and clung to tenuous resupply routes across the frozen waters of Lake Ladoga. Thereafter, German and Soviet strategic attention shifted to other more critical sectors of the Eastern Front, and Leningrad — its defending forces and its large civilian population — endured an 880-day siege of unparalleled severity and hardship. Despite desperate Soviet use of an "ice and water road" across Lake Ladoga to resupply its three million encircled soldiers and civilians and to evacuate one million civilians, over one million civilians perished during the ensuing siege. Another 300,000 Soviet soldiers died defending the city or attempting to raise the siege. In January 1943, Soviet forces opened a narrow land corridor into the city through which vital rations and supplies again flowed. Not until January 1944, however, did Red Army (q.v.) successes in other front sectors enable the Soviets to raise the siege. By this time, besieging German forces were so weak that renewed Soviet attacks drove them away from the city and from Soviet soil.

After November 1941, possession of Leningrad held only symbolic significance. The Germans maintained their siege with a single army, and defending

Soviet forces numbered less than 15 percent of their total strength on the German-Soviet front. The Leningrad sector was clearly of secondary importance, and the Soviets raised the siege only after the fate of German arms had been decided in more critical front sectors. Despite its diminished strategic significance, the suffering and sacrifices of Leningrad's dwindling population and defending forces inspired the Soviet war effort as a whole.

DAVID M. GLANTZ

Lepanto, Battle of

October 7, 1571

Lepanto was the largest naval engagement of early modern times, involving 160,000 men and 400 warships (mostly galleys). In 1570 the Ottomans (q.v.) launched one powerful expedition against the Venetian island of Cyprus and another to seize the Spanish protectorate of Tunis; early in 1571, Spain and Venice responded by signing an alliance with the papacy to create a Grand Fleet to relieve Cyprus. In the event, the Christians located their adversaries' navy in the Gulf of Lepanto (western Greece) and, thanks above all to superior firepower — 1,815 guns to only 750 — on October 7, 1571, they destroyed or captured some 200 of the 230 Turkish galleys, together with their artillery, stores, and some 30,000 men (many executed after the battle in cold blood). News of the vic-

BATTLE OF LEPANTO

tory sparked uprisings in Greece and Albania, which imperiled Ottoman rule there. It appeared to be one of the decisive battles of the century.

However, as a Turkish minister explained to the Venetians: "You have shaved our beard, but it will soon grow again, but we have severed your arm and you will never find another." And indeed, Lepanto failed to save Cyprus; in 1572, thanks to feverish work in shipyards all around the east Mediterranean, the Ottoman fleet again numbered over 200 galleys. Venice cut her losses and made peace in 1573. Spain regained Tunis but, crippled by the cost of suppressing the Dutch Revolt (q.v.), lost it again in 1574 and concluded an armistice with the Turks in 1577.

GEOFFREY PARKER

Leuthen, Battle of

December 5, 1757

The year 1757 was the first in the Seven Years' War (1756–1763) (q.v.) in which the league arrayed against Frederick the Great (q.v.) of Prussia had an opportunity to use its overwhelming strength. The summer and autumn were difficult for Frederick. The Russians invaded East Prussia and won a victory there at Gross-Jägersdorf (August 30). The Swedes invaded Pomerania, and the French conquered Prussia's ally, Hanover. The Prussians were forced to abandon their invasion of Bohemia, and the Austrians captured most of strategic Silesia, including its capital, Breslau.

Frederick saved the situation and stabilized the war by two victories. At Rossbach (November 5) he inflicted far greater losses on a much larger French army, which he attacked on the march and routed. Leuthen was a more difficult engagement. Frederick had a first-rate army of 35,000; Prince Charles of Lorraine 65,000 Austrians. Frederick, crucially, took and retained the initiative. Benefiting from the cover of a ridge, he turned the Austrian left flank while a feint attack led the Austrians to send their reserves to bolster their right. The Austrian left was unable to cope with the concentrated weight of the Prussian attack, and the cavalry of the Austrian left was also defeated.

However, Charles of Lorraine was able to wheel the Austrian army so that it formed a new south-facing front anchored on the village of Leuthen. The village was carried by the Prussians after bitter fighting, but the Prussian infantry became exposed to the Austrian

cavalry. This cavalry attack was preempted by the Prussian cavalry, and the battered Austrian infantry finally retreated. The Prussians lost 6,382 killed and wounded, the Austrians 22,000, including 12,000 prisoners. After their defeat, the Austrians abandoned most of Silesia. Leuthen made the Austrians far more cautious, paralyzing numerous Austrian initiatives later in the war. It did not knock Austria out of the war, but it played a major role in the "miracle" of Prussia's survival.

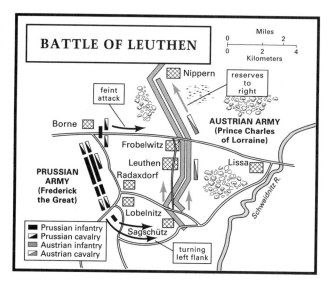

Leuthen was a victory that reflected Prussian firepower, Frederick's skilled exploitation of the terrain, the fighting quality of the Prussian cavalry, and the ability of Prussian commanders to take initiatives. It was the victory of a well-honed army over opponents who fought well but operated less effectively.

JEREMY BLACK

Leyte Gulf, Battle of

October 23–26, 1944

The aerial and naval battle conducted as Allied forces invaded the Philippines began with Leyte Island on October 20. Expecting an invasion, the Japanese fleet command ordered its forces to sea at the very first sign of Allied landings. Due to the effects of previous engagements and to Japan's precarious fuel situation, however, the Japanese fleet was deployed in a scattered fashion: carrier forces in Japan were training new pilots; battleship units near Singapore (close to the fuel sources) and some cruiser forces, formerly in

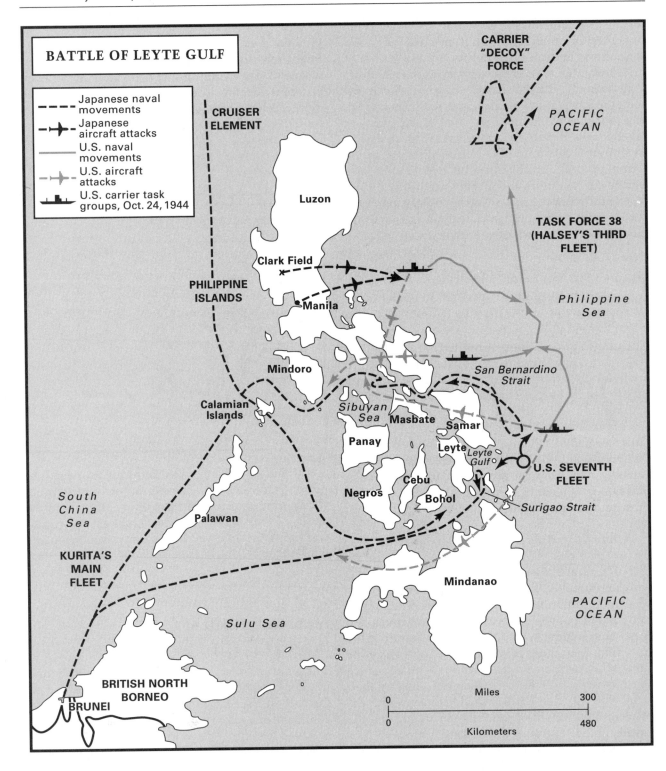

BATTLE OF LEYTE GULF

Japanese naval movements
Japanese aircraft attacks
U.S. naval movements
U.S. aircraft attacks
U.S. carrier task groups, Oct. 24, 1944

CARRIER "DECOY" FORCE

PACIFIC OCEAN

CRUISER ELEMENT

Luzon

TASK FORCE 38 (HALSEY'S THIRD FLEET)

Clark Field

PHILIPPINE ISLANDS

Manila

Philippine Sea

Mindoro

San Bernardino Strait

Calamian Islands

Sibuyan Sea

Masbate

Samar

Panay

Leyte

Leyte Gulf

U.S. SEVENTH FLEET

South China Sea

Negros

Cebu

Bohol

Palawan

Surigao Strait

KURITA'S MAIN FLEET

Mindanao

PACIFIC OCEAN

Sulu Sea

BRITISH NORTH BORNEO

BRUNEI

Miles
0   300
0   480
Kilometers

the northern Pacific, maneuvered in the wake of the Allied carrier strikes on Taiwan (October 10–12). When Japan ordered its fleet into Philippine waters, these forces had to sail separately and for the most part operated independently in the battle that followed.

Headed toward the Philippines, the naval command suggested that Admiral Kurita Takeo of the battleship unit detach an element of his fleet to enter Leyte Gulf through the Surigao Strait. He did send a force that way, which was annihilated in surface naval combat in a classic crossing of the "T" on the night of October 24–25. The cruiser element from the north tried to follow but recoiled before making contact. Japan's aircraft carriers successfully decoyed north the U.S. Third Fleet of Admiral William F. Halsey (q.v.), uncovering the San Bernardino Strait, through which Kurita's main fleet passed after turning away momentarily under the pressure of fierce U.S. submarine and air attacks. Kurita came closest to Leyte Gulf, in the process encountering several forces of small U.S. escort carriers, which the Japanese mistook for regular fleet carriers. Aircraft, however, made more and more powerful attacks on the Japanese as time went on, at length forcing Kurita to withdraw from Philippine waters.

Leyte Gulf was decisive in that it destroyed much of the remaining Japanese surface fleet while virtually ending Japan's ability to move resources from Southeast Asia to the home islands. Japanese losses included four aircraft carriers, three battleships, six heavy and four light cruisers, and eleven destroyers, along with several hundred aircraft and over 10,500 sailors. Allied losses were one light carrier, two escort carriers, two destroyers and one destroyer-escort. Despite overall failure, however, the Japanese showed that with determination they could still press home attacks against an Allied armada with huge technical and material advantages.

JOHN PRADOS

Liddell Hart, B. H.

1895–1970, *British Military Theorist, Journalist, and Historian*

Born in Paris of British parents but educated in England, Basil Henry Liddell Hart spent one year at Cambridge before being commissioned in 1915. He was badly gassed in the Somme offensive (q.v.) and spent the rest of the war in England, training infantrymen. He was invalided out of the army in 1924.

Liddell Hart made his reputation as a military theorist in the 1920s, developing ideas intended to prevent a repeat of the earlier trench deadlock: he outlined mobile offensive tactics such as the "expanding torrent" and, as strategy, advocated the "indirect approach," and a form of blitzkrieg involving both tanks and infantry. The indirect approach consisted of attacking enemy civilian populations by air, land, and sea.

However, by the 1930s Liddell Hart argued against a Continental commitment for the British army. Partly because of this, he now changed his mind and declared that the defense had become more powerful than the offense. As a result of the rapid German victory of 1940, his reputation as a theorist suffered. Nevertheless, Liddell Hart's extensive and influential publications established him as one of the important military theorists of the twentieth century.

TIM TRAVERS

Li Hung-chang

1823–1901, *Chinese Statesman*

Li Hung-chang gained power through military success and thus symbolizes the late Ch'ing shift away from civilian domination of politics, which paved the way for much of China's twentieth-century history. During the Taiping Rebellion (q.v.), Li's cooperation with foreign troops, known as the Ever Victorious Army under "Chinese" Gordon and others, convinced him of the potential advantages of importing military expertise and technology. He subsequently became a driving force in the late-nineteenth-century self-strengthening movement, focusing especially on developing China's ability to build modern armaments, ships, machinery, telegraphs, and railroads as the best means of resisting and then competing with foreign powers. His financial involvement in such modernizing enterprises led to accusations of corruption.

Li sponsored technical and military schools and laid the foundation for replacing the old Chinese army by organizing the Beiyang armies, which had modern weapons, foreign instructors, officer-training schools, and staff colleges; these forces also made Li almost unassailable in north China. His nearly 45,000-strong Anhui army was stationed all around China in the service of the Ch'ing dynasty, and the navy he controlled contributed importantly to coastal defense.

Involved in virtually every diplomatic incident for

thirty years, he negotiated the infamous Treaty of Shimonoseki (1894), ceding so much to foreigners that it sparked the first real rumblings of revolution in China. Thus Li's contribution to Chinese nationalism was somewhat ambiguous.

JOANNA WALEY-COHEN

Lincoln, Abraham

1809–1865, *Sixteenth President of the United States*

At the time of his nomination and election to the presidency in 1860, no candidate of a major political party had had so little administrative and legislative experience as Abraham Lincoln. In a country and at a time when military prowess was an asset for a successful political career, Lincoln had none. In 1832, he volunteered to serve in the Black Hawk Indian War and was elected captain of his company; his experience, however, was more reminiscent of comic opera than of a military campaign. It is ironic that an individual with no military experience should be fated to preside over one of history's bloodiest and costliest wars.

Born in Kentucky and reared in Indiana and Illinois, Lincoln pursued the twin professions of law and politics. As the former prospered, the latter languished, and Lincoln had to be content with several terms in the Illinois state legislature and a single term in the lower house of Congress. As a congressman (1847–1849), Lincoln disapproved of the Mexican War (q.v.), focusing his arguments on the controversy over the boundary between the two countries and the leadership of President James K. Polk, whom he accused of having deceived the American people by provoking an unnecessary and unconstitutional war. Other than a passive support to the soldiers in the field, he paid little attention to the conduct of the war.

During the 1850s, Lincoln found the key to political success in the growing sectional conflict over slavery when he adopted the position of the new Republican Party, which called for the restriction of slavery and its eventual abolition in the southern states. His unexpected nomination for the presidency in 1860 and his subsequent election triggered the secession of seven slave states (which later increased to eleven) and the organization of the Confederate States of America. The Confederate attack on Fort Sumter, six weeks after Lincoln's inauguration, opened the American Civil War (q.v.).

Lincoln met the challenge of war firmly and boldly, but not without opposition, as he defined the conflict, took steps to mobilize resources, raised an army composed of state militia units and volunteers, and increased the size of the regular forces, all without the input of Congress. Deliberately ambiguous in his view of the conflict, Lincoln insisted that it was a rebellion against the constituted authority of the Union, while he adopted policies that suggested it was a war between two belligerent nations, a pragmatic position that enabled him to prosecute the war with flexibility and freedom from the normal restraints of his office. Echoing his predecessors, Andrew Jackson and Polk, he argued that his oath to preserve, protect, and defend the Constitution gave him extraordinary war powers, including the power to bend the Constitution if necessary and the authority to exercise powers normally belonging only to Congress. In doing so, he expanded the limits of executive prerogative. At the same time, as an astute politician, he recognized the need to conciliate his political opponents, to maintain a unity of support, to retain the loyalty of the four slave states that remained in the Union, and to resist the demands of some in his own party that he follow a more extreme partisan course.

Throughout the war, Lincoln was unwavering in his insistence that the paramount war aim was the preservation of the Union and that the war could end only with the unconditional surrender of the rebels. Without compromising his own antislavery convictions, he rejected the appeals that the abolition of slavery should take precedence. As pressure to adopt an emancipation policy increased, Lincoln moved gradually to meet it, following his own agenda and exhausting the constitutional options while reaffirming the primacy of preserving the Union, finally issuing the preliminary Emancipation Proclamation on September 22, 1862 (to take effect on January 1, 1863). Limited in scope — freeing some slaves and not others — and of doubtful constitutionality, the proclamation was justified solely on grounds of military necessity. In his Gettysburg Address (November 19, 1863), Lincoln employed long-held notions of America's mission and destiny when he reiterated his belief that this "great civil war" was a test whether a nation "conceived in Liberty, and dedicated to the proposition that all men are created equal" could "long endure."

Because he had no military knowledge or experience, Lincoln relied heavily on the advice of his generals. Although sensitive to his responsibilities as commander in chief, he allowed his field officers a wide latitude of decision in matters of strategy and tactics, intervening only when popular opinion and congressional criticism demanded he do so. Plagued by a succession of incompetent generals early in the war, Lincoln suffered moments of utter frustration and deep despair that bordered at times on defeatism. It was not until the third year of the war that the prospect for victory brightened, with the double victories at Gettysburg (q.v.) and Vicksburg (q.v.). Lincoln's confidence was strengthened by Ulysses S. Grant's (q.v.) promotion to lieutenant general and his appointment as general in chief. Still, the war dragged on longer than expected, marked by stalemate and horrendous casualties. Lincoln's weariness with the "scourge of war" became apparent in his Second Inaugural Address (March 4, 1865), wherein he entrusted the outcome of the conflict to the "judgments of the Lord." The Civil War finally ended five weeks later when Robert E. Lee (q.v.) surrendered his army at Appomattox. Lincoln's relief was short-lived; five days after the surrender, he was felled by an assassin's bullet.

ROBERT W. JOHANNSEN

Mark E. Neely, Jr., *The Last Best Hope of Earth: Abraham Lincoln and the Promise of America* (1993).

Lin Piao

1907–1971, Chinese Communist General

Lin Piao, one of the three or four outstanding generals who fought for the Communist cause in China, was a superior practitioner of guerrilla warfare. Lin grew up near the city of Wuhan on the Yangtze River in central China as the son of a well-to-do factory owner. He became involved in radical student circles in the late 1910s and early 1920s, when he joined the Communists and entered the Whampoa Military Academy. Though the academy was officially Nationalist, Russian advisers taught there, and many Communists studied there until the breakdown of the United Front in 1927.

Using guerrilla tactics, Lin scored several crucial victories to secure the Kiangsi Soviet (1931–1934), the first sizable piece of territory under Communist control. It was also Lin who in 1934 led the famed Communist breakout from Chiang Kai-shek's (q.v.) encirclement that began the Long March, and who scored a famous victory over the Japanese at the Ping-hsing Pass near the Great Wall in September 1937.

Lin knew, however, that guerrilla warfare was the weapon of the weak. Close to Mao Tse tung (q.v.) and with a reputation for tactical and strategic brilliance, in 1945 he was appointed the commander of all Communist forces in Manchuria, where the fate of China was decided in the Chinese Civil War (1945–1949) (q.v.). Although initially forced to adopt guerrilla tactics, Lin gradually welded guerrilla units together into large armies capable of conventional warfare. Taking the offensive in 1947, he isolated Chiang Kai-shek's forces in the cities and put them out of action during the Liao-shen campaign of 1948. This was one of the great battles of the civil war period in which Lin showed off his tactical skills. His forces subsequently marched south, first taking Tien-tsin in a bloody battle and then securing the surrender of Peking. By the end of 1949, Lin's armies had marched through central China and taken the last major city in the south, Canton. Lin was only forty-two years old.

Lin today is much reviled. His reputation has suffered, perhaps because bouts of mental and physical illness kept him out of action during the Anti-Japanese and Korean (q.v.) wars. During the first, Lin was in Moscow between late 1938 or early 1939 and 1942, perhaps to recuperate from battle wounds, perhaps for other reasons. Between 1942 and 1945 Lin taught at the Resistance University at the Communist capital of Yan-an. In 1959 he became minister of defense and sought to strengthen Maoist principles in the army. He is famed for editing Mao's *Little Red Book*, requiring soldiers to study it endlessly, and he helped bring about the Cultural Revolution. In 1971 Lin attempted a coup d'état. Fleeing the country, he died when his plane crashed or was shot down over Mongolia.

HANS J. VAN DE VEN

Literature

See Memoirs of War *and* Representation of War in Western Literature.

Lloyd George, David

1863–1945, Prime Minister of Great Britain

A Liberal politician of advanced views, David Lloyd George acquired his vivid speaking style from Welsh churchgoing and his radicalism from his uncle, David Lloyd, who oversaw his education. First a lawyer, Lloyd George was elected to the House of Commons from Caernarvon in 1890. From 1905 he held cabinet office, notably as chancellor of the exchequer from 1908 into 1915, acquiring a reputation as a social reformer. A pacifist in 1914, he underwent a conversion after the invasion of Belgium, taking up the new Ministry of Munitions and transforming the nation into an arsenal. In 1916 he became war minister, upstaging the indecisive though once cunning prime minister, H. H. Asquith, architect of an ineffective multiparty coalition. British forces were then bogged down in a war of attrition in Flanders and in stalemate, at best, in the eastern Mediterranean.

When Asquith reacted to reverses with commissions of inquiry and continued tolerance of myopic and costly generalship, Lloyd George pressed for a small supercabinet to run the war. Although he preferred running a war cabinet to the more encompassing and unwieldy premiership, when Asquith declined a reduction to nominal prime minister, Lloyd George claimed both jobs in December 1916. He recruited efficient civilians to devise strategy and operations, proving to be a shrewd judge of talent. He persuaded key experts that Britain required a government that would prosecute the war with vigor and that he had the potential to lead. They took cabinet posts.

Overhauling the war-making machinery in Whitehall proved easier than remaking the bloodied expeditionary force in France. "Delay in war is as fatal as an illness," he charged. "An operation which may succeed today is no good six weeks later. . . . So in war." Although his war cabinet, with an effective secretariat under a former colonel, Sir Maurice Hankey, managed the fronts from London, Lloyd George was frustrated by his commanding generals, Douglas Haig (q.v.) and William Robertson, who — despite the butcheries at the Somme (q.v.) and Passchendaele — elicited steadfast loyalty from influential industrialists, politicians, press lords, and even the king. Lloyd George and Haig regarded each other as a misfortune. To Haig it was "a calamity for the country to have such a man at the head of affairs in this time of great crisis. We can only try and make the best of him."

The prime minister did rid the navy of Haig's counterpart, Admiral John Rushworth Jellicoe (q.v.), who opposed the convoy system, despite a hemorrhage of sinkings, and safeguarded warships from U-boats by keeping the Royal Navy uselessly close to home. Admiral David Beatty proved more aggressive at sea; but ashore, Haig continued the trench war of expensive

but minuscule movement until the spring of 1918, when necessity forced him into a unified command under Ferdinand Foch (q.v.). While the Germans exhausted themselves in last-ditch offensives, Foch held on to await the mammoth American buildup that would force the enemy into acknowledging that an armistice late in 1918 would be preferable to a defeat on German soil in 1919.

At Versailles, Lloyd George put his prodigious energies to winning the peace for Britain, but, although harsher on Germany than the idealistic American president, Woodrow Wilson (q.v.), neither could moderate France's appetite for retribution (see *Versailles, Treaty of*). Radical elements across the Rhine, notably Adolf Hitler's (q.v.) fascists, would prosper on promises to reverse Versailles. Lloyd George's near-dictatorial postwar ministry failed to exploit his wartime mystique. He retained office in December 1918 with a large Unionist majority but only 133 of his own Liberals. Although he negotiated an Irish settlement and influenced international disarmament treaties, external affairs caused his fall late in 1922 when his pro-Greek bluster in the Chanak crisis (see *Greco-Turkish War*) threatened war with Turkey and undid his coalition. He resigned that October.

His years as elder statesman were tarnished by a goatish sexual reputation and revelation of a traffic in honors to bolster party coffers. In 1940 he declined, on grounds of health, a war cabinet post under Winston Churchill (q.v.). Elevated to the House of Lords as Earl Lloyd-George of Dwyfor only in the last months of his life, he died two months before the second surrender of Germany, in 1945.

STANLEY WEINTRAUB

Logistics

Although logistics, the art of supplying and moving armed forces, do not possess the drama of battle, they underlay strategy and determine victory or defeat. As the old axiom goes, "Amateurs study tactics; professionals study logistics."

Navies evolved mechanisms of supply before armies did because sailors could not live off the land as soldiers could. Whatever a vessel and its crew required during its voyage, or at least until its next port of call, had to be stowed aboard from the start (see *Feeding Armed Forces*). Thus, navies developed arsenals and warehouses to take care of all of their needs

Vehicles move no more than two miles per hour on congested roads behind the American lines in France, 1918.

(see *Arsenals*). However, although navies existed in a more demanding logistical environment than did armies, they also enjoyed certain advantages. First, ships provided an excellent means to carry the very supplies their crews required, since water transport has always been the best means to move bulk cargoes. Second, a major logistical concern for armies — horses — was irrelevant to navies.

Armies too tried to exploit water transport when possible, but ultimately they had to rely upon overland communications. The simplest supply method required that men on foot carry their own foodstuffs, as did the Zulu (q.v.) of southern Africa, but since a man can lug only about sixty or seventy pounds at best, this method had inherent limitations. Pack and draft animals increased an army's carrying capacity but added the need for fodder to the army's already great need for food. Armies lessened some supply difficulties by living off the country, and until the twentieth century, this was common practice. In particular, the bulk and weight of fodder for animals prohibited its overland shipment in most circumstances; instead, it had to be gathered in the field during the spring and summer. Horse peoples of the steppe and central Asia raided widely on their grasslands but suffered when they moved into forested or arid lands. It was probably more the lack of sufficient fodder that stopped Attila (q.v.) than the Roman and German forces he encountered. In the early modern era, European armies dependent on horses for transport could campaign only while grass was in the fields, so as fall set in and fodder withered, armies retired to winter quarters.

Feeding men by living off the country was more risky than collecting fodder in the field. Ancient and medieval armies certainly understood the advantages of living off the enemy's resources, of making war feed war. Early modern European armies, however, discovered that as forces grew larger, living off the country could destroy discipline—that men sent out to forage often marauded and deserted. The excesses of foraging soldiers became legendary during the Thirty Years' War (1618–1648) (q.v.). By the late seventeenth century, armies undertook to supply their soldiers with food from regular magazines and field ovens, but this traded one problem for another, since maneuver became more constrained by supply lines. The armies of the French Revolution (q.v.) and Napoleon (q.v.) dispensed with umbilical cords of supply to some extent by again resorting to foraging for food.

The coming of steam-driven transport speeded the movement of supplies. Yet naval logistics became increasingly complicated as steam replaced sails, because ships now frequently called at port to refill their bunkers, and imperial powers required coaling stations prepared around the globe to ensure their mobility. Although the transition to oil-fired boilers in the early twentieth century simplified refueling at sea, the need for supply bases to feed engines as well as crews persisted.

Although ocean-going vessels accelerated long-range transport, river steamers and railroads could rarely bring supplies right up to an army on the move. Moreover, railroads were notoriously fragile supply lines, since rails and bridges made tempting targets for enemy raiders and could easily be destroyed as an army retreated. Thus, horses remained indispensable to link river ports and railheads with armies, and horse transportation still limited the speed of advance. During the Franco-Prussian War (q.v.), and even in World War I (q.v.), the advancing Germans outstripped railroads and wagons and thus relied very much on what they could take from French fields.

The internal combustion engine transformed the logistical environment of warfare on land more radically than steam power did. Trucks proved essential in World War I, which was probably the first war in which the main forces depended entirely upon supplies shipped in from the rear. Trucks, perhaps even more than tanks, made the mobile warfare of World War II (q.v.) possible. But although trucks opened up new possibilities they were not without limitations. When Erwin Rommel (q.v.) ground to a halt at El Alamein (q.v.), it had a great deal to do with the fact that he had exceeded the maximum range at which his trucks could ferry supplies to the Afrika Korps.

The emphasis on motorized transport created a whole new logistical need for armies: petroleum fuel and lubricants. For U.S. land and air forces in Europe during World War II, this amounted to 37 percent by weight of supplies shipped, making it the single greatest burden on the supply system. And modern armies also have increased needs for ammunition. Until the mid–nineteenth century, provided an army did not undertake a siege, it could probably conduct a campaign with the powder and shot it carried with it at the start. In contrast, modern weapons shoot off vast quantities of ammunition, making resupply a major logistical task.

Since World War II, air transport has helped to move troops and matériel. Göring's failed promise to supply German forces at Stalingrad (q.v.) by air in 1942–1943 demonstrated the inability of airplanes to keep up a steady flow of supplies before 1945. Today, although the great mass of war matériel must still move by water or overland, huge cargo planes can rapidly deploy the supply necessary for small forces or ship in selected key cargoes for larger forces; they did both during the Gulf War (q.v.). Still, aircraft have proved more valuable in moving troops than matériel, because the physics of air transport makes the carrying of bulk cargo difficult and expensive.

JOHN A. LYNN

John A. Lynn, *Feeding Mars* (1993); Martin van Creveld, *Supplying War* (1977).

Looting/Plunder/Booty

Today looting and plunder would be seen as immoral and dangerous to discipline (q.v.), but they have often been integral to the war effort as an incentive to troops and even as the handmaiden of operational plans.

At times when many soldiers did not fight for cause or country, the promise of material reward played a great role in convincing men to enlist in hopes of making their fortunes, or at least making a living in a world that provided them few opportunities. Commanders also used the hope of booty to gain compliance from their men in dangerous actions. The fruits of battle could be the riches in the enemy's baggage train or the wealth of the country laid open to exploitation by defeat. To some extent, desire for plunder explains why soldiers were allowed to sack towns that failed to surrender to besieging armies in a timely fashion. Men who undertook the deadly business of storming a breach deserved some expectation of booty, and the usual early modern practice was to allow them three days after a successful storming to do as they would.

The rapacious behavior of troops and the desolation they caused could play into a commander's goals. Allowing troops to sack a city that had held out too long made an example of it. Witnessing its sorry fate, other towns would think twice before resisting. Such was the case after the brutal sack of Magdeburg in 1631. The conduct of Spartan troops in Attica and the rapacious mounted raids, or *chevauchées*, carried out by English troops during the Hundred Years' War (q.v.) were designed to ruin the enemy's lands and draw him out from behind fortress walls. Organized devastation by troops can also be designed both to deny supplies to an enemy and to intimidate a hostile population. Both the devastation of the Palatinate (1688–1689) by Louis XIV (q.v.) and William T. Sherman's (q.v.) campaigns after the fall of Atlanta (1864–1865) appealed to such motives. Although such policies may have seemed brutally rational to those who formed them, they must have looked very much like senseless pillage to the victims of destruction.

Pillage also served the goals of policy by supporting armies in the field. European forces exacted contributions, or payments in money or kind imposed by an army upon a hostile or even neutral population unfortunate enough to lie in their path. Contributions amounted to little more than extortion enforced with the threat that uncooperative villages and towns would be burned. Once Albrecht von Wallenstein (q.v.) systematized the collection of contributions to support his army in the Thirty Years' War (1618–1648) (q.v.), they became a common military practice into the nineteenth century. German troops invading France during the Franco-Prussian War (1870–1871) (q.v.) imposed contributions on hapless towns. The practice of maintaining an army by looting extended far beyond Europe. In India, the Marathas led by their great ruler Shivaji (1630–1680) carried out looting raids against Mughal (q.v.) territory. His raids were part of his policy of imposing a tax on Mughal lands.

But if looting could be a tool of policy, it might also mark a state's incapacity to supply its troops. Unpaid and unfed troops turned ugly. If the soldier felt that he had entered a bargain that promised him pay and food in return for loyal service and obedience, then when the army failed to live up to its terms of the deal, there was no reason for the soldier to respect his commitment. Soldiers who defied their commanders and rampaged over early modern Europe, which occurred during the Thirty Years' War, usually rebelled because they were themselves the victims of hunger (see *Logistics* and *Feeding Armed Forces*). As states expanded their armies beyond the capacity of military administration to care for them, pillage seemed an inevitable result. So at times, soldiers who turned to pillage did so to escape their own misery.

Unfortunately, but not surprisingly, once soldiers turned to pillage, the bonds of decency tended to dissolve. When people defended their homes and harvests, they became the targets of violence — killing went hand in hand with the search for booty. Marauding soldiers intent on discovering hidden wealth employed torture to force information out of unfortunate victims. And beyond food and valuables, women also rated as booty (see *Rape*).

Although looting was more integral to military conduct in the past, it did not disappear in the twentieth century. Just as Napoleon plundered Italian art treasures and Egyptian antiquities during his victorious campaigns of 1796–1799, the Nazis seized artworks in countries that they occupied during World War II. Such theft may have been carried out in a more genteel manner, but it was theft nonetheless.

JOHN A. LYNN

John A. Lynn, *Feeding Mars* (1993); Fritz Redlich, *De praeda militari: Looting and Booty 1500–1815* (1956).

Louis XIV

1638–1715, French Monarch and War Leader

Louis XIV reigned over France during a period of French military preeminence. He came to the throne just before his fifth birthday. At first his Spanish mother served as regent, and the Italian-born first minister Cardinal Mazarin guided policy and effectively instructed Louis in affairs of state. When Mazarin died in 1661, Louis proclaimed that he would have no first minister; thus began his fifty-four-year personal reign.

On his deathbed, Louis confessed to his young successor that he had "loved war too much." Well over half his reign witnessed major armed conflicts, including the War of Devolution (1667–1668), the Dutch War (1672–1678), the War of the Grand Alliance (1688–1697) (q.v.), and the War of the Spanish Succession (1701–1714) (q.v.). In addition, many of the years of "peace" brought lesser struggles, such as when the French seized Strasbourg in 1681 and Luxembourg in 1684.

A search for glory drove Louis's foreign policy, but this was not as frivolous as it might seem, since glory resulted from accomplishment and brought international respect, and certainly Louis was not the only monarch of his day to pursue it. Glory at first demanded conquest, and his first two major wars were devoted to that end. After the Dutch War he was hailed both as Louis the Great and as the Sun King, in reference to the fact that he took the sun as his emblem. But after that war, he aimed more at creating defensible frontiers for his lands than at adding to them. However, he tried to secure his borders by seizing additional bits and pieces, and this gave his defensive policy an aggressive thrust: to the rest of Europe he seemed bent on hegemony. The War of the Grand Alliance began precisely when Louis grabbed one more fortress — Philipsbourg — and sought to bully the Germans into accepting previous acquisitions. The Sun King fought his last conflict, the War of the Spanish Succession, not to win new lands for himself but to secure the Spanish crown for his grandson, Philip of Anjou. In the sense that Philip secured the monarchy by the end of the war, Louis succeeded, although it cost France a great deal to put that Bourbon prince on the Spanish throne.

Immensely concerned with his army, Louis concentrated on the details of administration, drill, and siege warfare. So adamant was he to inspect his troops that one courtier called him "the king of reviews." He was served by the capable although brutal war minister, the marquis de Louvois (q.v.), who, along with his father and previous war minister Michel Le Tellier, did much to rationalize French administration and supply. Louis never commanded a field battle, but he attended many of the sieges conducted by his great military engineer, Sébastien le Prestre de Vauban (q.v.). Vauban suited Louis's desire to render France impenetrable. With Louis's strong support, Vauban buttressed the frontier between France and the Spanish Netherlands (Belgium and Luxembourg today) with the "pré carré," a term meaning both a square and a dueling field, designed by the great engineer as a double line of mutually supporting fortifications built in the elaborate star-shaped pattern associated with his name.

Louis made France the premier European power in the second half of the seventeenth century, but he left it exhausted and bankrupt by the time of his death.

JOHN A. LYNN

Andrew Lossky, *Louis XIV and the French Monarchy* (1994); John B. Wolf, *Louis XIV* (1968).

Louvois, François-Michel Le Tellier, Marquis de

1641–1691, *French War Minister*

Son of Michel Le Tellier, who was secretary of state for war during the minority of Louis XIV (q.v.) and later became one of his principal ministers, Louvois gradually replaced his aging father in both of these capacities. Arrogant, licentious, indefatigable, a believer in military power as a solution to everything, Louvois held ideas that coincided generally with those of the king, and where they did not, Louvois once summarized his philosophy in a letter to an overzealous subordinate: "His Majesty must not be served any better than he wants to be!" Yet Louvois built up a loyal following and encouraged independent experts such as Vauban (q.v.).

Louvois bears primary responsibility for some of Louis XIV's most heavy-handed policies, such as the reunions (annexations by judicial decree in peacetime of territories adjacent to France's eastern frontier), the dragonnades (quartering of unruly soldiers on his Huguenot subjects until they agreed to convert to Catholicism), and the devastation of the Palatinate (scorched earth policies by his army in Germany at the beginning of the War of the League of Augsburg). There are signs that the king became disenchanted with Louvois and with his conduct of this war, but it is doubtful whether Louis XIV would ever have had the courage to dismiss him, had he not succumbed to a heart attack in 1691.

PAUL SONNINO

Ludendorff, Erich

1865–1937, *German General*

Erich Ludendorff embodied the strengths and weaknesses of the imperial German army in the twentieth century. He is frequently described as representing everything negative in the rising generation of officers: bourgeois by birth, specialist by training, and philistine by instinct. Appointed head of the Mobilization and Deployment Section of the General Staff in 1908, he was a leading advocate of expanding the army. The War Ministry's reluctance to support that policy reflected concerns wider than the often-cited reluctance to risk diluting the officer corps with social undesirables. Ludendorff did succeed in getting army estimates increased in the face of a Reichstag whose parties, from Right to Left, above all disliked voting for taxes. He paid the price of his convictions in 1913 by being transferred to command an undistinguished regiment in the industrial city of Düsseldorf — a kind of punitive assignment frequently used to teach recalcitrants their manners.

When war broke out in August 1914, Ludendorff was restored to favor as deputy chief of staff to the Second Army. On August 8, he proved he was more than a desk soldier, rallying demoralized troops to play a crucial role in the capture of the Belgian fortress of Liège. On August 22 he was assigned as chief of staff to the Eighth Army in East Prussia.

Ludendorff's exact role in planning and executing the Battle of Tannenberg (q.v.) remains debatable. What is certain is his emergence as a national hero whose symbiotic relationship with Field Marshal Paul von Hindenburg (q.v.) seemed to symbolize the synthesis of the best of the old Germany and the new. Hindenburg supplied the character, Ludendorff the intelligence. Both men grew increasingly committed to an "eastern" solution to the strategic dilemma Germany faced by the end of 1914. Ludendorff had entered the war as a committed "westerner." But in the aftermath of the victories of Tannenberg, the Masurian Lakes, and in southern Poland, he could hardly be blamed for wondering what might be achieved with even a few fresh corps.

Personal ambition reinforced professional conviction. Ludendorff's increasingly open coveting of Erich von Falkenhayn's (q.v.) post as chief of the General Staff earned him widespread enmity among his colleagues and, in 1915, relegation to the sidelines as chief of staff to a mired German-Austrian army operating in a secondary theater.

But eventually, Falkenhayn proved the author of his own downfall when he launched the attack against Verdun (q.v.) in January 1916. Combined with the Allied offensive on the Somme (q.v.) six months later,

the result was the kind of attritional war that Germany had little chance of winning.

On August 29, 1916, Hindenburg was appointed chief of the General Staff with Ludendorff as his deputy. It was clear where the real power rested: Ludendorff was responsible for developing and enacting the Hindenburg Program, designed to put what remained of Germany's human and material resources entirely at the service of the war effort. Ludendorff took the lead in overhauling the army's tactical doctrines. Going in person to the front to discover what was going wrong, he sponsored a system of flexible defense that took heavy toll of the French and the British armies in 1917. Ludendorff also played an active part in German politics. His involvement was facilitated by the inability of Kaiser Wilhelm II to fulfill the role of a pivot figure, above the everyday frictions between soldiers and statesmen, and by the fierce rivalry among the political parties, which prevented the emergence of any effective civilian rival. In July 1917, Chancellor Theobald von Bethmann-Hollweg was dismissed. His nondescript successors did little but dance to Ludendorff's piping.

The general was for a time successful in orchestrating public support for the war effort. Trade unions and industrialists alike accepted an arms program so comprehensive that within months the impossibility of its execution was obvious. They accepted the starvation of their families in the Hunger Winter of 1917. They accepted the militarization of everyday life to a degree unthinkable in 1914. But this effort could be no more than temporary: the last spark of an exhausted system.

Ludendorff was committed less to ruling Germany than to winning the war. The defeat of the Italians at Caporetto (q.v.) in October 1917 and the collapse of Russia's provisional government at almost the same time offered opportunities for negotiation. Even the submarine campaign of 1917 might have been turned to advantage. At the start of 1918 Germany had the option of offering to end unrestricted submarine warfare and withdraw from all or part of its western conquests. Instead, with Ludendorff in the driver's seat, the Second Reich sought to integrate central and eastern Europe into an empire, a stable base for the next round of conflict for world power, while still fighting flat out in the west.

The German army had developed a set of offensive tactics that initially broke open every front to which they were applied. Ludendorff, however, possessed no equivalent strategic concepts. "Punch a hole and let the rest follow," the famous aphorism for the German offensive of March 1918, brought initial victories that neither troops nor generals could exploit (see *Ludendorff Offensive*). Instead, exhausted frontline units were driven back by massive Allied counterattacks. His artifice at an end, Ludendorff first called for peace, then argued for a fight to the finish, and finally on October 26, 1918, resigned his post and fled to Sweden. Apart from a figurehead role in the Munich putsch of 1923, his postwar political career was inconsequential.

From 1914 to 1918 Erich Ludendorff remained prisoner of his faith in the decisive battle. He refused to face the fact that a great power's armed forces could not be crushed by the combinations of mobility and firepower existing between 1914 and 1918; instead, he continued to insist that he had never been given quite enough resources to achieve the triumph glimmering over the horizon. For all his native ability and General Staff training, Ludendorff never rose above the mental level of an infantry colonel.

DENNIS E. SHOWALTER

Martin Kitchen, *The Silent Dictatorship: The Politics of the German High Command Under Hindenburg and Ludendorff, 1916–1918* (1976); Norman Stone, "Ludendorff," in *The War Lords: Military Commanders of the Twentieth Century* (1976).

Ludendorff Offensive

March 21–July 15, 1918

Quartermaster General Erich Ludendorff (q.v.) scheduled the beginning of Germany's great 1918 gamble for victory on the Western Front in World War I (q.v.) for the first day of spring, March 21. Success depended on delivering a knockout blow before the arrival of millions of Americans in the summer. The offensive, code-named Michael, struck the sector where British and French forces joined, and matched three fresh German armies against one overstretched British army and part of another. After an intensive and carefully phased bombardment, mixing high explosive and poison gas, elite storm troops went forward. Avoiding strongpoints, they headed for the rear, leaving the mopping up to the conventional infantry. A famously thick fog aided their progress.

By the third day of the battle, the Germans had opened a fifty-mile-wide gap and were pouring into open country: Ludendorff had broken the long trench stalemate — but he had not severed the connection between the Allied armies. Now heavy losses and fatigue took their toll; hungry soldiers stopped to loot British supply dumps. After a forty-mile advance, Ludendorff's tactical masterpiece faded to strategic inconsequence.

Meanwhile, on March 26, the desperate Allies agreed on a step they should have taken long before: putting their armies under a single commander, Ferdinand Foch (q.v.). He would deftly coordinate a defense that, several times in that menacing spring, seemed on the verge of collapse. Three German "Paris guns" with a seventy-five-mile range bombarded the capital. Ludendorff launched five more offensives, all on the March 21 model: Arras (March 28), which failed; the Lys River in Flanders (April 9), which threatened to force the British back to the Channel ports; and the breakthrough at the Chemin des Dames (May 27), which reached the Marne, just forty-odd miles from Paris. Americans helped to stop Ludendorff's exhausted divisions at Belleau Wood and Château-Thierry: he was clearly running out of time. His Oise attack (June 9) was a costly waste. Then, on July 15, Ludendorff made his final throw of the dice, seeking to pinch off Reims. This time the French turned his own defense-in-depth tactics against him, and his last offensive subsided in the chalky downlands of Champagne. Since March 21, Germany had suffered close to a million irreplaceable casualties — and the Americans were now arriving in France at the rate of 300,000 a month. For the Allies, it was the arithmetic of victory.

ROBERT COWLEY

M

MacArthur, Douglas

1880–1964, U.S. General

Douglas MacArthur was, to paraphrase Charles Dickens, the best of generals and the worst of generals. At his best, in both World War II (q.v.) and the Korean War (q.v.), he showed a mastery of the operational art unmatched by any other American general in the twentieth century. At his worst, he showed appalling lapses of strategic judgment and a disturbing lack of propriety in his relationship with the national command authority.

MacArthur was destined to be a military leader. His father was a general officer before him, and family connections eased his way to high rank. During World War I (q.v.), he earned a dazzling array of combat decorations. After the war, he became the youngest superintendent ever at West Point, and from 1930 to 1935 he was the longest-serving chief of staff of the army up to that time. Returning to the Philippines, where his father had been military governor and where he himself had already served three tours of duty, he spent his first period of retirement developing a Filipino national army.

The best and the worst were yet to come. In July 1941, as relations with Japan reached a crisis point, President Franklin D. Roosevelt (q.v.) recalled MacArthur to active duty as commander of U.S. Army Forces in the Far East. On December 8, 1941 (December 7 in Oahu), nine hours after the Pearl Harbor (q.v.) attack, a Japanese air raid destroyed most of his air force in the Philippines.

Though MacArthur was not wholly to blame for this debacle, he had badly misjudged Japanese capabilities and intentions, and he remained a remarkably passive commander on the fateful day. Yet, unlike the commanders at Pearl Harbor, he was not cashiered. The reason is not far to seek: in the subsequent resistance to the Japanese invasion of the Philippines, MacArthur's image had taken on heroic dimensions in the American public eye.

In truth MacArthur had mishandled the defense against the invasion as well, opting to meet Japanese amphibious assaults at the beaches, despite the grave qualitative deficiencies of the new Filipino army and despite the destruction of his air force. The result was yet another fiasco. MacArthur ordered a fallback to Bataan just in time, but supplies allocated forward were lost, thus diminishing the chances of a prolonged defense.

Roosevelt in March 1942 ordered the evacuation of MacArthur to Australia. Given command of Allied forces in the Southwest Pacific, the general stumbled in the initial operations to halt the Japanese advance in New Guinea, where he had little understanding of the difficult conditions that his soldiers faced. But he then hit his stride with a brilliant campaign in 1943 and 1944 that propelled his forces along the New Guinea coast and onto islands to the north.

MacArthur's success put him in a position to redeem his celebrated pledge of 1942 to return to the Philippines, though first he had to outmaneuver planners who wanted to bypass Luzon. For a long time MacArthur had complained about being starved of resources by Washington, but by the time that he reached the Philippines he commanded a force larger than the United States had committed to any operation in Europe before the invasion of France. Rather than simply contain strongholds of Japanese resistance on Luzon and other islands, he used his large force to carry out a bloody reconquest of the whole archipelago.

If the United States had gone on to invade Japan itself, MacArthur would have commanded the largest, and probably the bloodiest, American operation of World War II (see *Operation Downfall*). But the dropping of the atomic bombs made such an invasion unnecessary, and MacArthur, as the supreme commander of the Allied occupation of Japan, became a man of peace and reform among the Japanese. No American has had so much unmediated power over so many people as MacArthur did in Japan from 1945 to 1951, and for the most part he used that power beneficently, with positive effects that survive to this day.

Though the Japanese had long regarded the Korean peninsula as crucial to their security, MacArthur was not sensitive to the threat that loomed there. His occupation army in Japan was utterly unprepared for combat. When the Korean War broke out in June 1950, MacArthur was once again taken by surprise, and the forces under his command were once again outmatched.

This time it did not take long for MacArthur to bring about a reversal of strategic fortunes. His audacious operation at Inchon in September 1950 led to the near decimation of the North Korean army. Inchon, because of high tides and the configuration of its harbor, was among the worst places in the world for an amphibious assault. But precisely for that reason, the North Koreans were stunned by what hit them there.

MacArthur's success inflated his already swollen ego and encouraged a dangerous euphoria in Washington. There was now little question that MacArthur should drive into North Korea and reunite the peninsula under UN auspices. When President Harry Truman broached the issue of potential Chinese Communist intervention, MacArthur flatly dismissed the possibility. Once again, as in 1941, he badly misjudged the intentions and capabilities of an Asian adversary. When the Chinese did intervene, the result was the worst debacle in American military history.

MacArthur then lost his poise. Although General Matthew Ridgway (q.v.) was able to stabilize the military situation in Korea in early 1951, MacArthur insisted that there was no good strategic alternative to taking the war directly to China. After several months of vacillation in Washington, General Omar Bradley (q.v.), the chairman of the Joint Chiefs of Staff, delivered the prudent judgment that a wider war with China would be "the wrong war, at the wrong place, at the wrong time, and with the wrong enemy."

Meanwhile, MacArthur had lost all sense of propriety in his dealings with the Truman administration. Among his many acts of insubordination, MacArthur undertook military operations that went beyond those authorized; he made pronouncements to foreign leaders that undercut the foreign policy of his own government; and he openly appealed to domestic critics of his commander in chief, over Truman's head. It is no wonder that the president finally summoned up the political courage to fire MacArthur in April 1951.

MacArthur received a hero's welcome upon his return to the United States, where he had not set foot since 1937. In those fourteen years, he had become a Pacific Rim visionary, and in 1951 he was able to cause some embarrassment to the efforts of the Truman administration to sustain the Europe-first orientation of American policy and strategy. But MacArthur's meteoric career was over, at long last.

BRADFORD A. LEE

D. Clayton James, *The Years of MacArthur*, 3 vols. (1970, 1975, 1985); Gavin Long, *MacArthur as Military Commander* (1969); Michael Schaller, *Douglas MacArthur: The Far Eastern General* (1989).

Macedonians

The origin of the Macedonians is lost in the realm of myth. At some point they migrated out of the mountainous Balkan interior and settled in several areas of what is now northwestern Greece. By about 650 B.C., one group of Macedonians was organized under the leadership of the Argead family and became established in the plain just west of the later city of Thessaloniki. These lowland Macedonians eventually absorbed the highland Macedonians of the western mountains to become a formidable Balkan power.

The ethnicity of the Macedonians is a matter of dispute. Their language is unknown to us and may never have achieved written form, but, according to some ancient observers, it was sufficiently different from standard Greek to require translators. The overwhelming evidence from antiquity is that they were perceived by contemporary and later writers as a people different from the Greeks. Whatever the ethnicity of the Macedonians and their kings, some segments of their society, including the royal house, became Hellenized by the end of the fifth century B.C. Their new capital at Pella was graced by the work of Greek architects, artists, poets, and philosophers.

Beneath this facade of Greek culture were a tough

lot of farmers and mountain people. When one thinks of the Macedonian army, the superb fighting machine of Philip II (q.v.) and Alexander the Great (q.v.) comes to mind. Yet the Macedonian military forces before the age of Philip were nondescript, poorly disciplined, and ill equipped, a home force that was largely ineffective against Greek hoplites (q.v.) and neighboring Balkan tribal raiders. During the Peloponnesian War (q.v.) they fought erratically against Greeks who were intent on controlling Macedonia's rich timber resources. During the first half of the fourth century B.C., the kingdom was in a precarious state because of its vulnerability to invasion from neighboring city-states and tribes.

The potential for military success was realized with the emergence of Philip II. It is testimony to Philip's genius that within less than a decade (359–350 B.C.) he refashioned the army into a major military force loyal to him, and, for the first time, made the Macedonian army a tool for conquest. In turn, veterans were rewarded with booty and land. It was not only a personal army, but also one in whose service Macedonians achieved status and an expression of their nationality. Much of Alexander's success is due to the merging of his own military and personal skills with the superb force developed by his father.

The Macedonians responded well to this personal monarchy. In the five centuries of their independent history in antiquity, they were ruled by only two royal dynasties, which produced major figures such as Philip II, Alexander the Great, and Philip V, who in turn conquered the Greek city-states, eradicated the Persian Empire, and appeared to threaten Rome. After a prolonged struggle, the Romans ended Macedonian independence in 167 B.C. and absorbed the former kingdom into their expanding Mediterranean realm, thereby terminating the autonomy of what may have been Europe's earliest national state.

EUGENE N. BORZA

Machiavelli, Niccolò

1469–1527, *Italian Political Theorist*

This Renaissance Florentine was best known for his unblinking analysis of political power, *The Prince* (probably written in 1513; published in 1532). Frustrated as a government official with the Florentine Republic's relative helplessness during the Italian Wars (q.v.), from 1505 Niccolò Machiavelli experi-

mented with a homegrown infantry militia. Here his political concerns were as much internal as external; with this militia Machiavelli hoped to end Florence's dependence on mercenary captains. However, when put to the test against Spanish veterans at the siege of Prato in 1512, Machiavelli's militia failed miserably. The disaster ended the regime in Florence — and Machiavelli's active career. Exiled to his boring country farm, Machiavelli picked up his pen and wrote his way to fame. His *Art of War* (1521) argued for a return to Roman military virtues. Immediately successful, its then-novel theme is now a basic assumption: stable states require a disciplined military, based on citizens-in-arms.

THOMAS F. ARNOLD

Maginot Line

The Maginot line was named after André Maginot (1877–1932), a politician who served in World War I (q.v.) until wounded in November 1914. He used crutches and walking sticks for the remainder of his life. While serving after World War I as France's minister of war and then as president of the Chamber of Deputies' Army Commission, he helped complete plans for the defensive line along the northeastern frontier and obtain funds to build it.

The main fortifications of the Maginot line extended from La Ferté (thirty kilometers east of Sedan) to the Rhine River, but fortifications also stretched along the Rhine and along the Italian frontier. The fortifications on the northeast frontier included twenty-two huge underground fortresses and thirty-six smaller fortresses, as well as many blockhouses and bunkers. The French placed most of their largest fortresses in the northeast because of their desire to protect the large population, key industries, and abundant natural resources located near the Moselle valley.

The first attack by the Germans against the Maginot line itself occurred on May 16, 1940, and was directed against the isolated fortifications at La Ferté on the extreme western tip of the line. The Germans managed to capture the casemates only after four days of hard fighting, and with the support of large amounts of heavy artillery and high-velocity 88-mm fire. Despite the use of massive force, the Germans failed to capture a single major fortress before the armistice on June 25. Though designed to withstand attacks from Germany, the Maginot line fortresses could be defended against attacks from the rear; consequently, the Americans had no easy task fighting their way through the line in 1944–1945.

ROBERT A. DOUGHTY

Magyars

Moving west from Central Asia in the early 890s, the Magyars (Hungarians) entered the Carpathian basin, where the deep plain allowed them to support their nomadic lifestyle. Combining the strategic mobility provided by grass-fed ponies with battle tactics based on mounted archers using composite bows, the Magyars launched destructive raids that penetrated into northern Germany, France, and Italy from 898 to 954.

Ultimately, the Magyars were unable to solve the logistical problem of maintaining an adequate force of mounted archers on the limited area of deep plain available in the Carpathian basin. The success of Magyar raids therefore became dependent on political divisions in target areas, while their leaders increasingly relied on successful expeditions to maintain wealth and prestige. Declining forces and improved western European defenses finally forced the Magyars to seek a decisive battle (Lechfeld, 955 [q.v.]), which they lost. The survivors converted to Latin Christianity and established the kingdom of Hungary, providing western Europe with an effective buffer against further attack until the Battle of Mohács (1526) (q.v.).

EDWARD J. SCHOENFELD

Mahan, Alfred Thayer

1840–1914, U.S. Naval Historian

Alfred Thayer Mahan's father was Dennis Hart Mahan, who as professor at West Point was instrumental in framing the intellectual conceptions of many army officers who fought in the American Civil War (q.v.). Mahan the younger eventually decided on a naval career and graduated second in his class from the Naval Academy in 1859. Mahan's experiences in the Civil War were undistinguished: he spent most of the war on blockade patrols off the Confederate coasts — an experience that his writings on the Royal Navy's blockades of France would serve to justify.

In 1884 Stephen B. Luce, first president of the Naval War College at Newport, Rhode Island, persuaded Mahan to abandon sea duty for teaching. But Mahan's contribution to the U.S. Navy lay not only in the intellectual ferment that resulted from his famous studies on the contribution of sea power to British victories over the French from the late seventeenth century through Napoleon's (q.v.) defeat. He arrived at Newport to discover that Luce had been recalled to sea and that Mahan was now not only the college's chief instructor, but its president as well. And as such he played an important role in keeping the world's first naval war college in business.

Mahan also ran up against considerable opposition to the idea that naval officers might write books. But write Mahan did. The publication of his Newport lectures, reworked into book form as *The Influence of Sea Power upon History, 1660–1783*, launched the writing career of a man who was to have great influence on how navies and strategists thought about naval war in the twentieth century.

One should not make the mistake of considering Mahan a historian; even though he was president of the American Historical Association, he was not particularly interested in research or an unbiased analysis of the facts. Rather, in a number of forums, he propagated the idea that sea power was essential for great power status and emphasized, as had his father, the value of the central position and interior lines. But what navies, then and now, found particularly congenial was his emphasis on the concentration of naval forces into a main battle fleet, a dismissal of cruiser warfare (a raiding strategy), and an emphasis on the battleship. Consequently, according to Mahan, the destruction of the enemy's fleet was the main, if not the sole, objective of naval warfare.

It is doubtful, however, that Mahan's writings exercised a decisive influence over the direction that naval building took in the period from 1890 to 1914. Rather, his theoretical arguments provided reasoning that confirmed the inclination of admirals and naval-minded policy makers. Ironically, Mahan's greatest influence came in the conduct of submarine operations during World War I (q.v.) and World War II (q.v.). In those two conflicts his denigration of cruiser warfare negatively affected the adaptation of the British and American navies to the terrible threat posed by the German submarines. On the other hand, the German navy in both wars ended up minimizing the potential of the submarine in its preparations for war. Instead, following Mahan's arguments, the Germans emphasized the construction of a great battle fleet in the hope that they could win a decisive naval battle against their opponents. Thus, the German navy went to war with battle fleets that had little hope of winning such a battle and with submarine forces that represented a threat to which Allied navies could adapt — barely.

WILLIAMSON MURRAY

Mahmud of Ghazna

971–1030, Sultan of the Ghaznavid Dynasty

The Ghaznavids were the first slave group to establish its own dynasty (see *Slavery, Military*). In 998, Mahmud inherited from his father, Sebüktigin (a Turkish commander in the service of the Samanid dynasty of Bukhara), a sizable territory based in Ghazna in central Afghanistan. By the following year, his armies had occupied Khurasan (in eastern Iran), and he had asserted his independence from the Samanids. Over the next two decades, his military expeditions enabled him to expand into western Iran. He also seized territories as far east as Lahore and as far south as Sistan and even compelled southern Iran, including Isfahan, into accepting a tributary status.

With a base in Afghanistan, Mahmud next attacked North India and forced Indian princes to provide tribute. He campaigned repeatedly in the Punjab and the Sind and set the stage for the first substantial Muslim presence in India. His army was composed of slaves, mercenaries, and volunteers of diverse ethnic origins. He and later Ghaznavid rulers did not hesitate to recruit Arabs, Kurds, Turks, and Persians into their armies, whose greatest asset was their cavalry. Mahmud learned from the Indians how to use the elephant in warfare and in one battle reputedly employed thirteen hundred elephants to intimidate the enemy. By the end of his reign, he had carved out one of the largest domains in Asia, stretching from North India through Afghanistan and into Iran. His successors were unable to stave off new and more powerful Turkic groups, including the Seljuk Turks.

MORRIS ROSSABI

Manchus

In 1644, with the help of a turncoat Chinese general, the Manchus captured Peking from rebels who had already effectively overthrown the Ming dynasty (1368–1644). Although it took another forty years before they could convincingly assert legitimacy as the bearers of the Mandate of Heaven by reuniting China, including the south and Taiwan, under their control, the Manchus then ruled China as the Ch'ing dynasty until 1911.

Ethnically the Manchus were descended from the same Tungusic tribes, the Jürchens, who in the twelfth century had driven the Sung court south and ruled north China as the Chin dynasty. Sometimes erroneously confused with the Mongols (q.v.), whose record as an alien dynasty of all China they first emulated and later surpassed, the Manchus were not steppe nomads but came from a mixed pastoral, hunting and farming economy based in what is now known as China's "three northeastern provinces"; this region is sometimes called Manchuria, after the Japanese puppet state of Manchukuo established there during the 1930s.

As the Ming dynasty began to lose its grip toward the end of the sixteenth century, a young Jürchen nobleman named Nurhaci (1559–1626) gradually united the tribes across the northeast by conquest, diplomacy, and marriage alliance. In 1601 he organized his troops and their families into eight hereditary groups known as "banners," after the colors of the flags by which they were distinguished (yellow, white, red, and blue — four plain, and four bordered in a contrasting color). Later eight Mongol and eight Chinese martial banners were added to the original eight Manchu units. These were the Manchus' basic divisions of military and administrative organization and formed the nucleus of the Later Chin dynasty proclaimed by Nurhaci in 1616 as a declaration of intent to conquer China. The banner organization survived the 1644 conquest, and the bannermen, or members of the banner groups, became part of a hereditary Ch'ing elite separate from the scholar-officials whose high social position rested on examination success. Granted lands or stipends by the dynasty, and garrisoned in Peking and at strategic points around China, some bannermen gradually became impoverished and lost their special connection to imperial power. Accustomed to state support, many proved unable to support themselves by farming, and became parasites on society who were easy targets of anti-Manchu sentiment among the populace.

The sinicization of the Manchus was a matter of great concern to Ch'ing rulers, because the perceived erosion of Manchu traditions, especially the martial heritage, potentially threatened Ch'ing control in China. Yet Ch'ing rulers experienced great ambivalence about Manchu identity. For reasons of legitimacy they sought to present themselves as thoroughgoing Confucians whose authority stemmed primarily from their moral virtue, their scholarly attainments, and their benevolence as rulers, yet ultimately their power rested on military force. They wished the Manchus to be at once distinct from and merged with their Chinese subjects. Thus they severely punished perceived slurs directed at the Manchus in a "literary inquisition"; they encouraged the study of the Manchu language — Jesuit missionaries at the mid-eighteenth-century Chinese court found it absolutely necessary to learn both Manchu and Chinese — and they sponsored a series of works devoted to the heritage of the Manchus and other frontier peoples. At least until 1800, Ch'ing rulers actively encouraged physical activity such as horseback riding and archery. They staged elaborate hunts, which resembled military drills and were in a sense peacetime dress rehearsals for war. In the 1690s K'ang-hsi (q.v.), the last Ch'ing emperor personally to take part in a battle, made clear the connection between hunting and warfare when he openly sought to hunt down his adversary, Galdan, as though pursuing his prey for sport.

In the eighteenth century, Manchu emperors also devoted considerable effort to incorporating the martial heritage into the mainstream of Chinese cultural activity. Thus after the conquest of Sinkiang (Chinese Central Asia) they implemented a series of triumphal celebrations, involving ritual ceremonies attended by numerous foreign visitors as well as civil and military officials. Victories in battle, the conquests, and the celebrations themselves all were recorded in imperially commissioned commemorative paintings and inscribed monuments that were installed all over the country; the accompanying texts were frequently reproduced.

Yet by redirecting attention to their Manchu identity, the Ch'ing framed their own downfall, for they created among their Chinese subjects a sense of political resentment that, as massive internal rebellions and determined invasion by foreigners beset China during the nineteenth century, took the form of an inchoate nationalism whose first target was themselves (see *Taiping Rebellion*).

Their most lasting legacy to China was the militar-ization that began during the seventeenth-century conquest period and steadily spread throughout the Ch'ing dynasty before completely overtaking Chinese society in the twentieth century.

JOANNA WALEY-COHEN

Pamela K. Crossley, *The Manchus* (1996); Frederic Wakeman, Jr., *The Great Enterprise* (1985).

Manstein, Erich von

1887–1973, German World War II Field Marshal

Erich von Manstein, a captain in World War I (q.v.) who served mainly in staff positions, continued his career in the Weimar years and was a key figure in the German army. From 1935 to 1939 he held important positions in the army's General Staff. In 1939–1940, he contributed to changing the plan for invading the Low Countries, which shifted the main thrust from the northern to the southern wing, the operation that cut off Allied forces coming to aid Holland and Belgium (see *World War II*). After a part in the 1941 thrust toward Leningrad (q.v.), he commanded in the Crimea and in the summer of 1942 took the city of Sevastopol after a bloody siege. His assignment to take Leningrad ended in failure; his next mission, the relief and holding of Stalingrad (q.v.), ended in disaster. Alone of German army commanders, he had endorsed Adolf Hitler's (q.v.) belief that Stalingrad could be held and the surrounded army supplied by air; in his memoirs he covered this up by abundant fakery.

In spite of gaining Germany's last victory in the east in a counteroffensive in February–March 1943, Manstein was relieved a year later. He sat out the war, drawing bribes from Hitler. Massively involved in war crimes, including the mass murder of Jews — which he justified to his soldiers in a special order — Manstein was convicted in 1950 but served only two years of his eighteen-year sentence.

GERHARD L. WEINBERG

Mantzikert, Battle of

August 26, 1071

This battle was the first great Turkish victory over the Byzantines, one that resulted in the Byzantine loss of Anatolia and the settlement and emergence of the first powerful Turkish state there (see *Byzantium*).

On this well-watered site on a plain (today Malazgirt, in eastern Turkey), a decisive battle was fought between an unknown number of Seljuk Turks under the leadership of Sultan Alp Arslan and up to sixty thousand Byzantines under Emperor Romanos IV Diogenes. Romanos sought to drive the Seljuks from endangered Byzantine Anatolia but had not anticipated such a large Seljuk army under the personal leadership of the sultan. Inadequate preparation, logistical problems, ethnic tensions between Byzantines and Armenians, unrest among Byzantine mercenaries, and political and personal rivalries and treachery within the Byzantine forces weakened their abilities. Feigned flight, superior leadership, and mounted archers helped the Seljuks surround Romanos and his forces and compel them to surrender. The ensuing bloody Byzantine civil war resulted in the deposition and death of Romanos IV and opened the way for the Seljuk conquest of Anatolia within a decade and its ultimate transformation into a Turkish heartland.

WALTER E. KAEGI

Mao Tse-tung

1893–1976, *Chinese Revolutionary War leader*

Unlike Napoleon (q.v.), Mao Tse-tung never directly commanded a decisive battle, and he therefore cannot be classed as one of the world's great generals. Nonetheless, if Mao's contributions to Marxist theory and his performance as ruler have been disparaged, his reputation as a thinker about military affairs has remained intact. It was Mao who elaborated the principles of revolutionary war and provided the Chinese Communist Party with a strategy to seize power.

Mao's awakening to the importance of military power came in the late 1920s. Having grown up in comfortable rural circumstances, Mao attended a modern school in Changsha, the provincial capital of his native province of Hunan in south-central China. He became involved in radical student activities in the late 1910s and 1920s and was present at the founding of the Chinese Communist Party in 1921. Like all early Chinese Communists, he initially did not question that revolutions were brought about by uprisings in urban centers, as was true for the October Revolution in Russia. In 1926 and 1927, at the closure of a period of large-scale civil war when Chiang Kai-shek (q.v.), who had succeeded Sun Yat-sen as Nationalist leader, had deployed modern armies to seize power

and crush the Communists with whom he had first cooperated, Mao first concluded that China's countryside, and not its cities, was where China's revolution should begin. He also decided that "power comes out of the barrel of a gun." This opened the door to a strategy of Communist revolution integrated with military conquest.

The most salient aspects of revolutionary war are as follows. The party had to be in control over the military. Although the relation between the army and the party was never simply one of subordination, party control over the army was real. As soon as Mao set up guerrilla forces, he also instituted a commissar system. Soldiers were required to manifest Communist ideology in their behavior. The party always was the final arbiter over policy and military strategy.

From the fate of past peasant rebellions, Mao drew the conclusion that a band of guerrillas roaming the country could not secure revolutionary success. Base areas not only provided Communist armies with places for rest and the party leadership with a safe haven; at these locations, much of the population was drawn into a three-tiered system of local self-defense forces, militias, and regular armies, thus providing the military with an ample supply of personnel. Also, at base areas the movement's revolutionary social, economic, and political policies were put into effect. In Mao's words, base areas were "the buttocks of the revolution."

Revolutionary war also embraces a varied set of strategic and tactical principles for combat. Mao's principles stipulated that the goal of warfare was not the defense of territory, but the preservation of Communist forces and the collapse of those of the opponent. If a territory could not be held, it would be given up. Communists attacked only when they had significant superiority of troops, when they had the initiative, and when technical superiority could be nullified by close combat. Even though revolutionary war has been closely associated with guerrilla war, Mao Tse-tung always placed it in the context of mobile and conventional warfare.

Mao, for instance, argued in 1938 in "On Protracted War" that the fight against the Japanese would go through three phases. In the first phase of fighting the Japanese would advance to a standstill. Guerrilla warfare would be most important during the second phase of stalemate, after Japanese supply lines became stretched out and manpower scarce and when Chinese forces were building up their strength. Large armies fighting conventionally would destroy the enemy in the final offensive phase.

These ideas flowed naturally out of Communist experiences with Nationalist attacks on the Kiangsi Soviet in central China in the first half of the 1930s. The first attacks had been defeated by Mao's policy of mobile warfare and "luring the enemy in deep." Positional defense, however, was attempted. Even though other reasons contributed to the Communists' defeat, the Nationalists did force the Communists to leave the Soviet and begin the Long March in the autumn of 1934. Because Mao had led the Soviet's military during the first attacks but not the last, the defeat did give Mao the opportunity to oust his opponents and take charge again of military affairs at the Zunyi Conference of 1935. Mao then led the Communists to the safety of north China. It was a turning point in the history of Chinese Communism and the life of Mao.

Though developed specifically with reference to the Japanese invasion of China, Mao's principles could be applied also to the problems the Communists faced in the Civil War period (1945–1949) (q.v.). In broad terms, Communist warfare did develop along the lines indicated by Mao. But his military thinking did not defeat the Japanese; rather, the many campaigns fought by the Nationalists in China and, of course, by the Americans in the Pacific war did so. The Nationalists themselves had been exhausted during the war against the Japanese and were overwhelmed by the difficulties of taking charge once more of a vast country wrecked by decades of war and rebellion.

Mao Tse-tung was not only a military theoretician. He was the chairman of the party's military committee and deeply involved himself in military decision making. He was responsible for, or at least assented to, all the major strategic shifts that the Communists took on their way to power, including the decision to build base areas in north China, to conclude a second United Front with the Nationalists during the Anti-Japanese War (1937–1945), and to give priority to Manchuria during the Chinese Civil War (1945–1949). Manchuria's industry had been developed by the Japanese, and it was close to the Soviet Union. Sometimes Mao disregarded the advice of the military, as he did when he decided that China should join in the Korean War (q.v.). That decision was likely informed by the belief that the United States might drop a nuclear bomb on north China and Chiang Kai-shek use the Korean War to order his armies back to mainland China from Taiwan. Whether or not Mao's preemptive action prevented the occurrence of these events cannot be known. Mao, in short, was the revolution's chief of staff.

HANS J. VAN DE VEN

Mao Tse-tung, *Selected Works* (1977); Stuart Schram, *The Thought of Mao Tse-tung* (1989); Tien Chen-ya, *Chinese Military Theory* (1992).

Maps

In the recent European military tradition, war maps seem to have emerged soon after the fifteenth century. Before that time, military commanders had no crucial need of maps. It was possible to construct a satisfactory wall around a medieval city without the aid of a map, just as it was possible to direct an engagement between two bodies of horse, or between cavalry and a disorganized infantry, without cartographic help.

The growing importance of artillery and the emergence of a trained and powerful infantry arm changed all that. The improved guns led to the construction of bastioned traces, which could not be laid out in an improvised way as medieval walls could be, but had to be planned on paper from the start, to make sure that the fields of fire were interlocking and appropriate to the range of the weapons. The earliest plans of this kind probably date from Italy of the 1520s and 1530s; many survive from the 1540s in England.

As time went by, these fortification plans became ever more numerous, delineating cities, fortresses, and batteries in virtually all the countries of Europe, and indeed of the overseas territories conquered and fortified by the European powers. From the time of the publications of Albrecht Dürer (1527) and Battista delle Valle (1529), a large number of fortification manuals emerged, many of which were illustrated by plans (see Map 1, p. 282).

The other type of map that emerged from the

OPPOSITE:
TOP: *This fortification plan, "Plan of the Post of Black River" (1782), represents part of a British scheme to defend the island of Jamaica from the French.*
BOTTOM: *The Dürer woodcut* Siege of a Fortified Town *(1527) portrays ranks of pikemen, cavalry, artillery, supply carts, and — to complete the image — sacked villages burning on the horizon.*

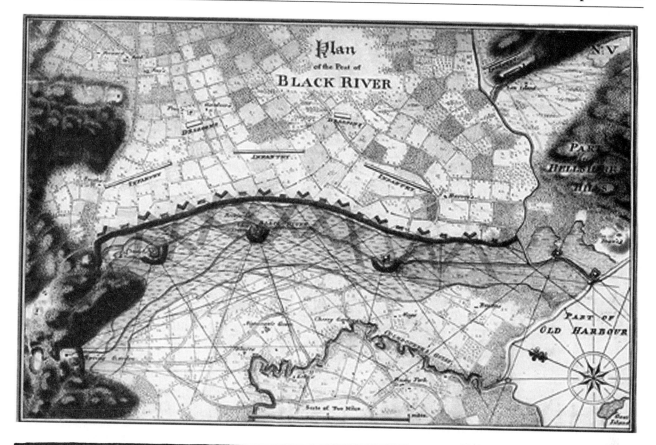

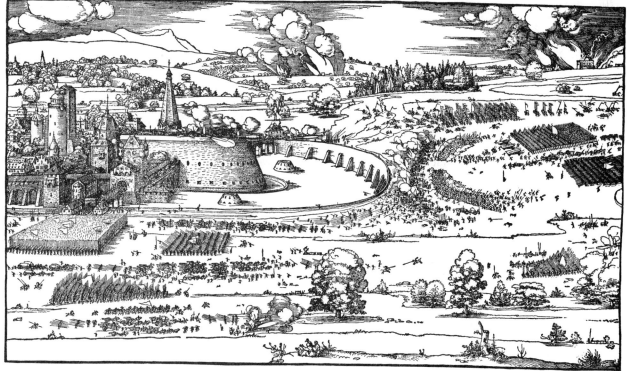

changes of the fifteenth century was the battle plan. The development of a newly powerful infantry meant that commanders now had to coordinate the activities of three arms (cavalry, infantry, and artillery) and relate them to the terrain. This led first to images drawn *after* battles, to show the disposition of the forces. Perhaps the earliest of these battle plans was Dürer's woodcut *Siege of a Fortified Town*, produced in 1527 (see Map 2, p. 282).

Throughout the sixteenth century, other artists followed the example of Dürer in offering images of this kind, summarizing the movements of armies on their campaigns. In the late seventeenth and eighteenth centuries, conventional signs began to replace the actual delineation of the arms; thus infantry might be signified by clear oblong blocks, cavalry by blocks with a diagonal slash, and artillery by gun symbols. These were all inserted onto topographical maps to show their positions at a certain stage in the battle; eventually, too, signs were used to show the way in which the various arms had maneuvered on the battlefield. To indicate the course of a complicated battle, a whole series of such plans was needed.

But these plans were all drawn *after the fact*, as historical documents. It took much longer for maps to serve commanders as actual bases for tactical judgments on the battlefield. From the time of the great atlas of Abraham Ortelius (1570), military leaders had in handy printed form a rough outline of the courses of the major rivers, the sites of the larger towns, and some idea of the topography. But maps at this small scale could play no part in tactical decisions, and it would seem that specially drawn manuscript maps remained for a long time very sketchy.

Maps that would be tactically useful had to await the completion of state programs that mapped whole countries at a relatively large scale. Such maps began to exist for France, for instance, in the late seventeenth century. For many of the German-speaking regions, such large-scale maps came into existence only during the course of the eighteenth century. Astute commanders could use these maps to gain decisive tactical advantages over less well equipped adversaries, and in countries such as France, whole cartographic staffs were created to provide maps of potential campaign areas; manuals were composed to codify the style of such battle maps. By the time of the American Revolutionary War (q.v.), each side had cartographic workshops whose maps were recognized as crucially important. Napoleon (q.v.), too, built up the cartographic branch of the French army, famously mapping Egypt in the course of his abortive campaign there (1789–1790).

By the middle of the nineteenth century, large-scale topographic maps existed of virtually all the countries of western Europe, and the Russians too had a well-developed military mapping agency. In the United States, whole areas lacked accurate large-scale maps at the beginning of the Civil War (q.v.), and so the activities of cartographers on both sides became very important. In all the wars since that time, large-scale maps have been regarded as indispensable at virtually all tactical levels; often they have been used with clear overlays, upon which the changing positions of units could be plotted with erasable crayons. Sometimes they have been supplemented by models, like those made by Louis XIV (q.v.) to help in the direction of sieges, or by General Dwight D. Eisenhower (q.v.) to help the Allied troops visualize the parts of Normandy that they were about to invade (see *D-Day*).

The most recent development in military mapping has been the emergence of satellite-operated, handheld ground position indicators, used to remarkable effect in the Gulf War (q.v.); they complement the electronic battlefield maps upon which the position of units can be plotted from minute to minute. The technique is dazzling, but the object is the same as in the days of Napoleon: to give troops on the ground a major advantage by allowing them to know exactly where they are in relation to the terrain, and to their objectives.

DAVID BUISSERET

John Hale, *Artists and Warfare in the Renaissance* (1991); J. B. Harley, Barbara Petchenik, and Lawrence Towner, *Mapping the American Revolutionary War* (1978); Martha Pollak, *Military Architecture, Cartography, and the Representation of the Early Modern European City* (1991).

Marathon, Battle of

September 490 B.C.

The first encounter on the Greek mainland between East and West took place on the small seaside plain of Marathon, twenty-six miles northeast of Athens. The Persian expeditionary force of Darius I was not large, perhaps numbering under thirty thousand. But it arrived confident after storming the nearby Greek city-state of Eretria. Moreover, no allies except the Plataeans joined the Athenian resistance of less than ten thousand troops, and some autocratic regimes in Attica supported the invaders in the hope of toppling the fledgling democracy.

To meet the larger invading force, the Athenian commander Militiades weakened his center and reinforced his wings, hoping that his hoplites (q.v.) could hold the middle while his flanks broke through the lighter-clad Persian infantry. In fact, the Athenian center broke, but it held long enough for the Athenians to rout the Persian wings and meet in the rear, causing a general panic among the invaders.

Almost immediately, the victory of "the Marathon men" captured the collective imagination of the Greeks. Ceremonial funeral mounds of the legendary 192 Athenian dead and the loyal Plataeans were erected on the battlefield. Epigrams were composed and panoramic murals were put on display. No wonder: it had been Athens's finest hour, when its democratic yeomen alone had beaten back the imperial might of Persia (see *Persian Wars*).

VICTOR DAVIS HANSON

Marching

See Drill/Marching.

Marines

Marines, or "soldiers of the sea," first appeared in the navies of ancient Greece and Rome. These fighting men launched rocks, flaming missiles, arrows, and spears at opposing galleys while the "sailors" (most often rowing slaves) powered the ship. Except for ramming, combat at sea resembled land battles. During the great naval campaigns of the seventeenth and eighteenth centuries involving Spain, Holland, France, and England, all of the belligerents still added soldiers to their warships to provide musketry and grenades to their vessels' close-quarters fighting power; most engagements, however, turned on the effects of naval cannon, so marines had only a supplementary role. Nevertheless, marines also provided the nucleus of a ship's landing party for raids on harbors, and they helped the captain preserve discipline among the era's unruly sailors, many of whom had been impressed into service. The English created the

first permanent regiment of infantry for maritime service in 1664; this force eventually evolved into the Royal Marines.

By the nineteenth century, France had expanded the missions of marines and, indeed, their very definition. Under the Bourbon monarchs, France governed its overseas colonies through the Ministry of Marine, which created both standing forces and militia for colonial self-defense. With uniforms that sported anchors rather than army insignia, such formations inevitably became "marines," although they had little connection with French naval forces. In addition, French marines assumed many coastal defense responsibilities, especially for naval bases, and thus created the *Corps Royal des Cannoniers Matelots*. Not until the early twentieth century did these French colonial regiments, called *troupes de marine*, transfer to army control. In the meantime, "real" French marines, like their English counterparts, were divided into three categories: ships' detachments of company strength, naval infantry organized as *regiments de marche* for expeditionary service or colonial policing, and naval artillery for either coastal defense or expeditionary duty.

In the English service, the marines were split into the Royal Marine Light Infantry and the Royal Marine Artillery, which also manned guns aboard warships. In the United States, marines of the Continental navy disappeared after the American Revolution (q.v.), but reappeared as the Corps of Marines in 1798 for service aboard warships. These marines also found themselves in the fore of landing parties and, after 1898, deployed to the Caribbean, Mexico, the Philippines, Central America, and China as colonial expeditionary troops. Imperial Germany organized European battalions of naval infantry for colonial policing. Imperial Russia used its naval infantry for shipboard service and landing parties.

The identification of marines with amphibious assaults had antecedents in the landing parties of the nineteenth century, but developed principally in the United States and Japan after World War I (q.v.). The postwar settlement left these two powers, competitors in the Pacific, with the problem of naval and air base defense and seizure in any future war. The Japanese developed two amphibious assault forces, one under army control, the other the Special Naval Landing Forces maintained by the navy. The U.S. Marine Corps, a separate naval service in the Department of the Navy, sought and received principal responsibility in 1927 for the development of amphibious assault doctrine, techniques, equipment, and tactics. It also assumed as early as 1921 that it would provide the expeditionary forces for a naval campaign against Japan, and in 1933 the U.S. Marine Corps designated its expeditionary forces the Fleet Marine Force (FMF).

World War II (q.v.), which saw amphibious operations conducted in every major theater, produced ample opportunity and justification for the permanent establishment of elite amphibious assault forces. The U.S. Marine Corps played the dominant global role of all marine forces in its amphibious campaign against Japan, forming six infantry divisions and four aircraft wings as well as specialized artillery, engineer, and amphibian tractor battalions. Its wartime strength reached almost 500,000. Other allied marines, largely associated with the British Commonwealth armies, served as the advance forces of amphibious operations and as seaborne "commando" raiders. Soviet and Japanese naval infantry played an intermediate role, usually participating in operations as reinforced regimental landing teams of three thousand to five thousand. Some marines provided specialized landing craft crews and beach-barrier destruction teams, although in American practice, teams of sailors and soldiers performed these missions.

Marine forces followed different postwar developmental patterns. The western European pattern, dominated by the British, French, and Dutch marines, followed the naval raiding, or "commando," path. Portugal, Spain, Turkey, and Italy followed suit with small battalions of marines for limited amphibious reconnaissance and raiding capabilities. Such corps of marines number less than ten thousand and are deployed in small battalions (from five hundred to eight hundred officers and men), which also provide some naval base security forces such as counterterrorism teams. The Royal Marines and their Dutch counterparts also specialize in arctic warfare operations, as the Royal Marines demonstrated in the Falklands War of 1982 (q.v.). France has three thousand *fusiliers-marins* for commando and naval security missions. The army *troupes de marine* have a marine division for rapid deployment and eleven small colonial infantry regiments (each employing eight hundred men).

Legitimized and protected by law after its stellar performance in the Pacific in World War II and in the Korean War (q.v.), the U.S. Marine Corps represents an entirely different modern marine tradition. The organization, training, and deployment of the FMF in air-ground amphibious task forces provides the U.S. Marine Corps with its central mission. Of the 177,000 marines of the 1990s, about 90,000 are in the FMF (three divisions, three aircraft wings), and most of the rest of the corps is preparing for FMF service. This force is heavily armed for air and ground combat; with more than eight hundred fighter-attack aircraft and helicopters, the U.S. Marine Corps fields one of the ten largest air forces in the world. The U.S. Navy provides an amphibious fleet of fifty to sixty specialized ships for beach assaults and vertical envelopments. Though not its primary mission, the U.S. Marine Corps also maintains nuclear weapons security teams, elite embassy guards, and other special forces.

Before the collapse of the Warsaw Pact, the Soviet Union and the German Democratic Republic maintained naval infantry divisions for amphibious operations; the remnant of the Russian naval infantry still has an official strength of sixty-two thousand. The naval infantry of the People's Republic of China's armed forces is small; the People's Liberation Army claims that it can mobilize up to forty-two regiments of armor, infantry, and artillery for landings.

Worldwide, the panache and historical elitism of marine formations has had lasting appeal, based on selective recruiting, arduous training, strict discipline, and demanding military missions. Marines of every nationality view themselves as guardians of traditional military virtues.

ALLAN R. MILLETT

M. L. Bartlett, ed., *Assault from the Sea* (1983); Allan R. Millett, *Semper Fidelis: The History of the United States Marine Corps* (1991); Robin Neilands, *By Land and Sea: The Story of the Royal Marines Commandos* (1987).

Marlborough, John Churchill, Duke of

1650–1722, *English Military Commander*

John Churchill, duke of Marlborough, commanded the British and Dutch forces in the Low Countries during the War of the Spanish Succession (1702–1713) (q.v.) and won an impressive series of victories over France; but he proved unable to turn these achievements into a decisive settlement of the war and was dismissed at the end of 1711. His appointment to command the army of the British state came when he was over fifty years old and seemingly at the end of a routine military career. Born into an impoverished and obscure family of the minor gentry, his ascent to social preeminence and eventually political and military power came through the turbulent world of later Stuart court politics: he was the last important military figure in English history to rise entirely through royal favor. He spent his early career in the service of Charles II and James II, but abandoned the Stuart monarchy at the Revolution of 1688. Ennobled by a grateful William III, he served the new British king only briefly before going into the political wilderness: in the mid-1690s he even spent a short period imprisoned in the Tower of London. However, his wife Sarah's close friendship with Princess Anne, who became queen upon William III's death in 1702, together with his own administrative abilities and unwavering support of the Protestant cause, led to his appointment as captain-general. When he secured supreme command in the Spanish succession struggle, he had limited military experience: he had served in only five Continental campaigns, and his sole independent command comprised a small force in Ireland in 1690.

Between 1702 and 1711, however, he held effective charge not only of British military strategy and diplomacy, but also of the allied war effort. Britain fought alongside the Dutch Republic and Austria, and the allied army also contained contingents of soldiers from smaller states, whereas France was supported only by the German Electorate of Bavaria. Yet the strategic position of Louis XIV's (q.v.) France was immensely strong, with an iron ring of fortresses protecting its northern and eastern frontiers (see *Vauban*). This near invincibility to invasion was supported by the French army's numerical superiority throughout much of the conflict. Marlborough was also handicapped by his own incomplete authority over the allied forces that he led: in 1706 he was given full command, but at times he was still unable to secure complete support from the Dutch, the Austrians, and even his own government in London.

He contributed to the war effort principally by imposing an aggressive and mobile strategy that aimed to defeat France in battle. This contrasted sharply with the attitude of the Dutch generals in particular, who adhered to the established conventions of warfare: the avoidance of battle unless victory could be guaranteed, a preference for sieges, and the protection of secure lines of communication down which an army might advance or retreat. Not without difficulty, Marlborough imposed an offensive strategy and, sometimes in partnership with the impressive

Austrian general Prince Eugène of Savoy, won a series of major victories over French troops. The duke's principal successes were in battles at Blenheim (August 13, 1704) (q.v.), Ramillies (May 23, 1706), and Audenarde (July 11, 1708), and these facilitated the reconquest of much of the Spanish Netherlands, thereby providing the Dutch Republic with some protection from a future French attack. Yet these battle honors, impressive in themselves and also the first major defeats suffered by the formidable French army since the 1650s, made little impact upon France's near-impregnable strategic position. The high cost in casualties aroused mounting criticism in England, where the number of Marlborough's political enemies was growing and where his wife's influence upon Queen Anne was rapidly waning. The bloody draw at Malplaquet (September 11, 1709) highlighted the inconclusive nature of the struggle. Little more than two years later (December 31, 1711), the duke had been dismissed, and in the next year he was forced into exile on the Continent. Though he returned at the accession of the house of Hanover in 1714, he suffered two disabling strokes in 1716 and died six years later.

Marlborough's trademark as a battlefield commander was his preference for flank attacks designed to create a local superiority and thus to force his opponents to move reinforcements to these areas, thereby weakening the center for a major and, he hoped, battle-winning thrust. This worked well in his great victories, but came to grief in the bloody encounter at Malplaquet, by which point the opposing commanders anticipated this stratagem.

The duke possessed an unusual ability to inspire his subordinates together with immense organizational skills: the logistical effort that made possible the march to the Danube and the victory at Blenheim in 1704 was of the highest order. He also had a shrewd eye for the topographical possibilities of a potential battleground, together with an appreciation of the crucial role of military intelligence. He was not an inspirational commander, but a well-organized, flexible, and personally courageous leader with a crucial belief in the possibility of victory over the seemingly invincible French.

Marlborough's military victories were perhaps less important than his diplomatic skills, which did much to keep the anti-French coalition together — particularly in the early years of the war — and to impose a unified strategy. But he could not overcome the strength of France's strategic position, which, together with its numerical superiority, turned the War of the Spanish Succession into an attritional struggle and denied the duke the dictated peace over Louis XIV of which he had always dreamed. He did not achieve the decisive victory that might have secured a place for him in the pantheon of great commanders: Napoleon (q.v.), when compiling his list of the seven greatest generals, found space for the duke's comrade-in-arms Eugène of Savoy, but not for Marlborough.

H. M. SCOTT

J. R. Jones, *Marlborough* (1993).

Marne, First Battle of the

September 6–13, 1914

The First Battle of the Marne was fought to the north and east of Paris in early September 1914 (see *World War I*). The opportunity opened for Anglo-French forces to reverse the hitherto victorious German advance through Belgium and France when First Army commander Heinrich von Kluck, who anchored the right wing of the German advance, swung north, rather than west, of Paris, across the front of Michel-Joseph Maunoury's French Sixth Army. Alerted by French air reconnaissance and radio intercepts, the first time either had been used in a major conflict, French commander in chief Joseph Joffre (q.v.) ordered an attack. On September 6, Maunoury, reinforced by troops, rushed to the front in requisitioned Paris taxis and buses — the first extensive use of motorized transport in wartime and forever celebrated as the "taxis of the Marne" — slammed into von Kluck's overextended army (see *Galliena, Joseph-Simon*). Surprised, von Kluck recalled his advanced guard and swung his forces to the southwest to meet Maunoury's attack. But in doing so, von Kluck lost contact with Karl von Bulow's Second Army on his left flank. The British Expeditionary Force (BEF) rallied together with elements of the French Fifth Army to surge into the breach von Kluck had opened in the German front. The tenacious defense of Ferdinand Foch's (q.v.) Ninth Army in the St.-Gond marshes against repeated attacks of the German Second and Third Armies frustrated German attempts to dislocate the French thrust by collapsing Joffre's right wing. On September 10, German chief of staff Helmuth von Moltke the younger (q.v.) ordered his forces to regroup on a front between Soissons and Verdun.

Joffre pursued into September 13, when French attacks failed to dislodge German positions north of the Aisne. Each army then began a series of flanking maneuvers known as the "race to the sea," which left in its wake a system of linked trenches protected by barbed wire.

The Anglo-French victory had been due in part to the fact that the Germans had outrun their logistics and their heavy artillery, used to crushing advantage in earlier battles. Moltke, whose command style has been compared to that of an orchestral conductor whose players disregarded his baton, lost control of his army commanders. But the real victory went to Joffre and the French General Staff, who took advantage of German overextension to snatch the strategic initiative from the attackers.

DOUGLAS PORCH

Marshall, George C.

1880–1959, *U.S. General and Statesman*

George Marshall remains, after George Washington (q.v.), the most respected soldier in American history. Yet he never had command of troops in battle, the customary path to greatness for a military leader. He excelled at many other tasks that a modern officer is asked to perform and then served capably in the civilian roles of diplomat and policy maker as well.

Marshall's rise to the top in the U.S. Army followed paths opened by reforms of the early twentieth century that emphasized professional military education, a new staff system to prepare for war, and closer coordination of the citizen soldiers of the National Guard with the regular army. As a staff officer in World War I (q.v.), Marshall was centrally involved in the planning of offensives by the American Expeditionary Force in France. Later, as assistant commandant of the Infantry School, he left a strong imprint on the tactics that the U.S. Army was to use in World War II (q.v.). Extensive work with National Guard units gave him exposure to the civilian world and experience in dealing with politicians that were unusual for officers of his time.

Though Marshall had never commanded a division, he became chief of staff on the day that World War II began in Europe. The U.S. Army in September 1939 had scarcely any modern weaponry and was roughly the size of the Dutch army that survived less than a week against the German blitzkrieg in 1940. By the time the U.S. Army began fighting the Wehrmacht in 1942, its effective combat strength had increased more than tenfold. Marshall was the architect of this remarkable buildup.

Marshall keenly appreciated that success in a multitheater coalition war required harmonious civil-military, interservice, and interallied relationships. He won the confidence of President Franklin Roosevelt (q.v.), worked effectively with his naval counterpart, Admiral Ernest King (q.v.), and ensured coordination of American and British military leadership through the Combined Chiefs of Staff and unity of command in combat theaters.

Marshall proved less sure-footed in his approach to the most important strategic choice facing the United States in World War II: when and where to employ American forces on a large scale. Marshall's support of a Germany-first strategic priority was on the mark, but his advocacy of an Anglo-American invasion of France in 1943 put him on shaky ground. Until American forces had gained more experience against the Wehrmacht, until command of the Atlantic was achieved in mid-1943, and until command of the air was secured in early 1944, an amphibious assault across the English Channel would have carried great military risk. And given that the British would have supplied the bulk of the troops for a 1943 invasion, military failure would have involved the political risk of undercutting Britain's commitment to the war effort. Franklin Roosevelt, although overruling the chief of staff on this crucial strategic issue, came to regard him as so indispensable in Washington that, when the cross-Channel assault was finally mounted in 1944, he could not let Marshall assume command of the invasion force. The general was sorely disappointed but characteristically never uttered a word of complaint.

Marshall was set to retire after the war when President Harry Truman sent him to China in late 1945 to avert a civil war between the Kuomintang government and the Communist Party. Even Marshall's force of character could not bring about a durable compromise between those antagonists, however. His experience in China did prove beneficial when he became Truman's secretary of state in 1947. For he could make a strong case that American military intervention in the Chinese Civil War (q.v.) would be a costly venture with only a dim prospect of success.

In the Cold War (q.v.), as in World War II, Marshall saw Europe as the top American strategic priority. The famous plan of foreign aid that bears his name helped protect friendly European countries from Communist subversion. Before he left the State Department in 1949, he also helped erect two other pillars of containment in Europe to stand alongside the Marshall Plan — a West German state and a Western military alliance: NATO.

After the outbreak of the Korean War (q.v.), Truman brought Marshall out of retirement once again, this time to serve as secretary of defense. The president hoped that Marshall would keep General Douglas MacArthur (q.v.) under control. But Marshall was not well suited for that role: although in principle he deeply believed in civilian control of the military, in practice he had also long believed that theater commanders should have considerable scope to act on their own judgment.

After Truman fired MacArthur, Senator Joseph McCarthy viciously impugned Marshall as a dupe of the Communists. But for almost all of Marshall's contemporaries, it was precisely his character and his patriotism that made him so worthy of respect.

BRADFORD A. LEE

Ed Cray, *General of the Army: George C. Marshall, Soldier and Statesman* (1991); Forrest C. Pogue, *George C. Marshall*, 4 vols. (1963–1986); Mark A. Stoler, *George C. Marshall: Soldier-Statesman of the American Century* (1989).

Martial Law

Martial law is not to be confused with *military government*, which refers to the administration of occupied territory, nor with *military law* or *military justice*, terms that refer to the governance of members of the armed forces and certain closely related civilians. Martial law is the maintenance of order and the protection of persons and property by and through military authorities and agencies under circumstances wherein the civilian courts and other agencies normally serving that purpose are unable to function for the time being. It may be imposed upon foreign territory by an invading army, in which case it in effect amounts merely to the will of the commander, tempered only by basic humanitarian rules of international law. A more difficult and interesting subject, and the subject of this article, is martial law within the home country.

Martial law of this nature is a concept in Anglo-

American law, corresponding in many respects to the "state of siege" recognized under French and other Continental law. Its principles have been more fully developed under American than under English law, reflecting the domestic tranquillity enjoyed by England since the seventeenth century. In the United States its principles derive mainly from the experience of the American Civil War (q.v.), together with "Dorr's Rebellion" in Rhode Island in 1842, the labor unrest of the late nineteenth and early twentieth centuries, and the post–Pearl Harbor (q.v.) period on the West Coast. There has been little or no experience with it in recent decades, while at the same time the U.S. Supreme Court has reinterpreted many constitutional guarantees during this period. A caveat to this article is therefore appropriate: quite possibly some of the principles described herein would not be reaffirmed by the Supreme Court today.

Normally, a state of martial law in an area is proclaimed by the executive authority: the governor of a state, or the president on the federal level. It is a prerequisite to martial law that the civil arm of the government be powerless and the courts unable to function, normally because of insurrection or invasion. It extends only to the area where the civil government is actually unable to function. Martial law is not to be confused with the mere calling out of the militia or other military forces to help preserve order when the ordinary police forces are overwhelmed by riot or other tumult, but the courts and other civilian agencies are still able to function.

Unlike the Continental "state of siege," in which the powers of the military authorities are defined in advance with some precision, martial law in American law is a flexible concept, measured by the degree of necessity. In general, the military authorities can do all acts reasonably necessary to restore and maintain public order. They can arrest or detain civilians without warrant on reasonable grounds for believing that they are engaged, or if not detained may engage, in insurrection or disorder; they can limit the right of assembly, impose curfews, forbid the sale of alcohol, and search for and seize weapons without warrant. Within uncertain limits they can suppress newspapers that encourage the disorder.

Although the military authorities administering martial law may in some circumstances try civilians in military tribunals, the extent of this power is not wholly clear. The better practice is to hold arrested persons until civil authority is reestablished and turn them over to the civil arm for trial in the ordinary manner — a procedure established by President George Washington (q.v.) in the suppression of the Whiskey Rebellion in 1794. In any event, the sentences imposed by military tribunals are no longer effective after the termination of martial law.

By the same token, consistent with the supremacy of the civil power and the flexible nature of martial law, once martial law has terminated, commanders can be required to justify acts prima facie illegal that were taken while it was in effect — the most notable example in our history being the fining of General Andrew Jackson for contempt of court in connection with his unduly prolonged maintenance of martial law in New Orleans after defeating the British in 1815.

THADDEUS HOLT

Charles Fairman, *The Law of Martial Rule*, 2nd ed. (1943).

Masada, Siege of

A.D. 73

Masada, site of the final action in the First Jewish War (A.D. 66–73), is a mountain fortress in southeastern Judaea, overlooking the western shore of the Dead Sea. It was first fortified to guard against nomads from the Negev by King Herod the Great (r. 37–4 B.C.), who hired Roman engineers to turn the mountaintop into an impregnable stronghold to serve as his last refuge in the event of a popular uprising.

Soon after the outbreak of the First Jewish War (see *Jewish Rebellions*), Jewish Zealots massacred the Roman garrison and seized Masada. After Jerusalem (q.v.) fell to the Romans in A.D. 70, Eleazer ben Jair, leader of the Jewish nationalist faction known as the Sicarii (daggermen), escaped with his men to Masada to continue the war. In the spring of A.D. 73, Flavius Silva, the legate commanding the Tenth Legion Fretensis and auxiliary soldiers totaling over 10,000 men, besieged Masada, which was defended by 960 Jews, including women and children. Flavius Silva conducted a model Roman siege, ordering first the construction of eight encampments and then a circumvallation to cut off Masada. Next, he raised a ramp to an elevation of 650 feet against the western approach and built a 90-foot moveable siege tower equipped with battering ram and encased in protective metal plates. As soon as the tower was pushed into place, archers atop the tower drove Jewish defenders from the wall while legionaries operating the battering ram undermined the wall's foundations. The resourceful Eleazar ordered a counterwall, faced with timber and containing loose earth, which would absorb the shock of the battering ram. By nightfall, Flavius Silva ordered his men to set fire to the counterwall. At dawn, legionaries stormed into the fortress to find that Eleazer and the defenders (save for two women and five small children hiding in the cisterns) had committed suicide.

KENNETH W. HARL

Maurice of Nassau

1567–1625, Captain General of the United Netherlands

Appointed to his post in 1588, four years after the assassination of his father, William the Silent, Maurice of Nassau successfully conducted the defense of the United Netherlands (or Dutch Republic) against Spain (see *Dutch Revolt*). A cautious and methodical field commander, always subjected to civilian control, Maurice favored positional operations. His importance in the evolution of modern war derives primarily from his transformation of a motley mercenary force into a smaller but well-trained and disciplined professional army in the service of the state.

Inspiration for reform came from classical models as well as practical necessity and included administration, training, and drill. Influenced by the neo-Stoic teachings of Justus Lipsius, his tutor, Maurice introduced a strict code of conduct, demanding that properly and promptly paid officers and men act as moral, disciplined servants of the state. Concerning tactics, his discipline and drill — based directly on Roman precedents and suggested to him by his cousin William Louis — made tactical deployment and infantry fire more effective. This enabled him to deploy smaller units, companies, and battalions, evenly divided between pike and shot, in linear formations only ten deep, the additional frontage enabling his units to maintain constant volleys. Maurice also improved siege operations, assigning both engineers and gunners to permanent roles in his army, and, profiting from the advice of Simon Stevin, the great mathematician, he applied scientific methods to sieges, with troops performing much of the labor. Finally, he standardized military equipment throughout the Dutch army.

The new tactics required trained officers to drill and lead subunits and introduced the formation of a command hierarchy, the foundation for the modern officer corps and modern military professionalism. The Dutch success in standing off larger Spanish armies and capturing fortified towns was widely admired, and soon similar practices were adopted by other European states — often under the direction of experts specifically requested from Maurice.

GUNTHER E. ROTHENBERG

McClellan, George B.

1826–1885, American Civil War General

Probably no military leader ever earned a more concise summing up than the observation of Abraham Lincoln (q.v.) that General George B. McClellan had a bad case of "the slows." McClellan had failed to follow up the Union stand at Antietam, Maryland (q.v.), in 1862, and Lincoln soon relieved him of command; he saw no service for the rest of the war.

This was a drastic comedown for the "Little Napoleon," who had served with distinction in the Mexican War (q.v.) and as a railroad official before the war. After an early, minor victory at Rich Mountain, he had been widely believed, not least by himself, to be the savior of the nation. As general in chief, he had snubbed President Lincoln and surrounded himself with sycophants. But his administrative talents had built the Army of the Potomac into a powerful force.

McClellan was not, however, a fighter. He failed to press his "Peninsular campaign" between the York and the James Rivers, though it took his army to the gates of Richmond in 1862 — a campaign stymied by Robert E. Lee (q.v.) in the Seven Days battles. Later that year, after the federal defeat in the Second Battle of Bull Run, McClellan again was placed in overall command and pursued Lee's army into Maryland. He could fight the Confederates only to a bloody draw at Antietam, however, and was relieved for good.

McClellan ran for president as a Democrat in 1864, losing to Lincoln. Later, he served as governor of New Jersey (1878–1881). Robert E. Lee called him the best general he had fought against — presumably because McClellan avoided total defeat in the Peninsular campaign. The "McClellan saddle," which he designed, is a claim to fame not marred by other authorities' low opinion of the Little Napoleon's war record.

TOM WICKER

McNamara, Robert S.

1916–, U.S. Secretary of Defense

As U.S. secretary of defense from 1961 until early 1968, Robert S. McNamara, the former president of the Ford Motor Company, introduced new techniques of weapons procurement and systems analysis into the Pentagon, supervised a massive buildup of strategic nuclear weapons, attempted to alter American nuclear targeting policy, oversaw large conventional military buildups during the Berlin crisis of 1961 and the Cuban missile crisis of 1962, and proposed the first American antiballistic missile system. His attempts to use systems analysis, which he learned as an executive at Ford, created enormous controversy in the Pentagon. His most important historical legacy, however, concerns his role in the Vietnam War (q.v.).

Faced with deteriorating military situations in both Laos and Vietnam during 1961, McNamara, together with Secretary of State Dean Rusk, put forth several proposals for American military involvement in Indochina during that year, but President John F. Kennedy rejected them. Instead, beginning in November 1961, McNamara took charge of an expanded American advisory effort in South Vietnam, including American tactical air support. By mid-1962, he had issued orders that the United States plan to complete this effort by 1965.

President Kennedy's assassination in November 1963 coincided with further deterioration of the military situation in South Vietnam. Within four months, McNamara had secured President Lyndon Johnson's agreement, in principle, to take military action against North Vietnam, but the president delayed action until after the November 1964 elections. Finally, in February 1965, the United States began both the bombing of the North and a sequence of ground deployments in the South. By late 1967, 500,000 American ground troops were fighting in South Vietnam.

McNamara seems to have decided by late 1966 — and certainly by May 1967 — that the United States was making no progress in its war against North Vietnam, that newly requested troop increments would make no real difference, and that the United States had to adjust its political objectives accordingly. Other senior officials still supported the war, however, and in late 1967, President Johnson nominated McNamara to head the World Bank and accepted his resignation as secretary of defense. Within a few months, McNamara's successor, Clark Clifford, had reached the same conclusion, and the escalation of the war came to an end. The strategy that McNamara had helped design had failed, and he had been unable to alter it. The publication of his memoir, *In Retrospect*, in 1995 ignited a new controversy over McNamara's role in the war.

DAVID KAISER

Medals and Insignia

For centuries, veteran military personnel have worn a variety of devices to mark their special acts of bravery and meritorious service or simply to identify their special status. Today, the uniform of even the rawest recruit is adorned with a number of such marks of honor and identity.

Decorations and Service Medals

Medals, commonly stamped or engraved metallic devices often decorated with enamel and precious jewels and suspended from bits of colored ribbon, may be divided into two main classes: decorations and service medals. Decorations, usually in the form of a cross or other distinctive shape, are presented to individuals for gallantry on the battlefield, for saving a life in peacetime, or for meritorious service in peace or war. Decorations reward outstanding performance in the past but also serve as incentives for valor and fidelity in the future. Service medals, usually in the form of a disk, are distributed to all military personnel who meet the established criteria for long and faithful service or participation in specific wars and campaigns.

The ancient Greeks often awarded a wreath of laurel leaves as a symbol of prowess in battle, but the Romans were the first to develop a comprehensive hierarchy of military decorations. For high officers, decorations took the form of crowns made of various materials as well as miniature standards and spearheads of silver. Any soldier or civilian who saved the life of a fellow citizen might receive the civic crown (*corona civica*) of oak leaves or later of gold, but the highest Roman decoration, a crown of grass (*corona graminea*) was reserved for senior commanders whose forces relieved a besieged camp or city. Centurions and soldiers of lesser rank were rewarded for valorous or meritorious deeds by crowns, collars, armlets, clasps, or *phalerae*, metal disks bearing the portrait of the reigning emperor or some other pertinent symbol. Usually awarded in sets of nine and arranged on a leather harness worn over the corselet, *phalerae* are the true ancestors of modern military decorations.

Most modern nations also have well-developed, hierarchical systems of military awards with one decoration prized above all others. The highest U.S. military decoration, the Medal of Honor (often improperly called the Congressional Medal of Honor), was authorized by Congress in 1861 and since 1904 has been awarded only to those individuals who have distinguished themselves in action against an armed enemy by "gallantry above and beyond the call of duty at the risk of life." The highest British military decoration for valor is the Victoria Cross, established by Queen Victoria in 1856 and struck (as it still is) from the bronze of Russian cannon captured during the Crimean War (q.v.). The French decoration corresponding most closely to the Medal of Honor and the Victoria Cross is the Médaille Militaire, established by Prince Louis Napoleon, then president of the French Republic, in 1852. However, the highest French decoration for valor or meritorious service is the Légion d'Honneur, established by Emperor Napoleon I (q.v.) in 1802 and awarded to both military personnel and civilians.

The modern practice of awarding a medal to all officers and enlisted men who participated in a given war or campaign was initiated by Oliver Cromwell (q.v.), who awarded a medal to all those who had fought against the Scots at Dunbar in 1650. The practice was revived with the issue of the Waterloo Medal in 1816 but did not become common until 1848. In France the practice dates from 1856. Republican and egalitarian sentiment in the United States retarded the establishment of service medals until 1898, when Congress authorized the presentation of the first such medal to all officers and men who had participated in the victory of Admiral George Dewey's fleet at Manila Bay.

Insignia

A wide variety of devices have long been worn by military personnel to identify their rank, service, unit of assignment, and military specialties. As with decorations, the use of military insignia can be traced back to the Romans. For example, the swagger stick carried by officers and senior noncommissioned officers of some modern armies recalls the *vitis*, a staff of hard vine carried by the centurion as a symbol of his rank and as an instrument for the punishment of offenders against military discipline.

From Roman times until the beginning of the twentieth century, officers could be identified clearly both on and off the battlefield by their distinctive uniforms. During the Middle Ages, leaders were marked by their better armor and often sought personal identification by the use of unique designs on their shields and the colors of their outer garments. Followers of a particular noble were often identified by wearing the distinctive colors of their leader. This practice was carried over with the introduction of uniforms in the late seventeenth century, and certain military units can still be distinguished by the color, cut, or unique adornments of their dress uniforms. In most modern armies the field uniforms of officers and enlisted personnel are quite similar, but officer dress uniforms are usually made from a higher-quality material, are better tailored, and include more elaborate adornments such as special sashes, epaulets, and buttons.

Each nation has its own unique system of military insignia, although the use of cuff stripes to indicate the rank of naval and air force officers and of chevrons to indicate the rank of enlisted personnel is common. However, the insignia of rank for army officers vary widely from country to country. For example, in the U.S. Army, a colonel wears a silver eagle, a colonel in the British army a crown and two "pips" (four-sided stars), and a colonel in the French army five gold stripes.

The additional hazards to frontline leaders on the modern battlefield have led many officers, beginning in World War I (q.v.), to hide their rank by dressing in enlisted uniforms and wearing their insignia under their outer clothing, if at all. During the Vietnam War (q.v.), the U.S. Army adopted the use of "subdued" (blackened) insignia of rank, branch, and unit on field uniforms for all ranks. The practice subsequently has spread to the armed forces of many other nations.

The various arms and services are usually associated with a special color, such as scarlet for artillery, yellow for cavalry, and light blue for infantry. Each arm and service is usually also distinguished by some unique metallic badge. Although each nation has its own system, crossed cannon or a flaming shell for artillery, crossed sabers for cavalry, and a bugle or crossed rifles for infantry are quite common. Distinctive regimental or corps badges, usually made of metal and incorporating various heraldic devices and often the motto of the unit, are designed both to aid identification and to foster esprit de corps. Cloth shoulder patches to identify units of division size or larger, common since World War I, serve the same purpose. Most armed forces also authorize a wide variety of metallic and cloth badges to designate the wearer's special skills and qualifications, such as aviator, diver, parachutist, explosive ordnance expert, driver, or marksman.

Many civilians, and even some soldiers, dismiss the insignia worn on the modern military uniform as ostentatious frippery, and decorations and service medals as mere baubles designed to enhance the self-importance of the military caste. However, medals and insignia serve important purposes — as the Emperor Napoleon I recognized upon the occasion of the establishment of the Légion d'Honneur, remarking that "... it is by such baubles that one leads men."

CHARLES R. SHRADER

Gilbert Grosvenor et al., *Insignia and Decorations of the U.S. Armed Forces* (1944); Robert E. Wyllie, *Orders, Decorations, and Insignia, Military and Civil, with the History and Romance of Their Origin and a Full Description of Each* (1921).

Medicine, Military

Organized military and naval forces in the West usually have provided some kind of medical care for their sick and wounded. Apart from the benefit of returning experienced personnel to duty, the morale factor has motivated this practice: abandonment of comrades does not enhance dedication to duty. Thus, it is not surprising that the oldest surgical text, the Smith papyrus of Egypt (from about 3000 B.C.) deals with the effects of wounds. Medical care of the sailor and soldier has usually been free of cost; in 1600 B.C. in Egypt, the law declared "on campaign, the sick are to be treated without cost to themselves."

Military medicine is commonly equated with treating the wounded. Certainly military historians have long accepted this definition and report "casualties" to mean the killed and (sometimes) the wounded. There is a long tradition for this view. The Hippocratic writings (400 B.C.) comment extensively on wound care, fractures, antiseptics, and bandages; the aphorism "He who would become a surgeon, let him join an army and follow it" urges the conclusion that war was the training ground for surgeons.

Battlefield medical care requires a structured system: the wounded must be moved from the place where they were hurt to a place of care. Data on such organization are scanty prior to the Roman army of the empire, in which physicians were assigned to the legions and enlisted soldiers (*capsarri*) were trained to dress wounds. Some evidence of transport of wounded and good evidence that military hospitals existed at the frontier posts has been found.

The general introduction of gunpowder weapons in the fourteenth century led to a change in wound care. Head, chest, and abdominal wounds remained overwhelmingly fatal; extremity wounds were contaminated by the material carried in by the musket ball, and amputation was thus the common major surgical procedure to prevent sepsis. This procedure was improved in the sixteenth century by Ambroise Paré, who added vessel ligature and the tourniquet to the operation. As armies became creatures of the organizing nation-states, the states paid for medical care. During the Reconquest (q.v.) in Spain, Isabella paid for hospitals. Charles V introduced an early version of an evacuation and treatment system in about 1550. From the 1550s, the Spanish army deducted one-thirtieth of each man's wage for medical care and in return provided surgeons and a field hospital. From 1585 the Spanish army of Flanders operated the first *permanent* military hospital (330 beds) at Mechelen.

By the late seventeenth and early eighteenth centuries, armies had surgical care stations, variously staffed by barber surgeons or — later — by men with some formal training. Field hospitals were common, but evacuation was delayed until the fighting stopped. Navies began the regular employment of ship's surgeons. The wounded were removed from the gun decks during battle and taken below to designated spaces for care. The naval surgeons and their patients did not enjoy the army's luxury of being moved out of the battle zone if wounded. This remains true today.

During the Napoleonic Wars, Dominique Jean Larrey (arguably the most famous military surgeon) introduced the "flying ambulance" — either a vehicle or a unit, depending on the context. His great contribution was forward surgical care at the battle's edge, with trained litter-bearers employed as an evacuation system and an organization of about 40 doctors and 250 soldiers to support every 10,000 troops.

However, the laypersons' and military commanders' emphasis for centuries on surgery as "military medicine" ignored the real causes of mortality and morbidity in war. Military historians have made the same mistake. From the medieval period to the late nineteenth century, many more soldiers and sailors died of disease than were killed in battle. Although empirical observations as early as Vegetius (q.v.) noted that camping near marshes and foul camp sites made soldiers sick, troop and ship commanders generally were unconcerned with preventive medicine measures. This attitude stemmed from several factors: class differences between officers and physicians, an inability to control the operational environment, lack of a sustainable theory of contagion, and the lack of predictability of illness in any given circumstance. In the Crimean War (q.v.), the British army became the model example of command indifference to medical care. In spite of this indifference, Florence Nightingale's (q.v.) sanitary approach to nursing care saved hundreds of lives and after the war had a major impact on the British army.

Some commanders, such as Marlborough (q.v.) and Napoleon (q.v.), saw tactical advantage in the illness of opponents; but, in general, although epidemic and endemic diseases were recognized as damaging to a campaign or a siege, they were viewed as uncon-trollable events. Sometimes camp hygiene was enforced for aesthetic reasons and because of the belief that miasmas arising from rotting organic material poisoned the air and caused disease. Some military physicians, Sir John Pringle in England in 1752, for example, wrote useful instructional texts on troop hygiene specifically for officers. But the urgings of these physicians of the eighteenth and early nineteenth centuries were generally ignored, even when commanders faced horrendous losses from tropical diseases during military explorations in Africa and Asia.

The health of sailors began to improve in the early nineteenth century with the elimination of scurvy through prophylactic lime juice, following the work of James Lind in 1754. Personal hygiene measures — "receiving ships" for recruits, better nutrition, and enforced ship cleanliness — did reduce disease deaths in navies by the end of the nineteenth century.

The seminal contribution to the health of all commands came from the discoveries of Louis Pasteur, Robert Koch, and their colleagues as germ theory and understanding of specific causation of disease entered medicine in the last quarter of the nineteenth century. This eventually led to laboratory diagnosis of disease, proof of contagion and of contamination of water and food, and, hence, predictability of disease occurrence. The proof of insect transmission of malaria, yellow fever, and other tropical diseases at the turn of the century provided additional practical methods of disease control.

Immunization began early in the military. George Washington (q.v.) ordered inoculation (with use of actual virus) for smallpox in 1777 in the American Revolution (q.v.), the first command-ordered immunization program. Although Edward Jenner's introduction of smallpox vaccination in 1798 was employed by some armies and navies, as late as 1870 the unvaccinated French army had thousands of smallpox cases in the Franco-Prussian War (q.v.), whereas the vaccinated Prussian force remained essentially free of the disease.

Surgical care of the wounded improved after 1847 when ether and then chloroform were introduced, but overall, better surgery had to await the "germ revolution" with Joseph Lister's introduction of antisepsis (1867) and its gradual acceptance and evolution into the aseptic surgery of today.

Management of medical support was perfected during the American Civil War (q.v.) by Major Jonathan Letterman of the Union Army Medical Corps. He

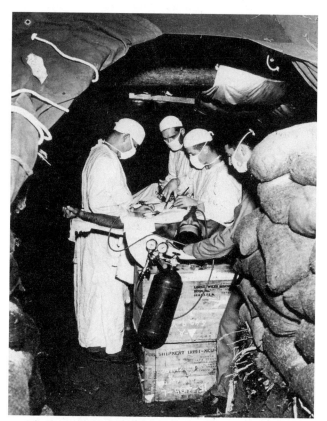

During World War II in Bougainville (the largest of the Solomon Islands) a combat surgical team of the U.S. Army Medical Corps operates in a jungle dugout.

developed ambulance units, field hospitals, use of medical inspectors, echeloned surgical care, and supply and record-keeping systems that ensured a controlled flow of patients from point of wounding to initial and then definitive surgical care. His essential, final contribution was to persuade the senior line commanders to place all of his system under *medical* command and control. Letterman's overall scheme has been adopted by all Western armies and improved by aeromedical evacuation and better surgical technology — but the system does not differ in concept.

The 1864 Geneva Convention (see *Laws of War*) and its subsequent modifications markedly changed and enhanced the status of medical personnel and their patients. The gradual provision of neutrality on battlefield and ocean, when offered by an enemy, simplified the evacuation and care of the wounded and sick. During the nineteenth century, the status of physicians was gradually transformed: formerly civilian participants, they became commissioned officers. Nurses, dentists, medical administrators, and veterinarians became officers during the twentieth century.

The first army to apply successfully all the technology of bacteriology, vector control, immunization, modern surgery, and echeloned care was the Japanese army in 1904–1905 in the Russo-Japanese War (q.v.). It was the first army to suffer more deaths from enemy action than from disease.

World War I (q.v.) brought all the new advances in civilian medicine to war: the x-ray, typhoid immunization, female nurse corps, automobile ambulances, blood transfusion, and major improvements in neurosurgery, wound care, and orthopedic and plastic surgery, for example. For the first time, psychiatry became a useful military medical discipline; it explained "shell shock" as a behavioral response rather than as cowardice or malingering. The airplane's entry as a weapon forced the development of the new physiological-clinical specialty of aviation medicine. Chemical warfare involved the medical disciplines in mask development and treatment of the chemically wounded. Mass weaponry produced mass casualties and the formal organization of triage as a medical procedure.

The interwar years saw the development of medical specialization, chemotherapeutic agents such as sulfa drugs and antibiotics, and marked improvements in specialized surgery. World War II (q.v.) became a great clinical laboratory, testing massive use of blood transfusion, DDT, aeromedical evacuation, antimalarial drugs, and the management of burns. The special medical problems of submarine crews and the management of casualties during amphibious assault were gradually and successfully solved. Psychic collapse became known as "battle fatigue" or "combat exhaustion" — language understandable to the line, and thus acceptable as a medical condition. The end result of this massive investment in medical support was a 4 percent died-of-wounds rate (statistics from U.S. and British forces) — the lowest ever in major war. As dependable preventive, prophylactic, protective, and sanitary control measures became available, medical staffs urged them on the line commanders. Not all commanders were as receptive as William Slim (q.v.) or Douglas MacArthur (q.v.). When commanders enforced hygiene, sanitation, the taking of prophylactic drugs, and so on, the disease rates fell. The troops of commanders who did not — such as Erwin Rommel (q.v.) and Omar Bradley (q.v.) — like the Japanese army, lost much of their fighting power because of disease, or in Bradley's case, to the cold of a European winter. Overall, World War II saw the death rates from disease fall markedly below the killed-in-action rates.

The more recent wars of the twentieth century have introduced technological changes that have benefited military medicine — the use of the helicopter for medical evacuation in Korea and Vietnam serves as an example. In spite of high-velocity and multifragment wounds, improvements such as faster evacuation, better ancillary support for surgery, and increased investment in military medicine have lowered the died-of-wounds rate to 2.5 percent. Much research has been devoted to the effects of radiation — happily, there has been no need to apply it. The hospital ship has become a true modern hospital afloat, and nursing and administrative specialists have assumed many of the tasks previously performed by physicians. Disease remains the greatest cause of morbidity, noneffectiveness, and temporary loss of manpower, in spite of increased use of immunizations, antibiotics, and control measures. It is necessary to continue teaching line commanders that they are responsible for the health of their command through their command of health.

Military medicine in the twentieth century in the West may be summarized as those aspects of medical practice and public health directed to diseases and injuries essentially restricted to combat. Line commanders have largely learned to understand and use the full capabilities of their medical support systems. Unfortunately, military historians still generally ignore the medical aspects of the campaigns and wars they report. Perhaps they will eventually accept the impact of medicine on war as at least as important as their discussions of weapons and tactics.

ROBERT J. T. JOY

Megiddo, Battle of

1468 B.C.

Megiddo has always been considered the key to northern Israel. Its location — twenty-two miles southeast of modern Haifa — at the head of a mountain pass along the Via Maris (an ancient coastal route that connected Egypt, Syria, and Mesopotamia) has allowed it to control lucrative trade traffic and to guard the fertile Valley of Jezreel (Esdraelon). It is also the site of the first battle in history to be recorded in detail.

In 1468 B.C., the Egyptian pharaoh Thutmose III (q.v.) faced a rebellion by a Canaanite league that included the king of Megiddo. The campaign was swift, and shortly after taking Gaza, Thutmose stopped to hold a council of war to determine which of three routes he should take to Megiddo. The most direct was through the Aruna Pass, a narrow mountain defile admirably suited for an ambush, or easily obstructed at its exit. Thutmose's commanders advised against it. In an inscription in the temple of Karnak recording the battle, they ask, "How is it to go through the pass which becomes narrow? When it is known that the enemy is there, waiting on the other side . . . ? Will not the horses have to go single file . . . ?"

Thutmose rejected their cautious advice and set out through the Aruna Pass at the head of his troops. The Canaanites, not believing their enemy would risk being ambushed, had divided their chariot forces to intercept the Egyptian army at the more easily accessible northern and southern routes. When they learned that Thutmose had come through the central pass, both wings sped back to attack his army, which had drawn up on the plains before Megiddo. In the battle that followed, the Canaanites were utterly routed, fleeing back to Megiddo in such disorder that the inhabitants had to pull their defenders to safety with ropes. Had the Egyptian army not stopped to loot the abandoned Canaanite camp, Megiddo would probably have been taken immediately. Instead, it withstood a seven-month siege before finally being captured.

This battle was far from the last for Megiddo. Because of its critical location, the site was fought for many times, and its possession or loss often signaled an ancient empire's rise or fall. Eventually, it became the symbol of humanity's final battle: the name Mount Megiddo, or Khar Megiddo in ancient Hebrew, was transliterated as Armageddon in the Book of Revelation.

IRA MEISTRICH

Memoirs of War

Recollections of war have been written since there have been wars to record and people who could write about them. Xenophon (q.v.) wrote his *Anabasis*, his account of the Greek expedition into Persia, in the fourth century B.C., and it is still one of the most vivid of war stories. Caesar's (q.v.) *Gallic Wars*, written three centuries later, is also a classic, though of a different kind: Xenophon was a civilian who was drawn into soldiering by circumstances; Caesar was a career commander, and a politician, as commanders often have to be.

This division of memoir writers has persisted through the centuries to the present day. On the one hand are the generals, who write about military strategy, large movements of troops, and battles lost and won, often with a good deal of self-congratulation for the victories and self-exoneration for the defeats. Caesar wrote like that, and two thousand years later so did William Westmoreland (q.v.), who commanded the U.S. troops in Vietnam (q.v.) (though he was not so good a writer). On the other hand are the ordinary soldiers, the junior officers and enlisted men. They see war at close range, with little sense of the larger battle of which they are a part. Their stories are about the strangeness and confusion of the fragment of war that they can see from their trenches, or down their gun barrels, and about fear and death. They rarely make broad moral or political judgments; they have little to say about courage and cowardice, or about victory and defeat. Their values are simpler: comradeship, endurance, good soldiering, and survival.

The small-scale stories that these ordinary soldiers tell are often sharply observed and intensely felt; they tell the reader how war looks and feels to a soldier in the midst of it. The best of them also tell what war does to young soldiers and how it changes them. Perhaps that is why so many war memoirs are written long after the events they narrate — the older, changed person can look back on youth and see the process of maturing in war. Most of the memorable narratives of World War I (q.v.) were written a decade or more after the war's end; roughly the same time lapse occurred between the Vietnam War and when men wrote their memoirs of it. Other veterans have waited longer: Elisha Stockwell was fifteen years old when he joined the Wisconsin Volunteers in 1861 and eighty-one when he wrote his recollections of the American Civil War (q.v.); Alvin Kernan waited fifty years to recall his experiences in the great aircraft carrier battles of World War II (q.v.) (in *Crossing the Line*).

Until the present century, the writing of war memoirs was limited by the fact that the majority of European soldiers and sailors were illiterate. For example, the best English account by a common soldier of the wars against Napoleon (q.v.), *The Recollections of Rifleman Harris*, had to be dictated: Harris could neither read nor write. A few remarkable memoirs did come out of Napoleon's armies — notably *The Memoirs of Sergeant Bourgogne*, a narrative of the march to Moscow and the terrible retreat, and *The Note-books of Captain Coignet*, which ends at Waterloo. But there are not many such books, when one considers how many men fought in those wars, because there were not many men who could write them.

American armies were better educated, and excellent memoirs were written by soldiers of both the Revolutionary War (q.v.) and the Civil War: from the Revolution, the writings of Colonel "Light-Horse Harry" Lee and Private Joseph Plumb Martin; from the Civil War, the works of General Ulysses S. Grant (q.v.), General Robert E. Lee (q.v.), Captain John Beatty, and Private John Ransom (whose story is of a prisoner of war in the Confederacy's Andersonville Prison). But still, the number of personal narratives of those wars is small in relation to the numbers of troops engaged.

In the early twentieth century this ratio changed because the class composition of armies changed. Nineteenth-century war had been fought by standing armies, mercenaries, and conscripts ("the scum of the earth," Wellington [q.v.] called them), commanded by professional soldiers of the traditional officer caste. The scale of World War I (q.v.) made such armies insufficient, necessitating recruitment from the middle class to fill the ranks of junior officers and men.

These middle-class soldiers — young, literate, idealistic, and recently civilians — wrote the personal

---

The Ten Best War Memoirs

Anabasis (Greece, third century B.C.) by Xenophon

Commentaries on the Gallic Wars (Rome, 53?-44 B.C.) and *Commentaries on the Civil War* (45 B.C.) by Julius Caesar

The Jewish War (Rome, first century A.D.) by Flavius Josephus

Personal Memoirs (United States, 1885) by Ulysses S. Grant

Storm of Steel: From the Diary of a German Stormtroop Officer on the Western Front (Germany, 1920) by Ernst Jünger

A Passionate Prodigality: Fragments of Autobiography (England, 1933) by Guy Chapman

Some Desperate Glory: The Diary of a Young Officer, 1917 (England, 1981) by Edwin Campion Vaughan

Alamein to Zem-Zem (England, 1946) by Keith Douglas

With the Old Breed: At Peleliu and Okinawa (United States, 1981) by E. B. Sledge

Dispatches (United States, 1968) by Michael Herr

---

narratives of World War I that are still read, books like Siegfried Sassoon's *Memoirs of an Infantry Officer*, Robert Graves's *Good-bye to All That*, Edwin Campion Vaughan's *Some Desperate Glory*, the German Ernst Jünger's *Storm of Steel*, the French Paul Lintier's *My .75*. Middle-class soldiers also wrote the poems and novels of that war that rank as classics of war literature. At this point the war memoir became a literary form in its own right — written by literary men who were self-conscious about what they were writing. Before this century, no war writer since Caesar had been a distinguished *writer*; now, for a time, many were.

Geography as well as class defined the canon of World War I memoirs. All of the books mentioned in the previous paragraph are centered on the Western Front: for their readers, that front *was* the war. But consider what that story leaves out: the entire Eastern Front (where far more men died than were killed in France); the Middle East (known to readers only through T. E. Lawrence's [q.v.] brilliant *Seven Pillars of Wisdom*); the fighting at Gallipoli (q.v.) and Salonika; all of Africa; the entire war at sea. The unrepresented armies include all the troops from the British and French colonies, whose memoirs exist but are not read, and the Americans (Hervey Allen's *Toward the Flame* should be considered a classic of the war, but it is not).

The war on the Western Front makes up the modern reader's favorite war story. World War II memoirs, by comparison, are far less popular, and no established canon of personal narratives has emerged. Why is that? Perhaps because of the war's enormous scale: it was bigger than World War I in every respect — more soldiers, more machines, more battlefronts, and more dead (including far more civilian dead). Perhaps readers' imaginations simply cannot encompass such range and variety. Or it may be simply that when the second war came along, the narratives of the first already existed: the soldiers' tales of what modern war was like had already been written and read.

Nonetheless, a great many memoirs of World War II were written, and the best of them differ in character from the narratives of the earlier war. What they add to the other war's story is the element of war's personal excitement. There are two possible reasons for this. One is that major battles of World War II were fought for the first time by machines, and that paradoxically these battles were romantic, because they seemed to be fought in single combats, like war in the *Iliad*. The Battle of Britain (q.v.) and the war of tanks in North Africa offer two examples. The best-known narrative of the air war, Richard Hillary's *The Last Enemy*, is not the best account of actual aerial combat; for that, one must turn to more modest books such as D. M. Crook's *Spitfire Pilot*. Keith Douglas's *Alamein to Zem-Zem* superbly narrates the tank combat in North Africa.

Perhaps another reason for the return of excitement in World War II memoirs can be explained by that huge war's often intimate scale — small, often secret units played an important role. It was as though the military planners regretted that World War I had so lacked individual high adventure and were determined to make up the difference in World War II with parachute drops into occupied France (*Hugh Dormer's Diaries*), commando attacks on Sardinia (John Verney's *Going to the Wars*), and Orde Wingate's irregular soldiering in Burma (Terence O'Brien's *Out of the Blue*).

Still, many excellent accounts were written of the large-scale, more anonymous battles: in Western Europe, Donald Pearce's *Journal of a War*; in Italy, Farley Mowat's *And No Birds Sang*, and John Bassett's *War Journal of an Innocent Soldier*; in the Pacific, E. B. Sledge's *With the Old Breed: At Peleliu and Okinawa*.

Although the world has seen many wars since 1945, only one has produced a significant body of war narratives. The Vietnam War marked another change in the constitution of a Western army: it was the first American war from which the middle classes were largely exempted. Soldiers were drawn primarily from the lower end of the social ladder — the rural and urban poor, the unemployed and unemployable, members of minorities. They were often hastily trained, and they went to the war for a short, fixed time — usually one year — so they scarcely had time to become seasoned soldiers or to coalesce into coordinated fighting units.

The war memoirs that these men have written tell of a troubling, fierce, and brutal war. They also tell of the troops' confusion about their reasons for fighting, their guilt at the civilian casualties they inflicted, and their resentment at their country's failure to stand solidly behind them. Some of the best accounts of that war are Philip Caputo's *A Rumor of War*, Tim O'Brien's *If I Die in a Combat Zone*, and Ron Kovic's *Born on the Fourth of July*. Kovic's book exemplifies one kind of memoir common among Vietnam veterans; he was paralyzed in combat, and much of his story is of the effects of that wound. The aftermath of Vietnam is an important part of the story of that war, and not all of the wounds inflicted in combat were physical.

The rise of popular journalism over the past century and a half has produced a new category of war memoir. From Winston Churchill (q.v.) in the Boer War (q.v.), Ernie Pyle in World War II, to Michael Herr in Vietnam, war correspondents have observed modern war at more or less close range and have recorded their impressions. More or less, because their nearness to the field of battle has depended on the degree of official censorship imposed: it was heavy in World War I, and there were no first-rate books by correspondents; it was light in World War II and in Vietnam, and there was much excellent reporting. It has been heavy since then, and there are no eyewitness accounts, by journalists, of the Battle for the Falkland Islands (q.v.) or the Gulf War (q.v.).

SAMUEL HYNES

Mercenaries

There is no general agreement on exactly what the term *mercenary* means. *The Great Soviet Encyclopedia* calls all professional armies, at least of capitalist countries, "mercenary armies." The word is often used to denigrate one's enemies — as when Kaiser

Wilhelm called Indian troops in British service during World War I (q.v.) "an army of mercenaries." On the other hand, the thousands of Canadian and Mexican citizens who served in the American army in Vietnam (q.v.) were clearly *not* mercenaries.

What then is a true mercenary? Essentially mercenaries are not part of the society for whom they fight nor a part of its regular forces; rather, they are specialists in warfare and are paid. Mercenaries provide a number of advantages to their paymaster, foremost being military skills not possessed by national troops. Mercenaries may be willing to serve when the paymaster's subjects may not be. They consequently often make better bodyguards than the national troops would; members of a given society may be swayed by politics or sentiment. As a seventeenth-century Scots mercenary who fought in the Thirty Years' War (q.v.) put it, "So we serve our master honestlie, it is no matter what master we serve."

Equally important is why a person becomes a mercenary. Although simple love of adventure and combat may be a factor, lack of economic opportunity is the chief motivator. Farmers, herders, and merchants who cannot earn a living, disinherited nobles, and others who simply know no other trade have always been the mainstay of recruitment. The supply of such men is as important as the demand.

Mercenaries have usually had an unsavory reputation, reflected in the old European saying that "Every soldier needs three peasants: one to give up his lodging, one to provide his wife, and one to take his place in Hell." Yet their use is almost universal in advanced societies, and they have often played key roles in history. Without them Carthage could never have challenged Rome, and Greek mercenaries were a crucial factor in the spread of Hellenistic civilization from Italy to Afghanistan after the death of Alexander the Great (q.v.).

Mercenaries were an essential, and underrated, element of medieval warfare. Flemish mercenaries, for example, allowed King Stephen of England (1135–1154) to fight off the Plantagenets for nearly twenty years. When Henry II came to power, he banished the Flemings, who were hated by the English — and promptly hired his own mercenaries. By the end of the medieval period, mercenaries were everywhere in Europe, from the famed Swiss pikemen to Italian *condottieri* like Sir John Hawkwood (q.v.). Mercenaries were heavily used elsewhere. In 755 the Chinese T'ang dynasty nearly fell when a Turkish general revolted and Indian pastoral tribes used military service to transform themselves into a warrior caste, the Rajputs, or "Sons of Kings."

The use of mercenaries by European powers continued; Hessian soldiers (q.v.) used by Britain in the American Revolution (q.v.) were a notable example. Before the creation of modern nation-states, most rulers found it convenient to use mercenaries. This era ended dramatically during the French Revolution (see *French Revolution, Wars of the*) with the massacre of the Swiss Guard in Paris. The modern concept of national sovereignty required the suppression of nonstate military activity. Foreign nationals would henceforth be uniformed, trained, and officered as units of the national army such as the French Foreign Legion and the British Gurkhas (q.v.). True mercenaries reappeared in the 1960s when new African states such as the Congo, lacking an indigenous military infrastructure, briefly employed such troops. The major market for mercenaries now seems to be drug cartels and private security companies.

W. SCOTT JESSEE

Mexican War

1846–1848

Regarded at the time as America's first foreign war and as the first real test of the military capability of a republic founded on democratic principles, the Mexican War coincided with a romantic American nationalism and a fervent expansionist spirit that would carry the United States to the Pacific Ocean. Relations between the United States and Mexico deteriorated, fueled by an unresolved claims issue against Mexico, by Mexico's refusal to recognize the annexation of Texas to the American Union, and by fears that Mexican lands on America's western borders would fall under British control. Following a futile effort to resolve the differences peaceably, undertaken by the administration of President James K. Polk, Mexican forces crossed the Rio Grande, Texas's traditional boundary, and engaged an American army under Zachary Taylor (q.v.). At Polk's strong urging, Congress recognized the existence of a state of war between the two countries (May 1846). Calls for volunteers to supplement the small American army were oversubscribed; naval units blockaded the Mexican coastline; and a massive effort to provide logistical support to a military force fighting on foreign soil far

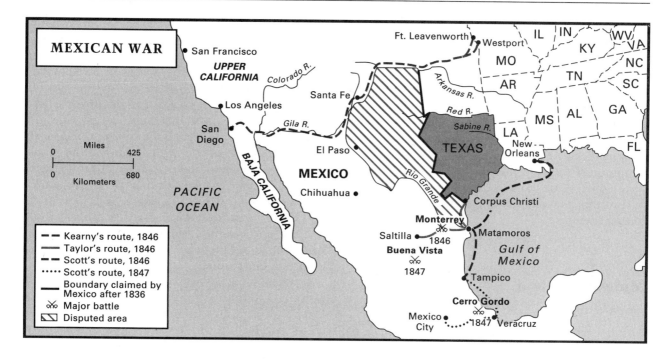

MEXICAN WAR

Miles
0 ——————— 425

Kilometers
0 ——————— 680

- - - Kearny's route, 1846
——— Taylor's route, 1846
- - - Scott's route, 1846
······ Scott's route, 1847
——— Boundary claimed by Mexico after 1836
⚔ Major battle
▧ Disputed area

from the nation's population centers was undertaken. Military operations were opened in three areas. Taylor's army moved into northeastern Mexico, taking Monterrey after a costly struggle and defeating a superior Mexican force under Antonio López de Santa Anna at the Battle of Buena Vista (February 1847). A smaller army, commanded by Stephen Watts Kearny, was sent from Missouri to occupy Mexico's northern borderlands, New Mexico, and California. Disappointed with Mexico's refusal to enter peace negotiations, Polk decided to open a third campaign against Mexico City. Commanded by Winfield Scott (q.v.), an army of regulars and volunteers landed on the Mexican coast near Veracruz, a virtually unprecedented logistical feat, and marched inland along the route of the sixteenth-century Spanish conquistadores (q.v.). Sharp engagements were fought at Cerro Gordo and in the environs of Mexico City, resulting in the occupation of the Mexican capital (September 1847). The Treaty of Guadalupe Hidalgo was signed (January 1848), by which Mexico recognized the Rio Grande boundary with Texas, and ceded New Mexico and upper California to the United States. The United States in turn paid Mexico fifteen million dollars to provide fiscal stability to the weakened and troubled Mexican government.

ROBERT W. JOHANNSEN

MIAs

Though the science of forensics is often enlisted to assist in the identification of remains, modern technology has increased the difficulty of determining whether a missing soldier (an MIA—missing in action) might still be alive. The extensive use of heavy artillery that began with World War I (q.v.), for example, greatly increased the chances that remains would be ploughed into the ground, scattered, or even pulverized. Similarly, the use of aircraft greatly increased the chances that there would be no witnesses to a soldier's death. These technical complications, however, pale in comparison to the political ones.

When armies were composed of "the scum of the earth enlisted for drink," the enumeration of casualties was simple. Finding the reason for any given loss was far less important than the fact of a gap in the ranks and was considered a far less pressing task than finding a substitute for the missing man. When, as in the case of modern industrial democracies, it became increasingly common for soldiers to be related to persons of influence in civil society, investigating the fate of those who failed to return home gained importance. After the end of U.S. involvement in the Vietnam War (1965–1975) (q.v.), for example, the fate of the two thousand or so Americans listed as "missing in action" became a matter of considerable public controversy.

Ironically, the interest displayed in accounting for all those who did not come home may have had the effect of increasing the number of those missing in action. Knowing that prisoners, remains, and even facts concerning missing men could be traded for thinly disguised foreign aid, some countries — including the Soviet Union after World War II (q.v.) and Communist Vietnam after the Indochina War (1946–1954) (q.v.) — tried to make the most of these assets by limiting the information they released to their former enemies.

BRUCE I. GUDMUNDSSON

Midway, Battle of

June 4–6, 1942

This fleet engagement between U.S. and Japanese navies in the north-central Pacific Ocean resulted from Japan's desire to sink the American aircraft carriers that had escaped destruction at Pearl Harbor (q.v.). Admiral Yamamoto Isoroku, Japanese fleet commander, chose to invade a target relatively close to Pearl Harbor to draw out the American fleet, calculating that when the United States began its counterattack, the Japanese would be prepared to crush them. Instead, an American intelligence breakthrough — the solving of the Japanese fleet codes — enabled Pacific Fleet commander Admiral Chester W. Nimitz (q.v.) to understand the exact Japanese plans. Nimitz placed available U.S. carriers in position to surprise the Japanese moving up for their preparatory air strikes on Midway Island itself.

The intelligence interplay would be critical to the outcome of the battle and began many weeks before the clash of arms. American radio nets in the Pacific picked up various orders Yamamoto had dispatched to prepare his forces for the operation. As early as May 2, messages that were intercepted began to indicate some forthcoming operation, and a key fact, the planned day-of-battle position of the Japanese carriers, would be divulged in a notice sent on May 16. By the time Nimitz had to make final decisions, the Japanese plans and order of battle had been reconstructed in considerable detail.

American combat forces took over where intelligence efforts left off. Scouts found the Japanese early in the morning of June 4. Although initial strikes by Midway-based planes were not successful, American carrier-based planes turned the tide. Torpedo bombers became separated from the American dive-bombers and were slaughtered (36 of 42 shot down), but they diverted Japanese defenses just in time for the dive-bombers to arrive; some of them had become lost, and now by luck they found the Japanese. The Japanese carriers were caught while refueling and rearming their planes, making them especially vulnerable. The Americans sank four fleet carriers — the entire strength of the task force — *Akagi, Kaga, Soryu,* and *Hiryu,* with 322 aircraft and over five thousand sailors. The Japanese also lost the heavy cruiser *Mikuma.* American losses included 147 aircraft and more than three hundred seamen.

Analysts often point to Japanese aircraft losses at Midway as eliminating the power of the Imperial Navy's air arm, but in fact about two-thirds of air crews survived. More devastating was the loss of trained mechanics and aircraft ground crews who went down with the ships. Some historians see Midway as the turning point in the Pacific theater of the war, after which Americans rode straight to Tokyo; others view it as a cusp in the war, after which initiative hung in the balance, to swing toward the Allies in

A Japanese cruiser tries to dodge American bombs in the June 1942 Battle of Midway, a turning point in the Pacific war.

the Guadalcanal campaign (q.v.). Either way, Midway ranks as a truly decisive battle.

JOHN PRADOS

Militarism

This term refers both to beliefs and patterns of behavior thought specific to the military, and more commonly to extreme influence or paramountcy in society of military ideas and organizations. Difficult to define precisely, the word appeared in English by the 1860s and acquired currency during the nineteenth century, as war itself was being transformed.

For analysts, the basic question has been whether militarism should be interpreted as a remnant of the past (for example, in the much-studied case of Germany, as fundamentally a legacy of Prussia) or instead as something distinctly modern, associated with industrialization or the rise of capitalism.

The first argument goes back at least to Jean-Jacques Rousseau, who saw the military and its technology as sources of excessive influence, which could be avoided by the democratization of forces, in particular through militia organization. This approach fed into the subsequent debate over standing armies, which Immanuel Kant and Johann Fichte criticized as "threats to peace and economic prosperity." In the nineteenth century, Herbert Spencer argued that militarism was fundamentally a process of regimentation, which spread from the army into the whole society. A generation later, Norman Angell began to draw a connection to economics when he contrasted the nonmilitary industrialism of the United States and Canada with the "stupid and sordid gold-braid" militarism on which he blamed the plight of Latin American countries and the militarized "struggle-for-survival" economic competition of the European states.

The second approach has become characteristic of Marxism, for which militarism raises the same issue as do force and violence (q.v.): first, how to explain the emergence of coercion from a system (market transactions) that is stipulated to be uncoerced; and second, and even more difficult, how to reserve primacy to economic factors and avoid imputing fundamental causal significance to military actions, even when the military has become paramount, as in fascist states.

On these issues Karl Marx is obscure and Friedrich Engels unhelpful; Vladimir Lenin adds little (the term *militarism* occurs in only fifty-nine passages in his collected works), but Leon Trotsky does invoke "Bonapartism" as an unexplained category. German radicals Karl Liebknecht, and then Rosa Luxemburg, however, elaborated the Marxist analysis in the early twentieth century, making militarism both product of and fundamental to capitalist class rule; Rudolf Hilferding and the Russian Nikolay Bukharin went further, associating stages of military evolution with specific phases of economic development.

The rise of fascist regimes in Europe starting with Italy, with their celebration of force and the military as basis, posed a serious challenge to such analyses. Initially the Marxists believed that these regimes were transitional — last gasps of capitalism to be quickly overthrown by revolution. But this approach was gravely undermined when events failed to unfold as predicted.

A concept related to militarism, that of the warlord, acquired wide currency when China confronted civil war in the 1910s and 1920s, and has since been borrowed by the West to refer in particular to chaotic situations in which groups of military figures divide a state, such as Lebanon or Somalia. The term goes back to German *Kriegsherr*, and reached Chinese through Japanese, being introduced in 1918 by the early Communist Ch'en Tu-hsiu. Ch'en was thoroughly familiar with the Marxist analyses outlined above, and used the word in a Marxist sense. The popularity of the term *warlordism*, however, rapidly raised the same questions as arose with *militarism* in the West. Like militarism, the concept is vague about causes: some in China saw the phenomenon as rooted in tradition and pointed to recurrent civil war at times of dynastic transition; others attempted to analyze it as a product of the economic dislocations caused by imperialism and the rise of capitalism.

Today the economic analysis of militarism has been largely discredited, as too has been the belief that military forces, by their nature, are power seeking. Even Francisco Franco, whose regime in Spain was a rather pure example of the military in charge, had power thrust into his (willing) hands by a crisis whose origins lay elsewhere. Hence the growing consensus today that militarism is a product of breakdowns of civilian rule, or failure of such rule to be firmly established. Such an approach was taken in China by the Columbia-trained philosopher Hu Shih and others who blamed warlordism on the failures of civilian politicians rather than on the military directly; in the West, it finds an echo in the work of the military historian Alfred Vagts, who contrasted militarism not with pacifism, but with genuine civilian control.

ARTHUR WALDRON

Volker R. Berghahn, *Militarism: The History of an International Debate, 1861–1979* (1982).

Militia

Militias, armed forces raised more or less ad hoc from civilian populations, began with the Greek hoplites (q.v.), who served their city-states in arms, as well as in political assemblies. In the Middle Ages, militias embodied the responsibility of towns and cities to conduct their own defenses and the pragmatism that led authorities in cases of emergency to summon anyone capable of bearing arms. China and pre-Tokugawa Japan followed patterns similar to those of the West, with laws and customs authorizing the summoning of peasants and townsmen when necessary. Traditional African states as well usually depended heavily on "hostilities only" mobilization of their peasantry.

In principle, most political systems, European and non-European, continue to require at least a theoretical military responsibility from fit males in their late teens to midforties, but in practice, militias have declined in appeal for several reasons. Politically, they represent at least a potential threat. Chinese rebellions were as a rule started and sustained by men with some military experience. Militias posed operational problems as well. From the Middle Ages onward, warfare demanded an increasing spectrum of skills that had no civilian counterparts: men lacking them were liabilities on the battlefield. Nor did militia units possess either the cohesion or the discipline to perform the evolutions and sustain the casualty rates on which early modern war depended. Finally, a point best highlighted by England's experiences in almost a century of conflict with American Indians and the French, militiamen could not be removed from subsistence economies without substantial risks of loss and disruption.

Militia units did often perform effectively in the Seven Years' War (q.v.) and the American Revolution (q.v.). Increasingly, however, their role became that of a feeder force for regular units. Wellington's (q.v.) peninsular army was largely sustained by replacements from the British militia. In the latter stages of the Napoleonic Wars, Austria and Prussia experimented with militias not only recruited but also officered from the general population and used as first-line troops. Prussia's military in particular performed effectively during the war. In the peace that followed, however, popular enthusiasm for the institution proved insufficient to maintain its effectiveness.

Britain and the United States developed alternate forms of militias in the nineteenth century. These comprised volunteer forces whose members committed themselves to systematic training on their own time and tended to acculturate as regular armies. The British Volunteers, later reorganized as the Territorial Force/Army, and the U.S. National Guard, made major contributions to the war efforts of 1914–1918 and 1939–1945. They remain part of their respective countries' military systems, though their operational roles have been eclipsed by their symbolic functions.

Militias, broadly defined, continue to sustain the political principle that citizens owe some form of military service, the economic virtue of relatively low costs, and the social benefit of minimally disrupting the participants' lives. Switzerland remains, however, the only state to place full reliance for its security on a militia force. In an age of high-tech war, amateurs, no matter how well intentioned, are seen as a liability where it matters most: in battle.

DENNIS E. SHOWALTER

Mitchell, William "Billy"

1879–1936, U.S. Army Officer and Proponent of Air Power

A pioneer airman, Billy Mitchell commanded the American Expeditionary Force's fledgling air force in World War I (q.v.). Mitchell proved himself a first-class leader in providing air support for John J. Pershing's (q.v.) offensives at St.-Mihiel and the Meuse Argonne. He successfully experimented with mass aerial bombing and was the first to use bombers to disrupt the enemy's retreat. Besides providing combat experience, the war allowed Mitchell to strike up a close acquaintance with the Royal Air Force leader, Sir Hugh Trenchard. Mitchell returned to the United States a hero and an advocate of air power. As such, he began a crusade to create an independent air force. In that effort, Mitchell became increasingly strident in attacks on the senior leadership of both the army and the navy, which he described as criminally incompetent. Such attacks from a serving officer were intolerable, and they eventually resulted in Mitchell's court-martial (1925) and resignation (1926).

By this time Mitchell had established himself as a prophet of air power, and on that reputation his historical importance rests. Like Hugh Trenchard and Giulio Douhet, he argued that aircraft would be *the decisive weapon* of the next war, because they could reach over armies and navies and strike at the heart of enemy military power — at industry and population. Moreover, he believed, air power represented a cheaper approach to war that would prevent recurrence of World War I's bloodletting.

In both these suppositions, history proved Mitchell wrong. But unlike his fellow theorists, Mitchell argued that the employment of air power demanded that air forces first defeat the enemy air force, and that therefore fighters would be a key component in the equation. Here history proved him right. In this sense his reputation as a prophet of air power is deserved, but his unprincipled attacks on the other services left bad blood well after his death.

WILLIAMSON MURRAY

Mobilization

The process of putting armed forces on a war footing can be as simple as hiring mercenaries (q.v.) or calling up civilian levies, whether peasants from the fields or armed and trained citizens like the Greek hoplites (q.v.). Mobilization in its modern Western context, however, began in seventeenth-century Sweden. That country's peacetime army was brought up to strength by men conscripted, left in their villages until summoned to the colors, and replaced by the community as they became casualties. The Prussian canton system, introduced in 1732, assigned regiments specific recruiting districts whose conscripts were furloughed most of the year and summoned to the colors only for refresher training. For most of the eighteenth century, however, Prussia remained the exception. Armies met their manpower demands by intensifying the recruitment of volunteers through promises of riches, glory, and regular meals, supplemented by alcohol.

The Wars of the French Revolution (q.v.) brought relatively few changes in traditional patterns. The patriotic volunteers of 1792 and the *levée en masse* of 1793 rapidly gave way to a conscription system with numerous loopholes. Neither successive revolutionary governments nor Napoleon (q.v.) himself were able to utilize in any systematic fashion the material resources of France, its clients, or its subjects. Nevertheless, over a million Frenchmen enlisted — not always from love of country. From Spain to Russia, Napoleon's armies came increasingly to resemble their predecessors of the Thirty Years' War (q.v.): rootless cosmopolitans sustained by hopes of plunder and dreams of glory.

It was Prussia that began the systematic planning that has been ever since regarded as the essence of mobilization. Initially the state focused on manpower. Successive conscription laws provided for limited terms of peacetime service in the active army, and its various reserves. For the Franco-Prussian War in 1870 (q.v.), from a peacetime army of 300,000, Prussia could raise over 850,000 men in a matter of days. Prussia's mobilization system also increasingly incorporated the systematic use of railroads to move troops and supplies to projected theaters of operation. The results proved so superior to the French improvisations that in succeeding years, every Continental army adapted its planning staff system to put as many of its citizens as possible into uniform and bring them to the frontiers in the shortest possible time.

Prior to 1914, relatively little attention was paid to economic mobilization. General belief in short, decisive wars produced a corresponding faith that anything not on hand when the shooting started would arrive too late to make a difference. The result during World War I (q.v.) was the inefficiency that inevitably accompanies improvisation, such as British shells that failed to explode. In the interwar years all the major powers, including Soviet Russia and the United States, were at similar pains to prepare contingency plans optimizing the use of human and material resources. In World War II (q.v.), Britain was probably the most successful in this process but paid the price of national exhaustion. Nazi Germany's administrative inefficiency seriously handicapped the Reich's war effort. In Joseph Stalin's (q.v.) Russia, the terror system more than made up for any structural weaknesses. The United States finished the war without breathing hard, but it was the exception.

Since 1945 nuclear weapons, guerrilla warfare, and increasingly complex military technologies have combined to make mobilization in the classic sense less important to the military policies of most nations. Israel and Switzerland are the principal exceptions. In recent years even those states have taken some steps away from the concept of the citizen-soldier whose existence makes mobilization necessary. Contemporary wars are expected to be waged from a standing start by professional forces presumably better able than uniformed civilians to cope with the demands of modern battlefields and high-tech weaponry.

DENNIS E. SHOWALTER

Moguls

See Mughals.

Mohács, Battle of

August 29, 1526

Following the capitulation to the Ottomans (q.v.) of the strategically important fortress of Belgrade in 1521, the rout at Mohács of a Hungarian army under King Lewis II Jagellon in only one and a half hours precipitated the division of Hungary into three zones. In their tactical use of "envelopment and annihilation," the Ottoman forces were able to take full advantage of the disarray of their opponents. The number of Ottoman troops has been estimated at approximately 60,000 regular and provincial cavalry troops, in addition to a like number of irregulars and auxiliaries, and between 25,000 and 40,000 for the Hungarians and their allies. After the battle Sultan Suleiman I (q.v.) and his army entered Buda, but returned home before the winter. This was the first occasion on which the Ottoman army had advanced into Hungarian territory, and marked the start of a long period of Ottoman land warfare in Europe.

The most significant outcome of the Battle of Mohács was the disappearance of the Hungarian kingdom. De facto partition between Hapsburgs and Ottomans, in the case of the latter through their candidate John Zápolya, led in 1541 to direct Ottoman rule of the central part of the country with the establishment of the Province of Budin (Buda); the Hapsburgs retained the northern and western parts of Hungary, while Zápolya's infant son was confirmed as Ottoman vassal in Transylvania.

CAROLINE FINKEL

Moltke, Helmuth Karl von

1800–1891, *Prussian and German Field Marshal, Chief of the Great General Staff*

Helmuth Karl von Moltke's importance to modern European history springs from two sources: As designer of the modern German General Staff (a system eventually adopted by all powers of consequence) he was and remains the preeminent military organizational innovator since Napoleon (q.v.). And as strategic architect of Prussia's victories over Denmark in 1864, Austria in 1866, and France in 1870–1871, he played a key role in restructuring the political map of Europe. Moltke was truly the Bismarck (q.v.) of the battlefield, forming with his fellow Junker the key political-military team of the nineteenth century.

Yet his character was hardly typical of the popular conception of narrow Prussian militarism. Deeply influenced by the broad learning and genteel mannerisms of his mother, Moltke as a young man did follow his somewhat less sophisticated father into military service; but literature, the classics, history, science, and languages all fascinated him. Indeed, while doing exemplary work as a young officer at the Prussian Kriegsakademie in Berlin (then under the direction of Carl von Clausewitz [q.v.]), Moltke managed to gain something very close to a traditional German liberal-humanist education.

In 1828, Moltke left his regiment for his first posting on the General Staff, but nonetheless found time to author popular fiction in magazines under a pseudonym. Always reticent — his sobriquet would soon become "the Man of Silence" — Moltke's interest in writing rather than speaking developed as his early army years went by. He soon translated Edward Gibbon's *Decline and Fall of the Roman Empire* into German; and when he was seconded to the Turkish army for a tour of duty in Egypt in 1835, he wrote a series of prose works about his travels.

In 1855 Moltke's military writings and performance were recognized when he became first adjutant to the Prussian crown prince, Friedrich Wilhelm. He was promoted to major general the following year. In 1857 he took over the duties of chief of the General Staff (a post that had declined into near irrelevance after the Napoleonic Wars, and his revolutionary contribution to both Prussian and world military history began to unfold in earnest.

"In war as in art," Moltke wrote, "there exist no general rules; in neither can talent be replaced by precept." The only way to ensure that narrow precepts did not rule within the Prussian officer corps, Moltke felt, was to train the officers of the General Staff to be cosmopolitan thinkers — much like their chief — who could be positioned throughout the army to spread the kind of philosophy and worldview that would encourage creativity and innovation. By then, Otto von Bismarck clearly intended to use the Prussian army to establish his kingdom's hegemony, first in Germany and then in Europe; and Bismarck's minister of war, Albrecht von Roon, had already begun to build an enormous new force (based on universal conscription and reserve service) to meet this political challenge.

Negatively impressed by what he read of the massive, lumbering armies and antiquated generalship of the American Civil War (q.v.), Moltke devised a system in which General Staff officers — steeped in a common philosophy — would be able to coordinate the actions of their units almost instinctively, without the need for specific orders from high commanders. The core idea behind this reorganization was *decentralization* of command structure in order to achieve greater *centralization* of forces on the battlefield. By exploiting modern innovations such as railroads and telegraphs, Moltke hoped to heighten this effect and bring even greater numbers of troops to bear at crucial junctures. As Moltke himself put it, "An order shall contain everything that a commander cannot do by himself, but nothing else."

Such a philosophy involved a break with Napoleon's emphasis on keeping an army concentrated between opposing forces — the so-called "inner line of operations" — and would allow movement in separated columns toward the enemy, leading to coordination at the final moment for a decisive strike. Mobility at the strategic level would thus be dramatically magnified.

Moltke first attempted to implement such a plan in Prussia's war against the Danes in 1864. But his directives were modified and even ignored by resentful Prussian commanders — who considered Moltke and his General Staff officers to be upstart, intellectual meddlers — and though Moltke's ideas were enough to ensure eventual victory, the action was not as swift and decisive as Moltke would have liked. The war with Austria in 1866, however, was totally different. Here, Moltke was allowed both to plan and direct the action. He outlined a scheme in which the Prussian army would enter Austria in three large, disconnected columns, defying the conventional wisdom of the past half-century. Moving swiftly, these columns were able to converge on the shocked Austrian enemy at Königgrätz (q.v.) on July 3, where they triumphed in one of the great battles of the century (see *Seven Weeks' War*).

Following the Austro-Prussian War, Moltke's stature heightened dramatically, and by the time Bismarck began to maneuver toward a war against France in 1870, no one in Prussia would have dared to argue with the chief of the General Staff's overall plan for the upcoming campaign. But Moltke, ever the innovator, stood his own Austrian triumph on its ear during this planning period and decided to drive into France with the Prussian army largely concentrated. Having studied railroad maps of eastern France, Moltke correctly divined that the French would be forced to concentrate their forces in two basic areas (around Metz and Strasbourg) and subsequently decided that the Prussians should drive one great wedge between these concentrations, destroying first one and then the other before they could join together. Having effectively killed off the principle of the "inner line of operations" at Königgrätz, Moltke apparently intended to revive it in France.

He succeeded. The first French army group was engaged in two great battles — Vionville–Mars-la-Tour and Gravelotte–St.-Privat — during which the Prussian high commanders made tactical mistakes that were counterbalanced by the almost uncanny ability of Moltke's General Staff officers to sense the plights of their comrades and come to one another's aid. The second French army group was pursued and engaged at Sedan (q.v.), but the strategic situation had already decided the result of this battle: separated from and unable to coordinate with the rest of their forces, the French were badly beaten.

Together, Moltke's victories in Denmark, Austria, and France allowed Bismarck to redesign radically the balance of power in Europe. But Moltke was far more than the military executor of Bismarck's political will. He took an active interest in politics throughout his life, and toward the end of that life he grew deeply distressed over the growing influence of the belligerent military clique that surrounded Kaiser Wilhelm. In 1890 Moltke spoke out against this group in the upper house of the German Reichstag, warning that when the war for which this group was agitating finally broke out, "its length will be incalculable and its end nowhere in sight . . . and woe to him who first sets fire to Europe, who first puts the flame to the powderkeg!"

Moltke died the following year, and his warnings against a general European war were not ultimately heeded by his inheritors. Still, his progressive innovations and broad intellect ensured his country's stability (and, arguably, that of Europe) for better than half a century — even as they created an instrument that would prove so devastatingly troublesome in less enlightened hands.

CALEB CARR

Cyril Falls, *The Art of War* (1961); Walter Gorlitz, *The History of the German General Staff* (1953); Michael Howard, *The Franco-Prussian War* (1961).

Moltke, Helmuth von (the Younger)

1848–1916, *German General and Field Marshal*

The younger Helmuth von Moltke, nephew of the man who directed Prussia's armies in the wars of German unification, was chief of the German General Staff from 1906 to 1914. A relatively conventional soldier, Moltke found himself heir to the boldest strategic conception of modern times, the so-called Schlieffen Plan (see *Schlieffen, Alfred von*), which he modified and implemented in line with his own cautious nature. The essence of the plan was an all-out attack in the west, with the right end of the German line sweeping around Paris to envelop the entire French army. Moltke reduced the weight of the German right to ward off an anticipated French offensive through Alsace and shifted additional troops to the east to counter an unexpectedly early Russian advance — two dangers that Schlieffen would have discounted. The net effect was to reduce markedly the striking power of the German attack in World War I (q.v.), though whether Moltke really deserves the lion's share of the blame for Germany's defeat on the Marne (q.v.), which he usually receives, may be doubted. Although the German right advanced less far and less fast than Schlieffen had intended, it was still exhausted and outrunning its supplies by the time it reached the Marne. Moltke's concern about the Russians was likewise reasonable, their military performance having improved considerably in the ten years since Schlieffen had perfected his work. In the end, Moltke's performance probably testifies less to the limitations of his own personality than to the larger truth of an adage coined by his great uncle: no

plan survives contact with the enemy for more than twenty-four hours. But "the Nephew," as he was called, was not the man to improvise a new plan when the old one had failed. The defeat on the Marne shattered his nerves and left him convinced, as he told the emperor, that Germany had lost the war. He was dismissed shortly thereafter.

DANIEL MORAN

Mongols

The Mongols, who created the largest connected land empire in world history, originated as a group in eastern Mongolia that in the early thirteenth century came under the leadership of Genghis Khan (q.v.). When they first appeared on the historical stage, they were pastoral nomads, migrating several times a year to find grass and water for their animals. The horse offered the mobility they required, and from an early age a Mongol learned to ride as well as to shoot a bow and arrow at full gallop. Their skill in horsemanship and archery translated into the development of a powerful cavalry, which made them a potentially formidable fighting force. However, their organization into tribes, each consisting of a relatively small number of members, meant that they could have only local or regional influence.

During the first three decades of the thirteenth century, the Mongols, led by Genghis Khan, occupied Northwest China, raided North China, and conquered much of Central Asia. Several of these campaigns, particularly in Central Asia, resulted in tremendous destruction and deliberate massacres, but the Mongol forces generally held themselves in check.

Their remarkable successes resulted from superior weaponry, tactics, and organization. They had developed a composite bow, made out of horn and sinew, and could shoot it accurately while riding a horse, giving them a significant advantage over their enemies. With a range of more than 350 yards, their bow was superior to the European crossbow, which was accurate only up to a range of 250 yards. Their small but extremely sturdy and fast horses also contributed strength to their feared armies. The Mongol cavalry, with its ability to traverse rugged terrain, was a vital asset in warfare. The Mongols' tactic of feigned withdrawal that lured their pursuers into a deadly trap, their use of dummies placed on horses to deceive the enemy about their numbers, and their positioning of captured enemy soldiers in the vanguard of their offense proved to be effective. The discipline they imposed on their forces and the sophisticated intelligence network they created before campaigns also contributed to their victories.

Genghis died in 1227, and two years elapsed before his son Ögödei was enthroned as the Great Khan. The Mongols pursued their military campaigns throughout Ögödei's reign, and their empire expanded even more dramatically. A large expedition overwhelmed the Russian states, reaching Kiev in 1240 and venturing into Poland and Hungary in 1241. Another force extinguished the Chin dynasty and overwhelmed North China by 1234. Other armies moved into Persia, Georgia, Armenia, and Korea. Throughout this time, the Mongols recruited foreigners into their military and employed non-Mongols to help them rule the vast territory they had seized. With the assistance of these foreigners, they conducted censuses, devised regular taxes, set up governments, and even constructed a capital city in Karakorum (in Mongolia).

However, Ögödei's death in 1241 set the stage for successional disputes, which weakened the Mongols and fragmented the Mongol domains. The Mongols had not devised a regular, orderly system of succession to the Great Khanate; an assemblage of the Mongol nobility (known as a *khuriltai*) met and selected new rulers from the Genghisid line. Disputes arose after Ögödei's reign, and several such contests flared up into open warfare. The Mongol domains were thus divided into four virtually autonomous khanates — the Golden Horde in Russia, the Il-Khanate in Persia, the Chaghadai in Central Asia, and the Yüan dynasty in China and the homeland of the Mongols.

These internal conflicts did not even temporarily halt the Mongols' seemingly inexorable expansionism but would eventually have a telling effect. In the 1250s, the Mongols compelled the submission of numerous Tibetan monasteries, defeated the kingdom of Ta-li in the modern Chinese province of Yunnan, and crushed the Abbasid caliphate, which enabled them to move into Baghdad and to contemplate further gains in the Middle East. Yet shortly thereafter the tide turned against them in the west. In 1260, partly due to the recall of their commander to Mongolia for the election of a new Great Khan and partly to conflicts with their fellow Mongols in the Golden Horde, a Mongol force at 'Ayn Jalut (q.v.) in Syria experienced a crushing defeat at the hands of the Mamluk rulers of Egypt. This battle not only ended any further expeditions in the west but also subverted the Mongols' mantle of invincibility. Though Kublai Khan (q.v.) engineered a stunning addition to the Mongol domains in the 1270s when he vanquished the most populous region in the world, Sung South China, the year 1260 represented the height of Mongol power; after that, the Mongols' internecine conflicts increased, making them more vulnerable both to their discontented subjects and to rival states.

Kublai Khan's conquest of South China was the last major Mongol military success. Kublai's expeditions against Japan (1274 and 1281), mainland Southeast Asia (1280s), and Java (1292–1293) were costly fiascos, which generated severe inflation in the Chinese economy. Succession struggles and economic problems bedeviled Yüan China and Il-Khanate Persia in the fourteenth century; the Chaghadai Khanate faced insurmountable obstacles in seeking to control the nomads and far-flung oasis dwellers of Central Asia; and the Golden Horde ultimately could not impose itself on the vast territory of Russia other than to demand tax and labor service. As the Mongols attempted to rule and started to settle down, some of their vaunted military skills began to erode, and their armies lost the power to intimidate. In 1368, the Ming, a native dynasty, overthrew Mongol rule; by the late 1330s, Il-Khanate Persia had fragmented into autonomous regions; by 1369, the Chaghadai Khan was a puppet in the hands of the Central Asian conqueror Tamerlane (q.v.); and Mongol control over Russia receded throughout the fourteenth century until the last limited trace of Mongol rule finally gave way around 1485.

Those Mongols who returned to Mongolia continued to be fractious and thus weakened themselves, but their cavalry, archers, and skillful commanders remained effective and offered several opportunities to revive and reestablish a Mongol empire. In 1449, Esen, a western Mongol leader, lured the Chinese emperor into a trap and captured him. In the late seventeenth century, Galdan, another western Mongol, challenged Ch'ing dynasty China until his final defeat and death in 1697. Disunity continued to plague the Mongols; their conversion to Buddhism began to dull their military skills; the expansion of the Russian Empire into Siberia and Central Asia impinged upon them; and new military technology, including the gun, vitiated their greatest strengths, their cavalry and their archers. Buddhist monasteries and Chinese merchants exploited Mongol herders, gradually impoverishing them. The Ch'ing dynasty ruled Mongolia in the eighteenth and nineteenth centuries.

The Soviet Union dominated Mongolia from 1921 to the early 1990s, and Inner Mongolia became part of China; the Russians have controlled the Mongols in Kalmykia, Buryatia, and Tannu Tuva. The military and political glories of the great Mongol Empire have faded considerably.

MORRIS ROSSABI

David Morgan, *The Mongols* (1986); Morris Rossabi, *China and Inner Asia* (1975).

Monte Cassino, Battles of

January–May 1944

Allied strategy in Italy during World War II (q.v.) centered on keeping the Wehrmacht fully committed so that its veteran divisions could not be shifted to help repel the cross-Channel invasion (see *D-Day*). However, the Allied high command mistakenly believed that the determined German defense of the invasion beaches of Salerno in September 1943 masked their preparations for retreat to the north. They never reckoned that the Germans would effectively use the weather and the terrain to turn the Italian campaign into a costly stalemate at the Gustav Line.

Mark Clark's (q.v.) disastrous attempt to split the Gustav Line in the Liri Valley died on the banks of the Rapido River ("the bloody Rapido") in January 1944, and when the Allied end run at Anzio (q.v.) also failed, there was now a stalemate on *two* fronts. In early February the U.S. Thirty-fourth Infantry Division failed to capture the western anchor of the Gustav Line, and one of the holiest shrines of Roman Catholicism, the abbey of Monte Cassino. A second offensive in mid-February again failed and resulted in one of the most hotly debated incidents of the war — the destruction of the abbey by Allied bombers.

The Third Battle of Cassino in mid-March was preceded by a thunderous artillery barrage from nine hundred guns and a massive aerial bombardment of the town. Follow-up ground attacks by New Zealand troops once again ended in failure. Only with the launch of Operation Diadem in May 1944 did the Gustav Line finally collapse when the Second Polish Corps succeeded in capturing the abbey on May 17, thus ending one of the longest and bloodiest engagements of the Italian campaign.

CARLO W. D'ESTE

Montgomery, Bernard Law

1887–1976, *British World War II Field Marshal*

Contenders for the title are few, but "Monty" was indisputably Britain's greatest soldier since Wellington (q.v.). He was better known for his outstanding professionalism and sense of "balance" than for his talents in getting on with his contemporaries — notably the American ones.

Fourth of nine children in a clerical Irish family of modest means, his early life suffered from a domineering mother. In October 1914, at the First Battle of Ypres (q.v.), Montgomery, a young lieutenant, was shot through the lung and nearly died. He received the Distinguished Service Order (an unusually high distinction for a junior officer). His wound led to an aversion for smoking — one of the first causes of friction with the chain-smoking Allied supreme commander in World War II (q.v.), General "Ike" Eisenhower (q.v.); he was also a strict teetotaler. The horrendous British casualties in 1914–1918 help explain Montgomery's caution as a commander twenty-five years later. (This once caused George S. Patton [q.v.], who hated him, to damn Monty as a "tired little fart.")

In the interwar period, Monty stood out for his dedication to professionalism. His uncompromising standards, and abrasiveness, were to affect his promotion. In 1927, at age thirty-nine, he married a war widow, Betty Carver, who tragically died of a rare blood infection in 1938. Monty never recovered, throwing himself even more fiercely into preparing for the new war with Germany.

In 1940, he led the Third Division, one of Britain's few elite formations, intact from Dunkirk. The next two years he spent retraining the British army, with utmost rigor, in southern England. When appointed to command the defeated Eighth Army in Egypt in August 1942, he was only Winston Churchill's (q.v.) second choice. El Alamein (q.v.), in October, the first major land victory the Allies won against Adolf Hitler (q.v.), made him a hero both in Britain and the United States; it also went to his head. Nevertheless — sporting the famed black beret with its unorthodox twin cap badges — he exploited popularity to inspire his men as did perhaps no other commander of World War II.

His insistence that the initial invasion forces be increased from three to eight divisions, of which three were airborne, was a historic contribution. It was essential to success on D-Day (q.v.) in 1944 — as was his role as ground commander of the Anglo-American forces under Eisenhower as supreme Allied commander. But failure to capture Caen in the first days marred his reputation in U.S. eyes. Rashly he insisted that everything was going "according to plan"; yet it was his basic strategy of wearing down the Germans on the left (British) of the line while Bradley's U.S. forces broke out in the west that led to victory in Normandy.

Relations with Ike, remarkably good up to D-Day, deteriorated beginning in September 1944, following Eisenhower's assumption of overall command over strategies to end the war. The bold but disastrous airborne coup at Arnhem (q.v.), the only battle Monty ever lost, further dented his reputation. In turn, he was tactlessly critical of the American reverse in the Ardennes of December 1944.

After 1945, Montgomery became chief of the Imperial General Staff — Britain's top military post — and later deputy to Eisenhower at NATO. The gulf between the two widened irretrievably in later years as both indulged in mutual recriminations on wartime strategy in their bitter "Battle of the Memoirs."

ALISTAIR HORNE

Morale

A spiritual quality thought to be desirable in soldiers, morale is a concept much beloved by generals and staff officers concerned with military action en masse. Morale is meant to describe a sublime, self-denying state of being that transpires when groups such as mobs or armies imbibe a sense of purpose that transcends the personal welfare of their members. The word *sacrifice* is usually found in the immediate vicinity.

Customarily, those who traffic in morale assume a positivist stance, expecting that if a fighting force actually has morale, it is good, or "high," morale, redounding to the credit of the commander's higher purposes, such as dying to the last man. No commander seeks to instill *low* morale, although military history is littered with commanders who have inadvertently done so. Morale is not always high, low, or even necessarily present in a fighting force. Even when a commander's vaporing reaches a fevered pitch, soldiers may not be in a mood to contemplate philosophically their victory, their defeat, or their

sacrifice. The temperament of a fighting force may turn less on rhetoric than on warm food, dry socks, and leaders who do not forget that they are human beings entrusted with responsibility to their own kind. Morale is thus not quite as straightforward as the casual investigator might imagine.

The history of morale is bound up with the history of cultural sensibilities and of how a society regards human life, whether as individual lives or as an aggregate. Whereas Frederick the Great (q.v.) wanted discipline from his forces, Napoleon (q.v.) put much stock in morale, and their styles of warfare reflected how much action each believed he could extract from his armies, and by what best means.

We can date modern military concerns with morale from the Enlightenment, when ordinary individuals were beginning to be thought of as counting for more than mere taxes or cannon fodder. Modern armies were to be made of soldiers who increasingly thought and acted for themselves. The reconciliation of the new individualistic mode of combat with the traditional demands of state was a neat legerdemain of the modern age, in which state became *la patrie*, a governing organism supposedly invested with the genius of its people.

In the nineteenth century, morale came dangerously close to subsuming the concept of morality itself. The justice of the cause being fought for came to be more significant than mere glory or honor. Now armies not only had to be technically proficient — they had to be good as well.

But how could one perform in the service of a bad cause, as soldiers often must? The answer eventually fixed upon by modern armies was professionalism (q.v.), in which the cause mattered less than loyalty to the military subculture itself. Morale could thus be detached from lofty purposes, safely quarantined from the religion of state. This form of morale can be found in its most extreme forms in Japan's samurai (q.v.) traditions and Western military formations laying claim to "elite" status, such as the French Foreign Legion.

Yet even today, morale is often confused with what is moral, with the implication that an army with morale is, a priori, fighting for a good and noble cause. Most Western armed forces would still prefer to believe this. But armed forces are, and have always been, moral eunuchs, fighting for any cause whatever. An army may possess high morale and fight very well for the most morally despicable of causes, as indeed did the armies of the Axis powers in World War II (q.v.). At the same time, a fighting force with high morale may in the end be useless to its masters, except in the aftermath of defeat, when the corpses are consecrated in the name of a lost cause. Famous defeats or "last stands," such as the Alamo, Isandhlwana, or Corregidor, are particularly useful for the recruitment of future victims. In these instances, morale was said to have persisted to the bitter end, surviving longer than resistance itself. Yet professional soldiers will insist that a direct correlation exists between the high morale of a military force and its performance.

To say that morale is a highly unscientific and quite elastic concept would be an understatement. Properly dissected, its innards would reveal a mixture of ancient tradition, chivalry, and unapologetic romanticism. Despite its insubstantial nature, morale seems to have survived intact the contest between romance and science to explain the nature of soldiers, sailors, and airmen in modern battle.

ROGER J. SPILLER

John Baynes, *Morale* (1967); John Keegan, *The Face of Battle* (1976).

Moscow, Campaigns for

1812 and 1941

Potentates who have sought to control Europe inevitably faced the necessity of confronting Russia. This was as true of Swedish king Charles XII (q.v.) in 1709 as of the United States during the modern Cold War (q.v.). Perhaps the most famous confrontations with Russia in military history are those of Napoleon (q.v.) in 1812 and Adolf Hitler (q.v.) in 1941. The high point in both cases would be campaigns designed to capture the Russian capital, Moscow. Though there are many differences between these experiences, there are some interesting similarities as well.

In both cases the campaigns against Russia represented relative power peaks that found France and Germany each at an apogee of strength. Napoleon mobilized 675,500 troops and 1,400 guns; Hitler massed almost three million soldiers. Both invading armies were multinational forces commanded by excellent leaders, Napoleon and his marshals in one case, the German field marshals and panzer leaders in the other. In 1812 the French crossed the Russian border on June 23; in 1941 the Germans invaded on June 22 (see *Operation Barbarossa*).

Russia expected a French attack in the first of these campaigns. Joseph Stalin (q.v.), the Russian dictator in 1941, seemed to have been taken by surprise. On the other hand, the German attack of 1941 was itself delayed by Hitler's decision to conduct a prior campaign in the Balkans. This delay contributed to a significant difference — in 1812 French forces arrived in the Moscow area during September, when the average temperature is fifty-two degrees Fahrenheit, whereas the Germans in 1941 began their Moscow area operations in November, when the temperature averages twenty-eight degrees.

Neither French nor German armies were able to enter Moscow unopposed. Napoleon fought a pitched battle at Borodino, seventy-five miles to the west, with 133,000 troops (a net 20 percent of the original force). By mid-November 1941, when the Germans began their final Moscow offensive, their cumulative casualties stood at 709,600 (24 percent of the original force). Although the 1941 invaders preserved their strength much better, in 1812 the French actually captured Moscow; the Germans never did. Despite his success, however, Napoleon did not feel he could winter in Moscow and left the city on October 19, 1812, little more than a month after he had entered it. Napoleon's army disintegrated during his retreat through the Russian countryside in the dead of winter.

Russian armies in 1941 stopped the Germans in front of Moscow, though in places Germans could actually see the spires of the city. In early December (average temperature, seventeen degrees Fahrenheit) the Russians began counterattacking with fresh forces, driving two hundred miles in some places. Like the French, the Germans suffered grievously in the cold, for they too were not prepared for winter. German losses between November and April numbered 900,000 men and over 180,000 horses.

"General Winter" clearly served Russians well in both these campaigns, but the immense size of Russia was also decisive. Uncertainty plagued both the French in 1812 and the Germans in 1941. Some of this uncertainty should be attributed not to the personality traits of commanders in 1812 and 1941 but rather to the sheer immensity of the task involved in combat with Russia.

JOHN PRADOS

Movies

See Representation of War in Film.

Mughals

The Mughals ruled over a powerful, wealthy, centralized empire in India, which dominated the subcontinent from the mid–sixteenth century to about 1720. The empire persisted as a declining regional power in the eighteenth century and was abolished by the British in the aftermath of the Indian Mutiny of 1857 (q.v.).

In spite of the claim of Babur (the founder of the lineage) (q.v.) to direct descent from Genghis Khan (q.v.), his band resembled dozens, even hundreds, of others in the late fifteenth century, roaming the broad steppes and mountains of the area north of present-day Afghanistan. Militarily, these bands consisted of heavy, mailed cavalry adept at the use of the reverse-curve, composite short Persian bow. In structure, the bands tended to be egalitarian (the leader would gain command by continuing to achieve success), readily distributed booty, and maintained a common dining table for all, at which stories were told, songs sung, and tactics discussed. Any such band hoped to gain long-term rights to some relatively wealthy trading city or agricultural area; such rights would have been promptly divided among leaders and men.

After two decades of failure to gain and hold such rights in his home area, Babur — from a base in Kabul — several times successfully invaded the plains of India, finally defeating the Afghan rulers of Delhi in 1526. The Mughals, when they arrived in India, were thus a composite warrior band, including Babur's kinsmen as well as leaders and men of many other lineages whose loyalty was to Babur personally. In his autobiography, Babur never enumerated his band; the one time he counted it, before the Battle of Panipat (q.v.), he merely commented that it was composed of fewer men than he had expected. An educated guess might put their number at ten thousand to twenty thousand.

The speed and success with which the Mughals adapted to rule an alien culture and environment were extraordinary. Within fifty years, Akbar (the third in the line) was ruling a centralized state, complete with tax-collecting bureaucrats, which was worlds apart from the egalitarian band of his grandfather. Three reasons are generally given for this success. First, the Mughals left in place many Indian governing institutions. Peasants expected to pay taxes on their produce; local militarized intermediaries (*zamindars*) had been collecting these taxes and paying them to Muslim rulers throughout the subcontinent for more than two hundred years. Second, the Mughals quickly adopted Indian dress and many Indian symbols of kingship, such as the umbrella, the sunshade, and use of the elephant. This process helped in securing alliances with indigenous military groups, such as the Rajputs. Third, Akbar was a genius at developing institutions that unified ethnically varied warrior followers and also strengthened the monarchy. He in fact turned the army into the state. One such institution was the *mansabdari* system, which ranked the pay of high leaders in the Mughal Empire according to the number of horses they commanded; it also separated this pay from rights in any particular area. Thus, pay, perquisites, and promotion became public, quantifiable, dependent on serving the king, and largely separated from family and ethnic considerations. Mughal rulers enhanced personal ties to this warrior elite (never more than three thousand men) by using household and discipleship imagery in their communication. Another institution introduced by the Mughal rulers was the written contract for service, spelling out pay, posting, and obligations — something unheard of in the earlier horde structure.

In the middle years of the Mughal Empire (roughly 1580–1660), its state was quite possibly the most opulent on earth. European travelers certainly thought so. The emperors and their nobles (both indigenous ones and immigrants from Persia, central Asia, and Afghanistan) were open-handed patrons of architecture, gardening, music, poetry, and art. Whole new cities, such as Fatehpur Sikri and Shahjahanabad (Old Delhi), and monuments, such as the Taj Mahal, were built.

Through the mid–seventeenth century, the Mughals maintained a primarily heavy cavalry army. As earlier, cavalry drill and training remained central. In camp, for example, men practiced with bow and arrow, hitting a moving target from a full gallop. They practiced wheeling and charging in formation. There was little reason to change strategy or tactics, as the Mughals were eminently successful against all indigenous armies in India. Gradually, infantry using muskets was added, and artillery (especially siege artillery) was developed. Honor and wealth, however, remained perquisites of cavalry leadership. In the border campaigns of the seventeenth century, the Mughals were quite capable of fielding and paying armies of thirty thousand men. Competing armies at times of succession were even larger.

It was only in the later seventeenth century that the Marathas, a local militarized group from western India, discovered that supply and terrain were the weaknesses of the larger, slower Mughal armies. They employed successful tactics, cutting off supplies, leading the Mughals into difficult, mountainous terrain where numbers were not an advantage, and simultaneously using superior mobility to raid deep into Mughal territory.

The rather abrupt military and bureaucratic decline of the Mughal Empire (1700–1750) provoked many causal theories at the time and has continued to do so ever since. Eighteenth-century theories centered on the degeneracy of the later emperors; nineteenth-century theories stressed the inability of Muslim rulers to command the loyalty of Hindus (a strand of thinking that continues today). Recent scholarship stresses that, as the Mughal Empire expanded, the all-important personal ties between the emperor and his commanders were much harder to maintain; the result was factionalization along ethnic, religious, and regional lines. Eventually, the commanders of large groups simply broke free, forming the successor states of eighteenth-century India. It was from these states that the English eventually wrested control of India.

STEWART GORDON

Bamber Gascoigne, *The Great Moghuls* (1971); William Irvine, *The Army of the Indian Moghuls: Its Organization and Administration*, reprint (1962); John F. Richards, *The Mughal Empire*, in *The New Cambridge History of India* (1993).

Music

See Music, Martial *and* Representation of War in Music.

Music, Martial

Prior to the industrialization of war in the nineteenth century, music served a number of major military functions. It served in conjunction with physical drill to enhance the effect of the latter, as a source of inspiration before battle, and as a device by which the morale of one's own troops was maintained or that of the enemy weakened during combat. In addition, musical signals were deployed as a means of command and control. In these capacities, music was a significant multiplier of fighting power. It also magnified the effect of military ritual and display, whose purposes could include military or political aggrandizement, recruitment, or entertainment. These noncombatant activities remained the principal justification for large investment in military music by the world's armed forces in the twentieth century, even after the advent of much more effective weapons and systems of conveying information had eliminated most of the battlefield utility of musical morale building and communications.

The war songs of primitive societies were probably the earliest form of military music. When sung by all fighting members of a tribe, the war song both fortified morale and generated fear in the enemy. Vocal music came to be augmented by instruments such as drums, bells, or trumpets. In the fifth century B.C. in China, drums were used to issue orders before battle, and drums and bells were played together during battle to impress friend and foe. Trumpets are known to have been used by Egyptian soldiers as early as 1415 B.C., and later by Assyrians, Israelites, Greeks, Etruscans, Romans, and Celts. The Greek trumpet appears to have been used for military purposes only, and trumpet playing as a military art, as in the case of javelin throwing, was a contest in the Olympic Games. To demoralize opponents, trumpets were used to make crude and loud noises that were not in a strict sense musical. The use of trumpets as a means of signaling, on the other hand, probably involved greater control and the production of distinct tune fragments. In medieval Europe, surviving Roman military musical practices seem to have been augmented after the Crusades (q.v.) by broad imitation of the Islamic military band, which consisted of winds, brass, and percussion.

During the Renaissance, the use of bands for military purposes was abandoned, and army music became restricted to trumpets for the cavalry, and drums, or fifes and drums, for the infantry. In the seventeenth century, the French and English armies formed regimental bands consisting only of woodwinds (oboes and bassoons). Brass instruments were

A bagpiper leads Seaforth Highlanders into battle positions at Normandy in 1944.

added to the woodwinds in the eighteenth century to create what became known as the classic military band, that is, an instrumental group that combined winds and brass. Not long afterward in the same century, cymbals, bells, triangles, and bass drums characteristic of the janissary bands of the Ottoman Empire, and for the most part played by Turks, were added to the winds and brass of continental European army musical organizations. English military bands, on the other hand, employed Africans as drummers and trumpeters, who developed a distinctly extravagant style of performance (see *Blacks in the Military*). Bagpipes had been adopted by Irish and Scottish military forces in the sixteenth century and later may have been regarded as an economical alternative to the brass and wind band, whose instruments were relatively expensive. Trumpets and drums were used by Mughal armies in India in the eighteenth century.

The exact reasons for the changes just described are not known but probably have much to do with advances in military technique. The greater use of gunpowder weapons created a need for progressively louder music — whose familiar sounds and regular cadence acted as a prophylactic against panic induced by fear, disorientation, and physical shock — that could be heard above or through the din of gunfire. In addition, control over the speed of movement of the new disciplined troop formations that were formed in the seventeenth century may have been improved by music played properly by specialists. It should be noted, moreover, that military trumpet calls increased greatly in number and variety beginning in the seventeenth century, almost certainly in order to meet the signaling requirements of tactically more flexible professional armies.

In the late eighteenth and nineteenth centuries, the advent of mass armies gave rise to the patriotic war song, of which "La Marseillaise" of revolutionary France was the prototype. In Germany and Japan in particular, military authorities made sure that singing was a regular part of army life as a means of improving the martial ardor of their conscripts. In the American Civil War (q.v.), songs such as "The Battle Cry of Freedom" lifted the spirit of Union soldiers on the march and in combat. But by the early twentieth century, the development of much more effective small arms and artillery meant that the outcome of a battle was determined to a much greater degree by firepower than by human determination. The military value of maintaining a certain kind of spirit in action thus dwindled, and with it, the fighting significance of music. As late as the mid–twentieth century, Chinese bugle calls unnerved American troops in the Korean War (q.v.), but did not spell the difference between victory and defeat. On the other hand, in the United States more is spent on the bands of the armed forces than on all professional orchestras combined, which may stand as testament to the high value still placed upon the utility of military ritual and display.

JON SUMIDA

Raoul F. Camus, *Military Music of the American Revolution* (1975).

Mussolini, Benito

1883–1945, *Italian Dictator*

Benito Mussolini's self-confessed "thirst for military glory" battled his acute intelligence, psychological acumen, and political shrewdness for control over his military policies. Originally a revolutionary Socialist, he abandoned his party to advocate Italian intervention in World War I (q.v.). Following the war, in which he served as a rifleman, Mussolini decided his destiny was to rule Italy as a modern Caesar and re-create the Roman Empire. He forged the paramilitary Fascist movement in 1919–1921, using it to march on Rome, become prime minister, and then to seize dictatorial power (1925–1926). By subduing Libya (1922–1932), pacifying Somalia (1923–1927), conquering Ethiopia (1935–1936), helping the Nationalists win the Spanish civil war (1936–1939) (q.v.), and seizing Albania (April 1939), Mussolini made Italy predominant in the Mediterranean–Red Sea region. But his military adventures in 1935–1939 left his armed forces exhausted.

National poverty, resource deficiencies, and scientific-industrial weakness, combined with inflexible commanders, plagued the Italian forces. The king, Victor Emmanuel III, provided monarchist officers with an authority figure to impede Mussolini's dominance of the armed services. An air power enthusiast, Mussolini did create an innovative, Fascist-minded air force. It performed well over Ethiopia and Spain but lagged technologically after 1935. Mussolini promoted Fascists to leadership positions and sponsored some new army thinking in the 1930s. But bitter interservice rivalry crippled joint planning. Mussolini lacked the understanding and power to solve

Mussolini (left) and Hitler take a break during negotiations at the Munich conference on September 29, 1938.

these problems. Thus, he pursued his imperial dreams with politically, strategically, and doctrinally incoherent forces.

Wishful thinking, megalomania, and Fascist ideology gradually overwhelmed Mussolini's common sense. He interpreted diplomatic victories over Britain and France during the Ethiopian and Spanish wars (1935–1939) as proof of his military genius. Because of his parents' and older brother's short lives, Mussolini expected to die young but considered himself uniquely capable of leading Italy to greatness. Therefore he perceived a fleeting historical opportunity (1935–1945) for spectacular Italian aggrandizement by pitting Fascist-Nazi power against French-British decadence. Mussolini decided to gamble for a Mediterranean-African empire through war with the west. Winning Caesarian glory would gain him the prestige necessary to abolish the monarchy and create a truly totalitarian state.

Mussolini slowly overcame his lieutenants' anti-German attitudes, and then allied himself with Adolf Hitler (q.v.) in May 1939. Mussolini expected coordinated policies to inhibit German initiatives until Italy's forces recovered from their recent exertions. Mussolini planned for war in 1943–1945. But Hitler started World War II (q.v.) in September 1939, giving only one week's warning to the Italians and forcing an enraged, humiliated Mussolini to declare "nonbelligerence."

Hitler's May 1940 successes persuaded Mussolini to intervene in a presumably short, parallel war. But Italy's cautious generals and admirals wasted brief opportunities in the Mediterranean and North Africa during June–October 1940. After Mussolini forced offensives in the fall, he suffered disasters in Greece and North Africa: only German military intervention in early 1941 preserved him from a military coup. Thereafter, Hitler dragged Mussolini in his wake, particularly once the German-Soviet war overwhelmed Axis strategy.

After the Allied victories of November 1942, Mussolini implored Hitler to make peace with Joseph Stalin (q.v.) and concentrate on defeating the British-American forces. Hitler's refusal and the Sicilian invasion convinced the king and high command to overthrow Mussolini in July 1943. Hitler rescued him, installing Mussolini as puppet dictator of northern Italy in September. Mussolini facilitated significant war production for the Germans and the creation of large, ruthless Fascist counterinsurgency forces. The

April 1945 German surrender in Italy forced Mussolini to flee. Insurgents captured and shot him.

BRIAN R. SULLIVAN

Mustafa Kemal

See Atatürk, Mustafa Kemal.

Mutiny

Notwithstanding its emotional baggage, mutiny is simply collective military insubordination. Because mutiny presents such a challenge to the stability of the state as well as a disgrace to the affected organization, the military and civil authorities try to use ambiguous euphemisms rather than the word *mutiny* itself: *strike, unrest, protest,* or *disaffection* are examples. Thus, the mutiny of the French army in 1917 — possibly the largest mutiny in history, involving as many as fifty-four divisions and many thousands of soldiers — was officially characterized as "collective indiscipline." The U.S. Army in Vietnam (q.v.) similarly referred to its mutinies as "battlefield refusals."

The mechanism of mutiny is usually less dramatic and certainly less bloodthirsty than fictional or cinematic accounts would have one believe. Granting the entertainment value of *Battleship Potemkin, Paths of Glory,* and *Mutiny on the Bounty,* they are less useful for the insights they provide us about the phenomenon.

Traditionally, the main sources of mutiny have been found in issues concerned with living and working conditions: food, pay, leave, discipline, and so on. The mutiny of the Royal Navy at Invergordon in 1931, for example, stemmed from drastic pay cuts that were perceived as unfair by the sailors. More recently, however, troops have been prone to mutiny for ethical, political, or moral reasons. Immediately following World War II (q.v.), American and British troops, originally conscripted for war service, protested the reason for, not the conditions of, their continued assignment to occupation duty. The numerous mutinies in the U.S. Army in Vietnam reflected a similar questioning of the fundamental nature of the military mission. And the mutiny on the U.S. aircraft carrier *Constellation* in 1973 had at its roots the issue of racial discrimination.

The enduring and uncompromising military ethic presumes that mutinies stem from poor leadership; as Napoleon (q.v.) is reputed to have said, "There are no bad regiments, only bad colonels." Therefore, military authorities traditionally hold commanding officers accountable for the mutinous behavior of their troops even though the cause may be found in circumstances utterly beyond their control. That said, there have indeed been mutinies in which the conduct of the officers was the determining factor — German naval outbreaks in November 1918, in which the ships' crews refused to accompany their officers on what was perceived as a suicide mission, serve as an extreme example.

Most mutinous outbreaks are ignited by a catalytic incident that galvanizes the seething discontent already present. However, there is often a discontinuity between the seeming unimportance of the catalytic incident and the seriousness of the ensuing uprising. The famous sepoy mutiny in India in 1857 (q.v.) had as one of its precipitating causes the rumor that newly introduced rifle cartridges were greased with pig fat, an offense to both Hindu and Muslim troops. The episode was quickly forgotten amid the passions ignited by the revolt and played virtually no role in the subsequent upheaval. Indeed, once in motion, most mutinies take on a life of their own, a life conditioned by any number of extraneous factors from the trivial to the profound, from the weather to the political situation.

The word *mutiny* frequently connotes violence, and some mutinies have produced their share of bloodshed: seven officers, including the captain, were killed on the *Potemkin* in 1905. Yet this is more of an exception than a rule; most mutinies involve little loss of life or even physical injury. In fact, most mutinies involve a passive refusal to perform duty rather than an active usurpation of authority. The industrial strike is the most reasonable civilian analogy to the military mutiny.

The duration of mutinies may be analyzed on the level of specific incidents or groups of related upheavals. Mutiny was an ever-present fact of life in the Spanish army in Flanders from 1570 to 1607, when over fifty major mutinies and countless minor ones took place. They lasted from one day to well over one year. In more contemporary times, groups of mutinies as well as individual mutinies tend to be much shorter. The mutinies that accompanied the Russian Revolution of 1905–1906 or the French army mutinies that followed the failure of the Nivelle offensive in 1917 endured over a period of months. But unlike the sixteenth-century Flanders mutinies, the typical modern individual mutiny is more likely to be measured in hours, occasionally days. Mutiny has self-limiting characteristics since modern Western soldiers and sailors exist in an environment in which all their physical and many of their emotional needs are provided for. Therefore, after an initial period of blowing off steam, there is usually a desire to bring the outbreak to some resolution, if only to provide the customary food and quarters.

Leadership in mutinies, like leadership in other social situations, gives rise to the chicken-or-egg conundrum of whether the leader makes the mutiny or the mutiny makes the leader. There is no clear answer. Leaders themselves typically assert that they assumed the leadership role through happenstance. The authorities, however, usually favor the conspiracy theory, tending to overemphasize the importance of a mutiny's leaders, contending that the mass of the troops were led astray by a few bad apples. The troops themselves tend to be a distinctly mixed bag, ranging from true believers to opportunists to swimmers-with-the-tide; some are simply intimidated, some want only to settle old scores.

The most immediate response to an outbreak comes from the officers of the units involved. Although there are instances of particularly stalwart officers facing down the mutineers, the evidence suggests that the larger the mutiny, the less likely are the officers to take any action that can possibly be avoided. Indeed, when the numbers are large, there is little that *can* be done other than to attempt to assert some moral authority. This rarely has much, if any, effect, and it is left to the threat, or more rarely, the application of force to resolve the issue. Troops are understandably reluctant to use arms against their own comrades, and when force has become necessary, it has usually been exercised by elite units or other formations least likely to show sympathy for the mutineers.

Classically, mutiny was the most serious crime a soldier or sailor could commit, punishable, in the military code of most countries, by death. In earlier times this was no doubt the case. But in the twentieth century there has been a trend toward greater leniency in military punishment. Execution was used through World War I (q.v.), but since that time the death penalty has been only rarely employed, and prison terms have become progressively shorter. The hesitation to use the word *mutiny* increasingly restricted the ability of the military to inflict legally stipulated penalties. Then too, in mutiny, as in other areas of life, there is safety in numbers. One simply cannot shoot a whole regiment or hang a whole fleet. The ancient expedient of executing every tenth man — from which the term *decimation* derives — would hardly be countenanced in today's world.

ELIHU ROSE

Elihu Rose, "The Anatomy of Mutiny," *Armed Forces and Society* (1982): 561–573; Geoffrey Parker, "Mutiny and Discontent in the Spanish Army of Flanders," *Past and Present* 58 (1973): 38–52.

N

Nagashino, Battle of

June 29, 1575

This dramatic engagement raised the harquebus (*tanegashima*) from an adjunct weapon to the key armament of early modern Japanese armies. The battle began when the warlord Takeda Katsuyori, leading fifteen thousand to twenty thousand troops, laid siege to Nagashino Castle in Mikawa Province; against this the warlords Oda Nobunaga (q.v.) and Tokugawa Ieyasu (q.v.) sent a relief force of thirty-eight thousand troops.

The common belief is that the Takeda army, arguably the finest of its age, was predominantly a cavalry force. But in actuality it centered on companies of spear-wielding infantry, led by officers on horseback and supplemented with men with harquebuses. To defeat it, Nobunaga built his strategy around his gunners, refining a tactic he had introduced at the Battle of Anegawa five years before. In his mobilization orders, he directed his commanders to prepare nets and wooden poles, from which he constructed a line of staggered palisades over a mile in length to the west of Nagashino. He positioned his army behind these, placing three thousand of his best harquebus men in the vanguard and directing them to fire in three-part volleys.

Baited into charge after charge and then devastated by disciplined musket fire and countercharges, by the end of the battle Katsuyori had lost some ten thousand men, including at least seven of his leading commanders. The Oda-Tokugawa army lost six thousand. The Takeda house, which, a scant two years earlier, had seemed to be on the verge of establishing a countrywide hegemony, never recovered from this debacle. Nobunaga's and Ieyasu's fortunes, however, continued to rise.

KARL F. FRIDAY

Nagumo Chūichi

1886–1944, *Japanese World War II Admiral*

Vice Admiral Nagumo Chūichi was a renowned torpedo and destroyer specialist, serving as president of the Naval Staff College when chosen by Admiral Yamamoto Isoroku (q.v.) to lead Japan's six-carrier strike force in April 1941. Nagumo has since been criticized by Japanese air officers for indecisiveness: first, because he did not order follow-up attacks against American port and fuel storage facilities during the attack on Pearl Harbor (q.v.), despite the need to cripple American operational capabilities; and second, for his handling of the Battle of Midway (q.v.), during which he vacillated before ordering a strike on American carriers that had appeared unexpectedly while his airplanes were attacking Midway Island, leading to the loss of his four fleet carriers. Nevertheless, acting under almost direct control of Yamamoto, Nagumo was given no clear strategic or operational orders, nor the freedom to act independently should unexpected events develop.

After Midway, Nagumo was relieved of sea command and served in several home island bases before being appointed commander of a small naval contingent in the Marianas in late 1943. Present on Saipan when the American forces landed (June 15, 1944), he committed suicide during the final stages of the battle.

THEODORE F. COOK, JR.

Napoleon Bonaparte

1769–1821, *General of the French Republic and Emperor of France*

Writing about Corsica, political philosopher Jean-Jacques Rousseau predicted, "One day this small island will astonish Europe." The speculation came true in the person of Napoleon Bonaparte, born on August 15, 1769, in Ajaccio, Corsica. He first set foot on French soil on Christmas Day in 1778, a nine-year-old aspirant headed for language training (he had previously spoken Italian) at Autun. He went on to a military preparatory school, was disappointed in an early desire to join the navy, and went on to the prestigious École Militaire, graduating with high honors in just one year.

Commissioned into an artillery regiment as a result of his proclivity for science and mathematics, Napoleon absorbed the theories of French military reformists, some of the best of whom were of the artillery branch of service. He spent time in Paris at the outset of the French Revolution, went for a time to Corsica in an effort to advance revolutionary precepts there, and returned to France in time to participate in a siege of Toulon in 1793, where French Royalists holding a base for a British fleet were beset and ultimately overwhelmed. Napoleon's handling of the revolutionary artillery in the siege earned him promotion from captain to brigadier general.

General Bonaparte spent part of 1794, the months of the Terror, on campaign as chief of staff to the French commander in Italy, then briefly fell victim to the vagaries of French politics; the fall and execution of figures to whom Bonaparte had been considered close (the brothers Robespierre) led to his arrest. It appears he was actually held only under house arrest and for a period of just ten days. The general was then released to help prepare a further French expedition against Corsica, which would be foiled by the British navy in April 1795. Subsequent months were whiled away awaiting assignment or avoiding ones he had no taste for. General Bonaparte spent some months as head of the Topographic Bureau, the technical heart of what passed for a general staff in France at that time, before appointment to command the army of Italy. His campaign against Austrian forces in Italy during 1796, including brilliant maneuvers and a succession of well-fought battles defeating often superior enemies or attaining difficult objectives (for example, the forcing of the Alpone River bridge at Arcola), marked the beginning of his military ascendancy.

In 1798, two years after defeating Austria, Bonaparte led an army to Egypt but was marooned when a British fleet under Admiral Horatio Nelson (q.v.) wiped out the French flotilla that had convoyed him to Egypt. For a time Bonaparte waged war against the Ottoman Empire, culminating at the unsuccessful siege of Acre (1799), but in August 1799 he abandoned the French in Egypt to return to the homeland. This abandonment and his callous treatment of his troops in the Holy Land prefigured what Napoleon would do in Russia when defeated there in 1812. In any case, he became one of three ruling "consuls" of France after a coup d'état in November 1799, subsequently emerging as the leading political figure of the nation. His rule would end only with French military defeat in Europe.

During renewed war with Austria in 1800, Napoleon outmaneuvered his enemies by leading a French army across the Alps. Thereafter he was declared "consul for life," but, dissatisfied with this exalted status, assumed the title emperor of the French in May 1804, later also declaring himself king of Italy. In the period 1800–1805, Napoleon devoted much attention to building a new "Grand Army" (la Grande Armée), a revitalized French military machine. Creating "corps" of troops from different combat arms (infantry, cavalry, artillery) permitted Napoleon's forces to operate in a dispersed fashion while retaining real striking power all along the front. The formation also enabled Napoleon to take his adversaries by surprise, such as in 1806, when he moved the Grand Army through the supposedly impassable Franconian Forest to defeat the Prussians at Jena. Innovations in logistics, by professionalizing French supply services and standardizing weapons and organizations, simplified Napoleon's arrangements to go on campaign. By having French armies live off the land as much as possible, Napoleon could cut himself loose from the traditional network of depots upon which armies had previously depended. The French also worked hard at accumulating basic information such as accurate maps of potential theaters of operations, a valuable form of intelligence that their opponents could seldom match. Altogether the Grand Army held numerous advantages.

Napoleon's campaigns were many and, for a long time, victorious. Only against England (1803–1805), where it proved impossible to negotiate the English Channel in the face of the Royal Navy, would an adversary prove impervious to French sallies. Napoleon defeated Austria again in 1805, went on to smash a combined Austro-Russian army at Austerlitz (q.v.), in 1806 defeated Prussia (Jena-Auerstedt), and in 1806–1807 did the same to Prusso-Russian forces (Eylau, Friedland). In 1808 he led a French army into Spain and forced the evacuation of a British army (Corunna) without fighting a major battle. The emperor first stumbled while again fighting Austria, in 1809, when an Austrian army fought him to a standstill, even a virtual defeat (Aspern-Essling), and then held up to a full-scale French onslaught in a follow-on battle (Wagram). The next big campaign was an invasion of Russia in 1812, where Napoleon fought an inconclusive battle (Smolensk) and then won a victory at excessive cost (Borodino), capturing Moscow but being effectively defeated by the Russian winter. The retreat from Russia destroyed the French army, and the forces Napoleon led into the field in Germany for the 1813 campaign never matched the quality of the earlier Grand Army. Russia, Prussia, Austria, Spain, Portugal, and Britain then forced Napoleon back with a certain inexorability in the campaigns of 1813 and 1814. Though Napoleon had successes (Lützen, Dresden, Hanau), his defeat at Leipzig (q.v.) in the biggest battle of the age determined the outcome. Allied armies fought their way into France where, despite minor defensive victories, Napoleon foresaw defeat and abdicated in April 1814.

Napoleon went into exile on the Mediterranean island of Elba, not that far from Corsica, where he functioned as ruler and even had a miniature army. But the former emperor tired of enforced idleness and determined to stake all on one more attempt to rule France. In early 1815 Napoleon took his small force and made it the nucleus of an army he landed on the French coast and with which he marched upon Paris, beginning the period known as the "Hundred Days." The former allies immediately started rebuilding their military forces to crush Napoleon, who had successfully driven the restored French king, Louis XVIII, from his seat of government in Paris. Anticipating allied military moves, Napoleon tried to steal a march by concentrating against just a part of their growing forces. This rapid campaign led to the twin battles of Ligny and Waterloo (q.v.) in June 1815, in which the French army, at first successful, suddenly disintegrated.

With his second abdication Napoleon was shorn of all power, and allies anxious not to repeat the mistake of Elba sent Napoleon as a virtual prisoner to the far-off South Atlantic island of St. Helena. There Napoleon spent his final years recalling the times of glory, French and European rulers and military leaders, his battles, and his friends and family. Napoleon died on St. Helena after a prolonged illness on May 5, 1821, at fifty-two years of age.

Perhaps some of the French feared the return of Napoleon because the emperor's actions while in

power had had a huge impact on every aspect of French society. Though Napoleon is often viewed simply as a great captain, political and social achievements rival his military ones and ought not to be overlooked. Patronage of the arts and letters was a mark of Napoleonic France. Napoleon reorganized French civil administration, the tax system, and the banking system; he encouraged industrial development, in many respects introducing practices that continue in France to this day. A number of these reforms started as ways to equip French armies or to finance Napoleon's wars, but this fact does not lessen their importance. A complete revision of the French legal system was achieved during this era, and the Code Napoléon remains the basis of French law today. In religious matters Napoleon negotiated a treaty with the Vatican that eased relations with the Catholic Church, at least through 1808, when Napoleon had Pope Pius VII arrested and imprisoned at Grenoble.

Another aspect of the period, which greatly contributed to the determination of the European monarchies to fight, was the impact of the French example upon nationalism, which, incidentally, brought minor allies to fight under the French banner. Napoleon made both positive and negative contributions here. The emperor's propaganda techniques, emphasizing the (actually rather indeterminate) "popular will," legitimated the notion of constitutional monarchy to which absolutist states in Europe one by one succumbed. Yet at the same time Napoleon overthrew kings and republics to establish brothers and friends as kings in their stead. Napoleon the Corsican Republican sounded a lot different by 1811, when he wrote in a letter, "The people must not be judge of its own rights."

Beyond the political, economic, and social events of Napoleon's reign, the emperor will always be known as a military leader. In this he had the advantage of coming upon the scene at a moment of technical and doctrinal transformation in military affairs. The question of the degree to which Napoleon simply benefited from these changes, or whether he initiated them, will remain a staple of argument. Recent scholarship tends to argue that, at least on the technical side, Napoleon was more beneficiary than innovator. In the French army, the changes in artillery practice and in tactical formations with which Napoleon is often associated were suggested by reformers predating him. Certain tactical changes were also forced on the French by the character of their Republican armies during the early years of the conflict. The General Staff procedures that Napoleon used to great advantage were championed by other French officers.

Napoleon's forte lay in recognizing quality, appreciating how innovations could help him, and institutionalizing the changes throughout the French forces. For example, it was characteristic of the French mass armies of the Republic that these forces outstripped their supply services, forcing soldiers to a greater extent to try to live off the land. Where previous generals had used slow-paced and (relatively) stylized patterns of movement to keep in tune with their supplies, Napoleon could take mass army dependence on the land and, deliberately dispensing with supply lines, make it the basis for much more ambitious maneuvers. In structuring his command system, Napoleon worked from a sense of how daily routines evolve, noting the patterns by which subordinate leaders typically got their troops into action, and then sent reports requesting instructions. Napoleon arranged his daily schedule so as to be available at the specific times of afternoon and late night that messengers tended to arrive with the most urgent matters requiring command decisions. This method optimized time, effectively giving Napoleon a tempo advantage over many of his adversaries.

In battle, Napoleon's proclivity for systems enabled him to conduct engagements to his best advantage. The use of certain techniques in Napoleon's battles — from massing artillery against some portion of the opponent's line, to extending the adversary's defenses by obliging him to defend against moves on the flanks, to the use of climactic assaults once he judged the moment propitious — was so often repeated that the tactics can only be seen as parts of a formula. This is not to say that other generals did not have their own formulas, but Napoleon's grand tactics proved so often successful that they inevitably set a new standard. Castiglione (1796) and Austerlitz (1805) are often considered Napoleon's prototype battles, but the emperor used his method on fields as far removed as Eylau (1807), Lützen (1813), Montmirail (1814), and even Borodino (1812). The method put a premium on careful timing and pacing of combat action, which meant personal control, and Napoleon frequently spoke of the capacity for coup d'oeil, essentially an ability to appreciate a situation and make the necessary decisions after just one glance. It is significant that Napoleon's great defeats or near-defeats, such as Leipzig (1813) and Aspern-Essling (1809), occurred in situations where the emperor was not on the battle-front, or else the front line had grown so lengthy it could not be surveyed from any one spot.

"The great art of winning a battle," said Napoleon on St. Helena, "consists in changing one's line of operations in the middle of the action." Battle was like a drama with a beginning, a middle, and an end: "The battle order . . . and . . . preliminary maneuvers . . . form the exposition. The countermaneuvers of the army which has been attacked constitute the dramatic complication. They lead in turn to new measures and bring about the crisis." A leader's role "consists in first calculating all the possibilities accurately and then in making an almost mathematically exact allowance for accident." Although, as Napoleon put it, "In war, nothing can be gained except by calculation," military genius lay in finding the balance between forecasting and accident, and in being constantly prepared to exploit accidents. "There is a moment in every battle," as Napoleon dictated in 1820, "at which the least maneuver is decisive and gives superiority, as one drop of water causes overflow."

Until late in his career, Napoleon successfully employed this theory of battle. Starting, perhaps, in 1809, the emperor's techniques became more brittle, more predictable, less alert for the moment of accident. At both Borodino and Waterloo, for example, Napoleon's timing in committing his Imperial Guard offered no particular advantage at all. It was as if the emperor wanted to make his own accident rather than take advantage of one. Still, Napoleon in person was almost always unbeatable, and opponents succeeded primarily by fighting French subordinates, not the emperor.

Probably Napoleon's greatest impact was as a strategist. Previous wars, including the first phase of the Wars of the French Revolution (q.v.), had been wars of position. In keeping with the narrow concept of supply constraints and the stylized notion of maneuver, generals most often fought their campaigns along well-defined land corridors, repeatedly fighting across the same rivers or besieging the same fortresses. Such methods were battle centered. Napoleon lifted his sight to war-winning strategies instead, maneuvering so as to gain secondary objectives that put the adversary at grave disadvantage if the latter refused to accept battle under conditions of the emperor's choosing. One must return to the duke of Marlborough (q.v.), or most recently Frederick the Great (q.v.), to encounter a strategist of equivalent vision. Indeed, Napoleon's performance proved so inspiring that it moved German theorist Carl von Clausewitz (q.v.) to codify a similar system of strategy in his text *On War*. In military affairs and other fields of endeavor, Napoleon Bonaparte has had an enduring impact upon our world.

JOHN PRADOS

Dorothy Carrington, *Napoleon and His Parents: On the Threshold of History* (1990); David D. Chandler, *The Campaigns of Napoleon* (1966); Vincent Cronin, *Napoleon Bonaparte: An Intimate Biography* (1971); Somerset de Chair, ed., *Napoleon on Napoleon: An Autobiography of the Emperor* (1992); J. Christopher Herold, *The Horizon Book of the Age of Napoleon* (1963); Robert B. Holtman, *The Napoleonic Revolution* (1967).

Napoleonic Wars

See Napoleon Bonaparte.

Naval Warfare, Theorists of

Theorists of naval warfare have been around for a long time. Thucydides, in Book One of his *History of the Peloponnesian War*, stresses the importance of sea power. The Chinese have an old (and little known in the West) series of treatises that include Chiang Chi's *The Myriad Stratagems* (including both naval and military ones), written in about A.D. 225; Li Chüan's *Manual of the Martial Planet* (that is, Venus) of 759; and the encyclopedist Tsêng Kung-Liang's *Collection of Military Techniques* of 1044.

The most famous early English work is probably the anonymous *Libelle of Englyshe Polycye* (1436?), which, in the context of the Hundred Years' War (q.v.), spoke of the need to control the Strait of Dover, a feat the king of England at that time probably could not achieve. The Elizabethan Sir Walter Raleigh (1552?–1618) stressed sea power and colonization as the best means of sapping Spanish strength by cutting off wealth from the New World. Spain's Alonso de Chaves (fl. 1530), Italy's Pantero Pantera (1568–1625), and France's Cardinal Richelieu (1585–1642) also produced treatises on naval warfare. One of Richelieu's celebrated maxims was "He who is master of the sea is master of the land." Most eighteenth-century works on naval subjects concern tactics, and most are now of no more than antiquarian interest. The golden age of naval theorists would come later, in the nineteenth century.

The name Alfred Thayer Mahan (1840–1914) (q.v.) is generally the first that comes to mind when discussing theories of naval warfare. An exasperated American secretary of war, Henry L. Stimson (q.v.), once even remarked during World War II (q.v.) that the Navy Department "frequently seemed to retire from the realm of logic into a dim religious world in which Neptune was God, Mahan his prophet, and the United States Navy the only true Church." Mahan had a relatively unspectacular career until 1890, when the publication of *The Influence of Sea Power on History, 1660–1783* made him famous. This was followed by several other influential works.

Mahan caught the imagination largely because of his grand scheme of certain principles of warfare at sea. He was one of the late-nineteenth-century theorists who liberated naval history from the realm of mere stirring tales of heroic adventures. Mahan believed that, first and foremost, the true objective in a naval war was always the enemy fleet. The traditional weapon of the weaker naval power, commerce raiding (*guerre de course*), would not be decisive without support of squadron warfare. Battle was to be carried through to a decisive finish, naval force was to be used offensively, and the fleet had to be concentrated and never divided. He considered capital ships (in Mahan's time, battleships) the most important vessels in the navy and found blockade (q.v.) valuable, a central position and interior liners advantageous, and proper overseas bases important for naval operations. According to Mahan, one obtained "command of the sea" by concentrating one's naval forces at the decisive point to destroy or master the enemy's battle fleet; blockade of enemy ports and disruption of the enemy's maritime communications would follow.

Mahan's work appeared at just the right moment, providing ammunition for navalists in Great Britain and Germany. In Germany the state secretary of the Imperial Naval Office, Alfred von Tirpitz (1849–1930) (q.v.), made sure that translations of Mahan were widely distributed as support for his naval bill. Tirpitz echoed Mahan in his emphasis on the decisive battle and primacy of battleships. Tirpitz's *Risikogedanke* (doctrine of risk) claimed that once the German fleet reached a certain size, the British would be deterred from attack lest they incur losses that would weaken their worldwide position. However, Tirpitz tended to consider a large navy and sea power to be primarily an expression of national greatness and a factor in diplomacy. Critics would later charge that Tirpitz never evolved a true strategy as to how the fleet would actually be used.

Mahan was certainly not alone in writing on naval affairs. In the 1880s the so-called *Jeune École* in France, associated with Minister of Marine Admiral Hyacinthe Aube (1826–1890) and publicist Gabriel Charmes (1850–1886) attracted much attention with its theories: the age of squadron warfare was over, and small, cheap torpedo boats and the *guerre de course* carried out by fast, light cruisers could bring the British to heel in a war with France, partially by raising insurance rates to prohibitive heights and thereby paralyzing trade. Mahan to a certain extent had written to refute these claims.

In Britain, Captain John H. Colomb (1838–1909) in a series of articles and lectures argued that the navy was the most important component of imperial defense; his brother, Admiral Phillip Colomb (1831–1899), sought to establish from history general rules applicable to modern naval warfare in his *Naval Warfare* (1891). But it was Mahan who captured the public imagination.

Mahan's most serious rival for professional status was probably Sir Julian Corbett (1854–1922) (q.v.), a civilian from a comfortable family who turned to naval history in his midforties. His lectures at the Royal Naval War College, Greenwich, eventually evolved into *Some Principles of Maritime Strategy*, published in 1911. Corbett's strategic thought was in some ways more subtle than that of Mahan; he emphasized the interdependence of naval and land warfare and tended to concentrate on the importance of communications (q.v.) rather than the battle. Communications governed both the movement of commerce and overseas expeditions; therefore securing one's own communications and disrupting those of the enemy formed important objectives. Combat at sea was not an end in itself; the primary objective of the fleet was to secure communications, not necessarily to seek out and destroy the enemy's fleet. Corbett's work as a historian also convinced him that an island nation like Britain with command of the sea would be able to isolate distant objectives and at the same time prevent the invasion of its home territory. Furthermore, raiding activity would be valuable against an enemy whose army was too strong to be attacked on the battlefield, and such raids should therefore be part of any strategic plan.

Mahan's and Corbett's theories faced a severe test in World War I (q.v.), which did not conform to prewar scenarios. The *guerre de course* in the form of the submarine campaign almost defeated the British — the blockaders in a sense were subjected to a blockade themselves. Corbett's ideas, which deemphasized the Mahanian concept of the great battle at sea, were viewed as heresy by many officers in the Royal Navy. Corbett was even blamed for John Rushworth Jellicoe's (q.v.) apparent caution at the Battle of Jutland (q.v.).

Yet Corbett received support from another well-known writer, Admiral Sir Herbert Richmond (1871–1946). Richmond had been highly critical of the Admiralty's conduct of the war; among other things, his historical study of eighteenth-century warfare had convinced him of the importance of trade defense and the convoy (q.v.) as a means to achieve this. Richmond had a high regard for the study of history and felt that all wars, both old and modern, were worthy of analysis — one should not be preoccupied merely with the most recent war. Richmond also downgraded the importance of the great battle and strongly believed in the importance of the general blockade. During the war he had advocated reducing the Grand Fleet's strength in destroyers in order to use them for the defense of trade. This might diminish the possibility of a tactical victory but would enhance the ability to win the war through the defeat of the German attack on trade. Richmond argued that it was important to determine what a navy would be used for, and in the early 1920s he opposed the construction of large battleships. They were expensive, too much effort would be concentrated on defending them, and British interests really required large numbers of cruisers and destroyers for the defense of trade. Richmond never wrote his planned volume on naval strategy, but his ideas appeared in his *Statesmen and Sea Power* (1943).

Mahanian concepts fitted well in a British or American setting. Continental theorists put a different spin on them. The German vice admiral Wolfgang Wegener (1875–1956) criticized the Tirpitz doctrine, with its emphasis on an eventual decisive battle. Wegener argued that even a German naval victory would not really shake British sea control. To achieve the latter, the Germans needed a flanking position to menace the British lines of approach. This meant that in the north the Germans should seize Denmark, southern Norway, and the Faeroe Islands, and in the south Brest or Cherbourg and eventually the Portuguese Atlantic islands. Wegener's critique earned him the enmity of the German naval establishment and premature retirement. When his *The Naval Strategy of the World War* was published in 1929, it was also purged to omit the aggressive references to Denmark and Norway, although they certainly foreshadowed German actions in 1940.

Vice Admiral Raoul Castex (1878–1968) sought to apply Mahanian doctrines to a navy such as France's, which was doomed to second-rate status by geography and France's obligation to maintain a large continental army. In his magisterial five-volume *Théories stratégiques* (1929–1935) — a sixth volume was published posthumously in 1976 — Castex did not discount the importance of the battleship or the battle, but regarded naval strategy as only part of general strategy. He also wrote much of the concept of *manoeuvre* (a term including plan of action or scheme, as well as movement), a complex of actions that the weaker fleet might use to alter the naval balance in its favor. Strategic *manoeuvre* was "a key element in the conduct of operations."

Many have judged that the experience of World War II (q.v.) was not flattering to naval theorists such as Mahan. The climactic battle between rival fleets never took place, and the submarine and airplane would significantly complicate Mahan's concept of command of the sea. The more nuanced approach of Corbett as well as the latter's emphasis on the importance of combined operations seemed closer to the mark. On the other hand, Mahan's rejection of the *guerre de course* was vindicated by the Allied defeat of the German U-boat offensive in both world wars, although in World War II the U.S. Navy conducted a devastating *guerre de course* with submarines against Japan. This did not necessarily contradict Mahan — he had made a distinction about *guerre de course* when backed by a regular fleet, in this case the powerful U.S. naval offensive.

It is not really profitable, however, to apply the doctrines of theorists from the classic age of naval theory to World War II. Technology had advanced beyond their wildest dreams, and, particularly in the case of air power, in an age of total war the distinctive position war at sea had formerly enjoyed was eroded. Even Castex, much younger than Mahan and Corbett, depreciated the potential of the aircraft carrier at the same time that he emphasized the importance of command of the air as well as the sea, and he accurately forecast a surprise attack on a naval base from the air. Nevertheless, in the broadest sense, the now

often-maligned Mahan was right — sea power against an island empire like Japan would prove decisive.

Bernard Brodie is a transitional figure. His *Sea Power in the Machine Age* (1941) appeared in the prenuclear era; his later work, notably *Strategy in the Missile Age* (1959), grapples with the new problems. Other nuclear strategists include Henry Kissinger and Robert E. Osgood. But in the scope and depth of their work, they are all a far cry from Mahan or Corbett. For similarities to Mahan, one might look to Soviet Russia and Admiral Sergei Gorschkov (1910–1988), commander in chief of the Soviet navy (1956–1985) and author of *The Sea Power of the State* (1976). Gorschkov's book lacks the brilliance and originality of the great naval theorists, but he led an unprecedented — and ultimately unsustainable — Russian buildup in both surface and undersea craft.

Theory of naval warfare is certainly not a dead subject. As the world's navies move toward the uncertainties of the twenty-first century, the interested reader can follow debates concerning naval strategy and tactics in publications such as the British *Naval Review* and the American *Naval Institute Proceedings*.

The classic age of theories of naval strategy probably ended with World War II. Post-1945 writers on strategy are abundant, but increasingly naval strategy has been merged with general strategy involving land and air warfare, and technology plays a dominant role in revolutionary means of propulsion, the development of guided missiles, and, of course, the dilemmas involved with the existence and possible use of nuclear weapons (q.v.).

PAUL G. HALPERN

Philip A. Crowl, "Alfred Thayer Mahan: The Naval Historian," in Peter Paret, ed., *Makers of Modern Strategy: From Machiavelli to the Nuclear Age* (1986); Theodore Ropp, "Continental Doctrines of Sea Power," in Edward Meade Earle, ed., *Makers of Modern Strategy: Military Thought from Machiavelli to Hitler* (1941); D. M. Schurman, *The Education of a Navy: The Development of British Naval Strategic Thought, 1867–1914*, reprint (1995).

Naval Weapons

The earliest fighting at sea probably involved no more than exchanges of antipersonnel missile fire with arrows and spears, followed by boarding and hand-to-hand combat with sword and pike. Beginning in about

The bow of a late-sixteenth-century Chinese barge is loaded with sea mines. The bow could be detached after a time fuse was lit, permitting the sailors in the stern to row away safely as the sea mines approached their target.

1000 B.C., galley warships were fitted with an underwater ram, which transformed the hull into a ship-destroying weapon. Boarding, however, remained the main means of reaching a decision. The Greeks later used catapults to launch grapnels and lines to draw enemy ships close enough for boarding. In the third century A.D., the Syracusans invented the *corvus* (crow), a boarding ramp with a hooked end that held enemy ships in place and provided a bridge that facilitated the attack of infantry. This innovation was used to great effect by the Romans. In the sixth century, the Byzantines developed a flammable liquid (Greek fire) that was squirted at enemy ships and used with deadly effect until the secret of its composition was apparently lost. In the twelfth century, the navy of the Southern Sung dynasty in China deployed armored, paddle-wheel small craft for riverine and canal warfare, and mounted heavy catapults on larger vessels. The advent of gunpowder artillery in the West in the fourteenth century further increased naval missile power. But boarding remained the principal means of winning a large-scale battle fought with galleys up to and including the Battle of Lepanto (q.v.) in 1571. The function of the *corvus* in the galleys of this period was assumed by a fixed, iron-tipped structure at the bow (the spur).

By the fifteenth century, European and Chinese sailing warships carried large numbers of light anti-personnel artillery and a few big-guns capable of causing substantial damage to ship structure. In the mid–sixteenth century, the replacement of fixed mountings by moving carriages — an English innovation — allowed guns to be reloaded more rapidly. When such weapons were mounted in numbers, suffi-

cient fire could be generated to inflict substantial damage on an enemy ship and cause many casualties. In 1588, English warships avoided boarding and used their superior artillery to defeat the Spanish Armada (q.v.). In 1592, large Korean vessels that were heavily protected by iron armor played an instrumental role in the defeat of an invading Japanese fleet, although their lack of seaworthiness and speed probably accounts for the short life of this innovation before industrialization (see *Yi Sun-Shin*). Over the course of the seventeenth and eighteenth centuries, naval ordnance and gunnery remained basically unchanged, although alterations in detail improved performance considerably. By the end of this period, the outcome of naval battles was determined by artillery.

In Europe and the United States, rapid innovation in ordnance followed industrialization. Explosive shells entered general service in Western navies in the 1830s. In the 1850s, the development of new methods of building guns in pieces rather than through whole casting opened the door to the construction of much larger and more powerful ordnance. Rifled ordnance that fired elongated projectiles also appeared at this time. Breech-loading small guns were introduced in the 1870s, breech-loading large guns in the 1880s, quick-firing medium-caliber guns and cordite charges in the late 1880s, more rapid-firing big-guns in the late 1890s, and armor-piercing explosive projectiles and high-explosive shells in the first decade of the twentieth century. Industrial technology also resuscitated old and created new weapons. The adoption of steam power gave vessels greater control over the speed and direction of movement, which revived the ram and otherwise transformed naval tactics, but reduced operational range. Advances in electrical and metallurgical science paved the way for the invention of practicable stationary and mobile underwater explosive devices — that is, the mine and the torpedo. And in turn, new warship types — the torpedo boat, destroyer, and submarine — were developed to serve as launching platforms for the latter device.

In the early twentieth century, the great extension of torpedo range by improved guidance and propulsion mechanisms forced navies to increase the effective range of naval artillery so that surface warships could fight at distances that minimized the torpedo threat. This resulted in the development of a plethora of sophisticated machines — including optical devices such as range finders, calculators that were capable of solving differential equations instantaneously, and complicated electrical data-transmission systems — that improved gun laying and sight setting. These developments in what was known as fire control prompted important changes in capital ship design, such as the all-big-gun battleship and battle cruiser. At the same time, improvements in the submarine and the advent of aircraft increased the poten-

The USS Missouri *fires three sixteen-inch shells toward the enemy coast at Hungnam, North Korea, in December 1950. In the Korean War, the United States possessed vastly superior naval firepower.*

tial of underwater and air warfare. The critical importance of the former, the possibilities of the latter, and the limitations of large fleets of surface fighting ships were demonstrated during World War I (q.v.), which set the stage for the major developments of the 1920s and 1930s.

During the two decades between the world wars, the offensive capabilities of large surface warships were greatly increased by improvements in guns, associated mechanisms, fire control equipment, communications, and auxiliary aircraft; their defensive qualities were enhanced by antisubmarine sensors and weapons such as sonar and depth charges, and antiaircraft sensors and weapons such as radar, fire control analog computers, fuse-setters, dual-purpose (surface and antiaircraft) medium artillery, and rapid-firing light cannon. On the other hand, the advent of the aircraft carrier and improvements in the speed, range, and payload of aircraft during the same period produced a weapons system whose potency rivaled that of the surface capital ship. And the power of submarines was also multiplied by the development of sophisticated analog computers that aimed gyroscopically guided torpedoes, improved engines and hull design, and more effective communications. As a consequence, by the outbreak of World War II (q.v.), all major navies were well on the road to the creation of forces that combined surface, underwater, and air elements, or "balanced fleets."

During World War II, advances in aircraft, among other things, tipped the scales in favor of the aircraft carrier over the battleship as the principal weapon of major navies. The advent of nuclear bombs then gave navies the capacity to devastate targets on land as well as at sea through aircraft strikes from carriers, or ballistic or cruise missiles launched from submarines. Air defense was vastly improved by the invention of guided missiles and various forms of electronic countermeasures. Nuclear propulsion allowed the construction of major warships with virtually unlimited operational range, which in particular enhanced the fighting capability of submarines. Advances in sensors and communications, and the concomitant development of bureaucratized information management (the combat information center) and electronic data processing, gave groups of warships and supporting air and space power unprecedented ability to cooperate and to coordinate their use of a variety of air, surface, and underwater weapons. The advent of highly compact digital computers also made it possible to replace voluminous files of paper on board ship with much smaller and lighter installations, freeing space for other purposes while improving the efficiency of administration and engineering maintenance.

JON SUMIDA

Navarino, Battle of

October 20, 1827

This naval engagement was fought in the bay of Navarino, located in southern Greece, between an Anglo-French-Russian fleet under the command of Sir Edward Codrington and a Turkish-Egyptian fleet led by Ibrahim Pasha. The Western powers were acting in support of the Greek revolt against the Ottoman Empire (see *Ottomans*), while the naval forces of the latter were operating to suppress it. The Western fleet pitted twenty-seven units, including eleven ships of the line, against an Eastern force of sixty-five vessels, including three ships of the line. The Turkish-Egyptian fleet occupied the bay and was supported by shore batteries. Both sides hoped to avoid hostilities, but following the uncontested entry of the Anglo-French-Russian fleet into the bay, skirmishing with small arms quickly escalated into an exchange of cannon fire. A general engagement ensued in which the numerically superior but outgunned Ottoman forces were practically annihilated. Navarino was the last major fleet engagement fought entirely under sail.

JON SUMIDA

Navies

Organizations whose primary function is fighting at sea, navies consist of warships and auxiliary vessels, their crews, and the shore maintenance and administrative establishments that support them. For two and a half millennia, navies have existed to protect or attack overseas lines of commerce or military supply and to maintain or contest control of certain waters, either in the defense of home territory or support of land operations on distant shores. In the twentieth century, the invention of aircraft carriers and submarine-launched ballistic missiles have given navies the power to strike deeply inland. The mobility, reach, and fighting power of navies are fundamentally dependent upon the characteristics of their matériel,

---

The Ten Most Important Sea Battles

Salamis (480 B.C.)
Actium (31 B.C.)
Defeat of the Spanish Armada (1588)
Virginia Capes (August 30–September 10, 1781)
Trafalgar (October 21, 1805)
Tsushima (May 27–28, 1905)
Jutland (May 31–June 1, 1916)
Battle of the North Atlantic (1939–1945)
Midway (June 4–6, 1942)
Leyte Gulf (October 23–26, 1944)

---

and they are thus highly sensitive to technological change. The building and servicing of warships require large expenditure, and the skilled labor needed to staff them effectively is also costly. Navies, for these reasons, have always been more capital-intensive than armies, and they may be regarded as archetypal mechanized fighting forces.

States have built navies in response to military and economic necessity. Insular Great Britain, for example, developed a navy as its primary defense against invasion and as a means of protecting extensive overseas trade and territory that were vital to its prosperity. Economic factors have had a major effect on the growth of navies in other ways. In preindustrial Europe, the English and Dutch navies were sustained by unique political-financial arrangements that gave their governments access to profits generated by commercial economies. In the industrial era, the naval armaments manufacturing capacity required to equip a major navy could be kept in existence only by regular large orders for new construction, which meant that governments built warships in order to meet economic as well as strategic necessities. And in certain cases, such as that of Wilhelmine Germany, satisfying the economic requirements of powerful naval industrial interest groups could secure their political support for the government.

The earliest known navies in the West were those of the Greeks, who in the fifth century B.C. possessed specialized warships fully staffed by fighting crews. The support of such forces imposed unprecedented fiscal burdens, and the Peloponnesian War (431–404 B.C.) (q.v.) may indeed have been the first conflict in which cash, which was required primarily to sustain

A depiction of the Royal Navy — "twenty-four miles of steel" — assembled for review by King Edward VII of Great Britain in 1907.

the Athenian navy, was of major importance. For the next nearly two thousand years, maritime trade for a variety of technical and economic reasons was restricted to coastal traffic. The attack and defense of merchant shipping by the navies of classical Greece and Rome — and the medieval navies of Asia and Europe — as a consequence were confined to waters in sight of land, as were of course all operations in support of armies. In Europe, by the fifteenth century, the invention of the compass, the advent of gunpowder artillery, and the improvement of the sailing ship had opened the door to the development of transoceanic trade and more effective methods of fighting at sea. By the sixteenth century, conflicts that were in part generated by competition over access to maritime wealth had led to the creation of navies that were equipped with large, gun-armed sailing ships.

The augmentation of coastal forces by those capable of operating on the high seas continued in the seventeenth century. During this period, the basic form of modern navies was established with the emergence of warships custom-built to perform one of three functions — combat with the strongest ships afloat (battleships), defense of trade routes over long distances (cruisers), and local patrol (flotilla). Battle fleet supremacy conferred immunity from seaborne invasion and strong cover for the activities of cruisers and the flotilla. Large fleets of battleships, however, were extremely expensive to construct and operate. The new model fleets also required skilled leadership and cooperation at many levels, which could be provided only by a permanent corps of well-remunerated officers. And the logistical support of larger, increasingly mechanized naval forces required the expansion of shore establishments. Navies thus placed heavy demands on the political, financial, and administrative organization of European states and were major contributors to the great changes made in these areas.

By the eighteenth century, European navies were fighting one another around the world. Financial exigency, however, often precluded pursuit of a strategy based on battleships and instead prompted certain naval powers such as France (and later, in the twentieth century, Germany) to resort to attacks on commerce waged by cruisers or armed merchantmen operating alone or in small groups as their principal form of naval warfare (*guerre de course*). Historically, these campaigns against commerce failed to achieve decisive results, but were probably worthwhile because they were contained only after the defending power had been compelled to expend much greater resources than those invested by their practitioners.

Navies were transformed by nineteenth-century industrialization, which, by accelerating the production of wealth and the development of new technology, made it possible to build fleets of much greater size and capability. The introduction of steam power, in particular, not only vastly increased the tactical flexibility of ocean-going warships, but also greatly improved the ability of smaller armed vessels to operate effectively off shore or on rivers. This enabled European naval forces to penetrate and control non-European littoral areas in a manner previously impossible, and they thus played a key part in the subjugation of much of the world to Western control. On the other hand, Japan's success in developing a Western-style navy preserved its sovereignty and enabled it to pursue a policy of colonial expansion in its own right.

In the great wars of the twentieth century, navies formed the main instruments of global power projection, which took place on an unprecedented scale. During these protracted conflicts, the disproportionately large consumption of industrial assets by first-class navies became a strategic issue of major significance. Improvements in amphibious warfare magnified the impact of navies on land operations; the dependence of twentieth-century industrial economies on imports amplified the effects of naval blockade (q.v.); and with the advent of the nuclear armed ballistic missile submarine, navies acquired the capacity to destroy any nation in a matter of hours. And given the enormous and still-expanding volume of international seaborne trade, the increasing dependence of the world economy on animal and mineral oceanic resources, and the possession of modern warships by all Western and non-Western maritime states, navies are likely to continue to play a major role in international affairs.

JON SUMIDA

Nelson, Horatio

1758–1805, British Vice Admiral

Horatio Nelson, first viscount Nelson, was the third son of a Norfolk clergyman and nephew of Captain Maurice Suckling, controller of the navy (1775–1778), with whom he first went to sea in 1770. Thanks to his uncle's patronage, he was made lieutenant in April 1777, commander in December 1778, and captain in June 1779. After ten years in the West Indies, he returned to England in 1787 with his new wife, Frances Nisbet, a young widow from Nevis, and spent four years in Norfolk on half pay. On the approach of war with France, he was appointed in January 1793 to command the 64-gun *Agamemnon* in the Mediterra-

nean. In this ship Nelson saw varied service, including in 1794 a leading part in the capture of Bastia and Calvi, where he was blinded in one eye.

In the next year, Nelson moved to the 74-gun *Captain* and was appointed commodore, commanding the squadron in the Gulf of Genoa. By this time the British position in the Mediterranean was deteriorating fast, as French armies overran northern Italy, forced Naples into neutrality, and pressured Spain into alliance; in the autumn of 1796 the Royal Navy began to withdraw from the Mediterranean. On February 14, 1797, Nelson took a brilliant part in the Battle of St. Vincent, turning out of line without orders to intercept part of the Spanish fleet, boarding the 80-gun *San Nicolas*, and from it the 112-gun *San Josef*. Now a rear admiral, a knight, and a public hero, he continued as second in command to Sir John Jervis, and in July 1797 he personally led an unsuccessful landing at Santa Cruz, Tenerife, where he lost his right arm.

In April 1798 he was sufficiently recovered to return to sea; in June, with fourteen ships of the line, he was ordered back into the Mediterranean in pursuit of the expedition of Napoleon Bonaparte (q.v.), which had sailed from Toulon for an unknown destination. Nelson guessed that the French were bound for the Levant, but he narrowly missed them on his passage to Alexandria and searched the eastern Mediterranean for a month before finally, on the evening of August 1, he found the French fleet at anchor in Abukir Bay at the mouth of the Nile. Admiral Brueys chose to fight at anchor, but his formation was loose and his ships ill prepared. Trusting to the tactical initiative of his captains, whom he had thoroughly imbued with his ideas, Nelson attacked at once; his leading ships passed inside the French line to achieve an overwhelming concentration, and by morning eleven (out of thirteen) battleships had been sunk or taken.

So decisive a naval victory was unprecedented; it played a considerable part in reconstructing the anti-French coalition, and Lord Nelson (as he now became) was greeted everywhere with adulation. Basing his squadron at Naples, he cooperated with the Neapolitan government against the French, and when they overran Naples in December, he evacuated the royal family to Palermo. In June 1799 a counterrevolution reestablished Bourbon rule, and in his capacity of commander in chief of the Neapolitan navy, Nelson was responsible for the execution of several Neapolitan officers for serving the French. Not everyone approved of this, and fewer approved of his infatuation with the wife of the British ambassador, Sir William Hamilton. Ignoring a direct order from George Elphinstone, Lord Keith, his new commander in chief, he remained ashore at Palermo for most of the next twelve months. In June 1800, accompanied by the Hamiltons, he left the fleet and returned overland to England. There his wife received him with understandable coldness, and they presently parted. For the rest of his life Nelson lived with Sir William and Lady Hamilton.

In February 1801 he sailed as second in command to Sir Hyde Parker with a squadron intended to break up the "Armed Neutrality" of Baltic powers. On April 1, while Parker with the biggest ships lay offshore, Nelson led his squadron to attack the Danish fleet before Copenhagen. Like the French at the Nile, the Danish ships were moored inshore; unlike the French, they were skillfully placed with shore batteries in support, and defended with great determination. The battle was desperate and for long doubtful; at the critical moment Nelson deliberately ignored Parker's signal to withdraw and was rewarded with a crushing if costly victory. He returned to England a viscount and spent the rest of the year commanding the flotilla watching French invasion preparations at Boulogne and elsewhere. On the return of war in May 1803, Nelson took command of the Mediterranean squadron, with the difficult task of blockading Toulon. On March 30, 1805, Pierre-Charles de Villeneuve's squadron succeeded in escaping to play its part in Napoleon's abortive scheme to concentrate a fleet in the West Indies, thence to return to the Channel and cover his invasion flotilla. Nelson followed Villeneuve across the Atlantic and back, and on July 18 he joined Cuthbert Collingwood off Cádiz, where Villeneuve had taken refuge. After a brief visit to England, he returned in October. On October 19 Villeneuve and his Spanish allies sailed, and three days later Nelson led his fleet to victory off Cape Trafalgar (q.v.), where he died.

Nelson's vanity and scandalous private life disgusted many who did not know him, but his charm seldom failed to work on everyone he met. In the navy he was adored by officers and men alike, and the success of his eclectic tactics owed much to delegation to trusted and informed subordinates, inspired by the example of an admiral who in actions of danger always led from the front. Nelson never invented a particular tactical system, nor did he alone break through the rigidity of the formal line of battle. He used a flexible combination of tactical ideas, relying heavily on the initiative of his captains. The object was always to break up the enemy fleet and bring a concentration of force on each part in turn. Trafalgar was the supreme example of his methods. His death in the hour of victory blotted out his failings and left a heroic memory to which subsequent generations added layers of myth.

N. A. M. RODGER

Carola Oman, *Nelson* (1947); Tom Pocock, *Horatio Nelson* (1987).

Neutrality

In 416 B.C., the hard-pressed rulers of the island of Melos discovered the weakness of principled appeals to neutral rights when they tried to persuade the Athenians that they should be left in peace, siding neither with them nor with the Spartans (q.v.). The Athenians replied that in this world "the strong do as they will and the weak suffer what they must." The Melians learned, too late, that the safest guard of neutrality is a defense so daunting that it is worth no belligerent's while to launch an attack. The doughty Swiss in two world wars made the prospect of occupying their country so uninviting that Germany refrained therefrom.

In ancient times as now, neutrals often tilt to one side, though they and their quasi enemies may find it convenient to pretend otherwise. Thus the Persians aided Sparta in the Peloponnesian War (q.v.), though they were formally at peace with Athens; similarly, the French supported the American colonists with arms and gold before formally recognizing the newly independent United States in 1778 (see *American Revolution*). A judicious neutrality can be profitable. Neutrals may let belligerents attempt to woo them into war with promises of material or territorial gain, as Italy did most successfully in the first year of World War I (q.v.) and, to a lesser degree, Turkey in World War II (q.v.). At the same time, pressure brought to bear on neutrals in the course of a war can breed new conflicts. Thus Great Britain in 1812 provoked a war with the United States by a severity of treatment that the Americans regarded as an unacceptable infringement of neutral rights.

Gradually, however, neutral rights and obligations have become well defined under international law, most notably in the Hague Convention of 1907, which, for example, requires that if ships of belligerent powers are in a neutral port, they may leave only at intervals of twenty-four hours from one another. Belligerent soldiers, sailors, and airmen were routinely interned during the nineteenth and twentieth centuries; more recently Iran benefited handsomely by confiscating Iraqi airplanes flown to Iran during the Gulf War of 1991 (q.v.). Modern rules of neutrality forbid the recruiting of combatant units to support either party to a conflict, or the movement of armed units or munitions through neutral territory — provisions known to have been violated, albeit usually under duress. In earlier times the rules were less restrictive (for example, regarding the recruitment of soldiers from neutrals), but the protection comparably less.

It may be in the strategic interests of one or even both belligerents in a conflict to have neutral states adjoining them. German war planners in 1914 directed their armies around Holland, believing that in the event of a prolonged war it would serve as Germany's economic "windpipe." Neutral states offer discreet surroundings for peace talks and, above all, points of access for intelligence services hoping to penetrate an opponent's security system.

The law and customs of neutrality harken back most to the optimistic hopes of the nineteenth century, during which it was possible to distinguish clearly between combatants and bystanders, and to hope that war could be contained, and even in some measure, civilized. The ideologically driven wars of this century, however, conducted with horrific disregard of humanity, let alone international law, make some of the rules appear slightly archaic. In an age of limited war, however, the laws of neutrality may acquire new vigor.

ELIOT A. COHEN

Roderick Ogley, *The Theory and Practice of Neutrality in the Twentieth Century* (1970).

Nightingale, Florence

1820–1910, *British Crimean War Nurse*

Reports in *The Times* from the Crimean War (1854–1856) (q.v.) and the British Hospital at Scutari painted a terrible picture of suffering endured by sick and wounded troops and urged the dispatch of nurses. Through personal connections, Florence Nightingale, who had no training in nursing or hospital administration, secured control of the nurses and the funds sent to comfort the British army.

Her formidable self-confidence and powers of persuasion secured her position. Nightingale's efforts at Scutari were quickly turned into popular legend by the newspapers, as an antithesis to the apparent incompetence of the military authorities. However, the bulk of all nursing, as it is understood today, was provided by male orderlies, restricting the nurses to cooking, cleaning, and spiritual comfort for the dying.

Manipulative, determined, and self-promoting, Nightingale rarely allowed the truth to interfere with her work. Her object was power and reputation; nursing was only the means to that end. Her real contribution to saving lives was the result of the superior order, cleanliness, and feeding she imposed.

After the war she campaigned for improved sanitation in army barracks and in India, and in particular popularized nursing, once considered a menial chore, into an honored vocation. Nightingale made an important contribution to care for the wounded and sick, and if she was never "the Lady with the lamp" of popular myth, she did raise the national consciousness and establish the role of the nurse in modern medicine.

A. D. LAMBERT

Nimitz, Chester W.

1885–1966, *U.S. World War II Admiral*

Admiral Chester Nimitz, as commander in chief, Pacific Fleet and Pacific Areas (1942–1945), led the greatest naval campaign of all time. The U.S. Navy's Pacific strategy in World War II (q.v.) was the product of Nimitz's cooperation with Admiral Ernest King (q.v.), chief of naval operations (CNO), and its execution was the responsibility of Nimitz and his combat commanders. The strategy of offensive sea control was simple and consistent: sail across the central Pacific, take island airfields, destroy the Japanese fleet, and sink its merchantmen until U.S. ships had a noose around the home islands. Pursuing this strategy, Nimitz relied on masterful subordinates, increasingly useful and well-used naval intelligence, and a fleet of ships and sailors, airmen, and marines, the extent of which the world may never again see.

Strategically, Nimitz and King were convinced that

there was more to be gained by a swifter, less costly attack through the central Pacific than by Douglas MacArthur's (q.v.) slow if steady march from the south. However, Nimitz saw how to use the whipsaw flexibility of the dual advance, moving carriers back and forth, keeping the Japanese off balance, denying them strong points in the South Pacific while mounting an offensive in the central Pacific. As he advanced, Nimitz hoped to provoke the Japanese fleet into a decisive engagement, but that never took place. Nimitz also understood all the other dimensions of contemporary offensive sea control. Submarines began an attrition strategy well before the navy established command of the sea. "Island hopping" left Japanese garrisons impotent and stranded as the offensive moved forward. The amphibious assaults of seaborne marines paved the way to Japan.

Though Nimitz missed the decisive battle, he and the navy accomplished everything American strategy required of them. One can understand his exasperation when an army officer, Douglas MacArthur (q.v.) was picked to accept the surrender of Japan, for if any service was to be singled out in the moment of victory, it should have been the navy. Nimitz, now fleet admiral, succeeded King as CNO in 1945, retiring from that post and from the navy two years later.

GEORGE BAER

Nine Years' War

See Grand Alliance, War of the.

Nivelle, Robert-Georges

1856–1924, *French General*

The man who perpetrated one of the great debacles of World War I (q.v.) was the very model of a general: as confident as he was brave, as imposing as he was arrogant. A mere regimental commander at the war's beginning, Robert-Georges Nivelle directed the captures of Forts Douaumont and Vaux in the Battle of Verdun (q.v.) in 1916. His celebrity was not to be denied, and he replaced General Joseph Joffre (q.v.) as chief of the French General Staff. *Élan* and *cran* (guts) were his watchwords. He charmed his British allies: here was a French Protestant who actually spoke English.

Nivelle immediately announced a war-ending plan that projected a vast rupture at the Chemin des Dames heights north of the Aisne. Everyone, including the Germans, knew its details. The Germans made a deliberate withdrawal, rendering irrelevant much of Nivelle's scheme. They prepared elaborate in-depth defenses. Nivelle persisted anyway. The uphill attack in the rain on April 16, 1917, against a well-prepared enemy made insignificant gains, cost more than 100,000 men, and left the war more deadlocked than ever. Nivelle grudgingly resigned. His successor, Philippe-Henri Pétain (q.v.), immediately had to deal with widespread mutinies in an army that now barely functioned. Luckier than the 32,000 who died on the fire-swept ridges of the Aisne, Nivelle retired to a face-saving command in North Africa.

ROBERT COWLEY

Nomads

The prime military assets of nomadism were mobility and manpower. Domestic animals (properly, by nomad standards, at least, one hundred sheep, including their equivalents in goats, cattle, and so on) provided subsistence and could move anywhere with suitable grazing and water. Nomad armies campaigning in, say, Inner Asia, the steppe between Hungary and Manchuria, employed simple logistics: the animals ate the grass, and the soldiers ate the animals. Animal management required little labor, freeing much manpower for war: perhaps 40 percent among Arabian camel-bedouin, and some 70 percent (nominally 100 percent) among Inner Asians, whose women and children managed the sheep, goats, and cattle. Moreover, nomad men considered themselves warriors and aspired to warrior virtues: endurance, ingenuity, bravery, and heroism.

Nomadism entailed some military limitations. Sparse grazing from aridity or incompatible vegetation complicated logistics. Pastoral dispersal inhibited assembly and training of troops. Migratory societies could not support technologies producing swords, metal armor, and, in later times, guns. And since nomad populations were much smaller than sedentary ones, greater mobilization might not yield higher numbers.

Some nomads had the advantage of numerous horses. Inner Asian and northern Middle Eastern steppes suit horse raising; most Arab and African lands do not. Nomads in the latter regions had little cavalry, and those were mostly lancers. Inner Asians, by contrast, kept perhaps ten horses per family and five per soldier, and fielded all-cavalry armies. Grazing gave this cavalry logistical freedom, but supported only pony-sized animals, more suitable for hit-and-run mounted archery than shock combat; and grazing took time, slowing the march of cavalry to fifteen miles a day. When whole nomad communities went to war, their grazing sheep set the pace of three to four miles a day. Camels could travel faster but were poor combat mounts. Cavalry made a difference in nomad society, since its effective employment demanded firm control and ready obedience. Inner Asian nomads had chiefs, autocratic leaders of political followings — tribes unrestricted by lineage or language, religion or race, and shaped for war. The term *tribe* in Arab and African nomadism, on the other hand, denotes an exclusive genealogical unit, acting — if at all — by consensus achieved through the cajolery of ad hoc leaders. The military power of nomads in Inner Asia tended to stalemate because of an overabundance of competing chiefs; it was negated in Arabia and Africa by the death of chieftains.

When their military and political limitations were overcome, especially by the appeal of some extraordinary undertaking to heroic idealism, nomads accomplished remarkable feats of arms. With inspiration, leadership, and organization supplied by the prophet Muhammad and his fellow townsmen of Mecca and Medina, mostly nomad Arab armies won Islam an empire. Turkish chiefs of the sixth through the eighth centuries A.D. claimed world rule, called for action in its establishment, and induced nomad warriors to overrun Inner Asia. The Mongols (q.v.) most conclusively demonstrated the congruence between nomadism and war. They used the idea of world conquest to challenge and attract both nomad and sedentary warriors; employed elastic, multicultural tribalism to array Turks, Persians, Russians, Chinese, Koreans, and many others alongside (or usually, in front of) their Mongolian soldiery; and with the mounted archers and lancers, infantry spearmen and crossbowmen, artillerists, engineers, and sailors that this diverse manpower abundantly provided, Mongol armies and navies conquered much of the known world: all of Inner Asia and the adjacent great powers — China, Russia, and most of the Middle East.

JOHN MASSON SMITH, JR.

Thomas T. Allsen, *Mongol Imperialism: The Policies of the Grand Qan Möngke in China, Russia, and the Islamic Lands, 1251–1259* (1987); Fredrik Barth, *Nomads of South Persia: The Basseri Tribe of the Khamseh Confederacy* (1986).

Normans

The Normans were perhaps the most dynamic and expansionist element in Europe during the eleventh century, a period noted for the crystallization of Western civilization. In the course of the century, the Normans left the confines of northwestern France to conquer England, southern Italy, Sicily, and Antioch in the Holy Land. Despite recent attempts to downplay their feats, it remains clear that the Normans had an enormous impact on European history. While capable of creatively harnessing the potent cultural, religious, and political currents of the day, their preeminence clearly lay in the mastery of warfare.

Nevertheless, many see the Normans merely as inhabitants of a typical French territorial principality with little, other than their military success, to distinguish them from any other part of medieval France. The Normans themselves, however, had no doubt that they were a breed apart, picked out by God to perform great deeds. Contemporaries who felt the sting of their might likewise saw them as an exceptional people: "cruel and inhuman in body and mind," as one resentful Italian put it.

The origins of the Normans were certainly ferocious enough. They began as Viking (q.v.) "pirates" who settled in the Seine River valley in the mid–ninth century. The Frankish nobility had abandoned this backward and impoverished territory, leaving a population of Frankish peasants to be dominated by the Norse warriors. As the pagan Normanni (Northmen) raided the surrounding territory, they earned the unremitting hostility of the Christian Franks. This hostility provided the central element of Norman identity: Normans were the warriors settled in an area called Normannia who, even though they soon adopted the French language and religion, were *not* Franks.

The danger from Frankish hostility (totally unjustified in the Norman view) was another key element. For security, the scattered war bands gradually acknowledged the leadership of the dukes of Rouen descended from Rollo, the Viking chief who had extorted acceptance of the Norse settlement from the Frankish king in 911. The dukes consolidated their control by marriage ties to the leaders of the major war bands throughout Normandy, whose descendants, warriors all and tied by blood and marriage to the dukes, formed the core of the Norman aristocracy. Their precarious military situation called for absolute loyalty to the duke within Normandy and extreme aggressiveness toward those outside its boundaries. This gave the Norman aristocracy of the eleventh century a sense of cohesion and discipline unmatched in Europe. Yet without warfare, and victory, the constantly growing demands for land and loot to reward warriors and kin could not be met.

This need provided the explosive force for Norman expansion, yet would have meant little without the Norman hallmark: superb military skill. The Normans adopted and perfected the techniques of warfare typical of northern France in the late tenth and early eleventh centuries. The new warfare did not center around the armored knight alone, but rather was a sophisticated combination of armed strongholds, siege operations, and the shock tactics of heavily armored cavalrymen. If well trained, the massed charge of heavily armed Norman cavalry could "pierce the walls of Babylon," it was said.

Training began early; boys were drilled, in groups of five to ten, to fight on horseback in small flexible units. The fact that Norman knights were united by kinship and had trained and fought together since childhood led to an extraordinary level of morale and discipline. The wealth needed for arming and training such troops led to the steady feudalization of Normandy and a great hunger for more land to provide the necessary estates and income.

The Norman ideal of leadership was personified by Duke William the Conqueror (q.v.), also known as "the Bastard." "I was brought up in arms from childhood," William is supposed to have said, and on the battlefield he earned the respect of warriors every bit as tough. After defeating Normans opposed to his rule at Val-ès-Dunes in 1047, William proceeded to establish the strongest government in France with the aid of aristocrats handpicked for their political and military skills and, above all, their loyalty. Believing England to be rightfully his, he crushed the English at the Battle of Hastings (q.v.) in 1066 and was crowned king. William then devoted his considerable political talents and ruthless energy to governing the new Anglo-Norman state.

Meanwhile Norman adventurers were carving out principalities for themselves in the Mediterranean. The most successful was Robert Guiscard. By his death in 1085, Robert was duke of Apulia, Calabria, and Sicily, capable of challenging the Byzantine Empire and a respected ally of the pope. The same desire for land and glory drove Robert's eldest son, Bohemond de Taranto. Disinherited in favor of a half brother, Bohemond joined the First Crusade (see *Crusades*) in 1096 with five hundred Norman knights and in 1098 led the crusaders' assault on the great city of Antioch. Once it was taken, Bohemond ruled the principality in his own right, establishing the strongest of the crusader states.

The Norman kingdom of Sicily came to an end in 1189, the English kingdom was permanently separated from Normandy in 1204, and Bohemond's principality of Antioch was extinguished in 1268. Although the inhabitants of Normandy still regard themselves as Normans, the descendants of the original Norman warriors elsewhere were soon assimilated by local societies.

Beyond the sheer drama of their conquests, the Normans were a creative force in European development. Their alliance with the papacy provided a vital bulwark for the reform movement that reshaped the church, while the Anglo-Norman kingdom laid the basis of the later history and culture of the British Isles. Their activities in the Mediterranean united southern Italy, brought it back into the fold of Latin Christendom, and regained Sicily from the Muslims.

W. SCOTT JESSEE

R. Allen Brown, *The Normans* (1984); David Nicolle, *The Normans* (1987); Eleanor Searle, *Predatory Kinship and the Creation of Norman Power, 840–1066* (1988).

North Atlantic, Battle of the

1939–1945

On the first day of Britain's participation in World War II (q.v.), a German U-boat torpedoed the liner *Athenia.* Thus began the longest battle of World War II, one that finally ended in May 1945. Neither side was ready for the war in the Atlantic: the Royal Navy had discounted the submarine as a menace, whereas the Germans had failed to emphasize U-boat construction before the war.

But once the Germans gained control of the French coast and its Atlantic ports after the fall of France in May 1940, their U-boats began to reach out ever deeper into the Atlantic. British losses had reached over 300,000 tons per month by late spring 1941, when British intelligence managed to break into the German navy's secret message traffic between the U-boat high command and its boats. Knowing the location of German patrol lines of U-boats, the British maneuvered their convoys around the threatened areas. Sinkings fell to manageable levels in the last half of 1941.

But in early 1942 the situation again changed in the U-boats' favor. Although they never recognized that their message traffic had been compromised, the Germans introduced additional complications to their enciphering devices in December 1941; it took British intelligence nearly a year to break back into the message traffic. By this time the United States had entered the war, and U-boats had begun to attack ships along its east coast. Moreover, the U.S. Navy had paid no attention to British experiences against U-boats, eschewing convoys and radio silence; ships silhouetted against the bright lights of the coast were easy targets. To German submarine skippers, the period was known as the "happy time," in many ways a greater strategic disaster than Pearl Harbor (q.v.). When the Americans tightened up their defenses, the Germans moved to the Caribbean, where they found equally lax defenses. Only when the Allies finally applied convoys and escorts did the struggle shift back to the North Atlantic.

Early 1943 saw over two hundred submarines available to the U-boat high command; but the Allies now could read the German ciphers and possessed vast numbers of escorts and long-range patrol aircraft to protect the great convoys that rolled across the Atlantic. In March 1943 the Allied defenses bent but did not break. Sinkings of Allied merchant ships approached three-quarters of a million tons; but by May the balance had shifted so much in favor of the Allies that the Germans lost nearly forty boats. Admiral Karl Dönitz (q.v.) called off the Battle of the North Atlantic, and the Allied sea lines of communications provided a broad avenue on which American production and manpower could flow to Europe and defeat the Third Reich. Victory in the Battle of the North Atlantic was the essential prerequisite on which the Allied victories in Europe of 1943 and 1944 would rest.

WILLIAMSON MURRAY

Nuclear Weapons

Weapons that harness the energy released by splitting or fusing atoms are termed nuclear weapons. Their destructive effects include blast, or overpressure; radiant heat; gamma, or short-term, radiation; the firestorm created by airbursts over cities, forests, and so on; alpha, or long-term radiation (both in the imme-

diate blast area and as wind-dispersed fallout); and electromagnetic pulse. Their enormous destructive capacities stem from the immense energies that bind together the subatomic particles of which atoms are made (in the case of fission weapons), and which are released when atoms combine to form new elements (in the case of fusion weapons). Although these energies are common to all atoms, only a handful of isotopes (atoms of a given element with the same chemical properties, but different atomic weights) lend themselves to nuclear weaponry. Only the very heaviest elements are fissile, and the cores of nuclear weapons depend on the U-235 isotope of uranium and the Pu-239 isotope of plutonium. Conversely, fusion can be induced in only the very lightest elements (the basic reaction is the fusion of two hydrogen atoms to produce a single helium atom, the reaction that fuels the sun), and isotopes of hydrogen and hydrogen-lithium compounds serve as fuel in thermonuclear, or hydrogen, bombs.

The explosive yield of "pure" nuclear weapons — that is, those depending on fission alone — is limited to about twenty to thirty kilotons (a kiloton is equivalent to a thousand tons of TNT [trinitrotoluene]). There is no theoretical upper limit on the yield of thermonuclear weapons, and weapons have been tested with yields in excess of eighty megatons, or eighty million tons, of TNT.

The development of nuclear weapons stemmed from the discovery on the eve of World War II (q.v.) that the nucleus of a uranium atom "split" by a free neutron gave off several neutrons, plus considerable energy. This raised the possibility of a self-sustaining chain reaction with enormous potential for destruction, though it was clear that immense theoretical and practical problems had to be resolved before — or if — fission weapons could be made. The most basic of these was to calculate supercritical mass, the size of a mass of uranium sufficiently large that enough free neutrons would strike nuclei before departing the mass to sustain an explosive chain reaction. The solutions to this and other associated problems, notably the production of fissile materials, were first worked out in the United States after British and American scientists convinced President Franklin Roosevelt (q.v.) that nuclear weapons were feasible and that Nazi Germany might develop them. Ironically, many key scientists in the American nuclear program, termed the Manhattan Project, were European émigrés, many of them Jews, who had fled Nazi Europe.

The ruins of Nagasaki, Japan, on September 24, 1945, six weeks after the second atomic bomb exploded over the city.

By mid-1943, Manhattan Project scientists working under the direction of General Leslie Groves and chief scientist J. Robert Oppenheimer were confident that an explosive chain reaction could be sustained in U-235 and in plutonium, an element created artificially in graphite-modulated nuclear reactors. But major obstacles remained: first, it proved extremely difficult to isolate the 235 isotope of uranium; second, although plutonium was more fissile than uranium, production progressed extremely slowly, and the chemistry of the new element remained unknown; third, the highly radioactive 240 isotope of plutonium constantly emitted free neutrons, thus dictating that the critical mass would have to be assembled extremely quickly to prevent a premature, partial nuclear detonation.

The Americans pursued two solutions: a "gun" weapon, which fired two subcritical masses of U-235 together to produce a supercritical mass; and an implosion weapon, which used shaped, high-explosive charges to compress a hollow sphere of plutonium into a supercritical ball. Their theories were validated when an implosion device was successfully detonated near Los Alamos, New Mexico, on July 16, 1945. A gun-type U-235 bomb was dropped on Hiroshima, Japan, on August 6, 1945, and a plutonium implosion bomb fell on Nagasaki three days later. Nazi Germany never came close to developing nuclear weapons, and Japan did not seriously try.

The awesome power of nuclear weapons dramatically reshaped the strategic realities of the postwar world, and it became clear that any nation with serious claims to great power status had to have them. First off the mark, in 1949, was the Soviet Union, helped by information passed on by spies within the Manhattan Project. Next, in 1952, came Britain (which had combined its program with that of the United States during the war), followed by France (1960) and China (1964). Several other nations have developed nuclear weapons, including South Africa (which subsequently abandoned them), Israel, and perhaps Pakistan; only India, which detonated a device in 1974, did so more or less openly. The United States tested its first thermonuclear device in 1952, the Soviet Union in 1955, Britain in 1957, China in 1967, and France in 1968. Nuclear weapons and the fission triggers for thermonuclear weapons were made progressively smaller, the key development being the increasingly efficient "squeezing" of subcritical masses of fissile material to supercriticality by using explosive shock waves to reduce the space between atoms. Today nuclear warheads can be carried in a field artillery shell . . . or a briefcase.

Perhaps ironically, the main strategic effect of nuclear and thermonuclear weapons, first carried by aircraft and then primarily as warheads on intercontinental and intermediate-range ballistic missiles, was deterrence (q.v.). Indeed, mutual nuclear deterrence was a dominant strategic reality of the Cold War (q.v.). Also, nuclear weapons have been a major spur to arms control and disarmament (q.v.) agreements; during the Cold War, these were highly politicized and highly technical, addressing not only numbers and yields of nuclear weapons, but also terminal effects and delivery systems. Following the Soviet Union's collapse in 1989, the primary strategic concern became the spread of nuclear weapons to terrorist organizations and "rogue" states such as Iraq and North Korea, a concern magnified by the existence of massive stores of formerly Soviet nuclear weapons. It is perhaps reassuring to note in this context that the shelf life of many radioactive components of nuclear weapons remains limited.

JOHN F. GUILMARTIN

Richard Rhodes, *The Making of the Atomic Bomb* (1986).

O

Oda Nobunaga

1534–1582, *Japanese Warlord*

Combining fierce ambition and unparalleled presumption with ingenuity and opportune timing, Oda Nobunaga rose from unremarkable beginnings to become master of central Japan and the most powerful daimyo (warlord) of his time. When he succeeded to his father's estate of Oda in 1551, the seventeen-year-old Nobunaga controlled about half of his native province. Nine years later he leaped into the circle of serious contenders for national power when, with only two thousand troops, he routed a twenty-thousand-man army under Imagawa Yoshimoto at the Battle of Okehazama, killing Yoshimoto in the fray. Within a decade of this, he clearly emerged as *the* major contender for countrywide hegemony. At the time of his death, at the hands of a recalcitrant vassal, he dominated nearly a third of the entire country, including the imperial capital of Kyoto.

A ruthless and even brutal campaigner, Nobunaga is popularly remembered as a destroyer, a reputation not entirely undeserved. Over the course of his career he unseated the last Ashikaga shogun (ostensibly the military overlord of the country, until that time), obliterated Buddhist monastic complexes, crushed dozens of daimyo houses, and abolished trade guilds and many other key political and economic institutions of medieval Japan. But historians today generally stress what he *created:* his tactical application of the harquebus in battles such as the one at Nagashino (q.v.) revolutionized Japanese warfare; his castle headquarters at Azuchi became the prototype after which all subsequent Japanese fortifications were modeled (see *Castles*); his policies laid the foundations for much of the political and economic structure of early modern Japan; and his enthusiastic patronage of the arts helped shape the high culture of his and the following age.

KARL F. FRIDAY

Offensive

From the earliest days of Western civilization, the offensive — the attack — has lain at the heart of the Western way of war. The *Iliad* is the tale of Greek warriors chasing across the Aegean to right a wrong one of their number had suffered at Trojan hands (see *Trojan War*). Yet it is well to remember that there are other human traditions: for example, tribes in pre-Columbian North America sometimes fought "battles" lasting a full day with no more than a few token wounded on each side. And prior to the arrival of the Europeans in the nineteenth century, the armies of Mughal India (q.v.) were such ponderous, poorly controlled arrays that they could seldom mount viable offensives. Likewise the Chinese — at least until the nomads arrived to teach them new lessons — tended to regard war as more a matter of subtle stratagems than of violent, uncompromising offensives.

But a ruthless, violent desire to overthrow one's opponents has characterized Western war; the ethos of the barbarian tribes that conquered western Europe in the fifth and sixth centuries only added to the disposition already inherent in Roman attitudes. And the only way to overthrow one's opponents in Western eyes lay in the offensive — a willingness to take the war into enemy territories. Perhaps only the Japanese have displayed a similar enthusiasm for the offensive; although Japanese politics and strategy were intricate indeed, the heart of Bushido, the code of the samurai warrior (q.v.), demanded total commitment to attack.

Certainly, in the Middle Ages the tactical offensive was almost mandatory for medieval European armies, based as they were on the shock action of heavy, armored cavalry. To win, knights had to charge. But the equation began to change with the introduction of missile weapons: the English kings of the fourteenth and fifteenth centuries launched strategic offensives into French territory, but remained on the tactical defensive to destroy attacking French chivalry (see *Hundred Years' War*). For a short period, gunpowder weapons allowed European monarchs to attack the castles of their rebellious nobility at relatively little cost. But introduction of the *trace italienne* in the sixteenth century — a form of fortification (q.v.) that robbed gunpowder weapons of much of their effectiveness — gave the defensive the upper hand.

But the advantage of the defense over the next two centuries did not prevent a few great captains from waging offensives that sought to overthrow their opponents. Gustavus Adolphus (q.v.) and the duke of Marlborough (q.v.) both took the strategic and tactical offensive in their campaigns, usually with devastating results. But in neither case were even these great commanders able to overthrow entirely their opponents. It was thus left to their successor, Napoleon (q.v.), to create a standard of offensive war that no other Western commander has matched since Alexander the Great (q.v.). Likewise, Britain's great naval commander in the early nineteenth century believed always in the attack. Summing up the attitudes of early-nineteenth-century war is Horatio Nelson's (q.v.) order at Trafalgar (q.v.): "No Captain can do very wrong if he places his ship alongside that of an enemy."

In the nineteenth century, interpreters of Napoleon concluded that the moral advantage of the offensive outweighed all other factors. The resulting "cult of the offensive" failed, however, to account for technological developments that restored the advantages of the tactical defense. In 1914, the French army's rigid adherence to this doctrine resulted in horrific losses in the 1914 Battle of the Frontiers. The Germans, meanwhile, held similar beliefs, although they were more concerned with the strategic and operational levels than with tactics. Count von Schlieffen's (q.v.) plan for the invasion of France via Belgium grew out of the assumption that the only way for Germany to survive the inevitable war was to launch a great, decisive offensive.

World War I (q.v.) represented a massive effort, at the cost of tens of millions of casualties, to return the offensive to the battlefield. Although the slaughter of 1914–1918 largely discredited the "cult of the offensive," military thinkers in the West sought new ways to strike directly at the heart of the enemy nation. Theorists such as Giulio Douhet, Hugh Trenchard, and Billy Mitchell (q.v.) forecast that air war waged against enemy nations would bring a quick halt to future wars. The German fixation with the offensive in ground war resulted in the creation of blitzkrieg (q.v.) tactics and operations that eventually led to the conquest of much of Europe by 1941. But German virtuosity on the offensive could not make up for flaws in German strategy — namely, a willingness to take on the whole world at once and a contempt for logistics and intelligence.

Even the arrival of the atomic bomb in 1945 could not change the emphasis on the offensive. Throughout the Cold War (q.v.), the sole Soviet strategy for a war in Europe remained a massive mechanized offensive accompanied by the laydown of hundreds of tactical nuclear weapons. The U.S. Army's response to the guerrilla war in Southeast Asia was an endless series of inept tactical offensives originally tailored for battles against Soviet forces. In the end, even deterrence rested on a willingness to use nuclear weapons on the attack. And in the uncertain post–Cold War world the offensive will probably remain the fundamental concept for Western armies.

WILLIAMSON MURRAY

Carl von Clausewitz, *On War*, ed. M. Howard and P. Paret (1976).

Okinawa, Battle of

April 1–June 21, 1945

Last and biggest of the Pacific island battles of World War II (q.v.), the Okinawa campaign involved the 287,000 troops of the U.S. Tenth Army against 130,000 soldiers of the Japanese Thirty-second Army. At stake were air bases vital to the projected invasion of Japan. Japanese forces changed their typical tactics of resisting at the water's edge to a defense in depth, designed to gain time. In conjunction with this, the Japanese navy and army mounted mass air attacks by planes on one-way "suicide" missions; the Japanese also sent their last big battleship, the *Yamato*, on a similar mission with a few escorts. The "special attack" kamikaze tactics the Japanese used on these

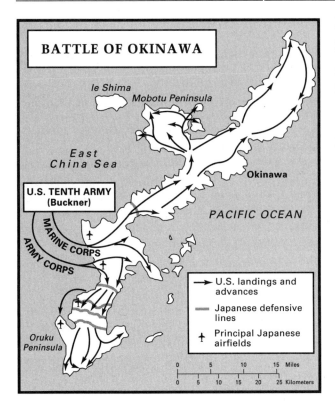

BATTLE OF OKINAWA

Ie Shima

Mobotu Peninsula

East China Sea

Okinawa

U.S. TENTH ARMY (Buckner)

MARINE CORPS

ARMY CORPS

PACIFIC OCEAN

Oruku Peninsula

→ U.S. landings and advances
— Japanese defensive lines
✝ Principal Japanese airfields

0   5   10   15 Miles
0   5   10   15   20   25 Kilometers

missions, although not especially sophisticated, were so determined that Allied forces perhaps faced their most difficult Pacific campaign. The net result made Okinawa a mass bloodletting both on land and at sea, and among both the island's civilian population and the military.

A series of defense lines across the island, both north and south of the American landing beaches, enabled the Japanese to conduct a fierce defense of Okinawa over many weeks. Using pillboxes and strongpoints, caves, and even some ancient castles, the Japanese defense positions supported one another and often resisted even the most determined artillery fire or air strikes. Mounting few attacks themselves, the Japanese conserved their strength for this defense. Caves or pillboxes often had to be destroyed individually with dynamite charges. This battle took place in an environment much more heavily populated than most Pacific islands, with civilian casualties of almost 100,000 and equally heavy losses for the Japanese army. "It was a scene straight out of hell. There is no other way to describe it," recalls Higa Tomiko, then a seven-year-old girl, who survived the battle.

The commanding generals on both sides died in the course of this battle: American general Simon B.

Buckner by artillery fire, Japanese general Ushijima Mitsuru by suicide. Other U.S. losses in ground combat included 7,374 killed, 31,807 wounded, and 239 missing in action. The navy suffered 4,907 killed or missing aboard 34 ships sunk and 368 damaged; 763 aircraft were lost. At sea and in the air, the Japanese expended roughly 2,800 aircraft, plus a battleship, a light cruiser, and four destroyers, with losses that can be estimated at upwards of 10,000.

JOHN PRADOS

Operation Aida

1942

Aida refers to General Erwin Rommel's (q.v.) drive to the Nile, his masterpiece. On May 26, 1942, Rommel set out from Sfax, Tunisia, for Alexandria, Egypt, with his Afrika Korps and the Italian Tank Division Ariete. In a textbook operation ("Theseus") featuring coordination of air, armor, and infantry, Rommel drove 380 miles through Cyrenaica in fifteen days and stormed Tobruk on June 21. The "Gazala gallop" cost the British Eighth Army seventy-five thousand men and one hundred tanks; Winston S. Churchill (q.v.) termed it a "hideous and totally unexpected shock."

On June 25, Rommel received permission to continue the "drive to Suez." The Afrika Korps advanced into Egypt in captured British clothing, driving British vehicles and eating British rations. But Rommel never reached Suez. Aided by three hundred Sherman tanks, one hundred self-propelled 105-mm howitzers, and six air groups from America, the Eighth Army halted Rommel and defeated him at El Alamein (q.v.) in November 1942.

HOLGER H. HERWIG

Operation Barbarossa

June 22, 1941–March 1942

On June 22, 1941, Adolf Hitler (q.v.) launched his armies eastward in a massive invasion of the Soviet Union: three great army groups with over three million German soldiers, 150 divisions, and three thousand tanks smashed across the frontier into Soviet territory. The invasion covered a front from the North Cape to the Black Sea, a distance of two thousand miles. By this point German combat effectiveness had reached its apogee; in training, doctrine, and fighting ability, the forces invading Russia represented the finest army to fight in the twentieth century. Barbarossa was *the* crucial turning point in World War II (q.v.), for its failure forced Nazi Germany to fight a two-front war against a coalition possessing immensely superior resources.

The Germans had serious deficiencies. They severely underestimated their opponent; their logistical preparations were grossly inadequate for the campaign; and German industrial preparations for a sustained war had yet to begin. But the greatest mistake that the Germans made was to come as conquerors, not as liberators — they were determined to enslave the Slavic population and exterminate the Jews. Thus, from the beginning, the war in the East became an ideological struggle, waged with a ruthlessness and mercilessness not seen in Europe since the Mongols (q.v.).

In Barbarossa's opening month, German armies bit deep into Soviet territory; panzer armies encircled large Soviet forces at Minsk and Smolensk, while armored spearheads reached two-thirds of the distance to Moscow and Leningrad. But already German logistics were unraveling, while a series of Soviet counterattacks stalled the advance. In September the Germans got enough supplies forward to renew their drives; the results were the encirclement battles of Kiev in September and Bryansk-Vyazma in October, each netting 600,000 prisoners.

Moscow seemingly lay open to a German advance, but at this point Russian weather intervened with heavy rains that turned the roads into morasses. The frosts of November solidified the mud, so that the drive could resume. Despite the lateness of the season and the fact that further advances would leave their troops with no winter clothes or supply dumps for the winter, the generals urged Hitler to continue. The Germans struggled to the gates of Moscow where Soviet counterattacks stopped them in early December. In desperate conditions, they conducted a slow retreat as Soviet attacks threatened to envelop much of their forces in a defeat as disastrous as that which befell Napoleon's (q.v.) Grand Army in 1812. In the end the Soviets overreached, and the Germans restored a semblance of order to the front; the spring thaw in March 1942 brought operations to a halt. But Barbarossa had failed, and Nazi Germany confronted a two-front war that it could not win.

WILLIAMSON MURRAY

Operation Downfall

Operation Downfall is the overall code name for the proposed U.S. invasion of Japan in World War II (q.v.). It would have been the largest amphibious operation in history. In the first phase (Operation Olympic), some 250,000 army troops and 87,600 marines would have assaulted Kyushu, the southernmost of Japan's home islands, in November 1945. They were to take the southern half of Kyushu, where air bases would be built for the invasion (Operation Coronet) of Honshu in March 1946. Most of the troops for that invasion would have been U.S. veterans of European fighting.

The planned invasion had historical significance, because President Harry S. Truman weighed the projected high casualty cost of the invasion against the use of the atomic bomb. General of the Army Douglas MacArthur (q.v.), who would have commanded ground forces for Downfall, initially estimated that battlefield casualties for the first ninety days of the Kyushu assault would total 95,050. Later he said that a Soviet invasion of Manchuria would greatly lessen casualties because so many Japanese troops would be unable to be deployed from the Asian mainland to the home islands.

By August 1945 Japanese had at least 370,000 ground troops and 575,000 home-defense forces on Kyushu, with defenders massed at the three beaches where U.S. troops would land. President Truman later said that he had been told an invasion "would cost at a minimum one-quarter of a million casualties." Critics of Truman's decision to drop the atomic bomb claimed he had inflated casualty estimates to justify his decision. But U.S. casualties undoubtedly would have been extremely high, especially because of the Japanese "Decisive Battle" strategy: kill so many Americans that the war-weary United States would negotiate a peace. The strategy would be carried out by more than two million troops on the home islands and thousands of kamikaze attacks on troop-filled transports. Japanese troop strength on Kyushu eventually rivaled the size of the invaders' forces, which, as an intelligence report to MacArthur said, "is not the recipe for victory."

THOMAS B. ALLEN

Operation Overlord

See D-Day.

Operations and Campaigns, Military

Standing alone, the term *operations* should not be confused with the terms *operational level of war, operational art,* or *grand tactics.* These latter terms usually refer to the employment of military forces at the independent or theater level of command. *Operations,* on the other hand, is a broadly used word in military affairs that can denote training, personnel administration, or almost any activity in land, naval, or air services. But in the context of describing a war, *operations* normally refers to battle maneuvers and dispositions that contribute to a military campaign. The term *campaign* usually describes a series of operations that are aimed at attaining a strategic goal.

Germany's great Western Front offensive of 1918 (see *Ludendorff Offensive*) might be used to differentiate between and illustrate the use of these terms. Berlin's *strategy* was to hold the Eastern Front and defeat the Allies in the west before America's potentially enormous resources would be brought to France. The German *campaign* was projected to be a thirty-to-sixty-day offensive effort that would split the French from the British and lead to Berlin's victory. German *operations* included air superiority, battlefield air interdiction, and close air-support efforts; sophisticated, brief artillery preparations; logistical support; and other such activities. The *tactics* of the 1918 German offensive included the employment of fast-moving, squad-size infantry penetration elements (storm troopers) that included light machine-gun or flamethrower teams.

In the Anglo-American tradition, the terms *campaigns* and *operations* have been in use for centuries, but neither word has had a solely military connotation. In the early seventeenth century, the word *champaign,* long having referred to a tract of woods or open country, spawned a military mutation. The new word, *campaign,* began to denote a distinct event in time. By the 1650s, it was common to hear soldiers speak of a summer's military expedition as a campaign, a leaving of winter quarters to fight engagements in the countryside during the warmer time of year. Battle in this era was often weather dependent. Not only were European summer road conditions more conducive to the traffic of large numbers of troops, cannon, and supplies, but there was also a great abundance of food and forage available along the way. Then, too, in those societies that depended on soldier-citizens, leaders had to accommodate the imperatives of the crop cycle. Awaiting the end of either the planting time or the harvest period before commencing military activities was normal. There was, therefore, a definite season for campaigns. But in the late 1880s, the American military lexicographer Edward S. Farrow noted that military campaigns had become less seasonal and more continuous.

The term *operations* has retained its original meaning and has enjoyed a broadened usage, one that long ago encompassed military endeavors. As early as the fourteenth century, *operation* meant work, action, a deed or performance. By the sixteenth century the word was used to denote surgery, and by the eighteenth century, it was being used to describe the concerted efforts of military units and naval fleets. In 1781, Edward Gibbon, for instance, described the actions of Rome's legions (q.v.) as operations directed by generals. The military sense of the term is not restricted to battle. It is appropriate to speak of logistical, training, or even administrative operations.

The relationship between military campaigns and operations is most often hierarchical and related to planning. Ideally, a military or naval leader will use violence to achieve a strategic goal by designing one or more campaigns in space and time that fulfill the desired political ends. The movements of forces and supporting elements during a campaign are plotted in a series of operations aimed at eventually defeating an adversary and placing one's own troops in a position to destroy or dominate the opponent. Operations are therefore usually subordinate to and supportive of campaigns. Conceivably, a war might be wholly described by recounting its various campaigns. Operations may be reduced to paper in the form of one or more "operations orders." But the written design for a campaign is usually referred to as a "campaign plan." It is appropriate to speak of operations in geographic or geometric terms. For example, Napoleon (q.v.), spoke of suddenly switching his "line of operations" as being a key to his success. Campaigns are sometimes differentiated by location: the 1863 Pennsylvania campaign (see *American Civil War*) or the Normandy campaign of 1944 (see *World War II*). On the other hand, operations are often differentiated by code names. For example, the planned but unexecuted 1945 invasion of Japan was named Operation Downfall (q.v.). Both campaigns and operations are occasionally differentiated by function. Air, naval, or ground campaigns might be directed and coordinated in such a way that an enemy is overwhelmed. Both operations and campaigns may be of an offensive, defensive, static, or mobile character. And there is no particular time limit on either. An operation or campaign may last for a few days or a few years.

As already noted, a reader often encounters the terms *operational level of war* and *operational art*. The first term denotes a level of action below the realm of the strategist but above the work of a tactician. For the past two centuries, the operational level has generally encompassed corps or theater maneuvers and plans but has not included divisional moves and actions. Both the operational and tactical levels are typically considered the proper preserves of uniformed professionals, whereas the strategic level may include both civilian and military experts. Operational art involves the methodology, technique, and style that particular generals or admirals employ at the operational level of war.

A recent trend threatens this linear, hierarchical thought pattern. During the Vietnam War (q.v.), it became common to refer to the allied pacification campaign, the effort to defeat the clandestine Communist infrastructure within the villages of South Vietnam, as "The Other War." It was so different in character from the allied campaign against the Communist regulars that it seemed to merit its own distinct category of conflict. This same reasoning began to be applied to the American bombing campaign against North Vietnam. By 1967, the aerial effort was commonly known as the "Air War." Many of those who described the 1990–1991 Gulf War (q.v.) made a similar distinction between the ground and air campaigns planned by General H. Norman Schwarzkopf (q.v.). These writers claimed there were two separate wars: the air war and the ground war. The American general, however, made no such distinction. To the allied commander, there were two coordinated campaigns he had planned to contribute to a single strategic objective: the defeat of the Iraqi armed forces.

Those who read military history should be on guard when operations and campaigns are detailed in print. The war or campaign described in tidy, organized, and coordinated segments is likely to have been, in reality, chaotic and confused. More often than not, historians can be justly criticized for imposing an artificial sense of order on military and naval events that were more influenced by happenstance than by plan or forethought (see *Chance*). This is a natural tendency on the part of writers who must sort out for themselves some connected flow of events before they try to make sense of them for the reader. It was, after all, the same Napoleon who spoke of logical, geometric certainties in conducting war who also said, "War consists of nothing but accidents."

ROD PASCHALL

Carl von Clausewitz, *On War*, trans. Michael Howard and Peter Paret (1976); J. Christopher Herold, ed. and trans., *The Mind of Napoleon: A Selection from His Written and Spoken Words* (1955).

Opium War

1839–1842

Triggered after Commissioner Lin Tse-hsü confiscated and destroyed much British opium in an attempt to ban the trade, the Opium War was the first of several aimed at opening China to international trade on terms acceptable to Western countries. It was marked by innovative Western technology and tactics, for instance, in the use of paddle-wheel iron gunships powered by sail or steam, which drew little water and could operate efficiently in very shallow coastal waters in all weather. The Chinese at once made replicas of these and other British warships with which to fight back.

British ships blockaded Canton and Ningpo and seized control of the entrance to the Yangtze delta before sailing north unopposed to threaten Tientsin, the port nearest to Peking. Subsequent negotiations achieved British withdrawal to Canton but were rejected by both sides. Further fighting around Canton preceded British bombardment and occupation of part of the city; the British fleet then returned northward, seized coastal cities including Shanghai, and sailed up the Yangtze to Nanking. Before the city could be attacked, the Chinese capitulated.

The 1842 Treaty of Nanking was the first of several that opened Chinese ports to foreign trade, residence, and later missions and manufacture; ceded territory, including Hong Kong; and involved large indemnities. The defeat hugely undermined China's national self-esteem and contributed to the continuing desire for global equality and for absolute autonomy as well as bringing new urgency to the military modernization already proposed by Chinese statecraft thinkers and encouraged by the military mind-set of earlier Ch'ing rulers (see *Manchus*).

JOANNA WALEY-COHEN

Organization, Rank, and Promotion; Military

In the Middle Ages in Europe, most fighting men owed their military rank to the weapons they carried and the way that they fought. The upper class of knights; the middle class of sergeants, archers, and men-at-arms; and the expendable proletariat of impressed peasants differed greatly from one another in terms of social status, pay, and even treatment when taken prisoners. On the battlefield, however, all served as individual fighters, responsible chiefly for their own behavior in battle. Promotion from one rank to another was possible and chiefly predicated on proven valor in battle, skill with certain weapons, the possession of certain kinds of equipment, and so on.

As medieval levies gave way to mercenary armies (q.v.) of the early modern era, rank became associated with authority over certain kinds of military units. The "head man" (*Hauptmann* in German, *capitano* in Italian) appeared as the military entrepreneur who rented the services of his "company" — the commercial sound of this term is no accident — to the highest bidder. This captain was assisted by a "place holder" (*lieutenant* in French) and a young nobleman (hence the Spanish *alférez* and the German *Fahnenjunker*) who bore the standard (hence the rank *ensign*). Additional help came from under-officers who held either the medieval title of sergeant or the new rank of corporal.

As the increasingly powerful states of the sixteenth and seventeenth centuries "nationalized" Europe's armies, mercenaries entered into more permanent relations with their employers. Companies were assembled into larger units — regiments, tercios, battalions, and the like — which, in addition to their tactical purpose, served as intermediaries for the business relationship between companies and the state. Command of these units was usually given to one of the captains of the component companies, who, in addition to discharging his duties as master of the field (Spanish *maestro de campo*), supreme captain (German *Oberst*), or captain of the column (Italian *collonella*, hence *colonel*), retained ownership of his own company. As considerable capital was often required to raise and maintain a multicompany unit, colonels tended to be wealthy men who regarded the day-to-day duties of command (q.v.) as a burden. They therefore appointed assistants with the titles of lieutenant colonel and major.

Like the command of large units, the command of early modern armies was initially given to one of the captains, who was often known as the captain general or, when he took the place of the sovereign, field marshal. As armies grew, the captain general (or simply "general") obtained assistants with the ranks of lieutenant general, major general, brigadier general, and, in the Austrian service, field marshal lieutenant.

By the eighteenth century, the basic rank structure that would be used for the next two hundred years was in place in nearly all armies of the European pattern. There were generals, field or senior officers (colonels, lieutenant colonels, majors), company or junior officers (captains, lieutenants, ensigns), and noncommissioned officers (sergeants and corporals). The last group was defined by the fact that its members were appointed by unit commanders rather than commissioned by the sovereign.

A wide variety of methods have been used to select and promote officers. From the beginnings of modern armies to the end of the eighteenth century, the most common means was direct appointment, in which a ruler or his designated subordinate gave military rank to a man who, by demonstrated merit or other means, had achieved favor in his eyes. Direct appointment was often made less capricious by the convening of formal boards to examine the qualifications of candidates. Less prone to favoritism was promotion by seniority, a system that became possible as ad hoc armies gave way to standing ones. In the eighteenth and nineteenth centuries, as the notion of military professionalism gained currency, formal military academies, which combined theoretical instruction with practical experience, were started to prepare future candidates for promotion. As none of the aforementioned systems of promotion was entirely satisfactory, most armies used, and continue to use, various combinations of them.

Obsolete methods of selecting and promoting officers include raising for rank, election, and purchase. Employed as a means of quickly raising units for conflicts such as the Napoleonic Wars and the American Civil War (q.v.), raising for rank granted both rank and command to those who had managed to recruit a certain number of men. Election, in which a military leader was selected in much the same way as any other holder of public office, was used extensively by nineteenth-century republics. In parts of eighteenth-century continental Europe (such as prerevolutionary France) and in Great Britain until 1872, many commissions and promotions could be obtained only by purchase. This remnant of the days when officers were the proprietors of their units ensured that only those men who had, in effect, posted a bond for their good behavior were trusted with command.

Throughout the modern period, a wide gulf had existed between commissioned and noncommissioned officers. In the eighteenth and early nineteenth centuries, this was a function of the notion that only noblemen were capable of command in battle. Later, the requirement that commissioned officers achieve high levels of formal education often limited the prospects of corporals and sergeants. Even in those countries, such as the United States, where the educational attainments of officers are modest, the need for credentials has often prevented talented soldiers from being promoted beyond noncommissioned rank. On the other hand, some of the most efficient armies of the twentieth century, including those of Finland and Israel, have taken pains to eliminate the barriers between commissioned and noncommissioned rank.

By the middle of the twentieth century, most non-Western armies had adopted the Western approach to military rank. In the 1860s, for example, the Japanese created a rank structure that, though lacking Western terminology, was nearly a carbon copy of that of the contemporary European armies. In the past decade, however, the most successful non-Western military organizations, such as those that drove the Soviet Union out of Afghanistan and the United States out of Somalia, have had ideas of rank very much at variance with those of the Western world.

BRUCE I. GUDMUNDSSON

Fernando Gonzalez de Leon, "The Command Structure of the Spanish Army of Flanders in the Eighty Years' War," *Tactical Notebook* (October 1993); "The German Army Enlisted Rank System on the Eve of World War II," *Tactical Notebook* (August 1992); Martin van Creveld, *The Training of Officers* (1990).

Origins of War

War seems eternal, apparently without a beginning and, by implication, without an end. Throughout history there has been a tendency to take it as a given, simply an extension of the intuitively obvious proposition that people have always fought and always will fight. This perhaps is true. But when we ask, "Is fighting synonymous with war?" it becomes apparent that we are talking about a special kind of fighting.

War, as we know it, is really an institution — a complex phenomenon that is premeditated and directed by some form of governmental structure, concerned with societal rather than individual issues, featuring the willing (though perhaps not enthusiastic) participation of the combatants, and intended to achieve lasting results. These characteristics point to a requisite level of social evolution and imply that warfare is a mechanism intended to perform certain functions, which have varied in range and intensity. Given such a definition, it becomes possible to differentiate simple blood feuds and extended acts of revenge from what is meant by war in historical terms. This distinction is critical, since it makes it clear that humankind was not born to war but eventually came to it as the result of fundamental shifts in our subsistence patterns.

But this raises some profound questions. Although it is possible to dismiss virtually all forms of hostility among animals as being not truly warlike, there remains one glaring exception . . . ants. Besides ourselves, they are the most social and well organized of creatures. Virtually all prerequisites for war are present in ant society — government, armies, politics, and lasting societal results — but the practitioners are automatons just a few millimeters long. Nonetheless, a number of creatures within the vast family *Formicidae* qualify as true war makers. Here, not among ourselves, we can find that true warfare originated as far back as fifty million years ago. That ants wage war flows logically from their highly organized way of life, much as it eventually would with human warriors — but there is one crucial difference. Individually, these ants are genetically predestined for a martial existence. They are haplodiploid reproducers, female offspring of a central queen, sharing three-fourths of their genes with their numerous sisters. Such creatures sacrifice for the group because it is their best chance to perpetuate their own genes; death in battle is trivial compared with the success of an army made up of genetic near-replicates.

We humans, of course, are not haplodiploid, but fully sexual reproducers. Virtually all mammals besides ourselves limit their sociality and self-sacrifice to close relatives. Therefore, it is not most pertinent to ask whether humans are inherently warlike, but instead to question why is it possible for us to wage war at all.

Although this issue is far from resolved, support has begun to emerge for a dual-inheritance model of human development, positing not only separate mechanisms for our genetic and cultural evolution, but also a subtle interplay of both to produce the most efficient behavioral patterns. This profoundly liberating evolutionary innovation, allowing us to rely upon the much more rapid and communicable medium of ideas rather than flesh, made us flexible and opportunistic in ways never before possible. And eventually it would permit us to wage war, not because our genes compelled us, but as a premeditated response to external conditions.

In the meantime, we had to eat. Humans evolved as hunters and gatherers, living for 97 percent of human history in pack-sized bands dictated by the availability of food sources and genetic affinity. Quite probably, the lives of our distant ancestors roughly mirrored the patterns revealed by recent hunting and gathering societies — a relatively low-key existence emphasizing personal independence, general equality among group members including women, consensus-based decision making, and freedom of movement particularly as a means of avoiding or resolving conflict. Weapons possession would have been virtually universal with males, but used for hunting, not for dominating the group or other groups.

It is unlikely that hunter-gatherers were any less aggressive, or less inclined to commit violence, than humans of later times. Indeed, hunting likely provided us with much of the behavioral raw material to build armies one day — small-unit cohesion, tactical planning, standards of courage, and effective use of arms. However, war as we have defined it would have been basically irrelevant in a world in which personal property had to be limited to what could be carried, seasonal diversity more than territory dictated the availability of food, and the genetic necessity for outbreeding made it advisable to avoid alienating other local gene pools.

In such an environment, our big brains evolved, along with speech and advanced sociality. And it stands to reason that we were deeply affected by this heritage. Yet our capacity for culture also left us, if not infinitely plastic, then at least capable of an unprecedented level of adaptation — able to undergo a transformation that in relatively short order would find us living in vast despotic societies that were at least broadly analogous to those of the social insects.

Plainly, the domestication of other lifeforms was critical to this change. However, contemporary scholars see this process as considerably more mutual and subtle than was previously thought; in a sense, other species domesticated us virtually to the same degree that we domesticated them. The first great change began to occur in about 10,500 B.C. in the Middle East, when humans began harvesting and eventually cultivating cereals. Before we knew it, we had become farmers; this new and abundant food source swelled human population to the point that there was no going back to hunting and gathering.

Shortly after, humans domesticated the beasts of the field. Pastoral animals were naturally kept toward the outskirts of farming communities where they could not eat or step on growing crops. In the Middle East, the herding of ruminant animals encouraged the development of the nomadic way of life, which contrasted with that of the village dwellers. Although both nomads and village dwellers would continue to share certain dependencies, considerable basis for antipathy emerged.

Beginning around 5500 B.C., numerous Middle Eastern farming communities began to build walls around their domiciles, probably to defend themselves against raiding nomads. To prevent pursuit, it is likely that these attacks would have been fairly brutal — terrifying enough to result in the gradual concentration of populations in fortified townships. Though sporadic and geographically irregular, these raids would have had economic and even ideological motivation sufficient to mark them as the beginning of something approaching true warfare among humans.

Furthermore, recent evidence from the Ukrainian steppe indicating that horse riding extends back to around 4000 B.C., along with remains of domesticated horses in the Middle East late in the fourth millennium, raises the possibility that by 3200 B.C., equestrian nomads had begun their own pattern of raiding. If so, their inherent military advantage could have been sufficient to spark further consolidation behind walled enclaves. This time frame also coincides with the rise of the state and the emergence of true urban societies in Mesopotamia.

But although true warfare may have begun in acts of theft perpetrated by pastoral nomads, war among the agriculturalists would become something considerably different. Focused behind walled fortifications, social development in the Near East intensified and accelerated. Armed male elites, the first true armies, rose quickly to prominence, fostering governmental structures, unequal access to resources, and coerced organization of labor. Population dynamics took on an entirely new aspect. On one hand, settled existence and an almost exclusively carbohydrate diet promoted fertility and population pressure. Yet close quarters also encouraged epidemic disease, which, when combined with intensified but famine-prone agriculture, produced demographies with roller-coaster ups and downs.

Wars and armies acted as stabilizing agents to balance these swings in population. During periods of overpopulation, armies could conquer new lands, or, at worst, face destruction and no longer have to be fed. And when numbers fell, new laborers had to be appropriated — this need explains the ancient traffic in slaves and the repeated, coerced transfers of entire peoples. Yet war was never more than a crude equilibrator; it was simply the most effective available, and it could be consciously applied.

In Sumer, this dynamic led eventually to a balance-of-power relationship among societies, an enduring political form. In such a system, war not only addressed a society's internal issues but also enforced a balance among competing groups. And because one power's military advantage could be quickly countered through an alliance of competing powers and opportunism, the net result of this pattern was usually a rough equilibrium . . . or general frustration.

The rise of great imperial, despotic societies was of profound significance, if for no other reason than that the bulk of humanity came to live in them. Ancient empires were precariously poised to rise or fall based on the balance of population growth with resources and technology. This also formed war's center of gravity — these societies were not necessarily the most adept militarily (they often met with disaster), but they were the most in need of the demographic results that war might bring. Soldiers were the tokens of exchange, and battles — orchestrated to produce their death, capture, or return with more labor or land — were key mechanisms by which energy was transferred from state to state.

But imperial societies (contingent upon their origins, location, and internal dynamics) varied considerably in their dependence on war. Thus Egypt, sheltered geographically and blessed with environmental factors that moderated the swings of demography, gave more attention to building monumental architecture. Assyria (q.v.), surrounded by enemies, came to be driven by war, pursuing it almost for its own sake until it was finally destroyed by belligerence. The very feature that made warfare a serviceable equilibrator — that it could be initiated as a matter of choice — also allowed it to become an all-consuming pursuit.

This was not China's fate. Here, the patterns of social and political evolution predisposed the Chinese to remain wary of the institution of war. Given the continuing pastoral threat from the steppe, the necessities of armies and defense could never be ignored. Yet they approached war gingerly, shackling it with all manner of intellectual and governmental restraints. There were costs, both in terms of military efficiency and demographic stability; but China would endure.

Perhaps most interesting from a theoretical perspective is the independent development of warfare in the Americas. Here the absence of a sufficient array of animals to support independent pastoralism, and the resulting urge among agriculturalists to huddle behind walls, caused social and political consolidation to take place in a less abrupt fashion, under conditions that reduced demographic instability. War was plainly part of the process, but its role was more exclusively political — a matter of conflict among elites, not peoples.

Finally, a few ancient societies, such as those of the Minoans and Phoenicians, clustered primarily along the Mediterranean littoral, managed to pursue a mercantile existence, retreating to the sea in the face of aggression. But the desirability of establishing and maintaining far-flung trade routes and entrepots logically called for some kind of protection, and this led to the development of navies. Yet these cultures appear to have resorted to force selectively and pragmatically — a sort of continuation of trade by other means. Though this approach might have set a sensible course for the future, in most parts of the world it was not an option. Large populations with access to only crude technology remained dependent on imperial agriculture; and thus war ground on, the clumsy balance wheel of this crude clockwork.

ROBERT L. O'CONNELL

D. W. Anthony, D. Y. Telegin, and D. Brown, "The Origin of Horseback Riding," *Scientific American* 265 (1991); Lawrence Keeley, *War Before Civilization* (1996); Robert L. O'Connell, *Ride of the Second Horseman: The Birth and Death of War* (1995).

Otto I (the Great)

d. 973, *German King*

German king (from 936), ruling consort to Adelheid, queen of Italy (from 951), and Roman Emperor in the West (from 962), Otto established the medieval German kingdom as the leading power in western Europe and the center of the revived Western Empire.

Militarily, Otto continued the program established by his father, Henry I (German king, 919–936), of relying on fortifications for territorial defense and supporting a highly trained professional army from royal and church estates. His activity included success in three civil wars that firmly established that the German throne would descend to a single heir rather than be divided among many; military and diplomatic interventions in Poland, Bohemia, and France, which demonstrated German leadership in Western Christendom; and the steady expansion of German control east of the Elbe. Otto's generalship displayed a superior ability to coordinate long-distance strategic movement and to keep forces from widely different regions working together. Both of these qualities marked Otto's most important campaigns: the defeat of the Magyars (q.v.) at the Battle of the Lechfeld (955) (q.v.) and two expeditions across the Alps (951 and 962) by which he secured control of Italy (especially Rome) and gained the imperial title.

Although this last achievement represented more a recognition of Otto's preeminent position in Europe than any increase in his actual power, Otto rather than Charlemagne (q.v.) was the direct institutional ancestor of the medieval Holy Roman Emperors. That Otto's achievement proved less than permanent is attributable to his far-ranging ambitions and the fact that his direct line of succession died out after two generations.

EDWARD J. SCHOENFELD

Ottomans

The Ottoman Empire began as one of several Muslim Turkish frontier principalities that emerged in western Anatolia in the late thirteenth century. At its greatest extent, in the late seventeenth century, the empire comprised contiguous territories from Hungary to Iraq, and from the Crimea to the Nile valley.

The Ottoman conquests were hard won — much of

their Anatolian territory was lost for a time following the defeat of Bayezid I by Timur (see *Tamerlane*) in 1402. The energetic campaigning of Mehmed II (r. 1451–1481) established the core Ottoman state of the Balkans and Anatolia, and his conquest of Constantinople in 1453 (q.v.) provided a renewed sense of mission and enabled the consolidation of the imperial dynastic state.

Tensions on the Ottoman eastern borders in Anatolia continued, however: the Safavid dynasty of Iran was beaten by Selim I (q.v.) in 1514 at Çaldıran (q.v.), and the Mamluk state of Syria and Egypt was annexed with the Ottoman victories at the battles of Marj Dabik (1516) and al-Raydaniyya (1517).

Sultan Suleiman I (1494–1566) (q.v.) conquered Hungary and Iraq, bringing Ottoman military might to its apogee; territorial expansion slowed thereafter. In the west, Ottoman-controlled Hungary and Bosnia formed a buffer against the Hapsburgs, while Transylvania, Moldavia, Wallachia, and the Crimea became dependent principalities. In the east, however, Georgia and Azerbaijan were annexed in the 1580s but were lost in 1618. Suleiman's conquests in Iraq were threatened with the fall of Baghdad to Iran in 1624; the vigorous Sultan Murad IV (r. 1623–1640) retook this province in 1638. The peace of 1639 with Persia lasted until 1723. By then, the Ottoman Empire had a new rival in an expansionist Russia.

The peace of Karlowitz in 1699 marked the Ottoman state's first formal acknowledgment of defeat. The Hapsburg-Ottoman wars of 1683–1699, precipitated by the Ottoman siege of Vienna (q.v.) in 1683, brought the loss of Hungary, Transylvania, and Dalmatia. During the earlier eighteenth century, some territories were regained, but war with Russia in 1768–1774 caused the loss of the Crimea and the northern Black Sea coast. The war of 1784–1792 confirmed Ottoman inability to stand against Russia.

In the nineteenth century, the great powers presided over the breakup of the Ottoman Empire: parts of the Balkans gained independence or autonomy in the first half of the century, and by its end, the empire comprised only Macedonia, Albania, Thrace, Anatolia, Syria, and Iraq. In the aftermath of World War I (q.v.), the empire was reduced to north and central Anatolia and Istanbul. The Turkish Republic was declared in 1923 after the reconquest of Anatolia in the War of Independence; in Thrace the Turks regained their prewar frontier.

In its "classical" form, the Ottoman army consisted

of (1) a majority of provincial cavalry funded by the dues collected from the state lands awarded to them; (2) an elite of salaried forces with well-regulated pay and rank structures of which the most prominent corps was the janissaries; (3) numerous auxiliary corps serving as logistic, garrison, and combat troops. In addition, crucial support came from the Crimean Tatars, Kurdish tribesmen, and others. The dramatic increase in recruitment of musketeers, especially from the time of the 1593–1606 war with the Hapsburgs, diluted the elite forces and also prompted a new development, the formation of companies of peasant mercenaries. The size of the Ottoman army stood at about 105,000 in 1473 and about 120,000 in the 1520s; figures for the Russo-Turkish wars of 1768–1774 (q.v.) range between 80,000 and 500,000. These and other estimates should be regarded with caution.

The Ottomans did not fear technical innovation: European renegades were freely employed, and all types of guns available to the Christian powers were cast. One explanation for the failures of the Ottoman army in Europe after 1683 was that they could not adjust to the field battles that were now the typical form of confrontation in this theater — the Ottomans had become more accustomed to siege warfare (q.v.) during the seventeenth century.

In field battles the classical tactical formation of the Ottomans was the crescent, with the provincial cavalry on the wings; the sultan (when present) in the center, protected by his guard and the janissaries armed with the harquebus or musket; and the other units of the standing army to left and right. In front of the janissaries stood the cannon, and in front of all, mounted raiders — the *akıncı*. Despite developments in army structure and weaponry, contemporary European accounts indicate that little change occurred in Ottoman tactical formation over the centuries.

The Ottoman army and navy were capable of operating in theaters at great range and of great geographic and climatic variation, thanks to strong logistical organization. Military confrontation took place on the peripheries of the state: a well-defined system of military roads, furnished with magazines at regular intervals, took the army through Ottoman territory to its destination. The government sent orders concerning mobilization, provisioning, and the supply of war matériel in advance of a campaign, and strove to distribute the burden equitably among the population. However, as the scale of military endeavor increased, so did the strain on both the local and broader economy. By the seventeenth century, the extraordinary taxes levied on subject populations were regularized.

Initial Ottoman naval activity against Genoa and Venice greatly expanded as the empire and Ottoman ambitions grew. Substantial resources were devoted to the development of the navy, and a number of talented admirals were employed; these efforts were rewarded with the conquest of Cyprus in 1570 and control of the eastern Mediterranean. Defeat in the Battle of Lepanto (q.v.) in 1571 was reckoned only a temporary setback, and the fleet was speedily rebuilt. It was not until the mid–eighteenth century that Russia began to challenge Ottoman control of the Black Sea. Operations against the Portuguese in the Indian Ocean were circumscribed by use of oared galleys rather than sailing ships; the potential of sailing ships was not exploited in Ottoman naval warfare until the mid–seventeenth century. Shortage of skilled manpower continued to be a problem, for no body of troops served exclusively at sea.

As the Ottomans withdrew from offensive conflicts in Europe in the eighteenth century, the intensive cultural exchange through Ottoman embassies to Europe stimulated recognition of the need for military reform. New corps and schools were established to train officers with the help of foreign experts; but not until the early nineteenth century was decisive action taken within the traditional army, which had never accepted these structural innovations. The janissary corps, bastion of conservative values, was annihilated in 1826. By that time, however, great power politics and the rapid pace of industrial and social change in Europe had irremediably widened the gap between the Ottomans and Europe.

CAROLINE FINKEL

P

Pacifism

The desire for peace has existed as a counterpoint to the appeal of war in every human society with a recoverable history. It exists in religions from Confucianism to Islam, and in literature from Lao-Tzu to Leo Tolstoy. Pacifism, however, is something different: a principled rejection of conflict as a means of settling disputes. Though much of its modern inspiration comes from philosophies such as Buddhism and philosophers such as Mohandas Gandhi, pacifism's roots are Western, traceable at least to classical Greece. On a peninsula racked by conflict, in a culture that arguably originated the concept of battles of annihilation, certain religious sites remained sacred to all, and certain religious rites were held in common even during war. In a political context, Greek theorists remained sympathetic to the concept of rules governing conflict among states, counterparts to those existing within the *polis* that made civic life possible.

Medieval Christian theologians and jurists sought to universalize the ad hoc ground rules of conflict that emerged from the decline of the Western Roman Empire. The truce of God and the peace of God, respectively forbidding battle on certain days and exempting specific groups from war's consequences, again may have been honored more in the breach than the observance. They are nevertheless important for integrating the appeals to natural law that were the classical world's heritage and the utopian concepts that remain Christianity's unique contribution to Western political culture (see *Laws of War*).

Natural law philosophies, however, found it increasingly difficult to agree on the nature of nature. German jurist Samuel Pufendorf saw nature as benign; English philosopher Thomas Hobbes considered it anarchic. In between lay a spectrum of positions rendered ever more complex in the sixteenth and seventeenth centuries as just war theories grew increasingly elastic. By the eighteenth century, the most common position, defended as much on pragmatic as moral grounds, held that states existing in a condition of anarchy could not be held to the same rules of conduct as ordered societies.

The eclipse of natural law justifications for pacifism opened the door to religious and ethical approaches. The Protestant Reformation proved a catalyst for biblically justified doctrines of nonresistance to violence and noncooperation with government, best exemplified on the Continent by the early Anabaptists and the Mennonites, and in England by the Quakers. Unlike their counterparts who increasingly tended to withdraw from the world, Quakers strove to reform society. On both sides of the Atlantic, their advocacy of peace among nations influenced other reform movements. Revolutionary wars and the Napoleonic Wars inspired numerous societies with the aim of promoting "permanent and universal peace." Some opposed all wars; others accepted defensive wars; most suffered tension between moderates willing to work with governments and radicals opposed to cooperation with political institutions.

What the peace societies had in common was support for arbitration, advocacy of international law supported by tribunals, and insistence on disarmament (q.v.). Although their basis was religious, they drew support as well from the Enlightenment, which dismissed war as unnatural and inhumane. As the nineteenth century progressed, principle was supported by organization. Though much stronger in Britain and the United States than on the Continent, which was influenced increasingly by nationalism and romanticism, the peace societies challenged the glorification of war. They received increasing support from liberals such as William Cobden, who regarded war as bad for business, and from radicals who supported various forms of popular revolution. Although Marxists rejected pacifism in principle, they did much to develop negative images of war as waged by capitalist states.

The outbreak of hostilities in 1914 seemed to demonstrate pacifism's irrelevance, as Europe's workers and intellectuals flocked to the colors in perceived defense of their respective countries. But the movement's roots remained solid, and four years of trench warfare made pacifism increasingly seem no more than simple common sense. After 1918, even in the face of totalitarianism, moral and utilitarian condemnation of war and preparation for it permeated Western civilization. Erich Maria Remarque's 1929 novel *All Quiet on the Western Front* became a central text of antiwar movements. Even the character of Nazi Germany did not essentially alter this mind-set. Resisting Adolf Hitler's (q.v.) Reich by force of arms was widely regarded as an aberration: necessary but temporary. Veterans of World War II (q.v.) were less eager than their predecessors to don uniforms again. Although pacifism may not have won great political victories, its principles increasingly shaped attitudes and behaviors after 1945. Even the Soviet Union in its final years could not ignore its people's hostility to the war in Afghanistan.

It was, however, the atomic bomb that made the question of war's legitimacy a central issue. Could either national interests or ethical values be served by recourse to nuclear armaments? Even theorists of nuclear warfare were uncomfortable with the implications of their subject. Pacifism was reinforced as well by the postwar emergence of liberation movements outside of Europe. The cause of self-determination seemed by its nature moral enough to deny any application of the justice of war. The brutality of most counterinsurgency (q.v.) operations made an increasing mockery of justice in war. By the 1970s, particularly in the West, growing numbers of citizens accepted pacifism de facto, reserving only the most abstract right to support certain specific conflicts: protest movements from Greenpeace in the Pacific to Rocky Flats in Colorado challenged military systems and military preparations. In Great Britain, the Committee for Nuclear Disarmament exercised influence far out of proportion to its numbers. Even in the USSR, the Afghanistan War generated popular resistance.

The end of the Cold War (q.v.) removed the immediate threat of nuclear apocalypse. The rise of professional armed forces diminished public involvement in conventional war. A paradox has resulted: one-time peace activists now demand intervention from Haiti to Bosnia for humanitarian reasons, whereas governments, ostensibly the loci of war making, grow increasingly reluctant to draw the sword under any circumstances. It seems, however, reasonable to speculate that the human costs of armed conflict at any level will continue to sustain pacifism's moral and pragmatic justifications even to critics of the pacifist witness.

DENNIS E. SHOWALTER

Peter Brock, *Pacifism in Europe to 1914* (1977); Peter Brock, *Twentieth-Century Pacifism* (1970).

Panipat, Battle of

1526

Invaders of India coming from the northwest, over the Khyber Pass, found no strong forts or natural obstacles on the Punjab plains en route to the rich capital of Delhi. Decisive battles were, therefore, fought between rulers of Delhi and invaders on the plains immediately west of Delhi. Several times these battles centered on the small town of Panipat.

In 1526, Babur (q.v.), founder of the Mughal Empire (q.v.) in India, and his seasoned heavy cavalry arrived on the Punjab plains, having fought and migrated from their home north of present-day Afghanistan down through Afghanistan and over the Khyber Pass. Babur adopted an unusual tactic for a cavalry that typically wheeled and charged. He used the town of Panipat to protect one flank and had his troops dig a wide ditch and fill it with cut brush to protect the other flank. They also commandeered carts from the surrounding villages and tied them together as a barricade at the front, with openings allowing the cavalry to sally. The Afghan ruler of Delhi arrived with a much larger army, but he constructed no defenses. Matchlock men, probably local recruits, opened the battle from behind the carts, assisted by a few small-bore guns. The battle was decided by Babur's "sweeping" tactic, which sent strong units to the sides and back of the Afghans. Babur's forces pressed from all sides, effectively using bow and arrow; the Afghan forces were so tightly packed that they could not effectively maneuver and thus were routed. This victory opened the way to Delhi and the establishment of the Mughal Empire in India, which lasted for more than two hundred years.

STEWART GORDON

Passchendaele

See Ypres, Battles of.

Patriotism

Devotion to one's country, patriotism (derived from the Latin *patria*, "fatherland") is today widely taken for granted as the basis for national cohesion in general, and required military service in particular. Yet it is not an easy phenomenon to define or explain. Even in the West, patriotism as we know it emerged slowly: ties to dynasty and to religion remained paramount in Europe until early modern times. But Western patriotism did at least develop out of traditional culture. In much of the rest of the world, modern patriotism is a cultural import that lacks roots in traditional social and moral understandings.

Western concepts of patriotism draw on the analogy, made by both Greek and Roman cultures, between moral obligations to family and those to the land of one's birth: as Horace most famously put it, *dulce et decorum est pro patria mori* — "to die for fatherland is a sweet thing, and becoming." (Homer had earlier expressed similar sentiments.) Yet although those Latin words are inscribed today in countless war cemeteries and memorials, an enormous cultural gap divides the Roman idea of the *patria* — literally "fatherland" — from the many modern words in European languages (*patrie* in French, *otechestvo* in Russian, *Vaterland* in German, and so forth) that, translated literally, have exactly the same meaning.

Loyalty to a native place is a powerful and basic emotion, but through most of history it has been subordinated to other claims. A royal house like the Hapsburgs might gather together with highly loyal persons who did not share native place, or even language or culture. Religion did the same: for Christians, the most important community is the Communion of Saints, which encompasses all believers, living and dead, regardless of native place. Christian-

ity, not patriotism, animated the Crusades (q.v.), and between 1530 and 1650 the rivalry between Protestantism and Catholicism proved more potent than national loyalties in the creation of European alliances and the initiation of wars.

Modern patriotism in the West developed alongside the nation-state, the *patria* to which it accords its primary loyalty. The nation-state as a political form appeared at the time of the French Revolution. Nation-states created new structures of administration that drew citizens into much closer relationship with government and fellow citizens, and produced as well a fundamentally new style of governmental legitimation, based not on dynasty or on religion but on nationalism. Thus in France devotion to the divine-right monarchy was replaced by the bond, stirringly evoked in "La Marseillaise," between *la patrie* — the fatherland — and its children.

This was more than an abstract change. Traditional rulers had often worried about arming the people and preferred small, loyal professional armies instead. But widely shared patriotic bonds made mass armies practicable. The military potential of such patriotically motivated armies was already clear in sixteenth-century Europe, for example, in the Dutch Revolt (q.v.) against Spain. Revolutionary France embraced the idea of patriotically driven universal service with the *levée en masse* of August 23, 1793. The mass armies that then came into being were fundamental to Napoleon's (q.v.) conquests, and his successes in turn forced other states to follow suit. In 1807, considering what to do after the disastrous defeat at Jena, the Prussian chief minister Baron von Stein looked for reforms that would "arouse a moral, religious, *and patriotic* spirit in the nation" [emphasis added].

Indeed, European state-builders of the nineteenth century were generally well aware both of the promise of patriotism as an organizing principle and also of the fact that it did not simply grow but had to be created. Institutional structures ran ahead of sentiment — or, as Massimo Taparelli, marchese d'Azeglio, is reputed to have remarked on the morrow of Savoy's triumph in 1861: "We have made Italy; now we must make Italians."

Mass warfare was one of the catalysts that intensified patriotic feelings. Robert E. Lee (q.v.) chose to serve Virginia, which he considered his true native place, rather than the Union, but the American Civil War (q.v.) nevertheless made most Americans into national patriots, who placed the country as a whole ahead of their individual states. Linguistic usage made this clear: before that war, "the United States" was treated grammatically as a plural; after the war, the term became singular.

In Europe, World War I (q.v.) probably witnessed the most complete realization of patriotism as an ideology, particularly in connection with military service. Indeed, during that war, death for country acquired, for the first time, a dimension of full religious sanctity, as churches (not without some debate) conferred on it some of the honor accorded to martyrdom for the faith. The *patria* and its people became, in effect, a Communion of Saints, and the (armed) soldiers who fell in their service were as blessed as (unarmed and unresisting) martyrs of the Church.

Even so, patriotism was never uniform or completely pervasive. Armies recruited on quite different bases — those of Austria-Hungary brought together soldiers of differing language and cultural backgrounds; postwar Europe saw a turn away from patriotism toward more inclusive ideologies, such as fascism and communism, and, after World War II (q.v.), European integration. Patriotism, moreover, has not always translated into support for the state that has espoused it: oppositions, too, have regularly waved the flag, and with success.

Nevertheless, the European model of patriotic mobilization remains very influential today. The institutionally weak states that followed colonialism have attempted, with varying degrees of success, to foster national patriotisms, although other more historical affiliations continually threaten the process: tribalism and communalism in Africa and South Asia, Islam in the Middle East, and so forth. More recently, the post-Communist states have also adopted patriotism: thus China, since the 1980s, has turned away from revolutionary ideology to official "patriotic education" to build loyalty, adopting a whole repertoire of Western inventions, such as solemn flag raisings — even though many of these lack cultural resonance.

So patriotism is far from the simple primary emotion for which it is often taken. Although a genuine sentiment rooted in personal identity and cultural loyalty, it becomes important historically only when bound, as it has become in the West through historical development, to larger structures of governance and belief. Precisely because it cannot be isolated from this complex matrix of historical structures, however, patriotism is difficult to foster or to manipulate.

ARTHUR WALDRON

John A. Armstrong, *Nations Before Nationalism* (1982); Harumi Befu, ed., *Cultural Nationalism in East Asia: Representation and Identity* (1993).

Patton, George S., Jr.

1885–1945, *U.S. Army General*

George Smith Patton, Jr., who was born in San Gabriel, California, the grandson of ancestors who fought for the Confederacy during the American Civil War (q.v.), was one of the most flamboyant, controversial, and exceptional officers ever to serve in the U.S. Army. As a youth, he was raised to believe it was his duty to become an army officer, and eventually a great general, but his education and future were clouded by a dyslexic condition that resulted in his being tutored at home until he was age twelve.

Determined to pursue a military career, Patton attended the Virginia Military Institute in 1903–1904 and the United States Military Academy in 1904–1909. Commissioned in the cavalry, he placed fifth in the modern pentathlon event in the 1912 Olympic Games in Stockholm, Sweden.

As a junior aide to John J. Pershing (q.v.) during the Punitive Expedition to Mexico in 1916, Patton gained national prominence after cornering and killing one of Pancho Villa's senior lieutenants. When the United States entered World War I (q.v.) in 1917, he accompanied Pershing to France, and after transferring to the newly formed tank arm, Patton organized and trained the American Expeditionary Force tank force in 1918. In less than a year, Patton rose from first lieutenant to lieutenant colonel and commanded a tank brigade during the St.-Mihiel and Meuse-Argonne offensives. In September 1918, he was gravely wounded near Cheppy in the Meuse-Argonne, whereupon he won the Distinguished Service Cross and promotion to colonel.

During the interwar years, Patton was demoted to major and returned to the obscurity of the peacetime cavalry for twenty years. Once again a full colonel, Patton was sent back to tanks in August 1940 by U.S. Army Chief of Staff George C. Marshall (q.v.). By April 1941 Patton was a two-star general in command of the

Second Armored Division at Fort Benning. During the 1941 Louisiana Maneuvers, he gained attention for a daring end run with his tanks, and in early 1942 Patton was promoted to the command of the First Armored Corps and established the Desert Training Center in southern California.

Patton commanded the Western Task Force during the Torch landings at Casablanca in November 1942; in March 1943 he was summoned by Dwight Eisenhower (q.v.) to command and revitalize the Second Corps in Tunisia after the American debacle at Kasserine Pass. His command of the U.S. Seventh Army during the Sicily campaign in the summer of 1943 brought him fame and left him the leading candidate to command American forces in the cross-Channel invasion of Normandy. However, after slapping a soldier he thought was malingering in a military hospital on two separate occasions, Patton's career very nearly ended in disgrace.

He was saved by Eisenhower, who gave him command of the Third Army, which spearheaded the breakout from the Normandy bridgehead in early August 1944 and raced across central France until running out of fuel in Lorraine. In the autumn of 1944, Third Army fought a prolonged battle of attrition that ended only when the Germans launched their great counteroffensive in the Ardennes. Patton's finest hour occurred during the Battle of the Bulge (q.v.) when he turned Third Army to the north in record time to relieve Bastogne and help ensure the failure of the German attack.

In 1945, Patton led Third Army to fresh triumphs during the final months of the war before Germany surrendered in May. As the postwar military governor of Bavaria, a position for which Patton was wholly unsuited, his clashes with Eisenhower over the use of former Nazis eventually led to his relief from command in September 1945. He died in Heidelberg, Germany, in December 1945 after an automobile accident left him paralyzed.

George S. Patton was the most outstanding American combat general of World War II. Known as much for his showmanship and eccentric behavior as for his boldness, Patton was an extraordinarily intellectual and cultured man who mastered his profession and employed his encyclopedic knowledge of history to fight his battles. Behind his profane public persona, Patton was intensely private; he wrote poetry, was obsessed with death, and overcame his own low self-esteem to become one of the most highly regarded generals in U.S. Army history. What separated Patton from his peers was an intangible, special genius for war that has been granted to only a select few, such as Robert E. Lee (q.v.) and German field marshal Erwin Rommel (q.v.). The Germans feared him more than any other Allied general.

CARLO W. D'ESTE

Martin Blumenson, *Patton: The Man Behind the Legend, 1885–1945* (1985); Carlo W. D'Este, *Patton: A Genius for War* (1995); Ladislas Farago, *Patton: Ordeal and Triumph* (1983).

Peace

In *The Devil's Dictionary*, Ambrose Bierce defined peace as "the interval of cheating between two wars." Alternatively, most religious and ethical systems regard peace either as humanity's natural state or as the ultimate goal for which we should strive. Military organizations find themselves locked in a permanent, if rarely explicit, struggle between these two conceptions.

Armies spend most of their existence at peace. Except in unusual times (say, the Napoleonic Wars [see *Napoleon Bonaparte*]) or among the constabulary of imperial powers (for instance, the French Foreign Legion in the nineteenth century), regular soldiering has very little to do with fighting. Even on campaign, actual military engagements may be relatively rare events, and even those may bring within their orbit a relatively small percentage of soldiers. By some calculations, for example, barely 10 percent of the American force in Vietnam (q.v.) saw regular intensive fighting — although this percentage would necessarily vary with circumstances and military technology.

Armies, therefore, live at peace but exist for war. A soldier is like a brain surgeon who is allowed to operate on real patients every twenty years or so.

What are some of the problems and perversities to which peace gives birth? One is the sheer physical impracticality of simulating actual combat maneuvers. In the era before the advent of firearms, it was easier to make simulations resemble real combat. Josephus famously described the rigorous Roman system of training by mock combat as bloodless battle, which had the effect of making their battles mere bloody drills. The more ruthless military organizations of the modern period have been willing to take casualties in training, but none are willing to stage full-fledged, two-sided combat. Moreover, as military operations become ever more costly and ruinous to the landscape over which they occur, large-scale maneuvers become prohibitive. Beginning in the early nineteenth century, and in some ways even earlier, a variety of substitutes began to be used: war games (q.v.), staff rides, and the like. Modern methods include advanced computer simulations, some with staggering visual fidelity. In some cases (naval warfare between surface ships is probably the best case) modern training methods can reproduce many features of combat. Still, no training methods can reproduce the *real* fears for life and limb, the anxiety born of responsibility, and the exertions of battle.

The prevalence of peace poses other subtler, but no less substantial, challenges to military organizations. Promotion practices may reward attributes (seniority, membership in a favored social group, political reliability, courtier skills) other than combat skill. War — "a harsh teacher" as Thucydides termed it — will tend to replace these criteria with meritocratic ones. A whole host of administrative routines arise in peace that may prove dangerously cumbersome in war: a persnicketiness about completion of paperwork is the best example of this. The upshot, as military historian Michael Howard once explained, is that all militaries will, to some extent, "get it wrong" in the initial battles of a war; the key question is who gets it least wrong, and who learns most quickly. It is a constant struggle for military organizations to instill in their members an awareness that wartime conditions differ dramatically from those of peacetime, and indeed, one good measure of military competence is the extent to which soldiers remind themselves and their subordinates of the artificialities of peace, and their struggles to cope with them.

The soldier's attitude to peace is, of course, determined by circumstance and culture. It is generally true that the younger and more aggressive fighters — particularly those who have never experienced combat — hanker for a testing of their skills and for opportunities for glory and promotion. By and large, however, it appears that senior officers are inclined to prefer peace. In some cases they fear a potentially disastrous test of their leadership and managerial skills. Most wars, they know, involve a wholesale sacking of commanders who do not prove up to the job. A more creditable and probably more prevalent attitude is one of a healthy awareness of the limitations on war's predictability and a sense of its costs. This last point is felt particularly keenly by those who have seen much war. The duke of Wellington (q.v.) is said to have remarked that the only sight more melancholy than a battle won is a battle lost. The soldier who turns to the ardent pursuit of peace, while retaining the warrior virtues, is not an uncommon figure.

In the West, at any rate, where warfare is credited as a normal or praiseworthy activity only in self-defense, military service is often justified by its contribution to maintaining peace. "Peace is our profession" was the motto of the branch of the American armed services responsible during the Cold War (q.v.) for large-scale nuclear warfare. And military preparedness can indeed preserve peace; Switzerland's record in the two world wars is at least partial evidence on behalf of such a conclusion. But the impulse to wage war can cause countries to disregard an opponent's military preparations, or at least to accept the losses that will result.

Peace among states is increasingly the norm. Interstate war, if not quite a relic of a bygone era, is ever more rare. But intrastate violence appears to be growing in many parts of the world. Whether as terrorism (q.v.), tribal genocide (q.v.), or mere banditry, the inclination to use violence remains a powerful force in national and international politics. Bierce's sardonic view of human nature, therefore, will probably continue to ring truer than civilized people would wish.

ELIOT A. COHEN

Geoffrey Blainey, *The Causes of Wars*, 3rd ed. (1988).

Peacekeeping

Peacekeeping per se is not a terribly mysterious activity. Whenever soldiers have been used to maintain domestic law and order or to keep various subnational groups from slaughtering one another, they may be said to engage in "peacekeeping." In contemporary usage, however, the term *peacekeeping* has acquired a different set of connotations. When British or French soldiers tried to prevent allied tribes of American Indians from going to war with one another, they were, in some sense, engaged in peacekeeping. Since World War II (q.v.), peacekeeping has been used to refer to the interposition of armed forces — usually, though not always, multinational units under the auspices of the

United Nations — between warring groups or states (see *San Francisco Conference*). This interposition, in response to a negotiated agreement among the parties or a mandate from a major international organization (such as the UN, the Organization of American States, or the Organization for African Unity) is usually limited in time and scope. It is therefore very different from the "peacekeeping" of imperial or national forces subduing unruly civilian populations.

Contemporary peacekeeping is, as one UN official has remarked, "no job for a soldier, but a job only a soldier can do." Peacekeepers operate quite differently from combat troops. Whereas normal tactical units camouflage their positions and put a premium on stealth, peacekeepers make themselves visible, often by painting their vehicles and installations a dazzling white. Whereas combat forces will try to maintain the security of their communications, peacekeepers will often use open lines to maintain "transparency" to all parties. Whereas fighting armies are, obviously, on one side of a political dispute, peacekeepers strive, or at least pretend to strive, for impartiality. Whereas normal units seek to destroy an enemy by fire and violent maneuver, peacekeepers regard use of their weapons as an absolute last resort, and extensive combat as a sign that the peacekeeping mission has failed. Thus, a Danish lieutenant general with an extensive background in peacekeeping notes that "when a UN patrol is fired at or threatened it does not fall down in a ditch by the side of the road" primarily because "the locals will think that the patrol is going into position to return fire."

Some peacekeeping operations have had a long history. The United Nations Truce Supervisory Organization in the Middle East dates back to 1948, and UNMOGIP, the UN Military Observer Group in India and Pakistan, is only a year younger. UN peacekeepers have, in recent years, monitored ceasefires, refugee movements, and elections from Cyprus to El Salvador, Rwanda to Macedonia. Although some peacekeeping operations have occurred outside UN auspices (most notably, the Multinational Force and Observers, which has operated successfully in the Sinai since 1982), most have occurred under its umbrella. Maritime peacekeeping is rare, though not unheard of: escort of shipping missions in war areas (by the U.S. Navy in the Persian Gulf during the Iran-Iraq War [q.v.], or by the Royal Navy in the Mediterranean during the Spanish civil war [q.v.]) are examples. Peacekeeping does not necessarily prevent wars.

UN forces in Lebanon watched helplessly for years as Israelis and Arabs shelled, mortared, and rocketed each other, and then simply hunkered down when Israeli forces occupied the southern part of the country in 1982. (Nor, it should be noted, did most UN forces attempt to interdict terrorist bands moving into Israeli territory either before or since.) Peacekeeping seems to work best when both sides see the need for an honest broker; peacekeeping then is a modest contribution to agreements already reached, not a cure for raging antagonism.

The humiliating and costly — though partial — failures of UN peacekeeping in Somalia and Yugoslavia between 1992 and 1995 suggest the limits of peacekeeping operations. UN forces there, as elsewhere, frequently found themselves at odds with the parties they were supposed to protect — civilian populations who felt themselves the victims of false promises. Impartiality in such circumstances was a sham: an intervention in a shooting war, if it is to have an effect, has to take sides. Also, large multinational forces, amounting to the equivalent of a very lightly armed division, posed enormous problems of logistics, command and control, and intelligence. National governments did not cede their authority to UN commanders, who frequently found themselves sharply limited in what they could ask their subordinates to do. More than one observer drew parallels with the occasionally farcical UN intervention in the Belgian Congo from 1960 to 1964, an experience that still suggests the limits of what is sometimes termed "peace enforcement," which might better be described as forcible pacification.

Yet peacekeeping activities look likely to grow. Pressure will come from the spread of so-called failed states whose populations suffer from murderous anarchy, the growing interest in various parts of the world in forcible attempts to change borders or the ethnic composition of populations within them, and the general reluctance of the major powers to act unilaterally. It is likely that more, and not fewer, men and women will find themselves wearing the blue helmets of UN peacekeepers and receiving orders not to look as if they are going to return fire when fired upon.

ELIOT A. COHEN

William J. Durch, ed., *The Evolution of UN Peacekeeping* (1993); United Nations, *The Blue Helmets: A Review of United Nations Peace-keeping*, 2nd. ed. (1990).

Pearl Harbor, Attack on

December 7, 1941

For the United States, World War II (q.v.) began at Pearl Harbor, Hawaii, then the advanced base for the U.S. Pacific Fleet, which was taken by surprise when a Japanese strike from aircraft carriers hit soon after dawn. Eighteen American warships were sunk or damaged, including eight battleships, of which the *Arizona* and *Oklahoma* were never recovered. More than twenty-four hundred Americans died, and 188 aircraft were destroyed. Losses from the six-carrier Japanese task force were minimal: 29 aircraft, perhaps a hundred sailors, and five midget submarines.

The events of December 7 triggered a succession of boards of inquiry and investigations, culminating in joint hearings by the U.S. Congress in 1946. Questions concerning the attack have never been fully resolved, and the desire to prevent future Pearl Harbors became a factor in the creation of the Central Intelligence Agency (CIA), America's first peacetime, permanent intelligence organization.

Pearl Harbor represented the largest mass use of aircraft carriers up to that time, the farthest-range conduct of a naval attack, the largest air attack against a naval target up to that time, and one of the most elaborate efforts to coordinate simultaneous attacks by aircraft and submarines. Despite these significant achievements, the Japanese failed to coordinate their surprise attack properly with diplomatic ultimatums to be delivered in Washington, D.C. Many analysts hold that the seemingly unprincipled surprise attack was self-defeating despite its tactical success, because it aroused the United States as few other actions could have.

JOHN PRADOS

Peloponnesian War

431–404 B.C.

The great war between Athens and Sparta lasted for twenty-seven years, destroyed the Athenian imperial system, and changed the entire course of Greek military history. After heroic roles in the defeat of the Persians (480–479 B.C. — see *Persian Wars*), for the next half-century Athens and Sparta assumed preeminence among the city-states, and their rivalry slowly led to the long-expected showdown. Thucydides, a contemporary historian, believed that the war broke out because of Spartan fear of the rising power of Athens, whose empire and capital increasingly isolated less imaginative and less adventurous rivals. Both were unusually powerful, atypical — and antithetical — Greek states that could afford to ignore the old rules of infantry warfare. Supported by nearly 200,000 Helots (serfs) who worked the farms of Messenia and Laconia, the Spartans (q.v.) fielded professional hoplites (q.v.), year-round infantry not subject to the normal restrictions that free agriculture placed on yeomanry in infantry battle.

Nor were the democratic Athenians comfortable with an artificial collision of oligarchical, armored farmers. In the wake of the Persian retreat (479 B.C.), Athens's fleet increased. Nurtured on the tribute of vassal states in the Aegean, Athens did not mothball its triremes; instead, they became a "benign" police force of sorts for its Greek subject allies overseas. Like the Spartans, imperial Athens too saw little need to limit warfare to a single afternoon, or indeed, given the success of its evacuation before Xerxes and subsequent naval response, to risk at all its hoplites in defense of the farmland of Attica. The majority of its citizens were not infantrymen and increasingly saw the navy as the bulwark of radical democracy.

Abandoning its countryside to Spartan invaders (431–425 B.C.), Athens understandably refused pitched battle with the crack hoplites of the Peloponnesian and Theban alliance. The strategy of attrition adapted by the Athenian leader, Pericles, depended on increased importation of food and material into the port at Piraeus, all the while sending out Athens's magnificent fleet to stabilize its maritime empire and to prevent Peloponnesian infiltrations, forgoing major land engagements at all costs. Sparta found its old strategy of ravaging cropland discomfortingly ineffective: its hoplites in Attica could neither draw the Athenian army out nor reduce the city economically. The Spartans' best ally was the unforeseen outbreak of plague inside the cramped walls of Athens, which killed Pericles and nearly one quarter of the citizenry. With stalemate in Attica, both belligerents turned to a variety of secondary theaters throughout the Aegean world and Asia Minor, as Sparta tried to turn Athenian subjects, and Athens in turn sowed insurrection among the Helots.

In these latter proxy wars, Athens used hoplites in combined maritime operations, whereas Sparta and its allies in time developed a competent fleet: during the entire course of the Peloponnesian War there were

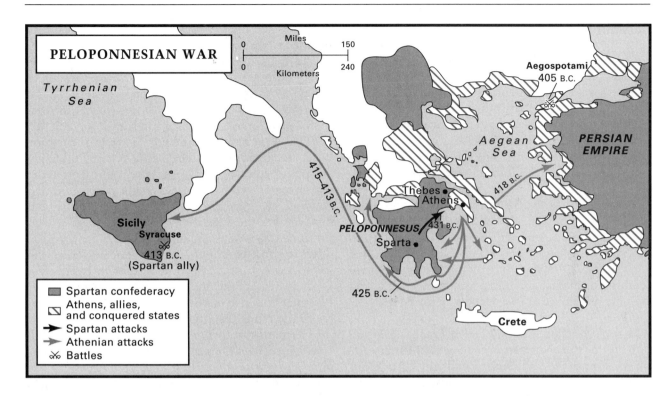

not more than three or four hoplite battles of the old style. Instead, mercenaries, lightly armed skirmishers, sailors, and siege engineers filled that void. All were expensive. And — disastrous for both sides — all apparently were incapable of ending an engagement decisively through a day's destruction or humiliation of an enemy's forces in the field.

Strategy became prominent for the first time in Greek warfare, as the Athenians made mostly inconsequential probes in and around the Peloponnesus. Their greatest success was the occupation of Pylos off the coast of the Peloponnesus (425 B.C.), where Spartan defenders were taken hostage and the way was made clear for Helot runaways. The subsequent failure of Sparta to reduce Athens in the first decade of the war led to a brief peace (421 B.C.).

But soon the Athenians intervened in the Peloponnesus (418 B.C.) and attacked neutral states in the Aegean. The folly of that aggressive policy culminated in the disastrous expedition to Sicily (415–413 B.C.), where nearly forty thousand Athenian allies perished a thousand miles from Athens (see *Sicilian Expedition*). Sparta now systematically garrisoned Attica with a permanent fort at Decelea (413–404 B.C.) to encourage desertions and local disruptions in commerce, all the while applying steady pressure to pry away tribute-paying Athenians and their allies in the Aegean, the lifeblood of the city's capital and military reserves. Unable to replace the manpower losses from the plague and the disaster at Sicily, the Athenian army and navy were routinely now outnumbered by the combined alliance of Sparta, Thebes, and Syracuse. Persian subsidies to this Peloponnesus-led coalition for the first time surpassed the financial reserves of Athens. After the final Athenian sea defeat off Aegospotami, the Long Walls down to the Piraeus were razed, and a Spartan garrison occupied the city.

Nearly three decades of constant fighting left Athens bankrupt, exhausted, and demoralized. But Sparta and its allies were in no position to maintain an even harsher military hegemony over Greece. In the detritus of the Peloponnesian War, the agrarian fighting of the old *polis* was ended. Warfare now meant expansion of conflict onto a variety of costly and deadly new horizons, where past protocol meant little. The Greek genius was freed to apply capital, technology, and manpower to war without ethical restraint, but in the process the old idea of a city-state was lost.

VICTOR DAVIS HANSON

Donald Kagan, *A New History of the Peloponnesian War*, vols. 1–4 (1969–1987); G. E. M. de Ste. Croix, *The Origins of the Peloponnesian War* (1972).

Pershing, John J.

1860–1948, U.S. World War I Army Commander

A mediocre student but a natural leader, John Joseph Pershing was president and first captain of the West Point class of 1886. Returning to the military academy as a tactical officer in 1897, he was nicknamed "Nigger Jack," or "Black Jack," by cadets who resented his iron discipline. The second of these nicknames, derived from his frontier service with the African-American Tenth Cavalry, stuck. In 1898, he went up San Juan Hill with his Black troopers, proving himself "as cool as a bowl of cracked ice" under fire from Spanish sharpshooters who killed or wounded 50 percent of the regiment's officers. Next came three tours in the Philippines, mostly in Mindanao, where Pershing displayed an ability to combine force and diplomacy to disarm the island's fierce Moro warriors.

In 1905 Pershing married Helen Frances Warren, daughter of the chairman of the Senate Military Affairs Committee. Pershing's friendship with President Theodore Roosevelt combined with this marital connection to vault him from captain to brigadier general in 1905, over the heads of 862 more senior officers. Eleven years later, his Philippines experience made him a natural choice to command the Punitive Expedition that President Woodrow Wilson (q.v.) dispatched to Mexico in 1916 to pursue Pancho Villa and his marauding army after they attacked American border towns along the Rio Grande. Although Pershing never caught Villa, he thoroughly disrupted his operations. Thus he became the president's choice to command the American Expeditionary Force when Wilson's neutrality policy collapsed in the face of German intransigence and America entered World War I (q.v.) in April 1917.

In France, Pershing rejected French and British demands to amalgamate his troops into their depleted armies. He insisted on forming an independent American army before committing any U.S. troops to battle and stuck to this position in spite of enormous diplomatic pressure from Allied politicians and generals — and awesome gains made by the German army in the spring of 1918. In June and July, however, he permitted his divisions to fight under French generals to stop the Germans on the Marne (q.v.). But on August 10, Pershing opened First Army headquarters, and on September 12, 500,000 Americans attacked the St.-Mihiel salient and quickly erased this bulge in the French lines, which the Germans had already planned to abandon.

The Meuse-Argonne offensive of September 26 was a very different battle. There, Pershing's doctrine of "open warfare," which was supposed to break the Western Front's stalemate with the American rifleman's superior marksmanship and rapid movements, collided with the machine gun, a weapon Pershing badly underestimated. The battle became a bloody stalemate, compounded by massive traffic jams in the rear areas as green American staffs floundered. On October 16, Pershing tacitly admitted failure and handed over the First Army to Hunter Liggett, who revamped its tactics and organization. Renewing the offensive on November 1, the Americans joined the advancing British and French armies in forcing the Germans to accept an armistice on November 11. Pershing was the only Allied commander who opposed the armistice, urging continued pressure until the Germans surrendered unconditionally.

In France, Pershing remained a disciple of iron discipline and constantly tried to shape the American Expeditionary Force to West Point standards. He ruthlessly relieved division officers who faltered under pressure. In a toast on armistice night, he paid honest tribute to how he had emerged from the cauldron of the Argonne a victorious general. "To the men," he said. "They were willing to pay the price."

Pershing served as army chief of staff from 1921 to 1924. He assisted in making his protégé, George C. Marshall (q.v.), chief of staff in 1940. "If he was not a great man," wrote one journalist who knew Pershing well, "there were few stronger."

THOMAS FLEMING

Persian Gulf War

See Gulf War.

Persian Wars

490 B.C. and 480–479 B.C.

Darius I of Persia crossed the Aegean in 490 B.C. to punish the mainland Greeks for their role in the failed Hellenic revolt in Ionia. After Darius's defeat at Marathon (q.v.), ten years elapsed before his son Xerxes could collect an immense land and sea force to descend into Greece. Almost immediately, King Leonidas and a small Spartan force were gloriously annihilated at the northern pass at Thermopylae in 480 B.C., as the Greek navy off the coast at Artemisium withdrew safely to the south. Nearly all of Greece north of the Peloponnesus was now captured or evacuated. The Athenians abandoned Attica, putting their last hopes in an impressive and proficient fleet of nearly two hundred triremes.

The allied Greek navy followed the advice of Themistocles to lure the Persian navy inside the narrow confines off Salamis (q.v.). After a brilliant victory there, Athens reclaimed Attica, and a grand army of national resistance was formed to crush the Persian invader in Boeotia. Xerxes retired to Asia with his ships, leaving his general Mardonius behind with an undefeated army of over 200,000 infantry and cavalry. But at Plataea, the largest army in the history of the Greek city-state — perhaps 40,000 hoplites and 60,000 auxiliary troops — under the Spartan general Pausanias routed the Persians, killed Mardonius, and chased the remnants northward.

These encounters all proved that the battlefield morale of the Greeks remained unquestioned — among the doomed three hundred at Thermopylae, the desperate rowers off Salamis, and the savage hoplites at Plataea — giving credence to the notion of an autonomous city-state governed by law and the free assent of its people. True, there were serious lapses in Persian strategic and tactical thinking; but ultimately the war hinged on the relative prowess and morale of the combatants themselves.

Until the invasions of Darius and Xerxes, the Greeks had been relatively immune from the turmoil of the eastern Mediterranean. But in the aftermath of the Persian debacle, Athens claimed hegemony over the Aegean and Ionia, collecting tribute and accelerating the process of both imperialism and democratization. Sparta used the hard-won prestige of Thermopylae and Plataea to collect an alliance of landed states within the confines of the Peloponnesus. Thus the Persian Wars led directly to both the Athenian renaissance and the increasing tension between Athens and Sparta, a fifty-year enmity that culminated in the disastrous Peloponnesian War (q.v.) and the decline of the city-state itself.

Militarily, the Persian Wars proved the superiority of Greek heavy infantry. After Thermopylae, hoplites (q.v.) were never again defeated by easterners, and the theater of east-west rivalry was turned permanently eastward from the Greek mainland. The lessons of Marathon and Plataea were not lost on generations of Greek infantry invaders. Xenophon's (q.v.) mercenary ten thousand, Agesilaus's expeditionary force in Asia Minor, and Alexander's (q.v.) Macedonians all marched east, rightly confident in the verdict of their ancestors a century prior.

VICTOR DAVIS HANSON

Pétain, Henri-Philippe

1856–1951, French World War I Field Marshal

Marshal Henri-Philippe Pétain endeared himself to the French nation during World War I (q.v.). Beginning the war as an obscure fifty-eight-year-old colonel in command of an infantry brigade, he rose quickly in rank, assuming command of the Sixth Division in September 1914, the Thirty-third Corps in October, and the Second Army in June 1915. From the start, he distinguished himself by his meticulous attention to detail, his careful preparation, and his reliance on artillery. His talents became most apparent when his Second Army played a large role in the September 1915 offensive in Champagne. Though the French failed to break through German defensive lines, Pétain's after-action report identified shortcomings in French methods and provided important ideas about future operations.

In February 1916, Pétain became commander of French forces at Verdun (q.v.). In the terrible destruction of what the French soldiers called the "furnace," he finally succeeded in halting the Germans. Though the French suffered huge losses, Pétain's careful husbanding of his troops avoided even greater bloodshed. Among his innovations, he introduced the "noria" system, which rotated divisions in and out of the trenches without permitting them to become ineffective in combat. (The noria system was named after a device used to raise water from a well, which consisted of a revolving chain of buckets that filled at the bottom of the well and emptied at the top.) Despite Pétain's success and his concern for his soldiers, General Robert Nivelle (q.v.) was chosen to replace Marshal Joseph Joffre (q.v.) as commander of French forces; he then brought France to the edge of disaster with his ruinous offensive in April 1917. With much of the army in mutiny, Pétain replaced Nivelle in May.

In subsequent months, Pétain revived the French army by meting out a combination of rewards and punishments, including about fifty-five executions (not the hundreds that some critics have alleged). He also insisted on limited offensives in which massive amounts of artillery prepared the way for the infantry. In October Pétain launched an attack on the fortress of La Malmaison in the Chemin des Dames, near where Nivelle's offensive had failed, and successfully seized this dominating piece of terrain. His success and his careful methods convinced French soldiers that he would not needlessly waste their lives. For the remainder of the war, Pétain remained in command of French forces, though General Ferdinand Foch (q.v.) leaped over him to become supreme commander of Allied forces. Other French leaders, including Foch, frequently criticized Pétain for his pessimism and caution, but he nevertheless established a particularly strong relationship with the American commander, General John J. Pershing (q.v.).

Pétain had a significant influence over French forces in the interwar period, but his role has sometimes been exaggerated. Others made greater contributions in structuring and preparing French forces for the next war. Nevertheless, he played an important part in the design and placement of the Maginot line (q.v.); he himself chose the best sites for its major fortresses. Later, during the mid-1930s, he served as minister of war for a brief period. As France fell before the German attack in May–June 1940 (see *World War II*), Pétain became premier a week before the capitulation. Subsequently naming himself the head of state in Vichy France, he headed a curious government that adopted "Work, Family, Country" as its slogan and sought a "National Revival." In April 1942, at the age of eighty-five, he passed real power to Pierre Laval, who pursued an openly collaborationist policy with the Germans.

Though Pétain later claimed that he had been playing a "double game," the harshest evidence of his having accepted German influence is his government's anti-Jewish measures. Vichy provided limited protection to native French Jews, but it adopted repressive measures on its own from 1940 to 1942, including property confiscation, dismissals from government service, and exclusions from professions and higher education. Though Jews had a better life in France than they experienced in other Nazi-occupied or Nazi-controlled countries, the Vichy government interned thousands of foreign Jews under primitive conditions, and as many as three thousand Jews may have died in camps under French control. The Vichy regime also rounded up foreign Jews in the unoccupied zone and handed them over to the Germans. The "savior of Verdun" cannot escape blame for these actions.

Tried in France after the war, Pétain was found guilty and condemned to death. After Charles de Gaulle (q.v.) commuted the sentence to life imprisonment, he was confined on the Île d'Yeu, where he died on July 23, 1951, at the age of ninety-six. Despite his wish to be buried among the fallen of Verdun, he remains buried on the small island off the coast of Brittany. His many contributions in World War I remain overshadowed by his actions in World War II.

ROBERT A. DOUGHTY

Richard Griffiths, *Pétain: A Biography of Marshal Philippe Pétain of Vichy* (1972); Stephen Ryan, *Pétain the Soldier* (1969).

Peter I (the Great)

1672–1725, Russian Emperor

Willful, vindictive, and mercurial in temperament, Peter the Great transformed the tsardom of Muscovy into the Russian Empire. The Great Northern War (q.v.) against Sweden (1700–1721) dominated his reign. After his initial defeat at Narva (1700), Peter instituted a series of reforms designed to modernize Russia and improve its armed forces. Increases in the tax burden helped defray the costs of the war, while the expansion of the country's mining and metallurgical industries eventually provided the army with sufficient cannon and muskets. Canals and roads were built expressly to improve military communications and supply. The nobility was bound to compulsory state service, hundreds of thousands of peasants were drafted, and an ocean-going navy was founded.

Russia's fortunes on the battlefield improved: from 1702 to 1704, Peter conquered most of Swedish Ingria. In the summer of 1709 he defeated Charles XII (q.v.) at Poltava (q.v.), and in 1714 the Russian navy capped the Finnish campaign with a conclusive victory at Cape Hangö.

It is overly simple to ascribe Russia's success against Sweden to Peter's "westernization" of Russia. Equally, Peter's army was more an improvisation than a "regular" force: fantastic rates of desertion and disease deprived it of institutional continuity. Central to Russia's victory was Peter's ruthless exploitation of autocracy and serfdom to squeeze more men, money, and resources out of Russia than any of his predecessors. Indeed, the oppressive system he created has been described as "totalitarian."

WILLIAM C. FULLER, JR.

Philip II

382?–336 B.C., King of the Macedonians

When Philip assumed the leadership of the Macedonian (q.v.) kingdom in 360–359 B.C., few could have foreseen that he would transform this Balkan backwater into a formidable European power. But Philip had two major resources at his disposal: a tough people inhabiting a land rich in natural resources and the force of his own personality.

Philip fashioned the Macedonian army into the tool by which he exercised his foreign policy, using the service of his troops as a means by which they expressed their loyalty to him and to the Macedonian cause. The army thus emerged as both a personal and a national military force.

It is not clear just when Philip developed the plan to invade Asia, but it appears that his policy toward the Greek cities intended to create an alliance whose security he would guarantee through his military hegemony, thereby freeing him to pursue his Asian expedition. The Greeks, of course, did not see it that way, being fearful that Philip's alliance would mean the end of Greek freedom. Philip normally preferred diplomacy to military force: he was too careful a commander to risk good troops unnecessarily. Perhaps the best proof of his intentions is that, after he defeated the Greeks at Chaeronea (q.v.) in 338 B.C., he created an alliance like the one he had offered the Greeks years earlier by peaceful means. One ancient writer described Philip as being prouder of his grasp of diplomacy than of his prowess on the field of battle. He was assassinated just before realizing his dream of invading Asia, but the task was brilliantly carried out by his son, Alexander the Great (q.v.).

EUGENE N. BORZA

Philippine Sea, Battle of the

June 19–20, 1944

This battle, the biggest in history between aircraft carriers, featured fifteen American aircraft carriers (956 planes) against nine Japanese (473 aircraft) and was fought over the Japanese effort to break up the American invasion of the Marianas Islands (Saipan, Guam, and Tinian) in June 1944. The Battle of the Philippine Sea resulted from one of the best-prepared Japanese naval sorties of World War II (q.v.), which had involved careful rehearsals and preplanned coordination between the carrier fleet, called the First Mobile Fleet, under Vice Admiral Ozawa Jisaburo, and the land-based First Air Fleet of Vice Admiral Kakuta Kakuji. The Japanese planned to take advantage of the longer flying ranges of Japanese aircraft, so that Ozawa's carriers would make strikes while still beyond the range of American aircraft. The Japanese planes were to land at bases in the Marianas and then return to the fleet after bombing the Americans again on their way back. Plans were hampered by the poor training of the Japanese pilots and air crews and by the delay between the first American attacks in the Marianas and the arrival of Ozawa's carrier fleet.

The American Task Force Fifty-eight under Vice Admiral Raymond A. Spruance (q.v.) completely dominated the battle despite Japan's careful preparations. For several days before the naval action, Spruance's carriers knocked out Japanese air bases in the Marianas and Kakuta's First Air Fleet. On June 19, when Ozawa made his air attacks, American radar and radio intercepts permitted coordinated defense by Task Force Fifty-eight fighters. Some 243 Japanese planes were shot down against 31 American ones, a lopsided result that led to the nickname "the Marianas Turkey Shoot." On the next day, Spruance continued with a dusk strike that sank the Japanese carrier *Hiyo* and damaged two carriers, a battleship, and a heavy cruiser. Submarines accounted for Ozawa's flagship, the carrier *Taiho*, and two scarce oilers. The worst U.S. losses were the 82 planes forced to ditch at sea when they could not find their carrier decks again that night. The Battle of the Philippine Sea broke the back of Japanese naval air power.

JOHN PRADOS

Piracy/Privateering/Letters of Marque/Prizes

Piracy — robbery at sea — dates from the beginnings of maritime commerce and is a global phenomenon. Imperial Rome swept the ancient Mediterranean of pirates (the word comes from Greek), but with Rome's collapse, piracy returned. In the recovery of seaborne commerce during the Middle Ages, European merchants overcame Muslim pirates but sparked new maritime conflicts. Governments hired ships from private owners to form fleets and licensed them in wartime to raid enemy commerce. Nascent international law recognized licensed commerce raiders, who came to be known in English as privateers, and outlawed unlicensed commerce raiders as pirates. Only legitimate sovereign powers could license privateers and issue the necessary letters of marque and reprisal (first mentioned in English law in 1354), which specified the ship, its officers, and what was fair prey, often with convenient vagueness. Admiralty courts of the licensing power regulated privateering, sold captured ships as prizes, and distributed the proceeds as prize money, with governments, captains, and crews receiving designated shares.

Navies (q.v.) owned and operated by states appeared gradually. Their commissioned officers regarded naval service as nobler than privateering. As strategists decided that command of the sea required disciplined navies, competition grew for seamen, who found privateering more lucrative. Moreover, when wars ended, privateers often turned to piracy.

In the dizzying sequence of war and peace during the sixteenth and seventeenth centuries, confusion grew concerning the distinction between privateering and piracy, most dramatically in the Caribbean. There, buccaneers (the name comes from a Carib device they used to cure beef) united as "Brethren of the Coast" and plundered Spanish commerce illegally in peacetime, but in wartime did so legitimately under French, Dutch, or English letters of marque. During the War of the Grand Alliance (1688–1697) (q.v.), when Louis XIV (q.v.) of France laid up his navy to cut costs and licensed privateers on a grand scale, buccaneers and French regulars served side by side.

With the return of peace in 1697, the European powers were determined to end the increasingly indiscriminate piracy their wars had spawned. The most celebrated victim was Captain Kidd, an Englishman licensed as a privateer in 1696 who turned to piracy when war ended and made British Indiamen his prey. Seized and convicted, he was hanged in 1701 on Execution Dock, London.

While vigilant navies and revived Spanish power curtailed Atlantic and Mediterranean piracy, privateering continued through the wars of the eighteenth century, the Napoleonic Wars, and the War of 1812 (q.v.). But Britain's big battle fleets ruled the waves, and technical developments permitted close blockades (q.v.). A strategy dependent upon commerce raiding seemed the desperate response of a weaker naval power. The Paris Conference of 1856 issued a declaration that abolished privateering. The United States did not subscribe because it required amending the Constitution (Article 1, Section 8). In the American Civil War (q.v.), the Confederacy licensed privateers, but they found more profit in blockade running and left the hounding of Union shipping to the tiny Confederate navy, whose *Alabama* captured over eighty merchantmen before being sunk off Cherbourg in 1864 by the USS *Kearsarge*.

The Hague Convention of 1907 refined the prohibition of privateering and set rules for taking prizes by warships. The United States now outlaws privateering through federal statute and, like most governments, has abolished prize money.

PETER O'M. PIERSON

Plains Wars

1840s–1880s

Although U.S. troops fought Indians on all types of terrain in all parts of the nation, the wars on the Great Plains have captured the public imagination. The befeathered horse-and-buffalo tribes who fought the army — mainly Sioux and Cheyenne in the North, and Kiowa, Comanche, Cheyenne, and Arapaho in the South — have come to personify all Indians.

Hostilities began shortly after the Mexican War (q.v.) of 1846–1848 and flared sporadically until the early 1880s, when the last of the tribes settled permanently on reservations. In both the North and the South, the principal cause of the wars was white encroachment on Indian homelands. In the North, conflict centered on the Platte River Road to Oregon and California and on the Missouri River corridor to the Montana gold mines. In the South, the focus was the Santa Fe and Smoky Hill trails across Kansas and the westward expansion of settlers in Texas.

To contend with protesting tribes, the army established a chain of outposts along the overland trails, up the Missouri, and along the Texas frontier from Red River to the Rio Grande. Troops patrolled from these bases and periodically launched large-scale offensives. Major conflicts in the South occurred in 1858–1860, 1864–1865, 1868–1869, and 1874–1875. Here the strategy of converging columns was inaugurated, aimed at harrying Indians from several directions un-

Warriors and their descendants have celebrated the Sioux and Cheyenne victory over Colonel George A. Custer and his cavalrymen at the Little Bighorn in drawings on animal skins, ledger books, and writing tablets. This example, by Amos Bad Heart Bull (Oglala Lakota), depicts Sitting Bull and Crazy Horse, the most prominent Indian leaders in the war.

til they despaired and accepted the reservation. The Red River War of 1874–1875 brought lasting peace to the southern plains.

In the North, comparable clashes erupted in 1855–1856, 1863–1865, 1866–1868, and 1876–1881. The last, also employing converging columns, featured the disaster to Lieutenant Colonel George A. Custer (q.v.) at the Little Bighorn in 1876. The final surrender of the Sioux leader Sitting Bull in 1881 marked the end of warfare on the Great Plains.

ROBERT M. UTLEY

Plassey, Battle of

1757

The wealthy, riverine Province of Bengal (in eastern India) effectively broke free from the declining Mughal Empire (q.v.) in the 1720s. By this period, various European trading companies had been competing for lucrative monopolies and privileges in the area for more than half a century. The successor dynasty in Bengal found itself, over and over again, embroiled with these companies over "special" trading privi-

leges, while the Europeans became deeply involved in the factional politics of the dynasty. In 1756, the new nawab of Bengal launched an ambitious plan to reduce the power and trading privileges of the European companies, especially the English one. The nawab's forces quickly captured the lightly defended English trading port of Calcutta. Robert Clive led a rescue operation of state-of-the-art company forces (trained infantry with muskets and bayonets (see *Sepoys*), supported by light artillery) by sea from Madras.

Because the nawab had alienated his own nobility, the actual battle was a meager affair, involving artillery volleys and an assault on the one unit of the nawab's army willing to fight. Most of the nawab's troops remained aloof. The nawab was deposed, and the British regained trading privileges. Military success brought the British compensation claims and formed the basis for the full British takeover of Bengal only some ten years later. Largely because of the wealth of Bengal, the British were able to finance the modern armies that eventually conquered the rest of India.

STEWART GORDON

Poitiers, Battle of

October 732

Franks under Charles Martel defeated Muslims from Spain under Abd al-Rahman between Tours and Poitiers, near the border between the Frankish realm and what was then the independent region of Aquitaine. Details of the battle and the exact number of combatants cannot be determined from the surviving accounts. Since the Muslims were engaged in a raid and Charles led a rapidly collected reaction force, estimates that the Muslims had over fifty thousand troops (and the Franks even more) are logistically impossible.

Previously accepted ideas about the importance of this battle have not been sustained by recent scholarship. Charles's victory did not represent a defense of Europe against an Islamic invasion; Leo the Isaurian's defense of Constantinople (717–718) (q.v.) and the Visigothic leader Pelayo's victory at Covadonga (718) in northern Spain already had stopped the Muslim advance. Nor did the victory at Poitiers end Muslim raids into Frankish territory: these continued sporadically until Charlemagne (q.v.) established the Spanish March after 797. Poitiers did not mark a radical change in Frankish military organization, which long had been based on bonds of personal loyalty between warriors and magnates. Still less did it signal any technical innovation: western European armies had begun to adopt the stirrup in the fifth century and did not complete the transition until the eleventh. The significance of the Battle of Poitiers lay in its demonstration of the need for the Frankish kingdom to be united in order to defend itself against attack, and the ability of Charles Martel and his successors in the Carolingian dynasty to provide that unity.

EDWARD J. SCHOENFELD

Poitiers, Battle of

September 19, 1356

The first phase of the Hundred Years' War (q.v.) was characterized by destructive English *chevauchées* (mounted raids) that left much of France in ashes. In 1356, Edward III of England's heir, the Black Prince, devastated much of Périgord, Limousin, Blois, and Touraine. Then, near Poitou, he encountered the French royal army — probably about fifteen thousand men. The French seemed more inclined to encircle and starve their enemies than to launch a direct attack, so the prince ordered a cautious withdrawal for his six thousand men (including two thousand longbowmen). Rather than risk his escape, the French marshals launched a hasty charge with two elite cavalry contingents. The English archers fought off this attack and then shifted their fire to help the English men-at-arms crush a division of miscellaneous infantry. The men-at-arms of the dauphin's division, advancing on foot by the advice of the Scottish soldier Sir William Douglas (an ally of the French), also suffered heavily from the archers' arrows. This, and the impact of the recoiling survivors of the first attack, cast their formation into disorder. After some hard fighting, the French were thoroughly defeated.

Seeing how the battle was going, a large portion of the duke of Orléans's division fled the field without engaging. The remainder joined the reserve force and advanced to meet the English, who had boldly gone over to the attack. The Black Prince's assault, combined with a surprise rear attack, crushed the French formation. In all, twenty-five hundred Frenchmen perished, including two thousand men-at-arms; like numbers were captured, including the French king himself.

The English victory was almost as decisive strategically as it had been tactically. After Poitiers — with the French king a prisoner in England and many other leaders captured or dead — plundering Free Companies, English and Navarrese garrisons, and rebel peasants ravaged the countryside and brought French society to the edge of collapse. The government could not restore order, much less prevent Edward III's follow-up invasion of 1359–1360. To buy peace, the French were forced to accept the Treaty of Brétigny, which provided for the transfer of a full third of France to English sovereignty. The huge ransom due for King John did much to establish permanent, regular, national taxation in France, a development of vast significance. Over time, the great costs of John's capture led French writers to reevaluate the role of the monarch on the battlefield, arguing that he was too valuable to risk in hand-to-hand fighting.

CLIFFORD J. ROGERS

Politics and the Military

The crucial question in the relationship between armed forces and political systems is why more states are not dominated by their armed forces. In complex societies, the military is the ultimate repository of effective deadly force. Militias, or police, to say nothing of armed citizens, are seldom capable of sustaining direct resistance to an army whose generals are determined to suppress that resistance. Countries whose secondary social institutions are weak (as in contemporary sub-Saharan Africa) or participate only to a limited degree in the political culture (as in postindependence Latin America) are correspondingly vulnerable to military intervention. In both of these regions, armies seldom capable of waging war against external opponents have regularly exercised formidable influence over political leaders afraid to challenge the generals directly.

Appeasement in such a context frequently seems preferable to confrontation. The French Republic in the late nineteenth century conceded a high degree of autonomy to its armed forces in good part because of fear of the man on the white horse, epitomized by General Georges Boulanger. Although his comic-opera attempt to seize the reins of government in 1888–1889 ended in ridicule and he eventually committed suicide on the grave of his mistress, a most astute, better-balanced candidate might have succeeded — or, even in failing, might have destabilized the Republic and threatened its survival.

Crises tend to exacerbate anxieties about the loyalties of men in uniform. During the Great Depression, Franklin D. Roosevelt (q.v.) referred to Army Chief of Staff Douglas MacArthur (q.v.) as one of the most dangerous men in America. Although this fear had more to do with MacArthur's flamboyant personal style (which antagonized many New Dealers) than with any demonstrable evidence that MacArthur saw himself as a potential dictator, such concerns are not always imaginary. When Germany's newly established Weimar Republic faced endemic revolts by right-wing paramilitary elements, Reichswehr chief Hans von Seeckt (q.v.) declared himself the only man in Germany who could make a successful putsch and promised he would not do so. This reassurance was at best limited comfort to his civilian superiors.

To a significant degree, military roles in politics are limited by force of habit. But should the stresses of war or domestic tension overstrain a system's capacity to respond, the possibility exists that even armed forces may regard themselves as called upon to save state and people from themselves. During the American Civil War (q.v.), General George McClellan (q.v.) saw himself as called by destiny to restore the Union in spite of the presence of Abraham Lincoln (q.v.). Perhaps, however, the clearest case study of the military's ability to influence politics involves Japan in the 1930s. The state did not face crises threatening to its existence. Nevertheless, a small number of low-ranking army officers were able to move their country toward a suicidally aggressive war by an explosive mixture of moral conviction and simple assassination. Mao Tse-tung's (q.v.) aphorism that political power grows from the barrel of a gun remains an uncomfortable truth at century's end — and a challenge to governments and societies.

DENNIS E. SHOWALTER

Poltava, Battle of

July 8, 1709

The Battle of Poltava is perhaps the most famous episode in the Great Northern War (1700–1721) (q.v.), Peter the Great's (q.v.) struggle to dispossess Sweden of its Baltic empire. Having dispatched Russia's Polish and Saxon allies, Sweden's great warrior king Charles XII (q.v.) tried to conclude the war by invading Russia itself in 1708. Peter's scorched earth policy and the brutal winter of 1708–1709 had resulted in the death of almost all the livestock and half the soldiers in the Swedish army before the battle was ever joined. In April 1709, Charles invested the fort of Poltava on the Vorskla River in Ukraine. Peter marched to its relief. On July 8, nineteen thousand Swedes assaulted the fortified camp, which was defended by Peter's forty-five thousand men. Russia's victory was virtually total. Charles fled to the Ottoman Empire, and the remnants of his army surrendered.

Although dramatic, the strategic significance of the battle was limited. Poltava did not decide the issue of the Great Northern War, which continued for another twelve years. It was the buildup of Russian naval strength in the Baltic Sea, leading to the enormous amphibious attacks of 1719–1721, that finally brought Sweden to its knees. Nonetheless, the psychological impact of the battle was enormous. News of Charles's defeat resounded through Europe and won Russia respect as a great power.

WILLIAM C. FULLER, JR.

Pontiac, Rebellion of

1763

The name is familiar, but it misleads. Pontiac was a local Ottawa chief who became prominent in the siege of Detroit, May–September 1763, which was the most publicized part of an Indian uprising that ranged from Fort Pitt on the Ohio River through Forts Niagara and Detroit up to Michilimackinac at the junction of Lakes Superior, Michigan, and Huron. The Indians rose because of deep-seated grievances aroused by occupying armies and seizure of their lands.

Historian Francis Parkman called it the Conspiracy of Pontiac, but the organizing tribe was the Senecas, who wanted especially to get British troops out of Fort Niagara. They were helped by the Delawares, whose objective was Fort Pitt. Neither succeeded. British reinforcements came across Lake Erie to Niagara, and Fort Pitt's garrison not only held off the besieging Delawares but infected them with smallpox. Other forts, however, fell to stratagem and surprise.

The mixed tribes besieging Detroit under several leaders, of whom Pontiac was one, hoped to infiltrate the place by a ruse, but Commander Henry Gladwin received warning and barred the gate. The Indians settled down to starve the garrison, meantime developing acrimonious dissension among themselves.

The Indians were defeated militarily but won a political concession in the Royal Proclamation of 1763, which banned colonial settlement in "crown lands reserved for the Indians." By ironical coincidence, occupying garrisons were soon withdrawn to suppress colonial tumults in eastern cities.

FRANCIS JENNINGS

Prisoners of War

Prisoners of war did not exist as such in antiquity; generally, defeated combatants were slaughtered or enslaved. During the Middle Ages, nobles carried gold into battle to use as ransom in case of capture; their vassals were released to make their own way home. History's most famous prisoner was King Richard I ("the Lion-Heart") of England (q.v.). He was captured in disguise in Vienna by the Austrians, whom he had offended in the Holy Land, and held to ransom for 150,000 marks, paid partly by the heavy taxation of his own subjects. He fared better, however, than his Saracen prisoners — he had slaughtered two thousand of them at Acre.

The concept of prisoners of war developed as the European state system emerged during the seventeenth century and as the Enlightenment fostered the idea of the dignity of the individual during the eighteenth century. Admittedly, the use of mercenaries (q.v.) assisted the development of this moral code; they sought to save their skins and often did so in prisoner exchanges. King George III of England threatened to treat the rebellious American colonists as traitors, but British behavior, never gentle, was nevertheless restrained by George Washington's (q.v.) warning to General Thomas Gage that he would treat British prisoners "exactly by the rule you shall observe toward those of ours now in your custody." In the Napoleonic Wars, the first to employ mass conscription, captured troops were often kept in prison camps and noisome offshore hulks for eventual exchange. Officers were exchanged or paroled in the countries that captured them; the British settled in a gambling colony at Verdun and the French at British spas, giving language lessons.

During the nineteenth and early twentieth centuries, elaborate rituals for humane treatment were codified through successive Hague and Geneva Conventions (see *Laws of War*). They were honored at least in principle during World War I (q.v.), flouted during World War II (q.v.), and politicized in the Cold War (q.v.), as might be expected during an ideological struggle. In the first protracted conflict after the Cold War, which took place in Yugoslavia, barbarities were visited on prisoners and civilians alike in the name of "ethnic cleansing" (q.v.).

The first formal code of conduct for dealing with prisoners of war was drawn up in 1863 during the American Civil War (q.v.) at President Abraham Lincoln's (q.v.) request by Francis Lieber, a German-born professor of constitutional law. It stipulated that captured troops had to be imprisoned, fed, and given medical treatment but not enslaved, tortured, or killed. In the world's first total war, this proved easier to promulgate than enforce, especially as the South was blockaded and starved into submission. But Lieber's ideas formed the basis of the code drawn up at the Brussels Conference of 1874, sponsored by Tsar Alexander II of Russia. Although never ratified, a version of the Brussels Code finally found its way into international law as the Hague Convention of 1899, which was revised in 1907 and then made binding on thirty-

A Chinese Communist guard (left) herds Turkish prisoners of war in Korea, 1951.

eight nations (not including the Soviet Union or Japan) as part of the 1929 Geneva Convention on the rules of war. This was clarified and strengthened in 1949, when the Soviet Union was one of the fifty-seven signatories.

The honorable treatment of POWs in World War I was idealized in the film *La Grande Illusion* of Jean Renoir, an appropriate title but not that far from reality, at least on the Western Front. World War II was a different matter. The death toll of prisoners was unprecedented: malnutrition, disease, slave labor, and mass murder took between six million and ten million prisoners' lives, predominantly among Russians and Germans held by each other. The death rate for American and British prisoners was about 11 percent, concentrated among prisoners of the Japanese, who did not believe in surrender and had contempt for Western nations that did. Prisoners were uniformly starved, maltreated, and occasionally executed. The most infamous incidents were the forced labor of British prisoners to build a railway for the Japanese through Burma, dramatized in the film *The Bridge on the River Kwai*, and the death march of American prisoners on the Bataan Peninsula after the Japanese capture of the Philippines, which covered 135 miles in eleven days — for five of those days, the prisoners received no food at all. In Germany, Western prisoners were subjected to harsh but not uncivilized conditions, whereas the humane conditions for German and Italian prisoners in England, where they were used as farm laborers, was a cause of complaint from the war-weary English. In Russia, thousands of German prisoners were held for years after the war, and in 1940 the Soviet secret police massacred twenty-four thousand Polish officers in the Katyn Forest to eliminate potential opposition to a postwar Communist regime.

But it was the Soviet Union's treatment of its own repatriated prisoners that politicized the issue in the Cold War. Joseph Stalin (q.v.) demanded and received from the Allies the enforced repatriation of thousands of Soviet soldiers who had been taken prisoner by the Germans, some to fight alongside them. Returned home, many were exiled, imprisoned, or executed — sometimes all three. Memories of their cruel fate conditioned American policy during the Korean War (q.v.), when more than 130,000 North Korean and Chinese prisoners were taken before the first truce talks began in 1951. By a ratio of four to one, they refused repatriation. Ensuring them a free choice prolonged the war by up to two years. To the consternation of their captors, Communist prisoners herded onto Koje Island off the southern coast of the Korean peninsula staged demonstrations and riots and at one point even seized the prison camp's American commandant as hostage, employing tactics that were carefully orchestrated by North Korean and Chinese truce negotiators. Meanwhile American and other allied prisoners held in brutal conditions in North Korea were inveigled, pressured, or tortured into making statements politically favorable to their captors.

These practices continued in Vietnam (q.v.), making the POWs a domestic political issue and enabling the Nixon administration to prolong truce negotiations on their behalf, which helped avoid the appearance of military defeat. The prisoners thus were converted into heroes to be celebrated upon their return, although their heroism was based on suffering, not conquest. Their homecoming eased the pain of the only major defeat suffered by the United States against foreign arms, but it also helped delay for years the resolution of this domestically divisive war by politicizing the unsolvable problem of those missing in action. The MIAs (q.v.) were presumed by some to have been hidden away in captivity; in fact, they were found to have been long dead when Vietnamese authorities opened their country to American investigators in order to restore relations with the United States in 1993.

LAWRENCE MALKIN

A. J. Barker, *Prisoners of War* (1975); Lawrence Malkin, "Murderers of Koje-do," *MHQ: The Quarterly Journal of Military History* (Summer 1993): 89–97.

Professionalism

Professionalism suggests two aspects of the occupational culture of military organizations. As applied to an entire armed service, it means that the service members are all volunteers (as opposed to conscripts) and seek together the highest standards of military effectiveness, principally in combat. Although many European military establishments had professionalist elements as early as the seventeenth century (for example, engineers and artillerists), the concept of a professional military establishment is really a post–World War II phenomenon; the pre-1945 armies depended upon large numbers of nonprofessionals to fill their ranks. Navies, on the other hand, could seek professional values anytime because they stressed mariners' skills and the distinct shipboard subculture. The air forces of the twentieth century also established professional values based on the demands of flight-crew service and the need for extensive training.

Professionalism also refers to the desire of the career officer corps to be accorded the power and status of other public service occupations like law, medicine, engineering, teaching, and the religious vocation. Members of a successful profession can control their definition of function, recruitment, self-regulation, and promotion. Military officers also hope to make admission and advancement a matter of merit, not a matter of family connections, civilian politics, and vested wealth or social status.

By 1914 all the armies of Europe, and Japan in Asia, had strong professionalist movements. Modern states encouraged professionalism for various reasons. It focused officers on preparing for war, not meddling in politics; it opened armies and navies to the middle class and democratic influences through the ideal of meritocracy; and it forced officers to learn about emerging technologies and managerial skills. A successful officer could no longer be simply a charismatic leader of great individual courage, but "a manager of violence." Out with El Cid (q.v.) and Suvarov (q.v.), and in with von Moltke (q.v.) and Kitchener (q.v.).

World War II (q.v.) demonstrated that military professionalization had brought the officers of all the major belligerents to a high state of strategic and operational expertise, managerial competence, and technological sophistication. It also showed that such competence did not necessarily create an equally high level of social responsibility. The senior officers of the European fascist powers accepted secret gifts, betrayed one another, lied, looted, and murdered; Japanese officers encouraged atrocities against fellow Asians. The Anglo-American strategic war against

Axis cities had its own moral dubiousness, and the Soviet armies pillaged their way into central Europe with the enthusiasm of the Mongols (q.v.).

The rise of new armies in new nations after 1945 raised more doubts about the value of military professionalism. Its very values, like the ideal of national service, propelled officers into politics, often revolutionary politics in nations such as Thailand, Brazil, Argentina, Syria, Iraq, and Indonesia. Military professionalism remains an appealing concept, if only to ensure military effectiveness, but it remains a conditional goal that carries political risks as well as functional promises.

ALLAN R. MILLETT

Bengt Abrahamsson, *Military Professionalism and Political Power* (1972); General Sir John Winthrop Hackett, *The Profession of Arms* (1962).

Propaganda

Propaganda in wartime, suggested a World War II expert, is as old as the pyramids — and certainly the hieroglyphic inscription celebrating a victory of the pharaoh Ramses II over the Hittites indicates that a monarch of the thirteenth century B.C. was as alive to the powers of propaganda as a modern dictator: "His majesty slew the entire force of the foe from Khatti. . . . his majesty slaughtered them in their places; they sprawled before his horses; and his majesty was alone, none other with him." But in a world where few had the freedom to travel, and even fewer could read, the audience for such megalomania was a small one. This, then, is the basic fact of propaganda history: though the impulse to propagandize is at least as old as Egypt, the ability to influence effectively and even control the thoughts and emotions of the general population has, until quite recently, been rather difficult. Thus two technological revolutions made propaganda a primarily modern phenomenon: first, the invention of the movable-type printing press in the fifteenth century A.D., and second, the exploitation of radio, film, and television in the twentieth. Before these revolutions, ancient and medieval propagandists used what techniques they could (inscriptions, ceremonies, monuments, coins, proclamations), but only a fraction of the population could be effectively engaged.

This essential limitation of premodern propaganda disappeared with the coming of printing, an innovation that preceded and assisted the collapse of Christendom into two warring confessional camps: Protestant reformers and Catholic counter-reformers. The very word itself — *propaganda* — comes from the papal office overseeing the religious reconquest of Europe, the *congregatio de propaganda fide* (congregation for the propagation of the faith). This propaganda struggle reached a crescendo in the Thirty Years' War (1618–1648) (q.v.), as both sides mobilized presses to churn out pamphlets and broadsheets by the thousands, extolling the victories of their coreligionists and blasting their enemies. One event alone, the destruction of Magdeburg in 1631 by a Catholic army, inspired at least 205 pro-Protestant pamphlets and 41 broadsheets. As always, atrocity stories, the more gruesome the better, were a favorite: in 1638 one sheet informed Englishmen that in Germany's wars "Croats eat children" and "noses and ears [are] cut off to make hatbands." Despite such sensationalism, ordinary people were now privy to the ideas and issues that brought rulers and ruled alike to conflict — and their hearts and minds had become a crucial theater of war.

The next great leap in war propaganda came with the Wars of the French Revolution (1792–1802) (q.v.) and the Napoleonic Wars (1805–1815). While fighting off Europe's monarchies, the French republican regimes focused an incredible propaganda effort on their frontline soldiers: special military newspapers and broadsheets aimed at the political education of the rank and file, and a billboard at the center of battalion camps posted a daily exhortatory *Bulletin*. The authorities also dispensed songbooks ("La Marseillaise" being the most enduring militant anthem), and even challenges and passwords (*liberty* or *Brutus*) reflected revolutionary ideals. Napoleon (q.v.), in propaganda as in all else, expropriated the revolutionary example. As emperor he manipulated the official record of his early career — such as at Marengo in 1800 (erasing his own errors, and minimizing the late afternoon intervention of General Desaix) — to emphasize his own omniscience, and he also controlled all knowledge and interpretation of the current military situation. Such prevarication in the soldiers' news sheets prompted the phrase "to lie like a bulletin."

By World War I (1914–1918) (q.v.), propaganda could no longer be a subsidiary effort: it was vital and necessary to bind a sophisticated populace (who were used to following politics in their daily newspaper, and who could often vote, too) to government policies. Therefore the governments of all belligerents marshaled every possible propaganda resource: posters encouraged recruits ("Daddy, what did *YOU* do in the Great War?" was the subtle but powerful message of one British poster) and advertised war bond drives; popular novelists churned out patriotic tomes; newspapers stepped into line; marches replaced peacetime music. In England, young women handed white feathers (symbolizing cowardice) to young men not in uniform. Atrocity stories shocked and horrified: the "rape" of "gallant" Belgium, with tales of German soldiers gaily bayoneting babies and ravishing nurses and nuns — fabrications based on frightened refugees' reports — dominated Allied propaganda early in the war. Propaganda was intended not only to galvanize the home front, but also to win over international and neutral opinion. At the opening of hostilities, there was already a German propaganda agency in the United States to woo American support. Later, anti-German propagandists successfully seized on the U-boat war and the sinking of the *Lusitania* to encourage U.S. intervention.

All the post–World War I revolutionaries (Benito Mussolini [q.v.] and Adolf Hitler [q.v.], Vladimir Lenin and Joseph Stalin [q.v.]) made propaganda the foundation of their political authority, using old techniques (posters, pamphlets, mass rallies, monumental architecture) as well as pioneering new ones (radio, film) to concentrate all power in their persons and parties. In the Russian Revolution and Civil War (1917–1920) (q.v.), Lenin's Bolsheviks developed the theory of "agitprop" — *agitation* plus *propaganda* — as a key war-winning revolutionary strategy. Later Communist revolutionaries, from Mao Tse-tung (q.v.) to Fidel Castro to Ho Chi Minh, showed that the mimeograph was as much a weapon of modern war as the machine gun. In particular, after World War I the new media of radio and film allowed charismatic leaders to connect directly and emotionally with their people. In Germany, the Nazi regime subsidized an inexpensive "people's radio set" to ensure the penetration of state propaganda: during World War II (1939–1945) (q.v.) millions tuned in to participate, from their living rooms, in Nazi rallies and to hear for themselves their führer's voice. As the war soured, and worried Germans searched the air waves for information, Allied broadcasts (such as that by a fictitious "SA Man Max Schroder") cleverly mimicked the tone of official

This Third Reich painting depicts Hitler in shining armor, associating him with the ideal of knighthood. The face was slashed by an American GI when the painting was captured by the U.S. Army.

Nazi radio to spread defeatism. Film, involving sight as well as sound, reinforced radio. Early in the war, weekly Nazi newsreels and feature films shared Wehrmacht and Luftwaffe victories with the people; at the bitter end, they prepared Germans for their Götterdämmerung, a last-ditch guerrilla war. Joseph Goebbels, Hitler's propaganda minister, aimed at nothing less than complete saturation, though a 1938 plan to place loudspeakers on the square of every German town had to be abandoned during the war (but North Korea has since proved such total propaganda coverage possible). Of course, World War II propaganda was not limited to totalitarian states, and both Winston Churchill (q.v.) and Franklin Roosevelt (q.v.) used radio to connect with their people; but in the Axis and Soviet regimes, propaganda was the web of life, linking everyone and everything to the politics and policies of the state.

Today, televisions, computers, and satellites make wartime propaganda a near-real-time process. During the Gulf War (q.v.), Iraqi officials showed video-camera teams "proof" that American bombers had hit civilian shelters and even an infant formula factory; the Cable News Network broadcast these reports internationally — and almost instantly. For its own part, the Pentagon released gun-camera footage demonstrating the incredible precision of "smart" bombs used against particular targets in Iraq. Such examples hint that as the telecommunications revolution shrinks the world in both time and space, the propaganda front remains crucial — and may even be growing in importance.

THOMAS F. ARNOLD

Prussians

Among European peoples, the military reputation of the Prussians is unparalleled in modern times. A small, impoverished kingdom strung across the northern German plain, Prussia emerged as a force to be reckoned with in European affairs during the reign of Frederick the Great (q.v.), who seized the Austrian province of Silesia during the War of the Austrian Succession (1740–1745), and then, to the astonishment of everyone, held on to it against the combined forces of France, Austria, and Russia throughout the Seven Years' War (1756–1763) (q.v.). The improbability of Prussia's survival, and the brilliance with which Frederick directed his forces in the field, won the admiration of Europe and secured Prussia a place among the great powers.

It was, however, the last place, and a century would pass before Prussia would improve its position. Only in the 1860s would Frederick find worthy successors in the persons of Prussia's minister-president Otto von Bismarck (q.v.) and its chief of staff Helmuth von Moltke (q.v.), who together conducted a series of short, violent, opportunistic wars — against Denmark (1864), Austria (1866), and France (1870–1871) — that transformed the European state system by placing a unified Germany at its center.

Whether Prussia can be said to have played an independent part in European history following its incorporation into the German nation-state may be disputed, though the predominance of Prussian values and institutions in Germany up to 1918 is clear enough. No less clear are the difficulties the Germans faced in harmonizing the disciplined, deferential elements of their Prussian heritage with the realities of a mass industrial society, which demanded more in the way of tolerance and egalitarianism than the Prussian past could supply. By the turn of the twentieth century, "Prussianism" was well established as a term of abuse among Germany's neighbors, having become synonymous with political reaction, blind submission to authority, and an alarming predilection to use force in the pursuit of national interests.

It goes without saying that the Prussian military experience included its share of defeats. Prior to its submergence in greater Germany, Prussia was by any reckoning an inherently weak state, without defensible frontiers or significant economic resources. During the Napoleonic period, when its armed forces fell into temporary decrepitude, Prussia was almost erased from the map of Europe by the vastly superior power of France. On the whole, however, Prussia managed to balance its material and geographical liabilities by cultivating a tradition of excellence at the operational and tactical levels of war, which went far beyond the proverbial *Kadavergehorsamkeit* (corpselike obedience) of Prussian soldiers.

The victories of Frederick and Bismarck occurred during periods when land warfare had become ponderous and indecisive, prone to logistical breakdown and inclined to stalemate and attrition. The ability of Prussian forces in both periods to mobilize and conduct operations more rapidly than their enemies, and to fight with greater determination once battle had been joined, were justly seen as exceptional — though hardly unique, since the armed forces and fighting doctrines of the major European powers have long tended to resemble one another. On the margins, however, Prussian armies almost always displayed more strategic flair and greater tactical flexibility than their opponents. When placed at the service of intelligent political leadership, these advantages could produce remarkable results.

The maintenance of armed forces capable of sustaining Prussia's place among the great powers was the paramount goal of the Prussian state. The effort this entailed was immense, as can be imagined if one considers that, at the end of Frederick's reign, the Prussian army was roughly equal in size to that of France, though its population was barely a fifth as large. Such disproportionate forces could exist only if all the economic, social, and moral resources of the country were mobilized in their behalf. The fiscal, political, and social arrangements required to accomplish this, rather than the martial qualities of the army itself, lay at the root of the "Prussianism" that outsiders found so worrisome.

Prussia was a military monarchy in the strictest sense. Its heavily aristocratic officer corps answered personally to the king and occupied the highest position in Prussian society. It could be subjected to politically responsible civilian control only with great difficulty, as Bismarck discovered to his chagrin in repeated run-ins with Moltke over how far military operations should be influenced by the demands of policy. The Prussian system of universal military service, to which virtually no exceptions were allowed, might in a different cultural environment have worked to democratize the army. In practice, however, the moral influence ran the other way, toward widespread popular acceptance of the army and its values as indispensable pillars of the social order.

The net effect of all this was effectively to inoculate Prussia against the claims of liberalism and democracy, which, apart from their inherent value, would increasingly come to be viewed as vital underpinnings of international peace. Both of the world wars of the twentieth century were deemed by the victors to be attributable in part to the persistence of the Prussian spirit in Germany, to the point where the Allied Control Council, seeking to eliminate all vestiges of "militarism and reaction," would find it symbolically useful even in 1947 to declare the Prussian state officially abolished.

Historians today would reject the most obvious implication of this action: it is wrong to equate the aristocratic values of old Prussia with the revolutionary nihilism of the Nazis. Nor is there anything in the historical record to suggest that, over the course of its history, Prussia went to war more often or more readily than its various opponents. But a society that, at great cost, bends every back in the pursuit of military power and celebrates the martial virtues at the expense of others no less worthy is likely to be judged differently from neighboring states on whom nature or history may have bestowed greater inherent strength. Few societies have risen so far by relying so exclusively on the excellence of their military institutions. None have paid a higher price in the end for having done so.

DANIEL MORAN

Gordon A. Craig, *The Politics of the Prussian Army* (1955); H. W. Koch, *A History of Prussia* (1978).

Psychological Warfare

Psychological warfare, which the *Oxford English Dictionary* defines as "achieving aims by acting on enemy's minds," connotes actions directed toward misleading the enemy or undermining the enemy's morale and dedication. The Chinese military thinker Sun Tzu (q.v.) of the fourth century B.C. strongly emphasized it in his *Art of War*. "To subdue the enemy without fighting," he wrote, "is the acme of skill." In its broadest sense, psychological warfare has been one of a range of techniques used from the beginning of organized war. When in 1400 B.C. Joshua marched around the city of Jericho (q.v.) for six days with trumpets and the Ark of the Covenant, it was as much to destroy the inhabitants' will to resist as to physically bring down the city walls. On the battlefield the use of elaborate armor, face painting, flags, banners, and military music have all been used at a tactical level psychologically to enhance the impact of an army. The battles of Marignano (1515) and Pavia (1525) became notorious for the noise of trumpets and kettledrums used to encourage weary troops and terrify the enemy. In 1950–1951, during the Korean War (q.v.), Chinese Communist forces advanced to the accompaniment of bugle calls, flags, and whistles, which were employed both for frontline communications and also (largely unsuccessfully) to unnerve the United Nations troops facing them.

The emergence in the modern world of mass ideologies underpinned the development of *strategic* psychological warfare. The notions of liberty and democratic national revolution, for example, were powerful weapons in Napoleon's (q.v.) armory, even though in this respect he always promised much more than was delivered. Technological advances brought the means of mass communication, which enabled governments to disseminate propaganda much more widely and effectively than hitherto. World War I (q.v.) saw the first systematic use of propaganda on a large scale. From the start of the war, the British aimed to undermine international support for Germany by publicizing German atrocities, such as the alleged attacks on defenseless Belgian civilians in 1914 or the sinking without warning of the passenger liner *Lusitania* in 1915. Both the French and the Germans produced propaganda news sheets targeted at soldiers and civilians in the frontline area. One German production, the *Gazette des Ardennes*, told stories of both Moroccan and British personnel fathering children by the womenfolk of French soldiers away at the war. Austrian attempts to undermine Italian morale with leaflets and agents provocateurs seem to have contributed to the disastrous Italian defeat at Caporetto (q.v.) in 1917. In the following year, Allied propaganda against the polyglot Austrian army did much to destroy its cohesiveness by encouraging anti-Austrian national feeling among Magyars, Czechs, Poles, and others.

Psychological warfare was further refined and expanded during World War II (q.v.). It was boosted above all by the development of mass radio communications, which provided a means by which propaganda could be directed specifically at both troops and civilian populations. William Joyce made English-language broadcasts for the Germans, and "Tokyo Rose" for the Japanese. Campaigns such as these — or the German *Silberstreif* (silver lining) operation of 1943 in which defectors were used to broadcast appeals to subvert the loyalty of Soviet troops — did not prove to be particularly effective. Joyce was ridiculed as "Lord Haw-Haw," whereas Tokyo Rose actually became something of an American forces' sweetheart. The most successful propaganda effort of the war — the BBC (British Broadcasting Corporation) broadcasts to occupied Europe — was not in fact aimed directly against the enemy. The BBC undoubtedly raised morale in the target countries, provided generally truthful information about the war, and transmitted information to resistance groups. Leaflets, too, were extensively used during World War II, and it has been calculated that some thirty leaflets for every man, woman, and child in Western Europe were dropped by American and British planes.

In the second half of the twentieth century, "psyops" has emerged as a distinct subdiscipline in military operations and planning. It took on a particular importance in counterinsurgency (q.v.) campaigns, especially against Communist-inspired uprisings. Mao Tse-tung (q.v.), the leading theorist of modern revolutionary war, laid down that the conflict was not merely military, but political and psychological as well. Above all, the mobilization and consolidation of popular opinion behind the revolutionary campaign was essential for success — hence Mao's celebrated analogy likening the civilian population to water and revolutionary troops to the fish that inhabit it; the latter cannot survive without the former. Faced with such a politico-military challenge, conventional state forces were obliged to enhance their psychological warfare expertise. In the 1950s in Malaya, where the British successfully countered a Communist guerrilla revolt, General Sir Gerald Templer coined the term "the battle for hearts and minds," which is at the core of psychological warfare. "The shooting side of the business," he asserted, "is only 25% of the trouble and the other 75% lies in getting the people of this country behind us." The French, as part of their doctrine of *guerre révolutionnaire*, established the Psychological Action and Information Service, which enjoyed some success in Algeria (q.v.) in the late 1950s.

Perhaps the most outstanding investment in psyops was that of the United States in Vietnam (q.v.), where personnel trained in civil and political affairs were attached to Special Forces units and where the Civil Operations and Rural Development Support (CORDS) organization aimed to secure the "pacification" of territory, promote rural reconstruction, and encourage supporters of the Viet Cong to defect to the South Vietnamese side. But — as is perhaps inevitable with psychological warfare — there was a continual tension between proponents of psyops and conventional soldiers, who have traditionally mistrusted the intangible basis of the former. The experience of the Vietnam War, too, demonstrated that psychological warfare, however sophisticated, is not sufficient for victory on its own. Properly integrated and coordinated in the wider war effort, however, it can powerfully contribute to ultimate success.

KEITH JEFFERY

Anthony Rhodes, *Propaganda, the Art of Persuasion: World War II* (1987).

Punic Wars

264–241, 218–201, and 151–146 B.C.

The three Punic Wars between Rome and Carthage (called after the Latin for "Carthaginian" — *Punicus*) saw the emergence of Rome as the dominant power in the Mediterranean world. Before the first war, its soldiers had never set foot outside peninsular Italy; by the end of the third, they had fought in what is present-day Sicily, Tunisia, Albania, France, Spain, Greece, Yugoslavia, and Turkey; had acquired for Rome its first provinces in Sicily, Spain, and Tunisia; and were about to acquire another in Greece.

The first war was for control of Sicily, which lay between Italy and the Carthaginian homeland (now Tunisia). Fought in and around the island, it was (apart from a disastrous Roman attempt to invade Tunisia in 256–255 B.C.) the longest continuous war in Greek and Roman history and one of the greatest naval wars ever fought. Possibly more men (over 285,000 — more than 138,000 Romans and 147,000 Carthaginians) took part in the Battle of Ecnomus off southern Sicily in 256 B.C. than in any other naval battle in history. The war ended with the defeat of the Carthaginian fleet off western Sicily, which compelled the Carthaginian forces in Sicily to come to terms.

The second war, chiefly famous for the part played in it by the Carthaginian general Hannibal (q.v.), was in complexity and number of states involved a "world war" in miniature. In ancient terms, Rome was a "superpower," and Hannibal's strategy was based upon the calculation that it could be defeated only if it could be deprived of the resources in manpower its confederacy in Italy provided. But this could be done only by victory in Italy — hence Hannibal's decision to march from his base in Spain across the Alps.

But though he proceeded to win a series of devastating victories, in the third of which — the Battle of Cannae (August 2, 216 B.C.) (q.v.) — he possibly inflicted worse losses (over 48,000 killed) on the enemy than those suffered by any other Western army in history in a single day, Rome's resolve never faltered.

With more than half its allies remaining loyal, not even Hannibal's genius could stem the tide. After defeating the Carthaginian armies in Spain, and confining Hannibal to the "toe" of Italy, the Romans invaded Tunisia under Scipio Africanus (q.v.), in 204 B.C. Hannibal was recalled, but only to be defeated by Scipio at Zama (q.v.) in October 202 B.C.

The peace treaty that ended the second war left Carthaginian territory in North Africa intact, but constantly subject to the aggressive pressure of Rome's erstwhile ally, Massinissa, king of Numidia (Algeria). In the end, urged on by the elderly statesman Cato, who took to ending all his speeches with the words "Carthage must be destroyed," the Romans issued a series of ultimatums, culminating in the requirement that the Carthaginians move their city ten miles from the sea. This spelled ruin for a great commercial power; provoked beyond endurance, the Carthaginians embarked on a third war, which they could not hope to win. After a desperate resistance, the city was finally destroyed in 146 B.C.

J. F. LAZENBY

Quebec, Sieges of

1759 and 1775–1776

The 1759 siege and battle of Quebec precipitated the end of the French and Indian War (see *Seven Years' War*) and changed forever the political complexion of the continent of North America. It also set the stage for the second siege and battle in 1775.

In July 1759, a British army invested the French fortress of Quebec. A fierce, ten-minute battle was fought outside the walls on September 13, and the besiegers entered the city in triumph. (Both commanding generals, James Wolfe and the marquis de Montcalm, were killed.) The peace treaty of 1763 left the British undisputed masters of North America.

The victory proved a mixed blessing, however; for even as Great Britain and its subjects in the lower thirteen colonies celebrated the removal of the French and Indian threat, those same colonists began to realize that they were no longer dependent on the protection of British redcoats. A large chunk of the cement that had bound America to England was removed, leaving an opening through which the Declaration of Independence roared thirteen years later.

At the outset of the American Revolutionary War (q.v.), a Continental army invaded Canada in order to deny the British their northern base for invasion. Quebec was besieged in November 1775 and attacked on December 31. The Americans were repulsed with enormous losses. Although the remnants of their army managed to maintain the blockade through the winter, the arrival of a British fleet in May forced them to withdraw from the city and, within the month, from Canada itself.

Had they captured Quebec, it is conceivable that Canada and the United States might now be one country. Failure, on the other hand, meant facing two British invasions from the north (1776 and 1777) and a prolongation of the war for another five years.

CLARE BRANDT

R

Ramillies, Battle of

May 23, 1706

The Battle of Ramillies was the duke of Marlborough's (q.v.) second great victory in the War of the Spanish Succession (q.v.). After his important initial victory at Blenheim (q.v.) in August 1704, the war in the Southern Netherlands became a stalemate, with the Anglo-Dutch army unable to make progress against France's defenses.

In 1706 Marlborough, who for the first time had full control over the allied forces, initially thought of marching to Italy, in order to assist Prince Eugène who was campaigning there, but French troops lay across his line of advance. Instead the duke directed his operations against northern France. Louis XIV ordered the leading French commander, François Villeroi, to engage the allies in battle, and so he ventured out from behind his fortified lines. The result was the engagement fought on the plain of Ramillies. The armies were of approximately equal size, but the French forces were drawn up over an extended front. The duke, whose own troops occupied a more compact position, first attacked Villeroi's flanks, forcing him to dispatch reinforcements there, and then made a decisive thrust against the weakened center, which carried the day. The overwhelming allied victory, at an exceptionally early point in the campaigning season, was brilliantly exploited by Marlborough who, in a spectacular military progress, conquered most of the Spanish Netherlands during 1706.

It seemed as if the deadlock in the War of the Spanish Succession had been broken, but within twelve months the stalemate had returned, and the war was to drag on for a further seven years.

H. M. SCOTT

Rape

Soldiers are trained to kill, but not to rape. Rape has usually been a sort of disreputable half-brother to the legitimate mayhem of war. No glory attends rape. Rather, rape after battle has been regarded as an ugly side effect, the spoils of war, Homeric booty: kill the men, take the women as prizes.

When the Yugoslav Milovan Djilas complained to Joseph Stalin (q.v.) about the rapes that Russians had committed in Yugoslavia, Stalin expressed a prevailing (male victor's) view of such brutalities: "Can't you understand it if a soldier who has crossed thousands of kilometers through blood and fire and death has fun with a woman or takes some trifle?" In 1945, Soviet soldiers raped two million German women as revenge for all that Germany had inflicted upon Russia.

But revenge is not always the motive. It cannot explain Nanking in 1937, for example: the Chinese had committed no atrocities against the Japanese, whose soldiers raped, and often murdered, tens of thousands of Chinese women.

Even sexual assault has its subtleties and protocols. In medieval and early modern Europe, the women of a besieged town taken by storm might be raped, but those in a town that surrendered on terms would not (see Laws of War).

Armies normally receive indoctrination on decent behavior and on which offenses, including rape, may result in court-martial. On occasion, however, as during the war in Bosnia-Herzegovina after the breakup of Yugoslavia in 1991, rape served as a deliberate instrument of war, a means of assaulting an enemy's solidarities, of shattering families and demoralizing the enemy. During the Bosnian war, a European Community team of investigators found that Serbs had committed mass rape as part of their expansionist policy of "ethnic cleansing" (q.v.). The investigators reported that "daughters are often raped in front of parents, mothers in front of children." Both sides in the Bosnian conflict — Serbs and Muslims — committed atrocities, including rape. Observed modern Balkan affairs scholar Mark Wheeler, "The idea of nationality in Yugoslavia is based on descent, and the greatest debasement is to pollute a person's descent."

In some societies, the taint of rape is indelible and toxic. In Indochina, rape meant the loss of a woman's sexual purity, the highest gift she can give her husband. The Cambodians have this saying: "A woman is cotton, a man is a diamond. If you throw cotton in the mud, it's always soiled. But if you throw a diamond in the mud, it can be cleaned."

By contrast, however, some women from Nicaragua and other parts of Latin America expressed pride in having been raped in war because their political beliefs taught them that they have given their bodies to the revolution.

But the diamond-and-cotton paradigm is the one that mostly prevails and makes rape an effective instrument in some wars. Rape lives on in the anger, grief, depression, and adhesive shame that it leaves behind — a moral and psychological scorched earth.

LANCE MORROW

Reconnaissance

Military commanders from time immemorial have fretted about the availability of useful information during a campaign, especially when they are operating in foreign lands and distant waters. *Reconnaissance*, the French military term for information gathering, entered the English military vocabulary sometime in the seventeenth or eighteenth century. This standing function of the exercise of command has been performed as long as armies and navies have existed.

Reconnaissance activities focus upon two categories of information: data on terrain and weather, and data about the enemy order of battle and activities. For environmental information, reconnaissance units would gather data on road conditions, bridges, tunnels, passes, civilian and military structures of all sorts, soil trafficability, economic resources (such as forage), potable water, obstacles, and significant terrain features such as lakes, mountains, forests, and deserts. Data for naval operations would include wind and tide information, weather conditions, the location of harbors and anchorages as well as shoal waters, and all sorts of landfall information.

Skilled reconnaissance should also provide information about the enemy, provided that enemy forces are within reach of the means of information gathering. An enemy's observable units and their activities can provide data on strength, force structure, general physical condition and state of morale, nature of weapons and equipment, logistical arrangements, pattern of activity in camp or on the march, deployment for battle, and security operations. The one thing reconnaissance observation cannot produce with confidence is insight concerning enemy intentions and plans — unless a reconnaissance unit captures knowledgeable prisoners or enemy documents and maps (see *Intelligence, Military*).

The instruments of reconnaissance have changed, even if its purposes have not. Stealth and established observation posts (usually on hills) favored the foot observer; coverage of wide areas and the rapid delivery of information required mounted scouts or "rangers." Skilled armies combined both types of reconnaissance units, but by the nineteenth century, light cavalry, accompanied by staff officers, performed the core reconnaissance functions. The maritime equivalent of light cavalry was the patrol boat and light, or "scout," cruiser, built for range and speed, not fighting ability.

The revolution in transportation and communications technology in the twentieth century expanded the capabilities of reconnaissance forces in geographic coverage, the recording of information, and the transmission of data to intelligence staffs. Army reconnaissance units by the time of World War II (q.v.) could be deployed in motorcycles, scout cars, and light armored fighting vehicles; light aircraft put observers above and beyond the battlefield. Radios allowed observers to report data without returning to command centers. Aerial photography made its debut in World War I (q.v.); Allied and German photoreconnaissance aircraft produced overhead and oblique aerial photographs of ever-increasing resolution, and photo interpretation entered the repertoires of intelligence staffs. Electronic reconnaissance became possible, first by producing sound-gathering devices that provided range and direction information about enemy artillery, and then by recording the direction

Developed in World War I, aerial photography became a major form of reconnaissance and damage assessment. RAF photoreconnaissance aircraft spotted German landing craft massed on the English Channel in 1940. Their subsequent destruction by RAF bombers contributed to the cancellation of Operation Sealion, Germany's plan to invade Great Britain.

and content of enemy radio communications. In the 1990s, whole families of satellites can take and transmit photographs, record electronic transmissions, and map the world with infrared sensings or the digitized reconstruction of elevations and depressions. The vast menu of technical means of data collection has almost swamped the ability of military staffs to analyze information, which, in turn, places an ever-increasing demand upon computerized data storage and analysis. In the field, reconnaissance elements have the advantage of night-vision devices, sensors, and satellite-linked radios that can be integrated with maps and electronic methods of determining one's position anywhere on earth in terms of latitude and longitude. Such instrumentation has been common aboard aircraft and ships since World War II.

The range, accuracy, and timeliness of reconnaissance information has reshaped concepts of operations for air, naval, and land warfare. Ground commanders employ the concept of "reconnaissance pull" (attributed to the German army of World War II),

in which highly mobile mechanized forces rush to exploit reconnaissance reports of enemy weakness. Such forces may enjoy overwhelming artillery support from guns and rocket launchers, linked to fire-support teams deployed with reconnaissance units. Airborne reconnaissance aircraft (light or heavy) can summon up fighter-attack aircraft or armed helicopters to destroy targets of opportunity. The destructive power of submarines, another twentieth-century innovation in gathering information, is so great that a submarine can not only attack enemy ships with torpedoes, but also strike land targets with cruise and ballistic missiles (q.v.). At the same time, all modern armed forces stress the destruction of an enemy's reconnaissance assets, including aircraft, satellites, and underwater sensor systems.

Reconnaissance units have traditionally considered themselves a military elite. European light cavalry regiments claimed special freedoms, usually relief from standard discipline and drills, and this elitism did not disappear with horses. Mechanized cavalry regiments, airborne reconnaissance units, special boat and swimmer units, and helicopter-borne scouts have laid claims to special training, discriminating personnel selection, and a richness in equipment and weapons that often stirs resentment within their armies and navies. Reconnaissance experts believe that they are unusually skilled and physically gifted — as they often are. The danger to a commander comes when his reconnaissance units substitute bravura for substance, a peril all armed forces have faced in the history of warfare.

ALLAN R. MILLETT

Tony Devereux, *Messenger Gods of Battle: Radio, Radar, Sonar: The Story of Electronics in War* (1991); Clark G. Reynolds, *Command of the Sea: The History and Strategy of Maritime Empires* (1974).

Reconquest of Spain

711–1492

The Reconquest, a term that refers to the centuries-long process whereby the Spanish Christians reconquered territories under Muslim domination, decisively influenced the history of Spain. In 711 the Muslims defeated the Visigoths at the Guadalete River, subsequently establishing their domination over virtually all of Spain, calling the acquired lands al-Andalus. It was only in 1492 — the year that Columbus reached the New World — that the Christians completed the Reconquest by taking Muslim Granada.

The process of the Reconquest as a whole is of conceptual significance. It defined the character of the Middle Ages in Spain, which differed from that prevailing elsewhere in western Europe. Forced to give precedence to war rather than letters for the better part of a millennium, the Spaniards were the military champions of the Christian faith. Spain became a society organized for war, with a greater percentage of its population positioned as nobles, knights, and warriors, as well as its own crusading ideals and military orders (q.v.). Yet at the same time the Moorish-flavored cultural legacy of the military Reconquest became evident in terms of architecture (for example, the cathedral-mosque of Córdoba and the "minaret" Christian churches of Aragón), irrigation (the *huerta* region of Valencia), and even to some extent in language, music, and literature.

The degree of acculturation depended on the chronology of the Reconquest. Moorish influence was less important in the north, which was insecurely held by the Muslims. The Christians soon reconquered a "no-man's land" down to the Duero River, and by the late eleventh century they had advanced to the Tagus (Toledo fell in 1085). Subsequently, after the Battle of Las Navas de Tolosa (1212) (q.v.), the way lay open for the reconquest of the rest of al-Andalus (Andalusia), a task mostly accomplished within the next fifty years: Córdoba was taken in 1236, Valencia in 1238, Murcia in 1243, Seville in 1248, and Cádiz in 1265, leaving only the Muslim kingdom of Granada.

The final phase of the Reconquest began with the capture of Alhama in February 1482. The Granadans were at a disadvantage because of discord within their royal family; Boabdil, who was proclaimed king in 1482 and was defeated and captured in April 1483, pledged fealty to the Catholic kings. By the spring of 1491 the Castilians completely surrounded the city of Granada, building the military base of Santa Fe within sight of its walls. The terms of a capitulation were agreed upon on November 25, and on January 2, 1492, Granada was occupied and the cross and the royal banner of Castile were raised over the Alhambra.

These successes were facilitated by new weaponry. There is evidence that the Muslims of Granada had used gunpowder artillery as early as 1331, as did the Christians before long. But during the final campaigns against Granada, its use and importance became particularly evident, above all in breaching the walls of castles and fortified towns. Without artillery, the final campaigns could not have been won within ten years.

ANGUS MACKAY

Recruiting/Conscription

Complex societies throughout the world have developed two patterns in the recruitment of armed forces. One is based on volunteers or mercenaries, usually limited in size and usually set apart from the societies they serve. The second approach links military service with citizenship, requiring in principle some combination of full-time duty and reserve service from every full-fledged member of the community.

In the West, the Greek city-states and the Roman republic began by depending on mobilized civilians. In Athens, for example, those who could afford the equipment served as hoplites (q.v.). Poorer men did duty as light infantry or as rowers in the galleys. These and similar systems broke down in the face of frequent or protracted wars. Not only did casualties mount; economic and social order suffered because too many key people served too long in the field. Warfare, moreover, grew increasingly complex. Part-time soldiers proved less and less a match for men who adopted military service as a career. The Macedonian army of Alexander the Great (q.v.) and the mercenary forces of China's Han dynasty (see *Han Wu-ti*) are familiar examples of the professionalization of warfare in the ancient world.

In medieval Europe, feudalism (q.v.) based land tenure on military service. These armies based on reciprocal obligation were more effective than is generally recognized. Nevertheless, as early as the twelfth century they were giving way to bands of paid fighters, as the growing complexity of weapons and tactics once more favored those willing to make their mastery a lifetime craft: the longbowmen of England, the light cavalry of Spain, the pikemen of Switzerland. The Ottoman Empire (q.v.) depended increasingly on its professional infantry, the janissaries, as opposed to the landholding *timars*.

Military enterprisers systematized this professionalization in Europe by agreeing with governments to raise certain numbers of men in return for specified compensation. It was these contract armies that dominated Europe's Thirty Years' War (q.v.). They

This marine recruiting poster of the 1920s evokes the excitement of encountering and mastering danger in exotic locales.

also demonstrated three problems common to the system everywhere: unreliable commanders, underdisciplined troops, and unexpectedly high costs of disbanding armies and then reraising them in a year or two. By the middle of the seventeenth century, the optimal military model from Mughal India (q.v.) to Louis XIV's (q.v.) France had become permanent armies maintained by central governments and recruited on a voluntary basis — usually with compulsion as an emergency backup.

Men brought into the ranks by this process became masters of a spectrum of skills increasingly foreign to the rest of the population; they were correspondingly difficult and expensive to replace. Under Gustavus II Adolphus (q.v.), Sweden introduced a system in which groups of farms provided and financed a soldier from their own resources. In the eighteenth century, Prussia adopted a "cantonal" organization for recruiting peasants. In the aftermath of the Seven Years' War (q.v.), the states of Europe sought ways of compelling their subjects to maintain their increasingly large armies. The Wars of the French Revolution (q.v.) emphasized voluntary enlistment as a symbol of patriotism (q.v.), but France rapidly resorted to a system of conscription systematic enough to bleed France white by 1814.

After the Congress of Vienna (q.v.), Europe's armies remained substantially larger than they had been in 1789 — too large to be sustained entirely by volunteers. At the same time armies preferred long-service soldiers as more politically reliable and more technically competent. A common compromise was a system of selective service with terms so long that lower-class conscripts often reenlisted for lack of career alternatives. Prussia (q.v.), with its smaller population, sustained the principle of short service based on universal conscription but was unable to implement it until the reforms of the 1860s.

Conscription was not always popular. During the American Civil War (q.v.), the North was shaken by major antidraft riots. Resistance to conscription in the Confederacy led to the virtual secession of some Southern counties. Nevertheless, in 1866 and 1870, Prussian draftees made such short work of their opponents that every European power of the Continent eventually introduced a similar system. Japan quickly followed suit. One major consequence was a growing emphasis on enthusiasm as a substitute for skill. The limitations of this choice became apparent during World War I (q.v.); its catastrophic casualties reflected the relatively low quality of the soldiers as well as their commanders. It should be noted, however, that Britain, which did not introduce conscription until 1916, faced similar problems with its volunteers.

After 1918 mechanization led theorists such as Charles de Gaulle (q.v.) to favor professional forces based on state-of-the-art technology. Experience showed the validity of the concept. While World War II (q.v.) was waged by conscript armies, in practice most of them had two layers: elite assault and mechanized divisions, and "straight-leg" infantry who did the dirty work.

Since 1945 the complexity of military technology and the prevalence of low-intensity warfare have increasingly favored professional soldiers. The United States through most of the Cold War (q.v.) operated a selective service system in which whether one actually donned a uniform depended heavily on such factors as educational, occupational, and marital status. This system broke down during the Vietnam War (q.v.), ostensibly because of its perceived unfairness, but also because of its failure to provide the kind of armed forces needed in an environment of limited wars. The European states that maintain conscription do so as much for political as military reasons. Even the Soviet Union before its collapse was seriously considering establishing professional armed forces with conscription as a supplement. It remains to be seen whether increased operational efficiency will be purchased at the price of the political reliability traditionally and legitimately associated with citizen armies.

DENNIS E. SHOWALTER

John Gooch, *Armies in Europe* (1980).

Red Army

Vladimir Lenin's government founded the Workers and Peasants Red Army (RKKA) in January 1918. Initially composed of Red Guards and revolutionary soldiers and organized on the militia principle, the RKKA became a conscript force in 1919 and grew to 5.5 million men by the end of the Russian Civil War (q.v.) in 1921. Although it was supposed to be authentically proletarian, the Red Army relied heavily upon expertise and traditions derived from the ancien régime. Possibly as many as 75,000 former tsarist officers entered its service from 1918 to 1921, either voluntarily or under compulsion. Nonetheless, the Red Army suffered throughout the war from chronic logistical shortages and mass desertion.

In January 1919, I. I. Vatsetis, the RKKA's first commander in chief, wrote to Lenin denouncing the vile sanitary condition of the "filthy and undressed" army. Later that summer Leon Trotsky would still be describing the Red Army as "barefoot, naked, hungry, and lice-ridden." A major reason for these conditions was the Bolshevik decentralization of the war economy, which made individual Soviet fronts responsible for acquiring their uniforms and growing much of their food.

Military service was unpopular in the villages that supplied the majority of the recruits. Draft evasion was common; the desertion rate mind-boggling. In 1919 alone, for example, the Red Army rounded up 1.7 million AWOL soldiers. As a result, the Red Army constantly experienced difficulty in bringing force to bear on the battlefield, despite its enormous paper strength. It has been estimated that no more than 11 percent of the Red Army was ever at the front, and less

than 3 percent ever saw action. In 1920, for instance, the Bolsheviks were able to mobilize only forty thousand men for their unsuccessful Polish campaign.

Yet the Red Army prevailed against the Whites notwithstanding. After the civil war ended, the RKKA played an indispensable part in suppressing anti-Communist peasant rebellions in Tambov, Penza, and Siberia. It was also instrumental in Moscow's re-annexation of vast territories in Central Asia and Transcaucasia.

The 1920s were a decade of contraction for the Red Army. The imperative need to reduce the defense burden caused the RKKA to decline to 516,000 men by 1923. At the same time the state emended the conscription statute: the majority of eligible males in any given age cohort were now drafted into the territorial militia, which was called out for active duty only in the summer months. The most important function of the Red Army in the period appears to have been the indoctrination of peasant recruits. A secret report of 1929 spoke of the expanding role of the RKKA as "a political-economic school."

At the end of the 1920s, the Soviet state decreed the collectivization of agriculture and adopted the first Five-Year Plan to accelerate the industrialization of the country. The RKKA was a prime beneficiary of the latter program: by 1932, the Soviet Union was manufacturing more armaments than any other state in Europe; by 1940 weapons would constitute 22 percent of total industrial output. Building up a domestic tank industry from scratch, the Soviet Union had produced a park of five thousand vehicles by 1932. Similar improvements in artillery and military aviation were achieved.

Further reforms in the recruiting statute deemphasized the territorial system and increased the Red Army in numbers. By early 1938, the RKKA had 1.5 million men in its ranks.

Progress was, however, checked in 1937. In June of that year, Marshal M. N. Tukhachevskii (q.v.) and seven other distinguished soldiers were tried and executed on false charges of treason. A full-blown purge of the Soviet officer corps ensued, resulting in the expulsion of thirty-five to forty thousand officers by 1940. The Soviet secret police (NKVD) imprisoned or shot many of those dismissed. Although the precise rationale behind the purge is still obscure, its undeniable effect was to cripple the Red Army.

Poor performance in the winter war against Finland (1939–1940) and the catastrophic losses suffered in the early phases of Germany's 1941 invasion of the

Soviet Union (see *Operation Barbarossa*) testified to the disorganization and demoralization of the Red Army. Nonetheless, it made an astonishing recovery and inflicted severe defeats on the Wehrmacht at Stalingrad (1942), at Kursk (1943), and in Belorussia (1944). Berlin fell to Soviet forces in May 1945. In 1946, the name Workers and Peasants Red Army was abolished and replaced by the Soviet Army as part of Stalin's reconstruction of the defense establishment after World War II (q.v.). This change in name implied a retreat from the proletarian and revolutionary traditions that, at least in theory, had animated the army since its creation in 1918.

WILLIAM C. FULLER, JR.

Francesco Benvenuti, *The Bolsheviks and the Red Army, 1918–1922* (1989); John Erickson, *The Soviet High Command: A Military-Political History* (1962); Mark von Hagen, *Soldiers in the Proletarian Dictatorship: The Red Army and the Soviet Socialist State, 1917–1930* (1990).

U.S. infantrymen march to the battle front in Korea in 1950, as South Korean refugees flee from it, taking the little they can carry.

Refugees

Refugees are a horrific fixture of war: frightened, bedraggled columns of civilians, disproportionately women, children, and the elderly, fleeing war as best they can, burdened with a few salvaged belongings. Though we think of such unfortunates as a modern phenomenon, they are in fact an ancient consequence of war. In all premodern societies, peasants responded instinctively to war, burying cash and grain in caches (farmers and road builders still regularly turn up forgotten coin hoards) and fleeing for the woods and hills with their animals. When the threatening army passed, the peasants returned to reclaim their lands, rebuild their torched barns and cottages — and take their revenge on straggling soldiers.

On the other hand, townspeople, with their concentrated, relatively immovable wealth, could not so easily escape: they built walls instead. But when those walls failed, sack or surrender could foreshadow expulsion and a grim time of wandering. The legendary Aeneas, who fled Troy's ashes to found Rome, testifies to the prehistory of the refugee. Besides such myths, antiquity gives documented historical examples. During the Peloponnesian War (431–404 B.C.) (q.v.), the desperate citizens of Potidaea negotiated a surrender to their Athenian besiegers, who allowed them their lives, the right to flee, a small sum of money, and one garment apiece — two for women. Such dispersals marked warfare down to modern times. Yet even in antiquity, refugee crises could threaten more than the refugees themselves: the Visigoths, the first of the German tribes to inundate Rome in the fourth century A.D., first entered the empire as refugees.

With the Industrial Revolution and the resulting leaps in urbanism, total population, and population density, the problem of civilians fleeing war exploded. Nineteenth- and especially twentieth-century wars proved to be mass events, with armies of millions fighting near-continuous battles along whole frontiers. Modern war both caught more innocents in its net and was much more difficult for civilians to avoid; roads and railways necessarily became rivers of refugees, who often had to flee enormous distances across borders and even over oceans. Simultaneously, the stakes and impersonality of modern war erased old reluctances to target civilians as combatants; therefore the Allied air war in World War II (q.v.) included a deliberate "dehousing" bombing campaign aimed at German cities — purposely making refugees of any survivors. Such revolutionary changes in the scale and nature of conflict created unprecedented massive refugee movements. As late as 1926 Europe still struggled with 9.5 million refugees created by World War I (q.v.) and the Russian Civil War (q.v.). In Europe alone, World War II produced an estimated thirty million refugees; into the 1950s there were still tens of millions of officially registered "displaced persons." Outside Europe, over two million Chinese fled to Hong Kong and Taiwan at the close of the Chinese Civil War (q.v.) in 1949. Refugees became a central disruption caused by modern war — and a principal concern of international diplomacy.

To try to cope with the post–World War I crisis, the League of Nations created a high commissioner for refugees in 1921, an office continued after World War II under the league's successor, the United Nations. The position remains one of the most visible and important in world affairs. Despite such high-profile attention, refugee crises only mount in intensity and intransigency. Today, apparently permanent refugee "camps" (those of Palestinians in the Middle East, or Cambodians in Thailand, now generations old) defy the settling of certain conflicts; they are institutional obstacles to true peace. Almost every recent "small" war — Vietnam, Afghanistan, El Salvador, Somalia, Rwanda — has created a human flood numbering in the millions. As an overpopulated and bellicose Third World threatens self-destruction, and as an equally unstable post-Soviet world veers toward many-sided civil war, the world may only now be approaching its greatest refugee crisis. Unlike imperial Rome — or imperial China — the West has responded to refugee crises with aid and diplomacy, not walls: but a change of strategy may only be a matter of time and urgency.

THOMAS F. ARNOLD

Religion, French Wars of

1562–1598

This series of at least eight distinct wars constituted part of a greater phenomenon of religious conflicts in Europe, but like the other struggles labeled as religious wars, they concerned more than questions of faith alone. The Catholic-Protestant split certainly drove passions and formed contending parties, but major noble families also fought over the pattern of power within France and vied with the monarchy over local and central authority. The struggle often involved not two, but three rival French parties — Catholic, Protestant, and royal.

There was nothing godly about the conduct of the wars. Fighting began on March 1, 1562, when a detachment of Catholic troops attacked, butchered, and burned Protestants at Vassy. Atrocities afflicted both sides. On Saint Bartholomew's Day in 1572, King Charles IX acceded to a Catholic plot to murder all the Protestants who had come to Paris to celebrate the marriage of Henry of Navarre, who escaped death only by a hasty conversion to Catholicism. Later Henry III ordered the assassination of Catholic champion Henry of Guise and his brother in December 1588, only to die by an assassin's knife himself in July 1589. Henry of Navarre now became Henry IV, and to accommodate his Catholic subjects, he converted to Catholicism once more in 1593. With his subjects behind him, Henry eventually outlasted the Spanish who had entered the war on the Catholic side, in an effort to gain the French crown. The wars ended in 1598 with the Edict of Nantes, which granted toleration to the Protestants, and with the Treaty of Vervins with Spain.

JOHN A. LYNN

Reparations

Successful belligerents throughout history have tried to profit at the expense of their defeated opponents, whether through conquest, pillage, ransom, or tribute. In the modern era this instinct found an ally in international law, which holds that nations violating legal norms have an obligation to pay an indemnity to the injured party. The result is the modern concept of reparations.

Legally, reparations are settlements (remedies) due for injuries sustained by a breach of the laws of war (q.v.) and related conventions. Economically, they can represent a way for the victors to recoup costs from the vanquished or hinder rivals' postwar economic activity. Politically, they satisfy the desire to punish enemies or control their postwar behavior. Since the mid–nineteenth century, their use has varied greatly depending on the specifics of each case and contemporary views about the lessons of history.

Prussia obtained indemnities from France after its victory in 1871 (see *Franco-Prussian War*); China was forced to pay reparations to Western powers after the Boxer Rebellion (q.v.); Japan sought satisfaction from

Russia in 1905 (see *Russo-Japanese War*). The unprecedented scale of World War I (q.v.) created new problems, however, as each belligerent found itself unable to afford the cost of the war. Britain and France, growing poorer and more indebted to the United States, decided to transfer as much of the burden as possible to Germany.

The legal basis for reparations originated in the Fourteen Points, which were accepted by the Allies, subject to the understanding that U.S. president Woodrow Wilson's (q.v.) idea for "restoration" of invaded territories be understood to mean "compensation [from Germany] . . . for all damage done to the civilian population of the Allies and their property." Just what this meant in practice was hotly debated ever afterward among the French, British, Americans, and Germans. An initial total of thirty-three billion dollars was set in 1921 (thirty-six times the French payment fifty years before). German failure to live up to the settlement's provisions led to French occupation of the Ruhr in 1923. The terms were eased by the Dawes Plan of 1924, but problems returned with the Great Depression. The Young Plan of 1929 reworked the terms again, but the entire structure collapsed in the early 1930s.

The reparations question involved practically every important issue in interwar economics and politics, and from the Treaty of Versailles (q.v.) onward, people have debated who was responsible for mishandling it, and from what motives. Certainly the failure to resolve it satisfactorily undermined stability in Europe and contributed to the rise of the Nazis and the onset of World War II (q.v.).

Trying to learn from this experience, Allied planners during that later conflict decided that postwar reparations should not involve cash payments and should not unduly undermine German stability. The Soviet Union, however, itself ravaged by the war and having little interest in German reconstruction, soon began to exact levies ruthlessly from its occupation sector — actions that contributed to the onset of the Cold War (q.v.).

In the 1950s, in a new twist on the concept, a resurgent West Germany voluntarily gave Israel roughly one billion dollars as compensation for actions by the Nazis.

GIDEON ROSE

Bruce Kent, *The Spoils of War: The Politics, Economics, and Diplomacy of Reparations, 1918–1932* (1989).

Representation of War in Drama

Drama, from the Greek word for action, employs actors who represent human action by impersonating characters on a stage. Plays and drama are nearly synonymous, starting with Greek masterpieces such as Aeschylus's *Agamemnon*, and *Peace* and *Lysistrata* by Aristophanes. The greatest English medieval mystery play, *The Second Shepherd's Play* (1385?), a dramatization of stories from the Old Testament, includes brilliant warlike depictions of the Harrowing of Hell as well as the Last Judgment, the latter an apocalyptic battle. Christopher Marlowe's *Tamburlaine* (1587) depicts a fourteenth-century Scythian shepherd, Alexander the Great's (q.v.) successor, whose impulse for absolute power leads him to conquer most of the known world. In such dramas, the topic of war allows comment on just and unjust rulers, or the ability of the weak to triumph over the strong, thanks to God's intervention.

Many of the world's greatest plays concern war, cynically defined by the American satirist Ambrose Bierce as "a by-product of the arts of peace." William Shakespeare wrote *Henry V, Richard III*, and *King John*; his play *Othello* concerns a great soldier undone by jealousy. War is rarely far from King Lear's mind. In more recent times, one thinks of the soldier in Georg Büchner's *Woyzeck* (published in 1879, though written in 1837), and George Bernard Shaw's *Arms and the Man* (1894), about war profiteers; *Heartbreak House* (1919), which ends with a Channel bombardment; or *Saint Joan* (1923), in which war and religious faith combine in the figure of Joan of Arc (q.v.). Lillian Hellman's *Watch on the Rhine* (1941), although not in *Saint Joan*'s league, urges war on Nazi Germany, thus combining art with propaganda. Other twentieth-century plays that deal with war, war disillusionment, and the impact of war include *Journey's End* by R. C. Sheriff (1928), *What Price Glory?* by Maxwell Anderson and Lawrence Stallings (1924), *The Human Comedy* by William Saroyan (1942), and *All My Sons* by Arthur Miller (1947). Ts'au Yu's *Thunderstorm* (1933) is one of China's most-produced plays (also filmed in 1936, 1962, and 1984), combining ample melodrama with the depiction of an industrialist whose mind-set makes him part of the continuing tensions of the Chinese Civil War (q.v.). Japanese classical Noh plays, most examples of which were written before 1600, reflect martial themes and have been adapted by Japanese filmmaker Kurosawa Akira with great success, in particular *Rashomon* (1951) and *The Seven Samurai* (1954).

One of the most-produced of all twentieth-century plays is Bertolt Brecht's *Mother Courage and Her Children* (1938), set in Germany's Thirty Years' War (1618–1648) (q.v.), but actually describing political courage, in feminine form, in the time of Adolf Hitler (q.v.). Some war drama addresses history, such as the alleged complicity of Pope Pius XII in the killing of the Jews, the subject of Rolf Hochhuth's *The Deputy* (1963), a play that occasioned protests by Roman Catholics in most European cities. No single play attacking America's Vietnam War (q.v.) had comparable impact, perhaps because almost all the playwrights attracted to this subject were so obsessed with the presumptive immorality of the war that they ended up writing little more than tracts indicting American policy makers. One of the continuing problems with the dramatic representation of war in the twentieth century is the tendency to offer generic denunciations of war per se. It is difficult for political tracts to be artistic successes.

Dramatic representations of war are found in many operas, which combine music and stage drama. Ludwig van Beethoven's *Fidelio* (1805) is a rescue opera, portraying the liberation of those unjustly imprisoned by a cruel despot. Alban Berg's *Wozzeck* (1925) includes a soldier who comments on the pointlessness of the military. Paul Hindemith's *Mathis der Maler* (1938) describes the painter Matthias Grünewald during the time of the Peasants' Revolt, but also comments on Germany in the 1930s. Dmitri Shostakovich's *Lady Macbeth from Minsk* (1934) comments on war and Stalinist terror as well. Krysztof Penderecki's *Ubu Rex* (1991) attacks political oppression, as the guarantor of ruinous war. The revolutionary "model operas" pioneered during China's Cultural Revolution by Madame Mao Tse-tung (Chiang Ch'ing) often dealt with military themes; *Shachiapang* (1967), an opera about irregular resistance to Japan, was also presented as a film and as a symphony.

DAVID CULBERT

Representation of War in Film

The Sands of Iwo Jima (1949) starring John Wayne is a war movie; it is also a World War II (q.v.) combat film that incorporates footage taken by American combat photographers of the Battle of Iwo Jima (q.v.).

The Ten Best War Movies

Battleship Potemkin (Soviet Union, 1925) directed by Sergei Eisenstein

All Quiet on the Western Front (United States, 1930) directed by Lewis Milestone

The Grand Illusion (France, 1937) directed by Jean Renoir

Casablanca (United States, 1942) directed by Michael Curtiz

The Best Years of Our Lives (United States, 1946) directed by William Wyler

Twelve O'Clock High (United States, 1949) directed by Henry King

The Cruel Sea (Great Britain, 1952) directed by Charles Frend

Zulu (Great Britain, 1963) directed by Cy Enfield

Apocalypse Now (United States, 1979) directed by Francis Ford Coppola

Kagemusha (Japan, 1980) directed by Kurosawa Akira

It is both fiction — a feature film — and propaganda for the American way of life: countless Vietnam veterans consider John Wayne the best army recruiter in American history. Yet the representation of war in film spans a much broader subject area than that of Hollywood war films — the topic also encompasses newsreels, comedies, documentaries, training and instructional films, propaganda, photoreconnaissance, musicals, and television news film. Some war film footage has been seen only by one or two archivists; some film images are familiar enough to be called, in Dorothea Lange's term, "visual cookie cutters." All these types of war film share a goal: to make the viewer see the face of battle, to experience vicariously what actual battlefront fighting consists of. This goal is almost never realized, in part because film makes use of only two of the five senses — seeing and hearing.

This failure is explained in part by technological limitations: yesteryear's heavy cameras on tripods, the need for floodlights to illuminate night fighting, and governmental restrictions on those seeking to film the front — especially filmmakers attempting to show footage not deemed entirely beneficial to the war effort. Official censorship, self-censorship, and propaganda ("the manufacture of consent") affect virtually all efforts to record the actual face of battle.

Thus, until recently, most wars have taken place far

Since 1930, the "reality" of trench warfare has been defined by the film version of All Quiet on the Western Front. *In this scene, German troops rush back to their own lines following an attack. Curiously, there was little actual combat photography in World War I.*

from the camera. This fact did not stop unscrupulous filmmakers from producing newsreels to "record" the battle front; in one of the earliest war newsreels (1898), Vitagraph's *The Battle of Santiago Bay*, the fact that the camera did not record the destruction of Admiral Pascual Cervera's Atlantic squadron proved no deterrent for film pioneer Albert Smith, as quoted by Raymond Fielding:

> Street vendors in New York were selling large sturdy photographs of ships of the American and Spanish fleets. We bought a set of each and we cut out the battleships. On a table, topside down, we placed one of Blackton's large canvas-covered frames and filled it with water an inch deep. . . . To each of the ships, now sitting placidly in our shallow "bay" we attached a fine thread to enable us to pull the ships past the camera. . . . The press said that the picture was even better than the battle itself.

Trickery, including all manner of editing tricks, led one disgruntled observer to comment that "the motion picture camera in particular is a natural liar." The most-acclaimed documentaries ("the creative treatment of actuality") have never succeeded in truly revealing actual battlefield experience — not Britain's pioneering full-length *The Battle of the Somme* (1916), whose over-the-top sequence took place in a staging area back home; not John Huston's *San Pietro* (1945), which featured sections restaged for the camera or photographed in places other than the scene of battle; not the most significant news film to come out of the Vietnam War, the execution by General Nguyen Ngoc Loan of a Viet Cong sympathizer (January 31, 1968) in front of two three-man network television camera teams plus an Associated Press photographer, Eddie Adams, who won a Pulitzer Prize for what was purported to be the instant of death (it was not). Loan told me his wife "gave him hell" for not destroying the footage. More conventional treatments of the Vietnam battlefront awaited Hollywood's helping hand—for example, *Apocalypse Now* (1979) and *Rambo* (1985).

More often, showing close-ups of death and destruction has been left to fiction, or feature, films. Here the quest of every cameraman and special effects person is to replicate the experience of combat, particularly the simulation of death or terrible injury. The most popular World War I–era feature films about the war, such as *The Kaiser: The Beast of Berlin* (1918), stressed the brutality of the enemy. Credulous viewers enthused about a film showing the Devil, replete with horns and a tail, advising Wilhelm II on some course of action. But World War I also saw the release of Charlie Chaplin's *Shoulder Arms* (1918), still genuinely hilarious.

The most important contribution of feature film to popular ideas of battle is *All Quiet on the Western Front* (1930), based on Erich Maria Remarque's novel. Historians have recently emphasized that relying on shots taken *above* scenes of trench warfare has shaped an impression of World War I combat that is inadequate and illusionary. If ironic, it is nevertheless true that the sincere Hollywood adaptation of this antiwar novel is the single most influential source of visual impressions about the reality of trench warfare—using trenches dug near Los Angeles, not Verdun.

Film is also a marvelous medium for revealing themes of war much broader than the instant of death on the battlefield. *The Best Years of Our Lives* (1946) portrays the experience of American veterans returning from war and coping with changes in their own families and American society as a whole. *The Grand Illusion* (1937) analyzes the meaning of war by focusing on French prisoners conversing with their cultured German commandant. *The Third Man* (1949) is Graham Greene's and Carol Reed's account of black market intrigue in post-1945 Vienna, a reminder of how often the Cold War (q.v.) has been used in film depictions of East-West tensions. Science fiction, depicting a different sort of war, has often dealt with themes such as the destruction of Earth by powers whose strength exceeds that of mortal humans. *The Invasion of the Body Snatchers* (1956), with its subtext relating to Senator Joseph McCarthy's witchhunts, shows the minds of people in one small American town taken over by an ideological foe, though physical exteriors remain unchanged. *The Day the Earth Stood Still* (1951) uses a polite alien, Rennie, to deliver an antinuclear warning.

Today war is covered visually by cable and satellite television. The recent Gulf War (q.v.), for example, represents the first time in history that a reporter (Peter Arnett) broadcast live from an enemy capital (Baghdad) while an air raid was in progress. On February 13, 1991, two "smart" bombs hit what surely was a bomb shelter in Al-Amariya. The American government found itself trying to provide spin control ("bunker," not "shelter") for battle footage provided by an enemy government, as interpreted live by CNN's Arnett. As a German photographer told Arnett that day, "We've just seen history."

The technological developments in television's ability to gather and transmit visual images in the 1990s assure unprecedented speed in viewing war, accompanied by no equivalent breakthrough either in assessing the validity of those images or in truly capturing the face of battle. Soldiers on frontline duty remain the experts on the experience of battle, and, occasionally, their experiences are successfully evoked in fictional film.

DAVID CULBERT

Raymond Fielding, *The American Newsreel, 1911–1967* (1972); Peter Maslowski, *Armed with Cameras: The American Military Photographers of World War II* (1993); Frank J. Wetta and Stephen J. Curley, *Celluloid Wars: A Guide to Film and the American Experience of War* (1992).

Representation of War in Western Music

The spectacle and political importance of war have made it a popular subject of music for the purposes of simple entertainment or the expression of deep sentiments. Long before recorded history, past combat has been celebrated or lamented in song. In such works, the verisimilitude of the narrative was probably on occasion reinforced by the inclusion of war cries, war songs, and onomatopoeia representing the noises of fighting. In the last case, vocal effects may have been supplemented by instruments and even the clatter of actual weapons.

European battle music as a written genre seems to have originated in Italy in the fifteenth century. The most famous example of Renaissance battle music was *La Bataille de Marignan* by Clément Janequin (1485?–1558), a four-part vocal piece published in

1528 that contained evocative imitations of trumpet fanfares and drum patter. It commemorated the ferocious engagement between the Imperial and French armies at Marignano near Milan in 1515 (see *Italian Wars*), at which the composer may have been present.

Heinrich Ignaz Franz von Biber (1644–1704) wrote in 1673 what is probably the most interesting battle piece of the baroque era. Entitled *Battalia*, this work described a generic battle by using a number of unusual techniques, such as dissonance worthy of a twentieth-century composer, to represent the rough singing of soldiers; paper was placed over the strings of the bass to produce sounds that approximated those of a military snare drum; highly chromatic antiphonal writing evoked the cries of the wounded.

In the eighteenth century, the Sinfonie *(La Bataille)* of Franz Christoph Neubauer (1760–1795), a precursor of the tone poems of the nineteenth century, exploited rich orchestration to re-create sonically the victory of a Russo-Austrian army over the Turks in July 1789 in Romania at Fokshani. Neubauer was outdone, however, by Ludwig van Beethoven (1770–1827), whose *Wellington's Victory* (see *Wellington, Duke of*), which celebrated the British defeat of the French in Spain at the Battle of Vitoria (June 1813), required muskets and cannon as well as a large orchestra. The use of ordnance was exploited even more effectively by Peter Tchaikovsky (1840–1893) in his *Year of 1812 Overture*, which recalled the destruction caused by Napoleon's (q.v.) invasion of Russia.

In the twentieth century, the musical battle piece was displaced by cinema as a means of providing entertaining battle commemoration. Serge Prokoviev (1891–1953), however, produced a vivid sound depiction of the Russian defeat of the Teutonic knights at the Battle of Lake Peipus (1242) in his film score to Sergei Eisenstein's *Alexander Nevsky* (1938), the materials of which became "The Battle on the Ice" movement in a cantata of the same name (1939). In the first movement of his Seventh *(Leningrad)* Symphony (1941), Dmitri Shostakovich's (1906–1975) musical portrayal of the German invasion of the Soviet Union is obvious, his disclaimer not to have written battle music notwithstanding. In his Eighth Symphony (1943), Shostakovich attempted to re-create the internal or psychological, as opposed to the external or physical, nature of the monstrous clash on the Eastern Front. Because the two symphonies were written while the conflict being depicted was in progress, by a composer who was a citizen of one of the hostile

powers, they were not remembrances but impressions of the event as it was being experienced, and perhaps in this regard, unique. And finally, the orchestral music written by Richard Rodgers and orchestrated by Robert Russell Bennett to accompany the American television series *Victory at Sea* (1952) replicates sonically many aspects of the fighting in World War II (q.v.); its length of thirteen hours probably makes it one of the longest orchestral compositions of all time.

JON SUMIDA

Representation of War in Western Art

What does war look like? The answer, as an artist confronts a square of canvas or a block of stone, is by no means obvious. A typical battle spreads over miles of countryside and unfolds over hours or even days. Capturing the psychological and historical essence of such an encounter with strokes of paint is a daunting task. With such issues in mind, the representation of war in art can be reduced to a single — but hardly simple — artistic problem: how does an artist condense the myriad events and emotions of war to a coherent visual image? In fact, artists responding to the challenge of representing war have produced some of the world's most important objects of art. What follows is a brief analysis of six notable works addressing a timeless subject: the famous battle. This survey gives an inkling of how inspired artists have manipulated shapes, colors, and composition to create distinctive and moving visions of war.

One way for an artist to convey both the personal drama and the larger historical significance of a given battle is to focus on a selected, heroic moment as emblematic of the battle as a whole. This is an ancient convention, as old as Greece. Unfortunately, little more than literary descriptions survive of Greco-Roman battle painting. There is one exception, from Pompeii: a huge Roman floor mosaic, a copy of an earlier Greek painting showing Alexander the Great's (q.v.) victory over the Persian king Darius at the Battle of Issus (333 B.C.) (see p. 12). Though damaged, it remains a breathtaking work. The original artist carefully and accurately recorded the Greek and Persian military kit as well as the expressions of men and animals. But beyond its exemplary detail, the artist's composition brilliantly reveals that this is the decisive moment, the crisis of the confrontation. Both

Companies of expensively equipped and mounted men-at-arms were the prestige units of Renaissance Italian warfare. They were organized and directed in battle by professional mercenary captains, the condottieri, and were hired by Renaissance city-states. Here, at the Battle of San Romano in 1432, the men-at-arms of the Florentine Republic (left) are about to rout the forces of their rival Tuscan city, Siena.

Paolo Uccello, The Battle of San Romano, *Uffizi, Florence, Italy*

Lady Butler made the charge of the Scots Greys at Waterloo a timeless vision of British valor. Never mind that the actual charge went too far and the Scots Greys themselves were almost annihilated: the Victorian public preferred the portrayal of war to be both heroic and poignant. As a French general said of another British cavalry charge, that of the Light Brigade at Balaclava in the Crimean War: "It is magnificent, but it is not war."

Lady Butler, Scotland for Ever!, *Leeds City Art Galleries, Leeds, England*

The static trench lines of the Western Front in World War I made it a siege writ large. While the men dug in to protect themselves, massed artillery batteries expended countless rounds in a spendthrift effort to root them out. Shellfire smashed the countryside, returning regions like Flanders to their ancient swampy form — seen here in Nash's evocation of the Passchendaele sector in 1917.

Paul Nash, The Menin Road, *Imperial War Museum, London, England*

Ten Famous Representations of Military History in Western Art

Alexander at the Battle of Issus (mosaic, Pompeii, first century B.C.)

The Bayeux Tapestry (embroidery, 1080s?)

The Battle of San Romano (3 of 4 panels are extant; those displayed in London and Florence, 1435?; in Paris, 1440?) by Paolo Uccello

Equestrian Portrait of Gattamelata (1445–1453) by Donatello

Charles V at Mühlberg (1548) by Titian

The Surrender of Breda (1634–1635) by Diego Velázquez

Ferdinand of Austria at the Battle of Nördlingen (1635) by Peter Paul Rubens

Napoleon Crossing the Alps (1805) by Jacques Louis David

The Execution of the Rebels on May 3, 1808 (1814) by Francisco Goya

Guernica (1937) by Pablo Picasso

Theodore Rabb

flee. Both the chaos of battle (the litter of shivered lances, discarded shields, dying men and horses) and the even fortune of the infantry encounter (note the raised crossbows in the near background) are routed with the single well-directed lance at the center of the piece, the sole strong horizontal line in the entire painting.

Uccello's painting can be compared with the Spanish artist Diego Velázquez's masterpiece *The Surrender of Breda*, painted to commemorate the 1625 capitulation of the Dutch city of Breda after an epic siege of almost ten months (see p. 143). Here the heroic moment is again at the center of the composition, but it is not an act of violence. Instead it is a magnanimous gesture by the victorious Spanish general, Ambrogio Spinola, graciously accepting the keys to the city while placing his hand on the shoulder of his defeated Dutch adversary. Breda itself, gently smoldering, is in the background. The circumstances are nonetheless crystal clear: to the left of the Dutch commander's head is a drooped, defeated Dutch tricolor; between him and Spinola, in the exact center of the painting, is an erect and victorious Spanish flag, white with a red St. Andrew's cross. The two sides of the painting reinforce the point and plainly contrast the two armies. On the left are the defeated Dutch, their faces slack or with averted eyes, their weapons negligently sloped. On the right rises a forest of victorious Spanish pikes. These pikes are so visually strong and so charged with symbolic meaning that the painting is known in Spain as *Las Lanzas*, "the lances." Though similar in appearance, these pikes' message (victory, not defeat) is very different from the upright lances in the upper right corner of the Uffizi's *The Battle of San Romano*. Velázquez's pikes can also be compared with those in the Alexander mosaic (note that it is impossible that either Uccello or Velázquez knew of the mosaic — it was buried between A.D. 79 and 1831).

Representing battle as a heroic encounter had lost none of its effectiveness by the Victorian era. Lady Butler's 1881 canvas *Scotland for Ever!* (see p. 391), to the prejudiced twentieth-century eye an embodiment of nineteenth-century sentimental nonsense, was actually inspired by the artist's indignation at the "unwholesome productions" of the avant-garde. It is perhaps the most popularly successful battle painting ever, endlessly reproduced on shortbread tins, tea towels, and the like. The subject is the charge of the Scots Greys at the Battle of Waterloo (1815). A viewer facing the enormous canvas (8.5 by 16 feet) stands

generals are present, their isolated heads elevated above the fray: Alexander, on horseback in the left center, boldly moves forward, his spear transfixing a Persian in his way; and Darius, in the right center, twists around in his chariot, clearly about to flee (his driver whips the horses on) but with one weak, weaponless hand vainly stretched back toward Alexander, as if to wave the conqueror away. We have further evidence that the tide has turned. In the background are the advancing pikes of Alexander's enclosing phalanx men — the Persian king has been caught between these infantry and the cavalry with Alexander at their head.

Centuries later, in the Italian Renaissance, Paolo Uccello similarly reduced the whole of a battle to certain heroic moments in a series of three paintings illustrating the Battle of San Romano (1435?) (see p. 391) between the cities of Florence and Siena. The center of the three panels (now in the Uffizi, Florence) depicts the Sienese commander struck from his horse by a well-couched lance. Uccello makes this incident a turning point, as the Florentine knights on the left of the panel (their lances canted forward, trumpets raised to proclaim the charge) prepare to sweep away the opposing Sienese men-at-arms to the right of the panel, their lances upright and irresolutely crossed, their backs and kicking mounts obviously turned to directly in the path of the impetuous gray chargers, their violent fury mirrored in the rolling gray clouds above. The troopers' faces, equally strained, are a catalogue of men's emotions in battle. The fact that the enemy are nowhere to be seen — they can only be imagined in front of, beneath, and trampled over — only adds to the power of the piece. Here the triumph is absolute, and the patriotism total: this is a victory as complete as both the Issus and San Romano.

What in England was widely acceptable as a representation of battle in 1881 was less so by the end of World War I (q.v.). The artist Paul Nash, a veteran of the 1917 fighting in Flanders, painted from personal experience. His 1919 painting *The Menin Road* (see p. 391) reveals a shattered countryside, a morass of flooded craters, shell-stripped tree trunks, mud, and assorted debris. Battle no longer seems capable of supporting the heroism implied in every brush stroke of *Scotland for Ever!* — unless survival on the Menin Road is heroic enough, making an Achilles and Ajax of the two scuttling figures at the center. Decision is even more absent than heroism. This battlefield is eternal, without context (and potentially without victory or defeat, winners or losers). It is shaped by immense and distant forces, artillery more than individual human feats of arms — the contrast between this landscape and the earlier paintings seems total. But connections remain. The smashed, limbless trees of *The Menin Road* echo the crooked stump in the Alexander mosaic, and their strong vertical forms, here conveying disaster and destruction, can be compared with the pikes and lances in *The Surrender of Breda* and *The Battle of San Romano*. And the battlefield litter in *The Menin Road* (corrugated iron, twists of wire, a half-submerged box) suggests chaos and waste in the same way as do the broken weapons in the foreground of *The Battle of San Romano* and the Alexander mosaic. Even *The Menin Road*'s dark mood, so redolent of twentieth-century disillusion, is no novelty: compare it with the exhaustion indicated in *The Surrender of Breda*.

A final work, Pablo Picasso's celebrated *Guernica* mural (see p. 437), unambiguously rejects the conventional heroic battle painting. An indictment of the 1937 Nationalist carpet-bombing of the Basque town of Guernica during the Spanish civil war (q.v.), there is no historical reference to the actual event: no planes, no bombs, no explosions. Instead, a tortured horse screams with a stabbing tongue. This anguished animal, like the frightened, excited horses in the Alexan-

der mosaic, *The Battle of San Romano*, and *Scotland for Ever!*, informs us that war is bestial and wild, but here the litter of war has swallowed the event entirely. Chaos, always a part of war, has completely vanquished heroism. What remain are shattered fragments: a wailing Madonna with lifeless child, a sacrificial bull, a broken sword. This rage reflects the circumstances of the painting's creation. It was an overtly political work, painted for the Spanish pavilion at the 1937 Paris World's Fair, and Picasso was a stalwart believer in the beleaguered Republican cause. *Guernica* therefore commemorates threatening political defeat as much as a specific atrocity, the brutal bombing of a provincial town.

There is a temptation to pronounce paintings like *Guernica* and *The Menin Road* — even *The Surrender of Breda* — as more realistic, more honest than *The Battle of San Romano*, the Alexander mosaic, and certainly *Scotland for Ever!* War, we know, is horrible. Yet part of war's horror is its glory, and the willingness with which men (and women — Lady Butler is an example) embrace its passion, its risk, and its heroism. Such emotions are no less honest and real, however we may judge them otherwise. That artists have seized upon the glory as well as the horror of war (sometimes in the same work) underlines their humanity as well as their artistic ability to manipulate a viewer's emotions as well as shapes, colors, and composition.

THOMAS F. ARNOLD

John Hale, *Artists and Warfare in the Renaissance* (1991).

Representation of War in Western Literature

Love and war, Eros and Thanatos, are the two great literary subjects, and although war is always lamented, the wars go on. Bosnia, Rwanda, Ireland, Israel today — where tomorrow? "Having done what men could, they suffered as men must": the Greek historian Thucydides spoke for all soldiers in describing a defeated Athenian army dying as slaves in the quarries of Sicily. From "the ringing plains of windy Troy" of about 1250 B.C. to the frozen slaughter of Stalingrad (q.v.) and the steamy jungles of Vietnam (q.v.), writers have depicted war through characters who try to preserve their humanity in the face of a savage energy that threatens to turn them to beasts and clods. The portrait gallery of these heroes of war is long, and viewing it is to see war in its many forms, Eastern and Western, from the furious and endless Chinese dynastic battles of the latter fifteenth century in *The Three Kingdoms* (Lo Kuan-Chung, 1330–1400) and the Japanese *Fire on the Plains*, to the eighth-to-tenth-century Anglo-Saxon warrior in the epic *Beowulf* and the stories of the Arthurian knights of the Round Table.

Homer's *Iliad*, the West's first epic, is also the West's first war story. During the Trojan War (q.v.), Achilles' dilemma — a long life without honor, or a short one with it — states the soldier's unchanging tragic problem. Angry at an insult to his *areté* (status), he tries to withdraw from the war, only to be pulled back to avenge his friend Patroclus; transformed by blood lust into a wild animal rather than a warrior, Achilles drags the body of his noble enemy Hector around the city walls behind his war chariot. In the end, however, after returning Hector's body to his father, King Priam, for honorable burial and accepting the inevitability of his own death, he sorrows with King Priam over humanity's common fate in death.

Something of the Greek sense of the warrior's tragic life remains in the Roman hero Aeneas, created by Virgil in the first century B.C. to portray the virtues needed by Augustus and his all-conquering legions to secure the Roman imperium. Aeneas escapes from Troy, carrying his father on his back, even as he must always carry his civic responsibilities, abandoning Dido and exterminating the wild Turnus and Camilla in order to found Rome.

Virgil's hexameters invest the soldier's duty with sadness, but the medieval epics of the armored knight on horseback exult simply in splitting pagan Moors from the helm to the saddle. Chevalier Roland's (q.v.) psychological complexity is minimal, and his code of truth, courage, friendship, and faith to his liege lords, Charlemagne (q.v.) and God, is unexamined. The honor he gains by refusing to blow the trumpet calling for help is as bleak as the gray rocks of the pass through the Pyrenees at Roncevaux, where he and all his friends in Charlemagne's rear guard die.

The heroic tradition of the warrior always had its light side — the soldier who valued his skin more than honor. This shadow hero appeared in classical literature in the comic *miles gloriosus* (braggart soldier). In the 1590s, the view that it is better to be a live dog than a dead lion walked the London stage in the person of Sir John Falstaff, telling the fire-eating Hotspur and Prince Hal, in Shakespeare's *Henry IV*, how little he likes such "grinning honour" as the dead have on the battlefield. Gunpowder, cannon, entrenchments, and professional armies made anachronisms of knights like Hotspur and Cervantes' Don Quixote, their heads filled with the romance of chivalry. Soldiers impressed from the urban slums and country villages were understandably as cynical about war's loud drums, bright flags, and spirit-stirring fifes as Sancho Panza and, in our own time, the "good soldier" Schweik, Jaroslav Hašek's drunken, lying, malingering, scrounging Austrian infantryman in World War I.

War's official image remained as bright as ever, but as the novel developed, more was seen of the rough soldiers who staffed the professional armies of the eighteenth and nineteenth centuries. William Makepeace Thackeray's *Barry Lyndon* (1844) features an Irish swaggerer who takes the king's shilling to escape hanging and ends up fighting in the Prussian army in the Seven Years' War (q.v.). Tough enough to endure the Prussian corporals' savage caning and to dress ranks in the full face of the cannon, he tells with pride how he killed a French boy officer with a smash of his musket butt and then was cheered by the army for robbing the body of its money and a silver bonbon box. Leo Tolstoy was himself a soldier, and the jingling spur and the swish of the cavalry saber still sound in *Sevastopol* and *The Cossacks*. The sweat still soaks through the red coats and the dust swirls around the parade of the British army of mercenaries in Rudyard Kipling's stories of lands where "there ain't no ten commandments."

Along with glory and patriotism, any sense of control by generals as well as soldiers over war disappeared in the *guerre à outrance* that arrived with conscription and the total state under arms. War was now, as General William T. Sherman (q.v.) perceived it, "Hell," and the hero was the soldier who, as the brutal Nathan Bedford Forrest said, "got there fustest with the mostest." In Tolstoy's *War and Peace* (1872), Napoleon (q.v.) at Smolensk, thinking he is controlling the fight, dispatches battalions into a field made invisible by gunpowder smoke, but the wiser Russian marshal Mikhail Kutuzov (q.v.), having placed his troops, leaves the fight to his peasant soldiers and retires to pray. A staff error sending Alfred Tennyson's light brigade to charge up the narrow valley into the Russian guns during the Crimean War (q.v.) turns courage to folly. Romantic innocence has no place on these modern battlefields. Stendahl's Fabrizio (*Charterhouse of Parma*, 1839) never quite knows whether he was at Waterloo or not. In *War and Peace*, Prince Andrey's wound at Austerlitz (q.v.) reveals to him the total indifference of the universe to human life. Stephen Crane's "Youth" (*The Red Badge of Courage*, 1895) at Shiloh ceases to think and is controlled entirely by instinct.

The war of total annihilation appeared in its full horror in World War I. Novels like Henri Barbusse's *Under Fire* (1916), poetry like Wilfred Owen's — "children ardent for some desperate glory" — and Robert Graves's bitter renunciation, *Good-bye to All That* (1935), were only a few of the cries *in extremis* from the mud, machine guns, and barbed wire of the Western Front. In the end the world chose two novels, Erich Remarque's *All Quiet on the Western Front* (1928) and Ernest Hemingway's *A Farewell to Arms* (1925), to represent the slaughter of millions. Both novels were burned in the same bonfire by the Nazis in 1933. Both are grimly despairing. Remarque's hero's statement, "While they taught us that duty to one's country is the greatest thing, we already knew that death-throes are stronger," parallels the American lieutenant Frederic Henry's desertion from glory and patriotism for love, only to find when Catherine dies in childbirth that Death rules the world everywhere.

When, twenty years later, the world was convulsed by a second world war, once again writers tried to solve the Homeric riddle of a short life with honor or a long one without. But where now was honor? The *succès d'estime* of World War II novels is Evelyn Waugh's *Sword of Honour* trilogy (1952–1961) about Guy Crouchback, the descendant of a Catholic family with roots in the Crusades (q.v.). Surrounded by grotesque malice and proud ignorance, Crouchback, like Waugh, is an inept soldier, but he serves and keeps the faith.

The book that has come to represent World War II for most is, however, the immensely popular black comedy *Catch 22*, by Joseph Heller. On an airfield on Sardinia, from which the B-25s bomb Italy, war is revealed as a series of absurd tautologies. If you ask to be relieved of flying because of stress, the asking shows you are still sane: "Returned to duty." If you don't ask, you are obviously crazy but go on flying anyway. That is the master catch, number 22. But war is one catch after another. The fluids drained from one end of a wounded aviator completely encased in plaster are reversed and poured back into him at the other. When the squadron commander, Major Major (his name itself a meaningless circle), is in, he is out; when he is out, he is in. Nothing makes sense. Everything goes round and round, maiming and killing as it goes. Only the bombardier Yossarian breaks out of the mad circle to discover a breathing, suffering human being when he opens up the gunner's flak suit and the gunner's insides come gushing out. "Save the gunner," he goes about crying.

The literature of war may have ended about here. Vietnam seems not to have its novel. But even as it was reported more powerfully on TV than in print, it does have its films, such as *Apocalypse Now*, *The Deer Hunter*, and *Born on the Fourth of July*.

ALVIN KERNAN

Ernest Hemingway, *Men at War: The Best War Stories of All Time* (1942); Samuel Hynes, *A War Imagined: The First World War and English Culture* (1990); Andrew Rutherford, *The Literature of War: Studies in Heroic Virtue* (1989).

Resistance

Conquered peoples usually assimilate with their conquerors over many generations; sometimes conflicts occur in the earliest stages, provided that a leader can be found to stimulate them. Although Spartacus's slave revolt (73–71 B.C.) was a class uprising rather than a national one and can be discounted, Boudicca's rising against the Romans in newly conquered Britannia (A.D. 61) was a genuine act of armed resistance, albeit doomed to a horrible defeat. Hereward the Wake roused parts of eastern England against the Norman Conquest of 1066 but seems in the end to have compounded with the conquerors; his name became synonymous with obstinate refusal to obey authority. Obstinacy, like courage, is one of a resister's leading characteristics.

Napoleon (q.v.) found in Spain that he could not command the obedience of the native population any more than he could in Russia; guerrillas continued to plague the lines of communication of his armies in Iberia for years, just as Cossacks (q.v.) pestered the Grand Army as it retreated from Moscow. The Spaniards had the advantage of support from an outside power, Great Britain: such support is always a solid advantage for armed resisters — where else are their arms to come from?

Occupying troops always consider armed resisters to be simply bandits or terrorists, and indeed, the line between a genuine bandit and a genuine resister is sometimes hard to draw, particularly because resisters may need to rob banks or pillage shops to keep themselves in money, food, and clothing. One of the marks of an unsettled society is that one can live there on banditry alone.

National resistance movements, such as the eighty-year struggle of the Dutch against the Spaniards (1568–1648) (see *Dutch Revolt*), are common. Elements of one against Napoleon could be traced in Germany in about 1810–1813, in what German historical myth cherishes as a *Befreiungskrieg* (war of liberation); myth and reality are, however, some distance apart. Later, the Prussians certainly administered short shrift to French attempts to sabotage their communications during the siege of Paris in 1870–1871. During World War I (q.v.), there was little scope for resistance, though some for banditry, in eastern Europe; in the Levant a serious attempt was made by the British to raise Arabs against Turks. The irregular genius of T. E. Lawrence (q.v.) provided plentiful diversions on the left flank of the Turkish army opposing British commander Edmund Allenby (q.v.) in Palestine.

The political consequences of the Arab revolt and the conflicting promises made to Arabs and to Jews continue to plague the area to the present day; this is the world's longest-standing armed quarrel, some millennia old. The next-longest quarrel, between the English and the Irish, which dates back to 1169, is also still unresolved. The anti-English Irish can rely on so much sponsorship from the Irish population of the United States to fuel their resistance efforts that no short-term solution is ever likely to stick.

Anti-Nazi resistance in occupied Europe during World War II (q.v.) was as widespread as pro-Nazi collaboration and has attracted much more media and propaganda attention on the winning side. In some countries, resistance was spontaneous — the Poles are proud of having never produced a Quisling; in others, resistance was organized from outside, by secret services devoted to the task. In the Soviet Union, the secret police, then called the NKVD, maintained strict watch over partisan bands, supplying them (when reliable) with arms and orders and ensuring that they followed the Communist Party's directions in all respects. The British Special Operations Executive, not formed until July 1940, and the American Office of Strategic Services, formed in June 1942, were much less politically involved but were rather more efficient in providing arms by parachute (or occasionally by ship) and advice on how the arms were to be used to forward Allied strategy. None of these three secret services could have achieved much of value without ample support from the local populations in which they sought to work; inside Germany, therefore, very little could be achieved by any of them.

Outside Germany, some material impact could be exercised. The nine Norwegian parachutists who scuppered Adolf Hitler's (q.v.) attempt to make an atomic bomb (by sabotaging the heavy water factory at Rjukan west of Oslo in 1943) provide the strongest example; the two Czechoslovakian parachutists who mortally wounded Hitler's Reichskommissar Reinhard Heydrich (at a fearful price in reprisals) provides another. German generals had no more control over their rear areas in France in 1944 than Napoleon's marshals had had over theirs in Spain in 1812. Ferocious reprisals by Heinrich Himmler's SS did not stamp out resistance — they only made resisters more angry.

In Poland the Home Army, sustained over five years by the government in exile in London and lightly armed by RAF parachute drops, welcomed the Soviet army as it invaded eastern Poland in 1944; its members were more roughly handled by the NKVD, who followed behind the leading troops. In Warsaw in August 1944, the Home Army tried to seize the city when Soviet troops approached the eastern suburbs and were left to the Germans' untender mercies, with catastrophic results.

From 1931 to 1945 the Chinese maintained lasting, if fragmented, resistance to the Japanese. The Afghans, emboldened by over one hundred years of skirmishing with the British on the northwest frontier of India, mounted sustained resistance to Soviet occupation (1979–1989) but with severe internal dissension.

Regular soldiers continue to distrust irregular warriors of all kinds, although a tremendous news myth has grown up about how splendid resisters are. To fit in with that myth, a resistance movement in Kuwait was postulated in news bulletins during the Gulf War of 1991 (q.v.). There were indeed a few acts of heroic resistance in that looted city, but there had been no time to organize a resistance movement properly.

In spite of the regulars' skepticism, resisters can usefully carry out four main tasks. They can provide intelligence of the enemy's doings, if there is an intelligence staff to which these data can usefully be supplied. They can mount sabotage against manufacturing and communications facilities, or actual attacks on troops, if they can be supplied with explosives or arms. They can help those opposed to an oppressive regime to escape; in particular, they can help downed air crews return to battle. And last, they can pass news round to each other about how the war is going, thus sustaining hope and morale. Morale factors are all-important in war, and resistance can aid morale mightily.

M. R. D. FOOT

M. R. D. Foot, *Resistance* (1977); Henri Michel, *The Shadow War*, trans. R. H. Barry (1972).

Revolution, Military

In the early modern period, Europe experienced a series of radical changes in the techniques and technologies of war. Although the precise causes, timing, nature, and implications of these changes have been vigorously debated, historians generally agree that, taken together, they constitute a "military revolution" that transformed not only European military institutions and practices but also European society as a whole.

The main components of this transformation are clear. The rise of infantry and of gunpowder artillery in the fourteenth and fifteenth centuries — whether revolutions in their own right or merely necessary preconditions for later developments — created a new style of warfare. Paid armies consisting mainly of common infantrymen, assisted by powerful siege guns, rapidly conquered territories from Normandy to Granada to Naples in the name of Europe's expanding "gunpowder empires." "Entire kingdoms," observed historian Francesco Guicciardini, "were conquered and captured in less time than it used to take to conquer a village." Italian architects, shocked by the success of the French invasion of 1494, developed a new style of fortification (q.v.) subsequently called the *trace italienne*. These new fortresses, characterized by thick sunken walls and a snowflake-shaped plan that enabled the defenders to sweep every foot of the walls with enfilading cannon fire, proved capable of resisting artillery bombardment and assault alike. Money, time, and methodical siegework, rather than battlefield victories, became the foundation of military success. To capture Hertogenbosch in 1629, for example, the Dutch had to spend over two months and construct twenty-five miles of siege trenchworks.

To ensure their control over these expensive, powerful, and strategically important fortifications, the central governments of Renaissance states increasingly garrisoned them with regular standing armies. For offensive operations, still more soldiers had to be found and maintained through long sieges and longer wars. To recruit, train, pay, and supply these troops required unprecedented amounts of money, larger military and fiscal bureaucracies, and correspondingly higher taxes. The military expenditures of the Spanish monarchy, for example, increased roughly twentyfold between 1500 and 1650, a 300 percent increase even after adjusting for inflation.

As armies expanded, states sought better ways to control their often unruly soldiers. Maurice of Nassau (q.v.), inspired by Roman precedents, developed the "Dutch system," which employed small units with more officers, linear tactics emphasizing gunpowder firepower, and (perhaps most important) regular drill (q.v.). Hapsburg and French rulers later made similar reforms. As perfected by Gustavus Adolphus (q.v.), these developments — combined with Europe's burgeoning economy and financial sophistication — made possible the truly explosive growth of armies (field forces and peacetime armies as well as wartime establishments) that began with the Thirty Years' War (q.v.) and continued to the end of the seventeenth century. The near-constant warfare sparked by religious and Franco-Hapsburg animosities made military expansion necessary. Over this short period, the armies of France, England, Sweden, and the Dutch Republic tripled or quadrupled, sending government expenditures rocketing upward. In some places, the vastly increased demands of war provided a strong impetus toward absolutism; in others, they boosted institutions like Parliament and the States General, which represented those people whose money the government so desperately needed.

All these changes, along with a concomitant revolution in naval technology (involving advances in navigational techniques and the development of strongly built, heavily gunned sailing ships far more powerful than any non-European vessels), radically altered the relationship of Europe to the rest of the world. In the sixteenth century, European soldiers and cannon-armed ships scored remarkable successes in the Americas, the Indian Ocean, and North Africa, and stopped the Ottoman advance into Europe. Late in the seventeenth century, Western armies finally gained clear superiority over Turkish and Indian opponents. By the end of the eighteenth century, Europe had produced the most powerful military entities the world had ever known.

CLIFFORD J. ROGERS

Rhodes, Sieges of

305–304 B.C., A.D. 600s, and 1522

Unlike its experience in the unsuccessful year-long siege of Rhodes by Demetrius I Poliorcetes ("The Besieger") in 305–304 B.C., Rhodes did in fact fall to besiegers in A.D. 654 and 1522. Byzantine tradition probably correctly attributes the first Muslim siege or attack on Rhodes to A.D. 654, although Muslim sources date it to 672–673. The ruins of the ancient Colossus of Rhodes were allegedly sold as scrap at the end of this raid, which followed Muslim seizure of Cyprus in 649. This attack was only one of the raids on the western coast of Asia Minor by Muawiya (governor of Syria, later caliph); the Battle of the Masts, the great Muslim naval victory over the Byzantines, was another. The intent of the siege of Rhodes was disruption of Byzantine control, seizure of captives and booty, and impairment of maritime commerce and

life on that as well as other nearby islands. Indeterminate numbers of combatants and casualties were involved; the raid probably terminated many continuities of ancient classical civilization on that island and reduced survivors to a difficult and marginal existence.

A second and more famous struggle between Muslims and Christians occurred in 1522. The Knights Hospital (see *Knightly Orders*) had fortified Rhodes since the fifteenth century. Their grand master, Philippe Villiers de l'Isle Adam, resolved to defend it against the maturing power of the Ottoman Turkish sultan Suleiman the Magnificent (q.v.), who believed that Rhodes strategically threatened Ottoman control of navigation routes in the Aegean and the eastern Mediterranean, and along the Anatolian coast. Suleiman besieged Rhodes in the spring of 1522. Only in December, when the Turks breached the defensive walls, did the defenders and civilians, facing starvation as well as assault, capitulate. The knights, including de l'Isle Adam, were allowed to depart, having taken heavy losses. This was one of Suleiman's greatest military achievements.

WALTER E. KAEGI

Richard I ("the Lion-Heart")

1157–1199, *King of England, Duke of Aquitaine and Normandy, and Count of Anjou*

Richard I ("the Lion-Heart") was already an acknowledged master of the art of war when he went on crusade in response to the capture of Jerusalem by the Egyptian leader Saladin (q.v.) in 1187. After meticulous preparation, he took an army and a fleet to the eastern Mediterranean. In 1191 he captured Cyprus, Acre, and Jaffa — strategically vital conquests. Although he eventually decided, on realistic logistical grounds, not to lay siege to Jerusalem itself, he twice defeated Saladin in battle, at Arsuf (September 1191) and at Jaffa (August 1192), thus winning great renown both as a commander and as a knight willing to risk his own life when he called upon his troops to risk theirs — hence the name by which his contemporaries knew him, "Lion-Heart."

Richard was captured in Austria on his way home; it took a king's ransom to secure his release (March 1194), and while he was in prison his fellow crusader, King Philip II Augustus of France, took the chance to seize some of his castles in Normandy. The rest of

Richard's life was devoted to their recovery. Key elements in his strategy of reconquest were building the naval base of Portsmouth and the great Seine valley fortress of Château Gaillard. He was killed at Chalus-Chabrol while fighting rebels who fought against his rule in Aquitaine.

JOHN GILLINGHAM

Richthofen, Manfred von

1892–1918, German World War I Fighter Pilot

Manfred von Richthofen began his career in World War I as a cavalry officer on the Eastern Front, but in 1915, when detailed for quartermaster duty, he rebelled: "I have not gone to war to collect cheese and eggs, but for another purpose." After initially failing his pilot's license, the future "ace of aces" saw action above Verdun (q.v.) and Kovel.

In August 1916, Baron von Richthofen joined a new fighter squadron at the Somme (q.v.) and recorded his first "kill" on September 17; his eightieth and last came in April 1918; on April 21 he was shot down, probably by ground fire over the Somme.

Richthofen's bright red Fokker aircraft earned him the nicknames "red knight," "red baron," and *diable rouge*," and his habit of moving the squadron, tents, and equipment from base to base gave rise to the sobriquet "flying circus."

The war in the air became Richthofen's blood sport. He possessed the courage to kill or be killed, flaunting his daring with reckless abandon and dispatching his victims in a brutal, pitiless manner. Preferring not to fight alone, he remained above his squadron in a dogfight until he spied his chance to swoop down, hawklike, upon unfortunate stragglers. "Everything in the air," he once boasted, "belongs to me." Many of his "kills" were, in fact, joint efforts, but were credited to Richthofen to enhance his stature as a national hero.

HOLGER H. HERWIG

Rickover, Hyman G.

1900–1986, U.S. Admiral

Hyman Rickover took the U.S. Navy into the nuclear age. He developed and closely supervised the building of the world's first nuclear-powered submarine, the *Nautilus*, and, by lobbying in Congress, got the money and authority to build the navy's first nuclear-powered surface ships. When Rickover died, more than 150 navy ships were sailing under nuclear power.

Rickover was the senior officer of a navy group sent in 1946 to a nuclear reactor research laboratory in Oak Ridge, Tennessee. There he began his campaign to introduce nuclear power in the navy — a change as revolutionary as the transition from sail to steam.

He became assistant chief for nuclear propulsion at the navy's Bureau of Ships and head of the Naval Reactors Branch at the Atomic Energy Commission (AEC). Skillfully manipulating both jobs, he persuaded the navy and the AEC to start construction of a nuclear-powered submarine. The *Nautilus* was launched in 1954.

Many of his superiors disliked him and his ranting, contentious style. He rarely wore a uniform, scoffed at navy tradition, and frequently denounced navy bureaucracy, especially in testimony before Congress. The navy failed to promote Rickover from captain to admiral in 1952, dooming him to forced retirement. He was promoted when Congress intervened. He was extremely influential in Congress, where he eloquently pleaded his case for what came to be called the "Rickover Navy."

Thanks to his friends in Congress, he remained on active duty until 1982, when the secretary of the navy, with the knowledge of President Ronald Reagan, ordered him to retire. In his farewell congressional appearance he denounced the arms race and said, "I'm not proud of the part I played in it."

THOMAS B. ALLEN

Ridgway, Matthew B.

1895–1993, U.S. General

A leading American battlefield commander during World War II (q.v.), Matthew Ridgway in the early 1950s exerted an extraordinary degree of influence over American military policy and strategy in Asia. Serving in the European theater from 1942 through 1945, Ridgway first commanded the Eighty-second Airborne Division, which dropped in Sicily and in Normandy on D-Day (q.v.), and then became commander of the Airborne Eighteenth U.S. Corps, which played a critical role in the Battle of the Bulge (q.v.).

Ridgway was serving in the Pentagon when the Korean War (q.v.) broke out, but on December 22,

1950, while American troops were retreating before the massive Chinese intervention in North Korea, he was appointed the commander of the Eighth Army in Korea. At that time, General Douglas MacArthur (q.v.), American supreme commander in the Far East, was arguing that the United States must choose between withdrawal from Korea and all-out war with China. But Ridgway quickly concluded, first, that U.S. forces could halt the Chinese advance, and then actually began a successful counterattack, retaking Seoul in February and crossing the thirty-eighth parallel by April. Then, on April 11, President Harry Truman relieved MacArthur of his command and replaced him with Ridgway. Ridgway always believed that the United Nations forces could have continued their advance successfully to the Yalu River, but that the United States would not have committed the forces necessary to hold that line, or to cross it. This showed an unusual awareness of the nature and demands of limited war.

Ridgway was chief of staff of the army in 1954, when the United States had to decide whether or not to intervene to prevent a French defeat in Indochina. While the chairman of the Joint Chiefs of Staff, Admiral Arthur Radford, argued that naval and air power alone might turn the tide, Ridgway replied that the United States would need a ground effort at least equal to that in Korea as well, and that this time, seeking a decisive victory was necessary. The United States decided not to intervene. Ridgway expressed pride in his memoirs (written in 1957) that he might have helped avoid American intervention in Indochina, and in 1966, in a prophetic magazine article, he argued the pitfalls of any new escalation of the U.S. role in Vietnam. Few American generals have matched Ridgway's combination of battlefield leadership and strategic grasp. He was both a fighting general whose battlefield presence won the confidence of his men, and a brilliant strategic thinker who trusted his own judgment.

DAVID KAISER

Ritual in War

Tradition, religious rite, and state protocol are usually needed to conduct war — an activity difficult to inaugurate and harder to conclude. The time, location, and conduct of early Western warfare (as was true of most other societies) were subject to careful rules and customs intended to confine killing to the combatants themselves and thus protect the middling citizenry of *polis*. In the early Greek city-state — almost exclusively agrarian and parochial — infantry battle may have first originated as conventional matches *(agones)* among elite corps or as individual duels between select champions *(monomachia)*, in which the battlefield verdict was accepted by both warring communities. Later fighting was the responsibility of a much larger warring class, but still defined solely as a formal collision of opposing phalanxes, during the summer in daylight, without the intervention of either true cavalry or missile troops (see *Hoplites*). Night attack, winter campaigning, ambush, and aggression without formal declaration of intent were outside the military protocol of the city-state. Before rivers could be crossed, foreign land entered, the enemy attacked, or booty distributed, the appropriate ceremony was required: early Greek seers, entrusted to beseech and repay godly succor, were as important as the board of amateur generals.

Yet soon ritual in the West evolved to facilitate and vindicate war making, *not* vice versa. Early Western warfare was fought violently over real objectives — disputed land, mostly — that were considered vital to the entire community. True, the race in armor, ritual dance in arms, collective oaths and feasts, public slaying of animals, and mock combat were frequent Greek cultural practices that sometimes marked the ascent of youth into adulthood or the formal inculcation of martial spirit and virtue. But such ritual activities in themselves were *not* war and had little to do with the ceremonial apparatus needed to bring off an actual collision of men on the battlefield.

The Peloponnesian War (431–404 B.C.) (q.v.) marked the transition to the Hellenistic and Roman military practice of applying capital and labor to war making without ritual restraint. Ceremony — the triumphal parade, declaration of war, and public sacrifice — was now entirely a question of pro forma approval of decisions based on sheer military expediency.

As such, Western warfare marks a distinct and historic break from what has sometimes been called "primitive" or "ritualized" war making. For concurrent with the rise of sophisticated warfare in Greece and Rome was another tradition, wherein military technology was limited to the bow and arrow, club, and spear. The cutting edges consisted largely of stone, and thus the degree to which mass killing was accomplished remained rather limited. In Africa, the Americas, and some areas of Asia, battle never evolved into a mechanism to annex land, achieve political hegemony, or ensure the extermination of rival societies. Consequently, complex strategic thought, technological advance, and logistics were not needed, and, in fact, largely ignored. Instead, battle remained centered around the raiding of rival livestock, the mass capture of women, or retribution to perceived slights against warriors' manhood.

As a means of ensuring internal social control or maintaining a rough ecological equilibrium between neighboring tribes, war's ends included captive torture, scalping, human sacrifice, and cannibalism, not the systematic slaughter of thousands through bronze and iron weapons. Anthropologists note, for example, that the Maoris of New Zealand seldom exterminated one another, simply because their warfare was focused on personal revenge and the need to take captives for ritual torture and cannibalism. Similarly, the Aztecs (q.v.) sought to capture, not kill, their adversaries to obtain a suitable supply of sacrificial victims for their own insatiable gods. Therefore, they never envisioned war outside the sphere of ritual religion — to the enormous advantage of the Spanish conquistadores (q.v.).

Of course, the distinction between ritual and sophisticated warfare was not always absolute, and some cultures, such as the Zulu (q.v.), at times have practiced both. Yet it remains a general truism that most societies can be characterized by the manner in which they fight. Those for whom ritual is simply a means to justify the mass military application of capital and manpower have evolved a dynamic and often terrifying practice of arms — in dramatic contrast to more localized raiding and plundering, in which rituals precluded true military evolution.

Thus, throughout later European warfare both religious liturgy and state sanction — the blessing of the troops, formal declaration of war, and legal truces — were commonplace. But these rites were nearly always used to legitimize, explain, defend, and facilitate fighting that served more worldly military and political objectives. Rarely, if at all, did ritual by itself either prevent campaigns that could be won or encourage fighting that was doomed — and that gave Westerners enormous military advantages over indigenous cultures who had no experience with the quite different — and terrifying — Greco-Roman idea of war.

VICTOR DAVIS HANSON

Yvon Garlan, *War in the Ancient World* (1975); Harry High-Turney, *Primitive Warfare: Its Practice and Concepts*, 2nd ed. (1971); John Keegan, *A History of Warfare* (1993).

Rocroi, Battle of

May 19, 1643

This battle, the key episode in the long Franco-Spanish War (1635–1659), pitted twenty-five thousand troops from the Spanish Netherlands under Francisco de Melo against twenty-three thousand French soldiers commanded by the young duke of Enghien, soon to be renowned as the Great Condé (q.v.). As the Spanish, having invaded France, besieged Rocroi, Enghien attacked them before they received reinforcements. On the morning of the battle, Enghien led the cavalry of his right flank and drove off the horsemen facing him. Learning that his own left had been beaten back, Enghien next swung his victorious horsemen entirely around the rear of the enemy army and defeated the Spanish right-wing cavalry. Now the Spanish infantry stood alone and defiant, but concentrated French fire nearly annihilated them.

Rocroi ranks as one of the major watersheds in military history; before this battle the Spanish army possessed an aura of near invincibility that it would never regain after its defeat by the French.

JOHN A. LYNN

Rokossovsky, K. K.

1896–1968, *Marshal of the Soviet Union*

Marshal Konstantin Konstantinovich Rokossovsky was one of the many officers who fell into the clutches of the NKVD (the secret police) during Joseph Stalin's (q.v.) military purges, which began in 1937. Fortunately for the Red Army (q.v.), he was released in 1939 — although his captors made clear that he was only on parole. Nevertheless, Rokossovsky displayed a strong sense of independence; in 1941 he went so far as to object to reintroduction of the commissar system. The German invasion (see *Operation Barbarossa*) proved his salvation in terms of life expectancy as well as career prospects. In 1941, he succeeded in pushing forces through to the Smolensk pocket so that some of those trapped could escape. He then played a significant role in Moscow's defense and subsequent counterattacks. At Stalingrad (q.v.) he had a relatively small part in the offensive that trapped the German Sixth Army, but then commanded the destruction of the pocket.

From 1943, Rokossovsky achieved the reputation as one of the foremost operational commanders in the Red Army. He commanded the assault on the Orel salient that helped bring the Battle of Kursk (q.v.) to an end. In June 1944, his forces opened "Operation Bagration" by breaking through and destroying the German Ninth Army; by the end of the summer offensive, nothing remained of the German Army Group Center. In January 1945 Rokossovsky commanded the Second Beylorussian Front, composed of five infantry armies and one tank army; his forces broke through north of Warsaw and then reached the Baltic, thereby isolating East Prussia before crunching through Pomerania.

At the end of the war he received honorary command of the victory parade in Red Square. In 1950 he became commander of Soviet forces in Poland, an appointment that caused considerable resentment because of the failure of his forces to support the Polish uprising in Warsaw in August 1944.

WILLIAMSON MURRAY

Roland

d. 778, *Frankish Hero*

Roland (Hrodulandus) was Frankish count of the Breton march and commander of Charlemagne's (q.v.) rear guard during the return from the Spanish expedition of 778, during which Roland's force was ambushed and destroyed by Basques while crossing the Pyrenees at Roncesvalles.

Roland's subsequent fame was based entirely on a highly fictionalized twelfth-century epic poem (*chanson de geste*), which transformed the rearguard action into a heroic last stand against impossible odds, the Basques into Muslims, and Roland and his companions into paragons of crusading chivalry. Historically, Roland is more important as an example of the system by which Carolingian rulers organized their border districts under a single civil and military governor (the march-count, or margrave) and, perhaps, as an early example of the tradition of entrusting major commands to inexperienced young aristocrats, often with disastrous results. (Roland was Charlemagne's nephew, and no military action at all is recorded during his tenure in the Breton march.) Even the *chanson* is highly critical of Roland's refusal to call for rein-

forcements in a timely fashion, a characterization of his command decisions (as opposed to combat prowess) that is best understood as an object lesson in how not to command a medieval army.

EDWARD J. SCHOENFELD

Roman-Persian Wars

For more than four centuries, the Romans and Persians fought a series of indecisive wars along their mutual borders in the Near East. In A.D. 229–233, Ardashir, first Sassanian shah, sought to expel the Romans from Asia and to restore Persian frontiers to their earlier limits. In a classic three-pronged counterattack, Severus Alexander threatened the Persian capitals Ctesiphon and Seleucia in Mesopotamia and compelled Ardashir to sue for peace. Shah Shapur I renewed the war in 238. The Roman emperor Gordian III took the field in 242–244 but was lynched in a mutiny masterminded by his prefect Philip, who, upon seizing the throne, purchased peace from Shapur for ten thousand pounds of gold.

In 253, Shapur invaded Syria and sacked its capital, Antioch. Emperor Valerian launched counteroffensives in 253–254 and 258–260. The second ended in Valerian's capture, but Rome's ally Odenathus of Palmyra rallied imperial forces, took Ctesiphon, and ended the war on favorable terms in 262. The emperor Carus (282–283), repeating Odenathus's march, was struck dead by lightning before Ctesiphon; the Roman army retired. Galerius commanded two campaigns against Shah Narses in 296–298; the second gained for Rome five strategic provinces beyond the Tigris. Shah Shapur II renewed the contest in 337. The emperor Julian (q.v.), seeking decisive victory by invading Mesopotamia in 363, missed capturing Ctesiphon and fell during the retreat. His successor Jovian had to relinquish the provinces gained in 298 and the strategic fortress of Nisibis. Since clashes in 421–422 and 503–505 produced no decision, Anastasius constructed Daras to counter Nisibis. The costs of the Persian wars drove emperors to debase their currency, thus sparking runaway inflation. Emperors countered Sassanian armies by massing forces on the Euphrates, perfecting logistics, fielding more cavalry, and reintroducing the phalanx.

In 526–532 and 540–545, Shah Khusrau I waged war against the emperor Justinian. The decisive victory at Daras by his general Belisarius (q.v.) in 530 enabled Justinian to negotiate the "Perpetual Peace" in return

This relief at Naqsh-e-Rustam shows triumphant Shah Shapur I receiving as supplicants the Roman emperors Philip, who signed a peace treaty in 244, and Valerian, who was captured in 260.

for paying eleven thousand pounds of gold. In 540, while Belisarius was reconquering Italy from the Ostrogoths, Shah Khusru invaded Syria, and Justinian repurchased peace in 545 and 562. Justin II terminated payments and ignited the war of 572–591, which the emperor Maurice Tiberius won by restoring the exiled shah Khusrau II. Upon the murder of Maurice by the usurper Phocas, Khusrau II, on the pretext of avenging his benefactor Maurice, overran Syria, Egypt, and Anatolia in 602–628. While Khusrau II besieged the imperial capital, Constantinople (q.v.), in 622–628, Heraclius landed on the Black Sea's northeastern shores, invaded Persia, and smashed four Sassanian field armies. Shah Ardashir III restored to Heraclius imperial territories, but the Roman and Persian Empires were so exhausted that they failed to halt the armies of Islam in 634–696.

KENNETH W. HARL

Rommel, Erwin

1891–1944, German World War II Field Marshal

Erwin Johannes Eugen Rommel gained immortality in the North African campaign of 1941–1943. Sent with a small German force to help the Axis against the British after the Italians had suffered severe defeat, Rommel — reaching Tripoli in February 1941 — was soon master of Cyrenaica and imposing his will on the enemy. For two years the opposing forces alternately advanced or withdrew over the desert, and Rommel's name became legendary — a master of mobile operations who was rapid, courageous, and audacious.

Rommel's supreme achievement was his defeat of the British at Gazala in May 1942, followed by the taking of Tobruk and a field marshal's baton. Nemesis came five months later at El Alamein (q.v.), when the British imperial army under Bernard Montgomery (q.v.) won a convincing victory. Rommel withdrew the survivors of his *Panzerarmee* to Tunisia. By then the British and Americans had landed in North Africa, the British Eighth Army had reconquered Tripolitania and was on the Tunisian border, and the Germans were hemmed in, isolated and facing overwhelming odds. Rommel left for Europe in March 1943. The African adventure was over.

Rommel has been criticized for lacking strategic sense, for excessive absorption in the tactical battle, for neglect of logistics, for periodic imprudence. These criticisms are shallow. Rommel's especial flair was undoubtedly for the battle itself, for the cut and thrust of maneuver, for personal leadership at the point of decision, above all for the speed and energy with which he decided and acted; but in his extensive writings and recorded conversations he showed a military perceptiveness and strategic insight that would have probably enabled him to shine with the brilliance of Erich von Manstein (q.v.) had he held high command on the larger scale of the Eastern Front. As to logistics, Rommel was acutely aware of them at all times — they dominated the African theater where all commodities had to be imported and transported over huge distances. He refused, however, to make excessively pessimistic assumptions or to overensure — or, as he put it, to allow the scope and pace of battle to be dictated by quartermasters. A more cautious approach would have often denied him victory. And although Rommel sometimes underestimated the timing and difficulties of an operation, he was one who believed war seldom forgives hesitation or delay. From his earliest days as a brilliant young leader in World War I, or as a panzer divisional commander crossing the Meuse against fierce opposition and racing across France in 1940, he had proved to himself the virtues of initiative and boldness. On the whole his decisions were justified by victory: and in Africa victory often against odds.

Rommel's last military appointment was in command of Army Group B, responsible in 1944 for much of northwest Europe. His energetic preparations reflected his conviction that the expected invasion had to be defeated near the coast, because Allied air power would nullify large-scale armored counteroperations after the landing. He believed, too, that the coming campaign should aim to defeat the invasion for one purpose: so that in the aftermath, peace might be negotiated in the west and a stalemate achieved in the east. Politically this was fantasy and militarily it failed; but for Rommel it was the only rational hope.

By then Rommel had lost all faith in Adolf Hitler (q.v.). Hitler had showed him favor, and Rommel was long grateful for what he saw as Hitler's restoration of German self-respect in the 1930s, but by 1944 he was disenchanted by Hitler's refusal to face strategic facts. After the Allied invasion had succeeded in establishing a front (see *D-Day*), Rommel — who believed that Germany must now inevitably lose a war on two fronts — tried again personally to confront Hitler with reality. He failed.

Rommel, therefore, was now determined to surrender the German forces in the west unilaterally. Before that could happen he was wounded in an air attack on July 17. At home on sick leave, he was visited by emissaries of Hitler on October 14 and offered the choice of trial for high treason or suicide — to be publicized as a heart attack — with guarantees for his family's immunity. He had never participated in the plot to assassinate Hitler, but his "defeatism" was known and his involvement presumed. He chose suicide and was given a state funeral.

Rommel has been variously described as a Nazi (because of long personal devotion to Hitler) or as a martyr of the German Resistance (because of the manner of his death). He was neither. He was a straightforward, gifted, patriotic German officer, a charismatic commander and master of maneuver, caught up in the disaster of the Third Reich.

GENERAL SIR DAVID FRASER

Roosevelt, Franklin D.

1882–1945, *President of the United States*

Franklin Roosevelt's historical claim to outstanding effectiveness is even greater in the realm of grand strategy during World War II (q.v.) than in the realm of domestic policy during the Great Depression. What made Roosevelt effective as a grand strategist was that he intuitively acted in line with Carl von Clausewitz's (q.v.) injunction that the primary duty of a statesman in a war is to understand the nature of the conflict. World War II was a coalition struggle that was waged across multiple theaters and that was bound to be protracted. In such a war, the side that can forge the most cohesive coalition has an immense advantage. To achieve strategic cohesion, the coalition partners must agree on who their primary enemy is and must then make sound decisions on the allocation of their military assets among the different theaters. Furthermore, if the will of the people in a democratic society is to withstand the stress of a protracted conflict, those who decide how to allocate the forces must be mindful of the need to generate periodic morale-boosting military successes. Roosevelt handled all these issues wisely.

The American president's choices were crucial to the formation and maintenance of a winning Grand Alliance. It was by no means foreordained that in mid-1940, as France fell and Britain came under direct attack at the hands of Nazi Germany, Roosevelt would begin to transfer to the British a substantial chunk of the firstfruits of the belated American rearmament. In choosing to do so, Roosevelt brushed aside the misgivings of his leading military advisers, who feared that Britain, too, was doomed to fall and that American forces would be left ill equipped. It was even less foreordained that in mid-1941, Roosevelt, along with Winston Churchill (q.v.), would embrace Joseph Stalin (q.v.) as a coalition partner after Germany attacked the Soviet Union. But the president saw that if the Soviets as well as the Americans were joined together with the British, it would be possible to defeat Hitler at a reasonable cost to the United States.

The unexpected Japanese attack on Pearl Harbor (q.v.) solved a political problem for Roosevelt by unifying American public opinion in favor of full participation in the war. But the attack complicated the problem of how to allocate American military assets against two first-rate adversaries in widely separated theaters of war. Despite the passion for revenge that Pearl Harbor aroused in American public opinion, Roosevelt affirmed the conclusion of Anglo-American staff talks earlier in 1941 that the war against Germany should have first priority. Still, in 1942 and 1943, he presided over the allocation to the Pacific theater of half of the still-meager American inventory of military assets. The result was a series of military successes that wore down Japanese power and buoyed up American morale. But the drain of American resources to the Pacific interacted with the British aversion to an early cross-Channel invasion to thwart the ardent desire of General George Marshall (q.v.), chief of staff of the U.S. Army, to strike at Germany through France as soon as possible. Brushing aside professional military advice once again, Roosevelt embraced what British prime minister Churchill had long wanted: a major Anglo-American operation in North Africa, where Britain was already heavily engaged. In making this pivotal decision, the president had in mind both the need to maintain coalition cohesion with the British and the need to sustain American public support for the war against Germany.

The main danger that Roosevelt perceived in this American detour to the Mediterranean was that it raised the odds of a Soviet defection from the Allies. To reassure Stalin about American steadfastness as well as to rally the American public, Roosevelt proclaimed unconditional surrender as the political objective of the war. Stalin was unmoved. The Soviet leader wanted two things from his allies: an immediate second front in Western Europe and acceptance of his expansionist ambitions in Eastern Europe. For a long time, Stalin could not be sure that he would get either. Then, at the first summit conference with Stalin at Teheran in late 1943, both Roosevelt and

Churchill proved accommodating on Eastern European issues, while Roosevelt and Stalin together levered Churchill into a commitment to a cross-Channel invasion in mid-1944.

As the Allied military forces converged upon Germany, the problems of coalition management finally overtaxed Roosevelt's skills. He wanted to ensure that Stalin would enter the war against Japan after the conflict in Europe ended. He hoped to keep together the Grand Alliance as the linchpin of stability in the postwar world. But he also hoped to influence Stalin's behavior in Eastern Europe through diplomatic finesse. It turned out that Roosevelt's leverage over his troublesome ally was quite limited. When Roosevelt died in April 1945, the end of World War II was imminent — but so was the beginning of the Cold War (q.v.).

BRADFORD A. LEE

Frank Freidel, *Franklin D. Roosevelt* (1990); Kent Roberts Greenfield, *American Strategy in World War II* (1963); Eric Larrabee, *Commander in Chief: Franklin Delano Roosevelt, His Lieutenants, and Their War* (1987).

Roses, Wars of the

1455–1485

These occasional, brief civil wars in England commenced in the 1450s with rebellions led by Richard, duke of York, who had been excluded from power at court by Henry VI of the house of Lancaster. From 1461 to 1471, the wars escalated into struggles for the throne between those who supported Henry and those who supported Duke Richard's son, Edward IV. A badge used by the house of York (the white rose) and the red rose adopted by the first Tudor king, Henry VII (to symbolize his claim to be rightful heir of the house of Lancaster) led to the coining of the phrase "the Wars of the Roses" in the nineteenth century.

The wars included more than sixty weeks of large-scale campaigning in England (with considerable fighting in Wales, and some too at sea, around English-held Calais and in Ireland). The many battles encompassed both skirmishes fought by small numbers (for example, St. Albans, 1455) and large-scale engagements involving heavy casualties (notably Towton, 1461). The principal strategic objectives were London, York, and Calais (which had the Crown's largest garrison). These places were well-fortified; but most

English and Welsh urban fortifications and castles had long been neglected, and so few important sieges occurred.

Kings and elites were unaccustomed to investing financially in fortifications and standing forces for domestic conflict (hitherto a rare occurrence). Their limited personal resources, and concern not to alienate their supporters by imposing taxation and by extortion, molded the character of the wars. Lords' kinsmen, officials, rural tenants, and clients rallied willingly for short periods; levies raised by cities, boroughs, and shires had a fixed term of service. These forces were sometimes reluctant and ill equipped: large-scale levying was hampered by its unpopularity, shortages of good recruits, and the need for rapid deployment. Both sides relied mainly on elite companies of knights and esquires — the long-term retainers of kings and nobles — and on foreign mercenary (q.v.) companies, such as the French and Scots who formed the backbone of Henry Tudor's army in 1485.

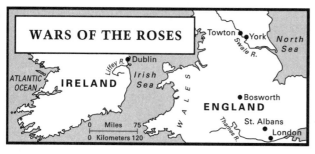

Tactics were traditional: mounted troops mostly fought on foot. The use by opposing sides of English longbowmen famed for their skill reduced the effectiveness of archery. Field artillery was often deployed, and companies of hand-gunners occasionally, but neither apparently to decisive effect. The social and economic impact of war was reduced by the shortness of campaigns (counted in weeks) and by the general concern of leaders to keep or win the support of civilians: the poor discipline of the Lancastrian army victorious at St. Albans (1455) produced crucial opposition in London to its entry into the city.

As civil conflicts, the Wars of the Roses were notable in that they did not produce widespread destruction and economic recession. The participants lacked the necessary muscle for prolonged warfare and could only have developed it, or resorted to terror tactics, at the expense of alienating public opinion. Attempts to revive dynastic rebellion against Henry VII, after his victory over Edward IV's brother Richard III at Bos-

worth Field (1485), were thwarted by the lack of convincing Yorkist candidates for the throne and by Henry's effective spy service and international diplomacy. Discontent was damped down by his use of revitalized Crown revenues to buy off potential opposition and to run a magnificent court, which attracted service to the monarch and propagandized the ethic of loyalty to the Crown.

ANTHONY GOODMAN

Ruses/Disinformation

Deception — feinting — is as old as combat, far older than war. Tricks can save lives on both sides and wind up conflicts quickly. The Greek wooden horse used to storm Priam's Troy may only be a legend, but it shows that ruses were an accepted form of warfare in Homer's day (see *Trojan War*). They were commonly used by Greek, Roman, and medieval armies.

As transport became more complicated, methods of deception multiplied. In 1704, the duke of Marlborough (q.v.) sent a bridging train up the right bank of the Rhine, to fix the attention of Louis XIV's (q.v.) commanders while he marched east to his victory of Blenheim (q.v.) in Bavaria. Two of his marshals, Murat and Lannes, secured for Napoleon (q.v.) in 1805 the only bridge across the Danube by which he could pursue his campaign against Austria and Russia, by riding across it in full uniform and deceiving the local Austrian commander into believing the bridge had been allotted to the French in a nonexistent armistice.

British rule in India rested on disinformation: the legend of the invincible distant Crown, which ensured the supremacy of the Raj.

Otto von Bismarck (q.v.) used the ruse of a Hohenzollern candidature for the throne of Spain to bring on the Franco-Prussian War (q.v.) in 1870, the necessary preliminary to the German Empire. Ruses of war multiplied when that empire's ambitions brought on World War I (q.v.). The Royal Navy, for example, used Q-ships — armed tramp steamers, not worth a torpedo — whose crews would abandon them when approached by a submarine, leaving a hidden crew on board who would sink the submarine when it surfaced to sink the steamer by gunfire. Feint land attacks were common, to direct enemy attention from where the real blow was to fall; by a series of ruses, British troops withdrew from Gallipoli (q.v.) at the end of 1915 with no worse casualties than one sprained ankle.

The propaganda ministries of Fascist Italy, Communist Russia, and Nazi Germany launched massive campaigns of disinformation, each seeking to exaggerate the strength and proclaim the invulnerability of the regime.

In World War II (q.v.), the Royal Air Force often mounted spoof raids, using a few light bombers to simulate the pathfinder force that preceded a major attack, and so diverted German night fighter controllers' attention away from the night's main objective. Commandos kept up a series of pinprick raids on the coasts of northwest Europe to distract the German high command's attention from impending major operations in the Mediterranean.

Shipping concentrations, often impossible to conceal, can give some warning of an enemy's intentions; hence the use of dummy battleships (invented by the magician Jasper Maskelyne) in 1941–1942 in the Suez Canal zone, and of dummy landing craft on the east coast of England and Scotland in the spring of 1944 as part of Operation Fortitude.

This major deception plan convinced Adolf Hitler (q.v.) that the main Allied landing would come south of Boulogne, and that the Normandy landings of June 6, 1944 (see *D-Day*), were only a feint. This enabled Dwight D. Eisenhower (q.v.) to seize a secure beachhead from which to pursue his advance. During the Gulf War (q.v.), Norman Schwarzkopf (q.v.) studied Operation Fortitude carefully and in 1991 persuaded the Iraqis that he was about to attack Kuwait from the sea, before mounting a crushing offensive on the opposite, landward flank.

M. R. D. FOOT

Russian Civil War

December 1917–November 1920

The Russian Civil War was the most costly internecine conflict of modern times: about 825,000 combat fatalities and over two million ancillary casualties resulted from starvation, exposure, and epidemics. When the fighting ended in 1920, the newly created Soviet Union was thoroughly devastated and a pattern of rule by terror firmly established.

War broke out in the immediate aftermath of the Bolshevik coup of October 1917 because the new Soviet government, then controlling only parts of European Russia, was determined to spread its rule throughout the former empire, while various elements of the imperial army, along with border peoples such as the Don Cossacks (q.v.), opposed the creation of a Communist state. Aside from anti-Communism, the different "White" (constitutionalist and monarchist) forces lacked common political and social aspirations. This put them at a disadvantage vis-à-vis the "Reds," who were unified in their goals, if not always in their strategies for attaining them.

The Russian Civil War was full of flux and confusion, with constantly changing fronts, units suddenly materializing and evaporating, wholesale desertion on both sides, atrocities aplenty, and periodic intervention by irregular forces who exploited the chaos for their own ends. Nonetheless, the war progressed through three fairly distinct phases and embraced three principal centers of action.

During the first phase (November 1917–November 1918), a southern front opened when two imperial army generals formed a "Volunteer Army" in the Don Cossack region on the lower Don River. Meanwhile, a band of ten thousand Czech soldiers, captured by the tsarist army in the war and on their way to a evacuation via Vladivostok, rebelled in Siberia when instructed to give up their arms and opposed the Bolsheviks along the Volga and in western Siberia. The Czechs were not repatriated until early 1920. Few significant military encounters occurred during this initial phase of the war because the Red Army proper (q.v.) came into existence only in the fall of 1918.

The second stage (March–November 1919) witnessed decisive battles between the rapidly growing Red Army and White forces. One contingent, loosely allied with the Don Cossacks, marched toward Moscow from the south; another advanced from Siberia; yet a third attacked Petrograd. Although successful initially, the White advances stalled largely because the various forces lacked coordination: each fought its own war. The Western powers sent soldiers and supplies to assist the Whites, but the intervention was far too small and poorly organized to have much impact.

The final phase was anticlimactic yet tragic: it involved a last-ditch effort by White forces to hold the Crimean peninsula. Devastated by hunger, typhus, and desertion, the survivors were evacuated by British and French navies in November 1920.

The Bolsheviks triumphed in this war not only because they had a unified command, but also because, like the North in the American Civil War (q.v.), they could draw on larger human and material resources than could the Whites. They also had the advantage of controlling the geographic center of the country. Ironically, the officers who won the war for the Reds were former imperial army officers who came from the same social backgrounds as their White antagonists. For many of them, their ultimate reward was to be imprisoned or executed by Joseph Stalin (q.v.) in the great purges of the 1930s.

DAVID CLAY LARGE

Russo-Japanese War

February 1904–September 1905

This war was fought between Japan and Russia for hegemony in northeast Asia, specifically for the control of Manchuria and Korea. As, in the Japanese view, this was a matter of national survival, the war was one for which Japan had prepared and Russia had not.

Russia, the world's foremost land power and the third-ranking sea power, could not easily bring its strength to bear in the Far East because of the great distances separating its military and naval forces there from European Russia. Russian armies in Manchuria depended upon the nearly completed single-track Trans-Siberian Railway, and the two naval bases at Port Arthur and Vladivostok were half a world away from the Baltic Fleet.

Thus, from the outset, as in the Sino-Japanese War (q.v.) ten years before, Japan correctly assumed that command of the sea would largely determine the course of the war on land and that Russian land forces

in the Far East must be beaten before they could be substantially reinforced from the West.

Without waiting for a declaration of war, therefore, Japan opened hostilities with a surprise attack on the main Russian fleet base at Port Arthur in February 1904. All Russian attempts to break the subsequent blockade of the port ended in failure. By spring 1904, Japanese armies had also begun to close in on the port, held by a forty-thousand-man garrison entrenched behind concrete forts, barbed wire, automatic weapons, and artillery. While Admiral Togo Heihachiro defeated an attempt to break out by the entrapped Russian fleet, investment of the hill-encircled base was begun by eighty thousand Japanese troops. Port Arthur fell in December 1904 after frightful losses on both sides: nearly sixty thousand Japanese casualties and over thirty thousand Russian. Not until Verdun (q.v.) would a single piece of ground claim so many lives.

In Manchuria proper, the Russians were forced into a series of enormous land battles and then were compelled to retreat northward as Japanese forces endeavored unsuccessfully to encircle and annihilate the Russian armies. The last and largest of these collisions — the three-week battle before Mukden — involved an unprecedented total of 550,000 men. Stalemated on land, the war ended when Russia's Baltic Fleet, which had sailed halfway around the world, was completely defeated at Tsushima (q.v.) by Togo in May 1905. Materially drained, both sides accepted American mediation and signed a peace treaty at Portsmouth, New Hampshire, in September.

The war demonstrated the defensive strength of entrenched automatic weapons and the offensive power of indirect artillery fire. Russia, in losing every battle on land and sea, betrayed ominous military deficiencies; Japan, displaying the professionalism of its armed services, vaulted to great power status and destroyed forever the myth of Western invincibility.

MARK R. PEATTIE

Russo-Turkish Wars

Russia fought nine wars with the Ottoman Empire (q.v.) between 1672 and 1878, either singly or with allies, in 1677–1681, 1695–1696, 1711, 1735–1739, 1768–1774, 1787–1792, 1806–1812, 1828–1829, and 1877–1878. In addition, Turkey took part in the anti-

Russian coalition during the Crimean War (1854–1856) (q.v.) and entered World War I (q.v.) against Russia in November 1914.

In the seventeenth and eighteenth centuries, Russia's conflicts with the Poles and the Crimean Tatars often engendered wars with Turkey as well. The Turks favored the maintenance of a robust Poland as a counterweight to Russia and consequently objected to Russia's numerous interventions there. Then, too, until its annexation in 1783, the Crimean Khanate was under the nominal suzerainty of the Ottoman Empire. For its part, Russia was interested in depriving Turkey of its possessions north and east of the Black Sea as well as in the Balkans. In the nineteenth century, St. Petersburg generally supported the continued existence of an enfeebled Turkey, in order to keep possession of the straits out of the hands of a stronger European power. When Russia did take the field against Turkey, it was often the outcome of an international crisis provoked by Turkey's mistreatment of its Christian subjects.

Russia's most successful wars against the Turks were those of the eighteenth century. Under the leadership of talented commanders such as Burkhard von Münnich, Nikolay Rumyantsev, Grigory Potemkin, and Aleksandr Suvorov (q.v.), Russia solved the logistical problems of campaigning in thinly populated territories and developed a unique style of war based upon aimed musket fire, skillful exploitation of the artillery, mobile infantry squares, and shock attacks. Such tactics often permitted a Russian army to defeat a Turkish force many times its size. Russian battlefield triumphs produced impressive political results: the spoils of Catherine II's two wars (1768–1774 and 1787–1792) included Azov, the Crimean peninsula, and vast lands between the Dniester and Dnieper Rivers.

WILLIAM C. FULLER, JR.

S

Sadowa, Battle of

See Königgrätz, Battle of.

Saladin

1137/38–1193, *Muslim Military and Political Leader*

On July 4, 1187, the Muslim forces of Saladin (Salah al-Din) decisively defeated the crusader army south of the Horns of Hattin (q.v.) in Palestine, capturing Guy, king of Jerusalem; Reginald of Châtillon, Saladin's enemy whom he personally killed; over two hundred Knights Hospitaller and Templar (see *Knightly Orders*) whom he ordered to be killed; and many crusaders whom he ransomed. The remaining captured Christians were sold on the local slave markets.

Born into a Kurdish, Sunni, military family, Saladin rose rapidly within Muslim society as a subordinate to the Syrian–northern Mesopotamian military leader Nur al-Din. Participating in three campaigns into Egypt (which was governed by the Shi'ite Fatimid dynasty), Saladin became head of the military expeditionary forces in 1169. After he was appointed *wazir* (adviser) to the Shi'ite caliph in Cairo, he consolidated his position by eliminating the Fatimid's sub-Saharan infantry slave forces. Finally, in 1171 the Shi'ite Fatimid caliphate was brought to an end by Saladin with the recognition of the Sunni caliphate in Baghdad. In the meantime, Nur al-Din kept pressuring Saladin to send him money, supplies, and troops, but Saladin tended to stall. An open clash between the two was avoided by the death of Nur al-Din in 1174.

Although Egypt was the primary source for his financial support, Saladin spent almost no time in the Nile Valley after 1174. According to one of his admiring contemporaries, Saladin used the wealth of Egypt

for the conquest of Syria, that of Syria for the conquest of northern Mesopotamia, and that of northern Mesopotamia for the conquest of the crusader states along the Levant coast.

This oversimplification aside, the bulk of Saladin's activities from 1174 until 1187 involved fighting other Muslims and eventually bringing Aleppo, Damascus, Mosul, and other cities under his control. He tended to appoint members of his family to many of the governorships, establishing a dynasty known as the Ayyubids in Egypt, Syria, and even Yemen. At the same time he was willing to make truces with the crusaders in order to free his forces to fight Muslims. Reginald of Châtillon violated these arrangements, to Saladin's annoyance.

Modern historians debate Saladin's motivation, but for those contemporaries close to him, there were no questions: Saladin had embarked on a holy war to eliminate Latin political and military control in the Middle East, particularly Christian control over Jerusalem. After the Battle of Hattin, Saladin, following the predominant military theory of the time, moved rapidly against as many of the weak Christian centers as possible, offering generous terms if they would surrender, while at the same time avoiding long sieges. This policy had the benefit of leading to the rapid conquest of almost every crusader site, including the peaceful Muslim liberation of Jerusalem in October 1187. The negative was that his policy permitted the crusaders time to regroup and refortify two cities south of Tripoli — Tyre and Ashkelon.

From Tyre, Christian forces, reinforced by the soldiers of the Third Crusade (1189–1191), encircled Muslims in Acre, destroyed the bulk of the Egyptian navy, and, under the leadership of Richard the Lion-Heart (q.v.), captured the city and slaughtered its Muslim defenders. Saladin, by avoiding a direct battle with the new crusader forces, was able to preserve Muslim control over Jerusalem and most of Syria and Palestine.

Saladin's reputation for generosity, religiosity, and commitment to the higher principles of a holy war have been idealized by Muslim sources and by many Westerners including Dante, who placed him in the company of Hector, Aeneas, and Caesar as a "virtuous pagan."

JERE L. BACHARACH

Malcolm Cameron Lyons and D. E. P. Jackson, *Saladin: The Politics of the Holy War* (1984).

Salamis, Battle of

late September 480 B.C.

The great naval victory over Xerxes' invasion fleet off the island of Salamis marked the turning point of the Persian Wars (q.v.) and ushered in the maritime supremacy of fifth-century B.C. Athens.

After retreating in the face of superior Persian power, the Greeks squabbled over the next point of collective resistance. On the advice of the Athenian general Themistocles, who had under his charge the alliance's greatest contingent of 180 triremes, the Greeks staked their national safety in a last-ditch sea battle in the channel between Salamis and Attica, within sight of occupied Athens.

The narrow straits hampered the mobility of the much larger Persian fleet, which may also have been more vulnerable to ramming by the heavier Greek ships. The decisive defeat of Xerxes' fleet prompted the king and his navy to abandon Greek waters altogether and ensured that the heroic defenders would never again fear enemy landings at their rear: Greece south of Attica was now safe. After Salamis, Greeks for the first time felt that defeat of the Persians was entirely practicable, and so in great numbers they joined a national army of resistance that drove out the Persian infantry the next year at Plataea.

In the battle's immediate aftermath, Greeks rightly saw the victorious rowers of Salamis as proof of the skill and courage inherent within the nascent democratic citizenry of Athens. But in the years subsequent, reactionary philosophers took a dimmer view. Plato and Aristotle traced radical democracy, Athenian maritime imperialism, and the collapse of

the traditional Greek values back to Salamis — a victory that had given enormous prestige to the poor and ill-bred of the fleet, and therefore in their eyes had made the Greeks "worse as a people." Few Greeks, however, shared their jaded appraisal, and instead rightly commemorated Salamis as the battle that had saved the West.

VICTOR DAVIS HANSON

Samurai

The samurai warrior class, which dominated Japan for nearly half the nation's recorded history, was born in a shift in imperial state military policy that began in the mid–eighth century and picked up momentum during the ninth. In keeping with a generalized trend toward privatization of government functions, the court supplanted and eventually replaced its conscripted, publicly trained military force with one composed of privately trained and equipped elites, creating a series of new titles that legitimized the use of personal military resources to serve the state. Government interest in martial talent dovetailed with growing private demands from the high court nobility for these same talents, making skill at arms an increasingly promising means for ambitious young men to get a foot in the door for careers in government or in the service of powerful aristocrats. The result was the gradual emergence of an order of professional fighting men in the capital and in the countryside.

For a quarter of a millennium, the members of this new order were content to fight the court's battles for it. And then, in 1180, Minamoto Yoritomo, a dispossessed scion of a leading warrior house, adeptly parlayed his own pedigree, the localized ambitions of provincial warriors, and a series of upheavals within the imperial court into the creation of a new institution, called the shogunate, or *bakufu* by historians, in the eastern village of Kamakura. This new regime was a government within a government, at once a part of and distinct from the court in Kyoto, charged with overseeing eastern Japan and the samurai class. Warrior power waxed steadily as shogunal vassals learned to exploit tensions between the court and the new shogunate. By the early fourteenth century, when Ashikaga Takauji's Muromachi shogunate replaced the Kamakura regime, warriors not only dominated the countryside, but also overshadowed the imperial court as well.

The steady unraveling of centralized authority and assertion of localized warrior power that began in the late twelfth century continued until real power in Japan had devolved to a few hundred feudal barons, called daimyo, whose rule rested first and foremost on their ability to hold lands by military force (see *Feudalism*). The fifteenth and early sixteenth centuries passed in almost continuous warfare as daimyo contested with one another to maintain and expand their domains. The spirit of this so-called Age of the Country at War is captured by two expressions current at the time: *gekokujō* — "the low overthrow the high" — and *jakuniku kyōshoku* — "the weak become meat; the strong eat."

But the instability of *gekokujō* could not have continued indefinitely. Daimyo discovered that the corollary cliché to "might makes right" is that "he who lives by the sword, dies by the sword," and that they spent as much of their time trying to defend themselves from their own ambitious vassals as from other daimyo. By the late sixteenth century, the most able among them were finding ways to reduce vassal independence. This in turn made possible the creation of ever larger domains and hegemonic alliances extending across entire regions. In the event, the successive efforts of three men — Oda Nobunaga (1534–1582) (q.v.), Toyotomi Hideyoshi (1536–1598) (q.v.), and Tokugawa Ieyasu (1542–1616) (q.v.) — eliminated many of the smaller daimyo and unified the rest into a nationwide coalition.

Under a new shogunate headed by the Tokugawa, Japan entered nearly three centuries of uninterrupted peace, with profound consequences for the samurai. Set apart from other classes by law, gathered in castle towns, and no longer engaged in battles, the samurai rapidly evolved from landed feudal warriors to stipended bureaucrats and administrators.

A combination of foreign pressure, changes to the nation's social and economic structure, and decay of the government itself eventually brought down the Tokugawa regime. In 1868 combined armies from two domains in southwestern Japan forced the resignation of the last shogun, and declared a restoration of all powers of governance to the emperor. This event, known as the Meiji Restoration, after the calendar era, marked the beginning of the end for the samurai as a class. Over the next decade they lost first their monopoly over military service, and then, one by one, the

This nineteenth-century Japanese woodblock print shows an armored samurai warrior dangling the head of a victim from his teeth.

rest of their badges and privileges of status: their special hairstyle, their way of dress, their exclusive right to surnames, their hereditary stipends, and their right to wear swords in public. By the 1890s Japan was a modern, industrialized nation ruled by a constitutional government and defended by a westernized conscript army and navy. The samurai had passed into history.

KARL F. FRIDAY

San Francisco Conference

April–June 1945

Nearly three hundred delegates representing fifty nations convened at a conference in San Francisco on April 25, 1945, to reach agreement on an international organization designed to keep the peace in the post-war world. The founding members of this organization were to be the states who were fighting the Axis powers and who had subscribed to the "Declaration by United Nations" of January 1942. Foreshadowing the future of the United Nations, the conference consumed seventy-eight tons of paper. The most important document was the Charter of the United Nations, adopted by the conferees on June 25, 1945.

Although Franklin Roosevelt (q.v.), the key architect of the charter, died shortly before the opening of the San Francisco Conference, his spirit lived on in the structure of the new United Nations. Hoping for success where both Woodrow Wilson (q.v.) and the League of Nations had failed, he had insisted that the authority to enforce collective security should rest firmly in the hands of the great powers, who would be permanent members of the UN Security Council. These "policemen" were also to have the right to veto any enforcement action unacceptable to them.

American, British, Chinese, and Soviet diplomats had reached substantial agreement on this collective security architecture at the Dumbarton Oaks Conference of August–September 1944. The main issue at San Francisco was whether or not the smaller powers would accept the "top-heavy" structure. In the event, the most remarkable feature of the conference proved to be how little dilution there was of the role of the great powers in the UN charter as it was adopted.

In the end, however, the United Nations did not fulfill Roosevelt's expectations. The new system could work only if and when concord existed among the great powers. Roosevelt's premise was that the Grand Alliance would survive the defeat of its common enemies; but, as Yogi Berra once declared, "The future ain't what it used to be."

BRADFORD A. LEE

Saratoga, Battle of

September 19 and October 7, 1777

The word *Saratoga* is shorthand for two battles that gave the coup de grâce to the 1777 British invasion from Canada during the American Revolutionary War (q.v.). After capturing Fort Ticonderoga with almost laughable ease, the British army, led by overconfident General John Burgoyne, crawled south at a tortoise pace, giving the rattled Americans time to regroup under Horatio Gates. To support him, General George

Washington (q.v.) sent Benedict Arnold (q.v.), his best infantry commander; Colonel Daniel Morgan and his crack regiment of Virginia riflemen; and two brigades of Continentals from the Hudson Highlands. They raised Gates's strength to about sixty-five hundred men. Equally important was Colonel Thaddeus Kosciusko, the Polish engineer, who built excellent field fortifications on Bemis Heights overlooking the Hudson River.

On September 19, Burgoyne attacked. The fiery Arnold prodded Gates out of his defensive mentality, winning permission to lead Morgan's men and Henry Dearborn's light infantry into the woods to block a British flanking column. For most of the afternoon, a furious struggle raged around and across a clearing called Freeman's Farm; Arnold poured in fresh regiments until the jittery Gates broke off the action, leaving the battered British in possession of the ground. After fortifying his camp and waiting in vain for reinforcements from New York, Burgoyne attempted another assault on October 7. Ignoring orders from the jealous Gates to remain in his quarters, Arnold joined the fighting and led an attack that captured key strong points, forcing the British to retreat to Saratoga (modern Schuylerville). There, surrounded by a belated outpouring of militia, Burgoyne surrendered ten days later.

THOMAS FLEMING

Sargon the Great

2334?–2279? B.C., *King of Akkad and General*

Sargon became a legend in ancient Mesopotamia for his extraordinary conquests, which created the first Mesopotamian-based empire. First conquering Sumer's ancient city-states, he then campaigned far beyond Mesopotamia, forging an empire that stretched over nine hundred miles from the Persian Gulf to the Mediterranean Sea and north into Asia Minor.

How he managed this is far from clear. His capital has never been found; records from his reign survive largely as later copies and as traditions preserved in omens, proverbs, and poetry. These report that he began as a royal cupbearer, became a ruler, and conducted thirty-four campaigns, ranging from Lebanon's forests to Iran's plains. Despite uprisings and attacks, his heirs ruled a vast empire for almost 150 years. From an ancient poem Sargon's challenge still echoes: "Any king who would rival me — let him go where I have gone!"

BARBARA NEVLING PORTER

Sargon II

r. 721–705 B.C., *King of Assyria and General*

Seizing the throne during an uprising, Sargon II went on to become one of Assyria's (q.v.) greatest warrior-kings. In his early years he subdued two successive revolts by western vassals, fought the rebel king of Babylon to a temporary standstill, and crushed an uprising against one of his eastern vassals. But Assyria's longstanding rival Urartu continued to foment rebellion from its remote mountain fortresses. Cutting paths through the mountains with pickaxes, Sargon's army approached Urartu from the rear, confronting the Urartians in a mountain pass some three hundred miles from Assyria. When the exhausted Assyrians faltered, Sargon attacked with his bodyguard, making "blood run down the ravines . . . like a river." The Urartian king retreated and then abandoned his capital; Sargon swept through Urartu, looting, burning, and crippling it permanently. Sargon's subsequent subjection of Babylonia made the Assyrian Empire essentially complete.

BARBARA NEVLING PORTER

Saxe, Hermann Maurice, Count de

1696–1750, *French General*

An illegitimate son of Augustus II of Saxony, Hermann Maurice, count de Saxe, enrolled in the Saxon army and fought at Malplaquet (1709) and then against the Swedes in Pomerania (1711–1712). He then entered Austrian service and served under Prince Eugène against the Turks (1717–1718); he was nearly killed at the Battle of Belgrade (1717). He entered French service in 1719, serving against Eugène in the War of the Polish Succession. Saxe played a major role in the War of the Austrian Succession, capturing Prague in a nocturnal storming (November 17, 1741). He became a marshal of France (March 26, 1743) and commanded the French force preparing for the invasion of England in the spring of 1744, but this scheme was thwarted by storms. Later that year he was appointed commander of the French army in the Low Countries. In 1745 he besieged Tournai and defeated the duke of Cumberland's relief attempt at Fontenoy (May 11, 1745): the battle demonstrated the strength of a defensive force relying on firepower and supported by a strong cavalry reserve. Saxe then captured Tournai and Ostend, and in 1746 he took Brussels and Antwerp and then defeated Charles of Lorraine at Roucoux (October 11, 1746). In 1747 Saxe outmaneuvered Cumberland when he sought to regain Antwerp and defeated him at Lawfeldt (July 2, 1747), where the British infantry, in defense of the village, inflicted heavy losses but were finally driven out. But Saxe failed to exploit his victory. In 1748, Maastricht fell to siege by Saxe and an army of over 100,000 men.

Saxe's generalship was instructive not only because of his battlefield ability to control large numbers effectively in both attack and defense, but also because of his determined espousal of a war of maneuver, as in his successful surprise convergence on Maastricht. Saxe's preference for bold maneuvers, emphasis on gaining and holding the initiative, and stress on morale contrast markedly with stereotyped views that mid-eighteenth-century warfare was indecisive. His *Mes Rêveries*, written in 1732 but posthumously published in 1757, criticized reliance on firepower alone and instead advocated a combination of firepower and shock (hand-to-hand fighting). Saxe preferred individually aimed fire to the "present method of firing by word of command," as the latter, he claimed, "detains the soldier in a constrained position," preventing "his levelling with any exactness." Saxe's military ideas embodied the contradictions of the eighteenth century. He was forward-looking, for example, in his stress on the use of light troops and the motivation of the soldiers, and yet also backward-looking: his idea of the legion as a unit and his interest in the reintroduction of armor were borrowed from ancient Rome. Saxe was important because he encouraged fresh thought about tactics and strategy.

JEREMY BLACK

Schlieffen, Alfred von

1833–1913, *German General Field Marshal*

Alfred, count von Schlieffen, chief of the German General Staff from 1891 to 1906, was the originator of the so-called Schlieffen Plan, with which Germany began World War I (q.v.). The plan sought to solve a complex set of tactical and strategic problems, most especially that of how to fight simultaneously against

France and Russia. Schlieffen's solution reversed that of his great predecessor, the elder Helmuth von Moltke (q.v.), whose experiences in the Franco-Prussian War (q.v.) had been sufficiently nerve-racking that he had come to doubt whether such swift success could be achieved again. Moltke had accordingly favored limited operations against France and a major effort against Russia. Schlieffen, in contrast, would seek immediate, all-out victory in the west by means of a massive attack through the Low Countries that would sweep south beyond Paris, trapping the entire French army against the Swiss frontier. German forces would then be shifted east by rail to counter the threat from Russia.

There was much to be said for this scheme, in theory. At the tactical level, the rapid advance of the German right wing would prevent the development of a static trench line and mitigate the difficulty of sustaining an attack against prepared defenses. By betting everything on a quick victory, Schlieffen also responded to widespread fears that industrial societies could not sustain long wars, but would break down rapidly once the markets and labor pools on which they depended were disrupted. That Germany, overmatched in manpower and cut off from world trade, would lose such an attritional conflict seemed obvious.

So too did the idea that the necessary rapid victory could be obtained only against France. There was no realistic chance of enveloping and destroying the Russians in the vast spaces of their homeland. France, moreover, was certain to attack quickly after declaring war and would exploit any disproportionate deployment of German forces in the east. The same could not be said of Russia, whose mobilization schedules — at least in 1900 — were markedly slower than those of France or Germany. The difference between the pace of Russian mobilization and the speed of the German advance across France represented a window of opportunity for Schlieffen, which he intended to exploit in order to win the next war.

Aside from its unparalleled audacity, the Schlieffen Plan had a number of striking characteristics that must, in the end, count heavily against it. Schlieffen was a professional staff officer par excellence, who felt no need to take account of political consequences: the likelihood that a gross violation of Luxembourgian and Belgian neutrality would draw Britain into war against Germany seemed to him a purely diplomatic (or possibly naval) problem. His plan also turned absolutely on one factor entirely beyond Germany's control: the speed with which Russia could launch an attack in the east, which was certain to improve as its armed forces modernized. Even assuming the available time was sufficient — which was barely true when war finally came in 1914 — this aspect of Schlieffen's plan effectively ceded to the Russians the decision of when Germany would go to war, a remarkable fact whose full significance became apparent only during the July crisis itself, when the speed of Russian mobilization exposed the barrenness of Germany's real strategic options: political retreat or war on two fronts.

Schlieffen worked ceaselessly to refine his strategic vision, which acquired its distinctive feature — a preemptive, enveloping attack against France — shortly after the Franco-Russian alliance of 1894, but never achieved the final, perfected form that is sometimes imputed to it. No fewer than forty-nine variants and revisions of the plan were prepared under Schlieffen's supervision, a process that continued under his successor, Moltke the Younger (q.v.). Moltke's changes were all in the direction of prudence, driven by concern for the improving military effectiveness of Germany's prospective opponents, and doubts about the logistical prodigies that Schlieffen had required to get his timetables to come out right. Schlieffen would certainly have joined those who found Moltke's conduct of operations in 1914 too timid. In the event, however, he did not live to see his work come to grief on the Marne (q.v.), having died the previous year at the age of eighty.

DANIEL MORAN

Schwarzkopf, H. Norman

1934– , U.S. Gulf War General

Part vain martinet, part selfless team player, General H. Norman Schwarzkopf, the most illustrious general of the 1990–1991 Gulf War (q.v.), will undoubtedly be remembered for his flawless coordination of an unlikely Muslim-Christian military alliance against an Arab foe. At West Point, Schwarzkopf gained an unwholesome reputation among his lower-class subordinates for handing out unnecessarily humiliating beratings over minor infractions. At the same time, out of uniform, he proved to be a kind, tireless mentor to younger cadets whom he coached in wrestling. But in the eyes of his superiors, the ambitious young officer was a comer. He succeeded in Vietnam and quickly rose above his peers to the rank of major general and commander of the Twenty-fourth Infantry Division. At lower levels, word that Schwarzkopf would callously hatchet subordinates caused those junior to him to seek assignments away from his command. Yet few doubted his effectiveness in building and maintaining high-performance fighting units.

The Gulf War brought out both sides of this complex man. Once in Saudi Arabia, he energetically courted the media, pushing a field soldier's image and vowing to show more concern for his troops' welfare than Vietnam-era generals had exhibited. Yet, some brother officers have contrasted his behavior unfavorably with the earlier leader General William Westmoreland (q.v.). For example, whereas Westmoreland usually welcomed dissenting views within his staff and from subordinate commanders, Schwarzkopf's intimidating demeanor often deterred the expression of opposing ideas. The best of Schwarzkopf was clearly demonstrated in his wielding of an ungainly, two-headed "Muslim and others" command into a victorious battlefield coalition. Following the war, claim of authorship to various parts of the allied plan came from several quarters. However, there is little doubt Schwarzkopf approved, directed, or shaped every aspect of the scheme and considerable skepticism that others would have claimed any ownership if the plan had failed. Rightly, he will be recalled as a skilled political general, an essential cog in multinational twentieth-century military endeavors.

ROD PASCHALL

Scipio Africanus (Publius Cornelius)

237–183 B.C., *Roman General*

Scipio Africanus, like the duke of Wellington (q.v.), combined patrician hauteur with the charisma of a born leader. Thus before assaulting Cartagena, he could persuade his troops that Neptune was on their side and afterwards put them through as rigorous a training program as any modern drill sergeant. As a tactician he was innovative, complex, and elegant, but he lacked Hannibal's (q.v.) deceptive but deadly simplicity, and he owed his victory over the latter at Zama (q.v.) to having the better army on the day.

His finest achievement was perhaps the defeat of the Carthaginian forces in Spain, where he accomplished in five years (210–206 B.C.) what his father and uncle had failed to accomplish in eight (218–211 B.C.).

But although his later strategy of invading Africa led B. H. Liddell Hart (q.v.) to describe him as "greater than Napoleon," it was pedestrian compared with the grandeur of Hannibal's invasion of Italy, being merely a repeat of what the Romans had already tried once before, in 256–255 B.C., and had been planning before Hannibal seized the initiative.

Scipio's career looked forward to those of men like Pompey and Caesar (q.v.) who were to destroy the Roman republic, though there was never any question of this in his case. Thus his appointment to Spain was an "extraordinary command," and after his victory at Baecula (present-day Bailén, Spain), he was allegedly the first Roman general to be saluted *"imperator"* by his troops.

J. F. LAZENBY

Scott, Winfield

1786–1866, *U.S. General*

During his fifty-three years of service, Winfield Scott made a significant impact on the professionalization of the army. During the first eighteen months of the War of 1812 (q.v.), he witnessed firsthand the problems inherent in a heavy reliance on ill-trained citizen militia. He rigorously trained American soldiers at Buffalo, New York, and in the summer of 1814 demonstrated what disciplined troops could do at the dexcisive victory near Chippewa Creek and the bloody stalemate along Lundy's Lane.

Taking advantage of the postwar nationalism, which caused many Americans to view the military more favorably, he assisted in pushing for a permanent army that adhered to standards of professionalism. In 1821 he wrote *General Regulations for the Army*, the first comprehensive, systematic set of military bylaws that set standards for every aspect of the soldier's life. He also wrote and periodically updated an infantry tactical manual. Well versed in military history, Scott patterned the American army after its European counterparts, which he greatly admired. Codification of army life along with his tireless advocacy of education and training were essential elements in bringing professionalism and tradition to the U.S. Army.

Not only did Scott work to create an American version of European armies, but he also tried to emulate their aristocratic officer corps. Born to a family of modest means and fatherless at a young age, Scott sought an upper-class lifestyle, and high rank in an institutionalized, professional army helped him attain that status. Several times in his career, however, his handling of funds led to controversy, which on one occasion resulted in his suspension from the army. He married into a wealthy Virginia family and was fortunate to have friends with power and means who sometimes helped him both politically and financially.

Although his character contained flaws, Scott's military ability was unquestioned. He reached the pinnacle of his career in the Mexican War (q.v.). In the Mexico City campaign in 1847, he repeatedly maneuvered his opponents out of their defensive positions. His chief engineer, Captain Robert E. Lee (q.v.), helped scout the route for some of these flank maneuvers, thus molding his own skills for a later war. Scott was not averse to using frontal assaults if necessary, but he preferred to win victories by siegecraft or turning movements. War to him was much like a game of chess that matched brains as well as brawn. His tactics were not always as glamorous as they might have been had he relied more on the bayonet charge, but neither were they as costly. Upon Scott's capture of Mexico City, the duke of Wellington (q.v.) proclaimed him the greatest living soldier.

Winfield Scott served as commanding general of the army from 1841 to 1861. He had a lifelong ambition to be president, but the closest he came was running as the Whig nominee in 1852. In 1861 he devised the Union strategy called the Anaconda Plan, which emphasized a coastal blockade and utilization of river systems. By maintaining constant pressure on the South, Scott intended to gradually squeeze the life out of the Confederacy. Although initially scoffed at, his method was eventually used to defeat the Confederacy (see *American Civil War*). Because of old age and infirmities he retired from the army in 1861, and he died at his beloved West Point in 1866.

TIMOTHY D. JOHNSON

Secret Weapons

They are the wild cards in war's deck, the arms equivalent of ambush, the essence of technological surprise: secret weapons. The very term conjures up images of ultrasecure laboratories, high science, esoteric technologies — the whole litany of what constitutes the state of the art.

Yet this is deceptive. There is nothing new in the concept of secret weapons, which reaches far back into history. Indeed, every arms innovation was in some sense a secret weapon when it was first used. Novelty always implies a measure of the unexpected, but the notion and intent of a secret weapon also suggest devastating surprise and foes rendered helpless in the face of something for which they have no defense.

Consequently, it also connotes ruthlessness and even desperation. For the dominant course of arms has been symmetrical — the matching of like-armed opponents testing their skill and valor within the context of certain at least implicitly agreed-upon rules of engagement. Secret weapons seek to upset the balance. The chief assumption is that if used unexpectedly, the weapon will prove particularly effective. But even among history's more successful secret weapons, this has not proved uniformly true.

Take, for instance, the case of modern chemical warfare. When first employed in 1915 by the Germans, who sought to break the stalemate that had developed on the Western Front during the first months of World War I (q.v.), a massive greenish yellow cloud of chlorine created almost instantly a four-mile-wide gap in French positions along the Ypres salient. But, by the very next day, Allied medical services had identified the gas and provided improvised face pads that enabled Canadian troops to hold their positions when similarly attacked. Poison gas would be used for the remainder of the war, with much more lethal varieties being developed. Yet by itself, it remained largely incapable of winning battles.

An analogous but more complex fate overtook several considerably more useful secret weapons. Equally intent on breaking the deadlock on the Western Front, the British in utmost secrecy formed a "landships" committee to develop an armored vehicle capable of overrunning trenches. The resultant "tank" (q.v.) — named to fool the Germans into thinking they were working on water-storage devices — was rushed into production early in 1916. While clandestinely perfecting the device, the British gave little thought to how it would be used. So, when the first few were ready, they were thrown into the Battle of the Somme (q.v.); the effect was as transitory as the first use of poison gas. These weapons had to be used en masse, and it was only much later, in 1917 and 1918, that the British employed tanks in sufficient numbers to make a difference. By this time, they were no longer secret.

A more flagrant and ultimately far more disastrous example of this phenomenon took place during the Franco-Prussian War of 1870 (q.v.). The French, ill

A fourteenth-century Byzantine warship directs its secret weapon, "Greek fire," a napalm-like concoction that might have contained quicklime, petroleum, and sulfur.

prepared and poorly led, placed great faith in the supersecret *mitrailleuse* — basically a hand-cranked machine gun. First tested in 1860 and produced six years later, the guns were purposely cloaked in such obscurity that when war came, hardly anyone knew how to operate them. Worse still was a tactical doctrine that called for *mitrailleuses*, a natural against infantry, to be fired at maximum range as artillery. Prussian cannon simply blew them up.

Nevertheless, once out in the open and properly used, both the tank and the machine gun proved to be excellent weapons, instruments that no serious army could afford to be without. And that was the problem — today's secret weapon had the nasty habit of becoming tomorrow's universal threat. And there could be no more monumental example of the syndrome than the nuclear devices dropped over Hiroshima and Nagasaki in 1945. Developed in complete security and used with decisive results, they seemed to epitomize the devastating possibilities of secret weapons. They actually ended a major war. They were viewed at the time and for the first few years after World War II (q.v.) as an American monopoly, truly representative of U.S. technological supremacy. But the Soviet Union, aided by scientist-spies from the United States, began a crash program of its own; in September 1949, an American research plane making atmospheric

tests detected unmistakable signs that the Russians had tested their own nuclear device. It was but the first of many shocks that would play out in an arms race (q.v.) destined to leave each competitor with literally tens of thousands of nuclear warheads aimed at virtually everything the other side held dear. Collectively, they made all-out war not only unwinnable, but absurd.

Yet strange outcomes are not just phenomena of the recent past. History provides examples of unintended consequences even among secret weapons sprung with great initial success on unsuspecting adversaries. In 260 B.C. the landlubber Romans, locked in a mortal struggle with maritime Carthage during the First Punic War (q.v.), found a unique means of evening the odds. They equipped their ships with a grapnel-based boarding bridge known as the *corvus*, effectively turning loose the major Roman military asset — swordsmen. It worked for a while, delivering a string of five consecutive victories in which the Romans managed to turn sea battles into land battles. Gradually the Carthaginians learned to apply their superior seamanship to ram the Roman boats at points where the *corvus* could not be deployed. By the end of the war the *corvus* had disappeared, and the victorious Romans had adopted Carthaginian tactics with surprising success.

More enigmatic was the fate of Korea's "turtle ships." Built in the last decade of the sixteenth century as a desperate measure to foil the invading Japanese under Toyotomi Hideyoshi (q.v.), these hundred-foot-long craft were entirely encased in a carapace of hexagonal metal plates virtually invulnerable to cannon shot. Handled with great skill by Korean admiral Yi Sun-Shin (q.v.), the turtle ships destroyed the main Japanese fleet in Hansan Bay on July 8, 1592. Surprised but apparently undaunted, Hideyoshi ordered supplies of iron plates, clearly intending to build a fleet of turtle-equivalents. But inexplicably the program was halted, as was the invasion after Hideyoshi's death in 1598. Indeed, from this point, Japan largely gave up naval warfare, entrusting its maritime trade to European crews. The turtle ships were rendered irrelevant.

Finally, a secret weapon of devastating initial effectiveness, continuing usefulness, and enduring confidentiality — the dream of all who seek this kind of military advantage — has existed; there is but a single unambiguous example, and once again the context is a struggle for survival. In A.D. 678 the Byzantine Empire was near extinction, its capital Constantinople besieged on land and sea by a massive force of Muslims (see Constantinople, Sieges of). Then, late in the year the Byzantines sent out a squadron of ships armed with siphons spewing liquid fire of such irrepressibility that it even burned in water. The Muslim fleet was torched, the siege was lifted, and Byzantium was saved. Forty years later the miracle was repeated. In 718 the citizens of Constantinople once again found themselves surrounded, this time by a much larger force of 200,000 soldiers and 7,500 vessels. The situation seemed hopeless, until Byzantine warships disgorging the same flaming substance staged raids on the Arab supply vessels and once again saved the city. The infernal liquid has come to be known as Greek fire, and seldom has a single weapon had such a decisive effect. It was no wonder. Like napalm, it stuck to everything and ignited practically anything — hulls, sails, rigging, and crew members, for whom even jumping into the sea failed to douse the flames. Byzantium became obsessed with guarding the secret, and legend has it that besides the emperor and his immediate family, only a single family, the direct descendants of its inventor, knew how to make the volcanic substance. Indeed, so successful were the Byzantines at keeping the secret of Greek fire that by 1204 it was lost, forgotten and never to be recovered. It was an ironic end to history's most enduring secret weapon.

The erratic course that secret weapons have cut through history is understandable — these engines were intended to destabilize the status quo and play upon the unexpected. It is logical, therefore, that they and their users should reap a whirlwind of unintended results. For on the battlefield, just as in life, change begets change.

ROBERT L. O'CONNELL

Bernard Brodie and Fawn M. Brodie, *From Crossbow to H-Bomb*, rev. ed. (1973); William H. McNeill, *The Pursuit of Power: Technology, Armed Force, and Society since A.D. 1000* (1984); Robert L. O'Connell, *Of Arms and Men: A History of War, Weapons, and Aggression* (1990).

Sedan, First Battle of

August–September 1870

During the Franco-Prussian War (q.v.), in August 1870, the French Army of Châlons was concentrated in the immediate vicinity of the city of Sedan on the Meuse. Under the personal command of Emperor Napoleon III, it was retreating from a failed attempt to lift the siege of Metz. Sedan lay in the path of two nearby German armies, and the Army of Châlons soon found itself surrounded.

Sedan is situated in the center of a bowl with a radius of about one thousand yards. Captured by the Germans, the heights that formed the rim of the bowl provided first-class positions for hundreds of artillery pieces. The Germans used these to bombard the closely packed (eighty-five thousand men in less than two square miles) French troops and assist the German infantry to beat back French counterattacks. By the afternoon of September 1, 1870, with no prospect of aid and German troops at the very gates of the city, Napoleon III decided to surrender. Thus ended France's Second Empire and the first phase of the Franco-Prussian War.

BRUCE I. GUDMUNDSSON

Sedan, Second Battle of

May 10–16, 1940

The Second Battle of Sedan began on May 10, 1940, when German forces advanced into Luxembourg and Belgium. By making their main attack through the Forest of the Ardennes, the Germans sought to avoid

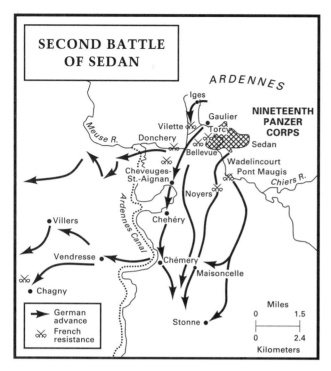

SECOND BATTLE OF SEDAN

ARDENNES

Iges

NINETEENTH PANZER CORPS

Gaulier
Vilette
Torcy
Doncherγ
Sedan
Bellevue
Cheveuges-St.-Aignan
Wadelincourt
Pont Maugis
Chiers R.
Noyers
Meuse R.
Ardennes Canal
Villers
Chehéry
Vendresse
Chémery
Maisoncelle
Chagny
Stonne

→ German advance
⚔ French resistance

Miles
0   1.5

0   2.4
Kilometers

the Allies' main strength and penetrate the light defenses along the Meuse River. Elements of the Nineteenth Panzer Corps, commanded by General Heinz Guderian (q.v.), reached the Meuse River near Sedan on the afternoon of May 12, and on the following day, after extensive aerial bombardment, they attacked. Including the action at Sedan, the Germans crossed the Meuse at three locations, and on the morning of May 16, they broke through the last of the rapidly assembling French forces.

Numerous myths have long surrounded the 1940 campaign. When the battle began, the Germans did not have a concept for what came to be known as the blitzkrieg (q.v.). Only after the successful campaign did the real potential of modern mechanized warfare become apparent to most German leaders. Much of the key fighting in the battle was waged by the infantry, whose skillful actions enabled German tanks to cross the Meuse River and continue moving despite spirited resistance at several locations south of Sedan. German aircraft made their most important contribution by weakening the will to fight of the French defenders along the Meuse: they actually destroyed few targets and failed to hold up French reinforcements.

The German victory at Sedan provided the opportunity for exploitation to the west and the swift defeat of

France. Few battles have provided such unexpected or decisive results.

ROBERT A. DOUGHTY

Seeckt, Hans von

1866–1936, Colonel General and Commander of the German Army

Hans von Seeckt, who laid the foundation for Germany's blitzkrieg (q.v.) tactics, was born to a noble Pomeranian family; his father was a general in the Prussian army. He was commissioned in 1887; in 1893 he was selected for the elite Kriegsakademie course and membership in the General Staff Corps.

Von Seeckt developed a reputation as a brilliant, innovative tactician in World War I (q.v.). His most notable successes were on the Eastern Front. As chief of staff of the German Eleventh Army, he masterminded the breakthrough of the Russian army at Gorlice in May 1915, which drove the Russians out of Poland. As an army group chief of staff, he executed successful campaigns in Macedonia and Romania.

In 1920, von Seeckt was selected as commander in chief of the army. He initiated a comprehensive study of the lessons of World War I and reformed the army doctrine and tactics. Von Seeckt believed that maneuver and mobility were more important than mass and firepower, so the German army was retrained in mobile, combined arms operations. Although Germany was virtually disarmed, von Seeckt created programs for aircraft and tank development and training. Seeckt's reforms of the 1920s created the foundation for the Wehrmacht and the blitzkrieg tactics of 1939–1940.

JAMES S. CORUM

Selim I

1470?–1520, Ottoman Sultan

Supported by the janissaries, Selim succeeded to the Ottoman (q.v.) throne in 1512 on the forced abdication of his father, Bayezid II, and consolidated his rule with the fratricide of his brothers Korkud and Ahmed and the murder of his nephews. Impatience at his father's tolerant attitude toward the Shi'ite "heretics" was apparent while he was governor of Trabzon, when he undertook raids eastward into the territory of the Iranian Safavid dynasty. After defeating the Safavid shah

Ismail at Çaldıran (q.v.), he imposed Ottoman allegiance on much of his eastern border.

Selim next destroyed the Mamluk state (the leading Muslim power and, like Safavid Iran, a threat to his frontier) by virtue of the battles of Marj Dabik near Aleppo (1516) and al-Raydaniyya near Cairo (1517). Syria and Egypt became Ottoman provinces, although not without continuing local disturbance. Before his death, Selim was preparing a further major campaign against Iran.

Selim greatly enlarged the Istanbul dockyards and in 1518–1520 ordered the building of a substantial fleet for a planned attack on Rhodes. The securing of the Mediterranean sea routes intensified after the conquest of Egypt, and Ottoman naval operations were also directed against the Portuguese in the Red Sea and Indian Ocean.

Selim's experience against the Safavids and Mamluks demonstrated the importance of firepower. With his support of orthodox Islam and his guardianship of the holy cities, achieved by his victory over the Mamluks, he had enhanced the moral prestige of the Ottoman dynasty, as well as ensuring that his state emerged victor in the struggle for power in the Middle East.

CAROLINE FINKEL

Sennacherib

r. 704–681 B.C., *Assyrian King and General*

With Assyria's empire extended to its practical limits and the last threat to Assyria (q.v.) removed by the defeat of Urartu by his father (Sargon II [q.v.]), Sennacherib was able to abandon the long-standing practice of annual campaigns, conducting no more than nine campaigns in his twenty-three years of rule and devoting himself instead to building a magnificent fortress-capital at Nineveh. Ironically, he is better known for besieging Jerusalem and sacking Babylon.

What happened at Jerusalem remains unclear. Sennacherib claimed to have suppressed a revolt by Judah and its western allies, taking booty and tribute, whereas the Bible reports an abrupt Assyrian withdrawal without taking Jerusalem, perhaps reflecting an unsuccessful second campaign that Sennacherib failed to mention. In Babylonia, repeated revolts led Sennacherib to create an Assyrian navy — unprecedented for this land-bound nation — to attack Babylonia's eastern ally Elam by sea. When Sennacherib's son was then assassinated, Sennacherib redoubled his attacks on Elam and Babylonia, finally sacking venerable Babylon.

Despite his other accomplishments — which included the building of Nineveh, the construction of a remarkable aqueduct that still stands today, and the invention of a new process for casting massive bronze statues (which was apparently the king's personal invention) — Sennacherib's fame rests on these two dubious military exploits.

BARBARA NEVLING PORTER

Sepoys

The name of these Indian troops serving under European discipline derived from the Urdu-Persian word *sipahi* (soldier). Most sepoys came from the same villages in northern India that had long provided volunteer soldiers to Muslim rulers such as the Mughals (q.v.). Until the 1740s, they also served the Europeans under their own leaders with traditional weapons, but thereafter they began to fight with muskets under the command of European officers and NCOs. By 1782 the English East India Company deployed almost 100,000 sepoys in India and occasionally used them abroad (above all in Burma and China). The Indian Mutiny of 1857 (q.v.), in which many sepoys withdrew their service from the company, marked a turning point. Although the British continued to employ Indian troops at home and abroad — Sikhs directed the traffic of Peking after the suppression of the Boxer Rebellion in 1900 (q.v.) — they now came from all over the subcontinent.

GEOFFREY PARKER

Seven Weeks' War

June–August 1866

The Seven Weeks' War (also called the Austro-Prussian War) pitted Prussia and Italy against Austria and most of the smaller German states. The war grew out of the increasing embitterment of Austro-Prussian relations since 1849, when Prussia tried to exploit revolutionary upheaval in central Europe to wrest control of the German Confederation from Austria. Despite the recent expansion and modernization of the Prussian army, most observers anticipated an Austrian victory — which made the speed and final-ity with which Prussia crushed its larger opponent all the more impressive. In the aftermath Austria gave up its rights in Germany and ceded Venetia to France, which presented it to Italy. Northern Germany was reorganized as a confederation under Prussian auspices, to which the southern kingdoms were bound by treaty.

Prussia's victory stemmed from a combination of political and military advantages. Otto von Bismarck's (q.v.) securing of French and Russian neutrality meant that Austria would fight, for practical purposes, alone. His opportunistic alliance with Italy was likewise useful in drawing Austrian forces away from Prussia. Years of planning by Helmuth von Moltke's (q.v.) General Staff in the use of railroads and telegraphy to move and control large forces also paid off, by allowing three independent Prussian armies to advance concentrically against a concentrated and static foe.

The decisive battle of the war occurred at Königgrätz (q.v.), where the Austrians narrowly escaped the envelopment Moltke had planned for them. Given the will, Austria might have fought on for months. To have done so, however, would have risked French intervention and even civil war, without doing anything to redeem Austria's preeminence in Germany, now lost forever.

DANIEL MORAN

Seven Years' War

1756–1763

The Seven Years' War essentially comprised two struggles. One centered on the maritime and colonial conflict between Britain and its Bourbon enemies, France and Spain; the second, on the conflict between Frederick II (the Great) of Prussia (q.v.) and his opponents: Austria, France, Russia, and Sweden. Two other less prominent struggles were also worthy of note. As an ally of Frederick, George II of Britain, as elector of Hanover, resisted French attacks in Germany, initially only with Hanoverian and Hessian (q.v.) troops but from 1758 with the assistance of British forces also. In 1762, Spain, with French support, attacked Britain's ally Portugal, but, after initial checks, the Portuguese, thanks to British assistance, managed to resist successfully.

The maritime and colonial war proved a triumph for Britain, a reflection of the strength of the British navy — itself the product of the wealth of Britain's expanding colonial economy and the strength of British public finances. The French planned an invasion of Britain, but their fleet was badly battered in defeats in 1759 at Lagos off Portugal (August 19–28) and Quiberon Bay off Brittany (November 20). These naval victories enabled Britain to make colonial conquests: Louisbourg (1758), Quebec (1759), and Montreal (1760) in North America; Guadeloupe (1759), Martinique (1762), and Havana (1762) in the West Indies; Manila (1762); and the French bases in West Africa. The British also prevailed in India, capturing the major French base, Pondicherry, in 1761. These campaigns around the globe demonstrated and sustained the range of British power.

The war in Europe began in 1756 when Frederick II invaded Austria's ally Saxony in order to deny a base for what he feared would be an Austro-Russian attack on him. The invasion was successful, but it helped to create a powerful coalition against Frederick. He pressed on to invade Bohemia, but the Austrians put up unexpectedly strong resistance and forced him to withdraw.

Frederick's survival was the product of good fortune and military success — not only a number of stunning victories, such as Rossbach and Leuthen (q.v.), but also the advantage of fighting on interior lines against a strategically and politically divided alliance. Russian interests centered on East Prussia, the Austrians were most concerned by Silesia, and the French increasingly devoted their efforts to the war with Britain.

Although Prussia survived the war, casualties were very heavy. Frederick discovered how exposed his dominions were, though their extent allowed him to abandon territory and thus to trade space for the vital time he needed to exploit internal lines, in order to defeat his opponents individually.

In 1757 East Prussia was invaded by the Russians, but Frederick defeated the French at Rossbach (November 5) and the Austrians at Leuthen (December 5). In 1758 the Russians captured East Prussia, but the bloody Battle of Zorndorf (August 26), in which Frederick lost one-third of his force and the Russians eighteen thousand men, blocked their invasion of the Prussian heartland of Brandenburg. In the following year, the Russians defeated Frederick at Kunersdorf (August 12), the Prussians losing nearly two-thirds of their force; but the Russians failed to follow it up by concerted action with Austria. In 1760–1761 the Austrians consolidated their position in Saxony and Silesia, while the Russians temporarily seized Berlin and overran Pomerania. Frederick was saved by the death of his most determined enemy, Tsarina Elizabeth, on January 5, 1762, and the succession of her nephew, Peter III. Frederick was his hero, and he speedily ordered Russian forces to cease hostilities. Isolated, Austria was driven from Silesia and obliged to sign peace at Hubertusberg on February 15, 1763, on the basis of a return to the prewar situation.

Frederick's difficulties stemmed in part from recent reforms in the Austrian and Russian armies. The Russians in particular fought well, and their formidable resources made a powerful impression on Frederick. To cope with these challenges, Frederick was obliged to change his tactics during the war: as everyone sought to avoid the mistakes of the previous year's campaigning season, warfare was shaped by the fluid dynamics of the rival armies. Initially, Frederick relied on cold steel, but after sustaining heavy casualties from Austrian cannon and musket fire at the Battle of Prague (May 6, 1757), he placed more emphasis on the tactics of firepower, for example, at Leuthen. Frederick became more interested in using artillery as a key to open deadlocked battlefronts. However, Frederick's success in avoiding decisive defeat at the hands of his opponents can distract attention from the extent to which they were able to innovate in order to respond to Prussian tactics. The Prussian oblique order attack (in which one end of the line was strengthened and used to attack, minimizing exposure to the weaker end) lost its novelty, and the Seven Years' War demonstrated the essential character of European warfare: the similarity in weaponry, training, and balance between component arms of different armies made it difficult to achieve the sweeping successes that characterized some encounters with non-European forces.

JEREMY BLACK

Sharpsburg, Battle of

See Antietam, Battle of.

Sheridan, Philip

1831–1888, *American Civil War General*

Philip Henry Sheridan graduated from West Point in 1853. Posted to the Northwest, he campaigned against the Yakima Indians and served for several years in Oregon, where he lived with a Rogue River Indian woman who taught him her native tongue.

A captain at the beginning of the American Civil War (q.v.), on May 25, 1862, he was made colonel of the Second Michigan Cavalry and on September 13 was promoted to brigadier general of volunteers. After distinguishing himself at Perryville and Murfreesboro, he was promoted to major general of volunteers as of December 31, 1862. He commanded a division at Chickamauga, and soon after, General Ulysses Grant (q.v.) gave him command of the Army of the Potomac's cavalry. He fought at the Wilderness, Spotsylvania, and Cold Harbor, and in May 1864, he raided the Confederate lines of communication around Richmond.

After Jubal Early's raid on Washington, D.C., in July 1864, Sheridan was given command of the 42,000-man Army of the Shenandoah, with orders to close the "back door on Washington." In September he drove Early back at Fisher's Hill, but when Early attacked his army at Cedar Creek, Sheridan was in Winchester on his way back from a meeting in Washington. Hearing the sounds of battle, he rode through the night to his command, retrieving victory from defeat, an exploit made famous by Thomas Buchanan Read in a poem, "Sheridan's Ride." On September 20, 1864, he was promoted to major general in the regular service.

The most anti-Southern of the Union generals, Sheridan turned the fertile Shenandoah Valley, the "breadbasket of the Confederacy," into a wasteland. He then rejoined the Army of the Potomac before Petersburg and played a major role in the operations leading to the surrender of General Robert E. Lee (q.v.) at Appomattox. Sheridan was a tough soldier who inspired fear and admiration in equal parts.

At the end of the war, Sheridan organized and directed campaigns against the Indians on the South Plains. In 1869 Sheridan, now lieutenant general, assumed command of the Division of the Missouri, which encompassed one million square miles from Canada to the Mexican border, and he did much of the planning for the Great Sioux War of 1876–1877 (see *Plains Wars*). Although widely credited with declaring that "the only good Indian is a dead Indian," he always denied having said this.

In November 1883, Sheridan became commanding general of the army, and in June 1888, two months before his death, he was made a full general.

BYRON FARWELL

Sherman, William T.

1820–1891, American Civil War General

Perhaps the originator and the first practitioner of what the twentieth century came to know as "total war," William Tecumseh Sherman in 1864 commanded the Union armies of the West in the decisive drive from Chattanooga to Atlanta and the famous "march to the sea" across Georgia.

In these campaigns and his later push northward from Savannah through the Carolinas, Sherman's troops carried the war to the Southern home front and blazed a wide path of destruction that delivered the death blow to the Confederacy's will and ability to fight. For the accompanying destruction, his name is still cursed in some parts of the South; but he is also recognized as a great strategist, a forceful leader, and — together with Ulysses Grant (q.v.) — the ablest Union general of the war. The partnership of William Tecumseh Sherman (known to friends as "Cump") with Grant helped bring both out of early obscurity, until Grant commanded all Union armies and Sherman led all federal forces in the West.

The careers of both men had been undistinguished between the Mexican War (q.v.) and the American Civil War (q.v.). When the South seceded, Sherman — West Point, 1840 — was superintendent of a military college that is now Louisiana State University. Aided by his brother John, a member of Congress from Ohio, he reluctantly left the South for a Union commission. Sherman commanded a brigade in the war's first major battle, at Bull Run in Virginia, and then a division in its first truly bloody encounter, at Shiloh; later, he led a corps in one of its climactic campaigns, against Vicksburg, Mississippi, and he commanded a federal army in the last battle of the war in the East, at Bentonville, North Carolina.

His military career had not always been so outstanding; as commanding general of the Department of the Cumberland, 1861–1862, he feuded with the press, displayed emotional problems, and suffered accusations of insanity. Only after this ordeal did he begin his long and fruitful association with Ulysses Grant. Sherman's influence, for example, helped stop Grant from resigning when the latter felt himself hamstrung by orders from Washington.

In the 1884 battles before Atlanta, Sherman's opponent was Joseph E. Johnston; but Johnston's skilled retreats before Sherman's turning tactics exasperated President Jefferson Davis, who replaced Johnston with the belligerent John B. Hood. Sherman soundly

The Ten Worst Generals

Alcibiades (Sicilian Expedition, 415 B.C.)

Julian (Persian Expedition, 363)

Ambrose E. Burnside (Fredericksburg Campaign, 1862; the Petersburg Crater, 1864)

Sir Douglas Haig (the Somme, 1916; Ypres, 1917)

Robert-Georges Nivelle (French Offensive, 1917)

Maurice Gamelin (Fall of France, 1940)

Mark Clark (Italian Campaign, 1943–1944)

Adolf Hitler (World War II, 1941–1945)

Chiang Kai-shek (Chinese Civil War, 1945–1948)

William Westmoreland (Vietnam, 1964–1968)

defeated Hood in several engagements and occupied Atlanta early in September 1864.

On November 15, in perhaps the boldest act of the war, he led an army of sixty-two thousand men in two wings, with thirty-five thousand horses and twenty-five hundred wagons, on an overland march to Savannah — cutting himself off from his line of supply and sustaining his army on the land. "The utter destruction of [Georgia's] roads, houses and people," he had written, "will cripple their military resources ... I can make Georgia howl!" Encountering little organized opposition, Sherman took Savannah on December 21, 1864, and later turned north for the Carolinas, covering 450 miles in fifty days.

The results of this remarkable march justified Sherman's strategic expectations and, together with Grant's victories in Virginia, destroyed the Confederacy's ability to carry on the war. It is still disputed, however, whether the burning of Atlanta, the later burning of Columbia, South Carolina, and the depredations of "Sherman's bummers" were either necessary or unpreventable.

For his military prowess, Sherman is justly renowned; he succeeded Grant as commander in chief in 1869 and remained in that post until 1883. Two memorable remarks of his also have entered history. Having written to Mayor Calhoun of Atlanta in 1874 that "war is cruelty, and you cannot refine it," he sharpened this definition in a commencement address at the Michigan Military Academy in 1879 to the oft-quoted phrase "War is hell."

Five years later, when he was frequently talked of as a prospective Republican nominee for president, Sherman sent the Republican National Convention of 1884 the most famous of all rejections: "I will not accept if nominated and will not serve if elected." Even today, "a Sherman" is well-understood slang for a firm refusal.

Perhaps the greatest tribute to William T. Sherman was paid by his old Civil War opponent Joe Johnston, who had fought him in Georgia and had signed with him an armistice after the Battle of Bentonville in April 1865. The two became friends. General Johnston attended Sherman's funeral in New York in 1891, stood in the rain to watch the cortege pass, and caught a cold. It caused Johnston's death two weeks later.

TOM WICKER

Sicilian Expedition

415 B.C.

In June 415 B.C., during a hiatus in the Peloponnesian War (431–404 B.C.) (q.v.), an enormous fleet set out from Athens on an eight-hundred-mile voyage to conquer Syracuse, a key ally of Sparta, and thereby gain control over the island of Sicily. Two years later, the campaign ended in abject failure, its generals dead, the plan's mastermind Alcibiades in service with the enemy, and most of nearly forty thousand Athenians and their allies captured or killed.

Ostensibly, the conquest of Sicily would have provided a rich source of revenue for the Athenian Empire, weakened Sparta, and opened possibilities for expansion into North Africa. In reality, Alcibiades' design to empty the city in hopes of destroying the only other large maritime democracy in the Greek world was lunatic from the beginning, and the Spartans (q.v.) immediately renewed the war with a permanent base within sight of Athens and a relief fleet sent to Sicily itself.

Exhausted and nearly defenseless, Athens managed to continue the war for another nine years, but the losses incurred at Sicily marked the end of its imperial aspirations and forced it into a desperate, largely defensive struggle that could not be won.

VICTOR DAVIS HANSON

Sieges

The siege constitutes the natural corollary of fortifications (q.v.), and until the advent of aerial bombardment a fortified location could be compelled to surrender in war only by employing one of four strategies.

The Ten Greatest Sieges

Jericho by the Israelites (1350? B.C.): The first recorded siege in history.

Troy by the Greeks (1190?–1180? B.C.): The longest recorded siege in history.

Constantinople by the Turks (1453): An early example of gunpowder artillery causing a fortress to fall.

Tenochtitlán by the Spaniards (1520–1521): The first full-dress siege in the Americas.

Yang-chou by the Manchus (1645): The bloodiest sack in history.

Vicksburg by the Union army of Ulysses S. Grant (1863): A turning point in the American Civil War.

Verdun by Germany (1916): The costliest siege of this century.

Leningrad by Germany (1941–1944): The longest siege of this century (nine hundred days).

Stalingrad by Germany (1942–1943): The turning point of World War II in Europe.

Dien Bien Phu by the Viet Minh (1954): Its fall marked the end of French colonial rule in Southeast Asia.

Geoffrey Parker

Many places, especially those containing a large civilian population, have fallen through hunger or thirst after a lengthy blockade (like Vicksburg, the last Confederate stronghold on the Mississippi during the American Civil War [q.v.], whose capitulation in 1863 cut off the western Confederate states). Others have been taken by a ruse (Troy, according to legend, fell to a group of soldiers intruded in a large wooden horse). Others still have succumbed through treachery (Jericho [q.v.], in the first recorded siege, was betrayed by information provided by "Rahab the harlot," the first spy — as well as the first prostitute — recorded in history). Finally, defenses have been demolished, either by artillery fire (as at Constantinople [q.v.] in 1453) or by the use of mines (see *Siege Weapons*), resulting in immediate assault and sack by the besiegers or in negotiated surrender.

Whatever the outcome, sieges normally caused huge loss of life. First, maintaining large concentrations of people in the same spot — whether inside the beleaguered stronghold or in the trenches around it — could easily create acute food shortages and serious epidemics that claimed numerous lives. Second, the fighting itself could cause heavy casualties, whether in hand-to-hand combat during attacks on the trenches and assaults on the town, or through the use

The storming of a fortified castle is depicted in a fifteenth-century French illuminated manuscript. Determined soldiers climb ladders with weapon in one hand and shield in the other while archers defend the castle from the battlements. Such sieges could last for years — wise castellans stored a year's supply of food and fuel in case of such an attack — and typically incurred enormous casualties (note the moat clogged with corpses).

of artillery and mines. Third, if the defenders rejected calls to surrender and then succumbed to a storm, according to the prevailing laws of war (q.v.), they might be slaughtered or enslaved: thus, after the capture of Yang-chou in China in 1645 by the Manchus (q.v.), a ten-day massacre left perhaps 800,000 dead, while all the women were raped, chained together, and deported. Knowledge of their likely fate if captured normally encouraged either hasty capitulation or else desperate resistance by defenders. Some sieges therefore lasted for years. Troy in the twelfth century B.C. defied the Greeks, according to Homer's *Iliad*, for ten years (see *Trojan Wars*); Leningrad in the twentieth century A.D. held out for nine hundred days — and even then starvation and repeated German assaults failed to subdue the Russian defenders, who knew the fate of other cities that had fallen.

Some sieges have been used to "bleed" an enemy. During World War I (q.v.), at Verdun (q.v.) in 1916, the German high command laid siege to a fortified com-plex that their adversaries were sure to defend at all costs in order to maximize their casualties. In the event, however, they lost almost as many men as the French defenders — the 400,000 killed and 800,000 wounded were split roughly equally between the two sides — and Verdun never surrendered. During World War II (q.v.), at Stalingrad in 1942–1943 (q.v.), al-though at one point the Germans held 90 percent of the city, the Soviets fed in enough fresh troops to keep the siege going until a decisive counterattack cut off some 200,000 of the exhausted besiegers. At Dien Bien Phu in 1954 (q.v.), French elite troops in Indo-china created a fortified complex in an isolated but strategically crucial location, in the hope of exhaust-ing the Viet Minh through a costly siege. Instead, however, arrangements for supplying the exposed gar-rison broke down and they eventually surrendered, in effect ending the war.

The frequency of sieges normally reflected the mili-tary geography of the theater of operations. Thus in Europe, areas with numerous towns close to a politi-cal frontier, such as Belgium, Hungary, or northern Italy, have traditionally invested heavily in fortifica-tions, so that battles became to some extent irrele-vant: defeating the enemy's field army only mattered if it led to the fall of fortified towns. In areas lacking modern defenses, however, such as England during the 1640s, field engagements proved both more com-mon and more decisive (see *English Civil Wars*). In other parts of the world, all urban centers might re-main unfortified: in Southeast Asia, Siberia, and sub-Saharan Africa, for example, until the arrival of the Europeans in the sixteenth century, even commercial and political capitals lacked fortifications, and the normal response to enemy attack was flight, since dwellings destroyed could easily be rebuilt. Sieges therefore remained unknown. But the creation of European artillery fortresses around the coasts of Asia and Africa introduced a new element to warfare and underpinned the rise of the West to global hegemony: until the fall of Singapore (q.v.) to the Japanese in 1942, no major European center overseas succumbed to a siege by non-European forces.

GEOFFREY PARKER

Siege Weapons

Just as humans from the earliest times sought to pro-tect themselves and their property with walls and ditches, so have their assailants sought the means to defeat those defenses. Archaeological evidence suggests that the earliest fortifications were hedges or wooden palisades and that fire was commonly used against them when treason, surprise, and escalade failed. Fire, however, was — and is — difficult to control and destroys as it defeats; moreover, walls of stone provided an effective defense against fire, so more sophisticated weapons were needed to launch a successful attack.

Though there is no direct evidence, the earliest of these was probably the battering ram, a beam of timber suspended from ropes and swung by a team of attackers to break down a wall or gate. By historical times, the heads of rams were often sheathed in metal, and rams were at times mounted in wheeled sheds, roofed to protect the operators from missiles, and suspended from the superstructure by ropes. By late antiquity, movable towers, covered with hides for protection from fire, were pushed against fortifications on rollers or wheels to gain fire superiority and serve as a jumping-off point for assault parties. Besiegers also attacked walls with sledges, picks, and pry bars, and by classical times, mining — digging a timber-shored gallery beneath the wall and burning the shoring away to collapse it — was an established tactic. Individual missile weapons were used to clear defenders away from the parapets, so attackers could work at the base of the wall or mount it with ladders. Torsion-powered mechanical artillery that could throw stone projectiles and javelins appeared in Hellenistic times and was used both offensively and defensively.

Much of the specialized European technology of siegecraft was lost with the fall of Rome. Greek fire, a self-igniting liquid incendiary of unknown composition, expelled from pumps, was important to the Byzantines as a defensive weapon. "Wild fire," probably red phosphorous, and liquid petroleum played minor roles as incendiary weapons. The crossbow, which reached Europe from China in late classical times, was the most important individual medieval missile weapon of siege warfare. Less accurate, of short range, and slower shooting than the Turco-Mongol composite bow or English longbow, the crossbow had limited value in field warfare but was useful in sieges for shooting through narrow embrasures and could be worked by defenders weakened by hunger or disease. Another Chinese development was the trebuchet, a stone-throwing engine worked by human traction or counterpoise. But the trebuchet was ineffective against stone walls, and, until the advent of gunpowder (like the crossbow and trebuchet, a Chinese invention), starvation and treason were the only generally effective means of defeating well-built, well-defended stone fortifications.

The first serious gunpowder siege weapon was the petard, a portable bomb used to blow in gates and doors. Although potentially effective, petards required tactical finesse, and unpredictable fuses — smoldering slow match and loose powder trains — led to the self-explanatory expression "hoist on his own petard!" Next came the advent of effective heavy gunpowder artillery, first in France from the 1420s, and then throughout Europe. From the mid–fifteenth century, the Ottoman Turks held the lead in very large siege ordnance, fielding guns capable of firing stone balls weighing in excess of one thousand pounds.

The French developed mobile siege guns by the end of the fifteenth century, marking a major watershed in warfare; except in remote and inaccessible locations, places defended by medieval curtain walls were now highly vulnerable. The explosive gunpowder mine appeared shortly thereafter and proved surprisingly long-lived: large subterranean mines were used by Union forces in the American Civil War (q.v.) at the siege of Petersburg, by all forces on the Western Front in World War I (q.v.), by Spanish Republicans at the siege of the Toledo Alcázar in 1936, and by the Viet Minh to break French resistance at Dien Bien Phu (q.v.) in 1954.

Bronze muzzle-loaders (called "cannon of battery"), typically firing a cast-iron ball of twenty-four to fifty pounds, remained the basic weapon of siege warfare from the early sixteenth century to the mid–nineteenth century. Change during this period was incremental and was as much tactical as technological. The barrels and carriages of siege and fortress ordnance became lighter and more efficient, and stone balls gave way to cast iron, first in the West and then in the East. As the numbers of guns increased, fortresses were armed more heavily, and garrisons were able to drive attackers back from the walls with cannon fire, forcing them to dig their way forward, advancing by saps and parallels. By the seventeenth century, the shovel was the besieger's most commonly used weapon, and the hand grenade was useful for close-in combat in the trenches. Walls were brought down far more frequently by mining than by battery.

This state of affairs changed dramatically with the appearance in Europe and America in the late 1850s of heavy rifled artillery that fired ogival rather than spherical projectiles. Capable of hitting accurately from ranges of several thousand yards, these quickly reduced masonry to rubble and forced another revolution in fortress architecture. The resultant fortresses of reinforced concrete, sunk low in the ground and defended by steel gun turrets, proved vulnerable in turn to heavy breech-loading ordnance firing high-explosive shells with time-delay fuses and sharply pointed noses of hard steel for penetration. This was an important lesson of the early days of World War I (q.v.), which saw the Belgian fortresses of Liège and Namur torn apart by heavy Krupp and Skoda siege mortars. The defender's solution was to rely on temporary earthworks, multilayered belts of trenches and dugouts defended by rifle and machine-gun fire and supported by artillery. Combat reverted to siege operations for most of the war, and the line between siege and field weaponry became — and remains — blurred. The flamethrower, fielded by the Germans in 1915 in response to the demands of trench warfare, proved effective against field fortifications in World War II (q.v.). Few specialized siege weapons have been built since, and most of those have proved a massive waste of resources, notably the German Kaiser Wilhelm Geschütz, which shelled Paris from the forest of Gobain at a range of some seventy-five miles in March 1918, and the monstrous Krupp Gustav railway gun designed in the 1930s to attack the Maginot line (q.v.) and used against Sevastopol in 1942. In a sense, the V-2 rocket of World War II — also a massive waste of resources in terms of German military priorities — might be considered a siege weapon, but it was really the first of an entirely new kind of weapon of more general utility, the ballistic missile.

JOHN F. GUILMARTIN

F. E. Adcock, "Cavalry, Elephants, and Siegecraft," in *The Greek and Macedonian Art of War* (1957); Charles W. C. Oman, "Siegecraft (1100–1300)," in *A History of the Art of War in the Middle Ages*, vol. 1 (1924); Charles W. C. Oman, "Siegecraft and Fortification," in *A History of the Art of War in the Middle Ages*, vol. 2 (1924).

Singapore, Battle of

February 1942

The Japanese conquest of Malaya, culminating in the capitulation of the Singapore garrison with more than 100,000 British and Empire troops in mid-February 1942, constituted a debacle virtually without parallel in British military history. Not since Cornwallis (q.v.) surrendered at Yorktown in 1781 (q.v.) had British arms suffered such a humiliating defeat. The blow to British prestige and morale was all the greater because Singapore had been long publicized as "the Gibraltar of the Pacific," an "impregnable fortress." Poor coordination between the services resulted in an ill-defined strategic concept that was further hampered by a lack of material support: few modern aircraft were available to support a defensive strategy based upon air power; the Royal Navy was unable to furnish adequate forces to protect the seaward flank; and there was not a single British tank in all of Malaya. The garrison commander, Lieutenant General Sir Arthur Percival, offered hesitant and ineffective leadership to a poorly integrated amalgam of British, Australian, and Indian troops, many of whom entered battle with only rudimentary training; some troops arrived in Singapore within a fortnight of their enlistment.

If the defense of Singapore was a textbook example of military incompetence, its conquest at the hands of the Japanese was exactly the opposite: a superbly planned and executed military operation under the command of Lieutenant General Yamashita Tomoyuki (q.v.). He early recognized the difficulty of a direct amphibious assault on Singapore Island and chose instead to advance upon the fortress from the Malay Peninsula. The success of this operation gave rise to the persistent myth that the fixed artillery on Singapore "faced the wrong way." All the major seacoast artillery did, in fact, traverse a full 360 degrees. But through a lapse of planning that characterized the entire defense, virtually all of their ammunition was armor piercing and therefore useless against any but naval targets.

ELIHU ROSE

Sino-Japanese War

August 1894–April 1895

This conflict marked the emergence of modern Japan on the international stage and heralded the onset of Japanese imperialism. As the culmination of ten years of Japanese planning for the strategic domination of Korea, the Sino-Japanese War was initiated by Japan for the eradication of Chinese influence there. Japan was quick to put an army ashore on the peninsula, but although it won a succession of decisive land victo-

In February 1942, a reconnoitering party of Soviet ski troops wear snow-camouflage hoods, cloaks, and gloves.

ries over Chinese forces — notably at Pyongyang and in the capture of Port Arthur — the most significant Japanese triumphs were scored at sea. Japan's strategy, though marked by caution, correctly assumed that command of the sea was critical to all that it hoped to achieve on land. It was imperative, moreover, that a decision at sea be quickly reached, since any prolongation of the war increased the risk of intervention by a European power. The Japanese Combined Fleet therefore swept into the Yellow Sea, where it utterly defeated China's Peiyang Fleet off the Yalu River at the outset of the war. The first fleet encounter since Italians and Austrians clashed at Lissa (1866), the battle underscored the superiority of the column formation, a homogeneous battle force, and the concentration of gunfire. The Japanese victory was followed up by the destruction of the remnants of the Peiyang Fleet at Weihaiwei. By the Treaty of Shimonoseki, which ended the war, Japan acquired Taiwan and Treaty Port privileges in China (although Korea eluded its grasp); thus Japan became the first modern Asian imperialist power.

MARK R. PEATTIE

Skiing, Military

The ski is extremely ancient, long used for hunting and transport across northern Europe and Asia. Traditionally, in most of Europe winter warfare was avoided because of the cold; but in Scandinavia, warriors have used skis for centuries, and the ski-equipped Swedish-Finnish army defended the frontier against Russia in 1656. The first military ski manual appeared in 1733 for the Norwegian army, which formed the first ski corps in 1747, supported by three-pounder mountain cannon mounted on ski ("winter") carriages. In mid-nineteenth-century Norway, interest in skiing broadened; the telemark ski was developed, and sport skiing emerged. Subsequent tactics and techniques were mainly patterned on Norwegian methods, and by World War I (q.v.), Switzerland, Germany, France, Austria-Hungary, Russia, Turkey, and Italy had ski units. In the winter war of 1939–1940, Finland fought with skillful guerrilla ski tactics, and the U.S. Army developed the Tenth Mountain Division (a skiing unit) during World War II (q.v.). — though this unit, which distinguished itself in Italy, rarely used its skis.

SCOTT HUGHES MYERLY

Slavery, Military

Slaves and ex-slaves have had a surprisingly widespread and varied career as soldiers throughout history, extending to times even within human memory.

Slaves in war can be divided into two types, ordinary and military slaves. Ordinary slaves were those valets, cooks, and field hands who found themselves in battle. They usually provided support behind the lines, reinforcements on the sidelines, or emergency help on the front lines; only rarely have they served as frontline troops. Ordinary slaves were not terribly effective, limited by their lack of training, by their owners' lack of enthusiasm (carrying arms has traditionally been considered a noble task), and mistrust (slave mutinies were never far from masters' minds). Still, the record shows that slaves generally fought faithfully; and why not, since for better or worse, once they appeared on the battlefield, they had cast their lot in with their masters? This reasoning even applied in the most extreme case, the American Civil War (q.v.), in which slaves accompanied their owners to fight for the Confederacy, though this meant they helped the very cause that kept them enslaved.

Ordinary slaves have fought in war from the time the first captives were taken alive on the battlefield and pressed into service until the early twentieth century. Outstanding examples include ancient Greece and Rome (where they formed autonomous units), ancient India (where they fought initial skirmishes before the main fighting began), and colonial Latin America (where, on some occasions, slaves were put in the front lines as cannon fodder).

To go beyond secondary tasks on the battlefield required military slaves, that is, men specifically acquired, trained, and employed for war: professional soldiers. Counterintuitive as it may sound, rulers, governors, and other powerful figures in many societies did see slaves as a useful addition to their forces. Slaves formed a significant proportion of the arms-bearing population in sixteenth-century Muscovy. Manchu (q.v.) rulers depended on battalions of Chinese slaves during their conquest of China for a few years after 1615. In the Napoleonic era, the British created the West India Regiments from specially recruited African slaves to do their fighting on Caribbean islands where tropical disease kept Europeans out. Thanks to the passage of the Negro Soldier Law, slaves began training to fight for the American Confederacy during the last, desperate month of the Civil War, though the war ended before they could see action. In Cameroon during the 1890s, German colonial administrators purchased slaves from Dahomey and relied on them as gendarmes.

In all these cases, slaves served in remote regions or in emergency circumstances. Only among Muslims did military slavery develop into a central and regular system of recruiting and employing soldiers. Muslim leaders depended on soldier slaves for roughly a thousand years (850–1850). Slaves performed critical military tasks from Spain in the West to Indonesia in the East; indeed, at some point they probably had a role in every Muslim-ruled territory. With the single exception of the Umayyads, in the very first century of Islam, every major Muslim dynasty in premodern times relied heavily on military slaves. In many of these dynasties, slave soldiers of Turkish origins tended to be the most highly prized and the most successful. The best-known instances of military slavery are the Mamluks of Egypt and the janissaries of the Ottoman Empire (q.v.).

Military slavery had two principal advantages for premodern rulers: they could acquire the most qualified soldiers (meaning those proficient on horses), and they could win their loyalty by bringing them in as teenagers and overseeing their education. Slaves began by serving as soldiers and performed so well, they quickly rose to become officers. Strong and loyal, they then took over political positions in both the provinces and the central government. Rulers brought them into the court, where they acquired enormous influence. In more than fifty instances, individuals of slave origins (including two women) became sovereigns. In several cases (most notably in Mamluk Egypt between 1250 and 1517; also in thirteenth-century India and in Ottoman Iraq) they formed dynasties in which one military slave succeeded another. Though these dynasties required a host of original and unlikely customs (for example, the exclusion of a ruler's sons in favor of his slaves), they unquestionably proved capable on the battlefield and succeeded in enduring politically.

DANIEL PIPES

David Ayalon, *The Mamluk Military Slavery* (1979); Daniel Pipes, *Slave Soldiers and Islam: The Genesis of a Military System* (1981).

Slim, William

1891–1970, British Field Marshal

Lord William Slim was of lower-middle-class origin; without World War I (q.v.), a career as an officer would have been unthinkable to someone with his background. But in 1914, Slim joined up and went to the Middle East, where he served with distinction throughout the war and earned a commission. Because of his family's lack of wealth, a career as an officer in the British army was out of the question; but the Indian army offered a respectable alternative.

Then war intervened again. After distinguished service as a brigadier in the Abyssinian campaign of 1941, Slim assumed command of a division in Iraq, helping to displace Nazi-leaning rulers and to secure the Iraqi oil fields. The disgraceful British collapse in Southeast Asia in early 1942 brought Slim his great opportunity; he had to lead shattered British forces out of Burma in a nightmarish retreat that ended at Imphal, where the Japanese ran out of steam. Once out of Burma, Slim tackled the job of restoring the fighting capabilities and morale of British and Indian troops. In his memoirs, Slim makes clear the principles on which his army operated:

1. The ultimate intention must be an offensive one.
2. The main idea on which the plan was based must be simple.
3. That idea must be held in view throughout and everything must give way to it.
4. The plan must have an element of surprise.

Over the next two years, Slim retrained his forces in Burma to a standard unmatched by other units in the British army.

In early 1944 the British hammered at Japanese positions in an attempt to break through, but the Japanese replied by invading India and in a lightening move surrounded British forces at Imphal. Flying supplies and reinforcements into the garrison, Slim mounted an overland campaign that gradually broke through to his besieged forces. Although the Japanese were able to get away, the prolonged fighting had wrecked their Fifteenth Army.

By early 1945, Slim's Fourteenth Army was poised to regain central Burma. In a swift move, the Anglo-Indian forces shifted well south of Mandalay, while the Japanese expected a crossing to the north of that city. After crossing the Irrawaddy, Slim's troops cut Japanese communications with Rangoon. The Japanese counterattack proved too little and too late; Slim was now in a race to gain Rangoon before the monsoon. His forces accomplished this on May 2, ending the most brilliant British campaign of the war. What is so astonishing about Slim's performance in command of the Fourteenth Army was his success in taking beaten, demoralized troops and, with virtually no support and few resources from Britain, turning them into an army that on both the tactical and operational levels met a standard that only the best of German troops equaled.

Slim went on to have a most successful career after the war. Over the vigorous protests of Bernard Montgomery (q.v.), he succeeded the victor of El Alamein (q.v.) as chief of the Imperial General Staff. He, more than any other individual, was responsible for changing the culture of the British army by emphasizing merit over connections. He completed his service to his country by serving as high commissioner of Australia. His memoirs rank with those of Ulysses S. Grant (q.v.) as one of the few honest testaments to the profession of arms by a great general.

WILLIAMSON MURRAY

Sluys, Battle of

June 24, 1340

In 1340, proclaiming his right to the crown of France, Edward III of England gathered an army to invade northern France with his Flemish allies. When his fleet neared Bruges, a French armada of over 200 vessels blocked its way. The 150-odd English ships closed and grappled, initiating the most important naval battle of the Hundred Years' War (q.v.). As usual in medieval sea fights, victory was determined not by superior seamanship or gunnery, but by ferocious hand-to-hand combat. The invaluable English longbowmen and Edward's sturdy men-at-arms carried the day, capturing an astounding 166 enemy ships — making Sluys more decisive, tactically, than Trafalgar (q.v.). More Frenchmen perished than at Crécy (q.v.) or Agincourt (q.v.). "If fish could talk," people said, "they would speak French."

Although the ensuing campaign accomplished little, the victory at Sluys greatly improved the English situation in the early Hundred Years' War. It ruined French plans to invade England and greatly facilitated the transport of the English troops whose *chevauchées* (mounted raids) brought Edward victory in the first phase of the war.

CLIFFORD J. ROGERS

"Smart" Weapons

"Smart" weapons, also called precision guided munitions (PGMs), alter their trajectories in flight to seek, or home on, their targets. Unlike conventional ballistic munitions, their accuracy does not normally diminish as range increases. The advantages of pinpoint accuracy have long been appreciated, particularly in aerial bombardment: the World War II (q.v.) dive-bomber was, in effect, a precision bombing system, and the Royal Air Force devoted two squadrons of Mosquito bombers to daylight, low-level, precision attacks on high-value targets such as Gestapo headquarters. In Vietnam (q.v.), U.S. Navy A-6s, and later U.S. Air Force F-111s, could achieve near-precision accuracy using radar offset bombing, aiming on the radar return of an object a known distance from the target. More recently, aircraft equipped with state-of-the-art bombing and navigation systems (taking advantage of sophisticated computer modeling of bomb-release aerodynamics, high-speed microprocessors, and laser range finders) can drop "dumb" bombs with precision accuracy. All of these methods, however, depend on low-release altitudes, thus putting the crew at risk. World War II Japanese kamikazes (q.v.) are the extreme example.

Attempts to replace human aiming with electronics date to World War II. Both the Luftwaffe and the U.S. Army Air Forces used radio-controlled bombs guided by a bombardier who tracked the bomb by means of a flare in its tail. In 1945 the Germans developed a visually tracked antitank missile that was guided by electrical inputs transmitted along thin wires played out by a spinning reel in the missile's tail. These weapons and an experimental U.S. Navy television-guided flying bomb were the ancestors of today's PGMs.

Generally speaking, PGMs are divided into four categories, according to their method of homing: command guidance, active, semiactive, and passive. Targets may be acquired and the munition tracked and guided optically, or by radar, sonar, or reflected laser light. Munitions using command guidance are steered to the target by a remote system or operator that performs all target acquisition, tracking, and guidance functions. Examples include optically tracked, wire-guided antitank missiles and most first-generation radar surface-to-air missiles, notably the Soviet SA-2. Active systems, such as antiship and air-to-air missiles with integral radar systems and homing torpedoes with on-board sonar, locate and home on their targets using emissions transmitted by the munition itself. Semiactive PGMs include most air-to-air radar missiles currently in service and laser-guided bombs; they home on energy bounded off the target by an external transmitter, usually aboard the launch platform. Passive systems home on energy emitted by the target; examples include heat-seeking air-to-air missiles, which home on infrared and ultraviolet energy in jet exhausts, and imaging infrared air-to-ground missiles, which home on a computer-memorized, infrared television image of the target. Long-range cruise missiles, notably the U.S. Air Force ALCM (air-launched cruise missile) and the U.S. Navy Tomahawk, do not fit cleanly in the above typology. The Tomahawk, the most successful and

The Patriot missile, a guided weapon equipped with radar in the nose, was originally designed as an antiaircraft missile. It was used in the Gulf War against Iraqi ballistic weapons.

widely used such missile to date, doesn't actually home on the target but uses on-board radar to generate midcourse guidance corrections for its inertial navigation system, whereas the ALCM flies to a precise set of coordinates using an inertial guidance system updated by Global Positioning System satellite transmissions.

JOHN F. GUILMARTIN

Soldiers

See The Common Soldier.

Somme, Battle of the

July 1–November 16, 1916

The Somme campaign in 1916 was the first great offensive of World War I (q.v.) for the British, and it produced a more critical British attitude toward the war. During and after the Somme, the British army started a real improvement in tactics. Also, the French attacked at the Somme and achieved greater advances on July 1 than the British did, with far fewer casualties.

But it is the losses that are most remembered. The first day of the Somme offensive, July 1, 1916, resulted in 57,470 British casualties, greater than the total combined British casualties in the Crimean, Boer, and Korean wars. In contrast, the French, with fewer divisions, suffered only around 2,000 casualties. By the time the offensive ended in November, the British had suffered around 420,000 casualties, and the French about 200,000. German casualty numbers are controversial, but may be about 465,000.

How did this happen? In early 1916, the French proposed a joint Franco-British offensive astride the river Somme. Because of Verdun (q.v.), the British army assumed the major role of the Somme offensive. Hence, on July 1, 1916, the British army attacked north of the Somme with fourteen infantry divisions, while the French attacked astride and south of the Somme with five divisions. In defense, the German army deployed seven divisions. The British attack was planned by Douglas Haig (q.v.) and Henry Rawlinson, GOC Fourth Army. The two differed about the depth of the offensive and the length of the bombardment, so the adopted plan was an awkward mixture.

The artillery was the key to the offensive, but it did not have the ability to cut all the wire, destroy deep

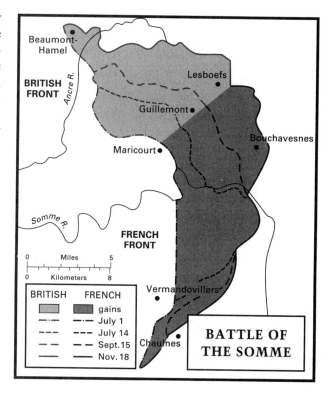

BATTLE OF THE SOMME

BRITISH FRONT

FRENCH FRONT

Beaumont-Hamel · Lesboefs · Guillemont · Bouchavesnes · Maricourt · Ancre R. · Somme R. · Vermandovillers · Chaulnes

BRITISH FRENCH
gains
—·— —·— July 1
——— ——— July 14
— — — — Sept. 15
——— ——— Nov. 18

German trenches, knock out all enemy guns, or provide a useful barrage for the infantry attack. And at zero hour on July 1, the artillery shifted away from the German front trenches too quickly and left the infantry exposed. But the French, with Verdun experience, had much more heavy artillery and attacked in rushes, capturing more ground and suffering less.

After July 1, a long stalemate settled in, with the German army digging defenses faster than Allied attacks could take place. Despite small advances, the Somme became a bloody battle of attrition, and Haig has been criticized for prolonging the campaign into winter, especially for the last six weeks. The Somme was an expensive lesson in how not to mount effective attacks, but the German army was also weakened and in February retreated to new, and shorter, defensive lines.

TIM TRAVERS

South American Wars of Independence

1810–1824

The Spanish-American independence wars were fought for almost fifteen years in one of the most extensive theaters of operations in modern history. The nature of the revolution, taking place simultaneously in many centers, demanded high mobility and resilience for movements over great distances and across rough terrain, often in appalling weather.

Fearful of social and economic upheaval in the wake of the French occupation of Spain, most independence revolutions began in 1810 in an effort to maintain the colonial status quo. Although at first the issues at stake were unclear because of political uncertainty in Spain, by 1814 — with a reactionary king back on the throne in Madrid — it became apparent that full independence of the Spanish colonies would be the only outcome.

Most serious fighting took place after 1815, when the insurgents had learned from earlier setbacks and put their political and military organization on a sounder footing, defining their goals and pursuing them with vigor. Important insurgent victories were won by José de San Martín at Chacabuco (1817) and Maipú (1818) in Chile, and by Simon Bolívar (q.v.) at Boyacá (1819) in Colombia, Carabobo (1821) in Venezuela, and Junín (1824) in Peru. The decisive victory over the royalists (with nine thousand men) was fought by Bolívar's lieutenant Antonio José de Sucre with six thousand men at Ayacucho in Peru, on December 9, 1824.

Independence fighters often specialized in hit-and-run and guerrilla tactics. High mobility and low population densities imposed severe limits on army size; they usually did not exceed five thousand men. In pitched battles, well-trained infantry tended to be decisive, but the scarcity of good foot soldiers gave cavalry a key role in most engagements.

Lack of provisions and equipment demanded considerable improvisational skills. Mules often replaced horses for cavalry, and knives and lances replaced guns. Compared to battles in contemporary Europe, artillery played a subordinate role. Insurgent officers were as good at improvising as their men since most lacked formal military training, with many rising through the ranks by merit and courage, whereas Spanish royalist officers were often trained according to European military practice and therefore found it hard to succeed in South America.

Armies were important social organizations at the local level. For many fighters, the army guaranteed survival and a livelihood for the female companions and children who often traveled with them. Successful, charismatic commanders often attracted many followers, regardless of the cause for which they fought. Many soldiers and officers switched sides frequently.

The independence wars can also be seen as a series of civil wars, in which each side had representatives from all social levels and national backgrounds. Thousands of foreign adventurers (English, Irish, German, French, and American) joined the insurgents. However, the majority fighting for each side was Spanish-American. From 1811 to 1820, some 43,000 fresh Spanish troops were sent to the colonies, and by 1820, regular Spanish troops in the colonies numbered more than 100,000 men, though most of them were by now Spanish-American natives.

Social and political consequences were far reaching. The wars ended the old colonial social system. The armies boasted a relatively democratic and open regime. In the weak successor states, control over important army units ensured political power and so contributed to frequent military coups and rebellions.

HANS VOGEL

Soviet-Polish War

1920

The Soviet-Polish War of 1920 was part of the upheaval surrounding the collapse of the Russian Empire and the Bolshevik Revolution. In April 1920, newly independent Poland, seizing the opportunity afforded by widespread chaos in Russia (see *Russian Civil War*), invaded Ukraine with the intention of establishing a pro-Polish regime there. Operating in tandem with nationalist Ukrainians, the Poles took Kiev on May 7, 1920. However, like the German invasion twenty-one years later, the Polish assault galvanized the Russians to patriotic resistance under the Communists.

In summer 1920, Soviet troops drove the Poles out of Kiev and launched an ambitious, two-pronged counteroffensive aimed at Lwów and Warsaw. Yet there was division among the Red leaders over whether to advance into Poland proper once Vilno and Minsk had been taken. Fearing intervention from the British and French, Leon Trotsky, commissar of war, advised against it. But Vladimir Lenin prevailed in pushing the invasion forward on the grounds that success in Poland might ignite Communist revolutions across Europe.

Colonel Theodore Roosevelt in July 1898 on the San Juan Heights with some of the Rough Riders whom he commanded — the Indian scouts, broncobusters, sharpshooters, and Ivy Leaguers of the First Volunteer Cavalry. On his hip, Roosevelt (center) sports a navy revolver salvaged from the wreckage of the battleship Maine, which blew up in Havana Harbor, setting off the Spanish-American War.

For a moment it looked as if this had been the right decision. By August the Soviet armies were advancing rapidly across Poland and seemed poised to take Warsaw. Joseph Pilsudski, the Polish leader, saw the Russian advance as "something irresistible, a monstrous and heavy cloud which no obstacle could halt." But believing Warsaw to be easily within his grasp, the Soviet commander Mikhail Tukhachevskii (q.v.) delayed attacking the city and divided his forces, thereby allowing a Polish army to spring into the gap. Caught by surprise, the Russians were badly mauled and beat a hasty retreat.

Yet this sudden reversal also turned out to be a miracle for the Soviets. Forced to forgo their quixotic pursuit of world revolution, the "Reds" were able to focus their full attention on the Russian Civil War. In losing Poland, the Bolsheviks saved their cause in Russia.

DAVID CLAY LARGE

Spanish-American War

April 21–August 12, 1898

Ambassador John Hay called it "a splendid little war," and in many ways it was. It lasted less than four months, and battle deaths were minimal; it brought the United States increased respect in the world community; and it ended almost four centuries of Spanish dominion of Cuba, Puerto Rico, and the Philippines.

The proximate cause of the war was the destruction of the U.S. battleship *Maine* in Havana Harbor on February 15, 1898, with the loss of 260 lives. A court of inquiry determined that a mine had initiated the explosion but did not fix responsibility. The yellow press, however, led by William Randolph Hearst and Joseph Pulitzer, blamed the Spanish. American outrage was also fueled by a fervent sympathy for Cuban insurgents who had begun a struggle for independence in 1895. Some 200,000 Cuban civilian supporters of the "revolution" had died in Spanish "reconcentration" camps.

President William McKinley's army was woefully unprepared for war, but the U.S. Navy, unlike Spain's, was honed to a fine edge. Admiral George Dewey captured Manila Bay in May, and an American fleet utterly destroyed a Spanish squadron at Santiago, Cuba, in July, thus relieving an American expeditionary force that clung precariously to the San Juan Heights, where Theodore Roosevelt, commanding the Rough Riders, had caught the public eye. As a naval officer put it, "An hour or two at Manila, an hour or two at Santiago, and the maps of the world were changed."

By the Treaty of Paris, Spain relinquished its last jewels of empire: Cuba, Puerto Rico, Guam, and the Philippines. Unfettered by colonial responsibilities, Spain made some progress on financial and political reform. A distinguished group of Spanish philosophers, artists, and writers called the "generation of '98" broke new cultural ground. The first U.S. overseas possessions seemed at first a bounty but in the end brought difficulties such as the bloody "insurrection" in the Philippines of 1899–1902.

MICHAEL BLOW

Spanish Civil War

July 18, 1936–April 1, 1939

The military rising of July 18, 1936, was the response of the Spanish Right to the reforming challenge of the Second Republic (1931–1936). The uprising succeeded in the Catholic agrarian provinces of León and

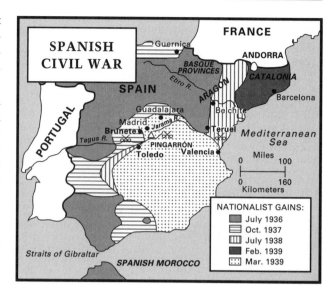

Old Castile, but was defeated by the workers in Madrid, Barcelona, and other northern industrial cities. In the south, the countryside fell to the Left, while in major towns such as Cádiz, Seville, and Granada, working-class resistance was crushed.

With untrained workers' militias facing untried conscripts, the rebels' advantage lay in the professional Army of Africa commanded by Francisco Franco, which was blockaded in Morocco by Republican warships. A further difference between the two sides was the rebels' success in seeking outside help. Hoping to cause problems for the French, Adolf Hitler (q.v.) and Benito Mussolini (q.v.) provided transport aircraft for an airlift of Franco's forces across the Straits of Gibraltar and turned a failing coup d'état into a long civil war. The Republic, in contrast, was abandoned by the democratic powers. Inhibited by internal political divisions and by British fear of a general war, the French government shrank from military aid for the Republic, which was forced to turn to the Soviet Union.

Once in mainland Spain, Franco's Moroccan troops advanced rapidly northward to Madrid while other forces cut off the Basque province of Guipúzcoa from France. On September 21, 1936, Franco was named commander in chief. He then diverted his columns to relieve the besieged garrison of Toledo, losing an unrepeatable chance to sweep on to a virtually undefended Madrid. Victory at Toledo clinched his own power, and a slower pace facilitated the bloody political purge of captured territory. Confirmed as head of state on October 1, Franco controlled a tightly centralized

Guernica, in the Basque region of Spain, was destroyed in an air raid in the first year of the Spanish civil war. The Germans, eager to test their military airplanes, bombed the town and machine-gunned the streets. Picasso's Guernica *(1937) memorializes — and condemns — the terror from the air.*

zone. In contrast, the Republic was deeply divided between the Communists and moderate Socialists, who made a priority of the war effort, and the anarchists, Trotskyists, and leftist Socialists, who wanted social revolution.

The Army of Africa resumed its march on October 7, but by then arms from the Soviet Union and the volunteers of the International Brigades (q.v.) had reached Madrid. Despite the assistance of the crack German Condor Legion, Franco's assault failed, and his attempt then to encircle the capital met with defeat at the battles of Boadilla (December 1936), Jarama (February 1937), and Guadalajara (March 1937). The Nationalists (as the rebels became known) still held the initiative, however, and between spring and autumn of 1937 easily captured northern Spain, where the Republicans were demoralized by German terror-bombing of towns such as Guernica.

The Republic tried to halt the Nationalists' inexorable progress by offensives at Brunete, west of Madrid, in July; at Belchite near Zaragoza in August; and at Teruel in December. Franco's advance was delayed, albeit at crippling cost in men and equipment, but each time the Nationalists brought up massive reinforcements before the Republicans could consolidate their early breakthrough. In early 1938, Franco launched a great offensive through Aragón toward the

sea, and by mid-April, his troops had cut off Catalonia from the rest of the Republic.

In late July, to relieve Valencia, the Republicans launched a diversionary assault across the River Ebro to restore contact with Catalonia, but after advancing twenty-five miles became bogged down. After three months of artillery and air bombardment, they lost all territory captured. Effectively, the Republic was defeated. Barcelona fell on January 26, 1939, and Madrid on March 27. The war ended on April 1, 1939, having cost 500,000 lives. About 400,000 Republicans went into exile to avoid the prison, torture, and executions that faced those left behind.

PAUL PRESTON

Spanish Succession, War of

1701–1714

During this struggle, a powerful European coalition at first humbled Louis XIV (q.v.), although he finally achieved his primary goal: the crown of Spain for his grandson. Louis XIV was not eager for another war; however, he and his heirs possessed the best claim to the Spanish throne as the sickly king, Carlos II, neared the end of his days. Attempts to avert a conflict by a diplomatic partition of Spanish lands failed when

Carlos willed all his holdings to the grandson of Louis XIV, Philip of Anjou, in 1700. Louis's aggressive behavior after he claimed the throne for Philip precipitated a general European war.

At the head of British and Dutch troops stood the duke of Marlborough (q.v.), perhaps the greatest English captain of all time, while the Hapsburg emperor — whose son was another claimant — found a commander of similar mettle in Prince Eugène of Savoy. They defeated French armies at the battles of Blenheim (1701)(q.v.), Ramillies (1706)(q.v.), Turin (1706), and Oudenarde (1708). Though less dramatic, numerous siege victories solidified the allies' hold on the Netherlands. Louis XIV now wished to escape from the war, but the overconfident allies proposed terms so extreme that the French king could not accept, and he resolved to continue the struggle.

In 1709 Louis found a general to match those of the allies, Marshal Claude-Louis-Hector de Villars. At Malplaquet on September 11, 1709, Villars collided with Marlborough and Eugène, and while the allies drove the French from the field, the French retired in good order. Allied losses were so high — as many as twenty-five thousand — that the cost outweighed the triumph. Marlborough did not fight another battle against Villars, and eventually a change in political winds blew Marlborough back to England in 1711. Eugène held on alone, but his forces were defeated at Denain (July 24, 1712). Villars followed this with a chain of successes as he seized city after city in the Netherlands and along the Rhine.

The conflict in Spain, the cause of the entire war, followed a seesaw pattern as Spanish and French forces now combined to battle Austrian, English, and Portuguese troops; Madrid changed hands twice. In the final act of the war, Barcelona fell to the French on September 11, 1714, and Philip was secure on his new throne. In North America, this conflict went by the name of Queen Anne's War. In the most important action of the war there, a British force seized Port Royal in Nova Scotia from the French in 1710, renaming it Annapolis Royal.

The Treaties of Utrecht, Rastatt, Baden, and Madrid of 1713–1716, which ended the war, transferred the Spanish Netherlands and Italian holdings, including Milan and Naples, to the Austrians, whereas Gibraltar and Minorca went to the British; however, Spain and its overseas possessions remained with Philip, although Louis promised that the crowns of Spain and France would never be united under one monarch.

The war was a classic dynastic struggle that Louis XIV won in terms of the interests of the Bourbon family but at an unacceptable price to the French state and people.

JOHN A. LYNN

Spartans

The ancient Spartans (or Lakedaimonians) were citizen-warriors who dominated the polis (city-state) of Sparta in the territory of Laconia in southern Greece. Spartans spoke a Dorian dialect; they apparently arrived in Greece in about 1200 B.C. By about 700 B.C. the Spartans dominated the other Laconians, who were divided into hereditary classes of serflike Helots and quasi-independent *perioikoi* (the "dwellers-around"). By about 650 the Spartans had conquered the neighboring Messenians, who were forced into helotry. At about the same time they adopted the "Laws of Lycurgus" (named for a legendary lawgiver), the strict code of education and social behavior that governed every Spartan's life, from infancy to old age. Spartans were renowned among the Greeks for their fanatical adherence to their Laws, an austere and standardized mode of life, "laconic" brevity in public speech, intolerance of foreigners and foreign ways, and military prowess.

The Spartans perfected the craft of hoplite (q.v.) warfare. They called themselves Homoioi (Similars), pointing both to their homogeneous lifestyle and to the discipline of the phalanx, which demanded that no soldier be superior or inferior to his comrades. Spartan education (beginning at age seven and continuing through age thirty) emphasized physical toughness, steadfastness in military ranks, and absolute obedience to orders. Because each Spartan man inherited the use of a plot of state land *(kleros)* and Helot labor to till it, he was a full-time, professional soldier. Being a Spartan meant being both a sturdy warrior and effective manager of Helot labor; the Spartan who flinched in battle or whose *kleros* failed to produce was ejected from the ranks of citizens. The harsh system worked well at first: by 500 B.C., some eight thousand Spartans dominated a league that encompassed the entire Peloponnesus (Greece south of the Isthmus of Corinth).

Along with Athens, Sparta's Peloponnesian League formed the core of Greek resistance to the Persian invasion of 480–479 B.C. The heroism of three hundred Spartans at the pass of Thermopylae allowed the Greek army to escape; Sparta's regiment fought to the last man, leaving a laconic epitaph: "Tell the Spartans we died for their Laws." Spartan leadership and hoplites ensured Greek victory in the decisive Battle of Plataea (479).

The Persian Wars (q.v.) represented Sparta's acme, but problems soon became apparent. Rumors that Pausanias, Sparta's general in northern Greece, was plotting treason led to his recall. Mopping-up operations and the organization of the postwar anti-Persian alliance were left to Athens. Sparta's recognition that its citizens were untrustworthy outside the jealous purview of the Similars precluded a proactive foreign policy; the eventual result was the consolidation of an Athenian empire and the disastrous Peloponnesian War (431–404 B.C.) (q.v.). Meanwhile, angered by systematic Spartan mistreatment (including a ritual in which Spartan youths crept about at night killing Helots and annual Spartan declarations of war against them) and encouraged by an earthquake in Laconia that killed numerous Spartans, the Helots of Messenia revolted (464 B.C.). The uprising was ultimately suppressed, but it underscored the powderkeg nature of Spartan society. During the Peloponnesian War the Athenians distracted Sparta by rousing the Helot population of Messenia, while Sparta preemptively murdered thousands of Helots, using spurious offers of freedom through army service to identify "overambitious" elements.

Sparta won the Peloponnesian War, but only by the desperate expedient of accepting Persian subsidies for a fleet capable of defeating Athens at sea; the price was Sparta's acquiescence to Persian takeover of the Greek cities of western Anatolia. The Spartans proved miserable postwar overlords for Greece; freed from the constraints of Sparta's disciplinary society, Spartan governors and field commanders proved brutal, treacherous, and incompetent. Spartan imperial policy soon led to new anti-Spartan leagues and new wars. With further Persian aid, Sparta initially held out, but the central Greek polis of Thebes (a former Spartan ally) proved a dangerous opponent. In 371, at Leuctra, Sparta gambled on a set-piece hoplite battle. Sparta's remaining three thousand hoplites were unequal to the challenge; the survivors fled. The Helots of Messenia were liberated, and Spartan power was broken forever. Subsequent attempts to revive the old ways were ephemeral; Hellenistic Sparta was at most a thorn in the side of the great states.

Demographic reality doomed Sparta's system, which allowed for mobility downward from the ranks of the Similars, but no upward mobility. In each generation fewer persons had a stake in the armed camp that was Spartan society. Sparta's later reputation may be attributed to the antidemocratic sentiments of ancient writers seeking a contrast to Athens's open society and modern nostalgia for an imaginary ideal *polis*.

JOSIAH OBER

Paul Cartledge, *Agesilaus and the Crisis of Sparta* (1987).

Special Operations

Since the earliest times, brave soldiers have put themselves forward to perform especially dangerous tasks in battle. At sieges, from Vauban's (q.v.) day to Wellington's (q.v.), parties called "forlorn hopes" would volunteer to lead the assault on prepared breaches; their casualties were enormous, but so was their glory. Less glorious and more practical work has been done in the present century, again by volunteers, in units specially formed for assault tasks.

Germany's final assault on the British lines in France during World War I, in March 1918, was led by storm troops, specially trained infantry who showed unusual initiative and enterprise. Similarly, in 1940 Winston Churchill (q.v.) formed the Commandos, men who became expert not only as marksmen, but also as battlefield athletes. Regimental commanders complained (as they always do in similar cases) that their best men were being taken from them: both storm troopers and commandos were simply ordinary soldiers trained to an extra pitch of excellence. So are parachutists, with whom the Russians began experiments in the early 1930s, followed by the Germans, the British, and later the Americans and the Japanese. Airborne troops, like shock troops and commandos, need extra gifts of initiative, self-reliance, and aggressiveness to outwit and outflank their opponents. Similarly, Bomber Command of the Royal Air Force formed its Pathfinder force in August 1942, and eventually these carefully chosen air crew were able to specialize in finding precise targets.

In July 1940, Churchill formed the Special Operations Executive (SOE), a secret service (one among eight) working throughout the world to disrupt the

Axis powers' grip, especially among Axis-conquered populations. SOE's total strength never exceeded thirteen thousand (three thousand of them women), with about forty thousand airmen in close support; but its influence was much greater than those numbers would suggest. In Poland, France, Denmark, Norway, Greece, Italy, Yugoslavia, Belgium, and Burma, it armed and sustained vigorous national movements of resistance. Given a little time and a lot of trouble, it was possible both to conduct sabotage coups against factories, railways, canal locks, and road bridges, and to form irregular armies who could at least attack Axis rear area forces and thus unsettle their hold on occupied countries. The service was closed in 1946, but it had succeeded in helping several nations defeated by Axis powers from 1939 to 1941 to regain their national self-respect and had inflicted severe damage on Axis rear areas and supply lines. The severity of this damage was not always appreciated by old-fashioned Allied commanders.

The special operations branch of the U.S. Office of Strategic Services, founded in 1942, imitated SOE closely and secured similar triumphs. For instance, fifteen men forming half an operational group in the Vercors rising in France in July 1944 fought so rigorously that the Germans took them for a battalion. It too was shut down at the close of the world war but was revived, in 1947, as part of the Central Intelligence Agency. If politicians allow such agencies to get on with their secret work in secret, they may do much good; they may also do much harm, and the problem of proper democratic supervision of them remains unresolved.

The British also developed during the war the Special Air Service (SAS) Regiment (rivals of the SOE), commando-type troops — sometimes airborne — who operated with success against Axis airfields and communications in North Africa in 1942–1943 and behind the German lines in northwest Europe in 1944–1945.

The Germans also had troops engaged in special operations: some of them were army criminals, sent as a punishment into the Brandenburg Regiment, working in Russian uniforms behind the Red Army's (q.v.) lines; others were volunteer parachutists — notable among them was Otto Skorzeny, who rescued Benito Mussolini (q.v.) (by a coup that SAS envied) in the autumn of 1943. In the Red Army, alleged criminals were put in punishment battalions, which were used to clear antipersonnel minefields by marching through them: a macabre special operation, but a useful one to an army with few manpower problems but scarce equipment.

After World War II, the Soviet secret police (KGB) became even more involved in politics than the SOE had been. Directly or indirectly, the Soviet secret services have influenced dissidence, disruption, and subversion all over the capitalist world. This sort of special operation is so unobtrusive that it often eludes the attention of later historians as well as that of politicians and commentators at the time.

Britain's SAS demonstrated in the Falklands (q.v.) campaign of 1982 and in the Gulf War (q.v.) of 1991 that their skills in fieldcraft and reconnaissance, honed in several obscure campaigns in southern Asia in the 1950s and 1960s, have exceptional military value. They were able to provide minute details of Argentine deployment in the Falklands and to locate numerous Scud missiles in western Iraq, thus notably assisting their own high command to assess what was going on and to secure victory.

M. R. D. FOOT

Spruance, Raymond A.

1886–1969, U.S. World War II Admiral

Had Congress permitted another admiral to have a fifth star, it would have gone to Spruance. A superb, unflappable battle commander, seasoned by years at sea before World War II (q.v.), he commanded the task force that stopped the Japanese advance across the central Pacific at Midway (q.v.) and headed the Fifth Fleet as it fought to victory in the bitterly contested islands of the Gilberts and the Marshalls. Spruance held the sea command during the invasions of Iwo Jima (q.v.) and Okinawa (q.v.) and would have landed the American army on Kyushu.

The only controversy in his brilliant career concerned his decision in June 1944 at the Battle of the Philippine Sea (q.v.) not to go on the offensive to engage the main Japanese fleet in decisive battle. The Japanese retired with six (of nine) of their carriers and all their battleships and heavy cruisers intact. Was Spruance correct in eschewing a Pacific Trafalgar?

The answer is yes, because his job was to support the invasion of Saipan, not to pursue the enemy fleet. His and Vice Admiral Marc Mitscher's carrier pilots did take a bold initiative and, in the "Marianas' Turkey Shoot," turned away the carriers of Vice Admiral

Ozawa Jisaburo, dealing Japanese naval air a blow from which it never recovered. Thereafter, Spruance was right not to take the offensive that might have been futile and would have exposed the expeditionary force about to land on Saipan. His battleship commander warned against night action, he did not know the disposition of the Japanese fleet, and prudence and an understanding of the navy's post-Mahanian attrition strategy correctly dictated standing by on the flanks of the largest invasion force ever assembled in the Pacific.

Spruance ended his career first as president of the Naval War College and then as ambassador to the Philippines. He deserved the fifth star.

GEORGE BAER

SS

See Waffen SS.

Stalin, Joseph

1879–1953, *Russian Revolutionary and Soviet Dictator*

Joseph Stalin was born Iosif Vissarionovich Dzhugashvili in the small Georgian town of Gori. After education at Tiflis Theological Seminary, he got involved in radical politics in 1898, was arrested in 1903, and was sentenced to administrative exile in Siberia. After a while he adopted the revolutionary alias "Koba" (after the name of a famous bandit) and then escaped and returned to Transcaucasia, where he joined the Bolshevik Party. During the revolution of 1905–1907, Stalin took part in terrorism and armed robbery, which led to further arrests and terms of exile.

On the eve of World War I (q.v.), Koba took "Stalin" (man of steel) for his new pseudonym. Although he became a member of the Central Committee of the party in 1917, he played an exceedingly modest role in organizing the October Revolution. During the Russian Civil War (q.v.), he was a member of the Revolutionary Military Council and served as a political commissar attached to various fronts. In 1922 he became the general secretary of the party, which served as his power base after Vladimir Lenin's death (1924).

From 1929 to 1932, Stalin forcibly collectivized Soviet agriculture, a program that led to the deaths of millions of peasants through execution, starvation, and deportation. At the same time his regime adopted the first Five-Year Plan, which proposed to increase the industrial output of the country by 250 percent. Political purges and terror intensified throughout the 1930s and claimed hundreds of thousands of victims.

In 1939 Stalin's foreign minister, Viacheslav Molotov, signed a nonaggression pact with Germany. This agreement, with its secret addendum partitioning eastern Europe, freed Adolf Hitler (q.v.) to attack Poland in 1939, thus touching off World War II (q.v.). For the ensuing two years, Moscow collaborated closely with Berlin in the economic sphere: the Soviet Union furnished Germany with 536 million marks' worth of goods — 7.8 percent of all German imports. Stalin took advantage of the pact to annex Bessarabia, the Baltic republics, and (in the aftermath of the winter war of 1939–1940) a slice of Finnish territory.

On June 22, 1941, Hitler invaded the Soviet Union (see *Operation Barbarossa*). Six months of military catastrophe followed, in which retreating Soviet armies lost 1.5 million killed and 3 million POWs. Hitler's advance was checked only at Moscow (November–December 1941) (q.v.). In the following year, Soviet forces thwarted the German effort to take Transcaucasia by destroying the German Sixth Army at Stalingrad (q.v.). In July 1943 the Soviet victory in the Battle of Kursk (q.v.) drove the Germans two hundred miles back to the west. The great Soviet offensives of the summer of 1944 obliterated German army group center and paved the way for the conquest of Nazi Germany in 1945. In August 1945, Stalin's forces attacked and overran the Japanese army in Manchuria, thus earning the Soviet Union a say in the postwar reconstruction of Asia.

In the second half of the 1940s, Stalin's communization of eastern Europe led to the Cold War (q.v.) with the West. His Berlin blockade stimulated the creation of NATO. Tensions between East and West heightened after Stalin approved Kim Il Sung's attack on South Korea in 1950 (see *Korean War*). The Soviet Union acquired the atomic bomb in 1949 and began a comprehensive arms buildup that same year.

Almost no one would dispute the fact that Stalin was a sociopathic despot. Nevertheless, one still meets occasionally with histories that present Stalin's diplomatic, political, and military activities in a favorable light. Such interpretations stress that rapid Soviet industrialization, although attended by horrendous human costs, gave the country the military potential that would be an indispensable precondition for victory in World War II. The pact with Hitler, it is said, was Stalin's desperate attempt to buy time in the face of British and French appeasement. During the war Stalin's leadership is supposed to have sustained the morale of Soviet troops and civilians alike, while his strategic genius was the guiding force behind battlefield victories. After the war Stalin is depicted as a shrewd and cautious statesman, carefully playing his hand to achieve the maximum political advantages for his country.

Such a brief for Stalin is, however, riddled with holes. First, although it is true that the industrial progress of the USSR did facilitate Soviet victory, two-thirds of all Soviet factories were conquered by Germany in the summer of 1941 and were consequently of no value for the war effort. With regard to the failure of collective security, evidence suggests that Stalin's commitment to forging a meaningful alliance with France and Britain was at best lukewarm. A deal with Germany was much more to his taste, since he supposed that the result would be a protracted war between the Nazis and the two Western democracies that would sap the strength of all three capitalist states.

Stalin probably did become a symbol of the Russian nation's resistance to the invader during the war, although doubt has recently been cast on how often Soviet soldiers *really* charged into battle with the slogan "For the Fatherland, for Stalin" on their lips. Likewise, although both Alkesandr Vasilevskii and Georgii Zhukov (q.v.) contended that Stalin exhibited ability as a grand strategist, particularly after 1943, nonetheless, he always remained a military amateur (a recent analysis of the annotations he penciled in the military books he read does not testify to insight or acumen). Further, it was the Red Army (q.v.) that had to pay with blood for Stalin's numerous errors: his purge of the Soviet officer corps (1937–1940) resulted in the intellectual decapitation of the armed forces; his disbelief in a German attack in 1941 virtually guaranteed the early success of Barbarossa; his prohibition of strategic withdrawal all that summer led to the capture of hundreds of thousands of Red Army men; and his order for a "general offensive" in the winter of 1941–1942 squandered the lives of thousands more. A large proportion of the Soviet Union's 26–27 million war dead probably perished because of Stalin's ineptitude. Soviet victory owed more to the achievements of the war economy, the emergence of a cluster of talented commanders, and the heroism and sacrifice of millions of common citizens, in and out of uniform, than it did to Stalin's leadership.

Finally, it could be argued that Stalin mismanaged his country's relations with its former allies after the war had been won. Far from encouraging divisions among the western European states and the United States, Stalin's policies united Europe and America in a solid anti-Soviet bloc.

WILLIAM C. FULLER, JR.

Albert Resis, ed., *Molotov Remembers: Inside Kremlin Politics, Conversations with Felix Chuev* (1993); Robert C. Tucker, *Stalin in Power: The Revolution from Above, 1928–1941* (1990); Dmitri Volkogonov, *Stalin: Triumph and Tragedy* (1991).

Stalingrad, Battle of

September 1942–February 1943

The Russians hailed it a "contemporary Cannae," and the Germans condemned it as a *Rattenkrieg* (rat war). Both descriptions were fitting. In the Battle of Stalingrad, Soviet forces surrounded and crushed an entire German army under General Friedrich Paulus, emulating Hannibal's encirclement and destruction of a Roman army under Aemilius Paulus in 216 B.C. For both sides, Stalingrad became a desperate ordeal of rodentlike scurrying from hole to hole.

This monumental battle is justly considered a turning point in the war on the Eastern Front and one of the most crucial engagements of World War II (q.v.). The invading Germans saw the conquest of Stalingrad as essential to their campaign in southern Russia, since from this strategic point on the Volga River they could launch further assaults in the Caucasus. The Russians were determined to defend the city as a vital industrial and transportation center. Both Joseph Stalin (q.v.) and Adolf Hitler (q.v.) understood the symbolic importance of the only city to bear the Soviet dictator's name.

On September 3, 1942, the German Sixth Army under Paulus reached the outskirts of Stalingrad, expecting to take the city in short order. But the Russians had built up their defenses and continued to bring in reinforcements. A very able general, V. I. Chuikov, took command of the main defending force, the Sixty-second Army, while Marshal Georgii K. Zhukov (q.v.), Soviet Russia's greatest general, planned a counteroffensive.

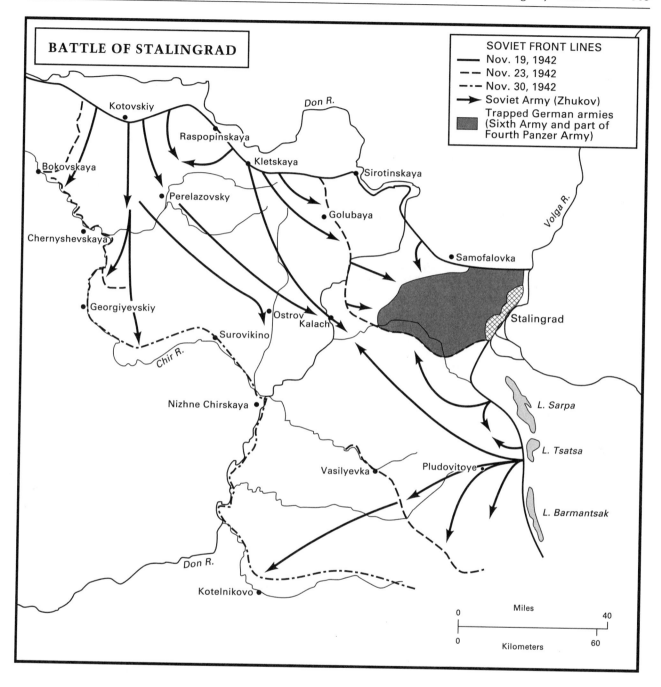

BATTLE OF STALINGRAD

SOVIET FRONT LINES
Nov. 19, 1942
Nov. 23, 1942
Nov. 30, 1942
Soviet Army (Zhukov)
Trapped German armies
(Sixth Army and part of
Fourth Panzer Army)

Kotovskiy
Don R.
Raspopinskaya
Bokovskaya
Kletskaya
Sirotinskaya
Perelazovsky
Volga R.
Golubaya
Chernyshevskaya
Samofalovka
Georgiyevskiy
Stalingrad
Surovikino
Ostrov
Kalach
Chir R.
L. Sarpa
Nizhne Chirskaya
L. Tsatsa
Vasilyevka
Pludovitoye
L. Barmantsak
Don R.
Kotelnikovo

Miles
0   40
0   60
Kilometers

In subsequent days the invaders fought their way into Stalingrad against fierce resistance. This was urban street fighting of the most bitter sort, occasioning tremendous losses on both sides. The blasted ruins of houses and factories began to stink as hot winds carried the smell of decaying corpses into every nook and cranny. By late September the Germans could raise the swastika flag over the Univermag department store in the center of town, but they could not dislodge the Russians from the sprawling industrial quarters along the Volga.

In mid-November, as the stalled invaders were running short of men and munitions, Zhukov launched his counteroffensive to encircle the enemy. At this point the Germans probably could have fought their way out, but Hitler would not allow them to: they

Soviet soldiers rejoice at the end of the epic Battle of Stalingrad in February 1943. Russians and Germans fought over and destroyed nearly every building in the city.

were ordered to hold their ground at all costs. Air Marshal Hermann Göring promised to resupply the Sixth Army from the air but proved unable to do so. As winter set in, Field Marshal Erich von Manstein (q.v.) mounted a rescue mission, but it was halted short of its goal, and the freezing and starving Germans in Stalingrad were forbidden to try to reach their would-be rescuers. On February 2, 1943, General Paulus surrendered what remained of his army — some 91,000 men. About 150,000 Germans had died in the fighting.

The Soviet victory at Stalingrad was a great humiliation for Hitler, who had elevated the battle's importance in German opinion. He now became more distrustful than ever of his generals. Stalin, on the other hand, gained confidence in his military, which followed up Stalingrad with a westward drive and remained largely on the offensive for the rest of the war.

DAVID CLAY LARGE

Stilwell, Joseph W.

1883–1946, U.S. Army General

Born in Florida and a West Point graduate, Joseph Stilwell served in Europe and the Philippines before being assigned to China, where he learned the Chinese language and served in a variety of posts from 1921 to

1945, most notably in the Burma campaigns in which he commanded largely Chinese troops, and as chief of staff to the Chinese leader Chiang Kai-shek (q.v.). Known as "Vinegar Joe" for his vitriolic tongue, Stilwell's debatable qualities as a soldier were manifested in the unsuccessful Burma campaign of March to May 1942 ("I claim we got a hell of a beating") and its victorious sequel of February 1943 to August 1944. But his relationship with Chiang Kai-shek — whom he unwisely ridiculed as "the Peanut" — proved less successful. No natural diplomat, as his diaries make clear, and overly confident of his own strategic wisdom, Stilwell took an adversarial approach that needlessly poisoned relations and brought about his own recall in 1944. Stilwell considered that Chiang's political concerns, about Communism in particular, prevented his seizing military opportunities; Stilwell believed that his own ideas should have been somehow forced on China by Washington. This assessment overestimates both Chiang's and Washington's power, while it fails to consider the complete circumstances.

Stilwell was a brave and dogged soldier, but he nevertheless lacked real strategic skills, and reached, according to Field Marshal Slim (q.v.), for "the sledgehammer to crack a walnut." His understanding of China in the 1940s, with its irrational animus against Chiang Kai-shek and his government, is increasingly recognized as at best partial.

ARTHUR WALDRON

Stimson, Henry L.

1867–1950, U.S. Statesman

Henry Stimson was born in New York City and educated at Yale and at Harvard Law School; his distinguished career included service as secretary of war for William Taft, secretary of state for Herbert Hoover, and secretary of war for Franklin Roosevelt (q.v.). But he is perhaps best remembered for his unsuccessful dealings with Japan before World War II (q.v.), for his contribution to the prosecution of that conflict as secretary of war (1940–1945), and for his key role in its conclusion. Stimson made the final recommendation to Roosevelt, in 1945, that nuclear weapons be used against Japan.

In 1931 Stimson denounced Japan's military occupation of Manchuria as a flagrant violation of the Washington Treaties guaranteeing China's territorial integrity, and he propounded the so-called Stimson Doctrine of American "nonrecognition," meaning diplomatic and legal condemnation without forceful action to reverse the situation. Japan's actions certainly violated international law, but Stimson's indictment nevertheless ignored Japan's legitimate grievances, accumulated over a decade during which China had flouted the provisions of the Washington Treaties of 1922, often with the acquiescence of the United States, which had turned aside repeated Japanese diplomatic representations. Stimson's hectoring yet toothless response is perhaps best understood against the background of the isolationism then strong in America. "Nonrecognition" had the twin disadvantages of locking Washington into an inflexible position that irritated Japan and emboldened China, while making manifest the United States' unwillingness to take substantial action. Franklin Roosevelt initially backed away from the policy but stopped short of fundamental change; the ultimate result, which reflected mutual miscalculations traceable in part to Stimson's ambiguous stance, was Pearl Harbor (q.v.) and the Pacific war.

As Roosevelt's secretary of war, Stimson coordinated the war effort's vast material mobilization and universal conscription, and he played key policy roles. When mass conventional bombing of Japan began, he insisted on military targets only and placed the ancient city of Kyoto off limits. In 1945 he called for atomic bombing of Japan "without specific warning, as soon as possible," but he also hoped for a "covenant" with the Soviets for future joint control of the technology.

The fifty-two volumes of Stimson's diaries are an invaluable historical source.

ARTHUR WALDRON

Strategic Bombing

At the outset of World War I (q.v.), unsophisticated airplanes, made mainly of wood and canvas and tied together with wire and string, were brought into service in a variety of military roles. As time went on, they became increasingly sophisticated, airworthy, and versatile. The intelligence advantages offered by an aerial perspective made airplanes a natural choice for scouting, artillery spotting, and trench mapping, and this led to dogfighting as pilots jockeyed for control of the skies over the battlefield. Dropping projectiles

and bombs from the air, which had been tested in a primitive way in the Italo-Turkish War (1911–1912), was also taken up. Modified and unmodified infantry weapons were hurled down on the fighting men below. The ability to go beyond the battlefield, however, gave aircraft their most revolutionary advantage.

In the long history of predictive literature that anticipated the development of aerial bombing, it was well understood that if explosives could be brought by air to enemy troops, they could be carried right to the heart of the enemy war machine — to the military, industrial, and commercial centers supplying and supporting the war effort. Such long-distance or "strategic" bombing, as it would come to be called, was envisioned from the outset as a way of undermining both the enemy's war-making capability and will to fight.

In late August 1914, as the German army neared the gates of Paris, a single German airplane dropped a bomb on the city. The French, who also showed an early interest in strategic bombing, ultimately offered their own response with bomber attacks on targets in Germany. In January 1915 the Germans used zeppelin balloons (named for their German inventor) to bomb Britain. The Royal Naval Air Service, which had been charged with defending the island, already was trying to stem the threat by aerial strikes against zeppelin sheds and factories. Other powers including Italy undertook some bombing as well; the Americans showed great interest in it at times, but entered the war too late to produce the machines required to carry out a strategic campaign.

In 1917 the Germans commenced raids against Britain with long-distance aircraft. These caused damage and hundreds of casualties, and triggered the development of a separate air service — which became the Royal Air Force (RAF). In the final year of the war, the British waged a bombing campaign aimed at German war industry and morale; they had plans for strikes against Berlin in 1919. By the time it ended, the war had revealed, in rudimentary form, all the ways in which aircraft would be used in later decades. As genuine "strategic" bombing had been small in scale and limited by early technology, however, nothing definite was proven about the theory that underpinned it.

By the mid-1930s, technical developments in both aircraft and air defense created a fluid and uncertain environment in which planners tried hard to cope

B-29 bombers based on Tinian in the Marianas fly past neighboring Saipan on the outward leg of their three-thousand-mile round trip to Japan. Each bomber was able to carry more than six tons of bombs.

with a future that was hard to predict. The early stages of World War II (q.v.) contradicted the prediction that the bomber would "always get through." The development of radar had given the British enough of a defensive edge over the Luftwaffe to foil Adolf Hitler's (q.v.) plans for an amphibious invasion of the island. Prompted by a request from President Franklin Roosevelt (q.v.), the belligerents made early pledges to restrict themselves to military targets; these constraints soon began to erode in light of the German bombing of Warsaw and Rotterdam. Having no other means for waging an offensive against Germany, the British sought to use their long-range bombers to undercut German war production and lower German morale. But economy-oriented interwar defense budgets and a lack of attention to the crucial technical details of strategic bombing had taken their toll. Inability to fly in daylight without suffering heavy losses forced British bombers to fly at night, but in the summer of 1941, the RAF discovered (through photoreconnaissance) that only about one in five of their planes was getting within five miles of its intended target. If they were to continue the offensive at all, it

would have to be waged against large, easily found targets. Thus the morale of German urban workers became the focus of the offensive, and the primary target became workers' housing.

The United States entered the war in Europe determined to wage a daylight bombing campaign against German industrial targets. The British tried to persuade the Americans to join the nighttime offensive, but the Army Air Forces were committed to their own way of doing things.

In practice, the effective prosecution of strategic bombing proved to be far more complicated and difficult than many of the interwar prophets had assumed it would be. Allied planners had made the mistake of assuming that the German economy was stretched to capacity at the outset of the war. It was not, and the Germans managed to maintain and even increase their industrial output through 1943. The Americans discovered that the B-17 Flying Fortress was not capable of penetrating deep into Germany without escort fighters. And the British discovered that German civilian morale was as tough as that of the British civilians who had lived through the London Blitz. As a result of a massive American aircraft production effort, the Allies gained the upper hand over the Luftwaffe in 1944, and the Germans were never able to recover fully.

Prior to D-Day (q.v.), Allied bombers were called upon to prepare the way for the invasion. Because of breakthroughs in target-finding techniques, British bombing was by this time as accurate — and at times more accurate — than American bombing, which was hampered by the frequent cloud cover of northern Europe. The head of Britain's Bomber Command, Air Chief Marshal Sir Arthur Harris (q.v.), was urged by his colleagues on the Air Staff to switch the focus of Bomber Command back to specific military targets, including oil production. But Harris generally resisted this pressure and continued to bomb German cities. The Anglo-American bombing that occurred late in the war, including the bombing of the refugee-packed city of Dresden, has been the subject of much postwar criticism and has caused the term "strategic bombing" to be associated, often incorrectly, with the terms "terror bombing" and "carpet bombing." The American strategic-bombing campaign against Japan, which by March 1945 was characterized by incendiary attacks on cities and by August had culminated in the use of atomic weapons against Hiroshima and Nagasaki, has also been the object of postwar moral criticism.

What strategic bombing accomplished in World War II is still hotly contested by historians. The defeat of the Luftwaffe made possible a successful Allied landing on the coast of France in 1944 and set the stage for the gradual erosion of the German military-industrial base. Civilian will did not prove a weak point in Hitler's Germany, and there is little evidence that the bombing of German workers' housing contributed very much to victory. The most effective targets proved to be those that inhibited the functioning and mobility of the German fighting forces. These included synthetic oil plants and the railway and transport lines on which the Wehrmacht depended for supplies and maneuver.

After the war, and with the advent of the Cold War (q.v.), most modern air forces turned their attention to nuclear bombing and nuclear deterrence. By the 1950s the U.S. Strategic Air Command (SAC) was a force of unprecedented destructive power, and by the 1960s SAC was capable of wreaking vast devastation on the Soviet Union. By that time, however, other strategic platforms — including missiles and submarines —

had been developed, and strategic bombing was no longer the exclusive preserve of the bomber pilot. The Soviets preferred to concentrate their strategic effort in missiles but maintained a nuclear bomber capability as well. The British nuclear deterrent was initially deployed on bombers but later was moved to submarines.

The United States employed strategic bombers, in a conventional mode, in the wars in Korea (q.v.) and Vietnam (q.v.). In neither case was their contribution decisive, however, because of the nature of those nations' economies, the nature of the wars themselves, and also the constraints imposed on those prosecuting the bombing campaigns. The hope that bombing would undermine the Viet Cong's will to fight proved unfounded. More recently, the U.S. Air Force used bombers to good effect in the Gulf War (q.v.). They helped to cut Iraqi communications, destroy and demoralize Iraqi fighting units, and undermine the ability of the Iraqi army to maneuver. In the end, however, the war was brought to a close by a swift, successful ground battle waged by coalition armor and infantry units.

TAMI DAVIS BIDDLE

Horst Boog, ed., *The Conduct of the Air War in the Second World War* (1992); Lee Kennett, *A History of Strategic Bombing* (1982).

Strategy

Theory

"Men do not understand [the coincidence of opposites]: there is a 'back-stretched connection' like that of the bow." Thus Herakleitos of Ephesus (500? B.C.), thought very obscure by the ancients, but for us his statement is quite transparent after the experience of nuclear deterrence, whereby the peaceful had to be constantly ready to attack, and nuclear weapons could be useful only if unused. Deterrence unveiled the paradoxical, seemingly contradictory logic of strategy, turning the "back-stretched" coincidence of opposites into a mere commonplace and vindicating Herakleitos, the first Western strategic thinker ("war is the father of all things"). Still, long before him, many a cunning fighter had won by surprising his enemy — a feat possible only when better ways of attacking — hence the expected ways — are deliberately avoided. In that particular coincidence of opposites, the bad way is the good way *because* it is bad, and vice versa. Nor is surprise (q.v.) in any form merely one advantage among many, but rather constitutes a suspension of the entire predicament of conflict, defined precisely by the presence of a *reacting* antagonist.

The Chinese word for strategy is *chan-lueh,* and we know that it encompasses the same logic because the first Chinese strategic thinker, Sun Tzu (q.v.), was just as paradoxical as Herakleitos ("those skilled in war subdue the enemy's army without battle"). The Roman tag "if you want peace, prepare for war" could have been Sun Tzu's.

The modern strategist, Carl von Clausewitz (q.v.), uncovered the processes of reversal that lead to the end point of the coincidence of opposites, showing, for example, how victory is transformed into defeat (beyond its culminating point, victory exhausts the will to fight, overstretches the victorious forces, and frightens neutrals into enmity and allies into neutrality) and how war leads to peace (war itself consumes the means and the will to persist in war, while war losses devalue the purposes of continued war; thus, for example, the abandonment of South Vietnam was accepted once enough American lives were lost).

Because the enemy is a reacting being, straightforward actions usually fail; yet "engineering" approaches that treat enemies as inert objects are persistently seductive. When Royal Air Force chief of staff Charles Portal submitted a mathematically compelling plan on September 25, 1941, that asked first call on all British resources to build a four-thousand-bomber force to defeat Germany in six months by bombing forty-three German urban-industrial centers "beyond recovery," Prime Minister Winston S. Churchill (q.v.) rejected the plan, pointing out that if the bombing *did* begin to succeed, the Germans would not passively await defeat, but would instead strengthen their air defenses and disperse their industries, for in war "all things are always on the move simultaneously." Twenty years later, Robert S. McNamara (q.v.) emulated Portal's error with his mutual assured destruction (MAD) scheme to stabilize deterrence and stop the nuclear arms race. McNamara's calculation that a reliable ability to destroy half the population and three-quarters of the other side's industrial capacity was ample to deter was unexceptionable, but he overlooked the possibility that Soviet leaders might not want what he wanted: the paralyzed stability of mutual deterrence.

Conflict unfolds at separate levels (grand strategic, theater strategic, operational, tactical), which interpenetrate downward much more easily than upward. Thus in World War II (q.v.), Adolf Hitler's (q.v.) choice of the wrong allies and the wrong enemies at the level of grand strategy could not be overcome by any number of German victories on the tactical, operational, or even theater levels (notably over France, in 1940). Had the D-Day (q.v.) landings been repulsed by some brilliant counteroffensive, Germany would not have won the war but would merely have become the first target of the atom bomb a year later, instead of Japan. As for the latter, given the complete inability of the Japanese to follow through by marching on Washington to impose their peace, the combat success of the Pearl Harbor attack (q.v.) was not even useless: it was counterproductive. Had Japanese pilots failed miserably on that day, evoking ridicule instead of hatred, the outcome of the war would have been the same, but at least the United States might have dealt less harshly with Japan. Again there is a parallel in Sun Tzu: "what is of supreme importance in war is to attack the enemy's strategy; next best is to disrupt his alliances; next best is to attack his army" — the strategic prevails over the tactical.

Practice

Given overwhelming superiority (material *and* moral), wars can be won and peace kept without need of strategy. Antagonists too weak to react significantly are, in effect, mere objects. War may still present huge difficulties of distance, terrain, and so on. But to overcome physical problems, it is not the paradoxical logic of strategy that is wanted, but rather the "linear" logic of sound common sense and of the relevant applied sciences. Hence, it is those fighting against the odds — the outnumbered, the beleaguered, and the overambitious — who have exploited the logic of strategy in their real-life practices. Naturally, more often than not, the great names of strategy, most notably Napoleon (q.v.), ultimately failed.

In all their variety, *grand strategies* can be compared by the extent of their reliance on costly force as opposed to the leveraging of potential force by diplomacy ("armed suasion"), by inducements (subsidies, gifts, honors), and by deception and propaganda. The smaller the force content, the greater the possibility of transcending the material balance of strength, to achieve more with less. During the Cold War (q.v.), the United States successfully protected many allies with relatively economical forces, little actual fighting, and a constant striving to uphold the armed suasion of nuclear deterrence. In this, Alexander the Great (q.v.) was a precursor, but the Byzantines remain the unsurpassed masters. Before his death, while retreating from a foolhardy attempt to invade India, Alexander had already earned millennial glory by conquering Achaemenid Iran, the only superpower for the Greeks. Although his tactics were "hard" (frontal attacks by the infantry phalanx and all-out cavalry charges), Alexander's diplomacy was "soft" and inclusive, as symbolized by the encouragement of Macedonian-Iranian marriages, to win over Achaemenid satraps and vassal peoples.

The East Roman Empire, which we call Byzantium, was least Roman in its strategy. Successively threatened from the east by Sassanian Persia, the Arabs, and finally the Turks, and from the north by waves of steppe invaders — the Huns, Avars, Khazars, Pechenegs, Bulgars, Magyars (q.v.), and Mongols (q.v.), the Byzantines could not hope to subdue or annihilate all comers in the classic Roman manner. To wear out their own forces (chiefly of expensive cavalry) in order to utterly destroy the immediate enemy would only open the way for the next wave of invaders. The genius of Byzantine grand strategy was to turn the very multiplicity of enemies to advantage, by employing diplomacy, deception, payoffs, and religious conversion to induce them to fight one another instead of fighting the empire (only their self-image as the only defenders of the only true faith preserved their moral equilibrium). Intercepted when still deep in the steppe by imperial envoys bearing gifts and misinformation, new arrivals were induced to attack the prior wave of invaders from the rear, or to stand against the next wave, or to bypass the imperial frontiers altogether. In this scheme of things, military strength was subordinated to diplomacy, instead of the other way around, and used preferably to contain or punish, rather than to attack or defend in full force. Other successful territorial empires in China, India, and Iran followed similar grand strategies.

The Roman, Ottoman, and Spanish empires by contrast relied more on force, all three commanding — and expending — the necessary resources. Even so, all three employed diplomacy to intimidate and win over potential enemies, and all three magnified their spheres of control cheaply, through client states, client tribes, or dependent principalities. For the Romans, the cost of empire increased when garrisoned frontiers replaced the client fringe (by the end of the first century A.D.), increasing much more when a defense-in-depth of mobile armies was also needed (from the third century A.D.) to counterattack enemies that penetrated the frontiers.

The grand strategy of the British naval ascendancy (fully formed by the early eighteenth century) certainly achieved power greatly in excess of material means. Its essence was to keep continental Europe divided and at war ("to uphold the balance of power," in self-serving British rhetoric) by persuasion, gold, and timely expeditionary interventions to prop up the weaker side. That forced the Continental powers to devote their resources to the upkeep of their armies, leaving little for their navies, which the British navy could then economically defeat. That in turn enabled the British maritime empire to exceed its Portuguese, Spanish, and Dutch predecessors and also the French colonial empire, without requiring a vast naval effort: British naval supremacy was actually secured on land, by the balance-of-power policy. In our own time, it was the Soviet Union that for a while acquired power greatly in excess of its economic capacity, by employing ideological propaganda to enlist devotees all over the world and sustain client regimes, deception to mask weaknesses, subversion to outmaneuver opponents, and espionage to transcend technological limits. It was only when the Soviet leadership decided to acquire an actual material, military supremacy (after the failure of the "Missile Gap" deception and the humiliation of the 1962 Cuban missile crisis) that their ambitions ruinously exceeded Soviet economic capacity.

Other substitutes for force at the level of grand strategy have included the penetration of enemy societies and the exploitation of inculcated fears. Exemplifying the former, Genghis Khan's (q.v.) Mongols captured walled cities though wholly lacking in siegecraft because merchants won over by their reliable, cheap protection of the caravan routes opened the gates to the invaders. The Arab invasion of the Byzantine Empire was likewise assisted by dissident Monophysite Christians, won over by Islam's promise of religious toleration. Exemplifying the latter, Tamerlane (q.v.) terrorized enemies into preemptive surrender by staging spectacular massacres. Adolf Hitler's (q.v.) blitzkrieg offensives were likewise preceded by fear propaganda (notably by newsreel) and featured "terror bombing," more demoralizing than physically damaging, against Warsaw (in 1939) and Rotterdam (in 1940), for example; but much more often they tactically employed dive-bombers whose sinister scream was especially contrived with a whistlelike device.

In all their variety through the ages, *military strategies* (comprising the theater and operational and tactical levels) can also be compared on the basis of a single criterion: their content of circumventing, disruptive maneuver, as opposed to force-on-force, destructive attrition. The smaller the attrition content, the less material strength is needed to achieve given results. But high-payoff maneuver methods tend to entail proportionate risks. Thus it is mostly the weak and the overambitious who have relied on maneuver, whereas the well provided through the ages have tended to rely on attrition.

With the vast resources secured by their organizational abilities, the Romans could generally afford the low-risk, low-payoff methods they much preferred. Actually, the entire Roman style of war was positively antiheroic (when charged with lacking aggressiveness, Scipio Africanus (q.v.), conqueror of Carthage, replied, "My mother bore me a general, not a warrior"). Relying on the routine skills of well-trained, salaried soldiers rather than the ephemeral fighting spirit of warriors, on sound procedures rather than the fortuitous talents of great generals, the Romans preferred to buy off enemies if it was cheaper than fighting them (*not* a decadent late-empire practice); if war still ensued, they preferred sieges to unpredictable battles, and then preferred to end them by starving out the enemy rather than by assault (the legion was a combat engineer force). Tactically, Roman warfare was mostly pure attrition, with enemies methodically cut down by the relentless advance of armored infantry. It was at the theater level that the Romans relied on maneuver, conquering by the vast encirclements of converging armies on a scale not achieved again until Napoleon. The Ottomans (q.v.) also had great organizational abilities, and they too relied on attrition; their janissaries were the first uniformed, drilled, rationed, and professionally commanded infantry since Roman times — complete with the first-ever military bands.

In our days it is the American style of war that has exemplified attrition; sometimes it has amounted to little more than the administration of firepower. Very successful against rigid fronts on land, against both German U-boats and Japanese fleets at sea once means became abundant, and sometimes successful in the form of air bombing even before the 1991 Gulf War (q.v.) advent of *routine* precision bombing, U.S.-style attrition failed badly only against guerrillas who stubbornly refused to assemble into conveniently targetable massed formations. But when Americans lacked material superiority, they did not lack for ingenuity: Douglas MacArthur's (q.v.) 1950 counteroffensive in Korea with its high-risk, high-payoff Inchon landings is a model of maneuver at the theater level.

Maneuver at any level is meant to disrupt and demoralize enemies by circumventing their strengths and exploiting their weaknesses; that is only possible if the enemy's ability to react is negated by surprise or outmaneuvered at each successive stage of combat by more rapid decisions and actions. Hitler's blitzkrieg of 1939–1941 achieved results far greater than German material strength. At the operational level, the long, thin, deep-penetration columns were theoretically very vulnerable to flank attacks, but they swiftly overran enemy forces, supply trains, and headquarters caught unprepared in the soft rear of pierced fronts. The Germans had little armor, but enough for tank spearheads to set a rapid pace; they had little air power, but enough to dive-bomb at critical points to open the way and to interdict flank attacks. At the theater level, the blitzkrieg disrupted by inducing hasty retreats: advance detachments pushed into the enemy's deep rear would lead to the hurried withdrawal of forces that might have prevailed if left in place, but that disintegrated while attempting to outpace the Germans to reconstitute linear fronts ahead of them. When the Red Army (q.v.) replicated and powerfully outmatched the German method, it did so with less tactical talent but much more real strength.

Deep-penetration maneuver had a long pre-1939 history, from the steppe horse nomads to Napoleon. Tactically, the horse nomads fought as they hunted. Enemies were outmaneuvered, trapped, and killed as game was, by the arrows of powerful sinew-and-bone compound bows (better than Napoleon's muskets). Able to live off the milk, blood, and flesh of their spare horses, with their families mounted also, the nomads had unlimited strategic mobility in grasslands. Attila's (q.v.) Huns first showed what horse nomads could achieve, if enough of them obeyed a single leader; but it was Genghis Khan who united entire horse-nomad nations to conquer on an Eurasian scale by fast, deep-penetration, all-cavalry advances that overran enemies before they could muster their defenses. Thus, few Mongols defeated many Russians and Chinese.

Just as the Arab invasions were propelled by a then highly functional religion whose very rituals taught discipline and drill and whose tenets positively required war for the conquest of non-Muslims while allowing the incentive of looting, Napoleonic warfare was propelled by a highly functional ideology. *Liberté, Egalité, Fraternité* attracted volunteers from all Europe, won over many of the educated in enemy societies — and allowed French officers to allow their ideologized men to skirmish ahead on their own without fear of mass desertions. To this, the organizational genius of Napoleon added efficient logistics and entire cadres of excellent subordinates, while his operational genius perfected the converging advance of separate columns that would force battle on a locally outnumbered, even if outnumbering, enemy.

One of those Greek words that the Greeks never knew, the pan-Western word *strategy* (*strategie, strategia*, and so on) derives from *strategos*, commonly mistranslated as "general," but in historical fact a combined politico-military chief, and thus a better source word for an activity equally broad. The Chinese language achieves the same generality by coupling the ideogram *chan* (indicating war) with further, specifying characters. It remains to be seen if strategy can be broad enough to accommodate the inability of low-birthrate, postindustrial societies to fight wars as they always did before, because of the novel refusal to tolerate even small numbers of casualties. As compared to that quandary, nuclear weapons are merely a technical innovation that offers an attrition potential that exceeds the culminating point of utility, thereby being too effective to be effective, as Herakleitos might have said.

EDWARD N. LUTTWAK

Suleiman I

1494–1566, Ottoman Sultan

Suleiman was the longest-reigning Ottoman sultan and led his army on thirteen campaigns starting with the successful siege of Belgrade in 1521; in 1526 he defeated the Hungarian king at Mohács (q.v.) and in 1529 undertook the first siege of Vienna (q.v.). Further campaigns resulted in the tripartite division of Hungary. The eastern front remained more fluid, although

Sultan Suleiman I, ruler of the Ottoman Empire at the height of its glory, watches his artillery destroy the Christians at the Battle of Mohács in 1526.

Iraq was annexed in 1534–1535 after military operations of great logistical difficulty.

Suleiman's naval operations began with the siege of Rhodes in 1522; by the end of his reign, the Ottomans (q.v.) were masters of the eastern Mediterranean, lacking only Malta and Cyprus. In 1526 an Ottoman presence was established in Yemen and in 1538 Aden was taken, but efforts against the Portuguese in the Indian Ocean brought no conclusive result.

Early in Suleiman's reign, rebellions occurred in the recently conquered provinces of Syria and Egypt as well as in eastern Anatolia, but these were swiftly contained. In the later part of his reign, succession disputes caused Suleiman to order the execution of his sons Mustafa and Bayezid, leaving the throne to his third son, Selim II.

Suleiman's energetic military endeavors — in all, he spent nearly one quarter of his long reign on campaign — expanded the borders of the empire almost to their greatest extent. Thereafter, gains were hard won and often of limited duration. His Turkish epithet, "the Lawgiver," reminds us that he is equally esteemed for presiding over the compilation of a body of law that would serve the empire in the future.

CAROLINE FINKEL

Sun Tzu

Sixth or fifth century B.C., *Chinese General*

Sun Tzu is the reputed author of *The Art of War* (*Ping-fa*), which some consider to be the best single book ever written on the subject. Of Sun Wu himself (Tzu is an honorific particle, meaning "master"), little is known beyond his birth in the state of Ch'i and service to King Ho-lu of Wu; he was a military specialist active during the turbulent late Chou dynasty. Recent excavations of ancient manuscripts of Sun Tzu in China have confirmed the great antiquity of the text attributed to him. Long studied in Asia, Sun Tzu's work became known in the West only in the late eighteenth century and was not properly translated until the twentieth.

Sun Tzu's approach to warfare, unlike that of Western authors, does not put force at the center: indeed, the Chinese character *li* (force) occurs only nine times in the text's thirteen chapters. This reflects the conditions of warfare in China at the time (force was then in fact of limited utility) as well as Sun Tzu's conviction that victory and defeat are fundamentally psychological states. He sees war, therefore, not so much as a matter of destroying the enemy materially and physically (although that may play a role), but of unsettling the enemy psychologically; his goal is to force the enemy's leadership and society from a condition of harmony, in which they can resist effectively, toward one of chaos (*luan*), which is tantamount to defeat.

Military action is presented by Sun Tzu in an implicitly Taoist frame of reference. The idea that terrain, weather, and enemy morale in effect have contours, through which the successful general finds the best ways (*tao*), thereby using the force inherent in them to support his purposes, is basically Taoist, as is the recurrent theme of transformation, from one state to another, as in the interplay he discusses between regular (*cheng*) and irregular (*ch'i*) forces.

But operationally, Sun Tzu's goal is psychological dominance and its exploitation, founded upon superior knowledge of the enemy (he lays great stress on the employment of secret agents) and *kueitao*, variously translated as "deception" or "unconventional means." Thus Sun Tzu commends operations that will harm enemy morale: splitting alliances, evading battle, attacking by surprise; he condemns those that may undermine one's own society, such as the attrition that might result from besieging a walled city. Some operations may be almost purely psychological in their purpose, such as setting fires, which Sun Tzu discusses in effect as a terror weapon. The height of military skill is to turn opposing plans to one's own uses by "attacking the enemy's strategy" (as the Germans did against the French in 1940), which at its best yields victory without fighting.

Sun Tzu, however, does not propose that combat can be eliminated. Rather, he is mindful of the tremendous risks attendant on any resort to force, especially bankruptcy and the social disintegration of the politically weak Chinese states of his time. So he urges that force not be squandered, but conserved carefully and used only when it may have decisive impact.

Sun Tzu writes about warfare within a single culture, wherein secret agents are difficult to detect and enemy thought processes differ little from one's own. One might question therefore the relevance of Sun Tzu in modern conditions, in which states are robust and force abundantly available, and in wars between nations, in which ethnic differences make spying difficult and enemy thought processes difficult to assess. Such concerns were probably more persuasive in the era of Carl von Clausewitz (q.v.) than they are today. For one thing, nuclear weapons (q.v.) have meant that the traditional Western road to victory — the application of massive, industrialized force — is now closed against a nuclear-armed adversary, and hence strategists must consider once again how to win without fighting, or at least without fighting too much. Force, as Vietnam (q.v.) showed, cannot alone win victory.

ARTHUR WALDRON

Roger Ames, trans., *Sun-Tzu: The Art of Warfare* (1993).

Surprise

The achievement of surprise on all levels of war — tactical, operational, and strategic — has always been considered one of the most important ingredients for success in war. As a fundamental principle of war, surprise allows the side that achieves it (usually the attacker, but possibly a defender) to concentrate superior forces unnoticed at the decisive point, and to catch the opponent unprepared (in terms of time, place, method, or new technologies). With his plans thus undermined, the opponent is caught psychologically off balance. Successful surprise enables the destruction of a larger proportion of the enemy forces at a lower cost or faster speed; a successful surprise therefore acts as a powerful force multiplier. At times, the achievement of surprise will provide a weaker side with the only hope of compensating for its deficiencies and the only chance to defeat a more powerful opponent. As a result, great efforts have always been made to achieve surprise through secrecy and concealment as well as through the extensive use of deception (q.v.) and diversions.

Throughout history, given the shorter time and smaller spaces involved in the lower levels of war, it was almost always possible to achieve tactical and operational surprise. Yet as Carl von Clausewitz (q.v.) observed, this was far less feasible on the higher strategic level of war. Since the beginning of the twentieth century, the increased mobility, speed, and range achieved by the introduction of railways, the combustion engine (cars), and ultimately, long-range air power and even ballistic missiles have made the achievement of strategic surprise practicable on the strategic level as well. In fact, almost all wars of the twentieth century opened with a surprise attack by the side initiating the war. The ability to achieve strategic surprise has also rendered obsolete the tradition of declaring war *before* the opening of hostilities. (Such official declarations of war (q.v.) were last made before the outbreak of World War I [q.v.]). States initiating a war did not want to lose the considerable advantages to be gained from achieving strategic surprise. Most modern wars are therefore launched by a strategic surprise, which is then sometimes followed by a formal declaration.

The ability to achieve a decisive strategic surprise in the opening stage of a war magnifies volatility in times of crisis; this reciprocal fear of surprise attack in turn creates strong incentives for making the first move or launching a preemptive attack.

Not only has strategic surprise become feasible in the twentieth century, but it has also, at the opening phase of war, become almost impossible to prevent despite the considerable improvement in the capabilities and performance of intelligence (q.v.) work. (In fact, despite all of the advances in intelligence, it has become even more difficult to prevent the achieve-

ment of surprise on the higher strategic and operational levels.) This is demonstrated by the following examples, in which strategic surprise was successful even when all sides were aware that war was likely: Port Arthur (1904); the German attack on Norway (April 1940) and in the west (May 1940); Barbarossa (1941) (q.v.); Pearl Harbor (1941) (q.v.); North Korea (June 1950); China in Korea (1950); Britain, France, and Israel (1956); Israel (1967); the Arab states (1973); the USSR's invasion of Czechoslovakia (1968) and of Afghanistan (1979); and Iraq's invasion of Kuwait (August 1990).

Larger-scale surprise could be achieved at sea in earlier periods (for example, Horatio Nelson [q.v.] at Copenhagen and the Battle of the Nile). Interestingly, in modern times, strategic surprise has been achieved despite the availability of more than enough intelligence information to indicate that a forthcoming attack was planned. Thus, for example, the United States knew before the attack on Pearl Harbor that the Japanese were seriously contemplating war and had read Japanese codes that gave some indication of the imminent attack. Joseph Stalin (q.v.) received literally hundreds of warnings before the German attack on Russia (June 22, 1941), which he chose to ignore. In the same way, the Israelis had plenty of warnings before the Arab attack in 1973.

This raises a number of serious questions concerning the value and limitations of modern intelligence, a subject that has received much attention, in particular from political scientists. Seven interrelated explanations are worth mentioning here:

Signals and Noise
Intelligence organizations find it difficult to separate correct information (reliable information or signals) from incorrect information ("noise").

Deception
Surprise is often preceded by elaborate deception operations designed to conceal the preparations, direction, or timing of an attack.

Theories of Perception and Misperception
This major field of inquiry demonstrates that the objective and accurate evaluation of intelligence is made extremely difficult by the interpreter's own ideas and prejudices, such as ethnocentrism, wishful thinking, defense mechanisms, the projection of one's own beliefs on the opponent, knowledge of the oppo-

nent, conditioning by past historical experience, and the paradoxical nature of risk assessment. It emphasizes the subjective nature of all intelligence work.

The Politicization of Intelligence

This theory argues that even when correct and accurate intelligence is obtained, leaders or organizations tend, either consciously or unconsciously, to ignore intelligence contradictory to their political interests, their earlier policies, or their plans and expectations for the future.

Organizational Behavior

Organizations tend to ignore or dilute intelligence because of poor inter- and intraorganizational coordination, the search for consensus, and the influence of the lowest common denominator, which smooths the path to consensus or reduces tension within or among organizations.

Complexity and Time

This factor, in a way, combines all the previous explanations. It demonstrates that even when perfect intelligence is received, untangling its complexities — how the preconception of each other's intentions and capabilities affects evaluations, the problems in correcting biases or misperceptions, the need to evaluate the quality of the information received, and exposing possible deception — demands so much time that it is usually impossible to make an accurate assessment in the time available.

The Paradoxical Nature of Risk Assessment

Intelligence work is riddled with paradoxical difficulties, tensions, and contradictions that have no simple, rational solution. One important paradox is this: the greater the risk, the smaller it becomes. When a course of action is considered too risky for the enemy to choose, the other side naturally considers it unlikely to occur and therefore does little to hedge against it. The enemy that actually opts for this course of action is therefore that much more likely to succeed. Examples include James Wolfe's plan of action at the Battle for the Plain of Abraham (1759), the landing in Normandy (1944), Douglas MacArthur's (q.v.) landing in Inchon (September 1950), and the Israeli raid on Entebbe (1976).

The possibility of deception casts doubt upon even apparently reliable intelligence as "too good to be true." Paradoxically, the more aware one is of the possibility of deception, the more one will question reliable intelligence.

When intelligence organizations are concerned about the possibility of a surprise attack, they may therefore be more ready in a worst-case analysis to alert the military. But an excessively sensitive alert system increases the number of false alarms (the "cry wolf syndrome"); this in turn eventually numbs the troops. On the other hand, the tendency to reduce the number of alerts, because they are so costly in both resources and psychological strain, may increase the probability of being caught by surprise.

This problem is exacerbated by yet another paradox. The opponent planning an attack may decide to cancel it if he observes that the defender is on the alert and mobilizing his troops. An alert or mobilization can thereby become a *self-negating prophecy* that creates a problem for intelligence gathering. Did the enemy postpone a planned attack because of the defender's alert, or was an attack not intended in the first place?

The problems for the intelligence community and political leaders multiply in response to the opposite problem, in which mobilization and alert occurring when the enemy was *not* actually planning to attack actually cause the enemy to mobilize its own troops in reaction. When the enemy's intentions are thus misconstrued, the result can be an unintended war. In this situation, mobilization, alert, and preparation become *a self-fulfilling prophecy*. Examples include the July crisis before World War I and the mobilization and crisis before the 1967 Six-Day War between Israel and its neighbors.

The aforementioned causes of strategic surprise demonstrate why it is practically impossible to avoid surprise even when reliable intelligence is available. A carefully prepared strategic (or operational) surprise is therefore a major element in achieving at least initial success in war. (Good examples of operational surprise include the landings in Sicily, Salerno, and Anzio [q.v.]; the German attack in the Battle of the Bulge [q.v.]; and MacArthur's invasion of Inchon.) The exploitation of strategic and operational command depends on many factors: meticulous planning, a decentralized military doctrine that encourages field commanders to use their initiative, proper training of the troops, and mobility and the full realization of the impact of surprise on the victim. The Germans in 1940 and 1941, the Japanese in 1941, and the Israelis in 1956 and 1967 were very successful in fully exploit-

A U.S. marine guards North Korean prisoners of war.

ing the surprise they achieved. In comparison, the British in Gallipoli (1915) (q.v.), after El Alamein (1942)(q.v.), and the British and Americans in Salerno, Anzio, and perhaps even Normandy were less successful. Yet a successful *initial* strategic surprise is not alone sufficient to bring about *final victory* in the war; this depends on political, economic, and military factors, which in the long run are not affected by the achievement of surprise.

MICHAEL I. HANDEL

Richard K. Betts, *Surprise Attack* (1982); Michael I. Handel, *War, Strategy, and Intelligence* (1989); Thomas L. Hughes, *The Fate of Facts in a World of Men: Foreign Policy and Intelligence Making* (1976).

Surrender

In earlier times a captured warrior's life was normally wholly forfeit to the captor. He might be enslaved (perhaps with some mutilation, such as blinding or castration) or killed, and in some cultures eaten;

among some North American forest tribes he might be ritually tortured to death. By the same token, voluntary surrender was not to be thought of. With the rise of chivalry in the Middle Ages, however, European society gradually accepted the proposition that it was not dishonorable to save life by yielding when resistance was hopeless and one had done everything within one's power; and by the same token, enslavement or killing of captives was abandoned, though they might be held for ransom. This general attitude now dominates modern international law, though as recently as World War II (q.v.) surrender was deemed absolutely unacceptable in the Japanese armed forces — an attitude that colored Japanese treatment of Allied prisoners of war. And in all military forces there still remains a fine line between surrender and desertion (q.v.).

Under the modern laws of war, any individual or body of troops is entitled to demand and receive "quarter" — that is, if they lay down their arms, surrender, and do not resist capture, the enemy must do nothing further to injure or kill them, and they are from that moment entitled to the rights of prisoners of war (q.v.). There are very limited exceptions. Quarter may be denied by way of reprisal for violations of the rules of warfare committed by the enemy. If a single soldier attempts to surrender while the rest of his unit continues to fight, the enemy is not obliged to recognize his attempt if it could not reasonably be accomplished without danger to the members of the capturing unit. The right to quarter is forfeited by a soldier who continues firing after the white flag has been hoisted. In past centuries, quarter could be denied to prisoners where the safety of the capturing force was vitally imperiled by their continued presence; nowadays, in such circumstances they must be disarmed and released.

The popular impression that, for example, a besieger may summon a city or fortress to surrender and declare that no quarter will be given if it is taken by storm, is quite wrong and reflects the comparative savagery of earlier days, especially of the religious wars from the Crusades (q.v.) through the Thirty Years' War (q.v.), as did the former rules that quarter could be refused to a weak garrison that obstinately and pointlessly persisted in defending a fortified place, and to the defenders of an unfortified place against an artillery attack. Under modern customary international law, confirmed by a specific provision of the Hague Regulations, it is specifically unlawful to declare that no quarter shall be given. Similarly, international law no longer permits the sacking of a captured city (see *Laws of War*).

Surrender — of an individual, a unit, a fortress, a city, a town, a district of the theater of operations, or a ship — may be unconditional (the technical term is "at discretion") or upon terms. Unconditional surrender of a force or defended place is signified by hoisting the white flag; of a vessel, by striking the national colors. A surrender upon terms naturally follows upon negotiations, customarily initiated by sending out a party under a white flag. The agreement embodying the terms is called a "capitulation." Unless there is an agreement to the contrary, the terms are presumed to include the understanding that members of the surrendering force become prisoners of war, and that all matériel of war and other public property are surrendered in the condition in which they existed at the time of the capitulation. But a capitulation may contain any terms that are within the authority of the commanders involved to grant. For example, the sur-

rendering force may be allowed to keep property that would otherwise be spoils of war, as at Appomattox in 1865 (see *American Civil War*). The surrendering force may be allowed to march out of its position with the honors of war, or some of them. In one extreme case, the surrender of Belfort to the Germans in 1871, the French defenders were permitted to depart with full honors, carrying their weapons and baggage, and rejoin the main French army unmolested (see *Franco-Prussian War*). Even an unconditional surrender may be embodied in a written agreement specifying details, as at Reims in 1945 (see *World War II*). The only limitation is that the terms must accord with the demands of military honor; that is, they must contain nothing personally degrading to the surrendering force, or require that they do such things as fight against their own country or commit acts forbidden by their country's laws or their conditions of service.

Only the commanders of the opposing forces have authority to enter into a capitulation, and their authority is limited to terms that can be fulfilled by their own forces or by superior officers. They are not presumed to have authority beyond the forces under their own command. In particular, they are not presumed to have any political authority, such as authority to cede places or territory, to agree that the surrendered troops will never again bear arms against the enemy, or to make terms that will take effect after the termination of hostilities. If a commander surrenders unnecessarily or shamefully, or in violation of orders, he may be punishable by his own government, but the capitulation is valid.

There is no fixed form for capitulations. They may be oral or written. Normally, of course, they are in writing. Their terms must be scrupulously observed. A serious breach by an individual without his government's authority is a war crime; an authorized breach is an international delinquency justifying renewal of hostilities and reprisals. If one party refuses to carry out any term, the other party may denounce the entire agreement.

THADDEUS HOLT

Morris Greenspan, *The Modern Law of Land Warfare* (1959); L. Oppenheim, *International Law* (Lauterpacht ed.), 5th ed., vol. 2 (n.d.); United States Department of the Army, *Field Manual FM 27-10: The Law of Land Warfare* (various dates).

Suvorov, Aleksandr

1730–1800, Russian General and Field Marshal

At age fifteen, Aleksandr Vasil'evich Suvorov enlisted in the Semenovskii Guards regiment as a private soldier. He rose through the ranks to become Russia's greatest eighteenth-century general — he never lost a battle. Commissioned an officer in 1754, he distinguished himself in virtually every campaign mounted by Russia over the ensuing half century. He took part in the Russian occupation of Berlin (1760) during the Seven Years' War (q.v.). When Russia intervened in Poland in 1772, Suvorov's capture of Kraków helped prepare the way for the first Polish partition. In the first Turkish war (1768–1774) (see *Russo-Turkish Wars*), he served in the Danubian army; during the second war (1787–1792) he won spectacular victories at Focşani, Rymnik, and Izmail. When Russia entered the War of the Second Coalition against revolutionary France (1798–1800), Suvorov became commander in chief of all allied forces in northern Italy. He defeated the French at Adda and in 1799 conducted an epic retreat through the Swiss Alps.

Suvorov was intensely pious, wildly eccentric, and extraordinarily accident-prone. He took a salutary interest in the well-being of his troops and insisted on making training as realistic as possible. When campaigning, Suvorov stressed the importance of coup d'oeil, speed, and shock. His famous saying *"pulia duraka, no shtyk molodets"* (roughly, "bullet is a fool but the bayonet is terrific") has caused some to conclude erroneously that Suvorov was the father of the cult of the bayonet in the Russian army. In actuality, Suvorov was notorious for his insistence upon aimed infantry fire.

WILLIAM C. FULLER, JR.

Swinton, Ernest

1868–1951, British Soldier and Military Theorist

The tank was the supreme military invention of World War I (q.v.), and although others, notably Winston Churchill (q.v.), explored similar ideas, Ernest Dunlop Swinton, an engineer officer with the substantive rank of major, is widely credited as its prime originator. Study of the Russo-Japanese War (q.v.) had given him "a machine gun complex," and in 1914 he rapidly concluded that the vigorous use of that weapon by the Germans required a more sophisticated response than massed infantry attacks, which seemed to him "about as hopeless as those of the Dervishes at Omdurman." He had combined soldiering with authorship, and it was this qualification that brought him into contact with the first campaigns. Journalists were barred from following the flag at this time, but the war secretary, Field Marshal Lord Kitchener (q.v.), recognized the public's thirst for news by dispatching Swinton to the Western Front, whence he reported home under the alias "Eyewitness." By October 1914 he had found a solution to the machine-gun problem; "it was as if," he wrote, "a ray of light had struck a sensitized plate."

He knew of the Holt Caterpillar tractor and envisaged an armored version of it that could defy and destroy machine guns and also cross trenches. Early "tell-tale" names for his concept included "landship" and "land cruiser"; asked to find a more generic term, he and a fellow officer proposed the simple monosyllable "tank" as "likely to catch on and be remembered"! He later trained the necessary tank personnel, but was not allowed to command in the field. However, his role was acknowledged by those who took his invention into battle; following the successful tank attack at Cambrai (q.v.) in 1917, the commander cabled him: "All ranks thank you. Your show."

Earlier, under the pseudonyms "Backsight Forethought" and "Ole Luk-Oie," Swinton had used the medium of fiction to raise debate about martial themes — even, in his short story "The Point of View," suggesting that in a future conflict, once a well-planned battle had begun, a general should leave the front and go fishing. He also anticipated mining, air balloons for artillery observation, and the military use of psychiatry, and he was the first to adapt the ancient phrase "No Man's Land" to a war context.

In appearance he was almost a Colonel Blimp, but no soldier was less conventional. He was eventually promoted to major general and became "Sir Ernest," but he always stood apart from the military establishment — an individualist with a distinct if sometimes underappreciated spark of genius.

MALCOLM BROWN

T

Tactics

A term of Greek origin, the word *tactics* describes how to achieve a battle task. The Greek word *taktika* meant "order of arrangement." *Tactic* can be used to characterize a single method or technique to accomplish an objective. Unlike strategy, wherein political considerations and national leaders are supreme, tactics lie within the purview of warriors. Tactics are concerned with the application of power, not the ultimate aim such power is expected to attain. Additionally, tactics are influenced by the personalities and professionalism of military and naval leaders as well as weather and terrain. Like *strategy*, the word has been appropriated by the business, sports, and political worlds, denoting methodology and techniques. When referring to the employment of military and naval units in combat, it deals with the maneuver and positioning of battle elements. The tactician's aim is to gain the best advantages for a friendly force while exploiting the vulnerabilities of an opponent.

Territorial protection and the aggressive techniques of the hunt are behavioral patterns shared between humans and many members of the animal kingdom. For example, pack animals such as wolves and hyenas often surround their prey and then attack. The same can be said about the defensive techniques of the herd, such as the formation of a compact mass to prevent the separation and isolation of individual members. Humans have learned and sometimes emulated animals' tactics during combat situations for many millennia.

Archaeologists have uncovered much of what is known about tactical evolution. Since defensive physical remnants are usually more substantial than the artifacts of offensive tactics, the archaeological record is perhaps a bit unbalanced. Jericho presents an early example of the defensive techniques associated with fortifications; its walls, estimated to have been built in approximately 8000 B.C., are twenty-three feet thick at base level. This structure included a moat and is believed to have required a defending garrison of five hundred to six hundred men.

Hand-thrown stones were perhaps the first missile weapons, and a simple stick, the initial thrusting weapon. Thrusting and club weapons suggest tactics of mass. All other factors being equal, the force with greater numbers would probably prevail. On the other hand, missiles such as arrows, permitting standoff attack, would have been particularly valuable to the early tacticians who could not attract large numbers into their ranks. Missiles, of course, offer the promise of deadly effect on an opponent while protecting one's own soldiers through the medium of distance. Shock tactics (overwhelming the opponents by a mass movement into their midst), featuring warriors wielding spears, swords, and clubs, or missile tactics, featuring soldiers armed with slings or bows and arrows, were crucial tactical options from at least 6000 B.C.

Mobility, over and above what could be achieved with one's own feet, became another tactical tool by at least 4000 B.C. in Sumer. The horse-drawn chariot eventually combined shock and missile tactics with charioteers armed with javelins or bows and arrows. By 1500 B.C., Egyptians were building highly capable, complex chariots, and they created sophisticated tactics to be used by their two-man crews. The Egyptian order of battle could include chariot formations that equaled almost one-half the army. By at least 1192 B.C., mobile tactics were extended beyond the land. A sea battle between Egyptians and Philistines has been dated to that year. This encounter, involving composite bows, sails, oars, and swords, probably amounted to little more than waterborne infantry combat.

Despite occasional naval actions and speeding chariots, warfare in this era was dominated by land struggles between closely packed groups of foot soldiers armed with spears, shields, and swords. The Sumerian phalanx of 2500 B.C. had an eleven-man front and a depth of six ranks. Infantry tactics involved head-on clashes where numbers, esprit, and training might win the day. Alternatively, envelopments might be used, an opponent's ranks being flanked by one or more similar formations. This sort of thrusting, stabbing, hacking mass encounter between dense formations of heavily armed men was a prime feature of warfare for over three thousand years.

Any example of early Western tactical prowess, however, would have paled before the strength, agility, professionalism, and superior weaponry of contemporary Chinese forces. Ch'in Shih-huang-ti (q.v.) fought for a decade, 230–221 B.C., unifying the seven kingdoms of China. The victor had his army immortalized in life-size terra cotta figures — horses and all — revealing a force of considerable tactical sophistication. Some of his infantry were organized into both heavy and light formations, equipped with spears, halberds, and cutting weapons. Both charioteers and cavalrymen were formed into separate groups, and there were bowmen as well as crossbowmen. Parts of this force were clad with extensive armor protection. Sun Tzu's (q.v.) *Ping-fa (Art of War)* gives a glimpse at how this force was likely employed. One array was to act directly and fix the enemy while another attacked by indirect, surprise means to complete the win. Leaders were advised, "A military force has no constant formation . . . the ability to gain victory by changing and adapting according to the opponent is called genius." These Eastern legions could be large. One campaign in the sixth century B.C. involved an enormous infantry and charioteer contingent and no less than 5,000 cavalrymen; it is believed that they together inflicted 400,000 deaths on an enemy in a single campaigning season.

In the West, the Roman era brought little tactical innovation. Rome's great talents lay in governance, logistics (q.v.), and engineering, not tactics. The sturdy legion was a formidable military tool, but was not much different in organization and employment than the Greek and Macedonian formations it replaced. And it was far less flexible and multifaceted than contemporary Chinese fighting forces. Rome's slow acceptance of the mounted arm and more flexible tactics contributed to the empire's collapse, but other factors were of greater import.

In the seventh century, the stirrup, a Chinese in-

Ten Examples of Tactical Brilliance

Megiddo (Thutmose III; Israel, 1468 B.C.)

Cannae (Hannibal; Italy, 216 B.C.)

Ramillies (Marlborough; Belgium, May 23, 1706)

Austerlitz (Napoleon; Czech Republic, December 2, 1805)

Chancellorsville (Jackson, Lee; United States, May 1–3, 1863)

Königgrätz (Moltke; Austria, July 3, 1866)

Beersheba (Allenby; Israel, October 31, 1917)

Khalkin-Gol (Zhukov; Mongolia, August 20–31, 1939)

Operation Aida (Rommel; Libya, May–June 1942)

Inchon (MacArthur; South Korea, September 15–26, 1950)

---

vention, began its journey westward, creating a tactical revolution. The device permitted a mounted archer to achieve greater accuracy and enabled a heavily armored horseman to keep his seat while wielding a sword. With the advent of the horseshoe and the stirrup, cavalry came to dominate tactics. During this period, tactics were still apt to be of the melee sort. One horde confronted another, there was an onrushing charge, and the entire mass dissolved into individual combats. This happened at sea as well as on land. Exceptions to these somewhat chaotic encounters were provided by the occasional employment of longbowmen and crossbowmen. Their speeding missiles could penetrate armor, bringing down the mounted knight. The bowmen, however, had to be protected, in some cases by driving sharpened stakes into the ground in front of their position. This tactic, providing a protected spot on the battleground for projectile launching, laid the methodological foundation for the employment of another Chinese technological marvel: firearms.

Firearms brought on a tactical revolution. The steady improvement of cannon eventually made above-the-ground fortifications obsolete and vastly changed naval warfare, transforming floating infantry platforms into wind-powered standoff weapons carriers. Gradually, naval tactics evolved into fleet battle dispositions of lines and columns, designed to make maximum use of one's own firepower while minimizing the effect of the enemy's guns. On land, cannon became increasingly mobile, providing tacticians with the means to support a cavalry or infantry attack by concentrating fire on an intended point of entry into an opponent's line. Alternatively, one could quickly shift the guns elsewhere, providing the means to thwart an assault by pouring shot and shell on an attacker. Individual firearms were also improved with increased ranges, lighter and handier designs, and steadily rising rates of fire. At first, tacticians interspersed firearms-bearing soldiers with others armed with pikes, spears, and cutting weapons. But by the eighteenth century, bows and arrows, crossbows, spears, javelins, and slingshots became identified with primitive peoples. Soldiers solely armed with cutting or thrusting weapons were largely confined to the cavalry arms of European states. Shock tactics, performed by horse soldiers, were only a part — a steadily decreasing part — of a greater array formed for missile delivery. And, since horse soldiers were already gaining firearms themselves, swords came to serve merely a ceremonial function. Tactics, therefore, were becoming a matter of placing missile platforms (riflemen, artillerymen, gun-wielding riders, warships, and so on) at the right spot at the right time and in sufficient numbers to make a difference.

The trend of missile tactics replacing shock tactics briefly changed during the Napoleonic era. Up to this point, technology and professionalism seemed to be the predominant engines of tactical change, but the Wars of the French Revolution (q.v.) brought sociopolitical factors into play. Revolutionary France was not only able to imbue hitherto unknown numbers with martial fervor, but also it could mobilize, equip, and move these masses to a distant battlefield with considerable speed. Vast numbers of infantrymen could be herded into a densely packed column and hurled at an opponent's line. Napoleon (q.v.) used the same technique, but often substituted cavalry for infantry as the battering ram, having carefully cleared the path for the assault by a skillful use of artillery. Shock tactics seemed to have regained ascendancy. However, within a few decades, as demonstrated by the American Civil War (q.v.), rifles replaced muskets as the infantryman's arm of choice. The foot soldier's dramatically increased effective range virtually destroyed the cavalry charge. Once again, missile tactics reigned supreme.

Although Napoleonic warfare had a modest effect on tactical change, it had a major impact in defining the parameters and limits of tactics as a subject of study through the outpouring of literature on Napo-

leon's campaigns and a growing field of military thought: strategy. Much of this writing in the nineteenth and early twentieth centuries centered on determining the difference between strategy and tactics. Carl von Clausewitz (q.v.) claimed tactics involved employing troops to win battles — strategy being the use of battles to win wars. A later nineteenth-century German writer, Count Colmar von der Goltz, more read in Britain and America than Clausewitz, said strategy had to do with generalship whereas tactics involved handling troops. An American widely read in Europe, Alfred Thayer Mahan (q.v.), called strategy the preceding actions that brought armies or fleets into contact. He said tactics comprised what one did with those armies or fleets in battle.

World War I (q.v.) had a serious impact on tactical development, literally adding a wholly new tactical dimension. Heretofore, tacticians confined their attention to the surface of the land or sea. The advent of air and submarine tactics took warfare into the third dimension. The appearance of the tank brought shock tactics back to the battlefield in a new, mechanized form. Toward the last of that war, missiles, in the guise of extremely long-range artillery projectiles fired from such weapons as Germany's "Big Bertha," were being aimed at cities many miles distant from launching positions.

Thus, World War I brought on vertical envelopment and long-range missile and air attacks. Although there was a successful submarine attack on a warship during the American Civil War, it was not until 1914–1918 that systematic use of submarines and the frantic search for a way to destroy them came about. Offensively, submarines were able to traverse an enemy's surface blockade by traveling under it and raiding its shipping, even in the enemy's "home waters." The most important tactic used against the submarine in World War I was the convoy (q.v.), surrounding transports with a circle of security rather than trying to create a zone of security the entire length of the transatlantic corridor. The tactics of attacking submarines increasingly relied on sophisticated electronic detection systems. Once a submarine was located, a simple use of explosives set to detonate at the correct depth could bring success. There was also a land version of vertical envelopment. The notion of parachuting thousands of troops deep in an opponent's rear occurred to the American air officer Billy Mitchell (q.v.) during the last phase of the 1918 campaign on the Western Front.

World War I featured distant attacks by aircraft as well by long-range artillery. Gradually, zeppelins gave way to multiengine airplanes as the airframe of choice for "bombers." Antiaircraft defensive tactics consisted of employing speedy, rapidly climbing interceptor aircraft, searchlights, and antiaircraft artillery. All of this became applicable to war at sea, resulting in a steady move to naval aircraft carriers in the 1930s.

World War II (q.v.) saw the aircraft carrier and its associated tactics assume first-order importance, displacing the battleship and naval gunfire. Radar allowed attack on targets invisible to the naked eye. Additionally, dispersal of ground troops, a needed tactical change derived from the brutal conditions of World War I, became possible in the 1940s. The light, portable radio permitted infantrymen to move in widely scattered but controlled small groups, a welcome relief from the requirements of trench warfare, in which visual contact with flanking soldiers units and supporting weaponry was essential in the attack. Thus, open-order tactics, a dream in 1914–1918, became a battlefield staple in 1939–1945. Radio-equipped, mechanically reliable, and faster tanks emerged as the prime instruments of penetration attacks, making the linear defense an increasingly doubtful choice; elastic defense became favored as an alternative. Elastic defense featured rear positioned, mobile armored formations used to suddenly overwhelm an opponent's forces once they had penetrated a thin forward defensive line. Also, the guided missile appeared during the latter phase of World War II. When this latter device was coupled with the atomic bomb, tactics of any sort seemed superfluous.

Unfortunately, war survived, and in the past one hundred years, it has become almost totally distanced from humanity's ancient hunting traditions. Since World War II, the trend toward dispersal and long-range attack has rapidly accelerated. During the Gulf War of 1990–1991 (q.v.), B-52 bombers took off from the United States, bombed targets half way around the world, and returned. Tanks in that war engaged targets at three thousand yards — and scored direct, devastating hits. Artillery is steadily giving way to rocket and missile fire, both types delivered from progressively distant locales. Additionally, use of night attacks has steadily increased, particularly by the American armed forces. Whereas Stone Age man was a daylight hunter and fighter, high-tech warriors of the late twentieth century wage battle around the clock. Throughout most of human existence, combat included physical or near-physical contact — proximity to an opponent today is a rarity. Tactics, the "how" of battle, have become a matter of impersonally delivering greater lethality at increasingly distant targets.

ROD PASCHALL

Robert Ardrey, *The Territorial Imperative: A Personal Inquiry into the Animal Origins of Property and Nations* (1966); Hans Delbrück, *History of the Art of War*, 4 vols. (1900–1920); Richard E. Simpkin, *Race to the Swift: Thoughts on Twenty-first-Century Warfare* (1985); Yigael Yadin, *The Art of Warfare in Biblical Lands* (1963).

Taiping Rebellion

1851–1864

The Taiping Rebellion was a major military and social movement to overthrow the Ch'ing dynasty of China (see *Manchus*) and establish a puritanical, egalitarian community based on the quasi-Christian beliefs of its leader, Hung Hsiu-ch'üan, the "Heavenly King." Perhaps twenty million people died in this war, which ranks among the bloodiest in world history; Chinese Communists later somewhat ambiguously claimed the Taiping as part of the revolutionary heritage of Chinese peasants.

Taiping armies originated in minority Hakka areas of rural Kwangsi; to overcome the prohibitions against private weapons construction, the honking of a large flock of geese, kept expressly for this purpose, disguised the sound of iron being hammered by would-be rebels, who also forged their own lethal, if crude, cannon and excavated illicit weapons buried nearly two centuries earlier. The Taiping's most remarkable military success was their capture of Nanking, which they occupied as their capital for eleven years.

Taiping military organization was based on an ancient, idealized model. Centered on a series of units of over thirteen thousand men each and employing a detailed command structure separated into strategic and administrative/training branches, it was both flexible and rigorous. Military planners distributed illustrated manuals of fighting formations, technical instructions on camp constructions, regulations for troops on the march, and an extremely strict military code, infraction of which was severely punished. This organization combined with Taiping utopian ideals to make them invincible against imperial forces. Hence the Ch'ing government authorized provincial leaders to assemble new armies, in a direct reversal of the longtime policy of forbidding independent military organization. These provincial armies, newly armed and aided by foreign mercenaries (q.v.), eventually defeated the Taiping, whose failure was also attributable first to defects of leadership, including the failure to coordinate with other contemporaneous uprisings elsewhere in China or to gain Western support, and second to the rebels' inability to implement many of their programs. Yet by undermining traditional principles such as a centralized military and by exposing and enhancing dynastic weaknesses, their long-term contribution to the Ch'ing downfall was unmistakable.

JOANNA WALEY-COHEN

Talas River, Battle of

July 751

The only major engagement ever fought between Chinese and Arabs, this battle was the product of a conflict between the rulers of Tashkent and Ferghana (both nominal vassals of China). After the Chinese intervened in support of Ferghana, the Arabs, who were competing with T'ang China for dominance in Central Asia, quickly became involved. An Arab army marched from Samarkand to attack the Chinese, and, at the town of Atlakh (near the Talas River in what is now Kirghizia), encountered an army of thirty thousand Chinese and allied troops led by the Korean-born general Kao Hsien-chih. The ensuing battle was lost by the Chinese when their Turkish (Qarluq) contingent defected. The Arabs remained the dominant power in Transoxiana for the next 150 years, and the region was brought firmly within the orbit of Islamic civilization. However, the withdrawal of T'ang China from Central Asia probably had more to do with the empire's chronic military weakness in the wake of the An Lu-shan rebellion (755–763) (q.v.) than the outcome of any single battle.

DAVID A. GRAFF

Tamerlane

1336–1405, *Central Asian Conqueror and Founder of the Timurid Dynasty*

Of Mongol (q.v.) descent, though a speaker of Turkic, Tamerlane galvanized an army initially composed of nomads to set forth on wide-ranging campaigns that rivaled and actually surpassed the conquests of Genghis Khan. However, he could never assume the title of khan because he was not directly descended from Genghis.

Born to a seemingly modest family within the Barlas tribe of modern Uzbekistan, in 1361–1362 he assumed control of the tribe. His next objective was leadership of the Ulus Chaghadai, the tribal confederation that constituted one-half of the Mongols' Central Asian empire. By the end of the 1360s, he had overwhelmed his other rivals; assumed the title of amir; installed a powerless figure, whom he could readily manipulate, as khan; and married a woman from the Genghisid line, thus bolstering his legitimacy by using the title *güregen* (royal son-in-law).

Having a sizable military force, Tamerlane now had to persist in expeditions in order to preserve the loyalty and support of his men. As his army grew, he recruited Turkic slaves as well as foreigners, and this multiethnic force, composed of Turks, Mongols, and Persians, among others, no doubt contributed to his success. He needed the military and administrative skills provided by his recruits from the sedentary world.

After a ten-year period during which he simply increased his eastern territory, Tamerlane initiated an astonishing series of successful campaigns over the next two decades. Starting in 1381, for about five years he led expeditions in Iran and Afghanistan that resulted in his occupation of Sistan (northern Afghanistan), Khurasan (eastern Iran), and northern Iran. In the late 1380s, his troops overran Armenia, Georgia, and Azerbaijan, territories the Mongols had conquered in the previous century. Hoping to buttress his position, he was about to return to Iran and Afghanistan when the Mongol khan of the Golden Horde, Tokhtamish, attacked his domain in Central Asia. He immediately headed back, and by 1390, he had expelled the khan from Central Asia, although sporadic fighting continued until Tamerlane routed Tokhtamish's forces in 1395. He destroyed Sarai, the Golden Horde capital; burned other important cities; and transferred the trade routes, with caravans coming from the East, to south of the Caspian, thus excluding the Golden Horde from this lucrative commerce.

In the last years of his life, Tamerlane campaigned on an even more expansive terrain. In 1398, he attacked North India and took Delhi; by 1402, his troops occupied Syria and defeated the Ottoman Turks (see *Ottomans*); and finally, in 1404, he made meticulous plans to conquer the largest empire in the world, China. In February of 1405, he died en route to China. He was buried in a tomb in Samarkand. In 1941, Russian scientists dug up his corpse and confirmed that his name, "Timur the Lame," was accurate.

His brutality has been overstated in the West: only if he met stiff resistance did he sanction the deliberate destruction of which he has been accused. His devotion to Islam, not simply a bloodthirsty drive for power, prompted some of his campaigns. His patronage of Islamic scholars and of poets and painters belies his image as a barbarian; and Samarkand, with its beautiful mosques, minarets, tombs, bathhouses, and central square (Registan) that he constructed, remains as one of his greatest legacies.

MORRIS ROSSABI

Beatrice Forbes Manz, *The Rise and Rule of Tamerlane* (1989).

T'ang T'ai-tsung

599?–649, *Chinese Emperor and General*

The second son of Li Yüan, who had seized the imperial throne and established the T'ang dynasty in 618, T'ai-tsung (whose personal name was Li Shih-min) quickly emerged as the leading T'ang field commander, in spite of his youth, in the chaotic civil wars of 618–623.

An outstanding leader, he was not content with a subordinate position; in 626 he ambushed and killed his two brothers (one of them the heir apparent) and usurped his father's throne. As emperor, T'ai-tsung presided over the defeat of the Eastern Turks in 630 and the T'u-yü-hun in 635, but was stymied in Korea in 645. In most of his campaigns, he employed essentially the same strategy of entrenching his army and avoiding a general engagement, while harassing the enemy's supply line with cavalry. As a rule, he would give battle only after the enemy had begun to weaken — but once the battle had been won, his pursuit was headlong and relentless. T'ai-tsung was not only a strategist but also a warrior who led cavalry charges and played an active part in the cut and thrust of the melee, and he once claimed to have killed more than a thousand men with his own hand during the course of his military career. At the same time, however, he was also a competent calligrapher and a reasonably good poet. In his own writings, T'ang T'ai-tsung repeatedly pointed to the need to strike a balance between the civil and military virtues, and his reign is remembered by the Chinese as an almost legendary period of virtuous and enlightened government.

DAVID A. GRAFF

Tannenberg, Battle of

July 15, 1410

In one of the largest cavalry battles of the age, the combined forces of the Poles and Lithuanians defeated the Order of the Teutonic Knights (see *Knightly Orders*). The Poles and Lithuanians, recently united politically, brought to the field an enormous army, perhaps 100,000 strong, including Moravian, Wallachian, Tatar, and Czech mercenaries and the clever military tactician and future leader of the Hussites, Jan Zizka (q.v.). The Knights' forces, estimated at eighty-three thousand, were supplemented primarily by German mercenaries. Although both sides brought crossbowmen and cannon, the battle essentially involved squadrons of light horse supported by reserves of mailed knights. Despite initial success, the Knights were ultimately defeated; their losses included the entire high command as well as the bulk of the field army.

The defeat was a great blow to the military might and prestige of the order, which lost its impetus as a crusading force. The image of Tannenberg, however, long remained in the German consciousness. When German armies defeated the Russians at Tannenberg in 1914, the high command portrayed it as revenge for the defeat of the order five hundred years earlier.

WILLIAM CAFERRO

Tannenberg, Battle of

August 25–30, 1914

The opening encounter between the Russian and German Empires in World War I (q.v.) ended in a major German tactical victory. The Schlieffen Plan (q.v.) left only a token force to defend the exposed province of East Prussia. The Russian plan of encircling the German Eighth Army with their overwhelmingly superior forces seemed on its way to success when German senior officers panicked after a local defeat on August 20. Instead, however, the Russian commanders delayed their advances and failed to coordinate their movements. This created an opportunity for Paul von Hindenburg (q.v.) and Erich Ludendorff (q.v.) to implement plans, already drafted by the Eighth Army's senior staff officers, for concentrating their entire strength against the Russian Second Army in the southern sector. After five days' hard fighting, fifty thousand Russians were dead or wounded, and over ninety thousand were prisoners of war.

Tannenberg has often been cited as a case study of Russian incompetence contrasted to German efficiency. In fact, the adversaries were reasonably well matched. The Russians' failure essentially involved attempting to fight on the Germans' terms, committing themselves to a strategy of maneuver that their field armies could not execute.

Tannenberg gave Germany two heroes, Hindenburg and Ludendorff, who would eventually become their country's de facto rulers. The battle also provided material for postwar legends of heroism and victory against the odds, which strengthened antidemocratic forces in the Weimar Republic and proved useful to Adolf Hitler (q.v.). Tannenberg's ultimate significance lay not in operations, but mythology.

DENNIS E. SHOWALTER

Taylor, Zachary

1784–1850, Mexican War General and President of the United States

Born in Virginia and raised in Kentucky, Zachary Taylor began his military career in 1808 with appointment as a first lieutenant of infantry, followed by frontier service in the War of 1812 (q.v.). Promoted to colonel by 1832, Taylor took part in the Black Hawk War, and five years later commanded the U.S. Army against the Seminole Indians in Florida, for which he was brevetted a brigadier general. In 1845, ordered to defend Texas against the threat of invasion by Mexico following its annexation to the United States, he moved his command to Corpus Christi and later took up a position on the Rio Grande. In May 1846 he repelled superior Mexican forces at Palo Alto and Resaca de la Palma, the first engagements of the Mexican War (q.v.), for which he was brevetted a major general. As volunteers augmented his small regular army, he mounted a campaign against northern Mexico, defeating the enemy at Monterrey and in February 1847 at Buena Vista. Widely celebrated as the war's hero,

Taylor was nominated and elected to the presidency of the United States in 1848. His rather undistinguished administration came to an abrupt end with his death in July 1850.

ROBERT W. JOHANNSEN

Technology

Technology is systematic, purposeful manipulation of the material world. It is a process: *power* is applied through a *tool or machine* to a certain *material* by employing a certain *technique*. The result is an artifact. The term *technology*, meaning the study of technics, appeared in the seventeenth century; before then, all was arts and crafts, passed on by apprenticeship.

Until modern times, the artifacts of war were built on a human scale, powered by muscle. By about 10,000 B.C., the major weapons of premodern warfare had appeared — the spear, sling, mace, knife or short sword, and finally the bow and arrow, arguably the first machine. These deadly instruments prompted development of defensive technologies, first body armor (q.v.) and then fortification (q.v.), the most important military technology before gunpowder. Walls precluded many wars and channeled the course of others.

There was a symmetry to the weapons employed in most wars fought before the modern era. The two sides deployed similar arms and armor. In such circumstances, the outcome was usually determined by strength in numbers, the fighting prowess of the combatants, or superior tactics, strategy, or leadership. Occasionally one side or another enjoyed a technological advantage, as did the chariot empires of the second millennium B.C. And occasionally arms races dominated, such as that between fortress building and siege techniques in the first millennium B.C. But there is no reliable evidence for secret military technologies in the ancient, medieval, or classical worlds, save Greek fire in the middle centuries of the Byzantine Empire; winning weapons were available to all.

Throughout the period when muscles powered war, weapons fell in two broad categories: missile and striking. Generally, missile weapons, such as the bow and arrow and the thrown spear, were the choice of mobile warriors, often mounted nomads and raiders such as the Scythians of Roman times. They used speed and surprise to throw the enemy off balance and

During the seventeenth century, the western European scientific revolution — particularly the study of physical laws applicable to matter in motion — introduced scientific and mathematical analysis to the waging of war. This illustration from a seventeenth-century treatise on the construction of siege guns depicts ballistics experts measuring the dimensions of a cannon.

inflict casualties without the risk of a toe-to-toe engagement. Striking weapons such as the sword, the mace, and the stabbing spear were the choice of infantry, who relied on discipline, formation, and mass to overpower and annihilate their enemy, as did the Spartans (q.v.) of classical Greece. The choice of weapons in such cases reflected deep-seated societal convictions about the nature of war and its role in society: a standing, professional army bent on offensive war might choose one set of weapons, whereas an amateur militia defending its homeland might prefer another. The weapons of choice also had to be appropriate to the context; cavalry, for example, was suited to the grassy steppes of Eurasia but not to the barren mountains of the Greek peninsula.

The gunpowder revolution that began in the West in the fourteenth century transformed warfare. Strength and skill gave way to machines. For the first time in the history of land warfare, equipment mattered more than men. On the battlefield of the late Middle Ages, for example, an uneducated, poorly trained, and uninspired gunman could bring down a mounted knight, the flower of European chivalry and the uncontested champion of the feudal battlefield.

What is more, larger versions of these same gunpowder weapons, when turned on fortress walls, could reduce the refuge to which the mounted knight had retired when faced with superior force and to which peaceful societies had turned throughout history when beset by predator bands. The muscle that had wielded the sword and raised the fortress wall gave way to the chemical power of the internal combustion engine, which powered the cannon. From there to the hydrogen bomb, it was a straight line.

Gunpowder weapons also transformed naval warfare. War at sea, since it first appeared in the second millennium B.C., has always been more technological than warfare on land. The ship, often the most complex artifact of its age, is a necessary precondition of this combat; it furthermore determines what the combat will look like. Throughout most of history, this combat involved oared vessels — galleys — which sometimes rammed each other but more often locked up in deadly embrace to support hand-to-hand fighting by marines. Unsuited to gunpowder weapons, the galley gave way in the sixteenth century to the European broadside-firing sailing vessel, which established Western hegemony over the world's littoral. This warship was in turn displaced in the middle of the nineteenth century by vessels incorporating steam propulsion, screw propellers, armor, rifled guns, and high explosives. These set off an arms race that spread in the twentieth century from battleships to submarines and aircraft carriers.

The Industrial Revolution that transformed naval warfare effected similar changes on land. From the American Civil War (q.v.) through World War II (q.v.), the great powers fought wars of industrial production. Often, the total resources of the state were mobilized; productive capacity, not battle, became decisive. The target of combat expanded accordingly, from the army in the field to the entire economic and industrial base of the enemy, including transportation, utilities, natural resources, and capital equipment.

World War II was the first war in history in which important weapons in use at the end had not existed when the war broke out. Jet aircraft, ballistic missiles, proximity fuses, and the atomic bomb were all invented and fielded in a frenzy of research and development. Since 1945, the quality of military technology has replaced quantity as the desideratum of modern war. The electromagnetic spectrum has become the most important locus of new military technologies, ranging from remote sensing devices and information technology to precision guided munitions and satellite-based navigation. The competition to prevail on this electronic battlefield has produced an international arms race (q.v.), military-industrial complexes in the United States and elsewhere, an unprecedented prominence for the military as a driver of civilian technology, and finally a search for dual-use technology that can serve both military and civilian purposes.

Nowhere are these phenomena more evident than in aerospace technology, the third dimension of warfare. A product of the twentieth century, air warfare, like naval warfare, is entirely dependent on technology. From the Battle of Britain (q.v.) in 1940 to the Gulf War (q.v.) of 1991, quality has consistently proved superior to quantity. Research and development drive the field and ensure that only the wealthiest, most technologically advanced states can be truly competitive. This same phenomenon is true in the latest arena of military technology — outer space.

ALEX ROLAND

William H. McNeill, *The Pursuit of Power: Technology, Armed Force, and Society since A.D. 1000* (1982); Lewis Mumford, *Technics and Civilization* (1934).

Tecumseh

1768–1813, Shawnee War Chief

Born at Old Piqua, a Shawnee village in Ohio, Tecumseh came of age during the American Revolution (q.v.) and fought against the Kentuckians in 1782–1783. Opposed to the American occupation of Ohio in the postrevolutionary period, in 1791 he led a scouting party against the Americans at St. Clair's Defeat and in 1794 fought against Anthony Wayne's army at Fort Recovery and Fallen Timbers. After the Treaty of Greenville he remained opposed to American expansion and used the religious revitalization movement led by his brother (the Shawnee Prophet) to forge a pantribal political movement; but in 1811, while Tecumseh was in the South, the Americans destroyed his village at Prophetstown. During the War of 1812 (q.v.) he was active on the Detroit frontier and fought with the British at the battles of Brownstown and Monguagon. He participated in the unsuccessful sieges of Fort Meigs and Fort Stephenson, and was killed in 1813 after his British allies fled at the Battle of the Thames. Admired by both the British and the Americans for his inspiring leadership, humane treatment of prisoners, and skill as an orator, Tecumseh has become an American folk hero, the most universally admired Indian leader in American history.

R. DAVID EDMUNDS

Terauchi Hisaichi

1879–1946, Japanese World War II Field Marshal

The oldest son of Terauchi Masatake (1852–1919), army minister in the Russo-Japanese War (q.v.) and prime minister (1916–1919), the younger Terauchi rose to command the Taiwan Army (1934–1935) and became a general (1935). He served as army minister after the aborted coup d'état by army officers in February 1936 and as inspector general of military education (1937) before becoming commander of the North China Area Army immediately following the outbreak of war with China in July 1937.

On November 5, 1941, Terauchi was named to command the planned Japanese offensive into the "southern resource area" and established his headquarters in Saigon on December 4. He oversaw offensives in Thailand, Burma, Malaya, the Philippines, and the Dutch East Indies.

More presiding potentate than hands-on theater commander, and famous for his deference to the opinion of subordinates and his staff, Terauchi was given the honorary rank of field marshal in June 1943 and remained in command throughout the war.

He was disabled by a cerebral hemorrhage in 1945, and, although unable to attend the Japanese surrender ceremony in Singapore, he personally surrendered to Lord Mountbatten on November 30, 1945, in Saigon.

THEODORE F. COOK, JR.

Terrorism

War is a terrifying business. Every fighting commander wants to frighten the opponents into giving in; the more frightened they are, the fewer casualties on both sides. A few generals in the ancient world — Alexander (q.v.), Pyrrhus, Hannibal (q.v.) — succeeded in using elephants for this purpose; but elephants could be made to panic and wreak terror on their own side.

In parts of France during the Hundred Years' War (q.v.), bands of pillagers called *écorcheurs* ranged over the countryside, looting and murdering anybody weaker than themselves — until they encountered more disciplined armed forces, who executed them in their turn.

Medieval rulers continued the Roman practice of public executions of criminals, intended to deter the populace from crime by terror; indeed, the practice went on, in countries that regarded themselves as civilized, until the mid–nineteenth century, and in a few countries (for example, Turkey) it survives today. Public executions by guillotine, in the heart of Paris and other large cities, formed part of the system of terror that accompanied the French Revolution. When Thomas Hardy watched a hanging in Dorset (by telescope) as late as 1862, as usual a large crowd surrounded the scaffold.

Government-sponsored terror has continued into modern times, often by sophisticated means. When Vladimir Lenin and Leon Trotsky seized power in Russia in November 1917, Feliks Dzerzhinski developed for them a system of terror through secret police that secured their party's power for seventy years and made the Terror of the French Revolution (q.v.) seem almost petty by comparison. The excuse for its use was that their opponents during the Russian Civil War (q.v.) of 1917–1922 had used terror against them;

An armed Muslim terrorist guards the open door of a hijacked TWA airplane in Beirut, in 1985.

whether White terror was any worse than Red terror, either in Russia or in Hungary (where both also had a fling), remains an open question. By undercover means, this secret police force — under various names, such as the KGB — was able to exert significant authority outside the state frontiers of the USSR; terror has played a large part in this sort of warfare without gunfire.

It has been practiced also, more hesitantly, by the British SOE (Special Operations Executive) and the American OSS (Office of Strategic Services) and CIA (Central Intelligence Agency), subversive secret services dealing in covert action, normally operating outside the conventional democratic controls. These services were thought necessary tools to deal with Adolf Hitler's (q.v.) and Joseph Stalin's (q.v.) dictatorships.

The Nazi Party secured power in Germany partly by frightening voters into voting for it, beating them up if they did not comply. Both in Hitler's Germany and in Stalin's Russia, almost everyone quickly came to realize that if they did not conform, they would be packed off to a concentration camp, the mere name of which was enough to deter them; the brutalities inside almost pass current belief.

German Gotha bombers had tried, quite without

success, to terrify Londoners into suing for peace in 1917. In 1939–1940, German Ju 87 dive-bombers, using bombs with cardboard attachments to make them howl as they fell, terrified some Polish, Dutch, and French troops into surrender; an air attack on Rotterdam drove the peaceable Dutch to give in promptly. But as a general rule, bombardment from the air angered, rather than terrified, the victims; this was the case in turn in Barcelona, London, and Berlin as terror bombing developed during the wars of 1935–1945. A refinement added to terror bombing by Germany in 1944 was the use of pilotless missiles, the V-1 and V-2, which might fall on anybody. Yet two American atomic bombs, dropped on Hiroshima and Nagasaki in August 1945, were terrifying enough to bring imperial Japan to its knees, because they demonstrated so far superior a class of explosive power that the Japanese felt they could honorably surrender to it.

Flame had been used as a defensive weapon in sieges since the early Middle Ages. In the winter of 1914–1915 the German army developed portable flamethrowers for use in trench warfare. They were crewed by firemen, who were more used to flame than their fellow soldiers, and were imitated by the British and French armies. A flamethrower mounted in a tank, developed by the British army by 1943, had indeed a terrifying effect against all but the steadiest soldiers. Tanks without flamethrowers, against troops unprepared to encounter them at close quarters, can also operate as terror weapons and are still more effective as such against civilians.

In the later twentieth century, terror has been used by disaffected national and political groups against established governments, sometimes with secret support from other governments who have provided training in the making of bombs and the use of small arms. A few determined fanatics can manage to set off a bomb or assassinate an individual almost anywhere; an imaginative terrorist can, for example, use a blowtorch (bought in any decent hardware store) as a portable flamethrower, to terrify information out of a captive and thus prepare an assassination. Only exceptionally vigilant security and intelligence systems will be able to stop attacks of this kind. Free societies face a standing dilemma: unless they limit freedom, they cannot provide security for their own leaders.

Moreover, the revised Geneva Convention of 1977 now seems to condone the use of terror weapons by "peoples struggling, and struggling rightly, to be free" (in an old phrase of Mr. Gladstone, who lost a favorite

nephew to a terrorist attack carried out with surgeons' knives in Dublin, in 1882). Terrorism is now inextricably bound up with the problems of nations that feel oppressed: one nation's terrorist is another nation's freedom fighter. Once oppression is severe enough for terror to secure broad popular support, freedom fighters proliferate, and their coups — the more terrible, the better — become popular.

M. R. D. FOOT

Tet Offensive

The Tet offensive is often considered to be the turning point in the Vietnam War (q.v.). It opened during the lunar New Year holidays in late January 1968, at a time when the conflict appeared to be at a stalemate. The Viet Cong, as the insurgent forces in South Vietnam were popularly called, were too strong to be defeated, but not strong enough to overthrow the Saigon regime or to drive U.S. troops out of the country. Communist leaders in Hanoi thus decided to launch a major attack inside South Vietnam with the objective of toppling the Saigon government and undermining public support for the war effort in the United States.

The offensive consisted of a series of sharp attacks on urban and rural areas throughout the country. Viet Cong forces were successful in seizing control of thousands of villages, thus giving them access to a vital source of provisions and recruits. Spectacular assaults took place on the U.S. embassy and on government installations in the capital of Saigon, while North Vietnamese regulars briefly seized the imperial city of Hue.

In the world media, the Tet offensive was generally portrayed as a defeat for the United States and the Saigon regime. In fact, it was a major setback for the Viet Cong. Casualties were high, and the local infrastructure in many areas was virtually destroyed. Still, the Tet offensive achieved one of its purposes by convincing many Americans that the existing U.S. strategy of attrition would not bring about final victory. In late March, President Lyndon Johnson called a halt to U.S. air strikes above the twentieth parallel in an effort to bring about peace talks with North Vietnam. Formal negotiations opened in Paris in November 1968. It was the first step in the deescalation of the Vietnam War, which would come to a final end after the U.S. withdrawal five years later.

WILLIAM J. DUIKER

BATTLE OF TEUTOBURG FOREST

GERMANY

0 ——— 80 Miles
0 ——— 80 Kilometers

■ Roman Empire, A.D. 9
✗ Battle

Teutoburg Forest, Battle of

A.D. 9

Arminius, prince of the Cherusci, annihilated three Roman legions under the command of Governor Publius Quinctilius Varus between the northeastern slopes of Kalkrieser Berg and the marshes just east of Bramsche. Varus, acting upon reports of a rebellion brewing among the tribes in northwestern Germany, was lured into the pathless Teutoburg Forest. German auxiliaries deserted, and legionaries, drenched by rainstorms and harassed by German skirmishers, lost cohesion under Varus's incompetent leadership and were slaughtered. Varus and his officers preferred suicide to capture.

The Germans failed to follow up their astonishing success by invading Gaul because they fell out among themselves in the wake of victory. Although prompt Roman action secured the Rhine bridges, the loss of three legions represented 10 percent of the empire's trained manpower. The ill-omened numbers (XVII, XVIII, and XIX) of Varus's legions were never again used, even after expeditions in the years 15, 16, and 41 recovered the lost legionary standards. Augustus concentrated eight legions — one-third of the imperial army — on the Rhine, and his stepson Tiberius conducted punitive operations in the years 10–12. Augustus, however, abandoned plans for a German province between the Rhine and Elbe Rivers, thereby perma-

nently fixing Rome's northern boundary on the Rhine and the Danube.

KENNETH W. HARL

Thirty Years' War

1618–1648

This conflict, which redrew the religious and political map of central Europe, began in the Holy Roman Empire, a vast complex of some one thousand separate, semiautonomous political units under the loose suzerainty of the Austrian Hapsburgs. Over the previous two centuries, a balance of power had emerged among the leading states, but during the sixteenth century, the Reformation and the Counter Reformation had divided Germany into hostile Protestant and Catholic camps, each prepared to seek foreign support to guarantee its integrity if need arose.

Thus in 1618, when Ferdinand II, heir apparent to the throne of Bohemia, began to curtail certain religious privileges enjoyed by his subjects there, they immediately appealed for aid to the Protestants in the rest of the empire and to the leading foreign Protestant states: Great Britain, the Dutch Republic, and Denmark. Ferdinand, in turn, called upon the German Catholics (led by Bavaria), Spain, and the papacy. In the ensuing struggle, Ferdinand (elected Holy Roman Emperor in 1619) and his allies won a major victory at White Mountain (1620) outside Prague that allowed the extirpation of Protestantism in most of the Hapsburg lands. Encouraged by this success, Ferdinand turned in 1621 against Bohemia's Protestant supporters in Germany. Despite aid from Britain, Denmark, and the Dutch Republic, they too lost, and by 1629 imperial armies commanded by Albrecht von Wallenstein (q.v.) overran most of Protestant Germany and much of Denmark. Ferdinand then issued the Edict of Restitution, reclaiming lands in the empire belonging to the Catholic Church that had been acquired and secularized by Protestant rulers.

Only Swedish military aid saved the Protestant cause. In 1630 an army led by King Gustavus Adolphus (q.v.) landed in Germany and, with a subsidy from the French government and assistance from many German Protestant states, routed the Imperialists at Breitenfeld (1631) and drove them from much of Germany. The Protestant revival continued until in 1634 a Spanish army intervened and at Nördlingen defeated the main Swedish field army and forced the

Protestants out of southern Germany. This new Hapsburg success, however, provoked France — which feared encirclement — to declare war first on Spain (1635) and then on the emperor (1636).

The war, which in the 1620s had been fought principally by German states with foreign assistance, now became a struggle among the great powers (Sweden, France, Spain, and Austria) fought largely on German soil, and for twelve more years armies maneuvered while garrisons — over five hundred in all — carried out a "dirty war" designed both to support themselves and to destroy anything of possible use to the enemy. Atrocities (such as those recorded in the novel *Simplicissimus* by Hans von Grimmelshausen) abounded as troops struggled to locate and appropriate resources. Eventually, France's victory over the Spaniards at Rocroi (1643) (q.v.) and Sweden's defeat of the Imperialists at Jankau (1645) forced the Hapsburgs to make concessions that led, in 1648, to the Peace of Westphalia (q.v.), which settled most of the outstanding issues.

The cost, however, had proved enormous. Perhaps 20 percent of Germany's total population perished during the war, with losses of up to 50 percent along a corridor running from Pomerania in the Baltic to the Black Forest. Villages suffered worse than towns, but many towns and cities also saw their populations, manufacture, and trade decline substantially. It constituted the worst catastrophe to afflict Germany until World War II (q.v.). On the other hand, the conflict helped to end the age of religious wars. Although religious issues retained political importance after 1648 (for instance, in creating an alliance in the 1680s against Louis XIV [q.v.]), they no longer dominated international alignments. Those German princes, mostly Calvinists, who fought against Ferdinand II in the 1620s were strongly influenced by confessional considerations, and as long as they dominated the anti-Hapsburg cause, so too did the issue of religion. But because they failed to secure a lasting settlement, the task of defending the "Protestant cause" gradually fell into the hands of Lutherans, who proved willing to ally (if necessary) with Catholic France and Orthodox Russia in order to create a coalition capable of defeating the Hapsburgs. After 1630 the role of religion in European politics receded. This was, perhaps, the greatest achievement of the Thirty Years' War, for it thus eliminated a major destabilizing influence in European politics, which had both undermined the internal cohesion of many states and overturned the

diplomatic balance of power created during the Renaissance.

GEOFFREY PARKER

Thomas, George H.

1816–1870, American Civil War General

"Most men diminish as you approach them," wrote an Ohio newspaperman in 1863; "General Thomas grows upon you." Stolid in build and outlook, George H. Thomas was a Virginian whose allegiance to the Union was as steadfast as it was unexplained. A West Point graduate and veteran of the Seminole and Mexican wars, Thomas led federal forces to victory at Mill Springs, Kentucky, in January 1862, helping secure that state for the Union. Often passed over for promotion early in the war because of suspicions about his loyalty, Thomas's stern sense of duty enabled him to serve without rancor under officers junior in grade. His stubborn defense of Snodgrass Hill saved William Rosecrans's army and brought him lasting reputation as the "Rock of Chickamauga," and his patient, calculated attack at Nashville in December 1864 virtually destroyed John Bell Hood's army. William T. Sherman's (q.v.) comment that Thomas was "slow, but true as steel" is an apt summary of a field officer magnificent in defense and deliberate in offense.

NOAH ANDRE TRUDEAU

Thutmose III

1490–1436 B.C., Eighteenth Dynasty Pharaoh, New Kingdom, Egypt

Thutmose III left the first detailed battle plan in history. Instead of simply declaring victory, as is commonly done in royal inscriptions, the story of the Battle of Megiddo (q.v.) carved on the wall of Thutmose III's temple at Karnak describes in precise detail the movements of his troops and those of the enemy, as well as the exact geography — the valleys, rivers, and rock formations — of the area of engagement (in what is now Israel), thus illustrating clearly how he was able to win the battle. In one of recorded history's earliest significant tactical moves, he led his army to victory through a narrow pass, the place least expected.

Thutmose III's reign followed that of his aunt Hatshepsut, the sole woman pharaoh in Egyptian history, who, by claiming power for herself after the death of her husband, Thutmose II, managed to keep Thutmose III from the throne for twenty years. When Hatshepsut died after a long reign of peace, Thutmose III defaced her monuments and attempted to eradicate every trace of her name. He then resumed the militaristic style of his male predecessors who had driven the Hyksos invaders back into Asia Minor and thus established the New Kingdom in Egypt.

During his long reign as pharaoh, he led seventeen military campaigns, extending Egypt's control far east into Asia across the Euphrates, and south into Sudan, creating for the first time an Egyptian empire.

SUSAN BRIND MORROW

Time

Time is the essential element in all military operations. The preparation for battle, the formulation of strategy, and the coordination of tactical movements and fire on the battlefield are all governed by considerations of time. Battles have been lost because a unit arrived late, the time a message was sent was uncertain, or a commander did not react quickly enough.

For centuries armies were regulated by "natural time." Campaigns were conducted in spring and summer; battles began at dawn and ended at sunset. As the size of armies, the sophistication of weaponry, and the complexity of military operations increased, more precise methods of timing their activities became necessary. The earliest mechanical clocks appeared at about the same time as the use of gunpowder, but for several centuries they remained too inaccurate and too clumsy for routine use in the field, although in his play *Richard III*, William Shakespeare alluded to the use of a "watch" on the eve of the Battle of Bosworth Field (August 1485) (see *Roses, Wars of the*). However, by the end of the eighteenth century, every prudent officer was equipped with a reliable timepiece. At sea, the perfection of reliable, rugged naval chronometers in the late eighteenth century made possible the accurate determination of longitude and thus facilitated the coordination of naval operations.

At the beginning of the nineteenth century, the emperor Napoleon I (q.v.) earned his reputation as a great military leader largely because he used time effectively to coordinate the movements of his forces. Napoleon frequently included time-related instructions in his orders and insisted that his generals put the hour, date, and place on all of their messages. By the mid–nineteenth century, the extensive military use of the railroads required precise and complex timing at all levels. During the American Civil War (q.v.) the use of mechanical timepieces reached down even to company level, facilitated by the availability of cheap, reliable watches. Even so, the coordination of forces remained somewhat ragged, and operations — notably James Longstreet's attack on the second day at Gettysburg (q.v.) in 1863 — frequently failed due to delays, premature advances, and general lack of coordination in time.

The importance of mechanical time in military operations is best illustrated by the large and complex operations of World War I (q.v.). All troop movements were coordinated by means of intricate timetables. Attacks were regulated by precise "zero hours" and by phase lines and objectives that were to be reached by a specified time. Artillery preparations, particularly the "rolling barrage," which was shifted forward on a detailed schedule, were timed to the second. If the barrage was lifted too soon, the enemy could recover and thwart an assault; if the barrage was not lifted in time, it was likely to fall on friend as well as foe. Amphibious operations, parachute assaults, and the coordination of air-ground operations in World War II (q.v.) required equally precise timing, as was demonstrated amply in the Allied invasion of France in June 1944.

One of the most familiar movie clichés is the scene in which officers synchronize their watches before an attack. The technique was first used by the French in their attack on Sevastopol in the Crimean War (q.v.). Before World War I (q.v.), watches attached to the wrist by a strap were worn only by women or "dudes," but the readily accessible wristwatch gained general acceptance among soldiers in the trenches in France and remains an essential accoutrement for both soldiers and civilians.

The military use of mechanical time has also had an impact on civilian usage. On March 19, 1918, the five familiar "standard time zones" were formally adopted in the United States, in part because of the need to coordinate World War I troop movements and other military activities. The concept of Daylight Savings Time (advancing clocks by one hour in the spring and falling back one hour in the fall) was also a World War I expedient that was codified by Congress in the Uniform Time Act of 1966. The equally familiar "military" system of the 24-hour clock (in which, for example, 6:30 A.M. is expressed as 0630 hours and 6:30 P.M. as 1830 hours) was adopted by the U.S. Navy shortly before World War I and was subsequently adopted as "standard" by the U.S. Army at 0400 hours, Greenwich Mean Time, on July 1, 1942.

Today the use of missiles, satellites, computers, and other modern military technology demands extremely precise determination of time, a need met by the use of electronic timepieces capable of measuring time in milliseconds. Modern technology has also significantly reduced the time required for a commander to react to events on the battlefield. Napoleon and Ulysses S. Grant (q.v.) could deal in days and hours; the modern commander must consider minutes and seconds. Thus, the efficient management of time has become an essential skill for the modern soldier at all levels, both on and off the battlefield. As the duke of Wellington (q.v.) noted in 1800, "In military operations, time is everything."

CHARLES R. SHRADER

Timoshenko, Semon K.

1895–1970, Soviet World War II Marshal

Timoshenko is generally regarded by military historians as a Stalinist toady and political general par excellence, although his colleague Georgii K. Zhukov (q.v.) considered him a competent and well-versed leader. Both estimates contain some truth. Timoshenko understood his craft and worked hard to reform the Red Army (q.v.) before World War II (q.v.), but he was too much Joseph Stalin's (q.v.) confidant to question the dictator's policies, even when he thought them misguided.

A veteran of World War I (q.v.) and the Russian Civil War (q.v.), in which he led a Red Army cavalry division, Timoshenko was one of the few representatives of the old guard to survive the purges of the late 1930s. He did so by becoming an accomplice in the operation: his job was to set up new commands to replace those wiped out by the dictator. He never questioned the logic or necessity of this disastrous enterprise.

The damage wrought by the purges was painfully evident in the Red Army's performance in the "Winter War" against Finland in 1940. Made defense commissar after this campaign, Timoshenko tried to correct the many deficiencies it had revealed but was unable to make much headway before the German invasion. He loyally accepted Stalin's "no provocation" policy vis-à-vis Hitler, which left Russia vulnerable to the German attack. Anxious to please Stalin, he ordered premature counteroffensives in spring 1942 that resulted in costly losses. Stalin relieved him of his command, and he spent the rest of the war as the dictator's representative on various fronts.

Awarded the Order of Victory by Stalin, Timoshenko served as chief of various military districts, including the Belorussian, from 1946 to 1960. From 1960 until his death he was an inspector general in the Defense Ministry and chairman of the Soviet Veterans' Committee. His remains were buried in the Kremlin wall.

DAVID CLAY LARGE

Timur

See Tamerlane.

Tirpitz, Alfred von

1849–1930, German Grand Admiral

Alfred von Tirpitz earned a reputation in the 1880s as an advocate of the torpedo boat service, and between 1892 and 1896 served as chief of staff of the naval high command; his last assignment at sea was in 1897 with the German cruiser squadron in East Asia, where he chose Kiaochow in Shantung Province as a German leasehold. A devout disciple of the naval philosophy of Alfred Thayer Mahan (q.v.), Tirpitz served as state secretary of the German Imperial Navy Office from 1897 to 1916, where he created the High Sea Fleet. He was responsible for the construction of a fleet of forty-one battleships as well as twenty large and forty light cruisers, which was to be completed by the early 1920s. This great host of sixty-one capital ships was to be replaced automatically every twenty years, thereby removing what Tirpitz called "the disturbing influence of the Reichstag" upon naval construction. Concerning the fleet's ultimate size, Tirpitz simply stated that Germany "must have a fleet equal in strength to that of England."

The fleet was built first and foremost for a clash with Britain "between Heligoland and the Thames." To camouflage these intentions, Tirpitz created the "risk" theory, according to which his fleet needed to be of such strength that not even the Royal Navy would risk challenging it. The risk concept was a subterfuge: Tirpitz designed the fleet as a "gleaming dagger" held ready at Britain's jugular vein. Britannia would either back down in the face of this threat and concede Germany its desired "place in the sun," or else Tirpitz was ready to stake the Reich's future in a naval Armageddon. Germany, he consistently argued, would either become a world power or sink to the status of a "poor agrarian land."

The "Tirpitz plan" suffered shipwreck by 1905–1906. The treasury could not sustain the cost of the naval race with Britain, the army became concerned that it received ever less of German defense outlays, Parliament worried about the diplomatic repercussions of Tirpitz's strident anti-British stance, and the Admiralty in London countered by building dreadnought-class battleships and battle cruisers.

In 1914 Tirpitz was eight battleships and thirteen cruisers behind schedule. For the first two years of World War I (q.v.), the grand admiral played a devious role: at times he demanded a decisive fleet encounter in the North Sea, and at other times he supported all-out concentration on submarine warfare. This inconsistency led to Tirpitz's dismissal in March 1916 by Kaiser Wilhelm II, with the comment: "He is leaving the sinking ship." Late in the war, Tirpitz cofounded the million-member, protofascist German Fatherland Party, which demanded a victorious peace and vast annexations. After 1918 the grand admiral was influential in right-wing politics, helping to persuade Paul von Hindenburg (q.v.) to run for the presidency in 1925.

A pure naval philosopher, skillful political manipulator, expert bureaucratic manager, and proven propagandist, Tirpitz never became a naval strategist. Indeed, his strategic horizon was restricted to the concept of an all-out battle against the Royal Navy in the North Sea. He never commanded a modern battleship — much less a squadron or fleet of capital ships. And he ignored the fact that sea power consisted of two things: a powerful fleet combined with a favorable geographic position.

HOLGER H. HERWIG

Tōjō Hideki

1884–1948, Japanese General and Prime Minister

Wartime leader of Japan's government, General Tōjō Hideki, with his close-cropped hair, mustache, and round spectacles, became for Allied propagandists one of the most commonly caricatured members of Japan's military dictatorship throughout the Pacific war. Shrewd at bureaucratic infighting and fiercely partisan in presenting the army's perspective while army minister, he was surprisingly indecisive as national leader.

Known within the army as "Razor Tōjō" both for his bureaucratic efficiency and for his strict, uncompromising attention to detail, he climbed the command ladders, in close association with the army faction seeking to upgrade and improve Japan's fighting capabilities despite tight budgets and "civilian interference." Tōjō built up a personal power base and used his position as head of the military police of Japan's garrison force in Manchuria to rein in their influence before he became the Kwantung Army's chief of staff in 1937. He played a key role in opening hostilities against China in July. Tōjō had his only combat experience later that year, leading two brigades on operations in Inner Mongolia.

Seeing the military occupation of Chinese territory as necessary to force the Nationalist Chinese government to collaborate with Japan, he continued to advocate expansion of the conflict in China when he returned to Tokyo in 1938 as army vice minister, rising to army minister in July 1940. He pushed for alliance with Germany (where he had served in 1920–1922) and Italy, and he supported the formation of a broad political front of national unity. In October 1941 he became prime minister.

Although Tōjō supported last-minute diplomatic efforts, he gave final approval to the attacks on the United States, Great Britain, and the Dutch East Indies in December 1941. Japan's early victories greatly strengthened his personal prestige and his assertion that there were times when statesmen had to "have faith in Victory."

When the war intensified, Japan's losses mounted, and its fragile industrial foundations threatened to collapse. Tōjō characteristically sought to gather administrative levers into his own hands. Serving as both prime minister and army minister, at various times he also held the portfolios of home affairs (giving him control of the dreaded "thought police"), education, munitions, commerce and industry, and foreign affairs. In February 1944, he even assumed direct command of army operations as chief of the Army General Staff. Yet despite all his posts, Tōjō was never able to establish a dictatorship on a par with those wielded by Adolf Hitler (q.v.) and Joseph Stalin (q.v.). He served constitutionally at the behest of the emperor, without support of a mass party, while crucial power centers, such as the industrial combines (known as *zaibatsu*), the navy, and the court, remained beyond his control. After the island of Saipan fell to American forces in July 1944, he was forced from power, despite arguments raised by some officials close to the throne that Tōjō should be left in office to the end to accept responsibility for the loss of the war so that a court official could "step in" to deliver peace.

After Japan's surrender the next year, Tōjō attempted suicide when threatened with arrest by occupation authorities, but he was tried and hanged as a war criminal on December 23, 1948. At his trial, he asserted his personal responsibility for the war and attempted to deflect attention from the emperor. In 1978, despite the protest of many citizens opposed to honoring the man they felt had brought disaster on Japan, Tōjō's name, along with those of thirteen other "class A" war criminals, was commemorated at Yasukuni, the shrine in Tokyo dedicated to the memory of warriors fallen in service to the imperial family.

THEODORE F. COOK, JR.

Tokugawa Ieyasu

1543–1616, Japanese Warlord

At birth the son of a minor daimyo (warlord), in death canonized by imperial decree as Tōshō-dai-gongen, a Buddhist avatar, this one-time subordinate ally of first Oda Nobunaga (q.v.) and then Toyotomi Hideyoshi (q.v.) accomplished what neither of his senior partners had achieved: institutionalizing his power in inheritable form and founding a dynastic military government that endured for nearly three centuries.

Ieyasu capped a military career that spanned six decades with a victory in the Battle of Sekigahara in 1600 that left him in effective control of the nationwide political confederation that Hideyoshi had forged. Nevertheless, although undeniably a shrewd politician, an exceptional general, and an insightful administrator, he owed his lasting success not to superior ability in any of these areas over Nobunaga or Hideyoshi, but to personal longevity and judicious institutional borrowing. Born within a decade of his erstwhile overlords, he outlived Nobunaga by thirty-four years and Hideyoshi by eighteen. He modeled his army and administration largely on those of his most dangerous enemy, Takeda Shingen (whom he

also outlived), and further shaped his national regime around policies introduced by Nobunaga and Hideyoshi.

KARL F. FRIDAY

Tondibi, Battle of

March 1591

Ahmed al-Mansur ("the Victorious") ruled Morocco from his crushing victory over European invaders in 1578 until his death in 1603. Aided by both Moorish fugitives from Spain and technical advisers from the Ottomans (q.v.), his army adopted gunpowder technology and possessed a formidable stock of cannon, muskets, and harquebuses. In 1590, learning of the weakness of the Songhai Empire south of the Sahara, reputedly full of gold mines, al-Mansur sent twenty-five thousand men (including four thousand musketeers) and ten cannon under the command of the Spanish-born Judah Pasha in a spectacular thousand-mile march across the desert. At Tondibi in March 1591 the Moroccans routed fifty thousand or more Songhai warriors, bereft of firearms, and took over the empire. Like the conquest of Mexico by Hernán Cortés (q.v.), Judah's campaign represented a devastating example of the power conferred by the "military revolution" (q.v.). Unlike Cortés, however, he found little gold.

GEOFFREY PARKER

Toyotomi Hideyoshi

1536?–1598, Japanese Warlord

The most celebrated parvenu in Japanese history, this son of a peasant conquered the whole of his nation and dreamed of subjugating Chŏson Korea and Ming China as well. Hideyoshi began his career as a foot soldier *(ashigaru)* in service to the warlord Oda Nobunaga (q.v.), but, thanks to his exceptional military talent, he climbed rapidly through the ranks to become Nobunaga's premier general. Following Nobunaga's assassination in 1582, Hideyoshi seized control of the Oda coalition. By 1591, with armies numbering 100,000 men, he had subdued the rest of Japan. A year later he launched the first of two unsuccessful attempts to conquer China and Korea (see *Korean War*).

Whereas earlier generations celebrated Hideyoshi's skill and cunning on the battlefield, historians today celebrate more his diplomatic and political acumen.

He was a brilliant alliance builder and a deft manipulator of men and symbols, bending vassals, enemies, religion, myth, the imperial court nobility, and the prestige of the imperial throne to the service of what he characterized as the restoration of peace in the realm *(tenka)*, under his own watchful stewardship. When Hideyoshi began his career, Japan was a political crazy quilt of squabbling, independent baronies; by the time he died, it was a united confederation under his hegemony.

KARL F. FRIDAY

Tradition

Since the time of the ancient Greeks and Romans, military institutions have depended on tradition to inculcate a sense of pride in individual soldiers and to encourage them to do their utmost on the field of battle. From start to finish, Spartan (q.v.) military training emphasized the tradition that the Spartan soldier either "came home with his shield or on it." The Romans were no less willing to emphasize past glories. For them the legion's eagle and the various insignia of the cohorts represented the heart of what soldiering stood for; there was no disgrace more horrible than the loss of the legion's eagle in battle. Individual awards for bravery encouraged even the common legionnaire to do his utmost.

Non-Western, premodern armies often relied upon strong traditions to inculcate military virtues and inspire men to fight bravely in battle. In ancient China, intellectual traditions based on Chinese political philosophy exercised a powerful influence on the conduct of battle; thus traditional military wisdom helped to bridge the gap left by the lack of any systematic training of officers in ancient China. Even fairly primitive societies such as the Afghan warriors of the nineteenth century could look back to their struggle with Alexander the Great (q.v.).

In the Middle Ages heraldry represented the embodiment of family traditions based on warrior nobility. Yet it was not until the reign of Gustavus Adolphus (q.v.) that European armies began to dress their armies in a uniform fashion (see *Uniforms and Military Dress*). By the beginning of the eighteenth century, armies had evolved into recognizable form based on strong military traditions. The current British regimental system and certainly the scarlet coats that still mark British dress uniforms reach back to earlier times and earlier successes.

With uniforms went the identification of certain units as possessing certain traditions. Honors won in battle identified particular regiments with heroic chapters in national history. Although individual soldiers may not have cared much about history in general, they certainly took great pride in the record of their own regiment in earlier times. As a British officer once observed: "Ships, men, and weapons change, but tradition, which can neither be bought nor sold, nor created, is a solid rock amidst shifting sands." Ernst Jünger, the great World War I (q.v.) novelist and highly decorated veteran of the worst battles on the Western Front, recalled with pride that the cap badge of his German Hanoverian regiment, the rock of Gibraltar, had been won in 1704 when his regiment, then serving with the English army, participated in the storming of the rock.

The American military, perhaps because of its egalitarian origins, has never displayed the same emphasis on tradition. In fact, during World War I, the U.S. Army waged a massive effort to strip away the traditions of volunteer regiments that reached back to the American Civil War (q.v.). Nevertheless, the American services do display their battle streamers on unit flags, while some U.S. Army divisions stress the record of their accomplishments in battle. But it is the U.S. Marine Corps among the American services that has emphasized tradition in its uniforms, training, discipline, and conception of itself. What to civilians may appear to be the idle emphasis on past glories in fact embodies the traditions that make the military so extraordinarily different from other professions: the profession of arms is capable of motivating men and women to fight for their country.

WILLIAMSON MURRAY

Trafalgar, Battle of

October 21, 1805

This battle was fought off the western mouth of the Straits of Gibraltar between a Franco-Spanish fleet of thirty-three ships of the line commanded by Vice Admiral Pierre-Charles de Villeneuve and Admiral Don Federico Gravina, and a British squadron of twenty-seven ships under Vice Admiral Horatio, Lord Nelson (q.v.). The allied fleet, steering north in a very irregular line, was attacked by the British in two columns, running before the wind from the westward. This was a dangerous tactic, exposing the leading ships to the risk of heavy damage, but Nelson correctly counted on superior British training and discipline, and on the initiative of captains whom he had thoroughly imbued with his ideas. He also placed his biggest ships at the head of the columns (rather than in the center, as usual), himself leading one in the *Victory,* while Vice Admiral Cuthbert Collingwood led the other in the *Royal Sovereign.* The result was to break up the allied line and expose its center and rear to overwhelming force, bringing a crushing victory in which nineteen ships were captured (though all but four of the prizes were wrecked, sunk, or retaken in a subsequent gale). The British lost no ships, but Nelson was killed.

This great victory brought to a halt Napoleon's (q.v.) elaborate scheme to concentrate an overwhelming fleet in the Channel to cover the invasion of Britain, but the scheme was unrealistic from the start, and Nelson commanded only one of several squadrons that stood in its way. Nelson's tactics have aroused controversy ever since, but attempts to derive universal principles from the battle are not persuasive. More important, Trafalgar fixed the image of invincible British sea power, which endured for more than a century thereafter, and apotheosized Nelson as the symbol of that invincibility.

N. A. M. RODGER

Training

Training soldiers to master the technical aspects of combat — the handling of weapons and movement as part of a formation — is as old as war itself. The idea of deliberately and systematically teaching the whole ensemble of the skills that a soldier needs to master is, on the other hand, relatively new. In armies that fought as compact bodies of men armed with close-range weapons — those of the ancient Romans and Chinese, the late medieval Swiss, European armies of the sixteenth through the early nineteenth centuries, and the nineteenth-century Zulu (q.v.) army — almost all formal military training took the form of drill (q.v.). Soldiers were taught to handle themselves, their weapons, and (in the case of horsemen) their mounts in the precise manner set down by increasingly detailed regulations. Everything else a soldier needed to know, from how to care for his uniforms to how to cook his rations, was taught as a sort of "folk wis-

dom." As long as armies maintained a sufficient proportion of "old soldiers," this system worked well enough. When, however, a large number of recruits joined the colors in a short period of time, the transmission of skills broke down. This happened to the French army of the last three years of the Napoleonic Wars. The heavy losses of the Russian and Spanish campaigns, as well as the policy of concentrating veterans in elite units, resulted in many battalions filled with men who lacked the definitive abilities of the French infantry of the period — skirmishing, foraging, and long-distance marching.

When, in the middle of the nineteenth century, armies in which common soldiers (q.v.) served for long periods of time were replaced by those composed of short-term conscripts or volunteers, the high turnover in the ranks made it impossible to rely on informal methods of training. At the same time, changes in weapons and tactics greatly increased the complexity of the skills that the ordinary soldier had to master. As a result, the drill that remained the foundation of most military training was heavily supplemented by lectures, demonstrations, and exercises designed to teach things such as range estimation, the use of cover, patrolling, and making reports. Even topics such as hygiene and patriotism (q.v.) became the subject of formal military training. These additional sessions, were, in turn, integrated into programs of instruction that were as carefully designed as any academic curriculum.

During World War I (q.v.), the pace at which tactics changed, as well as the unprecedented demand for new soldiers to replace the vast losses, demanded new approaches to military training. The method pioneered by the elite assault units of the German army made use of instructors with very recent combat experience and replaced the analytic approach — which broke down skills into their component parts — with a comprehensive one. Drawing heavily on techniques that the Germans had long used to educate officers, this approach employed free-play exercises that ranged from sandtable war games (q.v.) to unscripted mock battles using live ammunition. The great advantage of this approach, which might be called "just-in-time training," was that it was a very efficient means of preparing soldiers for the tasks they would most likely have to perform. The great disadvantage of just-in-time training was that — with the high value it placed on recent combat experience and other commodities rarely possessed by those in authority

— it failed to fit in with the way most twentieth-century armies were organized. The British, for example, were more comfortable with a system that was built around "battle drill" — stereotyped responses to given situations. Yet although battle drill ensured that a soldier would, even when under the intense pressure of combat, carry out specific, well-practiced actions, there was no guarantee that these actions would be appropriate — indeed, they might even be counterproductive. In World War II (q.v.), for example, soldiers taught to "hit the dirt" whenever fired upon were often easy prey for enemy snipers or mortarmen who had positioned themselves to take advantage of just such a reaction.

The approach used by the French (and later adopted by their American pupils) was to continue along the "analytic" path first used to train the short-term conscripts of the latter half of the nineteenth century. Drawing heavily from techniques used in industrial mass production, this military "Taylorism" (from American efficiency expert Frederick W. Taylor) broke down complex tasks into actions that were explicitly defined and thus easily taught. Though, in the wake of the disasters of 1940, the French abandoned "le Taylorisme," the approach became even more popular during the Cold War (q.v.), when both the U.S. and the Soviet armies were faced with the daunting task of teaching a wide variety of technical skills to soldiers with terms of service that rarely exceeded two or three years.

BRUCE I. GUDMUNDSSON

John A. English and Bruce I. Gudmundsson, *On Infantry*, rev. ed. (1994).

Treachery

Treachery under the laws of war (q.v.) is more usually called *perfidy*, implying a breach of faith. In general, when an express or tacit engagement to speak the truth to an enemy, to accord him certain treatment, or to behave in a certain fashion, imposes a moral obligation to do so, it is perfidy to secure an advantage over him by deliberate betrayal of trust. Perfidy is punishable as a war crime, because without some minimum sense of mutual trust, war tends to become internecine, and the basis for future amicable relations is undercut.

The distinction between perfidy and legitimate ruses and stratagems is a fine one, best perceived through examples of what is *not* deemed perfidious. It is legitimate to employ spurious radio transmission; to transmit false messages for the enemy to intercept or leave false documents for him to find; to set out dummy soldiers, weapons, vehicles, or installations; and to move landmarks. Ambushes, surprise attacks, feigned retreats, simulated activity or inactivity, the imitation of large formations by small ones, and deceptive supply movements are all legitimate ruses. It is lawful to mimic the enemy's signals and bugle calls, use his watchword, and create bogus orders apparently issued by his commanders. At sea, it is permissible to sail under false colors (the enemy's or those of a neutral) in order to pursue an enemy vessel, to escape, or to draw an enemy vessel into action; but before action, the national colors must be run up. It is perfidy to use an enemy's or a neutral's flag, uniforms, or insignia to deceive the enemy when actual fighting is involved.

Even direct lying is permissible when all that is involved is mere bluff against which an alert enemy should be on guard. Nor is it unlawful perfidy to bribe enemy officers or civil officials, or to induce enemy soldiers to desert or the enemy population to revolt. It is permissible to destroy fortifications, weapons, ships, and other public property pending negotiations for surrender (q.v.), but perfidy to do so after agreeing upon or signing a capitulation, unless the right to do so is reserved.

The most conspicuous examples of perfidy entail perversion of humanitarian rules of war such as the inviolability of hospitals and medical facilities, the sanctity of flags of truce, the protection of disabled enemies, and the duty to grant quarter to a surrendering enemy. Thus, it is perfidy to cloak any military activity under the Red Cross or any equivalent symbol, as by firing from structures so marked or using them for observation, signaling, quartering of troops or storage of supplies, or by moving active combatants or war matériel in hospital trains, ships, or airplanes. It is perfidy to use a flag of truce as a ruse to acquire military information or to play for time to retreat. Similarly, it is unlawful to claim falsely that an armistice has been signed, in order to gain a respite. A helpless enemy, or one who has laid down arms and surrendered, may not be killed or wounded. (This includes parachutists escaping from a disabled airplane, but paratroopers or others bent on hostile activity, such as spies or saboteurs, may be fired on while descending.) By the same token, it is perfidy to feign surrender or simulate death, wounds, or sickness in order to entrap an enemy. At sea it is unlawful to issue a false distress signal to entrap the enemy. It is unlawful to bring about the assassination of an enemy or to hire assassins for that purpose, or to declare his proscription or outlawry, or to offer a reward for him "dead or alive." (But this rule does not preclude attacks on individuals by normal means, as when the Americans deliberately and knowingly shot down Admiral Yamamoto Isoroku [q.v.] in 1943.)

Finally, apart from these specific situations, any deliberate breach of an agreement with the enemy — such as mounting a surprise attack during a truce or violating a safe-conduct — constitutes perfidy.

THADDEUS HOLT

Tribal Warfare

Anthropologists who study war most often focus on "tribal warfare," or war among peoples who are not under the rule of a state government. Their goals are to understand the place of collective aggression in the human condition, and the relationship between war and various aspects of cultural organization.

It seems likely that our ancestors always had the capacity to make war. Yet even though popular essayists have long spun bloody stories about our evolutionary past, all the archaeological evidence points the other way. Indicators of war — skeletal, technological, architectural, artistic — are uniformly absent in the oldest human remains. Signs of war begin to appear only well after the transition to a settled form of living. War has relatively shallow roots in human history, not because ancient ancestors were pacifists, but because there was less to gain by fighting and more opportunity to move away from conflict.

Among historically or ethnographically observed tribal peoples, some practice no war whatsoever, but the great majority do. Their wars encompass a huge range of practices. At its simplest, wars are equivalent to feuds, low-level violence among members of the same society. From that point, military practice expands in scale and sophistication, related to the size and complexity of social units, population density, terrain, weaponry, transportation (for example, canoes and horses), and objectives. Ambush and hit-and-run raids dominate some situations; open field fighting prevails in others. (Many Native American peoples went from battle lines to guerrilla tactics only

after the introduction of firearms.) Although mass killing by tribal peoples is not unknown, typically few individuals die in any combat. The loss of even one warrior often marks a raid as a failure, although as a percentage of the adult male population, war deaths may be very high over time.

War is not only a practice: it is both an expression and a condition of society as a whole. A local pattern of war interacts with many aspects of a people's way of life. If, for instance, a society is structured by intermarrying lineages, the patterning of both the lineages and the marriage ties will affect who will be considered allies or enemies. War affects relations with the natural environment, dispersing competitors for natural resources, but at the same time restricting the territory that can be exploited safely. On the psychological plane, conceptions of enemy "others" are related to understandings of human existence and the definition of "self."

One crucial connection between war and society lies in political organization. In simpler societies, war is carried out by local kinsmen, and participation is voluntary. Senior males who fill leadership roles — arguing for war or peace — have influence but not power. Decisions are by consensus, so to be acted upon, objectives must be generally shared, and a course of collective action must be renegotiated after every important event. As the scale and complexity of social groups increase, leadership roles become more central, often with distinctive war and peace leaders, yet these are still held in check by the need for consensus.

Leaders play an important role in negotiation and management of alliances, which in wartime can be critical for support, refuge, and information. Sometimes these arrangements are temporary, but in other situations they settle into traditions of enmity or alliance between specific groups. More permanent alliances develop into formal confederacies, peaceable within and cooperative in war, capable of fielding hundreds of warriors. Confederacies, in turn, can become tribes.

To this point, the term *tribal* has been used broadly to designate any people living outside the domain of a "state" — a bounded, centralized, stratified, and authoritative system of political rule. *Tribe* also has a more specific meaning: a type of political organization in which several local groups are joined as equals in a durable association and identity. Tribes frequently are warlike, and this external hostility contributes to their internal cohesion. Tribal authority, in war and otherwise, remains limited and typically is associated with a council. If leadership roles become more centralized and hierarchical, tribes become "chiefdoms." Chiefs may live in luxury and wield great influence, but still cannot command others to go to war. The ability to order subjects into battle, often at pain of death for refusal, is a hallmark of states and a critical watershed in the evolution of war.

Throughout history, but most dramatically over the past five hundred years, war as practiced by tribal peoples has been profoundly influenced by the proximity of states. Biological, economic, political, and ideological elements originating in states radiate far beyond their frontiers, transforming tribal social relations in a way that often increases local warfare and leads to formation of new tribes ("tribalization"). Such warfare is often a product and reflection of the colonial situation, related to population disruptions, political destabilization, and the introduction of new arms and material wants. For instance, the wars of the Yanomami of the remote Brazil-Venezuela border — long thought to be unaffected by the outside world — have been shown to be strongly connected to the penetration of missionaries and other westerners. Key to this fighting are antagonistic interests regarding access to steel tools and other manufactured products.

Recent use of the term *tribal warfare* in regard to wars in eastern Europe or sub-Saharan Africa is misleading. Comparative examination of these cases reveals that unlike tribal wars, which develop by consensus, recent violence has been instigated by stratified political elites — either in government or seeking to be — who are able to command soldiers to kill. The so-called tribal identities are often recent creations, deliberately manipulated by these elites to further their own ambitions.

R. BRIAN FERGUSON

R. Brian Ferguson and Neil Whitehead, eds., *War in the Tribal Zone: Expanding States and Indigenous Warfare* (1992); Jonathan Haas, ed., *The Anthropology of War* (1990).

Triple Alliance, War of the

1865–1870

The War of the Triple Alliance, fought between the allied forces of Brazil, Argentina, and Uruguay against Paraguay, was the longest and most destructive inter-

national conflict in the Western Hemisphere since the countries of the region attained their independence, and of all modern conflicts in this hemisphere, it was only exceeded in human cost by the American Civil War (q.v.). Losses on the allied side were 190,000 dead, of whom 100,000 were Brazilian. Paraguay lost 220,000, perhaps half the population, with the often-quoted resulting imbalance of four women to one man over fifteen years of age.

The causes of the war lay in the rivalries and boundary disputes of the River Plate states in the preceding decades, and the abandonment of the policy of Paraguayan isolation followed by the dictators Francia and Carlos Antonio López by the latter's son, Francisco Solano. His more assertive stance led him first into confrontation with Brazil and then with Uruguay and Argentina.

Paraguay had the advantages of interior lines, a strong sense of identity and discipline, and military preparedness; but these could not match attrition and isolation. Attempts at a negotiated peace failed in the face of Brazilian insistence on territorial gains and Paraguayan surrender.

The chief feature of the war was the prolonged Paraguayan defense of the southeastern gateway to the country, based on a system of entrenched forts dominating the river Paraguay, the skillful exploitation of marshy terrain, and prodigies of improvisation, particularly in artillery. The allies' naval superiority in gunboats eventually enabled them to outflank this resistance. After the fall of the capital Asunción, López fought on until cornered and killed in the remote northeast of his devastated country.

MALCOLM DEAS

Trojan War

Our only historical source for the Trojan War is a Greek epic poem, the *Iliad* of Homer, that was composed in its present form probably in the eighth century B.C., but incorporates material dating from many centuries before that. It tells us that Troy, a rich city on the coast of what is now Turkey, was besieged for ten years and finally destroyed by an army of some 100,000 Greeks who had arrived in an armada of exactly 1,186 ships. The poem's celebration of heroic martial values has made it an inspiration for warriors ever since; Alexander of Macedon (q.v.), in his campaigns in Asia, slept with a dagger and a papyrus copy of the *Iliad* under his pillow. His praise of it as a "handbook of the art of war," however, though prompted by his own fearless style of frontline leadership in combat, seems wide of the mark. The battles in the *Iliad* consist mostly of duels between heroes, who often address remarks to each other before engaging, while the chariots, those mobile platforms for archers armed with the composite bow — thirty-five hundred of them were deployed against the Egyptians at the Battle of Kadesh (q.v.) — are used by Homer's heroic warriors mainly as taxis to the front.

But the historicity of the Trojan War was never doubted by the Greeks of later ages; even Thucydides, though he conceded that Homer, as a poet, had exaggerated, accepted the tradition. And the belief that there was at least some kernel of historical truth in the legend remained prevalent until George Grote, in 1846, announced in his classic *History of Greece* that he would "begin the real history . . . with the first recorded Olympiad, or 776 B.C." Everything before that was "the legendary age." In 1870, however, Heinrich Schliemann began excavations on the site of ancient Troy and laid bare layer after layer of successive Bronze Age settlements. Meanwhile excavation in Greece had revealed an equally rich Bronze Age civilization at sites such as Mycenae and Pylos. The palaces there had been destroyed in the late thirteenth century; the layer at Troy labeled VIIA had been burned in midcentury. It soon became accepted doctrine that its destruction had been the work of the Mycenaeans, their last great exploit before their own extinction. In recent years, however, confidence in this scenario has begun to ebb. A colloquium of archaeologists and ancient historians held in 1981 came to the sober conclusion that "briefly and bluntly put, on present evidence there is neither room nor reason for Mycenaean hostilities against Troy."

BERNARD KNOX

Tromp, Maarten Harpertszoon

1598–1653, *Dutch Naval Commander*

Maarten Harpertszoon Tromp was the son of a sea captain, on whose ship he was captured by Barbary corsairs in 1611; after two years as a slave, he served in both Dutch merchantmen and warships, attaining the rank of captain (1624) and vice admiral (effective commander) (1637) of the Dutch navy. He led it to spectacular victory over a Spanish fleet at a battle off Dunkirk (1639), at which he drew up his entire fleet in a single line of battle — the first use of the tactic in European waters. The prizes taken in this and other actions brought Tromp wealth (in 1640 he valued his assets at ninety thousand guilders, at a time when an able seaman made ten guilders a month) and prestige (his wife came from one of the most notable families in The Hague); but he remained popular with his men, who nicknamed him "Bestevaer" (dear father). Tromp worked hard to professionalize the Dutch navy, advocating better training for the officers and heavier armament for the ships, but he died in action during the first Anglo-Dutch War (q.v.) before his plans could be implemented.

GEOFFREY PARKER

Tso Tsung-t'ang

1812–1885, *Chinese Military Leader*

National savior to the Chinese, genocidal murderer to the Sinkiang Uighurs, Tso Tsung-t'ang — with Li Hung-chang (q.v.) and Tseng Kuo-fan (1811–1872) — was one of three great leaders of late-nineteenth-century China. These men first became prominent because they raised, equipped, and trained the armies that eventually defeated the Taiping (q.v.).

Loyal but independent-minded, Tso fought the Nien rebels and then led the armies that crushed large-scale Muslim revolts in northwestern China (1862–1873), thereby enabling reunification for the first time since 1850. Early excluded from officialdom by examination failure, he studied frontier history and geography and experimented with various farming techniques, all of which helped him become expert in postwar reconstruction. His military strategy included establishing military farms to expand supplies, creating local arsenals, and using European weapons or their Chinese imitations. Competing for funds against those who favored coastal over frontier defense, he convincingly argued that the Russians sought land as well as the commercial concessions Westerners wanted, and that Sinkiang protected Mongolia and hence, indirectly, Peking. From 1874 to 1878 he campaigned bloodily against Yakoob Beg in Sinkiang, and as a result of his success, Sinkiang became a Chinese province in 1884 and the Russians withdrew from most of that region, though retaining a strong economic presence.

JOANNA WALEY-COHEN

Tsushima, Battle of

May 27–28, 1905

This culminating battle of the Russo-Japanese War (q.v.) was fought in the Korean Straits between the Russian Baltic Fleet under Admiral Zinovi Rozhdestvensky, who was attempting to link up with the Vladivostok Squadron and thus shore up Russia's sagging strategic position, and a Japanese fleet under Admiral Togo Heihachiro, who sought to annihilate Russian naval power in East Asia. Approaching the battle, the Japanese held a number of distinct advantages over their Russian enemy: operation from nearby bases, a compact force of modern battleships of uniform speed and firepower, thorough training and high morale of officers and men, and careful planning and intense training for critical strategic and tactical objectives.

Intercepting the cumbersome Russian force as it steamed northeastward on May 27, Togo undertook a daring maneuver that headed off Rozhdestvensky and brought his lead ships under devastating Japanese fire. In the next twelve hours of fighting between the battle lines, Japanese gunfire and torpedoes shattered the Russian fleet. By noon the next day, Rozhdestvensky surrendered; most of his ships had been sunk or captured, including all eight battleships. Togo lost only three torpedo boats.

Tsushima was one of the most annihilating victories in the history of naval warfare, and, as such, it became the model for Japanese naval doctrine. Following the battle, Russia dropped from third to sixth place among the world's sea powers, while Japan leapt to third place. Tsushima demonstrated the great increase in weapon range and appeared to confirm the principle of the all-big-gun battleship.

MARK R. PEATTIE

Tukhachevskii, Mikhail

1893–1937, Soviet Marshal

Of noble birth, Mikhail Nikolaevich Tukhachevskii started his military career as a guards officer in the tsarist army. Captured by the Germans in 1915, he was imprisoned in the same camp as Charles de Gaulle (q.v.). He escaped, returned to Russia, and joined the Bolshevik Party in 1918.

An active participant in the Russian Civil War of 1918–1921 (q.v.), Tukhachevskii acquired considerable command experience fighting the Whites, the Poles, and anti-Communist rebels. Tukhachevskii advocated a large, well-equipped, offensively oriented Red Army (q.v.), and in 1926, as the Red Army's chief of staff, he authored a secret report warning that technological inferiority was imperiling the defense of the country. Then, in the theoretical work "War as a Problem of Armed Struggle" (1928), he predicted mass wars of attrition, with each side trying to deprive the other of economic resources.

Joseph Stalin's (q.v.) industrialization of the Soviet Union led to steep increases in military spending. In 1931 Tukhachevskii became the Red Army's armament chief and deputy commissar of war, and he oversaw the mechanization and motorization of the armed forces. In 1935 he was promoted to marshal. In May 1937, however, Stalin ordered his arrest for treason; Tukhachevskii soon admitted to being a German spy. (His "confession" was partially spattered with his own blood.) On June 12 he was shot by firing squad. Tukhachevskii's fall was the beginning of the comprehensive purge of the Soviet officer corps.

Although it is possible to overrate Tukhachevskii as a theoretician, he made important contributions to Soviet thinking about combined arms war and deep battle. It was as the organizer and champion of mechanization, however, that Tukhachevskii best served his country. Tukhachevskii was rehabilitated in January 1957.

WILLIAM C. FULLER, JR.

Turenne, Henri de la Tour d'Auvergne, Viscount of

1611–1675, French Marshal

Turenne ranks among the greatest generals in French history. His family, though Protestant, was one of France's most exalted. It was linked with the house of Orange in the Dutch Netherlands, and he first learned his craft there. Entering French service in 1630, Turenne rose rapidly after the French came into the Thirty Years' War (q.v.) in 1635; the year 1643 saw him take command of French forces in Germany and receive his marshal's baton. When a civil war, the Fronde, struck France in 1648, he at first sided with the revolt but soon returned to the royalist camp to lead the army of the boy king, Louis XIV (q.v.). In this contest his great rival was Condé (q.v.), who joined the rebels in 1651. At the Battle of the Dunes in 1658, Turenne defeated Condé, who had taken up Spanish service, and brought the long war with Spain to a victorious conclusion.

As the young Louis XIV began his personal reign in 1661 and sought to master the military art, he turned to Turenne as tutor and adviser. In deference to his monarch and after much soul searching, Turenne converted to Catholicism in 1668. During the Dutch War (1672–1678), the marshal once again led an army in Germany and drove the Germans from Alsace in a winter campaign (1674–1675) that ranks as a true masterpiece.

Turenne was one of those rare generals who seemed to learn and improve. At the peak of his talents, he was hit by a cannonball at the Battle of Sasbach on July 27, 1675, and was killed. Turenne favored battle and maneuver with armies of moderate size, but siege warfare would predominate after his death. He once advised the young Condé: "Make few sieges, and fight plenty of battles; when you are master of the countryside the villages will give us the towns." After the French Revolution of 1789, his remains were disinterred and stored in a box, and its custodian sold his teeth as souvenirs.

JOHN A. LYNN

U

Uniforms and Military Dress

Those practicing the hard business of war have traditionally dressed in ways that set them apart from those engaged in peaceful pursuits. Even warriors of native tribes donned special apparel or marked themselves with paint or some other decoration to announce that they would now follow the ways of war. This may have been necessary to make it clear to the warrior himself and others that he had temporarily abandoned the codes of conduct that hold village communities together and had adopted the fierce code reserved for facing enemies. The differences between civilian and military life may explain the importance of uniforms to this day; to wear the uniform is to live in a different world.

The warrior's need to differentiate himself or herself from the nonwarrior is not restricted to "primitive" peoples. Of course, simply the carrying of weapons and the wearing of armor made clear a military purpose, but the issue here is clothing itself. Aristocratic medieval knights decorated themselves and their horses with elaborate coats of arms and other accoutrements that displayed their status, family, and martial purpose, as did the samurai (q.v.) of Japan. Common soldiers also dressed in ways that set them apart. Rank and file men of the sixteenth and seventeenth centuries dressed in garish, loose-fitting clothing, mimicking aristocratic styles even though they were commoners. They dressed in such a manner because it drew a line between themselves and the peasant class from which most of them had come, and peasants and soldiers harbored a strong loathing for each other.

Uniforms proper evolved in the seventeenth century. Spartans (q.v.) had worn red cloaks; Roman legionaries had put distinctive decorations on their shields (see *Medals and Insignia*) — but these precedents predated the evolution of modern uniforms by a millennium and more. Medieval nobles of stature might dress their staffs in their personal colors, but some saw wearing such livery as a mark of servitude. European soldiers did not wear uniform clothing until the seventeenth century. Before the adoption of uniforms, different sides in a battle often distinguished themselves simply by wearing some symbol, a sprig of some plant in the hat, or a sash or plume of a particular color. Colonels might choose a particular style or color for their men, but there was no general standard. Then, in about 1630, Gustavus Adolphus (q.v.) of Sweden tried to dress his regiments in blue, yellow, and green. The Parliamentary forces of the New Model Army of 1645 adopted red as their basic uniform color (see *English Civil Wars*), and it survives to this day, at least in full dress. French forces were slower to regulate appearance, but bit by bit French regiments too adopted uniforms before 1700. Infantry and cavalry donned white or gray coats, although royal regiments wore blue. Badges of rank evolved later than uniforms themselves, although epaulettes, chevrons, and sashes marked a man's authority in the eighteenth century.

Uniforms possessed many advantages. They enhanced appearance and the pride that went along with it. They also fostered group action and downplayed individualism; for this reason some say uniforms were a necessary adjunct to the mechanical drill of early modern armies. In addition, the standardized colors of uniforms made it easier to spot friend and foe in the haze of a black-powder battlefield.

Navies also standardized the dress of sailors, although the pressures to do so were less than those that drove for uniform dress among armies. Put bluntly, it was the ships and not their crews that announced

LEFT: *Like other early military uniforms, the elaborate costumes of these monumentalized Roman legionnaires would have served not only to identify them but to impress and intimidate the enemy in hand-to-hand combat.*

RIGHT: *This sepoy of the Madras army in 1825 wears European uniform better suited to cold climates than to the heat of South India. The only concession to indigenous dress is the turban-shaped headgear.*

allegiance, and it mattered little what the sailors on them wore. When naval uniforms appeared, they were surprisingly similar, almost always blue and white, with bibbed blouses and loose-fitting or bell-bottomed trousers.

Uniforms reached their ornamental peak in the first half of the nineteenth century. Napoleonic uniforms certainly had their glories, but the presence of war kept them from becoming too bizarre. However, the peace that followed allowed foolish extremes — jackets and cross belts so tight that they hampered breathing, pants so tight that one could hardly sit, and elaborate and awkward headgear that offered little protection. The practical necessities of midcentury wars put an end to the worst abuses.

In the late nineteenth century, the influence of colonial experience promoted camouflage colors, particularly in British service; *khaki* was in fact an Indian word for "dust" or "dust colored" (see *Camouflage*). By World War I (q.v.), the accuracy and high rate of fire of modern weapons forced soldiers to seek cover, and

the concealment made possible by earth-tone uniforms proved an advantage. Personal camouflage has become more and more effective, as witnessed by the brown-dabbled "chocolate and nuts" attire of U.S. soldiers in the Gulf War (q.v.). World War I also saw the return of armor in the form of the steel helmet, now intended to protect its wearer from shrapnel. This trend continued with the reintroduction of body armor, or flak jackets, in the 1950s.

As field uniforms became more utilitarian, greater contrast developed between combat clothing and full-dress uniforms. Fatigue outfits date back to the very origins of uniforms, when soldiers wore old coats or their regular issue turned inside out when performing manual labor. But it was hard enough to supply early modern soldiers with one set of clothing, let alone multiple sets for different purposes. This phenomenon was again a creation of the nineteenth century.

Elements of military clothing worn by successful forces have often been copied by other powers. Thus

U.S. soldiers wore French kepis and Zouave paraphernalia in the American Civil War (q.v.) and Prussian-inspired spiked helmets later in the century. The Japanese adopted the British uniforms of their advisers when they created their own modern navy.

As fascinating as the details of uniforms can be, there is a danger in the military buff's tendency to mistake a knowledge of buttons and brass for an understanding of military history. Such matters have more to do with parades than with warfare.

JOHN A. LYNN

Paul Martin, *European Military Uniforms: A Short History* (1968); John Mollo, *Military Fashion: A Comparative History of the Uniforms of the Great Armies from the 17th Century to the First World War* (1972).

V

Valmy, Battle of

September 20, 1792

At Valmy the French turned back a Prussian-Austrian invasion that sought to end their revolution. When war began in April 1792, French troops repeatedly broke before their more disciplined enemies; therefore, as the duke of Brunswick (q.v.) led this onslaught, many expected French forces to dissolve before him (see *French Revolution, Wars of the*). But Charles-François Dumouriez maneuvered brilliantly to hold up Brunswick at the Argonne Forest, and François-Christophe de Kellermann brought up his army just behind this barrier. When Brunswick finally broke through with thirty thousand to thirty-four thousand Prussians, he had to turn south to face Kellermann's thirty-six thousand troops at Valmy.

The battle itself consisted primarily of an extensive artillery duel, in which the superior French cannon proved their worth (see *Gribeauval, Jean-Baptiste de*). The Prussians tried to advance a few times, but were turned back. The French held solid with defiant cries of *"Vive la nation!"* Brunswick called off the attack, and after a week of fruitless negotiations, led his troops back into Germany. The retreat proved to be a disaster — disease decimated his army.

In terms of its political significance, the Battle of Valmy ranks as one of the world's greatest clashes, for the fate of the French Revolution, and thus of European history, lay in the balance.

JOHN A. LYNN

Vauban, Sébastien Le Prestre de

1633–1707, *French Military Engineer*

Born in Burgundy of a petty noble family, Sébastien Le Prestre de Vauban in 1651 began his military career under the legendary Condé (q.v.), and then in rebellion against young Louis XIV (q.v.). But by 1653 Vauban changed sides, acquiring a reputation as an engineer in the war against Spain, which ended in 1659. During Louis XIV's personal reign, which began in 1661, Vauban developed a close connection both with the marquis de Louvois (q.v.), the king's young secretary for war, and with Louis himself.

Vauban offered the king just what he wanted, a method of waging war elegantly and with a minimum of bloodshed. This method employed massive geometric fortifications, bastions, and outworks for the defense of strongholds (see *Fortifications*), and circumvallations, zigzagging trenches, and mines for their attack. The method was by no means Vauban's invention, having been developed by Italian and Dutch engineers in the course of the sixteenth century. But Vauban brought it to a high state of perfection in individual cases and applied it with strategic sweep, exploiting the munificence of his patron.

In 1667, during Louis XIV's War of Devolution against Spain, Vauban displayed his methods of attack in the sieges of Tournai, Douai, and Lille. After the war, between 1668 and 1672, he dedicated himself primarily to fortifying the irregular frontier between France and the Spanish Low Countries, an effort crowned by the intricate fortifications of Dunkirk and the magnificent citadel of Lille, which still stands today. But it should be noted that he had virtually nothing to do with *planning* Louis XIV's attack upon the Dutch Republic in 1672, which was intended to intimidate the Dutch into letting him complete his conquest of the Spanish Low Countries. It was only when this first campaign went amiss that Vauban, who had a habit of volunteering his opinions, began suggesting that the king should think about transforming his irregular northern frontier into a *pré carré* (a square field, or dueling field), by which Vauban simply meant a straightened out frontier, supported by a double or triple line of interconnected strongholds, which the enemy would find virtually impossible to penetrate. During the war, Vauban conducted most of the major siege operations, and since the war expanded and lasted until 1678, Louis XIV eventually adopted Vauban's defensive strategy, so to speak, by default, only after failing to expand the frontiers of France by conquering the Spanish Low Countries. During the 1680s, a period of increasing tensions between Louis XIV and the rest of Europe, Vauban elaborated on his defensive strategy by dotting France's frontiers, both land and maritime, with a chain of interconnected strongholds, some of which, such as Mont-Louis in the Pyrenees, can be visited today. But he had growing misgivings about the king's heavy-handed policies, including his domestic persecution of the Huguenots.

With the outbreak of the War of the League of Augsburg (see *War of the Grand Alliance*) in 1688, Vauban resumed both his conduct of the major siege operations and his unsolicited suggestions. He was so bold as to advocate, for example, that Louis XIV should abandon his persecution of the Huguenots. With the death of Louvois in 1691, Vauban lost his best friend at court. As the war continued, he grew increasingly critical of Louis XIV's new ministers, fearing that they were preparing to surrender too many key strongholds in order to achieve peace. Vauban, however, had no objection to the cession of Breisach on the right bank of the Rhine (which ran counter to his emphasis on a straight, thickly fortified frontier), and with the peace in 1697 he enthusiastically proceeded to construct one of his masterpieces, the stronghold of Neuf-Breisach on the left bank, which still stands.

In 1703, the second year of the War of the Spanish Succession (q.v.), Louis made Vauban a marshal of France, but he saw only limited service, devoting himself, among other things, to composing his definitive treatises on the attack and defense of strongholds. Shortly before his death, he published surreptitiously a sweeping proposal for a new universal tax. The king's council condemned the publication, but Vauban was allowed to spend his last days in peace. His professionalism, his humane approach to warfare, even his reservations about Louis XIV's policies have combined to give him a legendary status in French military history.

PAUL SONNINO

F. J. Hebbert and G. A. Rothrock, *Soldier of France, Sébastien Le Prestre de Vauban: 1633–1707* (1989); Sébastien Le Prestre de Vauban, *A Manual of Siegecraft and Fortification*, trans. G. A. Rothrock (1968).

Vegetius

Fifth century A.D., *Roman Military Writer*

Flavius Vegetius Renatus was a military writer of the late Roman Empire, writing sometime between A.D. 383 and 450, probably in the early fifth century. In modern times he has often been dismissed as unsophisticated, but in the Middle Ages and the Renaissance he was widely read. About 150 copies of his manuscript survived the Middle Ages, and his work was translated into French, English, and Bulgarian even before the invention of printing. The fact that he was the first Christian Roman military writer added to his popularity, and even in the eighteenth century he was widely read. George Washington (q.v.) owned and annotated a copy of Vegetius's treatise.

Although his *De Re Militari* contains sections on siege warfare and other military matters, his emphasis on the training of infantry dominates his work. He had little to say about cavalry, claiming correctly that the Romans were superior in cavalry warfare and that nothing need be said about it. He lamented the decline of the traditional Roman legions and argued that no one in his day had any firsthand experience with the old-fashioned Roman system of training and discipline. He clearly believed that the solution to the military problems of the late Roman Empire was the restoration of ancient Roman military techniques.

His description of those practices and tactics remains one of the best sources available today on the Roman army. Other Roman authors — Livy, Tacitus, and even Caesar (q.v.) — often failed to provide operational and tactical details about Roman military procedure. On many points Vegetius is the most reliable surviving source of information.

His work is filled with aphorisms, and they have helped maintain his popularity with readers. ("If you want peace, prepare for war" is a famous example.) Despite some modern criticisms, his work is dominated by common sense, and his emphasis on the need to strengthen Roman infantry is well taken. He should be read with greater care and appreciation than has been customary in the nineteenth and twentieth centuries.

ARTHER FERRILL

Verdun, Battle of

February 21–December 15, 1916

Only the World War I (q.v.) Western Front could have produced the rationale for the Battle of Verdun. In his so-called Christmas Memo of 1915, Erich von Falkenhayn (q.v.), the chief of the German General Staff, made a uniquely cynical proposal: not to take territory but to take lives, to cause the French army to "bleed to death" defending the fortress complex around Verdun on the Meuse heights.

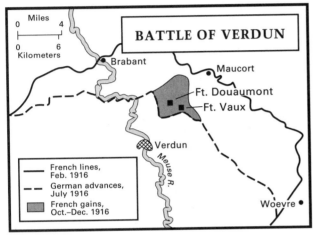

On February 21, 1916, more than 1,220 guns around an eight-mile perimeter opened fire. It was the sort of drenching shellstorm that would distinguish the battle. Verdun did act as a "suction cup": three fourths of the French Western Front divisions would eventually serve there. But even from the start, the "Meuse Mill" did not achieve the five-to-two kill ratio Falkenhayn had predicted. The attackers soon forgot this object. Orders went out to take French positions "without regard to casualties." At the end of the first week, the Germans had advanced six miles; a few men walked into an almost undefended Fort Douaumont and took possession. For the French, that marked the low point. Fighting degenerated into isolated struggles for shell-holes, forcing the French into an impromptu but successful defense-in-depth. At the beginning of June, the Germans took another key stronghold, Fort Vaux, after hideous subterranean melees. A few of their troops actually reached a point from which the twin towers of Verdun cathedral were visible, two miles away. Then, on July 14, the Germans called off their offensive. Falkenhayn was dismissed shortly after, largely for his failure at Verdun.

Now it was the turn of the French. In the autumn they retook Douaumont and then Vaux. By the time their advance ground to a halt in mid-December, they were close to the line where the battle had started ten months earlier. Casualties for both sides totaled between 600,000 and 700,000 and were roughly equal. (The total casualty figure for the entire war in the Verdun sector approaches 1.25 million.) Even today the skeletons of Verdun still surface, to be added to the towering bone piles in the basement of the Douaumont ossuary.

ROBERT COWLEY

Versailles, Treaty of

The Treaty of Versailles, signed in the Versailles Palace outside Paris on June 28, 1919, between the Allied and Associated Powers on the one hand and Germany on the other, brought World War I (q.v.) to an end. From the moment of its signature, the treaty ignited a continuing controversy over its treatment of Germany, with some arguing from the beginning that it was far too harsh, and others that it was too lenient to ensure a lasting peace.

The treaty, negotiated between January and June 1919 in Paris, was written by the Allies with almost no participation by the Germans. The negotiations revealed a split between the French, who wanted to dismember Germany to make it impossible for it to renew war with France, and the British and Americans, who did not want to create pretexts for a new war. The eventual treaty included fifteen parts and 440 articles. Part I created the Covenant of the New League of Nations, which Germany was not allowed to join until 1926. Part II specified Germany's new boundaries, giving Eupen-Malmédy to Belgium, Alsace-Lorraine back to France, substantial eastern districts to Poland, Memel to Lithuania, and large portions of Schleswig to Denmark. Part III stipulated a demilitarized zone and separated the Saar from Germany for fifteen years. Part IV stripped Germany of all its colonies, and Part V reduced Germany's armed forces to very low levels and prohibited Germany from possessing certain classes of weapons, while committing the Allies to eventual disarmament as well. Part VIII established Germany's liability for reparations (q.v.) without stating a specific figure and began with Article 231, in which Germany accepted the responsibility of itself and its allies for the losses and damages of the Allies "as a consequence of the war imposed upon them by the aggression of Germany and her allies." Part IX imposed numerous other financial obligations upon Germany.

The German government signed the treaty under protest. Right-wing German parties attacked it as a betrayal, and terrorists assassinated several politicians whom they considered responsible. The U.S. Senate refused to ratify the treaty, and the U.S. government took no responsibility for most of its provisions.

For five years the French and the Belgians tried to enforce the treaty quite rigorously, leading in 1922 to their occupation of the Ruhr. In 1924, however, Anglo-American financial pressure compelled France to scale down its goals and end the occupation, and the French, assented to modifying important provisions of the treaty in a series of new agreements. Germany in 1924 and 1929 agreed to pay reparations under the Dawes Plan and the Young Plan, but the depression led to the cancellation of reparations in 1932. The Allies evacuated the Rhineland in 1930. Germany violated many disarmament provisions of Part V during the 1920s, and Hitler denounced the treaty altogether in 1935. From March 1937 through March 1939, Hitler overturned the territorial provisions of the treaty with respect to Austria, Czechoslovakia, and Memel, with at least the tacit consent of the western powers. On September 1, 1939, he attacked Poland to alter that frontier, as well.

One can never know whether either rigorous Franco-British enforcement of the original treaty or a more generous treaty would have avoided a new war. Certainly the British and American governments after 1945 sought to avoid many of the problems that had been raised by the Treaty of Versailles, especially regarding reparations, and the division of Germany and the Cold War (q.v.) enabled them generously to rebuild the western zones and to integrate them into a western alliance without renewing fears of German aggression. Meanwhile, they deferred certain fundamental issues for so long that no formal peace treaty was ever written to end World War II (q.v.).

DAVID KAISER

Veterans' Organizations

Since the beginning of organized warfare, armed forces have faced the problem of what to do with their discharged soldiers. Ideally these men would return to their homes, shops, and farms. But what of those whose service had been so long that their civilian ties had vanished? Veterans of the Roman Empire often settled in military colonies that tended to cluster around the increasingly permanent legionary camps, greatly facilitating their evolution into urban communities. In imperial China, and the Muslim world too, old soldiers tended to prefer city life, often congregating by choice in the same neighborhoods.

These patterns, however, were informal; it is more accurate to distinguish between veterans' communities and veterans' organizations. The latter owe their existence to the rise of the citizen soldier and the emergence of the welfare state. The revolutionary and Napoleonic eras saw the emergence of organizations like the U.S. Order of the Cincinnati. These, however, were small in number and dominated by former officers. The American Civil War (q.v.) and the Wars of German Unification produced the first mass organizations of ex-soldiers. The Grand Army of the Republic and the United Confederate Veterans combined the activities and concerns of social club and interest group. After mutual waving of bloody shirts, both organizations also contributed to papering over the war's still-open wounds as leaders advocated and rank-and-file members accepted the necessity of reconciliation.

Imperial Germany's *Kriegervereine* were a different matter. Particularly after 1871, these associations, strongly supported by the government and the army, were intended to inculcate patriotism and national identity in a recently unified state that lacked a common heritage. Their militarism tended to be more public than private, particularly as their ranks filled with men who had done only peacetime service. Nevertheless, German veterans contributed disproportionately to the bellicosity that did so much to isolate the Second Reich from its neighbors.

World War I (q.v.), an experience as unique as it was unexpected, gave rise to the veterans' organizations of all the major Western combatants. The British Legion quickly developed into a welfare organization dominated by retired generals. Its political influence was correspondingly limited. On the Continent, veterans' groups tended to be identified with political movements covering the spectrum from moderate Left to radical Right. Across the Atlantic, the American Legion developed a reputation as a middle-class patrioteering body, which, although exaggerated, was not entirely undeserved.

The end of World War II (q.v.), by contrast, left many ex-soldiers unwilling to participate in veterans' organizations for other than social purposes. In Europe the social democracies that dominated postwar politics were sufficiently grateful to, and frightened of, their veterans to provide benefit packages generous enough to confine most organized activity to reunions. Ex-members of Germany's Waffen SS (q.v.) were more concerned with proving they had been "soldiers like all the rest" than with guarding the legacy of the Third Reich. In the United States, the American Legion and its sometimes friendly rival, the Veterans of Foreign Wars (VFW), had broader memberships and significant political agendas, usually conservative. Nevertheless, they too evolved as working-class and lower-middle-class counterparts to the country club.

Subsequent wars have been largely fought by professionals who in retirement prefer small private organizations to umbrella groups. Vietnam (q.v.) veterans represent the major exception. They, however, also tend to remain aloof from the Legion and the VFW, whose members fought "good wars."

DENNIS E. SHOWALTER

Vicksburg, Campaign for

November 1862–July 1863

Major General Ulysses S. Grant's (q.v.) Vicksburg campaign was one of the most successful examples of the operational art in the American Civil War (q.v.). In command of the Army of the Tennessee, Grant skillfully split two Confederate forces, defeated them in five different engagements, and captured the Vicksburg garrison.

Situated on bluffs that extended to the south and northeast, Vicksburg, Mississippi, dominated the Mississippi River. In December 1862, Grant tried to sneak William T. Sherman's (q.v.) men up the cliffs but failed. Over the next four months, he employed various schemes to position his army on the bluffs, where he could advance on the forty thousand defenders. None of them worked. Finally, the navy ran trans-

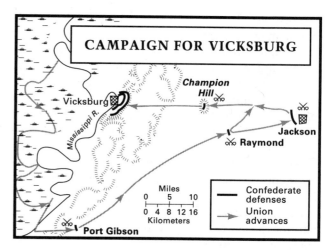

ports and supplies past the enemy guns at Vicksburg, and Grant marched his army of thirty-three thousand along the west bank to below the city and then shuttled it across the river. He hammered an opposing force to the north and marched swiftly eastward, driving off a second army from Jackson, the state capital. Grant then returned to pound back Vicksburg's defenders. After a six-week siege, the city and almost thirty thousand Confederates surrendered on July 4, 1863.

The Vicksburg campaign was one of the decisive events in the American Civil War. The victory secured a major strategic objective — control of the Mississippi River — and thus isolated a huge portion of the Confederacy. Coupled with the federal triumph at Gettysburg (q.v.), the fall of Vicksburg revived flagging spirits in the North. And by capturing the city and an army, Grant earned President Abraham Lincoln's (q.v.) lasting confidence.

JOSEPH T. GLATTHAAR

Vienna, Sieges of

1529 and 1683

Ottoman control of Hungary after Suleiman's (q.v.) victory at the Battle of Mohács in 1526 (q.v.) was threatened by Ferdinand, Hapsburg ruler of Austria, Bohemia, and Hungary, who demanded the return of all Ottoman conquests since 1521. Although the Danubian city of Vienna lacked strategic importance, in a bid to secure his northwestern frontier, Suleiman's army chased Ferdinand from Buda to Vienna, arriving before the city on September 26, 1529.

Vienna was well defended. The Ottomans (q.v.)

A Turkish depiction of the 1529 siege of Vienna by a Turkish army under Suleiman the Magnificent. Although outnumbered by at least two to one, discipline and technology enabled Western forces to ward off the invasion.

were unable to bring their heavy artillery before the city walls; two major assaults were unsuccessful, and the lateness of the season and inclemency of the weather led them to raise the siege. A significant result of the campaign was the confirmation of an Ottoman protégé, János Szapolyai of Transylvania, as king of Hungary. The Hapsburgs controlled only the western fringe of the kingdom.

In 1683, the Ottomans still governed much of Hungary, and Vienna, the capital city of the Hapsburg Empire, lay close to their frontier. The Ottoman-Hapsburg border in Hungary had repeatedly been contested since 1529, but the Ottomans stood at a disadvantage because of the distance that they had to travel to this theater, despite having forward bases in Belgrade and Buda, and they rarely proved able to retain the fortresses that they had won. However, in 1682 the Ottoman government went to war in response to the encouragement of both the Hungarian Protestant leader, Imre Thököly, and the Ottomans' French ally, and at the insistence of the ambitious grand vezir, Merzifonlu Kara Mustafa Paşa.

Sultan Mehmed IV and his army arrived at Belgrade on May 3, 1683; it was joined by the forces of the Ottoman vassals — the Crimean khan and the princes of Wallachia, Moldavia, and Transylvania — and continued along the Danube under the command of Kara Mustafa Paşa. Most inhabitants of Vienna, including the Hapsburg emperor Leopold, fled at the news of the Ottoman advance. By mid-July the city was surrounded: bombardment, mining, and assaults began. But on September 12, troops under the command of the Polish king, Jan Sobieski, who had earlier in the year allied himself with Austria, launched a decisive attack. Kara Mustafa Paşa had neglected to fortify his siegeworks, and the Ottoman army retreated in disarray, leaving behind booty that is still among the prized possessions of museums throughout central Europe. Mustafa was executed at Belgrade by order of the sultan.

From the mid–seventeenth century, Vienna was to the Ottomans the "Red Apple," symbol of their aspirations to hegemony in central Europe. Their defeat was in large measure due to cooperation among the Christian powers, who for once felt they had more to lose from the loss of Vienna than they had to fear from one another. The Holy League formed thereafter made substantial territorial gains and ended forever Ottoman expansion in central Europe.

CAROLINE FINKEL

Vietnam

Most Americans think of the Vietnam War as a phenomenon of the 1960s, when U.S. combat troops arrived in South Vietnam in an unsuccessful attempt to prevent a Communist takeover of the country. In actuality, for the Vietnamese people the conflict started long before that, when the Communist-dominated Viet Minh Front, led by the veteran revolutionary Ho Chi Minh, seized power in Hanoi from the defeated Japanese at the end of World War II (q.v.). After negotiations with returning French colonial authorities

U.S. Airborne Troops, Hill 873, 1967.

failed, full-scale war broke out in December 1946 (see *Indochina War*).

For the next eight years, the Viet Minh fought a guerrilla war against the French. Victory was elusive, so the latter turned for help to the United States. Concerned at the Communist victory in the recent civil war in China and the possibility of an expansion of the "red tide" into Southeast Asia, Washington began to provide assistance to the French in 1950. In succeeding years U.S. support increased, but after the major defeat at Dien Bien Phu (q.v.) in May 1954, the French decided to sign a compromise peace agreement at Geneva. The northern half of Vietnam was given to the Communists, the remainder to nationalist forces allied with the French.

The Geneva Agreement had called for national elections to unite the country, but South Vietnamese president Ngo Dinh Diem refused and began to suppress Viet Minh supporters in the south. In 1959, the Hanoi regime in the north decided to return to a strategy of revolutionary war and dispatched cadres southward to help strengthen the movement, now popularly called the Viet Cong (Vietnamese Communists).

By 1961 the insurgent movement had reached sizable proportions, and the United States decided to increase its support for the beleaguered regime in Saigon. The Kennedy administration assigned military advisers to train South Vietnamese soldiers in how to conduct counterinsurgency (q.v.) operations and "win the hearts and minds" of the local populace. Kennedy rejected a recommendation to send U.S. combat troops.

Under growing pressure from the Viet Cong, Diem continued to weaken, and in November 1963 he was overthrown by a military coup. Washington had hoped that new leaders would revitalize the war effort, but the Saigon regime remained political unstable, while Viet Cong strength increased in the countryside. In August 1964, responding to an attack by North Vietnamese patrol boats on U.S. naval vessels in the Tonkin Gulf, President Lyndon Johnson ordered air strikes on North Vietnamese territory and obtained congressional authorization to take necessary actions to protect U.S. interests in Southeast Asia.

Washington's effort to intimidate Hanoi failed. Communist leaders, now convinced that the Saigon regime was near collapse, stepped up infiltration and ordered a major effort to seek final victory in the south. But when Viet Cong forces attacked a U.S. camp at Pleiku in early February 1965, Johnson responded with a sustained campaign of air strikes (labeled Operation Rolling Thunder) and the introduction of U.S. combat troops to assist Saigon in the prosecution of the war. General William Westmoreland (q.v.), commander of the U.S. military in South Vietnam, drew up a strategy designed first to stabilize key areas in the Central Highlands and along the northern border and then to launch sweep operations to wipe out enemy base areas throughout the country. In the meantime, South Vietnamese forces would carry out pacification operations to root out Communist elements in the countryside.

As U.S. force levels increased, Communist leaders retaliated by sending substantial numbers of North Vietnamese regular forces into the south. Their strategy was to maintain constant pressure by launching selected attacks at vulnerable points throughout the country. This approach was costly, however, both in terms of casualties and morale. In late 1967, planners in Hanoi decided to launch a major offensive in the hope of bringing about the collapse of the Saigon regime and a withdrawal of U.S. military forces from South Vietnam. Known as the Tet offensive (q.v.), it was launched in early February 1968 and involved attacks throughout the countryside, along with assaults on major cities such as Hue and Saigon, where sapper teams (terrorist units) briefly seized government installations and the ground floor of the U.S. embassy.

From a military perspective, the campaign was a costly setback for the Viet Cong, who bore the brunt of the fighting and suffered heavy casualties. But Tet demonstrated the continuing vulnerability of the Saigon regime and undermined public support for the war effort in the United States. In late March, President Johnson called a halt to U.S. air strikes above the twentieth parallel as an inducement to bring about negotiations.

After considerable sparring, peace talks began in November, but neither side was ready to capitulate. Hanoi continued to hope that U.S. public opinion would force Washington to withdraw. To win the support of the "silent majority," President Richard M. Nixon directed the gradual removal of U.S. troops while simultaneously attempting to strengthen the Saigon regime. In 1970 he ordered a brief assault on Viet Cong sanctuaries inside the Cambodian border. Unfortunately, one consequence of the campaign was to extend the war into previously neutral Cambodia.

By the autumn of 1972, both sides appeared to recognize that total victory was unlikely. After a series of mutual concessions, a peace agreement was finally signed in Paris in January 1973. It provided for a cease-fire, the withdrawal of remaining U.S. troops, and provisions for a political settlement between the contending elements in South Vietnam.

For most Americans, the Paris agreement marked the end of the war. But the political settlement never took effect, and by the fall of 1974 heavy fighting had resumed. When Hanoi realized that the United States was too war-weary and preoccupied with the Watergate scandal to respond, North Vietnamese troops invaded the Central Highlands and finally seized Saigon on April 30, 1975. The country was soon unified under Communist rule.

The Vietnam War has usually been considered a defeat for the United States. In fact, the issue is not quite so clear-cut. Whereas both Cambodia and Laos were placed under Communist rule, the remaining states in the region were galvanized by the fall of South Vietnam to take action to protect their own security. In present-day Vietnam, Communist leaders are introducing market reforms, and the country ironically serves as the primary bulwark against possible future Chinese expansion into Southeast Asia.

WILLIAM J. DUIKER

William J. Duiker, *The Communist Road to Power in Vietnam* (1981); George C. Herring, *America's Longest War: The United States and Vietnam, 1950–1975*, 3rd ed. (1993); Stanley Karnow, *Vietnam: A History*, rev. ed. (1991).

Vikings

Scandinavian raiders, merchants, and explorers, the Vikings were active throughout Europe from about A.D. 780 to 1070. The term *Viking* derives from the Old Norse *vik*, meaning "inlet," either as the name for the home for some of the raiders (possibly Oslofjord) or from their use of inlets as bases for piracy and trade. In Old Norse the verb "to go viking" designated the activity, not the people who undertook it. Western European sources usually called them Northmen, or pagans, or simply pirates. In spite of their longstanding reputation as fierce warriors, trade and exploration were probably the most important elements of Viking activity.

Scandinavians had long traded throughout northern Europe, but in the late eighth century they began also to attack and plunder neighboring regions. The causes for this shift were probably internal, but archaeologists have ruled out simple population growth. The best explanation is that Scandinavian society was highly stratified, with intense competition between aristocrats for wealth and prestige, especially in the form of followers. (The picture of early Scandinavian society as a primitive democracy is a nineteenth-century Romantic fiction; the "free men" of the Scandinavian law codes were petty aristocrats with extensive holdings in land and slaves.) As kingdoms emerged, aristocrats who wanted to keep up in the competition for prestige turned to piracy as the quickest way to obtain the heroic reputation needed to attract a large following and the wealth in precious metals to support it.

While some losers in the domestic competition found viking to be a profitable activity while in exile, others found more opportunity overseas than at home and established lordships in Russia (Kiev), France (Normandy), and England (the Danelaw, stretching from Essex to Cumberland). From the late tenth century, Scandinavian kings took control of raiding activity as part of their own military policy. By that time, most lesser aristocrats either had become military followers of the kings and magnates or had turned to trade as a less risky way of maintaining their more modest positions.

Actual raids were normally small-scale operations; both the number of ships and their carrying capacity have been greatly exaggerated. Reliable data indicate that a fleet of thirty or so ships carrying no more than one thousand men was noteworthy. The so-called Great Army that invaded England in 865 may have included two or three such groups. Using clinker-built ships (made of overlapping planks) with shallow drafts, equally well suited to crossing the ocean and traveling up rivers, Viking raiders could appear literally out of nowhere, land at a completely unexpected site, and be gone with their plunder before a reaction force had arrived. Larger Viking forces sometimes seized beachheads and used stolen local transport to collect loot; eventually they began to negotiate huge payments (Danegeld) to leave a region.

The Vikings had the advantage of mobility, and the rapidity of their raids produced surprise and terror. They possessed absolutely no inherent battlefield advantage over the trained military forces of target regions, and confrontations with heavily armored soldiers in England and on the Continent resulted in defeat more often than victory. Famous Scandinavian victories, like that at Maldon (981), were caused more by stupidity on the part of defenders than by any extraordinary fighting ability of the Vikings. Similarly, Scandinavian bodyguards employed by the English kings and Byzantine emperors were valuable mainly because, as foreigners, they were unlikely to have local allegiances that might erode loyalty to their employer.

In fact, Vikings never successfully attacked well-organized political units. Their successes came almost exclusively in regions that were less developed (the Baltic and Russia), divided among petty kingdoms (Ireland and ninth-century England), or actively engaged in civil conflict (the Carolingian Empire in the ninth century). The one exception to this rule, late-tenth-century England, suffered from the neglect of basic military affairs under Aethelred the Badly Advised, whereas Viking forces were mainly large, well-organized fleets led by kings and would-be kings such as Olav Tryggvason. The Scandinavians stopped raiding and turned to trade whenever the target areas of Viking raids developed coherent territorial defenses under stable political leadership, as occurred in England under King Alfred, Germany under the Saxon kings, France under regional aristocratic leaders, and Ireland under Brian Boru. In the Baltic, such defenses and leadership were not in place until the thirteenth century.

The most lasting achievement of the Vikings was to expand and intensify the trade network of northern Europe. Mainly dealing in fur and slaves, Vikings established trade routes to Byzantium and the Near East. Their activity in eastern Europe sparked the development of Russian city-states such as Novgorod and Kiev. Similarly, Irish towns such as Waterford and Dublin were originally Viking markets. More important to the subsequent history of Scandinavia was the exploration of trade routes to the Arctic (the North Way) and in the Baltic Sea, which provided the economic foundation for the further development of Scandinavia.

EDWARD J. SCHOENFELD

Frans Bengtsson, *The Long Ships*, trans. Michael Meyer (1954); Magnus Magnusson, *Vikings!* (1980); Birgit and Peter Sawyer, *Medieval Scandinavia: From Conversion to Reformation, circa 800–1500* (1993).

Vimy Ridge, Battle of

April 9–12, 1917

For the first time in World War I (q.v.), the four Canadian divisions attacked together as the Canadian Corps, at Vimy in northern France. Some historians have seen this as a pivotal moment in the development of a Canadian identity. Vimy Ridge had defied previous attacks by the Allies, but in early 1917 its capture formed part of a larger battle, supporting a British attack at Arras, which itself assisted a major French offensive.

On Easter Sunday, April 9, at 5:30 A.M., the Canadian Corps swept forward in a sleet storm and took nearly all its objectives on schedule that day. Over the next three days, the last German defenses on the left were captured. This swift victory was achieved primarily through an excellent artillery preparation and creeping barrage, but also good infantry training and execution, effective infantry tactics ("leaning on the barrage"), poor German defensive plans, the sleet as cover, and the use of underground caves and tunnels contributed to the success. The Canadian Corps also outnumbered the defenders by 35,000 to 10,000, and, with flank support, deployed 1,130 guns. This latter concentration was more than double the density used at the Somme (q.v.).

Canadian casualties amounted to around 10,500, whereas the German defenders lost almost all their strength, including 4,000 prisoners. The capture of Vimy Ridge pointed to the future, where similar careful set-piece attacks in 1917 and 1918 established the Canadian Corps as a premier fighting force.

TIM TRAVERS

Virginia Capes, Battle of

See Yorktown and Virginia Capes, Battles of.

Waffen SS

The Waffen SS (Schutzstaffel) owed its origins to Adolf Hitler's (q.v.) creation of an elite guard unit within the body of the SA (Sturmabteilung, "storm-troopers"). In 1934, SS units proved particularly useful during the "night of the long knives," when Hitler purged the SA leadership. As war approached, the SS developed a number of semimilitarized units to protect the führer, guard concentration camps, and provide for internal security duties. However, both Hitler and Heinrich Himmler believed that these units needed to establish their credibility as future protectors of the regime by fighting on the battlefields of the coming war. But Himmler seemed also to have aimed at creating a force that could challenge the army as the bearer of arms in the future Nazi Empire.

By the time of the invasion of Poland, Himmler had formed these diverse units into combat regiments, armed largely with Czech weapons — the army was not exactly supportive — and named the Waffen SS. In the campaign, Waffen SS formations exhibited a fanaticism in combat and a disregard for military law that were to be the hallmark of their behavior throughout the war. Despite the army's opposition, a rapid expansion took place that saw the Waffen SS's strength grow from 28,000 men in 1939 to nearly 150,000 men by spring 1940. In the French campaign the Waffen SS provided the army with three divisions, and also several regiments. Senior army commanders proved quite receptive to the high level of enthusiasm and effectiveness that the SS troopers exhibited in combat. Even when soldiers from the SS Totenkopf Division — drawn from concentration camp guards — murdered more than one hundred British prisoners of war at the town of La Paradise on the Dunkirk perimeter in 1940, neither the army nor the SS took disciplinary action.

The Waffen SS came into its own during the campaign against the Soviet Union, beginning in June 1941 (see *Operation Barbarossa*). From the first, Hitler made the war in the east a war of ideologies — which perfectly matched the Waffen SS's fanatical, ideological orientation. Waffen SS troopers participated in innumerable atrocities against the "subhuman" races of the Soviet Union. The ferocious fighting in 1941 added to the impressive military reputation that Himmler's soldiers had earned, and another major expansion of Waffen SS numbers took place: by early 1943 the Waffen SS fielded a corps that played a major role in the successful recapture of Kharkov, during which the units involved suffered needless losses by disobeying orders, storming the city, and then murdering twenty thousand civilians.

In 1944, the Allies invaded Normandy and immediately ran into Hitler's ideological soldiers. On June 7–8, the soldiers of the Waffen SS division Hitler Jugend — consisting of sixteen- and seventeen-year-old fanatics from the Hitler Youth — dealt the Canadians a severe setback and proceeded to murder a number of their prisoners. At the same time the division Das Reich was moving from Limoges to Normandy; outraged by the actions of the French Resistance — which included the murder of a battalion commander — the SS troopers rounded up the entire village of Oradour-sur-Glane. They machine-gunned the men in barns and murdered all the village's women and children by burning down the village church where the SS troopers had driven them.

The Waffen SS represented a peculiar outgrowth of Nazi culture. Its soldiers were ferocious and effective on the battlefield. They may have taken more casualties than army commanders felt were justified, but even the German army had to admit that they were fighters. But they were also criminals, and their record of murderous behavior toward prisoners and civilians speaks for itself.

WILLIAMSON MURRAY

Wallenstein, Albrecht von

1583–1634, Imperial Generalissimo in the Thirty Years' War

Of Bohemian gentry stock, Albrecht Eusebius Wenzel von Wallenstein acquired large estates through marriage and used them to raise troops for the Austrian Hapsburgs against the Bohemian rebels (1618–1620). He subsequently acquired more lands, enabling him to raise an entire army for Emperor Ferdinand II in 1625 during the Thirty Years' War (q.v.). Wallenstein sustained his forces, which eventually numbered 150,000 men, through a "contributions system" — requiring communities to provide specified quantities of cash and supplies — which permitted better discipline and reduced desertion; but he remained highly unpopular, and after the defeat of Denmark in 1629, the emperor's allies forced his dismissal.

The invasion of Gustavus Adolphus of Sweden (q.v.) forced Wallenstein's recall to raise a new army that fought the Swedes to a standstill at Lützen. Now, however, the general turned politician and sought to broker a compromise peace; when, early in 1634, he required his colonels to swear to obey him — even against the emperor — Ferdinand declared him a traitor and had him murdered. Wallenstein, who had raised and commanded the largest military concentrations seen in Europe to that date, died at the head of only a handful of followers.

GEOFFREY PARKER

War

In essence it is possible to think of war in three ways, namely (1) as an instrument in the hands of policy, (2) as an end in itself, and (3) as both a negation and a combination of the two. Each of these ways leads to important conclusions as to the way in which war ought to be conducted.

The first, or instrumental, way of thinking about war is most often associated with the names of Thucydides and Carl von Clausewitz (q.v.); today, their line of thought is represented by the so-called

---

The Ten Greatest Military Disasters

Sicilian Expedition (Italy, 415 B.C.)

Cannae (Italy, August 216 B.C.)

Teutoburg Forest (Germany, A.D. 9)

Kosovo (Kosovo, June 28, 1389)

Mohács (Hungary, August 29, 1526)

Poltava (Russia, June 27, 1709)

Sedan (France, August–September 1870)

The Somme, First Day (France, July 1, 1916)

Singapore (Singapore, February 1942)

Stalingrad (Russia, September 1942–February 1943)

---

neorealists. This school looks at war from the top, as seen by the statesman or the commander. It considers that war is not a divine punishment, as people often thought during the Middle Ages, nor an accident that occurs without being subject to human control, nor some kind of game whose value lies in the entertainment that it offers. Instead it is, or should be, a deliberate act of policy rationally planned for the attainment of rational ends. Once the ends have been selected, one group of people, however organized, sets out to achieve them by killing the members of another group. Each side builds up its forces, arms them, trains them, and deploys them. The dictates of policy may demand that extremes be avoided, moderation exercised, and the enemy offered a way out; however, there is no room for half measures in the *idea* of war. The harnessing of all available strength results in the creation of a mailed fist, which is then launched in an attempt to break the enemy's will by destroying its armed forces. As a preliminary to this act of destruction, the fist may maneuver this way or that. Nothing prevents the commander from employing every possible stratagem in order to mislead the enemy and set it up for the final blow. In the end, however, and to quote Clausewitz's own words, "the best strategy is always to be as strong as possible; first in general and then at the decisive point."

As the above already suggests, both Thucydides and Clausewitz laid very great emphasis on physical strength while at the same time suggesting that moral strength is, when everything is said and done, even more critical. Clausewitz in particular presents war as the domain of uncertainty, friction, danger, deprivation, physical effort, suffering, pain, and death — to which he might have added long periods of boredom, which can be as corrosive to the military virtues as all other factors put together. However powerful they may be in other respects, no commander, army, or private soldier who is incapable of coping with these problems is worth a fig. Clausewitz's analysis of the moral forces that are needed — courage, determination, endurance, and possibly even a certain callousness that makes soldiers able to bear the sufferings of others and their own — is as admirable as it is brief. Nowhere, however, does he enter into a detailed discussion of the origin of those qualities. And indeed such a discussion is made a priori impossible by the very fact that he represents war as a rational instrument used to attain rational ends.

The excellence of the Clausewitzian way of thinking about war is evident from its widespread acceptance in all developed countries, including both Western ones and those of the former Eastern bloc. However, its emphasis on strength leaves one question wide open: why, over the last fifty years or so, has virtually *every* powerful, modern armed force in the world suffered defeat at the hands of ill-armed, ill-clad, ill-organized, often illiterate and barefooted militias, guerrillas, and terrorists — the French in Vietnam and Algeria, the Americans in Vietnam and Somalia, the Soviets in Afghanistan, the Israelis in Lebanon (except for a narrow strip of land along the border between the two countries) and the occupied territories, and the British in any number of places around the globe. Without exception, these defeats were suffered by people who acknowledged Clausewitz as their master — even if they never read a word he wrote. Without exception, too, they took place on the moral plane. From a material point of view, every one of the armies just mentioned remained intact, and indeed many of them barely even suffered a scratch.

These facts suggest that there is something fundamentally wrong with the Clausewitzian framework. No systematic alternative has ever been presented in the West, although hints as to the solution may be found in writers from Homer through Shakespeare all the way to Friedrich Nietzsche — none of whom is likely to be found on a modern officer's obligatory reading list. From Henry V in front of Harfleur to the *Übermensch* playing with danger, the starting point is the "romantic" idea that war does not consist primarily of killing; instead it hinges on the willingness *to die* if necessary. However, for a person to lay down

his life for his interest — let alone that of somebody or something else — is logically absurd. On this obstacle, Clausewitz's entire rational, "strategic" theory of war collapses like a house of cards.

For a soldier or army to lay down their lives they must be convinced, not merely in their brains but to the marrow of their bones, that the cause for which they fight is *just*. But it is impossible to be strong and just at the same time; to "fight" against the weak is unjust because it is *not* necessary. Under such circumstances he who kills is a criminal, whereas he who allows himself to be killed is merely a fool. As Vietnam and other examples have demonstrated, this dilemma is quite capable of making an army, even the richest and most powerful one in history, disintegrate, frag its officers, and go home in disgust.

The decisive question, then, is what makes the troops — who represent the vast majority of those involved — prepared to lay down their lives. To this question there can be only one answer: many of the greatest works of art of all history, as well as the entire field of sport and games, prove that coping with danger is a source of joy, and that war, which is not subject to rules and in which anything is permissible, is the greatest joy of all. To quote Nietzsche, a just cause does not make a good war; a good war makes a just cause. A good war, by definition, can be waged only against an enemy at least as strong as oneself — and the longer the conflict, the more true this becomes. The secret of victory is to wage war in such a way that soldiers can fight while at the same time keeping, even increasing, their self-respect as human beings. Only *after* that do numbers, organization, strategy, technology, and so on enter the picture.

These frameworks, the expressive and the instrumental, are diametrically opposed. Truth must combine them both — and, at the same time, negate them both. That is the achievement of the greatest of all writers on war, the Chinese Sun Tzu (q.v.). Sun Tzu, who *may* have lived during the second half of the first millennium B.C., belonged to the school of thought known as Taoism (from *tao*, best translated as "cosmic harmony"). Taoism knows neither ends nor means, justice nor injustice, let alone joy. The world is the product of necessity. The perfect philosopher's understanding-without-understanding is identical with the world. The latter floats his way, as it were, with no action on his part.

And now, to the real nature of war. It is neither a matter for self-expression nor an instrument, but an evil, not in any moral sense but because it disturbs *tao*. Nevertheless, owing to the willful actions of people who do not understand this, it is sometimes necessary; thus the question as to what makes the troops prepared to fight scarcely arises. From commander in chief to common soldier, everybody will do what is necessary, necessity being the one force that can make people prepared to risk their lives and at the same time justify their deaths. However, necessity is not for individual soldiers to judge on their own. When the emperor's concubines, whom he had formed into an army, disobeyed his orders, Sun Tzu had the chief concubine beheaded. Without iron discipline, backed by drastic punishment, no army can exist. Discipline (q.v.) is the commander's way of imposing necessity on the common soldier.

The most important questions having been both evaded and answered, the conduct of operations may now be discussed. The objective should be to restore *tao* by using the least force necessary, which presupposes "perfect knowledge of oneself and the enemy." "The best way is diplomacy; if you cannot use diplomacy, resort to dirty tricks [for example, assassinating the enemy commander]; if you cannot use dirty tricks, maneuver; if you cannot maneuver, fight a pitched battle; and if a pitched battle won't work, lay a siege [which is the most stupid way of all, since the enemy has every advantage on his side]." Contrary to Clausewitz, Sun Tzu states, "All warfare is based [less on strength than] on deceit"; it is a question of deliberately confusing reality and appearances to the point that the enemy no longer knows which is which and *then* of "throwing rocks at eggs." Needless to say, this requires immense intellectual and, even more so, moral gifts. On the other hand, the mere fact that one is constrained to fight proves that one's gifts were inadequate to maintain *tao*, the only perfect state.

Of the various frameworks for thinking about war, Sun Tzu's is the best as well as one of the briefest. Though there are four different English translations of *The Art of War* currently available, the book is ill understood, particularly by those who have accepted *On War* as their frame of reference. The impotence of the Russian Army in front of a few ill-armed Chechen is merely the latest proof that the developed world's "strategic" view of war is bankrupt. Sooner or later, those who cannot fight will find themselves forced to do so; let those who have ears to hear, listen!

MARTIN VAN CREVELD

Carl von Clausewitz, *On War*, eds. Michael Howard and Peter Paret (1976); Martin van Creveld, *The Transformation of War* (1991); Thomas C. Schelling, *Arms and Influence* (1966); Sun Tzu, *The Art of War*, trans. Thomas Clancy (1988).

War and Industry

The spread of modern methods of industrial production from Britain in the eighteenth century to much of the rest of the world ever since has had a remarkable influence on the conduct of war. Especially in conjunction with the innovation of mobilizing a nation's population that France pioneered during the 1790s (see *French Revolution, Wars of the*), industrialization has made possible enormous increases in the application of brute force. And the technological innovations at the heart of modern industrial revolutions have made possible new ways of waging war.

The most conspicuous type of war in the industrial age has been multitheater, protracted wars fought for such high political stakes that both sides mobilized the bulk of their resources. Though large-scale, protracted wars in the preindustrial era often took a great toll on life and property, the course of modern industrial wars has been marked by unprecedented destructiveness. The outcome of these "total" wars has seemingly followed a straightforward pattern: the state or coalition with the greatest industrial capabilities has won all such conflicts. The North in the American Civil War (q.v.), the Allies in World War I (q.v.), and the Grand Alliance in World War II (q.v.) eventually overwhelmed their opponents quantitatively. To be sure, such a result was not necessarily foreordained. In the global conflicts in this century, which states ended up on which side was the result of contingent choices, and a different alignment of coalition partners might have produced a different outcome in any given case. Moreover, in every case the losing side also made the disparity in the balance of industrial power worse by managing the mobilization of its resources less efficiently than the winning side.

There have also been wars of a very different type among industrial powers, wars of a much lesser scope and duration. When a power has achieved a quick, decisive victory in such a conflict, it often has derived its military success from the application of a new industrial technology. In the Seven Weeks' War of 1866 (q.v.), for example, General Helmuth von Moltke (q.v.), chief of the Prussian General Staff, used the mobility provided by a superior railway system to make possible a major battlefield victory over the Austrians. Because Otto von Bismarck (q.v.) kept the stakes of the war limited and kept the Austrians isolated from potential allies, that battlefield success was sufficient to bring the war to an early end. The Germans in 1914 tried, but failed, to win another quick, decisive victory. Their failure was partly due to the fact that, with the further evolution of industrial technique and technology, firepower had come increasingly to favor the defense. It was also due to the fact that the political nature of the war was quite different: the Germans now faced a coalition that saw the stakes of the war as much higher than the Prussians' adversaries half a century before. Then, in 1940, taking advantage of the industrial development of tanks and aircraft, Adolf Hitler (q.v.) won a surprisingly swift victory over the French. But in 1941 the Germans' "military-technical revolution" was not enough to overcome the Soviets, who not only had greater strategic depth, reserves, and resources than the French, but also saw the threat of Nazi conquest as more catastrophic.

A third type of war in the age of modern industry has pitted relatively advanced industrial states against less economically developed societies. In the nineteenth century, Western forces used the superior firepower made possible by industrialization to overcome relatively easily the military resistance of indigenous forces in Africa and Asia. But in the twentieth century, anti-imperialist insurgents were often able to use force successfully to reclaim national independence. By developing tighter political organization, devising more sophisticated military strategies, and arousing the passions of the masses, they could hope to resist an industrial style of warfare long enough to prevail in what became a contest of willpower more than of firepower.

With memories of the Vietnam War (q.v.) superseded somewhat by the experience of the Gulf War (q.v.) of 1991, some prophets now foresee the eclipse of industrial warfare not by a style of warfare based on revolutionary political ideologies but by one based on revolutionary information technologies. If history offers any guide to the future, however, the effectiveness of information warfare, like the effectiveness of industrial warfare in the past, will depend crucially upon the political nature of the conflicts to which it is applied.

BRADFORD A. LEE

Paul Kennedy, *The Rise and Fall of the Great Powers: Economic Change and Military Conflict from 1500 to 2000* (1987); Maurice Pearton, *Diplomacy, War, and Technology since 1830* (1984).

War Crimes Trials

The idea that there are legitimate versus criminal ways to conduct warfare has a long history (see *Laws of War*). After the American Civil War (q.v.), for example, Henry Wirz, commandant of the notorious Confederate prison of Andersonville, was hanged for mistreatment of Union prisoners. International war crimes trials, however, got off to a dismal start in 1918, after World War I (q.v.). The victorious Allies drew up a list of 4,900 alleged German war criminals. They soon thinned the list to 901 names. Of these, 12 were ordered to trial by a German court in Leipzig, four years *after* the war ended. Three of the 12 defendants did not bother to show up. Charges against 3 more were dropped. The remaining 6 defendants received wrist-slap sentences.

At the end of World War II (q.v.), the Allies were faced with far more staggering evidence of criminal wartime behavior: the fact that Nazi Germany had murdered six million to ten million innocent persons through the systematic extermination of the Jews and execution of hostages and criminal neglect of prisoners of war — mostly millions of Soviet POWs. Again, the cry went up for war crimes trials. The cry, however, was not universal. Joseph Stalin (q.v.), only half in jest, proposed shooting fifty thousand members of the German General Staff outright. Initially, both U.S. president Franklin D. Roosevelt (q.v.) and British prime minister Winston Churchill (q.v.) favored summary justice without benefit of trial. Eventually, however, the champions of law prevailed, arguing that if it was wrong for Germans to take lives without due process in wartime, it was no more right for the victors to do so in peacetime. In the fall of 1945, the Allies agreed on an international tribunal to meet at Nuremberg, Germany, composed of American, British, Soviet, and French judges, to try twenty-one surviving major Nazis. The defendants were accused not only of crimes against combatants and innocent civilians, but also of a new offense in international law: committing aggression. A year later, an eleven-nation international tribunal in Tokyo also tried twenty-eight alleged major Japanese war criminals.

Nazi defendants, including former air marshal Hermann Göring (standing in dock), hear their sentences at the world's first international war crimes trials at Nuremberg, Germany, in spring 1946.

From the outset, the legality of the Nuremberg trial was attacked, not only by those whose necks were at risk. Other opponents, for example, included the leading Republican U.S. senator, Robert Taft, who argued that the trial amounted to ex post facto law — that the crimes had been defined and a court had been created *after* the acts had been committed. Critics also asked under what jurisdiction an American prosecutor had the right to try a German national before a Russian judge for a crime committed in Poland. And why were only Germans on trial, since atrocities had been committed on all sides? And if aggression was a crime, why were the Russians sitting in judgment of the Germans, since they themselves had joined Germany to carve up Poland and had attacked Finland? Nuremberg, its critics said, was nothing but victors' vengeance. Even the chief justice of the U.S. Supreme Court, Harlan Fisk Stone, called the trial a "legal lynching."

Supporters of the trial argued that the Germans, by launching the war and conducting it barbarously, had violated international obligations that Germany had signed, the Geneva Convention, the Hague Rules of Land Warfare, the Pact of Paris outlawing war, and various peace treaties with its subsequently invaded neighbors. Consequently, the court was not ex post facto, but merely the legal machinery for enforcing existing international law. Furthermore, the Allies had had to assume jurisdiction because leaving justice in German hands had produced the farcical prosecutions of World War I.

The Nuremberg trial went forward, and of the original defendants, eleven were condemned to death, seven received lesser sentences, and three were acquitted. The most notorious of the condemned and second in command in Hitler's Germany, Reichsmarschall Hermann Göring escaped the hangman's noose by taking cyanide just over an hour before he was to mount the gallows.

After the main Nuremberg trial, hundreds of lesser Nazis were tried and some executed. In the East, several Japanese war criminals, including Japan's wartime prime minister, Tojo Hideki (q.v.), and General Yamashita Tomoyuki (q.v.), who had captured Malaya and Singapore, were convicted and executed. But with the coming of the Cold War (q.v.), Allied leaders became more concerned with opposing the Soviet Union than with punishing war criminals. By the 1950s, pardons and commutations of sentences were being handed out wholesale.

The Nuremberg trial, besides punishing the guilty, was supposed to set precedents for deterring future aggressors and war criminals. But in the approximately forty years following the trial, the world experienced 117 wars between nations, civil wars, wars of independence, and insurrections, costing 22,136,000 lives. Although these clashes included numerous acts of aggression, criminal warfare, and genocide (two million to four million Cambodians were exterminated by the Pol Pot regime), no international body tried a single war criminal because of these acts, though the United Nations had the power to do so using Nuremberg as its precedent. Not until 1993 did the United Nations vote to create a tribunal to prosecute atrocities committed in the former Yugoslavia.

Does the almost total lack of trials mean that the war crimes trials of World War II served no purpose? No. At a time when a movement is afoot to deny the occurrence of the Holocaust, no reasonable person can read the forty-two-volume Nuremberg trial record and doubt that the horrors charged actually happened. That is Nuremberg's greatest legacy.

Other trials followed later for Nazi crimes; Adolf Eichmann's in Israel and Klaus Barbie's in France were among them. Attempts have been made to bring alleged war criminals to trial for acts in the former Yugoslavia. However, clear-cut victory is almost a precondition for bringing the accused to trial. Negotiated settlements may produce peace, but where war crimes are concerned, they will not necessarily bring the perpetrators to justice.

JOSEPH E. PERSICO

Joseph E. Persico, *Nuremberg: Infamy on Trial* (1994).

War Finance

War finance, providing "the sinews of war," has usually determined a war's outcome. Fear of military defeat stimulates innovations in finance (among other reactions) that may have lasting consequences, whether victory or defeat follows. Many, if not most, of the lasting innovations in the way governments have collected taxes, managed the money supply, controlled wages and prices, serviced their debts, and regulated trade have emerged under the duress of war.

Innovations in war finance fall under the three ways governments can finance their expenditures — taxes, debt, and seigniorage (money creation). Perhaps the earliest example is the creation of coinage, originating in Lydia in the seventh century B.C. The use of coins allowed more efficient collection of taxes and tribute by military leaders. It also allowed governments to hire mercenaries (q.v.) instead of maintaining standing armies. It is a matter of conjecture whether coins or mercenaries came first, but it is indisputable that they spread together throughout Asia Minor and the Mediterranean. Coinage also facilitated the collection of taxes, including tribute from foreigners.

The first financial innovation to appear after coins was recoinage by the victor of an opponent's money supply, which could bring substantial payoffs. In the later Roman Empire and in medieval Europe, recoinage of one's own money was an occasional expedient of princes or cities under duress. During the military revolution (q.v.) of the sixteenth and seventeenth centuries, they relied upon it increasingly, culminating with the issue of fiat money (the value of which was determined by decree, rather than by the metallic content). This became standard by the end of the eighteenth century. Forerunners of fiat money were tokens issued on occasion in medieval cities, probably for use during sieges when coins were not available, but also available for daily transactions even in peacetime.

Credit had to be extended on occasion, even in the wars of antiquity, from the mercantile community. But it took the pressure of the military revolution in Europe during the sixteenth and seventeenth centuries to make credit the most important share of war finance. Spain's Philip II at first used foreign bills of exchange, backed ultimately by tax receipts, to maintain his forces combating the Dutch Revolt (q.v.). As the expenses of warfare grew, Philip II and his successors were forced into repeated bankruptcies. Essentially, they converted the accumulated short-term debt, *asientos*, into longer-term debt, *juros*, on which they had to pay only the interest. This eased the immediate liquidity problem of the Spanish rulers and enabled them to apply their extraordinary revenues to the next war. But used repeatedly — in 1560, 1575, 1596, 1607, 1627, 1647, and 1653 — these conversions inhibited merchants from giving credit again. During the Thirty Years' War (1618–1648) (q.v.), capital levies were imposed by both sides on cities and towns, which bore them indefinitely. The discovery that taxes collected regularly by any permanently existing governmental unit such as a city could be multiplied many times by assigning them to the service and repayment of a specific war debt (called "funded debt") laid the basis for far-reaching innovations in public finance throughout Europe in the second half of the seventeenth century. Non-Western societies were unable to imitate this practice because of the absence of credible commitment mechanisms to ensure continued debt service by the sovereign. Their failure in finance may have contributed to the rise of the West.

The "Glorious Revolution" of 1688 allowed the English Parliament to extend financial techniques previously confined to cities to an entire kingdom. Even so, modern national debt was not established until the traditional means of finance had failed in the War of the Grand Alliance (q.v.). The recoinage crisis of 1696, caused by the flight of silver from Britain to finance the war effort on the Continent, demonstrated that the British-funded debt, first held by the Bank of England established in 1694, had to be expanded. In the War of the Spanish Succession (q.v.) and thereafter, the national debt grew in each war to the extent that by the end of the eighteenth century, the British national debt far exceeded its national income. As a consequence, however, Britain won its "second Hundred Years' War" with France, and the restored Bourbon monarchy after 1815 quickly adopted the elements of British finance — a permanent national debt secured by specific taxes levied by a permanently constituted legislature.

Over the course of the nineteenth century, other emerging industrial nation-states followed suit — the United States with the Civil War (q.v.), Germany after the Franco-Prussian War (q.v.), and Japan after the Meiji Restoration in 1868 and victory in the 1895 Sino-Japanese War (q.v.). Many other states attempted to follow — tsarist Russia, Greece, and Spain to mention a few — but military defeats thwarted them.

In the twentieth century, the success of the Allies in World War I (q.v.) in mobilizing external finance, especially from the United States, stood in contrast to the experience of the Central Powers, whose domestic tax base was diminished by the war effort and whose access to foreign loans was nil. The result at the end of the war was a huge stock of inter-Allied war debts among the victors and an overwhelming stock of domestic debt owed by the separate Central Powers. Their domestic tax bases were further diminished by the terms of the peace treaties and the reparations (q.v.) demands. The refusal of the Central Powers to increase taxes to service reparations, combined with the efforts of the Allied powers to extract resources from their expanded colonial domains while reconstituting the gold standard, led to the financial collapse of the international economy in the 1930s.

The lessons learned were applied in World War II (q.v.). On the Allied side, the United States supplied war materials under the Lend-Lease Act to avoid inter-Allied debts at the end. On the Fascist side, heavy occupation taxes were levied upon each conquered country as well as levies of forced labor. At the conclusion of hostilities, the method chosen by the United States to minimize its outlay on occupation costs and reconstruction expenses led to the economic revival and miraculous export-led growth of Japan, West Germany, and Italy. Its European allies eventually learned the financial benefits of decolonization. American attempts to finance the Vietnam War (q.v.) with credit rather than taxes, however, led in 1971 to the collapse of the dollar as a standard for fixed exchange rates, which had been established after World War II. Meanwhile, the attempt of the Soviet Union to imitate the economic and financial policies of wartime Nazi Germany in its occupation zones in central and eastern Europe led ultimately to economic collapse in 1989.

Throughout the Cold War (q.v.), including both the Korean (q.v.) and Vietnam wars, the United States used its dominant economy to finance overseas bases and military actions, but relied increasingly on contributions from allies, especially Japan and Germany. These culminated in the Gulf War of 1990–1991 (q.v.), in which all outlays by the United States were covered by allied payments, reminding historians of the way the Athenian navy had been financed by the Delian League in antiquity.

LARRY NEAL

P. G. M. Dickson and J. G. Sperling, "War Finance, 1689–1714," in *The New Cambridge Modern History*, vol. 6, *The Rise of Great Britain and Russia (1688–1715/25)* (1970); Larry Neal, ed., *War Finance*, 3 vols. (1994).

War Games

The simulation of war through games is a military practice as old as organized warfare. Ancient board games — the Hindu Chaturanga, the oriental Go, and chess — all reflect societies that had maneuvering armies. Some sources also add Wei Hai, a game attributed to Sun Tzu (q.v.), the Chinese philosopher-general who wrote *The Art of War* in about 500 B.C. Wei Hai, played with colored stones representing armies, resembles modern war games, which stress the movements of large units.

In the European game of chess, the king, queen, castle, knight, bishop, and peasant pawn mirrored the world and the warfare of the era. By the seventeenth century, military chess, a German invention, appeared, and chess pieces evolved into specific battlefield figures, from marshal and colonel to captain and private. An eighteenth-century game was played on a board whose thirty-six hundred squares represented the terrain along France's northern border.

Not until the 1880s did gaming receive serious attention in the United States. The typical game of the time, played up to a level of sixteen companies, used topographical maps and colored blocks for troops. A roll of the dice decided issues that in real war would be decided at least somewhat by chance.

In 1889, at the five-year-old Naval War College in Newport, Rhode Island, the battlefield war game went to sea. The war college, which established many of the basic rules of American war gaming, assigned colors to game fleets. Blue became the permanent color of the U.S. Navy. The Royal Navy was red; the Japanese, orange. Of 136 strategic games played at the college between 1919 and 1941, 127 were played against orange.

Fletcher Pratt's Naval War Game became popular in the United States in the late 1930s, introducing a pastime that would become widespread by the 1960s. To determine whether a ship would be sunk, Pratt, a military writer, used a complex formula involving the thickness of a ship's armor, its speed, and the caliber and number of guns on each of the ships in an engagement. As proof of his formula, Pratt used the real-world fate of the *Admiral Graf Spee*, the German "pocket battleship" fatally damaged in 1939 during a running battle with three Royal Navy cruisers. "Rated on gun-power and armor," Pratt wrote, the *Graf Spee* "should have been more than a match for

the three British cruisers; but by the formula . . . they should have beaten her. They did."

For the Allies, World War II (q.v.) was not a milestone of gaming. But Japan and Germany made frequent use of gaming. In the fall of 1941, officers of the Imperial Japanese Navy played a game that climaxed in a surprise attack on Pearl Harbor. Other games covered plans for Japanese invasions from Singapore to the Philippines.

The most amazing German game was played in November 1944, when the staff of the German Fifth Panzer Army met to plan new moves in the defense of the Hurtgen Forest. The game had hardly begun, a participant remembered, "when a report was received that according to all appearances a fairly strong American attack had been launched" in an area exactly where the game was centered. Except for commanders of units under attack or directly threatened, the players continued playing, using messages from the battlefield as the basis for game moves. When players decided to throw a reserve unit into battle, the commander issued actual orders that paralleled his gaming orders. "The alerted division," according to a player, "was thereby set in movement in the shortest conceivable time. Chance had transformed a simple map exercise into stern reality." The moves in the game, reflected in the moves on the battlefield, sealed off the American penetration.

U.S. war gaming flourished during the Cold War (q.v.), which brought both civilians and military officers to highly secret games played in the Pentagon, think tanks, and academic institutions. War gaming, often aided by computers, became political-military gaming. Many players were academicians trying out theories, such as escalation and signaling — the idea that a U.S. move toward, say, more bombing would be seen not just as bombing but as a sign of impatience with secret negotiations. Mathematical models built into the games, wrote Paul Bracken, a defense analyst, "were based on an underlying blast damage calculus that had a powerful and pervasive influence on U.S. decisionmakers and their view of the entire U.S.-Soviet nuclear relationship." In other words, from models, strategists could envision real-world actions.

In the 1980s a creator of hobbyist war games began producing secret games for the Pentagon. The major one, involving nuclear confrontations between the United States and the Soviet Union, is called Strategic Analysis Simulation. Gulf Strike, a popular commercial game created in 1983, was used in January 1991 by

Players at the Naval War College in Newport, Rhode Island, set up a tactical war game in the mid-1950s.

U.S. military strategists setting up the ground war for the Persian Gulf War (q.v.). Pentagon players estimated that the ground war would go on for about ninety-six hours — almost exactly its real duration.

THOMAS B. ALLEN

Thomas B. Allen, *War Games* (1987); Peter P. Perla, *The Art of Wargaming* (1990).

War of 1812

1812–1815

The War of 1812 began after years of confrontation with Britain over that country's refusal to recognize the neutral rights of American merchant vessels and its policy of impressment. Because it was a war in which Americans sought to assert their rights and gain acceptance as an equal member of the world community, it is sometimes called the second war for American independence. Indeed, when Congress voted for war on June 18, 1812, what it sought more than anything else was respect.

Access to and control of waterways dominated the course of the war. The army's ability to operate around the Great Lakes was determined by the navy's ability to control those bodies of water: an American army under General William Henry Harrison successfully pursued and defeated the British at the Thames River only after Oliver H. Perry won control of Lake Erie in September 1813. Conversely, General Jacob Brown decided not to attack the British at Fort George, where the Niagara River empties into Lake Ontario, when he learned that he would not have the support of an American fleet under Isaac Chauncey. Although the Americans acquitted themselves well on the inland waterways, they could not compete with Britain on the open seas. Thus, the British could and did attack cities near the coast whenever they pleased.

The Treaty of Ghent officially ended the war in February 1815 with an agreement of the principle of *status quo ante bellum.* In 1814 the U.S. Army reached its peak strength of over thirty-eight thousand; only about twenty-two hundred Americans died in battle. Andrew Jackson's one-sided victory at New Orleans just as the war ended convinced many Americans of their martial superiority and helped generate a wave of nationalism. The war ushered in a new generation of political and military leadership, and it demonstrated that the United States deserved respect from Europe. It also led to one of the longest periods of uninterrupted peace in American history.

TIMOTHY D. JOHNSON

War Reporting

The idea that war news could be obtained by independent coverage rather than from government dispatches or letters from junior officers took a long time in coming. In an early attempt to collect news at the source, a Swiss newspaper, the *Zürich Zeitung*, published a report on the storming of the Bastille from its correspondent, Gottfried Ebel, on July 17, 1789, three days after the event: "One saw with amazement how on this day an almost naked and unarmed people, inflamed by boldness alone, attacked entrenched positions, armed itself with what it found, and in ten minutes conquered the first fortress of the kingdom."

When British correspondents began to follow their nation's armies in the Napoleonic Wars (see *Napoleon Bonaparte*), a quandary arose. Generals, and particularly the duke of Wellington (q.v.), did not want them around. The duke complained that in their reports they were giving away military secrets and did not allow them in his camp. As a result, there was no correspondent at Waterloo (q.v.).

Since war correspondent was a new profession, no one at first had any previous experience. The reporters were young men in search of adventure, or penny-a-liners who had previously covered the courts. No firm distinction was made between correspondent and soldier. When George Wilkins Kendall of the New Orleans *Picayune* covered the Mexican War (q.v.) in 1846, he rode into battle with McCulloch's Rangers on the Rio Grande and captured a Mexican flag.

The American Civil War (q.v.) was the first to be fully covered on both sides. The *New York Herald* alone had sixty-three men in the field. More than any other single development, the telegraph, which by then was widely used, changed war reporting. With

American war reporters rush copy down the Champs-Élysées to the press's wireless radio transmitter on the outskirts of Paris, in September 1944.

the wire came spot news — you could read what had happened yesterday. Newspapers became more competitive, and the scoop was born.

But one of the pitfalls of Civil War reporting, widespread on both sides, was a partisan slant. The correspondent became a propagandist for the army he was covering, an uncritical booster identifying with the men in the field and protective of the high command. In some cases, Civil War correspondents accepted favors and cash gifts from generals in exchange for favorable mention.

After the Civil War, with the rise in literacy and the growth of the popular press, no conflagration went unreported. In the Franco-Prussian War (q.v.), Archibald Forbes of the *London Daily News* was present at the surrender of Paris in January 1871, writing: "The whole city is haunted with the chaste odors which horse-flesh gives out in cooking . . . Half Paris seems converted into hospitals." There was an Associated Press (AP) correspondent with George Custer (q.v.) at Little Bighorn in 1876 and a *Times* correspondent with Charles George Gordon in Khartoum in 1885.

In another example of the war correspondent taking part in the action, James Creelman of the *New York*

Journal led a bayonet charge in Cuba in the Spanish-American War (q.v.) of 1898. This was also the first media-driven war, in which William Randolph Hearst and Joseph Pulitzer deliberately incited war fever as they vied to inflame their respective readers.

In World War I (q.v.), British and French censorship at first frustrated the best efforts of correspondents. Horatio Kitchener (q.v.), the British secretary for war, did not allow correspondents in the field. Those who showed up were arrested on sight. The French prevented them from visiting the front lines.

As a result, until 1917 many American correspondents covered the war from the German side, where they had better access. The lack of news from the Allied side distorted the coverage and did not give the American public an accurate picture of the war. Eventually the policy changed, and correspondents were taken to the front, wearing uniforms with green armbands.

One of my own experiences with censorship came during the Six-Day War (see *Arab-Israeli Wars*) in 1967, when I was clearing a story with the Israeli censor in Jerusalem, who read it and commented: "Banal but unexceptionable."

Clever correspondents occasionally used homemade codes to get past censors. On July 17, 1936, Lester Ziffren of the United Press Madrid Bureau filed a bulletin announcing the start of the Spanish civil war (q.v.) that began this way:

MOTHERS EVERLASTINGLY LINGERING ILLNESS LIKELY LARYNGITIS AUNT FLORA OUGHT RETURN EVEN IF GOES NORTH LATER . . .

The bulletin in full (formed from the first letter of each word) was translated as: MELILLA FOREIGN LEGION REVOLTED MARTIAL LAW DECLARED.

Sometimes a story earned expulsion. Frank Kluckhohn of the *New York Times* was ousted from Spain for reporting that German Junker bombers flown by German pilots had landed in Seville in August 1936. This was the first hard evidence of Adolf Hitler's (q.v.) aid to Francisco Franco.

Partisan reporting was again the rule in Spain, which was seen by those correspondents covering the Republican side as the place where fascism could be stopped. The *New York Times* prudently assigned a correspondent to each side, each of whom promoted the views of the people he was covering.

In my own case, I found that it was difficult not to become emotionally involved. Covering the war in Algeria, I saw some French Foreign Legion troops kill civilians in a village and I developed an anti-French bias. In the Six-Day War, I was with the Israeli brigade that took the old city of Jerusalem. When we came to the Wailing Wall, from which the Israelis had been barred since 1948, a soldier standing next to me, overcome with emotion, removed his helmet and kissed the wall. A Jordanian sniper shot him in the head and killed him. It takes inner vigilance to remain impartial in such situations.

In World War II (q.v.), as an improvement over censorship, the Allies developed the pool system, under which one reporter was allowed to witness the action, representing all the press. Thus AP's Joe Rosenthal was the pool photographer at Iwo Jima (q.v.) and took the picture of the raising of the flag.

The pool system was frustrating and sometimes led to poor reporting. The correspondents were expected to be cheerleaders, an arm of the war effort. Sometimes they were asked to suppress stories, as in the case when General George Patton (q.v.) slapped two soldiers in Sicily, or the failed Canadian raid at Dieppe on August 19, 1942. The best account of the Dieppe raid came from a German correspondent, who wrote: "As executed, the venture mocked all rules of military logic and strategy."

In spite of these restrictions, some of the great dramas of the war produced superb reporting. Alexander Werth of the Kemsley Group wrote from Stalingrad (q.v.): "And there seemed a rough but divine justice in those frozen cesspools . . . those horse's bones, and those starved yellow corpses."

William L. Laurence of the *New York Times* was aboard the B-29 that dropped the second atomic bomb on August 9, 1945, at Nagasaki — the only reporter ever to produce an eyewitness account of the destruction of a target by atom bomb. "The boiling pillar of many colors protruded through the white clouds," he wrote, "giving the appearance of a monstrous prehistoric creature with a ruff around its neck, a fleecy ruff extending as far as the eye could see."

World War II also saw the rise of the first soldier's advocate, Ernie Pyle, who took the part of the dogface against the high command. Pyle died from a sniper's bullet on a Pacific island. In deference to his work, Ernest Hemingway once called himself "old Ernie Hemorrhoid, the poor man's Pyle."

The long tradition of the war correspondent as cheerleader was buried in Vietnam (q.v.), where a band of young reporters in the early 1960s wrote that the United States was supporting a corrupt regime that did not have the will to fight. Against government pressure and accusations of near-treason, these correspondents continued to report the war as they saw it.

The tradition of personal involvement was also laid to rest, for when Peter Arnett of the Associated Press saw a Buddhist set himself on fire in 1963, he said: "I could have prevented that immolation by rushing at him and kicking the gasoline away. As a human being I wanted to, as a reporter I couldn't."

When Harrison E. Salisbury of the *New York Times* went to Hanoi in 1966 and reported that American pilots were bombing civilian targets, the Pentagon called him "Ho Chi Salisbury." Although the Pulitzer jury for international reporting voted four to one to give him the prize, the Advisory Board, which had final say, turned him down.

War correspondents have been accused and have indeed accused themselves of thriving on and profiting from death and destruction, but they have also taken the risks that go with the territory — in Vietnam, forty-five correspondents were killed.

I would not exactly call war reporting a noble calling — it is a distressing job, one that can lead to permanent combat fatigue — but I would agree with Herbert Matthews that "if you have not seen a battle, your education has been somewhat neglected for after all, war has ever been one of the primary functions of mankind, and unless you see men fight you miss something fundamental."

TED MORGAN

John Hohenberg, *Foreign Correspondence: The Great Reporters and Their Times* (1967); Phillip Knightley, *The First Casualty* (1975).

Washington, George

1732–1798, American Revolution General and President of the United States

From boyhood, George Washington had an intense desire to be a soldier. Succeeding his half brother, Lawrence, as adjutant of the Virginia militia in 1752, the six foot three inch Washington won praise by carrying a letter from the colony's royal governor across rain-swollen, ice-filled rivers and through the barren winter woods, warning the French to stop encroaching on British territory in the Ohio Valley. In the spring of 1754, as a lieutenant colonel, he and his men fired the first shots in what soon became the Seven Years' War (q.v.). After barely surviving British commander in chief Edward Braddock's defeat (1755), Washington spent three inglorious years guarding the western frontier, acquiring a bitterly realistic view of the American militia — and absorbing the Indians' tactics of surprise and ambush. In 1759, with victory and the French expulsion from Canada, he married Martha Custis, one of the wealthiest women in Virginia, and seemingly lost interest in military matters. But when Washington posed for a 1772 portrait by Charles Willson Peale, he put on his old uniform.

The upheaval of the American Revolution (q.v.) found Washington still Virginia's best-known soldier — and Massachusetts, eager to draw the largest of the thirteen colonies into the fray, proposed him as the commander of the embryo American army. In the next seven years, Washington won only three clearcut victories as a battlefield commander: at Trenton, Princeton, and Yorktown (q.v.). In seven other encounters — Long Island, Harlem Heights, White Plains, Fort Washington, Brandywine, Germantown, and Monmouth — he either was defeated or at best could claim a draw. He never won a major battle. Trenton was essentially a raid; Princeton was little more than a large skirmish; and Yorktown was a siege in which the blockading French fleet was an essential component of the victory.

Most contemporary Americans, even if unacquainted with these statistics, are inclined to see Washington as a figurehead, a somewhat empty-headed symbol whose dedication inspired his soldiers to endure starvation and neglect and persevere to victory. Both the statistics and this surprisingly widespread opinion are misleading. Without Washington's ability to think strategically in a crisis, the Revolution would have expired in 1776. As the American army reeled from defeat to retreat to defeat, he jettisoned the prevailing theory that the war would be won in one big battle — "a general action." On the contrary, he decided the Americans should "protract the war." He also scuttled Congress's reliance on militia. He demanded an army enlisted for the duration — one that would be able to "look the enemy in the face" and inspire the militia to turn out if they were needed.

Washington applied this new strategy to rescue prostrate New Jersey at the end of 1776. With his last twenty-five hundred ragged regulars, he smashed the Hessian garrison at Trenton and a few days later wheeled around the British flank to dispatch their rear at Princeton, forcing the mortified Royal Army to evacuate two-thirds of the state. When the British invaded from Canada in 1777, Washington shipped some of his best troops to the Northern Army, encouraging the militia to turn out and help force the invaders to surrender at Saratoga (q.v.). When the British shifted their main effort to the South, Washington once more sent a hefty portion of his dwindling supply of regulars to the region. A series of shattering defeats — the surrender of one army at Charleston, the rout of another force at Camden — would have shaken the nerve of a lesser man. But Washington responded by sending his best lieutenant, Nathanael Greene (q.v.), to apply the strategy once more. It paid off when a combination of regulars and militia destroyed the attacking British army at Cowpens in January 1781, and Greene built on this victory to drive the British out of the South. When their army retreated to the cul-de-sac of Yorktown, Washington pounced, and the war was over.

Washington handily defeated several threats to his authority as commander in chief. In 1778 the Conway Cabal, led by Horatio Gates, the victor at Saratoga, collapsed almost the moment he challenged it. Washington also rejected General Charles Lee's plan to disband the Continental army and fight a purely guerrilla war. Instead, he "stayed in the game" — one of his favorite phrases — letting time and distance slowly demoralize his opponents.

Yet Washington was no Fabius. Audacity runs like a bright thread through his career, from the all-or-nothing Christmas night attack on Trenton to the comeback Battle of Germantown in 1777, three weeks after the British thought they had thrashed him for good at the Brandywine. Even in winter quarters at Valley Forge, he retained the initiative against the British in Philadelphia, constantly skirmishing with their patrols and foraging parties, potshotting their sentries — and honeycombing them with spies.

Throughout the war, Washington was his own intelligence chief, running a dozen different networks simultaneously, using invisible ink, mail drops, double agents, and many other tricks of the modern espionage trade. In July 1780, for instance, the British commander, Sir Henry Clinton, decided to launch a preemptive strike on the French army that had just landed in Newport. It might well have succeeded — if Washington had not distracted him by allowing a British spy to capture some "secret" papers revealing American plans for an attack on New York (see *Ruses/Disinformation*).

Washington managed all these feats while maintaining a respectful attitude toward his appallingly inept political masters in the Continental Congress. He also displayed superb diplomatic skills in dealing with foreign volunteers, state governors, militia leaders, and his French allies. When his unpaid, outraged army tried to make him a king in 1783, he stopped the so-called Newburgh Conspiracy with a moving appeal to their patriotism and honor. Reflecting on his experience as army commander, he urged a stronger federal government and eventually presided at the Constitutional Convention of 1787. Washington proved his dedication to a government of free people by serving with distinction as the nation's first president (1789–1796).

THOMAS FLEMING

Waterloo, Battle of

June 18, 1815

When Napoleon (q.v.) returned to Paris from Elba in March 1815, the allied powers pledged 600,000 troops to crush him. The French emperor raised 360,000 men, but his field army hardly totaled 125,000.

An Anglo-Netherlands-German army of about 100,000 men under the duke of Wellington (q.v.) and a Prussian army of 120,000 troops under Marshal Gebhard von Blücher concentrated their armies around Brussels, awaiting the Austrian and Russian armies on the Rhine. Napoleon decided to strike immediately. He planned to separate and defeat Wellington and Blücher in detail. On June 16, he engaged and defeated the Prussians at Ligny, but Marshal Michel Ney, advancing to turn Blücher's flank, was contained by Wellington at Quatre Bras.

On June 17, Napoleon sent Marshal Emmanuel Grouchy to pursue the retreating Prussians while he joined Ney's troops and tracked Wellington to Mont-St.-Jean, south of Waterloo. Wellington decided to fight there if one Prussian corps would reinforce him; Blücher promised two corps.

Wellington deployed his troops on the reverse slopes to take advantage of the defensive terrain. On the morning of June 18, Napoleon delayed the attack until 11:30 A.M. because of the heavy rain of June 17. Napoleon ordered a feint attack on his left flank, hoping Wellington would shift troops from

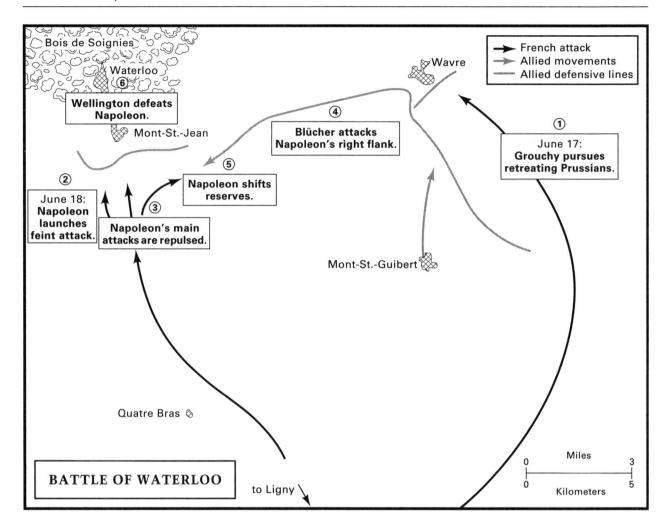

Bois de Soignies

Waterloo
⑥
Wellington defeats Napoleon.
Mont-St.-Jean

⑤
Napoleon shifts reserves.

④
Blücher attacks Napoleon's right flank.

Wavre

➤ French attack
➤ Allied movements
— Allied defensive lines

①
June 17:
Grouchy pursues retreating Prussians.

②
June 18:
Napoleon launches feint attack.

③
Napoleon's main attacks are repulsed.

Mont-St.-Guibert

Quatre Bras

BATTLE OF WATERLOO

to Ligny

Miles
0 — 3
0 — 5
Kilometers

his center. The British general was not deceived.

At 1:30 P.M. Napoleon launched the main attack on the British center. The French advance, poorly organized and unsupported by cavalry, was repulsed. Two hours later, Ney incorrectly assumed Wellington's army was withdrawing and launched an assault of five thousand cavalry without infantry support; the British infantry quickly formed into twenty squares and beat off each attack.

Grouchy's corps failed to contain the Prussians, so the first of Blücher's troops attacked the French right flank at about 4:30 P.M. As more Prussians arrived, Napoleon shifted his reserve to protect the right flank. By 6:30 P.M., Ney, employing both infantry and cavalry, made progress in the center and appealed for reinforcement, but Napoleon refused until his right flank could be stabilized. Finally, at 7:30 P.M. Napoleon unleashed the Old Guard, only to see it repulsed

by artillery and musketry. Blücher's army joined Wellington, and the French were driven off the battlefield. Allied losses totaled almost nineteen thousand, and the French suffered twenty-five thousand casualties and eight thousand captured. Waterloo ended Napoleon's military career and the Napoleonic Wars.

DONALD D. HORWARD

Wavell, Archibald

1883–1950, British General and Viceroy of India

Archie Wavell was famous for his silences and for being sacked from high command three times. In World War II (q.v.), it was his misfortune to fight a "poor man's war" when the ill-equipped Allies were disadvantaged. Between 1940 and 1943, Wavell directed fourteen campaigns. He was victorious against the Italians and the Vichy French, but against the Germans and Japanese he experienced defeat and humiliation.

Wavell had fought in the Boer War (q.v.) and the North West Frontier. In 1915, he lost his left eye in the trenches. In the vanguard of military mechanization, he pleaded the cause of the tank (q.v.) against the diehards who favored the horse. Wavell was also a military historian and an eminently quotable one. He divided generals into "great captains" and those of more average skills, whom he called *"les bons Généraux ordinaires."*

Military history taught Wavell the value of guerrilla warfare. When GOC Middle East, he encouraged the Long Range Desert Group and was impressed by Orde Wingate's ideas. He backed the formation of the Jewish Night Squads in Palestine and the Gideon Force in Abyssinia. In 1943 Wavell rescued Wingate from obscurity and supported the creation of the Chindits, special forces who conducted long-range penetration raids behind Japanese lines.

Wavell made mistakes. It was his advice to Winston Churchill (q.v.) in 1941 that led to the disastrous Greek campaign. When commander in chief in India, he underestimated Japanese military capabilities in Burma. One consequence was that his field commander, Lieutenant General William Slim (q.v.), had to retreat the length of Burma, over a thousand miles — the longest retreat in British military history.

Wavell could not handle politicians. Churchill sacked him twice, and his successor, Clement Attlee, dismissed him as viceroy of India, where he had served from 1943 to 1947.

ERIC MORRIS

Weather in War

For countless generations, weather has influenced the planning and conduct of military and naval campaigns. In his instructions to his generals, Frederick the Great (q.v.) wrote, "It is always necessary to shape operation plans . . . on estimates of the weather." Since soldiers and sailors in combat have little or no protection from the weather, commanders have often scheduled their campaigns for those periods when storms and weather were considered less likely to disrupt operations.

For centuries, commanders conducted their campaigns during seasons that allowed their soldiers and horses to forage for food and fodder. The onset of winter invariably halted campaigns and often resulted in armies' returning home or seeking shelter for the winter. Since armies lacked massive supply systems, commanders had little choice but to schedule their campaigns to take advantage of harvests. Napoleon (q.v.), for example, timed his invasion of Russia in 1812 so his soldiers could forage successfully. Though the emperor planned on using larger supply trains than in previous campaigns, he knew his huge forces could not carry all the food and fodder they required. Despite these preparations, Napoleon eventually lost more men to weather conditions, famine, and disease than to the Russian army.

The chance factor of weather has also influenced the result of individual battles. Weather played a key role, for example, in the Battle of Waterloo (q.v.), for the battlefield became so soaked by heavy rains that Napoleon delayed his customary early attack so the ground would dry enough for cannonballs to ricochet and for cavalry to have secure footing. That delay of only a few hours provided Marshal Gebhard von Blücher sufficient time to rush three Prussian corps forward and strike Napoleon's flank.

Throughout history, commanders have sometimes surprised their opponents by attacking when the season or weather caused them to lower their guard. During the winter of 1776, the British scattered their army in the American colonies in small garrisons, and on December 25, George Washington (q.v.) surprised the Hessian (q.v.) garrison at Trenton, New Jersey. He managed to get sufficient forces across the Delaware River, even though the weather was so severe that it kept some units from crossing. At the cost of four wounded, the Americans captured 948 Hessian soldiers and killed or wounded another 114.

During World War II (q.v.), weather forecasts played a decisive role in the scheduling of the amphibious landing in Normandy (see *D-Day*). The invasion was initially scheduled for June 5, but an unfavorable weather report anticipated thoroughly nasty seas and gales of up to forty-five miles an hour. A break in the weather on the next day enabled the Allies to land and, according to Dwight D. Eisenhower (q.v.), proved "the existence of an almighty and merciful God." An unanticipated benefit of the bad weather was that it helped the Allies achieve almost complete surprise.

In the Ardennes in December 1944, the Germans also used the weather to their advantage. Adolf Hitler (q.v.) coordinated the launching of the Battle of the

Bulge (q.v.) very carefully and did not initiate the attack until he knew stormy weather would cause the Allied ground troops to lower their guard and the Allied air forces to fly for fewer hours. Because of the extremely cold weather, some of the American commanders had left minimum forces in the forward foxholes of the previously quiet sector and let some of their soldiers find shelter in nearby houses. When the skies finally cleared, however, defeat of the German forces soon followed.

Weather has had a strategic effect, as well as an operational and tactical impact. It played a decisive role in the Mongol (q.v.) invasion of Japan in 1281 when Kublai Khan (q.v.) attacked Kyushu with some forty-four hundred ships and 140,000 troops. Before the entire invading army landed, a typhoon struck the coast of Kyushu and destroyed half of the ships and men. Most of the Mongols remaining on Kyushu were slaughtered by the Japanese or drowned as they attempted to flee on the small vessels that escaped destruction. The Japanese viewed the typhoon as a "divine wind" *(kamikaze)* sent by the gods to save Japan and concluded that Japan was a "divinely protected land."

Storms also greatly influenced the fate of the Spanish Armada (q.v.) in 1588. Weather affected the naval campaign early, for shortly after the Spanish fleet departed Lisbon in May 1588, a storm scattered the Armada; it took a month to reassemble the ships and to recondition them. Favorable winds carried the Armada through the English Channel, but skillful English fighting forced the ships to make their way into the North Sea. After the Spanish passed by the northern coast of Scotland and entered the Atlantic, thirty-five to forty ships foundered in heavy storms, and another twenty smashed against the rocky shore. The victors inscribed on one of their victory medals *Flavit Deus, et dissipati sunt* (God blew and they were scattered).

ROBERT A. DOUGHTY

Weinberger Doctrine

The Weinberger Doctrine was first made public by U.S. Secretary of Defense Caspar Weinberger on November 28, 1984. In a speech entitled "The Uses of Military Power" delivered before the National Press Club in Washington, D.C., Weinberger presented the doctrine in response to an ongoing debate between the secretary of defense and the Pentagon on the one hand, and Secretary of State George P. Shultz, the State Department, and members of the National Security Council on the other, concerning the presence of American troops in Lebanon and their contemplated use in Central America (in the civil wars in Nicaragua and San Salvador).

The proximate cause for the speech was the bombing of the U.S. Marine barracks at Beirut airport on October 23, 1983, a humiliating disaster in which 241 marines perished. This ill-fated U.S. peacekeeping mission in Lebanon had been undertaken despite the vigorous opposition of the secretary of defense and the Joint Chiefs of Staff, who argued that its purpose was never clearly defined and that the chaotic, violent situation in Lebanon could not be brought under control by any outside force. When dropped into the middle of this turmoil, the marine contingent would only, they insisted, become a convenient and prominent target for the various factions in the civil war.

The Weinberger address followed President Ronald Reagan's decision to withdraw the U.S. Marines from Lebanon and was therefore intended to summarize the lessons learned from this debacle in the hope that similar improper uses of American forces could be prevented in the future.

The more remote impetus behind the promulgation of the Weinberger Doctrine was the U.S. military's failure to win the war in Vietnam (q.v.). The Weinberger Doctrine reflects the collective lessons of the Vietnam War learned by the U.S. military with its resolution to avoid such quagmires in the future. All these lessons were distilled into the six points comprising the Weinberger Doctrine. They are as follows:

1. The United States should not commit forces to combat unless the vital national interests of the United States or its allies are involved.
2. U.S. troops should only be committed wholeheartedly and with the clear intention of winning. Otherwise, troops should not be committed.
3. U.S. combat troops should be committed only with clearly defined political and military objectives and with the capacity to accomplish those objectives.
4. The relationship between the objectives and the size and composition of the forces committed should be continually reassessed and adjusted if necessary.
5. U.S. troops should not be committed to battle

The Six Criteria of the Weinberger Doctrine: From Vietnam to Bosnia

Criterion	Vietnam	Grenada	Lebanon	Central America	Panama	Gulf War	Somalia	Bosnia
1. Vital U.S. interests involved	no	no	no	no	no	yes	no	no
2. Commitment to victory	no	yes	no	no	yes	yes	no	no
3. Clearly defined political and military objectives	no	yes	no	no	yes	yes	yes, at first — later, no	no
4. Continual reassessment of troop/objective ratio and of costs	no	yes	yes	yes	yes	yes	yes	yes
5. U.S. government mobilized public opinion before action	no	no	no	no	no	yes	yes, at first	no
6. Intervention/war was last resort	no	no	no	no	no	no	no	no
Decision for military intervention	yes	yes	yes, at first	no	yes	yes	yes	—
Success or failure	failure	success	failure	—	success	success	initial success	—

without a "reasonable assurance" of the support of U.S. public opinion and Congress.

6. The commitment of U.S. troops should be considered only as a last resort.

Although these six caveats make sense at first glance, they become problematic upon closer examination. First of all, it is not always clear exactly what constitutes a vital U.S. interest. Obviously, what is vital to some is not to others, and on some occasions, it may be wise to commit troops in order to deter an enemy from further aggression *before* truly vital interests are involved. Next, although the intention of winning should be present whenever relevant, not all wars can be won at a reasonable cost. The demand for clear political and military objectives is laudable, but one's original political and military objectives will often change once a battle or war has begun.

Furthermore, the third point contradicts the fifth point: the more ambiguous the objectives, the easier it is to mobilize a consensus. The continual reassessment of forces in relation to their objectives is essential, but also implies that if the cost becomes excessive, it makes sense to abort a mission (which contradicts item 2).

The fifth point, however, reflects the most important lesson of the Vietnam War: the folly of fighting without the support of American public opinion. Nevertheless, this point is as problematic as the first four. If vital U.S. interests are involved, the president might try to avoid a critical loss of time by committing troops to action before U.S. public support has been consolidated. Moreover, an initially supportive public can subsequently come to oppose military intervention after initial casualties and military setbacks have occurred. A major war, as Winston Churchill (q.v.) once commented, cannot be waged according to every fluctuation of a public opinion poll. Finally, it is unclear exactly what the last resort is; and, worse still, waiting for the last resort before taking action may be worse in the end.

In the years following the announcement of these guidelines, the United States has used force when no vital interests were at stake (in Bosnia), when political objectives were not clearly defined (in Somalia), and not necessarily as a last resort, as in the Gulf War (q.v.) (see table). In the final analysis, the paramount concern of the secretary of defense and the Pentagon in designing the Weinberger Doctrine was to allow the United States to fight only under conditions that would heavily favor and, if possible, guarantee success. Thus, *success*, not strict adherence to the six points, is what has mattered most.

In view of the United States' reluctance to commit troops to Bosnia or Rwanda, or its decision to withdraw its troops from Somalia (March 1994), there is no doubt that the logic behind the principles of the Weinberger Doctrine is still very much in place. Despite its imperfections and internal contradictions, the Weinberger Doctrine should continue to provide valuable guidance to U.S. civilian and military decision-makers in the future. If taken to its logical conclusion, the

Weinberger Doctrine provides persuasive reasons for the United States to avoid the commitment of troops to conflicts in which no direct vital interests are at stake. But since the United States also takes pride in its moral and ethical positions, we must consider Secretary of State Shultz's words of caution: "A great power cannot free itself so easily from the burden of choice. It must bear responsibility for the consequences of its inaction as well as for the consequences of its action."

MICHAEL I. HANDEL

Wellington, Sir Arthur Wellesley, Duke of

1769–1852, *British General and Statesman*

Sir Arthur Wellesley, one of England's greatest generals, received little formal military education. However, through a series of purchased promotions and judiciously applied family influence, he advanced through the ranks. By 1794, he served in the Netherlands as a lieutenant colonel of the Thirty-third Foot.

In 1796, when he accompanied his regiment to India, Wellesley began a program of self-education, especially in military tactics and strategy. Supported by his brother, Richard Wellesley, governor-general of India, he reorganized the commissariat and served as a divisional commander in the Mysore War; in 1803 he took the offensive and won the Battle of Assaye, although outnumbered seven thousand to forty thousand. Two months later at Argaum, facing thirty thousand of the finest native troops in India with less than eleven thousand men, he was forced to abandon the archaic infantry doctrine of western Europe that denied infantrymen the use of cover. To protect his troops from the enemy artillery, he ordered them to take cover or lie down for protection; this tactic proved highly successful and would become a characteristic of his future battles.

Wellesley returned to England in 1805 and served in the raid on Copenhagen two years later. When the French seized Portugal and occupied Spain in 1808, the Spanish changed sides, and Wellington landed a small army in Portugal and marched on Lisbon to confront a French army. Employing the tactics he had pioneered in India, he deployed his troops on the reverse slopes of hills and other topographic features to conceal them. When the French attacked, he surprised them with murderous firepower delivered from three lines of infantrymen. The French were decisively defeated at Vimeiro, and within two weeks negotiations had been completed for the withdrawal of the French army from Portugal.

Recalled to England, Wellesley returned to defend Portugal in April 1809. Within a month, he reorganized his army and took the offensive. Marching 130 miles, he slipped across the Douro River, surprised a French army at Oporto, and chased it from Portugal, inflicting five thousand causalities.

With Portugal liberated, Wellesley led his troops into Spain to cooperate with a Spanish army. Advancing toward Madrid, he encountered the French at Talavera, where he again deployed his forces to take advantage of the terrain. With the failure of the Spanish to support him, Wellesley, although victorious, retired into Portugal, convinced that the Spanish were incapable of joint operations at this juncture of the war.

In the fall of 1809, Wellesley, now Viscount Wellington, embarked on a defensive strategy that would revolutionize warfare. Convinced that Portugal could be mobilized and defended against the French, Wellington resurrected the Portuguese army and placed it under British officers; the militia was called up, and the *ordenanza*, all able-bodied men ages sixteen to sixty, was mobilized. The major frontier fortresses were repaired and resupplied, all invasion roads were destroyed, boats on the major rivers were registered for removal, and all means of transportation were withdrawn from the threatened areas. In effect, with the support of the Portuguese government, Wellington implemented the "scorched earth policy" as a national strategy for survival. Portuguese who ignored these orders were executed.

In addition, Wellington ordered the construction of the Lines of Torres Vedras across the Lisbon peninsula to protect the capital and the embarkation of his army, if necessary. As one of the earliest experiments in defense-in-depth, it proved to be crucial in the repulse of the French in October 1810. The mobilization of Portugal was a monumental achievement; it saved Portugal, encouraged continued Spanish resistance, and provided a sanctuary from which Wellington's army could attack the French in Spain.

Once the French had been driven from Portugal, Wellington besieged and captured the two main fortresses on the route into Spain — Ciudad Rodrigo and Badajoz — preparatory for the invasion of Spain. In the spring of 1812 he took the war to the French. Invading Spain, he attacked and defeated the French at Salamanca, inflicting almost thirteen thousand casualties. He temporarily liberated Madrid by this bold stroke and forced the French to retreat from Andalucía, thereby freeing all of southern Spain.

Although he retired to the safety of Portugal when the French forces united in late 1812, the following spring he invaded Spain for the last time. Supported by a massive flanking army to the north, Wellington drove the French armies back to Vitoria, where his forces united to win a climactic battle and captured the enemy baggage train. Once the last French strongholds in Spain were subdued, Wellington invaded France and chased the remnants of the French army to Toulouse, where he won the last battle of the Peninsular War.

A superb strategist, a master of tactics, and an astute politician, Wellington employed many of the same revolutionary "principles of war" that Napoleon (q.v.) pioneered. In addition, his battlefield instincts — his charisma, his judgment and composure under fire, his determination and focus, his courage and confidence — made him a worthy opponent of Napoleon and his marshals. No general in Europe other than Napoleon had more influence in determining strategy — both national and operational — than Wellington. His strategy in the Iberian Peninsula, seconded by the sacrifices of the Portuguese and Spanish people, eventually cost the French over 300,000 men and sapped the strength of Napoleon's empire.

Wellington, the "Iron Duke," fought his last battle at Waterloo (q.v.) in June 1815. Appointed to command the joint forces of England and the Netherlands, Wellington cooperated with Prussian forces near Brussels to oppose Napoleon's Armée du Nord. Containing the French left wing at Quatre Bras while the Prussians were crushed at Ligny on June 16, he retired to a position before Waterloo. On June 18, in the decisive battle of the Napoleonic Wars, Wellington repulsed the French attacks until the Prussian army arrived to ensure the final victory.

Wellington later served as a diplomat (1815–1828), as prime minister (1828–1830), and as statesman and commander of the army (1830–1852).

DONALD D. HORWARD

Paddy Griffith, ed., *Wellington as a Commander* (1983); Donald D. Horward, "Wellington as a Strategist," in *Wellington* (1990); Jac Weller, *Wellington in the Peninsula* (1962).

Westmoreland, William

1914– , U.S. General

After graduating from West Point and serving with the paratroops in both World War II (q.v.) and the Korean War (q.v.), General William Westmoreland arrived in Saigon, South Vietnam, in January 1964, and became commander of Military Assistance Command, Vietnam (MACV) in June of that year. He held that position for nearly four years, during which American forces in South Vietnam increased from about 20,000 men to over 500,000, and he directed the American ground effort until March 1968. The controversy over his strategy and tactics continues to this day.

Recently opened documents show that the Joint Chiefs of Staff and commander in chief, Pacific (CINCPAC) — Westmoreland's superiors in the chain of command — asked him to begin planning American ground deployments in August 1964, after the Tonkin Gulf incidents, and by March of 1965 he had laid out several courses of large-scale U.S. action to deal with various contingencies, including a North Vietnamese invasion of South Vietnam. On June 7, 1965, he formally requested new deployments amounting to forty-four U.S. and third-country battalions, signaling the beginning of an active American ground combat role. Until well into 1966, deployments seem to have proceeded as rapidly as logistics would permit, and American forces grew to nearly 500,000 by late 1967.

As Westmoreland himself made clear in his memoirs, he wanted American forces to focus upon the destruction of Viet Cong and North Vietnamese main-force units, while leaving the struggle against Viet Cong guerrillas and the security of villages — in his eyes, a secondary problem — to the South Vietnamese. He essentially regarded the war as a conventional struggle, and, like his superiors, sought to end the insurgency by destroying North Vietnam's will and capability to fight. He preferred to fight the enemy in remote areas near the borders of South Vietnam, rather than expose the civilian population to massive American firepower. Helped by an aggressive North Vietnamese strategy, Westmoreland succeeded in inflicting substantial casualties on North Vietnamese units in a number of major battles beginning in late 1965, but the enemy continued to control the tempo of the conflict and to inflict increasing casualties on American forces. Many major American search-and-destroy operations made only limited contact with the enemy, and the South Vietnamese made little progress toward the pacification of the countryside. Meanwhile, the enemy built up forces at least as rapidly as the United States.

By the spring of 1967, Westmoreland was pushing for a deployment of 600,000 to 700,000 troops, and for armed moves to engage enemy forces in their sanctuaries in Cambodia, Laos, and North Vietnam. The Johnson administration denied these requests, but Westmoreland continued to hope that they would eventually be met. In late 1967, he returned to the United States to assure the American people that they were, indeed, winning the war. Back in Vietnam, he concentrated American forces at Khe Sanh, near the Laotian border, where he believed the North Vietnamese planned a decisive battle. The enemy responded to the concentration of American forces by launching the countrywide Tet offensive (q.v.) in late January 1968.

The offensive failed militarily despite enormous casualties, but Westmoreland — prompted by Earle Wheeler, chairman of the Joint Chiefs of Staff — now argued that the new situation required the additional 206,000 troops he had long wanted in order to undertake more offensive operations. After a long reevaluation of the war in Washington, the administration denied most of the request, and on March 23, President Lyndon Johnson announced that Westmoreland would become chief of staff of the army.

In 1982, Westmoreland burst into the news again, when a CBS documentary claimed that he had insisted in 1967 that CIA intelligence estimates of Viet Cong strength be reduced, in order to imply that the United States was winning the war. Westmoreland filed a libel suit against CBS. In February 1985, after the defense called retired colonel Gains Hawkins, who testified that the general had indeed ordered him to reduce his own estimates of Viet Cong strength even before the controversy with the CIA, Westmoreland dropped the suit but claimed he had been vindicated.

Westmoreland's strategy remains the subject of heated debate. Critics suggest that he misunderstood the nature of the war, which required small-unit pacification operations rather than large-scale, main force attacks. Others continue to endorse his strategy, arguing that the civilian-imposed limits on operations (many of which the Nixon administration later lifted) led to its failure. In retrospect, Westmoreland's experience reflects a more profound dilemma: the problems faced by the United States in fighting a limited war on difficult Asian terrain as an exercise in containment. Historians may eventually conclude that no American strategy was likely to succeed.

DAVID KAISER

Westphalia, Peace of

Representatives of 194 European rulers, great and small, gathered at Münster and Osnabrück in Westphalia between spring 1643 and autumn 1648 to end the Thirty Years' War (q.v.). They resolved all the purely German problems first: the Holy Roman Emperor granted a large degree of sovereignty to all territorial rulers, a general amnesty to all outlawed princes, and toleration for both Calvinism and Lutheranism within the empire. They also abolished the Edict of Restitution. The participants further decreed that any change to the religious settlement could be achieved only through the "amicable composition" of the unequal Catholic and Protestant blocs, not by a simple majority.

These concessions did not lead to universal peace, however, because of the need to satisfy interested foreign powers. Eventually, in January 1648, Philip IV of Spain signed a peace that ended the Dutch Revolt (q.v.) by recognizing the Dutch Republic as independent and liberalizing trade between the Netherlands and the Iberian world. In August, Sweden made a separate peace in return for extensive territories in northern Germany, representation in the imperial legislature, and a war indemnity of five million talers. France, for its part, gained certain rights and territories in Alsace and Lorraine (October).

The Westphalian settlement, negotiated by the largest peace conference ever assembled to that date, inaugurated a new international order in Europe. A Swedish diplomat at the congress complained that "[Now] the first rule of politics here is that the security of all depends upon the equilibrium of the individuals. When one ruler begins to become powerful, ... the others place themselves, through unions or alliances, into the opposite balance in order to maintain the equipoise." This new European balance of power, with its fulcrum resting in a permanently fragmented Germany, proved so successful that no further war broke out in central Europe until 1740 (see *Frederick the Great*).

GEOFFREY PARKER

William I (the Conqueror)

1028?–1087, *Norman King of England*

An illegitimate son — hence known to contemporaries as William the Bastard — William was just a boy when he succeeded his father as duke of Normandy in 1035 (see *Normans*). His first achievement was to survive. He was nearly overwhelmed by a coalition of Norman rebels, and he owed his victory at the Battle of Val-ès-Dunes (1047) to aid from King Henry I of France. But in the 1050s King Henry switched sides and led several invasions of Normandy in support of rebels or in alliance with Count Geoffrey Martel of Anjou. In this hard school William learned the basic arts of war, capturing castles by blockade and defending his territory by shadowing and harassing invading armies.

In 1060 both Henry I and Geoffrey Martel died. The defensive first phase of William's military career ended, and the expansionist second phase began. He conquered the county of Maine and then turned his eyes to the greatest military enterprise of his life. By August 1066 he was ready to invade England. Had he sailed then, his landing would have been opposed by King Harold's naval and land forces, but not until late September did he cross the Channel. This delay enabled him to make an unopposed landing at Pevensey; by then Harold was in the north confronting — and at Stamford Bridge defeating — King Harold Hardraada of Norway. But if William was to make gains commensurate with the costs already incurred, he had to score a major success. His 1066 strategy was therefore a battle-seeking one — probably for the first time in his life. By ravaging Sussex he drew Harold south again and then by good reconnaissance — always one of his priorities — he seized the tactical initiative, forcing Harold to stand and fight. In the Battle of Hastings (October 14, 1066) (q.v.) William himself came close to death, but in the end it was Harold who was killed. William then seized Dover before embarking on the destructive march that soon brought the remaining English leaders to recognize him as king (December 1066). But it was to take another five years to complete the conquest in the teeth of a widespread, if ill-coordinated, resistance movement. As his castle-building program shows, his strategic priority was to control the major towns and the roads between them. He judged successfully when to be merciful and when to be ruthless. Where resistance burned most fiercely, in the north, he adopted the sternest method, the 1069–1070 "Harrying of the North" — the system-atic ravaging of an entire region, turning it into a wasteland and forcing its population to flee or starve.

In the third phase of his career, William was again forced back onto the defensive as he fought to retain his vastly extended empire, a task that grew harder in the face of challenges from the new rulers of France and Anjou. Despite setbacks at Dol (1076) and Gerberoi (1079) on the borders of Normandy, he died still holding all that he had conquered. Although rightly famous above all for his dominating part in the events of 1066; in the thoroughness of his political, diplomatic, and logistical preparations; in his strategic and tactical awareness; and in his personal courage and prowess, whether on reconnaissance patrol or in the front line at Hastings — throughout a long career he showed himself a master of the whole art of war.

JOHN GILLINGHAM

Wilson, Woodrow

1856–1924, *U.S. President*

Woodrow Wilson, president of the United States from 1913 until 1921, led the United States into World War I (q.v.) and tried, with very limited success, to create a new structure of international politics at the Paris Peace Conference of 1919.

An activist president in both domestic and foreign policy who involved the United States deeply in Mexico and the Caribbean, Wilson initially hoped to mediate among the warring European powers when World War I broke out. In May 1915, after the sinking of the *Lusitania* and the loss of hundreds of American lives, Wilson eventually declared that the United States would hold Germany to a "strict accountability" for further losses of life. Less than two years later, after Germany finally began unrestricted submarine warfare, this policy led Wilson to secure American entry into the war in April 1917.

Wilson insisted on maintaining a separate American political and military role during the war, labeling the United States an "associated" rather than an "allied" power, insisting that American troops fight separately in France, and planning a navy at least equal to any in the world. He made little or no attempt to direct the course of the fighting in France, but in January 1918 he issued his Fourteen Points, a plan for an impartial and lasting peace including freedom of the seas, an impartial adjustment of colonial claims, and greater freedom for many nationalities of eastern Europe. In September 1918 he suddenly became the key Allied leader when the German government asked him for an armistice based upon the Fourteen Points. His insistence upon changes in Germany's government helped lead to the German revolution and the armistice that followed on November 11, 1918.

At the Paris Peace Conference, Wilson tried to maintain the relatively impartial principles of the Fourteen Points against the demands of his allies, especially France and Italy. He successfully resisted the dismemberment of Germany, but the eventual Treaty of Versailles (q.v.) shocked many of his American supporters, who regarded it as a betrayal of his principles and an expression of French and British imperialism. Wilson suffered a stroke while campaigning for the ratification of the treaty in late 1920 and refused to make compromises that might have saved it when it came to a final vote in the Senate. The United States rejected both the treaty and the League of Nations, and Wilson's policies had been thoroughly discredited when he left office in March 1921.

DAVID KAISER

Women in War

For most of history, society has defined as nearly synonymous the military and the male roles. The Amazon legend (q.v.) flourishes in many cultures and portrays the military woman as an aberration, reinforcing traditional gender roles. Women dissatisfied with their circumscribed roles have sometimes disguised themselves as men and joined armies. Probably hundreds served during the American Civil War (q.v.). Much more often, women accompanied armies as "camp followers" who had auxiliary roles, serving as laundresses or as wives to the officers and noncommissioned officers, and drawing official rations. In Mexican military formations during the 1910s, "soldaderas" played auxiliary roles. Occasionally a wife might play a combat role; "Molly Pitcher" was the generic term for a woman who carried water to the artillery in battle and occasionally substituted for fallen men in the critical job of swabbing the insides of hot cannon barrels. George Washington (q.v.) tried to eliminate the auxiliaries in order to professionalize the Continental army; his partial success produced a decline in standards of cleanliness, hygiene, and discipline. By 1800, women had been excluded from auxiliary roles in most of the world.

Women often played active roles in guerrilla wars or resistance movements, but once the underground forces came to power, they typically relegated women to noncombat jobs (as in Israel and Vietnam) or ousted them from the military entirely (as in Yugoslavia and France). At Okinawa in 1945, the Japanese army drafted civilian women and used them in frontline auxiliary roles. Most were killed. Back in the home islands, the army prepared for the American invasion by training and arming large numbers of civilians, including women.

In established armies, women began making a comeback in the Crimean War (q.v.), when Florence Nightingale (q.v.) seized worldwide attention and created a new nursing profession out of the old auxiliary role. In the American Civil War, about 10 percent of the nurses on each side were civilian women. The invaluable role of 1,500 civilian nurses in the Spanish-American War (q.v.) led to the creation of the U.S. Army Nurse Corps as an auxiliary in 1901; the Navy Nurse Corps was established in 1908. The women were seen as specialized technicians, but not as soldiers. Their status in uniform guaranteed their availability in time of need.

The vast casualties of World War I (q.v.) necessitated the mobilization of women nurses. Germany used about 100,000 civilian women. Great Britain employed many civilians and expanded the ranks of its military nursing auxiliary to about 18,000. In the United States, the number of army nurses shot up from 400 in 1916 to 20,000 in 1918, and then receded to peacetime levels. Over 5,000 served on the Western Front, giving special attention to gas victims who needed around-the-clock nursing. The British army, uncertain that enough civilian volunteers would be available, experimented with numerous semiofficial and official women's units in 1914–1918. About 80,000 women served in uniform, in noncombat roles. Their main function was to perform roles that women were supposedly best at handling (such as telephone operator) and to replace men in service jobs so the men could be reassigned to combat units. The latter function was seen as highly threatening by many men (and their fiancées). The U.S. Navy and the U.S. Marine Corps enlisted about 11,500 women, with full military status, to handle clerical jobs. Known as Yeomen (F), these women were demobilized at the end of the war. An additional 300 women were attached to the American Expeditionary Force in France as Signal Corps telephone operators. After the tsar was overthrown in 1917, the provisional government established some all-female battalions; some 5,000 Russian women were involved. Two units engaged in active combat against the Germans in 1917, but nearby male units refused to support them, and they suffered heavy casualties. Perhaps their purpose was to shame men into volunteering for combat; one veteran, Maria Botchkareva, published her autobiography, *Yashka*, in New York in 1919. About 80,000 women served as auxiliaries in the Red Army (q.v.) during the Russian Revolution. Finland and Sweden developed "Lotta" auxiliary units.

World War II (q.v.) was a total war, and many nations had to reevaluate how efficiently their womanpower was being utilized. Recognizing that modern warfare required large numbers of soldiers to handle noncombat duties, General Staffs analyzed how they could fill these jobs with women and thereby release men for combat. However, total war also depended on the morale of the civilian population, who were essential to the production of munitions, which were consid-

British women of the Auxiliary Territorial Service in World War II march past one of the antiaircraft guns that they operated.

ered just as decisive as manpower. Women entered munitions factories worldwide in unprecedented numbers; in their roles as housewives, they were forced to handle severe controls, restrictions, and shortages as they struggled to feed and clothe their families and, in many cases, substitute as family head while the husband was in uniform. Ideology entered the calculus as well — Germany and Japan were reluctant to tear women away from traditional kitchens and bedrooms. At the other extreme, Joseph Stalin (q.v.) proved the most willing to experiment with new gender roles with scant regard for public opinion.

The British opted for a practical solution. Beginning in late 1941, Great Britain registered women and required national service. Most entered munitions work as civilians, but 125,000 were drafted into the military; 430,000 more volunteered. The largest of the women's units, the Auxiliary Territorial Service (ATS), began as a women's auxiliary to the military in 1938 and in 1941 was granted military status. With Luftwaffe bombers overhead, the Anti-Aircraft (AA) service went to the ATS to find women soldiers to serve alongside the men on the guns and searchlights. Prime Minister Winston Churchill (q.v.) was enthusiastic. He argued that any general who saved him 40,000 fighting men had gained the equivalent of a victory. By September 1943, over 56,000 women were working for AA Command, most in units close to London. The first mixed regiment to fire in action was the 132nd on November 21, 1941; the first "kill" came in April 1942. As one general observed, "Beyond a little natural excitement and a tendency to chatter when there was a lull, they behaved like a veteran party, and shot an enemy plane into the sea."

The United States entered the war more than two years after Britain, and Generals George C. Marshall (q.v.) and Dwight D. Eisenhower (q.v.) closely monitored the British experience. (Australia, Canada, and New Zealand also were using women in AA jobs.) They were impressed with what they saw; at the request of Marshall and the urging of Eleanor Roosevelt and other women leaders, Congress created the Women's Army Auxiliary Corps (WAAC) in May 1942. The navy bypassed the auxiliary stage in July and created the Women Accepted for Volunteer Emergency Service (WAVES), with the same status as male reservists. By November the U.S. Coast Guard had created SPAR (from the guard's motto, *semper parātus*); finally, the marines followed in February 1943. In all, over 350,000 American women served in uniform during World War II, with a peak strength of 271,000. The women were all volunteers and on average were better educated and older than the men who served. Although publicity focused on the traditionally male job assignments they sometimes handled, the great majority of servicewomen had clerical jobs as secretaries and file clerks, or worked as shopkeepers, technicians, and hospital orderlies. (The women did not cook for the men.) The WAVES were kept in the United States, but women who served in the army and the army air forces traveled worldwide, with duty in the South Pacific the most unhealthy and unpleasant.

In 1942 Marshall set up a secret experiment to see how well his WAACs could perform in antiaircraft combat. The results stunned the General Staff: mixed gender crews outperformed all-male crews. The women were more careful, paid more attention, and did a better job working the rather primitive radars and range finders. But Marshall refused requests to add women permanently — and publicly — to AA units. Although military efficiency called for such assignments, he feared public opinion was not ready for such a step. America thus drew the gender line against combat for women in 1943. Marshall kept the experiment secret and promised Congress that the U.S. Army would keep women out of combat. Reassured, in June 1943 Congress upgraded the auxiliary WAAC into the permanent Women's Army Corps (WAC) with full military status. The WASPs (Women's Airforce Service Pilots) flew airplanes for the air force during the war, ferrying bombers, testing fighters, and towing targets. The 1,074 WASPs had civilian status and never were integrated into the WAC. Since flying warplanes was the critical definition of a warrior in the air force, however, that service gained a special respect for women. In general, aviation has been much more supportive of women in new roles — including combat.

The posters that suggested a woman who volunteered for service could release a man for combat duty reflected the thinking of the generals and admirals, but it frightened many men who might get that combat duty. Their reaction was a whispered slander campaign that insisted women in uniform were sexually "abnormal" — either lesbian or morally loose. The allegations were false — the women were rather more prudish and vastly less sexually active than servicemen. Nevertheless, the rumors destroyed the image of heroic national service and caused volunteering to

plummet. The Pentagon never got a fifth of the million WACs it wanted, and women comprised only 2 percent of the personnel in uniform.

Despite Nazi antifeminism, the shortage of manpower by 1943 forced Berlin to enroll women volunteers; about 450,000 joined auxiliaries, in addition to the civilian units of nurses. By 1945, women were holding approximately 85 percent of billets as clerical workers, accountants, interpreters, laboratory workers, and administrative workers, together with half of the clerical and junior administrative posts in high-level field headquarters. As Allied strategic bombing grew ferocious, antiaircraft units became increasingly central to Germany's war effort. In mid-1943, Adolf Hitler (q.v.) relented, and eventually some 65,000 to 100,000 women served in AA units in Luftwaffe uniforms. Some searchlight units became 90 percent female. As did the British women, they bonded with the men as effective teammates. They emphasized their continued femininity:

> In spite of all the soldier's duties we had to do, we did not forget that we are girls. We did not want to adapt uncouth manners. We certainly were no rough warriors — always simply women.

The German women, like the British, were forbidden to fire the guns — training women to shoot at men was thought to be going one step too far. The Germans looked upon armed Soviet women as "unnatural" and consequently had no compunction about shooting such "vermin" as soon as they were captured. Referring to enemy females by degrading epithets made it easier for German soldiers to fight against these unladylike women.

The Soviets mobilized their women early, bypassing the auxiliary stage entirely. About 800,000 women served in the Red Army (q.v.), and over half of them were in frontline duty units. Many were trained in all-female units. About a third of the servicewomen received additional instruction in mortars, light and heavy machine guns, or automatic rifles. Another 300,000 served in AA units and performed all functions in the batteries — including firing the guns. When asked why she had volunteered for such dangerous and "unwomanly" work, one sergeant explained that her father had been killed and that she "wanted to fight, to take revenge, to shoot." She recalled the terror of battle: "The planes seemed to be heading straight for you, right for your gun. In a second they would make mincemeat of you. . . . It was not really a young girl's job." Eventually she became commander of an AA gun crew. Women made up about 8 percent of all Soviet combatants (not counting guerrillas and irregular units, which had a higher proportion of women). Over 100,000 were decorated during the war, including 91 who received the highest award for valor.

All the belligerents used women nurses, either as civilians or as auxiliaries. During World War II, 47,000 women nurses served in the U.S. Army and 11,000 in the U.S. Navy. In 1944 the Pentagon raised them from auxiliary status to full-status officers, with equal pay and rank — in theory. In practice, the doctors were nearly all men who were superior in rank and power to the nurses. Men were still prohibited from the nursing corps (until 1951), but 800,000 enlisted men joined Medical Corps, where they served as frontline medics and hospital orderlies. In one of the most unexpected role reversals in gender history, the women nurses, as officers, supervised the enlisted male orderlies. In no army were women nurses allowed in the front lines — the first medical intervention was the function of enlisted male medics. U.S. Army nurses served in combat zones. The policy was to keep them out of the enemy's artillery range, but to allow them to work inside the enemy's bombing range. Some became casualties, and 81 nurses were captured by the Japanese in the Philippines and Guam. Although the Japanese were extremely harsh toward male prisoners and executed some British and Australian nurses, they did not mistreat the American women.

After the war, most nations disbanded or drastically reduced their women's units. In the United States, however, the generals and admirals who had once been dubious about them proved enthusiastic. They demanded and received from Congress permanent women's units in each service. Ninety-eight percent or more of the military was still male, but women filled cadres that could be expanded enormously in case of another full-scale mobilization. In the mid-1970s, the feminist movement and the end of the draft forced the military to abolish the separate women's units and to integrate its women and men. Women were kept out of combat roles (including practically all infantry, armor, artillery, combat aircraft, and combat warship billets). In global perspective, the United States did, however, take the lead, passing the 12 percent female proportion in 1990 and systematically expanding the scope of women's activity. The first women reached flag rank in 1970 (army), 1971 (air force), and 1972 (navy), and they had command over significant numbers of men.

Sexual harassment has remained a serious problem, as exemplified by the navy's notorious "Tailgate" scandal and cover-up in 1991. Although official policy demanded equal treatment of women, many male soldiers thought the policy was artificial and political, covering up the basic "fact" that women could never be "real" combat soldiers. These men conceptualized combat in terms of individual performance, especially muscular displays that featured male upper-body strength. But senior officers have focused instead on team performance and, noting the outstanding record of mixed crews, insisted that women be accepted as teammates. Women served in Vietnam (q.v.) almost exclusively as nurses, but in the Gulf War (q.v.) of 1991, 41,000 women filled many noncombat jobs under harsh conditions and earned a grudging respect. Finally, in 1994 the Pentagon started assigning women to certain combat roles — as high-prestige pilots — for the first time.

D'ANN CAMPBELL

D'Ann Campbell, "Women in Combat: The World War II Experience in the U.S., England, Germany, and the Soviet Union," *Journal of Military History* (April 1993): 301–323; Nancy Loring Goldman, ed., *Female Soldiers: Combatants or Non-Combatants* (1982); Jeanne Holm, *Women in the Military: An Unfinished Revolution* (1992); Elizabeth Salas, *Soldaderas in the Mexican Military* (1990); Shelly Saywell, *Women in War: First-Hand Accounts from World War II to El Salvador* (1985).

World War I

1914–1918

World War I was the defining event of the twentieth century. Its unfinished political and military business laid the foundation for an even greater world war that began in 1939. Its impact on the great powers of Europe cleared the ground for the peripheral empires, the United States and the USSR, which in turn engaged in a third world war, a cold one (q.v.), that ended only in 1989. World War I marked the beginning of the end of Europe's moral and material hegemony over the world. It heralded the rise of managed economies. It opened the way to a technological revolution focused on electronics and internal combustion engines.

These and all the other results of the Great War were unintended consequences. Tensions among Eu-

British soldiers cross a duckboard bridge over the human-made morass at Ypres.

rope's major powers long antedated the actual outbreak of hostilities in 1914. War was not only expected: by the turn of the twentieth century, it was even desired in certain circles. The war's origins reflected economic and imperial rivalries and alliance systems that encouraged mutual belligerence. In that environment, rational calculation might reasonably accept war as the best feasible alternative to a state's political and military problems. Germany in particular believed by 1914 that a bid for continental hegemony and world power had a good chance of success. Germany's ally Austria-Hungary saw its survival contingent on destroying the South Slavic nationalism embodied in Serbia. The entente powers, France, Britain, and Russia, in turn decided that Germany could be stopped at reasonable cost. War thus became the continuation of politics by other means. The assassination of Hapsburg archduke Franz Ferdinand on June 28, 1914, in the Bosnian city of Sarajevo provided an excuse to settle fundamental issues of European politics.

World War I was also in part an accident. International rivalries were no worse in 1914 than in earlier years. Instead a generation of mediocre statesmen and second-rate soldiers proved unable to control the events that helped generate the crisis that followed the assassination. Indeed, worried about a belligerent public, they may have been less frightened of making war than of *not* making war. In a matter of days, from August 1 to August 4, the Central Powers (Germany and Austria-Hungary) and the Triple Entente (France, Russia, and Britain) sprang at each other's throats.

The participants agreed that the conflict would be short. Despite their differences, the great powers had enough in common socially, politically, and economically that the Great War at least began as a civil war rather than a mutual struggle for survival. Exponential increases in the destructive power of modern weapons were accompanied by a widespread belief that modern societies and modern psyches were too fragile to sustain the strain of war for any length of time. Commitment of Europe's armies to all-out strategic and tactical offensives were based on the premise that the war had to be won quickly or not at all.

But Germany's Schlieffen Plan (q.v.), the French Plan XVII, Austria-Hungary's invasions of Russia and Serbia, and Russia's two-pronged drive into Galicia and East Prussia all produced casualties on scales unknown in Western civilization. Almost 150,000 Russians were lost in the Battle of Tannenberg (q.v.) alone. French and German casualties in the war's first four months each exceeded 800,000. By year's end Russian troops had penetrated deeply into Austria-Hungary. Most of Belgium and much of northeastern France were in German hands. The conquests, however, were inconvenient: they were too small to convince the losers that there was no alternative to making peace, and too large to risk negotiation without making an effort to recover them by force.

The generals learned much between August and December of 1914. Railroad networks enabled the rapid movement of large forces over long distances, but once out of boxcars, soldiers still moved at foot speed. This fact by itself limited the impact of success since reserves could block breakthroughs faster than any momentary advantage could be exploited. Nor were victories easily won. Firepower had been gridlocking battlefields since the final years of the wars of Napoleon (q.v.). Magazine rifles, automatic machine guns, and rapid-firing field and heavy artillery gave the defense an advantage unknown in the history of warfare. The year 1914 introduced a new aspect to the problem. The sheer size of modern armies created force-to-space ratios so high that even in the wider reaches of eastern Europe, maneuver became almost impossible. Open enemy flanks could not be enveloped because they either did not exist or did not remain open for long. Nor did soldiers continue to stand heroically upright and charge forward with bayonets fixed. Instead they dug. By December 1914, a line of trenches no less formidable for being improvised defined the Western Front from the Swiss border to the English Channel, a distance of 470 miles. In the east, defensive systems were less comprehensive — because the front ran for almost double the distance — but proved almost as successful in defying attacks. Moreover, the avoidance of stalemate called for levels of genius foreign to the soldiers and the statesmen responsible for the war's direction.

The entente powers possessed a significant advantage in the resource race. Their control of the seas enabled them to draw on the entire globe, whereas Germany and Austria-Hungary were denied access to anything but their immediate conquests. The discrepancy, however, must not be exaggerated. Europe was still the focal point of the world's industrial system. Even the United States supplied more raw materials than finished goods to its French and British customers. In 1915 and for months to come, national mobilization primarily involved for all the combatants utilizing and developing their internal resources.

The question was, how could these resources best be used? Germany and Austria-Hungary, like poker players with a big stack of winning chips, were in a position to stand pat. During 1915 the Central Powers did seek to remove Russia from the war by diplomatic and military means. They inflicted over a million casualties and advanced up to three hundred miles — but Russia refused to give up. The moribund tsarist government could not afford the risks of making a separate peace.

France and Britain faced three more immediate dilemmas. The French army and the French government were committed to recovering their occupied territory as quickly as possible. At the same time Russia was making increasing demands for support from its allies, as much for morale purposes as from material need. Finally, Britain, which had initially hoped to limit its continental commitments, found itself constrained instead to raise the first mass army in its history, albeit through volunteering rather than conscription, to match the French commitment to the stalemated Western Front.

The next question concerned how best to employ this force. Throughout 1915 the French dashed their army to pieces in a series of attacks on increasingly sophisticated German trench systems. Their demand that Britain participate in the process was accepted by a British high command that believed the only way to end the war was to smash the German army in a direct confrontation. Their decision would condemn sixty thousand men to death or maiming in the autumn Battle of Loos. As casualties mounted, however, the search for a way around intensified. Winston Churchill (q.v.), then first lord of the Admiralty, argued forcefully, and convincingly, for an attack on the Dardanelles (see *Gallipoli Campaign*). This operation, directed against a ramshackle Ottoman Empire that had joined the Central Powers unenthusiastically in November 1914, would open a supply route to Russia, give the Allies a strong position in the Balkans, and convince Italy to enter the war in return for generous promises of territorial gains after the Central Powers' defeat.

It all seemed too good to be true — and was. The Anglo-French expedition bogged down on the Gallipoli Peninsula partly because of failures at high command levels, but also because of impassable terrain and unexpectedly effective Turkish resistance. The Allies suffered over a half million casualties before finally evacuating the survivors in December 1915. The Italian government, which had declared neutrality in 1914, finally joined the Allies despite substantial popular opposition in return for the promise of territory in the Adriatic Basin and the eastern Mediterranean. The Alps, however, proved a formidable obstacle to an inefficient Italian army that in 1917 was fighting no less than the Eleventh Battle of the Isonzo River (q.v.)!

By 1916, in short, the Great War was everywhere stalemated. Germany's colonies, with the exception of East Africa, were in Allied hands. Germany's principal overseas naval force had been destroyed off the Falklands in December 1914. But these were mere pinpricks. In the aftermath of the Dardanelles fiasco another British expeditionary force bogged down in Mesopotamia. The Turks surrounded ten thousand men of the Indian army at Kut and, after the longest siege in British history, forced them to surrender. An Anglo-French expeditionary force sent to the Balkans found itself so hemmed in around Salonika that the city was sarcastically dubbed the war's biggest internment camp. The civil war might have become a world war, but its focus remained in Europe.

With subtlety discredited, the major combatants again proposed to end the war by direct methods. Germany's chief of staff, Erich von Falkenhayn (q.v.), proposed to draw the French army into a killing ground around the old fortress of Verdun (q.v.), trading lives for lives until France was "bled white." Meanwhile, France and Britain planned a joint offensive along the Somme River — an offensive whose burden would be increasingly borne by the newly raised British armies. Both operations ended in mutual disaster. At Verdun, French and German losses totaled nearly 1.25 million, yet the lines in December 1916 remained almost where they had been when the German offensive began on February 21. The Somme offensive, lasting from July 1 to mid-November, gained a strip of territory about twenty miles wide and six miles deep at the price of 420,000 British casual-

ties and, often overlooked, 200,000 French. German casualty figures remain debated, but seem to have approached almost 500,000.

By the year's end French manpower resources were at the edge of exhaustion. The enthusiasm of Britain's volunteers was giving way to resignation and cynicism. The German army's superb cadre of regular officers and NCOs had been virtually destroyed: the Somme, one officer wrote, became "the muddy grave of the German field army." Yet this general war-weariness did not generate a will to end killing that had by now become a mechanical process. Efforts to initiate peace negotiations proved futile, not least because by this time all the combatants had set the stakes so high and suffered such huge losses that no one was willing to talk. It is often overlooked that Europe's upper classes sacrificed their own sons to a degree unknown before or since. Generals and statesmen were also grieving fathers who could not accept the argument that their children had died for nothing.

Instead, the combatants sought to increase the scale of the fighting. By 1916 thousands of guns firing millions of shells formed a necessary part of any attack. Battalions that had begun the war with two machine guns now had six, nine, or twelve. When sheer weight of metal did not produce decision, the combatants took to technical innovation. On the ground, poison gas and armored fighting vehicles took the field, yet neither could break the tactical stalemate. Above the trenches, aviation technology developed exponentially after August 1914, but the wire-and-strut biplanes were still too limited in their capacities by 1918 to be more than a limited auxiliary to the ground forces. At sea, the battle fleets built at such cost spent most of their time in harbor, occasionally emerging to engage in arm's-length duels like the Battle of Jutland (q.v.) on May 31, 1916, but never taking serious risks. This caution had psychological as well as military roots. When Winston Churchill called Grand Fleet commander Sir John Jellicoe (q.v.) the only man who could lose the war in an afternoon, he was recognizing that warships had become not merely fighting entities but symbols of their respective states.

The Allied blockade was inflicting increasing hardship on the Central Powers. Germany especially suffered the domestic consequences of exponentially declining living standards during 1916. But to seek victory through slow strangulation invited the question of whether the Allies might not crack first. Even as Verdun and the Somme raged in the summer of 1916, Russia mounted an offensive that produced significant initial gains but then, like all of its predecessors on every front, bogged down. In March 1917, the tsarist government gave way to a republic. Its premier, Alexander Kerensky, promised continued commitment to the war. Whether he could transform words to deeds was at best questionable.

Then, from across the Atlantic, a new hope emerged. The United States had initially sought to remain, in President Woodrow Wilson's (q.v.) words, "neutral in thought, word, and deed." However, a combination of emotional sympathy for the Allied cause, close economic ties with France and Britain, and clumsy German diplomacy convinced increasing numbers of Americans from the White House downward that a German victory would eventually prove disastrous for U.S. interests. Any lingering doubts were removed in January 1917, when Germany announced a policy of unrestricted submarine warfare, sinking any ship under any flag that approached the British Isles. In April, the United States declared war.

Seen in hindsight, the German decision seems a fecklessly applied recipe for disaster. In German terms it was a calculated risk. The United States possessed neither a balanced fleet nor a strong army. Even if the Americans could create a credible land force, German experts dismissed the possibility that it could be transported across the Atlantic at all, much less in time to save Britain from strangulation and France from itself.

Germany's prospects for victory seemed to increase as French and British offensives undertaken on the Western Front in 1917 proved more indecisive than Verdun and the Somme. In April 1917, the French army suffered such a one-sided disaster on the ridges of the Chemin des Dames that its hard-tried *poilus* mutinied. In the fall it was Britain's turn, as division after division vanished into the gelatinous mud of Flanders. The British Expeditionary Force lost another quarter million men in exchange for a few thousand yards of shell-churned ground and the ruined village of Passchendaele. German losses were almost as heavy. It was nevertheless clear that German defensive systems had become too complex, and German defensive tactics too sophisticated, to yield readily either to brute force or finesse. In the words of the new French field commander, Philippe Pétain (q.v.), it was necessary to wait for the Americans and the tanks.

But would either arrive in time to prevent Germany from springing through what seemed a final window of opportunity? Well before Lenin's Bolsheviks gave it the coup de grâce in November 1917, Kerensky's government was disintegrating. A Germany by now completely dominated by its generals saw this as an opportunity to create an eastern European sphere of influence impervious to blockade — an empire that would restore at least the material losses suffered since 1914. Troops poured eastward to occupy territories in Poland, the Ukraine, even Finland. But the process of acquiring and exploiting the new territories would take time, and time was something Germany no longer possessed.

In October 1917, a joint German-Austrian offensive shattered the Italian army at Caporetto (q.v.), inflicting 600,000 casualties — half of whom simply deserted. But once again this tactical victory produced no political gains; Italy remained in the war. Enough resources remained for one last blow. The German high command decided on a series of tactically focused attacks designed to split the French and British armies on the Western Front. Perhaps the British might retreat to the seacoast. France might consider peace on German terms. At worst, Erich Ludendorff (q.v.) expected so to cripple his adversaries that Germany would have time to consolidate its new continental position.

Hopes in this regard were enhanced when on March 3, 1918, a Bolshevik government concluded at Brest-Litovsk a treaty that gave Germany hegemony in central Europe. Eighteen days later, the German western offensive began. Employing innovative systems of artillery fire control combined with infantry tactics based on bypassing enemy strong points, Ludendorff's March 21 attack achieved initial successes that gave the Allies the courage of desperation (see *Ludendorff Offensive*). An April offensive against the British on the Lys River was briefly more threatening. For the first time the entente accepted a supreme commander. Marshal Ferdinand Foch (q.v.) proved more a coordinator than a generalissimo. Nevertheless, he was able to secure higher levels of mutual cooperation than had previously been the case — a particularly important factor given the insistence of the Americans that their rapidly growing army play an independent role in the war.

Meanwhile the German drive was coming to a standstill, as much from physical and moral exhaustion as from Allied countermeasures. By June the front had stabilized. In July the Allies counterattacked. First it was the turn of the tanks. At Soissons, exhausted French infantrymen — and American reinforcements — followed the increasing numbers of armored vehicles into German positions. On August 8, the British army used its armor to rip open the German lines around Amiens (q.v.). By this time the British had learned how to combine fire and movement in set-piece attacks that followed each other so closely that an exhausted German army had no time to counterstrike or rally.

Meanwhile the Americans had taken the field. The U-boats had been unable to stop their flow across the Atlantic. By July 1918 over a million American troops were on European soil with hundreds of thousands more arriving each month. In September, with French help, the American First Army pinched off the St.-Mihiel salient. In October it embarked on an offensive against far more formidable positions in the Argonne Forest. Clumsy tactics, poor commanders, and sheer inexperience led to high casualties, but the Americans' will and enthusiasm were the final blows to a German army that had long since exhausted both qualities. With defeat staring him in the face, Ludendorff called for peace. For a few days Germany had for the first time in its history a parliamentary government. Then a wave of revolt swept the country. Kaiser Wilhelm II abdicated. His senior generals sought retirement, leaving the newly established Weimar Republic to face a victors' coalition neither willing nor able to be generous in its days of triumph.

At 11:00 A.M. on November 11, 1918, the guns fell silent. About nine million men in uniform had perished. Millions of other human beings would die in an influenza pandemic whose impact owed much to the physical and emotional effects of a war that left Europe in shambles. The success of the Bolshevik Revolution, impossible without the war, drew an ideological line of demarcation between the new Soviet Union and its neighbors. The territorial changes in central Europe, largely a consequence of Austria-Hungary's dissolution, created a network of weak, unstable states. The Treaty of Versailles (q.v.), with its territorial, economic, and military demands, was widely viewed by Germans as imposing intolerable, immoral burdens on a country that had fought in self-defense. Adolf Hitler's (q.v.) promises to expunge the "disgrace" of 1918 contributed significantly to his rise to power — and to the launching in 1939 of a second war for the mastery of Europe.

Since the Great War, Europe has had neither the will nor the means to sustain the process of expanding its world influence that had begun in the fifteenth century. The mutual destruction that began in August 1914 continues to cast its shadow.

DENNIS E. SHOWALTER

World War II

1939–1945

After World War I (q.v.), the Germans, unreconciled to defeat, turned to a leader who prescribed a restructuring of German society along dictatorial and racial lines. Germany would fight wars to increase vastly its living space, and the soil, not the people living on it, would be Germanized. Adolf Hitler (q.v.) preached this program of demographic revolution in writings and speeches. Rather than continue ruling themselves, many Germans preferred to surrender their will to his; once lifted into power in 1933, he proceeded to fulfill his promises.

Germany initiated a rearmament program in 1933, anticipating these wars of expansion. The country was just beginning to recover from the depression, and this program drew on unutilized labor and capital resources; initially, it appeared to improve the economy without causing massive inflation.

Hitler's first military goals were to annex Austria and destroy Czechoslovakia. Weapons such as the tanks built during the 1930s were slated for the ensuing war with France and Britain, which was anticipated to be more difficult. The third war — against the Soviet Union — was expected to be quick and easy, and no special weapons systems were built to expedite it. The rapid conquest of the Soviet Union would provide vast lands for German settlers after the inhabitants had been killed or expelled. The fourth war, against the United States, was also predicted to be simple once battle had been engaged — the Americans were considered to be almost as weak and inferior as the Soviets. But because they were far away and had a large navy, preparations for *that* war began early. In 1937 orders went out for the development of the "American-Bomber" (the Me 264), which could fly from Germany to bomb the United States and return without refueling, and for construction of a fleet of superbattleships, which, together with other large surface ships, could defeat the American navy (keels

As American troops advance after heavy preliminary bombardment of Cologne, Germany, only the twin spires of the city's famous cathedral remain intact.

of the first 56,000-ton monsters were laid down in early 1939).

Why were these plans not nipped in the bud? Inside Germany, massive and increasing support for the regime among civilians and the military, combined with the controls of the dictatorship so many had wanted, muted any opposition. Outside Germany, the Soviet Union and the United States concentrated on internal affairs: the Soviet Union was in the throes of Joseph Stalin's (q.v.) push for industrialization and his great purges; the United States was recovering from the devastating Great Depression. Italy and Japan, which had been members of the World War I alliance against Germany, were now thinking of working *with* that country to satisfy their own imperialistic ambitions. This left France and Britain, the two countries that had suffered most in World War I. They would try to accommodate Germany's grievances, both before and after 1933, hoping thereby to avoid another war when they had not recovered from the past one, could not count on allies, and were not

certain they would win. In this, both governments were in accord with their publics, which during the depression had pushed for further disarmament rather than rearmament.

The Germans pulled back from war at the last moment in 1938 and were then determined *not* to hold back the next time. War against the western powers, which Hitler planned for the winter of 1938–1939, required a quiet eastern front: Lithuania, Poland, and Hungary had to be subordinated to Germany. Poland would not surrender to German demands, and it therefore had to be crushed as a preliminary to war against France and Britain. An alignment with the Soviet Union could speed that process. Hitler would give Stalin whatever concessions he demanded because once Germany had won in western Europe, a quick campaign in the east would reclaim those concessions and more as well. A Nazi-Soviet pact was signed on August 23, 1939, dividing eastern Europe between the two and assuring Germany of economic assistance from the Soviet Union.

Triumphant Japanese troops celebrate the surrender of American forces on Bataan in the Philippines early in 1942.

The Poles, fighting bravely, but isolated and lacking modern equipment, were quickly defeated in September 1939; but some of their soldiers escaped and fought on. Even before the German invasion of September 1, they had shared with the French and British their success against German code machines (the Enigma) and thereby provided a highly important — if long secret — intelligence weapon to the western powers, who declared war on Germany on September 3, 1939.

The use of armored thrusts to cut off substantial forces had been a feature of the German attack on Poland and was to be repeated in the west. Originally scheduled for November 1939, the attack was postponed primarily because of bad weather. During the pause, the Germans began the demographic revolution: the mass killing of the elderly, the handicapped, the mentally ill, and other Germans believed to be unproductive; in Poland they began killing the Polish elite and large numbers of Jews.

The invasion of Norway and Denmark in April 1940 at the urging of the German navy's commander, Admiral Erich Raeder, to gain better bases on the Atlantic, involved two innovations. First, it was aided by traitors within Norway. Their leader, Vidkun Quisling, gave his name to this type of activity. Second, the use of navy, army, and air force made this invasion a model of combined operations (q.v.) — showing that the rapid seizure of air bases was a central feature of such operations — but also led to the loss or damage of most major German surface warships. For the rest of 1940, Germany was practically without a surface navy. Thus, German victory in the west could not be followed up by an invasion of Britain.

The Germans had intended to attack in the west through Holland and Belgium at least since May 1938. They had originally hoped to seize bases in Belgium and northern France for the war against England, but they changed plans in order to cut off Allied troops, which might have moved forward to aid the Belgians and Dutch. The first of these measures worked: a German drive, led by armored divisions, punched through the French lines near Sedan (q.v.) in the Ardennes and rushed to the Channel coast in ten days. But then the effort to destroy the cut-off Allied forces collapsed. First the German air force and then the army failed to prevent evacuation of much of the British Expeditionary Force from Dunkirk, because the attack south against the French had priority and the Royal Air Force was able to batter the German Luftwaffe.

Though the new French government of Marshal Philippe Pétain pulled out of the war, the British fought on. At first the Germans did not believe their resistance would continue for long and turned their military preparations toward the next wars. Resumption of construction of the fleet for war against the United States was ordered on July 11. When Germany demanded bases in Spain for that fleet and its intended intercontinental bombers, the negotiation for Spain's entrance into the war as a German ally broke down. At Benito Mussolini's (q.v.) insistence, Italy had already come into the war, imagining that the main fighting was over. The Germans, however, were planning the war against the USSR, originally scheduled for the fall of 1940, but now set for 1941.

That invasion would provide the material basis (especially oil and steel) for war against the United States, enormous tracts of land for German farmers, and an opportunity to complete new stages in the demographic revolution: the killing of all Jews and the decimation of the Slavic population through sterilization or killing. This campaign (Barbarossa [q.v.]) was forecast to be quick and easy; the Germans began building weapons such as large tanks with heavy treads for the east only after they discovered that they had miscalculated the difficulty of the task. In the meantime they needed to defeat Britain, and an alliance with Japan appeared helpful when defeat in the Battle of Britain (q.v.) and lack of a surface navy made an invasion look too risky. That invasion had been planned in great detail — even the arrest list was printed in book form — but it had to be postponed because of the failure to obtain air superiority and the absence of a fleet. If Japan joined in, however, Germany could have a big navy on its side before it built its own. Therefore, as soon as Japan attacked the United States, Germany joined in its war.

The attack on the Soviet Union, which had tried to keep out of the war by helping Germany, at first appeared to go as the Germans hoped. A series of enormous victories was won by the Germans in June and July 1941, but they did not collapse the Soviet system. After the first weeks, the Germans pointlessly argued over whether to attack toward Moscow or the Ukraine, despite the fact that the Germans were logistically incapable of resuming the offensive toward Moscow. They overlooked the implications of Soviet control of the unoccupied country, from which Stalin could mobilize resources to fight on. And the murderous conduct of the Germans (for the first seven months they killed or let die about ten thousand prisoners of war every day) assured Stalin's government of the allegiance of most of the disaffected in the country. The first major Red Army (q.v.) counterattacks pushed back the Germans in August and September 1941, showing that the gamble on a quick Soviet collapse had been lost.

When the German offensives were halted and thrown back in November at the northern and southern ends of the front and in December before Moscow, even the Germans realized that their blitzkrieg (q.v.) strategy had failed. The Soviet Union and Japan had signed a neutrality treaty in April 1941. The Soviet Union would not allow the United States to bomb Japan from East Asian bases but could move some of its units from Siberia to Europe. On the other hand, the Germans watched in anger as American supplies poured into Soviet Far Eastern ports unimpeded by the Japanese. The Germans now intended to seize key Soviet industries and raw material and to inflict massive losses in order to win in 1942. This approach

failed disastrously; they blamed the allies they had dragooned into helping them in the Stalingrad (q.v.) and Caucasus campaigns for the defeat, which cost the Germans, Italians, and Hungarians one army each, and Romania two. A successful local German counteroffensive in February–March 1943 at Kharkov was followed by a final attempt to reclaim the initiative in July. Soviet victory in the great tank battle at Kursk (q.v.) instead shifted initiative permanently to the Red Army. Major victories in the winter of 1943–1944, in the summer of 1944, and finally in the winter of 1945 brought the Red Army to Berlin in April 1945.

The British government in 1940 had decided to defend itself against air attack and invasion, hoping to win the war eventually by attacking Germany by air, weakening Germany by blockade, and assisting expected uprisings in occupied Europe. When these measures had sapped Germany to the point of collapse, a small British army would return to the Continent. Before that happy moment, Britain had to maintain control of the sea-lanes and hope that reactions to German aggression would bring in allies.

The Soviet Union had not recognized the menace of Nazi Germany but was forced into war by invasion. The United States had become increasingly willing to provide aid; it was then pushed into the conflict by the actions of Japan, Germany, and Italy. Hoping to take advantage of Germany's victories in Europe and the assumed unwillingness of Americans to expend the blood and treasure needed to retake whatever Japan might conquer, the government in Tokyo opted for war against Britain, the United States, and the Netherlands in the summer of 1941. The Japanese occupied southern French Indochina as a base for new adventure — moving away from China, with which Japan had been fighting since 1937.

After seizing Manchuria from China in 1937, the Japanese continued to increase their pressure on the Chinese; major hostilities commenced in July 1937. In the subsequent fighting, they had occupied many of the ports and important industrial centers of the country but had failed to end the resistance of the Chinese Nationalist government. As if that fighting was not enough, the Japanese had also become involved in conflict with the Soviet Union over border issues in the summers of 1938 and 1939. In the latter case especially, they had suffered serious defeat at the hands of the Red Army (see *Khalkin-Gol, Battle of*). That experience, together with a lack of key raw materials unavailable in the Far Eastern provinces of the

Soviet Union, led Japanese expansionists to look to the south when the German victories in Europe in 1940 appeared to invite cheap expansion in that direction. Since the Philippines seemed to threaten the route to conquest in Southeast Asia, and the United States did not plan to leave its bases in those islands until 1946, a war with the United States was seen in Tokyo as a necessary part of their imperialist war.

But instead of keeping to their original plan — to seize an empire in Southeast Asia and then overwhelm the American navy as it headed across the Pacific, thereafter making peace with the United States — the Japanese navy in October 1941 accepted the Pearl Harbor (q.v.) plan of Admiral Yamamoto Isoroku (q.v.) when he threatened resignation. That attack, which damaged much of the U.S. Pacific Fleet (but not its aircraft carriers) was a tactical success but, as should have been anticipated, a strategic disaster for Japan. The majority of the U.S. ships were repaired, most of the crew members survived, and the outraged American public would pay any price for victory over a treacherous enemy.

The Japanese onrush conquered Malaya, the Dutch East Indies, the Philippines, Burma, and many South Pacific islands, but was then held back. Rather than try to meet the Germans across the Indian Ocean, Japanese forces postponed such a move and pushed to take Port Moresby in New Guinea; they were checked at Coral Sea (q.v.) in May 1942. The next month, another foolish scheme of Yamamoto's was adopted when he again threatened to resign. It involved seizing Midway (q.v.) and crushing the remaining American fleet. A major American victory followed, allowing Americans and Australians to counterattack on New Guinea and in the Solomons. The Japanese never thereafter developed a coherent strategy for a war they had started but had no way to finish. They simply hoped to make the war too costly for their enemies to continue it.

The Americans decided on an offensive on two axes: One was based on Australia and headed along the New Guinea coast and through the Solomons toward the Philippines and on to Tokyo, bypassing many substantial Japanese garrisons along the way. The other axis lay across the smaller islands of the South and Central Pacific to the Marianas, then to the Philippines, Formosa, or the China coast, and finally to the Japanese home islands. Basing an attack on Japan in China meant keeping that country in the war, a project that failed in spite of a massive airlift over

the Himalayas (called "the Hump") and victories in Burma by the British and Americans at the same time that Japan was crushing the Chinese Nationalist armies in 1944. The slow, bitter fight was therefore concentrated on the two American offensives, which culminated in landings on the Marianas in June and July 1944 and in the Philippines (q.v.) beginning in October. From there, the Americans moved to the Bonin Islands (Iwo Jima [q.v.]) in February and the Ryukyus (Okinawa [q.v.]) in April 1945.

In the meantime, the British and the Americans had argued over the best way to defeat Germany. They agreed that this had to precede the defeat of Japan and that priority had to be given to defeating Germany's submarines, a struggle in which Canada played an increasing role. But they disagreed concerning an early invasion of northwest Europe. The British thought of this as a last resort, emphasizing the Mediterranean — first, because it appeared to offer greater opportunities and fewer risks of disaster, and second, because they were committed to the defense of imperial interests there. But the Americans opposed a peripheral strategy, seeing no prospect of a decisive victory in the mountains of southern and southeastern Europe, and no hope of playing a major role in securing a permanent peace unless their power was projected into the heart of Europe.

In 1942 the Allies landed in northwest Africa, but the Pétain government's collaboration with Germany made it impossible to take Tunisia quickly and forced postponement of a landing in the northwest to 1944. Instead, they landed on Sicily and the Italian mainland. Their bombing of Germany, to weaken that country and assist the Soviets, was troubled by the German fighter defenses in the fall of 1943. But Allied long-range fighters turned this around and gave the Allies air superiority in 1944. With a large American army in England, control of the sea and air, and deception diverting German forces, the Allies succeeded in getting ashore in Normandy in June 1944 (see *D-Day*) and eventually breaking out into France. Supply shortages and German resistance made it impossible to finish the war in 1944; the Germans made one final effort with their last reserves in December (see *Bulge, Battle of the*). This Ardennes offensive failed, and in 1945 the Allies drove into Germany, meeting the Red Army and settling into occupation zones devised by the British. Germany had been crushed, and surrendered on May 7, 1945. But even before the end of fighting in Europe, both the Russians and the Americans had begun transferring forces to East Asia to finish the war against Japan. Poised to invade the home islands in November 1945, with the British intending to land in Malaya in September, the Allies instead ended the war in August by dropping atomic bombs and securing the entrance of the Soviet Union into the war. The large Japanese forces in the home islands and in control of much of China, Southeast Asia, and several Pacific islands obeyed the surrender orders from Tokyo on August 15 (a day earlier in the United States). To the relief of the Allies, the war came to an end in September 1945 with a number of official surrender ceremonies, the most famous of which occurred on the USS *Missouri*, in Tokyo Bay.

GERHARD L. WEINBERG

Xenophon

428?–354? B.C., Greek Soldier and Historian

An Athenian-born writer, student of Socrates, and mercenary soldier, Xenophon left a rich legacy of military and political history based largely on his own experiences. After his exile from Athens in 401 B.C., he joined an expedition of some ten thousand Greek mercenaries involved in a Persian civil war. After the betrayal and execution of his officers, Xenophon was one of those elected to lead the Greeks out of Asia Minor, a trek detailed in his *Anabasis.* Although this memoir lacks the grand themes of most Greek historical narrative, it provides an unusual and detailed account of the rigors of the march as experienced by the common foot soldier. Following his return to Greece, Xenophon settled on an estate near the Spartan frontier. He spent the rest of his life in the service of the Spartans (q.v.), whom he admired, and in writing several works on the history (including the wars) of his own time.

EUGENE N. BORZA

Y

Yamagata Aritomo

1838–1922, *Japanese Statesman and General*

Political and military leader of Japan for more than six decades, Yamagata Aritomo is often called the "father of the Japanese army." He also played a major role in building the political institutions of Meiji Japan. Born to a low-level samurai (q.v.) retainer in the feudal domain of Chōshū, he played a key role in the establishment in 1868 of the imperial regime headed by Emperor Meiji (r. 1867–1912). Yamagata was appointed assistant vice minister of military affairs following a year abroad to study European military systems, and in 1873 he assumed leadership of the new Army Ministry. He is credited with the enactment of the Conscription Ordinance of 1873 and with the reorganization of the army along Prussian lines in 1878. Yamagata resigned as army minister in 1878 and became the first chief of the General Staff. He drafted a series of regulations culminating in the Imperial Precepts for Soldiers and Sailors of 1882, which emphasized absolute loyalty to the emperor and enjoined soldiers to eschew politics. Nevertheless, Yamagata was named prime minister for the first time (1889–1891) in the same year he was promoted to the rank of full general. He was a field marshal when he led his second cabinet (1898–1900). During the Russo-Japanese War (1904–1905) (q.v.) he served as chief of the General Staff. For his services to the nation he was named prince (*kōshaku*) in 1907.

During his last twenty years, when he was often known simply as "the Grand Old Man," Yamagata was the most influential member of the group of elder statesmen known as the Genrō. From behind the scenes, he played an important advisory role in foreign affairs, spoke out on domestic issues through his disciples in the cabinet, and virtually dictated the selection of prime ministers until his death.

THEODORE F. COOK, JR.

Yamamoto Isoroku

1884–1943, *Japanese World War II Admiral*

Few modern Japanese military figures have been as admired, or as reviled, as this architect of Japan's naval strategy in the opening years of the Pacific war in World War II (q.v.). His early career showed him capable of both intellectual and professional flexibility and possessed of considerable diplomatic acumen, yet his performance at the highest level of command betrayed serious flaws in both vision and judgment.

Apologists for Yamamoto's strategic miscalculations have usually sought to place responsibility on others, claiming he was forced to war against his better judgment, let down by subordinates who lacked his vision, or betrayed by intelligence failings and ill fortune. Yet students of the Pacific war should recall that, as overall commander of Japan's naval resources, he produced no operational victory after the momentous achievements of the first four months of the war, in which Japanese air, land, and sea forces overran Southeast Asia, the East Indies, and much of the central Pacific. Moreover, from his position as commander in chief of the Combined Fleet, he may have been uniquely positioned to deflect Japan's government from a disastrous course, had he been willing to state flatly that Japan's navy could not win.

The sixth son of a school principal, adopted into the Yamamoto family, he went directly to the fleet on graduation from the naval academy and was wounded at the Battle of Tsushima (q.v.) in May 1905. Sent abroad to study in 1919, Yamamoto spent a year at Harvard University and another at the Japanese Embassy in Washington, D.C. He began his long connection to the navy's fledgling air service as executive officer at a naval air station before he was again posted to Washington (1926–1928) as naval attaché. He then returned to Japan to assume command of the aircraft carrier *Akagi* (1928–1929).

Yamamoto played a leading role at the London Naval Conference in 1930, strongly opposing extension of the Washington Treaty ratios that since 1922 had limited Japan's naval strength compared to that of the United States and Britain. Now a rear admiral, he was a dissonant voice in the chorus of believers who saw the battleship as the decisive weapon to win future struggles for control of the Pacific. As vice minister of the navy and then navy minister (1936–1939), Yamamoto was a strong proponent of naval air power incorporating both land- and carrier-based aircraft. He became head of the Combined Fleet in 1939 and took the lead in preparing the navy for war with Britain and the United States, although he had earlier argued that such a conflict would pose dangers for Japan.

In January 1941, Yamamoto initiated the idea of a carrier-borne air attack on the American base at Pearl Harbor (q.v.), to launch a war by disabling the American Pacific fleet, thus preventing its interference in Japanese operations in Southeast Asia. At the same time, Yamamoto reasoned, the attack would eliminate any direct American threat to the Japanese homeland early in the war. Some scholars claim that Yamamoto's political calculations led him to a belief that Americans would be demoralized by the blow, but it was less a strike with grand strategic purposes than the kind of operation that, once conceived, transfixes the planner's vision on a single course of action.

Although recognizing the awesome war potential of American industry, Yamamoto had little respect for the officers of the American navy; he also believed that rifts in American society could prevent the full mobilization of its industrial power in time to prevent Japan from achieving most of its objectives. Fiercely defending his idea, Yamamoto fought for the Pearl Harbor plan against most other naval leaders but never brought the plan to the army or any combined authority for review or assessment, ostensibly for fear of betraying the secret. The attack crippled the American battle fleet on December 7, 1941, but missed America's aircraft carriers, then at sea. Carriers thus became vital weapons of war in the Pacific, as Yamamoto had foreseen back in the early 1930s.

Following active American carrier efforts to thwart Japan's advances in the South Pacific at the Battle of the Coral Sea (q.v.) and the American bomber raid on Tokyo in April 1942, Yamamoto made the fateful decision to seek a decisive battle with the "remnants" of the American fleet. He chose this rather than the more circumspect course of remaining on the strategic defensive and taking advantage of numerical superiority in carriers supported by the extensive ring of island air bases lying across America's expected lines of attack in the central Pacific.

Known as a formidable poker player as well as an accomplished player of Japanese chess, Yamamoto's scheme for the Midway (q.v.) operation in the summer of 1942 was both risk-filled and elaborate, employing several task forces that ranged from the central Pacific to the Aleutians. He justified it as necessary to close a gap in Japan's defenses, planning to draw the Americans to fight at a place and time of his own choosing. Yet it was his own carrier force, under Vice Admiral Nagumo Chūichi (q.v.), that was taken by surprise and destroyed. Yamamoto learned of the disaster while at sea, where he was unable to coordinate his fleets as well as he might have done, had he remained in Tokyo. The extent to which Yamamoto's reach exceeded his grasp is clear from evidence that, had the Midway plan succeeded, he would likely have followed it with a landing in the Hawaiian Islands, extending even further an already indefensible perimeter.

In what may have been a strategic decision even worse than the Pearl Harbor operation, Yamamoto allowed himself to be drawn into a war of attrition following the American landings on Guadalcanal (q.v.) in August 1942. This battle at the periphery of the empire rapidly consumed Japanese fleet and air assets. Admiral Yamamoto was carrying out a strategic review of the theater when his plane was ambushed by American fighters alerted by intercepted and decoded messages to his inspection route. He was killed on April 18, 1943, near Bougainville. His state funeral in Tokyo included one of the last great wartime parades in Japan.

THEODORE F. COOK, JR.

Yamashita Tomoyuki

1885–1946, *Japanese World War II General*

A vigorous leader and risk-taker who graduated from the Military Academy the same year (1905) as Tōjō Hideki (q.v.), "the Tiger of Malaya" earned his nickname for his swift triumph over numerically superior British Empire forces in Malaya, culminating in the surrender of the fortress of Singapore on February 15, 1942. Yamashita Tomoyuki, a proponent of army air power, fully exploited Japan's air advantages in Malaya and based his "gambles" on excellent aerial reconnaissance.

Instead of a triumphant return to Tokyo, Yamashita found himself ordered to Manchuria to watch the border with the neutral Soviet Union, a location from which it was unlikely he could challenge Tōjō's position within the army. Arguably Japan's most effective combat leader was thus kept out of operations until his "exile" ended with Tōjō's fall in 1944.

Yamashita was now given the critical task of defending the Philippines, arriving to take up command of Fourteenth Area Army only days before Douglas MacArthur's (q.v.) landing on Leyte Island (q.v.) in October 1944, which denied him the opportunity to formulate his own plans for the archipelago's defense. Saddled with firm orders to hold Leyte, without joint command authority, Yamashita saw his forces on Leyte chopped up and eventually destroyed by January 1945, when the Americans invaded Luzon.

Despite tremendous handicaps, Yamashita fought vigorously, counterattacking U.S. forces, before he withdrew with his remaining troops into the mountainous interior of Luzon. He held out until September 2, 1945, when word of Japan's defeat finally reached him.

Yamashita was arrested by the U.S. Military Commission and charged with responsibility, as commander, for the atrocities committed by Japanese forces throughout the theater, even though they were in direct contravention of his own orders and occurred out of his effective operational control. After personal review of his case by General MacArthur, Yamashita was executed in Manila in February 1946.

THEODORE F. COOK, JR.

Yi Sun-Shin

1545–1598, *Korean Admiral*

One of two superintendents of the navy in Chŏlla Province at the start of the Japanese invasion launched by Toyotomi Hideyoshi (q.v.) in 1592, this innovative tactician emerged as the outstanding Korean commander of the war. Yi Sun-Shin's victories in a series of encounters off the southeast coast of the peninsula destroyed the Japanese supply lines and crippled their efforts to land reinforcements to their armies in the north. The "turtle boats" *(kŏkbuksŏn)* he is said to have invented were a crucial component of Yi's success. Although no reliable contemporane-

ous models or descriptions of these vessels remain, they are thought to have been armed with cannon mounted on all sides and defended by covered decks adorned with spikes to discourage boarders; some maintain they were iron-plated as well. Dismissed from his post for political reasons, Yi was returned to service to face the second invasion in 1597. He was killed by a musket shot in the final naval battle of the war (see *Korean War*).

KARL F. FRIDAY

Yorktown and Virginia Capes, Battles of

1781

When Charles, Lord Cornwallis (q.v.), British commander in the South during the American Revolutionary War (q.v.), retreated to the Yorktown peninsula in June 1781 to rest and reequip his battered army, George Washington (q.v.) was outside New York, preparing an assault on that British-held city with the help of the four-thousand-man French expeditionary force commanded by the count of Rochambeau. Then came news that the thirty-four-ship French West Indies battle fleet was heading for Virginia with three thousand infantry. (Rochambeau had urged the French admiral, de Grasse, to undertake this gamble.) Plans for New York were abandoned, and Washington executed a swift concentration of every available soldier before the little tobacco port on the Chesapeake. A trapped Cornwallis asked the British fleet and army in New York for help. The fleet sortied to clash with French ships of the line off the Virginia Capes in one of the most important least-known naval battles of history. The outnumbered British admiral, Thomas Graves, adhered rigidly to the conservative "Fighting Instructions," which prescribed a strict line of battle formation aimed at limiting losses. De Grasse battered several British ships in a two-and-a-half-hour clash, and Graves, after two more days of fruitless maneuvers for advantage, abandoned Cornwallis and returned to New York.

Meanwhile, a smaller French squadron under Admiral Barras slipped into the Chesapeake, carrying the French army's siege artillery. Trapped behind hastily constructed redoubts, without cannon heavy enough to match the French big guns, Cornwallis's army crumbled under night and day bombardment. On Oc-

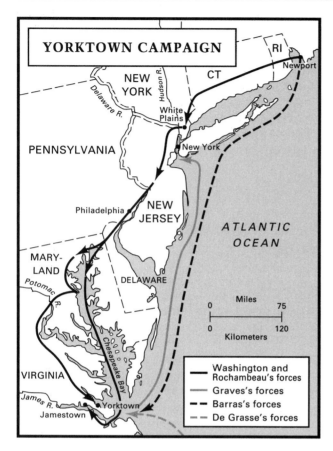

YORKTOWN CAMPAIGN

NEW YORK

Hudson R.

Delaware R.

PENNSYLVANIA

RI

Newport

CT

White Plains

New York

Philadelphia

NEW JERSEY

ATLANTIC OCEAN

MARY-LAND

Potomac R.

DELAWARE

Miles
0   75
0   120
Kilometers

VIRGINIA

James R.

Jamestown   Yorktown

Chesapeake Bay

Washington and Rochambeau's forces
Graves's forces
Barras's forces
De Grasse's forces

tober 14, two key redoubts were carried in a night assault. Three days later, Cornwallis surrendered. As his men marched out to stack their guns, their bands played "The World Turned Upside Down." In London, when Prime Minister Lord North heard the news, he cried: "Oh God, it is all over." So it was.

THOMAS FLEMING

Ypres, Battles of

October 1914–October 1918

During World War I (q.v.), four major battles between the Germans and the Allies were fought around the old Belgian town of Ypres — which became more important as a laboratory for war than for any strategic advantage it conferred on the opponents. Casualties probably totaled more than a million. The first great clash here occurred in October 1914, when Ypres presented the last opening in the Western Front. Time and again, the Germans hurled themselves against the

thinning ranks of British and French troops. The Germans actually sang, as much to maintain morale as to communicate and keep order in the thick mists of autumn. The Allies held, but just, and the Ypres salient took shape.

On April 22, 1915, Second Ypres began when the Germans discharged hundreds of cylinders of chlorine vapor, the first significant use of poison gas. French troops panicked, and the line broke. But the Germans never intended to take Ypres, which lay briefly open: they hoped merely to gain a local tactical advantage at minimal cost. It was only when they discovered the extent of the bite they had taken from the salient apple that they followed with more attacks, forcing the Allies back to the outskirts of town.

But the salient is best remembered for the Allies' three-and-a-half-month campaign called Third Ypres — better known as Passchendaele, after the pulverized village that became, *faute de mieux*, the final objective of General Douglas Haig's (q.v.) push. It began on July 31, 1917, and his objective was to drive the Germans from the Belgian coast. But unexpectedly bad weather, mud, and the new German defense-in-depth, centered on concrete pillboxes, impeded his advance. By mid-November, the Allies had gained a maximum of five miles; the combined losses for both sides exceeded 500,000. The following April, during the crisis of the German spring offensives, the British voluntarily gave up all those bitterly won gains. In September — Fourth Ypres — the Allies pushed out of the salient for good. The sieges of Ypres, Great Britain's Verdun (q.v.), had lasted just short of four years. But, for the record, the emotion-charged rubble heap that had been Passchendaele was finally taken, not by Empire troops, but by the Belgian army.

ROBERT COWLEY

Yüeh Fei

1103–1142, *Chinese General*

The conquest of North China by Jürchen invaders from Manchuria in 1126 set the stage for Yüeh Fei's career. A young man of humble origins who had already had some military experience as a junior officer, Yüeh reenlisted in the army and dedicated himself to the recovery of the lost territories (where he himself had been born). He rose rapidly in the service of the

Southern Sung dynasty, participated in several major offensive campaigns against the Jürchen between 1134 and 1140, and seemed close to success when the emperor Kao-tsung made peace on humiliating terms in 1141.

Yüeh had often bordered on insubordination in his dealings with the court, and once peace had been made, his ardent irredentism became a fatal liability; before long the general was arrested on trumped-up charges and put to death in prison.

Yüeh Fei is remembered by the Chinese as one of their greatest military heroes, but his fate also provides a striking example of the traditional Chinese preference for civilian control over the military even at the price of military weakness.

DAVID A. GRAFF

Z

Zama, Battle of

October? 202 B.C.

Zama, the decisive battle of the Second Punic War (q.v.), was actually fought near a place called Margaron, or Naraggara, probably somewhere near El Kef in western Tunisia. Numbers are uncertain, but Hannibal (q.v.) of Carthage possibly had thirty-six thousand infantry and four thousand cavalry to the twenty-nine thousand infantry and six thousand cavalry led by Scipio (q.v.) of Rome.

After an unsuccessful charge by Hannibal's elephants, Scipio's cavalry pursued their opposite numbers from the field, possibly as Hannibal had planned. Hannibal held back his third infantry line, consisting of his veterans from Italy, possibly hoping to catch the enemy in confusion after they emerged from defeating his first two lines — perhaps the first example of a true reserve in history. But Scipio was able to reorganize, and his cavalry returned in the nick of time to deliver the coup de grâce in Hannibal's rear. Hannibal escaped with perhaps a quarter of his men — Roman losses were between fifteen hundred and twenty-five hundred — to insist that Carthage make peace.

J. F. LAZENBY

Zenta, Battle of

September 11, 1697

On April 5, 1697, Prince Eugène of Savoy, arguably the best Hapsburg field commander, was appointed to lead the war against the Turks (see *Austro-Turkish Wars*). On September 11, with thirty-four thousand foot soldiers, sixteen thousand horsemen, and 60 guns, he won a complete victory over a Turkish army, led by Sultan Mustafa II, with double his numbers at Zenta, some 133 miles southeast of Buda. Catching the enemy as he was trying to cross the Tisza River, he inflicted over thirty thousand casualties and captured 146 guns, compelling the Turks to sign the Treaty of Karlowitz on January 26, 1699, ceding Hungary to the Hapsburgs.

This victory was one of the few that literally won a kingdom. It also marked the end of the Turkish threat to southeast central Europe and the beginning of the Ottoman decline. Militarily it demonstrated that the large but indifferently trained and disciplined Turks were no match for well-exercised European troops using controlled fire tactics and massed cavalry charges.

GUNTHER E. ROTHENBERG

Zhukov, Georgii K.

1896–1974, *Soviet World War II Marshal*

Georgii Zhukov was the most successful Soviet general of World War II (q.v.). His name is associated with the crucial campaigns to defend Moscow, lift the siege of Leningrad (q.v.), trap the Germans at Stalingrad (q.v.), and conquer Berlin. He is often portrayed as he sometimes portrayed himself: as a "soldier's soldier," the simple handyman of warfare. In reality, he was a gifted political operator and master of self-promotion. Distinguished as his battlefield exploits undoubtedly were, his career as a political soldier was at least as impressive and considerably more dangerous. An assessment of his place in military history must include — indeed must emphasize — his mastery of the political dimensions of the modern warrior's craft.

Zhukov was born in a village southwest of Moscow. His father was a poor shoemaker and his mother a farmworker. Zhukov's schooling was often interrupted by the necessity to help his parents. Yet he persisted with his academic studies even while learning the cobbler's trade, which was supposed to be his life's work.

He was saved from this fate by World War I (q.v.), in which he served as a private in a cavalry regiment. By ingratiating himself with his commander, he was allowed to study military tactics while other privates rode off to the slaughter. Eventually, however, he saw action on the Southwestern Front, where he won two St. George's Cross medals for bravery. In 1917 he showed early indications of a blossoming political talent by getting himself elected chairman of his squadron's Red Soldiers' Committee. He was not, however, directly involved in the Bolshevik Revolution, which turned out to be fortunate, for his later patron, Joseph Stalin (q.v.), resented soldiers who had distinguished themselves in the revolution.

During the subsequent civil war, Zhukov ascended the Red Army (q.v.) ladder with dizzying speed, going from volunteer private in August 1918 to squadron commander in 1922. Here his godfather was the great cavalryman Semen Budenny, in whose elite unit Zhukov served with distinction. In addition to piling up more commendations, including the Order of the Red Banner, he joined the fledgling Communist Party (March 1, 1919). Of this fateful decision he wrote tellingly in his memoirs: "Since then I have forgotten many things, but the day I was accepted into Party membership will remain in my memory throughout my life."

There is some confusion in the literature concerning whether Zhukov joined other Red Army officers at Berlin's War Academy during the rapprochement between Weimar Germany and the Soviet Union following the Treaty of Rapallo in the early 1920s. But whether or not he actually studied in Berlin, he certainly became exposed to General Hans von Seeckt's (q.v.) blitzkrieg (q.v.) doctrines, which helped turn him into a proponent of the mechanization of the Red Army.

Mechanization and military reform, however, were not Zhukov's main priorities in the next phase of his career. The name of the game became sheer survival, as Russia's paranoid dictator, Stalin, began in the mid-1930s to include leading officers in his vast purge of alleged "traitors" and "counterrevolutionaries." Now Zhukov's political skills were more necessary than ever, and few officers proved more adroit than he.

In essence, he survived by toeing the changing party line with a vengeance, making the division he commanded the most politically correct in the Red Army. He was later accused, perhaps justifiably, of denouncing fellow officers to protect his own political flanks.

Having negotiated the treacherous terrain of the Stalinist purges, Zhukov was dispatched in June 1939 to Russia's hottest military landscape: the disputed border region between Outer Mongolia and Japanese-dominated Manchuria. In the decisive campaign of Khalkin-Gol (q.v.), Zhukov employed a pincer movement to encircle and defeat a powerful Japanese army. This achievement was significant both for Zhukov personally and for the later evolution of World War II (q.v.). It earned him Stalin's admiration and foreshadowed the tactic he would use with equal success at Stalingrad; and it helped to deflect Japanese ambitions southward toward a confrontation with the Western powers in the Pacific.

Zhukov's military accomplishments in the Great Patriotic War, especially his role in the defense of Moscow, are well documented, not least by Zhukov himself in his memoirs. What is less well known is that in 1940–1941, Zhukov generally concurred with Stalin's disastrous decision to reduce Russia's western defenses as a gesture to placate Adolf Hitler (q.v.). The near loss of Moscow was as much the fault of political generals like Zhukov as it was of Stalin himself.

To his credit, however, Zhukov stood up to Stalin on several occasions during the actual defense of Moscow. He understood, and exploited, the dictator's growing dependence on his military expertise. He did so again in late 1942 when Stalingrad seemed about to fall to the Germans. Zhukov planned (though did not personally execute) the famous two-pronged counterattack that surrounded and ultimately crushed General Friedrich Paulus's Sixth Army on the frozen banks of the Volga.

Having "saved" Moscow and Stalingrad, and helped to lift the brutal siege of Leningrad, Zhukov quite naturally won the favor of leading the main assault on Berlin. A demanding military campaign, this was also an eminently political enterprise, involving as it did a race to control the postwar fate of Nazi Germany. Zhukov drove his troops relentlessly not only to ensure that the Russians got to Berlin first, but also that *his* army outran that of his Soviet rival, Marshal Ivan Konev (q.v.).

In his postwar career, Zhukov once again had to call upon all his political dexterity. Though appointed commander of the Soviet Occupation Zone in Germany in 1945, he was recalled a year later and charged by Stalin with exaggerating his part in the Great Patriotic War (an offense that he in fact shared with the dictator). For a time he was sent to languish in the provinces, but in 1947 it seemed that he might be jailed or even executed, when Stalin's secret police henchman, Lavrentii Beria, accused him of treason. Yet in the end, Stalin, mindful of all Zhukov's services, refused to sacrifice the great soldier.

After Stalin's death, Zhukov's star rose once again in the new political firmament of Nikita Khrushchev. In June 1957, as defense minister, he provided Khrushchev with crucial support against a cabal of old Stalinists who wanted to depose him. As a reward, Khrushchev made Zhukov an alternate member of the Presidium, the first time any military man had been so honored. Yet not long thereafter Khrushchev accused Zhukov of harboring "Bonapartist" ambitions for a military dictatorship and had him removed from office. Commenting later on this sad culmination of his career, Zhukov said revealingly: "There's no smoke without fire."

DAVID CLAY LARGE

Viktor Anfilov, "Zhukov," in *Stalin's Generals* (1993); Otto Preston Chaney, *Zhukov* (1971).

Zizka, Jan

1360?–1424, *Bohemian Military Leader*

The most imaginative military figure of the late Middle Ages, Jan Zizka first saw action as part of a band of noblemen guerrillas in southern Bohemia. Later he fought with the Polish army against the Teutonic Knights at the Battle of Tannenberg (1410) (q.v.), and at the defense of Radzyn. During the Hussite Wars, which began in 1420, he first designed an impregnable fortress on the heights of Mount Tabor and then went on to forge an army of peasants and townsmen that proved invincible in battles against a series of much larger armies. His first major victory — the Battle of Vitkov — was scored against the army of King Sigismund, who sought to capture Prague in the First Anti-Hussite Crusade. In all, five crusades were launched against the Hussites; all were sent packing.

Lacking cavalry, Zizka conceived a novel wagon-fort strategy. Each Hussite wagon — high-sided and stoutly planked — held up to fourteen men armed with flails, pikes, hackbuts, crossbows, and, later, howitzers. Circled and linked by chains, the Hussites' wagon train was a movable fortress bristling with an unusual array of firepower that could withstand — and break — cavalry charges. Once the assault was broken, Hussite troops within the circled wagons rushed out to rout the demoralized enemy.

Blinded in one eye in his youth, Zizka lost the sight of his other eye in battle of 1421 — after which he scored many of his greatest victories. He died undefeated.

JON SWAN

Zulu and the Zulu Wars

The African tribe known as the Zulu is believed to have emigrated to northern Natal, South Africa, from the central African lakes area in the fifteenth century. Until the eighteenth century it remained an obscure group, but through the organizing ability and generalship of Dingiswayo, an Abatetwa chief, and his successor, Shaka, who became chief in 1818, they terrorized their neighbors.

Shaka, born in 1787, merged the Abatetwa with the Zulu and is generally recognized as the founder of the Zulu Empire. During his reign he revolutionized warfare in South Africa by replacing the throwing spear with the stabbing *assegai* and by developing radical new tactics. Use of the short, stout *assegai* meant that warriors could no longer throw their spears and run, but had to close with their foes. His army in fighting formation was likened to the head of an ox; from either side of the main body came "horns," troops that ran ahead to envelop the enemy. He organized his regiments by age groups; no man could marry until he had washed his *assegai* in the blood of an enemy. Footwear was forbidden, and to make sure his warriors' feet were tough, he required them to dance on thorns; those whose dancing was not vigorous enough were clubbed to death.

In his wars, Shaka is estimated to have killed more than one million men. Captured enemy warriors were slaughtered; captured women were spared to become wives of his warriors. He absorbed land and peoples in an ever-expanding empire.

Military innovator Jan Zizka (on horseback) carries his famous knife-in-fist mace in this fifteenth-century woodcut. Blind in one eye since childhood — Zizka means "one-eye" — he lost the other eye in battle in 1421.

In the 1820s the wars of the turbulent Zulu gave rise to far distant ripples of fighting and disorder, as powerful tribes plundered weaker ones in widening circles of devastation. These troubled times were called the Mfecane (the Crushing), and the tens of thousand driven from their traditional homelands were called Mfengu (Homeless Wanderers), or, by most Europeans, "Fingos."

When white settlers arrived in Natal, Shaka established and maintained good relations with them and even presented them with large tracts of land. However, in 1828 he was assassinated by his half brother, Dingaan, who succeeded him. Less friendly to the white settlers, Dingaan sought to stop the Voortrekkers (Boers fleeing the British government in Cape Colony) from entering Natal. After he murdered the leaders of one group, the Boers declared war, and on September 16, 1838, on the Blood River, Boers under Andries Pretorius won a notable victory, the Zulu losing some three thousand, the Boers only a handful. Most of the tribe then moved north of the Tugela River, which came to be accepted as a natural boundary.

In 1840, Panda, a brother of Dingaan, led a revolution and, with the help of Boer commandos (Afrikaner yeomanry) made himself king. For thirty-two years peace was maintained, and in 1842 Natal became a British colony, but Panda's son Cetewayo, who succeeded him on his death in 1872, aroused considerable fear among the whites in Natal. As Cetewayo attempted to extend his authority over those who had fled his tyranny into Natal, friction on the frontier mounted.

On January 10, 1879, General Frederic Thesiger, viscount Chelmsford, led an army of 5,000 British and 8,200 African troops into Zululand in three widely dispersed columns. On January 22, while he was absent with a portion of his force seeking out the Zulu, his central column of about 1,800 British and 1,000 Africans camped at the base of a tall crag called Isandhlwana. There it was attacked by some 10,000 Zulu. All but 55 British and 300 Africans were slaughtered. No prisoners were taken.

At Rorke's Drift, a ford on the Buffalo River near Isandhlwana where the British had established a small hospital in a mission station, 4,000 Zulu led by a half brother of Cetewayo attacked on the night following the Battle of Isandhlwana. The station was successfully defended for twelve hours by 139 British soldiers, of whom 35 were sick. When the Zulu left the field, they had lost about 400 warriors; the British had lost 17. No less than 11 British soldiers were awarded the Victoria Cross for this fight, the most ever awarded for a single action.

Chelmsford, heavily reinforced, again invaded Zululand in March, and this time the Zulu were defeated. In August Cetewayo was captured by Lord Wolseley. The British then departed, leaving Zululand in turmoil as minor chiefs struggled for supremacy. In 1897 Zululand was annexed to Natal. The Zulu remained quiet until an uprising against British rule in 1906, when troops had to be called in to suppress it.

BYRON FARWELL

David Clammer, *The Zulu War* (1973); Donald Morris, *The Washing of the Spears* (1965).

Illustration Credits

MAP CREDITS

All maps created by Vantage Art of Massapequa, New York. In addition, credit is due the following sources: **Battle of Amiens** Adapted and reproduced by permission of Routledge, London, from Tim Travers's *How the War Was Won*, 1992. **Battle of Cambrai** Adapted and reproduced by permission of Routledge, London, from Tim Travers's *How the War Was Won*, 1992. **Battle of El Alamein** Adapted and reproduced by permission of Hodder & Stoughton, Ltd., London, from David Fraser's *And We Shall Shock Them*, 1983. **Battle of Gaugamela** Adapted and reproduced by permission from Major-General J.F.C. Fuller's *The Generalship of Alexander the Great*, copyright © 1960 by John Fredrick Charles Fuller. Reprinted by permission of Rutgers University Press. **Battle of Gettysburg** Adapted and reproduced by permission of Oxford University Press from James M. McPherson's *Battle Cry of Freedom*, 1988. **Waterloo** Adapted and reproduced by permission from Vincent J. Esposito and John Robert Elting's *A Military History and Atlas of the Napoleonic Wars*, New York, 1964.

PICTURE CREDITS

Air Strategy Courtesy U.S. Air Force Art Collection **Alexander the Great** Alinari/Art Resource, New York **Amazons** British Museum, London, neg. no. P5051292 **American Civil War** National Archives and Records Administration, neg. no. 165-SB-41 **Animals** Yale University Library, Maurice Durand Collection of Vietnamese Art **Arab-Israeli Wars** UPI/Corbis-Bettmann Archive **Armor (Western)** Art Resource, New York **Armor (non-Western)** Metropolitan Museum of Art, Rogers Fund, 1904 (04.4.2) **Artillery (mortar)** Corbis-Bettmann Archive **Artillery (trebuchet)** Corbis-Bettmann Archive **Aztecs** The Granger Collection, New York **Clara Barton** National Portrait Gallery, Smithsonian Institution, Washington (NPG.81.83)/Art Resource, New York **Blacks in the Military** National Archives and Records Administration, neg. no. 165-WW-127-12 **Blitzkrieg** Archive Photos **Boxer Rebellion** California Museum of Photography, Keystone-Mast Collection, neg. no. 73994 **Castles (Western)** Giraudon/Art Resource, New York **Castles (non-Western)** Private Collection **Cavalry, Early Modern to World War II (World War II)** UPI/Corbis-Bettmann Archive **Cavalry, Early Modern to World War II (Vietnam)** Corbis-Bettmann Archive **Charlemagne** Foto Marburg/Art Resource, New York **Children in War** UPI/Corbis-Bettmann Archive **Cold War** UPI/Corbis-Bettmann Archive **Command** National Archives and Records Administration, neg. no. 111-SC-194399 **Conquistadors** Corbis-Bettmann Archive **D-Day** National Archives and Records Administration, neg. no. 026-G-2343 **Disposal of the Dead** National Archives and Records Administration, neg. no. 165-SB-94 **Drills/Marching** Brown University Library, Anne S. K. Brown Military Collection **Dutch Revolt** Giraudon/Art Resource, New York **Education, Military** UPI/Corbis-Bettmann Archive **Engineers** *Caesar's Gallic War*, London: Allyn & Bacon, 1897 **Fortifications** Yale Beinecke Rare Book & Manuscript Library **Genghis Khan** Stock Montage, Inc. **Guerrilla Warfare** AP/Wide World Photos **Gulf War** Archive Photos **Hastings, Battle of** The Granger Collection, New York **Adolf Hitler** UPI/Corbis-Bettmann Archive **Hoplites** Scala/Art Resource, New York **Hussars** The Granger Collection, New York **Infantry** Archive Photos **Irish Republican Army** Archive Photos **Joan of Arc** Giraudon/Art Resource, New York **Kamikazes** The Granger Collection, New York **Knightly Orders** The Granger Collection, New York **Logistics** National Archives and Records Administration, neg. no. 111-SC-24644 **Maps (Dürer's)** The Granger Collection, New York **Maps (Black River)** The British Library **Medicine, Military** UPI/Corbis-Bettmann Archive **Midway, Battle of** Archive Photos **Music, Martial** Imperial War Museum, London **Benito Mussolini** National Archives and Records Administration, neg. no. 242-HCB-2209-1 **Naval Weapons (Chinese)** By permission of the Syndics of Cambridge University Library **Naval Weapons (U.S.)** National Archives and Records Administration, neg. no. 080-G-426954 **Navy** National Maritime Museum, London, neg. no. B3122 **Nuclear Weapons** National Archives and Records Administration, neg. no. 127-N-136176 **Plains Wars** The Granger Collection, New York **Prisoners of War** UPI/Corbis-Bettmann Archive **Propaganda** U.S. Army Photo **Reconnaissance** Imperial War Museum, London **Recruiting** The Granger Collection, New York **Refugees** UPI/Corbis-Bettmann Archive **Representation of War in Film** Springer/Corbis-Bettmann Archive/Copyright 1930 by Universal City Studios, Inc. Courtesy of MCA Publishing Rights, a Division of MCA Inc. All rights reserved. **Representation of War in Western Art (Uccello)** Alinari/Art Resource, New York **Representation of War in Western Art (Nash)** Imperial War Museum, London **Representation of War in Western Art (Butler)** Leeds Museums and Galleries, City Art Gallery, *Scotland Forever* by Lady Elizabeth Butler **Roman-Persian Wars** SEF/Art Resource, New

York **Samurai** The Granger Collection, New York **Secret Weapons** The Granger Collection, New York **Sieges** The Granger Collection, New York **Skiing, Military** AP/Wide World Photos **Smart Weapons** Archive Photos **Spanish-American War** Library of Congress, neg. no. LC-USZ62-7626 **Spanish Civil War** Giraudon/Art Resource, New York **Stalingrad, Battle of** Corbis-Bettmann Archive **Strategic Bombing** U.S. Air Force Association, Arlington, Virginia **Suleyman I** Giraudon/Art Resource, New York **Surrender** UPI/Corbis-Bettmann Archive **Technology** Corbis-Bettmann Archive **Terrorism** Reuters/Corbis-Bettmann Archive **Uniforms & Military Dress (Roman)** Giraudon/Art Resource, New York **Uniforms & Military Dress (sepoy)** Brown University Library, Anne S. K. Brown Military Collection **Vienna, Siege of** Giraudon/Art Resource, New York **Vietnam** UPI/Corbis-Bettmann Archive **War Crimes Trials** National Archives and Records Administration, neg. no. 238-NT-659 **War Games** Courtesy of the Naval War College Museum, Newport, Rhode Island **War Reporting** Corbis-Bettmann Archive **Women in War** Imperial War Museum, London **World War I** Imperial War Museum, London **World War II (ruins)** U.S. Army Photo **World War II (Japanese soldiers)** National Archives and Records Administration, neg. no. 111-SC-334265 **Jan Ziska** *Medieval Warlords* by Tim Newark, London: Blandford Publishing, 1987

Index of Contributors

General Index